Microsoft® Office 2000 Secrets®

Steve Cummings

IDG Books Worldwide, Inc.
An International Data Group Company

Foster City, CA ♦ Chicago, IL ♦ Indianapolis, IN ♦ New York, NY

Microsoft® Office 2000 Secrets®

Published by
IDG Books Worldwide, Inc.
An International Data Group Company
919 E. Hillsdale Blvd., Suite 400
Foster City, CA 94404
www.idgbooks.com (IDG Books Worldwide Web site)

Copyright © 1999 IDG Books Worldwide, Inc. All rights reserved. No part of this book, including interior design, cover design, and icons, may be reproduced or transmitted in any form, by any means (electronic, photocopying, recording, or otherwise) without the prior written permission of the publisher.

Library of Congress Catalog Card Number: 98-75531

ISBN: 0-7645-3262-6

Printed in the United States of America

10 9 8 7 6 5 4 3 2

1B/QS/QV/ZZ/FC

Distributed in the United States by IDG Books Worldwide, Inc.

Distributed by CDG Books Canada Inc. for Canada; by Transworld Publishers Limited in the United Kingdom; by IDG Norge Books for Norway; by IDG Sweden Books for Sweden; by IDG Books Australia Publishing Corporation Pty. Ltd. for Australia; and New Zealand; by TransQuest Publishers Pte Ltd. for Singapore, Malaysia, Thailand, Indonesia, and Hong Kong; by Gotop Information Inc. for Taiwan; by ICG Muse, Inc. for Japan; by Norma Comunicaciones S.A. for Colombia; by Intersoft for South Africa; by Le Monde en Tique for France; by International Thomson Publishing for Germany, Austria and Switzerland; by Distribuidora Cuspide for Argentina; by Livraria Cultura for Brazil; by Ediciones ZETA S.C.R. Ltda. for Peru; by WS Computer Publishing Corporation, Inc., for the Philippines; by Contemporanea de Ediciones for Venezuela; by Express Computer Distributors for the Caribbean and West Indies; by Micronesia Media Distributor, Inc. for Micronesia; by Grupo Editorial Norma S.A. for Guatemala; by Chips Computadoras S.A. de C.V. for Mexico; by Editorial Norma de Panama S.A. for Panama; by American Bookshops for Finland. Authorized Sales Agent: Anthony Rudkin Associates for the Middle East and North Africa.

For general information on IDG Books Worldwide's books in the U.S., please call our Consumer Customer Service department at 800-762-2974. For reseller information, including discounts and premium sales, please call our Reseller Customer Service department at 800-434-3422.

For information on where to purchase IDG Books Worldwide's books outside the U.S., please contact our International Sales department at 317-596-5530 or fax 317-596-5692.

For consumer information on foreign language translations, please contact our Customer Service department at 800-434-3422, fax 317-596-5692, or e-mail rights@idgbooks.com.

For information on licensing foreign or domestic rights, please phone +1-650-655-3109.

For sales inquiries and special prices for bulk quantities, please contact our Sales department at 650-655-3200 or write to the address above.

For information on using IDG Books Worldwide's books in the classroom or for ordering examination copies, please contact our Educational Sales department at 800-434-2086 or fax 317-596-5499.

For press review copies, author interviews, or other publicity information, please contact our Public Relations department at 650-655-3000 or fax 650-655-3299.

For authorization to photocopy items for corporate, personal, or educational use, please contact Copyright Clearance Center, 222 Rosewood Drive, Danvers, MA 01923, or fax 978-750-4470.

LIMIT OF LIABILITY/DISCLAIMER OF WARRANTY: THE PUBLISHER AND AUTHOR HAVE USED THEIR BEST EFFORTS IN PREPARING THIS BOOK. THE PUBLISHER AND AUTHOR MAKE NO REPRESENTATIONS OR WARRANTIES WITH RESPECT TO THE ACCURACY OR COMPLETENESS OF THE CONTENTS OF THIS BOOK AND SPECIFICALLY DISCLAIM ANY IMPLIED WARRANTIES OF MERCHANTABILITY OR FITNESS FOR A PARTICULAR PURPOSE. THERE ARE NO WARRANTIES WHICH EXTEND BEYOND THE DESCRIPTIONS CONTAINED IN THIS PARAGRAPH. NO WARRANTY MAY BE CREATED OR EXTENDED BY SALES REPRESENTATIVES OR WRITTEN SALES MATERIALS. THE ACCURACY AND COMPLETENESS OF THE INFORMATION PROVIDED HEREIN AND THE OPINIONS STATED HEREIN ARE NOT GUARANTEED OR WARRANTED TO PRODUCE ANY PARTICULAR RESULTS, AND THE ADVICE AND STRATEGIES CONTAINED HEREIN MAY NOT BE SUITABLE FOR EVERY INDIVIDUAL. NEITHER THE PUBLISHER NOR AUTHOR SHALL BE LIABLE FOR ANY LOSS OF PROFIT OR ANY OTHER COMMERCIAL DAMAGES, INCLUDING BUT NOT LIMITED TO SPECIAL, INCIDENTAL, CONSEQUENTIAL, OR OTHER DAMAGES. FULFILLMENT OF EACH COUPON OFFER IS THE RESPONSIBILITY OF THE OFFEROR.

Trademarks: All brand names and product names used in this book are trade names, service marks, trademarks, or registered trademarks of their respective owners. IDG Books Worldwide is not associated with any product or vendor mentioned in this book.

 is a registered trademark or trademark under exclusive license to IDG Books Worldwide, Inc. from International Data Group, Inc. in the United States and/or other countries.

Microsoft® Office 2000 Secrets®

ABOUT IDG BOOKS WORLDWIDE

Welcome to the world of IDG Books Worldwide.

IDG Books Worldwide, Inc., is a subsidiary of International Data Group, the world's largest publisher of computer-related information and the leading global provider of information services on information technology. IDG was founded more than 30 years ago by Patrick J. McGovern and now employs more than 9,000 people worldwide. IDG publishes more than 290 computer publications in over 75 countries. More than 90 million people read one or more IDG publications each month.

Launched in 1990, IDG Books Worldwide is today the #1 publisher of best-selling computer books in the United States. We are proud to have received eight awards from the Computer Press Association in recognition of editorial excellence and three from Computer Currents' First Annual Readers' Choice Awards. Our best-selling ...For Dummies® series has more than 50 million copies in print with translations in 31 languages. IDG Books Worldwide, through a joint venture with IDG's Hi-Tech Beijing, became the first U.S. publisher to publish a computer book in the People's Republic of China. In record time, IDG Books Worldwide has become the first choice for millions of readers around the world who want to learn how to better manage their businesses.

Our mission is simple: Every one of our books is designed to bring extra value and skill-building instructions to the reader. Our books are written by experts who understand and care about our readers. The knowledge base of our editorial staff comes from years of experience in publishing, education, and journalism — experience we use to produce books to carry us into the new millennium. In short, we care about books, so we attract the best people. We devote special attention to details such as audience, interior design, use of icons, and illustrations. And because we use an efficient process of authoring, editing, and desktop publishing our books electronically, we can spend more time ensuring superior content and less time on the technicalities of making books.

You can count on our commitment to deliver high-quality books at competitive prices on topics you want to read about. At IDG Books Worldwide, we continue in the IDG tradition of delivering quality for more than 30 years. You'll find no better book on a subject than one from IDG Books Worldwide.

John Kilcullen
Chairman and CEO
IDG Books Worldwide, Inc.

Steven Berkowitz
President and Publisher
IDG Books Worldwide, Inc.

Eighth Annual
Computer Press
Awards ≥1992

Ninth Annual
Computer Press
Awards ≥1993

Tenth Annual
Computer Press
Awards ≥1994

Eleventh Annual
Computer Press
Awards ≥1995

IDG is the world's leading IT media, research and exposition company. Founded in 1964, IDG had 1997 revenues of $2.05 billion and has more than 9,000 employees worldwide. IDG offers the widest range of media options that reach IT buyers in 75 countries representing 95% of worldwide IT spending. IDG's diverse product and services portfolio spans six key areas including print publishing, online publishing, expositions and conferences, market research, education and training, and global marketing services. More than 90 million people read one or more of IDG's 290 magazines and newspapers, including IDG's leading global brands — Computerworld, PC World, Network World, Macworld and the Channel World family of publications. IDG Books Worldwide is one of the fastest-growing computer book publishers in the world, with more than 700 titles in 36 languages. The "...For Dummies®" series alone has more than 50 million copies in print. IDG offers online users the largest network of technology-specific Web sites around the world through IDG.net (http://www.idg.net), which comprises more than 225 targeted Web sites in 55 countries worldwide. International Data Corporation (IDC) is the world's largest provider of information technology data, analysis and consulting, with research centers in over 41 countries and more than 400 research analysts worldwide. IDG World Expo is a leading producer of more than 168 globally branded conferences and expositions in 35 countries including E3 (Electronic Entertainment Expo), Macworld Expo, ComNet, Windows World Expo, ICE (Internet Commerce Expo), Agenda, DEMO, and Spotlight. IDG's training subsidiary, ExecuTrain, is the world's largest computer training company, with more than 230 locations worldwide and 785 training courses. IDG Marketing Services helps industry-leading IT companies build international brand recognition by developing global integrated marketing programs via IDG's print, online and exposition products worldwide. Further information about the company can be found at www.idg.com.

1/24/99

Credits

Acquisitions Editor
David Mayhew

Development Editors
Vivian Perry
Kenyon Brown

Technical Editor
Roy Stevens

Copy Editors
Robert Campbell
Michael D. Welch

Production
Foster City Production Department

Proofreading and Indexing
York Production Services

About the Author

Steve Cummings has been writing about computers since the early 1980s. Steve is the author of hundreds of published articles in magazines such as *PC Week, PC/Computing, Macworld,* and *Keyboard,* and he has been a database columnist for *PC World.* He has authored or coauthored more than ten books, including *VBA For Dummies* (IDG Books Worldwide).

Preface

Yes, you've found the book on Office 2000 you've been looking for. Between the covers of *Microsoft Office 2000 Secrets* lies a treasure house of the best in Office techniques, shortcuts, and undocumented features — secrets you need to get the most out of this incredibly rich software suite.

The printed manual that comes with Office introduces elementary topics clearly but in little depth. Beyond that, Microsoft relies heavily on the online Help files, along with supplementary electronic documentation on the Office CD-ROMs. While those files are extensive, the facts you need often remain buried in some obscure part of the Help system. In some cases, they aren't mentioned at all.

That's where *Microsoft Office 2000 Secrets* comes in. It flushes out this critical knowledge and serves it up in accessible form so that you can put it to work immediately. For each of the main Office applications — Word, Excel, Access, PowerPoint, and Outlook — and for every major task you can accomplish with the software, *Microsoft Office 2000 Secrets* highlights time-saving tips and techniques that might otherwise escape your notice.

Office is a vast product. At its core are five extraordinarily sophisticated applications that collectively can meet just about any computing challenge you can dream up. With a horde of supplementary components, full-blown Web page design tools, and a complete programming language to boot, Office has quite literally thousands upon thousands of features. To tell all its hidden stories would require a full shelf of Secrets books. Given its span of only one volume, *Microsoft Office 2000 Secrets* strikes a balance between surveying bread-and-butter concepts and skills on the one hand, and pinpointing truly advanced tips on the other.

Who This Book Is For

Like other titles in the IDG Books Worldwide Secrets series, *Microsoft Office 2000 Secrets* is meant for people who are comfortable with computers and are hungry for meaty information on real-world tasks. As a *Microsoft Office 2000 Secrets* reader, you're someone who already knows what the Office applications are for and how to get them started. You don't need to be told what a word processor is or why you'd want a database program in the first place.

Microsoft Office 2000 Secrets also assumes you know your way around Windows and are familiar with fundamentals such as installing and running application software, opening documents, using the mouse, and so on. I won't be explaining what a window is or how to OK dialog boxes. On the other hand, I may discuss changes you can make to the Windows Registry. Working with the Registry Editor (the Regedit.exe program) is another skill you'll have to bring to the table if you want to try these suggestions.

What's New in This Edition

Although *Microsoft Office 2000 Secrets* is based on an earlier book, *Office 97 Secrets,* all of the material has been reviewed and updated, and much is brand new — in fact, there are 14 new chapters.

Highlights of the improvements include:

- A new introductory chapter reviewing the innovations in Office 2000 and covering the new installation software, Office's multilanguage features, and more.
- Full treatment of the new HTML Help system.
- Beefed-up treatment of Web page authoring with Office, including a chapter on creating dynamic pages and one devoted to FrontPage.
- A completely rewritten, greatly expanded section on VBA — it now stands as a thorough introduction to this full-scale programming environment built into Office.
- New chapters on VBA programming in Word and Excel.
- Extensive revisions in the Access section, including new chapters on ADO — the latest and greatest component for writing database applications — and Access forms.
- Expanded coverage of Outlook.

And if it's sheer bulk that excites you, *Microsoft Office 2000 Secrets* is about a third again as long as the previous edition.

How This Book Is Organized

For roughly the first half of its pages, this book covers topics relevant to all the various Office applications. Parts I through VI include information about the following topics:

- **Part I** covers the Office user interface and other broadly applicable themes such as the Help system and using Office in conjunction with networks and the Internet.
- **Part II** thoroughly discusses the techniques you need to build Office documents, the end products of your work.
- **Part III** shifts the emphasis to managing those documents, with power strategies for working with disk files, locating documents, maintaining their consistency, and protecting them from harm.
- **Part IV** contains a full survey of Office's tools for authoring Web pages and building complete Web sites.

- **Part V** is all about using Office on networks and intranets, with tips on managing Office throughout an organization and collaborating on documents.
- **Part VI** provides a serious introduction to Visual Basic for Applications (VBA) programming.

In the remainder of the book, each of the five major Office applications receives the Secrets treatment in its own separate section. Space is limited, so Parts VII through XI cover each application according to its complexity and how commonly it is used:

- **Part VII**, the longest single section of the book, is devoted to Word. As the flagship of the Office suite, Word is far and away the most widely used application software in the world. Although writing letters and creating other basic documents with Word is easy, this program provides many great features that aren't obvious or that require special steps to achieve the desired results.
- **Parts VIII and IX** cover Excel and Access. Although more compact than the coverage of Word, these sections offer loads of high-end techniques for managing and analyzing data with two highly sophisticated pieces of software.
- **Parts X and XI** address PowerPoint and Outlook. While these applications are hardly simpletons, they aren't as complex as the other applications. Parts X and XI offer full introductions to the two programs, and plenty of advanced hints to boot, but are still relatively brief.

Uncovering Secrets — Conventions I Use in This Book

I've written *Microsoft Office 2000 Secrets* as a reference and browsing tool, so you can use it just to see what turns up. In every chapter, icons in the margin point out the most "secrety" secrets and highlight other items of special interest. The icons include the following:

The Secret icon highlights information that is not widely known or documented.

The Caution icon flags information that is important to your data, programs, or system as a whole.

The New icon signifies a new feature in this version of Office.

 The Macro/VBA icon indicates code you can use to speed, streamline, or customize your work.

 The On the CD-ROM icon draws your attention to software on this book's accompanying CD-ROM.

Typing Code and Commands

At various places in this book you'll find listings of the programming code for a macros (technically, VBA procedures) that can make your work more efficient or help you customize your Office applications. In addition, I occasionally suggest entries you should type at the DOS prompt, in a Windows shortcut, or in the Windows Registry Editor. When listed on separate lines, these items appear in a special font, as in the following example

```
Sub DoNothingProcedure()
    x = x
End Sub
```

Snippets of VBA code or brief commands sometimes appear within a paragraph, in which case they appear in `monospace` type.

Use the instructions in Chapter 19 to enter macros in the Visual Basic Editor. You should type them into a new module exactly as they appear in the text. Lines that end with an underscore (the _ character) have been broken up so they'll fit on the page. You can type these lines as they are printed—the underscore is VBA's line continuation character—or you can move up the text from the next line, deleting the underscore to make one longer line.

In a command or line of code that includes paired brackets, the brackets indicate an optional item. If you include that item, leave out the bracket characters when you type the command. Italics indicate an item for which you must supply a name, such as a filename or the name of a macro or command.

The *Microsoft Office 2000 Secrets* CD-ROM

Enclosed with *Microsoft Office 2000 Secrets* is a CD-ROM that collects many of the utility programs recommended in various places in the book, along with a slew of other useful software. See the appendix for details on the CD-ROM.

The Office Secrets Web Site and E-mail Address

You can find more secrets, as well as updates, amplifications, and corrections to the book, on the Office Secrets Web site. The address is:

www.seldenhouse.com/officesecrets/

The site also includes links to other Office-related information and to software mentioned in the book or included on the CD-ROM. I can't promise a glamorous, state-of-the-art browsing experience, but I will post useful information as it becomes available.

Feel free to e-mail me with suggestions, questions, or criticisms. I may not be able to reply to every message, but I do pledge to read your mail carefully and will try to respond to information requests either directly or via postings on the site. The e-mail address is:

OfficeSecrets@seldenhouse.com

Acknowledgments

For whatever is useful and coherent in this book, credit goes most to Vivian Perry, my development editor for this edition, and Susan Pines, who edited its predecessor, *Office 97 Secrets*. Contributors to the first edition deserve recognition, too. They include Jan Altman (Excel), Randy Byrne (VBA), Scott Lowry (Web page authoring), and Marshall Cummings (Outlook). I also want to thank Bob Cowart, Chris Van Buren, and Kristen Callahan.

Special praise is due to the marketing and sales staff at IDG Books Worldwide, whose work on behalf of this book has been and will continue to be critical to its success. These folks rarely receive the recognition they deserve.

Finally, I offer once again my deepest apologies, gratitude, and love to my family: Diana, Amy, Laura, Celia, and Irene.

Contents at a Glance

Preface vii
Acknowledgments xii

Part I: Office 2000 Power Secrets 1
Chapter 1: The Keys to the Office 3
Chapter 2: Mastering the Office Shortcut Bar 19
Chapter 3: User Interface Secrets 31
Chapter 4: Office Help Secrets 49
Chapter 5: Customizing Secrets: Office Your Way 61
Chapter 6: Office on the Internet 85

Part II: Building Great Documents with Office 2000 99
Chapter 7: Secrets of Polished Text 101
Chapter 8: Getting Graphical 135
Chapter 9: Secrets of Active Documents 171
Chapter 10: Sharing Information 179
Chapter 11: Printing Secrets 205

Part III: Secrets of Document Management 221
Chapter 12: Advanced Document Management 223
Chapter 13: Document Integrity and Security 259

Part IV: Monster Web Pages with Office 2000 271
Chapter 14: Essential Secrets of Web Page Development 273
Chapter 15: Building Dynamic Web Pages 305
Chapter 16: Building Great Web Sites with FrontPage 323

Part V: Secrets of Workgroup Productivity 347
Chapter 17: Networking Secrets 349
Chapter 18: Sharing and Collaborating on Office Documents 359

Part VI: Secrets of VBA 377
Chapter 19: Basic Visual Basic for Applications 379
Chapter 20: Using the Visual Basic Editor 393
Chapter 21: Writing Great VBA Modules 417
Chapter 22: Object-Oriented Programming with VBA 477
Chapter 23: Unbreakable Code: Debugging and Error Trapping 501
Chapter 24: Getting Interactive: Custom Dialog Boxes 527
Chapter 25: Building Power Applications 579

Part VII: Secrets of Word 2000 597

Chapter 26: Power Customizing 599
Chapter 27: Expert Editing 621
Chapter 28: Full-Speed Formatting 661
Chapter 29: Page Layout and Desktop Publishing 699
Chapter 30: Getting Organized with Tables and Outlines 727
Chapter 31: The Book of Numbers 747
Chapter 32: Creating Long and Technical Documents 769
Chapter 33: A Dream of Fields 797
Chapter 34: Word Power Programming 833

Part VIII: Secrets of Excel 2000 853

Chapter 35: Power Customizing 855
Chapter 36: Advanced Navigation and Selection 867
Chapter 37: Essentials of Editing, Formatting, and Printing 889
Chapter 38: Formulas and Functions 905
Chapter 39: Charting New Territory 931
Chapter 40: Analyzing Data 947
Chapter 41: Debugging Your Worksheets 967
Chapter 42: Excel Power Programming 977

Part IX: Secrets of Access 2000 991

Chapter 43: Getting Inside Access 993
Chapter 44: Fundamentals of Access 1015
Chapter 45: Secrets of Database Application Design 1041
Chapter 46: Working with Data Using VBA 1057
Chapter 47: Designing Access Forms 1079

Part X: Secrets of PowerPoint 2000 1097

Chapter 48: Powerful Presentations 1099
Chapter 49: Deeper PowerPoint Secrets 1117

Part XI: Secrets of Outlook 2000 1137

Chapter 50: Outlook Overview 1139
Chapter 51: Managing E-mail in Outlook 1169
Chapter 52: Managing Tasks, Schedules, Contacts, and Miscellany 1191

Appendix 1207

Index 1213
End-User License Agreement 1248
CD-ROM Installation Instructions 1254

Contents

Preface vii
Acknowledgments xii

Part I: Office 2000 Power Secrets 1

Chapter 1: The Keys to the Office 3

Office 2000 Innovations 3
    Better Office installation 3
    HTML as a universal document format 4
    International intelligence 4
Office Versions 4
Office Installation 4
    Installing and reinstalling Office 5
    Customizing the installation process in an organization 7
Command Line Options for Starting Office Apps 7
Setting Office Options 8
HTML Everywhere, Almost 9
The International Office 10
    Limitations in current versions of Windows 11
    Understanding the role of Internet Explorer 5 12
    Installing the MultiLanguage Pack 12
    Turning on language-related features 13
    Using other languages in your documents 14
    Understanding Unicode 16
Resources for Office Users 17
    About the Office Resource Kit 17
    Other resources 18

Chapter 2: Mastering the Office Shortcut Bar 19

Using the Shortcut Bar 19
    Shape-shifting the Shortcut bar 20
    Geography of the Shortcut bar 20
    Positioning the Shortcut bar 21
    Accessing the Shortcut bar 23
    Accessing buttons you can't see 23
    Refreshing a toolbar to bring the buttons up to date 23
Customizing the Shortcut Bar 24
    Creating new toolbars 24
    Reordering toolbars 25
    Adding new buttons to a toolbar 25
    Hiding and displaying toolbar buttons 25
    Moving toolbar buttons and adding space between them 26
    Renaming buttons and toolbars 26

Deleting toolbars	26
Restoring deleted toolbars	26
Deleting buttons	27
Changing Shortcut bar button icons	27
Shortcut Bar Tips	28
Fast access to the Windows desktop	28
Don't use the Programs toolbar	28
Changing the default folder for Office templates	28

Chapter 3: User Interface Secrets 31

Working with the Screen	31
Zooming in and out on your work	31
Using full screen view	33
Working with document windows	34
Keyboard Secrets	35
Keyboard control of the toolbars	35
How not to learn keyboard shortcuts	35
Working with Toolbars	36
Displaying and hiding toolbars	36
Working with docked toolbars	37
Working with floating toolbars	39
Floating fast	40
Using the tear-off submenus	40
Working with toolbar buttons	40
Mouse on Fire	40
Of mice and mouse alternatives	41
IntelliMouse? Can they be serious about that name?	42
Tuning in the Toolbar Tunes	43
Alternative Software Control and Input Techniques	44
Controlling Office and dictating information with speech-recognition software	44
The power of the pen	44
OCR software	46

Chapter 4: Office Help Secrets 49

Introducing Office Help	49
Installing Help	49
Understanding HTML Help	50
Using HTML Help	51
Working with the toolbar buttons	52
Navigating in the help topics	53
Using HTML Help with multiple Office applications	53
Opening HTML Help files outside of Office	53
Customizing the looks of HTML Help	54
Working with the Office Assistant	54
Taking control of the Assistant	55
Immobilizing the Assistant	56
Making the Help system available from the menu	56
Shutting off the Assistant altogether	57
Customizing the Help System	57
Creating your own Help windows using VBA	57

Creating custom help files 58
Programming the Office Assistant 59

Chapter 5: Customizing Secrets: Office Your Way 61

Creating Custom Commands with Macros 61
   When to use macros 62
   Recording macros 62
   Running macros 64
Customizing Office Toolbars 65
   Customizing the toolbars themselves 65
   Working with buttons on toolbars 68
   Customizing individual buttons 71
Customizing Office Menus 76
   Menu display options 77
   Moving menus with the mouse 78
   Customizing menu items 78
   Creating new menus 79
   Renaming menus 80
   Customizing the shortcut menus 80
   Restoring the original menus 82
Saving and Reusing Custom Toolbars and Menus 82
Customizing the Keyboard 82
   Quick keyboard shortcuts in any Office application 82
   Choosing the right shortcut key 83
Changing the Color Scheme 83
   Changing windows background and ScreenTip colors 84
   Using the Automatic color 84

Chapter 6: Office on the Internet 85

Office 2000 and the Internet 85
   Preparing to surf the Internet with Office 86
   Choosing a Web browser for Office 87
Internet and Intranet Backgrounder 87
   World wide wackiness 87
   About intranets 87
Accessing Web Pages in Office Applications 89
   How Office applications cope with Web pages 89
   Importing Web pages into Access 91
   Using the Web toolbar 91
   Setting your own start and search pages 93
   Navigating among hyperlinked documents 93
Internet Explorer and Office 94
   Working with Office documents inside Internet Explorer 94
   Jumping to Office documents via hyperlinks from within IE 96
   Editing Web pages opened in Internet Explorer 96
E-mail and Office 97
   Office's e-mail features 98
   Choosing e-mail software for use with Office 98

Part II: Building Great Documents with Office 2000 99

Chapter 7: Secrets of Polished Text 101

Perfect Spelling, Imperfect Grammar 101
   Spelling facts 102
   Managing the spelling dictionaries 105
   Working with on-the-fly spell-checking 109
   Grammar checking in Word 110
The Wordsmith's Tool Chest: Synonyms, Definitions, and Quotations 111
   Figuring out Word's built-in thesaurus 111
   Improving your references with Bookshelf 112
Lightning Text Entry with AutoCorrect 112
   Using AutoCorrect 112
   Making the most of AutoCorrect 114
Fonts and Typography 120
   Font mania 120
   Font aesthetics 132

Chapter 8: Getting Graphical 135

Line Art Graphics from Scratch 135
   Using the Drawing toolbar 137
Inserting and Editing Pictures 157
   Inserting pictures 158
   Managing clip art and other content with Clip Gallery 159
   Inserting images from a scanner or digital camera 162
   Working with PhotoEditor 162
   Modifying pictures 162
   Creating art with PhotoDraw 165
Objets D'art 165
   Adding graphs, org charts, maps, and equations 166
   Adding sound, video, and other objects 167
Formatting Objects: The Master Control Center 168
   Secrets of the Format dialog box 168
   Working with measurement units in Office 169

Chapter 9: Secrets of Active Documents 171

When to Use Active Documents 171
About Controls in Office Documents 172
About Forms in Word and Excel 173
   Word's Forms toolbar: Avoid it 173
   Excel's Forms toolbar: Try it 174
Working with Active AutoShapes 174
Adding ActiveX Controls 175
   Types of ActiveX controls 175
   Inserting ActiveX controls 176
   Using design mode 177
   Controlling controls with properties 177
   Making controls do magic—with and without programming 178

Chapter 10: Sharing Information 179

Power Clipboard Techniques and Utilities 180
    When to use the clipboard 180
    Using the Clipboard toolbar 180
    Alternatives to the standard Paste command 183
    Using the clipboard with specific types of data 185
Drag-and-Drop Information Transfer 186
    Left- and right-button dragging 187
    The secret way to drag and drop between applications 187
    Parking information in scraps 188
Secrets of the Import/Export Trade 188
    How to import 188
    Importing database and spreadsheet data 191
    Exporting data 192
    Generic import/export file formats 193
    Mass conversions 194
Sharing Information Using OLE 195
    The difference between linking and embedding 195
    The pros and cons of OLE 196
    Placing objects in your documents 197
    Working with objects in documents 201
Using Mail Merge to Send Form Letters 202

Chapter 11: Printing Secrets 205

Matching Print Orientation to Document Layout 205
Previewing Before You Print 206
    What you see in Preview 206
    Editing in Print Preview mode — only in Word 207
Printing Documents 208
    Shortcut and drag-and-drop printing 209
    Working with the Print dialog box 209
Application-Specific Printing Tips 211
    Word 211
    PowerPoint 212
    Excel 213
    Outlook 213
    Access 213
    Binder 214
Printing to a File 214
    Creating the print file 215
    Printing to a file automatically 215
    Printing a print file 215
    Show-off ways for printing print files 216
Hot Printer Utilities 216
Faxing Your Documents 218

Part III: Secrets of Document Management 221

Chapter 12: Advanced Document Management 223

Power Techniques for Document Management 223
    How do I create thee? Let me count the ways 224
    Secrets of the Open and Save As dialog boxes 225
    Saving documents 236
    Locating files 239
    Other search methods and utilities 246
Tracking Documents via File Properties 247
    Tips on using and setting properties 248
    Creating custom properties 248
Creating Compound Documents with Office Binder 249
    Running Binder 251
    Creating a binder 251
    Adding documents to a binder 252
    Working with documents in a binder 252
    Saving a binder 255
    Printing a binder 255
    Setting Binder options 257

Chapter 13: Document Integrity and Security 259

Using Templates to Ensure Consistent Documents 259
    Quick facts on Office templates 259
    What makes a template a template 262
    Using templates on a network 262
Keeping Shared Documents Up to Date 262
    Using Briefcase 262
    Other file-synchronizing utilities 264
There Ain't No Way to Hide Those Prying Eyes 264
    Office security 265
    Third-party security software 268
Protecting Documents from Disease and Accidents 268
    Coping with macro viruses 268
    Recovering documents after accidental erasure 270

Part IV: Monster Web Pages with Office 2000 271

Chapter 14: Essential Secrets of Web Page Development 273

Authoring Web Pages in Office 273
    Saving documents as Web pages 274
    Setting options for Web pages 275
Planning Your Site and Managing Your Files 276
    Determining the location for your finished site 276
    Making allowances for browser capabilities 276
    Managing files 277
Working with Hyperlinks 278

Using hyperlinks 279
Creating hyperlinks 279
Creating hyperlinks to existing pages and documents 280
Editing and removing hyperlinks 281
Jumping to specific locations in documents 281
Controlling the look of your hyperlinks 284
Word and hyperlinks 285
Access and hyperlinks 286
PowerPoint and hyperlinks 287
About Graphics in Web Pages 288
Working with GIF and JPEG images 288
Saving graphics in PNG format 289
Using vector graphics in Web pages 289
Editing HTML Code in Office 290
Web Page Authoring with Word 290
Basing new Web pages on templates 290
Using Word's Web Page Wizard 291
Editing Web pages in Word 292
Working with themes 293
Working with frames in Word 293
Building Web forms in Word 297
Web Presentations with PowerPoint 299
Creating a PowerPoint presentation for the Web 300
Saving a Web presentation 300
What you lose when viewing a presentation in a browser 302
Editing a Web presentation 302
Publishing Your Web Pages 302

Chapter 15: Building Dynamic Web Pages 305

Requirements for Office Interactive Pages 305
Publishing Spreadsheets on the Web 306
Choosing workbook elements to convert 307
Publishing interactive data 308
Database Publishing on the Net with Access 310
Exporting data to static Web pages 310
Storing databases on the Web server for dynamic pages 312
Creating server-side dynamic database pages 312
Working with data access pages 313
Enlivening Web Pages with Scripts 318
Working with scripting languages 318
Adding script commands to the toolbar system 320
Identifying scripts in Web pages 320
Editing code with the Script Editor 321
Using ActiveX controls on your Web pages 321

Chapter 16: Building Great Web Sites with FrontPage 323

Using FrontPage with the Rest of Office 323
Working with FrontPage 325
The FrontPage treasure chest 325
About FrontPage views 326
About FrontPage windows 327

Creating and Managing Webs in FrontPage 327
    Starting a new web 327
    Adding pages to a web 328
    Naming and renaming pages 329
    Working with folders and files 329
    Designing your web's navigation structure 330
    Managing hyperlinks 333
    Using the _private folder 335
    Managing complex web content using subwebs 335
Developing Web Pages in FrontPage 336
    Bringing content into a FrontPage web 336
    Editing pages in FrontPage 337
    Adding hyperlinks to pages 337
    Applying and customizing themes 338
    Using shared borders 338
    Working with navigation bars 339
    Inserting other components, doo-dads, and special effects 341
    Previewing pages 343
Publishing Your Web 343
    Choosing what to publish 343
    Publishing a web 344
    Republishing a web 345

Part V: Secrets of Workgroup Productivity 347

Chapter 17: Networking Secrets 349

Installing and Running Office on a Network 349
    Decisions, decisions 350
    Network installation 350
Customizing Office for Workgroups: Windows System Policies 351
    Features you can control with system policies 352
    Network requirements for system policies 352
    Using the Windows System Policy Editor 352
    Creating a system policy file 354
    Specifying which users or computers a system policy affects 355
    Defining individual system policies 355
    Details on how system policies work 356
    Using environment variables as system policy settings 356
Mapping Network Locations within Office 357
Installing Office Server Extensions 358

Chapter 18: Sharing and Collaborating on Office Documents 359

Storing and Finding Documents on the Net 359
    Opening and saving documents on your network 360
    Sharing documents on your hard drive with others 360
    Working with Web documents 361
    Working with documents on FTP sites 364
    Using workgroup template folders 365

Sharing Documents via E-mail 365
    Understanding MAPI and VIM 365
    Sending and routing documents from within Office 366
    Sending documents that aren't already open 367
    Posting documents to Exchange folders 367
Office Features for Collaborating on Documents 368
    Collaboration tools for all users, networked or not 368
    Discussing Office documents 368
    Subscribing to document-change notifications 370
Participating in Online Meetings 371
Sharing Documents between Different Versions of Office 374

Part VI: Secrets of VBA 377

Chapter 19: Basic Visual Basic for Applications 379
A First Look at the Visual Basic Editor 379
Writing a Simple Module 380
A VBA Backgrounder 382
    A brief history of VBA 382
    VBA as an industry standard 382
    Some VBA highlights 383
    What's new in VBA? 384
Getting Started with VBA 385
    Recorded macros are VBA programs 385
    Moving beyond macros 386
VBA: An Object-Oriented Development Tool 386
    Understanding objects 387
    Working with object models 387
ActiveX Technology and VBA 387
    ActiveX controls 387
    ActiveX automation 389
    About ActiveX servers 389
VBA Resources 390

Chapter 20: Using the Visual Basic Editor 393
Working with the Visual Basic Editor User Interface 393
    Out to lunch with Editor menus 394
    Tuning the toolbars 394
    Keyboard shortcuts 395
Managing the Windows 396
    Some windows are loners, some run in crowds 397
    Viewing and hiding windows 397
    Sittin' on the dock of the VB-ay 398
    Saving the screen layout 399
Managing Your Projects with Project Explorer 399
    Opening the Project Explorer window 400

Exploring the Explorer	400
Setting project properties	402
Using the Object Browser	404
Starting the Object Browser	404
Browsing objects	405
Searching for members	406
Using browsed items in your code	406
Coding Secrets	407
Opening Code windows	407
Creating new Code windows	407
Typing code	407
More Code window creature comforts	410
Using the Properties Window	414
Invoking the Properties window	414
Renaming a project or module in the Properties window	415
The Debugging Windows	415

Chapter 21: Writing Great VBA Modules 417

Program Building Blocks	417
A sample program	417
The VBA hierarchy	419
Programs defined	420
More about projects	420
Working with modules	420
Writing procedures	422
Scoping out the scope	427
Making statements	428
Manners, Please! VBA Etiquette	429
VBA naming rules	429
Naming conventions	430
Making your code legible	431
Remarks about comments	432
Working with Variables	434
Declaring variables	434
Where to declare variables	434
When to declare variables	435
Choosing and using data types	435
Specifying a variable's scope	438
Declaring multiple variables on the same line	439
Giving assignments	440
Expression-ism	441
Working with Constants	442
Declaring constants	442
The benefits of a constant approach	443
Using constants to represent attributes	443
Hello, Operators	444
Taking precedence	444
Comparing values	446
Stringing text together	448
Details on Data Types	448

- Converting between data types 448
- Understanding variants 448
- Choosing a numeric data type 449
- When to use Boolean variables 450
- Working with currency values 450
- Working with dates 451
- Stringing you along 452

Working with Arrays 453
- About the items in an array 453
- Array dimensions 454
- Declaring arrays 454
- Addressing elements in an array 455

Built-in Functions and Statements 456
- Where to find built-in commands 456
- Categories of built-in commands 457

Controlling the Flow 458
- Control structure anatomy 459
- Nesting control structures 459
- The road taken: using condition expressions 460

Using If...Then Statements 461
- The basic form: If...Then 461
- One-liners with If...Then 461
- Using If...Then...Else statements 462
- If...Then complexities 462

Using Select Case Statements 464
- Testing conditions in Select Case statements 464
- A sample Select Case statement 465
- The Case Else clause 465
- More about Case clause tests 465

Repeating Yourself with Loops 466
- Do-ing loops 467
- Quitting a loop early with Exit Do 470
- When to use Do without While or Until 470
- Repeating on Count with For...Next loops 471
- For Each...Next 474

Interrupting the Flow with GoTo 474
- A GoTo example 474
- GoTo caveats 475

Chapter 22: Object-Oriented Programming with VBA 477

So What's an Object? 477
- Objects can be components of a VBA application 477
- Conceptualizing objects can be hard 478
- A practical definition 478
- Object classes versus specific objects 479
- What's an object model? 479
- VBA forms are objects 481

Using Objects in Code 482
- What's your object? 482
- Getting and changing object properties 483

        Method acting 486
        Events 486
        Identifying the object you want to work with 487
        Creating object variables 489
        Creating new objects 491
        Efficient object coding using With statements 492
        Comparing object references 493
        Managing sets of data with Collection objects 493
    Do-It-Yourself Objects: Class Modules 497
        Creating class modules 497
        Components of a class definition 497
        Using your custom objects 500

Chapter 23: Unbreakable Code: Debugging and Error Trapping 501

    What Can Go Wrong, Will Go Wrong 501
        Fixing syntax errors 502
        Debugging for VBA programmers 502
    Seeing Data Tips 511
    Immediate Gratifications 512
    Keeping an Eye on the Locals (Window) 514
        Local mechanics 514
        Why edit variable values? 515
        How to edit variable values 515
    The Watch Window: A Key Debugging Tool 516
        What else is different compared to the Locals window 517
        Adding watch expressions 517
        Working with the Add Watch window 518
        Editing watch expressions 519
        Using watch expressions to define breakpoints 519
    Trapping Wild Bugs with On Error and the Error Object 520
        Where run-time errors come from 521
        How error-handling code works 521
        How to write error-handling code 521

Chapter 24: Getting Interactive: Custom Dialog Boxes 527

    Simple Interactions with the World 528
        Displaying message boxes 528
        Obtaining user input 531
    Designing Forms 532
        Running forms 532
        Forms and controls are objects — and they must be programmed 532
        Planning forms for your program 532
        Printing forms during the design process 533
    Laying Out Forms 533
        Creating the form 533
        Adding controls from the Toolbox 533
    Working with Form and Control Properties 535
        A tour of the Properties window 535
        Getting Help on properties 536
        Changing property settings 536

Don't forget to select the right item	537
Key form and control properties	537

Basic Control Editing 539
Working with the Grid 540
Formatting Controls 541
    Using the Format menu 542
    The UserForm toolbar 542
    Grouping multiple controls 542
    Arranging controls on top of each other 543
    Formatting multiple controls 543
    Other formatting choices 545
Working with Controls 546
    Setting the tab order for controls 546
    Assigning accelerator keys 547
Secrets of Specific Controls 547
    Sending messages with label controls 547
    Text boxes let you hear from the user 549
    Get things done with command buttons 551
    Frame controls group other controls 552
    Multipage controls 553
    Picking one item from a group with option buttons 554
    Turning options on or off with check boxes and toggle buttons 556
    Selecting options with list and combo boxes 557
    Selecting values with scroll bars and spin buttons 559
Form Programming 560
    Loading and showing forms 560
    Modal versus modeless forms 563
    Referring to forms using variables 563
    Hiding a visible form 564
    Removing a form from memory 564
Event Programming for Forms and Controls 564
    Common events 565
    Writing and editing event procedures 566
    Event procedure syntax 567
    Working with the Click event 567
    Responding to control changes 569
    Detecting keystrokes 569
Handling Common Form Programming Tasks 570
    Adding a Close or Cancel button 570
    Programming the OK button 571
    Validating entries 572
    Morphing forms and controls 574
Installing and Using New ActiveX Controls 575
    Adding new controls to the Toolbox 576
    Using ActiveX controls in your programs 577
    Some controls are invisible 577

Chapter 25: Building Power Applications 579

Building Custom Applications with COM Objects 579
    The Assignment 581
    Cross-application programming 582

Building Add-Ins 585
   Creating application-specific add-ins 585
   Creating COM add-ins 586
Using Custom Properties as Document Variables 586
Programming the Office Assistant 587
   Pulling the Assistant's strings 587
   Programming the Assistant's balloon 589
Securing Your Code with Digital Certificates 592
Locking Your Code 593
Using Office Developer 594
   Distributing your solution 595
   Building stand-alone Access applications 595

Part VII: Secrets of Word 2000 597

Chapter 26: Power Customizing 599

Startup Options 599
Selecting Word Options 600
Customizing the Screen 600
   Using the entire screen for your document in Full Screen view 601
   Customizing tips for special screen situations 603
Customizations, Templates, and Documents 605
   Customizing the toolbars and menus 606
   Customizing the shortcut menus 606
   Customizing the Word keyboard 606
Redefining Word's Built-In Commands 612
   Using Word templates 614

Chapter 27: Expert Editing 621

Setting Editing Options 621
Working with Files and Windows 623
   Opening previously used files 623
   Closing and saving documents: Quick tips 624
   Working with document windows 625
Advanced Navigation 626
   Mousing around 626
   Navigating with Document Map 627
   Navigation keyboard shortcuts 628
   Browsing by objects 629
   Go Back tips 630
   Optimizing the Go To command 630
   Bookmarks rule! 631
Find and Replace Secrets 635
   Where are the buttons? 635
   Find and Replace tips 636
   Advanced Find and Replace 1: Remember these features 637
   Advanced Find and Replace 2: Using special characters 637
Speeding Text Entry 646

AutoText secrets 647
Ditch the Spike for a clipboard enhancement utility 652
Using Repeat to clone text you just typed 654
Inserting the current date or time in one step 654
Quick Text Changes 655
Mouse text-selection shortcuts 655
Take advantage of the shortcut menus 656
Using the selection bar 656
Mouse moves—an alternative to drag and drop 656
A great secret keyboard move technique 656
Keyboard shortcuts for cutting words, lines, sentences, or paragraphs 657
Swapping characters 658
Improving on Word's case-changing functions 659

Chapter 28: Full-Speed Formatting 661

Formatting Basics: A Quick Review 661
Methods for applying formatting 662
Displaying formatting information 662
Setting the default measurement unit 663
Character Formatting 663
New font list 664
Tons of character formatting choices 664
The fastest way to apply character formatting to the current word 664
Removing character formats 665
Using Format Painter 665
Secrets of individual character formats: Quick reference 666
Using kerning and character spacing 667
Paragraph Formatting 670
What's so special about the paragraph mark 670
Reverting to the paragraph's original format 671
Setting indents 671
Advanced line-spacing considerations 674
Spacing between paragraphs 675
Working with the line and page break settings 675
Tabs 675
Using click and type for on-the-fly formatting 679
Tricks with borders and shading 680
Mastering Styles 685
Paragraph versus character styles 687
Displaying style assignments and previewing how they look 687
Applying styles 688
Keyboard shortcuts for applying specific styles 689
Customizing the shortcut menu to apply specific styles 689
Applying paragraph styles as character styles 690
Creating and modifying styles 691

Chapter 29: Page Layout and Desktop Publishing 699

Page Layout Secrets 699
The secret is in the sections 700
Starting a new section 700

Using the Page Setup dialog box 701
　　　Working with headers and footers 703
　Desktop Publishing with Word 707
　　　Complex page design in Word 709
　Working with Graphics 716
　　　Floating versus inline graphics 716
　　　Positioning graphics 717
　　　Understanding anchors 717
　　　Wrapping text around graphics 718
　Specialized Desktop Publishing Chores 721
　　　Designing fancy envelopes 721
　　　Designing labels and such 722
　　　Presentations on the cheap: Sharp slides for 50¢ apiece 725

Chapter 30: Getting Organized with Tables and Outlines 727

　Unraveling the Mysteries of Tables 727
　　　Unclassified table secrets 727
　　　Selecting table cells 728
　　　Inserting new tables 729
　　　Laying out and formatting tables 732
　　　Editing and formatting text in a table 740
　　　Data management in tables 741
　Working with Outlines 743
　　　Automatically collapsing body text 745
　　　Sorting a document by headings 745
　　　A macro for printing outlines 746
　AutoSummarize? Don't Get Your Hopes Up 746

Chapter 31: The Book of Numbers 747

　Numbering Pages and Sections 747
　　　Custom page numbering using Insert Page Numbers 748
　　　Using the Insert Page Numbers command for fancy page numbers 749
　　　Placing page numbers directly in a header or footer 750
　　　Counting page numbers in sections 750
　　　Skipping page numbers 751
　　　Including the total page count with page numbers 751
　　　Removing page numbers 751
　　　Printing both section and document page numbers 752
　　　Numbering chapters and sections 754
　Secrets of Numbered and Bulleted Lists 756
　　　What's new, and newish, in Bullets and Numbering 756
　　　Creating numbered and bulleted lists 757
　　　Why you should use automatic numbered and bulleted lists 758
　　　Maintaining a consistent format: Paragraph styles for automatic numbering and bullets 761
　　　Assign keyboard shortcuts to the numbering and bullets commands 761
　　　Bullet-specific secrets 762
　　　Numbering secrets 763

Chapter 32: Creating Long and Technical Documents 769
Adding Reference Information 769
Inserting captions 770
Fording cross-references 772
Adding footnotes and endnotes 774
Adding indexes, tables of contents, and other reference tables 778
Building Long Documents 784
Creating a master document 785
Creating reference tables, indexes, and cross-references in long documents 786
Group Document Development 787
Inserting comments 787
Reviewing documents 789
Using versions 793
Setting up a document to be reviewed 794
Network considerations in group document development 795

Chapter 33: A Dream of Fields 797
Working with Fields 798
Keyboard shortcuts for field commands 798
Using field commands on toolbars and menus 799
How fields work 800
Field anatomy 800
Inserting fields 801
Toggling between field codes and field results 803
Selecting a field 803
Updating fields 803
Locking a field to prevent updating 803
Converting fields into plain text 804
Working with field results 804
Formatting field results and field codes 804
Controlling the display of field results with switches 804
Using VBA with Fields 808
Field-related objects, properties, and methods 808
A procedure for finding fields 810
A Field Guide to Fields 811
Document information fields 811
= (Formula or Calculation) Field 816
Using Excel instead 817
Using bookmarks in formulas 818
Ask 818
AutoNum, AutoNumLgl, AutoNumOut 818
AutoText 819
AutoTextList 819
Barcode 819
"Bookmark" 819
Compare 820
Date 820
DDE and DDEAuto 820

Eq 821
Fill-in 821
GoToButton 821
Hyperlink 822
If 822
IncludePicture 823
Index 823
ListNum 824
MacroButton 824
Print 825
Quote 825
Ref 825
Section 826
SectionPages 826
Seq 826
Set 827
StyleRef 827
Symbol 828
TC 829
TOC 829
XE 830

Chapter 34: Word Power Programming 833

Understanding the Application Object 833
Accessing Word Documents in VBA 834
    Working with the active document 834
    Specifying a particular document 834
    Creating, opening, activating, and closing documents 835
    Working with document sections 835
Opening Windows with VBA 836
    Specifying windows in code 836
    Working with window panes 837
    Changing window appearance 837
    Using the View object 837
    Zooming in code 838
Working with the Selection Object 839
Understanding Range Objects 840
    Using the Range property 840
    Defining your own ranges using the Range method 841
Working with Text in Word VBA 843
    Selecting ranges, and creating ranges from selections 843
    Redefining ranges and selections 843
    Deleting, copying, and pasting text 845
    Inserting new text 846
    Formatting text 847
Finding and Replacing in Word VBA 847
    Working with found text 848
    Replacing text or formatting 849
    Finding and replacing formatting 849
Using Document Variables 850

Part VIII: Secrets of Excel 2000 853

Chapter 35: Power Customizing 855

Startup Options 855
    Controlling startup behavior with command line switches 855
    Opening workbooks automatically with startup folders 856
Setting Excel Options 857
Putting on a Pretty Face: Customizing the Screen 858
    Working with the color palette 859
    Using Full Screen view 859
    Storing a view of the current workbook 859
Recording and Using Macros 860
    Defining a keyboard shortcut for the macro 860
    Storing a macro 861
    Recording absolute versus relative cell references 861
    Running macros 862
Saving Custom Toolbar Layouts 862
    Creating global custom toolbars 863
    Attaching custom toolbars to a workbook 863
Using Excel Templates to Store Customizations 863
    Creating and saving workbook templates 864
    Inserting a new worksheet based on a custom template 864

Chapter 36: Advanced Navigation and Selection 867

On the Move 867
    Knowing your place 867
    Keyboard navigation 868
    Making a run for the border 868
    Jumping to a defined name 869
    Going out for a scroll 871
    Using workspace files 873
The Art of Natural Selection 873
    Shift magic 874
    Making multiple selections 874
    Back to square one 875
    Selecting from within a dialog box 875
    Navigating inside a selection 876
    A table of selection shortcuts 876
Details of Data Entry 879
    Single cell entries 879
    Home on the range 882
    Entering data in groups of worksheets 886
    Data validation 886
    AutoCorrecting as you go 888

Chapter 37: Essentials of Editing, Formatting, and Printing 889

Rearranging Information 889
    Life's a drag 889
    Right on the button 890

    Inserting within an existing range 890
    Going to another sheet in the workbook 891
    Resizing rows and columns 891
    Hiding rows and columns 891
    Finding and unhiding a hidden column 891
  Formatting 892
    Custom number formats 892
    Aligning data 894
    AutoFormatting 896
    Conditional formatting 897
    Pasting particular cell attributes 898
    Applying multiple formatting options quickly with styles 899
    Formatting shortcut keys 900
  Adding Comments 900
    Attaching a comment to a cell 901
    Viewing comments 901
    Editing comments 902
    Finding comments 902
    No comment at this time 902
  A Couple of Quick Printing Tips 902

Chapter 38: Formulas and Functions 905

  The Secret Formula 905
    Automatic versus manual calculation 905
    How does Excel calculate formulas? 906
    Viewing formulas instead of results 906
    The one great commandment for creating formulas 907
    Using the Formula palette 907
    Smooth operators for your formulas 908
    Referring to cells and ranges in your formulas 909
    Finding formula precedents with the Range Finder 912
    Working with 3-D references 912
    Performing complex calculations: VBA versus formulas 914
  Using Functions in Your Formulas 915
    Function anatomy 915
    Entering functions 915
    Nesting functions 916
    Creating custom functions 916
    Using the IF function 917
    A survey of Excel functions 917
  Formula Tips and Tricks 923
    Defining named constants 923
    The new millennium 923
    Out-of-range date arguments 924
    Creating dynamic data tables 924

Chapter 39: Charting New Territory 931

  Chart Speak 931
  Choosing a Chart Type 932

Worksheets à la Chart 933
    Using the Chart Wizard 933
    Viewing chart items 934
Changing the Chart Type 934
Adjusting Data 935
    Dragging points on the chart 935
    Goal-seeking using charts 936
    Modifying a chart's source data range 937
    Changing a chart's orientation 938
Formatting Charts 938
    Dabbling with your data 939
    Toying with your text 942
    Perspective and rotation 943
Mixing Different Data Types in the Same Chart 944
    Using combination charts 945
    Charts with secondary axes 945
Saving Chart Options to Use Again 945

Chapter 40: Analyzing Data 947

Filtering Data 947
    AutoFilter 947
    Creating custom filters 949
    Using advanced filters 949
    Removing filters 950
    Saving filters in shared workbooks 950
Handy Functions for Manipulating Lists 950
Pivot Tables and Pivot Charts 950
    When to use pivot tables 951
    Creating a pivot table 952
    Using the PivotTable toolbar and shortcut menu 955
    Fine-tuning pivot tables 955
    Creating pivot charts 958
Working with Add-ins 959
    Lookup Wizard add-in 960
    Analysis ToolPak add-in 961
    Solver 961
    Template Wizard with Data Tracking add-in 962
    Built-in forms for data tracking 963
Sharing Workbooks 963
    Keeping track of changes 963
    Merging changes 965

Chapter 41: Debugging Your Worksheets 967

Using the Auditing Toolbar 967
Depending on You 967
    Tracing with the Auditing toolbar 968
    The double-click trick 969
    For keyboard users 969
Cell Errors 970

Understanding cell error messages ...970
Tracing errors ...970
Auditing Data Validation errors ...970
Identifying circular references ...971
Finding errors in logic ...972
Error checking on the fly ...973

Chapter 42: Excel Power Programming ...977

Navigating the Excel Object Model ...977
Working with Cells in Code Using Range Objects ...978
    Specifying a Range object ...979
    Using the Cells property to define a range ...980
    Acting on cells en masse ...980
    Acting on individual cells in a range ...981
    Working with selections ...981
Programming Custom Worksheet Functions ...983
    Writing custom worksheet functions ...984
    Running custom functions ...984
    Testing your custom functions ...986
    Fancier functions ...986
Using Built-In Functions in Your Code ...986
Programming for Excel Events ...987
    Choosing the right object ...987
    Starting an event procedure ...988
    Reacting to worksheet changes ...988
    Programming dynamic charts ...990

Part IX: Secrets of Access 2000 ...991

Chapter 43: Getting Inside Access ...993

Getting a Grip on Access ...993
Power Customizing ...994
    Controlling startup behavior ...994
    Customizing the Interface and Other Options ...997
    Creating Macros in Access ...997
    Adding and Removing Components ...1000
Choosing a Database Engine ...1000
    The Jet engine ...1001
    Alternatives to Jet ...1001
    Considerations in choosing an engine ...1001
    Upsizing a database from Jet to SQL Server ...1005
Working in Access ...1006
    Expanding entries for easy editing ...1006
    Renaming database items ...1006
Optimizing Performance ...1007
    Using the Performance Analyzer ...1008
    Tweaking Jet settings in the Windows Registry ...1009
Optimizing Network Performance ...1012
    Housekeeping in Access ...1012

Chapter 44: Fundamentals of Access 1015

Database Concepts: The Short Course 1015
- Tables: Where the data dwells 1015
- Queries: Honing in on the data you want to see 1016
- Forms, pages, and reports: Tools for presenting and interacting with the data 1016
- Making things happen with macros and modules 1017
- Database objects 1017

Planning a Database 1018
- Start from the finish line 1018
- Designing tables and organizing fields 1018
- Designing table relationships 1019
- Defining fields in detail 1020
- Planning queries 1021
- Designing forms, data access pages, and reports 1022

Access Boot Camp: Database Construction Techniques 1022
- Using the Database window 1022
- Working with views 1024
- Creating and working with tables 1025

Getting Answers 1034
- Finding, sorting, and filtering data 1034
- Creating queries 1035
- Distributing reports 1038

Creating and Using Forms and Data Access Pages 1040

Chapter 45: Secrets of Database Application Design 1041

Understanding Access Applications 1041
- Planning and implementing the application 1042
- Choose the right tool: Access macros versus VBA 1043
- When not to use Access for database applications 1045

Applications by Magic: Using the Database Wizards 1047

Building Custom Applications in Access 1047
- Designing the user interface 1047
- Setting startup options and securing your custom interface 1051
- Maximum efficiency with minimum VBA code 1052
- Writing VBA code in Access 1054

Distributing the Application 1054
- Splitting a Jet database for network use 1054
- Database replication 1055
- Securing your files 1056

Chapter 46: Working with Data Using VBA 1057

An Introduction to VBA Database Programming 1057
- Using DoCmd in Access 1057
- SQL and VBA 1058
- All about database objects 1058
- Some related database technologies 1059

Writing Database Code with ADO 1060
- Error handling 1060
- Creating a reference to ADO in your project 1060

Establishing the connection 1061
Working with Recordset objects 1062
Using the Command object 1069
Working with SQL 1071
Avoiding SQL 1071
Understanding SQL dialects 1072
Inserting SQL statements in VBA code 1072
Writing SELECT statements 1072
Performing bulk updates and deletions in SQL 1077

Chapter 47: Designing Access Forms 1079

Access Forms: A World Apart 1079
About bound forms 1080
Form design tools — Access versus VBA 1080
Access's unique forms affect your development plans 1081
Designing Access Forms 1082
Using form views 1082
Access form anatomy 1083
Controlling form appearance with AutoFormat 1087
Binding a form to data 1088
Working with controls 1089
Working with forms in VBA code 1092
Working with subforms 1093

Part X: Secrets of PowerPoint 2000 1097

Chapter 48: Powerful Presentations 1099

Planning Great Presentations 1099
The virtues of simplicity 1100
Ensuring consistent presentations 1100
Starting New Presentations 1101
Disabling the Startup and New slide dialog boxes 1101
Choices for new presentations 1102
Creating Great Slides and Presentations 1103
Working with the PowerPoint user interface 1103
Arranging slides in a presentation 1105
Modifying the layout of individual slides 1105
Adding and formatting text 1107
Adding graphics, charts, and tables 1113
Creating tables in PowerPoint 1113
Inserting Word tables and Excel charts 1114
Copying formats 1114
Adding action buttons, interactive controls, and hyperlinks 1114
Multimedia madness 1115

Chapter 49: Deeper PowerPoint Secrets 1117

Working with the Options dialog box 1117
Using macros in PowerPoint 1118

Developing Custom Layouts and Formats 1119
    Working with masters 1119
    Working with color schemes 1122
    Working with templates in PowerPoint 1123
    Mixing slide designs within a presentation 1124
Putting Together a Complete Presentation 1128
    Checking your work with slide shows 1128
    Reordering and hiding slides 1128
    Animating slide transitions 1128
    Setting slide show timings 1129
    Creating custom shows 1130
    Overall slide show setup options 1130
Performing Your Presentation 1131
    Sending a presentation 1131
    Running a slide show from your computer 1132
    Printing handouts, outlines, and speaker's notes 1134
    Creating portable presentations with the Pack and Go Wizard 1134
    Choosing a display device 1135
    Live online collaboration 1135

Part XI: Secrets of Outlook 2000 1137

Chapter 50: Outlook Overview 1139

Getting Started with Outlook 1140
Startup Switches 1140
Customizing Outlook 1142
    Using the Tools➪Options dialog box 1142
    Customizing Outlook toolbars 1143
Working with Outlook Folders 1143
    Selecting a folder 1145
    Creating new folders 1146
Using Outlook Today 1146
Using and Customizing the Outlook Bar 1147
    Working with Outlook bar groups 1148
    Using the semisecret Outlook file manager 1149
Working with Views 1149
    Switching views 1150
    Types of Outlook views 1151
Adding and Editing Information Items 1151
    Working with items directly on a view 1152
    Deleting items from a view 1152
    Entering and editing items on forms 1152
    Working with forms 1153
    Assigning categories to items 1153
Customizing Views 1154
    Creating new and modified views 1154
    Defining views comprehensively 1155
    Adding and reorganizing fields in a view 1156
    Filtering a view 1157

Sorting a view 1158
Grouping related items 1158
Formatting choices 1158
Limitations on customizing views 1159
Outlook Housekeeping Secrets 1159
Using the Organize command 1159
Finding information 1160
Deleting items permanently 1161
Archiving Outlook information 1161
Compacting your Outlook folders 1162
Spell-Checking in Outlook 1162
Customizing Forms 1163
Opening a form for customizing 1163
Working with form pages in design mode 1164
Working with special design mode pages 1164
Displaying, hiding, and renaming pages 1164
Adding fields and controls to a custom page 1165
Adding default information to a custom form 1165
Saving forms 1165
Using Outlook forms 1167

Chapter 51: Managing E-mail in Outlook 1169

Setting Up Outlook for E-mail 1169
Setting up for Internet-only e-mail 1169
Setting up for networked e-mail services 1171
Working with Messages in Your Mail Folders 1173
Using AutoPreview to peek inside your messages 1174
Viewing mail with the Preview pane 1175
Selecting a view 1176
Flagging messages 1176
Managing your mail with the Rules Wizard 1176
Managing your junk mail 1177
Writing Messages 1177
Using special commands for messages 1178
Addressing a message 1179
Selecting an account for an Internet e-mail message 1182
Using message options 1182
Understanding message formats 1183
Using Word as your e-mail editor 1184
Including other information with e-mail messages 1185
Working with encoding formats for e-mail attachments 1186
Sending and Receiving Messages 1186
Working with the mail dialog box 1187
Sending an individual message 1188
Mailing on specific accounts 1188
Mail-handling options for networked computers 1188
Customizing Outlook's E-mail Settings 1188

Chapter 52: Managing Tasks, Schedules, Contacts, and Miscellany 1191

Keeping Up with Your Tasks 1191
  Viewing your tasks 1192
  Setting task-related options 1193
  Completing tasks 1193
  Entering tasks 1194
  Managing projects — you're mostly on your own 1195
  Delegating work 1196
  Responding to task requests 1196
Scheduling Appointments, Meetings, and Events 1197
  Navigating in the Calendar 1198
  Adding new calendar items 1198
  Moving calendar items 1199
  Scheduling meetings 1199
  Setting Calendar options 1200
Tracking Important People 1202
  Contacting your contacts 1202
  Working with Address Book 1203
  Speed dialing with Outlook 1204
Storing Miscellaneous Information 1205

Appendix 1207

Index 1213

End-User License Agreement 1248

CD-ROM Installation Instructions 1254

Part I
Office 2000 Power Secrets

Chapter 1: The Keys to the Office

Chapter 2: Mastering the Office Shortcut Bar

Chapter 3: User Interface Secrets

Chapter 4: Office Help Secrets

Chapter 5: Customizing Secrets: Office Your Way

Chapter 6: Office on the Internet

Chapter 1

The Keys to the Office

In This Chapter

- ▶ Hot enhancements throughout Office
- ▶ Efficient Office setup with the new Windows installer
- ▶ Start-up options for Office applications
- ▶ Where to find and change Office settings
- ▶ HTML as a universal format for Office documents
- ▶ Office goes international with multiple language support
- ▶ More resources for Office users

Keep your snoods on snugly, everyone. This chapter starts your intensive course in deep Office secrets. Here, you'll discover the benefits of the sweeping changes that apply to all of Office 2000 — and their pitfalls. You'll learn techniques for controlling the behavior of all Office applications. And you'll get connected to a host of sources of Office-related information and software.

Office 2000 Innovations

In addition to unleashing the obligatory flood of new specific features, Microsoft has made three fundamental changes that affect your work with every part of this gargantuan software suite. These are a new and perpetually active installation utility, the arrival of HTML as an alternative file format for Office documents, and big improvements in Office's support for different languages. The following brief descriptions of these new paradigms direct you to expanded coverage in other sections later in this chapter.

Better Office installation

Installing new software — and uninstalling it when it's no longer wanted — are hardly exciting tasks, but they're an unavoidable part of the computing experience. Office Setup has evolved into an extension of the Windows operating system that offers flexible installation options, lets you modify your Office configuration whenever you like, and automatically restores missing or damaged components. See the "Office Installation" section for details.

HTML as a universal document format

Office 2000 applications can store most documents as HTML files that preserve all the content and formatting you've added. As a result, people who don't have Office can view your documents in their Web browsers. For a full explanation, see "HTML Everywhere, Almost."

International intelligence

Office 2000 Premium includes major enhancements in features designed for viewing and editing documents in a variety of languages. The section called "The International Office" tells you what these features are and how to put them to use.

Office Versions

Microsoft makes Office 2000 available in more editions than any previous Office release. Most people pick between four distinct Office packages: Standard, Professional, Small Business, and Premium. In case you want to know how the software you bought compares to the other alternatives, here's a summary of the contents of each Office edition:

- **Office Standard.** Includes four of the five main Office applications—Word, Excel, PowerPoint, and Outlook—but omits Access.
- **Office Professional.** Includes all five main Office applications, plus Publisher for desktop publishing chores.
- **Office Small Business.** Includes Publisher but drops PowerPoint and Access.
- **Office Premium.** The complete package, it includes FrontPage (for creating and managing Web sites) and PhotoDraw (a sophisticated graphics editor) in addition to Publisher and all five core Office apps. Also provided is the MultiLanguage Pack, which lets you create and proof documents in a variety of languages.

While all of these four Office versions include the full-scale VBA programming environment, Microsoft markets a separate edition for serious software developers called, what do you know, Office Developer. Developer includes Office Premium plus a set of special programming tools and documentation, as summarized in Chapter 25.

Office Installation

With Office 2000, Microsoft introduces the Windows installer, a sophisticated utility designed to manage software installation and destined for integration into future versions of Windows. The first time you run the Setup program on the Office CD, it installs the Windows installer itself on your system. From that point on, the installer takes over.

Initially, the Windows installer's job is to copy needed files to your system and set up the correct keys in the Registry. But the installer has an ongoing role in maintaining the health of your Office installation: ensuring that all the necessary components are available and set up properly. And at any time, you can use the Windows installer to change the set of installed components or to remove Office altogether.

Secret

Don't be alarmed—but feel free to feel mildly peeved—if you see the Windows installer's little window when you start an Office application. The installer is just doing its job, checking to make sure that your Office files are in good order. (The initial message you see, "Preparing to install," is misleading, because no new installation steps are usually necessary.) The process does take a few seconds, which is something of a nuisance.

Installing and reinstalling Office

Office is most likely already set up on your system, and the installation process itself is straightforward, so I won't detail the steps required to install it. A few comments about installation may help you configure Office optimally, however, whether you're modifying an existing Office setup or installing Office for the first time.

The Windows installer for Office should run automatically whenever you put the first Office CD in the computer. If Office isn't yet installed, you'll be walked through the steps required. Remember, though, that you can run the installer whenever you want to examine or change your current configuration. If your CD is already in the drive, run the Installer from the Windows Control Panel by opening the Add/Remove Programs applet there. On the Install/Uninstall tab, select the item for Microsoft Office 2000. When you then click Add/Remove, the Windows installer starts up and displays the Office Setup screen in maintenance mode. To see how Office is currently installed, click the big Add or Remove Features button.

Whether you're installing Office initially or updating an existing setup, the installer's selecting features panel lets you see and change the parts of Office that are available on your computer, and where their files reside. To modify the setting for any component, click the graphic beside the component name and pick from the list of options for that component (see Figure 1-1). As shown in the illustration, the components are organized in hierachical groups. To work with components individually or as a group, you expand or collapse the hierarchy by clicking the *expand indicators*, the small square boxes that contain a plus or minus sign.

For fastest performance, pick the Run from My Computer choice, which copies the component's files to your hard disk. Selecting the Run from the CD option saves space on your hard disk but slows down file operation drastically. Also, it means you must have the Office CDs at the ready or the feature in question won't work. Use this option only for components that you use quite rarely, and for clip art and other content files that are just too large to store on your hard disk. The compromise choice, Installed on First Use, is discussed in the next section.

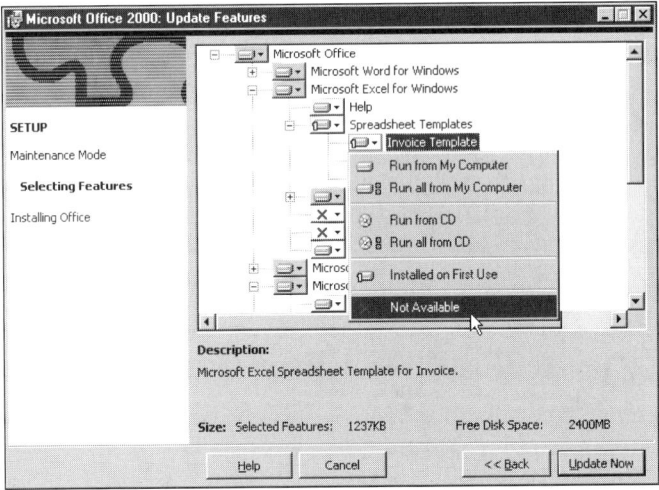

Figure 1-1: Use this panel in Office Setup to select features for installation and control how they're installed.

Using on-demand installation

Microsoft makes a big deal about the new Install on First Use option for installing Office components. Selecting this setting tells the Windows installer to wait before copying the necessary files to your hard disk until the first time you actually use the feature. As a result, you don't waste hard disk space on files you never need. But although the initial installation process runs a little faster, you lose more time than you gain when you do activate the feature. The installer has to start up and locate the needed files before it can copy them — and that assumes the Office disk is already in your CD-ROM drive. Bottom line advice: Select Install on First Use only for components that you're pretty sure that you're not going to use.

Manually repairing your Office installation

The Windows installer regularly verifies that your actual Office installation matches the configuration specified during the setup process. However, if you think something has gone wrong while you're working, you can instruct the installer to perform the examination whenever you like. In any Office applications, choose Help ⇨ Detect and Repair. Alternatively, start the Windows installer for Office and click Repair Office. With the latter method, you have the choice to reinstall Office in its entirety — avoid that option unless the less drastic repair procedure doesn't fix the problem.

Customizing the installation process in an organization

If you manage the installation of Office on other users' PCs, you can use a utility called the Custom Installation Wizard to modify Windows installer's default settings for the Office setup process. The Custom Installation Wizard is available in the Office Resource Kit (described in "Resources for Office Users" later in this chapter) and can also be downloaded from Microsoft's Web site. Among the installation options it lets you control are:

- The default path where Office 2000 files are installed on the user's hard disk
- Whether and how previous versions of Office applications are removed during setup
- The installation option for each Office 2000 component (in network installations, you can designate components that should be run from a server rather than the user's hard disk.)
- Custom Registry entries
- Shortcuts to be automatically created on the Start menu, on the Office Shortcut bar, and in other folders
- Outlook and Internet Explorer configuration options

Caution

One thing you can't do with the wizard is to specify different folders for different Office components on a user's computer. If your PC doesn't have enough space in a single disk volume to hold Office in its entirety, you must either delete other files, get a larger hard disk, or settle for fewer Office components.

Command Line Options for Starting Office Apps

Most Office applications let you control aspects of their behavior by entering optional *switches* on the command line when you start them. You can find tips on the specific switches available for each application in the relevant section of this book. In this section, I discuss the technique you need to put these switches to work.

Maybe you're trying to forget, but Windows still lets you start applications from the command prompt (also known as the "DOS box" in Windows 95/98). That means you can use the command line switches by typing them at the prompt after the name of the application, as in this example:

```
winword /a /n
```

But most people don't routinely start programs from the command prompt. To use these switches within Windows proper, type them into the Properties box for a shortcut to the application. To access the Properties box, right-click the shortcut you want to modify in My Computer or Explorer or on the Desktop. You can also right-click the button for an Office application on the Office Shortcut bar or, in Windows 98, a taskbar toolbar. From the shortcut menu, choose Properties and switch to the Shortcut tab in the resulting dialog box. As shown in Figure 1-2, the switches go on the line labeled Target, right after the program name and within the quotation marks.

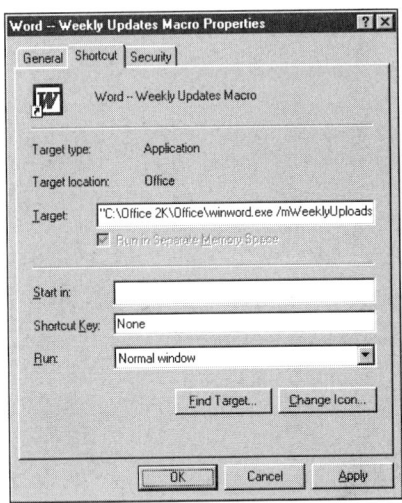

Figure 1-2: The Properties dialog box for a Word shortcut in Windows shows a command line switch that starts the macro named WeeklyUploads entered on Target line.

If you plan to use a particular command line switch every time you start the application, you can enter it in the existing shortcut for the program. More than likely, however, you'll want to use the switch only occasionally. In this case, make a copy of the original shortcut, naming it something descriptive (such as "Word — Weekly Uploads Macro"). After adding the switch to the new shortcut's Properties dialog box, you have instant access to Word with or without the switch, depending on which shortcut you use to start the program.

Setting Office Options

In every Office application, the Tools ⇨ Options dialog box is the central control panel for controlling a myriad of settings that govern all facets of the program's operations. Tabbed dialog boxes are commonplace in Windows, but Word's Options box takes the concept to an extreme with its 10 tabs. Elsewhere in Office, the Options dialog box isn't quite so overloaded — Figure 1-3 shows Access's version.

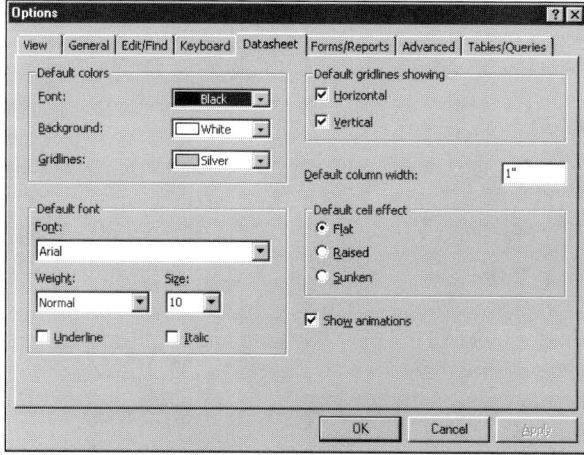

Figure 1-3: The Datasheet tab of Access's Tools ⇨ Options dialog box.

Although I touch on many of the available options in the chapters on the specific Office applications, I don't go through them exhaustively — many are self-explanatory, and many others are useful to relatively few people. For now, I simply recommend that you set aside a few minutes to acquaint yourself with how the Options dialog box is organized in each application and what it has to offer. Page through all the tabs, using the What's This help tool to explain any choices whose functions aren't clear.

HTML Everywhere, Almost

Office documents complete with all of their formatting can now be saved as HTML files, the kind used to define Web pages. By default, Office continues to store documents on disk in its proprietary file formats. However, the HTML option gives you an alternative that permits easier exchange of information with others, at least in theory. Because almost everyone has a Web browser, storing documents in HTML format provides nearly universal access to the document content, even for users who don't have their own copies of Office.

Caution

Before you get too excited about the using HTML as a universal file format, take stock of some real-world limitations. While the standard version of HTML is certainly gaining better formatting features, it gives you much less control over a document's looks than you have in, say, Word (by the way, Chapter 14 provides background on HTML). So when Microsoft tells you that you can save Office documents as HTML files, this doesn't mean that those documents will look the same when you open them in a browser.

What Microsoft has done is add special new features to HTML that provide the precise control over layout elements needed to reproduce Office documents faithfully. These HTML features enable Office programs to store and retrieve documents with their formatting intact. But browsers don't understand the new HTML codes all that well. Internet Explorer 5 — the browser that comes with Office — can display most Office documents pretty faithfully, but even IE5 falls down in places. Netscape Navigator and older versions of IE have more trouble.

But although HTML doesn't actually make Office documents as "universally viewable" as Microsoft claims, it does enable anyone with a browser to see much of their content. That's saying a lot, given the complexity of Office documents and their native file formats.

Office 2000 also beefs up tools for creating and editing documents intended for display as Web pages. Of course, the inclusion of FrontPage in the Professional version is one big step in support of Web site developers. Word and Access let you apply to their documents the same prefab design themes available in FrontPage. Part IV delves deeply into Web page development with Office.

The International Office

Office has long been available in separate versions for different languages. But Office 2000 vastly improves support for international use, offering components with the standard product for over 80 languages. This relieves headaches for software managers in global organizations, and it's also a boon for individuals who need or want to communicate in more than one language.

Microsoft has completely separated Office 2000's core software functions from the language-specific portions of the code, which plug into the core as needed. Because Office Premium comes complete with these plug-in language components, you don't need to buy anything when you want to work in another language, or even if you want to switch languages in which Office displays its menus and Help system. Figure 1-4 shows how Word looks in Chinese.

Office 2000's support for multiple languages includes the following elements:

- Compatibility with Unicode, a standard system for encoding language characters
- Fonts for languages such as Chinese and Arabic that don't use European alphabets, and new multilanguage versions of commonly used fonts such as Arial, Courier New, Garamond, and Times New Roman. These standard fonts now include the Euro currency symbol, too (see Chapter 7 to learn how to use it in your documents).
- Proofing tools such as spelling and grammar checkers and supporting dictionaries, thesauri, AutoCorrect lists, and hyphenation algorithms
- Templates and wizards customized for the supported languages
- Utilities for editing in and converting between various Asian languages
- Components for displaying the user interface in any supported language

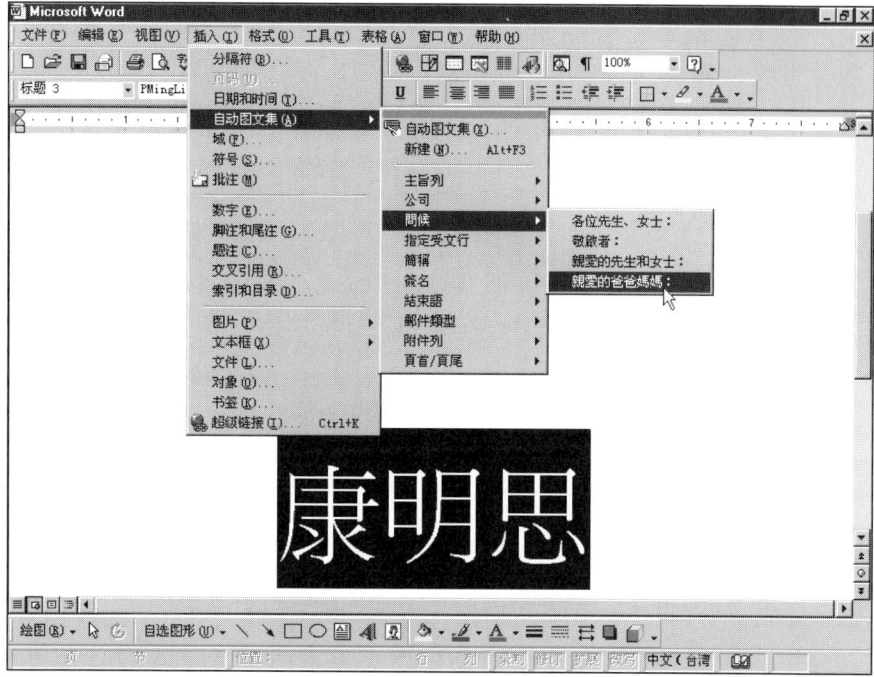

Figure 1-4: Word as it appears with the user interface set to display simplified Chinese.

The Office applications include commands unique to particular languages; the appropriate commands appear automatically on menus and dialog boxes when you enable a given language. As you'd expect, Word has the most support for multiple languages among the Office applications, and it is especially rich in language-specific commands. Even more impressively, Word is designed to automatically figure out which language you're typing in — and this feature usually works.

However, Office is still available in *localized* versions (a localized version is one version designed explicitly for a specific language and the date, time, and currency notation in use at a particular locale). That's because the language components provided with English version of Office don't cover every Office feature. Also, current versions of Windows won't let you use all the language features available in Office 2000, as the next section discusses.

Limitations in current versions of Windows

An important caveat: You will be able to take full advantage of the capability to switch languages freely only by running Windows 2000 — which isn't available as of this writing. Other versions of Windows set some limits. Until you install Windows 2000, then, you may need a localized version of Windows, Office, or both to work with some languages.

One obvious sore spot is in support for left-to-right languages such as Farsi, Arabic, and Hebrew. Localized versions of Windows are available for at least some of these languages, and with them, Office 2000 supports left-to-right editing. However, you can't use these languages with the English versions of Windows 95, 98, or NT 4.0. You may run into limitations with other languages as well, but as Figure 1-4 proves I've been able to display the Office user interface in Chinese on my English version of Windows NT.

Understanding the role of Internet Explorer 5

Office's capability to display the user interface in different languages depends partly on the presence of components that are part of IE5. (Might Microsoft have set things up this way to ensure that you use their browser? Ah, well, that's a discussion for another time.) At any rate, you must at least do a minimum installation of IE5 if the languages in question require different code pages. All Western European languages use the same code page, so IE5 isn't required for switching between them.

Caution

With IE5 installed, Active Desktop must be turned *off* in Windows if you want to be able to switch between different languages for the Office user interface. With Active Desktop on, you can only see the user interface in the language of your version of Windows.

Installing the MultiLanguage Pack

Office's language-related plug-in components are packaged as the MultiLanguage Pack on a separate set of CDs. To activate the capability to change language settings, install the MultiLanguage Pack by running its own Setup program. Once you've installed the pack, the main Windows installer takes over, installing any needed components when you change language settings in Office. Note that your Office CDs don't include files for every supported language — you may need to download files from Microsoft's Web site or order supplemental disks.

Secret

Language-specific components that have the same filename in every language are installed in folders named according to Microsoft's locale ID number for the language in question. If you're wondering why you have those folders named 1033, it's because 1033 is the locale ID number for U.S. English. The Help system includes a listing of the locale IDs for the languages Office supports.

If you no longer need to work in a given language, you should remove its files to free up space on your hard disk. To do so, rerun the MultiLanguage Pack's Setup program or use the Control Panel's Add/Remove Programs applet to get things started. When the Installer's dialog box appears, click Add or Remove Features to get to the list of installed languages, and set the ones you don't want any more to Not Available.

Turning on language-related features

The control panel for Office's language-related features is the Microsoft Office Language Settings dialog box, accessible in Windows via the Start ➪ Programs ➪ Office Tools folder. As shown in Figure 1-5, the box has two tabs, User Interface and Enabled Languages.

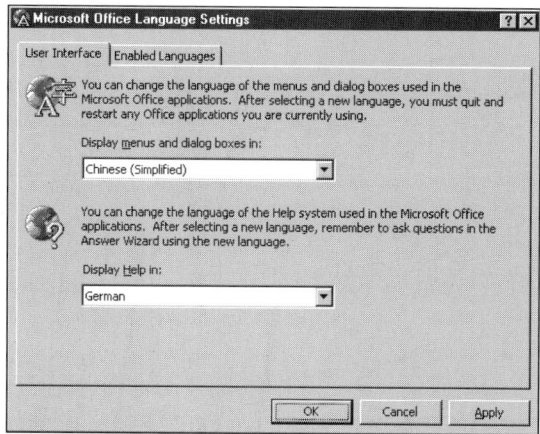

Figure 1-5: Control Office's language settings in this dialog box.

The settings on the User Interface tab determine the language in which Office displays text on menus and in dialog boxes, and which it uses for the Help system. You won't see this tab until you've actually installed language-specific user interface components from the MultiLanguage Pack, and the only choices offered are those of the installed languages.

Use the Enabled Languages tab to specify the languages in which you want to edit documents. You can have a field day here—all languages supported by Office are shown, whether or not you've installed them on your system. However, selecting languages you're not actually going to use has a downside: Commands unique to each selected language appear on the menus and dialog boxes in your Office apps, where they serve only to distract if you're not actually using that language.

Turning on keyboard support for other languages in Windows

All Windows versions let you switch between different languages at the operating system level. When you switch to a different *locale* (language), Windows notifies running applications of the change. Of course, many applications pay no attention, but Office adjusts itself accordingly. The locale setting also determines the layout of your keyboard (that is, the character Windows "sees" when you press each key). Although Windows provides a default keyboard layout for each locale, you can choose any layout you like for any locale. Note, however, that at least in Windows 95, 98, and NT 4, the list of available locales doesn't match the languages supported by Office 2000.

To add new locales to your Windows configuration, use the Keyboard applet in the Control Panel. Switch to the Input Locales tab and click Add, selecting a new locale from the lengthy list that presents itself. The "default properties" referred to in the Add dialog box simply refers to the keyboard layout associated with the locale. You can associate any locale with any available layout.

Adding support for Greek and Eastern European languages in Windows 95/98

If you're running Windows 95 and 98 and want to compose documents in Russian, Polish, Bulgarian, or a smattering of other languages — including Greek — you must install the Multilanguage Support component. Open the Control Panel, run the Add/Remove Programs applet, and switch to the Windows Setup tab. Check the Multilanguage Support box, and then click Details to select the specific languages you want to work with.

Using other languages in your documents

Once you've installed and enabled the language features in Windows and Office, you can start using them to view and edit documents. You don't have to do anything special to view documents — just open them in the appropriate Office application. Entering new information in a different language requires more work, however.

Switching locales

To access the characters of another language from your keyboard, switch to its locale in Windows. When you've installed more than one locale, an indicator appears in the taskbar. As shown in Figure 1-6, you can switch to another locale by clicking the indicator and picking the locale you want from the little menu. You can also use the keyboard shortcuts selected in the Control Panel Keyboard applet to switch locales.

Figure 1-6: Selecting a locale via the Windows taskbar.

Editing with alternative keyboard layouts

Often, the language for the active locale offers more characters than fit on the standard and shifted keys — this is the norm for European languages with accented characters. In such cases, you typically enter accented characters by pressing a two-key sequence starting with the accent key. In some layouts, still more characters are available when you hold down the right Alt key.

Using the Visual Keyboard utility

Included in the MultiLanguage Pack, the Visual Keyboard utility (see Figure 1-7) lets you see the keyboard layout for the locale that's currently active in Windows. Install Visual Keyboard by running the appropriate setup program located in the NT or Win9*x* subfolder in the Extras\Onscreen folder of the MultiLanguage Pack CD. In the prerelease version of Office, the installation routine doesn't seem to create a Start menu shortcut for Visual Keyboard, so you must make the shortcut yourself. (Hint: the setup routine places the executable program, Vkbd.exe, in the System folder of Windows).

Figure 1-7: Run the Visual Keyboard utility to see which keys you have to type to enter characters available in the active keyboard layout.

If you're working with a Windows keyboard layout that differs from the one shown on your real-life keyboard, Visual Keyboard shows you which key you must type to enter any given character into your document. Pressing Shift or clicking the on-screen Shift key shows the shifted version of the character set. To see characters that must be entered via a two-key sequence, press or click the key that starts the sequence (as shown in Figure 1-7, such keys appear in white on Visual Keyboard).

If you like, you can use the mouse to copy characters from Visual Keyboard to the clipboard. As you click characters on the keyboard graphic, they move to the utility's Editbox. Display the Editbox by choosing Show Editbox from Visual Keyboard's shortcut (right-click) menu. When you've accumulated the characters you want to enter in a document, click the key labeled Copy—it's where Enter should be—or choose Copy from the shortcut menu.

Editing documents in Asian languages

Although turning on support for an Asian language lets you view documents created in that language, you can't enter new ideographic characters directly. Instead, you need a special tool called an Input Method Editor (IME). Versions of Windows localized for a given language include the corresponding IME, or course, but only the one for that language. However, Office's Multilanguage Pack comes with limited IMEs (called global IMEs) for Japanese, Korean, and Simplified and Traditional Chinese, and these work in the English version of Office. Unfortunately, the global IMEs only work with Word and Outlook — you still need a localized version of the operating system if you want to enter and edit text in other applications.

Printing documents created in multiple languages

Complications can arise if you print documents created for different languages and locales. Chapter 11 discusses some of the potential problems and their solutions.

Understanding Unicode

The text-handling features of Office have been redesigned for Unicode, an international standard for numerically encoding the characters used in major languages. As you can see by taking a look at the Windows Character Map utility, conventional Windows fonts can only hold about 200 different characters. By contrast, Unicode can handle more than 65,000 different characters, and code numbers have already been assigned to about 40,000 letters, numerals, ideograms, punctuation marks, and other squiggles.

You won't see many fonts containing all possible characters — most Unicode fonts include one or more of the *subsets* that Unicode defines for specific languages and other purposes. The real point is that Unicode enables fonts and applications throughout the world to use the same code number for each character. This means that text prepared in any major language can be displayed accurately by other applications and on other computers, as long as the necessary fonts are installed.

About the huge Unicode font included with Office

Office 2000 does come with a complete 40,000-character-or-so Unicode font called Arial Unicode MS. You can use it to satisfy your curiosity about the vast range of characters people use to communicate their thoughts in writing. Practically speaking, though, its only value is in displaying multilanguage text in Unicode-aware applications that don't support font changes. For example, Access only allows one font in each database table. If you happen to have an Access table that lists translations for words for many languages, you need a Unicode font containing all the characters to display the table accurately.

The Arial Unicode MS font is located in the Windows\Fonts folder on the Office installation CD. You can install it from there using the Control Panel Fonts applet, or by starting the Windows installer for Office and selecting it under Office Tools ⇨ International Support. Just be aware that this font is huge — 23MB.

Secret

By the way, Word's Insert ➪ Symbol dialog box and the Windows Character Map utility in Windows 98 and NT both recognize Unicode fonts. When you select a Unicode font, use the Subset box to choose the range of characters you want to see, as illustrated in Figure 1-8.

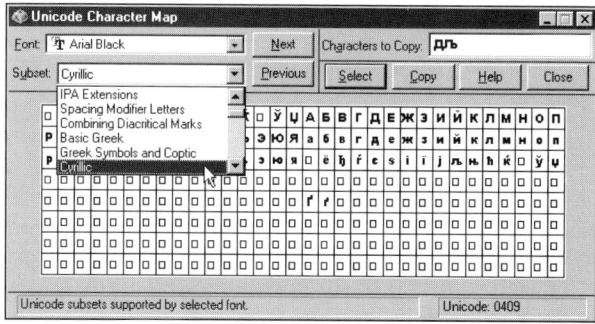

Figure 1-8: Using the Character Map utility to select and view a subset of Unicode characters.

Other Unicode fonts

Office 2000 also includes a number of Unicode updates for some fonts that you most likely already have on your system. These *big fonts* don't contain all the Unicode characters — not by a long shot — but they do offer multiple character sets covering many non-English languages. Big fonts included with Office include Arial, Arial Black, Arial Bold, Arial Narrow, Bookman Old Style, Courier New, Garamond, Impact, Tahoma, Times New Roman, Trebuchet, and Verdana.

Resources for Office Users

If you can't find the information you need in this book or in the Office Help system, you can turn to many other sources of Office lore.

About the Office Resource Kit

Microsoft's Office Resource Kit (ORK) comprises a huge collection of information about administering Office 2000 in organizations plus a bunch of supporting software tools. Although Microsoft explicitly intends the ORK for managers, not lowly "end users," the kit contains loads of details on topics such as custom configuration and file formats. The ORK is available as a separate product on its own CD, and you can buy the printed documentation as well. But you may also be able to download ORK files from Microsoft's Web site.

Other resources

Microsoft's Web site is stuffed to the gills with material on Office. You can read detailed descriptions of Office technologies, get advanced instruction on VBA programming and database development, find bug reports and answers to technical questions, and download additional templates, sample documents, utilities, and multimedia content. The quickest way to Microsoft's Office Web site is via the Help ⇨ Office on the Web command.

If you like your information in bite-sized chunks, consider subscribing to the PC World tip service at `www.tipworld.com`. You receive a daily tip on Office by e-mail. Most of the tips are actually pretty elementary, but they do remind you of useful features you might not use regularly, and occasionally you get a real Secret. Another source of Office tips and trivia is Woody Leonhard's Woody's Office Watch, a free weekly newsletter via e-mail (subscribe at `www.mcc.com.au/wow/`). And look for updates to this book as well as brand new secrets on my own modest Web site (`www.seldenhouse.com/officesecrets/`).

Conclusion

Microsoft Office 2000 Secrets is just warming up, but already you've been exposed to key details that affect the way all Office applications work. With Office installed on your machine to your specifications, and with an understanding of its suite-wide support for HTML and multiple languages, you've laid the foundation for your work with the individual components of this massive software edifice.

Chapter 2

Mastering the Office Shortcut Bar

In This Chapter

- Finding the Shortcut bar's hidden strengths
- Configuring the Shortcut bar to your preferences
- Customizing the Shortcut bar with new toolbars and buttons
- Using the Shortcut bar for immediate access to your desktop

The Office Shortcut bar is a simple tool, but it has some hidden strengths — and a few pitfalls — that you may not discover on casual use. Think of the Shortcut bar as an auxiliary Windows taskbar with complementary features. The taskbar displays the applications you're currently running, whereas the Shortcut bar gives you a one-click way to start programs in the first place — or to open documents or folders. For me, the Shortcut bar's Desktop toolbar is reason enough to install and use the Shortcut bar — see "Fast access to the Windows desktop" toward the end of this chapter for details.

Office Setup installs the Shortcut bar right along with the rest of Office. It may place a shortcut in the StartUp folder so that the Shortcut bar loads automatically whenever you start Windows. If you choose not to load the Shortcut bar automatically, you can run it when you please — you can find the Shortcut bar in the Microsoft Office Tools menu on the Start menu. If the Shortcut bar doesn't start automatically, or if you've turned it off, you can run it yourself by choosing Start ➪ Programs ➪ Microsoft Office Tools ➪ Microsoft Office Shortcut Bar.

Using the Shortcut Bar

At first blush, you might think that the capabilities of the Shortcut bar are devoted specifically to Office. After all, its default buttons trigger Office-related tasks: creating and opening Office documents, sending e-mail messages, scheduling appointments, writing notes, and making journal entries in Outlook.

But while the Shortcut bar works well with Office, it's actually a general-purpose Windows utility. Its essential functions duplicate those of the Start menu — both tools let you quickly access any folder, application, or document.

The Shortcut bar has some real advantages over the Start menu. For one thing, buttons that actually do something are right there — you don't have to click the Start button first. Two more important benefits: First, items on the Shortcut bar can be organized in any order you find helpful, and second, you can access their properties with a right-click, just as if you were working with the items on the desktop or in an Explorer window.

Shape-shifting the Shortcut bar

Like all other Office toolbars, the Shortcut bar can take two forms: floating in its own separate window that you can resize and drag anywhere on the screen, or docked in a stationary strip against any edge of the screen.

To move the Shortcut bar around on the screen, drag it using any part of the background as the handle. As you do, you see an outline of the shape and location the Shortcut bar would adopt if you parked it wherever you have dragged it so far. When you bring it close to a screen edge, it automatically flattens out into a narrow strip along that edge. Release the mouse button, and the Shortcut bar is docked.

Here's the fastest way to switch the Shortcut bar back and forth between the docked and floating configurations: Double-click the title bar (see Figure 2-1). No matter where you move the bar as a floating window, this technique docks it to the edge of the screen where it was before (and vice versa).

Geography of the Shortcut bar

Figure 2-1 illustrates the Shortcut bar and its various components.

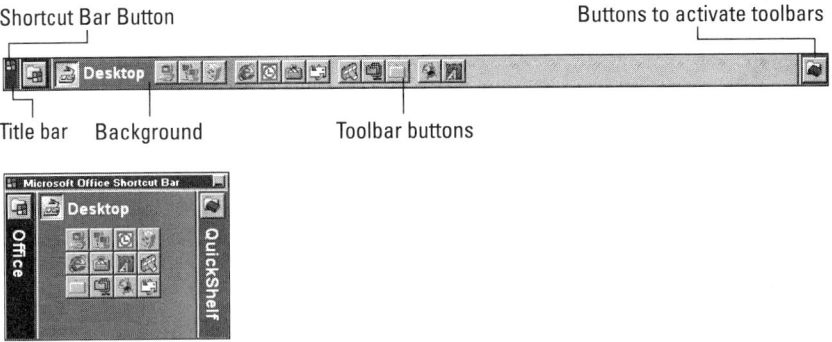

Figure 2-1: The Microsoft Office Shortcut bar is shown in both of its alternate configurations: floating and docked.

Though the Shortcut bar itself functions as a toolbar, Microsoft doesn't refer to it that way. Instead, it wants you to think of the Shortcut bar as a sort of shell containing a series of subsidiary toolbars. Only one toolbar's buttons are visible at a time. This active toolbar occupies the center of the Shortcut bar, while the other toolbars, if any, are condensed into narrow strips or squares at either side.

The first time you use it, the Shortcut bar contains only one toolbar, called Office. Several other toolbars come with the program, and you can create new toolbars of your own (see "Customizing the Shortcut Bar" later in the chapter). To show these other toolbars on the Shortcut bar, right-click the Shortcut bar background and select them from the list that appears. The little icon at the top left of the Shortcut bar is called simply the Shortcut Bar button. Click the Shortcut Bar button to display a menu offering help (Contents and Index) and various other options. Double-click the button to exit the Shortcut bar.

Like most windows, the Shortcut bar has a title bar. The title bar is obvious when the Shortcut bar floats in a separate window. When it's docked, though, the title bar is an inconspicuous strip of color next to the Shortcut Bar button at the top or left end of the Shortcut bar.

The background, of course, is any part of the Shortcut bar that doesn't contain a button. Typically, each toolbar has a different color background. Double-clicking the background displays the Customize dialog box, whereas right-clicking it brings up a shortcut menu.

Positioning the Shortcut bar

Usually, the best location for the Shortcut bar is docked at the top or bottom of your screen, opposite the Windows taskbar. Here's why: Most monitors are wider than they are tall, so docking the Shortcut bar horizontally provides room for more buttons.

Turning on Auto Hide

The Shortcut bar takes up room on your screen, so take advantage of the Auto Hide feature. This works just as it does with the Windows taskbar: With Auto Hide on, and with the Shortcut bar docked, the bar is invisible until the mouse pointer touches the edge of the screen where the bar is docked. As soon as you move the pointer away from the Shortcut bar, it disappears again.

Although there's an Auto Hide option on the View tab of the Shortcut bar's Customize dialog box, the fastest way to turn Auto Hide on is by clicking the Shortcut Bar button and choosing Auto Hide from the pop-up menu.

Windows won't let you place two toolbars with Auto Hide enabled — such as the taskbar and the Shortcut bar — along the same edge of the screen.

Placing the Shortcut bar in the title bar area

Secret

For fast access to the Shortcut bar, an alternative to Auto Hide is to glue the Shortcut bar to the top of the screen as a narrow strip as tall as a standard title bar. With this option on, the Shortcut bar is always visible and immediately available, without even the brief delay that occurs when you un–Auto Hide it. Figure 2-2 shows the Shortcut bar configured this way on top of Word.

To park the Shortcut bar in the title bar area, first dock it along the top of the screen. Double-click the background to display the Customize dialog box, and in the View tab, check the box Auto Fit into Title Bar Area.

Caution

This Shortcut bar configuration has some disadvantages besides its affront to screen aesthetics. The icons are smaller and harder to see. Of course, you can't see the title of the current document — in fact, depending on how many buttons the Shortcut bar contains, it may even obscure the name of the application. However, Microsoft has fixed a problem with Office 97's version of this Auto Fit option: If you've docked the Windows taskbar at the top of the screen as well, the Shortcut bar now gets out of the way when you display the taskbar. (This only works if the taskbar is set to Auto Hide.)

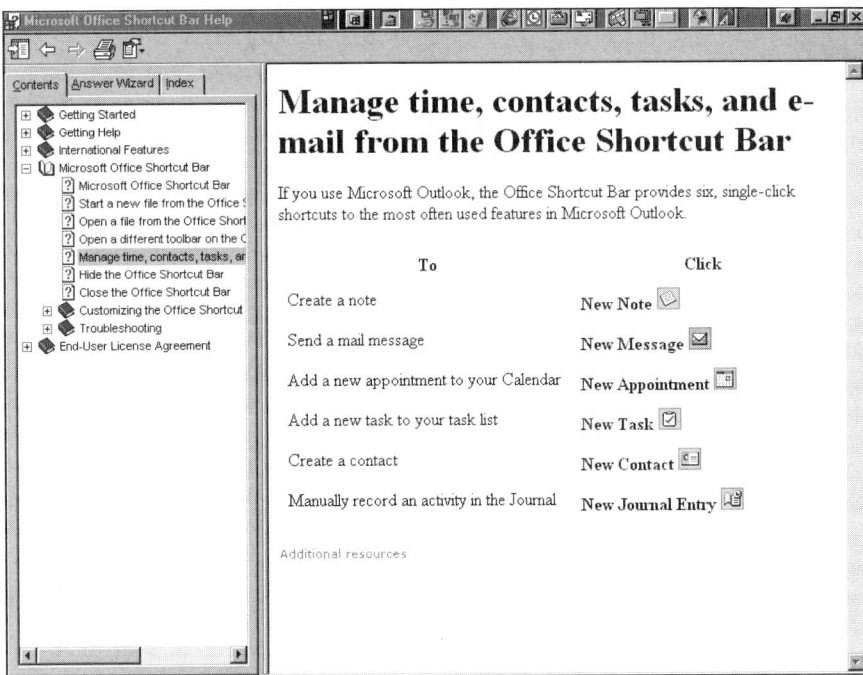

Figure 2-2: The Shortcut bar docked in the title bar area.

One other note: Don't be misled by the term "title bar area" for this Shortcut bar placement. The Shortcut bar is attached to the top of your screen rather than to the title bar, remaining there if you move all application windows down, or even if no windows are visible.

Accessing the Shortcut bar

The Shortcut bar is a mouse-dependent tool, more so than the Windows taskbar. Again, if the Shortcut bar is docked with Auto Hide enabled, display it by moving the mouse to that edge of the screen. If the Shortcut bar is floating, or if you've hidden it via the Minimize command on the Shortcut Bar button's menu, display it via the Windows taskbar.

Office provides no specific keyboard shortcut to display the bar when it's not already visible. The Shortcut Bar icon does appear in the box you see in the middle of the screen when you press Alt+Tab, the Windows keyboard shortcut for switching tasks. However, this only works when the Shortcut bar is configured as a floating window.

The one sure way to get to the Shortcut bar using the keyboard is to assign it a keyboard shortcut in Windows: Using My Computer or Explorer, navigate to the Start Menu\Programs\StartUp folder and locate the Shortcut Bar shortcut (good grief, what terminology — I'm talking about the icon labeled Microsoft Office Shortcut Bar). Right-click it and choose Properties, and then select the (what else?) Shortcut tab. Now, at Shortcut Key, press the keys for the keyboard shortcut you want to use to activate and display the Shortcut bar.

But why bother? Even when you can switch to the Shortcut bar using the keyboard, it doesn't do you much good. The problem is that you can't activate the Shortcut bar's buttons via the keyboard.

Accessing buttons you can't see

You can stop looking for a secret way to scroll through the buttons on the Shortcut bar when it's docked — there isn't any. If a toolbar's buttons don't all fit on the screen, the ones that you can't see are simply inaccessible. To get to them, you would have to haul the Shortcut bar out into the middle of the screen. But that's a lot of work for a "shortcut."

The take-home message here: Keep your toolbars short and simple (see "Customizing the Shortcut Bar" later in this chapter).

Refreshing a toolbar to bring the buttons up to date

Secret

Each time you start the Shortcut bar, it reconstructs its toolbars. That way, buttons representing folders and documents reflect any additions, deletions, or name changes made since the last time you ran the Shortcut bar, in case you closed it before shutting down Windows. Should the need arise, you can have the Shortcut bar perform this same reconstruction process at your command.

The Shortcut bar is usually able to keep up with such changes while it is running. For example, if you have added the Desktop toolbar to the Shortcut bar, saving a new file onto the Windows desktop immediately produces a corresponding button on that Desktop toolbar.

Occasionally, however, the Shortcut bar gets out of sync with the underlying documents and folders. In my experience, and for no reason I've been able to uncover, the icons on the buttons sometimes get replaced by question marks. Apparently, the Shortcut bar has somehow lost track of those files. If something like this ever happens to you, right-click the Shortcut bar background and choose Refresh Icons.

Customizing the Shortcut Bar

You can control most aspects of the Shortcut bar's layout and function directly with the mouse. For some customization tasks, you need the Customize dialog box, shown in Figure 2-3. The quickest way to display it is by double-clicking anywhere on the Shortcut bar background (you can also click the Shortcut Bar button or right-click the background, choosing Customize from either pop-up menu).

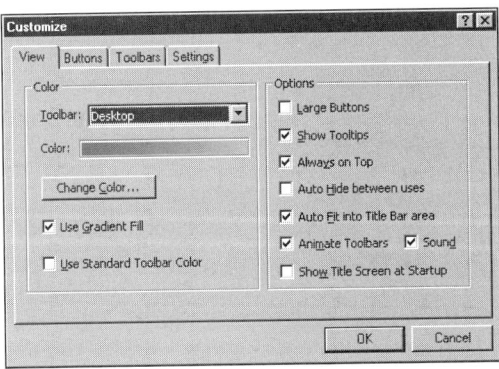

Figure 2-3: The Shortcut bar's Customize dialog box gives you control.

Remember that you must display a toolbar to see and use it on the Shortcut bar. If the toolbar you want isn't visible, right-click the background and select it on the resulting menu.

Creating new toolbars

To create a brand-new toolbar of your own, display the Customize dialog box, select the Toolbars tab, and choose Add Toolbar. In the next dialog box (see Figure 2-4), decide whether you want to create a new folder for this toolbar or add a toolbar representing a folder that already exists on your system. If you create a new folder, you need to type in its name. For an existing folder, choose Browse and select the folder in the usual Windows way.

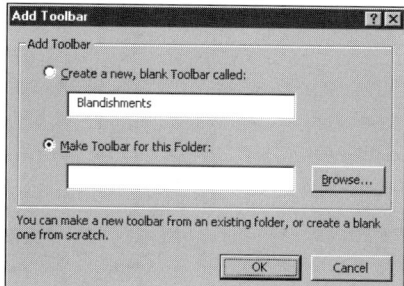

Figure 2-4: Use this dialog box to add a new toolbar to the Shortcut bar.

The folders for toolbars that you create from scratch, as well as for built-in toolbars such as Office, are stored in the Shortcut Bar folder. (The path is Windows\Application Data\Microsoft\Office\Shortcut Bar, and it can't be easily changed.)

Reordering toolbars

To change the order of the toolbars on the Shortcut bar, open the Customize dialog box, switch to the Toolbars tab, and use the arrow buttons to move a selected toolbar up or down in the list.

Adding new buttons to a toolbar

The fastest way to add buttons to a toolbar is to drag them there from My Computer or Explorer. You can't directly drag items such as disks and system folders (such as Control Panel or Printers) from the My Computer folder or from networked computers. Of course, the way to add a button for any of these items is to create a Windows shortcut for it first, and then drag the shortcut to the Shortcut bar.

By the way, the Shortcut bar comes with buttons for the Control Panel and Printers folders — they're just hidden. See the next section.

Hiding and displaying toolbar buttons

Secret

Except for the Office toolbar, each toolbar initially displays a button for every file (document, application, or shortcut) in that toolbar's folder. If a toolbar is too cluttered with buttons, you can hide the ones you don't need at present. To hide a button, right-click it and choose Hide Button (hiding buttons is different from deleting them — see "Deleting buttons" later in this chapter).

To display hidden buttons, you need the Customize dialog box. Select the Buttons tab, be sure the correct toolbar is selected in the Toolbar list, and then check the box for each button you want to display in the list at Show These Files as Buttons.

Moving toolbar buttons and adding space between them

The fastest way to change the order of the buttons on a toolbar is to hold down Alt while you drag each button to its new location. To add empty space between a pair of buttons, drag the button on the right farther to the right, again while holding down Alt. You can close up the space again by dragging it back to the left. You can accomplish the same tasks with the Buttons tab of the Customize dialog box, but why bother with it?

Renaming buttons and toolbars

Secret

The quick way to rename the buttons on the Shortcut bar: Right-click the button and choose Rename. Be forewarned, however, that renaming a button renames the underlying file, folder, or shortcut, too. You can rename an entire toolbar using the same technique. Just be sure to right-click the toolbar's button, given that right-clicking elsewhere on the toolbar won't work. Alternatively, you can rename the toolbar in the Toolbars tab of the Customize dialog box.

If you prefer to do things the slow way, you can go to the Customize dialog box and rename buttons or toolbars there.

Deleting toolbars

To delete an entire toolbar, open the Customize dialog box and switch to the Toolbars tab. Select the doomed toolbar and click Remove.

Restoring deleted toolbars

If you decide that you want to revive a toolbar that you've previously deleted, add it again with the technique detailed in "Creating new toolbars" earlier in this section. If you had created the deleted toolbar from scratch by choosing

Create a New, Blank Toolbar in the Add Toolbar dialog box, you can choose this same option. Then type in the name of the toolbar you previously deleted, spelled exactly as it had been before. When the Shortcut bar recognizes your entry as an old toolbar, you get a message asking if you want to restore it.

Alternatively, you can use the Make Toolbar for This Folder choice in the Add Toolbar dialog box. With this approach, you click Browse and navigate to the folder for the dormant toolbar — you'll find it buried in the Windows\Application Data\Microsoft\Office\Shortcut Bar folder.

Caution

You can't revive the deleted default toolbars such as Office, Favorites, Programs, Accessories, and Desktop. Although the Shortcut bar (sometimes) enables you to add your own toolbars by those names, they don't contain the buttons of the originals. The only way to restore the original toolbars is to reinstall the Shortcut bar. Reinstalling doesn't delete any custom toolbars you've created.

Deleting buttons

Caution

Deleting a toolbar button deletes the underlying file, folder, or shortcut and moves it to the Recycle Bin. Office warns you that this will happen and gives you a chance to cancel the operation, but you can still get into trouble if you're not sure whether you're working with a shortcut or the document it represents.

I recommend that you delete the items that buttons refer to via My Computer or Explorer instead. The Shortcut bar automatically detects that they're gone and removes the buttons. (If you insist on deleting buttons via the Shortcut bar, do so on the Buttons tab of the Customize dialog box.)

Changing Shortcut bar button icons

To change the icons shown on a Shortcut bar toolbar button, you must change the icon assigned in Windows to the underlying program, document, folder, or shortcut. You can do this from the Shortcut bar itself: Right-click the button whose icon you want to change and choose Properties from the shortcut menu. In the standard Windows Properties dialog box that appears, switch to the Shortcut tab and choose Change icon.

Secret

If you're daring, you can also change the icons for the special Shortcut bar buttons that identify and activate the various toolbars. These include the Desktop, Programs, Program Group, and Folder icons used by Windows, as well as the Shortcut Bar icons for the Office and Quickshelf toolbars.

The icons for the Office and Quickshelf toolbars are stored in the Shortcut bar program file itself, so you must edit these icons there. First, exit the Shortcut bar and make a backup copy of the program file, called

MSOFFICE.EXE, just in case something goes wrong. Using your icon editor, open the MSOFFICE.EXE file, locate the icons you want to change, and get artistic. When you save the modified MSOFFICE.EXE file and restart the Shortcut bar, you should see your new icons.

Because Shortcut bar icons can be displayed at several sizes, the program file contains several different versions of its icons. If you want to see your custom icons appear whether you're using the large or normal icons and whether or not you've placed the Shortcut bar in the title area, you must edit all the versions.

Shortcut Bar Tips

Here are some miscellaneous tips on using the Shortcut bar.

Fast access to the Windows desktop

In theory, the Windows desktop is a nice place to store all kinds of stuff that you use regularly: folders, disk drives, documents, and applications. The problem is, the desktop is inaccessible when you're doing anything productive with Windows (that is, when you're running any software).

Windows gurus have come up with tricks for making the desktop available from the taskbar, without having to resort to Minimize All Windows. See Livingston and Straub's *Windows 95 Secrets* or *Windows 98 Secrets* (IDG Books Worldwide, Inc.), if you're interested. But the Shortcut bar solves the problem much more elegantly. As soon as you turn on the built-in Desktop toolbar (as described under "Geography of the Shortcut Bar" earlier in this chapter), all the items on the desktop appear as buttons on the Shortcut bar for immediate, one-click access. As far as I'm concerned, this is enough to justify using the Shortcut bar.

Don't use the Programs toolbar

On the other hand, the prefab Programs toolbar isn't so helpful. It wastes space, simply duplicating the function of the Programs menu accessible via the Windows Start button. The only good thing you can say for this toolbar is that unlike the Start menu, the toolbar lets you position the buttons in whatever order you like.

Changing the default folder for Office templates

Office initially stores document templates in the Templates folder, located in the main folder where you installed Office. If you want to change the default location where all Office applications look for their templates (see "Using Templates to Ensure Consistent Documents" in Chapter 13), use the Shortcut bar.

Open the Customize dialog box and switch to the Settings tab. Select User Templates Location to change the main template folder. Alternatively, you can specify a secondary folder for Office templates by selecting Workgroup Templates Location. Either way, choose Modify to browse your system for the new folder.

Conclusion

This chapter taught the secret ways of the Office Shortcut bar. You now know how to position it, change its configuration (from floating to docked), and customize its appearance and the toolbars and buttons it contains. Most important, you have a good idea of when to use it and when not to. Chapter 3 digs beneath the surface of the Office user interface.

Chapter 3

User Interface Secrets

In This Chapter

- ▶ Zooming for just the right magnification on your work
- ▶ Navigating the toolbars and activating their buttons with keyboard shortcuts
- ▶ Working with the intricacies of the toolbars themselves
- ▶ Using mice and alternative pointing devices, including the new Microsoft IntelliMouse
- ▶ Turning on the music — working with sound in Office
- ▶ Using voice recognition software, pen technology, and optical character recognition (OCR)

Achieving the optimal screen view of your work, taking full control of Office's commands and toolbars, and moving information into documents smoothly are noble goals for any Office master-in-training. I'm not going to tell you how to work the menus or click the toolbar buttons, assuming you have those basics covered by now. But I *will* clue you in to some deeper truths about the Office user interface.

Working with the Screen

Most of this section is devoted to the intricacies of the zoom command, which lets you see more or less of your work on screen as necessary.

Zooming in and out on your work

As someone familiar with Office, you already know about the Zoom box, where you can select a magnification as a percentage of the document's actual size, or by description (as in Page Width or selection). Remember, though, that you're not limited to the options in the drop-down list — you can type in any whole-number zoom factor you like within the allowable range (in Word, 10 to 500 percent, in Excel, 10 to 400 percent).

If you have the Microsoft IntelliMouse, you can also zoom by rolling the wheel while holding down Ctrl. You can read more about the IntelliMouse later in this chapter.

Note that once the zoom factor is small enough, Word and Excel display multiple pages in Page Layout view. In other words, you don't have to switch to Print Preview (discussed in Chapter 11) to see several bite-size pages at the same time.

Secret

In Word, when you choose Page Width in the Zoom box while you're in Page Layout view, the magnification factor that Word sets for you lets you see the edges of the pages and even some of the surface they're resting on, too. In other words, you're zoomed out quite a bit, much more than necessary for most documents. As a result, your text may be hard to read. You can usually set the zoom factor manually to something approaching 100 percent and still see everything of interest on the page with the benefits of Page Layout mode.

Macro VBA

If you're interested in both detail work and the big picture, you typically switch back and forth between two zoom settings. Office doesn't provide a command that lets you toggle the zoom factor, but a macro does the trick. I know, what follows is long for a first macro, but it comes with the Secrets territory.

To create the macro in Word, choose Tools ⇨ Macro ⇨ Macros, enter ZoomToggle.ZoomToggle for the name, and choose Create to start the Visual Basic Editor. Type in the code as it appears here, check it carefully, and then choose File ⇨ Exit to save your work and return to Word (see Part VI on Visual Basic for Applications for details on these techniques). To spare yourself the work, you can find the macro in the Word Office Secrets template included on the CD-ROM. The CD-ROM also has a comparable macro for Excel.

Run the macro by highlighting it in the Tools ⇨ Macro ⇨ Macros dialog box and choosing Run, or assign it to a keyboard shortcut or toolbar button with the techniques described in Chapter 5.

```
Sub ZoomToggle()
Set objDocVars = ActiveDocument.Variables
With objDocVars

For Each aVar In objDocVars
    If aVar.Name = "StoreZoom1" Then num1 = aVar.Index
    If aVar.Name = "StoreZoom2" Then num2 = aVar.Index
    If aVar.Name = "ToggleFlag" Then num3 = aVar.Index
Next aVar

If num1 = 0 Then
    .Add Name:="StoreZoom1", Value:="0"
End If

If num2 = 0 Then
    .Add Name:="StoreZoom2", Value:="0"
```

```
        End If

        If num3 = 0 Then
            .Add Name:="ToggleFlag", Value:="0"
        End If

        If .Item("StoreZoom1").Value = 0 Then
            .Item("StoreZoom1").Value = _
                ActiveWindow.View.Zoom.Percentage
            GoTo Out
        End If

        If .Item("StoreZoom2").Value = 0 Then
            .Item("StoreZoom2").Value = _
                ActiveWindow.View.Zoom.Percentage
            ActiveWindow.View.Zoom.Percentage = _
                .Item("StoreZoom1").Value
            .Item("ToggleFlag").Value = 2
            GoTo Out
        End If

        If .Item("ToggleFlag").Value = 2 Then
            .Item("StoreZoom1").Value = _
                ActiveWindow.View.Zoom.Percentage
            ActiveWindow.View.Zoom.Percentage = _
                .Item("StoreZoom2").Value
            .Item("ToggleFlag").Value = 1
            GoTo Out
        End If

        If .Item("ToggleFlag").Value = 1 Then
            .Item("StoreZoom2").Value = _
                ActiveWindow.View.Zoom.Percentage
            ActiveWindow.View.Zoom.Percentage = _
                .Item("StoreZoom1").Value
            .Item("ToggleFlag").Value = 2
        End If

    End With

Out:
End Sub
```

Secret

In Word, another solution is to flip back and forth between two of the views, usually Normal and Print or Web Layout. Word remembers the zoom setting separately for each view.

Using full screen view

The View ⇨ Full Screen view, available in Excel and Word, devotes the entire computer screen to the document, hiding other window elements such as the toolbars — see Figure 3-1. Once you're skilled with the keyboard, you may want to spend most of your time in full screen view, where there's less distracting clutter on screen and lots more room for your documents. See Chapters 26 and 35 if you want to learn how to deep-six that little toolbar with the Close Full Screen button.

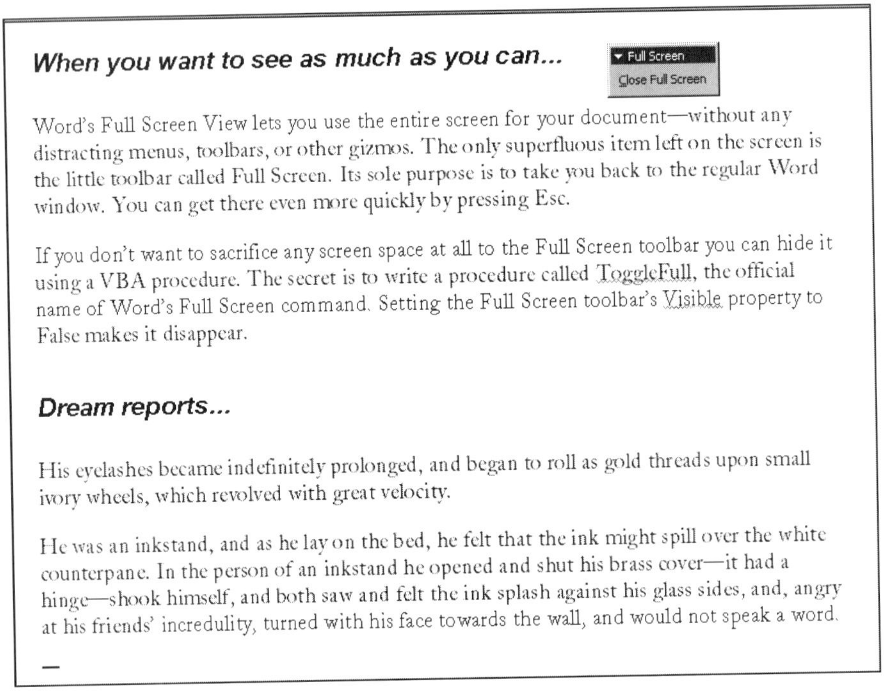

When you want to see as much as you can...

Word's Full Screen View lets you use the entire screen for your document—without any distracting menus, toolbars, or other gizmos. The only superfluous item left on the screen is the little toolbar called Full Screen. Its sole purpose is to take you back to the regular Word window. You can get there even more quickly by pressing Esc.

If you don't want to sacrifice any screen space at all to the Full Screen toolbar you can hide it using a VBA procedure. The secret is to write a procedure called ToggleFull, the official name of Word's Full Screen command. Setting the Full Screen toolbar's Visible property to False makes it disappear.

Dream reports...

His eyelashes became indefinitely prolonged, and began to roll as gold threads upon small ivory wheels, which revolved with great velocity.

He was an inkstand, and as he lay on the bed, he felt that the ink might spill over the white counterpane. In the person of an inkstand he opened and shut his brass cover—it had a hinge—shook himself, and both saw and felt the ink splash against his glass sides, and, angry at his friends' incredulity, turned with his face towards the wall, and would not speak a word.

Figure 3-1: Full screen view in Word

Working with document windows

In Word, Excel, and PowerPoint, each open document automatically has one window of its own. You can view different parts of the same document in separate windows by using the Window ⇨ New Window command to create additional windows for the document.

Although you can switch between document windows using the applications Window menu, Office 2000 gives you an alternative technique thats often easier and faster. In previous versions of Office, the Windows taskbar showed a single item for each Office application that was running, regardless of how many documents were open in the application. In Office 2000, by contrast, Word, Excel, and PowerPoint display a separate taskbar item for each document window thats currently open. If you open three workbooks in Excel and create a second window for one of them, you get four separate taskbar items. You can switch to the document you want by clicking its taskbar icon, or by pressing Alt+Tab or Alt+Shift+Tab to cycle through all taskbar items.

Keyboard Secrets

The trade-off for all the freedom a mouse gives you is a performance hit—taking your hands off the keyboard to pick up the mouse slows you down. For some tasks, of course, using the keyboard would be ridiculously cumbersome, and besides, breakneck speed can lead to emotional stress, physical injury, and more assignments from the boss.

Still, learning Office's keyboard commands can reduce your frustration level and increase your productivity. That's why this book mentions default keyboard shortcuts for most commands. When a default keyboard shortcut doesn't exist, or if the existing shortcut doesn't suit you, you can use the techniques discussed in Chapter 5 to create your own.

Keyboard control of the toolbars

Recent releases of Office give you keyboard control over a part of the user interface that was previously off-limits: the toolbars. Table 3-1 lists the keys you can use to push toolbar buttons without the mouse.

Table 3-1 Keyboard Control over the Office Toolbars

To Do This	Press
Activate the menu bar	Alt or F10
With the Toolbar System Active . . .	
Select the next button or menu	Tab or right arrow
Select the previous button or menu	Shift+Tab or left arrow
Select the next toolbar	Ctrl+Tab
Select the previous toolbar	Ctrl+Shift+Tab
Press a selected button or open a selected menu	Enter (down arrow also works for menus)
Display the toolbar shortcut (right-click) menu	Shift+F10

You may notice that as you press Ctrl+Tab, Office activates toolbars in an order that is different from how they appear on your screen. Thank goodness for little mysteries.

How not to learn keyboard shortcuts

Unfortunately, Office provides no master reference to all the default keyboard shortcuts it supplies. In Word, at least, you can use the List Commands command to prepare a document containing all keyboard shortcuts (see

Chapter 26). You can also print *custom* key assignments by selecting the corresponding choice from the Print What list in the File ⇨ Print dialog box.

Working with Toolbars

Every Office toolbar (including the main menu bar) can exist in one of three forms: hidden, docked, or floating. Hidden toolbars are hard to see, but Figure 3-2 shows both of the other types clearly.

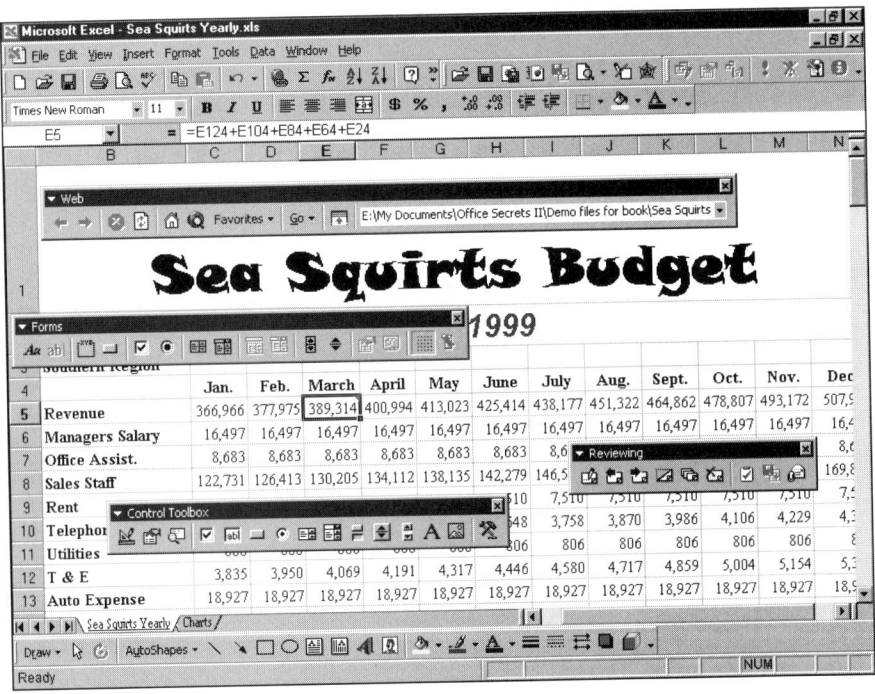

Figure 3-2: This window shows both floating and docked toolbars. Hidden toolbars are visible too; you just can't see them.

Don't forget that you can find out what any button does by holding the mouse pointer over the button for a second or two. In Office, the message that appears is called a *ScreenTip*. If you don't see the ScreenTips, turn them on by checking the appropriate box in the Options tab of the Tools ⇨ Customize dialog box.

Displaying and hiding toolbars

To display a hidden toolbar, or to hide one that's visible, right-click anywhere on any toolbar, picking the toolbar by name from the list that appears (also shown in Figure 3-2). If you're a keyboard kind of person, you can display the same menu by pressing Alt+V and then T to activate the View ⇨ Toolbars command, or by pressing and releasing Alt and then pressing Shift+F10.

Office displays some toolbars automatically when you enter a certain software mode. In Word, for example, the Outlining toolbar pops up like magic when you enter Outline view. These toolbars don't appear on the toolbar list except when you're using the special mode in question.

Secret

You won't find the menu bar on this toolbar list, so you can't hide it using this technique. In Word and Excel, however, you can use the View ⇨ Full Screen command to put the menu bar and all other toolbars out of sight, and then add back just the toolbars you want with the Toolbars tab of the Tools ⇨ Customize dialog box.

Working with docked toolbars

You can dock a toolbar along any of the four edges of the application window, as shown in Figure 3-3. Note that when a toolbar is docked on the left or right edge, menus and other buttons showing text are stood on end, while graphical buttons remain upright. Along each edge, toolbars can occupy as many parallel rows or columns as you want to devote to them. I call these rows and columns *docking slots*.

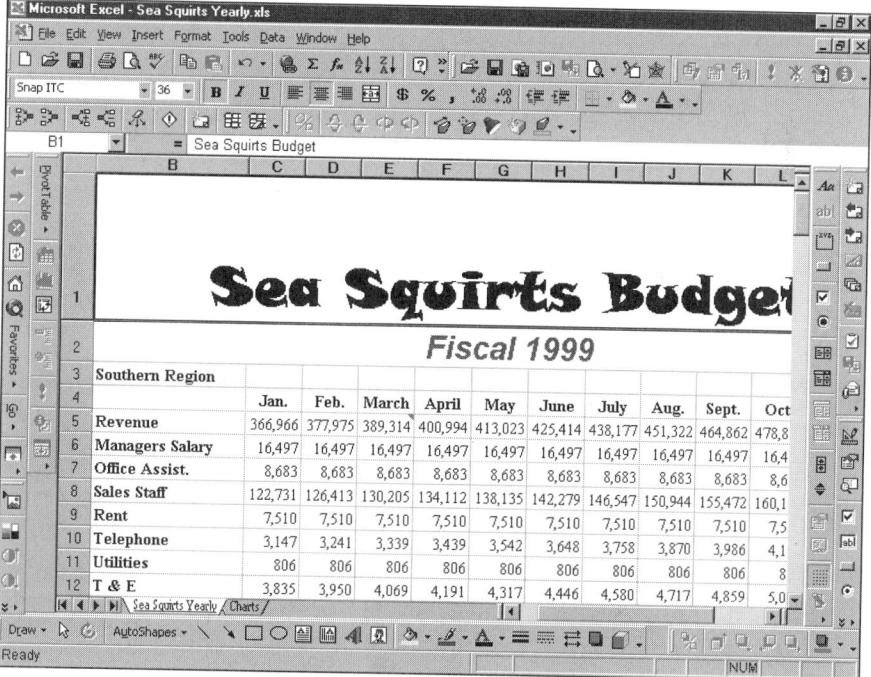

Figure 3-3: Toolbars docked along all four edges of the window

Moving docked toolbars

To move a docked toolbar, grab it by the move handle (that gray bar at the left or top of the toolbar). The mouse pointer becomes a four-headed arrow when you're in position. You can also drag using the toolbar's background, wherever there isn't a button. The background is most accessible over those little separator grooves between groups of buttons and along the edges of the toolbar.

If the toolbar is one of several in the same docking slot, you can move it within its slot by dragging it right or left, or up or down. You can place as many toolbars as will fit end to end with one another in the same slot. That can be quite a few, because Office will trim away space from existing toolbars in a slot to accommodate new ones you dock there.

By dragging the toolbar perpendicular to its slot, you can dock it in a different slot. If you drag the toolbar all the way out into the work area, it becomes a floating toolbar encased in its own little window. If you drag it still farther toward another window edge, it gets pulled in to dock there as if by a magnet. One restriction: You can dock the main menu bar in any slot, but it can't share a slot with any other toolbar.

By the way, don't bother with one of the new settings on the Options tab of the Tools ⇨ Customize dialog box, the box that causes Standard and Formatting toolbars to share one row. Checking this box is one way to make the Formatting toolbar jump up to the Standard toolbar's slot. However, turning on this option doesn't lock the toolbars in place there. You can accomplish the same end — or place these two toolbars wherever you want them — using the mouse.

Accessing all the buttons

When a docked toolbar is too long for all its buttons to fit across the screen in the room available, Office displays a slender button at the far right of the toolbar. This is the More Buttons button, marked with a double arrow pointing to the right. Click this button to see the toolbar's remaining buttons on an attached pop-up menu — see Figure 3-4.

Aside: If you don't see the double arrow, all the toolbar's buttons are already visible. On built-in toolbars, the More Buttons button always shows a single arrow pointing down. That's to indicate that the More Buttons pop-up menu includes a working Add or Remove buttons command, which is covered in Chapter 5.

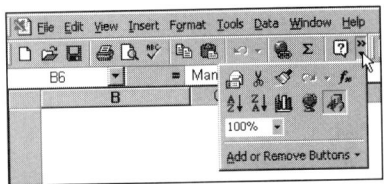

Figure 3-4: Use the More Buttons pop-up menu to access buttons that won't fit on a docked toolbar.

Anyway, if you click one of the buttons on the More Buttons menu, Office carries out the corresponding command, of course. In addition, though, Office adds the button you clicked back to the visible part of the original toolbar. Where does it get room for a button that didn't fit before? If another toolbar is parked in the same row or column, Office subtracts buttons from it and gives that space to the current toolbar. If no other toolbar has space to loan, Office substitutes the button you just clicked for some other button that was visible. Office is smart enough to keep track of which buttons you click most often, and it swaps out the buttons you haven't clicked recently.

Working with floating toolbars

Because a floating toolbar lives in its own discrete window, you can drag that window anywhere you like on the screen — even outside the borders of the Office application you're working with. Of course, that's possible only if the application isn't running in a full-screen (maximized) window — see Figure 3-5 for an illustration.

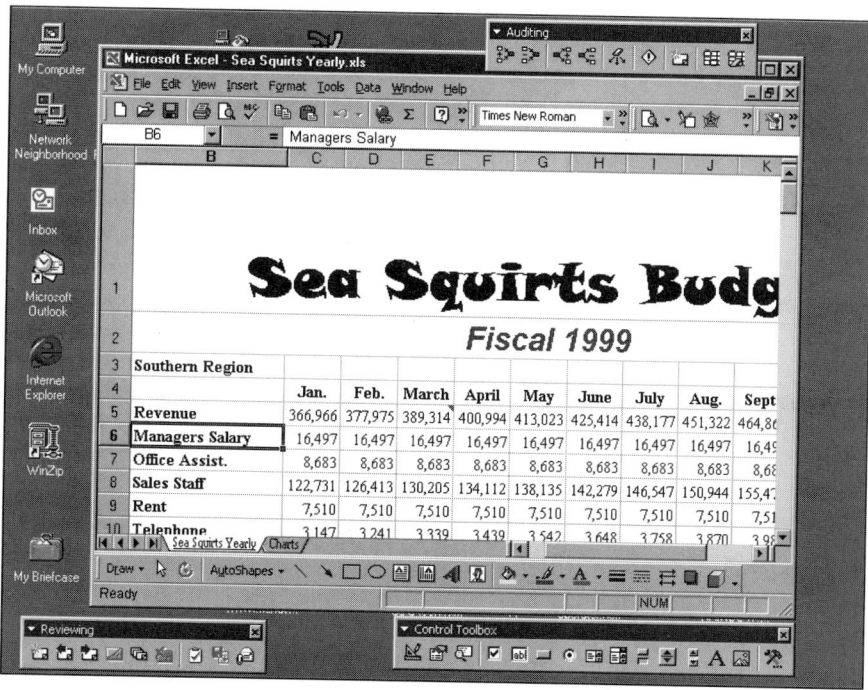

Figure 3-5: Floating toolbars positioned outside the application's window

Move a floating toolbar as you would any window, by dragging its title bar. You can hide a floating toolbar by clicking the Close button — the one with the X — at the right of the title bar. To resize a floating toolbar, hold the mouse pointer over one of its edges until it becomes a two-headed arrow, and then drag.

Floating fast

Secret

You can drag a toolbar to morph it from floating to docked or vice versa. But the quickest way to make the conversion is to double-click the toolbar anywhere that isn't directly over a button or the move handle. The toolbar remembers its old home, so each time you make the change, it reappears where it last was when previously in that form. Double-clicking doesn't work on the main menu bar when it's docked, however.

Using the tear-off submenus

You can convert many Office submenus into toolbars by dragging them away from the menu they belong to. You can recognize one of these tear-off submenus by the colored bar at the top. Gray normally, the bar turns blue when you point to it.

To tear off a submenu, drag it by the move handle. A submenu converted into a toolbar this way appears in its own floating window at first, but you can dock it like any other toolbar. See Figure 3-6 for an illustration of this process in action.

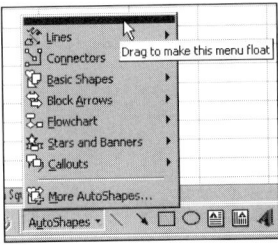

Figure 3-6: Tearing off a submenu to form a new toolbar

Working with toolbar buttons

Click a button, get a response — that's almost all you need to know about using toolbar buttons. For a few additional details see the next section, "Mouse on Fire."

Mouse on Fire

Point and click, drag and drop — everything you can do in Office, you can do with the mouse. Mouse technique is easy to master, but for the uninitiated, the following tips may prove helpful, or at least mildly diverting:

- Remember the power of the shortcut menu: Right-clicking almost anything produces a *shortcut menu* of choices specific to that item. This is often the fastest way to access commands when you're already using the mouse. (Depending on where you are in Office, Shift+F10 or the special shortcut key on Windows-aware keyboards usually pops up the shortcut menu, too.)

- In Windows, clicking a button while you hold down Shift on the keyboard sometimes produces different results than clicking the usual way. This is also true of at least one Office button: the Close button, which normally closes the current document. In Word and Excel, when you hold down Shift and click the Close button, *all* open documents close.

- Many Office buttons such as Font Color and the View button in Access are *split buttons*: Alongside the main part of the button they have a narrow gray bar with a little downward-pointing arrow. Click the main button and Office carries out the corresponding command immediately. Click the narrow bar, and if your aim is true, you get a drop-down panel offering various choices.

- Don't forget that you can use the Mouse applet in the Windows Control Panel to swap the functions of the left and right mouse buttons and to otherwise tinker with the settings of your mouse.

Of mice and mouse alternatives

Pointing device is the generic term for any gadget that lets you select options on the screen by pointing at them. The extensive catalog of variations on and alternatives to the standard mouse includes cordless mice, trackballs, touchpads, pointing sticks (both of the latter commonly found on notebook PCs), pen-like styli, and other gizmos too unique to categorize (anyone remember Felix?).

Chacun à son goût, of course, but be aware that certain pointing devices offer practical benefits, in addition to their appeal to your senses of fashion and ergonomics. In particular, if you like using a mouse more than using the keyboard, I suggest you consider pointing devices with more than two buttons.

A three- or four-button device like those made by Logitech is a start. The extra buttons can be programmed to act as a double-click or to perform whatever command you use most frequently. Microsoft's IntelliMouse has three buttons, all right, but the third button is a wheel—it rates special treatment in its own section later in this chapter.

If you spend a lot of time with your hand on the mouse, consider getting one that functions like a mini-keyboard. The UNIA (Vector Research Corp., 408-298-7898), for example, has a full numeric keypad embedded in the surface, and the keys can do double- or triple-duty for other functions. Alternatively, look at a keyboard from IBM with one of those little pointing sticks built right in. As long as you're comfortable with the way the pointing stick responds, you'll be able to use your "mouse" without moving your hands from the home position on the keyboard.

IntelliMouse? Can they be serious about that name?

Microsoft's IntelliMouse may not really be so smart, but it does offer some genuine benefits when used with Office, which was designed with the IntelliMouse in mind. The basic innovation is its rolling middle wheel. Clicking quickly straight down on the wheel is equivalent to clicking the middle button on an ordinary three-button mouse, but you can also give the wheel a roll to scroll (your document, that is), or to zoom.

In more detail, here's a survey of what you can do with the IntelliMouse in Office:

- Moving the wheel is like clicking the vertical scrollbar arrows — definitely more convenient than having to move the mouse pointer over to the scrollbar and then back again to the document.

- To smoothly pan the document without having to keep moving the wheel, drag while holding the wheel button down. The farther up or down the screen you drag from the vertical middle of the work area, the faster the scroll. Cancel this scrolling mode by clicking the mouse or pressing any key.

- To zoom in or out on the document, hold down Ctrl and move the wheel.

- Expand or collapse outlines in Word by pointing to a heading and then holding down Shift while moving the wheel. Similarly, in Excel, expand an outline by pointing to a summary cell and do a Shift+forward roll. Collapse the outline by Shift+backward rolling over a cell containing detail.

The IntelliMouse offers scads of software options for controlling the way it works. The quickest way to bring up its Control Panel — shown in Figure 3-7 — is by clicking the mouse icon in the system tray in the Windows taskbar.

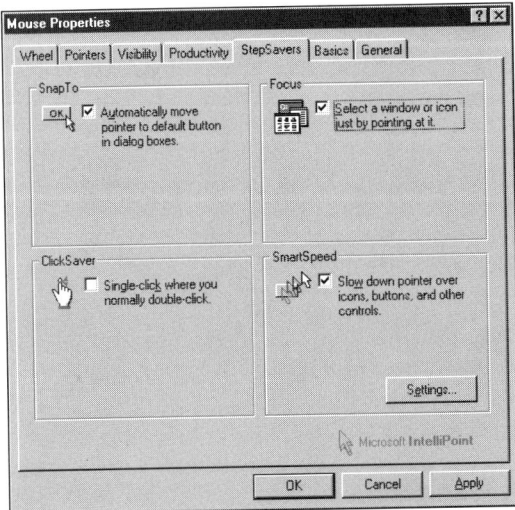

Figure 3-7: A tab on the IntelliMouse Control Panel dialog box

Tuning in the Toolbar Tunes

Whether your toolbars honk, bray, or sigh at you when you fiddle with them depends on an obscure setting on the General tab of the Tools ⇨ Options dialog box in Excel or Word. The control in question is named Provide Feedback with Sound. When this box is checked, sound is turned on for all events in all Office applications. Office can give you audible confirmation of many common events such as opening or saving files. You can turn on sound only if you've installed some required files first. However, these files weren't included in the prerelease version of Office 2000 available at press time. In the final version, they may be located on your Office CDs, or you may have to download them from the Office Update Web site (http://officeupdate.microsoft.com/).

Once you've installed Office sounds, you can change the specific sound you hear with each event using the Sounds applet in the Windows Control Panel. Open the Sounds Properties dialog box and scroll down the list until you get to the heading for Office. As shown in Figure 3-8, you can then locate the specific event you want to change and use the available controls to try out other sounds and assign them to the event.

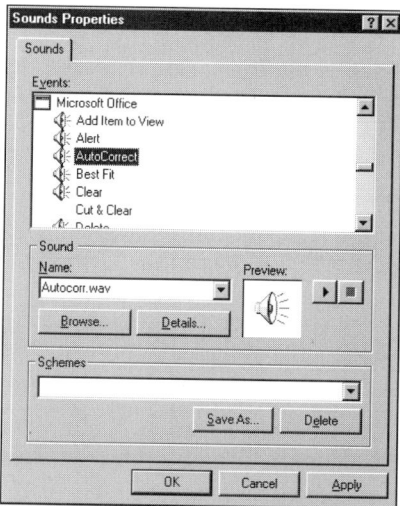

Figure 3-8: Assigning new sounds to Office events in the Windows Control Panel

Alternative Software Control and Input Techniques

The keyboard and mouse won't always be the main ways you interact with computers. The technologies described in this section already offer viable alternative ways to activate Office commands and move information into your documents.

Controlling Office and dictating information with speech-recognition software

Even by 2001 you won't be carrying on full conversations with computers, but your PC is already capable of understanding your monologues—if you equip it with speech-recognition software. Office 2000 was originally slated to include built-in speech-recognition, but as this feature was dropped you must buy a third-party product. Still, if you can talk faster than you can type, these products are well worth your attention.

While still not perfect, the current generation of affordable ($50 and up) speech software is impressively accurate at transcribing dictation. You no longer need to master a stilted speech style, and you can readily achieve dictation speeds of 60 to 70 words per minute, including correction time. These products also enable you to control software by spoken commands, such as "Open a file" or "Next window." All of them come already trained to recognize commands for common Office functions.

The names to know in this category are L&H's Voice Xpress, Phillips' FreeSpeech98, IBM's ViaVoice, and Dragon System's NaturallySpeaking. In my trials with Voice Xpress (see Figure 3-9) I've found that it recognizes speech accurately, and that it integrates well with Word. You can mix dictation with a comprehensive list of sensible, easy-to-remember commands for editing text (saying "undo that" activates Word's Undo command, for example).

The power of the pen

Pen technology was the darling of the venture capitalists 10 or 15 fads ago, but it has long since lost its appeal as a sinkhole for high-risk investment dollars. You may not hear much about pen-based PC systems these days, but hand-held machines equipped with pens are everywhere—in the form of those personal organizers so many people carry, and as specialized business tools, such as the little electronic notepads carried by Federal Express couriers. Even though pen products for mainstream personal computing are much less visible, they make a viable complement to the keyboard for some people.

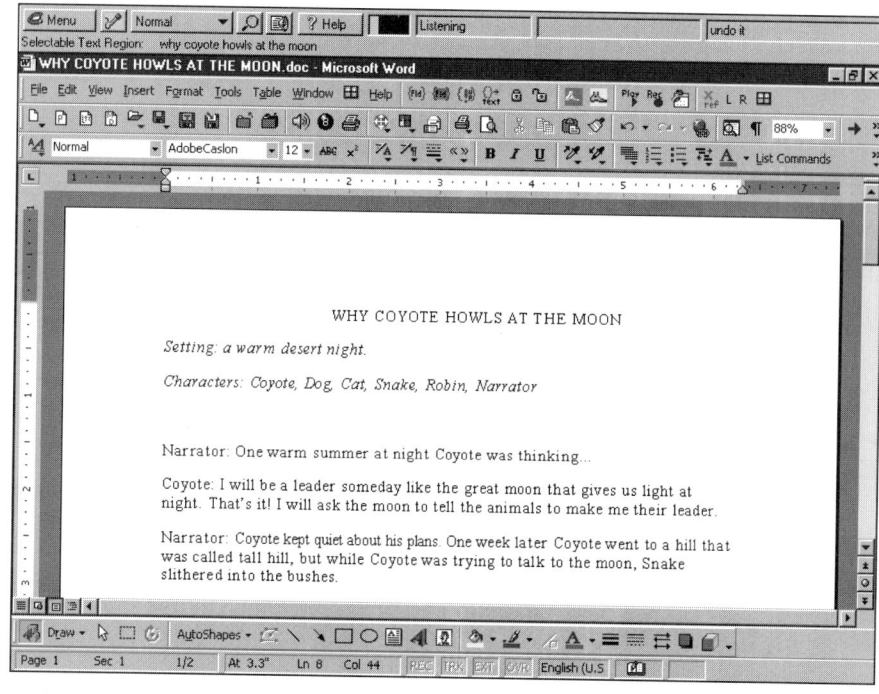

Figure 3-9: When Voice Xpress is running, it presents a toolbar at the top part of your screen that offers commands and status readouts.

By pen technology, of course, I'm talking about plastic styli that enable you to tap or write on special pads that electronically sense the pen's contact and motion. A pen makes an effective mouse-like pointing device, and it's fine for drawing text or graphics that get stored in bitmap form. But the big appeal of these products is supposed to be their capacity to recognize your handwriting. If the system works right, it converts the characters you write with the pen into the electronic codes used by Windows software to store text.

Venerable A.T. Cross Corp., a well-known manufacturer of conventional pens, makes the most popular pen add-ons for PCs. The Cross iPen consists of an electronic pen and accompanying tablet. In its basic operating mode, the iPen functions as a capable mouse substitute — you move the pen around on the tablet to move the mouse pointer and tap the pen on the tablet to click. Teamed with the smARTwriter handwriting recognition that comes with the system, the iPen recognizes handwriting with surprising accuracy. It's a strange and wonderful experience to watch your roughly scrawled letters vanish, replaced by perfectly formed characters all in a row (see Figure 3-10).

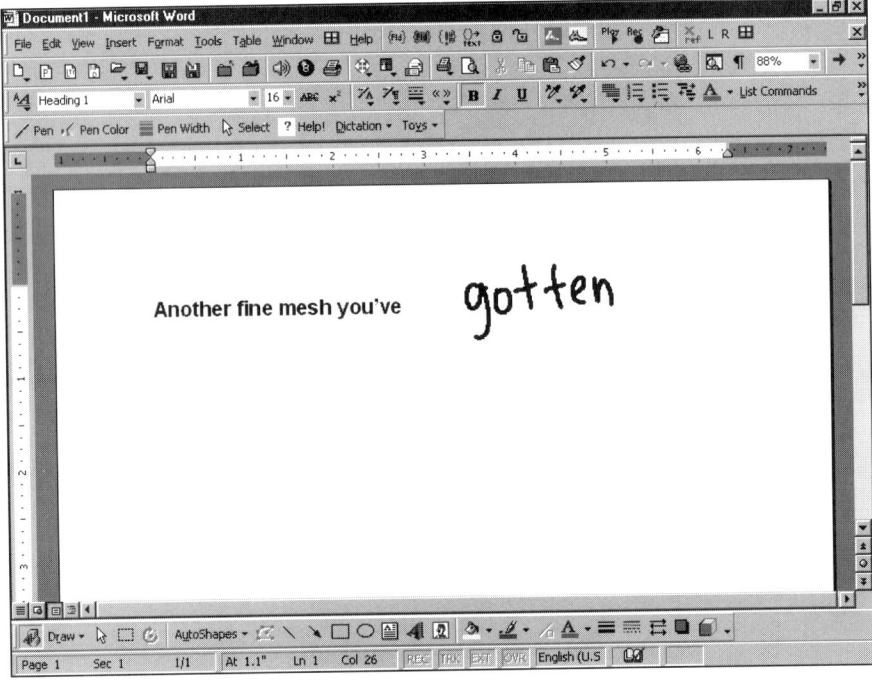

Figure 3-10: Handwriting-to-text recognition underway, courtesy of the Cross iPen Pro

Recognition isn't perfect, of course, and it takes some time to train yourself to use the system at top efficiency. Although you shouldn't expect the iPen to replace your keyboard for high-volume text entry into a Word document, the iPen works well for short notes and comments.

By the way, there's a Word command and corresponding button called Pen Comment. This inserts whatever you write with a pen as a graphical object directly in the document window, *not* as recognized text in the comments pane. Word doesn't add comment marks for these pen comments.

Another Cross system, the CrossPad, lets you write on ordinary paper as it simultaneously records your scrawlings in digital form. You can transfer the electronic version of your notes to your PC, where you can convert it to text.

OCR software

For anyone who works regularly with paper documents, the promise of optical character recognition (OCR) software is powerfully tempting. Theoretically, you feed a printed page into your scanner, run the software, and presto — within seconds, you have an electronic document containing the printed text in editable form. Once you've opened the document in Word or one of the other Office applications, you can sculpt the text to taste, just as if you had typed it yourself. In theory, OCR can work the same magic with virtual pages that have never been printed — text within graphics from downloaded Web pages, or faxes received via your PC's modem and stored on the hard disk.

When I first tried PC-based OCR software in the late '80s, scanners and computers were too slow to give OCR a real speed advantage over retyping. But even then, OCR software worked well. (Well, that is, as long as the documents you fed in were of fairly good quality, with conventional fonts printed in 10-point or larger type, and printed cleanly.)

OCR software accuracy has improved since then, but in my book, the big change has been in the hardware. With today's computers and scanners, you can transform printed documents into computerized text much more quickly than a human typist can. True, an OCR program makes many more mistakes than a good typist. But even when you factor in the time for correcting errors, OCR is faster. Chalk up another victory for the machine.

I've tested both of the two OCR market leaders in the versions available at press time — Caere's Omnipage and Xerox's TextBridge — because both claim to be designed to work with Office applications. As far as Office integration goes, Omnipage is the better choice. With either product, you can initiate OCR from within any of the Office apps. When the conversion is finished, the recognized text appears in your Office document. Pretty neat. With Omnipage, though, you can then check the conversion and correct errors with its proofing tools, right from your Office document. TextBridge only lets you do that in Word, which is probably adequate for most jobs, but could be limiting.

Omnipage is still slicker than TextBridge. It offers Office-style menus and lots of nice, tabbed dialog boxes. Omnipage's proofreading tools are easier to work with and more powerful overall, although TextBridge is more flexible when it comes to moving around in the original document while proofreading. In terms of raw OCR performance, TextBridge is as accurate as Omnipage and maybe even more so, at least in my tests. Both products do fine with professionally printed book and magazine pages, and they've both improved their handling of small and fuzzy type. Under the latter, less than ideal conditions, however, I still find that TextBridge makes fewer errors. At any rate, both programs are mature software tools, and either will serve you well for automated text input.

Conclusion

This chapter outlined features of the Office 2000 user interface that you might not have noticed on your early cruises through the software. It also covered a range of alternatives to the standard user interface, including speech-recognition software, pen input, and OCR products. If you want to put your own mark on the user interface and speed up your daily chores to boot, see Chapter 5 for an in-depth exploration of Office customizing.

Chapter 4

Office Help Secrets

In This Chapter

- Understanding HTML Help, the new standard for Windows help
- Finding information fast in HTML Help
- Getting the most from the Office Assistant — with the least distraction
- Creating simple custom Help screens in VBA
- Building custom help files using authoring tools

Office may not give you much in the way of a printed user's manual, but it does provide a truly massive amount of help information on your screen — via HTML Help, the new Microsoft standard for the Windows Help system. Because Office presents you with so many complex applications and supporting utilities, the ability to find the help you need and find it quickly becomes a vital skill.

Introducing Office Help

Office's Help tools include two main components: the HTML Help system, which contains the actual help information, as well as a system for finding the information you want to view; and the optional Office Assistant, which offers a small and friendly gateway to the main Help system.

Installing Help

You can select which help files to install when you run Office Setup, and the Installed on First Use option is available for those you're not sure you're going to need. If you're installing Office for an individual PC, not a network, I advise you to go ahead and install all the Help files directly onto your hard disk — you're going to need them, believe me. An exception would be the Word help file for WordPerfect users, which you can omit unless you have a WordPerfect background. If you've seen the Office Assistant in action and don't want to be troubled by it, change the setting for this item (listed under Office Tools) to Not Available. Chapter 1 discusses Office installation in more detail.

Understanding HTML Help

Although HTML Help looks a little different than the previous Windows help program, WinHelp, the two systems are quite similar from the user's point of view. Behind the scenes, however, they do vary in important ways.

As its name implies, HTML Help files are prepared in the same HTML format used for Web pages. Well, not exactly the same format — HTML Help extends standard HTML with special features for navigating complex information sets, such as a table of contents, an index, and controls for displaying lists of related topics and pop-up windows. At any rate, help authors can incorporate existing Web pages or use any HTML editor they like to prepare new content.

Because HTML Help relies on HTML as its file format, Help files can be placed on a Web page for easy viewing by anyone who can access the site — no direct network connection to a server is necessary. In fact, you can view any Web page using HTML Help, because it's really just a different face on Internet Explorer.

Although WinHelp enabled links to sites on the Internet, those sites opened in the user's browser. In HTML Help, when you click a link to content on the Internet or an intranet, the page opens within the HTML Help program and you can continue to navigate through the help system using its regular controls.

About HTML Help files

A complete HTML Help system can be stored in two forms: as a set of ordinary HTML files, one for each help topic, or as a single "compiled" HTML file. If Office is administered via a corporate intranet, the help system can be placed on a server in standard HTML format. That way, performance is optimized because only one topic at a time must be transferred to a user's computer. In addition, users who don't have HTML Help on their machines can still view help content.

By contrast, the compiled format is the best choice if you're storing help files on each person's computer. Compiled help files take up much less disk space and can wrap an entire help system into one file. Microsoft provides the Office help files in this format.

Compiled HTML Help files are stored on disk with the .chm extension. Related files used by the Office Answer Wizard have the .aw extension.

Contrasting HTML Help with WinHelp

Until Windows 98 arrived, Microsoft relied on a help viewer called WinHelp to deliver all help content to the user. WinHelp still works, or course, and Microsoft says they intend to continue including it with future versions of Windows for the foreseeable future. But from now on, all new software will use HTML Help instead.

I list some of HTML Help's advantages over WinHelp in the introduction to this section. In some respects, however, HTML Help falls short of WinHelp. HTML lacks all of the following features found in WinHelp:

- **Annotation.** WinHelp users can add their own additions or comments to any individual topic.
- **Font sizing.** WinHelp lets you adjust the size of the display font.
- **Bookmarks.** In WinHelp you can define bookmarks at any topic, and then jump directly there from whatever topic you're currently viewing.

Microsoft may eventually add these features to HTML Help. For now, though, you have to do without.

Using HTML Help

Unless you're running Windows 98, you may not be familiar yet with the look and use of HTML Help, the new Microsoft utility for displaying and searching online help. Figure 4-1 shows an Excel help topic as it appears in HTML Help.

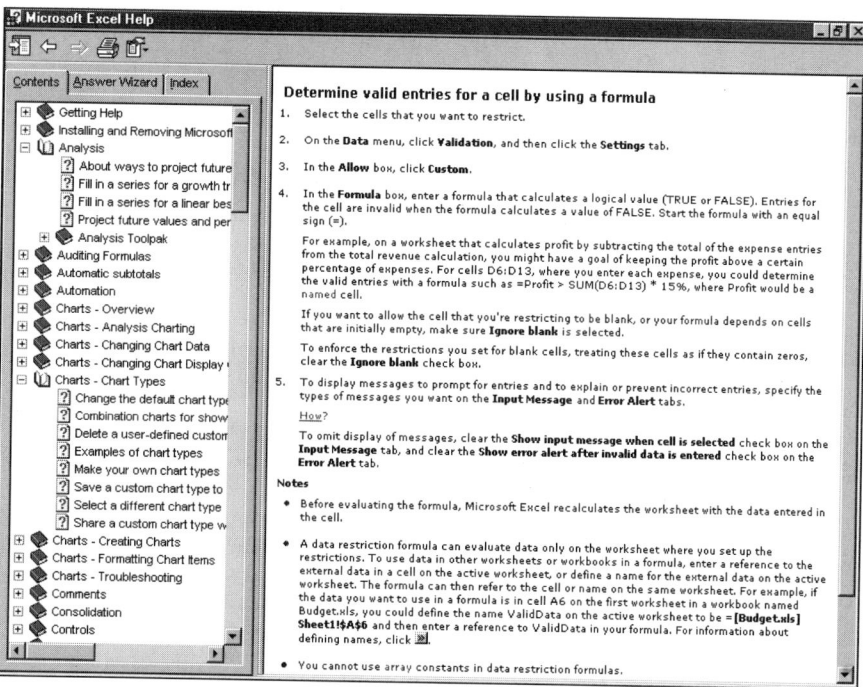

Figure 4-1: HTML Help for Excel.

To access the HTML Help program and display help information for the current Office application, you need to do one of two things:

- If the Office Assistant is turned on, click it and then type a question into its balloon or click one of the topics it suggests (see Figure 4-2). You're taken to the Help system, which displays the relevant information. Techniques for turning the Assistant off and on are detailed in the section on the Assistant, which follows this section.

- If the Office Assistant is turned off or hasn't been installed, press F1 or choose the menu item for the current application from the top of the Help menu (for example, Help ⇨ Microsoft PowerPoint Help). The HTML Help window appears, showing the first Help topic for that application. You can add a command to the menu to bring up the Help system even if the Assistant is on, as described in "Making the Help system available from the menu" later in this chapter.

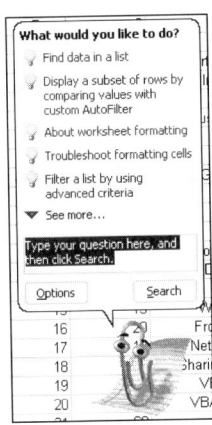

Figure 4-2: The Office Assistant with a sample balloon where you define your help requests.

Working with the toolbar buttons

HTML Help offers a simple toolbar at the top of the window. At the far left, the Show and Hide buttons determine whether the tabs frame is visible — it's the part that contains the Contents, Answer Wizard, and Index tabs. The Back and Forward buttons work like their counterparts in a browser. The menu revealed by the Options button includes commands that duplicate the main toolbar buttons, as well as four other choices:

- **Home** jumps to the home page defined for the help project, not to the home page defined for the Internet. If none is defined, nothing happens.

- **Stop** and **Refresh** perform the same way they do in your browser — use them with pages you jump to on the Internet or an intranet.

- **Internet Options** displays the same options you get from the Control Panel.

Navigating in the help topics

In Windows help documents, a *topic* is the information contained in the help window at one time. You may have to scroll to read the entire topic, but you don't have to use any other navigation tools. I'm sure you already know how to use basic navigation techniques in the help system — just click a colored link, or *jump*, to see the help information it refers to. Underlined jumps take you to other topics. Nonunderlined *pop-up jumps* display a tidbit of information — typically a definition of the jump term — in a pop-up box.

When HTML Help tabs are visible, they appear in a separate frame on the left side of the window. You use them to locate help topics of interest. In Office, the three tabs are:

- **Contents.** This tab displays the available help topics hierarchically, as organized by the authors of the help system. Click any item that displays a plus sign beside it to expand the list so you can see its subitems.
- **Answer Wizard.** Here, type in a question or just enter a few words describing the subject you want help with. The help topic deemed most relevant appears in the main part of the window, while related topics are listed below your query.
- **Index.** The Index tab lists the keywords designated as such by the authors of the help system. You can type in a term or select one from the scrolling list.

The Answer Wizard tab is unique to Office, or at least it's not present in standard HTML Help systems. In its place you normally find a Search tab. Search performs the same function as the Find tab in WinHelp. It locates topics containing any word that interests you, even when the help authors did not designate that term as a keyword.

Using HTML Help with multiple Office applications

If you have Help open with more than one Office application running, you can't switch directly from one application to another — at least that's the way things work in the late prerelease version of Office 2000. Let's say you're working in Word and want to switch to PowerPoint. If you click PowerPoint's button on the taskbar, or choose its icon using Alt+Tab, you'll see PowerPoint Help instead of PowerPoint itself. To get to the target application itself, click its taskbar button again, or use Alt+Tab to select its icon again.

Opening HTML Help files outside of Office

If you want to work with a help file for an application that isn't currently open, you can. Just double-click an HTML Help file in Explorer or My Computer to open it — after installation of HTML Help, the .chm file extension is associated with the HTML Help program. A caveat: If you display the main help file for any Office application with this technique, you can access the Contents only, not the Answer Wizard or the Index.

You can't start HTML Help by itself and then open a help file — try to do so, and you get an error message. Instead, you must supply the help file's filename as part of the command line that starts the HTML Help program. The HTML Help program is stored in a file called hh.exe in your main Windows folder. Therefore, you can open a command prompt window (DOS box) and type commands such as

```
hh jetsql40.chm
```

Customizing the looks of HTML Help

You won't find settings for font or colors in any obvious place on HTML Help's Options menu. Instead, HTML Help uses the settings you've chosen for such items in the Control Panel. The problem with this system is that if you do specify a font or color scheme for Help this way, your browser displays all Web pages in that font and color scheme. That is, the fonts and colors chosen by whoever designed the pages are always the same.

If you still want to alter your browser's look, you can access the Internet Options Control Panel applet from within HTML Help. Click the Options button and choose Internet Options. On the General tab of the resulting dialog box, click Accessibility to display a subsidiary dialog box, where you should check whichever of the top three boxes pertains to the settings you want to change (colors, font, and font size). You can then go back to the Internet Options box and use the Colors and Fonts buttons to specify the look you want.

Working with the Office Assistant

By now you've undoubtedly crossed paths with the point person of Office's Help technology, the Office Assistant. The Assistant is that animated graphic that steps in to answer your help queries and often to offer advice before you ask for it. The Assistant is one of those love-it-or-hate-it affairs. You can probably predict my feelings: Who wants a goofy paper clip taking up precious room on the screen, just so it can distract you with its constant writhing, grimacing, and jabbering?

Actually, the Assistant's help features would be, well, helpful if you could shut off that squirrelly picture and use them directly. But you can't.

The Office Assistant has two main roles:

- It offers tips. With software as large and complex as Office, it never hurts to be reminded of what you can accomplish and how to do it most quickly. The Assistant can display some of its tips automatically, as soon as you use a program feature that it thinks you should know more about. Others are available by clicking the light bulb when it appears in the Assistant window.

- It provides a friendly access point to the help system via the balloon displayed when you press F1 or click the Assistant window (refer back to Figure 4-2). Here, you can select from one of the topics that the Assistant thinks you might be wondering about — based on your most recent actions — or type in a question in ordinary English and choose Search.

Taking control of the Assistant

Even if you like having the Assistant around, it's probably going bother you from time to time. Whenever it becomes a nuisance or gets in your way, use the quick way to dismiss it from you screen: right-click the assistant and choose Hide.

To modify the way the Assistant works more permanently, choose Options in the Assistant's balloon. You see the large dialog box shown in Figure 4-3.

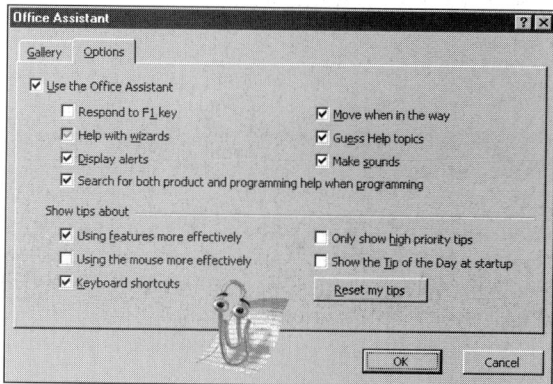

Figure 4-3: Control the Office Assistant from this dialog box. In the illustration, the Assistant is floating over the box.

The Options tab is for setting options, of course. I discuss a couple of these next. The Gallery tab lets you preview and select from the various personalities the Assistant can assume. If you really like this sort of thing, you can download still more Assistants from Microsoft's Web site.

Liberating the F1 key

In my book, the first change to make in the Assistant's behavior is to restore the standard function of the F1 key. By rights, F1 should display the full Help system. In the Options dialog tab, clearing the box labeled Respond to F1 Key does the trick.

Displaying tips at startup

Use the settings in the bottom half of the Options tab to control the display of tips. While these options are self-explanatory, I direct your attention to the box labeled Show the Tip of the Day at Startup. Check here to see a new tip each time you start the current program.

Immobilizing the Assistant

To keep the Assistant active but make it as unobtrusive as possible, choose the Assistant character that doesn't shimmy, shake, or even shimmer. In the Gallery tab of the Office Assistant dialog box, click Next repeatedly to get to the very last choice, the Office Logo with "Absolutely no moving parts."

If the immobile logo isn't present on your system, you can install it from the Office Resource Kit. Run ORK Setup. In the Select Features panel, find Motionless Office Assistant under Tools and change its setting to Run from My Computer. You can probably download this component from the ORK Web site at microsoft.com.

Making the Help system available from the menu

You may want to be able to use the Assistant and directly access the full Help system as well. To give yourself this flexibility, Step one is to set up the Assistant so that it doesn't respond to the F1 key, as described in "Liberating the F1 key." Step two: Add the Contents and Index command to the Help menu of each Office application. In the Tools ⇨ Customize dialog box, switch to the Commands tab and select Window and Help in the Categories list on the left. Then find the Contents and Index command in the list on the right and drag it to the menu (Chapter 5 details the customizing techniques you need).

If you don't see the Contents and Index command — it's missing from the prerelease version of Excel 2000 — you can write a tiny VBA procedure to bring up the Help system on your command. Chapter 19 covers the basic techniques for writing VBA procedures. Here's the code you need:

```
Sub HelpDisplay()
    Application.Help
End Sub
```

After you create the procedure, assign it to a new item on the Help menu using the customizing techniques described in Chapter 5. In Excel, be sure to store the macro in the Personal Macro Workbook so that it remains available no matter which workbook is active.

You can also use the Application object's Help method to display a specific topic of your choice from any Help file you like. Stay tuned for "Access to custom help information" later in this chapter.

Shutting off the Assistant altogether

If you regard the Assistant as just a big bother, shut it off altogether. Don't use Help ⇨ Hide the Office Assistant for this purpose — this command just hides the Assistant temporarily but doesn't deactivate it. Instead, right-click the Assistant, choose Options, and in the resulting dialog box clear the checkbox labeled Use the Office Assistant. You can revive the Assistant by choosing Help ⇨ Show the Office Assistant.

Customizing the Help System

Designing custom document templates and adding your own features by recording macros and writing VBA code are great ways to tailor Office to your unique needs. But you're going to need custom help files to match.

Creating your own Help windows using VBA

Instead of scribbling reminders on paper, you can use VBA to build yourself a simple electronic cheatsheet — a custom window containing brief reminders of the procedures and keyboard shortcuts you need regularly, but not so often you have already memorized them. Figure 4-4 shows an example.

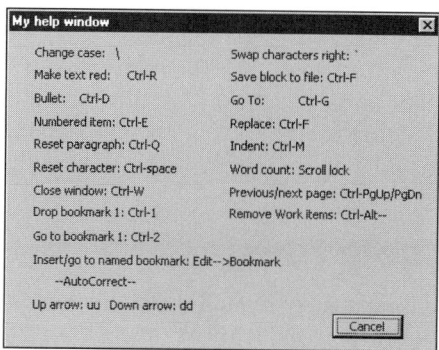

Figure 4-4: Use VBA to create a custom Help window like this one.

To create and display a window such as this, you need to do two things: design the window itself, and then create a tiny macro to display it. The instructions here are sketchy, so if you need more detail on VBA, consult Part VI.

The window is a simple example of a Visual Basic form. To design it, choose Tools ⇨ Macro ⇨ Visual Basic Editor, or just press Alt+F11. In the Visual Basic editor, choose Insert ⇨ UserForm. A blank form appears in the main work area.

Now you're ready to add text controls to the form to hold the help text. Locate the Toolbox, a floating toolbar that should be visible when you select the form. Define the boundaries for each item of help text by clicking the toolbox button for *label* controls (the one with the big letter A on it) and then dragging over the form. For a quick two-column help window, you need only two side-by-side text controls. After Shift+clicking to select both controls, you can use commands on the shortcut menu for these controls to align them and make them the same size. When the layout looks good, add your help text. Click a label control so that you see the flashing insertion point, and then type the text directly into the control.

If the form itself turns out to be too small, resize it with those handles around the right and bottom edges. Finish the form by giving it a suitable caption. In the Properties window, locate the Caption item in the left column. Click the right column in that row to edit the caption, which appears at the top of your form as you type. If you like, you can also change the name by which you refer to the form in macros. You can add an OK button to the form using the techniques discussed in Chapter 24, but this step isn't necessary — when the form is in use, you can close it by clicking the Close button in the upper-right corner or by pressing Esc.

Once the form is complete, it's time to code the macro needed to show it in your application. While still in the Visual Basic Editor, choose Insert ⇨ Module. In the code window, enter the following code, substituting the name of your form for `UserForm1`:

```
Sub MyHelpWindow()
    MyHelpForm.Show
End Sub
```

With this task finished, you can go back to the application you started from and use the Tools ⇨ Customize dialog box to place the macro on a toolbar, menu, or keyboard shortcut.

Creating custom help files

VBA is fine for one or two quick-and-dirty reminder screens, but beyond that you should create your own genuine help files. The process is straightforward as long as you have the proper tools for the job.

Help authoring software

One option for creating your own help files is the HTML Help Workshop that comes with the Office Resource Kit. Although fairly basic, this utility enables you to build complete HTML Help systems, including their tables of contents and indexes. By virtue of its Answer Wizard Builder, the Help Workshop can integrate your custom help files into the Office Answer Wizard, so that the topics you design appear with the standard Office topics in response to user queries.

Outside the Microsoft hegemony, various shareware and commercial programs can handle the dirty work of creating help files for you, leaving you free to concentrate on writing elegant explanatory prose. Many of these tools let you write and format a complete help document in Word, using headings as topic titles to designate the structure of your help system. You then run your document through the software and out pops a finished help file.

If you have a relaxed budget, consider the Cadillac of Help software, RoboHelp (BlueSky Software, 619-459-6365). RoboHelp is a complete help authoring system, enabling you to build both HTML and WinHelp systems from the same source documents. You can test your system while you're developing it.

CD

For those with little cash, an excellent Help authoring program is EasyHelp/Web, included on the CD-ROM bundled with this book. At press time the program supported only WinHelp, but a version for HTML Help should be available at www.eon-solutions.com by the time Office 2000 ships.

Access to custom help information

After you create a custom help system, you must integrate it into the relevant application, either by integrating your content into the main Office help system, or by creating a menu command or button that opens your help file directly. As I mentioned, the HTML Help Workshop that comes with the Office Resource Kit enables you to merge your own HTML help content into the main help system for any Office application, but only via the Answer Builder. In other words, your help topics don't appear in the Contents tab.

To display your help file directly from a menu or toolbar button, you must write a short VBA procedure and then assign the procedure to the menu item or button. The following example shows how this would look with an HTML Help file:

```
Sub HelpDisplayMyHelpFile()
    Application.Help "myhelpfile.chm"
End Sub
```

The same technique works for displaying WinHelp files, too — Windows uses the extension of the file you designate to activate automatically the correct help viewer for that type of file.

Programming the Office Assistant

If you're really gung-ho about preparing customized help for Office, consider commandeering the Office Assistant to provide on-screen answers. You can use VBA to display and hide the Assistant, to move it around on the screen, and to dictate what appears in its balloons. Techniques for programming the Office Assistant are discussed in Chapter 25.

Conclusion

No one can be expected to memorize the techniques required to get all of Office's myriad, complex features to do your bidding — face it, you need Help. More's the pity, you need help on Help itself. With the background information and skills you learned in this chapter, you're well equipped to get the most from Office's new HTML Help system.

Chapter 5

Customizing Secrets: Office Your Way

In This Chapter

▶ Streamlining repeated commands by recording them as one-click macros

▶ Customizing toolbars, buttons, and menus to match your work habits and aesthetic sensibilities

▶ Customizing keyboard commands and making them easier to use

▶ Defining your own color scheme (with tips on Office's Automatic color)

Out of the box, Office is an amazingly powerful software tool chest. Even so, you're sure to find places where it doesn't work quite to your liking.

Many people use some menu commands and buttons all the time and never touch others. Why not put your most-needed items where you can get to them quickly? Although Office provides commands for almost all tasks, it can't anticipate the order in which you'll use them. When you repeatedly employ the same set of commands, it makes sense to bundle them into one mega-command, or *macro*.

Fortunately, Office offers a deep level of customization. You can change and rearrange most aspects of the user interface, including the toolbar, menu, and keyboard functions. You can record frequently used command sequences and store them as macros for future use. When ordinary customization methods aren't enough, you can move on to Visual Basic for Applications (VBA), the Office programming language, to create complex custom commands and even complete, specialized applications of your own. Part VI of this book covers VBA.

Creating Custom Commands with Macros

To get anything done with an Office application, you must first issue a series of orderly commands. Because your work varies from day to day and document to document, the commands you use vary as well—if they didn't, you could hire a programmer to create software that does your work for you. But then you'd be out of a job.

However, you probably use certain sequences of commands time and again. This is where macros come in handy. Instead of executing each command in a sequence, you can record the sequence in a macro. Then you can carry out the sequence using the one command that runs the macro.

Although you can record and play back macros without inspecting their contents, you should know that macros and VBA programs are the same. The Office macro recorder is simply a way to convert your actions into VBA code without any effort on your part. You can edit a recorded macro or incorporate it into another VBA procedure by switching to the Visual Basic Editor, where you see the macro's underlying VBA code.

When to use macros

The word *macro* means big, of course. The term suggests the idea that you can accomplish big things with a macro, feats that would otherwise require a succession of little individual commands. But macros don't have to do big things. Any time you find yourself repeating even two steps, consider condensing the procedure into one macro. You can also use macros to do the following:

- Apply predetermined formatting choices to text, tables, or worksheets.
- Define keyboard shortcuts for standard menu commands. Office applications generally provide limited control over keyboard customization. If you want to use the keyboard simply to call up a particular dialog box, you may be able to record a macro that does so, assigning a keyboard shortcut to the macro.
- Redefine the standard menu and toolbar commands in Word. If you want Word to do something else automatically when you save a file, for example, create a macro that replaces the standard File ⇨ Save command.
- Use features that aren't available via the standard commands. While this requires VBA programming, it opens up a whole universe of customization possibilities.

You need VBA only if the task you want your macro to perform can't be accomplished via the standard Office commands. If you can do it with the menus and toolbars, you can record it in a macro. For a more complete discussion of when to record macros and when to write VBA code, see Chapter 19.

Recording macros

After all that hype, now comes the bad news: Only Word, Excel, and PowerPoint let you record macros. You can create macros of a sort in Access, but they aren't the same VBA-based macros provided by the other three applications (you create Access macros by filling in a special form as discussed in Chapter 43). And Outlook doesn't provide any direct macro-making capability. You can use VBA to create custom commands for all Office applications, but that's a different kettle of fish.

To record a macro in Word, Excel, or PowerPoint, choose Tools ⇨ Macro ⇨ Record New Macro. You see a dialog box in which you can assign a name to the new macro and make other choices, depending on the application you're using. Figure 5-1 shows the Record Macro dialog box for Excel.

The name you choose has to meet certain requirements. The first character must be a letter, and after that you're allowed only letters, numbers, and the underscore character, but no spaces or punctuation marks (Help_Me is acceptable, but Help_Me! is not).

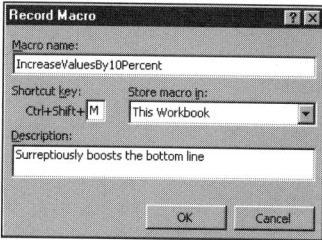

Figure 5-1: Excel's Record Macro dialog box lets you assign a macro name.

Secret

To replace one of Word's built-in commands with a custom macro, assign the new macro the same name as the command. You can find the name you need by selecting Word commands from the Macros In list on the Macros dialog box (see Figure 5-3). After noting the name exactly, close the dialog box and start recording your macro, giving it the same name as the Word command. Once you've recorded the macro, clicking a button or choosing a menu item for the original command executes the macro instead. In general, when you create a macro of this type you should record the original command as part of the sequence — in other words, the macro should enhance the existing command, not shut it off altogether.

As a simple example, let's say you want Word to display your document at a particular magnification (zoom) percentage every time you switch to Outline view. The name for the command that switches to Outline view is ViewOutline. So to create this macro you would name it ViewOutline and then record the two actions required: choosing View ⇨ Outline, followed by setting the magnification using the Zoom button. After you fill out the dialog box, choose OK to begin recording the macro. You see a little Stop Recording floating toolbar. Move it somewhere it won't get in your way, and then proceed to execute the commands you want to record. When you're finished, click the Stop Recording button on the toolbar. For an elaboration of this technique that requires VBA coding, see "Redefining Word's built-in commands" in Chapter 26.

Running macros

You can run any macro from the Macros dialog box: Choose Tools ⇨ Macro ⇨ Macros to display it, as shown in Figures 5-2 and 5-3. This dialog box looks a little different in the various applications, but it works essentially the same in all three.

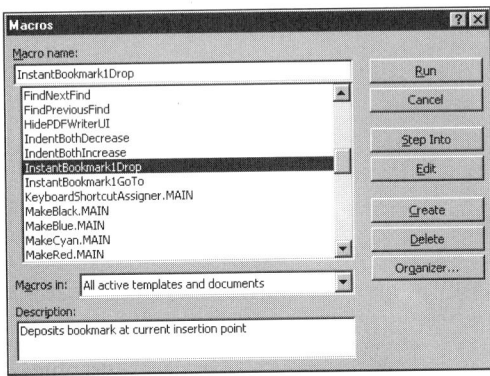

Figure 5-2: Word's Macros dialog box displaying macros

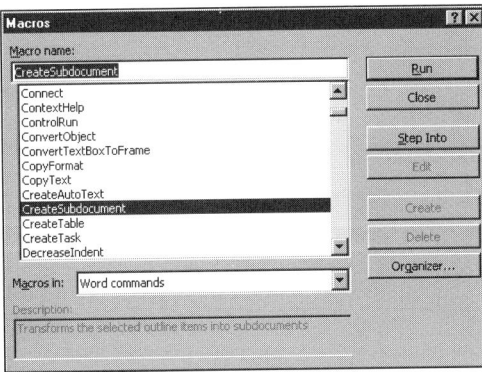

Figure 5-3: Word's Macros dialog box showing built-in Word commands

To run a macro, select it in the list and choose Run. To delete it, choose Delete. The Step Into, Edit, and Create buttons all take you into the Visual Basic Editor, so I leave them for Part VI.

Use the Macros In list to select the source for the macros you want to display. In Word, you can choose "All active templates and documents" to see all the currently active macros, or you can pick a single template or document from the list. In Excel and PowerPoint, you can display macros from all open documents (workbooks or presentations, respectively) or any one of the current documents.

Secret

In Word, the choice Word commands in the Macros In list is there to help you write (rather than record) VBA macros that replace built-in commands. See Chapter 24 for details.

Customizing Office Toolbars

All the Office applications now share a powerful drag-and-drop system for customizing toolbars. If you're used to the customizing system of Office 95 or earlier versions, you'll find that the new setup makes tinkering with the toolbar structure much easier, and therefore something you're more likely to put to regular use.

An equally big change is conceptual: Office applications no longer make a distinction between the menu bar and other toolbars. Someone at Microsoft must have had a minor epiphany one day, realizing that in a general way, a menu "button"—the place where you click to display a menu—does something when you click it, just like a toolbar button. Microsoft refers to menus and toolbars collectively as *command bars*.

True, a menu button can only be labeled with text, not a graphical icon, and when clicked it does something special, listing a bunch of other choices on a drop-down panel. But that doesn't make it fundamentally different from, say, the button that saves the current document to a disk file. In Office 2000, the main *Menu bar* is simply another toolbar that by default contains only menu buttons.

The upshot of this new concept is that you customize toolbars and menu bars using the same techniques. In addition, you can place menus onto toolbars containing graphical buttons, and graphical buttons onto menu bars.

Secret

Office doesn't carry the new paradigm all the way to its logical conclusion. You can't display a menu using a graphical button. And while the buttons for the individual items on a menu can include an icon with the text label, Office doesn't provide an option for displaying menu items as icons alone, without text (though you can accomplish this yourself if you like).

Customizing the toolbars themselves

This section covers in detail the techniques you need for customizing toolbars and their buttons. Although these techniques also apply to menus and the items listed on them, enough deserves saying about menu customization that it earns a separate section later.

Caution

One caveat is worth considering before you start experimenting with toolbar customization: The changes you make can't be reversed automatically by the Undo command. If you wind up with an unacceptably wacky toolbar or menu you have two alternatives. You must either put it right yourself, one button at a time, or use the Reset command for the item in question to restore it to its original state, obliterating all the changes you've made. If you need it, by the way, the Reset command is located on the shortcut menu for the item (see Figure 5-7 later in this chapter).

Putting toolbars where you want them

As described in Chapter 3, any toolbar can appear on the screen in two configurations: *docked* against an edge of the application window or *floating* in a separate window that you can move anywhere on the screen. You can dock a toolbar along any edge of the window, and yes, that includes the two sides. Chapter 3 offers tips on moving toolbars and parking them where you want them.

Displaying and hiding toolbars

The fastest way to display a toolbar that's not currently shown, or to hide one that is visible, is to right-click any toolbar and then choose the target toolbar's name from the shortcut menu. This shortcut menu lists most of the available toolbars, but not all of them. To display a toolbar that's not on the list, or to toggle more than one toolbar on or off, choose Customize at the bottom of the shortcut menu. The next section discusses the Customize dialog box.

Using the Customize dialog box

The Tools ➪ Customize dialog box, shown in Figure 5-4, is the command center for making changes to the toolbar structure in any Office application. Use it to hide, display, create, rename, or delete toolbars, and to add new buttons. With the mouse, the best way to display this dialog box is from the toolbar shortcut menu, accessed by right-clicking any toolbar. Office supplies no built-in shortcut key for this dialog box.

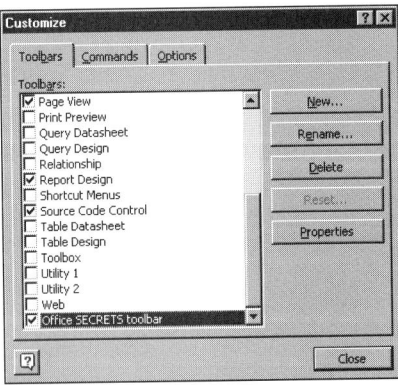

Figure 5-4: The Customize dialog box in Access

The list in the Toolbars tab shows all the toolbars available in the current application. Well, almost all — some toolbars appear in the list only when a particular mode of the program is active. In Word, for example, the Print Preview toolbar is listed only when you're doing a print preview. Anyway, check or uncheck the box by the name of a toolbar to show or hide it. Other things you can do with the Customize dialog box are covered in the sections that follow.

Creating toolbars from scratch

To add a new toolbar to the current Office application, open the Tools ⇨ Customize dialog box and switch to the Toolbars tab. Choose New and type in a name for the toolbar in the New Toolbar dialog box.

In the Word version of the New Toolbar dialog box, don't neglect that field labeled Make Toolbar Available To. Here, select from the drop-down list the template where you want to store the new toolbar: Normal.dot if you want the toolbar to appear in all your documents, or a specific template if Word should display the toolbar only in documents based on that template.

As soon as you OK the New Toolbar dialog box, the new, tiny, empty toolbar appears. Use the techniques covered earlier to add buttons to it.

Other toolbar options

Excel and Access offer unique toolbar-customization options unavailable in the other programs.

- In Excel, choosing Attach on the Toolbars tab of the Tools ⇨ Customize dialog box enables you to save your Custom toolbars with the current workbook file so that they are available to others who use the workbook.

- In Access, choosing Properties brings up another dialog box that lets you set a variety of options, such as whether the selected toolbar can be docked or altered. Who knows why Microsoft didn't provide these controls for the other programs, but you can accomplish the same goals via VBA routines.

Running out of room? Make some magic two-in-one toolbars

Push-button access to commands is great, but get carried away and you may wind up with so many toolbars that they crowd out your documents. Now that Office toolbars expand and contract dynamically, the space problem is a little less critical. Still, many of us can't get enough buttons, and with a little VBA programming you can create toolbars that seem to have twice as many buttons as the regular kind. Besides, even if you don't need *more* toolbars, the VBA procedure discussed here demonstrates how to display and position *different* toolbars as you need them. Again, VBA is covered in Part VI.

The technique actually requires two separate toolbars, each with a button that hides the current toolbar and displays the other one. In the macro code that follows for Word, substitute the names of your two toolbars for MagicToolbar1 and MagicToolbar2. Then, using the techniques described later in this section, create a button for the macro on both of the toolbars, placing it in the very first position (the far left).

```
Sub ToolbarSwapper()
For Each cb In CommandBars
    If cb.Name = "MagicToolbar1" Then
        With cb
            .Visible = Not (.Visible)
            If .Visible Then
' Try removing the comments from the next 3 lines
'           .Position = msoBarTop
'           .RowIndex = msoBarRowLast
'           .Left = 0
            Set myControl = .Controls(1)
            myControl.State = msoButtonUp
            End If
        End With
    End If

    If cb.Name = "MagicToolbar2" Then
        With cb
            .Visible = Not (.Visible)
            If .Visible Then
' Try removing the comments from the next 3 lines
'           .Position = msoBarTop
'           .RowIndex = msoBarRowLast
'           .Left = 0
            Set myControl = .Controls(1)
            myControl.State = msoButtonDown
            End If
        End With
    End If
Next

End Sub
```

Working with buttons on toolbars

In this section I discuss techniques for endowing each toolbar with just the buttons you want it to have, and only those buttons. To customize the buttons themselves, see the section "Customizing individual buttons" later in the chapter.

Relocating and deleting buttons

Aside from moving the toolbars themselves, the easiest customizing changes you can make are rearranging and removing buttons. To move a button to a new location, hold down Alt and drag the button to its new home on the same or another toolbar. To *copy* a button, drag it while holding down Alt+Ctrl. Note that this is consistent with the way Ctrl copies things in Explorer and My Computer. If the Tools ⇨ Customize dialog box is open, you can drag buttons around or off toolbars without pressing Alt, or copy them by dragging while holding down only Ctrl.

You can add or remove space (along with that little faux 3-D groove) between two buttons by Alt-dragging the button on the right sideways in either direction (Alt-drag the bottom button of the pair if you're working with a side-docked toolbar). To delete a button, Alt-drag it into the middle of the window, or up onto the title bar, releasing the mouse button when the pointer shows a big black X.

Secret

When space is really tight, you may be able to squeeze in an extra button on some toolbars by narrowing the special buttons that provide drop-down lists. On the Formatting toolbar, for example, the Style, Font, and Font Size buttons are all of this type. To narrow (or widen) a drop-down list button, open the Tools ⇨ Customize dialog box and click the button. When you then move the pointer to either edge of the button, it becomes a double-headed arrow. Drag the edge to change the button's width.

Adding buttons—the easy way

Office 2000 makes it easier than ever to enrich a toolbar's set of buttons, at least where the built-in toolbars are concerned. When any built-in toolbar is docked, clicking the thin More Buttons button at the far right drops down a menu offering the Add or Remove Buttons command, as well as any of the toolbar's buttons that aren't currently visible. Clicking here displays a secondary pop-up menu that shows all the buttons that might be suitable for the toolbar you're working with — Figure 5-5 shows what I mean. Click the buttons on this menu to add or remove them from the toolbar. Deactivated buttons remain on the menu, so you can add them back at any time. This is true even if you removed them by Alt-dragging them off the toolbar.

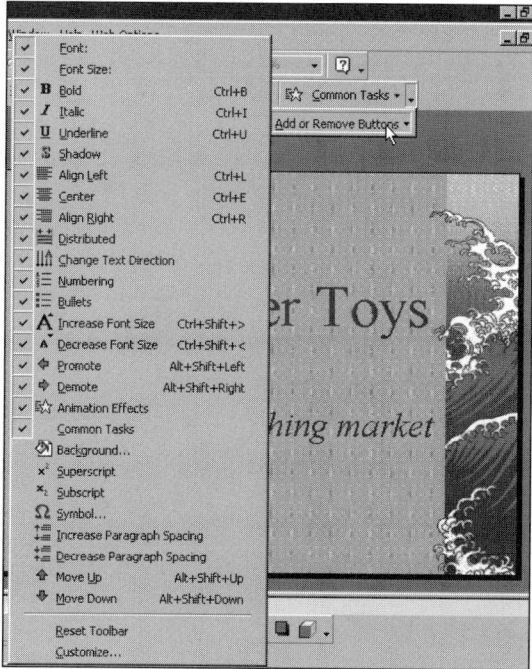

Figure 5-5: The Add or Remove Buttons menu for PowerPoint's Formatting toolbar

When a built-in toolbar is floating rather than docked, you access the Add or Remove Buttons command by clicking the little white arrow at the far left of the toolbar's title bar. Custom toolbars you create yourself don't have the Add or Remove Buttons command.

Adding buttons to toolbars

To place new buttons on your toolbars, start by opening the Tools ➪ Customize dialog box. Switch to the Commands tab, shown in Figure 5-6. The basic procedure for adding a button couldn't be simpler: You just drag the desired item from the Commands list on the right to its destination on any toolbar. The problem is finding the item you want on the list.

Note that items displayed with an icon in the Commands list become graphical toolbar buttons when you drag them to a toolbar, whereas those without icons are displayed as text-only buttons.

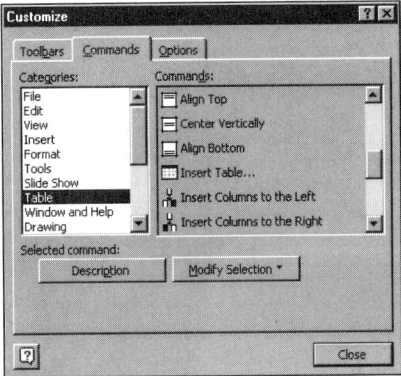

Figure 5-6: The Commands tab of the Tools ➪ Customize dialog box lets you add buttons to any toolbar.

Secret

Unless you get panic attacks when things are out of their proper places, you should take advantage of the empty space on the main menu bar: cram it full of buttons (take a look at Figure 5-10 later in the chapter).

Using the Commands tab

It pays to acquaint yourself with the way the Commands tab is organized. The key to finding the command or other item you want to put on a toolbar is to know — or more likely, guess — what category it belongs to.

The left side of the Commands tab lists its commands and other items under Categories, beginning with categories that more or less duplicate the standard menus (File, Edit, and so on) with some variations. When you select one of these categories, the Commands list on the right displays the standard commands found on that menu, along with other related commands.

Below the menu-related categories, the Categories list shows other categories that group together related commands that are not available on the default menus. Then toward the bottom of the list is a category for macros, and categories for items that you don't normally think of as commands: in Word, fonts and formatting styles; in Access, database tables, forms, and queries; and in all the Office applications, menus (for details on using the menu categories see "Customizing Office Menus" later in this chapter).

Secret

Word has a category titled "All commands" that puts them all in one very long alphabetical list. When you're not sure what category a command belongs to, don't waste time hunting through the less comprehensive categories.

What does that command do?

Up to this point, I've been assuming that you know the name of the command you want to assign as a toolbar button. But that's hardly a valid assumption. Office commands are named inconsistently and sometimes cryptically, so it's easy to be unsure about whether a given command will do the job you want it to do.

The Commands tab offers some guidance. Select a likely sounding command and choose Description to see a help message describing the command's function. Of course, you can always fall back on trial and error: Place the command on a toolbar, and then click the new button and see if it works the way you intended.

Customizing individual buttons

To change the look of a button, start by opening the Tools ⇨ Customize dialog box. You don't need the dialog box itself, but you have to display it to work with the buttons. At this point, right-clicking the button displays a shortcut menu full of options pertaining to the button's appearance (Figure 5-7).

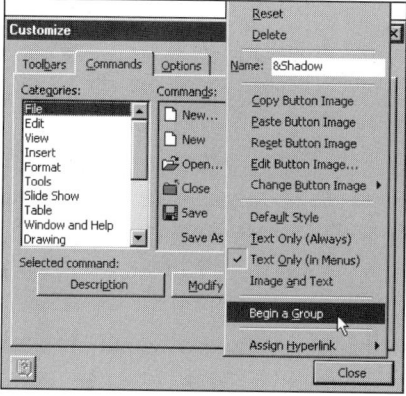

Figure 5-7: This shortcut menu lets you modify a toolbar button's look.

Office can display an icon, text, or both on the surface of any button (except for menu buttons, which only appear as text). You control this via a set of choices on the lower part of the shortcut menu:

- To display only the icon, or *button image,* for the command, check Default Style. Of course, this only works if the button has an associated image — otherwise, you see text.

- To display the button with descriptive text only, check one of the Text Only choices. Which one doesn't matter if you're dealing with a toolbar button, as opposed to an item on a menu list. The entry at Name on the shortcut menu is the button's text label.

- To display the button with both an image and text, check (hold your breath) Image and Text on the shortcut menu. You might want to do this while you're learning to associate the button's image with its function.

Changing or editing button images

To assign one of Office's built-in button images to a button, choose Change Button Image from the shortcut menu. Select a graphic from the pop-up bank of button tops. If none of the supplied button images rings your chimes, you can design a new image from scratch or modify the existing image. Choose Edit Button Image from the shortcut menu to bring up the Button Editor, shown in Figure 5-8.

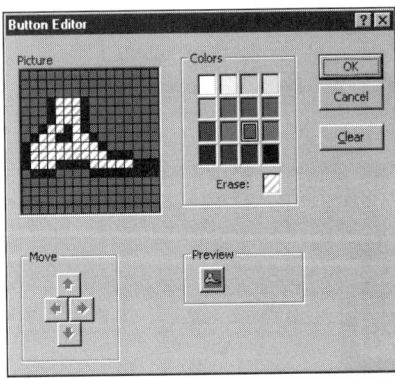

Figure 5-8: Edit the button image in this window.

The Button Editor is a crude painting tool, but it works OK for such small images. The main work area is the grid labeled Picture, where you paint a magnified version of the image. Each of the little squares represents a single pixel in the image and on the screen.

Squares with diagonal gray stripes are empty, meaning the background color shows through in the finished button. Clicking a square toggles it back and forth between empty and the currently selected color. As you work, the button image appears at actual size in the Preview area.

Choose Clear to erase the entire Picture area and start from scratch. Those four arrow buttons beneath the Picture move the entire image in case it's not aligned the way you want it.

Copying button images

Office makes it easy to copy images from one button to another. For example, you might be deploying a series of buttons for some related macros and want their images to look alike. For that matter, you might come across a button in Access that perfectly symbolizes a macro you've recorded in Excel. That's no problem, because the button-copying function works across all the Office applications.

To copy a button image to a new button, start from the application that contains the original version. Open the Customize dialog box and right-click the button you admire, choosing Copy Button Image from the shortcut menu. If necessary, switch to the destination application and open its Customize dialog box. Now right-click the button to receive the copied image and choose Paste Button Image. If the copied image requires modifications, edit it by choosing Edit Button Image.

Importing button images from other sources

Because the Paste Button Image command relies on the Windows clipboard, you can feed it any bitmap image. That means you can create a suitable bitmap image from scratch using a paint program such as Windows Paint or Paint Shop Pro (included on the CD-ROM that comes with this book) and then paste it onto a button.

Better yet, you can pilfer graphics from anywhere in Windows via a screen capture program. Anything you see on the screen can be converted into a button image. If you don't have screen capture software, you can capture a screen image to the clipboard by pressing the PrintScreen key, alone or in combination with Alt.

The key to good results with imported button images is to make them the right size: The button image grid is 16 · 16 pixels. If the image you paste is some other size, Office makes a gallant effort to scale it to fit, but the results generally look terrible. When you capture the image from the screen, it's hard to get the size right at the time. Don't try—instead, capture a larger area, pasting it into Paint or another bitmap editing program. There, you can select the best 16 · 16–pixel area, copying it back to the clipboard for pasting onto the button.

CD

If you plan to do any serious work with icons, get the right tool for the job— an icon editing and management program. The shareware programs IconForge (on *this book's* companion CD-ROM) and Microangelo are great choices.

Displaying ScreenTips for toolbar buttons

ScreenTips are those little yellow message boxes that pop up when you hold the mouse pointer for a second or two over an item. ScreenTips for toolbar buttons should be turned on and probably already are. But if they're not, open the Tools ⇨ Customize dialog box, switch to the Options tab, and check the box labeled Show ScreenTips on Toolbars (see Figure 5-9).

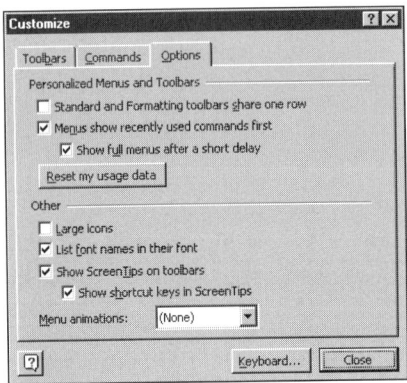

Figure 5-9: The Options tab of the Tools ⇨ Customize dialog box lets you control the display of ScreenTips and menus.

No matter which application you use to set this option, it applies throughout Office. In Word, PowerPoint, and Access (but not in Excel) a subsidiary option in the same dialog box tab lets you decide whether each ScreenTip includes the button's keyboard shortcut, if there is one.

Choosing button names

Although graphical buttons are space-efficient and add zest to your screen, you may find use for a few buttons labeled with text instead. Often you just don't have the time to locate a suitable button image for a command that doesn't already have one or to draw an image of your own. In addition, the text can tell you what the button does, which is certainly nice to know.

Every button has a name, and by default, its name is the label you see on the button when you set it to display as text (the available options for button display are discussed at the beginning of the "Customizing buttons" section earlier in this chapter). To change the button's name, open the Tools ⇨ Customize dialog box and then right-click the button. In the shortcut menu that appears (refer back to Figure 5-7), edit the entry at Name.

Secret

If you have a really great visual memory, you can squeeze lots more buttons onto your toolbars by giving them very short names and displaying them as text only. The results may not be pretty, but you'll have one-click access to tons of commands. And if you're willing to do a little work in VBA with the technique described in the text that follows, you can have the ScreenTip display a full description of the command.

Labeling a button with text is also a quick way to create a keyboard shortcut for that command. See "Quick keyboard shortcuts in any Office application" later in this chapter.

Normally, the ScreenTip for a button just displays its name, so a default ScreenTip doesn't supplement a short, cryptic button name with further information. However, if you're willing to go to the trouble of writing brief VBA routines, you can define long ScreenTip explanations of each button's function with its TooltipText property. Part VI has details on writing VBA modules. Here, I'll just present the code you need for an example routine that defines a custom ScreenTip for an imaginary Excel button:

```
Sub This_Button_Needs_A_ScreenTip()
CommandBars("Mr. GoodBar").Controls(2).TooltipText = _
    "Format cell: centered, bold, currency"
End Sub
```

The `Sub` and `End Sub` statements are just wrappers for the procedure—the one starting with `CommandBars` performs the work. Analyzing it from left to right, it identifies the toolbar you're working with—in this case a custom toolbar named Mr. GoodBar. It then specifies a particular button, the second one on the toolbar in question. Finally, it selects the TooltipText property. The text following the equal sign redefines that property.

To prepare your version of this routine, substitute the name of the toolbar that contains your button for the name in quotes. Enter the button's position, counting the first button on the left as 1, in the parentheses after `Controls`. Your new ScreenTip text goes in quotes after the equal sign.

You only have to run this procedure (macro) once. Because Office stores the new ScreenTip with the template or document file you're working with, you can delete the procedure immediately.

Resizing list buttons

You can widen or narrow toolbar controls containing lists, such as the Font button in Word, Excel, and PowerPoint. Right-click over any toolbar and choose Customize to open the Customize dialog box, and then click the control in question. Move the mouse to either end of the control until the pointer becomes a two-headed arrow. You can then drag to change the control's width.

Creating buttons that activate hyperlinks or insert graphics

Office 2000 now lets you easily assign a hyperlink to any button or menu item on any toolbar or menu (I'll refer to toolbar buttons and menu items collectively as "buttons"). The same feature also enables you to create buttons that each insert a specific picture into your documents—a good trick for keeping your logo or scanned signature handy.

Begin by opening the Tools ⇨ Customize dialog box. Because assigning a hyperlink to a button deactivates its original function, you probably want to add a new button to the toolbar system—use the techniques discussed in

"Adding buttons to toolbars" earlier in this chapter. With the target button visible, right-click it to display its shortcut menu (Figure 5-7). Choose Assign Hyperlink and then one of these items:

- **Open.** Creates a hyperlink to an Internet site, Web page, or disk file. After you close the Customize dialog box, clicking the button causes the assigned item to appear in the appropriate application or in your browser.
- **Insert Picture.** Creates a link to a graphic file (available only in Word, PowerPoint, and Excel). When you click the customized button, the application inserts the specified picture into the current document.

Both commands open the Insert Hyperlink dialog box. The dialog box and hyperlinks in general receive full treatment in Chapter 14.

You can restore a hyperlink button to its original function by choosing Assign Hyperlink ⇨ Remove Link from the button's shortcut menu. Note that you can't convert a menu, submenu, or drop-down list button into a hyperlink.

Customizing Office Menus

Though one-click graphical buttons are fast, menus have their own set of strengths: They pack lots of commands into very little space, and each command has a descriptive name. Use them for the commands you don't need constantly.

To repeat, menus are now just specialized buttons that display a list of commands. The listed items themselves are usually commands just like the buttons on a toolbar, although they can also be submenus, menu buttons that produce subsidiary lists of commands. At any rate, you use the techniques just described, with a few modifications, to customize menus.

The methods covered in "Relocating and deleting buttons" work to move entire menus to other locations on the same toolbar or to any other bar. But in addition, these same techniques let you move a menu itself, or any of its commands, onto another menu. Likewise, a submenu can be moved off its current parent menu and out onto a toolbar to become independent.

Secret

What we're talking about here is the ability to radically customize the entire menu system. If you're well versed in the keyboard shortcuts and toolbar buttons, you probably hardly ever use the menus. In that case, you can delete the menu items you never use and condense the rest into a single menu button listing all the standard menus as submenus. You can still fall back on the menu commands when you need them, but now you have the rest of the menu bar free for more one-click buttons. Check out Figure 5-10.

Contrariwise, if you need a certain submenu all the time, haul it out onto the menu bar (or onto some other toolbar) where it's easier to get to.

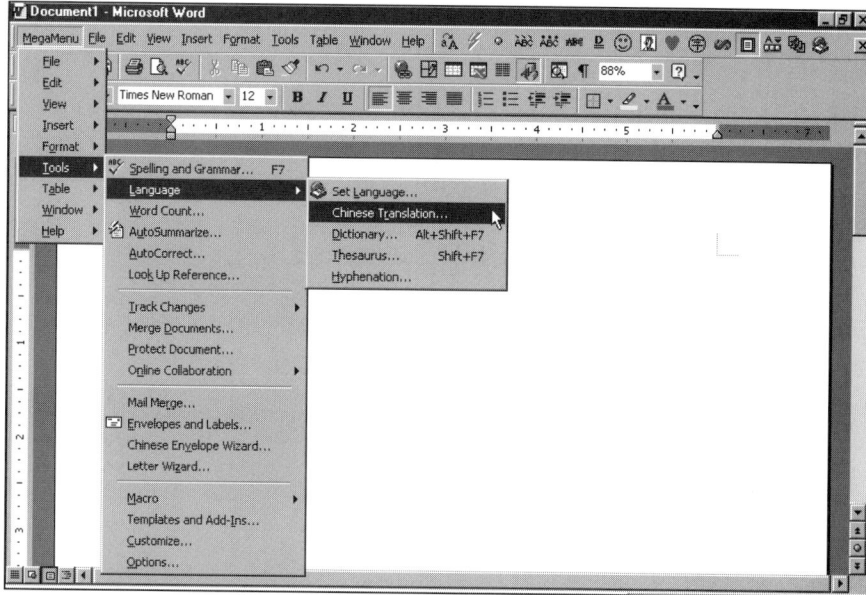

Figure 5-10: The menu bar in Word with added graphical buttons and a custom menu containing all the standard menus

Menu display options

To shorten the time you spend hunting for commands, Office applications now give you an option to display only the menu commands you've recently used. Turn on this feature by checking the box labeled Menus Show Recently Used Commands First in the Options tab of the Tools ⇨ Customize dialog box (refer back to Figure 5-9). With the feature in effect you can still see the entire menu by holding the mouse over the little double-arrow at the bottom of the menu for a second or so. The commands that weren't on the shorter version appear recessed on the complete menu that appears so that you can see what has been added (see Figure 5-11).

Other pertinent settings in the Options tab of the Tools ⇨ Customize dialog box include:

- **Show full menus after a short delay.** Check this box if you don't want to exert your mouse hand at all to see the complete menu. It appears automatically if you just wait two or three seconds.

- **Reset my usage data.** Click here if you want to access the complete set of menu commands again. Office immediately resumes tracking the commands you do use and will soon start hiding the ones you don't.

- **Menu animations.** Fond of screen distractions? This setting forces Office to display menus gradually rather than all at once.

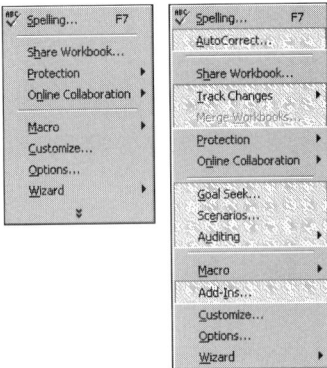

Figure 5-11: The short and long forms of an Excel menu as they appear when the "Show recently used commands first" setting is turned on

By the way, all the menu display settings apply throughout Office, regardless of which application you use to change them.

Moving menus with the mouse

You can move existing menus (the individual menu buttons, not the menu bars they belong to) with the Alt-drag and Alt+Ctrl-drag techniques. To make a menu into a submenu on another menu, Alt-drag its button over the second menu so the latter opens, displaying its list of items. While still holding down Alt, continue to drag the first menu down the list until you get to the desired position. To place a submenu on the menu bar or other toolbar, you must open the Tools ⇨ Customize dialog box and then drag or Ctrl-drag the submenu to its destination.

Customizing menu items

The Alt-drag technique doesn't work for moving items on menus to new locations, and of course you can't use it to add new items to menus. To accomplish these goals, you have to open the Tools ⇨ Customize dialog box first.

Once the Customize dialog box is open, clicking a menu button displays the entire menu. You can then drag any item (including submenus) to a new position on the menu, onto a different menu, or to a toolbar as an independent item. Note that you must release the mouse button after clicking the main menu button—if you try to drag from the menu button down to the list of menu items, you succeed only in moving the menu to another toolbar or deleting it altogether.

To add a new menu command, find the item in the Commands tab of the dialog box (see "Using the Commands tab" earlier in this chapter). Then drag it into place on the menu du jour.

To add a 3-D groove and a little space between any two menu items, indicating a new group of items, just drag the lower item down a bit. You can remove the groove by dragging the item back up. Right-clicking the item and selecting Begin a Group is an unnecessarily cumbersome alternative.

Only one version of each built-in menu is allowed

Caution

Changes you make to the items on any of the standard menus appear in all copies of that menu, if for some reason you have created more than one. If you want to build two File menus that list different items, don't copy the standard File menu. Instead, create a new menu and rename it "File."

Displaying a graphical image with a menu item

A command listed on an Office menu can be displayed with a graphical image alongside the item's text, assuming an image is associated with the item. Some of the items on Office's standard menus are set up this way. When a default menu item has an associated graphic, it's the same one that appears on the toolbar button for that command. (However, menu buttons, the ones that open menus or submenus, can't be given images.)

To add a graphic to a menu item, or to replace the graphic it already has, open the Tools ⇨ Customize dialog box. Click the menu containing the item, and then right-click the item itself to display the shortcut menu. You can then use the Edit Button Image, Paste Button Image, and Choose Button Image commands to add the image you want.

The image appears in the menu alongside the item text if Default Style or Image and Text is checked in the shortcut menu. To turn off the image display, check either of the Text Only choices.

Creating new menus

To place a new menu on the menu bar or any other toolbar, start from the Commands tab of the Tools ⇨ Customize dialog box. At the bottom of the Categories list, you find two relevant items: Built-in Menus and New Menu.

- If you select Built-in Menus, the Commands list displays the menus found on the standard menu bar, along with a number of others, depending on the application (many of these are submenus from the standard menus). You can drag the built-in menu of choice onto any toolbar (where it opens with its complete list of commands), and then further customize it there.

- If you select New Menu, the only choice in the Commands list is the obscure New Menu. Dragging this to a toolbar creates a new empty menu, to which you can add items with the technique covered in the previous section.

Renaming menus

To rename a menu, use the same technique you would for other buttons: With the Tools ⇨ Customize dialog box open, right-click the menu to display the shortcut menu, and then edit the entry at Name. Type an ampersand (&) immediately before the character that should be underlined in the menu name. This character indicates the key that opens the menu with the standard Windows keyboard technique — when you press the key after or while pressing Alt.

Note that one difference between menu buttons and other buttons is that Office won't let you assign a graphical button image to a menu button, a submenu item on a menu, or any button that produces a list of items (such as the AutoText button). Can't do it.

Customizing the shortcut menus

In addition to customizing all the regular menus, Office lets you fiddle around to your heart's content with the context-sensitive shortcut menus that pop up when you click the right mouse button on something in your document.

Let me tell you, there are a lot of these shortcut menus. Don't plan to make a thorough revision of the options Microsoft has provided for you, or you'll be spending days on the project. However, if a particular shortcut menu cries out for a command that it doesn't possess, you can add it.

The technique for editing a shortcut menu starts with an awkward first step — you get the feeling that the software designers at Microsoft came up with it at the end of a long day. But hey, it works and you can see the logic behind it if you squint.

Here's how to start the process: In the Tools ⇨ Customize dialog box, start by switching to the Toolbars tab. Scroll the Toolbars list to find a Shortcut Menus item. Check its box to display a special toolbar intended solely for customizing shortcut menus, shown in Figure 5-12.

This is the awkward step I was referring to. How are you supposed to know that you need to turn on a toolbar called Shortcut Menus before you can customize shortcut menus? Every other toolbar in the list actually functions in your applications, and you check its box to display it on the screen after you close the Customize dialog box. By contrast, this artificial Shortcut Menus toolbar has no independent life. At the least they could have named it the Customize Shortcut Menus toolbar.

Chapter 5: Customizing Secrets: Office Your Way

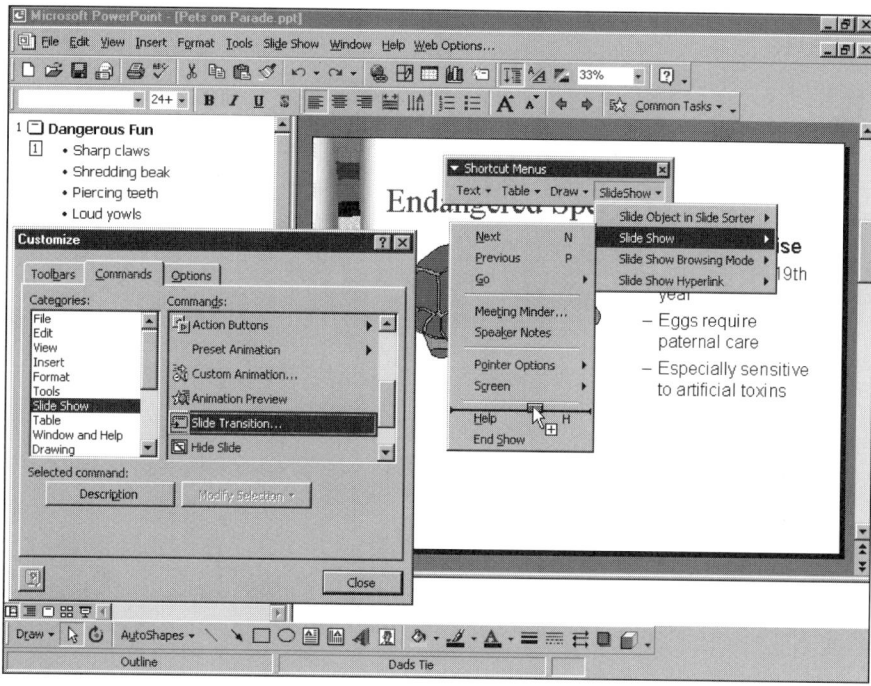

Figure 5-12: Customizing a shortcut menu in PowerPoint

Enough of my grousing. To access a shortcut menu, you click one of two or three special menus on the toolbar, which group together the shortcut menus for the current application in categories. The shortcut menus are submenus of these toolbar menus. When you've found the one you want, click it to display the actual list of menu items. (Remember, you must click and release each menu and submenu button in turn to display the menu lists — you can't drag your way through the hierarchy.)

The rest of the process works just like customizing one of the regular menus. You switch back to the Commands tab in the Customize dialog box and then move items from the list there to the target shortcut menu. The only problem, and it can be a big one, is this: By the time you've worked your way through the menu hierarchy, the shortcut menu often covers up the Customize dialog box, at least on a standard VGA screen. Don't be surprised if you have to repeatedly reposition the dialog box, the toolbar, or both before you can access all the tools you need at the same time.

Restoring the original menus

Secret

If you get too far afield in your forays into menu customization, don't fret. To bring back the original configuration of a built-in menu is easy, but you have to know how. Open the Tools ➪ Customize dialog box, and then right-click the menu and choose Reset at the very top of the shortcut menu. The restoration happens immediately, and there's no going back. Resetting a menu is an all-or-nothing proposition. If you want to preserve customizations of individual menu items, copy them to another menu or toolbar first.

Saving and Reusing Custom Toolbars and Menus

Different custom toolbars, menus, and buttons may be appropriate for different situations or documents. Word and Excel let you store sets of these items so that you can activate the right set when you need it. In Word, you use templates; in Excel, you store them in settings files (.xlb files). The specific techniques required are covered in the sections on the individual Office applications.

Customizing the Keyboard

In contrast to the powerful control they provide over toolbar layout and function, most Office applications limit your keyboard options. The obvious exception is Word, which lets you define and redefine keyboard shortcuts with complete abandon—for any command, macro, font, or special character (see Chapter 26 for details).

Keyboard customization in Excel and Access is much more limited and cumbersome to set up, and isn't allowed at all in PowerPoint and Outlook. Still, it's worth using the tools that are available. Keyboard customization for Word, Excel, and Access is covered separately in the sections for those applications.

Quick keyboard shortcuts in any Office application

Secret

The trick that follows gives you a quick-and-dirty keyboard shortcut for any command in any other Office program. It relies on the standard Windows method for opening menus using the Alt key (first you press Alt, and then the menu shortcut key, or you can press both Alt and the menu key at the same time). Because toolbar buttons and menu buttons are now essentially the same, you can "open" a button with an Alt-key menu shortcut, as long as you display the button's name.

To create a keyboard shortcut for any command in any Office program, do the following:

1. Start by assigning the command to a toolbar button as described in the previous section. If a button for the command already exists, skip this step.
2. Once the button is in place, open the Tools ➪ Customize dialog box (as shown back in Figure 5-6).
3. Right-click the button to display its shortcut menu (Figure 5-7).
4. Here's the key step: The entry at Name is the label that appears on the button if you display it as text, or if it has no button image. Here, type an ampersand (&) immediately to the left of the shortcut key (which triggers the command when pressed in combination with Alt).
5. To activate the shortcut, you must display the name on the button. The name will be displayed if Default Style is checked on the shortcut menu only if there is no associated button image. If the button has an image, check Text Only or Image and Text to ensure the name appears on the button.

Choosing the right shortcut key

Choosing the right key for the shortcut in Step 4 can be difficult. Most, if not all, of the built-in commands already have a shortcut key defined in their name. You can accept this default, but it often makes sense to change it.

Ideally, of course, you would prefer a mnemonic letter suggestive of the command, such as *F* for the Font command. Trouble is, you don't want to duplicate the shortcuts for existing buttons, including the standard menus such as File. (If you do specify a duplicate shortcut key, nothing catastrophic happens—but to use your shortcut, you have to press the shortcut repeatedly until the desired button is selected, and then press Enter.)

The other point to consider when naming a button is that most text labels make the button wider than it would be with an image alone. Try to shorten the name to the minimum text necessary to remind you of the button's function. If you're sure you have the shortcut memorized, change the button's name to the shortcut character alone.

Changing the Color Scheme

You can control the color of items you add to documents—such as text, graphics, borders—within each Office program. But what about the color of the window itself? To change that, you need the Windows Control Panel.

Changing windows background and ScreenTip colors

To change the colors of the work area, open the Display applet in Control Panel and switch to the Appearance tab. Click in the main work area of the sample window labeled Active Window, so that Window appears in the Item field. Then choose Color to select a new color.

You can also change the ScreenTip color in the same Display Properties dialog box (see "Displaying ScreenTips for toolbar buttons" earlier in this chapter). Select the Tooltip option in the Item drop-down list.

Using the Automatic color

Secret

When you assign a text color in Word or Excel, one of the choices is Automatic, hardly a self-explanatory description of color. What Microsoft means is "Windows default window text color." Text assigned to the Automatic color appears in whatever window text color is currently selected in the Appearance tab of the Control Panel's Display applet. To change this color, select Window at Item, and then change the Color (to the right of the Font field).

In PowerPoint and Excel, the Automatic color choice is also available for slide and chart elements, such as text and backgrounds in PowerPoint slides, or bars and lines in Excel charts. In this case, it refers to the default color for the selected element. If you change the defaults, elements assigned to the Automatic color change hue automatically.

Conclusion

Customizing Office takes time and effort, but the payback comes quickly. With macros, toolbars, menus, and Help screens tailored to your specific work habits, you'll produce finished documents faster and with less frustration. It's kinda fun, too.

Chapter 6

Office on the Internet

In This Chapter

- A quick primer on the Internet, intranets, and the World Wide Web
- Office's blizzard of features for Internet and intranets
- How to use Office applications and your browser jointly to access documents on the Web and on the desktop
- Navigating among hyperlinked documents — whether they're stored on the network, the Web, or your own hard disk
- Viewing and editing Office documents in Internet Explorer 5.0
- All about Office's e-mail features

No one can have missed the explosive growth of the Internet and its most visible component, the World Wide Web. No longer is the question whether the Internet or some permutation will become a central feature of our culture and economy, but just how pervasive its influence will be. Office 2000 consolidates and extends Microsoft's efforts to integrate communications on the Internet and corporate intranets with personal computing.

Part IV covers Office tools for publishing and managing information on the Web. The focus of this chapter is on using Office and Internet Explorer together to access information browser-style, whether the documents in question reside on your own computer, a network server, or out there on the Web.

Office 2000 and the Internet

Internet features are rampant in Office. The list includes:

- You can insert hyperlinks directly into your Office documents — Word even converts Web addresses into hyperlinks automatically as you type them. Office hyperlinks can refer to Web pages and other Internet addresses, but also to documents on your network or on your own computer, and to e-mail addresses as well. Clicking a hyperlink takes you to the specified location either through your Internet software or by directly opening the document. See "Working with Hyperlinks" in Chapter 14.

- You can also jump to Web pages and other Internet addresses via the Web toolbar, available in all the Office applications. The Web toolbar is described in detail later in this chapter.

- All Office applications except Outlook let you open Web pages (HTML files). (Access extracts tabular data from HTML files, ignoring formatting and other content.)

- Word, Excel, and PowerPoint let you save any document in HTML format for distribution as a Web page, yet reopen it with content and formatting intact in the application that created the document. Chapter 1 has background on this new capability. In Access you can save datasheets, reports, and form data as Web pages, with the option to enable people viewing the pages to interact dynamically with the database. Outlook sends and opens e-mail messages in HTML format.

- Office 2000 Premium includes FrontPage, a full-fledged tool for Web page design and complete Web site publishing and management. It's easy to transfer Office documents into a FrontPage Web site, and FrontPage shares its design themes with Office programs.

- Office now includes a set of new ActiveX controls intended for use on the Web pages you design. With a compatible browser, anyone opening these pages can interact with worksheets, pivot tables, charts, and Web databases. Office also lets you add VBScript or JavaScript code to Web pages with a new script editor.

- If you use Outlook or other compatible e-mail software, you can send Office documents as e-mail messages. In Word, you can start a new message by clicking a hyperlink to the recipient's e-mail address. Office's e-mail features are summarized later this chapter, and Chapters 18 and 51 offer detailed coverage.

- Outlook provides a prefab field for the Web page of each of your contacts right along with the name, address, phone number, and e-mail address information. An Explore Web Page command takes you directly to the person's page.

- From within an Office application you can jump directly to Microsoft's Office Web site.

Preparing to surf the Internet with Office

To use Office in conjunction with the Internet, you need to start with a connection to the Internet, of course. Most individual users rely on dial-up modem connections to an Internet service provider (ISP). In business, educational, and government organizations, much faster connections are often available via the institution's network. You must also have installed a browser, software that enables you to see (and hear) the contents of Web sites and to jump from site to site at will. The browser must also be set up properly in Windows so that Office will recognize its presence.

Choosing a Web browser for Office

Using Microsoft's Internet Explorer (IE) as your browser is definitely the path of least resistance for anyone with Office. IE is included with Office, and some Office features don't work properly unless you install the new version of the Microsoft browser. Office and IE share similar user interfaces, with the buttons on the Web toolbar in Office copied from their counterparts in IE.

However, if you're already hooked on Netscape Navigator or some other browser, Office won't make you switch and will generally work well with what you have. In point of fact, there are some good reasons to consider the Netscape browser. This isn't the place for a detailed comparison, but among Navigator's strengths are its availability on more platforms and its unambiguous support of Java, a less proprietary programming technology than Microsoft's ActiveX.

Internet and Intranet Backgrounder

The Internet is a sort of metanetwork of thousands upon thousands of computers and smaller computer networks located across the planet, connected to one another over fast telephone lines. The history of the Internet's evolution from a military enterprise to a communications tool for academia and, now, to a locus of frenzied commercial activity is a fascinating story.

World wide wackiness

Of course, it was the World Wide Web that brought the Internet to the attention of the general public. The Web added two crucial elements to the Internet. First, it gave users direct, on-screen access to multimedia documents containing formatted text, graphics images, and, more recently, sound and video. And it provided hyperlinks—text and graphics hot spots that let you jump from one document to another regardless of where the documents are located on the Internet.

About intranets

An *intranet* is a private network within a corporation or government agency based on the same network protocols used by the Internet. Because these include HTTP, the organization can set up its own internal Web, enabling users to find and distribute information using exactly the same browsers and Web page authoring tools used with the Internet. An intranet can be connected to the Internet, giving users seamless access to all the resources on both the intranet and the World Wide Web. For the most part, references I make to the Internet apply equally to an intranet. I'll spare you from cumbersome phrases like "Internet/intranet."

Internet Services and Protocols

Because the Internet connects computers of all types running many different operating systems and application programs, platform-independent standards had to be developed to make Internet communications possible. A protocol is the term for a standard governing the way software programs interact. The protocols you hear about most often include:

- **TCP/IP (Transmission Control Protocol/Internet Protocol):** This is the low-level protocol that lets computers connected on the Internet talk to one another intelligibly in the first place. Other Internet protocols such as HTTP and FTP build on and require TCP/IP.

- **FTP (File Transfer Protocol):** As the name implies, this older protocol simply enables you to download files from a computer on the Internet to your own computer, and, if you have privileges to do so, to transfer files from your machine to the other computer. Public FTP sites enable anyone to log in as an "anonymous" user, although they usually require your e-mail address as a password. Office includes special features for working with files on FTP sites, as described in Chapter 11.

- **HTTP (Hypertext Transfer Protocol):** This is the protocol that sets the Internet standards for creating, displaying, and hyperlinking multimedia documents on the World Wide Web.

- **HTML (Hypertext Markup Language):** This is a specialized programming language of sorts. HTML can also be thought of as a file format for documents, comparable to the formats used by Word and other Office applications for storing their files. As described in Chapter 14, HTML consists of codes that describe the content and layout of Web pages.

Other Internet services, each based on its own protocol, include Telnet, which lets you run programs on another computer, and Gopher, an Internet search tool that presents the item in a text format that can be viewed with Web browsers or other search interfaces.

Internet Addresses

Every Web page, FTP site, and other location on the Internet is identified by a unique address called a URL, or Uniform (or Universal) Resource Locator. Now that even the corner grocery store has a Web site, everyone recognizes addresses such as

    www.idg.com

Although today's browsers automatically interpret Internet addresses as Web sites, a complete URL actually begins with the protocol that must be used to access the site (HTTP, FTP, or what have you) followed by a colon. After a pair of forward slashes, the URL then lists the site or *domain* name followed by the name of the specific document or folder, as in these examples:

    http://www.microsoft.com/
    ftp://oak.oakland.edu/
    gopher://gopher.micro.umn.edu/

Accessing Web Pages in Office Applications

All five Office applications provide commands for viewing Web pages. Here are the methods you can use:

- To open a Web page (HTML document) in your browser, type its Web address (URL) or path and filename in the Address box of the Web toolbar. If the current Office document contains a hyperlink to the Web page you want to open, just click the hyperlink to display the page in your browser. You can also open Web pages in your browser by double-clicking them in My Computer or Explorer.

- To open a Web page in the current Office application, select it in the File ⇨ Open dialog box. This works in all Office applications except Outlook, but the results you get depend on the circumstances, as discussed in the next section. In Access, the Open dialog box lists Web pages only if you manually select Web Pages at Files of Type.

Secret

Be sure to check out the reverse technique, accessing Office documents from within your browser (see "Working with Office documents inside Internet Explorer" later in this chapter).

How Office applications cope with Web pages

What happens when you try to access a Web page with an Office application's Open command? Well, that depends. The details are as follows.

If you open a "regular" HTML file, Office imports the page into the current application. The results you see vary based on the constraints imposed by the application in question. In Excel, each paragraph of text occupies a set of merged cells in a single row of the worksheet; table cells in the Web page are converted to individual worksheet cells. If you import a page of any size into PowerPoint, the program valiantly tries to separate it into separate slides — but the results aren't always pretty, as Figure 6-1 illustrates.

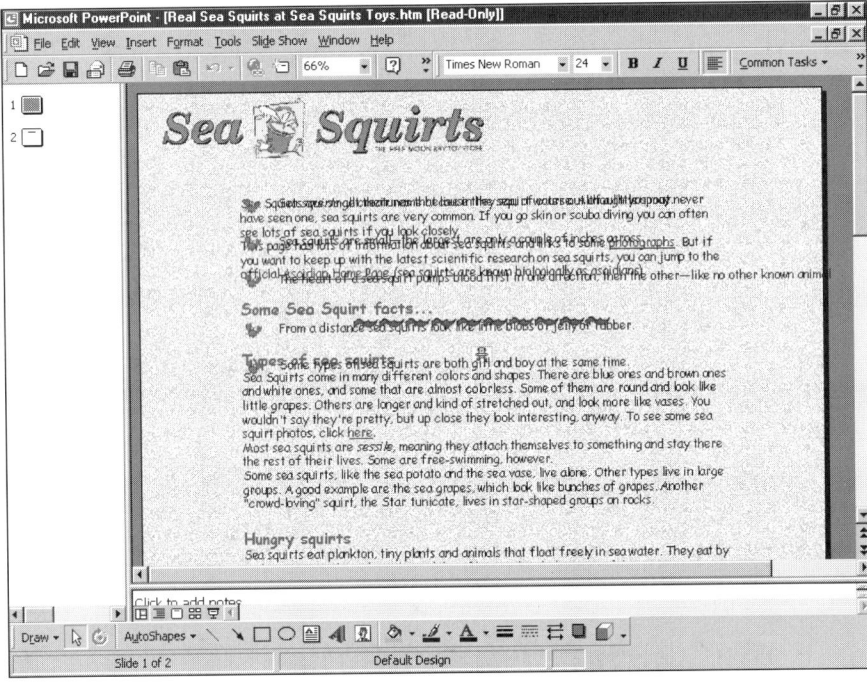

Figure 6-1: A downloaded Web page opened inappropriately in PowerPoint

However, if you select a Web page created by an Office application, the page opens in the application that made it. Note in Figure 6-2 that ordinary HTML files appear in file management dialog boxes with the icon of your default browser, but HTML files created by Office have unique icons that tell you which application they were saved by. (These special icons appear only in Office file management dialog boxes, and not in My Computer or Explorer. In the latter windows, double-clicking a Web page created in Word causes it to open in your browser, not Word.)

Secret

Once you've opened a Web page in an Office application, jumping to it from a different application or your browser takes you to the application in which you first opened it, not your browser.

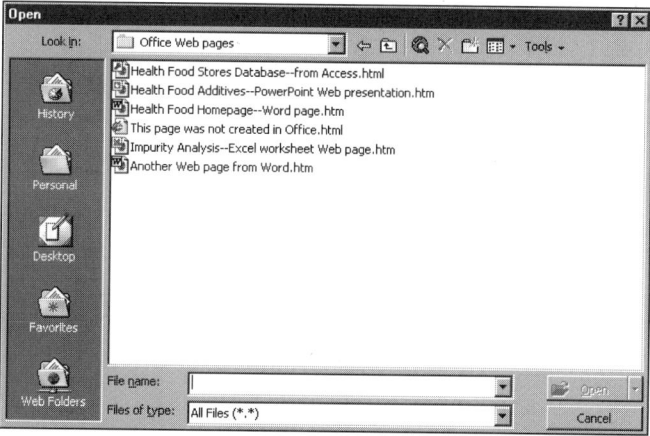

Figure 6-2: File icons for Web pages created by Office identify the application that created them.

Importing Web pages into Access

Access can open Web pages directly or import them into an existing database or project. Here are the techniques required (see Chapter 15 for details on the special features of Access Web pages):

- To open a Web page as a separate entity, not as a part of a database, use the Files of Type list in the File ⇨ Open dialog box to specify Web Pages, and then open the file. Practically speaking, you would do this to modify a previously saved data access page.

- To import an existing Web page into a database as the basis for a new data access page, select Pages in the Database window, and then double-click the choice labeled Edit Web Page That Already Exists.

- To import tabular data stored in an HTML table or list, choose File ⇨ Get External Data ⇨ Import.

Using the Web toolbar

Each Office 2000 application has a Web toolbar. Obviously, you use the Web toolbar to work with documents located on the Web. It's useful for any documents that contain hyperlinks, whether those documents are located on your own hard disk, are accessible via your network, or are out there somewhere on the Internet. Figure 6-3 shows the Web toolbar. As with most toolbars, the quickest way to display it is by right-clicking any visible toolbar and then selecting it on the shortcut menu that appears.

Figure 6-3: Office's Web toolbar

Most of the buttons on the Web toolbar duplicate the ones they resemble in IE5. For example, the Back arrow button at the far left jumps to the last document you viewed via hyperlink, whereas the Forward button reverses directions, if you've already gone backward. As in IE, the corresponding keyboard shortcuts are Alt+Left Arrow to go back and Alt+Right Arrow to go forward. The Start Page and Search the Web buttons take you to the same pages or documents as the Home and Search buttons in IE (see the section "Setting your own start and search pages" later in this chapter).

As shown in Figure 6-4, the Go button drops down a menu that mostly duplicates the functions of other buttons on the Web toolbar. For example, its Open command brings up a dialog box with an Address field offering the same history list as the main Address button on the Web toolbar. Those items at the bottom of the menu are documents in the hyperlink sequence — see "Using the file list at the bottom of the Go menu" later in this chapter. All this makes Go a good item to add to the main menu bar if you're short on space for toolbars. However, the Go menu does have some tricks of its own to offer. It lets you change the start and search pages, and it lists documents you've opened via hyperlinks (see "Navigating among hyperlinked documents" later in this chapter). But don't expect much from the check box in the Go ⇨ Open dialog box, the one labeled Open in New Window — for me, at least, documents opened with the Go ⇨ Open command always open in new windows, even if the check box is cleared.

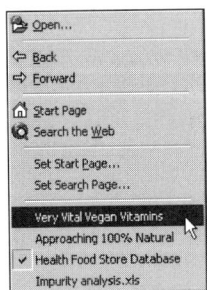

Figure 6-4: The Web toolbar's Go menu

The Web toolbar's Show Only Web Toolbar button is supposed to hide all the other toolbars, and it works that way at first. But if, while it's pressed in, you unhide one or more other toolbars, those toolbars will be allowed to stay on your screen the next time you turn the button on.

The Address button on the Web toolbar shows the Internet address (URL) or path of the current document, and it provides a drop-down history list of the most recent pages you've accessed on the Web or documents you've opened by jumping to them from hyperlinks. Standard documents you open via the File ⇨ Open dialog box aren't displayed here. (As far as I'm concerned, Microsoft really should provide a similar history button for ordinary files — nine files on the File menu aren't enough.)

Setting your own start and search pages

You can change the Web pages that Office jumps to when you click the Start Page and Search the Web buttons on the Web toolbar. Actually, either button can load any Web page or, for that matter, any ordinary Office document.

Your start page (home page) is supposed to be the one you use as a home base, from which you venture out into the wilds of the Web and to which you return when you get tangled up after pursuing one too many links. The search page is meant to give you one-click access to your favorite search tool on the Web. The default is typically the All in One search page on MSN (although this may vary depending on where you bought your computer). From it, you can access the most popular search engines on the Web. To change the page for either button, the key step is to start by opening the page you want to jump to with that button. Then choose Go ⇨ Set Start Page or Set Search Page.

Office and Internet Explorer share the same start and search pages. Setting the start or search page in an Office application changes the start page in Internet Explorer, and vice versa. If you pick an Office document instead of a Web page for your start or search page, clicking the relevant button opens the document in its home application, whether or not that application is currently running.

Navigating among hyperlinked documents

Chapter 14 covers inserting and modifying hyperlinks in your Office documents, because they're so vital to Web page design. Here, I offer a couple of tips on managing documents you've opened via hyperlinks, including any you've opened on the Web.

Using the Back and Forward buttons

You use the Back and Forward buttons on the Web toolbar to move between Office documents you've jumped to via hyperlinks (in other words, documents that opened in an Office application, not in your browser). Again, the equivalent keyboard shortcuts are Alt+Left Arrow and Alt+Right Arrow, respectively. If the next document in the sequence belongs to a different Office application, you'll be taken to that application. If the link is to a Web page, you're taken to your browser.

Using the file list at the bottom of the Go menu

The bottom of the Go menu lists Office documents that you opened via hyperlinks or with the Address bar. You can switch to any document on the list by selecting it.

Secret

Documents are listed at the bottom of the Go menu by title, if one exists, or by filename otherwise. You can change a document's title in the File ➪ Properties dialog box.

Note that the bottom of the Go menu lists the documents in your hyperlink sequence only when you're currently viewing one of them. In other words, if you've switched to another document that isn't in the hyperlink sequence — perhaps by opening a new document — you can't get back to the sequence via the Go menu. Instead, you have to go up to the Window menu and choose the document in the hyperlink sequence there.

Internet Explorer and Office

Internet Explorer 5 comes on the Office CD and shares key software components with Office. This section concentrates on the integration of IE with Office, but it also includes a sidebar with some tips on using IE effectively.

Working with Office documents inside Internet Explorer

In theory, one of the coolest ways to integrate the Internet with Office is to use IE as a kind of shell from which you access all your Office documents. In this capacity, IE functions much like Binder (see Chapter 12). An Office document appears in IE as it would in its originating application, with all the associated toolbars, keyboard shortcuts, and macros available to you (see Figure 6-5). In Microsoft's jargon, IE is acting as an ActiveX container to display ActiveX documents.

You can open Word, Excel, and PowerPoint documents via IE's File ➪ Open command or by dragging files from an Explorer or My Computer window onto the IE toolbar area. You can tell that IE is displaying an ActiveX document rather than a regular Web page by looking at the Windows taskbar — the IE icon changes to that of the contained document.

Once you've opened one or more Office documents in IE, you can switch between them and between any Web pages you've visited using the Back and Forward toolbar buttons. Alternatively, you can pick a specific open file or Web site from the list on IE's Go menu.

Chapter 6: Office on the Internet

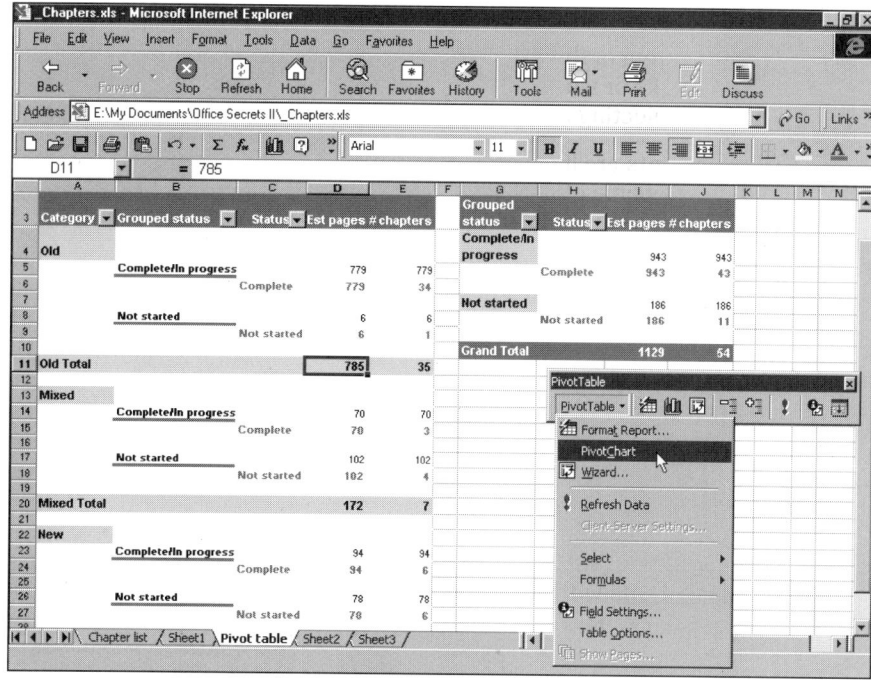

Figure 6-5: Editing an Excel worksheet in Internet Explorer

Secret

When you first open an Office document in IE, none of the toolbars of the originating application may be visible. To display them, select them from the View ⇨ Toolbars submenu. Once at least one toolbar is on the screen, you can display more by right-clicking the toolbar and selecting others from the menu that appears.

Caution

Editing documents inside of IE isn't quite like working in the originating application. For one thing, the File menu remains that of IE. That means you can't access some very important commands — such as File ⇨ Save, for example (however, the File ⇨ Save As command and the Save toolbar button do work). And IE's File ⇨ Open dialog box is *still* a wimpy little thing with none of the amenities you're accustomed to in Office. The Close command is unavailable, but this is consistent with the way IE works — you close one document by moving to another. Other commands, such as Customize, are disabled as well. And to access Help for the application instead of IE, open the submenu at the bottom of the main Help menu.

Jumping to Office documents via hyperlinks from within IE

Secret

While you're working in IE, clicking a hyperlink to an Office document opens that document in the browser, not in the Office application. If you would prefer to open such documents in Office instead, go to Explorer or My Computer. In the View ⇨ Options dialog box switch to the File Types tab. There, select the type of file you want to have open in the originating application, and click Edit. In the resulting Edit File Type dialog box, clear the check box labeled Browse in same window. You must repeat this procedure for each type of file you want to modify.

Editing Web pages opened in Internet Explorer

IE5 lets you edit any Web page open in the browser with push-button ease. Click the big Edit button at the right side of the main IE toolbar to open the page in the application that IE thinks is most suitable for editing it — typically, this is Word. You can click the skinny right side of the button to see and select alternative editing applications that may apply (see Figure 6-6). If you edit the page in Notepad, you see the complete HTML source code.

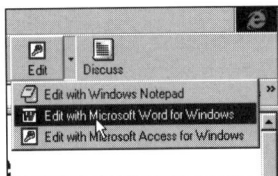

Figure 6-6: Click IE's Edit button to open the current Web page in another application for editing.

Internet Explorer Secrets

You can speed up your use of Internet Explorer with the following handy tips:

- **IE keyboard navigation shortcuts:** Press Tab to move to the next link on the current page, Shift+Tab to back up to the previous one; Enter activates the selected link. Press Ctrl+Tab or Shift+Ctrl+Tab to move from one frame to another.

- **More keyboard shortcuts:** Ctrl+D adds the page to your Favorites folder (instantly, with no opportunity to rename it). Alt+Left or Right Arrow duplicates the functions of the Back and Forward buttons. To select the Address bar, press Alt+D. Drop down the Address bar list by pressing F4. When you're typing an address, Ctrl+Enter adds www to the beginning and .com to the end.

- **Remember your history:** Get in the habit of displaying the history pane for easy access to sites you've previously visited — just click the big button with the sundial on it. The history pane records every page you've viewed, not just primary addresses as in the Address bar list. Put away the history pane when you're not using it by clicking the button again so that you can see more of the current page.

- **Organize your favorites:** Don't clutter up the Favorites folders with bazillions of Web site shortcuts. Instead, use the Favorites ⇨ Organize Favorites command to place them into subfolders within your Favorites folder. These subfolders then appear on cascading submenus of the Favorites menu.

- **Take advantage of IE's shortcut menu:** Right-clicking the page you're viewing pops up the shortcut menu shown in the accompanying figure. Use the shortcut menu to select and copy text and to save individual graphics.

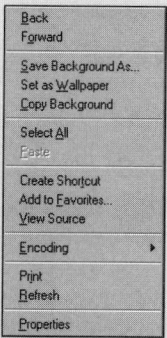

Internet Explorer's shortcut menu

- **Batching it:** If you prefer the direct approach, create a batch file called WebGo to take you to any Web site from DOS or the Start menu's Run command. The batch file just needs one line:

    ```
    start http://www.%1.com
    ```

    To go to a site called http://www.whashakin.com, type **WebGo whashakin**. With this batch file, you don't need to type the http:// preface or the .com suffix. Obviously, you would have to create a different batch file for Web sites that end, for instance, in .org or .edu.

- **File management with IE:** You can use IE as a limited stand-in for My Computer to manage files. Just type a path (such as C:\Windows) into the Address box. When you're viewing a disk folder, the main toolbar offers buttons for file management rather than Internet access.

- **You can take it with you:** Don't forget to take along your preferred Internet addresses when you travel. In IE5, choose File ⇨ Import and Export. In successive panels, select Export Favorites, choose the Favorites folder you want to include, and pick a destination filename for the exported list. Once the file is saved, you can copy it to your other computer and import it into IE there.

E-mail and Office

For most people, communicating by electronic mail is at least as important to their professional and personal lives as the ability to browse Web sites.

Office's e-mail features

Recognizing the centrality of e-mail in the digital age, Office integrates many e-mail features, including:

- A full-featured e-mail management system in the form of Outlook. I devote all of Chapter 51 to Outlook and e-mail.

- The ability to use Word as your editor for e-mail messages. This option is available if you use Outlook or Microsoft Exchange as your e-mail client (the client is the software individual users run to manage their e-mail, as opposed to the server software, which an organization runs to route mail to and from all the users). With Word as your editor, you can take advantage of all of its editing power and your own Word customizations, and you don't need to learn any new commands. If the receiving party also owns Word or has a copy of the Word viewer, that party can see the message with all of its formatting and graphics.

- Automatic recognition of e-mail addresses you type in your documents. All Office applications except Access convert the addresses into hyperlinks automatically. When you then click an e-mail address hyperlink, your e-mail editor starts with a blank message addressed to that person. (You can turn off the automatic detection of hyperlinks in Word using the AutoFormat As You Type tab of the Tools ⇨ AutoCorrect dialog box. In other applications, use the Undo command immediately after the automatic conversion to convert your entry back to ordinary text.)

- The ability to send any open Office document as an e-mail message via the File ⇨ Send To command (see Chapter 18).

Choosing e-mail software for use with Office

Of course, many people and organizations will have already chosen their e-mail software by the time they install Office. Although you can keep using whatever software you already have, be aware that your e-mail software must meet certain requirements to take advantage of many of Office's e-mail integration features. To be able to send Office documents directly, your e-mail software must be MAPI- or VIM-compatible. And if you want to use Word as your e-mail editor, you have to use Outlook.

Conclusion

Even if you never publish your own Web pages, Office has plenty of Web-related features that improve the experience of working with Web documents and communicating with other people. To delve deeply into the tools for Web site design and management, flip to Part IV of this book.

Part II
Building Great Documents with Office 2000

Chapter 7: Secrets of Polished Text

Chapter 8: Getting Graphical

Chapter 9: Secrets of Active Documents

Chapter 10: Sharing Information

Chapter 11: Printing Secrets

Chapter 7
Secrets of Polished Text

In This Chapter

- Spell-checking documents in all your Office applications
- Using Word's grammar checker without getting burned
- Making the best of Word's built-in thesaurus
- Accessing Bookshelf conveniently, so that you actually use all those great reference materials
- Performing full-speed text entry with AutoCorrect
- Managing large font collections
- Inserting symbol characters into your documents using six different techniques
- Using fonts tastefully, plus other typographic tips

Whether you're talking about a simple business letter, a long, complex report, or a presentation that has to convince, the core vehicle for communicating your ideas *and* impressing your audience is your text, nine times out of ten. You have to choose the right words, get them into your documents efficiently, spell them correctly, and then dress them up presentably in your document. This chapter touches on all these bases.

Perfect Spelling, Imperfect Grammar

From a writer's perspective, one of the coolest new features in Office 95 was Word's capacity to unobtrusively but unmistakably mark misspelled words, by underlining them with little wavy red lines. Since then, the on-the-fly spell-checker has been added to PowerPoint, too, and Word now boasts a similar as-you-work grammar checker (though of dubious value).

Word's Spelling and Grammar dialog box displays the misspelled word in context (meaning with its entire sentence). You can accept changes suggested by the spell-checker, or edit the word (or for that matter, any part of the sentence).

On-the-fly spelling checks still aren't available in Excel or Access. Still, all Office applications bestow the benefits of manual spell-checking. And they all share the same dictionaries, so you can be sure your results are consistent from application to application. Choose Tools ⇨ Spelling to start the process. If Office finds any spelling errors, you see the Spelling and Grammar dialog box shown in Figure 7-1 (if you're using Word) or a Spelling dialog box similar to the one in Figure 7-2 (if you're using another Office application).

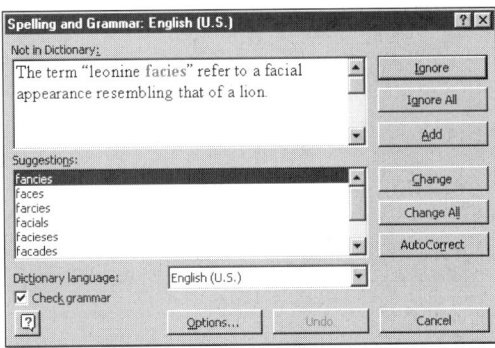

Figure 7-1: Use this dialog box to check spelling and grammar in Word.

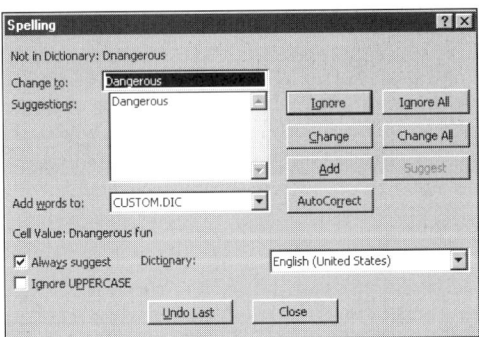

Figure 7-2: The Spelling dialog box, Excel style

Spelling facts

Here's a set of quick tips and secret facts about checking spelling in Office.

What gets checked

Make sure Office checks what you want it to. Keep in mind the following points:

- If you select text before you start the spell-check, Office checks only the selected text and then asks if you want to check the rest of the document. Take advantage of this technique to avoid being taken to far-off places in the document when all you want to do is check the current word.

- In Excel, with nothing selected, almost everything in the current worksheet gets checked: cell values and comments, charts, text boxes, headers and footers, and even buttons. However, formulas and the text that results from them aren't checked, nor are protected worksheets. If you check spelling while you're working in the formula bar, only the formula bar contents get checked.

- In Access, you *must* select something — a form, table, or query, or some data within one of those — to check.

- In Outlook, the spell-checker can only be activated when you're editing an item (a task, journal entry, or contact, for example) and then only when you're working in fields where you enter text in bulk (such as the task description or an e-mail message in a contact item).

Ignoring technicalities

How do Ignore and Ignore All work, you ask? That depends on the application.

- In Word, choosing Ignore makes the spell-checker skip this occurrence of the misspelled word from then on, even if you recheck the document. Choosing Ignore All skips the word everywhere it appears in the document; and again, you won't see it the next time you do a spell-check. If you decide you have Ignored some words that you really should have corrected, go to the Spelling and Grammar tab of the Tools ⇨ Options dialog box and choose Recheck Document.

- In PowerPoint, Ignore and Ignore All are permanent — after you've told the spell-checker to ignore a word, you can't get the spell checker to notice that word again in the current document.

- In Excel, Ignore and Ignore All only affect the current spell-check operation. The next time you check spelling, the ignored words will again be flagged as misspelled.

- In Word and PowerPoint, you can edit your document while the Spelling dialog box is open. If you do, the Ignore button changes to Resume, which you must click to restart the spell-check.

Correcting misspellings

To correct a misspelled word in the Spelling dialog box, you choose Change. If you like one of the suggestions, select it and then choose Change to make the substitution and move on to the next misspelling.

If you don't like the suggestions, edit the text yourself. Now when you choose Change, Office rechecks your entry (or the whole sentence in Word). If the edited text contains new misspellings, you'll get an appropriate warning. Change All works the same way but corrects every occurrence of the misspelled word automatically.

Turning off spell-checking for specific text

In Word and PowerPoint, you can skip over any text that would otherwise earn poor marks from the spell-checker, perhaps because it's full of proper names, technical mumbo-jumbo, or foreign language terms. That way, the rest of the document will still be checked.

The trick: Select the text, choose Tools ⇨ Language ⇨ Set Language (in PowerPoint, just Tools ⇨ Language) to open the Language dialog box. Then, in Word, check the Do not Check Spelling or Grammar box, or in PowerPoint, select "(no proofing)." See "Checking spelling in other languages" later in this chapter for details about the way this dialog box works.

In Word, you can turn off spelling and grammar checking for paragraph styles, too. This way you can banish the spell checker's red pencil by applying a style.

If you regularly work with goofy spellings, the command to shut off spell-checking for specified text only deserves a keyboard shortcut or a place on your toolbars. This requires a one-step macro that you can record. Choose Tools ⇨ Macros ⇨ Macro ⇨ Record New Macro, assigning the macro to a toolbar or the keyboard. With the macro recorder running, open the Language dialog box and select the option that turns off proofing as described earlier. As soon as you OK the dialog box, stop the macro recorder.

To use the recorded macro, you must first select the text that should not be checked and then click the macro's button or press its keyboard shortcut. In Word, if you want the macro to apply to the current word automatically when no text is selected, create it as follows in the Visual Basic editor (see Part VI):

```
Sub ProofingShutOff()
   If Selection.Type = wdSelectionIP Then
      Selection.Words(1).LanguageID = wdNoProofing  ' see below
   Else
      Selection.LanguageID = wdNoProofing
   End If
End Sub
```

To shut off proofing for the *paragraph* containing the insertion point instead of the current word, substitute the following line for the third line in the preceding macro, the line with the "see below" comment:

```
Selection.Paragraphs(1).Range.LanguageID = wdNoProofing
```

Managing the spelling dictionaries

Office checks spelling by comparing the words in the document against entries in its dictionaries. These dictionaries are really just lists of correctly spelled words. Office comes with a giant (words in the U.S. English version) dictionary containing officially approved spellings. You can install dictionaries for other languages, and you can create your own custom spelling dictionaries for special words you use regularly.

Working with custom dictionaries

You probably use lots of words that aren't in the standard spelling dictionary, whether these come from the specialized technical jargon of your profession or the caverns of your own mind (as in, "Blast! More telegraffiti guzz in my e-mail!"). If you *intend* to use such words, make sure they're spelled correctly by adding them to your custom dictionary. You can also obtain prefab custom dictionaries containing common technical terms (one source is mentioned in "Checking spelling in other languages" later in this chapter).

All your Office applications use the same custom spelling dictionaries, but you must use Word to control which of them are active. Use the Custom Dictionaries dialog box (Figure 7-3) for this job.

Figure 7-3: The Custom Dictionaries dialog box

Two routes take you to this dialog box: If the Spelling and Grammar dialog box is open, choose Options and then Dictionaries. Otherwise, open the Tools ⇨ Options dialog box, switch to the Spelling and Grammar tab (it shows the same set of options), and choose Dictionaries there.

Activating and deactivating custom dictionaries

If your documents cover a wide range of topics, it may make sense to keep separate custom dictionaries for each topic and mix and match the dictionaries depending on which documents you have open. Up to ten custom dictionaries can be active simultaneously. Select which custom dictionaries you want activated by checking their boxes in the Custom Dictionaries dialog box.

Adding and removing custom dictionaries

The Custom Dictionaries dialog box also lets you add more dictionaries to the list (if you already have one somewhere on your hard disk), create new dictionaries from scratch, or retire existing dictionaries from the list. The obvious buttons, Add, New, and Remove, perform these tasks.

When you choose Add, you get a standard Office file dialog box with which you can locate and open the correct dictionary file. By default, dictionary files have the .dic extension. But that isn't a requirement, so if you're looking for a custom dictionary with a different extension, select All Files at Files of Type.

You can store custom dictionary files anywhere accessible to your system, but they're normally kept with the other proofing tools. In the case of single-user PCs, that location is C:\Program Files\Common Files\Microsoft Shared\Proof, while for a PC with user profiles, it's Application Data\Microsoft\Proof in the main folder for your user profile. Your custom dictionaries from old versions of Office or Word will work fine; they're likely to be located in C:\Windows\Msapps\Proof.

Secret

Because dictionary files are just plain, ordinary text files, you don't need the New button to create a new custom dictionary. Just use a text editor to create the file, typing a single word on each line (follow each word with a carriage return and line feed pair).

Adding words to a custom dictionary

You can add words to a custom dictionary in two ways:

- Individually, during a spell-check.
- In groups, whenever you feel like it.

You must make separate entries in your custom dictionaries for singular and plural forms, as well as for possessives. Also, capitalization makes a difference. The rules work like this:

- Enter the word in all lowercase letters if you want Office to accept it in your documents in lowercase, initial caps, or in all caps.
- Enter it with an initial capital letter if Office should accept it capitalized or in all caps.
- Enter it with special capitalization (all caps or with capitalization such as "OfficeSecrets") if Office should accept it only as written.

Adding words during a spell-check

In the Spelling dialog box, choose Add to add the highlighted misspelled word to a custom dictionary. In Word and PowerPoint, you can also choose Add from the shortcut menu of a misspelled word marked by the automatic spell-checker.

Secret

In Word and Outlook, if more than one custom dictionary is active, the new word goes into the dictionary selected at Custom dictionary on the Spelling and Grammar tab of *Word's* Tools ⇨ Options dialog box. In Excel, Access, and PowerPoint, you can choose which custom dictionary receives added words from a drop-down list in the Spelling dialog box.

Adding — or deleting — words en masse

From within Office, you have to use Word to freely edit a custom dictionary, whether you want to add a set of new words or remove or edit existing words. In Word's Tools ⇨ Options dialog box, switch to the Spelling tab and choose Dictionaries. Select the dictionary to which you want to add words and choose Edit. This opens the dictionary in Word, where you can now type your new words, one on each line. You can use the opportunity to delete words you no longer want in the list, or to edit the current entries.

When you finish, save the file without changing its format (again, it's an ordinary text file). When you edit a custom dictionary, Word shuts off automatic spell-checking, so you have to turn it on yourself after saving the dictionary.

Secret

If Word isn't already running, a text editor does the trick just as well for editing custom dictionaries. The files can be edited while you're using Office applications. The Edit button is grayed out and unavailable when you open the Custom Dictionaries dialog box from the Spelling and Grammar dialog box.

Creating an exception dictionary

Secret

You can't edit the main spelling dictionary that comes with Office, but you can do the next best thing — you can tell Office to consider specific words as misspelled, even though they're in the main dictionary. How? Use an exception dictionary.

You might want to do this when a word has two or more variant but correct spellings. If you want to be sure that you use one of these spellings consistently, add the spelling you *don't* want to use to the exception dictionary.

For example, say you're writing about winter and relying heavily on the word grey, which you prefer to the more modern-looking gray. If Office considered both words as properly spelled, you would place gray in the exception dictionary. From then on, the spell-checker would think gray was a misspelling.

As it turns out, in most cases Office has already decided which of the variant spellings should be enforced. It likes gray, not grey, for example. When you want to use the less common variant in this situation, you have to add it to a custom dictionary, in addition to placing the alternative in the exception dictionary.

Another use for the exception dictionary is to catch words that you often misspell correctly, as it were. If you mean nicer but often type ricer (which passes in Office and is defined by Bookshelf as "a kitchen utensil used for ricing soft foods by extrusion through small holes"), put ricer in the exception dictionary.

Okay, enough theory. To create an exception dictionary, use Word or a text editor to list the exception words one per line, just as for custom dictionaries. Save the file as a text file (in Word, choose Text Only at Files of Type in the Save As dialog box). The name and folder location for this file are both critical:

- Place it in the same folder as the spell-checker and other proofing tools. On a single-user PC, this is C:\Program Files\Common Files\Microsoft Shared\Proof. If your computer has user profiles, the file belongs in the Application Data\Microsoft\Proof folder in the main folder for the user profile.
- The name should be identical to that of the main dictionary for that language, but with the extension .exc. If you're using the U.S. English dictionary, you should call it mssp2_en.exc.

Checking spelling in other languages

Chapter 1 discusses the MultiLanguage Pack that comes with Office Premium.

Using dictionaries for other languages

After you install a dictionary for another language, you can set it up as the default main dictionary for all your Office documents. Alternatively, you can use it to check the spelling of selected text in Word or PowerPoint, or — only in Word — the spelling of specific paragraph styles.

To spell-check a portion of a document using an alternative dictionary, select the text written in that language. If you want to change the default language for all documents in all Office applications, it doesn't matter whether anything is selected. Choose Tools ➪ Language ➪ Set Language to open a dialog box listing all the available languages (in PowerPoint, Tools ➪ Language will do). Figure 7-4 shows the Word version of this box. Pick the language for the selected text and choose OK, or choose Default to change the default main spelling dictionary.

Working with language settings in Word

Note that in Word a language setting assigned to selected text works just like other kinds of character formatting except that you can't see it. You can transfer the language setting to other text with the Format Painter. Also, the Reset Character Formatting command (Ctrl+Space) removes it and restores the default language.

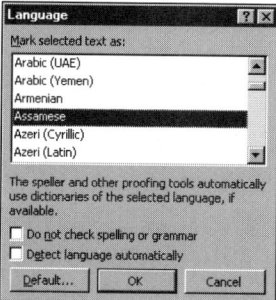

Figure 7-4: Use this dialog box to choose the language for your text, and Office spell-checks it with the corresponding dictionary.

Caution

The Language command isn't available in Excel or Access. The workaround: Use Word or PowerPoint to change the default main dictionary. In Access, you can also switch to a different dictionary by choosing Options from the Spelling dialog box and picking from the Dictionary list.

Secret

In Word, you don't need the Language dialog box to check spelling in multiple languages. Instead, you can set up paragraph styles for the other languages you use. The spell-checker automatically switches to the corresponding dictionaries when it checks these paragraphs. Open the Format ⇨ Style dialog box, choose New or Modify, and then Format.

Word knows whether you have explicitly chosen a language for a given paragraph style. If you have, the style's language setting doesn't change when you set a new default language. But styles that have not been assigned to a specific language always match the default language set in the Language dialog box.

Working with on-the-fly spell-checking

In Word and PowerPoint, when the automatic spell-checker flags a misspelled word with that wiggly red line, right-clicking the word brings up a spelling shortcut menu. It provides everything you need to fix the problem right there: a list of suggested corrections and the same Ignore All, Add, and AutoCorrect commands found in the Spelling dialog box.

Secret

In Word, consider enriching the shortcut menu for misspelled words. It lacks the Cut, Copy, Paste, and formatting commands found on the shortcut menu for regular text, deficits that I find frustrating. Use the techniques for customizing shortcut menus described in Chapter 5 to add any of the missing commands to the Text ⇨ Spelling menu on the Shortcut Menu toolbar.

Spell-checking in Word without leaving your document

By virtue of the automatic spell-checker, you don't need the Spelling dialog box in Word. Double-clicking the icon of a book toward the right end of the status bar jumps you to the next word or phrase Word has marked as a spelling or grammatical problem.

Turning off automatic spell-checking

Can you think of any good reasons for turning off automatic spell-checking entirely? A few possible scenarios come to mind:

- You write in a language for which a spelling dictionary isn't available.
- Your document is full of technical terms that are marked as misspelled even though they're correct.
- You spell so poorly that the document is riddled with those wiggly red underlines, and your self-esteem takes a nosedive.
- Your PC is so slow that automatic spell-checking slows it down unacceptably.
- You simply prefer to focus on your ideas and don't want to be distracted by the wiggly lines, so you check the spelling after finishing the writing.

To shut off the red lines for the current document, or to turn off the whole system, use the appropriate boxes on the Spelling and Grammar tab (just Spelling in PowerPoint) in the Tools ⇨ Options dialog box. The status of the Hide spelling errors in this document box is saved with each document.

Grammar checking in Word

Microsoft has spent a lot on efforts to improve Word's grammar checker, but the results still leave a lot to be desired. In my tests, it has consistently found errors where there were none and failed to find glaring intentional mistakes.

But I'm not saying you should shut off the grammar checker altogether. Although it doesn't handle complexities such as subject-verb agreement very well, it can point out some boo-boos — such as too many spaces between words or sentences — with unfailing accuracy. It also does a fair job of pointing out passive constructions, the bane of the manic modernist writer. To customize the grammar checker so that it works within its limits, choose Tools ⇨ Options, select the Spelling and Grammar tab, and then choose Settings to produce the dialog box shown in Figure 7-5.

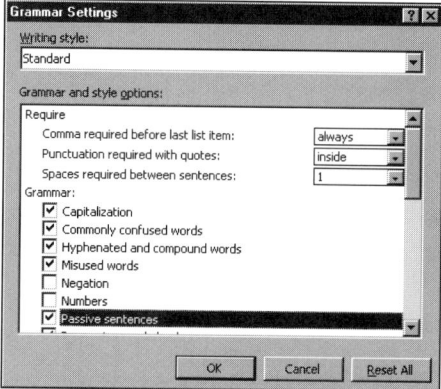

Figure 7-5: Use this dialog box to set options for grammar checking in Word.

In the list at Grammar and Style Options, a minimal set of grammar-checking features to turn on might include the following: Capitalization, Hyphenated and Split Words, Numbers, Possessives and Plurals, and Punctuation. Other candidates to consider, depending on your writing style, include Negation, Passive Sentences, Phrases, and the various Style settings. The options in the Require section of the dialog box also have merit.

The Wordsmith's Tool Chest: Synonyms, Definitions, and Quotations

Spelling is drudgery, but picking out words that express your thoughts and feelings with precision and grace — now that's sublime (when you're not on deadline). The core Office applications offer some help, but when you want more, consider adding a separate reference product such as Microsoft's Bookshelf.

Figuring out Word's built-in thesaurus

Word's built-in thesaurus remains one of its weakest features, which I guess you could say is praising with faint damnation. Anyway, the dialog box is confusingly organized and you can't trace your steps through a series of synonymic lookups. And worse, the thesaurus doesn't understand different word forms well and it just doesn't offer a rich enough collection of synonyms. Here are a few tips on using the built-in thesaurus:

- You don't have to select a word to look it up in the thesaurus. Word automatically selects the word nearest the insertion point for you.

- The keyboard shortcut for the thesaurus is Shift+F7. If you're serious about synonyms, memorize it early. Consider adding the Thesaurus command to the standard Text shortcut menu (see Chapter 5 on customizing shortcut menus) or to the main Tools menu (so you don't have to go through the Language submenu to get to it).
- To look up a new word once the Thesaurus dialog box is open, type it into the Replace with Synonym box, and then choose Look Up.
- To return to a previously looked up word, use the Previous button or select the earlier word from the drop-down list at Looked Up.

Improving your references with Bookshelf

Sadly, Office 2000 no longer comes with Bookshelf, which you can still buy separately, or even Bookshelf Basics, the truncated version that was included with Office 97. If you have Office 97, you can still install and use Bookshelf Basics with Office 2000. Otherwise, do consider getting a copy of Bookshelf for key references including *The American Heritage Dictionary of the English Language* and *Roget's Thesaurus of English Words and Phrases*. Bookshelf's thesaurus puts the stock thesaurus in Word — which isn't even accessible in the other Office apps — to shame. Bookshelf is integrated with Office, enabling you to look up definitions of selected words in the dictionary.

Lightning Text Entry with AutoCorrect

AutoCorrect is an umbrella term covering various automatic changes Office can make as you type. It's available in all the Office applications except Outlook. Figure 7-6 shows the AutoCorrect dialog box where you can toggle on or off the various settings. Most of the lower half of the AutoCorrect dialog box is occupied by the *AutoCorrect list*. When you type an entry in the left column in your document, Office substitutes the entry in the right column.

Using AutoCorrect

AutoCorrect jumps into action the moment you complete a word by typing a space, by typing a punctuation mark, or by pressing Enter. It checks each word against its list, instantly making any indicated substitution. AutoCorrect has two main functions: correcting spelling and usage errors automatically, and expanding little shorthand codes (I refer to them as abbreviations) into lengthy, complete words or phrases or into special symbols. The default list corrects many common errors such as "adn" for "and," "isn;t" for "isn't," "their is" for "there is," and even "blase" for "blasé."

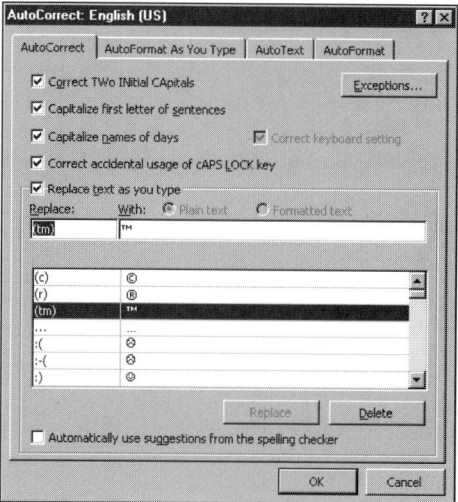

Figure 7-6: Set AutoCorrect options in this dialog box.

To add a new item to the AutoCorrect list, type the misspelling or the abbreviation in the Replace box. The correct spelling — or the word, phrase, or symbol to be substituted for the abbreviation — goes in the With box. If your document already contains the text that belongs in the With box, select it before you open the AutoCorrect dialog box — Office automatically places it in the With box for you.

AutoCorrect sports several important benefits aside from its availability throughout all the major apps. For one, you can define AutoCorrect entries that contain spaces (in other words, AutoCorrect now recognizes and replaces more than one word), and in Word, paragraph marks. In Word, control over the AutoCorrect list via macros has also been beefed up.

Note that Word has several other AutoCorrect-like capabilities not found in the other Office applications. New in Word 2000 is the capability to use the suggestions of the spell-checker to automatically correct misspelled words as soon as you type them — the change is made only if the software is fairly certain that it knows which word you really intended. You can turn this option on or off with the check box below the AutoCorrect list. The rest of Word's special features come under the heading of AutoFormat As You Type and are covered in Chapter 27. For that matter, AutoCorrect itself is enhanced in Word, where it can store formatted text and fields. All this is discussed in Chapter 27, too.

Although AutoCorrect works in text boxes, it's inactive in WordArt objects (see Chapter 8 for info on both text boxes and WordArt). In Excel, AutoCorrect works on any text you enter into cells, cell comments, embedded charts, text boxes, buttons, and headers and footers. It does not make its substitutions in protected worksheets, formulas, or text that results from a formula.

Making the most of AutoCorrect

When you're ready to move beyond the basics, use the tips and tricks covered in this section to add octane to AutoCorrect.

Expanding abbreviations with AutoCorrect

Marketed as an automatic proofreader, AutoCorrect does more than correct mistakes in your typing. Certainly, it's a good idea to add to the AutoCorrect list any words that you commonly misspell or mistype. But you can and should exploit AutoCorrect to convert shorthand abbreviations into complete words or into symbols that would be hard to enter otherwise.

If you work for the Department of Health and Human Services, that's quite a handful to type several times a day. Go to Tools ➪ AutoCorrect, create an entry that replaces the name with a shortcut, such as "dhh," and click Add. The next time you type "dhh" and a space, Office expands the entry.

Sharing AutoCorrect entries between Office applications

All the Office applications that support AutoCorrect share the same AutoCorrect list. Changes you make to the list in one application immediately (usually) show up in the other programs' AutoCorrect dialog box.

Secret

Remember, though, that only Word allows AutoCorrect entries containing formatted text, which it stores in the Normal template. Such entries don't show up in the other programs' AutoCorrect lists.

Caution

In Excel, PowerPoint, or Access, be sure you don't define AutoCorrect entries that match entries containing formatted text in Word. You won't see Word's formatted-text entries on the AutoCorrect list in the other programs, and you won't be warned when you define new entries with matching abbreviations. Bye-bye formatted-text entry.

Using the default AutoCorrect symbol substitutions

The AutoCorrect list that comes with Office includes shorthand codes for symbols you need all the time: trademark symbols, arrows, and the ellipsis. In case you didn't realize this, a true ellipsis is a special one-character mark, not three consecutive periods. Codes for not-so-useful little faces are yours as well.

In Word, if you check the Symbol characters with symbols and Borders boxes in the AutoFormat as you type dialog box, AutoFormat creates special dashes and borders when you type the right sequences. Table 7-1 catalogs these default substitutions.

Table 7-1 Built-in AutoCorrect and AutoFormat Symbol Entries

To Place This in Your Document	Type This
AutoCorrect	
©	(c)
®	(r)
™	(tm)
→	-->
←	<--
➔	==>
⬅	<==
⇔	<=>
… (ellipsis character)	... (three consecutive periods)
☺	:-) or :)
😐	:-| or :|
☹	:-(or :(
AutoFormat as you type (Word only)	
— (em or long dash)	-- (two hyphens between two words, or after a word at the end of a line)
– (en or short dash)	-- (two hyphens with a space on either side)
(thin horizontal border spanning width of paragraph)	--- (three or more consecutive hyphens)
(thick border)	___ (three or more consecutive underscores)
(double border)	=== (three or more consecutive equal signs)

Undoing unwanted AutoCorrect and AutoFormat "corrections"

Secret

There's a quick way to reverse any change made by AutoCorrect (or by Word's AutoFormat as you type): Just press Ctrl+Z (the keyboard shortcut for the Undo command) as soon as Office has made the substitution. You can use the Undo button or Edit ➪ Undo if you prefer. If you meant to type some wacky spelling that happens to be on the AutoCorrect list, Undo gives you back the intentional goof after AutoCorrect has fixed it. Once you've really gotten this concept (that any AutoCorrect or AutoFormat-as-you-type change can be undone), you'll want to leave most of the AutoCorrect and AutoFormat features on all the time.

Turning off automatic exceptions

If you check the appropriate boxes in the AutoCorrect dialog box, AutoCorrect automatically capitalizes the first word of every sentence and ensures that only one consecutive letter at the beginning of any word is capitalized. AutoCorrect lets you specify exceptions to its rules, because these features don't always give you the results you want. For example, the period that ends an abbreviation shouldn't be seen as the end of a sentence, so an AutoCorrect exception keeps Office from capitalizing the next word automatically. To add or modify the exception list, click the Exceptions button on the AutoCorrect dialog box.

In Word, if you've turned on automatic corrections via the spell-checker, you can tell AutoCorrect to allow specified misspellings to remain without automatic correction. Use the Other Corrections tab of the AutoCorrect Exceptions dialog box to enter words to leave uncorrected. Be careful, because the words in this list are ignored altogether by the spell-checker.

Secret

So far, so good. But by default, AutoCorrect automatically adds new exceptions based on how you edit your text. Its intentions are good, but it can't tell whether you really typed an abbreviation or decided not to capitalize the next word for some other reason. My advice: Add exceptions manually and turn off the automatic additions feature. To do this, choose Tools ⇨ AutoCorrect and then Exceptions. Uncheck the Automatically Add Words to List box in both the First letter and INitial CAps tabs (and in Word, the Other Corrections tab). These are independent settings.

Using a different AutoCorrect list

You might want to keep one AutoCorrect list for technical documents, another for personal correspondence, and so on. Unfortunately, Office doesn't let you select an alternative AutoCorrect list, as you can with custom spelling dictionaries, nor does the AutoCorrect list appear in the File Locations tab of the Options dialog box. Nevertheless, there are ways to switch between two or more AutoCorrect lists, although Office 2000 is less flexible in this regard than Office 97.

The easiest way to do this is to set up a separate user profile for each AutoCorrect list you want to maintain and log in as a different user when you want to switch lists. This is something of a nuisance, especially if you have a single-user system and don't normally log in, but it's easier and more reliable than the alternative — manually copying alternative AutoCorrect lists from backup locations.

If you're willing to write VBA code, you can use Word's AutoCorrect object to fine-tune the AutoCorrect list for every situation. To add, modify, or delete entries, you need statements such as the following:

```
AutoCorrect.Entries.Add Name:="secerts", Value:="secrets"
AutoCorrect.Entries("wihs").Value = "wigs"
AutoCorrect.Entries("npo").Delete
```

Secret

AutoCorrect lists are stored in files with the .acl extension. Office places AutoCorrect lists in the Application Data\Microsoft\Office folder, which you can find in your main Windows directory (for single-user computers) or in your user profile folder (for multiple-user systems). The active AutoCorrect list for U.S. English — the one containing your own changes to the stock list, if any — is named `mso1033.acl`. The original list that came with Office is stored in `mso1033.bak.acl`. AutoCorrect lists for other languages are also identified by language number (see Chapter 1 for information on how Office works with various languages).

Caution

The AutoCorrect Utility macro for Word included with Word 97 (in the Macros8.dot template) is supposed to create and restore backup copies of the AutoCorrect list. Unfortunately, the version of the macro included on the Office CD-ROM doesn't work if your AutoCorrect list includes formatted entries containing paragraph marks. The problem is that the macro stores the list in a Word table, and mistakenly creates new cells when it encounters those paragraph marks. Subsequent entries are in the wrong columns.

Adding words to the AutoCorrect list during a spelling check

If you repeatedly misspell the same word in the same way, it makes sense to add your habitual boo-boo to the AutoCorrect list. You can do this during a spelling check, as soon as you figure out that you're likely to make the same mistake in the future. Here are two methods:

- Using the Spelling dialog box, select the correct spelling from the suggestions Word offers, or type it in. Then click the AutoCorrect button.

- If you're using automatic spelling in Word, the shortcut menu that appears when you right-click a misspelled word (one with a wavy red line under it) offers an AutoCorrect choice. Select this, and then select the correct spelling from the suggestions.

Turning AutoCorrect off and on

AutoCorrect is great for most conventional prose. However, if you also use Word to prepare technical manuals, computer programs, or other specialized documents, it can get in the way, "correcting" punctuation and peculiar capitalization schemes when you don't want it to. While the AutoCorrect dialog box is fine for turning on and off the individual AutoCorrect options, there should be a single command that shuts down or revives the entire AutoCorrect mechanism.

Alas, no such command exists, but you can create your own with a macro. Type in the following code. You can customize the macro for your own AutoCorrect needs by changing some of the False items to True. The macro won't work in other Office programs.

```
Sub AutoCorrectShutOff()
    With Autocorrect
        .CorrectInitialCaps = False
        .CorrectSentenceCaps = False
        .CorrectDays = False
        .CorrectCapsLock = False
        .ReplaceText = False
    End With
    With Options
        .AutoFormatAsYouTypeApplyHeadings = False
        .AutoFormatAsYouTypeApplyBorders = False
        .AutoFormatAsYouTypeApplyBulletedLists = False
        .AutoFormatAsYouTypeApplyNumberedLists = False
        .AutoFormatAsYouTypeApplyTables = False
        .AutoFormatAsYouTypeReplaceQuotes = False
        .AutoFormatAsYouTypeReplaceSymbols = False
        .AutoFormatAsYouTypeReplaceOrdinals = False
        .AutoFormatAsYouTypeReplaceFractions = False
        .AutoFormatAsYouTypeReplacePlainTextEmphasis _
            = False
        .AutoFormatAsYouTypeReplaceHyperlinks = False
        .AutoFormatAsYouTypeFormatListItemBeginning = False
        .AutoFormatAsYouTypeDefineStyles = False
    End With
End Sub
```

Adding special characters to AutoCorrect entries

As you can read about later in this chapter, AutoCorrect is one good way to add special characters that aren't on the keyboard to your documents. But how to get those special characters into an AutoCorrect item?

The easiest way is with Word's Insert ⇨ Symbol dialog box (see Figure 7-7). Select the character for which you want to create an AutoCorrect entry. Then choose AutoCorrect to display the AutoCorrect dialog box, with the selected symbol already entered at With. Note that by default, the Formatted text button is selected. This is the way to go if you're creating an Autocorrect entry for a symbol available only in a special symbol font such as Wingdings. However, if you're creating an AutoCorrect entry for a symbol found in ordinary text fonts, select the Plain Text button in the AutoCorrect dialog box. The entry will work throughout Office. (See Chapter 27 for further discussion of using formatted versus plain text for AutoCorrect entries.)

However, if you're creating an AutoCorrect entry containing more than one symbol, this technique won't work. You have several alternatives: In Word, you can enter special characters directly into the With field of the AutoCorrect dialog box using the same keyboard shortcuts available in your documents. This includes shortcuts you have defined yourself. In any application you can also enter symbol characters in the AutoCorrect dialog box by code number. With Num Lock on, hold down Alt and type the character's four-digit ANSI code as shown in Table 7-2 later in this chapter.

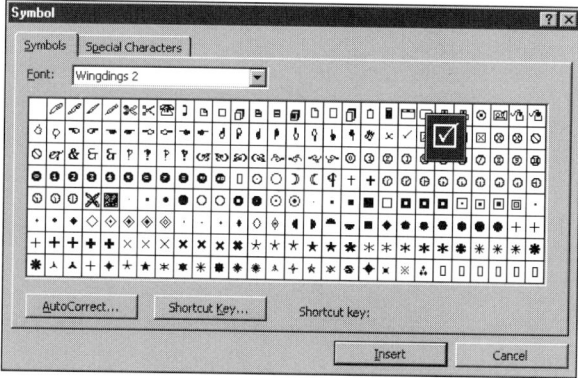

Figure 7-7: The Insert ⇨ Symbol dialog box in Word

In Word, yet another method, and probably the easiest, is to copy the symbols from a document. Dismiss the AutoCorrect dialog box and go back to your document. There, enter the complete replacement text (the text that AutoCorrect will insert in place of what you actually type) using the Insert Symbol command to place the special characters. Select the replacement text you just entered and choose Tools ⇨ AutoCorrect again. The replacement text will appear in the With field automatically. You can now type in the text to be replaced in the Replace field. If you want to include special symbols in the Replace field, you can do this by typing the text in the document, cutting or copying it to the clipboard, and then pasting it into the field.

Automatic dashes in all Office applications

Caution

Consider adding AutoCorrect entries for em and en dashes. True, the Symbol feature in Word's AutoFormat as you type converts pairs of hyphens into em or en dashes automatically. But aside from the fact that this feature isn't available in the other Office apps, it has other problems.

AutoFormat's dash substitutions only appear if you type hyphens between two words, and then only if you type no more than one space between the words. In fact, they don't appear until after you finish the second word, which can be unnerving. And AutoFormat sometimes refuses to convert the two hyphens at all, if you add them after the fact, between two existing words. A separate problem is that you always get spaces surrounding the en dash. In my copy of the *Chicago Manual of Style*, en dashes are typeset with no surrounding spaces.

Word already provides keyboard shortcuts for em and en dashes: Alt+Ctrl+– and Ctrl+–, respectively (both of these shortcuts require the dash or minus sign key on the numeric keypad, not the one in the top row of typewriter keys next to 0). But if you want the convenience of entering them via hyphens, set up the following AutoCorrect entries:

Replace	With
-- (two hyphens)	— (em dash)
—- (em dash+hyphen)	– (en dash)

Note that with these two entries active, you actually type three consecutive hyphens to produce an en dash. AutoCorrect converts the first two hyphens into an em dash. When you type the third hyphen, it converts the whole thing into the en dash.

Fonts and Typography

In personal and professional business situations, much of the allure of personal computing stems from its power to create documents that look professionally produced. That's why, no matter what your job title, it pays to acquaint yourself with the fundamentals of font management, typography, and document design. I assume you know what you want to say and how to say it.

Font mania

You're in good company if you feel frustrated by fonts. Libraries of hundreds of high-quality fonts such as a typesetter once could hardly have imagined are now within the reach of ordinary schmoes. But keeping track of all those myriad fonts, finding the one that looks right for your document, putting it into play without half an hour's work, and accessing its special symbols conveniently — ah, these are the problems of the wealthy. Of course, even if you do tame your font collection in a technical sense, you still face the deeper challenge: when and where to use them in your documents.

Font formats, and the coming Pax Fontana

Microsoft and Adobe have announced their mutual intention to end their war over *scalable* font formats. Scalable fonts, of course, are those that can be *scaled* to any size for display or printing. The two major types of scalable fonts are TrueType, the official Microsoft/Windows kind, and Type 1, an earlier format that is part of PostScript, the widely used page description language for complex graphical designs.

Current versions of Windows directly support TrueType only. If you want to use Type 1 fonts you must install Adobe Type Manager (ATM) to scale them. As a result of the Adobe-Microsoft rapprochement, however, a new font format called OpenType has been promised. OpenType is supposed to be a superset of Type 1 and TrueType formats, so that the font data in either existing format can be transferred wholesale into a new OpenType font.

Because the conversion process will be so easy, the commercial type vendors should be able to convert their libraries almost immediately.

In addition, the OpenType format fixes some limitations in existing font formats — in particular, it supports ligatures and alternate characters within a single font (see "Using expert font sets" later in this chapter). And it will enable embedding of compressed font information within documents, permitting Web page designers to use specific fonts and still have pages open in the reader's browser with reasonable speed.

Windows will still be able to handle existing TrueType fonts and apparently will be able to scale current Type 1 fonts by converting them first into TrueType data. It's not clear whether Windows will be updated to include built-in native scaling for Type 1 fonts that aren't converted into the OpenType format. You may still need to buy ATM for that. And when will all this happen? Dates are conspicuously absent from the press releases, and no specific OpenType products have yet been announced.

When to use Type 1 fonts

While a few technical differences exist between TrueType and Type 1 fonts, they are functionally identical in most situations. Because TrueType is the Windows standard, your decision is whether to use Type 1 in addition, or not. Consider these issues:

- Are the fonts you like available in TrueType format? These days, most font design companies sell their offerings in both formats, but so far, Adobe still makes Type 1 fonts only.

- Might you print the document on a different printer later? The spacing of text formatted with a TrueType font can change when you change printer drivers, which can ruin a perfect layout. Spacing of text that uses Type 1 fonts remains the same regardless of the printer.

- Will you be sending out documents to a service bureau or desktop publishing shop for output (usually on film via a high-res PostScript laser typesetter)? If so, you should match your fonts to the ones available at the service bureau. Many service bureaus prefer Type 1 fonts, and some still can't handle TrueType. The previous comment also applies.

- Will you be sharing documents with Macintosh or UNIX users? Although both TrueType and Type 1 are available on the Mac, Type 1 fonts predominate there. UNIX platforms only support Type 1 fonts.

Drowning in fonts

Anyone who accumulates more than about 50 fonts needs a system for managing them — and this means you, because with Windows and Office alone you already own about 200 fonts. If you have too many fonts installed at the same time, your font menu will be overwhelmingly long, and the performance of your whole system suffers.

Secret

In case you hadn't noticed, the Valupack folder on the Office CD-ROM includes a subfolder called MSFonts, containing 150 or so fonts.

The simplest font-management system is to throw away the bulk of your font collection. I'm serious. Most people aren't graphic designers, and fiddling around with fonts is a great way to waste time while showing off your amateur standing. Choose one font for body text, one font for headings, and no more than five other fonts for spice. Of course, you must also keep the standard Windows fonts: Arial, Times New Roman, Courier New, Symbol, and Marlett, as well as Tahoma and other fonts that Outlook and Office require.

Okay, so the ascetic, toss-'em-out solution is no fun. If you're stuck on your font collection, get some font-management software. What you need is a utility that can keep track of your fonts in named groups rather than as individual files, installing and removing these groups as required by your active documents. It will also show you samples of the fonts on-screen before you install them and print specimen pages.

If you want or need to use Type 1 fonts, picking a font manager is a no-brainer. You must buy Adobe's ATM Deluxe in order to use Type 1 fonts at all, at least until Microsoft releases an OpenType update to Windows. But in addition to handling Type 1 font scaling, ATM Deluxe is an excellent font manager for both Type 1 and TrueType fonts. You should know about one drawback, however: while it prints specimen sheets, ATM Deluxe can't print complete character charts showing all the characters in a font and their associated code numbers.

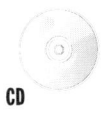
CD

If you use TrueType fonts exclusively, or if you're not satisfied with ATM's font-management features, you'll find plenty of alternative font managers to choose from. High-quality shareware font managers abound — check out especially MyFonts, included on the CD-ROM that comes with this book.

Secret

Unique among font managers, the Font Handler/Font Sentry duo (from QualiType, www.qualitype.com) automatically installs the TrueType or Type 1 fonts needed by the documents you're currently working with. When you open a document containing text formatted with an uninstalled font, Font Sentry steps in, installing the needed font. Of course, it permits manual installation when you need fonts that aren't already in use in the document. This system doesn't work with all software — desktop publishing applications in particular may block Font Sentry's access to Windows' font black box — but it does perform well with Office apps.

Using special characters

Windows fonts promise an infinity of special characters for every imaginable occasion, and then some. Aside from the ordinary letters, numbers, and punctuation marks found on the keyboard, you can find professional typographic marks; foreign language letters; symbols used in business, math, and science; and loads of hard-to-classify ornaments, dingbats, and doohickeys.

Tables 7-2 and 7-3 list the most commonly useful of such characters found in standard text fonts and the Symbol font that comes with Windows.

Table 7-2 Special Symbol Characters by Category

Symbol Category	Symbol	Character Code (* = key to type)	Word Keyboard Shortcut (if available)
For symbols that are available only in special fonts, the font required is indicated in parentheses.			
Symbols marked by asterisks (*) can be entered by typing the indicated key rather than a character code.			
Dashes			
	— (em dash)	0151	Alt+Ctrl+– (on numeric keypad)
	– (en dash)	0150	Ctrl+– (on numeric keypad)
	- (nonbreaking hyphen)		Ctrl+_
	(optional hyphen)		Ctrl+ -
Spaces			
	(nonbreaking space)		Ctrl+Shift+Space
	em space (space the width of the letter *m*)		By default, em and en spaces are only available via the Insert Symbol command
	en space (space the width of the letter *n*)		
Business-Related Symbols			
	©	0169	Alt+Ctrl+C
	®	0174	Alt+Ctrl+R
	™	0153	Alt+Ctrl+T
	¢	0162	Ctrl+/,C
	£	0163	
	¤	0164	
	€	0128	Alt+Ctrl+E
	¥	0165	

Continued

Table 7-2 *(continued)*

Symbol Category	Symbol	Character Code (* = key to type)	Word Keyboard Shortcut (if available)
Typographical Marks			
	... (ellipsis character)	0133	
	¶ (paragraph mark)	0182	
	§ (section mark)	0167	
	• (bullet character)	0149	
	' (open single quote)	0145	
	' (close single quote)	0146	
	" (open double quotation mark)	0147	
	" (close double quotation mark)	0148	
	†	0134	
	‡	0135	
Ligatures (available in expert fonts only)			
	ff		V *
	fi		W *
	fl		X *
	ffi		Y *
	ffl		Z *
Math and Science			
	× (multiplication sign)	0215	
	÷	0247	
	° (degree symbol)	0176	
	±	0177	
	≤	0163 (Symbol font)	
	≥	0179 (Symbol font)	
	≠	0185 (Symbol font)	
	⁰	0186	
	¹	0185	
	²	0178	

Symbol Category	Symbol	Character Code (* = key to type)	Word Keyboard Shortcut (if available)
	³	0179	
	π	p (Symbol font) *	
	∞	0165 (Symbol font)	
Fractions			
	¼	0188 (standard or expert fonts)	
	½	0189 (standard or expert fonts)	
	¾	0190 (standard or expert fonts)	
	⅛	0192 (expert fonts only)	
	⅜	0193 (expert fonts only)	
	⅝	0194 (expert fonts only)	
	⅞	0195 (expert fonts only)	
	⅓	0196 (expert fonts only)	
	⅔	0197 (expert fonts only)	
Arrow Characters (available in Symbol font only)			
	↔	0171	
	←	0172	
	↑	0173	
	→	0174	
	↓	0175	
	⇔	0219	
	⇐	0220	
	⇑	0221	
	⇒	0222	
	⇓	0223	

Table 7-3 Non-Keyboard Characters (Normal Text)

Symbol	Code Number	Word Keyboard Shortcut (if available)
‚	0130	
ƒ	0131	
„	0132	
…	0133	
†	0134	
‡	0135	
ˆ	0136	Ctrl+^, space
‰	0137	
Š	0138	Alt+Ctrl+^, S
‹	0139	
Œ	0140	Ctrl+&, O
'	0145	Ctrl+`, `
'	0146	Ctrl+', '
"	0147	Ctrl+`, "
"	0148	Ctrl+', "
•	0149	
–	0150	Ctrl+– (on the numeric keypad)
—	0151	Alt+Ctrl+– (on the numeric keypad)
˜	0152	
™	0153	Alt+Ctrl+T
š	0154	Alt+Ctrl+^, s
›	0155	
œ	0156	Ctrl+&, o
Ÿ	0159	Ctrl+:, Y
¡	0161	Alt+Ctrl+!
¢	0162	Ctrl+/, c
£	0163	
¤	0164	
¥	0165	
¦	0166	

Symbol	Code Number	Word Keyboard Shortcut (if available)
§	0167	
¨	0168	Ctrl+:, space
©	0169	Alt+Ctrl+C
ª	0170	
¬	0172	
-	0173	
®	0174	Alt+Ctrl+R
¯	0175	
°	0176	Ctrl+@, space
±	0177	
²	0178	
³	0179	
´	0180	Ctrl+ ', space
µ	0181	
¶	0182	
·	0183	
¸	0184	Ctrl+,, space
¹	0185	
º	0186	
»	0187	Ctrl+`, >
¼	0188	
½	0189	
¾	0190	
¿	0191	Alt+Ctrl+?
À	0192	Ctrl+`, A
Á	0193	Ctrl+ ', A
Â	0194	Ctrl+ ^, A
Ã	0195	Ctrl+~, A
Ä	0196	Ctrl+:, A
Å	0197	Ctrl+@, A
Æ	0198	Ctrl+&, A

Continued

Table 7-3 *(continued)*

Symbol	Code Number	Word Keyboard Shortcut (if available)
Ç	0199	Ctrl+,, C
È	0200	Ctrl+`, E
É	0201	Ctrl+', E
Ê	0202	Ctrl+^, E
Ë	0203	Ctrl+:, E
Ì	0204	Ctrl+`, I
Í	0205	Ctrl+', I
Î	0206	Ctrl+^, I
Ï	0207	Ctrl+:,
Ð	0208	Ctrl+', D
Ñ	0209	Ctrl+~, N
Ò	0210	Ctrl+`, O
Ó	0211	Ctrl+', O
Ô	0212	Ctrl+^, O
Õ	0213	Ctrl+~, O
Ö	0214	Ctrl+:, O
.	0215	
Ø	0216	Ctrl+/, O
Ù	0217	Ctrl+`, U
Ú	0218	Ctrl+', U
Û	0219	Ctrl+^, U
Ü	0220	Ctrl+:, U
Ý	0221	Ctrl+', Y
Þ	0222	
ß	0223	Ctrl+&, S
à	0224	Ctrl+`, a
á	0225	Ctrl+', a
â	0226	Ctrl+^, a
ã	0227	Ctrl+~, a
ä	0228	Ctrl+:, a
å	0229	Ctrl+@, a

Symbol	Code Number	Word Keyboard Shortcut (if available)
æ	0230	Ctrl+&, a
ç	0231	Ctrl+,, c
è	0232	Ctrl+`, e
é	0233	Ctrl+', e
ê	0234	Ctrl+^, e
ë	0235	Ctrl+:, e
ì	0236	Ctrl+`, I
í	0237	Ctrl+', i
î	0238	Ctrl+^, i
ï	0239	Ctrl+:, I
ð	0240	Ctrl+', d
ñ	0241	Ctrl+~, n
ò	0242	Ctrl+`, o
ó	0243	Ctrl+', o
ô	0244	Ctrl+^, o
õ	0245	Ctrl+~, o
ö	0246	Ctrl+:, o
÷	0247	
Ø	0248	Ctrl+/, o
ù	0249	Ctrl+`, u
ú	0250	Ctrl+', u
û	0251	Ctrl+^, u
ü	0252	Ctrl+:, u
ý	0253	Ctrl+', y
þ	0254	
ÿ	0255	Ctrl+:, y

Expert techniques for inserting special characters

It sometimes seems as if a glass wall stands between you and all those special characters — you can look but you can't use. Actually, the problem is one of inconvenience. Non-keyboard symbols often don't get used because the common techniques for accessing them are too much bother.

Part II: Building Great Documents with Office 2000

To tell the truth, there is no perfect solution. But Table 7-4 lays out a variety of ways to access special characters, and their advantages and drawbacks.

Table 7-4 Techniques for Inserting Special Characters

Method	Pros	Cons	Comments/Tips
Choose Insert ⇨ Symbol and select the desired character from the chart in the Symbol dialog box (works in Word and PowerPoint).	Requires no additional software. In Word, you can select symbol characters from a list of descriptions (use the Special Characters tab of the Symbol dialog box), as well as from a chart. Lets you insert characters from different fonts in the same pass.	Not available in Excel, Access, or Outlook. Although you can insert as many characters as you like, the window is so big; it usually covers up the insertion point, so that you can't see that you've actually inserted the correct characters in the correct order. Characters may not show up in files exported to other formats.	
Use the Character Map accessory that comes with Windows (Start ⇨ Accessories ⇨ Character Map).	Lets you select multiple characters before inserting them, enabling you to edit the sequence before pasting it into your document. Works with all Office (and Windows) applications.	Hard to use because the characters in the chart are *tiny*. You can only insert characters from one font at a time.	
Use AutoCorrect.	Super-fast — just type an abbreviation and the desired symbol appears in your document. Works in all the Office applications except Outlook.	You have to set up a separate Auto-Correct abbreviation for each special symbol. You also have to remember all those abbreviations. Works only in Office.	The fastest way to set up an Auto-Correct entry for a special symbol is via Word's Insert ⇨ Symbol command. See "Adding special characters to AutoCorrect entries" earlier.

Method	Pros	Cons	Comments/Tips
Use a Windows utility that works like AutoCorrect.	Your abbreviations will work in all Windows applications. You can organize the entries by category, not just in alphabetical order.	These utilities aren't as sophisticated as AutoCorrect: They can't store formatted text and they don't recognize punctuation as the end of an entry (if a special character falls at the end of a sentence or before a comma, you have to hit the Spacebar to expand the abbreviation, and then go back and type in the punctuation).	Shareware programs enable you to set up AutoCorrect-like abbreviations that convert automatically into expanded text passages. Check out ShortKeys (included on the CD-ROM).
Create a keyboard shortcut or toolbar button for each symbol you use frequently.	Keyboard shortcuts are as fast as AutoCorrect. Toolbar buttons (on an open toolbar) give you immediate visual access to the symbol.	Setting up a keyboard shortcut or toolbar button for a symbol character requires a macro or VBA programming, except in Word. Keyboard shortcuts may be harder to remember than AutoCorrect abbreviations.	
Type in the keycode for the character (see Comments).	Fast and reliable, if you know the codes (for some people, memorizing a numeric sequence is no worse than memorizing an AutoCorrect abbreviation).	Typing numeric codes may put you off or make you feel like a computer nerd. No visual guidance.	Here's the technique: Hold down Alt while typing the four-digit ANSI code on the numeric keypad (NumLock must be on). When you release Alt, the corresponding character appears in your document in the font currently active at the insertion point. If necessary, select the character and change its font.

Font aesthetics

Once you've mastered the mechanics of fonts, you still have to know how to use your fonts artistically. This book is hardly the place for a treatise on typography or graphic design, but a few suggestions are in order. Using text in graphical effects with WordArt is covered in Chapter 8.

Don't break up the family

Fonts come in families. In addition to the mama font (the standard version of the font, which may be called regular, roman, or book), there's a papa font (the bold version), two babies (italic and bold italic versions), and sometimes various aunts, uncles, and cousins (light, heavy, condensed, and expanded versions are common). The characters belonging to each of these family members were designed separately for best appearance. Although Windows can thicken any TrueType font to make it bold or slant it for *faux* italics, the results look second-rate. You need a separate font file — regular, bold, italic, and bold italic — for every member of a family.

Using expert font sets

To lend a professionally typeset look to your documents, invest in a font set that includes an *expert set*. The fonts in an expert set are variations on the regular versions of the same family with special characters used by the pros. Adobe is the main purveyor of expert sets, but several other font design companies also sell them.

Among the various types of characters included in expert sets, the following are the most important:

- **Ligatures.** Certain letter combinations beginning with lowercase *f* are set by typesetters as special single ligature characters, not a series of separate letters. Ligatures prevent unsightly clashes between the *f* (its curved top and the bar through its middle) and the character that follows. Here are examples of ligatures and the character combinations they replace (in each pair, the ligature appears on the right):

Ligature Pair	Example
ff	ff
fi	fi
fl	fl
ffi	ffi
ffl	ffl

Chapter 7: Secrets of Polished Text

- **Small caps.** When setting a word in all capitals, a typesetter avoids overwhelming the surrounding text by using small uppercase letters specially designed for this role. Here's an example:

    Published by IDG BOOKS . . .   Published by IDG BOOKS . . .

    Word can convert ordinary capital letters into small caps via a check box in the Format ⇨ Font dialog box, but the results look misproportioned to the practiced eye. Expert sets include honest-to-goodness small uppercase letters designed to harmonize with mixed-case text of the same font size.

- **"Old-style" numerals.** In most Windows fonts, the numerals are designed so that they'll line up properly in tables and spreadsheets. But they're harder to read than mixed-case letters.

    Unlike the proportionally spaced characters of the alphabet, standard numerals are monospaced — each numeral occupies the same amount of space horizontally, along the line of text. And like uppercase letters, they're monotonously tall and lack *descenders*, the portions of letters as in *g* or *q* that fall below the baseline on which most letters sit. In the following example, compare the standard numerals on the left with the old-style numerals on the right:

    Call me any old time: Beechwood 4-5789   Call Jenny: 867-5309

    The old-style numerals in expert sets are analogous to lowercase letters: their heights and widths vary from character to character, making them easier to distinguish and giving your work a très distinguished look.

Sources for cool fonts

If you're in the market for top-quality and distinctive fonts, you'll want to browse the catalogs of the major digital type foundries, including Adobe, Bitstream, and Monotype. But don't overlook the offerings of smaller type-design outfits, where you can find some of the most elegant, original, and offbeat fonts. Try the following sources:

Emigre, Inc.
www.emigre.com

Judith Sutcliffe: The Electric Typographer
Available from www.will-harris.com/store.htm.

Letter Perfect
www.letterspace.com
www.gsl.com/UTF/UTF.html

Vitatype
www.primenet.com/~jeffib/index.htm

The following two Web pages have links to tons of font designers:

www.typeindex.com
www.microsoft.com/typography/links/

The Top Ten Font and Layout Rules

Never, ever break any of the following ironclad, hard-and-fast imperatives:

1. Use a maximum of three fonts per document, not counting italic and bold variations — and try to get by with two. Settle on one font for the body text, one font for the headings and fine print, and optionally, a third for the main title or banner headline.

2. Select simple fonts with clean lines for the body text and headings. Reserve those fancy font designs (*display* fonts) for judicious use in the title or headline, selecting the one that best evokes the right mood in your reader.

3. Match the type size to the importance of your message, but above all, size the text so that it's easy to read. It should be big enough so that the reader doesn't have to squint, but not so large as to look crowded. Make the headings noticeably larger than the body text. You can set your two main fonts in a few different sizes in distinct areas of the document, but again, go easy on the variety. (Font size is measured in points. See Chapter 8 for a discussion of measurement units in Office.)

4. In body text, *use ordinary italics for emphasis* — avoid underlining or using ALL CAPITALS. Use bold cautiously in body text, because it can draw too much attention. But headings often look best in bold.

5. Except in the most formal of publications, left-align body text rather than fully justifying it. This goes double for columnar layouts or narrow text boxes.

6. Be generous with white (empty) space on the page. If space is limited, cut the text to preserve breathing room — otherwise you'll lose potential readers.

7. Except in fiction, use lots of subheadings to break up the visual monotony.

8. Be sure that each subhead is visually linked with the text that follows. Leave more space above the subhead than below. Ruling lines are best placed *above* a subhead, setting the new section off from the text above.

9. Strive for consistent spacing and alignment between the page elements. Spacing variations and misalignments irritate the reader.

10. Use restraint with visual elements such as ruling lines and borders, rotated text, and 3-D effects. A little goes a very long way.

11. Try breaking these rules.

Conclusion

At the heart of most Office documents, text deserves careful attention, both as to looks and content. The techniques covered in this chapter will help you enter your words quickly, accurately, and attractively.

Chapter 8

Getting Graphical

In This Chapter

- Creating and editing graphics with Office's powerful drawing tools
- Drawing and refining complex freehand shapes
- Using text graphically with text boxes and WordArt
- Speeding up the drawing process with custom toolbar modifications
- Dressing up your documents with pictures — and where to find more clip art
- Accessing the secret Office applets to add graphs, organization charts, and equations to any document
- Laying out any graphical object to your specifications

Text may be your communication vehicle, but if your message lacks rakish fins, a bold grille, and a shiny hood ornament, no one will be watching when it arrives. Polished documents need graphical elements to illustrate their points, to summarize key information in immediately understandable form, and simply to break up the monotony.

Office lets you beautify your documents with pictures of all sorts, from the simplest lines and boxes to complex illustrations, from charts and graphs to scanned photographs. The new drawing tools built into Office approach the power of those in professional graphics software. And if they don't do the trick, you can add artwork from essentially any paint, photo-editing, or line art application. Office's features for manipulating imported and embedded graphics have been improved as well. And for that matter, you can add other kinds of embellishments to your documents, such as video and sound clips.

Line Art Graphics from Scratch

In three of the Office applications — Word, Excel, and PowerPoint — you can embellish your documents with graphics of your own design with Office's drawing tools. Now we're not talking about just a few simple shapes and lines, maybe with some basic patterns. Office 2000's drawing tools give it much of the power of the major-league drawing programs for creating line (vector) art. Professional graphic artists are still going to want stand-alone applications such as Corel Draw or FreeHand, but you can often accomplish comparable results with Office alone.

In addition to the traditional set of simple lines, rectangles, and ovals, Office comes with a whole palette of prefab *AutoShapes* that you can add to your document with a couple of quick clicks. You can choose from polygons, hearts, arrows, flowcharting symbols, scrolls, and even those word balloons you see in cartoons (see Figure 8-1 for a few examples). And for the first time, Office offers a full set of features for drawing freehand complex shapes. After laying down a shape with one of three freehand tools, you can edit the points that define its perimeter one by one, the kind of control that you need to work seriously in the line-art medium.

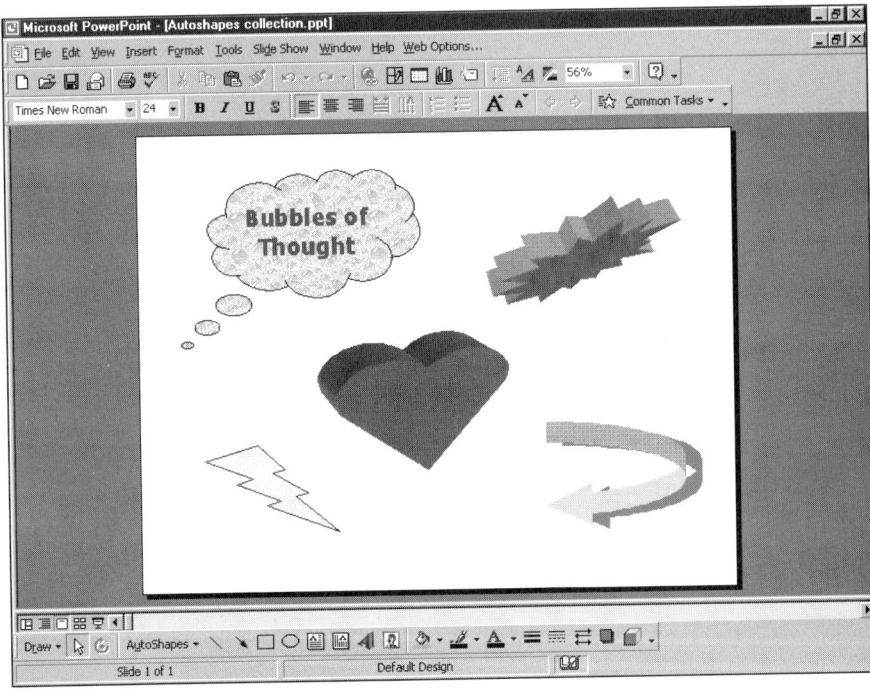

Figure 8-1: A few of the AutoShapes available in Office, some after special effects have been applied

Once you've created a shape, Office lets you enhance it with a set of new special effects. The 3-D effect is especially powerful: You can apply the illusion of three-dimensional depth, perspective, and lighting to almost any shape, rotating the shape freely in imaginary 3-D space. Simpler shadow effects are also new in this version. For the first time, you can freely rotate any shape. And you can use text as visual spice, adding text to any AutoShape, and making sophisticated graphical effects with WordArt.

Using the Drawing toolbar

All of the Office drawing tools are accessible from the Drawing toolbar, one of the standard toolbars. Shown in Figure 8-2, the Drawing toolbar looks exactly the same in all three applications in which it is available — Word, Excel, and PowerPoint. If it's not already visible, you can display it by clicking the Drawing button. This button toggles the Drawing toolbar on and off. You can also show the Drawing toolbar by right-clicking any toolbar and selecting Drawing from the shortcut menu.

Figure 8-2: Use the Drawing toolbar to add your own graphics and edit imported clip art.

Starting from the left, the first section of the toolbar has the tools for selecting and editing existing shapes. Next comes a section devoted to laying down new shapes and text elements. The buttons in the third section let you select colors, patterns, and line width, and turn on the shadow and 3-D effects.

Adding drawing shapes to a document

To insert drawing shapes into a document, start by clicking the button for the shape. The buttons for the basic shapes (line, arrow, rectangle, and oval) appear on the Drawing toolbar. Access the buttons for the other prefab shapes on the AutoShapes menu, described in the next section.

Once you choose a drawing shape, the mouse pointer changes to a simple cross. Click in the document to produce the shape at a predetermined size. Drag the pointer in to size it to your own requirements, releasing the mouse button when the shape takes on the right size and proportions.

To create an object within a perfectly square boundary, hold down Shift while you draw it. Use this technique to add impeccable squares and circles, isosceles triangles, and perfectly proportioned hearts, stars, and whatnot. Holding down Shift while you draw a line or arrow constrains a line to preset angles — this is especially useful for drawing true horizontal or vertical lines.

Hold down Ctrl while you draw to have the new object expand out symmetrically in the opposite direction, like a mirror image of what you draw. To center an object on a particular spot, begin drawing from that location using this Ctrl-drag technique.

Secret

Ordinarily, the mouse pointer reverts to normal as soon as you've drawn a shape, enabling you to select shapes or return to editing your document. To draw multiple shapes of the same type without having to reactivate the tool each time, *double-click* the button for the shape. To bail out of this repeat-draw mode, click it once more, right-click anywhere, or press Esc.

Inserting AutoShapes

To insert an AutoShape, choose AutoShapes on the Drawing toolbar and select from one of the submenus (see Figure 8-3). You can also insert AutoShapes from a toolbar by that name, or from toolbars for each of the AutoShapes submenus. To display these toolbars, tear them off from the AutoShapes menu by dragging the colored bar at the top of each menu or submenu. You can also choose Insert ⇨ Picture ⇨ AutoShapes to display the AutoShapes toolbar.

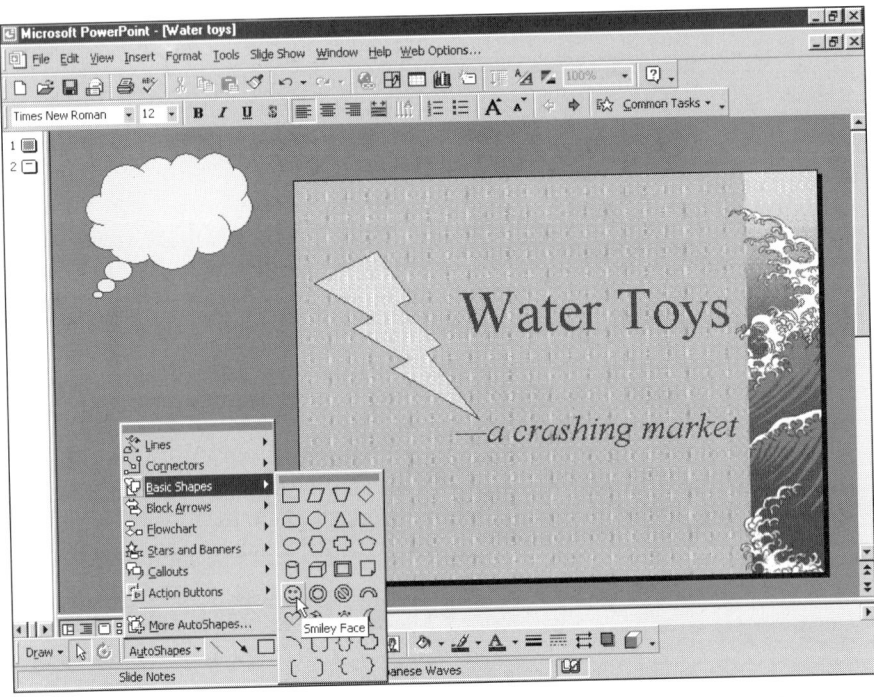

Figure 8-3: Place AutoShapes in your documents by selecting them from the menu system on the Drawing toolbar, shown on the left, or from the AutoShapes toolbar on the right.

Caution

You can't double-click the buttons on the AutoShapes submenus. If you want to draw any of these shapes repeatedly, you must first tear off its submenu to make it a floating toolbar. You can then double-click the shape's button.

More AutoShapes?

The shapes accessible via the More AutoShapes item on the AutoShapes menu or toolbar aren't really AutoShapes. Instead, the More AutoShapes command displays the Clip Gallery, discussed in "Managing clip art and other content with Clip Gallery" later in this chapter. Items in the Clip Gallery are ordinary pictures, not AutoShapes. You can't size them as you're inserting them as you do with other toolbar shapes, you can't add text to them, and you can't reshape them as you can with most AutoShapes.

Special AutoShapes: action buttons and connectors

Note that PowerPoint's AutoShapes menu, shown in Figure 8-3, has more options than the versions in Excel (which lacks action buttons) or Word (which is missing both action buttons and connectors). Action buttons and connectors have built-in smarts. *Connectors* connect objects, staying attached when the objects get moved. An *action button* does something, such as display another slide, when you click it in a PowerPoint presentation.

You can add action buttons and connectors, minus their intelligence, to a document created in another Office application. Place the shape into a PowerPoint document and then move it to its destination via the Clipboard.

Selecting drawing objects

As is the norm with drawing software, you must select a shape before you can change it. You can tell when a shape has been selected by the little white squares (the *sizing handles*) arranged in a rectangle around the shape. When a shape containing text is selected, the bounding rectangle appears shaded.

Immediately after you draw a shape, Office selects it automatically. Thereafter, you can select it by clicking anywhere over it. Alternatively, you can activate the Select Objects tool first (the Drawing toolbar button with the arrow pointer on it). This approach is useful in the following situations:

- To select objects that are behind text or other objects, or if other elements in the document make it hard to see what you're doing. See "Organizing and aligning graphics" later in the chapter.

- To select groups of objects by dragging to enclose them in a selection rectangle. You can also select two or more objects by Shift-clicking them one at a time.

- To work only with drawing objects and pictures. The Select Objects button is a toggle, and as long as it's pressed in, the selection pointer is active. You can then be sure that you're only selecting graphics objects.

Moving, resizing, rotating, and duplicating graphics objects

As usual, you have multiple options for altering the size or position of a graphics object. Table 8-1 summarizes the available techniques.

To move an object, just drag it where you want it to go. You don't need to select it first, but if text or objects are in the way you may need to use the Select Objects tool to do the dragging.

You know you're in position to drag-move an object when the mouse pointer becomes a four-headed arrow. For most objects, including WordArt objects, you must drag over the enclosed parts of the shape or its outlines, not the bounding rectangle marked by the selection handles. For an object that contains editable text, drag by the object's outline, or by the shaded rectangle surrounding the object.

Table 8-1 Keyboard and Mouse Actions with Graphics Objects

To Do This	Use This Mouse Action	Or This Keyboard Action
Select an object.	Click the object with the standard mouse pointer or with the Select Object pointer.	After first selecting an object with the mouse, press Tab or Shift+Tab to select the next or previous object.
Select multiple objects.	Shift-click each object in turn, or drag a selection rectangle around all the objects using the Select Object pointer.	
Move an object.	Drag over the shape or its outline; or drag with the right button to the new location, selecting Move Here after releasing the button.	Select the object, and then press the arrow keys (Ctrl+arrow to move in smaller increments).
Move an object in horizontal or vertical directions only.	Hold down Shift while dragging the object.	
Duplicate an object, moving the new copy.	Hold down Ctrl while dragging the object; or drag with the right button to the new location, selecting Copy Here after releasing the button.	Select the object; press Ctrl+C and then Ctrl+V; now move the duplicate object.
Resize an object.	Drag a sizing handle.	
Resize an object, preserving its proportions.	Hold down Shift while dragging a corner sizing handle.	
Resize an object from the center outward.	Hold down Ctrl while dragging a sizing handle.	
Resize an object from the center outward, preserving its proportions.	Hold down Ctrl+Shift while dragging a corner sizing handle.	
Resize an object without the settings for the grid and guides.	Hold down Alt while dragging a sizing handle.	
Specify a new location or size by precise numeric measurements.	Double-click the object.	Select the object. Then choose Format followed by the type of object at the bottom of the format menu; or display the shortcut menu and choose Format at the bottom.

Chapter 8: Getting Graphical **141**

To Do This	Use This Mouse Action	Or This Keyboard Action
Rotate an object.	Select the object, click the Free Rotate button, and then drag over any of the circular green rotation handles.	Select the object, then choose Draw ⇨ Rotate or Flip. Choose a rotation or flipping option from the menu.

You can also use the keyboard to move an object once it's selected. Each press of an arrow key nudges the object in the arrow's direction. Hold down Ctrl while you press an arrow key to move the object in smaller increments. And you can position objects at precise locations using the Format dialog box, described in the section "Formatting Objects: The Master Control Center" later in this chapter.

Resize a selected object by dragging on the sizing handles (the white boxes along the edges of the selection rectangle enclosing the shape). You can also enter new measurements in the Format dialog box.

Reshaping AutoShapes

Secret

Experiment with dragging those yellow diamonds you see when you select many AutoShape objects. Depending on the object, you can use this technique to change the width, contour, or rotation of parts of the object without affecting its overall size (see Figure 8-4).

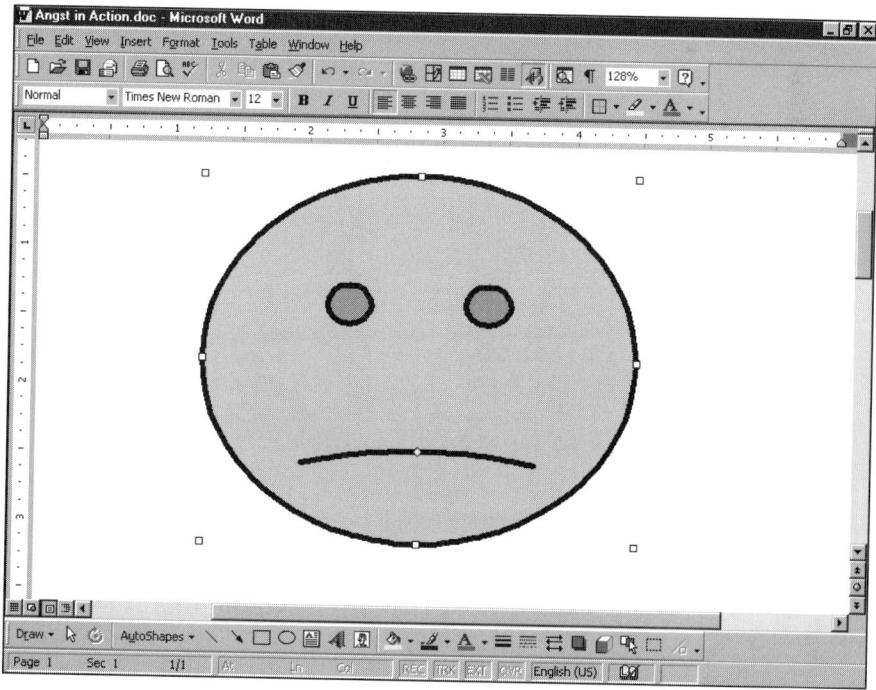

Figure 8-4: The face of anxiety, produced by dragging a happy face's diamond handle.

Secret

Transforming AutoShapes

You can transform just about any enclosed AutoShape into any other. After selecting the object, open the Draw menu on the Drawing toolbar, choose Change AutoShape, and pick out the new shape you want from the submenus. This works for text boxes and other shapes containing text. It doesn't work if the original shape was drawn freehand using the tools on the AutoShapes ⇨ Lines menu. (Text boxes and freehand drawing are covered later in this chapter.)

Precision work with the grid and guidelines

In Word, you can turn on an imaginary grid of evenly spaced horizontal and vertical lines, to which your objects stick when you draw, move, or resize them. With the grid on, you can't position an object in between two adjacent gridlines — it's as if a magnet pulls the object edges so that they always line up on the grid.

You can also rig things so that objects automatically align with one another. With this option turned on, the rectangular boundary of an object you're moving or resizing seems to cling to the boundary of any object it passes over.

To control these auto-alignment settings, choose Draw ⇨ Grid on the Drawing toolbar. In the Drawing Grid dialog box (Figure 8-5), check Snap objects to grid to turn on the overall grid. You can then define exactly the grid you need with the spacing and origin settings below. Check the Snap Objects to Other Objects box to make objects' edges stick to one another as you draw.

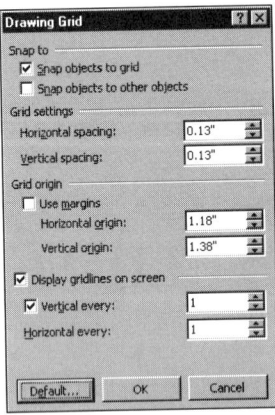

Figure 8-5: The Drawing Grid dialog box

Secret

Holding down Alt while you work disables the snap-to features.

Working with text boxes and callouts

Text boxes are just what the name implies: rectangles ready to receive text. You can place a text box anywhere you want on a document, overriding the basic layout.

The Drawing toolbar has a separate button for creating text boxes. After you click the button, you can insert the text box by clicking or dragging in your document, just as with other drawing toolbar shapes.

However, almost any enclosed AutoShape can contain text. To add text to, say, an AutoShape heart, activate the Text Box tool and then click the shape. Alternatively, select the shape, display its shortcut menu, and choose Add Text. As soon as you do, a rectangle representing an attached text box encloses the shape on the screen. You can't add text to plain lines or freehand shapes, however. Note also that text added to an AutoShape is constrained by the attached rectangular text box — you can't type within the entire shape.

Using callouts

A *callout* is just a text box with a line, called a *leader,* connecting it to another location in your document. Use a callout to add text commenting on another item, as shown in Figure 8-6. The free end of the leader remains stationary as you move the callout shape around on your document, so that the callout always points where it did to start with. Via the AutoShapes menu, callouts come in a multitude (well, 20) of shapes and line configurations.

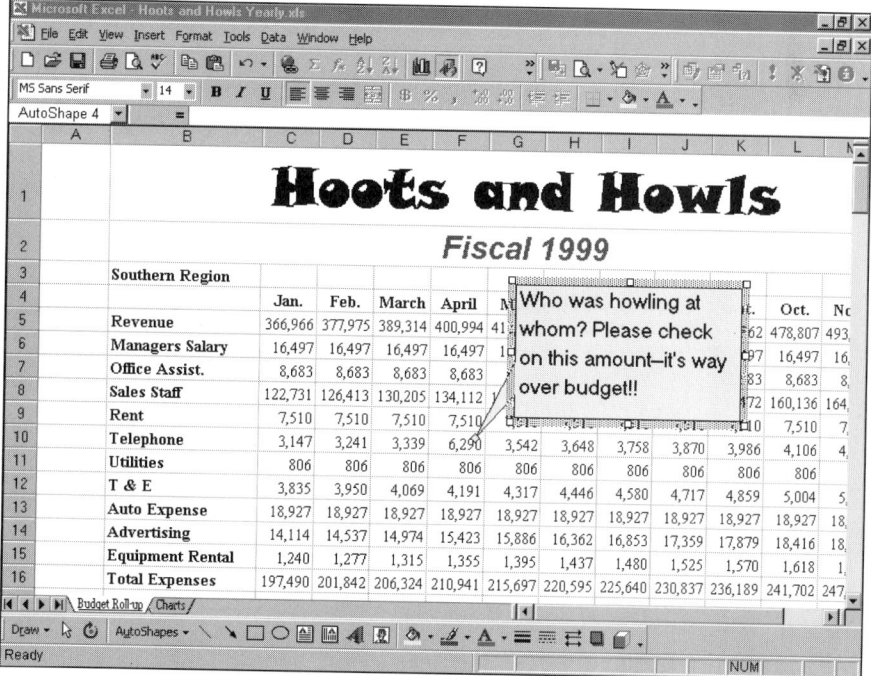

Figure 8-6: A callout in action

Once you've inserted a callout, you can modify the leader by dragging on the yellow handles that define the leader's endpoint and the points where it bends, if any. To see these handles, you must select the callout itself by clicking the rectangle, not the space inside, where text goes.

For all but the first row of shapes on the AutoShapes ⇨ Callouts menu, you can also change the leader's configuration, the gap between the leader and the callout shape, the side where the leader attaches to the callout, and so on. Right-click the callout, choose Format AutoShape, switch to the Text Box tab, and choose Format Callout.

Formatting text boxes and the text inside them

You can do anything to text in a text box, callout, or AutoShape that you can do to text elsewhere in your documents. In Excel and PowerPoint, you can apply character formatting (see Chapter 28 for a definition). In Word, however, you can also set paragraph alignment, control the spacing between lines and between paragraphs, add bullets or numbers, and apply paragraph styles, just as with text in the body of the document. Word text boxes can also be linked together, letting text added to one box flow through a series of boxes (this time, see Chapter 29 for more info).

Because text boxes are drawing objects, however, you can also apply to them most of the Drawing toolbar's formatting options. Detailed later in this chapter, these include fancy backgrounds as well as alignment and grouping commands.

Secret

To format a text box itself, as opposed to the text it contains, click directly on the rectangle that defines it (note that formatting applied to nonrectangular AutoShapes affects the shape, not the text box rectangle). Conversely, to work with the text, click the text area to display the insertion point, and if that doesn't work, choose Edit Text from the object's shortcut menu. See the section "Formatting Objects: The Master Control Center" at the end of this chapter for more text box formatting secrets.

You can rotate the text in a text box in all three applications, but you do it a little differently in each program. Here are the tricks:

- In Word, you select the text box and then click the Change Text Direction button on the Text Box toolbar.

- In Excel, select the text and choose Format ⇨ Text Box. In the resulting dialog box, select a text rotation format from the list of buttons. Note that one of the options is for vertical text without rotation—the letters that would normally be in a line are arranged in a column, but each letter is still oriented the normal way.

- PowerPoint works like Excel except that you can only rotate the text in by degrees. Check the relevant box in the Format ⇨ Text Box dialog box.

Drawing and editing freehand shapes

Modeled on the features of high-end drawing applications like Corel Draw, Office's trio of freehand drawing tools — curve, freeform, and scribble — are quite powerful. Don't get the wrong idea — you wouldn't want to rely on Office for a major design project. But the drawing tools let you make acceptable freehand sketches (see Figure 8-7).

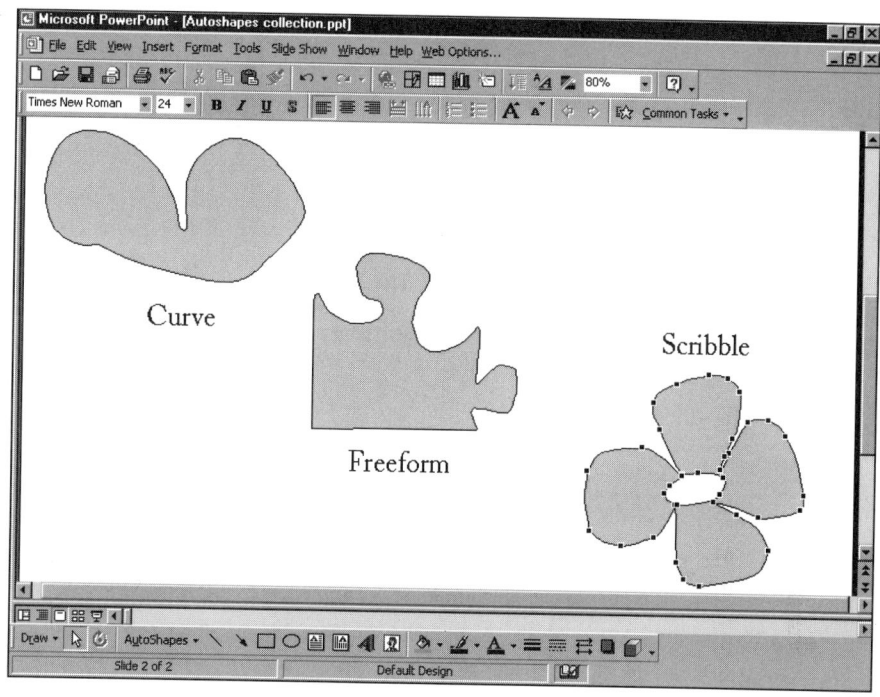

Figure 8-7: Sample freehand shapes drawn with the curve, freeform, and scribble tools

The Office drawing tools provide a critical capability: You can edit what you draw. Drawing with a mouse is hard, to put it mildly, and you can't expect to lay down lines where you want them. But as long as you can go back and push them into place, you can gradually sculpt the curve you had in mind. In Figure 8-7, the scribble shape on the right has been selected for editing the points that define the line.

Before starting work on a freehand drawing object, magnify your work by at least a 200 percent zoom factor. Then to draw the object, choose AutoShapes ➪ Lines to display a graphical menu of six line-drawing tools. The top row contains ordinary straight lines, but clicking one of the tools on the bottom row starts a new freehand drawing. Here's how they work:

- **Curve.** Imagine you're playing with a really long rubber band that you can pin down anywhere you like on the drawing surface — that's sort of how this tool works. Click and release the mouse button to pin down the starting point. Moving the mouse pointer now extends the line straight out from that point. When the free end reaches a place where the curve should bend, click again to pin down the rubber band there. When you stretch the line out from that spot in any new direction, the line curves smoothly accordingly. You can remove previous direction-change points in reverse order by pressing Backspace. Finish the curve by double-clicking the final anchor point.

- **Freeform.** This tool lets you draw shapes that include both straight and curving lines. Click and release the mouse button to define the endpoints of straight segments. Drag the mouse to draw freehand curves.

- **Scribble.** Drag with this tool to draw freehand shapes with the finest possible detail. When you draw with this tool, Office detects and records in the drawing smaller changes of direction than when you draw freehand with the freeform tool. As a result, scribbles are likely to look more jagged than freeform shapes unless you're a good mouse artist.

Editing freehand shapes

I've never met a freehand shape that I didn't have to edit. Of course, you can perform any of the basic manipulations available for AutoShapes: resizing, rotating, adding a fill, changing line color or size, and even adding shadows and 3-D effects.

But the real action is in editing the shape's contour itself. To edit a freehand shape, select it and then choose Edit Points from its shortcut menu or from the menu of the Draw button. (By the way, the technique described here works for imported line, or vector, graphics too, including clip art — but to apply it, you need the tip in the section "Editing line art" later in this chapter.)

When Edit Points is turned on, you see black squares along the shape's outline, one for each point where the line changes direction. Microsoft refers to such a direction-change point as a *vertex*. It's really critical that you zoom in on the object to work with the points comfortably. It also helps to distinguish the points from the line by setting the line width to 0 points. With the shape selected, click the Line Style button on the Drawing toolbar, choose More Lines, and then enter 0 for the Weight setting. You can change back to the correct line style after you finish the edits.

Once you've taken care of these preliminaries, you can

- Move a point by dragging it.

- Delete a point to smooth out an overly wiggly stretch by holding down Ctrl while you click the point.

- Add a new point by clicking at any point-less location along the curve.

- Change the degree and direction of deflection for the segment passing through a point. Click the point to select it, and then drag its *tangent handles*. This is an extremely powerful technique for shaping and smoothing freehand lines, so be sure to familiarize yourself with how it works — see the next section.

Working with tangent lines

As shown in Figure 8-8, the tangent handles are those white boxes you see when you select a point. Microsoft calls them *tangent points*, but if you use that name you'll mix them up with the direction-change points on the freehand line.

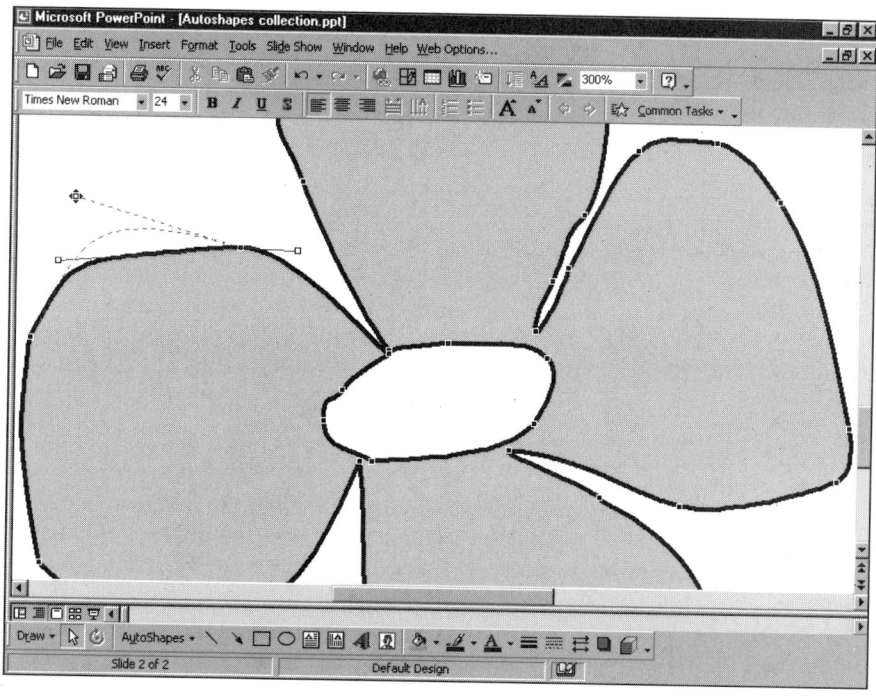

Figure 8-8: Reshaping a freehand line by dragging a point's tangent handle

Dragging the tangent handles controls the pair of blue *tangent lines* to which the handles are attached. The *angle* of one tangent line to the other determines the direction of stretch it places on the curve. The tangent line's *length* determines how far that part of the curve gets stretched. If you see only one handle, it means that the segment on the other side of the point is a straight line and can't be bent (but see "Changing a segment's type" later).

Of course, the line that takes shape as you work with the tangent handles also depends on the location and types of the points (vertices) on either side of the one you're working with. Practice — you'll see what I mean.

Changing point and segment types

To further refine the contour at a specific point, right-click along the outline to display a shortcut menu. The choices listed in the second menu group vary, depending on whether you right-clicked directly over a point or elsewhere along the outline (see Figure 8-9).

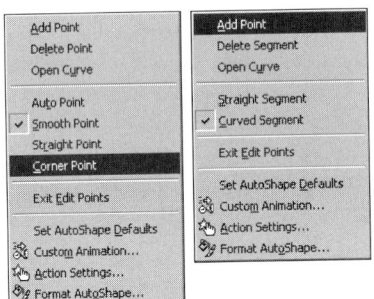

Figure 8-9: On the left, the shortcut menu of an individual direction-change point in a freehand shape; on the right, the shortcut menu for the segments between points

Changing a point's type

On the shortcut menu for a specific point, the important choice is the type of point. Four point types are available:

- **Auto Point.** Creates a smooth curve through the point automatically. Office decides for you how to bend the outline, and you can't see tangent handles or lines when the point is selected.

- **Corner Point.** Creates a sharp corner at the junction of the two segments that meet at the point. You can vary the length and angle of each tangent line independently.

- **Smooth Point.** Select this type of point to have the outline curve smoothly through the point, but with customizable deflection. You can bend the outline at will by dragging either tangent handle, but the two tangent lines always extend equally in opposite directions (you can't vary the angle between them).

- **Straight Point.** Use this point type when you want the segment on one side of the point to be "flatter" than the segment on the other, but you don't want a sharp corner. You can stretch the two tangent lines by different amounts, though they always extend in opposite directions. Nota bene: You don't need a straight point to create a straight line passing through the point — a smooth point will work just as well, so long as you stretch the tangent lines far enough.

More weird facts about editing curve points

You can convert a straight point or smooth point to a corner point by holding down Shift while you drag a tangent handle. Likewise, hold down Ctrl to change a corner point or straight point into a smooth point. If you hold down both Shift and Ctrl, Ctrl wins.

You can pop up the points shortcut menu by right-clicking a tangent handle. Selecting a new point type from the menu changes the handle's point accordingly. But if you choose Add Point, you get a new point at the current location of the handle.

When you first draw a shape with the Curve tool, all the points are AutoPoints. However, scribbles and freeform shapes have corner points.

Changing a segment's type

With a freeform shape's points showing, right-clicking over a portion of the outline between two points (a *segment*) displays a shortcut menu with two items of note: Straight Segment, and Curved Segment. You can see in the menu which type of segment you're dealing with, and you can convert the segment to the other type by selecting it on the menu.

A straight segment connects two points with a straight line, of course, one that can't be bent no matter what type of point lies at either end. If you turn on point editing and select one of the points, you'll see that it lacks tangent handles on the side toward the straight segment.

Curved Segments sometimes look perfectly straight, depending on how the shape was drawn and edited, but they *can* be deformed by pulling on the tangent handles of the points at either end of the segment.

Closing and opening freehand shapes

One more option is available on the shortcut menu when you're editing the points of a freehand outline: If the shape is closed (with a continuous outline), choose Open Curve to break it apart at the direction-change point nearest where you right-clicked the outline. If the shape is an open line with a beginning and an end, choose Close Curve to have Office connect the two endpoints.

WordArt for designer text

If you like graphically powerful text effects, WordArt is for you. This feature takes any text of your choosing and warps it to one of many shapes, adding 3-D effects in the process. Sample results are shown in Figure 8-10.

WordArt is incorporated into the Drawing toolbar. To add a WordArt object, click the corresponding button to display the WordArt Gallery dialog box. If the Drawing toolbar is hidden, you can choose Insert ⇨ Picture ⇨ WordArt instead. You shouldn't have trouble picking out a style or entering and editing the text you want displayed.

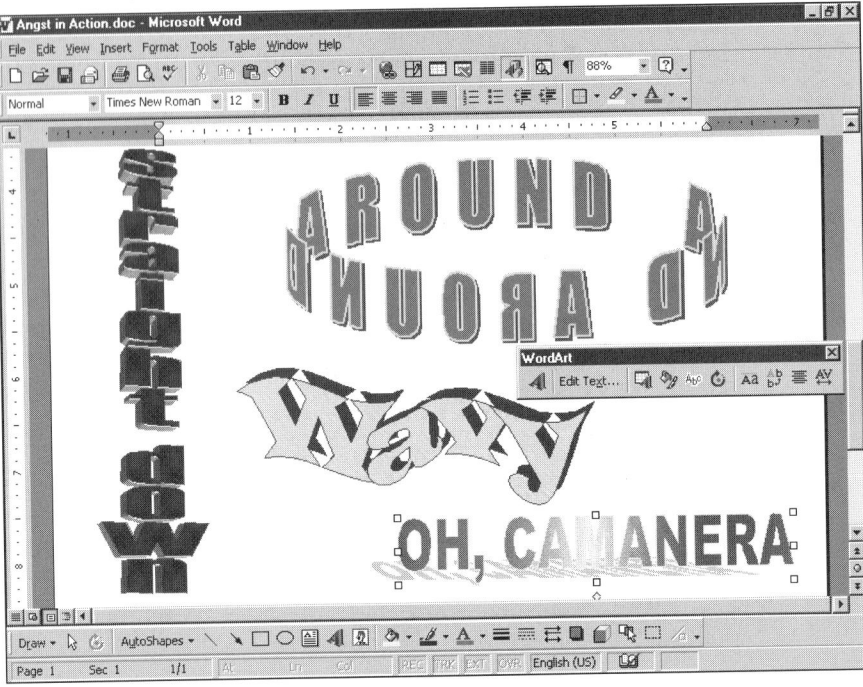

Figure 8-10: Samples of WordArt

Don't overlook those yellow diamond handles that appear when a WordArt object is selected. As usual, they let you change the shape of a curve, but this time you're working with the invisible curve along which the WordArt text is stretched and bent. Dragging the yellow diamond further distorts the characters, or straightens them out.

Note that when you select a WordArt object, a special toolbar appears automatically. You can use the buttons here to alter the basic WordArt settings for the object, including the shape it's based on, the text it displays, and whether the text appears horizontally or vertically. You can also adjust such fine points as letter height, character spacing, and paragraph alignment.

Working with color, line, and texture

You can control the width and color of the line defining any drawing object, and you can fill most objects with a color, simple pattern, textured background, or clip art image or other picture.

Most of the objects you can draw are *closed*, meaning that they have a continuous outline around an enclosed area. When Office refers to the line of a closed shape, it means this outline. Of course, you can also draw ordinary *open* lines, the kind with two free ends. Either way, a line can be straight, jagged, or smoothly curving. In addition to the techniques covered in this section, you can also control fill and line options from the Format dialog box, described in the section "Formatting Objects: The Master Control Center" later in this chapter.

Filling objects

To fill an object, select it (of course) and then click the Fill button. Click the main portion of the button to fill the object with the currently selected color. If you want to change colors or apply a pattern or texture, click the vertical bar at the right of the button to display a pop-up menu of colors. You can choose from these, but if you want an even fancier fill, select More Fill Colors or Fill Effects.

Secret

The dialog box displayed when you choose More Fill Colors is the secret residence of the Semitransparent check box. Checking this box allows text or other documents behind the object to peep through a bit. This setting is also available on the Format dialog box, described in the section "Formatting Objects: The Master Control Center" later in this chapter.

The Fill Effects choice brings up the Fill Effects dialog box, shown in Figure 8-11.

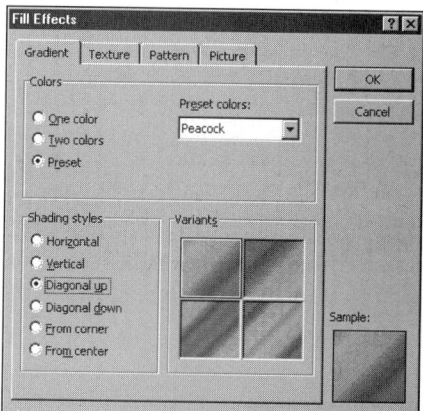

Figure 8-11: The Fill Effects dialog box

Here, select among four types of complex fills by switching to the corresponding tab, as follows:

- **Gradient.** Creates a fill with a gradual transition between two or more colors. The One Color option blends the chosen color into black or white, depending on the setting of the Dark/Light slider. You can select the colors involved and control the geometric pattern of the transition.

- **Texture.** Fills the shape with a pattern designed to imitate a textured surface. You can select a texture from the available presets, or choose Other Texture to pick an image in a disk file. The chosen image has to be small so that it can be displayed at full size within shapes. Office tiles copies of the image so that the shape is completely filled.

- **Pattern.** Fills the shape with one of 48 simple preset patterns. You can select foreground and background colors for the pattern.

- **Picture.** Fills the shape with an imported picture. The picture is scaled larger or smaller as necessary to completely fit the shape.

Secret

Note that you can "fill" lines that don't completely enclose an area. Office adds the fill on one side of the line.

Controlling line options

Use techniques similar to those described in the previous section to change the color, width, or pattern of the selected shape's outline. Click the main part of the Line Color button to apply the line color shown on the button. Click the vertical bar beside the button to select a different color or to choose a patterned outline from a dialog box.

The pop-up menu displayed when you click the Line Style button lets you select the line width and whether you see a single, double, or triple line. To create a broken line, select one of the choices on the Dash Style menu. The Arrow Style menu is only available if the "shape" you're working with is a line (not a closed shape).

Secret

The Line Style pop-up menu lacks a choice for lines of no width at all. If you want an selected object to have a fill but no outline, you must open the Format dialog box — clicking Line Style ⇨ More Lines is one method for doing so. On the Colors and Lines find the Line section in the middle and click Color. Now choose No Line on the drop-down menu.

That's a lot of work for such a simple operation. Word and PowerPoint have hidden commands that turn the visibility of selected lines on and off. These commands are DrawLineToggle (in Word) and Line On/Off (in PowerPoint). Use the techniques covered in Chapter 5 to place their buttons on the Drawing toolbar.

In Excel, you need the following simple macro to do the same job. After you create it in the Visual Basic Editor — see Chapter 19 for instructions — place a button for the macro on the Drawing toolbar with the technique covered in Chapter 35.

```
Sub LineMakeInvisible()
    Selection.ShapeRange.Line.Visible = msoFalse
End Sub
```

Adding shadow and 3-D effects

Office art can be deep, really deep — if you use shadow or 3-D effects. To get started, you just select the object and then click the appropriate button, Shadow or 3-D, on the Drawing toolbar. This pops up a menu of preset effects shown as little graphical examples. Click one of these, and your shape takes on the settings of the chosen preset.

But who wants to be stuck with presets? The illusion of depth is enchanting, and no one can resist playing with shadow and 3-D effects. The keys to controlling them yourself are the Shadow Settings and 3-D Settings toolbars.

Display them by clicking the corresponding choice at the bottom of the pop-up menu displayed by the Shadow and 3-D buttons.

By the way, you can add shadows to just about any object, including placeholders for multimedia clips. But you *can't* add the Drawing toolbar's 3-D and shadow effects to selected text. When you add 3-D to a text box, the text itself remains flat, and it just sits there as you tilt the 3-D object. To place 3-D text in a 3-D shape, slap a WordArt object on top of the graphical one. (In Word, you can add shadow, embossed, and engraved effects to selected text via the Format ⇨ Font dialog box.)

Secret

Both the 3-D and Shadow toolbars have On/Off buttons at the left that toggle the relevant effect. The object remembers its most recent settings for both effects, so you can turn an effect on or off or switch back and forth between 3-D and shadow effects without losing your previous work. By the way, you don't need the On/Off buttons to switch between 3-D and shadow. Clicking any button of the other effect's toolbar immediately restores that effect with its previous settings.

Secret

The Shadow effect includes presets that make the selected object look embossed or engraved. Choose Style 17 to apply the embossed effect, Style 18 for an engraved look. Both effects remove any existing border.

Customizing shadow and 3-D effects

The Shadow Settings toolbar has buttons for moving the shadow relative to the object itself as well as one for changing the shadow's color. These tools are adequate, but the 3-D Settings toolbar is a lot more fun. The tools include the following:

- Four tilt buttons for rotating the *faux* 3-D object about its horizontal and vertical axes. Note that you're allowed only 180 degrees of rotation. For example, you can stand an object on its face, so that the back side of the 3-D effect becomes its top, but you can't turn the new top surface closer toward you.

- The Depth button, for determining how far, in points, the 3-D effect extends out from the original drawing. Remember, there are 72 points to an inch. So if you're entering a custom depth and you think in inches, multiply the depth you want by 72. The 0 pt. setting doesn't actually produce a flat object, just one with very little depth. Use it to display the object as a planar surface (changing the 3-D color can make the edges more obvious). When available, the Infinity setting extends the 3-D effect off toward the horizon, although the shape may stop before it reaches the edge of the page.

- The Direction button, which lets you determine which way (left, right, up, or down) the 3-D effect extends from its object. In addition, you can control the manner in which the effect extends. Select Perspective to give it an artist's perspective, with all the lines converging toward a single point in the distance. Choose Parallel to have the lines extend parallel to one another — this option doesn't give the illusion of reality, but it's the usual technique in technical drawings.

- The Lighting button, for selecting the brightness and direction of the imaginary lighting source. As you pass the mouse over a direction button on the pop-up menu, the cube in the center gives you an idea of how that choice would look. Click the center cube to light the object directly from the front.

- The Surface button, which lets you select from three options controlling how reflective the surface of your 3-D shape will appear. Matte gives it a dull look, whereas Metal supposedly makes it look like polished metal, with Plastic somewhere in between.

- The 3-D Color button, for choosing the color of the 3-D effect. Select Automatic to have Office choose the color for you based on that of the original object (use the standard Fill Color and Line Color buttons on the Drawing toolbar to change the object's color even when a 3-D effect is in place).

Organizing and aligning graphics

Be sure you're aware of the many options Office provides for working with groups of objects. These fall into three basic categories of commands: alignment, grouping, and ordering.

Aligning objects

It's bad enough trying to get a picture to hang straight, but the human nervous system is sorely inadequate to the task of lining up two or more graphics objects on a screen using a mouse. One alternative, typing in numeric coordinates, takes too long. The solution can be found on the menu you get by choosing Draw ⇨ Align or Distribute (Figure 8-12).

Before you open this menu, select the objects that you want to bring into relationship with one another, or with the page they're on. It doesn't matter which order you select them in. Then display the menu of alignment tools. In Word or PowerPoint, if you want to align or distribute the objects relative to the whole page rather than to one another, turn on the Relative To option at the bottom of the menu (to Page in Word, to Slide in PowerPoint).

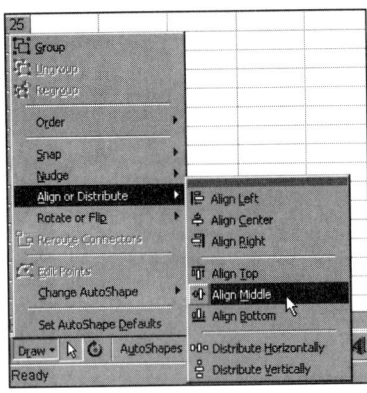

Figure 8-12: The Align or Distribute menu

Secret

The basic functions of the alignment options should be self-explanatory. What may not be so obvious is that objects are moved so that they line up with the one that's already located farthest in the selected alignment direction. For example, if you select three objects and choose Align Left, the object that is farthest left remains in place, while Office moves the other two objects so that their left sides line up with it. Also, remember that Office aligns the objects based on the imaginary rectangles that surround them.

The distribution choices arrange three or more selected objects at equal distances from one another. The two objects at the top and bottom of the page remain in place, while the ones in between divide the intervening space evenly. If the Relative to Page option is on, distributing two or more objects moves them all so that they're evenly spaced on the page.

Grouping objects

You can and should group objects together to preserve their relative positions and sizes, during moving and resizing operations, or if you know you'll always be applying the same effects to all the objects. All you have to do is select all the objects and choose Draw ⇨ Group. The selection handles are removed from the individual objects but appear around the entire group, which you can now move, size, or color as a unit.

To work with the objects individually again, select the conglomerate object and choose Draw ⇨ Ungroup. This is the only way to edit the points of a grouped freehand object, for example. After making any changes you like, you can reconstitute the last group you ungrouped by choosing, well, Draw ⇨ Regroup. This works even if you have moved the objects onto different pages — Office will bring all the chickens home to roost on the same page when you use the Regroup command. The trio of grouping commands is also available from the Grouping menu on an object's shortcut menu.

You can group smaller groups of objects into larger groups for as many levels of organization as you like. The Ungroup command only breaks apart the top-level group. If a drawing is composed of groups of grouped groups, you have to use the Ungroup command repeatedly to get to the individual shapes so you can edit their points. In Word, however, the DrawDisassemblePicture command — available from the Tools ⇨ Customize dialog box — can ungroup all the groups in one fell swoop.

Ordering objects

We're talking order as in sequence of placement, not as in, "I'll have two objects to go, hold the tacky fill patterns." Anyway, as in all drawing programs, Office graphics objects are ordered in an imaginary stack, one on top of the next. You only notice this when two objects overlap, or when you place an object on top of text. The object on top covers up the one below it, although if the top object has no fill color, you can still see the object below.

Use the Draw ⇨ Order menu to change a selected object's position in the stack (the menu, shown in Figure 8-13, is also available from an object's shortcut menu). You can do this to change the look of the object landscape, but also just to retrieve an object that's buried underneath others.

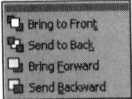

Figure 8-13: Use the commands on this menu to bury an object beneath a pile or pull it out again.

On the menu, the Bring to Front and Send to Back commands move the selected object to the very top or bottom of the pile, whereas the Bring Forward and Send Backward choices just promote or demote it by one level. In Word, the menu also lists commands to move the object in front of or behind the document text, which is initially at the bottom of the stack of objects.

Toolbar modifications for efficient drawing

You have room on the standard Drawing toolbar for a few more buttons. Don't hesitate to fill up that space with any tools you find useful (see Chapter 5 for information on customizing toolbars).

Aside from obvious choices such as the Alignment and Grouping commands, some suggestions include:

- **The EditPoints command.** If you do any work with freehand shapes, for example, by all means add this button. Turning on point-editing via the shortcut menu is cumbersome, and it's too easy to mistakenly turn it off. (For that matter, a keyboard shortcut for this command might come in handy too.)

- **The Select Multiple Objects command.** Clicking this button displays a dialog box with a list of the shapes in your document by type. Click the shapes you want and OK the box to select them.

- **In Word, the DrawMarquee command.** This lets you select multiple graphics just as you can with the pointer tool. However, it shuts off as soon as you release the mouse button. You can't use it to select objects by clicking.

- **The command to turn outlines on or off.** See the section "Controlling line options" earlier in this chapter.

Secret

If you work extensively with special effects, customize your toolbar setup so that the buttons of the Shadow Settings and 3-D Settings toolbars are automatically available whenever you draw. That way, you won't have to manually display them each time you start working on a shape.

You can do this in two ways:

- Create a custom toolbar and fill it with the buttons found on both of the Settings toolbars — just Ctrl-drag the buttons from the existing toolbars to your new one. If you regularly use any particular depth, direction,

- lighting, or surface settings, you can drag out their buttons onto the custom toolbar for one-click access. Then dock the new toolbar so that it's always at the ready.

- Create a VBA procedure (macro) that displays the Shadow Settings and 3-D Settings toolbars automatically whenever you turn on the Drawing toolbar. Here's the code you need in Word:

```
Public Sub DrawingToolbarsToggle()
Dim boolDrawingBarVisible As Boolean
With CommandBars("Drawing")
.Visible = Not (.Visible)
boolDrawingBarVisible = .Visible
End With
CommandBars("3-D Settings").Visible = boolDrawingBarVisible
CommandBars("Shadow Settings").Visible = boolDrawingBarVisible
End Sub
```

Assign the macro to a button on one of your standard toolbars in place of the standard button for the Drawing toolbar. You might as well use the same button image. If you like, create a custom toolbar like the one just described and display it instead of the stock Settings toolbars — just refer to it by name in quotation marks in a statement patterned after those shown here just above the End Sub statement. If you want to get really fancy, you could toggle *off* the toolbars you use for editing text whenever the Drawing toolbar is active for more room to work on your drawings.

If you do keep the 3-D Settings and Shadow Settings toolbars (or their buttons) at the ready, you can dispense with the 3-D and Shadow buttons on the main Drawing toolbar and use their slots for other buttons. With an object selected, clicking on any of the 3-D Settings buttons turns on the 3-D effect, which you can then tweak to taste.

Setting defaults for fill, line, and special effects

To set up defaults for all future shapes you draw, format an object in your document with all the options you want as your defaults for fill color, line color and style, and 3-D or shadow effects, if any. Select this object of your affections and choose Set AutoShape Defaults from the Draw button's menu or the selected object's shortcut menu. From here on in, every shape you draw will take on those same characteristics.

Inserting and Editing Pictures

When the built-in drawing tools won't suffice, adorn your document with graphics from other sources. Office uses the term *picture* to mean any type of graphical image you acquire from a source other than the built-in drawing tools. This encompasses both paint-type *bitmaps* and draw-type (vector art) *metafiles* in any format Office recognizes.

Pictures are, of course, *objects*, the general term for anything from an external source placed in its original form into an Office document. Chapter 10 covers the basics on how objects behave and how you can manipulate them in Office. Here, the focus is on a survey of specific types of objects you're likely to use to make your documents presentable, as well as the commands used to format objects once they reach an Office document.

Inserting pictures

The standard way to add pictures created in other software is the Insert ⇨ Picture command. Use the two choices at the top of the submenu, Clip Art and From File. (The other items, some of which vary depending on the application you're using, don't insert pictures in the sense that Office usually uses that term. They are covered elsewhere in this chapter.)

The Insert ⇨ Picture ⇨ From File choice brings up a fairly standard Office file dialog box of the type discussed in Chapter 12. As shown in Figure 8-14, however, the Insert Picture dialog box lets you preview images rather than documents before you select them.

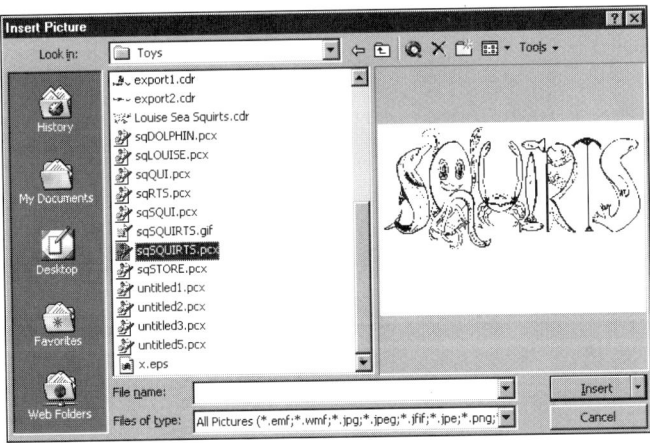

Figure 8-14: The Insert Picture dialog box gives you a preview of the images you might want to place into your document.

Choosing Insert ⇨ Picture ⇨ Clip Art summons the Clip Gallery, described in the next section. But keep in mind that the only real difference between clip art and other pictures in Office is where you find the graphics. Once in your document clip art pictures function just like ones you insert from a file or by scanning them in.

Secret

You can create a button that always inserts a specific picture into the current document. See "Creating buttons that activate hyperlinks or insert graphics" in Chapter 5.

Managing clip art and other content with Clip Gallery

The Clip Gallery program has been given a major makeover for Office 2000 that is consistent with Microsoft's "browser everywhere" philosophy. Figure 8-15 shows the new Clip Gallery window.

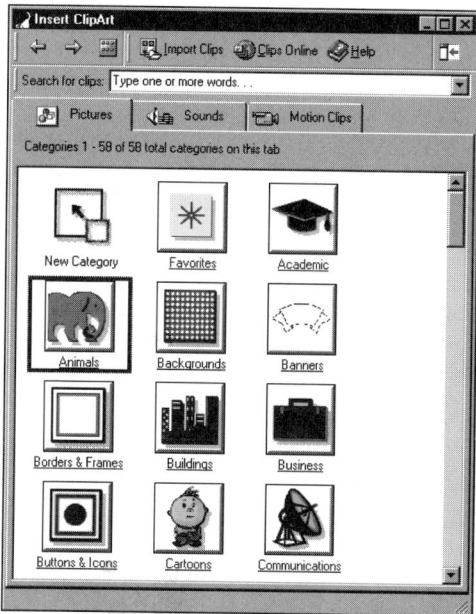

Figure 8-15: Microsoft Clip Gallery now features controls reminiscent of Internet Explorer.

You should become familiar with Clip Gallery because you'll see it frequently — it appears not only when you're inserting clip art *per se*, but also when you insert horizontal lines or picture-based bullets in Word; when you add shapes to a document using the More AutoShapes command; and when you insert various other graphical items in Office. The title of the Clip Gallery window, along with the images you can access, varies depending on which command you use to display Clip Gallery. But the mechanics of working with it are consistent.

The main part of the Clip Gallery window is divided into three tabs, for pictures, sound, and video. When you use Insert ⇨ Picture ⇨ Clip Art to open Clip Gallery the window shows a graphical listing of the categories contained in your clip art collection. These categories can contain items from any of the three types of content, so you see the same categories no matter which tab you're viewing.

Quickly, here's how to maneuver in Clip Gallery:

- To see the individual content items in a category, click the category once. If it contains any items of the content type you're viewing—pictures, sounds, or video—they appear in the window.
- To browse through content you've already viewed, use the browser-type Back and Forward buttons or their keyboard shortcuts, Alt+Left arrow and Alt+Right arrow.
- To return to the main category display, click the All Categories button or press Alt+Home.
- To search for content items by subject, type the keyword for the subject in the Search for Clips box and press Enter. The results you get depend on whether the clip items have been assigned matching keywords— see "Organizing your clips" later in this section.

Like the typical program window, Clip Gallery has Minimize, Maximize/Restore, and Close buttons in the upper-right corner. But you get additional control over window size with the Change button in the toolbar just below the three buttons just mentioned. Clicking here alternates between a very narrow window and a middle-sized one, enabling you to quickly redistribute space between Clip Gallery and your Office application without covering up the entire application window. The keyboard shortcuts for shrinking and widening the Clip Gallery window are Ctrl+Shift+< and Ctrl+Shift+>.

Using content items in Clip Gallery

Inserting a clip art image or other content item from Clip Gallery couldn't be easier. Clicking the item displays the four-choice graphical menu shown in Figure 8-16. Click the top button to place the item in your document.

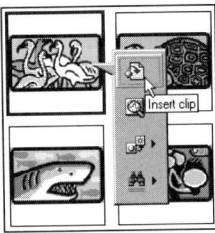

Figure 8-16: Insert content items by clicking the top button on this pop-up menu.

Clip Gallery always inserts the chosen item into the application from which you started the program. If you switch to a different Office application and then insert an item, it still appears in the original application, even though the second app is the one visible on your screen behind Clip Gallery.

To preview a picture in a larger window before you insert it, or to hear a sound item or see a video clip, click Preview clip, the second button on the pop-up menu.

Organizing your clips

A collection of clip art, sounds, and video clips can quickly become overwhelmingly large. Clip Gallery has simple but solid tools to help you keep track of all the content. These all depend on *clip properties* you assign to the individual content items.

To work with a clip's properties, right-click the item and choose Clip Properties. The three-tab dialog box shown in Figure 8-17 appears. The tabs work as follows:

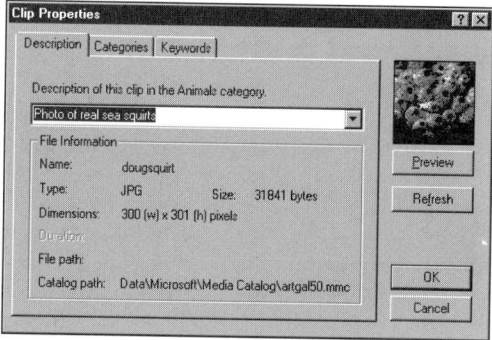

Figure 8-17: Use the Clip Properties dialog box to add descriptions and keywords to content items and to assign them to categories.

- **Description.** Type in a name or description for the item that will jog your memory. Your description appears in Clip Gallery when you hover the mouse over the item for a second or so. You may want to include technical information such as the number of colors the image contains or the file format "flavor" (subtype). The description you see automatically includes the main file type (GIF, WMF, BMP, or what have you) and the file's size.

- **Categories.** You can assign any image in your collection to an existing category by switching to this tab and checking the boxes for the categories where it belongs. To create a new category, you can of course use the New Category button just below the category list. Alternatively, a big New Category button is available as the first item in the main Clip Gallery window when you're working with categories rather than individual clips.

- **Keywords.** Use this tab to assign and remove keywords to the clip. These are the words that Clip Gallery matches when you type in a search.

If information about the clip, such as its size or dimensions, isn't visible in the Description tab, clicking the Refresh button should display it.

Adding new images to the Clip Gallery

If you're not much of an artist yourself, it's easy to expand your library with other people's creations. To supplement your clip art library with items accessible on your hard disk or a network, click Import Clips. Another source is the Internet: from Clip Gallery, choose Clips Online to connect to a site from which you can preview and download loads of new images. After you retrieve a content item with either method, Clip Gallery displays the Clip Properties dialog box described previously. Be sure to assign the imported item to at least one category or you might have trouble finding it again.

Inserting images from a scanner or digital camera

To place an image into an Office application using your scanner or digital camera, choose Insert ➪ Picture ➪ From Scanner or Camera. A small dialog box appears in which you can select the specific device you want to use to harvest the image and set the image resolution. Click Insert to turn on the device and place the image in your document.

Working with PhotoEditor

Bundled with Office is PhotoEditor, a reasonably capable program for scanning images and modifying the resulting bitmap pictures using a variety of special effects. Comparable in function to Adobe Photoshop, PhotoEditor doesn't claim to have as many bells and whistles, but it does a decent job within its limits. PhotoEditor isn't installed by default, so if you want to try it out you should rerun Office Setup and select an appropriate installation setting for it.

If you install PhotoEditor, it automatically opens when the image has been scanned. You can posterize the image, emboss it, or otherwise add special effects, as well as perform more mundane adjustments to brightness, contrast, and color. Once the picture looks right, choose File ➪ Exit and Return To (your document).

Caution

Although you can create "new" pictures in PhotoEditor, this isn't a paint program — it offers no tools at all for adding new dots to a bitmap image.

Modifying pictures

Once you've inserted a picture, you aren't stuck with the way it looks. Office lets you fuss with all sorts of picture characteristics, depending on the type of picture you're working with:

- You can resize or move the picture, of course. With the mouse, you use the same techniques as you would for a graphic object created with the built-in drawing tools (see "Moving, resizing, rotating, and duplicating graphics objects" earlier in this chapter).

- You can add a border, a line, and a fill color for portions of the picture that aren't already colored.

- You can crop the picture, covering up parts of it that you don't want to show in the document.

- You can adjust the picture's brightness and contrast.

- If the picture is a line art (vector) image, you can convert it into individual shapes that you can then edit with Office's built-in drawing tools.

- If the picture is a paint (bitmap) image, you can remove one of its colors. You ask why? See the next two sections.

- If need be, you can go back to the application in which the picture was created and edit it there. Assuming the other software is installed on your system, this process is as simple as double-clicking on the picture — if you have linked or embedded it instead of simply importing it wholesale.

Using the Picture toolbar

When you select a picture, the Picture toolbar (Figure 8-18) pops up automatically. You can display it at other times too, as you would any other toolbar. The Picture toolbar has most of the controls you need for modifying your digital art.

Figure 8-18: The Picture toolbar lets you manipulate art.

From left to right, the buttons on the Picture toolbar work as follows:

- **Insert Picture.** Duplicates the Insert ⇨ Picture ⇨ From File menu selection.

- **Image Control.** Offers four presets for settings affecting the picture's appearance. Choose Grayscale to convert the picture's colors to corresponding shades of gray. The Black & White option converts all colors to either black or white. Watermark makes the image bright and low-contrast so that it can be placed behind the rest of the document, simulating a watermark (use the Draw ⇨ Send to Back command). Select Automatic to let Office decide the settings.

- **More Contrast** and **Less Contrast.** Raises or lowers the color *saturation* (intensity), decreasing or increasing the gray content.
- **More Brightness** and **Less Brightness.** Adds white or black, making all the colors lighter or darker.
- **Crop.** Hides the edges of the picture as though clipping them away. To crop the picture, click the Crop button and then drag a sizing handle.
- **Line Style.** Same as the Line Style button on the Drawing toolbar. It applies a border around the picture itself (or in Word, around the picture boundary).
- **Text Wrapping.** Controls the flow of text in the underlying document around the picture. Only available in Word.
- **Recolor Picture.** Only available if the selected picture is a draw-type image, not a bitmap. Click it to change the picture's existing colors.
- **Object.** Displays the Format Picture dialog box. See the section "Formatting Objects: The Master Control Center" later.
- **Set Transparent Color.** Only available for bitmaps, this tool makes one color in the image transparent, letting the document behind it show through. Click the button, and then click the color you want to strip away. The color becomes transparent throughout the image, not just where you clicked. It's a neat effect, but see "Transparent pitfalls" later.
- **Reset Picture.** Removes cropping from the selected picture; restores it to its original size; and returns the color, brightness, and contrast controls to their original settings.

Transparent pitfalls

The Set Transparent Color tool on the Paint toolbar is handy for removing a one-color background from a bitmap picture so that the foreground art work stands out. Images with transparent areas are commonly used in Web pages to make the graphics look embedded directly in the background. However, you should be aware of some caveats pertaining to the Set Transparent Color tool.

For one thing, some bitmaps already include transparent areas, and if these are present you can't use the tool. For another, the really cool bitmaps you probably want to use have palettes of 256 colors or more. With that many colors available, you'll rarely find large areas of all one color. Because you can make only one color transparent, you'll end up with a field of pinholes rather than a transparent background. And finally, it's common to find the background color in the foreground design — in which case you'll have holes in the foreground as well.

A caveat on imported bitmap pictures

Office usually converts inserted bitmap pictures into enhanced metafiles, a newer Windows picture format. In the process, the original data is changed. If you cut or copy such a picture from an Office document back to the clipboard, and then into another application, it won't be readable as a standard Windows bitmap. You can't paste it into Paint, for example. If you do find a program that will accept the pasted metafile, the image looks different from the original.

Editing line art

Secret

You can edit the underlying shapes in imported draw-type pictures just as if you had drawn them with Office's built-in graphics tools. The only trick is, you have to break up the picture into its component shapes and edit each one individually. For example, you can rearrange parts of the image, change fill and line colors, and even edit the points of the individual shape outlines. This technique also lets you combine parts of two or more images.

The basic technique is simple: You just select the picture and choose Ungroup from the shortcut menu or the Draw button's menu (see "Grouping objects" earlier). What you're likely to discover, though, is that the picture consists of groups of grouped objects. In other words, you'll have to Ungroup a succession of objects until you finally expose the individual shapes for editing.

When you're done making changes, you can put the whole image back together by using the Group command on the individual elements. Regroup won't work, because it only reassembles the last set of ungrouped items.

Creating art with PhotoDraw

Some versions of Office 2000 come with Microsoft PhotoDraw, a full-scale application for creating and modifying graphics of all types. PhotoDraw combines paint (bitmap) and draw (line or vector) tools, fancy templates for everything from flyers to Web buttons, and hordes of sophisticated special effects. The program supports Adobe PhotoShop plug-ins for even more advanced effects. All this is wrapped up in a set of menus and toolbars that parallel those of other Office applications, so you should feel at home quickly. Still, this is a sophisticated, rather complicated program — it comes on two separate CDs — and if your needs are more basic, you may be better off with PaintShop Pro, included on the Office Secrets CD-ROM.

Objets D'art

In Office, all pictures are objects, items that function semiautonomously within a document. But depending on how you insert a picture, it may or may not enter your document as an *OLE* object. OLE objects retain their connection to another application, while an ordinary picture object is a loner image that takes up residence, for a time at least, in an Office document.

When you bring in a picture with the Insert ➪ Picture ➪ Clip Art command, the picture arrives as a Clip Art OLE object. That's why double-clicking it takes you back to Clip Gallery. By contrast, pictures inserted via the Insert ➪ Picture ➪ From File command normally aren't OLE objects — if double-clicking them does something, that something happens within Office.

You *can* insert a picture with a link to the file it came from, the simple type of OLE connection, by checking Link to File in the Insert Picture dialog box. If the information in the linked file later changes, Office will then update your document to show the revised image. Of course, it's also possible to insert a picture as an embedded OLE object. You must use the Insert ⇨ Object command, choosing a suitable Object type from the list. Chapter 10 has the scoop on OLE and the Insert ⇨ Object command.

Besides pictures, you can use lots of different types of objects to gussy up a homely document. Office itself comes with several applications for creating visually compelling document building blocks — see "Adding graphs, org charts, maps, and equations" — and you can use similar third-party programs to handle other special-purpose illustration chores. In addition, multimedia resources such as sound and video clips are fodder for any Office document.

Adding graphs, org charts, maps, and equations

Office comes with four separate specialized applications for creating graphs, organization charts, maps, and formatted equations, which you can then add into any of your documents. Space won't permit detailed discussions of the applications themselves, but a few words on what they are and how to use them are in order.

All four applets are designed to function as OLE servers. As Chapter 10 spells out in more detail, OLE servers enable you to create their objects from directly within the main Office applications. To edit the object, you just double-click it, and the applet's menus and toolbars appear in place of the main application's.

Most of these applets are scaled-down versions of commercially available third-party products. In a way, they're come-ons: Although the "light" versions included with Office are reasonably capable, many important features are missing. Oh, well.

Using applet objects in your documents

The simplest way to insert a graphical object using one of the included applets is by way of the Insert ⇨ Picture menu. Depending on which Office application you're using, this menu lists one or more of the items you can create with the applets. In PowerPoint, for example, you can choose Insert ⇨ Picture ⇨ Organization Chart.

However, you can't access all the applets in all the Office applications this way. But no matter which application you're using, you can add an object from any applet via the Insert ⇨ Object command. The official names of these applets are Microsoft Graph 2000, MS Organization Chart, Microsoft Map, and Microsoft Equation. You need these names to locate them in the Insert ⇨

Object dialog box. To insert an equation object into a Word document, for example, choose Insert ➪ Object, and on the Create New tab, select Microsoft Equation from the list.

Secret

As OLE servers, all the Office applets are available in *any* OLE container application. If you want an equation from Microsoft Equation in a WordPerfect document, that's just fine.

Just a suggestion: Don't use Microsoft Graph

Secret

Office provides two separate ways to insert charts and graphs into your documents: the Microsoft Graph applet and Excel's own charting function. Outside of Excel, the Insert Chart toolbar button and the Insert ➪ Picture ➪ Chart command both add Microsoft Graph charts. While this makes Graph the convenient choice, I recommend against using it; instead, I suggest relying on Excel charts for all of your Office charting needs.

My reasons are as follows:

- Excel offers significantly more sophisticated charting features than does Graph. While you may not need them all the time, they're available when you do. And simple Excel charts are no more difficult to construct than Graph ones.

- You won't have to learn two separate charting programs. You're going to be using Excel's charts in Excel worksheets, so why not practice the skills you need there in other Office documents? While Graph and Excel are quite similar, they do have their differences — it doesn't make sense to spend your intellectual energies memorizing these details.

To insert an Excel chart in any Office document, choose Insert ➪ Object, select Microsoft Excel Chart, and click OK. Not too hard, eh? If you use lots of charts, record a macro that does it in one step. Charting with Excel is covered in Chapter 39.

So why is Graph included with Office? Its main value is for VBA programmers, who can create and distribute applications that contain charting functions based on Word or Access. With Graph, the programmer doesn't have to worry whether the recipient of the program has Excel installed.

Adding sound, video, and other objects

Office places no limits on the types of objects you can insert in your documents. All the loud fuss over multimedia has long since blown over, but there are definitely times when it makes sense to illustrate a document with a video clip or some recorded speech or music.

As noted before, the Clip Gallery can house such objects for your ready retrieval according to category or keyword. You can also insert these items directly from disk via the appropriate commands on the Insert menu.

Formatting Objects: The Master Control Center

Whether you're working with a drawing object you created with the Office drawing tools, a picture, or any other type of object, the Format dialog box consolidates a comprehensive assemblage of settings with which you can control the object's appearance in your document.

The settings you see when you select an object and choose Format ⇨ Object vary, depending on the type of object and the Office application you're working in. You can also get to the dialog box from the object's shortcut menu. Figure 8-19 shows a representative sample.

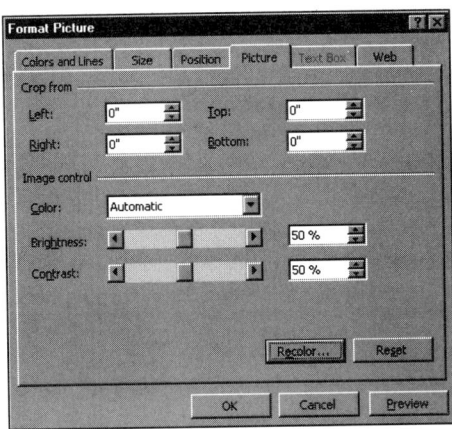

Figure 8-19: The Format Picture dialog box

Secrets of the Format dialog box

Get to know the Format dialog box. The Size, Position, and Picture tabs enable you to control the object spatially with much more precision (though more slowly) than you can with the mouse. Tabs on this key dialog box include:

- **Colors and Lines.** You don't need this tab if you use the Drawing toolbar — it duplicates the Fill Color, Line, and Arrow Style buttons there.
- **Size.** This tab lets you specify the object's size in absolute units (with the Size and Rotate settings), or as a percentage of the object's current size (using the Scale settings). For picture objects, you can check Relative to Original Picture Size to scale the picture based on its original size rather than its current size (in PowerPoint, you should also specify your slide show monitor's resolution). Whether you use the Size or Scale settings, check Lock Aspect Ratio to maintain the object's original proportions as you change either height or width.

- **Position.** In PowerPoint, use this tab to specify the object's position on a slide. Use the From settings to indicate the starting point for the measurements you enter. Word no longer has the Position tab. Instead, you must switch to the Layout tab and then click the Advanced button to bring up the Advanced Layout dialog box and there, switch to the Picture Position tab (see Figure 8-20).
- **Properties.** In Excel, you can select one of three options governing how the object changes as its underlying cells move or change size (handy for sorting tables containing pictures).
- **Layout.** In Word, this tab specifies how text will wrap around the object. See Chapter 29.
- **Picture.** This tab lets you crop a picture object and set brightness and contrast with numeric precision.
- **Text Box.** In Word, this tab lets you set the margins between the boundaries of a text box and the text it contains. PowerPoint adds controls for fine-tuning the look of your text boxes. You can duplicate most of these functions with Word's more sophisticated formatting options. Still, Word lacks the PowerPoint setting Resize AutoShape to Fit Text, which automatically resizes the box and any attached shape as you add or delete characters. Excel has this setting too, but it's on the Alignment tab of its special Format Text Box dialog box, where the setting is labeled simply Automatic Size.

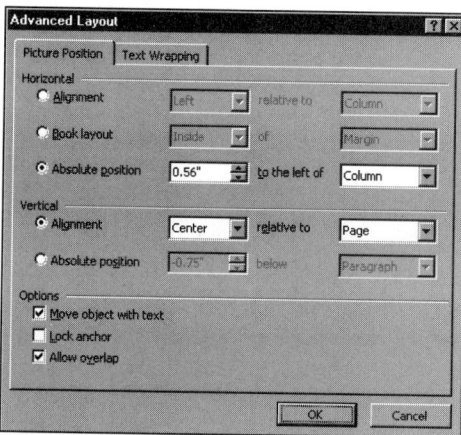

Figure 8-20: In Word, positioning an object with numeric precision requires the Picture Position tab of the Advanced Layout dialog box.

Working with measurement units in Office

Any time you change size, spacing, or position, Office expects you to enter the information using one of the measurement units it understands. Here are the measurement units and the corresponding abbreviations you should use when typing them into a dialog box.

Unit	Abbreviation	Sample Entry
Inches	in	.25 in
Inches	"	.25"
Centimeters	cm	.1 cm
Points	pt	18 pt
Picas	pi	1.5 pi
Lines	li	2 li

(Points and picas are typographic units. A point is approximately $1/72$-inch and a pica contains 12 points — so an inch contains about 6 picas.)

You can't use every measurement unit with every formatting choice. When you're setting font size, for instance, Word only accepts an entry in points, not inches or lines. However, in many Word dialog boxes, you can type in new values in your choice of several units. If you're not using the default units, you just have to include the abbreviation for the units you've settled on. In Word, you can change the default units on the General tab of the Tools ⇨ Options dialog box.

Conclusion

Enriched tastefully with graphics, an Office document makes its point more clearly and is a pleasure to read. With Office's wealth of sophisticated graphics tools, you have a complete graphics arts studio at your fingertips.

Chapter 9

Secrets of Active Documents

In This Chapter

- ▶ About active documents and controls
- ▶ When to use controls in your documents
- ▶ How to convert ordinary AutoShapes into active controls
- ▶ How to insert ActiveX controls into a document
- ▶ Practical techniques—with and without programming—for putting ActiveX controls to work

Although people still tend to think of a document as a sheaf of papers, many Office documents never make it to the printed page. A document that spends its entire existence in disk files or on screen is less portable than a paper counterpart—but it has advantages of its own. In particular, you can build actively responsive Office documents by filling them with *controls*—push buttons, check boxes, scroll bars, and the like—that alter the document's appearance or content or that trigger under the user's control. And by the way, you *can* print a document containing controls—the controls and any information they contain appear on the page, but obviously they lose their magic powers there.

This is the shortest chapter in the book. That's because many of the techniques that make the controls in your documents actually do things are covered elsewhere—specifically, in Chapters 14 and 24. In this chapter, after an introduction to the concept of active documents, you learn how to add controls to the documents you create with Office and how to control their appearance and behavior without programming.

When to Use Active Documents

By now, Web pages have introduced everyone to the concept of active documents. But you don't need to have a Web site to take advantage of them with Office. You might create an exclusively electronic document for your personal use, storing it on your own PC in a file that you open whenever you need to see the document. You might send copies of the document file on disk or via e-mail to other people, who can then display it on their own computers — faster than they could access it on the Web.

One typical use for an active document is as an on-screen form. Controls make it easy to create a document with fill-in-the-blank entry fields and boxes for checking off options. While you can accomplish the same end using custom-crafted dialog boxes (the VBA forms described in Chapter 24), why go that route when you can embed controls directly in a document? Figure 9-1 shows an example.

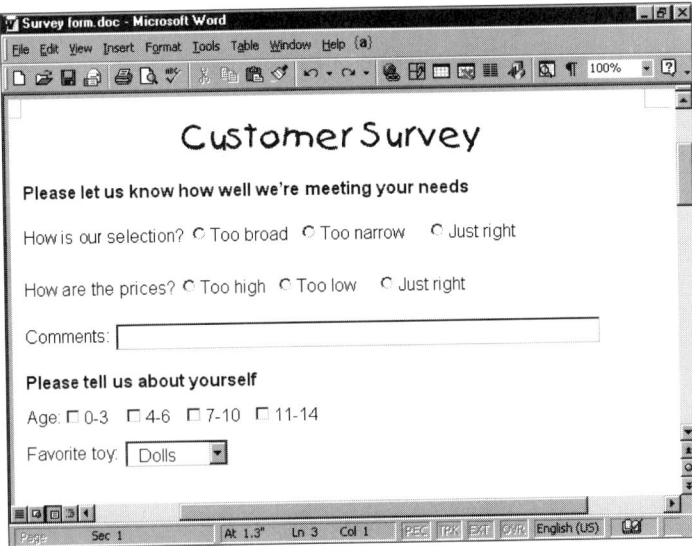

Figure 9-1: This Word document looks and functions like a paper form.

But you don't need to build an entire document around controls — a few simple check boxes can enhance many on-screen documents.

About Controls in Office Documents

You can think of a control as any element in an on-screen document that reacts to a user action such as a mouse-click. In a printed document, controls supply check boxes and entry blanks where the user can enter responses to questions or fill in information. The controls at your disposal as a document author fall into a number of overlapping groups, as follows:

- **Hyperlinks.** Hyperlinks are hotspots that when clicked take you to another location in the current document, to a different document, or to a Web page. You can use hyperlinks to make any Office document interactive. Simple text hyperlinks — the kind that typically appear on a Web page in blue type with an underline — are the most common. You can also assign a hyperlink to any picture (graphic) you insert in a document. Hyperlinks are covered in detail in Chapter 14, the chapter on Web page development, not here. But be sure you understand that they work just as well in ordinary Office documents as in Web pages.

- **HTML controls.** In Word only, the Web Tools toolbar lets you insert standard HTML forms controls directly into documents destined to be Web pages. Because these controls only work on Web pages, they're covered in Part IV.

- **"Forms" controls.** The Forms toolbars in Excel and Word provide various controls unique to these two applications. These are discussed in the next section, "About Forms in Excel and Word."

- **AutoShapes.** AutoShapes were introduced as graphical document elements in Chapter 8, but you can turn them into active push buttons via simple menu commands. In Word, PowerPoint, and Excel documents they can serve as hyperlink buttons. In Excel, you can assign macros to AutoShapes. PowerPoint AutoShapes have special talents — when clicked, they can perform actions such as navigating to another slide or playing a sound. See the section "Working with Active AutoShapes" later in this chapter.

- **ActiveX controls.** ActiveX controls are standard software components that can be used in applications developed with programming tools such as VBA, Visual Basic, or C++. Office lets you place these same controls directly into your Word, Excel, and PowerPoint documents and then add VBA code "behind" them to get them to do tricks.

About Forms in Word and Excel

In Office, the term *form* means different things in different contexts. Generically, of course, a form is any document that has blanks, check boxes, or other areas with which users of the document are expected to interact. However, other uses for the term are more specific. The custom dialog boxes and other windows you can build with VBA are technically called *forms*. Web pages can contain HTML forms, which you can readily create with Word. And Word and Excel have their own special sorts of forms.

Long before VBA and HTML became universal Office tools, the forms tools in Word and Excel were making it possible to build active documents. You can still access these tools by displaying the Forms toolbar in either application. These toolbars provide various controls you can insert into your document, along with related buttons that help in forms design.

Word's Forms toolbar: Avoid it

Caution

In Word, the "old-style" controls on the Forms toolbar are few in number, limited in functionality, and really quite obsolete — everything you can do with them, you can do with ActiveX controls. They're provided only so you can display and edit documents created in older versions of Word.

Excel's Forms toolbar: Try it

Secret

In Excel, the controls on the Forms toolbar provide an easier way to create interactive on-screen worksheets, compared to the ActiveX controls described later in this chapter. The reason: No VBA programming is required to make them work.

After you add a control to a worksheet, you can then build a formula that produces results based on the current value of the control. This requires that you link the control to a worksheet cell and then refer to the linked cell in your formula. To specify the linked cell, right-click the control and choose Format Control on the shortcut menu. In the resulting dialog box, switch to the Control tab. Then, in the Cell Link box, specify the cell that will display the current entry in the control as follows:

- For a check box, the linked cell displays either TRUE or FALSE.
- For a list or combo box, the linked cell displays the number of the item selected in the list.
- For spinner and scroll bar controls, the linked cell displays the numeric value selected by the control.
- In the case of a set of option buttons, the linked cell shows the number of the selected button.

To specify the items that are to appear in a list or combo box, type them into a worksheet column, and then open the Format Control dialog box, switch to the Control tab, and enter the column in the Input Range field.

Secret

Although Excel controls aren't ActiveX controls, you can write VBA code for events, such as mouse-clicks. that occur to the control. To add code, select the control by right-clicking it, and then click the Edit Code button on the Forms toolbar. VBA event procedures for Excel controls appear in standard VBA code modules, whereas code for ActiveX controls embedded in a worksheet goes in the special code module for that worksheet. See Chapter 24 for details on writing event code for controls.

Working with Active AutoShapes

Secret

The basic technique for creating an active AutoShape — one that does something when you click it — requires two steps: First you add the AutoShape to your document using the techniques discussed in Chapter 8. With the AutoShape selected, you then assign an action to it.

To make an AutoShape into a hyperlink, select the AutoShape and choose Insert ⇨ Hyperlink. Alternatively, right-click the AutoShape and choose Hyperlink from its shortcut menu. Use the techniques described in Chapter 14 to specify the hyperlink's destination.

To assign a macro to an AutoShape in Excel, right-click the shape and choose Assign Macro. The resulting Assign Macro dialog box lets you choose an existing macro for the shape or record a new one.

In PowerPoint, AutoShapes are more capable than in Word or Excel. I guess that makes sense, because PowerPoint documents are usually presented rather than printed. At any rate, in addition to triggering hyperlinks PowerPoint AutoShapes can navigate to other slides, play sounds or video clips, run macros or other applications, or perform any actions permitted by OLE objects inserted on the slide. None of this requires any programming—see Chapter 48 for details.

Adding ActiveX Controls

AutoShapes are great for graphical hyperlinks and triggering simple functions, but they can't display information themselves. ActiveX controls are far more flexible and powerful. The controls that come with Office represent most of the standard types you see in Windows programs, and you can choose from a cornucopia of other ActiveX controls from Microsoft and third-party developers.

In Word, PowerPoint, and Excel you can use ActiveX controls directly in documents and also on the custom VBA forms discussed in Chapter 24. By contrast, in Access and Outlook you can *only* place controls onto custom forms. However, Access and Outlook forms aren't standard VBA forms, and Access and Outlook forms are distinct from one another to boot. These variations can seem very confusing at first, but you can take heart that you use the same basic methods to work with ActiveX controls in all applications.

Types of ActiveX controls

Table 9-1 lists the standard ActiveX controls included with Office, along with their uses.

Table 9-1 Office ActiveX Controls

Control Name	Button on Toolbox	Use
Check Box	☑	Indicates one of two possible values, such as yes or no, or on or off.
Text Box	abl	Provides a place to type in text or information.
Command Button	▭	Lets the user click the button to activate a hyperlink or VBA procedure.
Option Button	⊙	Used in groups, lets the user select one of several choices (also known as radio button).
List Box	▤	Lets the user select one of several preset choices.
Combo Box	▤	Lets the user select one of several preset choices or type in a new entry from scratch.

Continued

Table 9-1 *(continued)*

Control Name	Button on Toolbox	Use
Toggle Button		Switches back and forth between two settings.
Spin Button		Contains two buttons that raise or lower a setting's value each time it's clicked.
Scroll Bar		Like a spin button, but with a bar between the buttons that displays the relative value of the setting graphically (also known as a slider).
Label		Displays text specified by the creator of the document.
Image		Displays a graphic that can be clicked.

Inserting ActiveX controls

To place an ActiveX control in a Word document, Excel worksheet, or PowerPoint slide, begin by activating the Control Toolbox, a special toolbar shown in Figure 9-2. The button for the Toolbox is located on the Visual Basic toolbar, but you can also display the Toolbox directly via the View➪Toolbars menu.

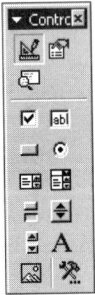

Figure 9-2: Use the Control Toolbox to insert ActiveX controls into Office documents.

With the Toolbox on your screen you can get down to the business of inserting the control. In Word, start by placing the insertion point where you want the control to appear. The location must be in the main part of your document — you can't place controls inside tables or text boxes. You don't need to select a location first in PowerPoint or Excel.

Now click the Toolbox button for the type of control you want. Word automatically places the control near the insertion point, but in the other two programs you must then click in the document where you want the control to go.

To insert an ActiveX control that's installed on your system but not visible on the Toolbox, click the More Controls button. A scrollable list of the available controls appears from which you can select any control you desire. Chapter 24 goes through the technique for installing new ActiveX controls.

Using design mode

As soon as you insert an ActiveX control, Office switches to *design mode* — you can tell because the Design Mode button looks pressed in. When design mode is off, clicking a control triggers some response from the control. But when design mode is on, clicking a control selects it so that you can change its look or behavior. Use the handles (the little black squares) bordering a selected control to resize it, just as you would a graphical object. Drag anywhere else over the control to move it to a new location. To turn design mode on or off manually, just click the Design Mode button.

Secret

Word inserts each new ActiveX control into the document "in line" with the text at the insertion point — that is, as if the control is itself a text character. Although you can move the control around in the text, you can't position it freely anywhere on the page. To gain this freedom, right-click the control and choose Format Control from the shortcut menu. In the Format Control dialog box, switch to the Layout tab and click a Wrapping style other than In Line with Text — Tight or Square is usually the best choice. You can then move the control around in the document with abandon.

Controlling controls with properties

To change the look or behavior of a selected control, use the Properties dialog box. This box appears when you click the Properties button on the Control Toolbox. Although the properties available depend on the type of control you're working with, common ones include the foreground (text and arrow) and background colors, the font for text that appears on the control, and properties determining the control's size and location. Control properties are discussed in much more depth in Chapter 24.

Secret

Normally, all the option buttons you insert in a document are part of one group — if you click one option button to turn it on, all the other option buttons get turned off. However, you can set up more than one group of option buttons in the same document using the GroupName property. To assign option buttons to a particular group, just type the identical text in each button's GroupName field. The buttons in each group then function independently, so that each group has its own active button.

Making controls do magic — with and without programming

As soon as you add any control to a document and leave design mode, the control is ready to react to mouse-clicks. But these reactions aren't usually useful by themselves. For example, clicking a command button makes the button look pressed in but doesn't do anything else, unless you write VBA code that responds to the click event. Likewise, you can drag the thumb in a scroll bar control to a new position, but to make that change do something useful in a document you must write code that carries out some action in response.

To get started writing a VBA procedure that dictates a control's behavior, select the control and click the View Code button on the Control Toolbox. You're whisked to the control's Code window in the Visual Basic Editor, where you can type in the code. Chapter 24 covers the details on writing VBA code for controls.

However, some of Office's ActiveX controls respond in useful ways without any programming, especially because their current settings are saved with the document. These include the check box, option button, and text box controls.

When you click a check box control, for example, you see a check mark alternately appear and disappear in the box. You might insert a check box to enable an editor to indicate whether he or she has finished reviewing the document. Similarly, clicking an option button activates it and deactivates the previously active option button. And when you click a text box, a blinking insertion point appears in the box and you can start typing text. Because Office saves the current control settings and text, you can use these controls to give users a way both to highlight current information in a graphically interesting way and to store it directly in the document. To store control values in a database, however, requires the programming techniques discussed in Chapters 46 and 47.

Conclusion

Active documents aren't for every situation, but they can make your on-screen documents much more interactive and more fun to use. Even if you don't want to delve into VBA programming, consider adding some AutoShape buttons and ActiveX controls to your electronic documents.

Chapter 10

Sharing Information

In This Chapter

- Why the clipboard can still be the best way to transfer information between two documents
- Transferring information between applications with drag-and-drop
- Importing and exporting information in disk files
- Add-on data conversion software that lets you access file formats Office doesn't recognize
- Viva OLE! When to use OLE and how to answer that burning question: To link or to embed?

Opening up the barriers of divergent file formats to let the information within flow free can be a challenge. Though no perfect solution exists, Office places at your disposal three main methods for transferring information between documents:

- Through the clipboard, the old fashioned cut- or copy-and-paste way, or via drag-and-drop
- By exporting and importing the information to and from disk files
- Using Object Linking and Embedding (OLE) so that you can edit the information in the destination document with the commands of the application the information came from

Each of these methods receives the Secrets treatment in this chapter. But the list omits one of the most powerful information-sharing techniques: automated data-passing using VBA techniques. To scratch the surface of that deep mother lode, consult Part VI. Related topics include Binder's ability — described in Chapter 12 — to build compound publications containing component documents from Word, Excel, PowerPoint, and Microsoft Project. You might also want to look at Chapter 18, which discusses sharing Office documents via e-mail.

Power Clipboard Techniques and Utilities

The standard Cut and Copy commands send information from a source document to the clipboard, a temporary holding area available to all Windows applications. Any type of data—text, graphics, sound files, or what have you—can be sent to the clipboard. From the clipboard, you can then paste the information into any application that understands that data type.

When you use the Edit ⇨ Paste command to place the clipboard contents into a destination document, the information becomes merged into the document with no connection to its source document or to the source application. (This is in contrast to data sharing via OLE, in which such a connection is maintained.) The pasted data can be edited with whatever tools the destination application provides.

Of course, you already know all about these clipboard basics. But Office applications introduce some wrinkles. A new Clipboard toolbar gives a boost to cut- or copy-and-paste operations. Special paste commands enable you to control the way the receiving application inserts the data. And for all the effort Microsoft has made to integrate the Office applications, each handles clipboard data transfers a little differently.

When to use the clipboard

Transferring information into a document using the conventional cut- or copy-and paste commands via the clipboard makes sense when:

- You want the fastest possible method for transporting the data from one location to another.
- You're sure that you won't need to update the data in the future.
- You plan to share the document with someone who doesn't have access to the application that created the information you're transferring (in which case an OLE connection wouldn't work).
- Your computer is too slow or has too little memory to use OLE efficiently.

Using the Clipboard toolbar

New in Office 2000, the Clipboard toolbar gives a major boost to information transfers via the Cut, Copy, and Paste commands. Office now stores cut or copied items in 12 separate slots in its own Office clipboard for later retrieval when you need them. What's more, the Office clipboard can receive these items from any Windows program. Figure 10-1 shows the Clipboard toolbar.

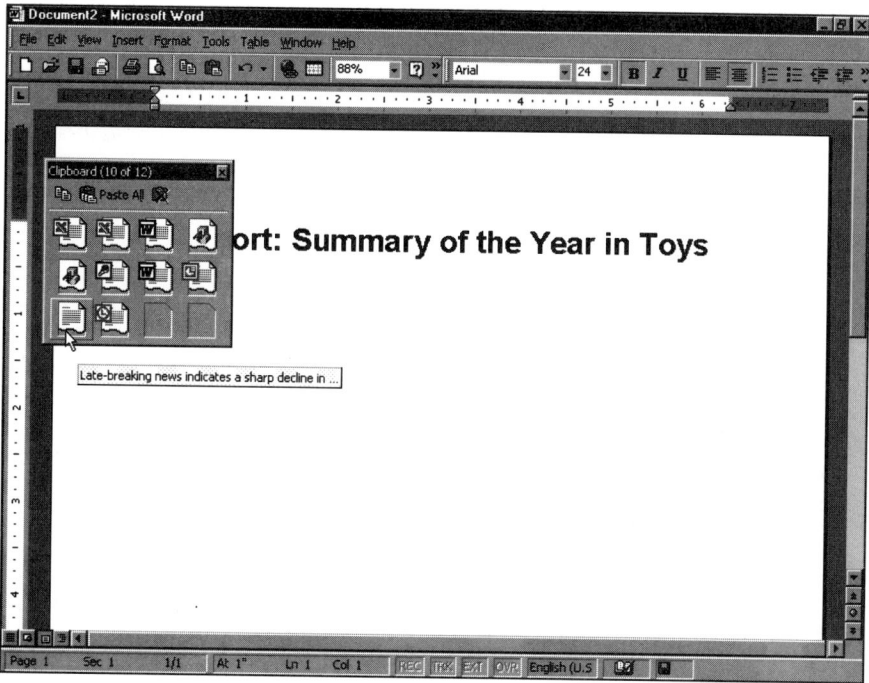

Figure 10-1: The Clipboard toolbar shows several chunks of data from different Office programs, ready to be pasted whenever and wherever you need them.

Below the toolbar buttons a set of rectangles represent the slots for data that you've placed on the Office clipboard. Each occupied slot appears as an icon illustrating the source application. If you hold the mouse pointer over the item, you see a ScreenTip describing the information (if the item is text, the ScreenTip contains the clipboard text itself). To deposit an item from the Clipboard toolbar into a document, position the insertion point or otherwise select the location where you want it to go, and then click the item on the toolbar. You can paste all of the items on the Office clipboard to one location with the Paste All button.

Secret

When you paste an item from the Clipboard toolbar into a document, that item is passed to the Windows clipboard. In other words, you can paste the same item again and again using the standard Windows Edit ⇨ Paste command or its Ctrl+V shortcut.

Pasting items from the Clipboard toolbar into a document is easy enough, but how do you get those items onto the Office clipboard in the first place? No special techniques are required — anything you cut or copy in any Windows application automatically enters the Office clipboard, as long as the item is stored in a format recognized by Office. In Office applications, you can click the Copy button on the Clipboard toolbar to transfer in selected information, but the toolbar isn't visible when you're working in non-Office programs.

The Take-Home Message: Get a Clipboard Enhancement Utility

One of the best ways to spend your software dollars is on a clipboard utility for Windows, one like the ClipMate program included for your evaluation on the CD-ROM that comes with this book (see the accompanying figure).

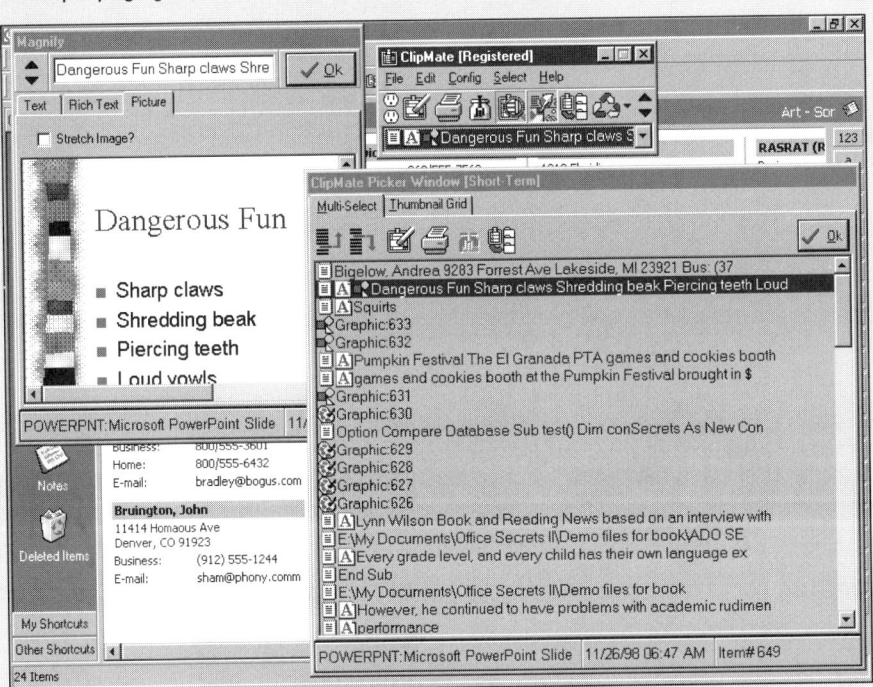

ClipMate's three windows. The smallest one is the main control center for the utility.

Unassisted by such a utility, the standard Windows clipboard is actually pretty pathetic. Its main limitation: It stores only one chunk of data at a time. Each time you cut or copy anything to the clipboard, its previous contents vanish forever. Even the new Office Clipboard toolbar can store only 12 items at once.

ClipMate provides the recall the clipboard lacks, automatically storing everything placed on the clipboard. You can reuse items that you previously cut or copied any time, by picking them out of the list that ClipMate keeps. You can prune the list, reorder the items in it, or glue items together so that they can be pasted together in one shot. ClipMate is a great program — once you start using it, you'll never want to be without it.

Alternatives to the standard Paste command

Office provides two variations on the plain old Paste command for placing clipboard data into an application: the Edit ⇨ Paste Special and Edit ⇨ Paste as Hyperlink commands.

Specialty pasting

When an application places information on the clipboard, it often does so in more than one form. That way, the receiving application (or the person using it) can decide which form should go into the document.

In all five Office applications, the Edit ⇨ Paste Special command lets you control how clipboard information reaches the destination document.

Figure 10-2 shows the Paste Special dialog box as you see it when information from another application is on the clipboard (in Excel, the Paste Special dialog box looks completely different when you're pasting information placed onto the clipboard from within Excel itself).

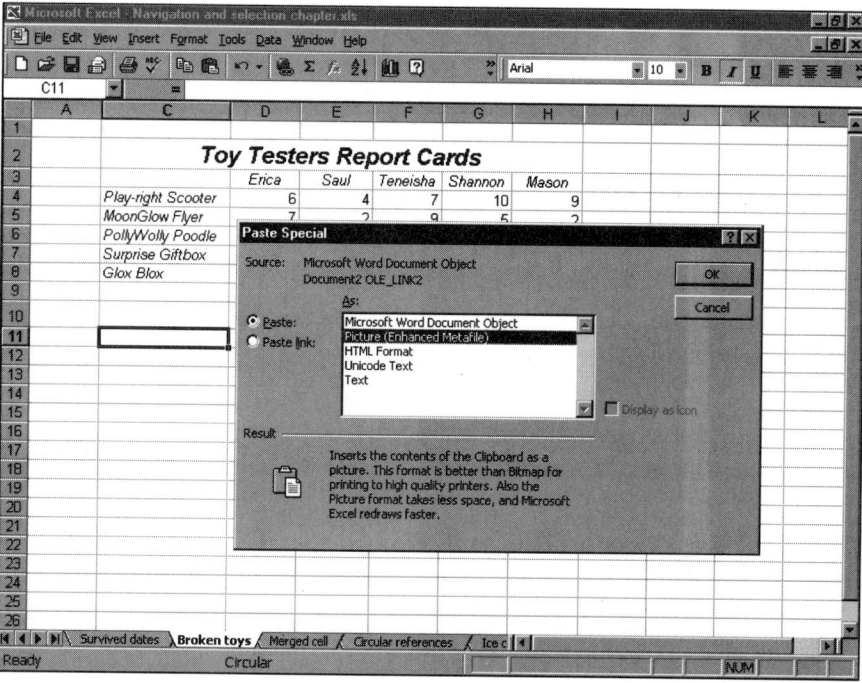

Figure 10-2: Pasting Word text into Excel with the Edit ⇨ Paste Special command

The Paste Special dialog box is also one route to placing OLE objects into your document. See "Specialty pasting, part II: Pasting objects" in the section on OLE later in this chapter.

Pasting data as a hyperlink

In all the Office applications except Outlook, you can create a hyperlink to another document by pasting data from the source document. Once the hyperlink is in place, one click on it jumps you to the original document. There, the Web toolbar automatically appears, so you can return to the document containing the hyperlink by clicking the Back button. (Hyperlinks are covered in detail in Chapter 14.)

To insert a hyperlink this way, place text or numeric information on the clipboard and switch to the destination application. There, use the Edit ➪ Paste as Hyperlink command instead of doing a regular paste. This isn't an OLE link — the pasted data are treated as if pasted the regular way (Excel cells become a table in Word, for example). But they appear with the telltale underlined blue characters of a hyperlink (see Figure 10-3).

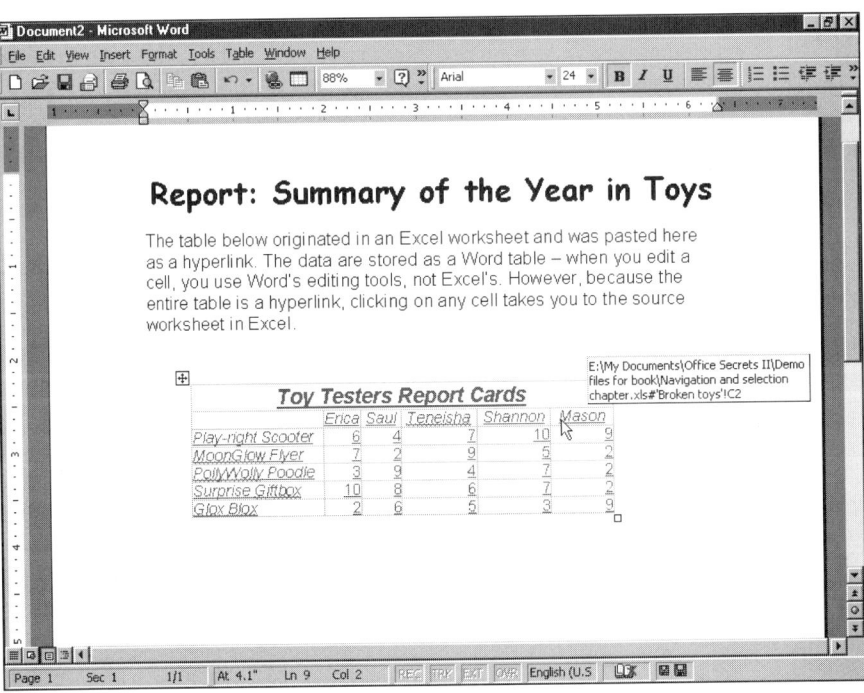

Figure 10-3: A selection from an Excel worksheet pasted as a hyperlink into Word. The ScreenTip message gives the path of the originating workbook.

One important first step: The source document must have been saved first — otherwise, the receiving application won't know how to find it again.

Using the clipboard with specific types of data

Office applications often differ in their treatment of information transferred through the clipboard, either on the sending or receiving ends of the transfer. The next few sections describe some of these variations on the cut-copy-paste theme.

Transferring Word text to other Office applications

Caution

PowerPoint, Excel, and Outlook both recognize character formatting in pasted text originating in Word. But all formatting is lost when you paste text from Word into Access, which converts pasted text into its default font.

Transferring tabular data into Word

When inserted via the ordinary Paste command, information from an Excel worksheet or Access database ends up in Word as a table. The table is formatted as it was in the originating application. In Figure 10-4, the bottom table originated in Access, where the column headings were given that nice gray shading.

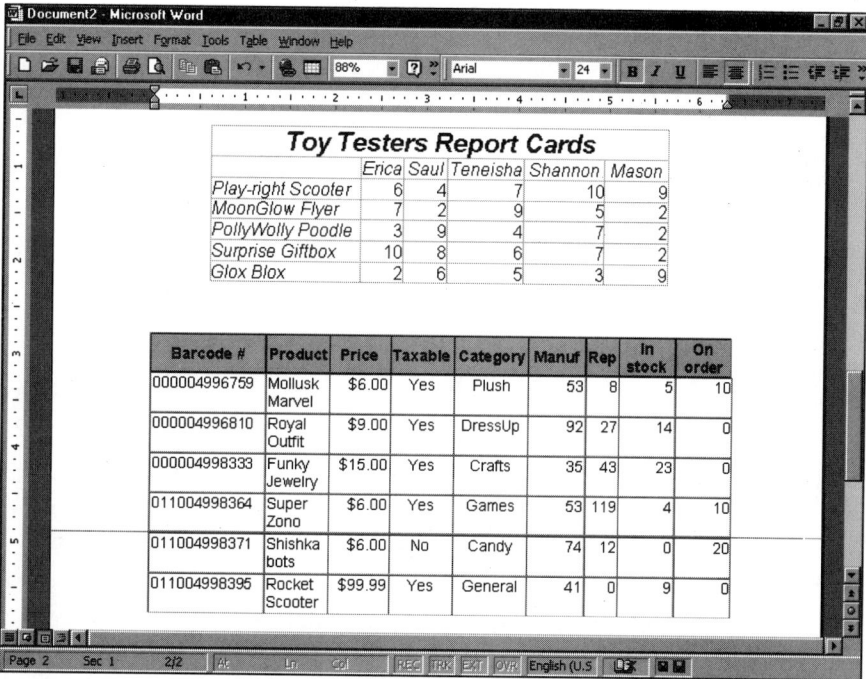

Figure 10-4: Word created the top table from pasted Excel data, the bottom one from Access data.

Inserting information into Access

Chapters 45 and 46 cover importing and linking information in Access in considerable detail. Here, and in the next section, I discuss simple clipboard transfers to and from a database. To bring information into Access from another application, the data must be organized in tabular format. Sources that Access accepts include Excel worksheets, Word tables, and text manually formatted in tabular form, with a tab between each column.

To paste the information into an Access datasheet (a table, a query, or a form displayed as a datasheet), select enough rows or columns to hold all the incoming data. Of course, the order of the columns in the source information should match that of the destination datasheet. You can choose whether to replace current records or add the pasted data in new records. To replace existing records in the datasheet, select their rows and choose Paste. To add the data as new records at the bottom of the table, choose Edit ➪ Paste Append.

Secret

Pasting into a form that displays a single record at a time is a little trickier. In this case, Access checks the data you're transferring in, comparing the entries in the top row of each column to the names of the controls on the form. If they match, Access pastes the data. If not, Access inserts the data into the form according to its tab order. You can select a record in a form with the record selector at the form's top-left corner or, if that's not visible, by choosing Edit ➪ Select Record.

Transferring Access data to other applications

When placed on the clipboard, information from Access is formatted with tabs between each field, as you'd expect. The field names are always included in the data as the first row. Rich Text information is also included, so simple formatting such as bold and italics will show up in the receiving application, if it can read Rich Text data. Access info slides smoothly into Excel complete with formatting information. If you do a standard Paste operation in Word, you get a Word table.

Drag-and-Drop Information Transfer

If you have a truly huge screen, drag and drop is the ideal way to move information from one application to another. You can keep the windows of all the applications you use open to a decent size, each in a separate corner of the screen. When you want to transfer information from one application to another, you can just select it and then pull it across with a quick drag-and-drop operation.

Office permits just such super-easy information transfers. Anything you can place on the clipboard, you can drag to another application where you can drop it into place. That goes for graphics as well as text or worksheet cells. Take a look at Figure 10-5.

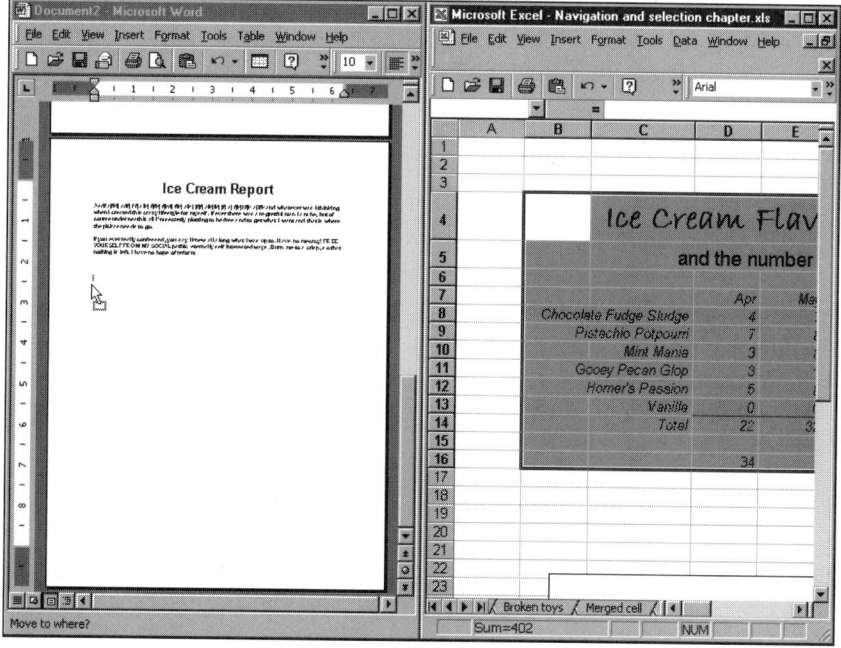

Figure 10-5: Dragging part of an Excel worksheet into a Word document

Left- and right-button dragging

Left-dragging *moves* the selected item from the source document to the destination. Hold down Ctrl while you left-drag to copy the item instead. Note that depending on which two applications are involved and where you start, the information may be transferred as ordinary clipboard data or as an embedded object (see the "Sharing Information Using OLE" section later).

If you right-drag, you get a shortcut menu when you release the button at the destination. From the menu, you can choose whether to copy or move the information, or to paste it in various other forms such as an embedded object or hyperlink. When you start in Excel, you can hold down Alt as you drag toward the window border to prevent the worksheet from scrolling. Remember that in Excel, you move or copy selected cells by dragging on the outline of the selected area.

The secret way to drag and drop between applications

Secret

In real life, of course, few screens are big enough to permit the luxury of multiple side-by-side windows of any size. Most people work with only one application at a time, keeping its window maximized to fill the whole screen. If that's your practice, you can still take advantage of drag and drop. The key is the Windows taskbar. Select the information you want to move or copy, and drag it to the icon on the taskbar for the destination application. Keep the mouse button held down there, *until the second application appears on the screen*. You can now deposit the information packet in its new home.

Parking information in scraps

The Windows desktop or any other folder can serve as a holding area for random chunks of information that you intend to use later in other documents. Make a selection, then drag it to the desktop or a My Computer or Explorer folder window. You'll have to expose a bit of the desktop first, if that's your destination. If the target is a folder window, however, the secret just described works. Later, you can assemble a new document from your scraps by dragging them back to the original application (in which case they enter as ordinary data, as if pasted from the clipboard) or into a different application (in which case they enter as embedded objects — see "Sharing Information Using OLE" later in this chapter).

As an alternative to drag and drop, you can create scraps by copying or cutting a selection, displaying the desktop, and choosing Paste from its shortcut menu.

Secrets of the Import/Export Trade

When you need to add to a document large amounts of data created in another application, the best approach is often to *import* information stored in a disk file. In Office, importing information stored in a foreign file format is as simple as opening the file, via the File ⇨ Open, Insert ⇨ Picture, or (in Word) Insert ⇨ File commands. The only catch is, you must have installed a *converter* for that file format. Also known as *filters* or *translators*, converters are software plug-ins that perform the translations between foreign data formats and that of the Office application you're using.

Office comes with converters for a large number of common file formats of various types: word processor documents, database and spreadsheet files, graphic images, and files of personal information managers (Word even has an import converter for Excel worksheets). Some of these converters are automatically installed, but you can select among many optional converters when you run Office Setup.

To see whether a converter for the import file's format is installed, look at the list at Files of Type in the Open or Insert dialog box. File types are listed either by the name of the source application (as in WordPerfect 5.*x*) or by description (for some graphics file formats, and generic formats for tabular data).

How to import

Secret

The easiest way to import any file is simply to try to open it, without specifying what format it's in. Select All Files at Files of Type, locate the file, and choose Open or Insert. Office can usually figure out what format the data is stored in without any help from you.

If you like, you can select the correct format — assuming its converter is installed — at Files of Type. When you do, Office modifies the file list to show only files with the extensions typically associated with files of that type. The main value of this step is just to help you pick out the file you want to import in a sea of other files. Sometimes, however, Office needs your help in determining how to convert the file. So if choosing All files doesn't work, this is the next step to try.

Access and Outlook have special commands for importing data. In Access, choose File ➪ Get External Data ➪ Import. Outlook comes with an Import and Export Wizard for converting to and from the formats of other Personal Information Manager (PIM) software. Use File ➪ Import and Export to start it.

The import process goes smoothly most of the time. But what if the import file's format isn't listed at Files of Type? What if you can't see the import file in the file list? And worst of all, what if Office bungles the import process, so that the incoming data appears in your document as gibberish?

Installing additional file format converters

If you don't see the import file's format in the list at Files of Type, don't get too excited until you've checked to see whether you just forgot to install the necessary converter. To see what's available, run Setup and select a custom install. In the resulting dialog box, the Converters and Filters choice houses most text and graphics converters (see Figure 10-6). However, the Setup items for Word, PowerPoint, and Excel each offer one or more miscellaneous converters as well.

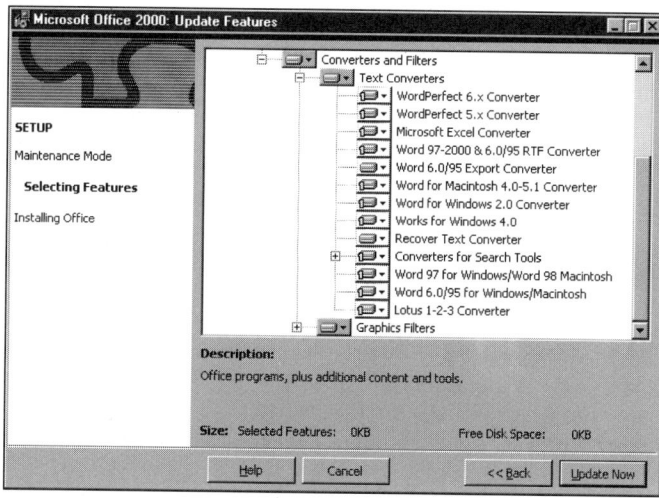

Figure 10-6: Use this item in Setup to install your choice of the many text converters provided with Office.

In addition to those available through Office Setup, you can find additional converters in the Office Converter Pack, which comes with the Office Resource Kit (ORK) discussed in Chapter 1. More may be available on Microsoft's Office Web site:

www.microsoft.com/msoffice/

If you don't see your files when trying to import them

When you select a specific file format in the Open or Insert dialog box, Office displays only files having the extension it thinks files of that type ought to have. If your import file has a different extension, it won't appear in the file list. You can deal with this in two ways:

- Rename the import file, giving it the extension Office prefers. You can do this directly from the Open or Insert dialog box by selecting All Files (*.*) at Files of Type, locating the file, and choosing Rename on its shortcut menu.

- After selecting the proper format at Files of Type, enter the import file's extension into the File Name box, as in ***.art** or ***.cog**, pressing F5 or Enter to refresh the display. A caveat: If the import file has a filename extension that Office recognizes as belonging to a different format, Office may get confused about which converter to use. If necessary, rename the file to match Office's expectations.

If the import converter is missing or doesn't work

Despite the wealth of converters that come with Office, at times you will want to import a type of file that your Office application can't convert properly. This may be because the import file was created in VisiCalc, MacWrite, or some other long-forgotten or extremely alien program, and a converter for that file format just doesn't exist. In some cases, however, it's because the Office converter isn't as accurate as it ought to be. Recent versions of Word, for example, are well known for making goofs when importing files created in Word for DOS.

Whatever the cause, this problem can be remedied — if you're lucky — in one of two ways:

- By using the source application to *export* the information into a format that the destination application does understand. Even the most obscure software usually provides an export command that will generate a file Office can read. Of course, this only works if you have access to the source application.

- By using third-party utilities to convert the file from its current format to one that the destination application can read. See "Mass conversions" later in this chapter.

Importing database and spreadsheet data

Using the File ⇨ Open command, you can quickly import a database object (usually a table) into Word or Excel. The problem is that *all* the information in the object enters your document or worksheet, leaving you to delete columns or rows that aren't germane to your purposes at the moment. Also, this only works with database objects that are stored in their own separate files — you can't open a single table residing in an Access database, for example.

You need other tools to reach inside complete databases and extract specific information from one or more of its objects. Office comes with *data source drivers* for many different database formats, including dBase, Paradox, 1-2-3, and, through ODBC, many others, including high-end, networked databases such as Oracle.

To import via these drivers in Word, click the Insert Database button on the Database toolbar and choose Get Data. In the Open Data Source dialog box, you can activate MS Query, an add-in program for extracting specified data from database files, by choosing its button (you only see the button if the program is installed). Otherwise, pick the type of database file you're importing at Files of Type, browse to and select the file itself, and choose Open. You'll still be able to design a simple query via the Query Options button on the Database dialog box.

Office sometimes provides more than one driver for access to the same database type. For example, you can place Access data into Word via either a Dynamic Data Exchange (DDE) link or ODBC. After selecting an Access database file from Files of Type in the Open Data Source dialog box, check the Select Method box. When you then choose Open, Word asks you to pick the method you want to use to get at the data, ODBC or DDE (see Figure 10-7). DDE activates Access itself to manage the data transfer. This technique enables you to use queries stored in the database as your data source, so you're not limited to a single table. Alternatively, you can use the ODBC driver to avoid starting Access — but in this case you can only select data from one Access table unless you use MS Query.

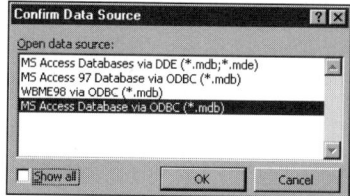

Figure 10-7: Selecting an ODBC driver as your access to Access

Although Excel can import a variety of database files by opening them with the File ⇨ Open command, you need MS Query to focus in on records meeting your criteria or to import data relationally. The command required is Data ⇨ Get External Data ⇨ New Database Query command.

Secret

MS Query is a visual data analysis tool similar to the query designer in Access. Although I don't have enough space to plumb its mysteries here, you can get clues about it in Chapter 44.

Exporting data

You can look at the data transfer problem from either end — the source or the destination. When your data are bound for another program, you can be sure they'll get there by exporting them to a file format that you know the other program can read.

Even within Office, exporting is sometimes useful for data transfers between applications. More often, though, you'll be exporting to share your information with others who don't use Office 2000. Fortunately, with the exception of Access, the Office 2000 applications use the same file formats as did their Office 97 and Office 98 (Mac) predecessors, so applications that can read those formats should be able to import your files directly. However, many people use software that doesn't recognize the current Office formats. Exporting your data to a file format their programs recognize will help them out.

Here are some tips on exporting from Office:

- In most Office applications, you export using the File ⇨ Save As command. In the Save As dialog box, select the format for the export file from the list at Save as Type. As with importing, you may need to install additional converters to export the data in the desired format (see "Installing additional file format converters" earlier in this chapter).

- If you routinely share files with users of another program, you can set Excel, Word, and PowerPoint to save automatically in any supported format you choose. In the Tools ⇨ Options dialog box, go to the Save tab (for Excel, the Transition tab). Make your selection from the Save As drop-down list.

- In Access, to export a table, report, or other object with formatting intact to an Excel worksheet, choose Tools ⇨ Office Links ⇨ Analyze It with MS Excel. Likewise, the Publish It with MS Word command places the information into a Rich Text Format (.rtf) file, opening it in Word. Choose Merge It with MS Word to start a new mail-merge document based on the source table.

- Alternatively, you can use Access's File ⇨ Save As/Export command to export an Access object. Your choices for the format of the exported information are numerous. You can create an Excel worksheet (Excel can open that, of course), a Rich Text Format file (which Word and other word processors can import with preservation of the tabular database layout), or a plain text file. You can also export the object in a database or Web format.

- In Outlook, you export to other personal information managers via the File ⇨ Import and Export command.

- Because Office files are so sophisticated these days, what with all the formatting information, versions, comments, and so on, it's a near certainty that some elements in your document will be left behind when you export the information. C'est la vie; but if you want to be sure that at least all the text in a document gets to its destination, you may have to manually copy items to the clipboard and then into Word for export.

Generic import/export file formats

When more sophisticated converters are unavailable or don't work properly, you can usually transfer textual data from one application to another in one of several generic, lowest-common-denominator formats.

- At the very lowest level, it's usually possible to extract the raw text from a document without too much trouble. Most applications store text in linear fashion, so you can import the document into Word as a text file and then use Find and Replace supplemented by manual editing to remove extraneous garbage. Better yet, open the file in Word by first selecting Recover Text from Any File at Files of Type in the Open dialog box. This choice tells Word to comb the chosen file for data that's recognizable as text and import only that information.

- Nearly every spreadsheet and database program can read and write (import and export) comma- or tab-delimited files. Word and many word processors can handle these files too. They're stored in plain text format, but the data are organized in a structured way. Each row of the table occupies a single line of the file, and the columns within a row are separated by commas or tab characters. These files contain no formatting, but they work well for transferring the essential information from one application to another.

- Most up-to-date word processors understand the Rich Text Format. RTF files contain very sophisticated formatting information, but they are stored as ordinary text, with special bracketed codes representing the font and layout instructions (see Figure 10-8). RTF files have a two-sided appeal. If the destination application understands them fully, the document should translate with formatting preserved. If not, because these are stored as standard text files, it's relatively easy to extract their text.

- All Office applications now allow you to import and export files in HTML format. See Part IV, especially Chapter 14, for a discussion of HTML and the process of exporting Office documents to this format.

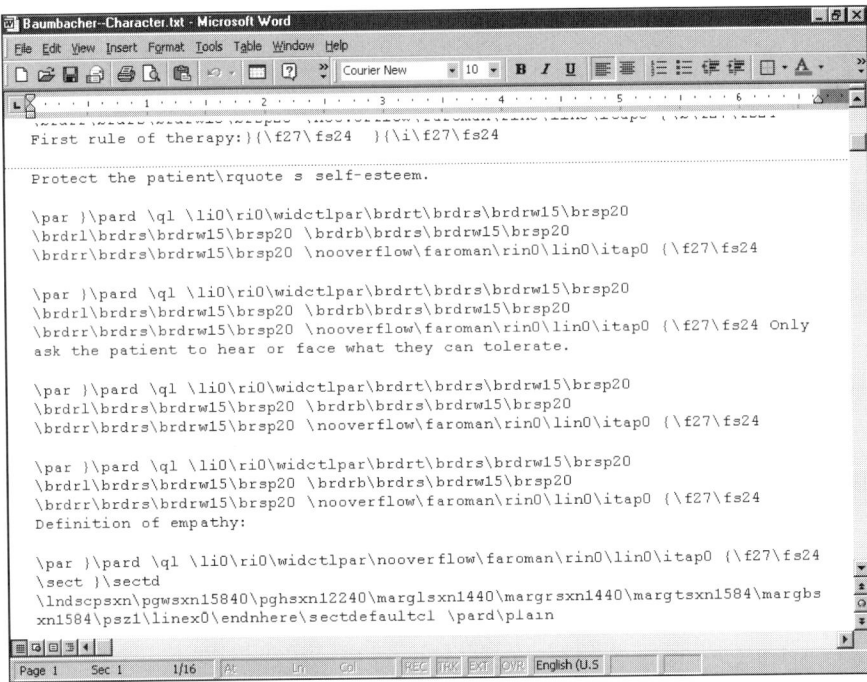

Figure 10-8: A Rich Text file opened as an ordinary text file in Word. Those unintelligible codes in the curly braces are formatting instructions.

Mass conversions

When Office mangles data you're trying to import, or if it lacks an export converter for a desired file format, investing in a utility to handle the translation may make sense. Here are products to look into:

- **General.** To convert from or to almost every common format, check out Conversions Plus (DataViz, www.dataviz.com). It contains converters for most PC and Macintosh word processors. Graphics, spreadsheet, and database formats are well represented as well. In addition to the converters, Conversions Plus includes a viewer that lets you peek into any file of a supported file type from My Computer or Explorer, and MacOpener, a tool that lets you open Mac-formatted disks (including SCSI hard disks, Zip and SyQuest cartridges, and CD-ROMs).

- **Graphics.** While Conversions Plus converts a number of graphics file formats, Paint Shop Pro (included on the CD-ROM that accompanies this book) handles many more and is a great choice for this specific need. In my tests, Paint Shop Pro has been flawless at converting one image format into another.

- **Database.** Data Junction (DataJunction, 800-580-4411) is a powerhouse conversion tool for tabular data from just about any source, from structured text files on up to mainframe database tables. It handles complex data structures that can gag the importing routines in Office, and it supports far more file formats. The same publisher markets Cambio, a remarkable tool for extracting information stored in unstructured text files and organizing it into tabular format.

Sharing Information Using OLE

Microsoft's document-centric philosophy becomes practical reality through a software technology called Object Linking and Embedding. As a sexy acronym, OLE never really caught on, and it isn't mentioned much any more in the Office documentation or help files. But OLE technology is still very much alive in Windows and in Office 2000.

OLE permits a document to serve as a kind of container for distinct hunks of information created in other applications. In the obvious Office example, a Word document can contain — interspersed with text created in Word itself — an Excel worksheet, a PowerPoint slide, and via DDE — a predecessor of OLE — the results of a query of an Access database.

Instead of being merged into the destination document, each of these information hunks remains an independent *object* — like an apple bobbing in a bucket of water — and retains its connection with the source application. As a result, the information within an object can't be edited with the tools of the destination application (Word's, in this example).

By virtue of OLE, however, you *can* open the object for editing. When you do, the source application's menus and toolbars appear, and all of its functionality is at your disposal. But as Figure 10-9 shows, you haven't left the container document — you can still see the rest of the document, and the title bar still bears the destination application's name.

The difference between linking and embedding

Office 2000 may not say much about OLE, but it does talk about *linking* and *embedding* a fair amount. Although both of these OLE techniques place objects created in one application into documents created in another, there's a key difference.

An embedded object exists only in association with the destination document and can only be opened there. Think of embedding as a connection to the source *application*. Embedding is the default type for most OLE connections in Office.

A linked object represents a gateway to all or part of a source *document*, stored independently in its own disk file. You can open a linked object from within the destination document, yes, but you can also open the file it represents with the object's source application. If you make changes to the document in the source application, those changes appear in the destination document — after all, the linked object in essence *is* the source document, or at least part of it.

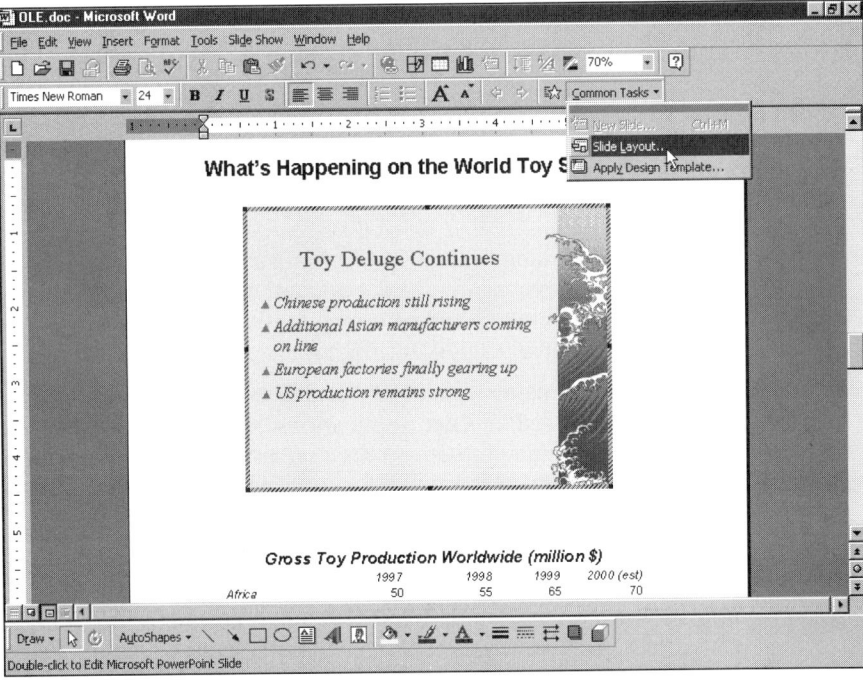

Figure 10-9: OLE objects from Excel and PowerPoint inside a Word document

So insert a linked object if you want to be able to edit it separately with the source application, even when the destination document isn't open.

The pros and cons of OLE

OLE offers huge benefits, but they don't come free. The cost/benefit analysis appears in Table 10-1.

Table 10-1   Counting the Blessings and the Cost of OLE

Advantages	Disadvantages
Allows mixing and matching of information from different applications.	Must have continuous access to the source application.
Places information from another application into the document without any loss of formatting.	If the object is linked, the source document must remain accessible and must not be moved or renamed.
Allows later editing of the object with the full functionality of the source application.	Slows down the system, requires lots of memory.

Placing objects in your documents

If you decide OLE is for you, you can take any of several routes to your destination, as usual:

- The Edit ⇨ Paste Special command
- The Insert menu. Relevant commands include Insert ⇨ Object, Insert ⇨ Picture, and Insert ⇨ Chart, among others.
- Application-specific commands (for example, you can send a PowerPoint slide as an object to a Word document using a menu command)

Specialty pasting, part II: pasting objects

Probably the simplest way to embed or link an object is with the Edit ⇨ Paste Special command. If the information on the clipboard is packaged as an object, one of the choices on the Paste Special dialog box will let you insert it in that form.

For example, when you copy Excel cells to the clipboard, Excel bundles them up as an object. In Word, the standard Paste command ignores the object packaging, inserting the cell data as a Word table. But on the Paste Special dialog box, you have the choice of pasting the same information as a Microsoft Excel Worksheet Object, as shown in Figure 10-10.

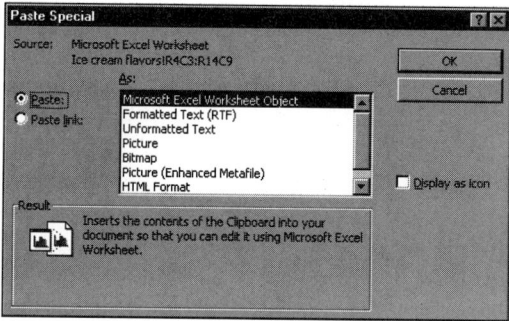

Figure 10-10: The Paste Special dialog box in Word, as it appears when Excel data is on the clipboard

Secret

Whether information on the clipboard winds up in the destination document as an embedded object, a linked object, or ordinary merged information depends on your choice of settings in the Paste Special dialog box, and also on the information itself.

To embed an object, choose the Paste radio button. This button's behavior is a little tricky. With ordinary clipboard information — that isn't packaged as an object — choosing the Paste radio button inserts the information without any connection to the source application. When an object is on the clipboard, the same Paste button embeds the object. How can you tell which type of information you're dealing with? The item name listed at As should give you a clue, but look at the help text listed at Result — if it says ". . . you can edit it with (*source application*)," the item will be embedded.

To link the object, choose Paste Link, which is available only if the clipboard contains an object. The wrinkle here is that you can often paste the object as a link in any of the formats listed in the Paste Special dialog box, when embedding is possible only with the standard object type. For example, Word lets you paste an Excel object as a link in plain text format. You can then edit and format this text within Word. Because the text you're working with is actually a LINK field, however, updating the field (F9) removes your edits and displays the current values from the source file. You can also select the field and choose Edit ➪ Linked Object to edit the object using the source application.

Inserting objects

If you don't already have the source application running, creating an object by inserting it is often the way to go. The relevant commands on the Insert menu in Word, Excel, and PowerPoint include Picture and Object. (To insert objects in Access, you must use the Insert ➪ Object command, the Unbound Object Frame tool, or an image control, depending on issues too complex to discuss here.)

Inserting items named on the Insert menu

When is an inserted item not an object? When you choose Insert ➪ Picture ➪ From File or in Word, Insert ➪ File. The inserted information enters your document as if you had used the standard Paste command, not as an embedded or linked object that you can edit with the source application. However, if you check the Link to File box, a link *is* established between the picture and the source file — that is, any changes you make to the file in the source file object will show up in the object inserted in your document.

Other items listed on the Insert menu and on the Insert ➪ Picture submenu are always inserted as objects, almost always as *embedded* objects. These items vary from application to application. Excel has an Insert ➪ Map command, whereas PowerPoint offers Insert ➪ Chart and Insert ➪ Movies and Sounds. In Word, the Picture submenu lets you insert a chart or a scanned image. In Excel and PowerPoint, you can insert organization charts from the same submenu.

Secret

That these items are objects isn't obvious, in that the source applications are often the hidden applets included with Office. Clip art, charts, WordArt text effects, maps, equations, organization charts, and all drawing objects created in Office work this way. Because you can't run the applets as stand-alone applications, you can only *embed* their objects. You can't store the objects in separate files, so linking is impossible.

Inserting objects of any type

The Insert ⇨ Object command is a fallback technique for placing any type of object into your document. The resulting dialog box (Figure 10-11) has two tabs, one for creating a new object from scratch, the other for inserting an existing file as an object.

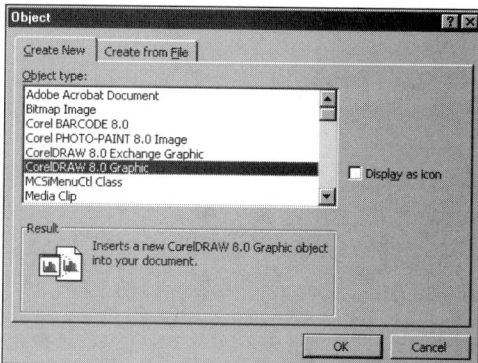

Figure 10-11: The Object dialog box gives you many options.

The Create New tab inserts *embedded* objects only. It lists all the object types registered on your system. When you select an object type, the corresponding application starts up with a new item at the ready. Add and edit information to taste, and then select File ⇨ Exit. You'll be back in your own document where the newly embedded object should be visible.

You can embed or link objects with the Create from File tab. Just locate the file with the Browse button, and then specify whether the inserted object should be embedded or linked by clearing or checking the Link to File box.

Secret

You can insert any file as an object of sorts, but you can only edit the object within your document if its file type supports OLE, as registered with your system. A non-OLE file appears in your document as an icon (Figure 10-12). If the file type is associated with an application (non-OLE), you can open the file in its source application in a separate window by choosing Edit ⇨ Package Object ⇨ Activate Contents. You aren't automatically returned to your document when you close the file.

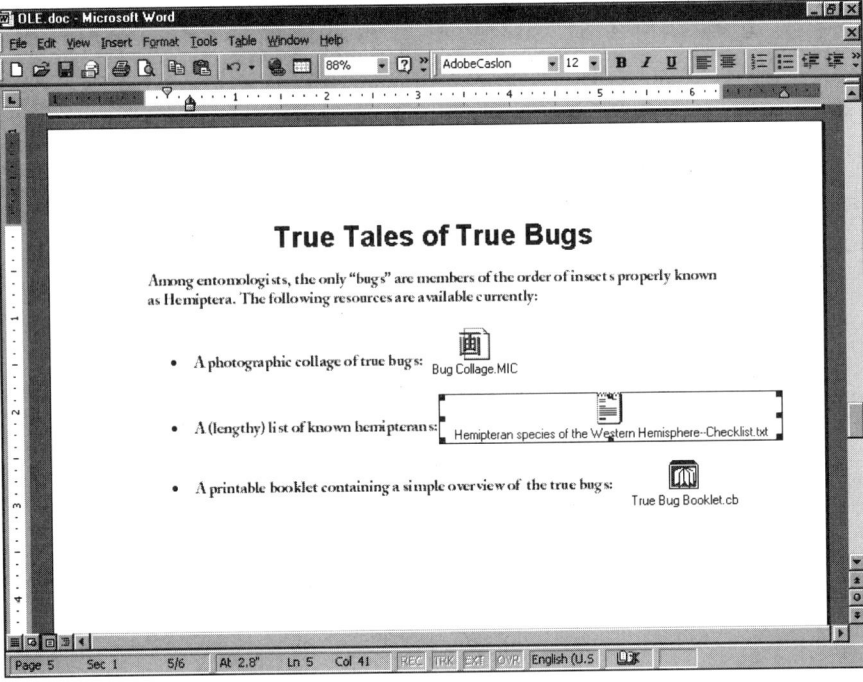

Figure 10-12: The icon represents a file created in a non-OLE application packaged as an object.

Other ways to place objects in documents

Depending on the Office applications you're working with, you may be able to tap special commands for transferring objects from one application to another. The list includes these possibilities:

- In PowerPoint, the File ⇨ Send To ⇨ Word command creates a new Word document containing the current PowerPoint slide or presentation. To insert a PowerPoint slide into an existing Word document, you must start from the Outline view, where you copy the chosen slide to the clipboard. Then, in Word, use the Edit ⇨ Paste Special command.

- In Access, you can create an Excel PivotTable object to analyze information in your Access database. Select Forms in the Database window, click the New button, and in the New Form dialog box choose PivotTable Wizard.

- In Word, you can insert an updatable Access database using the Database toolbar. After displaying the toolbar, click the Insert Database button, select the data and a table format, and then check the Insert data as Field box in the Insert Data dialog box. (Actually, this sets up a DDE connection rather than an OLE link. The data in your Word document will be kept current with the corresponding Access file, but you can't edit the Access file from within Word.)

Working with objects in documents

Once you've placed an OLE object into a document, editing its contents is as simple as double-clicking the object. You can also choose Edit ⇨ Object ⇨ Edit or Object ⇨ Edit from the object's shortcut menu — and you must use the menu method with multimedia objects, which play when you double-click them. When you edit an embedded object, the title bar doesn't change, but the menus and toolbars become those of the source application. Return to the main document by clicking somewhere outside the object.

If you prefer, you can edit the object in the source application's own window. Choose Edit ⇨ Object ⇨ Open, or from the object's shortcut menu, Object ⇨ Edit. When you're through making changes, choose File ⇨ Close or File ⇨ Exit.

Secret

Linked objects can only be edited in the source application. The Edit Link and Open Link options on the Object submenu are equivalent.

Converting an object to another type

You can sometimes convert an object to another type of object that you can then edit using the application associated with that object type. I've found very few cases where this works, but now at least you know what the Edit ⇨ Object ⇨ Convert command is supposed to do. You *can* convert clip art objects into editable graphics, as discussed in Chapter 8.

Secret

You can convert an existing embedded object into a linked object if the source application runs independently (which is not the case for the chart, draw, map, equation, and organization chart applets included with Office). Here's how: Open the object in its source application. There, choose File ⇨ Save Copy As to save the object in a separate file. When you exit the source application back to your main document, delete the embedded version of the object. Choose Insert ⇨ Object, select the Create from File tab, locate the new file, and check the Link to file box before choosing OK.

Displaying an object as an icon

You don't have to display the content of an object. If you simply want a way for readers to easily see related material, drop in the object as an icon. When the icon is opened or edited, the object's content appears.

You can display an object as an icon at the time you insert it, by checking the Display as Icon box in the Insert ⇨ Object dialog box. To display an existing object as an icon, select it and choose Edit ⇨ Object ⇨ Convert and on the resulting dialog box, check Display as Icon.

Managing links

If a document contains any linked objects, you can use the Edit ⇨ Links dialog box to view and modify those links (see Figure 10-13).

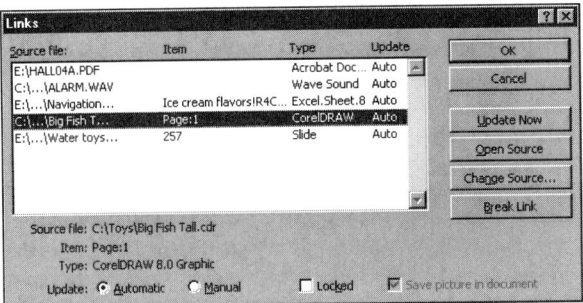

Figure 10-13: Manage linked objects in the Links dialog box shown here.

The box lists the current links and provides various options for controlling them, which include:

- **Update Now.** Updates the selected link using the current contents of the source file. Useful if the object is set to manual updating (see last bullet).

- **Open Source.** Opens the object in the source application.

- **Change Source.** Lets you replace the current link with a different filename, which is most useful for reconnecting the link after the source file has been moved (this command isn't the same as Edit ⇨ Object ⇨ Convert — think of it as "change source file," not "change source application").

- **Break Link.** Removes the link between the object and the source file. What you end up with is just a picture of the original data as it appeared at the time you broke the link. (In Word, you can perform the same conversion on a linked or embedded object right in the document with the Unlink Fields command — the shortcut is Ctrl+Shift+F9.)

- **Update.** Choose Automatic to keep the data in your document always current with the source file, or choose Manual if you want it updated only on command. Checking the box labeled Locked prevents updates of either type.

Using Mail Merge to Send Form Letters

If you reach your audience via mass mailings, you need a way to fill boilerplate form letters with information that's unique to each recipient (typically a customer's name, address, and other personal details). You write the letter in Word, but those names and addresses are stored in an Access database, an Excel table, or the Outlook contacts folder — or perhaps in a data file in some other format. The software tool you need to combine the variable information with the form letter text is called *mail merge*.

You may already have a collection of names and addresses stored in one of those locations. Otherwise, deciding where to keep that information is the first step in setting up for mail merge. In making up your mind, you should give some thought to what you plan to do with those names and addresses besides just sending mail to them. Outlook is probably easiest to use, and it's definitely the tool of choice for keeping track of people to whom you send e-mail. But for large lists of names, an Access database is the way to go.

In outline, the mail merge process is simple. You identify a main document in Word to serve as a container for the text and graphics that will appear in every letter. After telling Word where the names and addresses are stored, you go on to add content to the letter, indicating the locations where each piece of variable information goes by inserting a merge field. Here's the technique in more detail:

1. To start a form letter in Word, open an existing letter, if you have one you want to work from, or start a new one. You may want to pick one of the letter templates in the Letters & Faxes tab of the File ⇨ New dialog box.

2. Choose Tools ⇨ Mail Merge. In the resulting dialog box, choose Create, then Form Letters, and then Active Window. This sets up the current document as the main document for a mail merge.

3. Choose Get Data. Here's where you tell Word where to find your names and addresses. If they're stored in a worksheet, database, or for that matter, another Word document, choose Open Data Source. If they're in an Outlook or Exchange address book, choose Use Address Book instead.

4. Choose Edit Main Document. Word deposits you back in its main window, where the Mail Merge toolbar should now be visible.

5. Type in your letter and add any appropriate graphics. Wherever an item of variable information belongs, click the Insert Merge Field button and select the field you want at that location.

6. When the letter is ready to go, click the Mail Merge Helper button, or just choose Tools ⇨ Mail Merge again. Choose Query Options if you want Word to create the actual letters in order according to one or more fields in the source data, or to create letters only for those items in the data source that match your criteria.

7. Now choose Merge to go ahead and create the individual letters. You can specify whether to immediately print them or send them via e-mail, or to place them in a new document for your review. In the latter case, Word creates a separate section for each letter, which lets you print out selected letters by listing their sections in the Pages field in the File ⇨ Print dialog box.

Conclusion

Information is far more useful when you can use it anywhere you need it instead of its being locked inside a single document. This chapter covered the gamut of strategies and techniques for transporting data between Office applications, and between them and programs and documents in the wider computer universe.

Chapter 11

Printing Secrets

In This Chapter

- Previewing your printouts to save time and paper, and the secret of editing Word documents in Print Preview
- Printing documents in Office: The Print button versus the Print dialog box, details on how both work, and making a button out of the Print dialog box
- Printing via a file's shortcut menu or by drag and drop
- Printing to a file so you can send your output to an unconnected printer or reprint the file at the fastest possible speed
- Great printing utilities for booklets and graphics

Producing printed documents is an everyday task and, fortunately, one that usually isn't very complicated. That's why this chapter is short. But you can still find here some clandestine nuggets that are bound to help you feel less put out by your output chores.

Matching Print Orientation to Document Layout

You take it for granted that your monitor is wider than it is tall, unless you have one of those fancy pivoting models. People designing worksheets in Excel and forms and reports in Access or Outlook tend to do the natural thing, laying them out to fit the available screen real estate. But when you print such a document, you're likely to end up with the contents running off the right side of the page or squashed to illegibility at the top.

To avoid such embarrassments, you should train yourself to set each individual document's orientation when you first create it, choosing portrait (tall) or landscape (wide) as appropriate. But if you work primarily with worksheets and forms, consider setting the default print orientation to landscape using the printer's Properties dialog box (available in Office from the Print dialog box, or in Windows proper, via Start ➪ Settings ➪ Printers folder).

Previewing Before You Print

All Office applications except PowerPoint let you see what your document will look like on paper before you actually print it, using the File⇨Print Preview command or the corresponding button. The case for using print preview? It saves time and resources, not to mention wear-and-tear on your printer. The trees you spare will thank you.

What you see in Preview

Each Office application has a different Print Preview screen — Excel's being the most rudimentary, style-wise, lacking cool graphical buttons (see Figures 11-1 and 11-2). But they all work in essentially the same way.

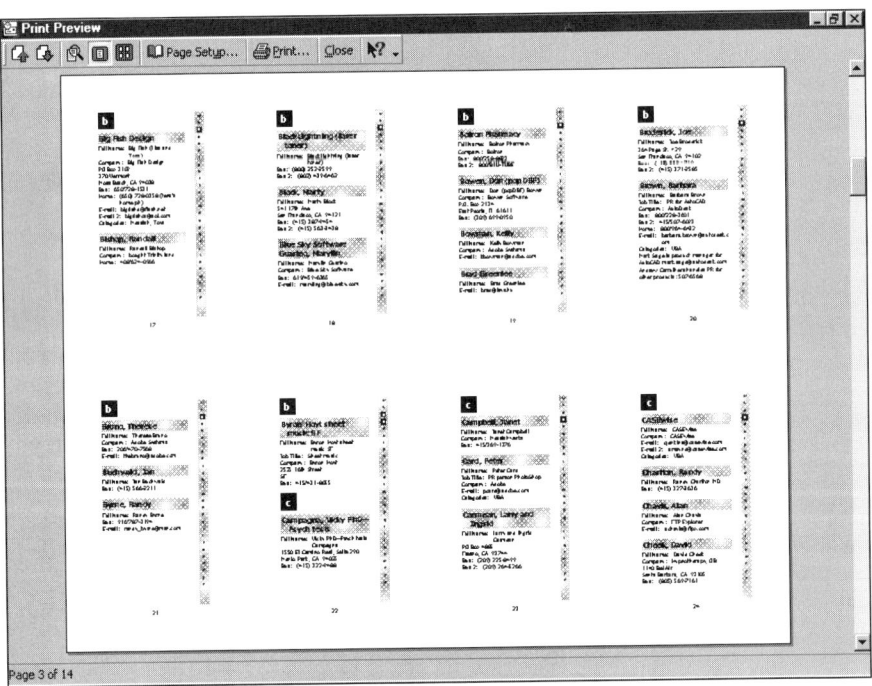

Figure 11-1: Outlook's Print Preview, with lots of neat-o buttons

The view of your document in Print Preview mode shows exactly what your Office application intends to print, except that resolution is lower on the screen than it is in print. Document elements that in other views you can't see (or can't see well), such as headers and footers, appear in their proper locations and in the proper color.

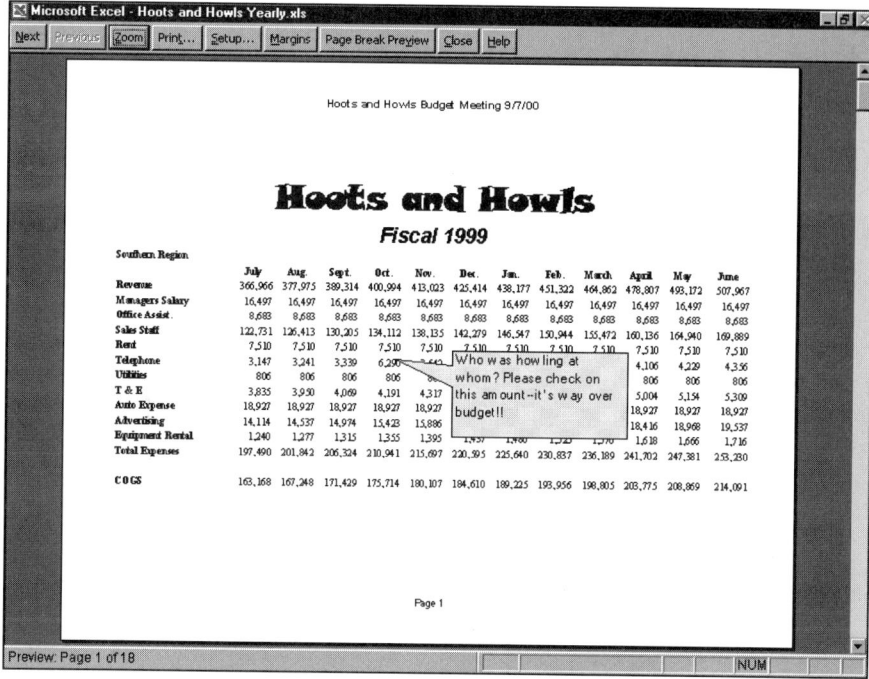

Figure 11-2: Excel's pedestrian Print Preview window

Each program provides one or more buttons to toggle between a full-size view of the document and at least one zoomed-out view that shows the whole page at once. In Word and Access, the Multiple Page button on the Print Preview toolbar lets you display a variable number of pages. If you've ever used the Insert Table button in Word, you should find the workings of the Multiple Pages button familiar. You click the button and then use the mouse to sweep an area in the displayed grid to select the number of pages to be previewed and their arrangement, in rows and columns.

There's a limit to how many pages you can display with this technique, although it varies with the document and the resolution of your monitor. Of course, the more pages you display, the less detail you see. Displaying multiple pages is useful mainly for getting a crude overview of your pages. It can also help you find one specific page of interest quickly.

Editing in Print Preview mode — only in Word

Only Word lets you edit a document in Print Preview. In the other applications, you can look, but you can't touch.

Secret

How to edit in Word's Print Preview is hardly obvious. When you enter Print Preview, the Magnifier button is pressed in, enabling you to switch back and forth between full size and whatever alternative zoom setting is active. To edit, click the Magnifier button so that it pops out. Now you can click your document and edit away.

Printing Documents

Out of the box, Office programs give you two ways to print: by clicking the Print button to print directly or by choosing File ⇨ Print to bring up the Print dialog box (pressing Ctrl+P also displays the Print box).

The Print button bypasses the Print dialog box, sending the document immediately to the printer you last selected with the settings you last chose. If you're not sure which printer is currently selected, hover the pointer over the Print button for a moment, and you see the printer name on the ScreenTip that appears.

Secret

For one-click access to the Print dialog box, place the File ⇨ Print menu command on a toolbar. See Chapter 5 for the techniques required to place menu items on toolbars (a quick hint: You must open the Tools ⇨ Customize dialog box). One suggestion seems appropriate here: Place a *copy* of the Print menu command on the toolbar, rather than moving the command off the menu — so hold down Ctrl when you drag the command. You'll find that the button image for the Print dialog box looks exactly like the one for the standard Print button, so a paint job (editing one of the twin button images) is in order — again, Chapter 5 covers the technique.

For guaranteed one-click printing on a specific printer, record a macro for that printer. Using the method discussed in Chapter 5, start recording the macro, naming it something like PrintToNetworkLaserPrinter and assigning it to a button. Next, open the Print dialog box and select the desired printer. The other options in the dialog box will also be recorded, so change them to whatever settings you want in your macro. After you choose OK to start the print job, stop the macro recorder (you can cancel the print job too unless you actually want to print the current document).

CD

If you want a button that opens the Print dialog box with a specific printer already selected, you need to write the macro in VBA as shown here. Substitute the name of the printer as shown in the Name box in the Print dialog box for *printer name* (don't forget the quote marks).

```
Sub PrintUsingPrinterName () ' Word version
    ActivePrinter = "printer name"
    Dialogs(wdDialogFilePrint).Show
End Sub
```

In Excel, you must explicitly state the Application object (it's understood in Word), and you must also include the port on which the printer is connected as in this sample:

```
Sub PrintUsingPrinterName()  ' Excel version
Application.ActivePrinter = "HP LaserJet 4 on LPT1:"
Application.Dialogs(xlDialogPrint).Show
End Sub
```

Shortcut and drag-and-drop printing

A tip that works for many Windows applications: If all you want to do is print a document, you don't have to bother opening it in its application and then choosing the print command. Instead, locate the document in My Computer or Explorer and right-click it, choosing Print from the shortcut menu. After the computer tucks its shirt in and straightens its tie, the document appears on screen within its application, but only long enough to prepare the print job. With that complete, the application gracefully exits.

Secret

You can use the preceding trick from within Office's file-related dialog boxes, such as Open and Save As. You never see the document or its application on your screen, except that you may be asked to specify what to print. If you want to work your mouse a little harder, and if you have more than one printer available on your system, drag and drop can save you some time. Drag the document's icon from a My Computer or Explorer window, dropping it onto the icon of the printer you want to use or into the printer's window (the one displayed when you double-click the printer icon). Unless you keep the Printers folder open, you must first create a shortcut to the target printer by dragging the printer icon from the Printers folder to the Desktop.

Working with the Print dialog box

If you've seen one Print dialog box in any of the Office applications, you've seen them all, more or less. Figure 11-3 shows one example.

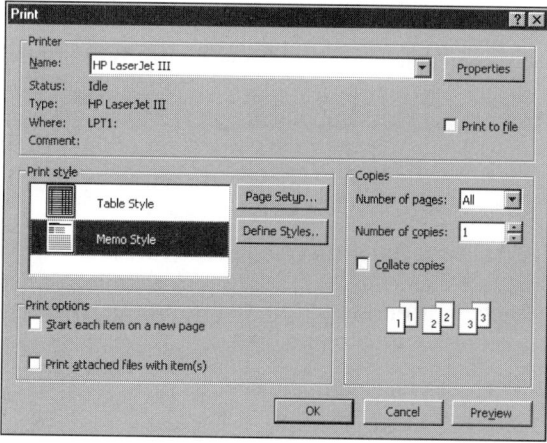

Figure 11-3: Outlook's Print dialog box. Note that Outlook lets you select from various print styles, a choice not available in other Office apps.

Secret

One basic fact to tuck away in your bio-RAM regarding the Print dialog box is that the settings you select remain in effect *during the current session* until you change them again. The next time you run the program, the settings revert to their defaults.

Controls in common

The Print dialog boxes of all the Office applications have a set of controls in common. Click the Properties button to change setup options for the printer currently displayed in the Name field. If you have more than one printer installed on your system, you can select the one you want to print to by dropping down the Name list. The printer initially selected is the one set as the Windows default in the Printers folder of the Control Panel. Other controls common throughout Office include Print to File, Number of Copies, and Collate. These controls are covered later in the chapter.

The typical Office Print dialog box also has some way to specify a print range: which pages, worksheets, binder sections, and so on to print.

If you select something before calling up the Print dialog box, you often get a chance to print only the selection. In Word, you can include noncontiguous pages in the print range by separating the pages with a comma. To print pages 3, 4, 5, 7, 8, and 9, enter 3–5, 7–9. You can also specify pages within a specific section, an entire section, or noncontiguous sections, as follows:

What You Want to Print	Example Entry in Print Dialog Box
A complete section	s2
Noncontiguous sections	s3,s6
Specific pages in a section	p30s2–p40s2
Specific pages spanning two or more sections	p30s2–p65s5

Secret

Weird Office facts, continued: In PowerPoint and Word, you can print items in reverse order by typing the print range backward, as in 3–1. In Word, however, this trick isn't necessary: the Print Options dialog box (see "Application-Specific printing Tips" later in this chapter) has a Reverse print order check box.

Collating

If you check the Collate box, Office prints the entire document all the way through for as many times as you've specified by the entry at Number of Copies. That way, each copy emerges from the printer in proper page order, and you have nothing to do but clip or staple.

This is dandy, so Collate is checked by default. But you should turn off collation if:

- The file you're printing contains complex graphics that take a long time to translate into a page image.

- You're printing multiple copies of a one-page file.
- You're printing to a file.

Need some explanation? One downside of having Office do the collating can be slower printing. This applies to page printers such as lasers. It takes time for the print information for a page to be transferred from your PC to the printer, and still more for the printer to convert those bytes into an image of the page. Once the page image has been formed, however, the printer can make any number of copies at top speed. When you turn on collation in the Print dialog box, the data transfer-translation process must be repeated for every single page. This makes no sense whatsoever for a one-page file, and it's also very time-consuming if the pages contain complicated graphics or many fonts.

Printing to a file can also be affected. Generally, when you print to a file you want to generate the smallest file you can. If collation is on, the file contains as many copies of all the page information as you requested. See "Printing to a file" later in this chapter.

Application-Specific Printing Tips

Each Office application has a few wrinkles of its own when it comes to printing.

Word

Secret

In the Word Print dialog box, the Options button brings up the same print-related settings you get when you select the Print tab from the Tools ⇨ Options dialog box. You can also print items other than the current document, including lists of styles and custom keyboard assignments, by selecting them from the Print What list.

Knowing what you're printing in Word

It's time to print — do you know where your insertion point is?

Selecting the Current Page option from Word's Print dialog box prints the current page, of course. But wait — which is the current page? It's *not* (necessarily) the page you see displayed behind the dialog box. For printing purposes, the current page is the one that contains the insertion point. But when you scroll with the mouse, the insertion point stays behind until you click the document. For this reason, the current page may be at one end of the document, while the page you see on your screen is at the other.

So if you plan to print only the page on the screen, make sure the insertion point is blinking somewhere on that page before you call up the Print dialog box. If you forget to check the location of the insertion point before you get to the dialog box, you can look down at the status bar to see which page is current.

Printing booklets in Word

Word has a great new feature for converting regular documents into compact booklets or drafts. In the Zoom section of the File ⇨ Print dialog box, change the setting at Pages per sheet from 1 to any of the available values up to 16. When you print, Word shrinks each page appropriately. With a typical document, a setting of 2 gives you reasonably legible text and uses only half the paper. Higher settings are usually best for previewing the document's overall layout. ClickBook, described in the "Hot Printer Utilities" section later in this chapter, is a lot better for booklets, but this feature is a start.

Shrink a Word document to fit on the page

If you originally laid out your document for a specific page size and now plan to print it on smaller sheets, you may not have to reformat the whole thing. Instead, try the new Scale to Paper Size setting in the File ⇨ Print dialog box (Zoom section). You can condense a document intended for legal paper so much that it fits onto an envelope, but don't blame me if no one can read the results.

Word's Shrink to Fit command has been around longer and works differently. Use it when a document is just a bit too long for a single page, with a little bit of leftover text flowing over onto the next page. Actually, it works on documents of any length. Shrink to Fit automatically reformats the document so that it fits on one page fewer than its current length, changing type size and line spacing. Don't expect miracles or typographic elegance from the Shrink to Fit command, but it does shorten your document. The Undo command restores the document to its previous condition if the results are just too ugly.

The only trick about using this command is knowing where to find it: By default, it's only available via a button on the Print Preview toolbar. If you don't routinely use Print Preview, you can place the ToolsShrinkToFit command on another menu or toolbar or assign it to a keyboard shortcut with the customizing techniques presented in Chapter 5.

PowerPoint

PowerPoint too has a Print tab in the Tools ⇨ Options dialog box. Among other choices, it lets you fix some print settings for the current document, overriding the current settings in the Print dialog box when you print by clicking the Print toolbar button.

In PowerPoint's File ⇨ Print dialog box, use the Print What list to specify whether you want to print slides, paper handouts, speakers notes, or an outline.

Excel

Excel locates additional print-related settings on the Sheet tab of the File ⇨ Page Setup dialog box. Here, you can control the sequence in which different sections of a worksheet print, and thus the order in which those sections are numbered. You can find additional Excel printing tips in Chapter 35.

Outlook

Outlook's Print dialog box lets you select a print style for the item you're printing. The options depend on the type of item you're printing. For instance, if you're printing a calendar, you can pick from styles such as daily, weekly, monthly, and so on. The Page Setup button duplicates the File ⇨ Page Setup command. It displays a dialog box chock-full of controls for specifying the size and format of printed items (Figure 11-4) based on settings dictated by the styles. You can define new styles at your whim.

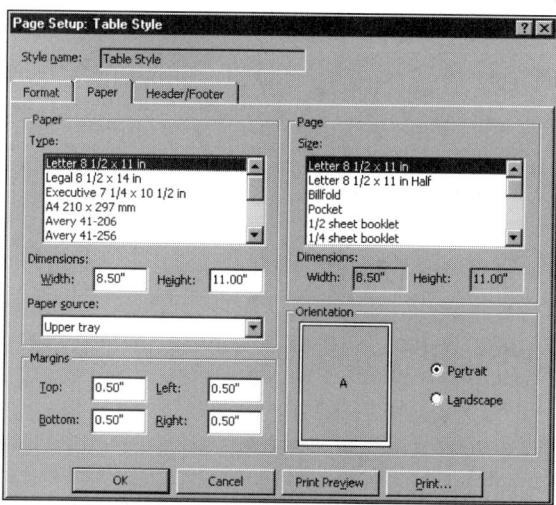

Figure 11-4: Outlook's Page Setup dialog box, used to define the format of printed items

Access

In Access, you must print each object, such as a data table, form, or report, separately. It follows that each object has its own print settings. To define margins and columnar layouts, you can either choose File ⇨ Page Setup or click Setup in the Print dialog box. However, only the File ⇨ Page Setup dialog box lets you designate a specific printer for a given form or report. If you use a fast laser printer to print out your financial reports but rely on a dot matrix printer to produce invoices or receipts, use this feature to ensure that each item always comes out of the correct printer.

Access forms and reports have two print-related properties: When Layout for Print is set to Yes, the text Access displays on your screen conforms to the spacing it will have when printed, even if your screen fonts don't match your printer fonts. The text may look distorted on the screen, but at least you know it's in the right place. Setting the Fast Laser Printing property to Yes causes Access to substitute underscore and vertical bar text characters for real lines, which makes printing quicker — but only on laser printers.

Binder

In Binder, the File ⇨ Print dialog box lets you choose whether to print the entire binder or selected sections only. You can also control how sections of the binder mega-document are page numbered at print time — consecutively throughout all sections or starting over at the beginning of each section.

Printing to a File

If you check the Print to File box, your Office application saves on disk the entire stream of instructions and information that it would normally send to the printer. If all goes well, you can then copy the resulting print file directly to a printer at any time without opening the original application (see "Printing a print file" later in this chapter). Because every printer speaks a different language, you must specify the type of printer you plan eventually to use when you create the *print file*.

Why go to the trouble of preparing a print file? For either of the following two reasons:

- You want to be able to reprint the document frequently without running the application that spawned it. Copying a print file to the printer is considerably faster than running the application, opening the document, and then printing.

- You want to output it on a device that isn't available to your system. One possibility is that you're preparing documents for output on high-end equipment on slides or film, the kind used by professional printing shops. You can print to a file and then send that file to the service bureau that produces the final product. (Note, however, that most service bureaus want a copy of the document itself in case something goes wrong.) In another scenario, a friend or someone in your company might give you physical access to a fancy color printer, but you can't connect to the machine from your PC, directly or via a network link. A simple solution is to print to a file, take that file on a floppy disk to the computer connected to the printer, and copy it from that computer to the printer.

To print to a file bound for a printer that isn't already installed on your system, you must first install the necessary printer driver. Use the Add Printer icon in the Printers folder (Start ⇨ Settings ⇨ Printers). Realize that you can install a driver for any printer any time — the printer doesn't have to be connected. And see "Printing to a file automatically" later in this chapter.

Secret

Printing to a file also gives you an alternative way to export information crudely. By installing (in Windows) the Generic/Text Only printer driver you can produce text files by "printing" them to a file.

Creating the print file

In the Print dialog box, select the driver for the destination printer. Again, Windows doesn't care if the printer isn't accessible to your system. Then check the Print to File box. You can choose other options as usual, but see the comment on the Collate box in the "Collating" section earlier in this chapter.

When you print, you get a dialog box asking you to enter a name for the print file. The extension .prn is customary for most print files, while .ps is usually used for PostScript files (remember that you must type quotation marks around a filename to save it with a nondefault extension — see Chapter 12). However, if you create print files intended for two or more different printers or other output devices, choose different extensions for each printer.

If the print file is destined for a printer unavailable on your system, you can copy it to a floppy disk or other removable medium as soon as it hits the hard disk. Then either send the floppy to the service bureau or use it to copy the file to a computer connected to the printer. Alternatively, send the file via the Internet or by direct modem transmission to its destination.

Printing to a file automatically

Secret

The Print to File check box in Office applications is always available, but you have to remember to use it. If you use a particular printer driver only for creating print files, set up the driver to print to a file automatically. In Windows, just select FILE as the port for that printer when you first install it, or later, on the Details tab of the printer's Properties dialog box.

Printing a print file

Once you've gone to the trouble to create a print file, your next challenge is sending it to the intended printer. Not much of a challenge, really, as long as you're comfortable with simple DOS commands.

At the DOS prompt, type

```
copy /b filename.prn lpt1
```

substituting the correct printer port for lpt1.

Secret

Most printers can print plain text files using this technique. If you need a quick printout of a Read.me file or some such file, just use the preceding DOS command to put the file on paper.

Show-off ways for printing print files

Secret

Windows plays dead if you drag and drop a print file onto the corresponding printer icon, but you can teach it to do better tricks. Try either of the following training techniques.

For printing print files by drag and drop:

1. Use a text editor to write and save a batch file called PRNTFILE.BAT containing the following line:

   ```
   copy /b %1 lpt1:
   ```

   (If necessary replace *lpt1* with the printer port to which your printer is connected.)

2. On the Windows Desktop or in any convenient folder create a new shortcut for the batch file. Name it something like Send File to LaserJet.

3. After the new icon appears, right-click it, and then select Properties. On the Program tab, select Minimized in the Run field, and check the Close on Exit box (leave it unchecked if you want to see and then close a DOS box on your screen while printing is in progress).

Once the shortcut is ready, you can send *any* file to the printer by dragging it and dropping it onto the shortcut icon. Alternatively, you can select the file, choose Copy from its shortcut menu, and then choose Paste from the shortcut menu of the new icon.

For printing print files via the *file's* shortcut menu:

1. Create the PRNTFILE batch file and its shortcut as in the preceding Steps 1 through 3.

2. Make a copy of the shortcut in the Send To folder (in the main Windows folder).

Now when you right-click any file, you can choose Send To ⇨ Send File to Printer (or whatever you named the shortcut in the Send To folder).

Hot Printer Utilities

Anyone with a printer needs a copy of ClickBook, an incredibly useful utility that automatically formats and prints documents as booklets, and in lots of other special layouts as well (BlueSquirrel, 801-523-1063, `www.bluesquirrel.com`). One of ClickBook's windows is shown in Figure 11-5.

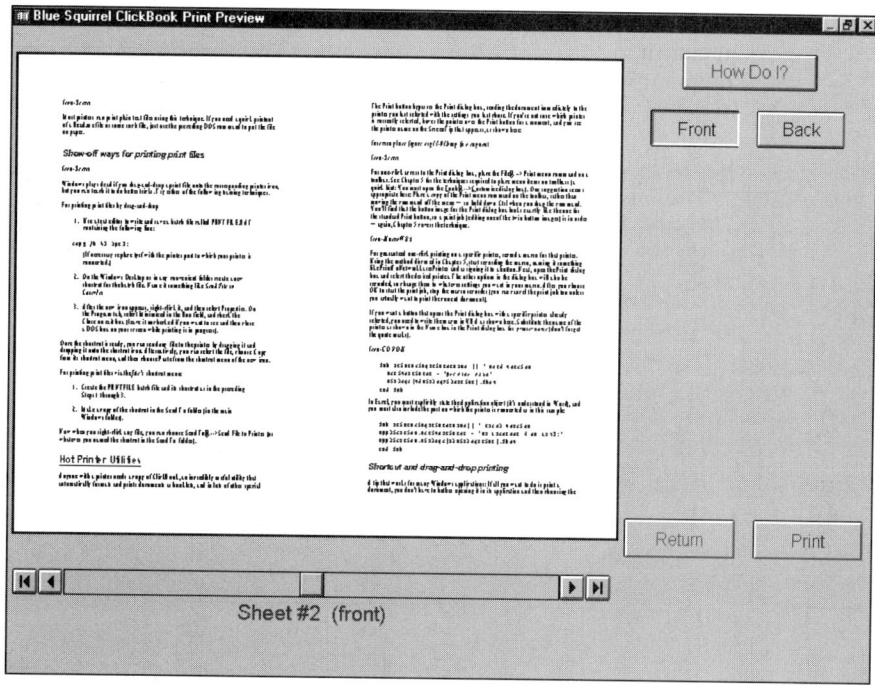

Figure 11-5: ClickBook lets you select specific pages to print in this preview window, which also illustrates how the utility squeezes two Word pages onto one sheet of paper.

In a booklet, each side of each sheet of paper is printed with a pair of side-by-side miniature pages. You might think there's nothing much to printing a booklet in Word — just lay out a landscape page in two columns and print away, flipping the pages over to print the other sides. But you're forgetting that booklet sheets are stacked on top of one another and then folded.

As a result, the order of the little page images is quite different from the order of pages in the folded book. In even the simplest example, a one-sheet booklet, pages 1 and 4 fall on one side, with pages 2 and 3 on the other.

Futzing with the page order in Word would be bad enough, but imagine trying to print a booklet from Excel. With ClickBook, you create your documents on individual pages at regular size without worrying about the booklet layout at all.

ClickBook installs a series of new printer drivers, each of which sits, metaphorically speaking, between your Windows applications and one of the original printer drivers already on your system. When you select a ClickBook driver at print time, the program banks the raw output information, rearranging all the pages in proper booklet order. In the process, it shrinks your pages down as necessary so that two (or more) fit onto a single sheet. When everything is just so, ClickBook sends the resulting data on to the original printer driver that in turn passes it to the printer.

All this has worked flawlessly in my tests. The constraints of the physical plane dictate that you have to accept mild distortion of text proportions, or put up with smaller text and larger empty areas. These are exceedingly tiny concerns.

Another specialized printing utility, SuperPrint, claims to speed up printing by replacing the hybrid 16/32-bit Windows 95 print system with fully 32-bit software, with a finely tuned print spooler, and on networks, by sending compressed metafiles rather than raw printer data to the print server.

But SuperPrint's most compelling benefits relate to graphics flexibility and print quality. Most impressively, it can interpret Level 2 PostScript output (the kind with lots of fancy colors and special effects), translating the information into a form that can be printed by a destination non-PostScript printer. You can preview the results and capture them to the clipboard, making SuperPrint a PostScript import and file conversion utility (Chapter 10 discusses file conversions in more depth).

The program also offers manual and automated features for improving the quality of printed graphics. And it can convert print output from any Windows application into a bitmap, which you can then incorporate into Web pages. Another Zenographics product, InterPrint, lets you print to any printer by sending e-mail. (Contact Zenographics at www.zeno.com.)

Faxing Your Documents

Two truths: In Office, printing documents is one way to fax them. Conversely, faxing documents is one way to print them.

If you have a fax modem — and assuming you've installed the fax services that come with Windows or comparable faxing software — you can fax any document by printing it. Just choose the name of your fax software driver in the Print dialog. This works in any Windows application. If you install Outlook and no other fax program, the "printer" to choose is either Microsoft At Work (if you chose Outlook's Corporate or Workgroup configuration) or Symantec Fax Starter Edition (with the Internet Only configuration).

In Excel, Word, and PowerPoint, you can also fax documents using the File ⇨ Send To ⇨ Fax recipient, which is probably a bit simpler. In Outlook, you can send messages by fax instead of e-mail by selecting the appropriate version of the recipient's name from the address book, as in Sue Smith (Business Fax) or Jane Jones (Home Fax). If you travel with a notebook PC but without a printer, remember that you can always produce a paper copy of any document by faxing it to the nearest fax machine using either of the preceding methods.

Conclusion

Make the printing experience as luxurious as it can be. Take advantage of print previews, macros for quick printing with your favorite settings, and the custom settings in the Print and Print Options dialog boxes. And don't neglect the fine arts of printing to a file, faxing by printing, and printing by faxing.

Part III

Secrets of Document Management

Chapter 12: Advanced Document Management

Chapter 13: Document Integrity and Security

Chapter 12

Advanced Document Management

In This Chapter

- A catalog of techniques for creating and opening documents
- Arcane tricks for navigation and file management with the Open and Save As dialog boxes
- Tips for finding files anywhere
- A critical appraisal of the hidden file indexing application, Find Fast
- Office Binder: pros, cons, and power tips

In Office, as in Windows itself, the *document* reigns supreme—not the software you use to create it, and not the operating system that permits that software to run. After all, when you build a chair, you concentrate on the wood, the fasteners, and the finish. You pick up tools as you need them, but your eyes, mental and physical, remain on the piece of furniture emerging before you.

This idea of a document-centric computer universe is a few revolutionary paradigm shifts old by now, but it still makes sense. Documents are the reason to use Office, and the reason to learn Office secrets. This chapter looks at techniques for working with documents as complete units, and for integrating component documents into larger ones via Office Binder.

Power Techniques for Document Management

If you're going to be making documents, you need to know how to create them, store them, name them, organize them, and find them when you need them. Building on your knowledge of basic Windows skills, this section leads you through a more advanced discussion of document management in Office.

How do I create thee?
Let me count the ways

Windows and Office combine to give you a profusion of ways to start new documents and open existing ones. But which one is best? Lame as it may sound, you have to decide for yourself, based on your work habits, aesthetic preferences, and shoe size.

To create a new document, you have these choices:

- From the Start menu, choose New Office Document, and then select and open a template for the type of document you want to create.
- Click the New Office Document button, located on the Office toolbar of the Shortcut bar.
- In almost any My Computer or Explorer folder, or on the Desktop, display the shortcut menu (right-click or press Shift+F10) and choose New. Then select the type of document you want to create from the submenu. The only time this won't work is if you're viewing My Computer itself or a special folder such as Printers or Control Panel.
- In a My Computer or Explorer folder, open an Office template directly (double-click the template icon, or highlight it and press Enter).
- From any running Office application, choose File ⇨ New. Then select and open a template.

To open an existing Office document, you have these choices:

- From the Start menu, choose Open Office Document. This brings up the Open Office Document dialog box, the mother of all Open dialog boxes, set to list all the standard types of Office document files (the next two sections in this chapter have lots of tips on using the Open dialog box).
- From the Start menu, choose Documents to list your most recently used documents. Choose the one you want to reopen. A shareware program called Recent Documents 97 helps you manage your Documents menu, making it a much more useful tool — it's included on the CD-ROM that accompanies this book.
- Display the Shortcut bar and click the Open Office Document button on the Office toolbar.
- In a My Computer or Explorer folder, locate and double-click the document, or highlight it and press Enter.
- In any running Office application, choose File ⇨ Open and then select and open one or more documents.
- In any running Office application, choose from the list of recently used documents at the bottom of the File menu. In Word, you can also select files from the Work menu choice, if you've added it to your menus (see "Opening previously used files" in Chapter 27).
- Use the Web toolbar, as described in Chapter 6.

Note that when you open a new or existing document by any of these techniques with the corresponding application already running, the document opens in that application's current window. If for some reason you want to open the document in a separate copy of the application, you must first start a second instance of the program and then open the document from there.

Secrets of the Open and Save As dialog boxes

Once you're working in an Office application, you open existing documents and save new ones via a pair of similar dialog boxes labeled Open and Save As, of all things. Nearly all Windows 95 and NT applications use versions of these dialog boxes, but in Office, they're souped up with special features.

When you choose File ➪ Open to access existing documents, the Open dialog box appears as shown in Figure 12-1. The dialog box looks quite a bit different from its counterpart in Office 97, but it has all of the old features and then some. Similar or identical dialog boxes appear when you use any command that accesses existing files, such as Insert ➪ File or Insert ➪ Object in most Office applications, Section ➪ Add from File in Binder, or Format ➪ Apply Design in PowerPoint. The Save As dialog box looks much the same, just a little less complicated.

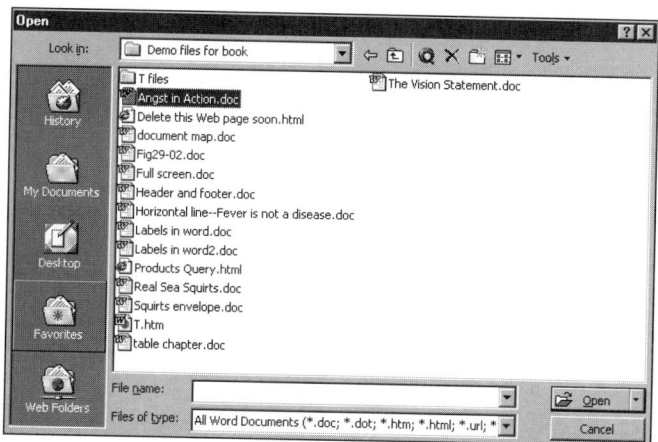

Figure 12-1: The File ➪ Open dialog box. You see essentially identical dialog boxes with different names when using various file-related commands in Office.

The *file list*, where the file and folders are displayed, consumes the bulk of each dialog box. Of course you're familiar with the basic operations of these dialog boxes, but you may not have appreciated all you can do with them. The section "Locating files" covers the fine points of finding and displaying groups of files that meet specific criteria in these dialog boxes. This section gives you the inside story on their other powerful hidden features.

Selecting multiple files in the Open dialog box

As in My Computer and Explorer, you can select two or more files at once in the Open dialog box, and then choose Open to open them at the same time. You can make two kinds of multiple-file selections:

- **Select two or more files in a continuous range.** With the mouse, click the first file, hold down Shift, and click the last file. Using the keyboard, highlight the first file in the sequence, hold down Shift, and extend the selection by pressing any of the standard cursor movement keys (the arrows, PageUp, PageDown, Home, or End).

- **Select files randomly.** With the mouse, click the first file, hold down Ctrl, and click the remaining files one at a time. If you mistakenly select a file, be sure you're still holding down Ctrl and then just click the file again.

Secret

Because you can only save one file at a time, the Save As dialog box doesn't permit multiple selections. Which leads to a tip: If you want to perform Windows file-management chores from within Office, use the Open dialog box, not Save As.

More keyboard tricks in the Open and Save As dialog boxes

Aside from selecting multiple files at random, anything you can do with the mouse, you can probably do faster with the keyboard — once you have the necessary keyboard shortcuts burned into your brain (see Table 12-1). Note that an item in a dialog box is said to *have the focus* when it accepts keyboard input, as is made evident by a faint dashed rectangle around it or by a blinking insertion point.

Table 12-1 Keyboard Shortcuts in the Open and Save As Dialog Boxes

Task	Keyboard Shortcut
Select a file	Space (to select the file marked by a dotted rectangle); cursor keys (to move the selection highlight to another file)
Rename a file	F2 (The file has to be selected first. Learn this one — it's definitely easier than using the mouse!)
Press (activate) any of the dialog box toolbar buttons	Alt+1 through Alt+9 (see the "Buttons in the Open and Save As dialog boxes" section that follows)

Task	Keyboard Shortcut
Open the Look In list (when file list has the focus)	F4 (also drops down any list that has the focus)
Refresh the list of files (in the Open dialog box, search for files using the current search criteria — same as Find Now)	F5
Go up one level in the disk/folder hierarchy	Backspace (when the file list has the focus)
Display a shortcut menu for selected file (same as right-click)	Shift+F10
Display a shortcut menu for the current *folder* (not a specific file), in order to see the folder's Properties, or to use the Paste command	Shift+F10 with no file selected (to deselect all files, press Alt+N to activate the File Name list, in which you type *; then press Tab to switch back to the list)
Display properties for a selected file or folder	Alt+Enter
Display properties for the current folder	Alt+Enter with no file or folder selected
Move selected file(s) to the Recycle Bin	Delete
Delete selected file(s)	Shift+Delete

Buttons in the Open and Save As dialog boxes

The Open and Save As dialog boxes are both equipped with one-click buttons for common functions. These include the big new folder management buttons in the vertical bar along the left side of the dialog box, along with the toolbar buttons across the top. Although some of these buttons duplicate functions available through other keyboard shortcuts or the shortcut menu, others supply unique capabilities that you should take advantage of — see Table 12-2 for details.

Secret

Clicking a button works fine, but you can also activate any of the buttons along the top of the Open or Save As dialog boxes by pressing Alt plus the number key corresponding to the button's position on the toolbar, starting with 1 for the Back button. Use the typewriter number keys along the top row of your keyboard, not those on the numeric pad.

Table 12-2 Buttons in the Open and Save As Dialog Boxes

Button	Button Name	Function
Navigation buttons		
	History	Displays the Recent folder, into which Office automatically places shortcuts for the documents you've opened and the folders you obtained them from. A gotcha: Folder shortcuts are listed in the currently active sort order, rather than at the top of the list.
	My Documents	Takes you immediately to the My Documents folder, or another "home base" folder you've specified for documents in the Windows Registry (see the sidebar "Changing the My Documents and Favorites folders" later in this chapter).
	Desktop	Takes you directly to the Windows Desktop.
	Favorites	Switches to the Favorites folder. See "Using the Favorites folder to access frequently used items" later.
	Web Folders	Switches to the Web folders.
	Back	Moves to the folder or disk you were last using.
	Up One Level	Moves to the parent folder or disk.
File Management buttons		
	Search the Web	Opens your browser's default search page (see Chapter 6).
	Delete	Deletes the currently selected file or files. Hold down Shift when you click this button to delete the file permanently rather than send it to the Recycle Bin.
	Create New Folder	Creates a new subfolder in the current folder.

Button	Button Name	Function
Views button and menu		
(same as next one)	Views	A split button. Clicking the main part of the button cycles between the List, Details, Properties, and Preview views described next. To switch directly to a specific view, click the thin bar on the right part of the button and choose from the drop-down menu.
	List view	Displays filenames.
	Details view	Displays the name, size, type, and date of each file. See "Tips on Details view" later.
	Properties view	Displays the properties of the selected file in the right pane.
	Preview view	Shows you a preview of the selected file in the right pane. This works on just about any type of file you can open in Office, including documents from the other Office applications, text files, files from various word processors and spreadsheets, and even pictures (but see the Secret that follows). One drawback to using this button is that displaying documents takes a lot longer than simply listing a bunch of filenames. When this view is active, use the mouse to move from file to file, because scrolling via the keyboard takes too much time. Another problem: You can't delete a file you're previewing, because it is technically open in Windows, and Windows protects open files from deletion.
Tools menu		
	See Figure 12-4 later for the Open dialog box Tools menu	Displays a menu of relevant choices (see the section "The Tools menu," which follows shortly).

Tips on Preview mode

Among the modes accessible through the Views button listed in Table 12-2, the Preview and Details views deserve further comment. Preview mode, entered by pressing the Preview button described previously, is actually fairly complicated.

- In Office applications except Word, you can only preview graphics files and Office documents. But you can only preview those Office documents saved with the Save Preview Picture box checked in the File ⇨ Properties dialog box (Summary tab). Checking this box stores in the document file a little graphic image of the first page. This *preview picture* graphic is what you'll see when you preview the file.

- In Word, you can preview many files without the preview picture. This works for most file types that Word can import, such as text, HTML, or Excel files (Chapter 10 discusses the text and graphics converters necessary for importing files). Note that you can't preview PowerPoint files saved without a preview picture.

- If you save a *Word* document with a preview picture, you see only that tiny, barely recognizable picture when you preview it, even in Word — not the entire document in a small scrollable window, as you otherwise would. Therefore, it may make sense to save preview pictures only when you want to preview your Word documents in other Office applications (but see "Tips on using and setting properties" later in this chapter). Although you can decide whether to save the preview picture for each document independently, this setting is stored in Word's templates. Templates are discussed in Chapter 13.

Tips on Details view

Details view in the Open and Save As dialog boxes — the view you see if you click the Details button described in Table 12-2 — works just like its counterpart in My Computer. Each file appears on a separate line, with columns for the file's name, size, type, and date modified. As in My Computer or Explorer, you can change the width of these columns by dragging the separators between them.

Secret

Which leads me to a tip: To make more room for important information — namely, long filenames — change the way Office documents are listed in the dialog boxes. In the Type column, Office documents are always preceded by the Microsoft moniker, as in "Microsoft Excel Worksheet," "Microsoft PowerPoint Presentation," and even "Microsoft HTML Document." The point is that self-important naming style eats up way too much room, leaving less for the filenames.

To remove those superfluous *Microsoft*s, open My Computer or Explorer (it doesn't matter which folder you display) and choose View ⇨ Options. In the Options dialog box select the File Types tab so that the dialog box appears as shown in Figure 12-2.

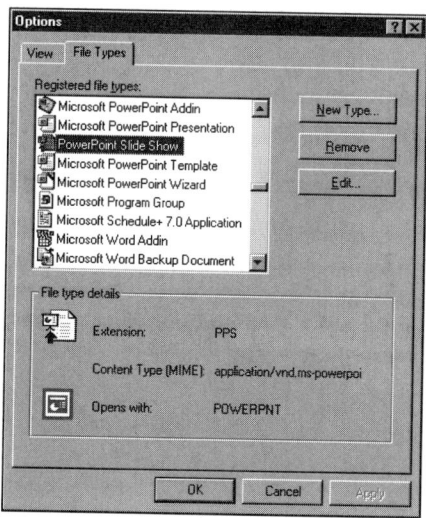

Figure 12-2: The File Types tab of the Options dialog box in Explorer

Here, scroll the list of Registered File Types until you get to the long section of those that start with *Microsoft*. Select one of the common types, such as Microsoft Word Document, and click Edit to bring up the dialog box shown in Figure 12-3. In the box at Description of Type, delete the word *Microsoft*. If you like, shorten the entry further, so long as you can understand it (Word Doc would probably do). Click OK to return to the Options dialog box, where you can repeat the procedure for as many types of files as your patience permits.

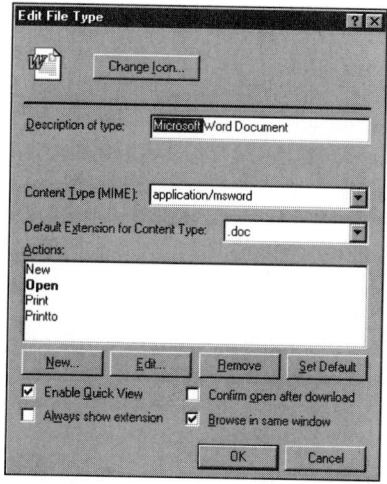

Figure 12-3: Edit file type descriptions in this dialog box.

The changes take effect in Details view the next time you use each Office application. Removing the "Microsoft" from Office document descriptions has another benefit: It's easier to pick out the different types in the Details list when they don't all start with the same word.

Sorting the file list

To sort the file list, click the arrow on the Views split button. Then choose Arrange Icons followed by the sort type you want (by Name, Type, Size, or Date).

Displaying files in subfolders in the Open dialog box

Normally, the Open dialog box shows you only the files in the current folder, the one displayed at Look In. To see those files *plus* all those in the current folder's subfolders, click the Tools menu, choose Find to display the Find dialog box, and check the box labeled Search Subfolders. Without making any other changes, click Find Now to return to the Open dialog box.

Protecting a document's contents with special file-opening options

Secret

You can open a disk file in several different ways in the Open dialog box. To select one of the alternatives, use the split button labeled Open at the lower right of the dialog box.

Clicking the arrow at the right of the button drops down the list of variations on the standard Open command. The commands you see depend on the type of file selected and the Office application, but can include:

- **Open.** The standard opening method, this opens the file under its current name and lets you edit it.
- **Open Read-Only.** Although you can edit the file, you can't save the changes using the original name (if you try to save the file you'll get a warning followed by the Save As dialog box).
- **Open as Copy.** Office first makes a copy of the file in the same folder, naming it "Copy of *original filename*," and then opens the copy for editing.
- **Open in Browser.** For HTML and other Web page files, you can choose to open the file in your browser rather than the Office application you started from.
- **Open in *application*.** Opens the file in the specified Office application, no matter which application created it.
- **Open Exclusive.** In Access, choosing this command opens the database for your exclusive use — other users can't open it even if they have access to it on the network.

- **Open Exclusive Read Only.** Opens an Access database for your exclusive use and as a read-only version. Unlike the other Office apps, Access won't allow you to make any changes to a read-only document.

You can access these same commands more quickly from the shortcut menu for one or more files.

Caution

Take note: A document opened as read-only in Office is only treated that way during the current use. Once you have closed it, you can open it again the regular way later (although you will get a reminder that you last opened it as read-only). The file's operating system read-only attribute is *not* set, so other programs can modify it as well.

Use these alternative file-opening methods when you want to be sure that the original file won't change. Open the file as read-only if you simply want to review it, or if you want to copy information from it to another document. If you plan to edit the document contents and save the changes, without disturbing the original document, open it as a copy.

Secret

To protect a file from modification by Office or by any other program, turn on the read-only attribute using My Computer or Explorer: Select the file, display its properties (Alt+Enter), and check the Read-Only box on the General tab. Although you can display the Properties dialog box from within an Office file–related dialog box such as Open or Save, the attribute choices are grayed out and inaccessible. If you want to be able to change attributes within Office, look for a freeware utility called Properties Plus (www.ne.jp/asahi/cool/kish), which lets you toggle attributes via an item on the file's shortcut menu.

The Tools menu

When you open the Tools menu, you get a little list of special commands and options. Figure 12-4 shows the version of this menu you get in the Open dialog box.

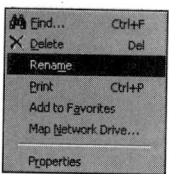

Figure 12-4: The Tools menu of the Open dialog box

Choices on the Tools menu in the Open dialog box

The items on the Tools menu are as follows:

- **Find.** Displays the Find dialog box, previously called Advanced Find. Here you can specify criteria for documents that Office should find and display in the main dialog box. See the section "Locating files" later in this chapter.

- **Delete.** Erases the selected file or files, of course. The Delete button on the main dialog box toolbar is faster.
- **Rename.** Performs the obvious function.
- **Print.** Prints the selected document without opening it (see Chapter 11).
- **Add to Favorites.** Adds a shortcut to the selected item (file or folder) to your Favorites folder.
- **Map Network Drive.** Lets you connect to a drive on your network. See Chapter 17.
- **Properties.** Displays the selected file's Properties dialog box. If you select more than one file, you only see the first file's properties. The keyboard shortcut to display the Properties dialog box is Alt+Enter.

Tools menu choices for the Save As dialog box

In the Save As dialog box, the Tools menu omits the Find and Print commands but adds a set of save-related choices. Depending on the application you're running, these may include:

- **Web Options.** This command displays the Web options dialog box, discussed in Chapter 14.
- **General Options.** In Word and Excel, choose this command to bring up a dialog box of save-related settings. Word offers the same Save options you can access in the Tools ⇨ Options dialog box.
- **Save Version.** In Word, this option lets you save the current state of the document along with other versions you may have saved previously in the same file. See Chapter 32 for details.
- **Embed TrueType fonts.** In PowerPoint, selecting this choice tells the program to include TrueType fonts used in your presentation in the document file. That way, you can distribute the presentation without worrying that the recipient might not have the necessary fonts.

Using the Favorites folder to access frequently used items

Favorites is a subfolder created automatically in your main Windows folder (on single-user PCs) or in your user profile folder (on systems that support multiple users). The Favorites folder serves as a kind of hyperspace jump gate, if you'll excuse the sci-fi metaphor, enabling you to navigate instantly to any location available to your system.

The idea is to fill up the Favorites folder with shortcuts to the drives, folders, and individual documents that you access most often. When the shortcuts are in place, a click on the Favorites button gets you to its folder, and another click on the shortcut and you're there.

Because Favorites is just a folder like any other, you can put shortcuts into it in the usual Windows ways using My Computer or Explorer. But by far the fastest way to place a shortcut in the Favorites folder is with the Open dialog box in any Office application. Navigate to the item the old-fashioned, impulse engine way (I know, I'm getting my TV shows mixed up) and then choose Tools ⇨ Add to Favorites. When you make your choice the deed gets done — a shortcut to the item will now be listed every time you display the Favorites folder. And the best way to do that, of course, is by clicking the big Favorites button.

Changing the My Documents and Favorites folders

Suppose you think that My Documents is a pretty dorky name and you want to keep your main document stash in a folder called Strange, Rare, and Peculiar. Well, you're free to do so — but you'll run into trouble in Office's Open and Save As dialog boxes. They don't provide a way to redirect the navigation button to your chosen folder. However, you can specify a folder of your own. The surest way to do so is by tinkering with the Windows registry. If and only if you know how to recover from a registry meltdown, run the Registry Editor — using File ⇨ Export to make a copy of the registry, please, before you change anything. Then search for the following registry branch:

```
[HKEY_CURRENT_USER\Software\
Microsoft\Windows\
CurrentVersion\Explorer\
User Shell Folders]
```

Within the User Shell Folders branch, identify the Personal key and replace the existing value with the correct path for your new documents folder. Close the Registry Editor and test the changes by opening an Office Open or Save As dialog box. You should see a button labeled Strange, Rare, and Peculiar (or whatever folder you selected) in place of the original My Documents button. Use the same basic technique to specify a different Favorites folder by changing the Favorites key in the same registry branch. In this case, the name of the button doesn't change in the Open and Save As dialog boxes.

Playing many favorites: Fast access to specific folders

If you store documents regularly in any of several different folders, you can save lots of time and dialog box–fiddling by writing little macros that display the Open or Save As dialog box open to a specific folder.

The example shown here is for Word's Open dialog box. In your version, substitute the full path of the target folder within the quotation marks on the line beginning with .Name. Be sure to include the final backslash! Substitute **wdDialogFileSaveAs** for the term in parentheses for a Save As macro.

```
Public Sub FolderOpenPuppyTales()
With Dialogs(wdDialogFileOpen)
    .Name = "E:\Puppy Tales\"
    .Show
End With
End Sub
```

Here's the comparable macro in Excel. (No, VBA isn't as consistent across the Office applications as Microsoft promised to make it.)

```
Public Sub FolderOpenBudgieBudgets()
Application.Dialogs(xlDialogOpen).Show ("D:\Budgie Budgets\")
End Sub
```

Use **xlDialogSaveAs** in the parentheses for the Save As dialog box.

Disk housekeeping with the Open and Save As dialog boxes

If you dislike leaving the safe haven of the Office environment, the Open and Save As dialog boxes give you a serviceable alternative to My Computer or Explorer for tidying up your disks and all their folders and files. In either dialog box you can:

- **Move or copy files.** Select the files and on the shortcut menu, choose Cut (for a move) or Copy. Then open the destination folder, display the shortcut menu (with no file selected), and choose Paste. Alternatively, if the destination folder's icon is visible in the file list, select it and choose Paste from its shortcut menu.

- **Rename files.** Select a file and press F2; or wait a second and then click again (don't double-click); or choose Rename from the shortcut menu.

- **Delete files.** Select the files and then press Del or choose Delete from the shortcut menu to move them to the Recycle bin, or press Shift+Del to rid yourself of them more permanently.

When Open is open, you can perform move, copy, and delete operations on more than one file at a time. That's not allowed in Save As, but the latter dialog box lets you create new folders. If you like the idea of managing your files within Office, you should also check out Outlook's special features for this purpose, described in Chapter 50.

Saving documents

Once you've saved an Office document for the first time in the Save As dialog box, further saves require only a quick Ctrl+S. Practice that key combination so frequently that it becomes an automatic finger twitch, and you'll never have to wail, "I just lost an hour's work!"

Saving documents in other formats

Whether you're working with a brand-new document or one that's been around the block a few too many times, you have the option of saving it in a format other than the standard, or *native*, one used by preference by its Office application. To change the format, choose File ⇨ Save As (of course, Save will work with a new, previously unsaved document). Then use the drop-down list at Files of Type to select an alternative format for the document. More information about file formats and conversions can be found in Chapter 10.

Saving documents with a custom extension

Secret

To save a document with a different extension from the default Office supplies for the chosen format, enclose the whole name in quotation marks. For example, to save a Word document called My Summer.Fun, you would type "My Summer.Fun" in the File Name field. If you just type the name without the quotes, Office appends the default extension to the name. In this example, you would end up with a file called My Summer.Fun.doc.

Setting Save options

Excel, Word, and PowerPoint offer various options for fine-tuning the way they save your documents. You can display these settings by choosing Options from the Save As dialog box, or in Word and PowerPoint, displaying Tools ⇨ Options and selecting the Save tab. Some available options include the following:

- **Allow Fast Saves.** Available in PowerPoint and Word, this setting speeds up the saving process, often dramatically, but makes your files bigger. When it's on, the application records at the end of the file the changes made to the document since the last save, without removing previously saved information. Eventually a limit is reached and the current contents of the document get saved in their entirety. Although it's generally best to leave this setting active, turn it off if you want to ensure the file is as compact as possible, perhaps to send it over a modem. This also allows the file to be read by text editors and viewers that can't translate the Office file formats.

- **Allow Background Saves.** Another speed-up option but only available in Word, this setting sends information to the disk in bits and pieces while you work instead of forcing you to wait until the entire file is saved. It's a little risky, because if the computer happens to crash while the background save is in progress, you may lose your work.

Crash protection

Several Save options specifically relate to protecting your work against human error or computer crashes. These are:

- **Always Create Backup.** Available in Word and Excel, this option renames the existing file first (using the .wbk extension in Word, .xlk in Excel) and then saves a new copy of the file. In Word, this setting applies to all documents, and is found on the Tools ⇨ Options dialog box; you can't do fast saves if this option is active, which makes sense, if you think about it. In Excel, you can turn it on or off for each document independently in the Save As dialog box. Go to the General Options choice on the Tools menu. An alternative backup strategy is to use a macro to force your application to make two copies of your file each time you save it. The results are different — you can't recover a previously saved version, but your current version is more secure.

- **Save AutoRecover Info.** Available only in Word and PowerPoint, this setting causes the application to automatically save the document's current contents at the interval you specify, placing them into a folder designated in the File Locations tab of the Tools ➪ Options dialog box (at least in the case of Word). If the computer quits on you unexpectedly, which it's bound to do from time to time, your application should automatically load the AutoRecover version of the document. See "Recovering from AutoRecover, and other tips on handling crashes" later in this chapter.

- **Read-Only Recommended.** If this box is checked, the file can't be saved under its current name. This is a weak form of security, but it's adequate when you and your coworkers know what you're doing. See also the discussion in "Protecting a document's contents with special file-opening options" earlier in this chapter.

Recovering from AutoRecover, and other tips on handling crashes

Caution

The AutoRecover feature can bail you out when your computer crashes, but it doesn't always work as you might hope. If you've trained yourself to save your documents frequently anyway, the AutoRecovered version of a document may actually be older than the one stored in the original file.

So don't replace the original file with the AutoRecover document until you've inspected both files to see which is really more current. Fortunately, using the Save command on an AutoRecovered document doesn't automatically wipe out the original file. Instead, choosing File ➪ Save brings up the Save As dialog box. If you want to replace the original file you must enter its name yourself at File Name, and you must then confirm the replacement in a warning dialog box.

Secret

When you restart your application after a crash, it may fail to load one or more of the AutoRecovered documents. If you're pretty sure they should be there, you can just open them yourself using the File ➪ Open dialog box. In the case of Word, you find them in the folder designated in the Tools ➪ Options dialog box (File Locations tab). PowerPoint AutoRecover files seem to be stored in the Temp folder (or whatever folder is designated on your system for temporary files), but this may change by the time the final version of Office is released.

Word AutoRecover documents are always named AutoRecovery save of *filename*. If you don't know which folder holds the files, you can use the search capabilities of the Open dialog box to find them. Set Look In to My Computer, enter **AutoRecovery*** at the File Name box, and then choose Find Now.

You only get one chance to manually recover these AutoRecover files — they are deleted when you quit the application.

Locating files

Often, Windows' long filenames tell you enough about your documents' contents that you can pick out the files you want to work with in the Open dialog box. But plenty of times arise when you need more help finding the right files. The document you want to open may have been stored in one of a jillion different folders, and the question is, "Which one?" This problem is compounded if you have more than one hard disk, and it gets really serious if you're accessing files on a network or over the Internet.

Besides, even if you know which folder to look in, you may have trouble picking out the correct files by name alone. You may remember that you once reported on last year's failed investment in an eggshell recycling project, burying the details somewhere below a minor sub-subheading in a document. When suddenly eggshells become a vital constituent in a premium clean-burning gasoline, searching for your write-up in a sea of documents with names such as "Quarterly report 3, Fall 1996" gets old in a hurry. Instead, tell Office to look for files containing the word *eggshell* and the right document appears in moments.

In the Open dialog box, the four boxes at the bottom covered in the next section are usually all you need to track down the files you need and show them in the file list. More complicated winnowing requires an advanced search, covered in "Constructing advanced searches" a bit later.

Specifying files in the Open and Save As dialog boxes

When you first use the Open or Save As dialog boxes, they are set to show you all documents in the current folder that belong to the Office application you're using. But with only a little effort you can filter the file list to display a more limited group of files.

Caution

Office 2000's new Open and Save As dialog boxes do away with options for finding files based on date, contents, or properties. I guess Microsoft thought these choices were too confusing, but their loss inconveniences us power user types. Anyway, you can still use advanced finding options described later in this section to use such criteria in your search for files.

Using the File Name box

In both the Open and Save As dialog boxes, the File Name box does double duty, depending on what you type in it:

- If you enter a complete filename at File Name, pressing Enter opens that file (in the Open dialog box) or saves the current document using that name (in Save As).

- If you type in a filename containing wildcards, or a disk path and then press Enter, the file list displays files matching your entry, opening the requested folder if you specified a new path.

Secret

Don't overlook this second function of the File Name box—it can save beaucoup time when you're trying to display files of a certain type or navigate to a particular folder. See the next section for a complete discussion of this trick.

Displaying groups of files using wildcards

The Open and Save As dialog boxes come with the obligatory drop-down lists for specifying file types (these lists are labeled Files of Type in the Open dialog box and Save as Type in the Save As dialog box). Although you can use these lists to filter the file list so that it shows only a particular kind of file, wildcards give you more flexibility. Besides, you can type them just as fast as you can pick an item from the list. Note that entries in the File Name box override the selection at Files of Type or Save as Type.

Wildcards in the File Name box work much as they do (no, not did) in DOS, only better. The * character represents any number of characters, whereas a ? represents any single character. For example, to display files that include the word Access at the beginning of the name, type **Access*** at File Name. To display all files of a given type, say, .prn files from an old copy of Lotus 1-2-3, type ***.prn**. You don't have to type the * to show filenames that contain a given bit of text. If you want to find files with *Office* anywhere in the name, just type **Office** (actually, **office** will do).

You can even combine two or more requests on the same line by separating them with a semicolon. To see PRN and NRP files only, type ***.prn;*.nrp**. To see all files whose names contain either the word *monitor* or the word *printer*, type **monitor; printer**.

Unfortunately, this technique can fail if you combine filename extensions listed in the Files of Type drop-down with unlisted extensions. In this situation, only the files with the listed extensions appear in the dialog box. Combining two or more unlisted file types works, as does combining two or more listed types.

Secret

Here's another little-known Amazing Fact: You can display files from two or more folders on completely separate paths. Type in each path, separating the entries with a semicolon. You might, for example, type **c:\consultations;e:\references**. Only the first folder named appears in the Look In field, but all the files from all the folders are there.

Navigating with the File Name box

If you're a decent typist, and if you know DOS conventions and your hard disk hierarchy, typing entries in the File Name box zooms you directly to your destination at another folder or drive. Just type the destination path, as in **C:\My Documents**. You don't have to enclose the path in quotation marks.

Secret

What's really cool about the File Name in the new Office file dialog boxes is that it completes your entry for you. Start to type a file or folder name, and it fills in the first matching item it finds. It manages this trick even if you begin by specifying a different disk, for example, by typing D:\.

With this improvement, keyboard navigation to a buried subfolder becomes truly practical, even if all the folders have long names. After you type the first character or three of the top-level folder, Office should find the right match. Press right arrow to move beyond the entry it supplies and start typing the subfolder at the next level down. Again, Office will find the match. Keep going like this, remembering to press right arrow after every match so that you don't erase the entry Office has supplied.

You can also use DOS-type special path characters and conventions to shorten your typing. Try the following:

To Move	Type
To the root folder of the current drive	Backslash
To the parent folder of the current folder	.. (two periods)
Up the folder hierarchy a specific number of levels	Two periods plus another period for each level you want to move (to move up to the third level above, type five periods)
To a subfolder in the current folder	The subfolder's name, followed by a backslash

You should definitely use this technique to switch to another drive. Instead of hunting for the drive in the Look In list, just type its letter name and a colon at File Name. When you press Enter, the active folder on the new drive opens in the dialog box (by active folder, I mean the one that Windows registered as the last one used). If you don't want to type any more, you can now use the file list or the Look In list to navigate to the right folder.

Secret

Using this technique you can toggle back and forth between folders on different drives in one step — without having to navigate to the destination folder each time as you would using the Look In list.

Constructing advanced searches

If you can't locate the files you need using the controls of the main Open dialog box, choose Tools ⇨ Find to display the Find dialog box, shown in Figure 12-5. For the uninitiated, this dialog box can be a bit daunting, but you can master it if you take it slowly.

The large area at the top of the Find dialog box contains the current list of file search criteria. You can't type entries directly into this area, so don't try. Instead, let Office construct them for you based on your selections in the lower part of the dialog box. Below this area on the right, the Delete button removes selected lines from the list, while the New Search button clears them all.

242 Part III: Secrets of Document Management

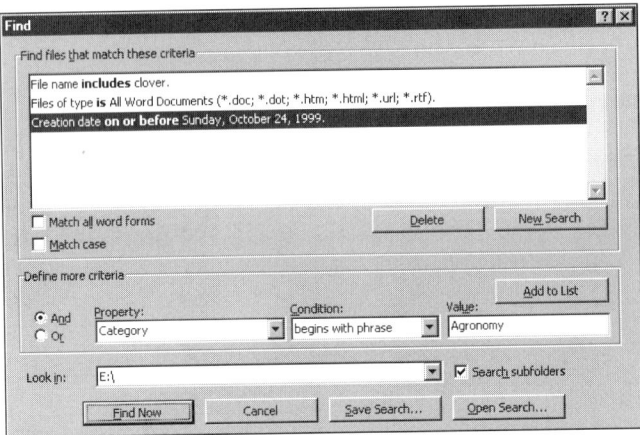

Figure 12-5: The Find dialog box, available from any Office Open dialog box

Defining search criteria

The heart of the dialog box is the area marked Define More Criteria. To create a new file search criterion, do the following:

1. At Property, select the type of information on which to base the search. The list here includes all the properties listed in the Properties dialog box (see "Tracking Documents via File Properties" later in this chapter), with various properties that don't appear there but are maintained automatically, plus other items that aren't strictly speaking document properties. These include "Files of Type" (which duplicates the box of the same name in the main Open dialog box) and "Text or Property" (which lets you search for document contents).

2. At Condition, select an entry from the list for the type of comparison Office will perform when deciding whether a file meets the search criteria. This list includes all sorts of comparisons, such as "includes words," "is (exactly)," "any number between," "last month," and so on. The list items available change depending on what type of property you've picked, but even so, some of the choices may not be applicable to the selected property — be careful to select one that's germane.

3. At Value, type in the word, number, date, or logical term (*yes* or *no*) against which Office should compare the chosen property's contents. To enter times or dates, use the abbreviations *m* for minutes, *h* for hours, *d* for days, and *w* for weeks. Specify months by typing the month's number (you can't specify years without entering the complete date). If the Condition specifies a range "anytime between" or "any number between," type the word *and* between the two items that define the range.

4. With the search criterion definition complete, select one of the radio buttons And or Or. Choose And if you want to display only files that meet

this criterion *and* the last one you entered, or choose Or if you want to see files that meet either this criterion or the previous one.

5. The boxes Match All Word Forms and Match Case just below the criteria list apply to all the criteria you enter. Check Match All Word Forms to display files whose text or properties contain other versions of the words in your search criteria, such as plurals or different verb conjugations or tenses. Check Match Case to locate files whose text or properties exactly match the capitalization in your search criteria. The two boxes are mutually exclusive—you can only check one at a time (they aren't displayed as radio buttons because you can uncheck both boxes).

You can go on adding new criteria till the cows come home.

Selecting a search location

Once your search criteria are defined, use the Look In box to select the path that Office will hunt through for matching files. Checking the Search Subfolders box makes Office search for documents in all subfolders in addition to the folder listed at Look In.

Displaying files containing specified text

It's easy to locate files containing a particular word or phrase: Just type the text for which you're searching at Text or Property in the Open dialog box. To list two or more words, enclose the whole phrase in quotation marks, as in "carrot and raisin salad." When you press Enter, the file list displays only those files containing the search text, either in the document itself, or anywhere in its properties (document properties are discussed in a later section).

Displaying files matching a chosen date

To locate files according to date, select Creation Date, Last Modified, or Last Printed in the Property list. With a date property active, the Condition list offers a slew of date-related choices covering every conceivable past date. If you want to see all files modified over the last ten weeks, choose "anytime between" in the Condition list and type in the limiting dates separated by the word *and*.

Saving, reusing, and renaming an advanced search

Once you've gone to the trouble to put together an advanced search, don't waste all that work—save the search criteria so you can use them again later. Choose Save Search and enter a descriptive name for the search (such as "Last year's Word, RTF, and PowerPoint documents on North Atlantic fisheries"). You can save a practically unlimited number of different searches.

To recall a previously saved search in the Find dialog box, choose Open Search and select it from the list in the resulting dialog box. You can rename or delete a search in this dialog box using the appropriate buttons. One sour note: Saved searches are only available in the application in which you created them.

Working with Find Fast

When you want to find information in a big book, you turn to the index and look up the page number where the topic is covered. The alternative, scanning through the pages one by one, is much too slow.

That's the concept behind Find Fast, a document-indexing utility included with Office. True, computers are uncomplaining, tireless, and much faster readers than people. But if you ask your PC to look for the word *needle* in a haystack of files, a word-by-word search can still take quite a while. If instead the computer can look up the term in an index, the search time will be much less.

Find Fast is installed automatically with the rest of Office, and it runs automatically whenever you start Windows after you turn it on. Every so often (every two hours by default), Find Fast sneaks around on your hard disk looking for new or changed files. When it finds one, it adds the new information to the index.

All this work pays off for you when you search for files in the Open dialog box of any Office application. Rather than rummaging through every file in the folder to see if it matches your search criteria, Office consults the Find Fast index, looking up the criteria there. The downside: Every time Find Fast begins indexing, your computer slows down considerably.

Maintaining Find Fast indexes

Because the indexing process is automatic, there's usually no need for you to deal with Find Fast at all. But there are several situations where you need to manage the indexes yourself:

- To index folders on other computers on the network
- To change the types of files included in the index
- To update an index prior to an important search
- To select optimal indexing options for your search needs

To open the Find Fast program, open the Control Panel and double-click its icon there. The rather nondescript Find Fast window appears, as shown in Figure 12-6.

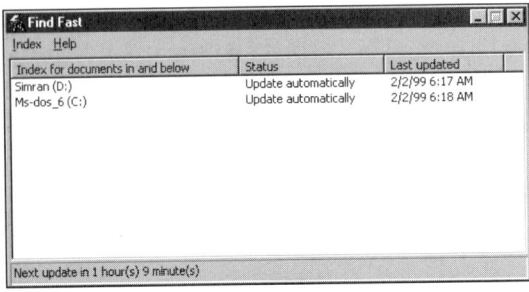

Figure 12-6: Find Fast's main window

Indexing new folders

To index a drive or folder that isn't already listed in the Find Fast window, choose Index ⇨ Create Index. Enter the drive or folder you want indexed in the resulting dialog box, selecting available shared network items. Be prepared for some prolonged hard disk activity when you create a new index, as the indexing process isn't a trivial task.

Choosing which file types and locations to index

By default, Find Fast indexes almost every type of document associated with Office, plus plain text (.txt), RTF, and HTML files. If you want to change the types of files included in the index, you must first delete the existing index (select it and choose Index ⇨ Delete Index). Then create a new index for the same disk or folder, choosing from the options available in the Of Type list.

So why change the file types in the index? One possibility: If your index files are too large and you usually only need to search for information in a particular type of Office document, you can limit the index to that document type.

Caution

Conversely, you can use the Find Fast index to locate information in non-Office documents by choosing to index All Files (*.*). In general, an index that covers all files will be really large and full of lots of useless junk, such as references to program code and the pixels in bitmap files. Because you can confine indexes to specific folders, you might think an all-files index would work for specific folders that you know contain documents consisting largely of text, such as WordPerfect documents. But believe me, other indexing utilities make better choices for indexing non-Office files.

As you see if you create a new index (see "Indexing new folders" earlier in this chapter), you can control which drive or folder an index covers, and whether or not the index includes subfolders. Find Fast works most efficiently if you let it create indexes for entire drives rather than for individual folders. However, if you do decide to change the types of files included, or if for some reason you want to exclude specific folders from an index, you can create new indexes for specific folders. Because each folder can only be represented in a single index, you must delete its existing index before you create the new one.

Updating an index

Although Find Fast reindexes your documents every couple of hours automatically, you can order an early update by choosing Index ⇨ Update Index. Do this if you want to be sure that the index is completely current before you conduct a critical search. Select the drive or folder you want updated at In and Below.

Interrupting indexing

Although indexing takes place in the background while you work with other applications, your computer slows down while it's in progress. If you notice the drag on performance, or if you realize you have specified the wrong parameters for the indexing operation, you can pause or stop the procedure.

Choose Index ⇨ Pause Indexing to temporarily interrupt all index creation and updating. This command is a toggle, so repeat it to restart Find Fast's normal operations. In any case, it turns itself on the next time you start your PC.

To stop a specific indexing task, select it in the main Find Fast window. Then choose Index ⇨ Cancel Selected Task. If you stop an index as or before it is created, Find Fast does the sensible thing and deletes the index (or never creates it in the first place). If you stop an index update, further updates are postponed until you restart the process, but the existing index remains intact.

Changing the automatic update interval for indexes

Adjusting how often Find Fast does its updates lets you balance your need for up-to-date indexes against the performance hit of the indexing process. Choose Index ⇨ Update Interval and enter whatever time suits you. Your entry applies to all Find Fast indexes.

Secret

If an up-to-date index is your highest priority, set the update interval to 0. Find Fast reindexes your files continuously (meaning as soon as it detects any changes).

Indexing phrases

If you frequently need to locate documents by searching for phrases (words with spaces between them) or words in proximity to one another (using the "includes near" search condition), consider optimizing your Find Fast indexes for such searches. I say consider, because such "optimized" indexes are much larger than the standard-type index — they can take up almost a third as much disk space as the documents themselves. If you decide in the affirmative, choose Index ⇨ Create Index and check the Speed Up Phrase Searching box.

Other search methods and utilities

Office's built-in finding capabilities are generally adequate, but it never hurts to know about other options. You can use Windows' own Find utility (Start ⇨ Find ⇨ Files or Folders) or the version that Outlook places on the same menu (Using Microsoft Outlook). Then there are text-indexing utilities that provide even more sophisticated searching choices than Find Fast does. And Part IV discusses finding documents on the Web or an intranet with Web Find Fast.

Tracking Documents via File Properties

Part and parcel of every Office document is an attached set of *properties*, named items that hold identifying information about the document. In any Office application, to display or edit the *active* document's properties, choose File ⇨ Properties. To work with *any* document's properties sheet, select the document in the Open or Save As dialog box and choose Properties from its shortcut menu.

Either way, you'll get the dialog box shown in Figure 12-7. You can also see this dialog box by displaying the file's properties in My Computer or Explorer, but you can't edit the Office-specific properties there.

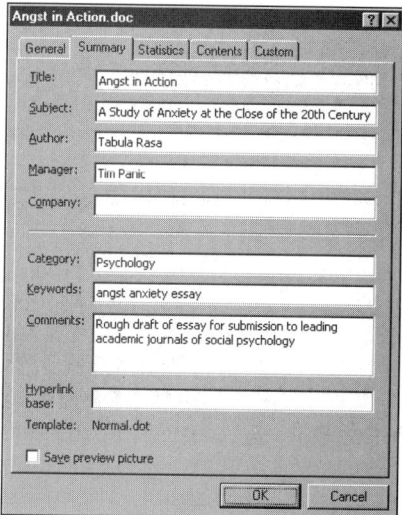

Figure 12-7: The Properties dialog box

Office maintains a set of *automatically updated* properties containing current data on such items as the number of words and characters the file contains, and the dates it was created, last used, and last printed. You can inspect these in the Statistics tab of the properties dialog box. The filename and path also fall into the automatic category, of course, and are displayed on the General tab.

Other properties can be edited to hold whatever information you think is appropriate. Of this type, Office implements more than a few *preset* properties. It records default information into some of these automatically, such as the title and author's name, while in other cases it leaves the properties blank until you fill them in. An example is the Keywords property, which lets you specify a series of words related to the document's contents or function. You can also create any number of *custom* properties, filling them with information directly, or linking them to an item in a document, for example, via a Word bookmark.

Once you've entered the relevant information, you can search for documents based on their properties. That topic is covered in the "Locating files" section earlier in the chapter.

Tips on using and setting properties

To improve the odds that you'll actually fill in the Properties dialog box, you can have Office applications display it automatically when you first save each document. This is a setting on the Tools ⇨ Options dialog box. Open the dialog box and switch to the Save tab (in Word or PowerPoint) or the General tab (in Excel). Check the box labeled Prompt for Document (or workbook, or file) Properties.

The Contents tab is filled in for you, sometimes with useful information. In Excel, it displays the names of macro sheets in Microsoft Excel. In Word, it shows you all the headings in the document (if you've used the standard heading styles) — but only if you have also checked the Save Preview Picture box on the Summary tab.

In Word, the AutoSummarize command — which I don't recommend — fills in the keywords and comments properties automatically. If you use AutoSummarize against my advice but don't want it to replace your own keywords and comments, choose Tools ⇨ AutoSummarize and when the process is complete, clear the Update document statistics box.

Unlike the other properties, the preset property Hyperlink Base (on the General tab of the Properties dialog box) actually does something. Enter here the base address for relative hyperlinks in the document. See Chapter 14 for information on relative versus fixed hyperlinks.

Creating custom properties

If the preset properties supplied by Office aren't enough to satisfy your need to pigeonhole things, just create some more properties of your own. In the Properties dialog box, select the Custom tab shown in Figure 12-8.

Microsoft has already thought of many of the custom properties you might want to use, and these semicustom properties are available in the list at Name. If you don't find a suitable name in the list, type in your own. Then select a Type for the new property (text, date, number, or yes or no). After entering the information you want assigned to the property at Value, choose Add to store the custom property with the information.

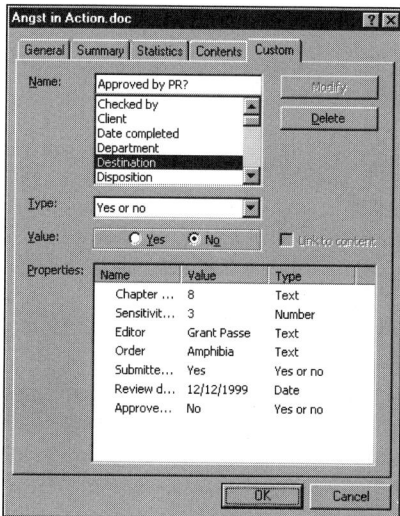

Figure 12-8: The Custom tab of the Properties dialog box

To link a custom property to content in an Office document, start by defining the content in the document itself. In Word, bookmark the text that should be inserted into the property. In Excel, name a cell or cell range. In PowerPoint, just select whatever text you want assigned to the property.

With the content ready, create a custom property as described previously. Instead of typing in a Value, however, check the Link to Content box. If your document contains more than one linkable item (bookmark or named range), choose the correct name from the list at Source. The new property appears with its current value in the list that follows with a little link icon beside it. (See "Bookmarking text in PowerPoint" in Chapter 48 for a tip on using a custom property as a bookmark in PowerPoint.)

From now on, the property automatically contains the current document content referred to by the link. However, if you delete the linked bookmark (in Word), named range (in Excel), or text (in PowerPoint), the property retains its last value, and this can't be changed. The Properties list shows it with a broken link icon.

Creating Compound Documents with Office Binder

Sophisticated documents such as business reports or scientific papers often require the combined capabilities of several Office applications. The text for the bulk of the document takes shape in Word, of course, but you need Excel to lay out the raw numbers and to summarize them in charts. If you're going to present your work to a group, the complete document may include a slide show created in PowerPoint.

With Office, you have two main routes to producing compound documents of this type. You can build the main document in one of the applications, usually Word, placing in it links to documents from the other applications. That approach is covered Chapter 10.

The alternative? You can combine all the individual documents into one virtual compound document using Office Binder. And what is a Binder document called? A binder, of course.

Binder gives you a central control station for these binders, from which you can edit each component document using the full power of the originating application. When you're in a Word portion of a binder, Word's menus, toolbars, keyboard shortcuts, and macros are all at your fingertips. When you switch to an Excel portion, Binder takes down the Word scaffolding and puts up Excel's. Binder's window is shown in Figure 12-9.

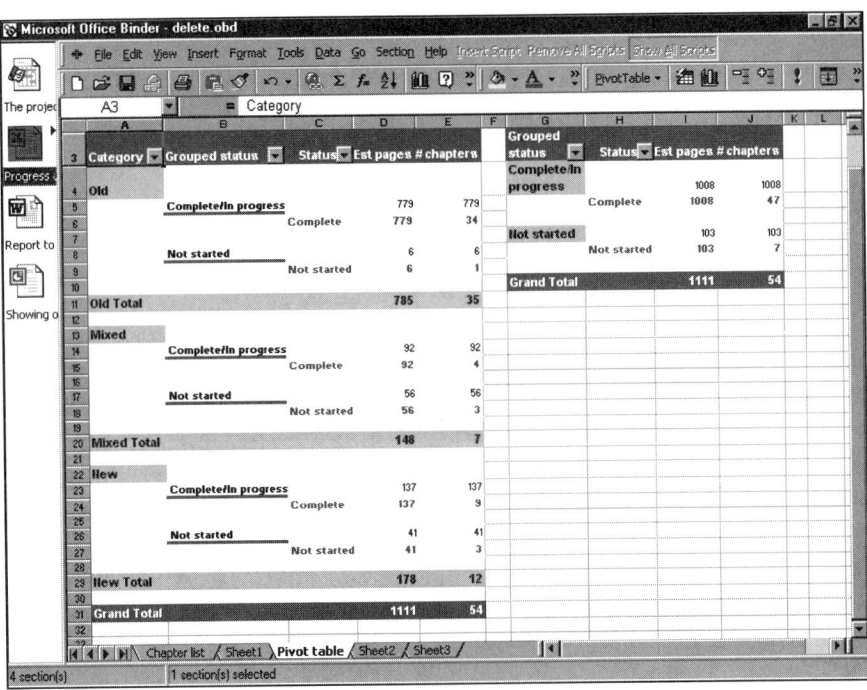

Figure 12-9: The Binder window showing an Excel worksheet as the active document

As you can see, the toolbars are those of Excel. The menu combines Excel's menu with Binder's own Go and Section menus. The Binder window is divided into left and right panes. The left pane shows icons for each component document in the current binder, while the right pane shows the document that's currently active. The status bar of the document's application isn't visible in the Binder—Binder has its own status bar, which you can turn on or off via the File ⇨ Binder Options dialog box.

Binder is an effective tool, but it still has some significant limitations. You can create a single header and footer for an entire binder document. In a similar vein, Binder has its own Print Preview command—you can see how the whole binder will look on paper, moving smoothly from one component document to the next. Binder is also fully network-savvy—you can open and save binders in any accessible folder on the network.

But don't expect too much of Binder. Word, Excel, and PowerPoint documents can be incorporated into a binder, and so can Microsoft Project documents, but not Access reports. Also, the headers and footers and Print Preview features apply only to Word and Excel documents. Still, because most composite documents are built in Excel and Word, Binder will often do the trick.

Running Binder

You can start Binder in all the ways you use to work with other Office applications:

- Via the Start menu or by double-clicking a shortcut to Binder in any My Computer or Explorer window.
- By starting a new binder document via the Start a New Document button on the Office toolbar of the Shortcut Bar
- By opening an existing binder document (for example, from the Documents menu on the Start menu, or by clicking the Open a Document button on the Shortcut Bar.

Creating a binder

Like other Office apps, Binder opens a new, blank document when you start it without specifying another document, using the first technique described. To create this sort of empty-vessel binder via the Shortcut Bar method, select the General tab from the New dialog box and open the Blank Binder template. Likewise, if Binder is already running, choose File ⇨ New Binder, select the General tab, and choose Blank Binder.

You can also base a new binder on a template. Binder templates are simply collections of template-like documents from the allowed Office applications arranged in a particular order. To start with a template, click the Start a New Document button on the Office toolbar of the Shortcut Bar, or if Binder is already running, choose File ⇨ New Binder. Either way, choose a template other than Blank Binder. Depending on how Office was installed, you may find a few prefab Binder templates in the Binders tab.

Adding documents to a binder

Each component document in a binder is called a *section* (that's why Binder has a Section menu). There are three ways to add sections to a binder:

- **Add existing documents.** Choose Section ⇨ Add from File and open the files you want to add. Drag-and-drop works too: From My Computer, Explorer, or the desktop, drag the document icon to the left pane.

- **Add a *portion* of an existing document.** Select a portion of a document and drag that to the binder, dropping it in the left pane. Or drag a document scrap from the desktop to that same area. Dragging and dropping between applications and document scraps are both covered in Chapter 10.

- **Create the section from scratch within Binder.** Choosing Section ⇨ Add displays what amounts to a New dialog box, enabling you to select a template for the new document. However, you only have access to a few template folders, namely the main Templates folder and only those beneath it containing Word templates. This severely limits your freedom to create new Excel and PowerPoint documents in the binder.

Caution

Be sure to remember that documents that you add to a binder from existing files are *copies* of the original documents. Binder preserves no link between the original document and the binder section based on it. In other words, when you edit the original document in its own application, the changes you make *don't* appear in the binder. The converse is also true.

Working with documents in a binder

To activate a specific section (document) in a binder, just click its icon in the left pane of the Binder window. You can also choose Next Section or Previous Section from the Section menu to move through the sections one by one.

Once the correct section appears, you can devote the whole screen to it by clicking the Show/Hide Left Pane button at the top far left of the menu bar. The button, whose image is a two-headed arrow, is located where the document icon would be if you were working in the underlying Office application. If you can't see the button, see "Setting Binder options" later in this chapter.

You can now use the full power of the underlying application to work on the section. All the toolbars, macros, and keyboard shortcuts that would normally be available are at your disposal.

However, the menu bar is a little different from the one that goes with that section's application. The Binder's Go and Section menus are added to the menu bar, while the Help menu is that of the underlying application, with the Binder Help submenu tacked on at the bottom.

Some of the most important changes are in the File menu. As you can see in Figure 12-10, the items on it are Binder commands, not Word, Excel, or PowerPoint commands, and they apply to all the documents in the current binder. When you choose File ⇨ Save, for example, you're saving the entire Binder.

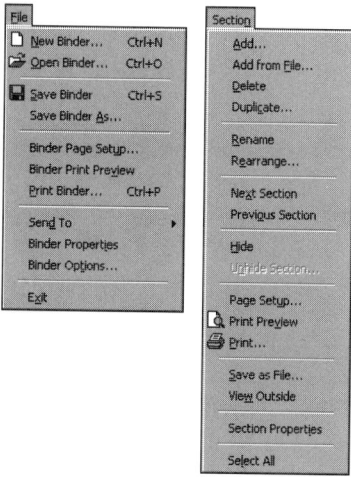

Figure 12-10: Binder's File and Section menus

The Section menu, also shown in Figure 12-10, is where you find the commands from the File menu of the underlying application, those available in Binder, anyway (these include Print, Print Preview, Page Setup, and Section Properties). The remaining Section menu commands have to do specifically with Binder. All commands on the Section menu apply only to the active section.

A few commands available in a document's originating application can't be accessed in Binder. If you run into one of these, use the Section ⇨ View Outside command to edit the document in the real application, not the slightly altered version you get within Binder. To return to Binder, choose File ⇨ Update (which replaces the Save command on the File menu) and then File ⇨ Close & Return to Binder. A couple of Excel commands, Share Workbook and Track Changes, won't work even with this tactic.

The Binder's Go menu, for navigating the Internet, your organization's intranet, or hyperlinked documents, duplicates those found in the other Office applications. See Chapter 6 for details on the Go menu.

Selecting sections

Selecting a single binder section displays it in the Binder window, where you can edit it. It's sometimes also useful to select two or more sections, such as when you want to print or move only those sections.

Working in the left pane, you use the standard Windows mouse-and-keyboard conventions to select sections. To select a single section, just click it. To select adjacent sections, hold down Shift while you click them in turn. To select sections at random, hold down Ctrl instead. You can select the entire binder with all its sections by choosing Section ⇨ Select All.

Copying and reordering sections within a binder

To add an exact copy of the current section to your binder, choose Section ⇨ Duplicate. Use the Insert After box that appears to specify where Binder should insert the new copy.

You get two ways to rearrange sections within a binder: via a dialog box or with the mouse. I recommend the mouse method. With the left pane visible, just drag the section icons where you want them. You can instead choose Section ⇨ Rearrange and then use the Move Up and Move Down buttons to relocate each selected section.

Hiding sections

You can hide sections that you don't want to see or print if you decide to keep them around to hold supplemental information or maybe for sentimental value. To hide the active section, choose Section ⇨ Hide. To show a hidden section, choose Section ⇨ Unhide Section and select the section to be revived from the list that appears.

Moving sections to another binder

Moving one or more sections from one binder to another requires only a little drag-and-drop action. The key is to situate the two Binder windows so that the left panes are visible in each. Then all you have to do is select the sections and drag them out. Standard left-dragging moves the section, removing it from its previous binder. If you right-drag, you get a little menu asking whether you want to move or copy the section to the destination.

Unbinding sections

You can also move sections from the confines of a binder out into the sunshine of their own independent existence. Again, just drag the sections you want to release from the left pane, this time to a suitable drag-and-drop destination such as Explorer, My Computer, or the Desktop.

If you want to save a copy of the current section as an independent document, leaving the version in the binder intact, choose Section ⇨ Save As File. You can also make independent copies of all sections in one swell foop, but you have to do it outside of Binder. Locate the binder file in question in My Computer or Explorer, or in an Office Open or Save As dialog box. When you choose Unbind from its shortcut menu all its sections are copied into separate documents in the same folder (the binder itself is unaffected).

Saving a binder

When you save a binder, the contents of all component sections are stored in a single binder file on your disk. This includes any sections you added to the binder from existing files — the original files are left intact, and any changes you've since made are incorporated into the binder file.

To save the binder as a template so that you can reuse its structure and content as the starting point for other binders, just select Binder Templates at Save as Type in the File ⇨ Save Binder As dialog box. Be sure to save the template to the folder in which you store Office templates, or one of its subfolders.

Printing a binder

You can print an entire binder document, any combination of its sections, or a single section. Printing a single section individually is the only way you can control which specific pages get printed. You can choose from the following:

- To print the entire binder, choose File ⇨ Print Binder. In the Print Binder dialog box leave the All Visible Sections button selected. As this option indicates, Binder only prints *visible* sections — hidden sections are ignored.

- To print selected sections, start by selecting them in the left pane of the Binder window. Then choose File ⇨ Print Binder and select the Section(s) selected in left pane button. You can make this the default by choosing File ⇨ Binder Page Setup, selecting the Print Settings tab, and choosing the Section(s) selected in left pane button (see "Setting Binder options," later in this chapter).

- To print a single section, switch to that section and then choose Section ⇨ Print. You see the standard Print dialog box for the application of that section.

The Start Numbering At box isn't too useful if you restart numbering for each section: It applies to every section in the binder. It's rare you'll want to start every section on Page 4.

Creating binder headers and footers

One of the most compelling reasons to use a binder instead of preparing each document separately is that you can set up and print a header and a footer that apply across all sections. Binder comes with a whole bunch of prefab headers and footers (that is, header and footer text) ideal for draft printouts. You can also enter your own custom headers and footers. At print time, you get to decide whether page numbering should restart with each section or be continuous throughout the binder.

Caution

Before you get too excited about Binder headers and footers, let me clue you in to their weaknesses. In essence, these are Excel's headers and footers, not the far more flexible ones in Word. You can't use pictures or text boxes in Binder headers and footers.

Adding a header and footer to the binder

To create binder-wide headers and footers:

1. Choose File ⇨ Binder Page Setup and select the Header/Footer tab.

2. Decide whether the header and footer will apply to the entire binder or just to selected sections via the radio buttons at the top of the dialog box. If you select Only Sections Selected Below, check the boxes for the sections you want to include the header and footer.

3. Okay, now you're ready to create the header and footer. To select prefab header or footer text, choose it from the drop-down lists at Header and Footer. The chosen text appears in the box below the list, formatted as it will look in the printed document.

4. To customize the header or footer, click Custom to display the dialog box shown in Figure 12-11, with separate boxes for left-, center-, and right-justified text. If you've already selected prefab text, it will appear in the appropriate box(es). You can now type in new text, edit existing text, or insert fields for date, time, and so forth using the buttons at the top left. The button at the far left labeled with an A lets you change the font of selected text. Because pressing Enter closes the box, you can start a new line of text by pressing Ctrl+Enter.

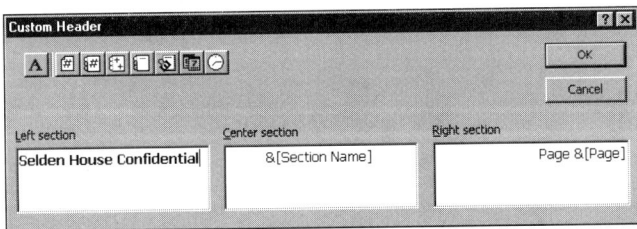

Figure 12-11: Use this window to create custom binder headers and footers.

Creating separate headers and footers for each section

Any given section can have its own header and footer, independent of the binder's. Here's how this works: When you specify a binder's header or footer, Binder transfers the header or footer information to the header or footer within each section. Once that information is in place, you can edit it on a section-by-section basis, using the header and footer commands for each section's application. In Word, you can create separate headers or footers for odd and even pages, or attach graphics or text boxes to the header or footer (use the View ⇨ Header and Footer command). If the section is an Excel document, choose Section ⇨ Page Setup in Binder and select the Header/Footer tab.

When you edit an individual section's header or footer, Binder deselects that section in the Header/Footer tab of the File ⇨ Page Setup dialog box. From now on, changes you make to the binder's header or footer won't affect the header or footer in that section (when you work with a Microsoft Project section, you must deselect the section yourself in the dialog box). Likewise, it's safe to add documents containing their own headers or footers to a binder that has a header or footer already. To replace a section's header or footer with the binder's, go back to the File ⇨ Binder Page Setup dialog box and apply the binder header and footer to the section.

Caution

Be careful not to apply a binder header and footer to a section that has its own unless you're sure you want to replace the existing header and footer. Once you've connected the binder header and footer to the section, the section's independent versions are replaced. You can't restore them via the Binder Page Setup dialog box. Trusty Undo will bring them back, but you'll lose any other changes to the document made since the binder header and footer were applied.

Setting Binder options

Unlike other Office applications, Binder places its Options on the File menu. Choose File ⇨ Binder Options to display the dialog box shown in Figure 12-12.

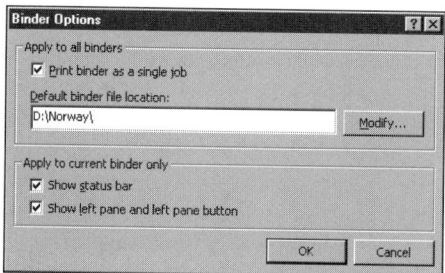

Figure 12-12: The Binder Options dialog box

Here, you can change the default location for binder documents, decide whether to display the Binder status bar, display or hide the left Binder pane and its button, and specify whether the entire binder prints in one pass or as separate jobs. Select the latter option if your printer gags when you ask it to print an entire binder.

Other options affect printing by setting defaults for settings on the Print Binder dialog. These are found on the Print Settings tab of the File ⇨ Binder Page Setup dialog box. These include a pair of radio buttons for deciding whether to print all the visible, unhidden sections or just those currently selected; and another pair governing whether page numbering restarts with each section or is continuous throughout the binder.

Conclusion

Office has powerful, flexible tools for creating, finding, and cataloging your documents, and for combining documents created in different applications into complete works. If you want to make your long days with Office really productive, start by learning and applying the deep Office knowledge presented in this chapter.

Chapter 13

Document Integrity and Security

In This Chapter

- Maintaining consistent documents with Office templates
- Synchronizing documents between desktop and laptop
- Protecting documents with passwords and encryption within Office
- Securing your documents and e-mail messages with third-party privacy software

This chapter serves as a shoebox to hold several important miscellaneous topics related to ensuring the consistency, contemporaneousness, and confidentiality of your documents, as well as the confidence you can place in their contents. I can see I'm going to run into conflicts with my editor, so I'll get right to the particulars.

Using Templates to Ensure Consistent Documents

In every Office application, *templates* help you enforce a consistency in the appearance, layout, and content of your documents. For example, a Word template specifies page layout and text formatting settings, along with stock text and graphics such as headers or footers that you want to appear in all documents of that type. A document or other item based on a template automatically takes on all the characteristics of the template, although you can modify the document to taste.

In general, you specify a template when you first create a new document, although you can change templates in Word and Access. In addition to dictating document layout and contents, templates in Word, Excel, and PowerPoint can store macros and, in Excel, custom toolbars.

Quick facts on Office templates

Table 13-1 summarizes key facts about templates in the various Office applications. See the Word, Excel, and PowerPoint sections for more detail on their templates.

Table 13-1 A Summary of Office Templates

Application	Template Extension	Default Name Template	Where Stored	Contents Stored in Template
Word	.dot	`Normal.dot`	`Normal.dot` and other standard templates: \Application data\Microsoft\Templates; - Global templates: \Application \Microsoft\Word \Startup	Page setup options, boilerplate text and graphics, paragraph and character styles, macros, AutoText entries, custom toolbars, menus, and shortcut keys
Excel	.xlt	`Book.xlt` (default for new workbooks) `Sheet.xlt` (default for new sheets inserted with the Insert ⇨ Worksheet command) **Note:** These templates aren't required, but if present, new workbooks and worksheets are based on them.	Default templates: \Application Data \Microsoft\Excel \XLStart (`Book.xlt` and `Sheet.xlt` must not contain - macros or they won't work as default templates); Other templates: \Application Data \Microsoft \Templates folder	Protected or hidden portions; boilerplate text, numeric data, formulas, and graphics, macros, custom toolbars, shortcut keys, and hyperlinks. In a workbook template, the number and type of sheets and calculation and window options
Outlook	.oft extension	(Not applicable)	Templates stored as individual files: \Application Data \Microsoft\Templates. Templates can also be stored in Outlook folders and in library files (see Chapter 50).	Form design and content, including fields and their layout, color scheme and other formatting, plus any information saved with the item (for example, the content of the Subject field)

Chapter 13: Document Integrity and Security

Appli-cation	Template Extension	Default Name Template	Where Stored	Contents Stored in Template
Power-Point	.pot	Blank Presentation.pot This template isn't required, but if present, new presentations are based on it. It doesn't have to be blank.	\Application Data \Microsoft\Templates; Design templates: \Templates \Presentation Designs folder in the main Office folder; Content templates for AutoContent wizard: \Templates\1033 in Office's main folder (for English-language content)	Color schemes, font selections, slide and title masters, as well as any included individual slides with their content and format
Access	n/a (not a separate file)	Normal (default name of the form and report templates, not their filenames)	In the Access workgroup information file (System.mdw), which is located in the \Office folder in Office's main folder	Settings for forms and reports, including default property settings and the number and layout of the sections they contain. Use the Forms/Reports tab of the Tools ⇨ Options dialog box to specify a form or report in the database as a template for new objects or the same type.
Binder	.obt	n/a (New Binder choice on the New dialog box does not represent a template)	\Application Data \Microsoft \Templates	The documents constituting the sections of the binder, with all their contents.

Note: Unless otherwise specified, folders referred to in the Where Stored column are located in the main Windows folder (on single-user systems) or in your user profile folder (on systems that support multiple users).

What makes a template a template

Secret

Although template files are usually identified by the special extensions listed in Table 13-1, what actually distinguishes a template is simply *where* it is stored. You can convert any Excel, PowerPoint, or Word document file into a template by placing a copy of the document—or even just a shortcut to it—in the Templates folder, or in one of its subfolders. No special extension is required.

Using templates on a network

Extending the preceding Secret is one way to solve the problem of sharing templates on a network, without constantly having to worry about whether each user has the most recent version. Place shared templates in any folder that is accessible to everyone on the network. Each user should then place a shortcut to that folder, or to any of the individual template files, in the Templates folder on his or her own computer. Whoever is responsible for the templates can modify them individually, or add or delete templates to the folder, and these changes will show up in every user's copy of Office via the shortcuts.

Another means to the same end is to define the shared folder as your workgroup templates location. If a workgroup templates folder is specified, Office programs look there for templates as well as in the regular user Templates folder. You can do this on the Settings tab in the Shortcut bar's Customize dialog box (see Chapter 2), or via the File Locations tab in Word's Tools ➪ Options dialog box.

You don't have to be on a network to define a workgroup templates folder. As an individual user, if for some reason you want to keep templates in two separate places, you can specify any folder on your system as the workgroup templates location.

Keeping Shared Documents Up to Date

Whenever the same document gets used on two or more different computers, making sure that each computer always has the most current version becomes a real chore. Maybe you shuttle your work between your home PC, an office computer, and a laptop. Or maybe you share files with someone else who isn't on your network. In either scenario, you should take advantage of a utility designed to handle all the file housekeeping chores for you, ensuring that you always work with the most up-to-date version of the document.

Using Briefcase

One obvious option is the Briefcase utility that comes with Windows. Briefcase is a sophisticated tool that synchronizes the files on your hard disk with copies stored on another computer over network or direct cable connections, or via floppy disk or other removable intermediaries.

To synchronize files with Briefcase, you must first copy the files you want to keep up to date into a special briefcase folder (you can create as many of these briefcases as you need). Note that I said *copy* the files, not move them. Your original document files stay put, so you don't have to change the way you've organized them, or learn new folder locations.

But this is a weakness as well as a strength. It means you must set aside double the disk space for every file you place in a briefcase. And it just makes things complicated, especially if you don't use Briefcase all the time.

Anyway, once you set up a briefcase, you use it as a way station for the files you plan to work with on other computers:

1. Start by copying the whole briefcase to a floppy disk (or disks, as necessary).

2. Take the floppy to the second computer and copy the briefcase to that computer's hard disk.

3. There, leaving the files inside the briefcase, edit them as you like. In the meantime, you can also edit the files on the first computer.

4. Reverse the process: Copy the briefcase on the second computer back to the floppy, and then copy the briefcase from the floppy back to the first computer.

5. Now let the Briefcase utility do its magic. Open the original briefcase folder on the first computer and choose Briefcase ➪ Update All. Briefcase locates the newest version of each document, whether it's in the briefcase or in the original folder. It copies that version to the other location, replacing the older version there. If both versions have been changed since the file was first placed in the briefcase, nothing happens, and you get an appropriate message (see Figure 13-1).

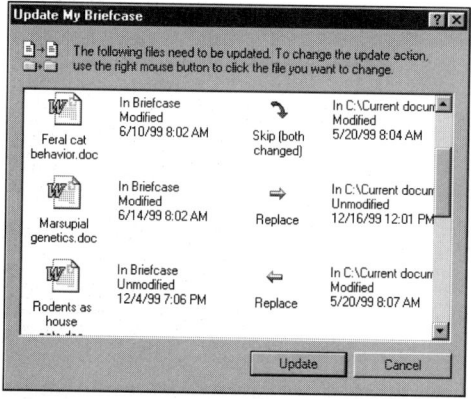

Figure 13-1: Briefcase reports on the status of the files in the briefcase folder before the update.

Other file-synchronizing utilities

Briefcase is an effective tool, and it's hard to quarrel with the price. Still, it does have drawbacks. In addition to eating up disk space on the home base computer, it works only with Windows 95 and NT 4.0, not with earlier versions.

CD

Alternatives to briefcase include LapLink, a comprehensive file transfer program (Traveling Software, www.travsoft.com) and various shareware utilities. You can find an evaluation copy of one of these, Second Copy, on the CD-ROM that accompanies this book (see Figure 13-2). Second Copy dispenses with a separate folder for the files it tracks, simply comparing and synchronizing files located in two folders. These synchronizing features are actually icing on the cake — the program is primarily marketed as an all-purpose automated backup utility.

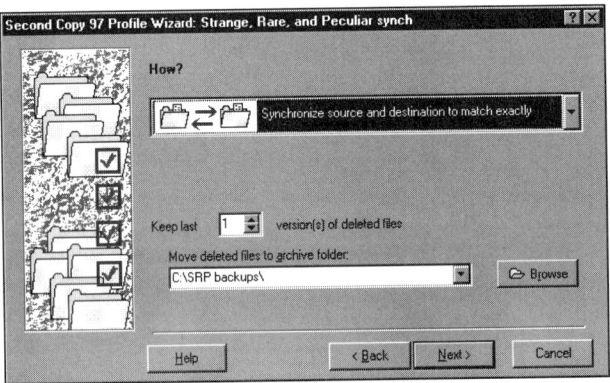

Figure 13-2: Using Second Copy

There Ain't No Way to Hide Those Prying Eyes

If you're singing the refrain in this heading to somebody with access to your computer, this section is for you. Now that everybody has a portable computer, is on a network, or both, "personal computing" no longer means "private computing." If your laptop gets lost or stolen, or if your network's security system is less than impenetrable, your sensitive personal or business data may fall into the wrong hands.

Office itself has simple features that will keep novice users from opening or modifying your files without your permission. If your organization uses Microsoft Exchange Server for e-mail, Outlook lets you protect messages sent to others in the group. But to keep out thieves and determined snoops, and to secure all of your e-mail, you need stronger security measures in the form of special software designed for that purpose.

Office security

Details, details. While all Office applications (except PowerPoint) provide basic password protection for their files, each goes about it in a slightly different way. One consistent feature is that in Office, passwords are case-sensitive. They must be typed exactly as originally entered.

Password protection has been improved in Office 2000. Now, passwords are a good way to protect your files from unauthorized modification (with the caveat that a malevolent intruder can always delete a file altogether) and they also keep information hidden from spies. When you protect a file with a password, Office 2000 now encrypts it, scrambling its contents to make it completely unreadable to those without the password.

Password-protecting Word documents

Assign password protection to Word documents with the Save tab on the Tools ➪ Options dialog box. To require a password for any access to the document, enter a password at Password to Open. Once this type of password is assigned, a user entering the correct password can open and read the document but can't save it under the current name, so it can't be modified (the File ➪ Save As command works, however). To allow only authorized users to save changes to a document, enter a password at Password to Modify.

Security in Excel

Excel lets you password-protect entire workbook files or selected portions of their contents.

Password-protecting Excel workbooks

Set a password for an Excel workbook by saving the file. In the File ➪ Save As dialog box, choose Tools ➪ General Options. You see a small dialog box in which you can enter two kinds of passwords:

- If it's OK for people to open the workbook and view its contents, but you don't want just anyone to make changes, type a password at Password to Modify.

- If you want to prevent unauthorized users from opening the workbook in the first place, type a password at Password to Open.

Controlling modifications to Excel data

Excel gives you precise password control over which elements in worksheets or workbooks other people can view or modify. Use the options on the Tools ➪ Protection submenu for this purpose:

- For a single worksheet, you can protect its contents, objects, and scenarios, in any combination. With the contents protected, for example, a user without the password can't change the cell entries except for those cells that you specifically unlocked prior to protecting the sheet. Hidden formulas, rows, and columns can't be unhidden.

- Once you password-protect a workbook, the password is required in order to see hidden worksheets, or to change the worksheets in any way, including moving, deleting, hiding, renaming, or adding new ones. You can make recording macros off-limits, and you can even prevent users from moving, resizing, or closing workbook windows.

- To prevent changes to the sharing settings of a shared workbook, use the Tools ⇨ Protection ⇨ Protect and Share Workbook dialog box. Check the box at the top and then assign a password so that nobody else can alter this setting without your permission.

No passwords in binders

To add a password-protected document to a binder, you must enter the password at the relevant prompt. Once the document enters the binder, however, its password protection is removed. And believe it or not, you can't password-protect binders.

Password-protecting Access databases

Access provides two kinds of passwords, one restricting the opening of a database, the other preventing access by unauthorized users, even when the database is already open.

Setting up a database password

To require a password each time a database is opened, set up a *database password*. Start with the closed database file (all users must close it). In the File ⇨ Open Database dialog box, click the part of the Open button on the right with the arrow to drop down a short menu. Here, choose the Open Exclusive box (which prevents anyone else from opening it while you're using it). Then click the main part of the Open button to retrieve the database. Once the database is open, choose Tools ⇨ Security ⇨ Set Database Password and type your password.

Setting up user passwords

A database password will prevent unauthorized users from opening the database in the first place, but once it's open, anyone with network access can use it freely. You need to set up a *security account password* for each user to prevent someone else from logging in under that user's name, and to define exactly what each user can and can't do with the database.

To set up security account passwords, begin by defining a password for the default user account, called Admin. (Until you define this password, Access doesn't require a login procedure, and anyone can open and modify the database.) Then go on to define additional passwords for other authorized users.

In brief, here's how you define a security account password: Start Access from the workgroup containing the user account for which you're creating the password, logging in with the correct user name. After opening the database, choose Tools ⇨ Security ⇨ User and Group Accounts. Enter the new password on the Change Logon Password tab. You can then go on to define the user's privileges in the Tools ⇨ Security ⇨ User and Group Permissions dialog box (see Figure 13-3).

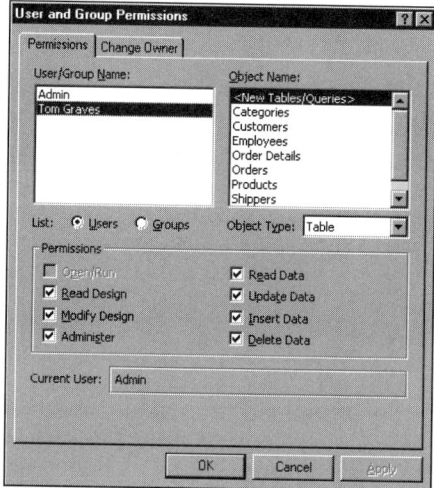

Figure 13-3: In addition to requiring an individual password, you can control a user's access to database features and objects with this dialog box.

Encrypting a database

Encrypting a database is the only way to ensure that a knowledgeable hacker can't extract the information in the file, even if you've password-protected the database. After a database has been encrypted, Access can still work with it normally, without any special steps on your part — it decrypts the information on the fly as needed.

To encrypt an Access database, start with the database closed (all users must close it). Then choose Tools ⇨ Security ⇨ Encrypt/Decrypt Database. Enter a name and path for the encrypted copy. You can replace the existing file with the encrypted copy by entering the name of the current file.

Encryption only protects the contents of the file when you're *not* using Access to examine them. Password protections remain in effect, however.

Security in Outlook

Outlook's security features pertain to messages you send to or receive from other users, not your own Outlook items. The relevant settings are on the Security tab of the Tools ⇨ Options dialog box. They fall into three categories, as follows:

- **Secure e-mail.** Provides security for the messages you send over the Internet based on digital IDs. A digital ID is used to verify that messages actually came from the person who claims to have sent them and that they have arrived unaltered. You can encrypt (scramble) messages sent with a digital ID to prevent their contents from being read until they get to the intended recipient.

- **Secure content.** Enables or disables active content in the e-mail messages and Web pages you receive, content that could monkey with your disks and files such as ActiveX controls, scripts, and Java applets. You select a named *security zone* for your messages corresponding to the degree of confidence you place in your sources. You can change the security settings of the zone you select, but note that the changes apply in any program that uses the zone — Internet Explorer being the main example.

- **Digital IDs.** Enables you to obtain a new digital ID via the Web and to move existing IDs to or from other computers.

Third-party security software

If you're at all worried about your privacy, the confidentiality of your e-mail messages, or the security of your business data, the password protection built into Office probably won't give you much peace. Consider buying a third-party software package.

Several such products are available, among them PGP Security (McAfee Software, www.mcafee.com), Norton Your Eyes Only (Symantec, www.symantec.com), and Encrypted Magic Folders (RSE Software, www.pc-magic.com). All of these shareware programs provide advanced, convenient protection for daily use with your Office documents. Their on-the-fly encryption technology integrates with Windows so that once you type in the right password, you can open and save secured files as if they weren't encrypted. All you have to do is designate specific folders as secure, and all files in them get the magic treatment.

Protecting Documents from Disease and Accidents

After giving birth to a fledgling document and spending untold hours of hard work nourishing it to robust maturity, no one wants to see the child of their labors get sick or die. As we all know, the real world is a dangerous place, but you can take measures to rescue your documents from infections and major trauma.

Coping with macro viruses

Unleashed on an innocent world in 1995, the Concept virus was the first known example of a *macro virus*, a computer infection carried through macros rather than executable programs. Wouldn't you know it — the Concept virus infects Word documents. It displays a cryptic message box containing only the numeral 1.

Before Concept came along, people generally thought only their programs were vulnerable to attack by viruses — documents were considered safe. But because macros are very much executable programs — and because Office applications can be made to execute macros automatically when documents are opened or closed — a document containing macros makes a perfect virus vehicle. Since Concept, many more macro viruses have shown up, with names such as DMV, Nuclear, Colors, Hot, Wazzu, and Laroux.

Because documents are so often copied from user to user, even organizations that don't allow individual users to install new programs are vulnerable to infection. And while Concept wasn't much more than a nuisance, causing no serious damage to your system, it could easily have been programmed to modify or wipe out files. Depending on the programming involved, Office macro viruses can act like those swine flu germs that infect both people and pigs — they are potentially infectious across platforms (that is, on the Mac OS, and any version of Windows).

Preventing infection

As a preventive measure, good computer hygiene is virtuous but not really practical — so many files come and go that you can't hope to evaluate the health of each one. But there are steps you can take to cut your risk of viral infections.

Because macro viruses depend on the capability of Office applications to execute macros automatically, the basic prevention technique is to shut off automatic macro execution. In Word, to disable the autoexecution of macros for all documents, all the time, create a macro of your own named Autoexec, with the following code:

```
Sub DeepSixAutoMacros()
WordBasic.DisableAutoMacros
MsgBox "AutoMacros have been shut down", 64, "Office SECRETS Message"
End Sub
```

If you have created your own automatic macros, however, this technique disables them, too. In this situation, you can manually disable automatic macros in documents with suspect pedigrees by holding down Shift while you open or close a document.

Another step you can take is to set the default templates (`Normal.dot` in Word, `Book.xlt` and `Sheet.xlt` in Excel) to read-only status. Because macro viruses typically attack these templates, this stops them in their tracks. The drawback here is that your programs then can't automatically save changes you make on purpose to the template.

Word, Excel, and PowerPoint display a warning message every time you open a document or template containing macros, and therefore possibly a macro virus (see Figure 13-4). Though your Office programs don't actually check the new document or template for macros, this message can be mildly helpful in jogging your memory that yes, you do need to think before opening just any document. You can turn this feature off, if you like, in the Tools ⇨ Options dialog box.

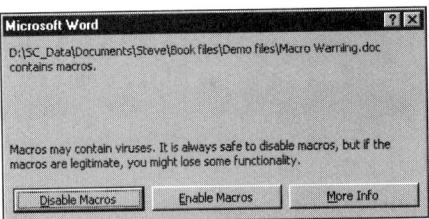

Figure 13-4: Word displays this warning when you open a file containing macros.

Disinfecting your documents

Once a macro virus takes hold on your system, you can remove it from your documents manually by deleting the macros from each infected document individually. After opening the document, choose Tools ➪ Templates and Add-Ins ➪ Organizer. After switching to the Macro Project Items tab, delete the document's macros (which should be listed in the left pane of the Organizer dialog box).

A better solution is third-party virus disinfection software such as McAfee VirusScan (McAfee Software, 408-988-3832, www.mcafee.com) or Norton AntiVirus (Symantec, 800-441-7234, www.symantec.com).

Recovering documents after accidental erasure

Consider buying a copy of Symantec's Norton Utilities or McAfee's Nuts&Bolts for their "unerase" utilities. By copying to the Recycle Bin files you delete using Explorer, My Computer, or the Office Open and Save As dialog boxes, Windows does help prevent accidental, permanent loss of precious documents. But there are easy ways to circumvent the Recycle Bin. Files deleted while you're working in DOS don't go there, nor do files deleted from within some applications. And you can bypass the Recycle Bin by pressing Shift when you delete any file from Windows or Office. Both the Norton Utilities and Nuts & Bolts have tools to rescue these erased, nonrecycled files, as long as you realize your mistake before putting new files in their place.

Conclusion

Introduced in this chapter, templates are important tools for maintaining consistent documents and eliminating repetitive busywork. Keeping different versions of your documents up to date with one another and protecting documents, whether from unauthorized users, viruses, or accidental deletions, are other key priorities also given their due here.

Part IV

Monster Web Pages with Office 2000

Chapter 14: Essential Secrets of Web Page Development

Chapter 15: Building Dynamic Web Pages

Chapter 16: Building Great Web Sites with FrontPage

Chapter 14

Essential Secrets of Web Page Development

In This Chapter

- Saving Office documents as Web pages
- Understanding HTML — the language of the Web
- Planning your site and managing your files
- Working with hyperlinks
- Authoring Web pages with Word
- Creating frames and forms in Word Web pages
- Creating Web-based presentations in PowerPoint
- Publishing your Web site

If you're a Web page designer, you need look no farther than Office 2000 for the tools you need to put gorgeous pages on the Web or your intranet. Office now makes very little distinction indeed between Web pages and other types of documents. For Web page design, you have at your disposal Office's complete cornucopia of sophisticated features for text editing, graphics design, and document layout.

This chapter covers background information on using hyperlinks in Office documents, building Web pages, and managing Web sites. Fundamental techniques for creating Web pages in Word and PowerPoint also receive plenty of attention. Chapter 15 ups the ante with coverage of more advanced topics such as spreadsheet and database Web publishing and the Office script editor.

Authoring Web Pages in Office

Web page design tools have been rapidly maturing, and Office is no exception. Until recently, you couldn't escape writing your own HTML code to produce pages of any sophistication, even if you were using one of the visual tools (see the sidebar "HTML: The Language of the Web" for a brief introduction to HTML). Today, the story is very different. While coding directly in HTML still has merit at times, you can now turn out pages of remarkable elegance in Office, without ever laying eyes on an HTML tag.

Saving documents as Web pages

In Word, PowerPoint, and Excel, you can save as a Web page any document that can be displayed in a browser. No special preparation is required — all you do is choose File ⇨ Save As Web Page and supply a filename, and the deed is done. Microsoft has struggled mightily to turn HTML into an alternative standard file format for Office documents. When you save a document as a Web page, all the content and formatting is preserved in the HTML file. Even if some elements don't appear correctly when the page is displayed in a browser, the document should function properly again when you reopen it in the original application.

Understanding XML

When saving a document as a Web page, Office relies on the Extensible Markup Language, or XML, to represent formatting, content, and other elements that can't be converted faithfully into conventional HTML code. XML is a simple standard format for representing structured data using ordinary text. In an Office document stored as a Web page, XML code is embedded into the body of the HTML file within HTML comments. When a browser that doesn't understand XML opens the file, it ignores these comments, but their content remains intact and can be read by Office applications.

Previewing documents in your browser

In Excel, Word, and PowerPoint, you can view any open document in your browser to see how it will look as a Web page. You don't need to save the document first. Choose File ⇨ Web Page Preview to start the browser and load it with a temporary Web page version of the document.

Changing Web page titles

A Web page's title appears in the browser's title bar when you're viewing the page. The browser also stores the title on the history and favorites lists. Because the title will be publicly visible, give it some thought. If you don't assign a title of your own, Office uses the document's filename for that purpose. You can change the title in the Summary tab of the File ⇨ Properties dialog box, or by clicking the Change Title button in the Save As Web Page dialog box.

HTML: The Language of the Web

Hypertext Markup Language (HTML) is the language of the Web. It consists of instructions called tags, which are placed into the body of a simple ASCII text file. Files containing these tags are called HTML files, naturally enough, and are identified by the .htm or .html extension. When a Web browser such as Microsoft Internet Explorer or Netscape Navigator opens an HTML file, it translates the tags and other information the file contains into a formatted document on your screen. A Web page you open with your browser corresponds to an HTML file.

Most HTML tags are paired, enclosing the information that the tag relates to. As a simple example, in the sequence <B>great</B> the characters in angle brackets are the paired tag for bold type. They enclose the word *great*, telling your browser to display that word in bold.

The HTML language includes scores of different tags encompassing a wide range of functionality. Some govern the appearance of elements on Web pages, making a word bold, displaying a table, or telling the browser to display a specific graphical image. Some tags control placement of text and graphics. Other tags define links to other HTML files (pages) or other sites. Form-related tags define Web page fields that can be filled out by the reader, enabling your pages to receive, store, and analyze various types of information. Still other tags activate other programs to perform functions such as returning information from a database. You can even use tags to play sound files in the background or display video clips.

Regardless of the operating system on which a browser is running, a given Web page appears basically the same. Thus, you can create and publish a single HTML document on the Web, knowing that millions of people can view it and that each of them sees what you designed, as you designed it. (There are exceptions, but this is the theory and intention of the Web's designers and of the HTML language.)

If you're interested in learning more about the HTML language, you'll find dozens of books on the subject. Of course, the Web itself is an excellent resource for this information. Go to one of the popular search sites, such as Yahoo!, and search for html — you'll find listings for the overseer of the HTML language, the World Wide Web Consortium (W3 Consortium), along with many other sites that offer specifications, training, tips, and other information about HTML.

Setting options for Web pages

Each Office application provides settings that control the way its documents are converted into Web pages. For example, you can decide where to store supporting files, select a format for graphics files, and choose an encoding scheme so that the correct characters are displayed in non-English Web pages. These settings are located on the Web Options dialog box. Reach it by opening the Tools ➪ Options dialog box, switching to the General tab, and clicking the Web Options button.

Some settings on the Web Options dialog box vary from application to application, but many of them are common to multiple Office programs. When this is the case, changing the settings in one application changes them throughout Office.

Planning Your Site and Managing Your Files

Before you begin work on your Web site in earnest, take a few minutes to sketch the overall plan for your site. It won't hurt to define your goals for the site briefly but in writing, so you can be sure that your efforts are concentrated where they belong. Every page in your site should make a contribution that is consistent with this informal mission statement.

Determining the location for your finished site

You should know in advance where the finished site will be housed. The capabilities of the computer or *server* on which the site resides determine what content you add to your pages. If you have a direct connection to the Internet and are setting up the site on your own NT-based server, limitations will be few. But if you use an ISP or plan to place the site on a private intranet, you should check with the powers that be to identify content that will and won't play on the server. Ask specifically about support for forms, image maps, Active Server Pages, ActiveX controls, and the FrontPage and Office Server Extensions (the latter topics are covered in Chapters 16 and 17, respectively).

Making allowances for browser capabilities

The capabilities of the browser can also place limitations on what content the user can successfully access. It's important to plan your pages accordingly. HTML is a dynamic and rapidly evolving language. New tags are added to the language with each version, adding features that allow for increasingly sophisticated Web sites. The downside of this progress is that older browsers are unable to interpret the new commands. HTML pages produced by Office include many of the latest HTML tags, designed for viewing with up-to-date browsers. In most cases you can view pages containing the newer tags with older Web browsers, but they may look significantly different, and some of the content may not appear at all.

If you're publishing your Web site to a private intranet in a tightly standardized organization, every user should have the same browser. In this case, your work is simplified — you can plan your documents according to the features of the target browser and Office sees to it that your pages contain the correct features. (In PowerPoint and Word, you can set options that automatically adapt your documents to the demands of specific browsers.)

By contrast, browser chaos reigns on the Internet, and at many institutions, too. While Netscape Navigator and Microsoft Internet Explorer own the vast majority of the browser market, plenty of people do use other browsers. More important, older versions of Navigator and IE are still in wide use. A lowest-common-denominator strategy is one solution. Office doesn't give you much help in this regard, because the Web Options dialog box doesn't let you dumb down your pages to the version 3 level of Navigator and IE. Instead, you have to educate yourself as to which HTML features are supported in the browsers you've chosen to represent the lowest common denominator.

The problem with accommodating only the lowest common denominator is that you limit the potential appeal of your site and may alienate those who do have up-to-date browsers. In many cases your best choice is to go ahead and use all the features that you like and leave the users to worry about their browser's capabilities. After all, browsers are free and easy to get. Someone who chooses not to update his or her browser is probably not too concerned about the latest and greatest features. I do recommend that you inform your audience that you're using features that require one or more particular browsers — a small "best viewed with" message will do.

The most ambitious approach is to build code into your pages that determines which browser is running and displays the appropriate content accordingly. That option requires lots of work but is the best solution for highly visible sites. You'll have to consult books or other resources on HTML for the techniques required.

Managing files

If you're developing or working with a Web site of more than several pages, you should do some planning to avoid confusion as the site grows.

Planning your site's folders

To plan a logical hierarchy for your site, sketch it out using an organizational chart format. For example, let's say that you have a site with pages under the headings of Our Company, Personnel, Products, Employment Opportunities, and Feedback. You might set up a file structure on your hard disk consisting of a main folder called Web Pages, with subfolders named for each of these headings and perhaps another subfolder for images. As you create your pages, save them in the appropriate folders and place the images you'll be using in the Images folder.

Software that specializes in Web site management can help you organize your site and make sure that every file is in its proper place. The obvious choice is FrontPage 2000, bundled with Office Premium and the subject of Chapter 16.

Caution

You may not have free rein to organize your site as you see fit — your organization, or your Internet service provider, may enforce standards as to the folders your site should contain, and which types of files belong in which folder. Be sure you're aware of any such mandates before you start work in earnest.

Dealing with Office's automatic support folders

When you save a document as a Web page, Office automatically creates a subfolder for the page's supporting files. Located in the folder where you save the page itself, the subfolder is named after the page's filename. If you save the page as HomePage.htm, the support folder will be called HomePage_files. In this subfolder go all the graphics, sound and video clips, and whatnot — all the elements that belong to the page but are housed in separate files. These files receive filenames automatically, if they don't already have them. (If you prefer to store the support files in the same folder as the page, clear the Organize Supporting Files in a Folder check box on the Files tab of the Web Options dialog box.)

Office keeps up with its housekeeping as your page evolves. If you delete a graphic from the page, the corresponding file is automatically removed from your disk the next time you save the page. You're on your own, though, if you move or copy the page to another location. You must also move or copy the supporting subfolder and its contents (or the files only, if you aren't using a subfolder) to the same destination.

Caution

Although Office's automated file management system for Web pages prevents chaos on your hard disk, it's likely to conflict with the one you choose for your site as a whole. Typically, you're going to be using some graphics on many different pages. Instead of storing separate copies of their files in each page's subfolders, you should place the common images in a folder shared by all pages. Also, you may simply prefer to organize support files by type or content. Unfortunately, you can't specify alternative locations for support files individually. For that matter, you can't supply your own names for the support files. To take matters into your own hands, you need a dedicated page editor such as FrontPage, or you must edit the HTML code for the page yourself.

Working with Hyperlinks

Hyperlinks are hot spots that let the user of a Web page or other document navigate to another page or file on the local hard disk, the network, or the Web. Ordinary Office documents can contain hyperlinks — the document doesn't have to be saved as a Web page. Although most hyperlinks simply take you to the top of the target page or document, hyperlinks can zero in on particular locations within a page, including the one you're currently viewing (see "Jumping to specific locations in documents" later in this chapter).

Hyperlinks enable the reader of a document to explore related information. Activating or *following* a hyperlink typically leads to a more complete description or explanation, or to a page or document on a related topic. Hyperlinks can reference any document type. For instance, a report you create in Word might contain a link to an Excel spreadsheet, one to a graphics file, and another to a public Web location. A hyperlink can also function as a live e-mail address, automatically opening a new message in your e-mail program with the address referred to in the link already entered in the To field.

Using hyperlinks

By now, everyone knows how to use hyperlinks in Web browsers, but Office introduces a minor variation or two. A hyperlink's visible hot spot in the document can be any text or image. Passing the mouse pointer over a hyperlink changes the pointer to a pointing finger, figuratively pointing to another location. In Office, if ScreenTips are turned on, a box containing the address or filename of the destination appears when you hold the mouse over the link for a second or two.

To activate or *follow* a hyperlink, you click the link or select it with the keyboard and press Enter. Doing so starts the application program associated with the address or file, which then opens the item. When you click a hyperlink in an Office document, the Web toolbar appears. The toolbar enables easy navigation between linked files with buttons much like those found on the Microsoft Internet Explorer Web browser (see Chapter 6 for details on the Web toolbar).

Creating hyperlinks

To create a hyperlink, select the text, worksheet cell, or graphic that is to identify the hot spot that the user must click to get to the linked destination. If you don't select something first (or if the selected worksheet cell is blank), the hyperlink's default text in your document is the destination address or filename.

With your selection made, click the Insert Hyperlink button or choose Insert ➪ Hyperlink. Either technique opens the Insert Hyperlink dialog box (see Figure 14-1). The box at the top lets you enter or change the text of the hyperlink to be displayed in your document — it automatically contains any text you selected before opening the dialog box.

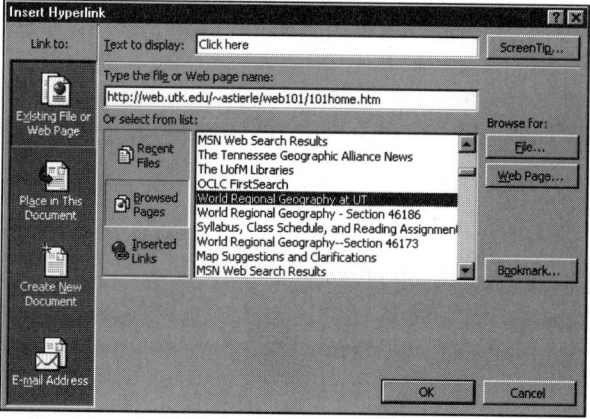

Figure 14-1: Use the Insert Hyperlink dialog box to define hyperlinks to Web sites, other Internet URLs, and documents on a local or network disk.

Arranged vertically along the left side of the box, the large Link To bar contains buttons for selecting the type of hyperlink you want to create. When you click a button, the options in the main part of the box change accordingly. The Link To buttons are:

- **Existing File or Web Page.** See the next section, "Creating hyperlinks to existing pages and documents," for details.

- **Place in This Document (in Access, Object in This Database).** This button's function is better expressed as "Create a hyperlink to another location in the current document" — not "Insert a hyperlink into the current document." See "Jumping to specific locations in documents" later in this chapter.

- **Create New Document (in Access, Create New Page).** Click here if you want to start a new document as the destination for the hyperlink you're inserting.

- **E-mail Address.** Click this button if you want the hyperlink to start a new e-mail message using your default e-mail program.

Creating hyperlinks to existing pages and documents

Hyperlinks can jump to and activate any document file accessible on your system, your network, or the Internet. The only requirements are that the application that opens that file type is present on your system and that the file type is associated in Windows with that application. For Web pages, of course, the requisite application is a browser.

Using the Insert Hyperlink dialog box, identify an existing Web page or document as the hyperlink's target by clicking the Existing File or Web Page button if necessary. Then use one of these three methods:

- Type in a URL or a path and filename yourself.

- Choose the target from one of the lists controlled by the three buttons just to the right of the Link To bar. Recent Files displays files you've opened or inserted in Office. Browsed Pages displays Web pages that you've viewed in your browser recently by title, if the title is available. Because the HTML Help program is really just Internet Explorer with a different face, all the Help topics you've viewed show up here — this is usually a distracting nuisance. Inserted Links lists the Web site URLs you've entered in your browser's address box, as well as links you've actually inserted previously in the current file.

- Click one of the Browse For buttons to locate a filename or Web address. Clicking Web Page starts your browser. When you find the page you're looking for, you must manually copy its URL from the browser's address box back to the Insert Hyperlink box.

The Bookmark button lets you specify a named location in the target document as the hyperlink's destination. See "Jumping to specific locations in documents" later in this chapter.

Editing and removing hyperlinks

To edit an existing hyperlink, right-click over the link. Choose Hyperlink ⇨ Edit Hyperlink on the shortcut menu to open the Edit Hyperlink dialog box. Its controls are identical to those of the Insert Hyperlink dialog box described earlier, except for the Remove Link button at the bottom left.

The quick way to delete a hyperlink is to right-click it and choose Hyperlink ⇨ Remove Hyperlink on the resulting shortcut menu. If you've already opened the Edit Hyperlink dialog box, clicking the Remove Link button there accomplishes the same goal. Removing a hyperlink doesn't delete the text or graphics that held the link in your document, just its hyperlink functionality.

In Excel, to delete a hyperlink that was created with the HYPERLINK workbook function, use the arrow keys to select the cell that contains the formula, and then press Del.

Changing the text displayed by a hyperlink

The surefire way to edit the text a hyperlink displays is in the Edit Hyperlink dialog box. Just type in the changes in the Text to Display field. In Word and Excel, you can run into trouble if you try to edit the hyperlink text directly in the document—you have to be careful not to click the hyperlink, because that activates it. Instead, click right next to the hyperlink (in Excel, for example, in an adjacent cell) and then use the arrow keys to move to the hyperlink itself. Once you're there, you can use standard editing commands to make your changes. In Excel you can edit the characters in the formula bar or press F2 to edit them in the cell itself.

Editing hyperlinked graphics

Secret

If you want to edit the graphic on which a hyperlink resides, Ctrl+click the graphic to select it without activating the hyperlink. You can then resize the graphic, move it around in the document, or right-click it to pop up the shortcut menu with options such as Format, Change, or Edit, depending on the graphic type.

Jumping to specific locations in documents

Although many hyperlinks just take you to the beginning of a Web page or document, your hyperlinks can jump to particular places within those same files. You can create hyperlinks to specific locations in the current document or in any other document. These locations can be Word bookmarks, Excel worksheets, cells, or named ranges, PowerPoint slides, or bookmarks in Web pages. Specific Access database objects can be hyperlink destinations, but only when you're placing the hyperlink into an Access database.

You can call on three different methods to create these well-aimed hyperlinks: dragging and dropping the hyperlink content, copying and pasting it, or using the Insert Hyperlink dialog box. The first two methods are quick and easy, especially because they don't require you to first create named locations in the target document (the one the hyperlink will jump to). The Insert Hyperlink dialog box lets you work with documents that aren't currently open; it seems to be the only reliable route to hyperlinks that jump to named locations in Web pages.

Secret

Before you can create a hyperlink to a specific location in a document, you must save the target document first. This isn't a safety step—the method only works if the file is saved first.

Dragging Office content to create hyperlinks

The easiest way to create a hyperlink within an Office document or from one Office document to another is via drag and drop. Here are the steps required:

1. Open the target document if necessary, and be sure to save it.

2. Select the destination text or graphics in the target document. At this step, you're choosing the specific location that will appear when the user clicks the hyperlink. (If the destination is a PowerPoint slide, you can select any text or graphic, because hyperlinks to individual items on a slide aren't allowed.)

3. Using the right mouse button, drag the selection to the document that is to contain the hyperlink. Unless you're creating a hyperlink within the target document, or unless both documents are visible simultaneously on the screen, you must drag the selection to the Windows taskbar, holding the mouse pointer over the icon for the target application or document until the application itself appears. Without releasing the button, continue dragging into the body of the document.

4. When you get to the location where you want the hyperlink to appear, release the mouse button. On the shortcut menu that appears, choose Create Hyperlink Here. (If you're creating the hyperlink within a PowerPoint presentation, release the mouse button over the destination slide in the outline pane.)

Creating a hyperlink via the clipboard

To create a hyperlink to a specific location via the clipboard, open the target document, or create and save it. Select the destination text or graphics in the target document and copy the selection to the clipboard. Switch to the document that is to contain the hyperlink and choose Edit ⇨ Paste as Hyperlink.

Creating location-specific hyperlinks using a dialog box

The Insert Hyperlink dialog box is the refined way to create a hyperlink to a particular spot in an Office document or Web page. The target document should already be saved in an accessible location, but it doesn't have to be open. In the document where you're placing the hyperlink, choose Insert ➪ Hyperlink to bring up the dialog box. Proceed as follows:

- If the hyperlink's destination is in the same document, click the Place in This Document button (in Access, the button is Object in This Database). You're presented with a list of locations in the current document.

- If the destination is in a different document, stick with the Existing File or Web Page button instead. After you locate the target Web page or Office document, click Bookmarks. A dialog box containing linkable locations in the document appears.

This technique works well, as long as the location you want to jump to appears in the list of bookmarks. In Word and Excel, you can create your own named bookmarks or ranges as destinations.

Bookmarks in Word documents

To create a bookmark in a Word document — or in a Web page that you're creating in Word — position the insertion point where you want the bookmark to go and then choose Insert ➪ Bookmark. The Bookmark dialog box opens, enabling you to enter a Bookmark name (see Figure 14-2). Chapter 27 has more on Word bookmarks.

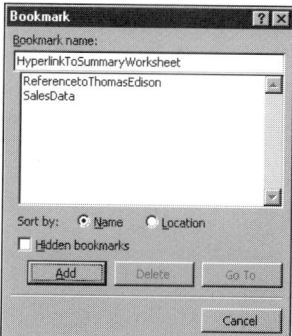

Figure 14-2: Use Word's Bookmark dialog box to insert a bookmark that is then available as a hyperlink destination.

Hyperlinks provide the next best thing to cross-document bookmarks in Word. Word lacks a command to "Go To" specific hyperlinks. But if you bookmark the hyperlink itself, you can use the Go To command to jump to the hyperlink (actually to its bookmark) and then click the hyperlink to get to your final destination in another document.

To get to the destination without having to click the hyperlink yourself, use the following VBA module. First, it opens the GoTo dialog box. When you then select the bookmark for a cross-document hyperlink — and after you press Esc to put away the dialog box — the module jumps to the hyperlink and activates it for you:

```
Sub CrossDocBookmark()
    b = Dialogs(wdDialogEditGoTo).Show
        If b = -1 Then
            If Selection.Hyperlinks.Count >= 1 Then
                Selection.Hyperlinks(1).Follow
            End If
        End If
End Sub
```

Bookmarks in Excel worksheets

Create a "bookmark" in an Excel worksheet by naming a range of one or more cells. Highlight the cell(s) you want to mark and then choose Insert ⇨ Name ⇨ Define. The Define Name dialog box opens, enabling you to enter a name for the selected cells, which are also specified in the Refers To: entry (see Figure 14-3). You can read more about named ranges in Excel in Chapter 36.

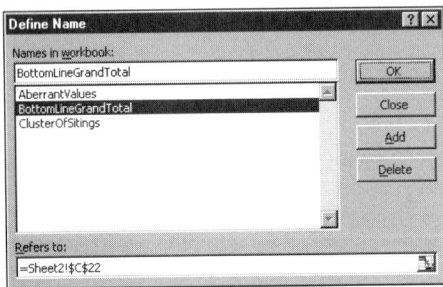

Figure 14-3: After naming a range of cells in this dialog box, you can set up a hyperlink that jumps to the named range.

Controlling the look of your hyperlinks

Office programs give you varying degrees of control over the appearance of hyperlinks. Depending on the application, you can dictate color, font, and underlining style for hyperlinks as they appear before and after they've been followed (clicked).

Formatting hyperlinks in Word and Excel

Use styles to control the look of your hyperlinks in a Word document or throughout an Excel workbook. In either application, choose Format ⇨ Style to open the Style dialog box. In the list of styles, the ones you want are

Hyperlink, for links that haven't been followed yet, and FollowedHyperlink (in Word) or Followed Hyperlink (in Excel), for those that have (note that the latter style becomes accessible in Excel only after a Hyperlink has been followed). After selecting the style you want to work with, click Modify to change its formatting settings. All Word text effects are available. This might be one suitable place for animated text, though text animation won't be visible if you save the document as a Web page and display it in a browser.

In Word and Access, themes provide a great alternative to styles for formatting Web pages that include hyperlinks. See "Working with themes" later in this chapter.

Setting hyperlink appearance in PowerPoint

In PowerPoint, the text color of your hyperlinks is determined by each slide's color scheme. To change or customize the color scheme, use the Format ⇨ Slide Color Scheme dialog box. Switch to the Custom tab to locate the individual items for specifying colors for hyperlinks and followed hyperlinks. See Chapter 48 for details on the PowerPoint color schemes.

Changing hyperlink options in Access

To set the color of hyperlinks in an Access database, open the Tools ⇨ Options dialog box. There, switch to the General tab and click Web Options. In Access, this dialog box is devoted entirely to the appearance of your hyperlinks. You can choose a color for regular and followed hyperlinks, and turn underlining on or off.

Word and hyperlinks

This section treats a couple of hyperlink-related features that are unique to Word.

Automatic hyperlinks in Word

By default, Word automatically converts URLs and filenames into hyperlinks as you type them in your documents. This behavior can be a bit disconcerting when you're writing a book about the Web, but if you actually plan to use the hyperlinks that you type, it's very handy. To turn automatic hyperlinks on or off, open the AutoFormat as you Type tab of the Tools ⇨ AutoCorrect dialog box and check or clear the box labeled Internet and Network Paths with Hyperlinks. To convert an existing document's text into live hyperlinks, use the Format ⇨ AutoFormat command, choosing Options before proceeding to be sure the conversion setting is turned on.

Using HYPERLINK field switches in Word

A hyperlink inserted into a Word document is placed there in the form of a HYPERLINK field. You can manually insert switches in the field after the linked filename or URL to control the hyperlink's behavior. See Chapter 33 for details.

Access and hyperlinks

In Access, you can store hyperlinks as data directly in a database table using a Hyperlink data field, and you can assign hyperlinks to buttons or other controls on a form. These two methods have different functions in an Access database.

Storing hyperlinks in fields

When you want to keep track of the hyperlinks themselves as part of each record in a table, create a field in that table and assign it to the Hyperlink data type. Once the hyperlinks have been entered into the table, you can access any hyperlink by clicking it in the table itself. In addition, just as with any Access field, you can display a hyperlink field on a form by binding it to a text box. That way, the hyperlink associated with the current record is always visible as you flip from record to record.

This approach is appropriate if you happen to be designing a Favorite Web Sites table, but you can also use Hyperlink data type fields to store e-mail addresses or personal Web pages in a Contacts table. Also, because hyperlinks can jump to regular documents as well as to Web content, you can use hyperlink fields to create document archiving and retrieval databases with live links to the actual documents. The user just clicks the hyperlink to see the document and doesn't have to go hunting for it in a folder based on keywords or a description.

Adding a hyperlink field to a table

Create a hyperlink field by adding a new field to the table in Design view and setting its DataType to Hyperlink. In Datasheet view, add a new hyperlink field by choosing Insert ⇨ Hyperlink Column. You can enter a hyperlink URL or UNC path in an ordinary text field, but Access won't recognize the entry as a hyperlink. Clicking it lets you edit the text, but nothing more.

Binding a hyperlink field to a form text box

To add to a form a text box bound to a hyperlink field, start by opening the form. To be on the safe side, check the form's `RecordSource` property, which should be set to the table with the hyperlink field, or to a corresponding query. Now you're ready to place the field onto the form. Just click the Field List button on the Form Design toolbar. Locate the field containing the hyperlink data and drag it from the list onto the form. Figure 14-4 shows a form with a bound hyperlink field.

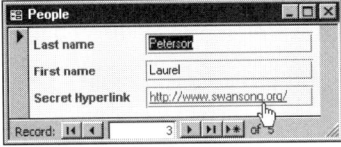

Figure 14-4: This form lets you browse records containing a hyperlink field.

Placing hyperlinks on controls

Often it makes sense to give users a stable jump gate to one Web site, document, or database object — a hyperlink that points to the same target no matter which record they're working with on the form. To set this up, use the control's HyperlinkAddress and HyperlinkSubAddress properties. After placing the control on the form in Design view, you can set these properties to point to the URL or document you want the control to jump to. When you select either HyperlinkAddress and HyperlinkSubAddress in the control's Properties dialog box, the button that appears to the right of the field (shown in Figure 14-5) pops up the Insert Hyperlink dialog box.

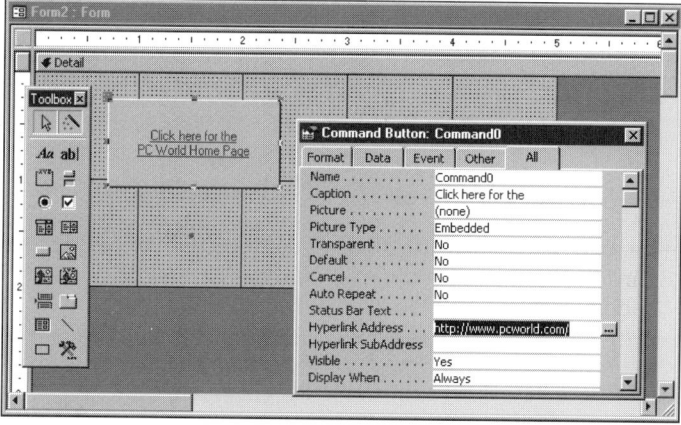

Figure 14-5: Click the little button to the right of the field for the HyperlinkAddress property to display the Insert Hyperlink dialog box.

To create a hyperlink button, you must add the button to the form and then add the hyperlink to the button. You can insert a label containing a hyperlink in one step: Click the Insert Hyperlink button or choose Insert ⇨ Hyperlink. After creating a hyperlink control, you can edit the text displayed on the control without affecting the underlying hyperlink. To change the text, you can click the text directly so that a blinking insertion point appears, or use the control's Caption property.

When a hyperlink on a form is clicked, Access displays the Web toolbar, which stays on the screen even when you close the form. If this offends your sensibilities (or consumes space on the screen unnecessarily), you must write VBA code to hide the toolbar for the form's OnClose event.

PowerPoint and hyperlinks

Hyperlinks in a PowerPoint presentation are active for one-click jumps only when you view the presentation as a slide show. To follow a hyperlink in a slide you're editing, right-click it and choose Open near the top of the resulting shortcut menu. As discussed in Chapter 48, PowerPoint action buttons provide an alternative way to insert hyperlinks. You assign hyperlinks to an action button using the Action Settings dialog box that appears at the time you insert it, or when you right-click the button and choose Hyperlink ⇨ Edit Hyperlink.

About Graphics in Web Pages

When you save an Office document as an HTML file, the application stores each graphic in the document in a separate file. The file format used to store a given graphic depends on the type of image, the number of colors it contains, and settings in the Web Options dialog box. The file format chosen has an impact on performance and image quality, so it pays to be aware of these technicalities.

Working with GIF and JPEG images

Traditionally, Web browsers have been capable of displaying two types of image files, GIF (.gif) and JPEG (.jpeg or .jpg). Both of these are bitmap (raster) formats, which represent the individual dots that compose the image. Both GIF and JPEG compress the original image, but in different ways, and they have other differences as well. Here's a summary of their characteristics:

- To compress files, GIF finds and records where large blocks of the same color are located rather than specifying each dot in these blocks individually. GIF files can be interlaced, so that the browser first displays every other line of dots and then fills in the missing lines. Interlacing lets the user see the entire image sooner, albeit fuzzily at first. You can also specify a transparent color in a GIF image, so that the Web page underneath the image shows through everywhere that color appears. This is great for making it look like you've placed an irregularly shaped object directly onto a page, rather than on a rectangular field that blots out the page beneath. Finally, GIF files support simple animations by storing multiple images that are displayed in succession.

- JPEG compares the color value of adjacent pixels and records the differences between them. JPEG compression can be adjusted to ignore different degrees of color difference between pixels. The greater the difference that it ignores, the less information it records, resulting in smaller files but reduced image quality.

The bottom line: GIF is best suited for images such as logos and icons, and JPEG is best for images with many colors such as photographs, or illustrations that contain smooth gradations.

When you import an image in either format, Office preserves that format when it saves the page. If you import an image in a different format, however, Office chooses the format that best suits the image.

Saving graphics in PNG format

Portable Network Graphics (PNG) is a newer bitmap format that produces images of high quality but smaller size than JPEG or GIF. However, PNG isn't a good choice for use on the Internet at this point, because only the newest browsers can display PNG files. If you know that all your users have IE5 or another PNG-savvy browser, enable this format in the Pictures tab of the Web Options dialog box. There, check the box labeled Allow PNG as an Output Format. From now on, Office stores Web page graphics in the PNG format, except for those images you import as JPEG or GIF files.

Using vector graphics in Web pages

Vector (line) graphics represent images by describing them mathematically, rather than by storing information about individual dots. They are superior to bitmaps in two important ways: they're smaller, so they download faster, and they are resolution-independent, so they maintain a sharp appearance as you zoom in or out. Despite these benefits, HTML hasn't supported vector graphics until the advent of Office 2000 with its Vector Markup Language (VML).

A VML graphic appears in the code for a Web page as an HTML tag. Within the tag, data describing the graphic's shape, color, and other characteristics are stored using XML coding conventions. In other words, the graphic data are part and parcel of the Web page itself, and are not stored in a separate file as they would be with a bitmap picture. Here's an example of the VML code for a simple blue oval:

```
<v:oval style='width:150 pt;height:75 pt' fillcolor="blue">
</v:oval>
```

Although you can create graphics by writing VML code, most Office Web page designers aren't that masochistic. Office automatically generates VML code for graphics you create using the standard Office drawing tools covered in Chapter 8.

Vector graphics are great, but once again, the big drawback to adopting an Office 2000 innovation is incompatibility. Although Microsoft has proposed VML as a Web standard for vector graphics, at this point, only Internet Explorer 5 can display VML images. If all your users have standardized on IE5, you can turn on VML support in the Pictures tab of the Web Options dialog box. Check the box labeled Rely on VML for Displaying Graphics in Browsers. With this box checked, Office won't generate bitmaps for images that it can represent using VML.

Editing HTML Code in Office

Office apps make it easy to view and edit the HTML code representing a document. Once you've saved or opened a HTML-format document, the View ⇨ HTML Source command becomes available. Choose this command to open the code in the Microsoft Script Editor, described further in Chapter 15. Opened using the HTML Source command, the Script Editor displays a simple two-window layout — the source code pane occupies most of the screen, but the Project Explorer window is also visible. Close the Project Explorer to see more code. The Script Editor displays HTML code in various colors to designate tags, attributes, and values. You can edit the code as you would in a typical Windows text editor.

If the HTML Source command isn't listed on the View menu, add it from the Commands tab of the Tools ⇨ Customize dialog box. Select View in the Categories and then scroll the Commands list until you find the HTML Source command. Drag it up to the View menu or another suitable destination. The Script Editor is also available from the Tools ⇨ Macro submenu, but its layout is busier when you activate it that way.

Web Page Authoring with Word

Word is a natural as a Web page editor. After all, tasks such as text editing, graphics design, and layout apply equally to print and electronic documents, and Word performs all these tasks superbly. Add in a panoply of special Web page authoring features, and Word should satisfy your need for a powerful, all-purpose page development tool.

You face no special challenge when turning any document into a Web page that can be viewed in a browser. A quick trip to the File ⇨ Save As Web Page dialog box is all that's required. If you haven't yet created the document, however, Word provides a set of templates to further ease the design process, and a wizard to help you construct an entire Web site in no time flat.

Basing new Web pages on templates

To create a new blank Web page, choose File ⇨ New and then double-click the template labeled simply Web Page. All you're really doing is starting a new empty document based on the Normal template, and switching to Web Layout view. However, Word also offers templates that include some content to help you get started with a new page's design. Find these templates in the Web Pages tab of the File ⇨ New dialog box. When you access a template this way, you can't see what a page based on the templates will look like until you create the new document — when you use the Web Page Wizard, you get to see a sample document ahead of time (read on).

Using Word's Web Page Wizard

Word 2000's "Web Page Wizard" is misnamed — it's really a Web site wizard. You can use it for single pages, but it's most useful when you're undertaking a brand new multiple-page site. To begin, open the File ⇨ New dialog box, switch to the Web Pages tab, and double-click Web Page Wizard.

The wizard starts by asking you for the title of your new Web site and the folder where you want to store it. Simple enough. The next wizard panel, shown in Figure 14-6, lets you choose whether to include automatic navigation frames in your pages, and if so, how they should be oriented (frames are introduced in "Working with frames in Word" later in this chapter).

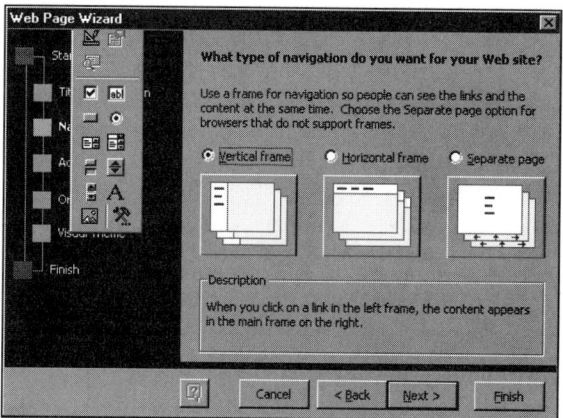

Figure 14-6: Working with Word's Web Page Wizard

In the third panel you get down to the business of adding pages to your new site. The buttons here let you create new blank pages or new pages based on Word templates, or add extant pages already available on your disk or the network. When you click the Add Template Page button, Word displays a secondary dialog box listing the available templates. As you select the different templates in this box, Word shows you how a document based on the selected template would appear, which makes it a lot easier to choose the template that's best suited for your design goals. Because you're going to be modifying the page with your own information, don't worry if you don't find exactly what you want among the selections available.

Secret

The Add Existing File button works fine for Web pages created in Word or outside of Office. However, if the page you're trying to add was created in another Office application, opening it the usual way won't add it to your new Web site — instead, that other application will try to open it. You must select the page, click the arrow bar at the right of the Open button, and choose Open in Microsoft Word.

After you've assembled the pages, the next panel in the wizard lets you shuffle their order. You can't create a multiple-level hierarchy of pages, but you can specify the order in which pages appear in the navigation frame created by the wizard.

The final wizard panel lets you choose a theme for all the pages in the site. Themes are discussed in "Working with themes" later in this chapter. When you've made your selection, choose Finish. All the Web pages you've created open for editing in Word.

Editing Web pages in Word

Although you can save a Word document from any view, Word 2000's new Web Layout view is the one to use if you want to work on the document pretty much as it will look in a browser. Web Layout view disables formatting features that don't work in Web pages, and it enables Web-specific components such as frames. If you create or save your document as a Web page, Word restricts it to features that browsers can display. However, aside from the unavailability of some formatting features, you can use all of Word's standard editing and layout capabilities to author your Web pages.

Specifying a target browser

If you know that your users have standardized on a particular browser, get Word to help tailor your Web pages for that program. On the General tab of the Web Options dialog box, select the browser(s) that your users have. Thereafter, Word disables formatting that won't display properly in the target browser. You have only two choices here, one for Internet Explorer 4.0 and Netscape Navigator version 4.0, the other for Internet Explorer 5.

Adding tables to your Word Web page

You create and modify Word tables for a Web page in the same way as you do other documents, as detailed in Chapter 30. Although many tables in Web pages have the same function they do in print documents — to display information in an orderly fashion — they also serve a critical role in formatting. Text, graphics, and form elements placed directly on a Web page get moved around by the browser according to factors such as the size of the window and the fonts in use. By inserting those elements in a table, however, you can keep them where you want them. Tables are often used to create columnar layouts in Web pages, because true columns aren't available in HTML.

Inserting horizontal lines

Horizontal dividing lines are a commonly used formatting element in Web pages. To add one to your Word document, place the insertion point where you want the line and choose Format ⇨ Borders and Shading. Clicking the Horizontal Line button in the resulting dialog box opens the Clip Gallery, where you can choose from over 30 graphical lines. You can repeatedly insert the same line by clicking the Horizontal Line button on the Tables and Borders toolbar.

Adding scrolling text

To have text scroll across your page like a marquee sign, click the Scrolling Text button on the Web Tools toolbar. Enter the text in the dialog box that appears. After you OK the box you can change the font and other formatting for the scrolling text. First click the Design Mode button on the Web Tools toolbar. You can then select the scrolling text element and access the relevant commands on the Format menu.

Working with themes

In the Office lexicon, a *theme* represents a comprehensive design template for Web pages. A theme dictates the page's color scheme, specifies the graphics used for the background image, horizontal lines, and bullets, and determines the fonts to be used for each text style (body text, headings, bulleted points, and so on). By applying a theme to a Web page, you set the look of all these design elements in one step. And if you use the same theme for every page in your site, you automatically ensure that all the pages share a consistent look.

Themes are available in Access and FrontPage as well as Word, which gives you a no-hassle way to stick to a common design in all three programs. And although Office comes with loads of prefab themes, you can design your own using FrontPage — see Chapter 16 for details.

In Word, apply a theme to any document by choosing Format ⇨ Theme. The Theme dialog box lists the available themes and displays a sample of the one currently selected in the list. Note that each theme has three optional variants: vivid colors, active graphics, and background image. You can turn these on or off independently using the relevant check boxes. Don't click the Style Gallery button. Doing so displays Word's Style Gallery, which lists and shows samples of Word templates, not themes, and you can't get back to the Themes dialog box directly.

In Access, you can assign themes only to data access pages, which are covered in Chapter 15. A quick tip: You must be in Design view to choose the Format ⇨ Theme command. FrontPage lets you assign themes from any view, and you can apply the chosen theme to an entire Web or to selected pages.

Working with frames in Word

Frames divide the browser window into sections that act independently of one another. In the most typical configuration, a header containing a logo and other static information appears in a frame at the top of the browser window, a menu of navigation hyperlinks is shown in a frame on the left, while the page of interest is shown in a frame on the right. Technically, each frame displays a separate Web page. That's why frames are so handy for navigation — while one frame displays a constant page containing navigation links, another can show different pages according to which link has been clicked. A *frames page* is a special page that serves as container for the various frames to be displayed. Opening the frames page displays the frames it contains and their contents.

Word 2000 knows how to build frames and frames pages, so if you want to use them, you can quite easily do so. But while frames have their advantages, they have drawbacks, too. Chief among these is that some Web zealots love to hate them and love to let you know how strongly they feel. As the Web has become a mainstream experience, such passions are receding, but don't be surprised if your gorgeous frame-based page design draws harsh words from some inspired, articulate critics.

Using the Frames toolbar and menu

Shown in Figure 14-7, the Frames toolbar gives you access to most of the commands you need to create and tweak frames in Word. It appears automatically when you work with a frames page. The same commands appear on the Format ⇨ Frames submenu.

Figure 14-7: Word's Frames toolbar

Creating a frames page

Word's Web Page Wizard offers an easy path to creating a simple frames page containing two frames. If you want a different or fancier design, you can create a new frames page from scratch, or modify the wizard's work.

To create a new frames page based on the document that's currently open in Word, choose Format ⇨ Frames ⇨ New Frames Page. It doesn't matter whether the document you start from is a Web page or an ordinary Word document. Word creates a new document — this is the frames page — and opens it in Web Layout view. At this point, the new frames page contains only one frame. Because that frame fills the whole window, and because the frame in turn contains the document you started with, you probably won't be able to tell that anything has changed. If you look at the title bar, however, you'll see the title of the new document, not that of the document you started with.

You use standard editing and formatting techniques to edit a document displayed in a frame. Save the frames page as you would any other Word document. When you do, Word saves the frames page itself and the documents in all of its frames.

Secret

You can save only the document contained in an individual frame to give it a different name or store it in another location. Right-click in the frame and choose Save Current Frame As. The standard Save As dialog box appears.

Adding and deleting frames on a frames page

Add frames to a frames page by clicking one of the New Frame buttons on the Frames toolbar or by using one of the corresponding commands on the Format ⇨ Frames menu. Word creates a new document for each new frame, automatically assigning it a name when you save the frames page. To delete a frame, click inside it and then click the Delete Frame button.

Working with frame properties

Formatting options and other settings for frames are few in number and easy to learn. You control them in the Frame Properties dialog box, shown in Figure 14-8. To display it, click the target frame to select it. Then click the Frame Properties button at the right of the Frames toolbar or choose Format ⇨ Frames ⇨ Frame Properties.

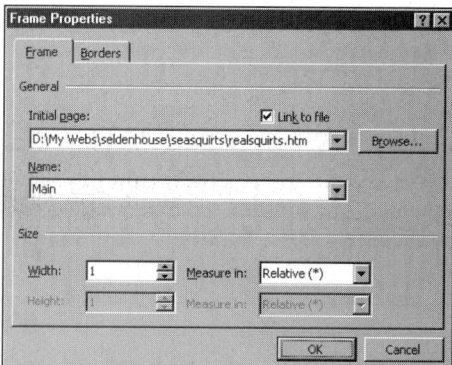

Figure 14-8: The Frame Properties dialog box lets you control the content and format of Web page frames.

Specifying a frame's name and initial Web page

Each frame has a name. You need the name to control the frame's content by hyperlinks you insert into another frame. Word assigns to each frame a name for you, but you can change the name in the Frame tab of the Frame Properties dialog box. Also on the Frame tab, the Initial page field lists the page or document that's currently displayed in the frame. To display a different page when the frames page is opened, enter its filename in the Initial page field.

Formatting frames

To size a pair of adjacent frames in Word, drag the frame border, if it's visible, to a new position. If the border is hidden, or if you want more precise control, you can use the Width and Height settings on the Frame tab of the Frame Properties dialog box to specify a frame's size. Settings that directly affect the borders themselves are on the Borders tab of the Frame Properties dialog box. You can choose whether or not the borders are visible, how wide they are, and their color. Clear the Frame Is Resizable box if you don't want users to change frame size. Scrollbar options for the selected frame are also located here.

Inserting hyperlinks in frames

Because frames are most often used to provide Web site navigation, mastery of the techniques required to fill them with hyperlinks won't hurt. In the typical scenario, a page containing a series of hyperlinks occupies the frame on the left; clicking one of these hyperlinks displays a particular page in the frame on the right. Working in the left-hand frame, here's how to set up each of its hyperlinks:

1. **Identify the location for the hyperlink.** If you want to use a graphical button for your hyperlink, insert it into the left frame and select it. For a text hyperlink, just click in the frame where you want the hyperlink to reside.

2. **Open the Insert Hyperlink dialog box.** Use the Insert ⇨ Hyperlink command, or click the corresponding toolbar button. When you're working in a frame, the dialog box looks a bit different than it does otherwise — as shown in Figure 14-9, it includes a thumbnail of the frames page at the bottom.

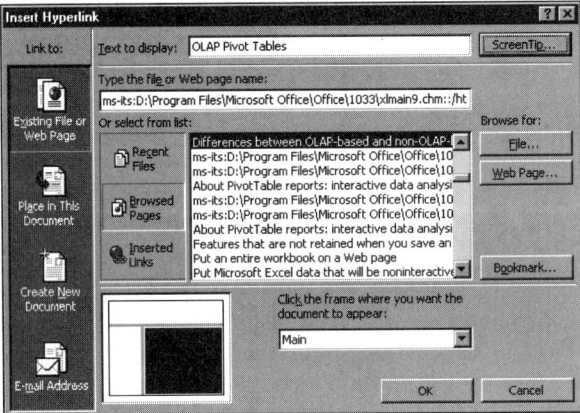

Figure 14-9: The Insert Hyperlink dialog box as it appears when you create a hyperlink inside a frame

Chapter 14: Essential Secrets of Web Page Development

3. **Create the hyperlink.** Type in the hyperlink text and identify the page or other document that you want it to open in the right-hand frame — use the techniques detailed in the "Working with Hyperlinks" section earlier in this chapter.

4. **Specify the frame where the target document will be displayed.** Use the drop-down list at the bottom of the dialog box to identify the frame by name. If you forget the name of the frame, hold the mouse pointer briefly over the corresponding part of the thumbnail to see its name in a ScreenTip.

Building Web forms in Word

Forms are standard components of Web pages — if you've spent any time on the Web, you're bound to have come across many examples. They enable users to interact with your Web site through controls (also known as form elements) such as option buttons, check boxes, and text boxes. Figure 14-10 shows a Web page form created in Word.

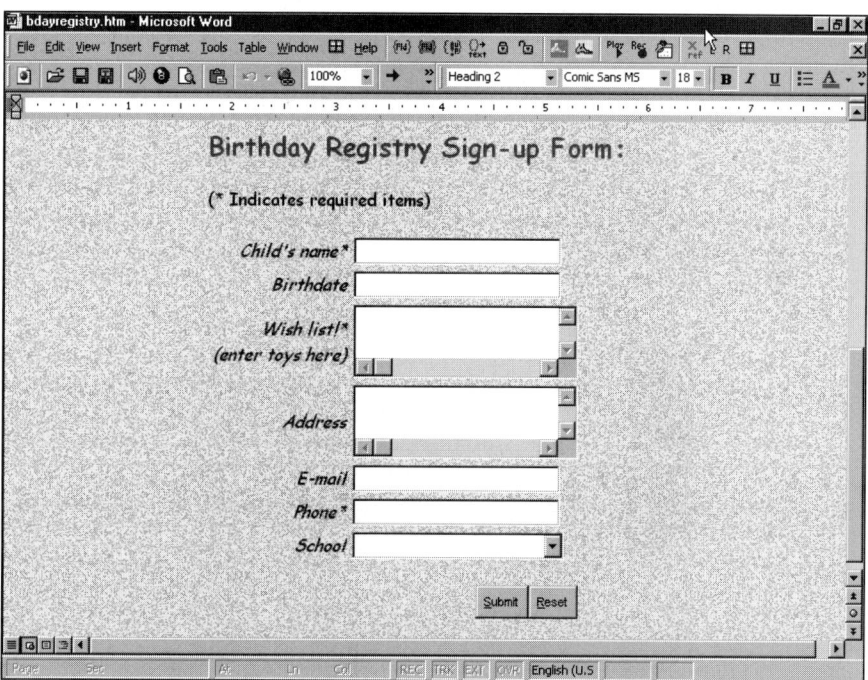

Figure 14-10: This Web page shows a typical use of Web forms.

Empowering your form with scripts

Although a form control can respond visually to user interaction without any programming, it won't do much of anything useful until you endow it with a *script,* a kind of miniprogram that tells it what to do. Office 2000 includes a sophisticated script editor for creating these little programs. It is introduced in Chapter 15.

Caution

Word has the tools you need to create Web forms, all right, but to get your forms to work properly, you must know how to write scripts that power them, and how to hook those scripts up to your forms. If you have FrontPage, you're much better off creating forms with that program — FrontPage handles all those details for you, based on your entries in dialog boxes.

Creating forms

To add a form to a Web page, start by displaying the Web Tools toolbar. It contains buttons for all the standard HTML forms controls and related functions. To insert a control, position the insertion point where you want the element to be placed, and then click the button for that element on the Web Tools toolbar. Word creates a form area in the document as soon as you insert a control from the toolbar.

Like their counterparts on VBA forms, HTML form controls have properties that you can set to govern their behavior. To set a control's properties, select it and click the Properties button at the top middle of the Web Tools toolbox. Most controls have the Value property. Be sure to set this — it determines the data that the control represents. In the case of a check box or option button, this is the value that appears in the form if the user selects the box or button. For list and drop-down boxes, the Value property contains the items in the list, while it specifies default text for text box and text area controls.

Adding a Submit control

Every form must have one control that the user clicks to submit his or her entries. Use the Submit control to place a standard command button on the form, or the Submit with Image control to use a graphic as your submit button. In either case, the control's Action property should be set to the name of the script that should run when the form is submitted. Set the Method property to Post instead of Get unless you want to limit the form results to 255 characters.

Using tables to format forms

Secret

A simple way to control the spacing of form elements, so that the page appears exactly as you want, is to create a table inside the form. The elements are then placed in cells of the table.

Here's how to be sure that the table is inside the form:

1. Place the insertion point where you want the top of the form and insert any control there by clicking the appropriate button on the Web Tools

toolbar. Word creates a form area in the document and adds the control there.

2. Immediately delete the new control. The form itself remains, as indicated by lines representing its top and bottom borders.

3. Insert a table within the form. You can alter details of the table's layout as you add the controls.

Web Presentations with PowerPoint

PowerPoint presentations transfer smoothly from your computer to the Web or your company intranet. When you use the Save as Web Page command, your presentation is instantly converted into a set of Web pages, all accessible via a single master page and complete with buttons and links to navigate the site. Figure 14-11 shows a sample presentation saved in HTML format.

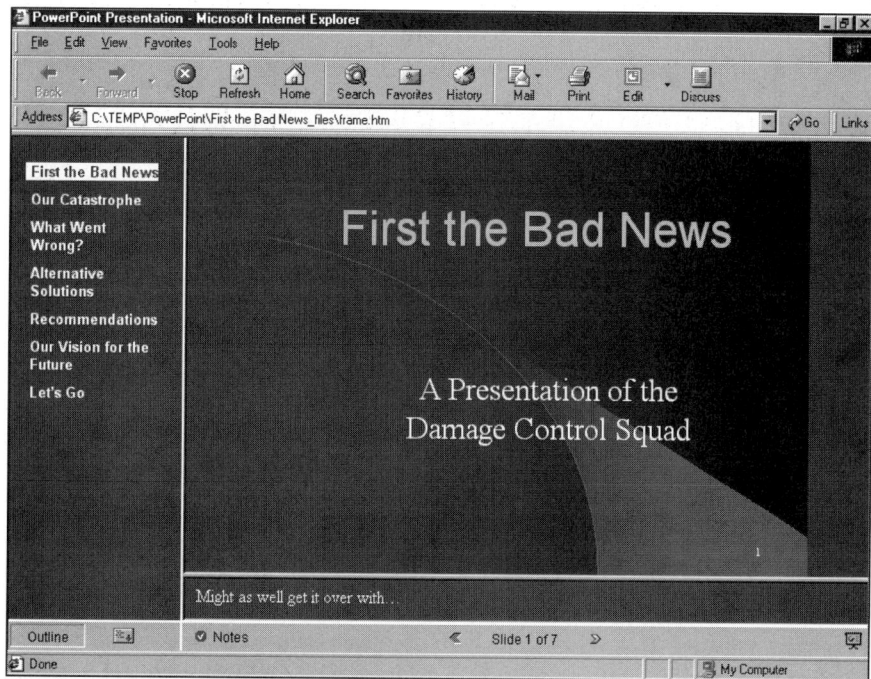

Figure 14-11: A PowerPoint presentation saved as a Web page

Note that the browser window is divided much like the Normal view in PowerPoint. The main part of the window displays the slide. A navigation bar on the left carries the titles of all the slides in the presentation — click a title to see that slide. An area below the slide is reserved for speaker notes.

Running across the entire window at the bottom is a bar containing viewing controls. From left to right, these are:

- **Outline button.** Hides or displays the outline frame.
- **Expand/Collapse Outline button.** Expands the outline to show subsidiary points under the slide titles, or collapses it again.
- **Notes button.** Hides or displays the speaker's notes frame.
- **Previous and Next buttons.** Takes you to other slides in order.
- **Full Screen Slide Show button.** Displays the presentation on the entire screen, as you would usually see it from within PowerPoint. The outline and speaker's notes are hidden.

Creating a PowerPoint presentation for the Web

Before you generate the PowerPoint Web pages, your first step is to get your presentation to the point where you're satisfied with it as a slide show presentation. If you're creating a new presentation, begin by choosing File ⇨ New and double-clicking AutoContent Wizard. After the wizard opens and you choose the presentation type, the wizard asks if the presentation is for Presentations or the Internet. When you select Internet and press Next, the wizard gives you the opportunity to include additional items on each page, including a copyright notice, the date the page was last updated, and a link to your e-mail address. If you're modifying an existing PowerPoint presentation for the Web, you can manually enter these items on each page.

Once you are finished with the AutoContent Wizard, the presentation outline appears and you can begin producing the presentation that you've envisioned. Use PowerPoint's slide show function until you're satisfied that the presentation delivers the message that you're after. You're now ready to convert your presentation for viewing on the Internet or your organization's intranet.

Saving a Web presentation

Converting an ordinary PowerPoint presentation to one for the Web is as simple as choosing the File ⇨ Save as Web Page command, typing in a filename, and clicking Save. You do have options governing the way PowerPoint creates the resulting pages. To access most of them, click Publish in the Save As dialog box. The Publish As Web Page dialog box is shown in Figure 14-12. Additional settings unique to PowerPoint appear in the Web Options dialog box, which you can access from the Publish box or from the General tab of the Tools ⇨ Options dialog box.

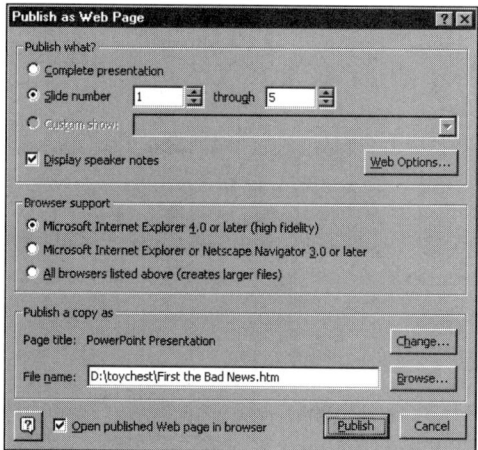

Figure 14-12: Use this dialog box to set options governing your Web presentations in PowerPoint.

Your considerations when saving a Web-based presentation include:

- **Which slides to include.** You can include the entire presentation, select a series of slides, or choose from among the custom slide shows you've defined for the presentation, if any.

- **Whether to include speaker notes.** To exclude notes, clear the obvious box on the Publish dialog box.

- **How to handle the outline pane and control bar.** You can exclude the outline and control bar from the presentation, but don't do so casually — doing so means you can only display the first slide in the presentation. If you want to proceed, open the Web Options dialog box, and on the General tab, clear the box labeled Add Slide Navigation Controls. If you do include the outline and control bar, you get to select its color scheme using the drop-down list beneath the checkbox.

- **Which browser(s) to support.** You can select a target browser to tell PowerPoint how to translate presentation features into HTML code. The All Browsers choice adds code that figures out which browser is running and displays the pages appropriately.

- **Whether to include animation effects.** Why not, if you've taken the trouble to add animation in the first place? Maybe because you're publishing the presentation on the Internet, where animation effects won't be so impressive for users with dial-up connections. Another problem is that some animation effects don't work right or don't work at all in browsers. If all that doesn't dissuade you, go to the General tab of the Web Options dialog box and check the Slide Show Animation While Browsing box to turn on animation in the Web presentation.

What you lose when viewing a presentation in a browser

Lots of slide show features don't work properly in Web presentations, at least when you view them in a browser. These include many animation effects and action settings, as well as automatic updates of the date or time and some text formatting elements. Fewer shortcut keys for browsing the show are available. If you reopen the HTML presentation in PowerPoint, however, everything should still function.

Editing a Web presentation

You can open the Web version of a presentation in PowerPoint, edit it, and save the changes. Just remember that a Web presentation may represent a subset of the original PowerPoint document, because you can select specific slides when you first save the Web presentation. If you didn't include the entire presentation in the Web version, you're probably better off making any changes in the original PowerPoint document and then recreating the Web version from that.

Publishing Your Web Pages

When you're finished creating all of your Web pages, it's time to post them to a Web server on your intranet or the Internet. If the server supports the Office Server Extensions, you can copy the files using Web Folders, described in Chapters 17 and 18. Alternatives include FrontPage, which includes a full-service Web site publishing feature, or one of the File Transfer Protocol (FTP) programs available on the Internet and elsewhere.

Your only real problem is to make sure that all the files involved in your Web site wind up on the server in the proper locations. Remember that most Web pages refer to a number of elements besides the HTML file, most commonly image files for photos, illustrations, charts, buttons, lines, and so on. There may also be sound and video files or other files that you're providing to your users for downloading.

All of these files must be stored on the Web server or in a location that the server has access to. They must also be in the exact location specified in the Web page (.htm file) that you've created, relative to the page being viewed. If they are not where they are supposed to be, you will have a broken link, where an image doesn't appear, another page doesn't open, or something else that was expected doesn't take place.

After you've published your Web site, be sure to test all the pages in a Web browser. Check to see that all the graphics are visible. If you see a red X where a graphic should be, it means that a supporting image file didn't make it to the server. If you have direct access to the page via Web Folders, you can open it in Office to correct the problem. Display the Web Options dialog box, and on the Files tab, check the box labeled Update Links on Save. Saving the page back to the server should fix the problem. If you aren't able to use Web Folders, try publishing the site again with whatever method you used previously, double-checking to make sure that you copy all the support files to the correct locations.

Conclusion

Why buy a specialized authoring tool when Office lets you create gorgeous Web pages with no additional software? Even if you need to incorporate interactive spreadsheets and databases into your pages, Office can handle the challenge — Chapter 15 bears that out.

Chapter 15

Building Dynamic Web Pages

In This Chapter

- Using Office components for interactive Web pages
- Saving spreadsheets as Web pages — interactive or otherwise
- Creating Web pages with live links to your Access data
- Adding custom functionality to your Web pages using scripts

Interactivity and immediacy are the essence of the World Wide Web experience. When you're ready to move beyond hyperlinks, Office provides advanced tools for making your pages responsive to their users. Excel and Access let you put together dynamic, data-intensive pages with a minimum of extra effort. And when you need full control of what happens when someone browses your page, the new script editor stands ready to support your forays into custom Web page programming.

Requirements for Office Interactive Pages

A small but uniquely powerful set of interactive, Web-enabled controls make their debut in Office 2000. Called collectively the Office Web Component controls, these controls include a spreadsheet control that works like a mini-Excel; a PivotTable list control, for viewing and manipulating pivot tables on a Web page; and a chart control, for working with interactive charts. Plug them into your Web pages, and people who browse your Web site gain moment-to-moment control over the information they see. Figure 15-1 shows the spreadsheet control in action in a Web page.

The only trouble is, many people won't be able to access pages that contain these components. For one thing, they work only in Internet Explorer versions 4 and 5. This requirement right away eliminates all the hordes of people who use other browsers. Next, a user must also have these components installed on his or her system. Otherwise, Web pages that contain them will show big empty areas where the controls belong, even in IE. Departing from its usual practice for add-ons, Microsoft isn't distributing the Office Web Components for free. Instead, only those who have licensed Office 2000 can legally use them.

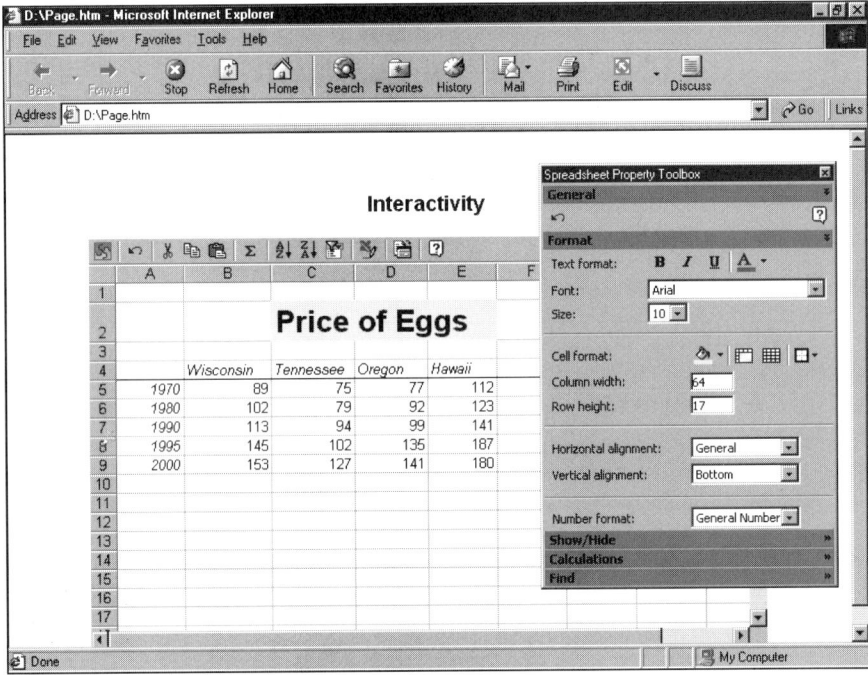

Figure 15-1: An Office interactive spreadsheet control goes live in this Web page.

The upshot of these restrictions is that until Office 2000 is as universal as the Web itself, publishing pages containing the Office Web Components will remain a dubious proposition, at least on public Web sites. If your organization standardizes on Office 2000, however, you can put them to use on the local intranet with carefree abandon.

Publishing Spreadsheets on the Web

Converting any part of an Excel workbook to a Web page is as easy as saving the document in HTML format using the File ⇨ Save as Web Page command. You do face a few choices, the most important being whether to convert the entire workbook or only a part of it, and whether to save the page in static or interactive form. To an extent, you can control these alternatives from the Save As dialog box itself. For a richer range of options, however, click the Publish button in the Save As box. When you do, the Publish as Web Page dialog box appears in place of Save As (see Figure 15-2). Note the check box that opens the page in your browser as soon as it's saved.

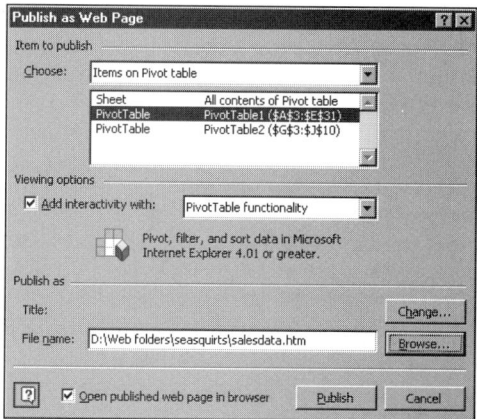

Figure 15-2: The Publish as Web Page dialog box gives you control over what part of your workbook to convert to a Web page and how to make the conversion.

Caution

Unlike Word documents and PowerPoint presentations, Excel workbooks can lose some functionality or formatting when you convert them to Web pages. Although Excel can open the resulting HTML files again, they may not look the way they used to or contain all the original information. This limitation is especially true when you save interactive data, but some features get lost even when you save an entire workbook as a static Web page. For this reason, always save your workbooks in the standard .xls format before saving them as Web pages.

Choosing workbook elements to convert

In the Save As dialog box you can choose whether to save as your Web page the workbook as a whole, or whatever was selected before you opened the dialog box. Use the two radio buttons in the Save area to make your choice. Note that if you choose Selection rather than Entire Workbook, you can save the selection *only* as a Web page — the alternative file formats that would otherwise be listed at Save as Type become unavailable.

If you want fast action, then, select the part of the workbook you want in your Web page before you open the Save as Web Page dialog box. Just be sure that you select the item in its entirety, because redefining the selection requires you to leave the dialog box. To save a pivot table, for example, select it by choosing Select ⇨ Entire Table from its shortcut menu. If you want to save a single worksheet, it's best to explicitly select it by clicking the Select All button at the top-left corner of the worksheet.

Once you're in the Save As dialog box, if you decide that your Web page should contain a part of the workbook that you didn't select ahead of time, click Publish. You can now pick items in the Choose area to identify just about any discrete element in the workbook. First, use the drop-down list to select one of the sheets by name, or pick the Previously Published Items or Range of Cells choices. Then, if your selection has more than one element that can be saved, choose the element you want in the list box just below the drop-down list. If you selected a Range of Cells in the drop-down list, you must type in a range or click the Collapse Dialog button to select the range with the mouse.

Publishing interactive data

The distinction between interactive and static spreadsheet-based pages is simple: In an interactive page, users can play with the data in their browser, while in static pages, the data just sits there. Users of interactive pages get to modify values, sort or filter the information, and enter formulas to perform calculations that give the results they want to see. In the case of pivot tables, users can reorganize the component fields and choose the level of detail to see in grouped fields. Interactive charts can be altered by changing the underlying data in the accompanying datasheet.

Although interactive Web pages are a lot more fun for users, they aren't the right choice for every situation. You may want to be sure users see the correct values, and you may not want to distract them with gee-whiz interactive controls.

To save a workbook element as an interactive Web page, just click the Add Interactivity check box in the dialog box you use to save the data, either Save as Web Page or Publish as Web Page. The Save as Web Page dialog box automatically determines the type of interactive page you save (spreadsheet, pivot table, or chart). In the Publish as Web Page box, you get more control — you can choose to save worksheets or ranges as interactive pivot tables, or to save pivot tables as interactive spreadsheets.

Secret

You can't turn an entire workbook into an interactive Web page. However, you can save each sheet individually in interactive format and then create a frames page in Word (see Chapter 14) to display the sheets in one frame under the control of navigation button in another frame.

Preparing to publish interactive workbook data

Some prep work may be required to realize the intended results in interactive Web pages based on Excel workbooks. Consider these points:

- If the worksheet or data range you're converting contains external data, saving it as a Web page "freezes" the data. If you want the Web page to retrieve current data each time it's opened, you must incorporate the data into a pivot table and then save the pivot table in interactive form.

- If you're saving an interactive pivot table, remove custom calculations and set the data fields to use one of the following four summary functions: Sum, Count, Min, or Max. You can save an interactive pivot table that you've already formatted, but don't bother formatting it for purposes of the Web page—all custom character and cell formatting vanishes (see Figure 15-3).

- If you're saving an interactive chart, confine yourself to chart types and elements that translate properly to Web pages. Surface and 3-D chart types in particular are off limits. If the chart resides on a worksheet, save it separately rather than as part of the sheet—charts are removed when you save sheets with interactivity.

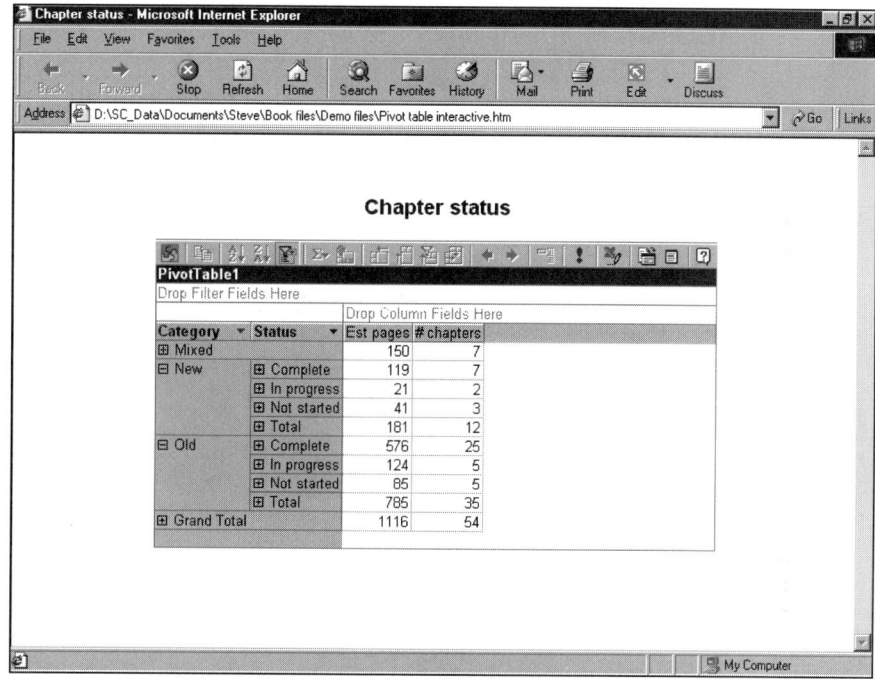

Figure 15-3: This Web page illustrates the simple formatting applied to all interactive pivot tables.

Formatting interactive pages

Cell and text formatting is retained in interactive spreadsheets, but not in pivot tables. If you open a page containing an interactive spreadsheet in Excel, changes you make to cell formatting are retained when you save the page and will appear in the browser when the page is opened there. However, you have to use the spreadsheet control's property toolbox to apply formatting to the cells in the control—Excel's usual formatting commands don't work.

Excel isn't a stellar performer as a page layout program. Microsoft recommends that you apply formatting to the rest of the page—the parts not occupied by the interactive control—using Word, Access, or FrontPage.

Working with interactive data in a browser

Opened in a browser, an interactive spreadsheet behaves much like a scaled-down version of Excel itself. The user can edit cell data or type in new values or formulas. Most built-in Excel functions are available, so formulas can perform sophisticated calculations. The toolbar across the top of the spreadsheet provides buttons for sorting and filtering the information, among other tasks (see Figure 15-4). Clicking the Property Toolbox button, second from the right, displays a range of other controls. Among these are a bunch for changing font, color, and other formatting characteristics of the cells (refer back to Figure 15-1 to see the Spreadsheet Property toolbox).

Figure 15-4: The toolbar of the interactive spreadsheet control

Interactive pivot tables work much like pivot tables in Excel, except that you can't change their formatting. Users can't modify an interactive chart directly with the mouse, but a spreadsheet containing the underlying data appears below the chart and those data can be sliced and diced there.

Database Publishing on the Net with Access

Access provides several ways to distribute information over the Internet or an intranet. The easy way is to export database objects such as tables and queries as ordinary HTML documents, which you can then post to the Web or wherever. With a bit more work, however, you can make live Web pages that display current information from your database for all those data-hungry surfin' fools who browse your site.

Secret

In VBA code or macros, use the `OutputTo` method to export database information in any supported format, including HTML.

Exporting data to static Web pages

Exporting a database object as an ordinary Web page is child's play. The drawback is that the resulting file retains no link to the original data. As soon as your database changes, your Web page is out of date until you export a new version of the file. Another problem: When you export a form, only its datasheet winds up in the Web page — not the formatted form you laid out so carefully.

If you can live with the prospect of early obsolescence and minimal formatting, export the currently selected object by choosing File ⇨ Export. In the Export dialog box, select HTML Documents in the Save as Type box. Check the Autostart box if you want Access to start your Web browser and open the exported document there so you can see the results.

After you choose Export, a diminutive HTML Output Options dialog box appears. If you want to merge the exported data with an HTML template to enhance the otherwise Spartan output from Access, specify the template name here. (An HTML template is a text file you create that specifies the location and appearance of common elements in an Access-based Web page — for details, search in Access Help for "HTML template"). Then choose OK to go ahead and save the exported HTML document.

Access exports each selected datasheet and each printed page of a report as a separate HTML file, adding the page number to the end of each filename. If you save a report with multiple pages, Access supplies basic navigation controls in the form of First, Previous, Next, and Last text buttons (the HTML template you specify can include placeholders for these navigation controls). During the export, Access generates the appropriate hyperlinks for the navigation buttons on each page.

Using report snapshots on the Web

If ordinary exported datasheets look too plain, use report snapshots for fancier-looking Web pages based on static Access data. A report snapshot is a file that encapsulates an Access report as it appears when you display it in Print Preview — that is, with the current data and full formatting you see on the screen. You can distribute these snapshots to anyone, even those who don't have Access (a 32-bit version of Windows is required). A Snapshot Viewer program is required to display report snapshots. The Viewer comes with Access and is available freely from Microsoft.

Creating a report snapshot is as simple as exporting the report. In Access, select or open the report you want to use and choose File ⇨ Export. After you select Snapshot Format in the Save as Type list and click Save, Access asks you for any parameters required by the report. When the snapshot has been saved, it appears automatically in the Snapshot Viewer, where you can proofread it before distributing the file.

One distribution method is to simply send the snapshot file on disk or via e-mail. Recipients can then run Snapshot Viewer as a stand-alone program and open the snapshots within it. Alternatively, however, you can include a snapshot in a Web page using either of the following techniques:

- Insert a hyperlink to the snapshot file onto the page. When the user clicks the link, the snapshot opens in the browser (with Internet Explorer 3 or above) or in a separate window.

- Add to your Web page the Snapshot Viewer ActiveX control, also included with Access, and set its `SnapshotPath` property to the URL of the snapshot file. When the page is viewed in a browser, the snapshot appears within the control. Obviously, this method works only with browsers that support ActiveX controls. If the Snapshot Viewer control isn't already installed on the user's computer, the browser downloads it from your Web site the first time a page containing the control is opened.

Storing databases on the Web server for dynamic pages

Your organization's Web server may not be the computer where the company databases reside. In this situation, one solution is to place a copy of the database on the Web server so that dynamically generated Web pages can locate the data they need. The problem, of course, is that you must keep updating the database copy to reflect changes in the original. Use Replication Manager, a software tool that comes with Office 2000 developer, to automate this process.

Creating server-side dynamic database pages

If you want users to be able to interact with your database in any browser, you can export database information in either of two dynamic data formats: IDC/HTX (Internet Database Connector/HTML extension) and ASP (Active Server Pages). Both formats work by inducing your Web server software to query the database on the fly. The server generates an HTML file containing the requested data and sends that file to the browser. As a result, the data displayed by the browser in this dynamically generated Web page are always current. You can export tables, queries, and form datasheets, but not reports, to either format.

Server requirements for dynamic database pages

Compared to static data pages, which you must constantly update, dynamic database pages require much, much less maintenance. However, because the IDC/HTX and ASP formats rely on nonstandard enhancements to HTML, they work only when published on compatible servers. Server requirements are:

- **For IDC/HTX files.** Any version of Microsoft Internet Information Server (for Web servers running NT Server) or Personal Web Server (for servers running NT Workstation or Windows 95).

- **For ASP files.** Microsoft Internet Information Server 3.0 or greater with ActiveX Server controls, running on NT Server.

Choosing a format

Of the two formats, ASP is the most versatile. Because they support ActiveX Server controls, Active Server Pages enable users to add, modify, and delete records in the database, assuming they have permission. (By the way, the Help file for the Microsoft Script Editor contains a great deal of reference information on Active Server Pages. The Script Editor is discussed in the last major section of this chapter.)

Exporting dynamic database pages

Exporting your database objects in either IDC/HTX or ASP format requires only a smidge more work than creating static pages. Choose File ⇨ Export, select the desired output format at Save as Type, and click Save. However, when you specify one of the dynamic formats in the Save As dialog box's Save as Type field, the Output Options dialog box prompts you for a number of additional entries. Figure 15-5 shows this dialog box as it appears when you save pages in the ASP format.

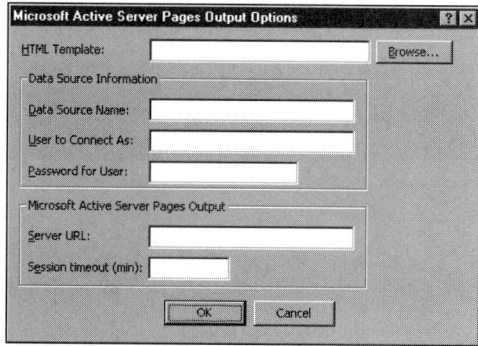

Figure 15-5: Fill out this dialog box when you export to an ActiveX Server page.

In addition to the path to an HTML template, you must specify the ODBC DSN (data source name) needed to connect to the database, along with user connection information including a user name and password. When you're saving to the ASP format, you must give the URL for the server where the exported ASP page is to be stored during Web access. To connect to your database with either type of file, the Access Desktop driver must be installed and the correct ODBC DSN for the database must be set up. You can find information on the steps required in Access Help.

Working with data access pages

On an intranet, Access 2000's new data access pages enable users to work with live, formatted data in their browsers — as long as they're using Internet Explorer 5. Unfortunately, because data access pages require users to have IE5 and the Office Web components, they aren't a general solution for interactive database access over the Internet.

Understanding data access pages

Unlike other objects in an Access database, data access pages are stored in individual files, separate from the database itself. In the Database window, the data access page icons represent shortcuts to these files.

You can create data access pages that function as:

- **Interactive reports.** Unlike a printed report, a data access page lets users determine how much detail they see and enables them to sort and filter the data.
- **Data entry forms.** When you add, edit, or delete a record on a data access page, the changes are entered in the underlying database.
- **Data analysis tools.** Data access pages can include interactive spreadsheets, pivot tables, and charts that summarize data and help you identify trends.

Each user is free to change the way data are displayed in his or her browser without affecting the data access page stored on the server. Changes made to the data themselves, however, are real — they are posted to the database on which the page is based.

Creating data access pages

Create data access pages as you would other Access database objects. Switch to the Pages button in the Objects bar. There, your options include:

- **Creating a page (semi)automatically.** Click the New button and choose AutoPage: Columnar in the resulting dialog box. Select a table or query on which to base the page, and click OK to open the page.
- **Running the Page Wizard** to guide you through the process of choosing, grouping, and sorting records in the page. Click Create Data Access Page by Using Wizard.
- **Starting a new data access page from scratch in Design view.** Click Create Data Access Page in Design View.
- **Converting an existing Web page to a data access page.** Double-click Edit Web page that already exists. When Access opens the page you specify, you must indicate the database you want to connect it to. You can then add interactive elements as you would to any data access page. Saving the page creates a corresponding shortcut in the Database window.

Designing data access pages

You use the same basic techniques for laying out a data access page as you would when designing an Access form or report.

Figure 15-6 shows a new data access page opened in Design view. The *body* of a data access page constitutes the page's work area, onto which you place all visible elements. When the page is viewed in IE, the body adjusts its size to fit into the browser window. The body contains two preformatted text areas, one for typing a title, the other for explanatory text or instructions. You can place controls such as labels, buttons, and check boxes into the body, but more often they go into a *section*, a defined rectangular area intended for form-type layouts.

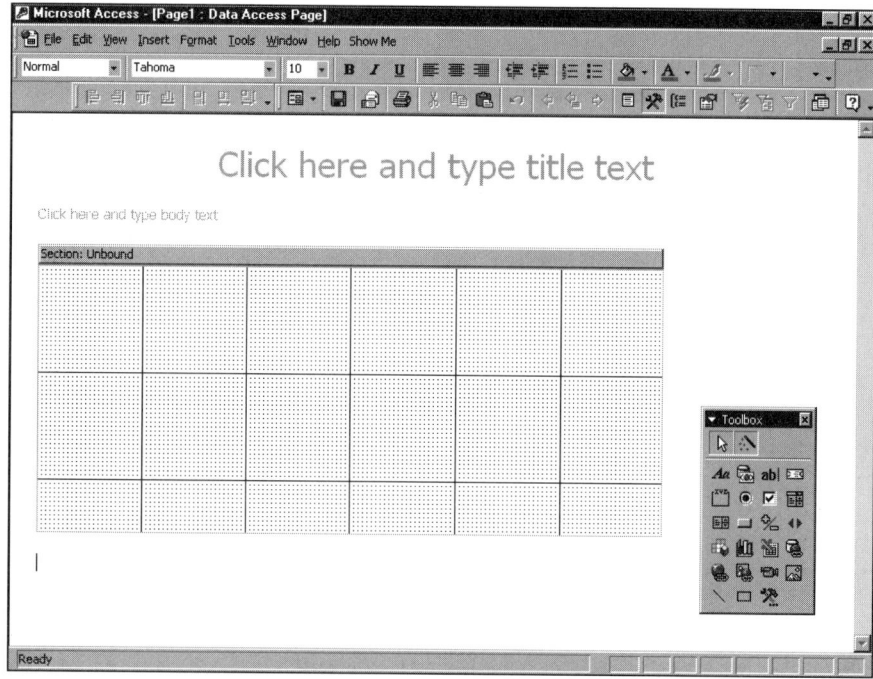

Figure 15-6: Starting a new data access page in Design view

You can add controls to the form by dragging them from the Field List, a window listing all the tables and queries in the database and their fields, or by using the Toolbox toolbar. Adding a field from the Field List produces a text box control bound (linked) to that field. Chapter 47, on Access forms, explains how bound controls work, and the techniques described there for laying out controls work in data access pages, too. You can add all the fields from a table or query en masse by dragging the corresponding table or query item from the Field List to the page.

Working with grouping levels and sections

A new, blank data access page like the one in Figure 15-6 opens with a single unbound section (that is, it isn't linked to any table or query in the database). Once you bind a database object, sections are defined by the way you group the data. For example, if your data access page displays sales data grouped by month and then by state, you have two *group levels*, each with its own sections. Four sections are available in each group level, although you use only the sections appropriate for your needs. The sections are:

- **Group header.** Misleadingly named, this section is used to display individual records as well as for elements you might expect to see in a header.

- **Group footer.** Displayed directly above the record navigation section, the footer is used to display calculated totals for the group.

- **Record navigation.** This section automatically displays the record navigation control for the group level and appears after the group header section. You can add unbound controls to it as well.

- **Caption.** Place text boxes, labels, and other unbound controls in this section, which appears above the group header. Bound controls are off-limits here, too.

Secret

In data access pages used for data entry, you can have only one group level, and the Group footer section isn't available.

Setting up group levels

You can create as many nested group levels as you need. When you use the Page Wizard to create a data access page, you can set up grouping levels on the page with the wizard's help. Otherwise, you have to do it by hand.

To create the first group level in a new blank page, bind a database object to the unbound section. All you have to do is drag a field that belongs to the desired table or query from the Field List to the section. This step creates a field on the page and simultaneously binds the section to the table or query containing the field.

The technique for adding additional group levels depends on whether you're grouping by an individual field in the same table or query, or by one of two separate tables or queries. Shown in Design view, the data access page in Figure 15-7. is grouped first by the Region field of the Customers table, then by the rest of the Customers table, and then by the Orders table.

Here are the details on setting up each type of group:

- **Grouping by a field in the same table or query.** A field that contains the same data in many different records makes a useful "group-by" field. In a table of addresses, for example, you might want to group by the state fields, because the database probably contains multiple records from each state. To group by an individual field, add it to the section, make sure that it's selected, and then click the Promote button on the Page Design toolbar.

- **Grouping by a table or query.** You can add fields from more than one table or query to the same data access page. When two tables or queries have a one-to-many relationship, Access lets you group by the item on the "one" of the relationship. For example, if the database has a Categories table and a Products table related by a shared CategoryID field, you would group by Categories, producing a page that shows the products in each category. To set up the groups, add the fields you want to display from both tables to the section. Then select any field from the table you want to group by and click the Group by Table button on the Page Design toolbar.

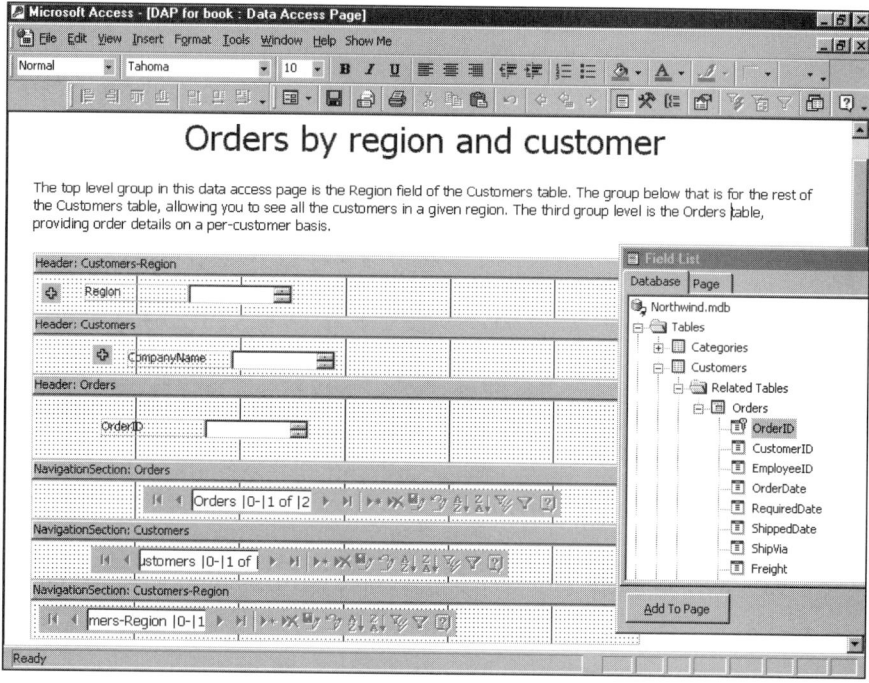

Figure 15-7: A budding data access page showing multiple group levels

Once you create a new group level, Access automatically adds new sections to the page for that group. Which sections you see depends on settings in the Sorting and Grouping dialog box, described next.

Modifying group level settings

You can see and modify the settings for each group level by choosing View ➪ Sorting and Grouping. In the resulting dialog box, select the group level you want to work with by clicking it in the Group Record Source section. You can then fiddle with the group's properties as displayed in the lower half of the box. Turn on or off any of the group's four sections using the first four properties.

Creating data entry data access pages

To create a data access page for entering and editing data, you must observe one essential rule: Create only one group level for the page.

Secret

You can't use group levels to work with two related tables in a single data entry data access page, but you can stitch together a workable solution using *two* pages. Bind each page to one of the tables. Then place a hyperlink from the page on the "one" side of the relationship to the other page. If you're feeling ambitious, you can then create a frames page in Word (see Chapter

14) or FrontPage, loading the two pages into its frames. With some layout elbow grease and some luck, the result should work like a single page and enable you to see and edit data from either table simultaneously.

Using data access pages within Access

A data access page is live in the Access database where you create it — you don't have to view it in Internet Explorer. Data access pages serve essentially the same functions as forms and reports. You may want to use an existing data access page rather than go to the trouble of building a comparable form or report from scratch.

Enlivening Web Pages with Scripts

Scripts are small programs attached to a Web page that provide snippets of custom functionality. Because scripts are embedded in the page's HTML code, they are downloaded to the browser when the user opens the page. This means the script program runs on the user's computer, not the server.

Scripts make your Web pages come alive, manipulating the page to produce animations or other changes the user can see. Scripts can run when the page opens, or in response to what the user does with the mouse and keyboard, and in response to other events. As a simple example, a script might determine the number displayed on one of those counters that shows how many times a page has been opened.

From out of nowhere, it seems, Office 2000 has added a full-blown development environment for viewing, writing, and testing Web page scripts. Shown in Figure 15-8, the Microsoft Script Editor is actually a complete HTML editing toolkit, and is available in all the Office applications except Outlook (choose Tools ➪ Macro ➪ Microsoft Script Editor to run it). The illustration shows a new script skeleton in the Source tab — that blank line in the middle of the window is where you would type the script's code, and the lines immediately above and below it identify it as a script. Note that the window's title bar displays the Script Editor's alternate name, the Microsoft Development Environment.

Working with scripting languages

Power has its price, and with scripts, that price is learning how to write script code. Two scripting languages are in common use on the Web: JavaScript (called JScript by Microsoft) and VBScript. Learning to program in either language is no trivial ambition, but the challenge is well within reach for a Secrets reader. However, because a worthwhile introduction to either language would eat up 50 pages or so, I must ask you to look elsewhere for details on JavaScript and VBScript coding. An excellent place to start is the Script Editor's Help file, which contains complete tutorials and reference information on both JavaScript and VBScript. I can offer brief remarks on the languages themselves.

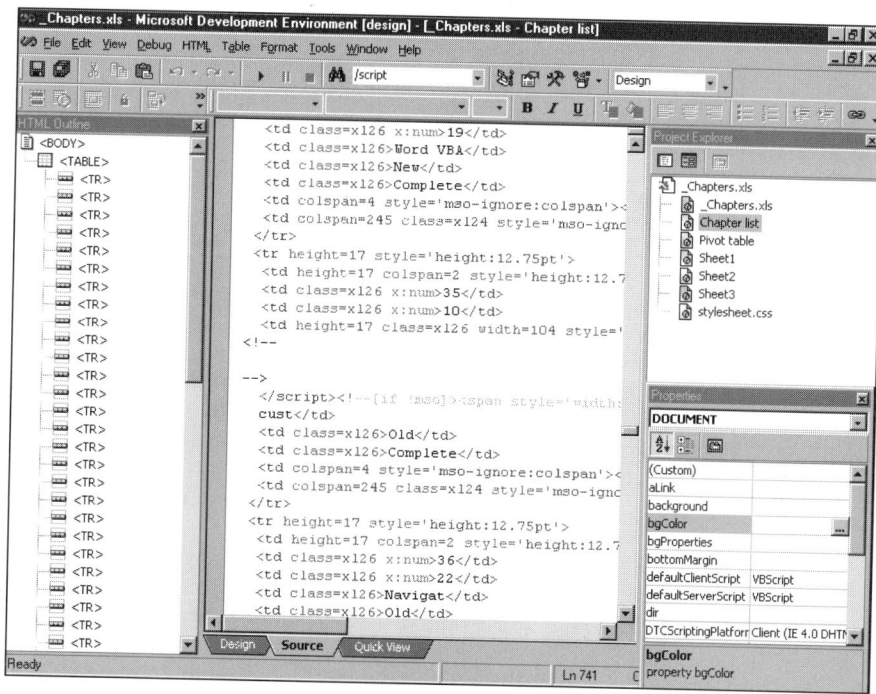

Figure 15-8: The Microsoft Script Editor lets you edit not only scripts but the HTML code for the entire document.

Comparing VBScript and JavaScript

Formally known as Microsoft Visual Basic Scripting Edition, VBScript is a scaled-down version of the Visual Basic language that powers VBA and receives extensive coverage in Part VI of this book. Because it's so similar to VBA, VBScript is a natural for Office developers. The problem is that browsers other than Internet Explorer (version 3 and later) can't execute VBScript code. Use VBScript only if all your users have IE.

JavaScript enjoys much wider support among browsers than does VBScript. That makes it the scripting language to use in pages you publish on the World Wide Web, or anywhere they will be opened by users who get to choose their own browsers. By the way, JavaScript bears no direct relationship to the Java programming language, although the two languages have some similarities.

Selecting a default scripting language

You can choose either scripting language, VBScript or JavaScript, as the default for the Web pages you work on in the Script Editor. To change the default scripting language, locate the `defaultClientScript` property in the Properties window. Alternatively, display the View ⇨ Property Pages dialog box, and on the General tab, select the preferred language in the drop-down list provided (this dialog box is just another way to access the same properties available in the Properties window when the entire page — the document object — is selected).

Adding script commands to the toolbar system

If you're at all serious about using scripts, equip yourself with some related commands that are missing from Office's default menus and toolbars. The commands are Insert Script, Show All Scripts, and Remove All Scripts. Using the customizing techniques covered in Chapter 5, place them on the menu or toolbar of your choice: Open the Tools ⇨ Customize dialog box, switch to the Commands tab, and select Tools in the Categories box. Now you can locate the three commands in the Commands box and drag them, one at a time, to the destination. You have to repeat this process for every Office application where you use scripts.

Identifying scripts in Web pages

You can tell where the scripts are embedded in a Web page by the presence of *script anchors* visible when you open the page in Office (see Figure 15-9). Script anchors may not be visible, however — show or hide them using the Show All Scripts command (add it to the toolbar system as described in the previous section). Here are some script anchor tricks:

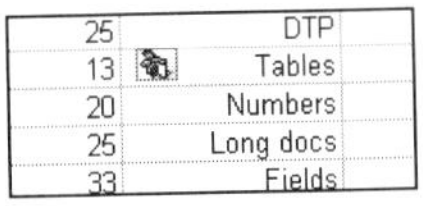

25		DTP
13		Tables
20		Numbers
25		Long docs
33		Fields

Figure 15-9: This little icon is a script anchor and is shown in an Excel workbook.

- Rest the mouse pointer on a script anchor to see the first 50 characters of the script in a ScreenTip.

- Double-click a script anchor to edit the script in the Microsoft Script Editor.

- Click a script anchor to select it. You can then press Del to delete it, or cut or copy it to the clipboard and then paste it elsewhere, even on a different document.

- Drag a script anchor to move the script to a new location in the document. Dragging with the right mouse button lets you make a copy of the script at the destination, preserving the original script.

Caution: Many scripts work fine no matter where they are placed in any Web page, but some are location-dependent — they won't work correctly when moved from their original location.

Editing code with the Script Editor

To open the current Office document in the Script Editor, choose Tools ⇨ Macro ⇨ Microsoft Script Editor. If the document isn't already a Web page, it's converted into HTML code. You can scroll through the document to view the HTML and scripts, and if you know what you're doing, you can type in new scripts anywhere you like in the code. Again, to display a specific script in the Editor, double-click its script anchor in Office.

Opening a document in the Script Editor creates a separate copy tied only loosely to the original. The code you type in the Script Editor doesn't automatically affect the original document, and likewise, changes you make back in the original document aren't automatically reflected in the code in the Script Editor. When you modify either version of the document and switch to the other, the Refresh toolbar appears. Click Refresh to bring the two versions into synch, or click Don't Refresh to keep them distinct.

Inserting scripts

To add a script to a specific location in an Office document, you need the Insert Script command, one of the three script-related commands you should install on a menu or toolbar (see "Adding script commands to the toolbar system" earlier in this chapter). Select the target location and click the button or menu item for the Insert Script command. The document opens in the Script Editor, with the skeleton of a new script at the appropriate place in the HTML code.

Previewing pages in the Script Editor

Click the Quick View tab at the bottom of the Script Editor window to see a mock-up of your document roughly as it would appear in Internet Explorer 4. The page is live, so you can test your scripts visually. The Design View tab lets you edit a Web page graphically rather than as HTML, much like you would in Word or FrontPage. To use it, however, you must open the page directly from its disk file, rather than from an Office application.

Using ActiveX controls on your Web pages

You can adorn your Web pages with the same ActiveX controls used to power VBA forms (see Chapter 24). ActiveX controls provide extraordinary capabilities, but be aware of two potential problems. First, they tend to be relatively large chunks of software, so they can really slow down pages that contain them. However, users feel this performance drag only the first time a page is downloaded — opening the page automatically installs its controls on the user's system, and thereafter, those controls are available for immediate use with any Web page. Second, ActiveX controls work only inside Internet Explorer — users who have Netscape Navigator are out of luck without special third-party plug-ins.

If you're not dissuaded, here are the steps required to place an ActiveX control on an Office Web page:

1. Starting with your document open in its Office application, display the Toolbox, the toolbar containing ActiveX controls (in Word, this toolbar is called the Control Toolbox).

2. Click the Toolbox button for the ActiveX control you want to use, and then click in your document to insert it there.

3. Resize the control to taste.

4. Click the Properties button on the Toolbox to display the Properties window. Use it to set the initial appearance and behavior of the control.

5. Write event procedures for the control. To create an event procedure, click the Insert Script button to start a new script in the Script Editor. Although you enter the procedure code directly into the page, you should pattern the procedure itself after the event procedure you would use in a VBA code window (see Chapter 24 for a complete discussion of event procedures). The following example shows a simple procedure for the `Click` event that changes the caption of a command button control:

```
<script language="VBScript">
<!--
Sub cmdBigButton_Click
    cmdBigButton.Caption = "You clicked me!"
End Sub
-->
</script>
```

6. Switch to the Quick View tab to test the event procedure.

    Nota bene: At Step 5, be sure you don't choose View Code from the control's shortcut menu. Doing so would take you to the Visual Basic Editor for VBA. VBA code runs on your computer, not the user's.

Conclusion

If you can master the complexities of spreadsheet and database design, you won't have any problem publishing Office data in interactive form on the Web or an intranet. And with the new Script Editor and some programming know-how, you can pull out all the stops to create dynamic Web pages that respond to the user just as you want them to.

Chapter 16

Building Great Web Sites with FrontPage

In This Chapter

- Creating Web sites with FrontPage
- Adding and importing pages to a FrontPage web
- Creating a navigation structure for your web
- Editing Web pages
- Using shared borders, navigation bars, and other special components
- Publishing complete Web sites to a server

Included with Office 2000 Premium is FrontPage, the leading software tool for Windows-based Web page development and Web site management. Even with the advanced page authoring features in Office proper, you're likely to find FrontPage a boon for some editing and formatting tasks. But FrontPage's main appeals to the Office aficionado lie in its abilities to organize a set of pages into a complete, coherent Web site, and to publish the entire site to a server.

Many of FrontPage's neatest features are available on servers running the FrontPage Server Extensions. The Extensions are available as software plug-ins for operating systems other than Windows, so you may be able to access them even if your organization or ISP uses a UNIX server. Just be sure to check on this before you go hog-wild with FrontPage's special capabilities.

Using FrontPage with the Rest of Office

It's fitting that Microsoft now bundles FrontPage 2000 with Office, because this is the first version of the program to be fully integrated with Word, Excel, and all the others. Functionally and cosmetically, FrontPage and Office go together like fingers on the same hand.

The availability of common themes for Web page design in Word, Access, and FrontPage demonstrates this tight coupling. Because the three applications share the same themes, you can create a given page in whichever program is most appropriate, yet maintain stylistic harmony throughout your site with no special effort.

Because you can store Office documents in HTML format, and because you can directly save and open Office documents in webs, you face no import-export hassles. When stored in HTML in a FrontPage web, Office documents *are* pages of the web, automatically. Office documents serving as Web pages don't lose their identity, however. When you're working on FrontPage and you click a page created by another Office application, the page opens in that application for editing.

Of course, FrontPage's user interface has been brought into line with the rest of Office, too (see Figure 16-1). The Views bar that lets you switch from one main function of the program to another looks and works like the Outlook bar and the Objects bar in Access. The Options and Customize commands on the Tools menu bring up dialog boxes similar to their counterparts in the other Office apps. The toolbars are now Office standard issue, and you can customize them with the techniques covered in Chapter 5.

Figure 16-1: FrontPage 2000's user interface is patterned closely after those of its Office suite-mates.

FrontPage has even gained full-bore VBA support. Understand, though, that you use VBA in FrontPage to automate the process of page design and web organization—not to add interactivity to your finished Web pages. To create pages that respond to user input in a browser, you can add prefab FrontPage components, such as a hit counter, and add custom scripts using the same script editor available elsewhere in Office (see Chapter 15).

Working with FrontPage

At the outset, you should understand a bit of jargon: the term *web* (with a lowercase *w*), as it's used in FrontPage. Speaking practically, a web corresponds roughly to what most people would call a Web site. In other words, it's a collection of Web pages hyperlinked together to make a coherent whole, along with the graphics and multimedia content the pages contain, and any downloadable files they make accessible. However, a FrontPage web isn't really a Web site until you *publish* it, that is, transfer all this content to a Web or intranet server. What's more, a finished Web site can contain content from more than one FrontPage web (see "Managing complex web content using subwebs" later in this chapter).

From another standpoint, a web constitutes the document in FrontPage. Understood this way, FrontPage webs are analogous to Excel workbooks or PowerPoint presentations. You use commands on the File menu to create new webs and open existing ones, just as you would work with documents in other Office applications. The web document is a record of the various files and folders you have added to the Web site you're developing. It doesn't directly contain the site's content itself, which resides in the HTML pages and associated files.

This web-as-document idea has a couple of holes in it, true. For one thing, FrontPage webs aren't stored in individual disk files but as a series of folders and the files within them. For another, when you use FrontPage as a Web page editor, the page is a document in its own right. Still, I hope it gives you a sense of the what's going on behind the scenes when you work with FrontPage webs.

The FrontPage treasure chest

FrontPage wraps together a comprehensive set of tools for Web site development. These include:

- **A Visual Web page editor.** Use FrontPage's specialized components to add navigation functions and visual consistency to the pages you create in other Office applications. If you develop a fondness for FrontPage's design tools, you're free to develop Web pages from scratch.

- **An HTML editor.** You can edit the HTML code for any Web page within FrontPage, and switch back and forth between the page and its HTML at will. FrontPage color codes the various HTML elements so that they're easy to distinguish visually, and it sees to it that the code is consistently formatted.

- **A Web site organizer.** FrontPage shows you the structure of your web as a simple hierarchical list with icons for individual pages. To modify that structure, you just drag the page icons to new locations in the hierarchy.

- **A hyperlink manager.** As your web grows and evolves, the links within it and to other sites are bound to become stale. FrontPage lets you see the network of links in your site and sniffs out broken ones for you.
- **A Web site publishing utility.** Once your FrontPage web is set up to your liking, a single command transfers the entire site to the server for public consumption.

About FrontPage views

Because FrontPage encompasses a welter of disparate functions, it must use a variety of visual devices to present them effectively. Rather than risking screen chaos by providing a separate window for each of these functions, Microsoft has chosen to limit you to one function at a time, each in its own *view*. To switch to the view you want to use, just click its icon in the Views bar, shown again for easy reference in Figure 16-2.

Figure 16-2: Use the Views bar to switch to the FrontPage view you want to work with.

FrontPage's views are:

- **Page view.** Used to view and edit individual Web pages (in previous versions of FrontPage, these functions were consigned to a separate program, the FrontPage Editor).
- **Folders view.** Provides an Explorer-type look at the organization of your web on disk, with icons for all the pages and other files, as well the folders that contain them.
- **Reports view.** Lets you see all kinds of information about your web via a host of predefined lists, error readouts, and diagnostic analyses.

- **Navigation view.** Used to organize the pages of your web.
- **Hyperlinks view.** Shows pages and other items linked to and from a chosen page or document, enabling you to inspect them for links that go nowhere.
- **Tasks view.** Keeps track of your to-do list of web-related tasks.

If you want to devote the screen real estate occupied by the bar to something more practical, such as viewing page content, right-click the bar and choose Hide Views Bar. You can then change views using the choices on the View menu.

About FrontPage windows

Although the main FrontPage window won't let you break up its contents into separate subwindows as you can in Excel and PowerPoint, you *can* open as many main FrontPage windows as you like. Each of these is accessible via the Windows Taskbar and in the Alt+Tab cycle. To open an additional main window you can:

- Open another web or create a new one. FrontPage automatically displays each open web in a separate main window.
- Choose Window ⇨ New Window. FrontPage opens another window for the current web. You can now display the same web in different views simultaneously.

By the way, the rest of FrontPage's Window menu lets you switch back to any Web page that's open in Page view. Pages stay open even when you switch to another view, so you can jet back to a specific page by selecting it from the Window menu.

Creating and Managing Webs in FrontPage

Before you can start adding pages to a FrontPage web, you must first explicitly create the web. FrontPage lets you create either *disk-based* webs, which you must later publish to a server, or *server-based* webs, which you develop on the server from which your audience accesses them. You should create server-based webs only if you're running FrontPage on the server — accessing a web's content across an intranet or Internet connection slows you down.

On disk, FrontPage stores each new web in a separate folder. It automatically creates several subfolders and some required support files within the web's main folder.

Starting a new web

Because FrontPage is both a Web page editor and a Web site manager, a single New command won't suffice. To create a new web, choose File ⇨ New ⇨

Web, or click the right-side bar on the New split button and choose Web on the resulting menu. Either action displays the New dialog box, which offers templates and wizards to get the new web started.

Before you make a selection, be sure to name the web-to-be in the box labeled Specify the Location of the New Web. If you don't name the web yourself, FrontPage supplies a dorky generic name such as MyWeb2.

Secret

Although the New dialog box doesn't make this clear, a web's name *is* the folder name or URL you supply as the location of the web. Be sure to choose the name that you want people to use for accessing your web. If you're planning to publish your little web on the big World Wide Web, observe the naming limitations in force there: Use only letters, numerals, and ordinary punctuation marks, and don't include spaces in the name.

Once you've named the new web, you can select one of the templates or wizards. The lower-right quadrant of the New dialog box carries a description of the currently selected item. When you double-click your choice or click OK, FrontPage creates the new web immediately (in the case of a template) or starts the selected wizard, which presents you with a series of choices via which you can begin to define the web's structure and some of its content.

Adding pages to a web

When you use the Empty Web template to create a new web, FrontPage sets up the web folders and support files and leaves you with the job of creating the web's pages. With any of the other templates and wizards, a new web contains at least one page to get you started. Either way, though, you're bound to need additional pages. To add a brand-new page to a web you can:

- Choose File ⇨ New ⇨ Page.
- Click the main part of the New button (you don't have to worry about opening the button's drop-down menu when you're creating a new page).
- Right-click anywhere in the Folders or Navigation views, or over the folder list in Hyperlinks view, and choose New Page from the resulting shortcut menu.

Any of the preceding actions create a new page file in the current web. If a page hasn't already been opened for editing, switching to Page view automatically creates a new page — but you have to save it in your web's folder before it becomes part of the web, and you can save it elsewhere if you prefer.

You can also add existing Web pages to a FrontPage web. See "Bringing Content into a FrontPage Web" later in this chapter.

Naming and renaming pages

Each page in a FrontPage web has three names: its filename as stored on disk, its name in FrontPage for navigation purposes, and its title, the name displayed in the title bar when it's opened in a browser. Here's how to edit each of these:

- When you create a new page in Folders view, FrontPage assigns it a default filename but assumes you're not going to like its choice—the filename is automatically selected for editing. You can change the filename at any time by selecting the page and pressing F2.

- To change a page's name for navigation, switch to Navigation view and click the page icon in the navigation pane (not in the Folder List) to select it. Press F2 to start editing the name.

- To change a page's title, right-click the page in the Folder, Navigation, or Hyperlinks views and choose Properties from the shortcut menu. Edit the title in the General tab of the resulting dialog box.

Secret

Select titles for your pages with care—make them brief but informative. The title is the name under which a page is stored in the browser's History list and Favorites folder.

Working with folders and files

FrontPage's Folders view works like Windows Explorer, so you shouldn't have any trouble using it to navigate the constituent files and folders of your web. A few points bear comment, however.

You can select any arbitrary set of files in the Folders view Contents pane (the big section on the right) to carry out cut, copy, and delete operations; to find and replace text in the selected files; and to apply themes or specify shared borders. Shift+click to select a series of consecutive files, or Ctrl+click to select or deselect any file individually.

As in Explorer, double-clicking a file opens it. By default, Web pages created in another Office application open in that application, while those created in FrontPage or stored in generic HTML open in FrontPage's page editor (Page view). Image files open in the application with which they're associated in Windows, except that GIF and JPEG files open in Internet Explorer, if IE is running. You can change these defaults in the Configure Editors tab of the Tools ⇨ Options dialog box. All the editors you thus configure are available when you right-click a file and choose Open With.

Note that Folders view's icons for pages are informative. You can see at a glance which Office application created the page, because a mini-icon for the application is overlaid on each page's icon. Generic HTML pages saved by IE, a text editor, or some other Web page editor have icons without any identifying mini-icon. Also, when a page is open in the FrontPage editor, a little pencil—I guess that's what it is—gets added to its icon in Folders view.

Finally, be aware that the Folder List navigation bar, a fixture of Folders view, is optionally available in the Page, Navigation, and Hyperlinks views as well. It works a bit differently here, listing files as well as folders but enabling you select only one file at a time. Use the View ⇨ Folder List command or the corresponding toolbar button to turn it on or off in these views.

Designing your web's navigation structure

Once your web contains its pages, it's time to organize those pages into a hierarchical structure for navigation purposes. Use Navigation view for this chore. Shown in Figure 16-3, Navigation view presents your web on a sort of pasteboard on which you can arrange and rearrange the pages to clarify their relationships.

You're supposed to use Navigation view in concert with *navigation bars* you insert in your pages. A navigation bar is a FrontPage component that automatically adds the appropriate navigation buttons to the page, based on the location of the page in the navigation structure. But even if you eschew navigation bars, Navigation view can help you turn a hazy mental picture of your site's organization into a definite road map.

Secret

It's important to understand that placing a page in the navigation structure does *not* automatically add links to any other pages in the structure. FrontPage creates links for you only if you add navigation bars to the page.

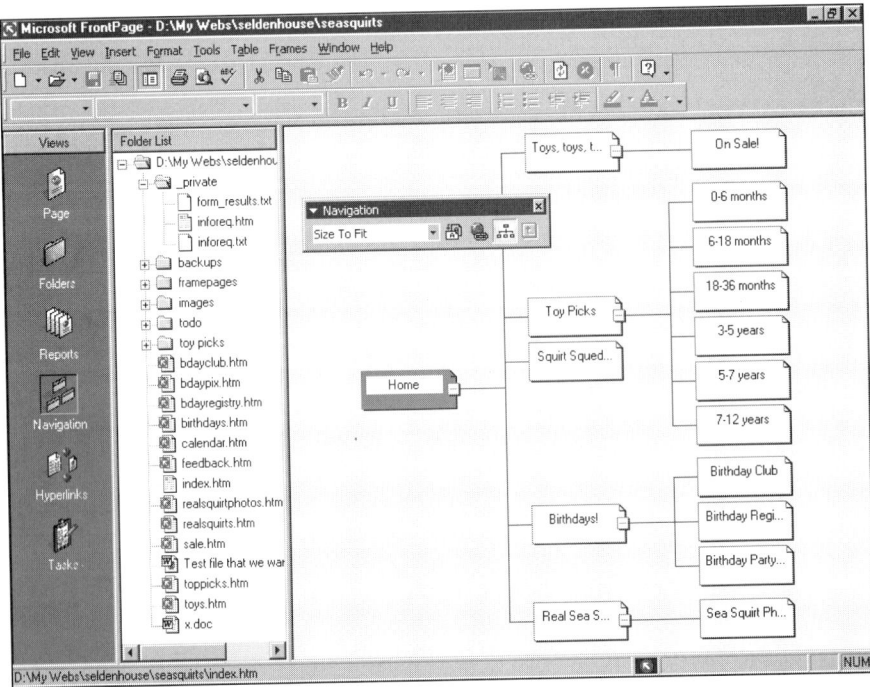

Figure 16-3: Navigation view helps you organize your web (shown here rotated so that it fits better on the screen).

Working with pages in the navigation structure

A web's home page is the only one automatically included in its navigation structure. To add an additional page, drag it from the Folder List to the location in the structure where you want it to reside. To position the page where you want it, watch the location of a fuzzy line that connects the icon of the page you're adding to an existing icon on the structure (see Figure 16-4). Let the fuzzy line guide you as follows:

- If you don't see the fuzzy line, the page can't be added to the structure at the current location. Drag on until the line appears.

- To add a page to the *top level* of the web — the level of the home page — the fuzzy line should extend from the top of the home page icon (or the left side, if you're viewing the structure in the rotated portrait orientation).

- To add a page at a subsidiary level to an existing page, drag the icon for the new page until the fuzzy line connects it to the bottom of the existing page's icon (the right side in rotated view).

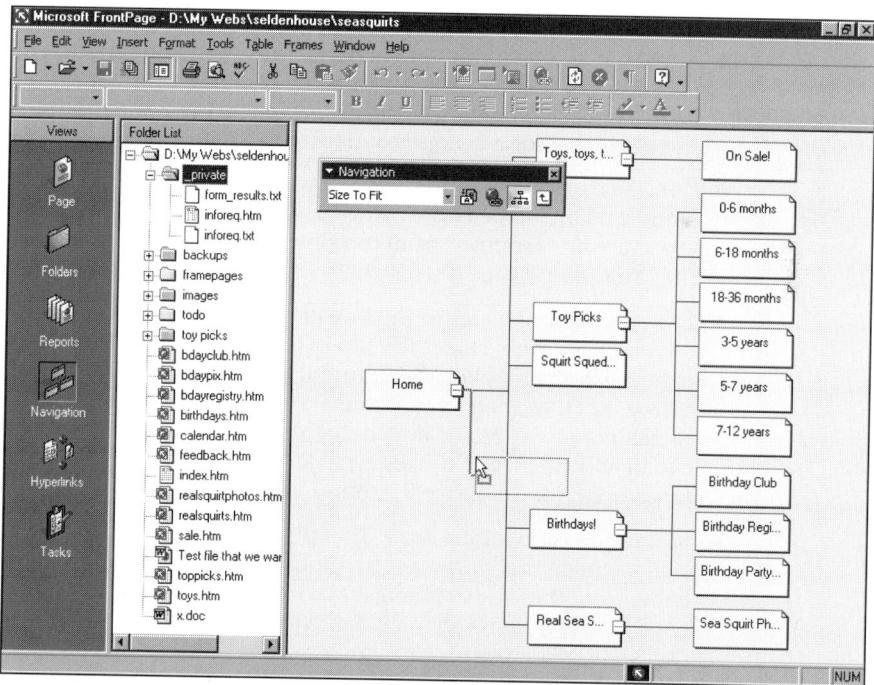

Figure 16-4: While you drag a page icon in the navigation structure, a fuzzy line shows you where the page will drop in.

You can add a page to the structure only once.

To revise the navigation structure, just drag page icons around on the screen. The fuzzy line continues to serve as your guide to their placement. You can delete a page by clicking it to select it and pressing Del, or via its shortcut menu. In the resulting dialog box, you can tell FrontPage to delete the page from the navigation structure only, or to remove it from the web itself, erasing the page's file.

Caution

If the page you're deleting has subsidiary pages in the navigation structure, deleting it removes all of the subsidiary pages as well.

Using the Navigation toolbar

As shown in Figure 16-5, the Navigation toolbar appears automatically when you enter Navigation view. By default, it's a floating toolbar, but you can dock it to get it out of your way if you prefer.

Figure 16-5: The Navigation toolbar lets you adjust the appearance of Navigation view.

From left to right, the controls on the Navigation toolbar include:

- **Zoom.** Lets you adjust the magnification by selecting one of several preset zoom factors. Size To Fit is my preferred setting. If you zoom out, a page's entire name may not fit in the icon. Hover the mouse pointer over the page icon for a second to display the name in a ScreenTip.

- **Portrait/Landscape.** Click here to toggle back and forth between the standard landscape (wide) view, in which the levels of the navigation structure are arranged from top down, and a portrait (tall) view, in which they're shown from left to right.

- **External Link.** To add to the navigation structure a page or file located outside your web, select the page to which you want to connect the external item and click the External Link button. In the Select Hyperlink dialog box that then appears, use the graphical buttons at the lower right to navigate to a Web or intranet address or a disk file, or to enter an e-mail address. Once the external link is part of your navigation structure, you can move it around just like a page from your web.

- **Include in Navigation Bars.** This button appears pressed in when you select a page that you want to appear where appropriate in navigation bars. To exclude a particular page from your navigation bars, click the page to select it and then click this button so that it no longer looks pressed in. The page icon changes color.

- **View Subtree Only.** Use this button to focus in on a single branch of the navigation structure. Begin by clicking the page at the top of the branch, one that has subsidiary pages attached to it. When you then click the View Subtree Only button, you see only the chosen branch. Click the button again to see the entire navigation structure.

To *hide* the details of a given branch of the navigation structure, click the little white box containing a minus sign at the bottom or right side of the page at the top of the branch. All the subsidiary pages disappear. Clicking the box again — it now contains a plus sign — restores the hidden pages.

Managing hyperlinks

FrontPage's Hyperlinks view automatically analyzes your web, displaying graphically the links connecting a selected page to other pages, files, and URLs. To subject a page to the analysis, just click it in the Folder List. As shown in Figure 16-6, the chosen page appears in the center of the view. Pages containing links to it are on the left, while those that it contains links to are on right.

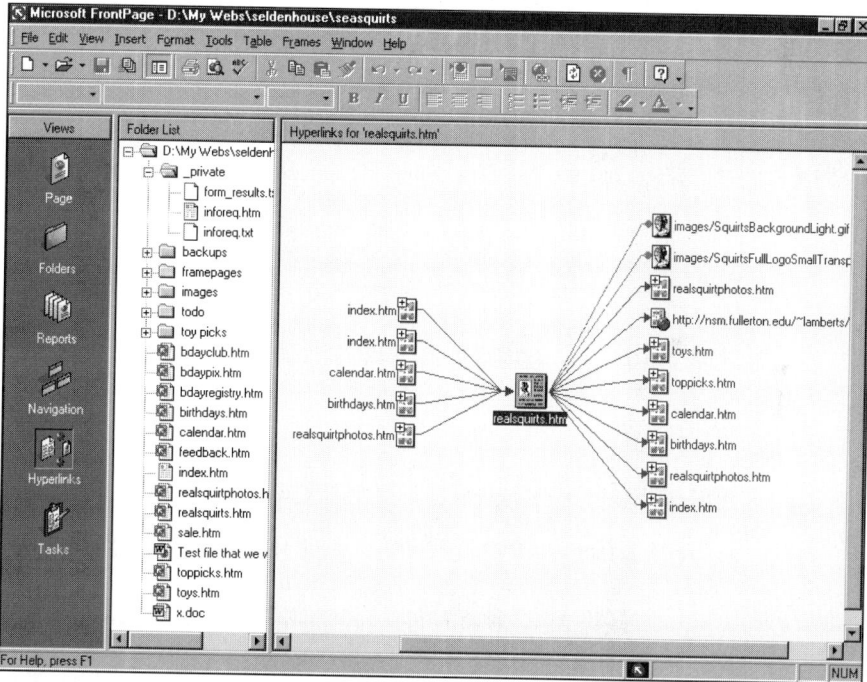

Figure 16-6: Use Hyperlinks view to see links involving a selected page.

You can follow a chain of links as it branches out through a succession of pages in either direction — just click the little plus signs on pages that have them to open the next set of links. Don't get carried away — because pages are often linked to each other, you can easily produce an infinite chain of links in which the same pages appear over and over.

Hyperlinks view displays broken links — that is, links to pages that don't exist in the current web — as broken lines. Although this visual cue is helpful, you may miss it. To prevent embarassing and annoying dead links, be sure to check the status of your links with a Broken Hyperlinks report (Figure 16-7). In Reports view, choose the report by name from the Report drop-down list (Reporting toolbar). The View ➪ Reports submenu gives you immediate access to any report from anywhere in FrontPage, so choosing View ➪ Reports ➪ Broken Hyperlinks is another way to display this report.

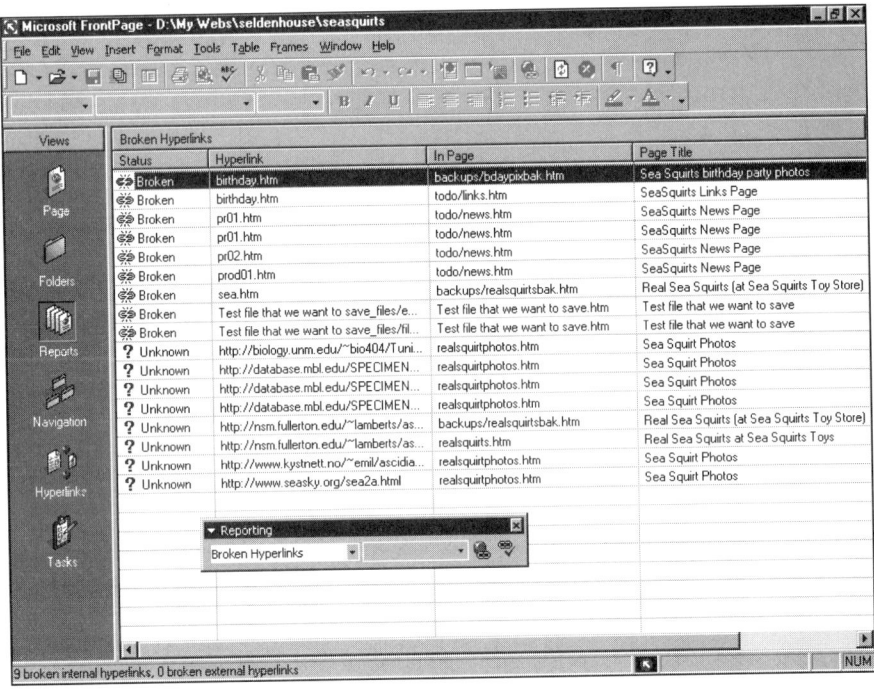

Figure 16-7: Display a Broken Hyperlinks report to track down dead-end links in your web.

A Broken Hyperlinks report lists both truly broken links and unknown ones, that is, links to external URLs (FrontPage can't verify these). To correct the bad links directly from the report, double-click an item. The Edit Hyperlink dialog box that appears lets you replace the existing hyperlink with a new one. If you want to see the broken link in context before you make changes, right-click the item in the report and choose Edit Page. Of course, the problem may be that the link is correct but the file it points to is missing from your web. In that case, you can simply locate the missing file and add it to your web, or create it if it doesn't yet exist.

To see a list of files contained in your web that aren't linked to any pages, display the Unlinked Files report. You can then decide whether to add links to these files, delete them from the web, or keep them in your web unlinked, for possible future use.

Using the _private folder

FrontPage webs always include a folder named _private. Files contained in this folder are inaccessible to visitors to your Web site. Use the folder to store form results and other information you want to keep to yourself. You can add subfolders to the _private folder to keep the material organized — everything in them remains off-limits to your visitors.

Managing complex web content using subwebs

Secret

If you're creating a web of significant size or complexity, you may want to break it down into sections that you develop separately. By dividing a large web into *subwebs*, you may find it easier to keep track of related portions of the content. Subwebs are especially helpful when you want to house several separate Web sites at a single domain (I used them to create the set of modest Web sites at my domain, `seldenhouse.com`). You can also use subwebs to break up the workload by assigning a different author to each subweb. Finally, because you can assign distinct security settings to each subweb, you can use subwebs to limit access to portions of your site.

A subweb is just like a regular web except that it resides within another web (the *parent web*). You work with a subweb in its own FrontPage window. It inherits basic settings from the parent web, including the theme and security permissions, but you can change these as appropriate. You can create subwebs within subwebs within subwebs, if your site requires them.

To create a subweb in the current FrontPage web and open it for editing follow these steps:

1. Add a new folder to the web. In Folders view, right-click the Folder List and choose New Folder, changing the default folder name to whatever name you've chosen for the subweb (remember to avoid spaces and most punctuation marks in the name).

2. Right-click the new folder and choose Convert to Web. FrontPage displays a warning, but you can disregard it because the new folder contains no files yet. When you dismiss the dialog box, the folder's icon gains a tiny faux globe.

3. Double-click the subweb's folder to open the subweb in a separate FrontPage window.

Secret

Importing a web doesn't convert it into a subweb. Instead, FrontPage just adds the web's files and folders to the current web. To convert an external web into a subweb, create and open the subweb first using the preceding steps and then import the external web into the subweb. The next section discusses the importing process in more detail.

By default, subwebs aren't published when you publish the parent web. When you publish a web containing subwebs, be sure to check the Include Subwebs box in the Publish Web dialog box (you must display options for the dialog box to get to the check box—see the "Publishing Your Web" section later in this chapter).

Secret

An alternative way to create a subweb: add an existing web to one that you've already published to your intranet or the World Wide Web (or to a server-based web). All you need do is publish the web that's destined to become a subweb to the URL of the parent web.

Developing Web Pages in FrontPage

Even if you rely primarily on the other Office applications to create and edit your Web pages, you should be familiar with FrontPage's specialized features for composing pages that look good and work properly when viewed in a browser. Adding FrontPage elements to pages you create in Word or Excel is simple, and you can continue to edit the pages in the original application after you do.

Bringing content into a FrontPage web

The easiest way to add pages and other files to a FrontPage web is simply to save or copy them to one of the web's folders. In Office applications, you can save documents as Web pages to the target folder. Use standard Windows file management techniques to copy in existing files using My Computer, Explorer, or the command prompt.

If you're already working in FrontPage, you can add existing files to a web by importing them. Start by opening the folder into which you want to import the files. You can then choose File ⇨ Import to display the Import dialog box. Here, you can assemble any number of files for import in one step. Click Add File to select files individually, or click Add Folder to add a folder and all the files it contains to the import list.

As you're building an import list, be sure *not* to click the From Web button— use it instead of the top two buttons. It dismisses the Import dialog box and starts the Import Web Wizard, which lets you add another web in its entirety (or a disk folder and all its subfolders) to the web you're currently working with. Panels in the wizard let you specify the URL of the foreign web and how much of it you want to import.

Adding files to a web doesn't automatically make them available to someone browsing the web—you must insert hyperlinks to the imported files into your pages.

Editing pages in FrontPage

To open a page for editing in Page view, you can double-click it in Folders view, select it from the File ➪ Recent Files submenu, or choose File ➪ Open and locate it anywhere on your hard disk, your network, or any accessible location on the Internet. Page view presents three separate renditions of the page you're working with. The Normal tab lets you edit the page graphically. The basic techniques for adding, editing, and formatting page content in the Normal tab are familiar to any Office expert. In the HTML tab, you can access the underlying HTML source code for the page. Preview tab displays the page as it will appear in a browser. Switch among these choices by clicking the tabs at the bottom of the window, or by pressing Ctrl+PgUp or Ctrl+PgDn.

Adding hyperlinks to pages

As in the other Office applications, you add hyperlinks to a page in FrontPage by pressing Ctrl+K, right-clicking and selecting Hyperlink, or choosing Insert ➪ Hyperlink (select text or a graphic first to convert the selection to a hyperlink). FrontPage's Create Hyperlink dialog box looks different than the corresponding box found elsewhere in Office — compare Figure 16-8 to Figure 14-1. Though it has the same basic function, the FrontPage version doesn't list recently visited files or previously used links, but it does provide a Parameters button for creating hyperlinks based on database queries.

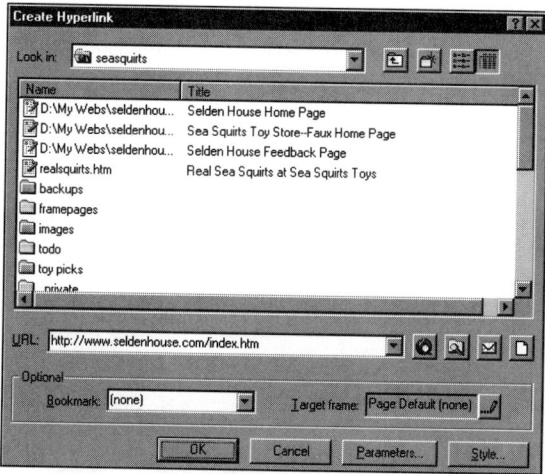

Figure 16-8: FrontPage's Create Hyperlink dialog box

You can edit a text hyperlink directly, just as you would regular text. To change a hyperlink itself, right-click the item and choose Hyperlink Properties from the shortcut menu. The Edit Hyperlink dialog box looks exactly like the Create Hyperlink box. When you're working in the Normal tab of Page view, Ctrl+click a hyperlink to follow it.

If you want to create a hyperlink to a particular spot on the same page—useful when the page is long—use the Insert ⇨ Bookmark command first to bookmark the location. The bookmark then appears in the Bookmark drop-down list in the Create/Edit Hyperlink dialog box.

Applying and customizing themes

Although *themes* are defined and introduced in Chapter 14, they originated in FrontPage, emerging in Word and Access only with the advent of Office 2000. In FrontPage, you can apply a theme to an entire web, to any set of pages selected in Folders view, or to the page that's currently open in Page view. However, you can't use FrontPage to apply themes to pages created in Word or Access—you have to reopen the page in the original application and apply the theme there.

Only in FrontPage can you modify an existing theme or create a new one of your own. To customize themes, choose Format ⇨ Theme to get to the Themes dialog box. There, click Modify to display a series of buttons under the theme sample, as shown in Figure 16-9. Each button opens a secondary dialog box where you can customize the corresponding elements of the theme. When you're done making modifications, click Save to store the changes using the original theme name or Save As to create a new theme. To delete a custom theme, select it in the theme list and click Delete. You can't delete the prefab themes supplied with Office.

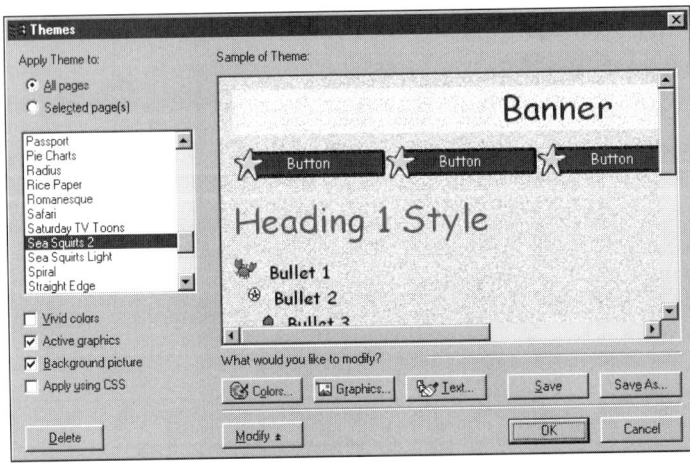

Figure 16-9: Modify existing themes or create new ones in the Themes dialog box.

Using shared borders

Although FrontPage provides a complete set of tools for adding HTML frames to your pages, it offers a simpler alternative that works well for many Web sites: shared borders. Shared borders are four special regions containing content that appears in every page to which they are applied. Shared borders are especially useful as containers for navigation bars, which are covered in the next section.

You can choose a default configuration for shared borders that applies to the entire web, but you can still control which of the shared borders appear on a page-by-page basis. Work with shared borders by choosing Format ⇨ Shared Borders. The resulting dialog box lets you turn on or off each of the four shared borders — top, left, right, and bottom. You can apply the changes as a default for the entire web by selecting All Pages, or to one or more individual pages (if you want to change the shared borders for a group of pages en masse, select them in Folders view before opening the Shared Borders dialog box).

Secret

Shared borders are easy to use, but you can quickly run into their limitations, especially in complex webs. For more control over content that appears repeatedly on more than one page, use the Include Page feature, discussed in "Include pages: repeating content" later in this chapter.

Working with navigation bars

Without doubt, the quickest way to provide a page with links to the other pages in your web is by inserting a *navigation bar*. A navigation bar consists of a set of hyperlinks generated for you by FrontPage, based on the web structure you set up in Navigation view. You have control over which pages appear on the bar, whether the links appear as graphical buttons or text, and whether the bar's orientation is vertical or horizontal.

Inserting a navigation bar

To add a navigation bar to a page, place the insertion point where you want the bar and choose Insert ⇨ Navigation Bar. FrontPage confronts you with the dialog box shown in Figure 16-10.

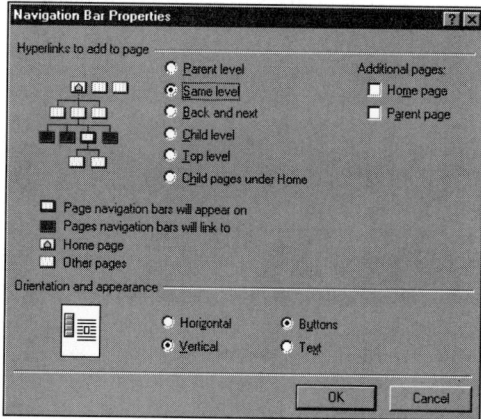

Figure 16-10: Select options for navigation bars in the dialog box shown here.

The top-left portion of the dialog box lets you select which set of pages to list in the navigation bar. What you have to understand is that the icons on the diagram represent not actual pages, but their locations relative to the current page in the navigation structure. Suppose you choose the Parent Level option button, for example. In this case, the navigation bar will contain a button or text link for each page one level higher in the navigation structure. If you later modify the navigation structure by adding or removing pages, the navigation bar updates its links to reflect those changes. Play with the option buttons while you watch the little sample graphic, and you should understand the links each choice generates.

Secret

By the way, selecting the Back or Next Option button provides links to the pages on either side of the current page in the navigation structure — it doesn't duplicate the Back or Next button in your browser. This choice is a good one when you want to encourage people to view pages in a specific sequence.

Using navigation bars with shared borders

Although you can insert navigation bars anywhere you like, they work especially well when placed within shared borders. Because the content of a shared border appears on every page, you need to insert the navigation bar only once, into the shared border. Each time a new page is displayed, FrontPage generates the proper links based on that page's relative location in the navigation structure.

Although one-step automatic navigation bars for an entire web sounds like a great boon, you won't get off that easily in most webs. Remember, you can only define one set of shared borders for an entire web, which means that each border contains the same navigation bar setup. Unfortunately, relative links that are ideal for a page at one level of the navigation structure often aren't appropriate at other levels.

Secret

In simple webs with only two levels, you can achieve satisfactory results using navigation bars in both the top and left shared borders. The bar in the top border contains links to top-level pages, while the bar in the left border has links to pages at the same level. You can then shut off the left shared border on the home page, inserting a separate navigation bar set to link to child pages.

The more complicated your web gets, the less helpful are navigation bars in shared borders. However, you may be able to find settings that work well for the majority of pages. Try adding two navigation bars to the left shared border, one set for same level and one for child-level pages. If you stack them on top of one another, they'll look like one bar in a browser. You can then turn off the shared border on pages where it doesn't give the desired results.

Secret

To create an imitation shared border, turn the page into a giant two-cell table with the left column the same width as the shared border. You then can place a custom navigation bar or individual links into the left column, while the rest of the page's content goes into the right column.

Inserting other components, doo-dads, and special effects

FrontPage offers tons of specialized prefab gadgets and gizmos that you can plug into a page to enhance its content, functionality, or looks. Find these elements on the Insert and Format menus. Be sure to acquaint yourself with the Component, Database, Form, and Advanced submenus of the Insert menu — they offer rich repositories of such items. I don't have space to cover these elements in depth, but the remainder of this section points out some of the highlights.

Page banners

The Insert ⇨ Page Banner command places an automatic title or logo across the page. Usually consisting of text on top of a graphic, banners are typically used as page titles, and you can drop one in the top shared border if you want every page to have a banner title. As in the case of navigation bars, you see a banner only if you include the page in the navigation structure. You can choose a graphical or text-only banner, but graphical banners can have text, too. The banner graphic that actually appears is determined by the theme you apply to the page. Finally, you can edit the banner text on a page-by-page basis, even when you place a banner in a shared border.

Office components

The Office Web components introduced in Chapter 15 — the Spreadsheet, PivotTable, and Chart controls — are all available for use in FrontPage from the Insert ⇨ Component submenu.

The hit counter component

The Insert ⇨ Component ⇨ Hit Counter command adds a fully functional hit counter to the page, enabling you to display the number of visitors to your site without any programming. You can select from five prefab hit counter graphics or supply your own. To create a custom counter, use a graphics program to design a picture containing the numerals 0 through 9 evenly spaced side by side, each the same height and width. Save the picture in GIF format to the Images folder in your web, naming the file `custom.gif`.

Include pages: repeated content

The same content often appears on more than one page in a web. The wrong way to go about adding that content would be to create it from scratch on each page — that would cost you way too much time, and you would have to update each page individually with every content change. Shared borders are one possible solution, but they have limitations. Shared borders can only appear around the edges of a page, and you have to use the same shared borders throughout a web.

If you want complete control over repeated content, use the Insert ⇨ Component ⇨ Include Page command instead. Place the insertion point where you want the subsidiary page to appear, and then launch the command. In the shrimpy dialog box that pops up, use the Browse button to locate the page you want to incorporate. When you click OK, the content from the included page appears immediately (but only its content — its formatting is set by the theme of the receiving page).

Tables of contents and site maps

FrontPage can automatically build a comprehensive navigation control center for your entire web. Place a table of contents component at the insertion point via the Insert ⇨ Component ⇨ Table of Contents command. The result is an outline of hyperlinks to the pages in the web. The outline's hierarchy is based on the web's navigation structure and on other pages containing hyperlinks.

To generate a site map organized by categorical headings, follow these steps:

1. **Create the categories.** Display the Properties dialog box for any file in the web (choose Properties from the shortcut menu that appears when you right-click any page or file icon, or in Page view, when you right-click the page itself). Switch to the Workgroup tab and click Categories. In the subsidiary dialog box, add your custom categories to the list.

2. **Categorize the files that you want to list on the site map.** In each file's Properties box, check the categories to which the file belongs. You can verify that you've categorized all the files correctly with a Categories report (choose View ⇨ Reports ⇨ Categories). You can examine individual categories by selecting them one at a time in the Report Setting list on the Reporting toolbar.

3. **Insert into your site map hyperlinks to the files in each category.** Create or open the page where the site map is to reside. For each category, type the category name onto the page. Positioning the insertion point beneath the category name, choose Insert ⇨ Component ⇨ Categories, check the category's box, and click OK. You have to repeat this process for each category — if you insert more than one category, the files belonging to all the categories are mixed together in the resulting list.

The DHTML Effects toolbar

FrontPage offers a few canned DHTML effects for easy application to text in your pages. Choose Format ⇨ Dynamic HTML Effects to display the DHTML Effects toolbar (Figure 16-11). In Page view (Normal tab), place the insertion point in the paragraph that you want to receive the effect. Then work your way from left to right through the controls on the DHTML Effects toolbar. In the On list, choose which event will trigger the effect. Next, in the Apply list, pick the type of effect you want. The choices depend on which event triggers the effect — you have many more effects to work with during page loads than with any other event. Finally, if the chosen effect has optional settings, the

Choose Settings list becomes active. Make your selection and then check out your handiwork in the Preview tab.

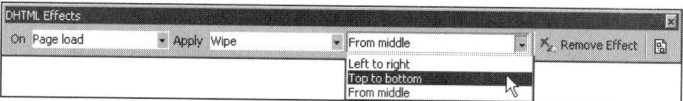

Figure 16-11: Use the DHTML Effects toolbar to make text dance.

Previewing pages

Page view's Preview tab lets you see the page you're editing roughly as it would appear in a browser. It's always best to save your page before switching to the Preview tab, because even then, items such as hit counters won't work — you have to publish the page to a server before they become active.

Except for the caveat just mentioned, pages previewed in the Preview tab appear almost exactly as they will in Internet Explorer 5. However, if you want to see how a page will look in your browser — or a browser that you expect your audience to use — click the Preview in Browser button or choose File ⇨ Preview in Browser.

Secret

The Preview in Browser button automatically sends the page to the browser designated as the default on your computer. However, the File ⇨ Preview in Browser command brings up a preliminary dialog box in which you can choose which browser to use and specify the window size in which the page will appear. You can designate additional browsers by clicking the Add button and entering each program's name and the command line needed to run it.

Publishing Your Web

Unless you create your web on the server from which users will access it, you must *publish* the finished web to make it available to the world at large, or at least to your target audience. Publishing is just a fancy term for copying all the web's files and folders to the server. But FrontPage makes the publishing process painless, ensuring that all the files arrive on the server and that they make it to their proper locations.

Choosing what to publish

FrontPage lets you control which files in your disk-based web reach the server when you publish. To keep a file out of the published web, open its Properties dialog box by right-clicking the file icon or an open page and choosing Properties. On the Workgroup tab — who knows how this option wound up there—check the box labeled Exclude This File When Publishing the Rest of the Web. If you need to view or set this option for many files, open the Publish Status report (choose View ⇨ Reports ⇨ Publish Status). As shown in Figure 16-12, this report lists all files in your web, displaying each file's status in the Publish column. To change the setting in the Publish column, click the file once to select it, wait a moment (don't double-click), and then click the Publish column. In the drop-down list that appears, choose Publish or Don't Publish as appropriate.

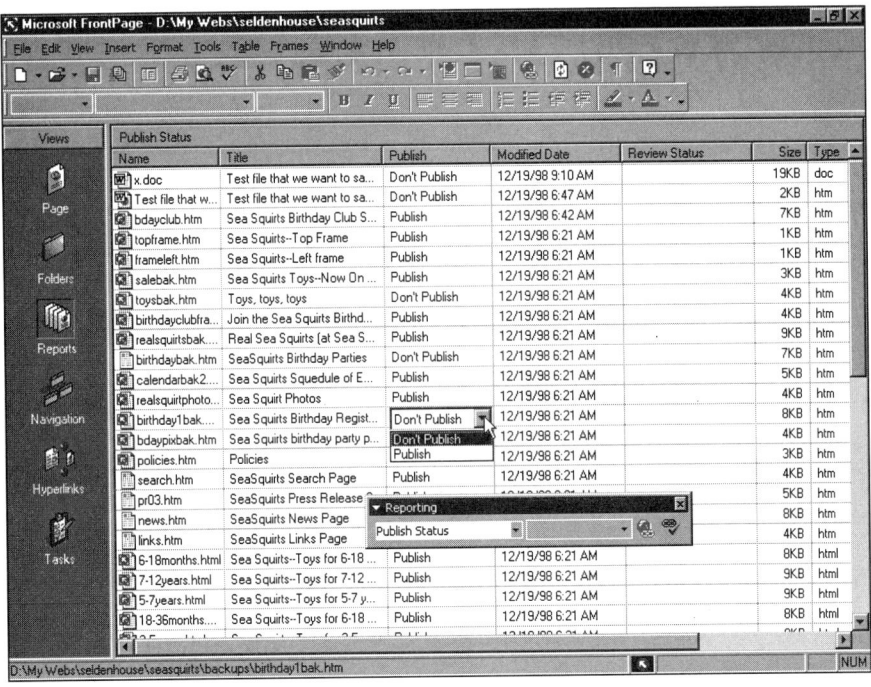

Figure 16-12: The Publish Status report lets you control which files get transferred to the server when you publish your web.

Caution

After you first publish a web, be sure you exclude from future publishing files whose content is changed by interactions with users on the server. If you republish the original files from your disk-based web, they will replace the versions with the user changes.

Publishing a web

To publish the current web, click the Publish Web button or choose File ⇨ Publish Web. The dialog box that appears is shown in Figure 16-13. The illustration shows the dialog box after the Options button has been clicked to reveal an important set of option buttons and check boxes—do check these out.

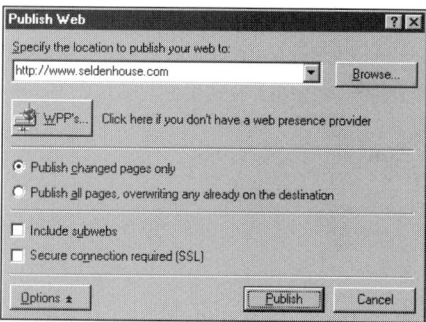

Figure 16-13: Use this dialog box to publish your web to a server.

Your main task, however, is to enter the URL of your server at the top of the box. If the server is running the Front Page Extensions, you can publish via HTTP; otherwise, you must use FTP, but the results will be the same. You can make a copy of a disk-based web by specifying another folder on your own computer or a network share instead of a URL. Click Publish to get the ball rolling. During the process, FrontPage provides a continuous report on its progress.

Republishing a web

Whenever you make changes to a web, send these changes to the server by publishing it again. FrontPage keeps track of what has changed and what hasn't since the last time you published, so it only needs to update the changed files each time you publish. If you want to ensure that all the files on the server match those on your disk-based web — perhaps because other people have had access to them on the server — select the Publish All Pages option button in the Publish Web dialog box.

Conclusion

FrontPage's sophisticated tools for Web site management and publishing are a perfect complement to the Web page design features of the other Office applications. Add in its special Web widgets and formatting tricks, and you have compelling reasons to learn and use this powerful Web site–making machine.

Part V
Secrets of Workgroup Productivity

Chapter 17: Networking Secrets

Chapter 18: Sharing and Collaborating on Office Documents

Chapter 17

Networking Secrets

In This Chapter

▶ Installing and running Office on a network
▶ Using system policies to ensure that Office works the way you want it to on networked computers
▶ Accessing network locations from within Office
▶ Installing Office Server Extensions

Networking is a complex and often very technical topic, but it deserves your attention in this era of intranets and workgroup computing. I can't promise that you'll leave this chapter a networking guru, but at least you'll get a better sense of what's possible with Office in a networked environment. For detailed information on the technicalities of installing and administering Office on a network, be sure to get Microsoft's Office Resource Kit, described further in Chapter 1.

Installing and Running Office on a Network

In a workgroup setting, Office can be installed on each user's individual computer — locally — or on a network server for shared access. The decision should take into account the following factors:

Where Office Is Installed	Advantages
Local computer	Faster — Office applications perform better when installed on a local computer than when accessed over the network.
	Always available — When the network or the server goes down, the individual user can still run Office.
Network server	Saves disk space on the local computer
	Provides for more convenient support and updates.

Actually, the choice is a little more complicated—you're not locked into one or the other of these options. You can decide to install some Office components on the local computer and others on the server. If Windows itself is being shared over the network, many of Office's big DLLs and other support files must be placed on the Windows server, even if you install the rest of Office on each local machine.

Decisions, decisions

If you plan to share all or part of Office on the network, Office must be set up on each PC through a special network installation process described in the next section. If you plan instead to install Office in its entirety on each PC, you have two choices:

- You can use the same installation process required for sharing files over the network but specify that all the Office files be copied to each local computer.
- You can always run Setup on each local computer.

Network installation

If you choose to install Office from a network server, you get to decide whether to install Office components on users' computers or have them run on the server. You can make this selection separately for each component. Just remember that if any Office features are set to run from the network, the server must always be online and accessible to users—when the server is down, those features won't be available to the users. That goes for components for which you select the Install on First Use option, too.

Installing Office via the network involves two main steps:

1. **Administrative setup.** Set up the administrative installation point on a network server accessible to all workstations that will be running Office. You need to specify a folder (share) on a drive accessible on the network and containing more than 560MB of free disk space. All the Office files are copied to this server during this step.

2. **Client setup.** On each workstation, install Office onto that computer by running Setup from the administrative installation point. During this part of the setup process, you can specify the location for the various Office components (server or local computer).

Preparing the installation point and customizing Setup

The key to initiating a shared installation of Office is to run Setup using command-line options. Using the Windows Start ➪ Run command, type **[drive letter]:setup /a install.msi** in the Open box. Setup asks you to enter your

CD Key and organization name—the entries you make will be supplied automatically during user installation—and the server and share you created.

After Setup copies all the files from the Office CD to the server, you must then:

- Give your users read-only access to the share.
- Customize Setup for the installation options and default Office settings you want to specify. You can customize Setup by entering options on the command line, by supplying your settings in the Setup.ini file, or by using the Office Custom Installation Wizard included with the ORK to create a *transform*, a special file that controls Setup's behavior.

Running Setup to install Office on user PCs

Once you have created and customized the administrative installation point, users can install Office by running Setup from the root folder of the server share. Users can run Setup themselves using the command line options, settings file, or transform that you have chosen; or you can run Setup for them through a network login script or a systems management product such as Microsoft Systems Management Server.

When you're in charge of installing Office on a network, you can decide how much control to give to users during the client setup portion of the installation process. If you trust your people, you can let them perform an interactive installation, selecting which Office components should be installed and where.

Otherwise, you can write a custom script that dictates all installation options when the user runs Setup. Or for total control over the procedure, you can write a script that installs Office automatically on a workstation the next time that user logs into the network. The Office Resource Kit includes the utilities you'll need to create such scripts. Alternatively, you can use Microsoft Systems Management Server to perform the installation on remote computers.

Customizing Office for Workgroups: Windows System Policies

To ensure consistency in the way Office applications behave on all the computers on your network, use Windows system policies. A system policy defines the value of a key in the Windows Registry. Office, of course, uses the Registry to store the settings for its many options, such as those in the Tools ➪ Options dialog boxes.

Because system policies change Registry values, you can use them to wrest control over the way Office works from your users. This is handy if you're power-hungry, true, but the real point is to improve efficiency in the group.

When Office works the same way on each workstation, a user can work at any computer without encountering unfamiliar toolbars or keyboard shortcuts, and you'll have an easier time giving technical support.

A set of system policies is stored in a system policy template, a file kept on the network server. Each time a user logs into the network, Windows automatically downloads the system policy file to the user's computer, which updates the Registry settings accordingly (the file can be set for manual downloading).

Be aware that because system policies tinker with the Registry, you can really foul things up if you don't know what you're doing. Be sure to back up your Registry files before you try out system policies.

Features you can control with system policies

System policies enable you to:

- Disable (or enable) any program command and the corresponding toolbar button.
- Disable (or enable) any keyboard shortcut.
- Specify a host of application settings, such as most of those in the Tools ⇨ Options dialog box.

Caution

System policies can control an Office application's global settings, but not settings that pertain to a particular document. You can't set document properties, for instance. In Word, you can't control whether spell and grammar checking are active for a particular document.

Network requirements for system policies

On a Windows NT network, system policies can only be downloaded automatically if Client for Microsoft Networks is the primary network login client and a domain is defined. Likewise, on a NetWare network, the primary login client must be Microsoft Client for NetWare Networks, and a preferred server must be defined. You can only download system policies manually on NETX and VLM networks.

Using the Windows System Policy Editor

Use the System Policy Editor utility to create or modify a system policy template. Shown in Figure 17-1, this program is included on the Windows CD-ROM.

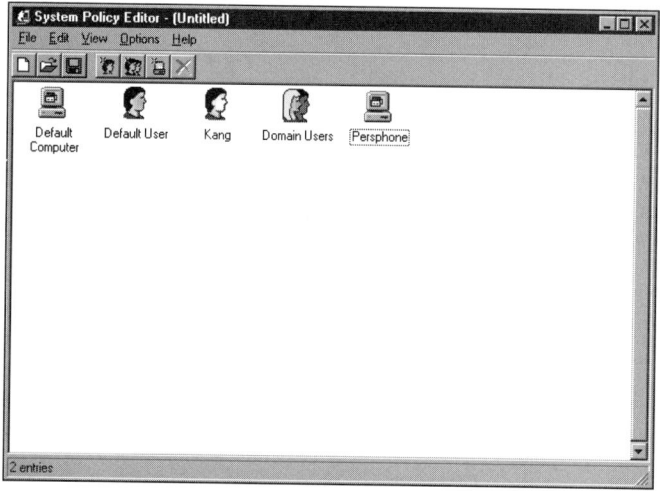

Figure 17-1: Use the System Policy Editor to set options for Office users on a network or shared machine.

However, the version of the System Policy Editor you want is the one that comes with the Office 2000 Resource Kit (if you don't have the ORK, you can download the System Policy Editor and the necessary template files from Microsoft's Web site). For one thing, the Editor itself has been improved, as follows:

- **The process of setting policies is easier to understand.** With this version of the Editor, you first decide whether a given setting is to be enforced by the policy or not. If you choose an enforced setting, you then specify its value.

- **Policies are more strictly enforced.** If a user changes an option, the setting dictated by the policy is restored whenever the user restarts the application.

- **Users' original settings can be restored.** If you clear a policy, each user's previous setting for that option automatically comes back, whether the setting had been customized or was simply the application's default.

- **Policies accept environment variables.** Instead of preordaining folder names or filenames or other settings values, you can now assign environment variables to your policies. Because environment variables can be changed readily from the command prompt, you can quickly switch back and forth between different policy settings by running login scripts or batch files that change the environment variables in question. See "Using environment variables as system policy settings" later in this chapter.

Another advantage of the System Policy Editor that comes with the Office 2000 ORK is its predefined template files for Office — with them, you don't have to build new policy files from scratch. The ORK includes separate templates for shared Office settings, the five major applications, Publisher, Clip Gallery, and the Windows installer.

Secret

System policies created with the version of the System Policy Editor that comes with the Office 2000 ORK are stored in the Windows Registry in the HKCU\Software\Policies key. This is a new location.

Creating a system policy file

To create a system policy file:

1. Start the System Policy Editor.
2. Choose Options ⇨ Policy Template. Figure 17-2 shows the resulting Policy Template Options dialog box.

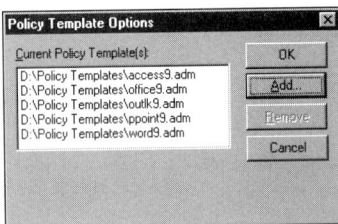

Figure 17-2: The Policy Template Options dialog box (note that it's so narrow you can't see the template name if the path is more than about 30 characters long)

3. Choose Add and then select one or more of the policy template files supplied with the ORK (if they're not already listed).
4. Choose File ⇨ New Policy to create the policy document.
5. Choose the computer, group, or user to which you want to apply the policies in the file (see the next section). Then define the individual policy settings you want to control (see "Defining individual system policies").
6. Choose File ⇨ Save As. The default name for the policy file is Config.pol. Save the file to the Netlogon folder of the primary domain controller (on NT networks) or the Public folder of the preferred server (for NetWare networks).

Secret

You can use the System Policy Editor to change policy settings for the computer you're working on at the moment — even if it's not on a network — to ensure a set of custom settings that persist from session to session, or to assign environment variables to your program options.

Specifying which users or computers a system policy affects

You can set system policies for all client computers, for all users, or for a specific computer, user, or group of users:

- **User policies.** These system policies govern the user currently logged into Windows (that is, the person who is going to be running Office when the system policies are activated—not you when you're running the System Policy Editor). These policies are stored in the HKEY_USERS branch of the Registry and the USER.DAT Registry file on disk. You can define user policies for all users or for a single user.

- **Group policies.** These policies determine the settings for all members of a particular group and also stored in HKEY_USERS and USER.DAT.

- **Computer policies.** These policies control settings for all client computers or for any one computer on the network. They go in the Registry branch HKEY_LOCAL_MACHINE and are kept in the SYSTEM.DAT Registry file.

User policies only work if user profiles have been enabled on each client computer. To use group policies, you must first install groups on each client computer.

Use the icons in the SPE's main window to specify which users or computers the policy you're defining will control. Initially, the window contains only Default User and Default Computer icons, but you can add icons for specific computers, users, or groups, by choosing Add Computer, Add User, or Add Group from the Edit menu.

Defining individual system policies

Once you've created the icons you need, double-click the one for the user(s) or computer(s) you want. As shown in Figure 17-3, the Properties dialog box lets you define the specific policies available.

Each system policy in the Properties dialog box has a check box that can have one of three settings:

- **Checked.** This means that you want your policy setting to be enforced on the user. If you check this box, a subsidiary check box or text field becomes available below it, enabling you to enter the setting that you want enforced. When the user logs in, the local Windows Registry changes to match your policy setting.

- **Cleared.** The policy and its settings should not be used. If it was previously implemented, its settings in the Registry are excised, and the settings the user previously had made are restored.

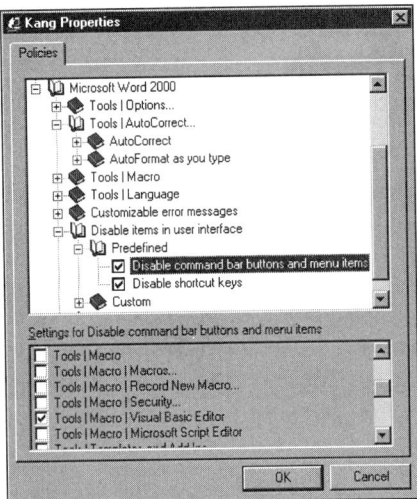

Figure 17-3: Use the Properties dialog box to define specific system policies.

- **Grayed (unavailable).** The policy hasn't been changed. All policies are in this state initially. With the check box in this state, the Editor makes no modifications to the user's configuration settings, or to any previous changes made by the Editor. You shouldn't change a policy to this state — clear the check box instead if you want to allow the user to control the setting.

Details on how system policies work

Each time a user logs in, Windows locates and downloads any system policies that apply to that user, entering the policy settings into the Registry as follows: If user profiles are enabled, any policies specific for that user are applied first. If Windows does not find user-specific policies, it applies any policies specified for the Default User (see "Specifying which users or computers a system policy affects" earlier in this chapter). If group policy support has been installed, and if there are no user-specific policies, group policies for all groups the user belongs to are downloaded and applied in order of increasing priority. If present, computer-specific policies are also applied. If not, Windows applies any policies defined for the Default Computer.

Using environment variables as system policy settings

As noted earlier in this section, Office 2000 recognizes environment variables as valid system policy settings. To use an environment variable as a system policy setting, place the variable between percent signs in the text field that becomes available when you check the box for the setting itself. Here's an example:

```
%ProjectFolder%
```

As the example intimates, a great use for an environment variable is to specify the default file location. This makes it easier to use a different folder for each project. Create a login script or batch file that creates the environment variable you've chosen and sets it to your project folder. When you use the Open command, it automatically opens the folder for the current project as specified by the environment variable.

Mapping Network Locations within Office

For easy access to a networked computer, or one of its folders, map it so that it appears as a drive letter under My Computer and on the Look In list inside Office dialog boxes. Although you can map network drives and folders from Explorer or My Computer, you don't have to leave Office to do it. Instead, in the Open or Save As dialog box, click the Tools button, the one at the far right of the button strip. When you choose Map Network Drive, the dialog box shown in Figure 17-4 appears. You don't have to leave Office to map a disk drive.

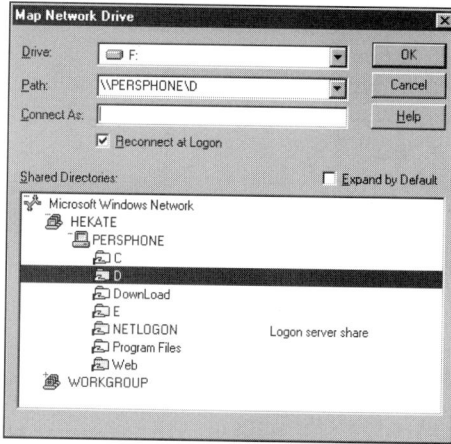

Figure 17-4: The Map Network Drive dialog box in NT 4

The Drive drop-down list should show the next drive letter available on your computer. You can change this default if you want. In the Path box, enter the path of the drive you want to map, including its computer name, in the following format:

```
\\server\share
```

Here, *server* is the name of the computer and *share* is the name of the disk and folder or directory (this terminology is the official lingo used in the UNC, or Universal Naming Convention, for network computer locations). You can extend the path after *share* as necessary to identify the proper folder.

If you've previously connected to the folder you're after, you may find it listed in the Path drop-down list. Check the Reconnect at Logon box to map the chosen drive automatically each time you start Windows.

Installing Office Server Extensions

If your organization runs an NT-based Web server, installing Office Server Extensions (OSE) enables Office users to take advantage of special features for document management and collaboration. Chapter 18 discusses these features in detail, but briefly, they include:

- Search and navigation capabilities for documents on OSE-server Web sites
- Discussions of Office documents located anywhere on the network — any user on the intranet can participate
- Automatic e-mail notification of changes in documents stored on the server

The Office Server Extensions require Internet Information Server (IIS) version 4 on NT Server, or Peer Web Services on NT Workstation. Assuming you've installed and configured the Web server software, you can then add the Office Server Extensions from the appropriate Office CD (this is disk 3 in Office Premium Edition, at least in the prerelease version).

Conclusion

Office 2000 integrates smoothly into today's networks, providing network managers with the tools they need for setting up and managing this software behemoth, as introduced in this chapter. Chapter 18 covers networking from the user's perspective: how to take advantage of the network and Office features to develop documents collaboratively with others in your workgroup.

Chapter 18

Sharing and Collaborating on Office Documents

In This Chapter

- Accessing documents on an organization's network
- Opening and saving documents on a Web and FTP sites
- Sharing Office documents via e-mail
- Collaborating on documents with coauthors and reviewers
- Sharing documents with others who have different versions of Office

Many documents represent the combined efforts of several coauthors. Even more commonly, documents are passed around an organization — or to the boss — for review and comment before the final edited version gets distributed. Recognizing the obvious, Microsoft has blessed Office 2000 with a slew of features that provide for sharing documents on a network and actively collaborating on developing their content.

By the way, don't pass over this chapter just because your PC isn't connected to a network. The sections on e-mail distribution of your documents, Office features that support collaboration, and sharing documents with those who have earlier versions all offer tricks that should be useful even if you don't have a network connection.

Storing and Finding Documents on the Net

Group collaboration on creating or editing documents requires that you be able to open and save Office documents where they are accessible to everyone in the group. Office provides plenty of help to that end. Even if your organization has a traditional, nonintranet network, you can readily share documents and you can link them together via hyperlinks placed within them. But if your network does support intranet protocols, you can take advantage of Office's more advanced features for network document management.

Opening and saving documents on your network

If you work on a network, you already know this: In Windows, any site accessible on your network appears in file-related dialog boxes just as local disks and folders do.

In Office dialog boxes such as Open and Save As, you open the Network Neighborhood item in the Look In list to navigate to computers on the network and their folders (see Figure 18-1). Once you've opened the right folder, you can store and retrieve documents on another computer exactly as you would those on your own PC.

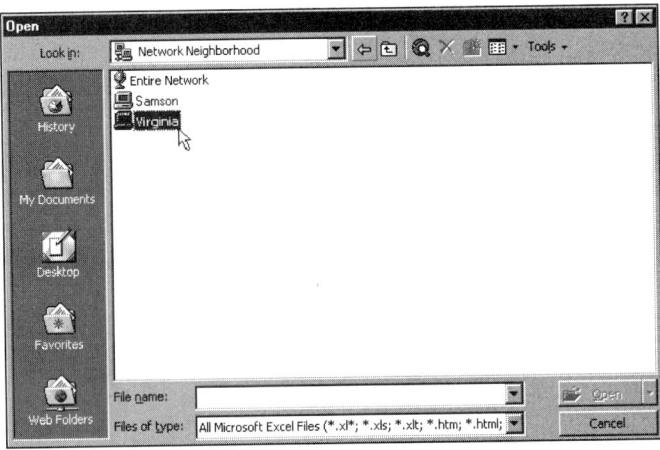

Figure 18-1: Navigating to a networked computer (on a very small network)

Sharing documents on your hard drive with others

Rather than saving your documents to a site on another computer on the network, you may decide to give others access to your documents where they're stored on your own PC. If you (rather than your network administrator) have control over such things, you can expose any disk or folder to other users on the network. Tact still demands you notify the administrator of your plans, of course.

In Windows 95 or 98, the first step is to enable network sharing. In the Windows Control Panel, open the Network applet. On the Configuration tab, choose File and Print Sharing, and in the resulting dialog box check the box labeled "I want to be able to give others access to my files."

Once you've enabled sharing in general, if necessary, you must then specify the folders or disks you want to make accessible. Do so in My Computer. For each disk or folder you want to share, select Sharing from its shortcut menu.

In the resulting Properties dialog box, choose Shared As to activate sharing for the item and specify which type of access network users can have.

Working with Web documents

Because Web sites have become a standard way to organize and disseminate information, it makes sense that Office 2000 provides the ability to store, retrieve, and manage Web documents painlessly. Because Office applications can store documents in HTML format without losing content or formatting, you can choose to use either the standard Office file formats or HTML for documents you place on Web sites. Of course, HTML is the way to go if the documents are to be browsed by people who don't necessarily have Office themselves.

Using Web Folders to manage files

Office 2000 enables you to open and save files on organization Web sites just as you would work with files on your own PC or a network computer. Web Folders is a sort of virtual folder containing shortcuts to Web sites located on servers on the Web or your intranet. Just be aware that Web Folders only works with servers running the Office Server Extensions, the FrontPage Server Extensions, or the DAV protocol.

In My Computer, Explorer, and Office file–related dialog boxes, the Web Folders item appears at the same level as your disk drives — just below the My Computer item itself. The shortcuts it contains are based on Web site URLs, but you can give them sensible names such as "Edna's Web site" or "Protean Polyphonies, Inc." Figure 18-2 shows the File ⇨ Open dialog box in an Office application with Web Folders selected on the Places bar. Note the special icon that signifies a Web site shortcut.

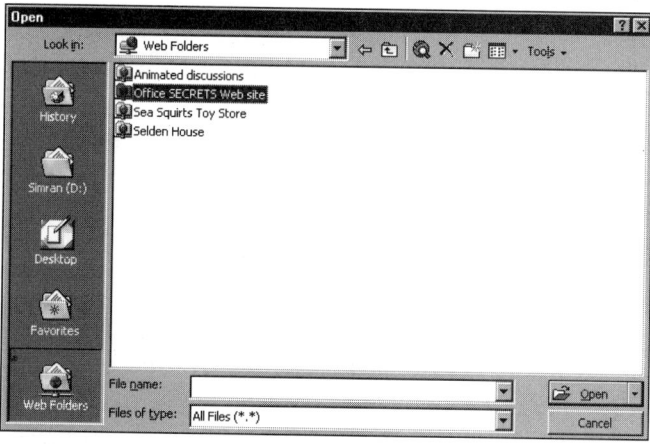

Figure 18-2: When you click the Web Folders button on the Places bar, Office file–related dialog boxes display Web site shortcuts you've created.

Secret

In Windows 2000 (NT 5), Web Folders and Network Neighborhood are both replaced by a new item called My Network Places, which contains shortcuts to Web folders, UNC locations, and computers accessible on your LAN.

Adding shortcuts to Web Folders

Use the Add Web Folder dialog box shown in Figure 18-3 to create new Web Folders shortcuts. Connect to the Internet or your intranet before you begin. Then, to open the dialog box in Office file–related dialog boxes, click the Create New Folder Button. In My Computer or Explorer, double-click Add a Web Folder.

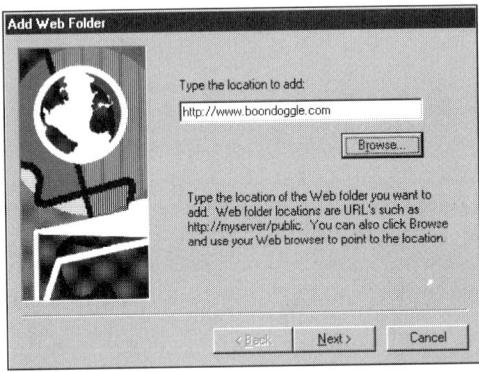

Figure 18-3: Create new Web Folders shortcuts with this dialog box.

In the Add Web Folder dialog box, you can type in a URL or use the Browse button to locate the URL yourself. If you take the latter route, your Web browser opens, enabling you to navigate to the site you want to add to Web Folders. When you have the target page displayed in your browser, switch back to the Office application where you started. There, the URL for your page has been entered in the Add Web Folder dialog box.

Secret

Office apps automatically add a new Web Folder shortcut every time you open or save a file to a Web address (an HTTP URL). The address of the shortcut includes only the name of the server and its top-level directory.

Managing files in Web Folders

Opening a Web Folders shortcut gives you access to all the folders and files it contains. Standard file management techniques work for navigating and for moving, renaming, and deleting these items and for creating new folders. In Explorer or My Computer, you can copy files to any folder on the site by dragging them there.

Caution

Just so you're clear, when you work with Web site folders and files that you access from a Web Folders shortcut, you're working with these items directly—not with shortcuts to them. In other words, if you rename or delete a file, the change occurs to the actual file on the Web site.

Caution

Users who have access to a Web site through a Web Folders shortcut can view and modify any of its files. If you don't want an item to be visible, use NTFS permission settings on the file to keep it from appearing when other people browse the site.

Working with Office documents accessed through Web folders

Within Office, you can open and save documents to any folder listed in Web Folders. In the appropriate dialog box, Open or Save As, just select the file or type in its name. Remember, however, that opening an HTML file takes you to the application that created it. For example, if you're working in Word and try to open a Web page created in FrontPage, the page opens in FrontPage, not Word. To open it in Word, right-click it and choose Open in Microsoft Word.

If you're using IE5, you can work offline on Office documents stored on a Web site. That way, you can work with the document at top speed, without having to send information back and forth across the network as you edit the file. This technique is especially valuable for saving time if you have a dial-up connection to the Internet.

To work with a document offline, start by opening Web Folders in an Office file–related dialog box. Navigate to the file, right-click it, and choose Make Available Offline. The file is transferred to your computer. From then on, when you open it in Web Folders, you're actually working with the replica stored on your own PC.

When you're through editing the file and want to update the "real" version on the Web site, right-click the file and choose Synchronize. The changes you made offline are incorporated into the file on the Web site. The Synchronize command can also be used to ensure that the replica of the file on your computer contains any changes that have been made to the original version by other users. If you're trying to synchronize a file that you've edited but that has also been changed by others, you're notified and asked how to deal with any conflicts.

Web Find Fast

On an organization's intranet, a version of the Find Fast indexing tool described in Chapter 12 can be installed to radically speed up searches for Office and HTML documents on the network. Web Find Fast enables you to search the entire network for documents containing specified words or phrases, or with particular properties. It indexes the content of all servers and shared folders on the network.

Web Find Fast works on Windows NT, Novell NetWare, and some other network operating systems. The computer on which you install it must be set up as an HTTP server. When Web Find Fast is installed, the network administrator provides each user with access to a custom search page used to initiate Find Fast searches. Tools in the Srvpack folder can help you build your search page. Then to connect to the search page conveniently, make it the default at each workstation. On the Web Toolbar, choose Go ⇨ Set Search

Page to specify a new search page, as discussed in Chapter 6. That way, it appears when you click the Search button on the Web toolbar or in the File ⇨ Open dialog box.

Working with documents on FTP sites

If your company has an intranet, you can retrieve and store Office documents on its FTP sites via the Open and Save As dialog boxes (saving only works if you have access rights, and if the FTP site permits it). You can also browse any FTP site on the Internet that permits anonymous logins, although you may or may not be able to open the files there.

Adding FTP sites to the Open and Save As dialog boxes

In Office, the painful way to access a document on an FTP site is to type its URL in the File Name field of the Open dialog box. Ease the pain by setting up your Office programs with the FTP sites you frequent. Once you've added an FTP site, you connect to it by selecting it in the Look In list. After Office makes the connection, you can then browse the site's files and folders with the standard navigation techniques.

To add an FTP site, drop down the Look In list and choose Add/Modify FTP Locations down toward the bottom. In the dialog box that appears (see Figure 18-4), enter the site name, select a login method, and enter your password. Most sites that allow anonymous login require your e-mail address as the password.

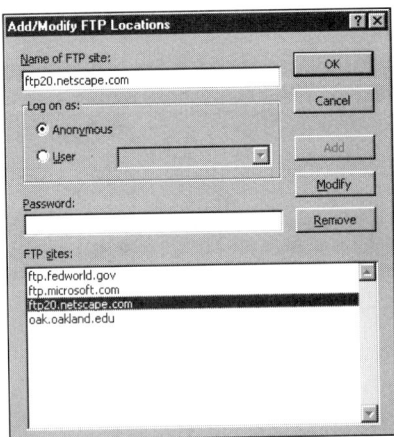

Figure 18-4: Adding an FTP site for access via the Open and Save As dialog boxes

More facts about FTP access

After you add an FTP site, Office remembers the address and login information. From then on, the site appears near the bottom of the Look In list under FTP

Locations in the Open and Save As dialog boxes. To connect to the site, just select it from the list.

You can use a system policy to add up to 10 FTP sites to the Look In list for multiple users. Using the System Policy Editor as discussed in Chapter 17, set the following policy:

User\Office\Internet\FTP Sites\Add FTP Sites

Secret

Include the extension when you save an Office document to an FTP site. If you're saving an Excel workbook, type in the .xls extension — for some reason, Excel won't supply the extension for you as it does when you save to a local disk or your network.

Using workgroup template folders

Office applications let you specify two different folders for document templates: one for user templates, the other for workgroup templates. See the section on templates in Chapter 13 for details on how these folders work.

Sharing Documents via E-mail

As an alternative to sharing your documents directly over a network, consider exchanging them using e-mail. Obviously, this makes sense when the intended recipient isn't accessible on your organization's network. But it also enables you to control more tightly who sees the document and when they get their hands on it.

To share documents using e-mail, you simply need any e-mail program capable of sending binary files as attachments — in other words, any recently released e-mail program will work for this purpose. However, if your e-mail software is MAPI- or VIM-compatible, you don't have to attach the files yourself. Instead, you can take advantage of special features that permit you to e-mail your documents directly from within Office.

Understanding MAPI and VIM

MAPI, or Messaging Application Programming Interface, is a 32-bit software protocol that Microsoft introduced with Windows 95 and Exchange. It provides a common conduit between client e-mail applications such as Exchange client and Outlook and the services they connect to, like Exchange server, Microsoft Mail, MSN, and Internet mail servers. VIM, or Vendor Independent Messaging, is the comparable protocol in the 16-bit world, and is used by Lotus cc:Mail.

Because you own Office and Windows, you have MAPI-compatible e-mail software in the form of Exchange and Outlook. Whether you use that software is another matter — your organization may have adopted e-mail software not based on either MAPI or VIM.

Sending and routing documents from within Office

If Office detects a MAPI- or VIM-compatible e-mail client on your system, the File ⇨ Send To menu in Excel, Word, and PowerPoint offers the Mail Recipient and Routing Recipient commands. Use them as follows:

- Choose Mail Recipient when you want to send the document to one person, or to multiple recipients simultaneously. This is the best choice when you have only one recipient, and it's certainly the simpler approach at send time. But if you're seeking comments from multiple reviewers, you'll get back a separate copy of the document from each of them, which can definitely be an inconvenience.

- Choose Routing Recipient to specify a series of recipients who should receive the document one at a time. That way, each of them gets to see the comments of the previous reviewers. Only one copy of the document is in circulation, so you get back a single copy containing all the comments and changes. Routing also lets you receive e-mail notification each time the document gets forwarded to a new recipient, and you can have the document automatically returned to you when the last reviewer completes work on it.

Sending a document (without routing it)

When you choose File ⇨ Send To ⇨ Mail Recipient, your e-mail software starts a new message containing the current Office document as an attachment. (Before the message opens in Exchange or Outlook, you are first asked to specify a profile if the e-mail program hasn't yet been started and if you don't have a default profile.) Enter the recipient's name and a subject, type in any text for the message body, and send the message.

Routing a document

To route a document to a series of recipients, choose File ⇨ Send To ⇨ Routing Recipient. Again, you may have to specify an Exchange profile before proceeding. At the Routing Slip dialog box, select recipients for the routing list by choosing Address. The order of recipient names in the To list determines the order in which they receive the document. If necessary, change the order by selecting a name and clicking the arrow buttons to the right. Another point: Although you can specify a group alias as the recipient for a routed document, everyone in the group will receive the document simultaneously. If that's not what you intend, specify the people in the group individually.

Fill in a subject and any text you want in the message separate from the attached document. At the bottom of the dialog box, specify whether you want the document to be sent to each recipient in sequence or to all of them simultaneously. This latter option is similar to selecting multiple recipients with the Send To ⇨ Mail Recipient command. However, it lets you use the special features of the routing command to track the document's status, and in Word, to protect the document from unauthorized changes.

Check Return When Done if you want to get the document back automatically after the last reviewer finishes with it, and check Track Status if you want e-mail notification as it makes its rounds from recipient to recipient.

In Word, the Protect For field at the bottom right is important. It determines what in the document recipients can change. Choose:

- **Comments.** To allow recipients to add comments but prevent them from making any changes in the document's contents.
- **Tracked Changes.** To force revision marking to be turned on, which tracks all changes the reviewers make in the document.
- **Forms.** When the document is a form that you want the recipients to fill in. They won't be able to alter the form itself.
- **(none).** To allow recipients to freely change the document. Their changes won't automatically be tracked, though they can turn on change tracking manually.

To send the document to the first recipient immediately, choose Route. If you prefer, however, you can close the dialog box without sending the document by choosing Add Slip. When you later decide to send the document, choose File ➪ Send To ➪ Next Routing Recipient.

Sending documents that aren't already open

If the Office document you want to send isn't currently open, you can still dispatch it to the intended recipient easily. Start from within an Office Open or Save dialog box—or in My Computer, Explorer, or Outlook's own file manager, described in Chapter 50. Right-click the document and choose Send To ➪ Mail Recipient. Outlook creates an e-mail message containing the document as an attachment. Actually, this works with all types of documents, not just Office ones.

Secret

Although you can attach documents to an Outlook message that's already open, using the Send To command on a document's shortcut menu as just described is often faster. If you send documents by e-mail with any frequency, teach yourself this trick.

Posting documents to Exchange folders

If you don't want to e-mail a document to a large number of recipients, you may have an alternative: You can make it available to anyone who has access to an Exchange public folder. However, posting a document to an Exchange folder only works if your group is using Exchange Server (if you're not running Exchange Server, you can post a document to an Exchange folder on your own computer, but that isn't much good for document sharing).

With the document open, choose File ➪ Send To ➪ Exchange Folder. A list of Exchange folders appears. Specify the destination folder and you're done.

Office Features for Collaborating on Documents

Once you have a handle on the mechanics of sharing Office documents, you and the members of your team can actually work on their contents together. Office already had a number of features to help you keep track of what has changed in a document and who did the changing. In Office 2000, though, you get new tools specifically designed to facilitate collaborative document development on a network.

Collaboration tools for all users, networked or not

You don't need a network to take advantage of Office features for working on documents with others — these features are equally appropriate for documents you share via e-mail or on floppy disks. Here's a quick rundown:

- Word has several distinct features that support group collaboration on documents. It lets authors and reviewers attach comments to selected text and see those comments by simply holding the mouse pointer over the text. You can have Word display the additions and deletions made by each collaborator in a different color, and compare or merge together different versions of the same document. Finally, different versions of the document can be stored in the same file, each version identified as to when it was saved and by whom. All these features are discussed in Chapter 32.

- Excel supplies similar help for groups building worksheets. Comments can be applied to specific cells. A changed cell appears with a border color indicating the person who changed it. The shared-workbook feature allows access to the same workbook by different users, preserving all of their changes in separate versions stored in the same file. See Chapter 40 for more on these features.

- PowerPoint's group document features are crude by comparison. Anyone who works on a presentation can add comments via the Insert ➪ Comment command or the corresponding button on the Reviewing toolbar. Comments aren't attached to specific text or graphics on your slides, and all comments are either hidden or showing. By way of consolation, you can move a comment box around on a slide and reformat its text.

Discussing Office documents

New in Office 2000, the Discussions feature enables all collaborators to add their own two cents worth with a minimum of hassle. The discussions feature requires an Office-extended server.

Comments from all participants are stored in a separate document on the server, whereas the original document can be stored in any accessible location on the network. This means that you don't need to send the document around to one reviewer at a time (route it) — everyone can comment on it at any time, without having each person having a separate copy of the document. In addition, your group can discuss read-only documents, ensuring that the original isn't modified. Office discussions are *threaded* — that is, they're divided into topics, with replies and further comments about a given topic grouped together.

Preparing for discussions

Before you can jump into a document discussion, you must specify the server that is (or will be) managing the discussion. Choose Tools ⇨ Online Collaboration ⇨ Web Discussions. In the dialog box shown in Figure 18-5, type in the name of the Office-extended server your workgroup is using, and give it a simple name if you'd like to make it easy to refer to later.

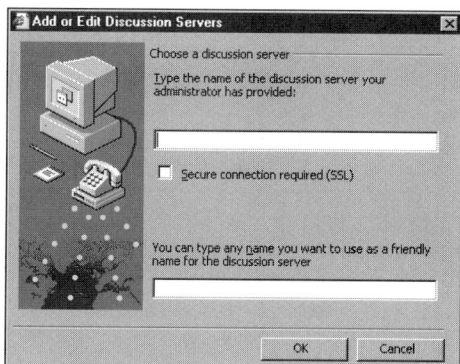

Figure 18-5: Specifying a server for Office document discussions

Typically, a group uses only one Office-extended server for managing discussions. Different groups within a department or company might have occasion to discuss the same document independently, in which case each group requires a different server. If your institution does have more than one discussion server, take pains to ensure that each user specifies the correct server.

Starting a discussion thread

To kick off a discussion about a document, begin by opening the document in Office. In Word, Excel, or PowerPoint, you can initiate a *general discussion* about any aspect of the document. In Word only, you can also start an *inline discussion* tied to a particular part of a document (in this case, position the insertion point appropriately). By the way, inline discussions work even in Word documents stored in the standard Word file format (.doc files), and in HTML or RTF files as well.

To start the discussion, click the Discussions button on the Collaboration toolbar, select Insert about the Document (for a general discussion) or Insert in the Document (for an inline discussion in Word). Type in a subject for your discussion thread, enter the text of your comments, and click OK when you've said your piece. You don't need to sign or date your remarks — the server keeps track of this information automatically.

Participating in a discussion

When you open a document that's the subject of a discussion, the Collaboration toolbar appears automatically. Reviewers' comments appear in a separate discussion pane, which you can display by clicking the Show General Discussions button on the toolbar. In the case of inline discussions in Word, an icon appears in the document at the location under discussion. Click it to open the discussion pane with the relevant comments.

In the discussion pane, each remark is identified by its subject, the discussant's name, and the date it was entered. Click the Filter toolbar button to display only remarks made by a particular person or during a particular time period. Clicking the button to the right of the item brings up a menu enabling you to reply to the item, or if you wrote the remark, to edit or delete it. If you have the proper permissions, you can delete an entire thread via a choice on the button's shortcut menu. The OSE Configuration Wizard enables you to create an Admins group with permissions to edit or delete all discussion remarks.

You can participate in a discussion using your Web browser instead of Office. In IE4 or IE5, choose View ⇨ Explorer Bar and choose Discussions to display the Discussions toolbar at the bottom of the browser window. Then open the document being discussed in Web Folders. In IE3 or Netscape Navigator, you have to go to the OSE Start Page on your server and open the document from there.

Subscribing to document-change notifications

Busy people don't always have time to make the rounds on the server just to check if someone has changed a document. With the new Web Subscriptions feature, Office will tell you instead. As a subscriber, you will receive an e-mail message from the server when various changes occur. You can request notification of changes to folders, individual documents, or document discussions. Because the server sends out notices in batches, you get a single e-mail message containing all the changes that have occurred during each period.

To set up a subscription from an Office application, choose Tools ⇨ Online Collaboration ⇨ Web Discussions. You can also subscribe using IE4 or 5 by choosing View ⇨ Explorer Bar ⇨ Discussions. After you choose Subscribe, you can select a file or folder, enter your e-mail address, and specify how often and under what conditions you want to be notified about changes to the selected items. You can view and delete subscriptions by clicking Manage Subscriptions on the Office Server Extensions Start Page.

Participating in Online Meetings

Office 2000 includes Microsoft's NetMeeting software for online conferences, and lets you participate in these meetings directly from within Office applications. NetMeeting covers most of the bases:

- You can talk to other participants (literally, using your computer's sound card, microphone, and speakers, or by exchanging typed text).

- You can share a document so that others can see what you're working on, and even allow others to edit the document.

- All participants can sketch ideas and type notes simultaneously using NetMeeting's Whiteboard.

Online meetings are brokered through special *directory servers* set up for that purpose. Participants log into the directory server, where they can see everyone else currently logged in. When two or more people agree to meet, the server routes their communications to and from each other. The only requirements for participants in an online meeting are that they each must be running NetMeeting and be logged into the same directory server only the host of the meeting needs to have Office installed.

Setting up NetMeeting

Before you use NetMeeting for the first time from within Office, take a few minutes to get acquainted with the full NetMeeting program and set it up to your specifications. If NetMeeting is installed, you can run it from the Start menu (Start ➪ Programs ➪ NetMeeting). The first time you do, a wizard walks you through the basic setup steps. You're asked to enter your name and e-mail address, choose the *directory server* you plan to use for your meetings, and set up your sound card and microphone. All participants in a meeting must use the same directory server. To change these settings later, and to fine-tune others, use NetMeeting's Tools ➪ Options dialog box.

Starting a meeting

Before you try to participate in an online meeting, be sure that you're connected to the Internet or an intranet on which a directory server is accessible. Then, if you're the one hosting the meeting, start it by choosing Tools ➪ Online Collaboration ➪ Meet Now from within any Office application. If NetMeeting is able to connect to the directory server you've chosen, you see the Place a Call dialog box shown in Figure 18-6. It lists the people currently logged into that server, and it lets you call them, one at a time, by picking from the list.

Secret

To allow others to work with your documents when you host online meetings you must enable application sharing in NetMeeting. To do so within the NetMeeting program, choose Tools ➪ Enable Sharing. If you haven't enabled sharing and you try to start a meeting from within Office, you are asked to do so. In any event, enabling sharing requires you to restart your computer, so be prepared for this interruption.

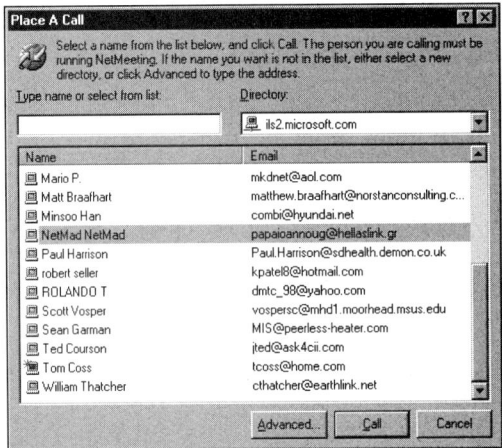

Figure 18-6: Select the names of the people you want to participate in your meeting from this dialog box.

Once you invite the first person to join the meeting, the Online Meeting toolbar appears, shown in Figure 18-7. You can ask others to join the meeting at any time by clicking the Call Participant button. As soon as those you "call" respond to your request, your meeting is in progress.

Figure 18-7: The Online Meeting toolbar provides buttons that let you control the meeting.

Scheduling online meetings in advance

To schedule an online meeting in advance, choose Tools ➪ Online Collaboration ➪ Schedule Meeting. An Outlook meeting item opens, enabling you to specify the participants and details such as the time, the subject, and the document that you plan to discuss. When you save the item, Outlook automatically generates e-mail invitations (meeting requests) for each participant.

Participating in an online meeting

As a potential participant in a meeting that someone else is hosting, you may be invited to join in one of two ways: by receiving a "call" to join a meeting about to begin or in progress, or by receiving an Outlook e-mail meeting request for a meeting scheduled in the future.

Before you can receive an online meeting call, you must already be running NetMeeting and be logged into the proper server. When the call comes in — in the form of a Join Meeting dialog box announcing the invitation — click Accept to participate or Ignore to go on with your own business.

In the case of a meeting scheduled via an Outlook meeting request, it's easy to let the meeting host know whether you plan to participate. Open the meeting request item in your Outlook inbox and click Accept, Tentative, or Decline, as the case may be. When you then save the item, Outlook automatically generates an e-mail message to the host containing your response.

Secret

To send your meeting request as both an e-mail and an Outlook calendar item that automatically appears in the recipient's calendar, choose Actions ➪ Forward as Calendar.

Later, shortly before the meeting is to start, Outlook displays a reminder message. Unlike ordinary Outlook reminders, this one includes a Start NetMeeting button. Click it to log into the server in preparation for joining the meeting.

Collaborating in an online meeting

As soon as an online meeting is in progress, you can talk with other participants using your PC's microphone and speakers, and see video images of them if they're using a video camera. To chat by typing messages to other participants, click the Display Chat Window button on the Online Meeting toolbar. To work with the Whiteboard, click the Display Whiteboard button. The Chat window and Whiteboard are shown in Figures 18-8 and 18-9, respectively.

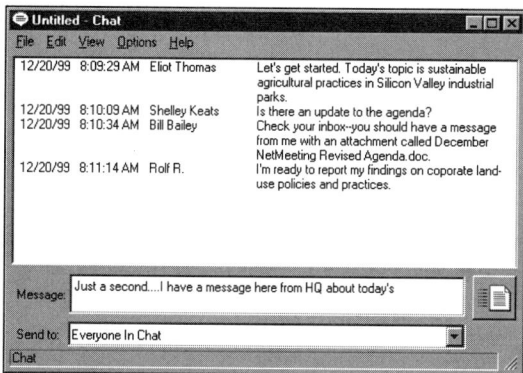

Figure 18-8: Exchange typed messages with other NetMeeting participants in the Chat window.

If you're hosting the meeting, you have sole control of the document the group is discussing until you give others access. To allow other people to edit the document, enable *collaboration* by clicking the Allow Others to Edit button on the Online Meeting toolbar. From this point on, other participants can take control of the document by double-clicking it. As a participant works with a document, the mouse pointer shows his or her initials on all participants' screens. To take back control of the document, click in it (anyone who has previously had control can resume editing by single-clicking). As the host, you can shut off collaboration by clicking the Allow Others to Edit button again, or, if you don't currently have control, by pressing Esc.

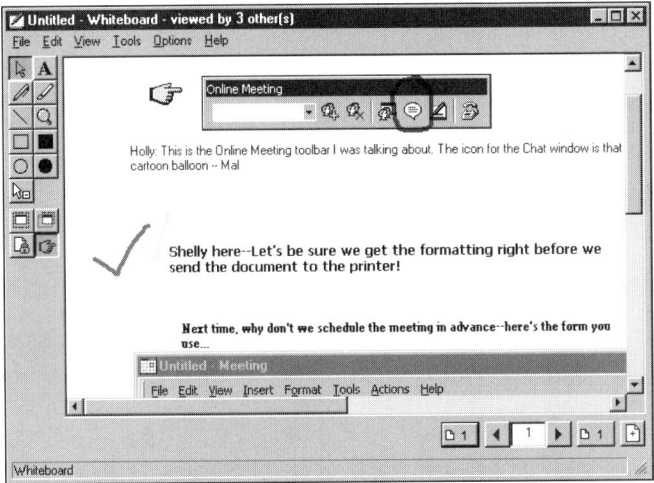

Figure 18-9: The Whiteboard, a souped-up version of Windows Paint, lets the entire group draw and type messages at once.

The host of an online meeting can send any open Office document to meeting participants. Choose File ⇨ Sent To ⇨ Online Meeting Participant to begin the transfer. Despite the singular used in the menu choice, all participants receive the document. To send the document to selected individuals, you have to use ordinary e-mail. If you're not hosting the meeting, or if you want to send a file that isn't open, switch to the NetMeeting window and choose Tools ⇨ File Transfer ⇨ Send File.

Sharing Documents between Different Versions of Office

Despite the continual push for standardization, many organizations field personal computer armadas that vary widely in vintage and pedigree. One workgroup may be outfitted with a set of hot Pentium II boxes, while elsewhere in the same building, another group is making do with a motley assortment of older PCs and Macintoshes.

When such circumstances prevail, working collaboratively on documents can be difficult. Fortunately, the file formats used by Office 2000 applications except Access are the same as those of Office 97 and Office 98 for the Macintosh. Still, some types of content that can be stored in Office 2000 files aren't recognized when the files are opened in Office 97.

The formats used by earlier versions of Office are incompatible with those of Office 2000, so your documents can't be opened directly by those who have the older versions of the software. On the other hand, Office 2000 can open files created by earlier Office versions and can save its own files in the earlier formats. The only foolproof collaboration strategy, then, is to settle on the lowest common denominator, the file format everyone's software can understand. This approach is easy to implement, because Office automatically saves a document in the format in which it was opened (although you may get a little warning message the first time you save). You won't be able to use new document features, but at least everyone can contribute. If you really need to use features that are available in Office 2000, you can do so at the end of the editing process, after other users have made all the other changes. At this point, use Save As to save the file in the standard Office 2000 format.

I lied a little when I said that earlier versions of Office couldn't read Office 2000 files. The Office Resource Kit CD-ROM comes with Converter Pack software containing utilities that allow earlier versions of Word, Excel, and PowerPoint to open Office 2000 documents.

If you trade files with Macintosh users who aren't on your network, using floppy disks to transfer the files is your only option, short of hooking the computers up directly with a cable. For years now, all Macs have been able to read and write files on standard PC floppies. Because PCs don't provide the reverse capability, it makes sense to ask the Macintosh users to put up with your floppies as vehicles for the shared files. Alternatively, several PC utility programs enable Windows machines to read Mac floppies. Try MacOpener, which is available separately or bundled with the Conversions Plus product mentioned in Chapter 10 (DataViz, 800-733-0030).

Conclusion

One of the most important reasons to use a network is to collaborate with others on documents. Whether you rely on a company LAN, an intranet, or Internet e-mail, Office provides the features you need for accessing documents on the Net and for working on them together with members of your workgroup, professional colleagues, and friends.

Part VI
Secrets of VBA

Chapter 19: Basic Visual Basic for Applications

Chapter 20: Using the Visual Basic Editor

Chapter 21: Writing Great VBA Modules

Chapter 22: Object-Oriented Programming with VBA

Chapter 23: Unbreakable Code: Debugging and Error Trapping

Chapter 24: Getting Interactive: Custom Dialog Boxes

Chapter 25: Building Power Applications

Chapter 19

Basic Visual Basic for Applications

In This Chapter

- An introduction to the Visual Basic Editor
- First try: a simple VBA module
- A quick survey of Visual Basic for Applications (VBA)
- What's new in VBA for Office 2000
- When to record macros and when to write VBA code
- About objects in VBA
- ActiveX technology and VBA
- Useful resources for working with VBA

As feature-rich as the Office applications may be, they can't meet every software need. If the point-and-click customizing techniques laid out in Chapter 5 don't go far enough, Office includes a full-fledged software development toolkit called VBA. Visual Basic for Applications — that's what VBA stands for — lets you cook up everything from simple yet intelligent customizations for any Office 2000 application all the way to complete custom software solutions that can tap the features of the entire Office suite. I don't claim that programming in VBA is as easy as clicking buttons on a toolbar, but it's something anyone in the Secrets club can undertake successfully.

CD

I've collected the VBA code for the example procedures listed in this section (Chapters 19–25) in an Excel workbook called VBA examples.xls. It's included on the CD-ROM that accompanies the book. To work with the sample code, open the workbook in Excel and the choose Tools ➪ Macro ➪ Visual Basic Editor. Using the Project Explorer as described in Chapter 20, open the Modules folder to see the code modules.

A First Look at the Visual Basic Editor

Figure 19-1 shows the Visual Basic for Applications Editor. Get used to this window, because you're going to be spending lots of time here if you use

VBA. As an added bonus, you won't have to relearn all the commands and shortcut keys if you also plan to develop in Visual Basic.

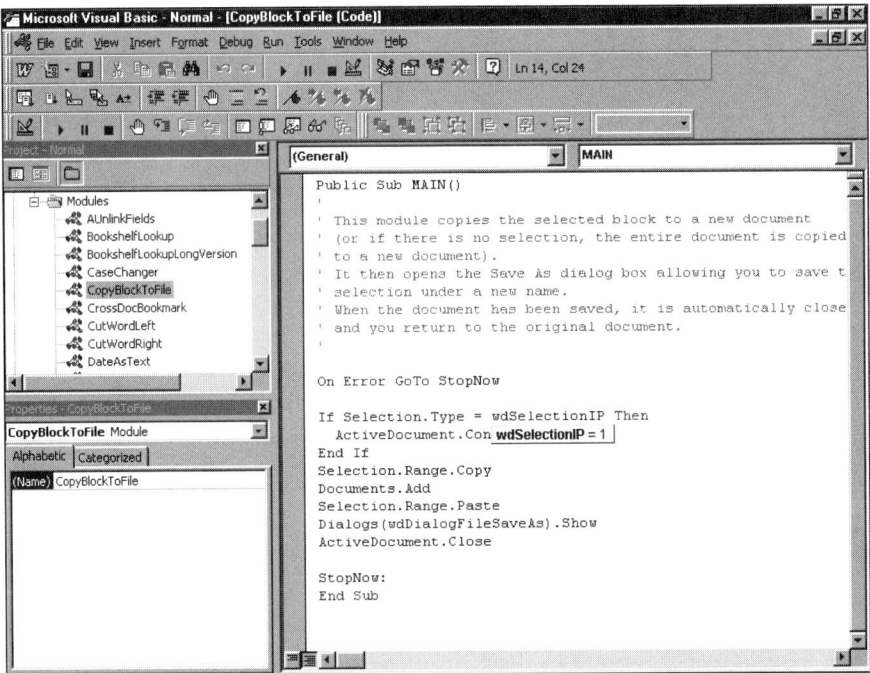

Figure 19-1: The Visual Basic Editor showing Project, Properties, and Code windows; the Quick Info pop-up help window; and the VBA toolbar

Chapter 20 discusses using the Visual Basic Editor in detail. For now, just be aware that you must start the Editor from within an Office application (or other VBA app) — you can't run the Visual Basic Editor all by itself. On the screen, the Visual Basic Editor acts as a separate application in a completely separate window from that of the *host application*. However, because the Editor operates within the same memory space, changes you make in your VBA code are immediately available when you run the code in the host application.

Writing a Simple Module

Just to familiarize yourself with VBA, try writing this very simple one-line module. (Simple as it may be, it actually does something modestly useful.) Follow these steps:

1. Start Word.
2. Press Alt+F11 to start the Visual Basic Editor.

Chapter 19: Basic Visual Basic for Applications

3. Click the Normal item (corresponding to Word's Normal template) in the Project Explorer window.

4. Choose Insert ⇨ Module to insert a module into the Normal template. This module will most likely be named Module1.

5. In the Module1 code window, type **Sub DisplayAppVersion** and press Enter. This tells VBA you're writing a sub procedure.

6. Notice that the editor has provided parentheses following your typing and also has added an End Sub statement on a separate line. The blinking insertion point appears between the two lines. Now type the following two additional lines of code exactly as written, including the underscore at the end of the first line:

```
MsgBox "Version/Build: " & application.version & _
    "/" & application.build
```

7. Press Enter. Notice that after you do, VBA automatically capitalizes the words `application`, `version`, and `build`.

8. Press F5, the keyboard shortcut for running modules in the Visual Basic Editor. As shown in Figure 19-2, you should see a message box displaying the Build and Version numbers of the copy of Word you're running.

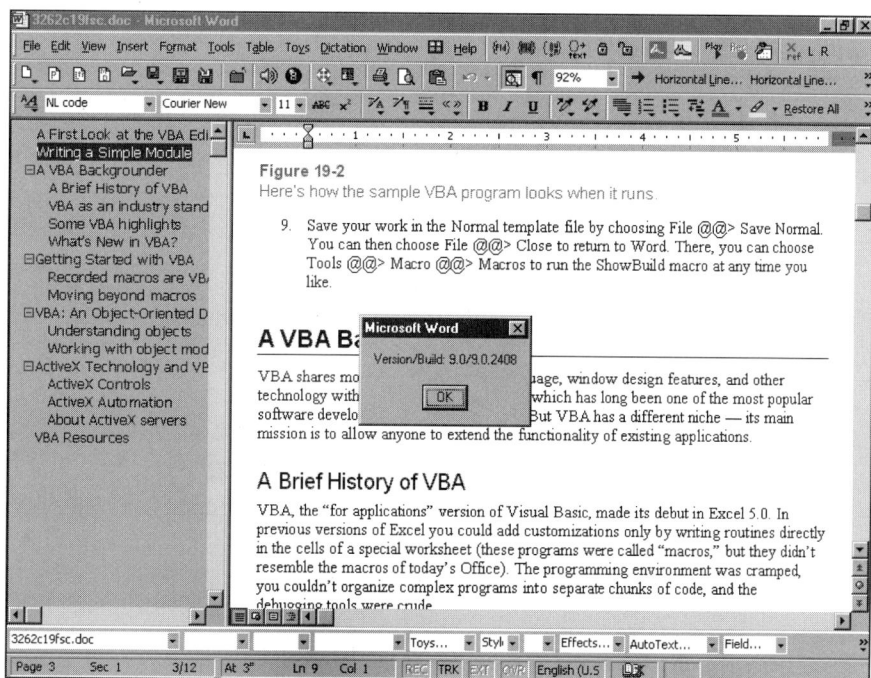

Figure 19-2: Here's how the sample VBA program looks when it runs (it's that small dialog box in the middle of the Word window).

9. Save your work in the Normal template file by choosing File ⇨ Save Normal. You can then choose File ⇨ Close to return to Word. There, you can choose Tools ⇨ Macro ⇨ Macros to run the ShowBuild macro at any time you like.

CD

By the way, I've provided this procedure on the CD-ROM accompanying this book in both Office Secrets.dot (Word template) and VBA examples.xls (Excel workbook). In each document, the procedure is stored in the module called Chapter 19.

A VBA Backgrounder

VBA shares most of its programming language, window design features, and other technology with Microsoft's Visual Basic, which has long been one of the most popular software development tools on the planet. But VBA has a different niche — its main mission is to enable anyone to extend the functionality of existing applications.

A brief history of VBA

VBA, the "for applications" version of Visual Basic, made its debut in Excel 5.0. In previous versions of Excel you could add customizations only by writing routines directly in the cells of a special worksheet (these programs were called "macros," but they didn't resemble the macros of today's Office). The programming environment was cramped, you couldn't organize complex programs into separate chunks of code, and the debugging tools were crude.

All of that changed radically with the advent of VBA. VBA offered the ability to organize code into logical chunks (procedures and functions) accessible in a separate software "environment" tailor-made for the software development process. VBA gradually gained momentum, appearing next in Microsoft Project, then in Access. Finally — with the arrival of Office 97 — VBA arrived in Word and PowerPoint, replacing the older application-specific Access Basic and WordBasic languages.

VBA as an industry standard

But the VBA universe doesn't stop at the borders of Microsoft Office. VBA was always envisioned as an industry standard programming tool, and it has finally started to live up to that billing. More than 200 other software developers have licensed the VBA technology from Microsoft, and VBA appears in such well-known applications as Visio and AutoCAD. Although each application provides a unique set of programming resources with which you must acquaint yourself, the core VBA tools — the language and the Visual Basic Editor — are identical in nearly all VBA applications.

Secret

For that matter, VBA and the stand-alone version of Visual Basic are nearly identical as well. The main difference between VBA and Visual Basic is that a VBA program can only run in conjunction with its host application, whereas programs built with Visual Basic proper run independently as stand-alone applications.

Also, and disappointingly, the forms and controls that come with VBA aren't the same as those you get with Visual Basic, so you can't convert a VBA application to Visual Basic without redesigning its windows and dialog boxes. On the plus side, your VBA development skills transfer directly to Visual Basic.

Some VBA highlights

Here's a quick listing of some of the major features of VBA as implemented in Office 2000:

- All Office applications — now including Outlook — host VBA.

- All the Office 2000 applications share a (reasonably) consistent object model and most can act as either Automation servers or Automation controllers (object models, servers, and controllers are discussed later in this chapter). Some objects, such as the CommandBar and Assistant objects, are common across all Office applications. VBA itself acts as an Automation server, encouraging the development of add-ins for its own programming environment.

- The Visual Basic Editor provides an integrated development environment (IDE) in which you develop and test your VBA modules and forms in separate windows — see Chapter 24 for details. The Visual Basic Editor is almost identical to the IDE found in Visual Basic.

- All full-fledged VBA applications — including all the Office applications except Access — support a common system for designing custom dialog boxes and windows (called *forms* or UserForms in VBA). The benefits to you include a standard set of design tools, and standard controls that work the same way in each application. In addition, you can design a form in, say, Word and reuse it in Excel without any changes. The controls that ship with VBA applications are powerful enough for sophisticated, great-looking forms (see Figure 19-3). If these aren't enough, VBA enables you to plug in ActiveX controls from other sources (see the section on ActiveX controls later in this chapter).

- You can create your own objects in VBA using class modules. Your custom class modules promote code reuse and shrink the time required to develop a project.

- Your Office documents can access data stored in a variety of sources using ActiveX Data Objects, or ADO. ADO is a new programming standard for retrieving and storing information whether it resides on your own PC's hard disk, a workgroup server, or the corporate mainframe. Besides providing a uniform method for accessing data wherever it's located, ADO is easier to use, faster, and more compact than data access tools available in earlier versions of Office, such as DAO and ODBC Direct. See Chapter 46 to learn more about ADO.

- Conditional code compilation lets you develop applications localized for different languages, for example. You can also use conditional code compilation to run selective blocks of code during debugging.

- If you need features VBA can't provide, your VBA programs can directly access the features of Windows itself via calls to the Win32 API (the Windows application programming interface).

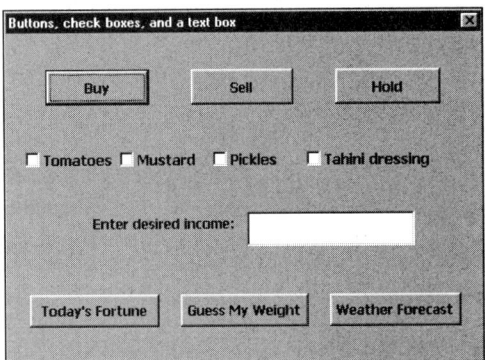

Figure 19-3: A sample dialog box (VBA form) loaded with the ActiveX controls that come with VBA

You may have noted that I described VBA as "reasonably consistent" in all Office applications. For all the effort Microsoft has made to bring harmony into the VBA universe, some tasks still require coding variations depending on which application you want them to run in. As a simple example, you refer to Word's built-in File ⇨ Save As dialog box as wdDialogFileSaveAs, but the corresponding dialog box in Excel is called xlDialogSaveAs. (Note that the Excel version doesn't mention the File menu.) More problematic is that, compared to Word, the other applications allow significantly less control over their built-in commands via VBA. Be prepared to cope with such differences.

What's new in VBA?

The millennial version of Office enhances VBA with a raft of new features. Some of the most important of these include:

- **The Visual Basic Editor in Access and Outlook.** In Access 97, you had to make do with a scaled-back VBA development environment that was far more primitive than the Visual Basic Editor. This was a real hardship, because Access VBA programs tend to be larger and more complex than those in the other Office apps. Now, Access developers benefit from all the creature comforts and debugging tools of the full-fledged Visual Basic Editor. In Outlook 97, you couldn't use VBA at all but were limited to a scaled-back version of VBA called VBScript.

- **Modeless UserForms.** In previous versions of VBA, all your screen forms had to be *modal*. In other words, they acted like a garden-variety dialog box, which you must close before you can get back to working with the program. This is often a desirable limitation, but not always. With a modeless form, by contrast, you can go back and forth between the host application and the form — Word's Find dialog box provides a good example. A modeless form's entries remain intact and aren't finalized until you close the form. Chapter 24 covers forms in detail.

- **Improved security for VBA programs and add-ins.** You can set Office to check for "digital signatures" to verify that VBA programs you acquire from others are from a trustworthy source. See Chapter 25 for more on security issues and VBA.

- **COM add-ins.** Strictly speaking, this isn't a VBA feature, but it offers a major advance in Office programmability. COM add-ins are custom programs that you create with a separate programming tool such as Visual Basic or C++. COM add-ins and other advanced programming topics get attention in Chapter 25. See "ActiveX Technology and VBA" later in this chapter for an overview of COM itself.

Getting Started with VBA

VBA is a rich enough programming environment to appeal to the professional developer. However, even if you don't have a programming background, VBA can give you a big boost by helping you automate repetitive tasks in your daily work.

Recorded macros are VBA programs

The easy way to get your feet wet with VBA is by using the macro recorder available in Word, PowerPoint, and Excel. The mechanics of macro recording are covered in Chapter 5.

The point to make here is that the macros you record are stored as VBA code, just like the kind you type in yourself. To examine the code corresponding to a recorded macro, choose Tools ⇨ Macro ⇨ Macros, select the macro by name, and choose Edit.

Note that each recorded macro is a single VBA *procedure*. (To get technical, a macro is a Sub procedure that takes no arguments.) By default, Office stores all recorded macros as separate procedures in a single *module* (a unit of code that can contain one or more procedures) within the current document. Procedures and modules are discussed fully in Chapter 22, "Object-Oriented Programming with VBA."

Moving beyond macros

Macros are fine for speeding up a set of commands that you use repeatedly in exactly the same order. The problem with a recorded macro, though, is that it's dumb — it always does the same things in the same sequence. To create a software routine that can modify its behavior to suit current conditions, you need to "hand-code" it in VBA.

Here are some other reasons to graduate from the macro recorder to VBA:

- **To create custom dialog boxes and windows.** VBA lets you design anything from simple Yes-No-Cancel message boxes to complex interactive windows containing multiple tabbed pages — all without any programming. VBA is a *visual* software tool expressly because you lay out forms on the screen by drawing them with the mouse. To make your forms do useful work, however, you do have to write code.

- **To retrieve data from file-based databases such as Access, Dbase, or FoxPro, or from a back-end relational database management system accessible via OLE DB or ODBC.** While you can use Microsoft Query to view data from these sources, you have to write VBA code if you want to manipulate those data in your own custom routines.

- **To add error handling to your VBA routines.** Even a recorded macro can benefit from a little code that steps in when errors occur, allowing the routine to make a soft landing instead of crashing violently. Error handling code is especially vital if you distribute your VBA programs to other people, in that they will be running your software under conditions you can't control. VBA offers robust error trapping comparable to that available in Visual Basic.

- **To create custom Help messages.** With VBA, you can add context-sensitive help to your program and display appropriate error messages when the user makes a mistake. You can even program the Office Assistant to coach your users through a complex process.

- **To protect your programs from unauthorized tampering or copying.** Password-protecting your VBA code encrypts it securely so that no one can view the code without the password.

VBA: An Object-Oriented Development Tool

Purists will tell you that VBA doesn't meet all the criteria for a true object-oriented programming language. They may be right, but objects still play a fundamental role in VBA — and you need to understand how they work to use VBA effectively. Chapter 22 discusses VBA objects in detail, but you deserve a brief introduction to these important concepts here.

Understanding objects

If you're new to object-oriented programming, the easiest way to think about objects is as parts of the host application and the documents you create with it. In Excel, for instance, each worksheet cell is an object, each named range of cells is an object, a chart is an object, an entire worksheet is an object, and so is a complete workbook.

But objects can be more abstract. Sticking with Excel, the CustomView object represents a workbook custom view. A custom view isn't something you can see on the screen but instead is a group of settings that define the look of the workbook and its print options. In all VBA applications, a Collection object represents any group of variables or other objects that you want to work with as unit, regardless of their type.

Working with object models

Each VBA object fits into a hierarchy of other objects as defined by the host application and VBA itself. The object at the top of the hierarchy has its own properties, methods, and events, but it also acts as a *container* for other object types, those that are beneath it in the hierarchy. These objects in turn contain other subsidiary ones, and so on.

At the top of the object hierarchy is the *application* object. Below the application object come derivative object collections such as documents, paragraphs, characters, bookmarks, dialogs, and so on.

The *object model* of a VBA application encompasses the specifics of these hierarchical relationships between objects, along with the characteristics of the individual objects. Figure 19-4 illustrates a portion of the Word object model. Because VBA itself has objects that are available in all VBA applications, VBA has its own object model, too.

ActiveX Technology and VBA

ActiveX is a Microsoft marketing term for a variety of technologies all having to do with interchangeable software components. The individual ActiveX technologies are actually quite distinct, but you can think of them together as a set of standards for software building blocks. These building blocks can be linked on a mix-and-match basis to produce powerful customized applications.

ActiveX controls

Controls are the individual doodads on dialog boxes and toolbars that a software user can click or type text into to produce a response from the software. Examples of controls include buttons (the push-button type), radio buttons for picking one of several predetermined options, and text boxes in which you can type or edit entries.

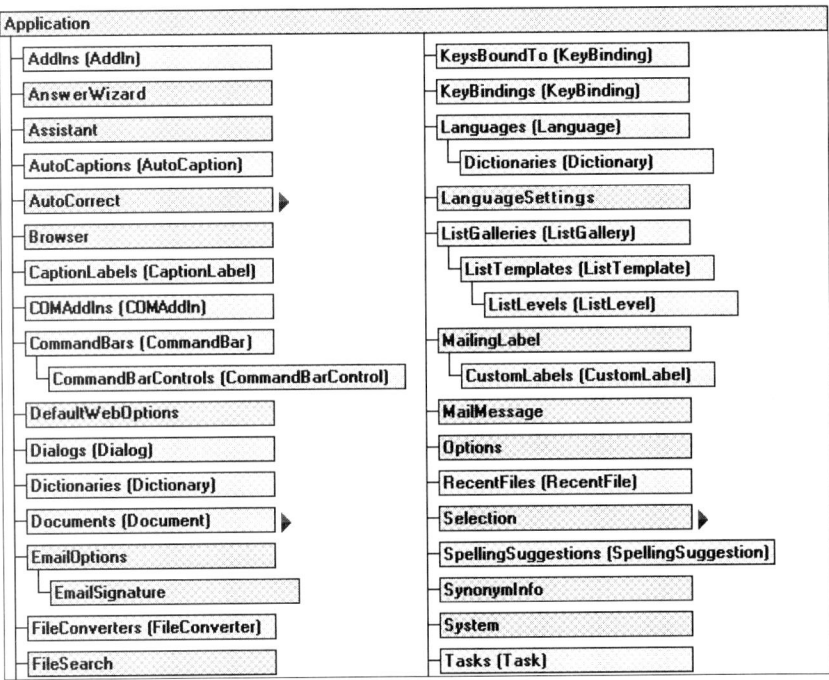

Figure 19-4: The picture represents part of Word's object model diagrammatically.

The Microsoft standard for *ActiveX controls* means that you're not limited to the controls that come with VBA. ActiveX controls are interchangeable software widgets that you can plug into your programs as you see fit, and they work in Visual Basic, C++, and Java, as well as VBA. If you need a control that doesn't come with VBA, hundreds of other ActiveX controls are available as shareware and from commercial software vendors. You can even create your own ActiveX controls (using the Control Creation Edition of Visual Basic), if you're so inclined. Figure 19-5 illustrates a VBA form with a variety of third-party ActiveX controls.

Although controls are usually thought of as items you can see on a dialog box or toolbar, some ActiveX controls have no visual presence. Instead, they provide plug-in units of software functionality, performing specialized services such as financial calculations on demand.

As you can learn in more detail in Chapter 24, ActiveX controls are also portable across computers and operating systems when used in Web documents. From within an Internet browser that supports the ActiveX standard, users can see and interact with any ActiveX control that appears on the page. Consequently, ActiveX technology extends the component software model across boundaries imposed by different operating systems and network topologies.

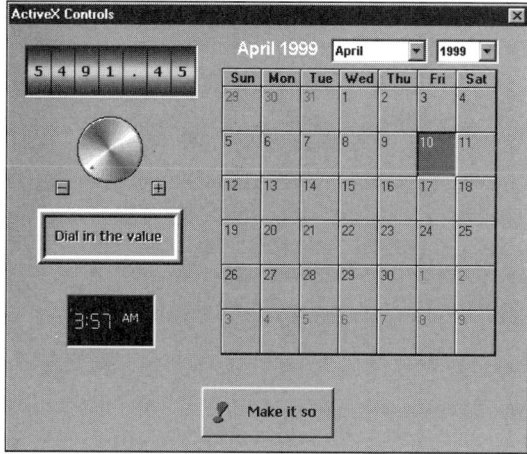

Figure 19-5: A dialog box studded with ActiveX controls that *don't* come with VBA

ActiveX automation

Your VBA programs aren't limited to the objects in the host application. Instead, you have access to the objects of any application or software component that adheres to Microsoft's *Component Object Model* (COM) standard. The COM specification details how objects should be defined within applications and how those objects are *exposed* so that they can be used by other applications. The term *automation* refers to the ability of one COM-based application to automate — that is, to activate and control — the objects of other applications.

Automation and COM open up fantastic possibilities for custom VBA applications of tremendous scope and power. If you're really ambitious, you could put together a single application that combines and processes information from Word documents, Excel worksheets, Access and Outlook databases, PowerPoint presentations, Visio diagrams, AutoCAD technical diagrams, and so on. A custom software solution can display all this information on your own custom forms and also in the windows of the individual applications automated by your program. Using the DCOM (Distributed Component Object Model) technology, the ActiveX components can be maintained and distributed across networks — no matter whether those networks are LANs or enterprise-wide intranets.

About ActiveX servers

Applications that expose their objects to manipulation by other programs are called ActiveX Automation *servers*. Conversely, an application that can control another application's objects is called an ActiveX Automation *controller*. Every application in Office can function as both an Automation server and an Automation controller.

VBA Resources

This book is big enough for a rich introduction to VBA, but if it whets your appetite for more you need to look elsewhere. One good place to start, if I do say so myself, is *VBA For Dummies* (IDG Books Worldwide), by yours truly. Although the material is presented at the introductory level, it offers more detail than you find here.

Resources for VBA programmers abound on the Internet. Begin at the beginning, with Microsoft's VBA and Visual Basic Web pages:

- www.microsoft.com/vba/
- www.microsoft.com/vbasic/

You can also find lots of VBA-related info at microsoft.com in the areas for the individual Office applications and in the Microsoft Knowledge Base.

Other Web sites to explore include:

- www.download.com/PC/Activex/
- www.geocities.com/WallStreet/9245/
- www.web2.airmail.net/gbeene/visual.html
- www.inquiry.com/techtips/thevbpro/index.html
- www.cgvb.com/

Print periodicals that cover VBA include:

- *Microsoft Office Developer's Journal*

- *Automating Office with VBA*
  ZD Journals
  800-223-8720
  www.zdjournals.com

- *Microsoft Office & Visual Basic for Applications Developer*
  Informant Communications Group, Inc.
  10519 E. Stockton Blvd., Suite 100
  Elk Grove, CA 95624-9703
  916-686-6610
  www.informant.com

- *Visual Basic Programmer's Journal*
  Fawcette Technical Publications
  209 Hamilton Ave.
  Palo Alto, CA 94301
  650-833-7100
  www.windx.com

Conclusion

Programming in Visual Basic for Applications is decidedly an advanced Office skill — as far as I'm concerned, even an introduction to VBA takes you into Secrets territory. Still, the Visual Basic Editor, the advanced forms design tools, and Microsoft's improvements in consistency between Office applications make the trip look a lot more tempting.

Chapter 20

Using the Visual Basic Editor

In This Chapter

- Where to find commands in the Visual Basic Editor's menu system
- Displaying, moving, and customizing the Editor's toolbars
- How docking works in toolbars and windows
- Grappling with the multitudes of Editor windows
- A cheatsheet of keyboard shortcuts available in the Visual Basic Editor
- A bird's-eye view of your VBA projects with the Project Explorer
- Investigating project objects with the Object Browser
- Writing code — and having it written for you — in the Code window

A carpenter has her workshop, a baker his kitchen, and you, well . . . now you have the Visual Basic Editor. The Visual Basic Editor is the official term for VBA's integrated development environment, the digital studio in which you sculpt your own software creations. It's an integral part of all five major Office applications.

In this chapter, you learn how to tame the resources of the Visual Basic Editor — I sometimes refer to it simply as the Editor. First you get an orientation to the components of the Visual Basic Editor including its toolbars, menus, and windows. Then comes a tour of the individual windows and the unique contributions each one can make to your programming projects.

Working with the Visual Basic Editor User Interface

The Visual Basic Editor's user interface is standard Microsoft fare — the menus, toolbars, and keyboard shortcuts look and work just like those in other parts of Office. You should feel right at home.

Out to lunch with Editor menus

I realize you already know how to use menus. What you might be interested in, though, is where to find certain commands on the Visual Basic Editor's menus.

For the most part, the Editor's commands are organized logically. When you want to display a particular window, for example, you shouldn't have trouble locating the necessary command — it's on the View menu, of course. A few items aren't so obvious, however. The following little table clues you in on some of the Editor's hidden menu commands:

When You Want to Do This	Use This Menu Command	Comments
Control the settings for an entire project.	Tools ➪ Project Properties	This is an odd location for a command pertaining to the VBA project you're working with — I expected to find it on the File menu.
Customize the Visual Basic Editor itself.	View ➪ Toolbars ➪ Customize and Tools ➪ Options	
Turn on Design mode.	Run ➪ Design Mode	The Design Mode command sounds like it's intended for laying out forms, so why is it on the Run menu? Because it stops any running program. What exactly it's good for, I still haven't figured out.

Tuning the toolbars

If you're familiar with Word, Excel, or PowerPoint, you're probably plenty comfortable with the way toolbars work in the Visual Basic Editor. If not, a few brief comments should suffice.

The included toolbars

The Editor comes with four prefab toolbars. They are:

- **Standard.** This is the only toolbar visible when you first run the Editor. It includes buttons for a broad range of functions, including saving your work, inserting new forms and modules, editing, and running your programs.

- **Edit.** The buttons on this toolbar are handy when you're editing code. They duplicate commands on the Edit menu.

- **Debug.** This toolbar contains buttons for commands you're likely to need while tracking down errors in your programs.
- **UserForm.** Use this toolbar for forms design. Most of the buttons duplicate commands on the Format menu for aligning, ordering, and grouping controls on forms.

Monkeying with the menus, toolbars, and buttons

Like other Office toolbars, those in the Editor can exist in one of three states: hidden, docked, or floating. You use the same techniques covered in Chapter 3 to display, hide, or move the toolbars, and to convert them from floating to docked and vice versa. Likewise, you can customize the Editor's menus (including the shortcut menus), the toolbars, and their individual buttons using the standard Office procedures covered in Chapter 5.

Keyboard shortcuts

Table 20-1 summarizes keyboard shortcuts available in the Visual Basic Editor. You can also use the standard Windows keyboard commands for cursor control and text editing. Remember also that Shift+F10 pops up the shortcut menu for the window or other item that's currently active — just as if you had right-clicked the item.

Table 20-1   Keyboard Shortcuts in the Visual Basic Editor

To Do This	Press
Displaying windows	
Display the Code window for the selected form or control	F7
Display the form or control corresponding to the active Code window	Shift+F7
Move to next Code or UserForm window	Ctrl+Tab
Activate the Object Browser window	F2
Activate the Properties window	F4
Activate the Immediate window	Ctrl+G
Activate the Call Stack window	Ctrl+L
Working with code	
Jump to the definition of the item at the insertion point	Shift+F2
Display the Find dialog box	Ctrl+F
Find Next (find next occurrence of Find text)	F3
Find Previous	Shift+F3
Replace	Ctrl+H

Continued

Table 20-1 *(continued)*

To Do This	Press
Working with code	
Jump to the line previously edited	Ctrl+Shift+F2
Undo	Ctrl+Z
List properties/methods	Ctrl+J
List constants	Ctrl+Shift+J
Display Quick Info about the variable or object at the insertion point	Ctrl+I
Display parameter information for the function at the insertion point	Ctrl+Shift+I
Complete the word you're typing automatically	Ctrl+Space
Working with properties	
In the Property window, move to the next property in the list that begins with a particular letter	Ctrl+Shift+<letter>
Running programs	
Run the procedure or UserForm in the active window	F5
Pause code execution and enter break mode	Ctrl+Break
Debugging	
Execute code one line at a time (step)	F8
Execute statements one line at a time without stepping into procedure calls	Shift+F8
Run, stopping at line containing the insertion point	Ctrl+F8
Specify (set) the next statement to be executed	Ctrl+F9
Run the error handler code or return the error to the calling procedure	Alt+F5
Step into the error handler or return the error to the calling procedure	Alt+F8
Toggle breakpoint in code line with insertion point	F9
Clear all breakpoints	Ctrl+Shift+F9
Add watch for the item at the insertion point	Shift+F9

Managing the Windows

Unless you have a really gargantuan monitor, plan to spend lots of time moving windows around in the Visual Basic Editor. None of those windows are there just for looks — each has something very valuable to contribute to your programming effort. The problem is, it's not practical to keep them all open at once — you won't have enough space left for your VBA code and forms.

By the way, this chapter only discusses the mechanics of working with windows, not the functions of the windows themselves. Later in this chapter each of the individual windows are discussed in some depth.

Some windows are loners, some run in crowds

One Basic Fact to understand about Visual Basic Editor windows: You can have as many Code and UserForm windows as you need, but only one each of the other window types. This may make perfect sense to you already, but it took me a while to figure out how the system works.

You need multiple Code and UserForm windows because you're likely to create more than one form and one VBA module. With a window for each, you can keep all your forms and modules in memory and available for quick access.

Some of the remaining windows — the Properties and Locals windows, to name names — change their contents automatically when you switch to a different Code or UserForm window. It's like getting multiple windows for the price of one. Others, such as the Object Browser, the Project Explorer, and the Immediate window, apply to everything you do in the Editor, so only one of each is necessary.

Viewing and hiding windows

Most Editor windows have their own keyboard shortcuts, which means you can pop up a window that isn't currently visible without taking your fingers off the keyboard. Table 20-1 lists the shortcuts you need. If you can't remember the shortcut, though, you can display any window via the View menu.

Perhaps unfortunately, the keyboard shortcuts *aren't* toggle switches. If a window is already open, pressing its key combination doesn't hide it. To put a window back to bed, you have to click the window's little Close button (at the far right on the title bar).

To display a specific window that is open but buried, you can choose it by name from the Window menu. Only nondockable windows are listed there.

Secret

As in many Windows applications, two keyboard shortcuts exist for switching from one window to the next: Ctrl+Tab and Ctrl+F6. In the Visual Basic Editor, however, only nondockable windows become active in sequence as you press the shortcut keys repeatedly. So what is a nondockable window? That's the topic of the next section.

Sittin' on the dock of the VB-ay

Like the toolbars, most of the Editor's windows are *dockable* — you can attach them along any of the four edges of the main workspace where they can't cover up other windows. Of course, docking a window makes the workspace smaller. Figure 20-1 shows the Editor with all visible windows docked.

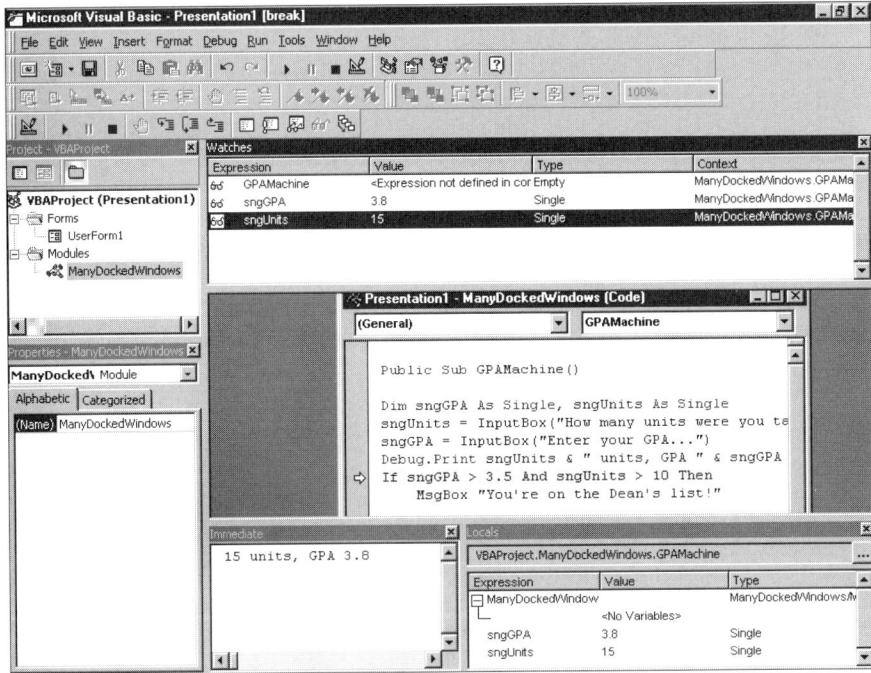

Figure 20-1: As you dock windows along the edges of the Visual Basic Editor window, the space available for editing code and designing forms grows smaller.

Alternatively, you can let your windows float freely in the breeze. Floating windows leave you more room for writing code and designing forms, but they often cover up other windows. If you have a big monitor, you might prefer to display the Visual Basic Editor at less than maximum size, and then move individual floating windows outside the Editor altogether.

No docking allowed . . .

Certain windows can't be docked. Docking is completely out for the Code and UserForm windows. In addition, you can make any other window "nondockable." To check or set docking status for all window types (except Code and UserForm windows, of course), choose Tools ⇨ Options and click the Docking tab. You can also make a dockable window nondockable, or vice versa, by right-clicking the main part of the window and choosing Dockable from the shortcut menu.

More docking factoids

Secret

Here are some hidden docking truths to ponder:

- A Code, UserForm, or any other nondockable window can be maximized, minimized, or "restored" (Microsoft jargon for windows of user-determined size). Nondockable windows have the standard buttons for these functions at the right side of the title bar.

- You can tell whether a window is currently dockable by looking at the title bar. Dockable windows have only a Close button there, whereas nondockable windows have the Minimize and Maximize (or Restore) buttons.

- When you maximize any nondockable window, it fills whatever space is left over by any other windows that are currently docked in the work area.

- To move a floating window to the edge of the work area without docking it, you must first make the window nondockable.

- All open, nondockable windows are accessible in sequence via the Ctrl+Tab keyboard shortcut. They're also listed on the Window menu.

Saving the screen layout

The Visual Basic Editor automatically preserves the layout in effect at the time you exit. The locations of your windows, menus, and toolbars don't change from one Visual Basic Editor session to the next. The layout remains the same even you switch from one Office application to another. This only holds true, however, when you close one application before starting the next.

Managing Your Projects with Project Explorer

In VBA, a *project* is all the code and forms that belong to one document, along with the document itself. In the Visual Basic Editor, you use the Project Explorer window for a bird's-eye view of all projects currently open in your application — and more important, to navigate quickly to the Code or UserForm window you want to work with.

Secret

To save the project you're currently working with — the one selected in the Project Explorer, as described later in this section — click the Save button on the Visual Basic Editor's Standard toolbar. In other words, you don't have to go back to your VBA application to save the document with its associated code.

Opening the Project Explorer window

The Project Explorer should already be visible when you first open the Visual Basic Editor. If it isn't, you can make it appear with any of the following techniques:

- Press Ctrl+R.
- Click the Project Explorer button on the Standard toolbar.
- Select View ➪ Project Explorer.

Exploring the Explorer

If you've ever used the Windows Explorer to manage your disks and files (oops, documents), you'll be right at home in the Project Explorer. The Project Explorer gives you a branching hierarchical look at your open projects. Figure 20-2 shows an example.

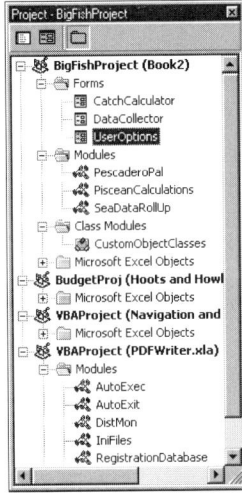

Figure 20-2: Here's the Project Explorer in Excel, showing several active projects open simultaneously.

At the top of the hierarchy are the individual projects themselves. They're listed furthest to the left in the Project Explorer window.

Each document that's open in your application automatically has a project. That's true even if you haven't written any code or created any forms for its project so far. By default, a project takes on the name of its associated document, but you can change the name via the Project Properties dialog box or in the Properties window (see "Renaming a project or module in the Properties window" later in this chapter).

The next level in the hierarchy are groups of related objects: forms, code modules, *references* to other object libraries, and objects from the underlying application. Normally, the Project Explorer displays a folder for each of these groups. At the bottom of the hierarchy come the individual objects themselves.

Navigating the Project Explorer window

The Project Explorer gives you the fastest way to find and activate the modules, forms, and other objects you want to work with. Just like the Windows Explorer, the Project Explorer displays a little box beside each item, or *node*, in its list. When only the project itself is visible, and its contents are hidden, this box, the *expand indicator*, contains a plus sign. If the nodes at lower levels of the hierarchy are visible, the expand indicator displays a minus sign instead.

Here are the techniques you use to work with the Project Explorer:

- To expand a node, displaying items lower in the hierarchy, click the expand indicator when it contains a plus sign, or highlight the node and press the right-arrow key.

- To collapse a node, hiding subsidiary items, click the expand indicator when it contains a minus sign, or press the left-arrow key.

- To open the UserForm or Code window corresponding to a module, form, or class module item in Project Explorer, double-click the item or highlight it in the list and press Enter.

- To activate a form's Code window, highlight the form in the list and press Shift+Enter.

- If you can't remember the difference between Enter and Shift+Enter, you can fall back on those buttons at the top of the Project Explorer window, just below its title bar. They work like this:

 The View Code button displays the Code window for the highlighted item.

 The View Object button shows you the highlighted item itself. If the item is a form, you see it in its UserForm window. If the item is a document, you're switched back to the underlying VBA application with that document active.

 The Toggle Folders button turns on or off the middle level of the project hierarchy. Normally, the Project Explorer separates the forms, code modules, and document objects into separate folders. If you click this button, those folders disappear and you see all the individual objects in each project in one alphabetical list. Click the button again to turn the folders back on.

Using the Project Explorer shortcut menu

The Project Explorer's shortcut menu, shown in Figure 20-3, gives you yet more ways to get up close and personal with the elements of your project. These commands are all available via the menus, but the shortcut menu provides faster access when you're already working with the Project Explorer.

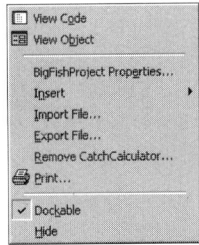

Figure 20-3: The Project Explorer shortcut menu

Setting project properties

The Project Properties dialog box lets you change the name of your project, add a brief description, attach a custom help file, and protect the project from unauthorized snooping or changes. Until you're a fairly advanced VBA developer, though, most of these options aren't terribly useful.

But anyway, at least now you know this dialog box exists. To display it, choose Tools ⇨ *Project Name* Properties, or right-click the Project Explorer window and select *Project name* Properties from the shortcut menu. Figure 20-4 shows the General tab on the Project Properties dialog box.

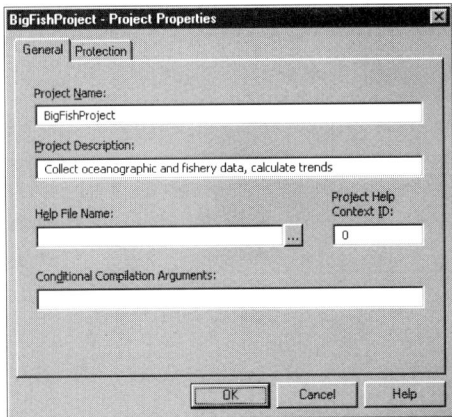

Figure 20-4: The General tab of the Project Properties dialog box

Renaming a project

The Project Explorer and the Object Browser list projects alphabetically by name. This means you can move a project in either window by changing its name. Of course, you may also want to change a project's name for purely artistic reasons.

The easiest way to change the VBA-supplied generic project name is in the Properties window. When you highlight the project in Project Explorer, the Properties window displays its name. You can edit the name to taste right there in the Properties window. You can also change the project's name on the General tab of the Project Properties dialog box, if you have it open for other reasons.

Protecting your project

If there's any chance someone else might get onto your computer and mess around with your programs, consider protecting your VBA projects with a password. To raise your security fence, display the Project Properties dialog box and switch to the Protection tab, shown in Figure 20-5.

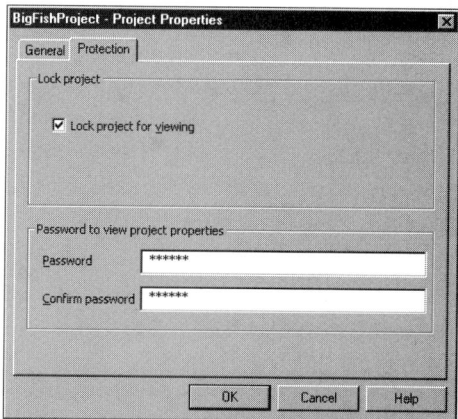

Figure 20-5: The Protection tab of the Project Properties dialog box

Here's how the settings on this tab work:

- **Lock Project for Viewing.** Checking this box completely locks out anyone who doesn't have the password. They can't even view the project without the password. If you don't check this box, your password prevents anyone else from opening the Project Properties dialog box — and this prevents them from locking *you* out of your own work.

- **Password.** Type in the password you've chosen for your project.

- **Confirm Password.** Type it again — this guarantees that you entered the password correctly the first time.

Unless your memory is infallible, write down the password and put it somewhere you can find it. VBA encrypts the project quite stoutly. Forget the password and you will have to recreate the project from scratch.

Using the Object Browser

Although it looks different and has more bells and whistles, the Object Browser has a lot in common with the Project Manager. Like the Project Manager, it lets you navigate quickly through the hierarchy of objects available to your VBA programs.

Cosmetics aside, though, a fundamental difference is that the Object Browser displays only one project at a time but lets you access *all* objects available to that project, not just the ones that belong to the project itself. In other words, besides your project's code modules and forms, you can also view the objects provided by your application, by VBA itself, and in other object libraries you may have opened.

The Object Browser's other great advantage is that it can track down the procedures, methods, events, properties, and so on from any of these object libraries.

Starting the Object Browser

The F2 key is your quick trigger command for displaying the Object Browser. Slower routes to the same destination include clicking the Object Browser button on the Standard toolbar, or choosing View ➪ Object Browser. Figure 20-6 shows the Object Browser window.

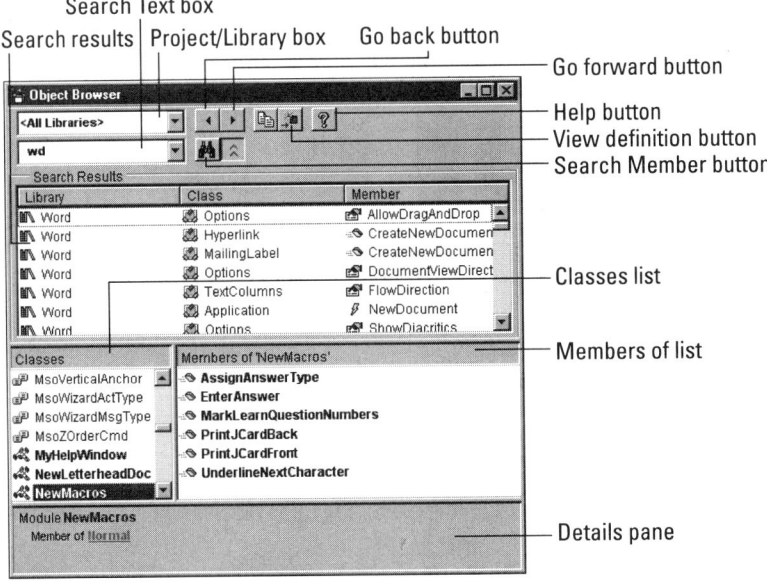

Figure 20-6: The Object Browser

Browsing objects

Caution

Before you do any serious work with the Object Browser, be sure you're browsing the right project. All you have to do is select the project you want to work with in the Project Explorer.

With that precaution out of the way, clicking the Project/Library list box at the top left displays the libraries available in the chosen project. (Your project should be there in the list — if it's not, go back to the Project Explorer and make sure it's selected.) By choosing <All Libraries> in the Project/Library box, you can browse all the objects available to your project (that is, the objects of all libraries that are referenced in your project). To home in on a particular library, just select it in the list. To cruise the objects of other libraries, add a reference to them using the Tools ⇨ References dialog box (see Figure 25-3).

Browsing panes

The Classes list occupies the left pane in the middle of the Object Browser window. It displays all the objects, collections, modules, forms, and constants available in the selected library or project. Clicking any one of these items displays its members in the pane on the right, the Members Of list. The members may be procedures, methods, properties, events, or individual constants.

Secret

Want to know where your VBA code lives? Just look for items displayed in bold in either the Classes list or the Members Of list.

In the bottom or Details pane of the Object Browser window, information about the currently selected object appears. The display lists the item's type and the object it belongs to (if you can't see all of this information, drag the separator at the top of the pane up or use the scroll bar at the right). Clicking the object the item belongs to displays that object in the Browser.

The Object Browser is pretty accommodating when it comes to your layout preferences. You can resize any of the panes (or the columns in the Search Results pane, which I'll cover in a bit) by dragging them into place.

Surfing the projects

The Object Browser works a lot like a Web browser. As in a Web browser you can follow hyperlinks to related items — clicking the underlined object in the Details pane (at the bottom) displays it in the Object Browser.

And as in a Web browser, you can retrace your steps. To revisit objects you've previously examined, click the Go Back button at the top of the Object Browser window. Of course, there's also a Go Forward button, which reverses direction again, eventually returning you to the object you were looking at when you first clicked Go Back.

Instant access to your code

If the item you've selected in the Object Browser is a module or procedure from your own code, just press Enter to bring up its Code window. Mouse lovers can click the Show Definition button for the same service.

Help in the Object Browser

Pressing F1, clicking the Help button, or choosing Help from the shortcut menu is supposed to bring up a Help topic on the object, method, property, or event you've selected in the Object Browser. In fact, it usually works this way. If your thinking style is more freeform than regimented, randomly nosing around with the Object Browser and displaying Help for any item that catches your eye is a great way to learn VBA painlessly.

Searching for members

Suppose you're not sure which of your code modules contains a particular procedure, or which object "owns" a particular method or event. Rather than comb through your modules in Project Explorer, or rummage through the Help system, you can get the Object Browser to locate the item for you.

1. Set the Library/Project drop-down list to <All Libraries> if you need to search the entire project, or to a specific library. If you select the wrong library, you might find something, but it won't be what you were looking for.

2. Enter the text you want to search for in the Search box. You can repeat any of your last four searches by reusing it from the Search box's drop-down list of items.

3. Press Enter or click the Search button (the binoculars). After the obligatory hard disk rattle, matching items appear in a new Search Results pane above the list panes. You can resize any column that's too small for the item displayed.

4. To close the Search Results pane, click the double up-arrow button next to the Search button. Click the same button (which now displays a double down-arrow) to redisplay the Search Results pane.

Using browsed items in your code

Secret

The Object Browser does more than satisfy your curiosity about the objects in your project — it can be a modestly practical coding aid. Once you locate an item that you actually want to use in your own code, you can press Ctrl+C or hit the Copy to Clipboard button to place the term on the clipboard. Then after switching to the appropriate Code window, paste the clipboard contents into your program. This technique ensures correct spelling — any little typo, and your code will run amok, or never get running in the first place.

Coding Secrets

Code windows are the heart of the Visual Basic Editor. It's here that you construct the VBA statements that actually perform useful work. In this chapter, I'm not going to say anything about the content of those VBA statements — well, not much, anyway. Instead, I focus on how to get the most out of the Code window when you're entering code.

Opening Code windows

The Visual Basic Editor gives you lots of different ways to open the Code window of an existing module, class module, or UserForm. First, you have to locate and select the item in the Project Explorer. Once you have it in your sights, any of the following techniques brings up the corresponding Code window:

- Press F7.
- Click the View Code button at the top of the Project Explorer window.
- Right-click the object and select View Code from the shortcut menu.
- Open the View menu and choose Code.
- For modules, double-click the item or just press Enter (this doesn't work for forms).

If you're currently viewing a UserForm window, pressing F7 or choosing View ⇨ Code displays that form's Code window.

Creating new Code windows

Inserting a new module into your project automatically opens a new Code window for that module. Chapter 21 walks you through the process of starting new modules. When you create a new form, a Code window is automatically created for it (you won't see it until you use one of the techniques just listed).

Typing code

VBA Code windows are in essence simple text editors, but they include loads of special features designed for writing VBA code. You type your VBA statements just as you would in a word processor, using the same cursor control and editing keys that are standard in Windows (you know, pressing Home takes you to the beginning of a line, whereas Ctrl+Home takes you to the top of the window — like that). You can select text with the mouse or by holding down the Shift key while you move the cursor.

Like every self-respecting text editor of the late twentieth century, the Code window supports drag-and-drop editing.

After you select the text you want to work with, you can:

- Move it, by dragging it into position and dropping it there.
- Copy it, by holding down the Ctrl key as you drag and drop.

You can drag text to another location in the same Code window, to a different Code window, or to the Immediate window or Watch window (the latter are covered in Chapter 23). If the destination is in a different Code window, you must arrange the two windows so that both the original text and the destination are visible before you start.

Secret

The Code window also lets you undo previous changes you made to your code. Each time you press Ctrl+Z or choose Undo from the Edit menu, another change is reversed. The Edit menu does provide a Redo command as well — to undo the effects of the Undo command — but Redo has no keyboard shortcut in the Visual Basic Editor.

The ideal coach

Like that perfect servant you always wished for, the Visual Basic Editor is constantly but unobtrusively checking and correcting your work in these ways:

- If you indent one line of code, the following lines are automatically indented to match (you can shut off this feature in the Tools ⇨ Options dialog box by removing the check from the Auto Indent box).

- If the editor recognizes a VBA *keyword,* it automatically capitalizes it according to VBA conventions (if you type an if...then...else statement, the Editor changes it to If...Then...Else). In addition, keywords are automatically colored blue so that they stand out from the other items you type (you can change the Editor's color scheme in the Tools ⇨ Options dialog box).

- In Code windows, you create a new procedure by typing Sub or Function followed by parentheses and an argument list, if required. When you do, the Visual Basic Editor automatically supplies the required closing statement for you, either End Sub or End Function.

- Finally, and most importantly, typing a VBA statement that is obviously incomplete or otherwise at odds with proper coding syntax provokes a warning message from the Editor (see Figure 20-7). With this immediate notification, you can correct the problem while you still remember what you were trying to accomplish with the statement in question. Even if you dismiss the warning for now, the Editor displays the statement in red to remind you that something serious is wrong.

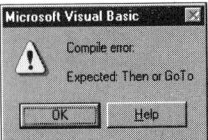

Figure 20-7: You get a warning message like this one when a line of VBA code doesn't follow correct syntax.

Navigating in a Code window

When you create a program of any complexity, a single Code window can contain pages and pages of code. Scrolling up and down randomly to find the section you're looking for would be much too primitive in such elegant surroundings.

Instead, take advantage of those two drop-down list boxes at the top of the Code window. They zoom you directly to the procedure you want to see or edit, as follows:

- The list box on the left is the *Object box*. In a module window, this contains only (General), and you don't need to worry about it. But when you're working with the Code window for a form, this box lets you pick out a specific control on the form (or the form itself). When you do, the Code window displays the default procedure for that object.

- The list box on the right is the *Procedures/Events box*. Here, selecting the Declarations section (for the entire window) or a specific procedure displays the code for the selected item. If you're working in a form's Code window, this box lists only the events available for the item you chose in the Object box. When you select an event, the Code window displays the corresponding procedure for that event.

Bookmarking your code

It's 3:00 A.M. Your eyelids are so heavy they're falling on your typing fingers, but the deadline looms and you keep on knocking out line after line of fairly routine code. Suddenly, inspiration strikes — you've just realized how to solve a major programming problem you were working on yesterday morning.

Before you jump to that other module to implement your brilliant idea, drop a *bookmark* where you're now working. That way, when it's time to get back to this module you can make like Hansel and Gretel and find your way home in a flash.

To place a bookmark on a line of code (well actually, alongside the code — see Figure 20-8), click the Toggle Bookmark button. All the bookmark-related buttons appear on the Edit toolbar, so you'll have to display this toolbar if you want access to them. Alternatively, you can use the corresponding menu command (Edit ➪ Bookmarks ➪ Toggle Bookmark), but it's much slower. (Cruelly, Microsoft omitted keyboard shortcuts for the bookmark commands.) You can lay down as many bookmarks as you want.

Of course, a bookmark does you no good by itself. Click the Next Bookmark or Previous Bookmark button to jump in sequence from one bookmark to the next until you arrive at your destination.

To remove a single bookmark, place the insertion point on the line containing the mark and again click the Toggle Bookmark button. If you've accumulated so many bookmarks that the Next and Previous Bookmark commands work like scrollbar buttons, you can wipe them all out by clicking the Clear All Bookmarks button.

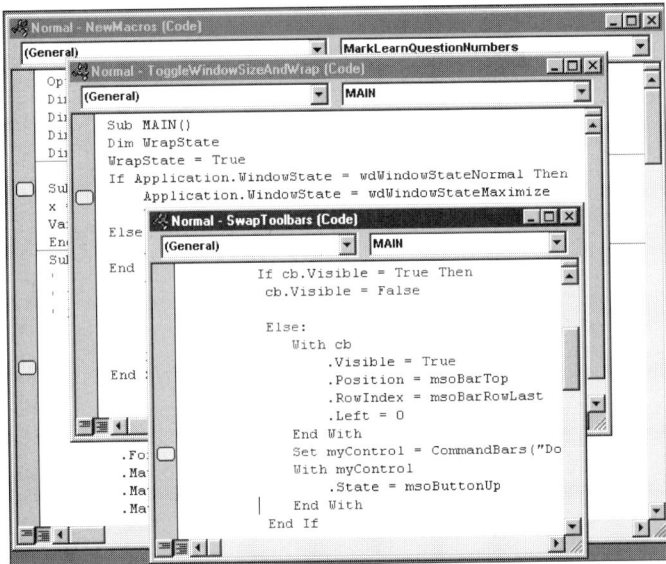

Figure 20-8: Those light ovals along the left side of the Code windows represent bookmarks. They appear in light blue on a color monitor.

Splitting a code window

You can split any Code window into two separate panes (see Figure 20-9). This enables you to see code in different parts of the same module at the same time. It also gives you an easy way to cut and paste between sections of your code.

To split a Code window, use the split bar — it's that little gray bar just above the top right scrollbar arrow. Drag the split bar downward until the panes are sized to suit you. To reunite them, remove the split bar by double-clicking it, or by dragging it back to the top of the window.

More Code window creature comforts

Why write code when you can have someone else type it for you? The Visual Basic Editor pampers you by automatically entering those wacky VBA terms for you at just the right time. Not only does this minimize your typing, it guarantees accurate spelling.

Several related Editor features, all found on the Edit menu, provide these amenities. They are:

- The List Properties and Methods feature
- The List Constants feature
- The Complete Word feature

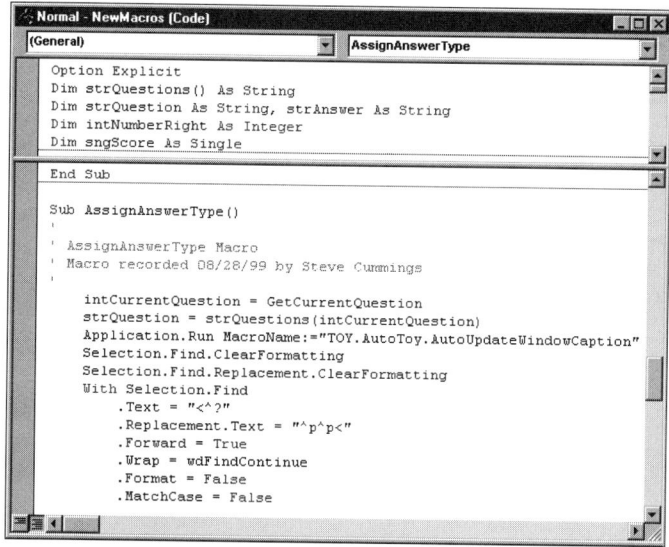

Figure 20-9: This Code window has been split.

Using the List Properties and Methods feature

Of these, the List Properties and Methods feature sees the most use. Here's how it works: To do anything useful with a VBA object, either you change the setting of one of the object's properties or you activate one of its methods. To identify the property or method you want to work with, you type the object's name, then a period (the *dot* operator), and then the property or method name, like this:

```
ActiveWindow.Selection.Group
```

(See Chapter 22 for the full story on working in code with objects and their properties and methods.)

With List Properties and Methods, all you have to type is the object name and the dot. As soon as you do, a little list of all the available properties and methods for that object pops up in the window. Figure 20-10 shows this list in action. To find the correct property or method, you can scroll the window using the arrow keys or type the first letter or two of the item's name. Once the right item is highlighted, hit the Tab key to insert it into your document.

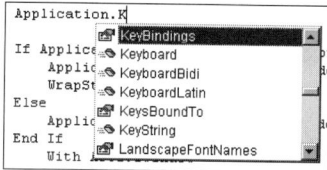

Figure 20-10: The List Properties and Methods feature gives you a power assist when entering — what else? — properties and methods in code.

The List Properties and Methods feature performs similar service when you're declaring a variable (defining its type). When you start typing a statement such as

```
Dim Muesli As CerealObject
```

a list of all the available data and object types pops up just when you finish typing the word "As." Just as before, you pick from this list by scrolling or typing a letter or two and pressing Tab. By the way, Chapter 21 covers declaring variables.

Secret

List Properties and Methods works not only with built-in VBA objects, but also your own object variables — *unless you haven't explicitly declared them as such*. This gives you a good reason to explicitly define variables.

Oh, one other point. The Properties and Methods list pops up automatically only if the proper setting is turned on in the Options dialog box. If you don't get the list, choose Tools ⇨ Options and be sure the box labeled Auto List Members is checked. You can pop up the list manually with the appropriate command on the Edit menu, or using the keyboard shortcut, Ctrl+J.

Listing constants automatically

The List Constants feature works just like the List Properties and Methods feature, except that it displays the names of the predefined constants for the property you're working with. This list pops up just after you type the = in a statement such as

```
Muesli.Crispness = Mushy
```

It's beyond me why this is considered as a separate command rather than just another part of the List Properties and Methods. But because it is, it requires a slightly different keyboard shortcut: Ctrl+Shift+J.

Completing words automatically

The Visual Basic Editor's Complete Word feature will enter just about any valid VBA term for you. To activate it, press Ctrl+Space. This pops up a list that looks and works just like the one provided by the List Properties and Methods feature described previously. The difference is, this list includes just about everything you might want to type: objects, functions, procedures, constants, methods, properties, and your own variables. One exception is the keywords for built-in data types, such as Integer and Variant.

Secret

Typing a letter or two before you press Ctrl+Space limits the list to items starting with those characters. Better yet, if you've typed enough letters to match only one item, the Editor inserts it for you as soon as you press Ctrl+Space — the list itself never appears.

Getting into arguments

Many VBA procedures require you to specify one or more *arguments* when you execute the procedure in your code. Such a procedure bases its calculations (or does whatever else it does) on the information you supply in these arguments. Many object methods require arguments just as procedures do.

The Visual Basic Editor won't type the arguments for you — it can't, because it doesn't know which specific values you want the arguments to have. However, it will pop up a little bitty window containing a kind of cheat sheet — it tells you which arguments the function requires, which are optional, and the type of information each argument represents. Figure 20-11 shows an example.

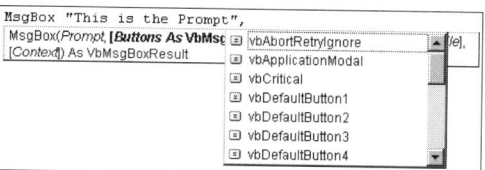

Figure 20-11: The Quick Info window in action

This is the Quick Info feature. If the Auto Quick Info box is checked in the Tools ⇨ Options dialog box, the Quick Info window will appear automatically as soon as you type the name of a function, method, or procedure that requires arguments. If you shut off this automatic response, you can still display the Quick Info window by pressing Ctrl+I.

Many functions and procedures require multiple arguments. To help you keep track of where you are in the list of arguments, the Quick Info window displays the argument you're currently typing in bold. As soon as you type the comma that indicates the end of one argument, the next argument turns bold in the Quick Info window.

Quick Info versus Parameter Info

The Parameter Info feature complements Quick Info when you get into heavy VBA coding. It often happens that you want to use one function to determine the value of an argument required by another function, as in this simple example:

```
MsgBox(Str(AnIntegerVariable))
```

Here, the Str function converts the integer value stored in the variable AnIntegerVariable into a text string. This string is then used as the argument to the MsgBox function (it becomes the prompt you see when VBA displays the message box on your screen).

But because you can *nest* functions within functions within functions in this way, the Quick Info window isn't enough. It always shows you the argument list for the function containing the insertion point. An extra helper, the Parameter Info feature displays the argument list for the "outermost" function, the one within which all the other functions are nested. The keyboard shortcut for the Parameter Info feature is Ctrl+Shift+I.

Using the Properties Window

The Properties window lets you view and edit the properties of whatever object (project, module, form, or control) is currently active in the Visual Basic Editor. If you look at Figure 20-12, you can see that the title bar of the Properties window shows the name of the active object, which also appears highlighted in the Project Explorer (if the selected object is an individual control on a form, only the form itself is listed in the Project Explorer).

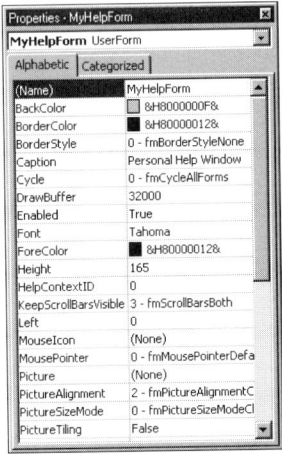

Figure 20-12: The Properties window for a form

When a project or module is the selected object, the only property listed in the Properties window is the project name. With form and control objects, however, the window gives you access to a myriad of properties governing the appearance and behavior of the selected object.

Because the Properties window is primarily useful for designing forms, I've postponed a full discussion of how it works to Chapter 24. For now, I'll just show you how to display the window and use it to rename projects and modules.

Invoking the Properties window

You can do any of the following tricks to display the Properties window:

- Press F4.
- Click the Properties button on the Standard toolbar.
- Open the View menu and choose Properties Window.

Once the Properties window is visible, switching to a Code or UserForm window or clicking an item in Project Explorer displays that item's properties in the window.

Renaming a project or module in the Properties window

Projects and modules have only one property each: a name. But regardless, you still use the Properties window if you want to change that one property. To rename a project or module, follow these steps:

1. Select the project or module in the Project Explorer.
2. Display the Properties window, if it isn't already visible.
3. Activate the Properties window, if it isn't already active (clicking it will do, or you can press F4).
4. Type the new name. Because this is the only property, you don't have to click the row for the (Name) property before you start typing.

The Debugging Windows

Chapter 23 covers debugging, so the windows you use to detect and correct errors in your code are described there. For now, just be aware that four windows are designed for debugging: the Immediate, Locals, Watch, and Call Stack windows.

Conclusion

Accessible from Word, Excel, Access, and PowerPoint, the Visual Basic Editor adds a powerful custom software development tool to Office. Mastering the many windows and controls of the Visual Basic Editor is a necessary first step on the path to creating your own intelligent macros and custom applications.

Chapter 21

Writing Great VBA Modules

In This Chapter

▶ Getting straight on the components of VBA programs, and how they relate to each other

▶ Creating modules and procedures

▶ Naming elements in your programs

▶ Working with variables, named storage bins for your data

▶ Using arrays to manage multiple items of the same data type

▶ Calculating with VBA operators

▶ Using control structures to branch, loop, and keep your programs well organized

▶ Avoiding unnecessary programming with built-in commands

Now that you've been exposed to some VBA concepts and know your way around the Visual Basic Editor, it's time to roll up your sleeves and start writing code. This chapter introduces essential programming and testing techniques for all VBA programmers.

Program Building Blocks

A VBA program isn't just a random collection of instructions to the computer. Rather, it's a highly organized random collection of instructions. Lines of code are collected into procedures, which reside in modules, which, in turn, are housed within projects.

A sample program

To make the discussion of this hierarchy of VBA elements a little less abstract, you can refer to the following module of code. It contains all the elements I mention except a project, in that modules go inside projects rather than the other way around. The sample module presented here searches the selected cells in an Excel worksheet, formatting those containing values greater than 1000 so that they stand out in boxed, bold, red type. It then tells you how many cells it changed (see Figure 21-1).

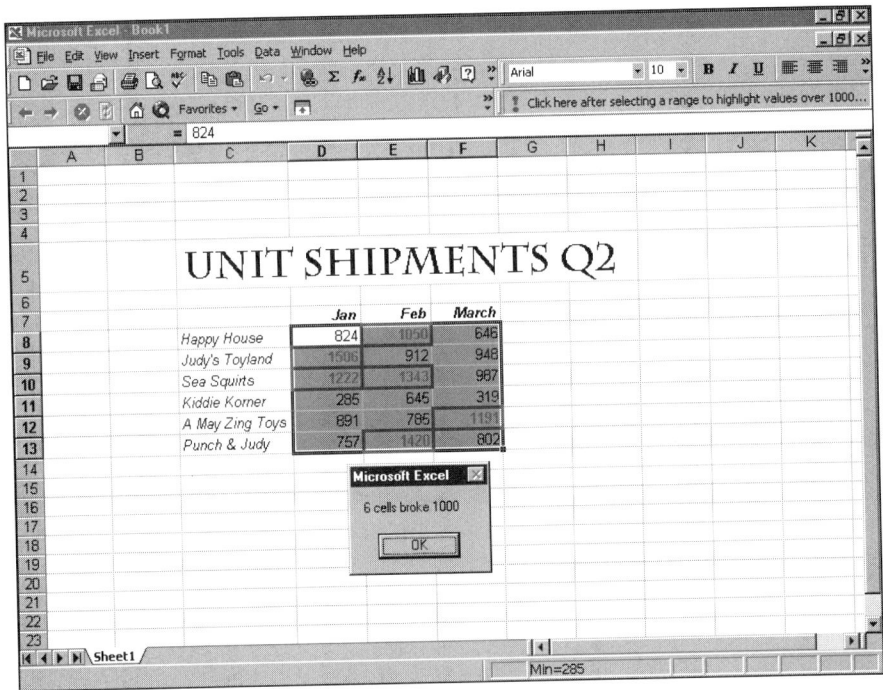

Figure 21-1: Here's what an Excel worksheet looks like when the sample module runs.

If you want a satisfying hands-on experience with the sample, start in Excel, open a new worksheet, and type in numbers in a block of cells — some values should be less than 1000 and some greater. Select the cells with the numbers. Then press Alt+F11 or choose Tools ⇨ Macros ⇨ Visual Basic Editor to enter the Editor. Display the Project Explorer and Properties windows by pressing Ctrl+R and F4, respectively. Choose Insert ⇨ Module to open a completely empty code window, your blank canvas for the new module.

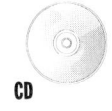

CD

A generic name for the module appears in the code window's title bar, in the Name field of the Properties window, and in Project Explorer's tree list. To change the module's name, select the current name in the Properties window and type in one of your own. I suggest `HighlightBigNumbers` for the sample, but use any name you like as long as it starts with a letter and contains no spaces — see the information on naming rules and conventions later in this chapter. Back in the code window, type in the following code. If you don't want to type, you can just open the Big Value Highlighter.xls workbook on the CD-ROM and switch to the Visual Basic Editor, where you can find the code in the `HighlightBigNumbers` module.

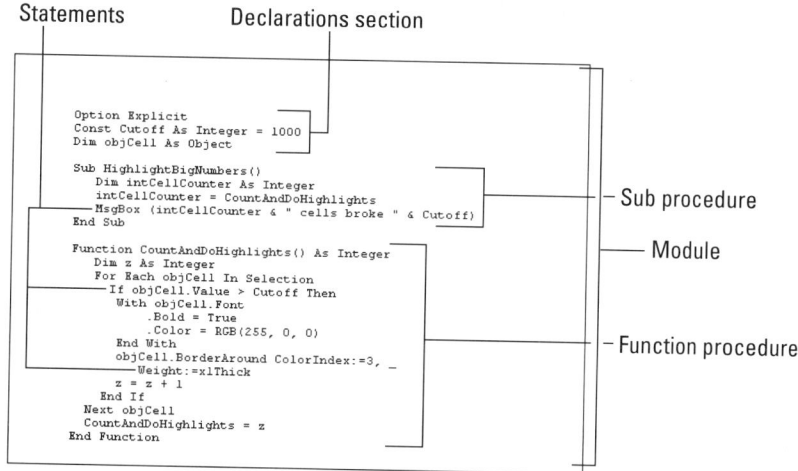

The VBA hierarchy

With the sample program in mind, you should be better able to understand the following definitions and descriptions of VBA code building blocks.

A *statement* is the smallest unit of VBA code that can accomplish anything. A statement may be used to declare or define a variable, set an option of the VBA compiler, or carry out an action in your program. A valid statement is a lot like a complete sentence — it has to include the proper "parts of speech" or it isn't really a statement at all.

A *procedure* is the smallest unit of code that you refer to by name. It's also the smallest unit of code that you can run independently. VBA recognizes two main types of procedures: Sub procedures and Function procedures. A procedure of either type consists of one or more statements, sandwiched inside two special statements: the procedure's declaration at the top, and the End Sub or End Function statement at the end.

A *module* is a named unit consisting of one or more procedures, plus declarations common to all procedures in the module. Although VBA allows you to place all your procedures in a single module, it makes sense to divide related procedures into separate modules to make it easier to keep track of them.

Two types of modules are available in VBA. By far the most common is the *standard module*, the kind you use for the code you want to run. The other type of module, the *class module*, is used to define custom objects and their properties and methods.

A *project* consists of all the modules, forms, and application-related objects associated with a particular document, plus the document itself.

Programs defined

So what's a *program*? Conceptually, a program is a complete, functioning (or malfunctioning) software totality. A program consists of one or more statements that execute in the order defined by the programmer.

But a program isn't an official VBA entity. VBA recognizes by name procedures, modules, and projects, but not programs as such. A VBA program requires at least one procedure — because VBA only executes statements within procedures — but it can encompass two or more procedures, within one or more modules, spanning one or more projects.

More about projects

You never have to do anything to create a project. Every document from a VBA application is a project automatically. Of course, a document's project doesn't contain any code or forms until you create them in the Visual Basic Editor or record macros in the application. The section on the Project Explorer in Chapter 20 covers the techniques you need for working with projects as a whole.

Working with modules

The module comes just below the project in the hierarchy of VBA code elements. A module provides storage for one or more VBA procedures, along with a Declarations section containing statements that apply to the entire module.

Planning your modules

Deciding how your modules should be organized doesn't have to be a big deal. It does make sense to think about how many modules you should create and which procedures each one should contain. The basic points to remember are these:

- Your procedures can *call*, or run, procedures stored in other modules. You can use variables declared in another module too.

- However, it's slightly more complicated to use procedures and variables from other modules. For example, to call a procedure in another module, you enter it with module's name, as in `OtherModule.DoSomethingNow` (see Chapter 23 for more information on accessing items stored in different modules or projects).

In general, you should place related procedures together in a single module. Typically, a module contains all the procedures for one complete VBA program — and no extraneous procedures. That simplifies your programming, because you don't have to deal with the little complications involved in accessing procedures or variables in other modules.

However, if you create procedures that you plan to use in more than one program, you can organize them in modules according to type, as in MyMathProcedures or TextHandlingRoutines. You might also create modules called BrandNewProcedures or OldProceduresIMightNeedSomeday.

Adding a new module to a VBA project

To create a new module in the Visual Basic Editor, start by making sure you're working with the correct project. In the Project Explorer, select the project itself or any of the objects it already contains (this can be a form, an application object, or an existing module — it doesn't matter). You can then use any of the following techniques to insert the new module:

- Click the Insert Module button. This is a split (multifunction) button for inserting various items. If the module icon isn't visible, click the narrow bar with the arrow to the right of the main part of the button and choose from the menu.

- Right-click the Project Explorer window — make sure you do it over the correct project — and choose Insert ➪ Module from the shortcut menu. If you prefer the main menu bar, choose Insert ➪ Module.

The Visual Basic Editor automatically opens the new module's Code window. It also christens the module with a generic name. To change it, type a new name in the Properties window (see "Renaming a project or module in the Properties window" in Chapter 20).

What goes where in a new module

The Code window for a brand-new module has only one section, the Declarations section. You can tell which section you're in by looking at the list box at the top right of the Code window.

You can enter two types of statements in a module's Declarations section. These are:

- Declarations of variables, constants, and user-defined data types. These tell the compiler the name and type of each item (but not its value). Variables and constants declared in a module's Declarations section can be used in any procedure in that module.

- Compiler options that control the way VBA compiler operates.

What you can't place in the Declarations section are assignment or executable statements — statements that actually do something when the code runs. For example, you can't specify the *value* of a variable in the Declarations section. That requires an assignment statement, which must go inside a procedure elsewhere in the module. (The differences between executable statements, assignment statements, declarations, and compiler options are clarified, hopefully, in the section "Making statements" later in this chapter).

Secret

Statements in the Declarations section are also referred to as *module-level code*. Each procedure you add to the module is considered a separate section. After you've added a procedure, its name appears in the list box at the top right of the Code window, enabling you to jump directly to that procedure by selecting its name in the list.

Standard modules and modules with class

The garden variety VBA module is a standard module (standard modules were known as code modules in older versions of VBA and Visual Basic). They contain statements that declare variables and constants, define custom (user-defined) data types, and set compiler options, as well as executable statements that actually get things done. You can make use of any existing objects you have access to in a standard module, but you can't create new object types in this type of module.

You use class modules, by contrast, to define your own custom objects. After creating a class module for the custom object, you fill it with the code for the object's properties and methods. This done, code in other modules can access the object's properties and methods, just as if it were a built-in VBA object. Writing your own classes is a powerful VBA programming technique; it's covered in Chapter 22.

Writing procedures

Procedures are critical functional units of your VBA code, because code must be stored within a procedure or you can't run it. VBA procedures fall into two everyday types, Sub procedures and Function procedures (see the "Procedure Types" sidebar). Here are two simple procedures, one of each type:

```
Public Sub SubMarine()
    MsgBox "Up Periscope!"
End Sub
Public Function FunkShun (Birthdate As Date)
    FunkShun = DateDiff("yyyy", Birthdate, Date)
End Function
```

As you can see, each procedure comprises an opening declaration statement, one or more lines of code, and a terminating End statement. I'll go into these elements fully in the sections "Sub procedures in detail" and "Function procedures in detail."

Creating a new procedure

Before you can start a new procedure, you have to first open the Code window for the module in which you're going to store the procedure. Create a new module with the steps laid out earlier in this chapter, or open an existing module by double-clicking it in the Project Explorer.

Once the module's Code window is open and active, you're ready to begin the new procedure. Your initial task is simply to insert into the module the procedure's declaration statement, and its complement, the End statement that signals the end of the procedure. You can accomplish this in two ways: via the Insert ⇨ Procedure dialog box, or by typing the statements yourself.

Typing versus the dialog box

I recommend typing in the procedure's "shell" yourself, simply because the dialog box method doesn't save any time unless you're a *really* slow typist. The do-it-yourself approach also lets you control where in the module to place the procedure, which you can't do with the dialog box. All you have to do is click where you want the procedure to go and type the procedure's declaration statement and hit Enter. You don't have to type the parentheses or the closing End Sub or End Function statement—the Visual Basic Editor adds them for you.

Completing the procedure

The real work in writing a procedure is in typing a series of VBA statements between the declaration and End statements. This isn't the place for details on what to type. Suffice it to say that the statements within a procedure are executed in the order in which they appear, except when your code instructs VBA to jump to another location.

Procedure Types

Here's a summary of the various function types:

- A Sub procedure is a general-purpose procedure for getting things done in VBA. Sub procedures are the only type you can run independently. However, one Sub procedure can also run, or *call*, another.

- A Function procedure can execute any VBA statements you like. However, it differs from a Sub procedure in that it calculates a value and then *returns* that value to the procedure that activated the Function in the first place.

- An Event procedure is a special type of Sub procedure used to respond to events that occur to forms and to application objects such as documents and the application itself. Chapter 24 covers the particulars on event procedures.

- A Property procedure is used to determine or assign the value of a custom object's property. Property procedures are covered in the section "Do-It-Yourself Objects: Class Modules" in Chapter 22.

A VBA macro is, technically speaking, a Sub procedure that *takes* (requires) no arguments. Macros are the only kind of Sub procedures you can run directly, by name, in the Visual Basic Editor or your VBA application. To run a Sub procedure that does take arguments, you must call it from another procedure.

Sub procedures in detail

In some programming languages, "subprocedures" or "subroutines" are those that are called by main procedures. In VBA, while a Sub procedure can be called by another procedure, the main procedure of a program is itself *always* a Sub procedure. Here's a sample Sub procedure, with the declaration at the top, the terminating End statement at the bottom, and a few statements in between:

```
Public Sub ASweetProcedure()
   Dim ANiceMessage As String
   ANiceMessage = "Have a nice day!"
   Msgbox ANiceMessage
   (more statements)
   ...
End Sub
```

Items in a Sub procedure declaration

In the procedure's declaration statement, the first term, Public, specifies the procedure's scope. This can be Public or Private. Public is the default, so you don't need to include this keyword. However, doing so makes the scope obvious so that you don't have to wonder. I discuss scope in "Scoping out the scope" later in this chapter.

Next comes the Sub keyword, which simply indicates you're declaring a Sub procedure. After that is the procedure's name, which can be anything you like, as long as it conforms to the standards given in "VBA naming rules" later in this chapter.

About arguments

Closing out the declaration is a pair of parentheses. They are there to hold *arguments*, if the procedure has any. In this case, the procedure has no arguments, so nothing appears inside the parentheses. Arguments are discussed in "Winning arguments," which follows the section on Function procedures.

Calling Sub procedures

You can run, or *call,* any Sub procedure — whether or not it takes arguments — from another procedure. To call a Sub procedure, just include a statement consisting of the name of the Sub procedure you want to call, as in this code fragment. The line reading WashMyOldCar calls the WashMyOldCar Sub procedure:

```
...
MyOldCar = "Valiant"
WashMyOldCar
NumberOfCarwashTrips = NumberOfCarwashTrips + 1
...
```

Function procedures in detail

A Function procedure can conduct general business just like a Sub procedure, but its main *raison d'être* is to calculate a value. When the Function completes its work, it returns that value to the calling procedure, which can use it in further computations.

Here's a sample Function procedure:

```
Public Function DeFunct(x As Integer, y As Integer)
    Dim z As Integer
    z = x + y
    DeFunct = x ^ z
End Function
```

This line raises x to the *z*th power

Obviously, the basic form of a Function procedure is much like that of a Sub procedure. The declaration begins with an optional keyword defining the procedure's scope (in this case Public). Next comes the Function keyword, then the procedure's name, and finally its arguments. A function ends with a terminating statement, End Function.

The difference between Function and Sub procedures

There is one critical difference between Sub and Function procedures: somewhere in a Function procedure, at least one statement specifies the value of the function itself. It does so by using the name of the procedure as if it were a variable. In the preceding example, this occurs in the line DeFunct = x ^ z. After this line executes, DeFunct holds the value that will be returned to the calling procedure.

Calling Function procedures

Normally, you call a Function procedure by setting a variable equal to the name of the function. In the first executable statement in the following example, the variable ZPower receives the value returned by the DeFunct procedure. Note that the arguments required by the DeFunct procedure are passed in parentheses following the procedure name:

```
Sub DoDeFunct()
    ZPower = DeFunct(3, 4)
    MsgBox Zpower
End Sub
```

Built-in VBA Functions

VBA comes with numerous built-in *functions*. Like a Function procedure, a VBA function returns a value to a calling procedure. Also, you use the same technique to call both functions and Function procedures. The names vary, but the only difference between Function procedures and functions to the person using them is that you don't have to write code for functions. The section "Built-in Functions and Statements" offers an overview of the functions available in VBA.

Winning arguments

Arguments represent values that VBA is to transfer, or *pass,* from one procedure to another. The second procedure is said to *take* the arguments. You build arguments into a procedure when you want the procedure to modify its behavior based on values you supply at the time you call the procedure.

Refer to the sample Function procedure DeFunct shown in the earlier section "Function procedures in detail." It takes two arguments, x and y. As the DeFunct illustrates, a procedure's arguments are declared as part of the declaration of the procedure itself. They always appear in parentheses following the name of the procedure. In this *argument list*, you declare individual arguments just as you would variables of the same type except that you leave out the Dim or similar keyword (see "Working with Variables" for details on declaring individual variables).

A procedure that takes arguments requires those arguments to do its job. Within the procedure, arguments serve exactly the same role as variables that you declare in the usual way. Look again at the DeFunct procedure. After declaring a variable z for its own use, the procedure calculates z's value as the sum of the two arguments, x and y. Then, to calculate the procedure's own return value, the next line of code raises the x argument to the power of z. As you can see, x, y, and z all have similar roles. If you wanted, you could have raised z to the power of x instead of the other way around.

So why argue?

So if arguments are so much like variables, why use arguments at all? Actually, you don't have to — you can use ordinary variables to accomplish everything you can do with arguments. But arguments have the following advantages:

- When you're reading through your code, arguments make it clear which outside values a procedure requires to do its job.

- When you're writing code, arguments help you minimize the number of variables you need to create outside of procedures (in the Declarations section of the module).

- When you call a procedure that takes arguments, VBA *forces* you to state values for those arguments. This helps ensure that the procedure gets the correct values it needs.

Calling procedures that take arguments

The way you call a procedure that takes arguments depends on the situation:

- When you use a Function procedure to return a value, you place the arguments in parentheses separated by commas:

    ```
    ProceedsFromOldCar = SellOldCar ("Rambler Classic",1962)
    ```

- When you call a Function procedure by itself, ignoring its return value, and whenever you call a Sub procedure, state the arguments without parentheses:

    ```
    SellOldCar "Studebaker", 1957
    ```

Scoping out the scope

Each VBA procedure has a defined *scope*. The scope determines the parts of your program from which you can call that procedure. If you have a visual imagination, think of it this way: A procedure's scope decides which parts of your program can "see" the procedure.

Procedures can have three different scopes:

- By default, VBA procedures (except event procedures) are *public* in scope. That means that you can call them from any part of your program — from the same module, from another module, or even (if your program includes multiple projects as discussed in Chapter 19) from a different project.

- When it suits your programming needs, you can create procedures that are *private* in scope. Private procedures are visible, if you will, only within the same module. In other words, you can call a private procedure from another procedure in the same module, but not from procedures in any other modules.

- In a VBA program that includes more than one project, you can create procedures that are accessible to all the modules within a given project but off limits to other projects.

Variables have scope, too, and scope works in a similar way for them. See the section "Specifying a variable's scope" later in this chapter.

Specifying a procedure's scope

To specify the scope of a procedure, all you have to do is place the `Public` or `Private` keyword at the beginning of the procedure's declaration. Look at these examples:

```
Public Sub IKneadYou()
... (procedure statements)
End Sub

Private Function IKneedYou()
... (procedure statements)
End Function
```

Because ordinary (non-event) procedures are public by default, you don't have to include the `Public` keyword to give a procedure public scope. If a program contains any private procedures, however, I recommend that you explicitly declare the public procedures so that you can tell at a glance which is which.

To restrict the scope of a public procedure to its project only, so that it is inaccessible to other projects, place the statement `Option Private Module` in the Declarations section of the module in which you declare the procedure. See the "Declarations" and "Compiler options" sections later in this chapter for details on working with such statements.

Using private procedures

Making a procedure private helps prevent errors. Because you can only call the procedure from within the same module, you can more easily control the conditions in effect at the time the procedure gets called (conditions such as the values of variables that the procedure uses).

Making a procedure private in scope is easy enough, but why bother? After all, VBA doesn't *demand* that you call a procedure from another module, just because that procedure is public.

Well, the reason is self-protection. You may forget that you designed a procedure so that it should only be called from within the same module. If the procedure is private, VBA won't let you call it from another module even if you try to. As a bonus, in programs of substantial size and complexity, limiting the number of access points to a given procedure helps you better keep track of the program's organization.

Making statements

Procedures are made up of statements, the smallest viable units of code. Most statements occupy only one line of code, and a line of code usually has only one statement — but not always, as you'll see later in this section. VBA distinguishes four different statement types: declarations, assignment statements, executable statements, and compiler options.

Declarations

A declaration statement announces to the VBA compiler your intention to use a named item — a variable, constant, user-defined data type, or procedure — in your program. The declaration goes further, specifying which type of item it is and providing any additional information the compiler will need to make use of the item. Once you've declared an item, you can use it elsewhere in your program.

The following statement declares the variable named `MyLittleNumber` as an integer variable:

```
Dim MyLittleNumber As Integer
```

This statement creates a string (text) constant named `UnchangingText` and consisting of the characters "Eternity":

```
Constant UnchangingText = "Eternity"
```

The following statement declares a Sub procedure named `HiddenProcedure`:

```
Private Sub HiddenProcedure()
```

Assignment statements

Assignment statements set a variable, or a property of an object, to some specific value. These statements always have three parts: the name of the variable or property, an equal sign, and an *expression* specifying the new value (see "Expression-ism" for a discussion of expressions).

The following statement sets the value of the `MyLittleNumber` variable to sum of the `SomeOtherNumber` variable and 12:

```
MyLittleNumber = SomeOtherNumber + 12
```

This statement sets the `Color` property of the AGraphicShape object to Blue, which has presumably been defined as a constant:

```
AGraphicShape.Color = Blue
```

Executable statements

Executable statements do things.

For example, this statement executes the `Rotate` method of the AGraphicShape object:

```
AGraphicShape.Rotate(90)
```

This statement performs the `Sqr` function — which calculates a square root — on the current value of the `MyLittleNumber` variable, placing the result into the `SquareRoot` variable:

```
SquareRoot = Sqr(MyLittleNumber)
```

Compiler options

Instructions that control the VBA compiler's behavior constitute the last class of statements. Of the four compiler options statements, the main one to learn is

```
Option Explicit
```

See the section "Choosing and using data types" for information on the `Option Explicit` directive.

Manners, Please! VBA Etiquette

In the service of readable, understandable, working code, this section covers rules and conventions for naming VBA items, formatting your code for legibility, and adding comments.

VBA naming rules

VBA enforces rules for naming program elements including variables, constants, data types, procedures, modules, forms, controls, and projects. If you try to enter a name that violates any of these rules, the Visual Basic Editor will warn you as soon as you move the insertion point off that line of code. Here are the rules:

- Names must begin with a letter, not a numeral. After the first character, however, you can use numerals and the underscore character, as in

    ```
    Hidden_Variable3
    ```

- Aside from the underscore character, punctuation marks are off limits altogether in VBA names. Off-limits characters include:

  ! @ & ' $ # ? , * . (period) { } ( ) [ ] = + - ^ % / ~ < > : ;

- Names can't include spaces.
- You're limited to a maximum of 255 characters (40 characters for forms and controls).
- A name can't duplicate a VBA keyword, function, or statement.
- You can't use the same name more than once in the same scope. For example, all procedures in the same module must have different names. A procedure and a module-level variable — one declared in the Declarations section of a module — can't share the same name, However, you can use duplicate names for variables declared inside different procedures. The section "Specifying a variable's scope" tries to clarify the muddy issue of scope.

VBA ignores the capitalization of names but preserves the capitalizations you use.

Naming conventions

As long as you live by the rules listed earlier, you can give any name you like to any item in your program. Nevertheless, you can make your programming life a lot easier by sticking to a logical naming scheme. One method that many people use is to start each name with a short prefix that indicates the type of item and follow that with a capitalized brief descriptive name. Table 21-1 lists suggested prefixes for the most commonly used VBA items. You can make up your own or use them as suffixes if you prefer. The important thing is to use them consistently.

Table 21-1 Suggested Prefixes for Naming VBA Items

Use This Prefix	To Name This Type of Item	Example
Variables		
byte	Byte	byteDaysInMonth
bool	Boolean	boolClearedStatus
int	Integer	intWeeksOnChart
lng	Long integer	lngPopulation
sng	Single	sngRadius
dbl	Double	dblParsecs

Use This Prefix	To Name This Type of Item	Example
Variables		
cur	Currency	curUnitPrice
str	String	strLastName
dat	Date/Time	datBirthdate
var	Variant	varSerialNumber
obj	Object	objStampCollection
Controls on forms		
txt	Text box	txtEnterName
lbl	Label	lblAnswerMessage
cmd	Command button	cmdCalculateInterestRate
mnu	Menu	mnuTools
cmb	Combo box	cmbToyCategory
fra	Frame	fraHabitat
opt	Option button	optGasolineGrade
chk	Checkbox	chkCaseSensitive
Other items		
bas	Module	basTextFormatFunctions
frm	UserForm	frmOptionsDialog

Making your code legible

This section offers a few simple suggestions for writing code that you can decipher when you come back to it tomorrow, next week, or next year.

Judicious indenting helps organize your code

Develop and practice a consistent indenting style. The VBA compiler ignores blank space at the beginning of a line. This means you're free to use indentation to set off related lines of code. So which lines of code should you indent, and by how much? Your indenting goal is to indent related statements by the same amount, so the relationship between them is visually obvious. More specifically, statements that are executed only when some condition is in effect should all be indented together.

For example, VBA executes the statements within an If...Then...Else construction or inside Do...Loop and For...Next loops as a group, so they should have the same indentation. Here's another example:

```
Do While intC <> 20
    intA = intA + 1
    If intA = intB Then
        intA = 5
        intB = 10
    Else
        intA = intB
        intC = 20
    End If
Loop
```

Note that *control structures* like Do...Loop and If...Then...Else always consist of at least two statements: one that starts the structure, the other that terminates it. For Do...Loop, the terminating statement is Loop; for If...Then...Else, it's End If. Statements that are part of a given control structure itself should all be indented by the same amount. This enables you see clearly the outline of the structure, and which other statements fall inside it.

Secret

To cut your workload to a minimum, the Visual Basic Editor automatically indents each new line of code to match the previous one. When you get to a line that requires a smaller indentation, just press the Backspace key to back up. If you don't like the assistance, you can shut off automatic indenting in the Editor tab of the Tools ➪ Options dialog box.

No scrolling! Use the line continuation character

Although shorter statements are easier to understand and debug, it's perfectly acceptable to extend a single statement over multiple lines in the Visual Basic Editor. Obviously, each line will be much easier to read if it all fits into the visible portion of the Code window, so you don't have to scroll sideways.

To continue a statement onto another line, place an underscore, _, at the end of the line. For example, the following three lines together constitute one statement:

```
sngWackyNumber = Cos(12 * 57.5 / Sqr(intMyTinyNumber + _
intMyBigNumber) + CustomDataMassage(sngrawinfo, 12) + _
(bytFirstTuesdayInAugust * curLastPayCheck) + 1)
```

Caution

Be sure you remember to type a space before the underscore (also called the *line continuation character*) on every line where you use it. Otherwise, VBA will give you an "invalid character" error message. Another cautionary note: Don't place the underscore within a pair of quotation marks that enclose a string of text.

Remarks about comments

Like all serious programming languages, VBA lets you add explanations to your code. Comments enable you to record the purpose of each statement or group of statements. Please be lavish with comments. The comments you type are totally ignored by the VBA compiler. They live only in the text file representing the contents of the Code window, not in the compiled program.

They don't make the compiled program any longer, nor do they slow it down in any way. Comments cost you nothing except a minuscule amount of disk space, so use them freely.

How to make comments

A comment begins when you type an apostrophe. Everything you type to the right of the apostrophe on that line of code is part of the comment. You can place comments on lines all by themselves, or you can add comments after a line of active code. Figure 21-2 shows a Code window with lots of comments interspersed among the active code statements.

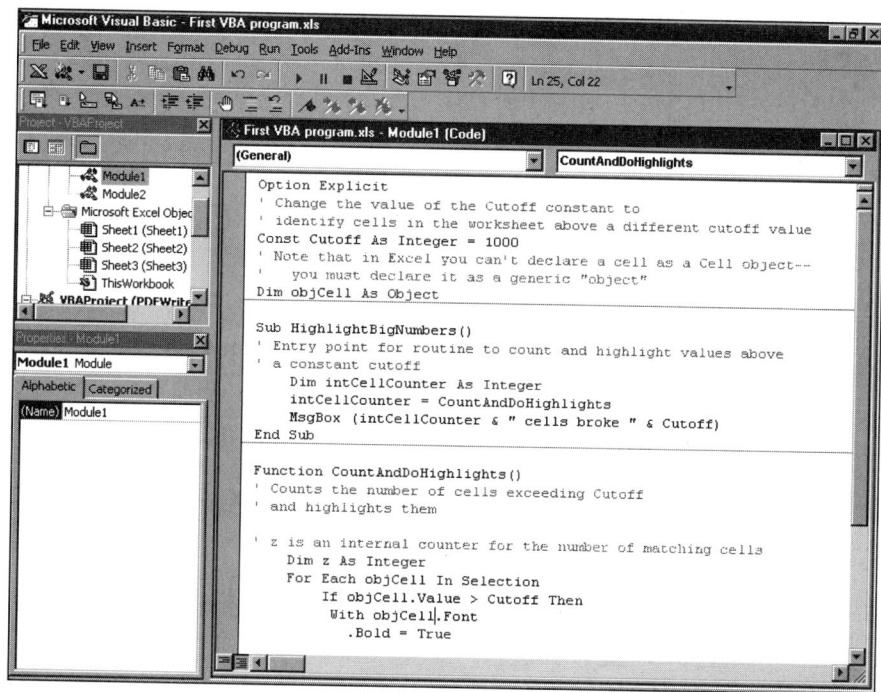

Figure 21-2: Comments, please?

Secret

Commenting is a good way to take real code statements out of active duty without deleting them for good. This can come in handy when you want to try two alternative approaches to the same coding problem, or to shut off code that you know contains an error while you test another part of the same module.

Long-winded comments

To include a long comment spanning two or more lines in your code, you must place an apostrophe at the beginning of each line. But fortunately, VBA provides a one-button command for commenting blocks of lines in bulk. You can also "uncomment" a block of lines that currently begin with apostrophes. Select the block and click the Uncomment Block button. Using the Comment

Block and Uncomment Block buttons, you can quickly deactivate and reactivate any code block.

Secret

One little note about the way these buttons work is in order. If a line already starts with an apostrophe, the Comment Block button adds a second apostrophe to it, and so on. Likewise, each time you click the Uncomment Block button, only one apostrophe is removed. This means that when you comment and then uncomment a block of active code, you don't lose any "real" comments that it contained.

Working with Variables

To tap the full potential of VBA, programs require *variables* to store information that can change. Variables are the key to writing programs that alter their own behavior based on up-to-date information or other changes in prevailing conditions. In essence, a variable is an ID tag for a chunk of information stored by your program. It's like when you go to the theater and leave your hat at the hatcheck. The attendant puts your hat away somewhere in a back room — you couldn't care less where, as long as it's safe. In return, you get a slip with a number on it. When you leave, you give the attendant the number and you get your hat back. At the next performance, the staff uses that same number for somebody else's hat.

Declaring variables

One of the most common uses of declaration statements is to declare variables. Variable declarations look like this:

```
Dim varAnyOldVariable
Private intIntegerVariable As Integer
Static strNewYearsResolution As String
```

Most variable declarations are Dim statements. The `Dim` keyword is short for dimension, used as a verb. The idea is that the Dim statement gives VBA the dimensions for the storage area the variable refers to. You can also use the `Private`, `Public`, and `Static` keywords to declare variables and at the same time specify their scope. Read about scope in "Specifying a variable's scope."

Where to declare variables

You can declare a variable in either of two places in your program:

- The Declarations section of the module (at the module level)
- Anywhere within a procedure (at the procedure level)

The choice of this location helps determine which procedures can access the variable, or in other words, the variable's scope. In general, if you declare the variable at the module level, any procedure in the module can use the variable. If you declare it in a particular procedure, it can be used only in that procedure. You can also use the `Public`, `Private`, and `Static` keywords to specify a variable's scope. For additional info on scope, see "Specifying a variable's scope" later in this chapter.

Although VBA won't object if you interleave variable declarations with executable statements within a procedure, your code will be clearer if you declare all the procedure's variables at the very beginning. Note how the following procedure follows this practice:

```
Public Sub VariableProcedures ()
Dim strChildsName As String
Dim intToyCount As Integer
Dim curAllowance As Currency
strChildsName = InputBox ("Enter the child's name:")

' in the next two lines, CountToys and NewAllowance
' are Function procedures presumably defined elsewhere
' in your code
intToyCount = CountToys(strChildsName)
curAllowance = NewAllowance(strChildsName, intToyCount)
End Sub
```

When to declare variables

Secret

All the experts agree that declaring variables ahead of time, before you use them in your program, is the best practice. One simple reason for doing so is to make your code easier to understand. Other advantages come into play when you use the `Option Explicit` compiler directive, covered in "Force yourself to use explicit declarations" later in this chapter.

By default, however, VBA permits you to use variables without declaring them first. If you type A = 7 anywhere in your code, VBA dutifully creates a variable named A and stores the value 7 in that variable. Variables you create without declaring them are automatically defined as variant variables, which are discussed in the next section.

Choosing and using data types

When you write a variable declaration, you can simply name the variable. The following statement tells VBA to set aside storage space for a variable named `varIable` but does not say what sort of information that variable should hold:

```
Dim varIable
```

Alternatively, you declare the variable's *data type* explicitly. The statement

```
Dim sngMyOldSocks As Single
```

declares the variable `sngMyOldSocks` as of the *single* data type, meaning that it holds a relatively small floating-point number (the kind written in scientific notation with a decimal point and an exponent, as in $6.02 \cdot 10^{23}$).

VBA recognizes a variety of other distinct data types for your variables, including helpful types like Date and Currency. Familiarize yourself with the available types because collectively they are an important key to writing code that works right. Table 21-2 summarizes key facts about the data types. The last part of this chapter offers tips on working with many of the specific types.

Table 21-2   VBA Data Types

Data Type	Explained	Range of Permitted Values
Boolean	Logical true or false	True (–1) or False (0)
Byte	Small whole number	0 to 255
Integer	Smallish whole number	–32,768 to 32,767
Long	Large whole number	–2,147,483,648 to 2,147,483,647
Single	Single-precision floating-point value	–3.402823E38 to –1.401298E–45 for negative values; 1.401298E–45 to 3.402823E38 for positive values
Double	Double-precision floating-point value	–1.79769313486232E308 to –4.94065645841247E–324 for negative values; 4.94065645841247E–324 to 1.79769313486232E308 for positive values
Currency	Large, precise number; 19 significant digits, including four fixed decimal places	–922,337,203,685,477.5808 to 922,337,203,685,477.5807
Decimal	Even larger, more precise number with 29 significant digits and up to 28 decimal places	+/–79,228,162,514,264,337,593,543,950,335 with no decimal point; +/–7.9228162514264337593543950335 with 28 places to the right of the decimal
Date	Dates and times	January 1, 100 to December 31, 9999
Object	VBA object	Any object reference
String (variable-length)	Sequence of text characters of variable length	0 to approximately 2 billion
String (fixed-length)	Sequence of specified number of text characters	1 to approximately 65,400
Variant	Anything goes	Any numeric value up to the range of a Double; same range as for variable-length String

Data Type	Explained	Range of Permitted Values
User-defined (requires the Type statement)	Group of variables used together as a unit	The range of each variable in the group corresponds to its data type (see preceding entries).

Pros and cons of using specific data types

Secret

Depending on whom you talk to, declaring a variable as a specific data type — that is, as a type other than *Variant* — is either a great idea or a bad one. The practice definitely makes for smaller and faster programs, but in most cases, the speed and size improvements probably aren't significant.

Here's the background: When you declare a variable's data type carefully, you can select the type requiring the smallest amount of storage space needed to hold the information you plan to keep there. The alternative is to declare it as a Variant, a catch-all type that can hold any kind of data. (If you don't declare the type, you get a Variant variable by default.)

Variants consume more memory than variables of other types, and accessing their information slows down your program. However, these effects are trivial unless you work with very large numbers of variables. And by declaring all variables as Variants, you can reduce errors and make your code easier to write, more flexible, and less complicated to modify. I don't have room to explore this issue in detail, but you should be aware that some very good programmers recommend coding exclusively with Variants.

Secret

You can declare Variants just as you would variables of other types, as in this example:

```
Dim varTootSuite As Variant
```

However, because Variants are the default data type, you can get by with simply listing the variable name in your Dim statement, as shown here:

```
Dim TootSuite
```

Force yourself to use explicit declarations

Whether you decide to declare each variable as a specific data type or use Variants for all your variables, you should set VBA to force you to declare them. When you place the statement

```
Option Explicit
```

in the Declarations section of a module, VBA displays an error message every time you try to use a variable that you haven't declared. Duly reminded, you can go back and add the necessary declaration.

Requiring explicit declarations in this way produces an even more important benefit: It prevents spelling errors from introducing major problems in your code. Imagine this scenario: You decide to wing it without the Option Explicit statement in your module. Still, good little programmer that you are, you declare a variable explicitly. Somewhere in the body of a procedure, however, a random finger spasm strikes while you're typing the variable name. When the VBA compiler encounters this line, it thinks you've just designated a new variable and cheerfully creates it for you. Your program may still run, but don't be surprised if it turns all your text purple or tells you that the world's population just hit 12.

Secret

Rather than typing the `Option Explicit` directive in every module, you can have VBA insert it automatically. Go to the Tools ⇨ Options dialog box. On the Editor tab, check the box labeled Require Variable Declaration.

Specifying a variable's scope

A variable's scope — that is, where in your program the variable is accessible — depends on two interacting factors:

- The location where you declare the variable (either inside a procedure or in the Declarations section of a module — see "Where to declare variables" earlier in this chapter)
- The keyword you use to declare the variable (`Dim`, `Public`, `Private`, or `Static`)

If you declare a variable inside a procedure using `Dim`, you can only use that variable inside that procedure. Elsewhere in your program, VBA won't recognize the variable. Variables declared with `Dim` in the module's Declarations section are accessible throughout the module — but not from other modules.

Private variables

The `Private` keyword works exactly like Dim. The two declaration statements shown here function identically:

```
Private strLouie As String
Dim strLouie As String
```

Secret

Because `Private` and `Dim` work the same way, you can forget about `Private` if you like. You may want to use `Private` instead of `Dim`, however, to remind yourself when you read the code that the variable is accessible only in the current module or procedure.

Public variables

Declaring a variable with `Public` makes the variable accessible throughout your entire project. Here's an example:

```
Public intBeulah As Integer
```

However, `Public` has its special power only if you declare the variable in the Declarations section of a module. Although VBA accepts `Public` declarations within procedures, the variables so declared are still inaccessible outside the procedure where you declare them.

The Static advantage

Secret

Use `Static` to declare a variable within a procedure when you want the variable to remain in memory — and even more important, to retain its value — even when the procedure isn't running.

In the following example, the variable `intLastingVariable` acts as a counter, recording the number of times the procedure runs:

```
Sub TransientProcedure()
   Dim strTransientVariable As String
   Static intLastingVariable As Integer
   strTransientVariable = Format(Now(), "Medium Time")
   intLastingVariable = intLastingVariable + 1
   MsgBox "The time is " & strTransientVariable & _
      ". " & "You have executed this procedure " & _
      intLastingVariable & " times."
End Sub
```

In the example, the statement `intLastingVariable = intLastingVariable + 1` adds 1 to the value of the variable each time the procedure runs. If you declare `intLastingVariable` with `Dim` instead of `Static`, the variable always starts with the same value (zero) with every pass through the procedure — which means the procedure is essentially worthless.

You can only declare `Static` variables within a procedure. If you want *all* the variables in a procedure to remain intact even when the procedure isn't running, declare the whole procedure as Static. In the procedure declaration, place the keyword `Static` immediately before the `Sub` or `Function` keyword that defines the type of procedure you're declaring. Here are a couple of examples of this technique:

```
Private Static Sub DoItAll ()
Static Function DontDoVeryMuch(intTimeToWaste as Integer)
```

Note that `Static` comes after `Private` or `Public` in the procedure declaration, if you include either of these optional scope-related keywords.

Declaring multiple variables on the same line

To conserve space, you're free to declare more than one variable on the same line of code. You only have to type the `Dim` keyword once per line. A comma should separate each variable. Just remember to specify the data type for *each* variable that you declare — even if all the variables on the line are of the same type. Here's an example of the right way to do it:

```
Dim intA As Integer, intD As Integer, intL As Integer
```

Mixing data types on the same line works, too:

```
Dim curNetWorth As Currency, datSecondTuesday as Date
```

Caution

Declaring multiple variables on the same line increases the likelihood you'll accidentally fail to specify a data type. Any variables on the line for which you don't supply a data type are automatically registered as variants. If your declaration reads

```
Dim strX, strY, strZ As String
```

`strX` and `strY` are treated as variants, not string variables.

After you've declared a variable, the next thing you do with it, usually, is fill it with information (putting known information into a variable for the first time is called *initializing* the variable). To place information in a variable, you *assign* the value of the information to the variable. Whenever it suits your purposes, you can store different data in the variable by assigning a different value to it.

Giving assignments

To assign a value to a variable, all it takes is one little equal sign. For instance, to store the number 3 in a variable named `intC`, just type

```
intC = 3
```

In VBA, an *assignment statement* consists of an equal sign between a variable on the left and an *expression* specifying the variable's value on the right. In the example, the expression is simply the number value, 3. Values you specify directly like this are called *literal* values. (See "Expression-ism" for the definition of expressions.)

Take a look at another assignment statement:

```
strQuote = "Ask not what your country can do for you," _
    & " ask what you can do for your country."
```

In this case, the statement assigns all the text to the right of the equal sign to the variable `strQuote`. As before, the information in this statement's expression consists entirely of literal values — the actual text you want to place in the variable. However, the statement is broken up over two lines, so the text expression has to be divided into two separate strings. That & sign tells VBA to join them together. No matter how many parts an expression has, VBA computes its overall value and *then* assigns that value to the variable.

Secret

Understand that until an assignment statement actually executes, it isn't a statement of fact. In math, when you write an equation such as 2 + 2 = 4, you're proclaiming that the values on either side of the equal sign are actually equal. By contrast, a VBA assignment statement *compels* the variable to become equal to the expression's value. Another assignment statement can change the variable's value at any time.

Using variables in assignment statements

You can assign a variable a value based on other variables as well as on literal values.

The statement `curSalePrice = curCost * sngMargin` multiplies the `curCost` and `sngMargin` variables together and assigns that result to the curSalePrice variable. VBA makes the necessary calculation based on the current values stored in those variables.

Using functions in assignment statements

Functions and Function procedures can also be used in assignment statements, as in this example:

```
strFavorite = InputBox("What's your favorite flavor?")
```

Each function or Function procedure returns a value. In this example, the InputBox function displays a little dialog box with the specified message and provides space for the user of your program to type in a response. That response is the value returned by the function, in the form of a string (more on the InputBox function in Chapter 23).

Expression-ism

An *expression* is a portion of a VBA statement that can be evaluated to give a value, such as a number, a text string, or a reference to an object. It can consist of one or more of the following, in any combination:

- Variables, such as bytMonth or boolWinter
- Literal values such as 1234 or "This is only a test."
- Constants, which stand in for literal values and are covered later in this chapter
- VBA functions such as InputBox() or Sqr()
- Function procedures in your code

If the expression has more than one of these elements, they are joined with *operators* such as the + sign, or in some cases, by nesting functions and Function procedures inside other functions and Function procedures. Note that if an expression has more than one component, each component is itself an expression — it has a value.

What's in a variable before you assign it a value?

When VBA runs a procedure, it creates storage space for each variable and assigns an initial "nothing in here" value to the variable. Most of the time you assign your own information to a variable before using it in any other statements. But it's quite possible, and sometimes useful, to access a variable before you know for sure whether it contains any of your own data.

Suppose that your program has a procedure that runs only under certain conditions. Suppose also that this procedure assigns a value to one of the program's variables. In this situation, another procedure might check to see whether the variable contains a value as a way to see whether the first procedure has already been executed.

Table 21-3 lists the values that your variables contain before you assign any values to them yourself.

Table 21-3 Default Values of Data Types

Data Type	Initial Value
All numeric data types	0
String (variable-length)	A string of zero length ("")
String (fixed-length)	A string of the specified length consisting of ASCII character code 0 — which isn't a visible character
Variant	Empty (a special value indicating a variant with no contents)
Object	Nothing (a special value indicating that no object reference has been assigned to the variable)

Working with Constants

When your program uses a value that *doesn't* change, you don't need a variable to represent that value. Although you can always place literal values in the meat of your procedures, declaring *constants* to represent these values is usually better.

Declaring constants

Use a `Const` statement to declare constants:

```
Const cstrPetsName As String = "Foo-foo"
Const cdtmTargetDate As Date = #6/23/98#
Const cblnUp As Boolean = True
```

Note that this technique is quite similar to the way you declare variables. The difference is that you specify the value of the constant when you declare it. You can declare constants as any of the same data types you use for variables except object, user-defined, and, for now, decimal (refer to Table 21-2).

Notice also that I declared the name of each constant with an initial lowercase c (standing for "constant," of course). This method is the simplest way to indicate that a declared name is a constant rather than a variable. However, you can choose another meaningful prefix if you prefer.

You might follow the example of VBA itself and choose a prefix based on your name, or on the name of your VBA project. VBA and Visual Basic identify constants with the prefix vb, as in `vbBlue` (representing the code number for the color blue, 16711680) or `vbKeyTab` (representing the code for the Tab key, 9). VBA applications often name the constants they define using an application-specific prefix, as in the Excel constant `xlBarStacked` (representing the code for a stacked bar chart, 58).

Secret

By the way, you're free to use the constants defined by VBA or your VBA application in your own programs. You can use the Help system or the Object Browser to locate information on these predefined constants (see Chapter 20 for a discussion of the Object Browser).

The benefits of a constant approach

After you declare a constant, you can use it by name in your program wherever you would have entered the corresponding literal values. For instance, let's say that you write a program that determines an employee's salary based on his shoe size. One way to code a part of the program would be

```
If bytShoeSize > 12 Then
    curJoesSalary = 75000
End If
```

One problem with this approach is that it "hard-codes" the exact salary amount in your program. If a rising cost of living increases salaries across the board, you have to dig through your code to find the amount that needs changing. And if you use the same value more than once in the program, you have to change each occurrence — and you run a bigger risk that typing errors will creep in and gum up the works.

Here's the same code written with a constant:

```
Const CcurTopSalaryStep As Currency = 75000
...
If bytShoeSize > 12 Then
    curJoesSalary = CcurTopSalaryStep
End If
```

With this solution, it's easy to locate the constant declaration at the top of the module or procedure. Change the constant's value there, and you instantly alter your code to match at every place the constant appears. As a bonus, the code is much easier to understand. Instead of asking, "What does this number 75000 represent?" you know at a glance that Joe is due the top step of the salary scale if he wears size 12 shoes.

You *could* use a variable to gain the advantages of a constant. However, variables take up space in memory, and more important, you run the risk of accidentally changing the variable's "constant" value in your program.

Using constants to represent attributes

Constants are handy for working with a group of named elements or characteristics such as days of the week (Monday, Tuesday, and so on) or tastes (sweet, salty, sour, and bitter). Instead of manipulating the names of these items as text strings in your program, an easier approach is to pick a number to represent each item and then declare a constant equal to that number based on the item's name. From then on, you can refer to the items by name rather than number. Here's code that uses this technique:

```
Const cbytSweet = 1, cbytSalty = 2
Const cbytSour = 3, cbytBitter = 4
Do While intTaste = cbytSour
    AddSweetener
    intTaste = CheckTaste()
Loop
```

Hello, Operators

In VBA, an *operator* is a special symbol or keyword in an expression that combines two values (subexpressions, if you will) to give a new result. The two values are listed on either side of the operator. In the following expression, the + (addition) operator adds 3 to the value of the `intA` variable.

```
intA + 3
```

VBA includes operators in three main categories, arithmetic, comparison, and logical, plus a few miscellaneous operators such as the ones for string *concatenation*.

Caution

When used with text strings, the + operator performs concatenation, not addition — it joins the two strings together. But it's better to use the "real" concatenation operator, the & symbol. VBA interprets the expression

```
"My name is " & "Ellie."
```

as "My name is Ellie."

Here's a comparison operator at work:

```
Tan(sngAngleA) <> 1.4
```

The <> symbol is the "not equal to" operator. It tests to see whether the two values in the expression are unequal, returning a result of True or False. If the tangent of `sngAngleA` is *not* equal to 1.4, the result of this expression is True. Otherwise, the result is False.

Taking precedence

In fancier expressions that include more than one operator, VBA has to figure out which operation to perform first, second, and third. Take the expression

```
intA + intB * intC
```

It contains two operators, + (the addition operator) and * (the multiplication operator). In English, you would read the entire thing as "intA plus intB times intC."

Although the * symbol is the second operator in the expression, it has *precedence* over the addition operator. VBA first multiplies `intB` times `intC` and then adds this result to `intA`. As this example illustrates, VBA follows a fixed sequence in evaluating the parts of an expression when it contains more than one operator.

You can use parentheses to override the predetermined precedence order by which operators are processed. If you type

`(intA + intB) * intC`

VBA first adds the first two variables and then multiplies `intC`'s value by that number.

Without parentheses to guide it, what rules does VBA follow when deciding which operator to process first? If the expression includes two or more categories of operators, VBA evaluates all the operators in each category in the following order:

1. Arithmetic and concatenation operators come first.
2. Comparison operators follow.
3. Logical operators are processed last.

Within a category, VBA applies preset rules to determine which operator comes first. Arithmetic, comparison, and logical operators are processed according to the order shown in Table 21-4. VBA takes comparison operators as they come, working from left to right. If two or more operators at the same level of precedence appear in an expression, VBA processes them from left to right as well.

Table 21-4 VBA Operators and Their Precedence Order *

Operator	Operation Performed	Details, Comments
Arithmetic		
^	Exponentiation	Raises the preceding value in the expression to the power of the value that follows.
−	Negation	Reverses the sign of the next value.
* or /	Multiplication and division	
\	Integer division	Divides but discards any fractional part of the answer rather than rounding it up or down.
Mod	Modulus arithmetic	Divides but returns only the *remainder* of the division as the result.
+ or −	Addition and subtraction	
Concatenation		
&	String concatenation	

Continued

Table 21-4 *(continued)*

Operator	Operation Performed	Details, Comments
Comparison		
=	Equality	
<>	Inequality (not equal to)	
<	Less than	
>	Greater than	
<=	Less than or equal to	
>=	Greater than or equal to	
Like	String comparison to pattern	
Is	Test if two items refer to the same object	
Logical		
Not	Logical not	See the Secret in "When to use Boolean variables" later in this chapter.
And	Logical and	
Or	Logical or	
Xor	Logical exclusive or	
Eqv	Logical equivalence	
Imp	Logical implication	

* Within each category, operators are processed in the order listed.

Comparing values

VBA has six all-around comparison operators for comparing numeric and string values, plus two special-purpose comparison operators, `Like` (for strings) and `Is` (for objects). (The comparison operators are summarized in Table 21-4). Note that VBA uses the equal sign, =, as a comparison operator as well as to assign values to variables in declarations.

Secret

The result of an expression based on any of these operators is always either True or False. For example, here's an expression based on the <= (less than or equal to) operator:

```
intX <= 11
```

If the value of `intX` is 12, the result of the expression is False, because 12 is not less than 11.

Comparing strings

You can use the comparison operators to compare strings of text as well as numbers. The expression `"Sweetpea" = "Daffodil"` gives False as a result — obviously, these two strings are not equal. But in other cases the results of a string comparison aren't so easy to predict. To get the results you want when comparing strings, you have to understand the rules VBA uses to decide whether one string is "greater than" another one.

Unless you specify otherwise, VBA uses a "binary" comparison method. The two strings are compared on the basis of the numeric codes in which the characters are actually stored in your program. In this coding system, common punctuation marks have the lowest numbers, followed by numerals, uppercase letters, lowercase letters, and then accented characters. Because the code numbers for lowercase letters are larger than those for uppercase letters, the expressions `"a" > "A"` and `"a" > "Z"` both give True results.

Secret

To use a different, more intuitive method for comparing strings, include the statement `Option Compare Text` in your module's Declarations section. With `Option Compare Text` in force, the strings are compared alphabetically, ignoring case (accented letters are still treated as higher in value than the corresponding unaccented versions). Under these conditions, the following are all True expressions:

```
"a" = "A"
"a" < "Z"
"Aunt Hill" < "Žunt Hill"
```

When comparing two strings, VBA starts by comparing the first characters in each string. If these characters differ, the "greater" string is the one with the greater character. If the first characters in each string are the same, VBA then compares the next, and so on.

The `Like` operator compares a string to a wildcard pattern rather than a specific set of characters. Use it to see whether a string falls within, or outside, a given range. I don't have room here to explain the many details involved in using this operator, but you should know that it exists — it's a powerful tool for handling text.

Using comparison operators in code

The results of a comparison operation can be stored in a variable, typically one of the Boolean data type, using a standard assignment statement:

```
boolTheAnswerIs = 5 > 4
```

Because 5 *is* greater than 4, the result of the greater than operation is True, and in turn VBA assigns True as the value of the `boolTheAnwerIs` variable.

Secret

The `True` and `False` keywords are actually built-in VBA numeric constants, representing the values –1 and 0, respectively. You can assign the result of a comparison to any numeric variable.

Comparison operators are frequently used in conditional statements to decide whether or not to execute a particular branch of code:

```
If intP <= intQ Then
    SomethingWentWrong 'call error-handling procedure
End If
```

Stringing text together

The concatenation operator, &, joins strings together. You can use it with literal strings, string variables, or any function that returns a string value. You can use it repeatedly to construct a long string from multiple string values, as in this example:

```
strA = "You answered " & InputBox("Type an answer:") & _
    " . The correct answer was " & strAnswer & "."
```

After this statement executes, strA might contain "You answered Portugal. The correct answer was Spain."

Note

When assembling large strings from smaller ones, don't forget to build in the spaces and punctuation marks needed in the final string.

Details on Data Types

This section offers tips on when and how to use the garden-variety VBA data types. The object data type is crucial but quite complex, so it rates special treatment in Chapter 22.

Converting between data types

Data types are a convenience for human beings — VBA actually stores all information in numeric form. That being the case, conversions between different data types aren't a big challenge for VBA. VBA comes with many functions for converting one data type to another under your control. Realize, however, that whenever possible, VBA automatically converts between different types of data as the context suggests. For example, the + operator adds the number in a string to a numeric value, as long as the string contains only numerals. Similarly, if you assign a decimal value to an Integer variable, VBA automatically rounds off the value for you.

Understanding variants

The Variant data type provides a one-size-fits-all container for your data storage needs. Variants can hold any kind of data you can use in VBA, including numeric values, strings, dates and times, and objects. What's more, the same variable can store different types of data at different times within a single program. The following code is perfectly acceptable, though hardly very productive:

```
Dim varAnythingGoes as Variant
varAnythingGoes = 3
```

```
varAnythingGoes = "I suppose."
varAnythingGoes = #12/31/99 11:59:59 PM#
```

Not only does VBA permit such statements, but it also figures out and keeps track of the type of data you're placing in the Variant. After that last statement in the preceding series, for example, `varAnythingGoes` is cataloged as a Variant/Date variable. You can find out which type of data VBA is currently storing in a Variant, using the `TypeName` function, as in

```
strVariantType = TypeName(varAnythingGoes)
```

After this statement executes, the value of `strVariantType` is `"Date"`.

Because they're so flexible, Variant variables are very convenient. Instead of worrying about which data types to use, all your variables can be Variants, and you can stash any type of data in them as the need arises. However, conventional wisdom has it that Variants cost too much in terms of storage space and speed. For a discussion on this point, see "Choosing and using data types" earlier in this chapter.

Choosing a numeric data type

If you declare data types explicitly, you should choose the smallest possible data type for each variable — your programs will be faster, smaller, and more likely to work properly. Of course, the variable should have enough storage capacity to accommodate the range of values that it may contain. However, any extra room is just wasted space. Table 21-2 summarizes the value ranges for each numeric data type.

Caution

If your program does calculations with the numbers in a variable, it may be necessary to choose a data type large enough to hold the *result* of those calculations. This can be so even if you don't assign the calculation results to the variable itself.

Here are some tips on specific data types:

- Use the Boolean, Byte, Integer, or Long data types to hold whole numbers (the kind without decimals).

- Use the Single and Double data types to store floating-point numbers of up to 15 significant digits and their exponents. Though the range of values is huge, be aware that rounding may introduce errors — and these may be significant in operations on values of very different sizes. To assign a floating-point value such as $4.72 \cdot 10^{-22}$ to a Single or Double variable, use the following format (VBA assumes the exponent is positive if you leave out a + or – sign after the letter E):

    ```
    sngFloating = 4.72E-22
    ```

- If you need more precise calculations, the Currency data type gives you up to 19 significant digits, and with the Decimal type you can have as many as 29 (neither type provides exponents). In the current version of VBA, however, Decimal isn't a stand-alone data type — in other words, you can't declare a Decimal variable. Instead, Decimal is only available as a subtype of the Variant data type. To ensure that a number is stored as a decimal variant rather than one of the floating-point types, use the `CDec` function in the assignment statement.

When to use Boolean variables

Variables of the Boolean data type can only hold one of two values: True (stored as –1) or False (0). Declare a Boolean variable whenever you need to know which of two alternative conditions currently prevails. For example, you might have a variable called `boolIsOn`, whose value would be True if whatever it is, is on, and False if it's off.

Another way to use Boolean variables is to define other constants with the same values as True and False. Your variable names can then be neutral, while the constants explicitly refer to the two alternative conditions. This is definitely easier to show than to explain, so look here:

```
Dim boolBellyButtonStyle as Boolean
Const Innie As Boolean = True
Const Outie As Boolean = False
If boolBellyButtonStyle = Outie Then
    TickleLightly
End If
```

Secret

To toggle the value of a Boolean variable or object property to its opposite, use the `Not` operator. In Word, for example, you can turn on the document map if it's off, or turn it off if it's on, with this line of code:

```
ActiveWindow.DocumentMap = Not ActiveWindow.DocumentMap
```

Working with currency values

The main reason to use the Currency data type for financial work is to ensure accurate results. True, the floating-point data types Single and Double can store numbers with decimal points — which is basically what currency values are. However, calculations involving floating-point values often produce small errors, and these drive the bean counters crazy.

Regardless of whether you're working with money, you can use variables of the Currency type any time you need to store larger numbers than you can fit in a Long integer variable, or make calculations on them with more precision than you could get from the floating-point data types. Currency values can have up to 19 significant digits, 15 to the left of the decimal point and 4 to the right (the decimal point is fixed).

Secret

You don't need to declare a variable as Currency to display it as a properly formatted money amount. Use VBA's `Format` function with the "Currency" format to automatically dress up any numeric value as dollars, francs, or whatever is appropriate locally.

Working with dates

Use the Date data type to work conveniently with dates, times, or both. Behind the scenes, VBA encodes a date or time as a number such as 35692.9201273148 — apparently meaningless to mere mortals. But you can ignore this detail and work with dates and times in your programming as you would on paper or in a word processor.

The one trick you have to remember is that you must always type date and time values — date literals — between paired number sign characters. For example, the following statements declare two Date variables and assign them values:

```
Dim datWeddingDay As Date, datTimeOfCeremony As Date
datWeddingDay = #4/20/99#
datTimeOfCeremony = #3:15:00 PM#
```

As with currency, VBA automatically outputs dates according to local formatting customs. The expression Format (#10/24/89#, "Long date") gives the string "Tuesday, October 24, 1989" in the United States, but "Terça-feira, 24 de Outubro de 1989" in Brazil.

Entering date values

You can type date literals in just about any format that appeals to you. The following are all acceptable:

```
#09/1/1998#
#Sep 25, 93#
#Janua 9 1905#
```

If the Visual Basic Editor recognizes your entry as a valid date, it converts it into the "short form" date format specified in the Windows Control Panel. If you omit the year, VBA adds the current year for you. The conversion happens as soon as the insertion point moves off the line, before you run your program.

Time has value

Enter time literals in the format #*hours:minutes:seconds symbol*#, where *symbol* is AM or PM. Examples include:

```
#10:45:00 PM#
#2:3:30 AM#
```

You don't have to type in leading zeros, as in #01:02:03 PM#; VBA adds them for you when you move the cursor to another line of code. Similarly, you can omit portions of the time value you don't need, but VBA fills in the blanks. For example, you can enter seconds alone by typing something like #0:0:23#, but VBA changes such an entry into a complete time value, in this case #12:00:23 AM#.

Date and time math

Adding or subtracting dates with the standard VBA arithmetic operators is *possible*, but unfortunately it doesn't work the way you would expect. For example, #3/19/2005# - #3/19/2004# does not equal "1 year," but

#12/30/1900#. The explanation has to do with the way VBA stores date data, which I won't trouble you with here. All you really need to know is that VBA has two functions, DateAdd() and DateDiff(), that handle all your needs for date math. For details, look them up in Help.

In contrast, you *can* do time calculations fairly easily with the regular arithmetic operators. Take a gander at the following expressions:

```
#07:15 AM# + #12:00# ' = #07:15:00 PM#
#07:15:00 AM# - #0:15 AM# ' = #07:00:00 AM#
#07:15:15 AM# + #0:0:30 AM# ' = #07:15:45 AM#
```

The examples show the minimum entries you can type. As always, VBA converts your entries into complete time literals — #0:0:30 AM# becomes #12:00:30 AM#, for example.

Stringing you along

Because VBA so freely converts between different data types, you may need string variables less often than you think. If all you need to do is display a nonstring value in a form that humans can read, you don't need to convert it into a string first. Instead, you can use a number or date — or a variable containing one — as the argument to a function or as the value of an object property that by rights should be a string.

What you *really* need string variables for is to work with nonnumeric characters, that is, letters and punctuation marks. You can't get these out of number values, not no way, not no how.

Secret

Careful programming practice dictates that you explicitly convert numeric values into strings before manipulating them as such. If you follow this advice, you're likely to make fewer errors and produce code that's more understandable. Still, it's nice to know you can output variables with so little work.

Along the same lines, you don't really have to use those quote marks when you assign values to a string. Ever the pampering parent, VBA makes its best effort to convert numeric, date, or currency values into strings. If your program executes this code:

```
Dim strGString As String
strGString = #July 22, 1904#
```

the strGString variable will contain the string "7/22/1904" until some other statement changes it. But it's better to assign the actual text in quotation marks to make sure that the variable contains exactly what you intend.

Secret Use VBA's `Chr` and `Asc` functions to convert a numeric value representing an ANSI character code to the corresponding text character and vice versa. `Chr` lets you place characters you can't type, such as quotation marks, in your strings. `Asc` returns the numeric code of the *first* character in a string.

Working with Arrays

Frequently, you need to work with similar chunks of information together as a group. That situation calls for an *array*, a structured storage compartment for multiple data elements of the same type. (An alternative to an array for working with a set of items is a Collection object, discussed in Chapter 22.)

Suppose you have a list of numbers representing prices, test scores, or the distances of certain astronomical objects from Earth. Imagine that you type that list on a piece of paper, with each item on separate row. What you wind up with is a simple array. Here is an example:

Surefire winning lottery numbers

214236

891982

545273

000000

371453

941241

With a list of very similar items like this one, the individual items have unique values but otherwise lack special identifying characteristics. If you want someone else to ponder an item, you say something like "it's the third item in the lottery number list." VBA arrays work exactly this way.

About the items in an array

Each VBA array has a name, corresponding to the title of the paper list. To work with an individual item in the array, you refer to it by the array name and an *index*, a positive integer number specifying its "slot" in the array. For example, the expression `intLottoArray(3)` refers to the third item (or fourth, depending on the numbering system in effect) in the array called `intLottoArray`. As you can guess, the "int" at the beginning of the array name lets you know that this is supposed to be an array of integer values. Therefore, it's a safe bet that the data stored in `intLottoArray(3)` is an integer.

You should be clear about two key points regarding arrays:

- You can create arrays of any data type. VBA will happily store strings, dates, currency values, and any numeric data type in arrays.
- However, an array can hold only one data type. You can't build an array with separate slots for both Date and String data type values. However, the Variant data type can store any kind of VBA data, and arrays of Variants are perfectly okay.

Array dimensions

An important concept concerning arrays is that they can have multiple *dimensions*. The simple list in the preceding example is a one-dimensional array. A table or spreadsheet with rows and columns corresponds to a two-dimensional array. VBA arrays can have up to 60 dimensions.

Declaring arrays

Like ordinary variables, arrays must be declared before you can use them to store data. Fortunately, declaring an array is just like declaring a variable, with one addition to the declaration statement: You add parentheses following the variable name. The parentheses can be empty, if you want to define the array's dimension later. Alternatively, they can contain values specifying the size of each dimension in the array.

This example declares an array of Currency data but doesn't set its size or dimensions:

```
Public curPriceQuotes () As Currency
```

The next statement declares a one-dimensional array of 12 items of Date data:

```
Dim datTimeOfImpact (12) As Date
```

This statement declares a four-dimensional array of Integer data:

```
Dim intArrayOfIntegers (34, 13, 29, 4) As Integer
```

The total number of individual data elements in an array is equal to the product of the sizes of each dimension, of course. Multiple-dimension arrays can be very large data sets.

How array elements are numbered — and how to determine how big your array should be

Secret

Unless you specify otherwise, the elements in an array are numbered beginning with 0 — or to put it slightly differently, element 0 is the first one in the array. Because this is so, the value you enter when sizing an array should be one less than the number of elements you want to store. If the array is supposed to hold 10 elements, enter 9 as the size.

When you later access the individual data elements in the array, you must keep in mind this numbering system. A reference to `intArray (1)` is actually a reference to the second element in the array. If you don't like counting from 0, you can start numbering your array from a different number — which would usually be 1. To set things up so that VBA numbers all arrays in the current module starting from 1, place the statement Option Base 1 in the module's Declarations section (before any procedures). This statement only affects arrays in the same module, so you must include it in every module if that's how you want to number all your arrays.

Declaring fixed and dynamic arrays

If you specify the size of the array when you declare it, its size remains fixed — your program can't make the array smaller or larger later. To declare a *fixed array*, include the size of each of the array's dimensions in the parentheses in the declaration statement. Fixing the size of an array when you declare it can be good practice if you know for sure the array size won't change.

To declare a *dynamic* array, just leave out the array's size when you declare it. Declare your array as a *dynamic array* if you:

- Don't or can't know the size of your array before your program runs.
- Know the array's size will change during the course of your program.
- Want to free up the memory it occupies for other variables after you're through using the array. A large array can use lots of memory, which you can liberate if the array is dynamic.

Secret

A dynamic array can't hold any data until you actually create the array by specifying its size. Use the ReDim ("redimension") statement to do so, as in this example of a one-dimensional array:

```
Redim datBirthdays (intNumberOfBirthdays - 1)
```

You can re-ReDim a dynamic array as many times as you like, completely redefining the number of dimensions it has and their sizes. Just keep in mind that ordinarily, resizing an array destroys its current contents.

Addressing elements in an array

To work with a particular element in an array in your code, list the array name followed by the element's *index* in parentheses. The index contains an integer value for each array dimension. For example, the expression strSayings (4,6) uniquely identifies the string data at row 4, column 6 in a two-dimensional array of strings.

With this system, you can use array data elements just as you would variables. You can

- Assign a value to an array element. In this example a value is assigned to a single storage slot in a 3-D array of Currency values:

    ```
    curBigDough (5,8,19) = 27.99
    ```

- Assign a value stored in an array to another variable:

  ```
  datThatDate = datTheseDates (25, 10)
  ```

- Use the value of an array element in an expression:

  ```
  intA = 35 * (intB + intCounts (3,2))
  ```

You're not restricted to literal values in the index. It's often crucial to code the index with variables, and let your program decide which array element you need at the moment. The last line of the following program shows this method in action:

```
Dim strTodaysFortune (29)
Dim intUserChoice As Integer
... ' Code assigning strings to the array goes here
intUserChoice = InputBox ("To see your fortune, enter" _
    & " a number between 1 and 30")
msgBox (strTodaysFortune (intUserChoice - 1))
```

Built-in Functions and Statements

Before you get rolling on writing your own procedures from scratch, be sure you're not reinventing the wheel. VBA comes equipped with a little arsenal of built-in commands that can blast through many common tasks. Covering these functions and statements would take space I don't have. About all I can do is point you in the direction of the VBA help files and reference books on VBA or Visual Basic.

Secret

By the way, although Excel's large collection of worksheet functions aren't VBA functions, you can use them in any VBA program if you first add to the project a reference to the Excel object library. Chapter 25 tells how to add object references, and Chapter 42 gives techniques for working with Excel functions in VBA code.

Where to find built-in commands

Keeping in mind that an action may fall into an unexpected category, VBA gives you three types of built-in commands for doing useful work. They include:

- **Statements.** Although the term "statement" usually encompasses a complete programming directive, VBA also refers to individual keywords for specific chores as statements. Some of these statement keywords function as complete statements in themselves. For example, the statement

  ```
  Beep
  ```

  sounds the computer speaker. (Please, don't go overboard with that one.) Other statement keywords must be used as part of a complete statement. For example, the `ChDir` (change directory) "statement" is useless unless you include with it an argument specifying the directory, or folder, you want to change to

```
ChDir("\Documents about Dreams")
```

- **Functions.** The built-in functions act just like the Function procedures — that is, they return a value. Often, you use a function by assigning its value to a variable, as in this example with the `Tan` (tangent) function:

```
dblTangent = Tan(dblAnyOldAngle)
```

Functions are also used to provide values in more complex expressions, or in conditional statements, such as

```
If Tan (dblAcuteAngle) < 45 Then
```

- **Methods** of built-in objects. The curious one in this group is the `Print` method, the Debug object's only one. You use it to direct output to the Immediate window in the Visual Basic Editor with a statement such as

```
Debug.Print(strMessageFromMars)
```

Table 21-5 lists examples of built-in VBA commands drawn from all three categories (statements, functions, and methods).

Table 21-5 Examples of Built-in Functions, Statements, and Methods

Command	Type	What It Does
`Randomize`	Statement	Initializes the random number generator.
`Sqr (number)`	Function	Returns the square root of *number*.
`Format (string)`	Function	Formats string according to your specifications.
`Date`	Statement	Sets the system date.
`Date`	Function	Returns the current system date.
`Err.Raise`	Method of Err object	Generates a run-time error by ID number.

Categories of built-in commands

VBA's built-in commands fall into the following categories:

- **Formatting data.** VBA's `Format` function formats any of the built-in data types for display or print purposes according to a pattern you specify. Via the `Format` function, you can easily output a date variable — which VBA actually stores as a unintelligible number — in any of many different typical formats such as 11/09/99, or Friday, July 9, 2001. If none of the built-in formats will do, you can create your own formats for reuse with the `Format` function.

- **Converting data.** Although VBA converts between different data types on the fly, automatically, VBA includes many explicit conversion functions. They're useful for ensuring that VBA performs the correct conversion, performing conversions that VBA won't do automatically, and making your code self-explanatory. Examples include `CByte`, `Fix`, `Hex`, and `Val`.

- **Manipulating strings.** VBA offers a rich collection of statements and functions for formatting text strings and extracting portions of them that you may find especially mesmerizing.

- **Working with dates and times.** VBA offers a panoply of statements and functions for finding out what day or time it is now, making date-related calculations, and extracting from a date variable the component of interest, be it the year, the day of the week, or the hour.

- **Interacting with the user.** The `MsgBox` and `InputBox` functions display simple dialog boxes that let you talk to the program's users, and let them talk back.

- **Performing mathematical and financial calculations.** VBA comes chock full of prefab functions for manipulating numbers. These perform chores ranging from the very simple (such as returning an absolute value or a number's sign) through the staple computations of algebra and trigonometry. If the bottom line is sinking, VBA's healthy dose of financial functions may be just what you need to float the business boat again.

- **Handling miscellaneous chores.** You can tap a wide array of commands for working with files on disk, inserting and examining entries in the Windows Registry, manipulating variables, and other chores.

Controlling the Flow

Control structures are code statements that determine what the procedure will do next, based on some condition that is in effect at the time the code runs. VBA offers a healthy assortment of powerful control structures falling into three main groups: *conditional statements*, *loops*, and the `With` statement:

- A conditional statement determines which branch of code to execute based on whether a condition is True or False. VBA conditional statements include `If...Then`, in several permutations, and `Select Case`.

- A loop repeatedly executes a block of code, either a fixed number of times or until some condition becomes True or False. When you know in advance how many times to execute a loop, use a `For...Next` loop. If your code needs to test some condition to see whether to continue running the loop, use the `Do...Loop` statement, available in multiple flavors. And to repeat actions on the objects in a collection, use a `For Each...Next` loop.

- The `With` statement enables you to perform multiple actions using the same object without having to name the object in each action.

Control structures lend clarity, organization, and, well, structure to your program. They make it relatively easy to trace the branches of the path that your program may follow as it runs.

Control structure anatomy

What makes a control structure a "structure" is that it's not just a single statement, but rather a whole block of them. Your basic `If...Then` statement will serve as a model for all control structures:

```
If a < b Then       ' If a is less than b, then
    b = a           '    set b equal to a
    a = c           '    and then set a equal to c.
End If              ' That's all—proceed with the program.
```

The skeleton of this structure is an opening statement that identifies its type and sets up a condition, and a statement that tells VBA where the structure ends. Sandwiched in between is the meat of the structure, the statements that actually *do* something.

All control structures have this general outline, except that in some of them, the structure's condition comes in the last statement rather than the first.

Nesting control structures

When you're talking about control structures, *nesting* means to place one structure inside another, above the statement that marks the end of the first structure. VBA enters the second structure before it finishes executing the first. Nesting is a necessity for solving many complex, real-life programming problems. You can nest control structures to as many levels as you think necessary.

In the following example, a `Do While...Loop` structure is *nested* inside an `If...Then` structure, and another `If...Then` structure is nested inside the `Do While...Loop`:

```
If a < b Then
    Do While b > c
        b = b - 1
        If c > d Then
            d = a
        End If       ' End of inner If...Then
    Loop             ' End of Do While
End If               ' End of outer If...Then
```

The road taken: using condition expressions

Making choices is fundamental in software as in life. Although simple in concept, decision-making control structures are some of the most powerful programming tools at your disposal. "All" they do is to choose which of two or more different blocks of code to execute. But after one block executes and the other does not, you will say with Frost, "And that has made all the difference."

To decide whether to execute a block of code, three of VBA's control structures evaluate a *condition expression* that you write. These include the Do...Loop looping structure as well as the two explicitly named conditional statements, If...Then and Select Case. I devote the rest of this section to discussion of the condition expressions used in all three of these structures. Two other decision-making controls structures, For...Next and For Each...Next, don't use condition expressions.

How condition expressions work

If...Then, Select Case, and Do...Loop structures all decide what to do based on one simple test: Is the condition True, or is it False? The condition in question can be any VBA expression. (And remember, 0 is equal to False in VBA. All other values are considered True.) Most often, condition expressions are built around a comparison operator that compares the values of two subexpressions. VBA's set of comparison operators are listed and discussed earlier in this chapter. However, you can get the basic idea by looking at the sample statements in the following table:

Expression	Translation in English
a < b	Item a is less than b.
b = c	Item b is equal to c.
colTBears("Henry") Is objCurrentBear	The object stored in the colTBears collection under the key "Henry" is the same one now referred to by the ojbCurrentBear variable.
sqr(1/x * 29.3234) >= CDbl(strNumber) + 12	The square root of the quantity 1 divided by x times 29.3234 is greater than or equal to the numeric value of the string variable strNumber plus 12.

Using logical operators in conditions

A logical operator evaluates two subexpressions separately as True or False and then combines them according to a set of rules to produce a final value—also True or False—based on a set of rules. The most important logical operators—or at least the ones that are easiest to figure out how to use—are And, Or, and Xor. Here's how they work:

Operator	Returns True	Examples	Result
And	Only if *both* subexpressions are True	3 * 2 = 6 And 12 > 11	True
		2 + 2 = 4 And 4 - 2 = 1	False
Or	If *either* subexpression is True	10 > 20 Or 20 > 10	True
		5 < 4 Or 6 < 5	False
Xor	If only one subexpression is True (False if both expressions are True or both are False)	5 + 5 > 9 Xor 5 + 5 = 10	True
		5 + 5 > 9 Xor 5 + 5 = 10	False
		5 + 5 < 9 Xor 5 + 5 <> 10	False

Using If...Then Statements

By far the most commonly used conditional statements are If...Then and its variations, If...Then...Else and If...ElseIf.

The basic form: If...Then

At its most basic, an If...Then statement executes a special block of code if the condition you feed it is True, but simply does nothing if the condition is False. The syntax is

```
If condition Then
(statements to execute if condition is True)
End If
```

When VBA executes an If...Then statement, if *condition* is True, it plows through the statements between If and End If. If *condition* is False, it skips over them, continuing with the next statement in your program. Note that the Then keyword goes on the same line as If and the condition expression. Be sure to include the End If statement, or you will get an error message.

One-liners with If...Then

When an If...Then structure only needs to execute a single statement if the condition is True, you can put the entire thing on one line. In that situation only, an End If statement isn't required — in fact, it's illegal. The following statement:

```
If curPrice > 20 Then MsgBox "Warning! Price too high!"
```

functions identically to this structure:

```
If curPrice > 20 Then
    MsgBox "Warning! Price too high!"
End If
```

Using If...Then...Else statements

If you want your program to choose between two alternative blocks of code based on a condition, you need an `If...Then...Else` statement. In this case, one block is executed if the condition is True, and a completely different block is executed if the condition is False. Here's the syntax:

```
If condition Then
(statements to execute if condition is True)
Else
(statements to execute if condition is False)
End If
```

If `condition` is True, VBA executes the first block of statements and then skips over the rest of the structure to the line of code following the `End If` statement. On the other hand, if `condition` is False, only the statements in the block following `Else` get executed.

In the following example, the condition expression checks to see whether the control on a VBA form is a command button. If so, it paints the button's background color red. All other controls are painted cyan (sky blue).

```
If TypeOf ctlCurrentControl Is CommandButton Then
    ctlCurrentControl.BackColor = &HFF&    'Red
Else
    ctlCurrentControl.BackColor = &HFFFF00    'Cyan
End If
```

In the example, you can assume that the `ctlCurrentControl` variable already holds an object reference to a particular control on the form. The `TypeOf` keyword enables you to check whether the object referred to by a variable or other object reference is of a specific type, in this case a CommandButton object. Forms and controls are discussed in Chapter 24.

If...Then complexities

Frequently you need to test two or more conditions before you know what path your program should take. It's just like in real life. If you were writing a book, you might be thinking something like, "If I finish by the deadline and if I don't run out of money before then, and if the dollar holds its value against the peso, then I can go to Mexico for two weeks in October. But if the dollar falls, I'll have to settle for Turlock." Depending on the specific tests involved, you may need to include `ElseIf` clauses in your `If...Then` structure, or to nest one or more levels of `If...Then` statements.

Complexities part I: using If...ElseIf statements

Use the `ElseIf` keyword to test a new condition when you want to execute certain statements only if the first condition *isn't* True. The syntax is as follows:

```
If condition1 Then
   (statements to execute if condition1 is True)
ElseIf condition2
   (statements to execute if condition1 is False but condition2 is True)
ElseIf condition3
   (statements to execute if condition1 and condition2 are both False but
    condition3 is True)
... (additional ElseIf clauses)
Else ' optional clause
   (statements to execute if all of the conditions are False)
End If
```

Only one `ElseIf` clause is required, but you can have as many as you like. The `Else` clause is optional.

Secret

In an `If...ElseIf` structure, only the statements associated with the first true condition are executed. After they run, any remaining `ElseIf` and `Else` clauses are skipped over. The `Else` clause is optional, but if included, it must be the last one in the structure — which makes sense, if you think about it logically.

Complexities part II: nesting If...Then statements

Nested `If...Then` statements are sort of the opposite of `If...ElseIf` statements. Use them when you want to test a second condition to decide whether to execute a block of code, but only if the first condition is True. Nesting two `If...Then` statements is like saying, "If X is true *and* Y is true, then I'm going to do A, B, and C."

You can nest `If...Then` statements of any variety — `If...Then...Else`, `If...ElseIf`, or garden variety `If...Then` — in any combination. In schematic form, here's a pair of nested `If...Then` statements:

```
If condition1 Then
   If condition2 Then
      (statements that execute if both condition 1 and
       condition2 are True)
   ElseIf condition3 Then
      (statements that execute if condition1 and condition3
       are True but condition2 is False)
   End If     ' Ends the inner If...Then block
   (other statements that execute if condition1 is True,
       regardless of condition2)
Else
   (statements that only execute if condition1 is False
End If
```

The following simple example of nested `If...Then` statements displays a congratulatory message box for high grades achieved with at least a nominally full-time schedule:

```
If sngGPA > 3.5 Then
    If sngUnits > 10 Then
        MsgBox "You're on the Dean's list!"
    End If
End If
```

Complexities part III: using logical operators in conditions

Using logical operators in condition expressions can be a more elegant alternative to `ElseIf` clauses and nested `If...Then` structures — but only when just one branch of a multiple-condition path has the statements you want to execute. For example, look at the code fragment just before the heading of this section. You could accomplish exactly the same goal with a single `If...Then` statement, as follows:

```
If sngGPA > 3.5 And sngUnits > 10 Then
        MsgBox "You're on the Dean's list!"
End If
```

Using Select Case Statements

`If...ElseIf` and nested `If...Then` statements are ideal for testing different expressions before deciding which block of code to execute. If, however, you need to test the *same* value against different conditions, a `Select Case` statement is usually the way to go. The syntax is

```
Select Case value
Case test1
(statements to be executed if value meets test1
   criteria)
Case test2
(statements to be executed if value meets test2
   criteria)
... ' additional Case clauses
Case Else ' optional
(statements to be executed if value meets none of the
   above criteria)
End Case
```

Testing conditions in Select Case statements

The `Select Case` structure doesn't directly use complete condition expressions of the type outlined earlier. Instead, you have to break up each condition into two parts, represented by *value* and *test*n in the preceding syntax. If the equivalent condition expression is

```
a + b > c
```

you can think of *value* as the part to the left of the comparison operator (a + b) and *test*n as everything to the right, including the operator (> c).

A sample Select Case statement

You definitely need an example to illustrate how a "real" `Select Case` structure might look. In the code that follows, objRollOfFilm is an object representing a roll of film and has a `Type` property corresponding to the type of film. Here's the listing:

```
Select Case objRollOfFilm.Type
Case "Slide"
    intCountSlide = intCountSlide + 1
Case "ColorPrint"
    intCountColorPrint = intCountColorPrint + 1
Case "BWPrint"
    intCountBWPrint = intCountBWPrint + 1
Case Else
    MsgBox "Not a known type."
End Case
```

At this point in your program you're only concerned about one value, that returned by the `Type` property, but it must be compared to several possible alternatives. The `Select Case` statement is perfect for this situation. The example's first Case clause is equivalent to writing `If objRollOfFilm.Type = "Slide" Then`. That is, if the object's `Type` property is "Slide," then the program executes the next statement; if not, it moves on to Case clause number 2. Notice, though, that the = operator you'd expect is missing from the tests in all three Case clauses. That's because in `Select Case` statements, equality is assumed to be the comparison you're making.

The Case Else clause

If the value of the `Type` property isn't equal to the tests in any of the `Case` clauses, control falls to the `Case Else` clause, always the last one in a `Select Case` structure — in this case, the `Case Else` clause displays an error message. A `Case Else` clause is optional, because you may not want anything to happen if none of the criteria are satisfied. As in the example, though, it's often wise to include the `Case Else` clause if only to alert you to unexpected values stored by your program.

More about Case clause tests

The tests performed by the Case clauses in the preceding example are sweet, simple tests of a single equality, as in "Is the Type property equal to such and so?" But you can do much more sophisticated testing with each Case clause.

This is easiest to illustrate with a numeric example. Suppose your `Select Case` statement opens with the following line of code:

```
Select Case intPatientAge
```

In this case, the value being tested is an integer variable that represents the age of a patient at a medical clinic. This is the value being tested in the examples shown here:

- You can test the value against a range:

    ```
    Case 18 To 35
        Messages("YoungAdult").Print
    ```

    Note that you place the `To` keyword between the values defining the bounds of the range. The range includes both values as well as everything in between.

- You can test the value using a comparison operator other than =:

    ```
    Case Is > 65
        Messages("OlderAdult").Print
    ```

    Here, you're supposed to use the `Is` keyword before the comparison operator. Actually, you don't have to type Is — VBA puts it in for you if you omit it.

- You can perform multiple tests in the same Case clause:

    ```
    Case 0 To 5, 15, Is > 55
        Messages("ImmunizationReminder").Print
    ```

    Be sure to separate the tests with commas. By the way, a Case clause with multiple tests is equivalent to an expression built on a series of `Or` expressions — if the value passes *any* of the tests, the following statements get executed.

Repeating Yourself with Loops

Use a loop control structure to execute the same block of code more than once. This is a fundamental chore when performing many mathematical computations, extracting smaller data items from larger ones, and repeating an action on multiple items in a group.

VBA offers three main types of loop structures. Here they are, and what they're for:

Loop Type	How It Loops
`Do...Loop`	While or until a condition is True
`For...Next`	A specified number of times
`For Each...Next`	For each object in a collection

Secret

When working with nested loops, remember this simple truth: the inner loop finishes looping before the outer loop.

Do-ing loops

The various versions of the `Do...Loop` statement all are designed to repeat a block of code indefinitely, until a condition is met. To determine whether to continue looping, a `Do...Loop` statement evaluates a condition expression of the same type described earlier in this chapter and used in `If...Then` statements. Uses for `Do...Loop` structures are legion. Some include:

- Displaying an error message repeatedly until the user makes a valid entry in a dialog box
- Reading data from a disk file until the end of the file is reached
- Searching for and counting the number of times a shorter string occurs within a longer one
- Idling your program for a set period
- Performing actions on all items in an array
- With `If...Then` statements, performing actions with multiple items that meet criteria in an array or collection

Types of Do...Loop statements

VBA offers the `Do...Loop` in five flavors, but all of them work very much alike. Here they are:

Statement	What It Does
`Do...Loop`	Repeat the block indefinitely, exiting when a conditional statement within the loop executes an `End Do` statement.
`Do While...Loop`	Begin and repeat the block only if the condition is True.
`Do...Loop While`	Execute the block once, and then repeat it as long as the condition is True.
`Do Until...Loop`	Begin and repeat the block only if the condition is False.
`Do...Loop Until`	Execute the block once, and then repeat it as long as the condition is False.

Using the Do While...Loop statement

The prototypical `Do` structure is `Do While...Loop`. The syntax is

```
Do While condition
(statements that execute while condition is True)
Loop
```

When it encounters a `Do While` statement, VBA begins by evaluating *condition*. If it turns out that this expression is False, it ignores the rest of the loop, skipping to the program statement following `Loop`. But if *condition* is True, VBA executes the statements in the block. When it reaches the `Loop` statement, it jumps back up to the `Do While` statement to test the condition again.

Typically, one or more statements in the body of the loop can change the value of *condition*, so it may now be False. If so, VBA terminates the loop and skips over it. But if *condition* is still True, the loop statements again get executed.

The whole process repeats until at some point, *condition* becomes False. In other words, there is no set limit on how many times the block of statements in the loop get executed. Assuming an infinite power supply and a computer that never breaks down, the loop will repeat forever if *condition* never becomes False.

A Do While...Loop example (two examples, actually)

The following example relies on two `Do While...Loop` statements to reverse the digits in a number selected by the user. It has no practical value but illustrates how `Do` loops work:

```
Sub ReverseTheDigits()

Dim intOriginalNumber As Integer
Dim intOneDigit As Integer, strBackwardsNumber As String

Do While intOriginalNumber < 10
    intOriginalNumber = _
        InputBox("Type in an integer greater than 9.")
Loop

Do While intOriginalNumber
    intOneDigit = intOriginalNumber Mod 10
    strBackwardsNumber = strBackwardsNumber & intOneDigit
    intOriginalNumber = int(intOriginalNumber / 10)
Loop

MsgBox strBackwardsNumber
End Sub
```

The example explained

The first `Do` loop checks the value of the number typed in by the user of the program to make sure that it's not a negative number, and that it has at least two digits — otherwise, why bother reversing them? The first time the program encounters this loop, the value of the `intOriginalNumber` variable is zero, because nothing has been assigned to it so far. Zero is less than 10, so the condition is True and VBA enters the loop.

The loop contains one statement, an input box asking the user to type in a suitable number. Once this is done, the `Loop` statement sends VBA back to the top of the loop, where the number entered is checked. Only when a valid number has been entered does the loop terminate. (Note that this example omits important validity checks, such as whether the number is an integer and whether it's not larger than the maximum value for an Integer variable.)

Once VBA confirms a valid entry, it's on to the next loop. The condition for executing this loop is that the variable containing the number must be greater than zero. Because a nonzero value is True, you can simply write `Do While intOriginalNumber` instead of `Do While intOriginalNumber > 0` — either version works identically.

In the loop proper, a simple three-step procedure takes apart the digits of the original number working from right to left, using them in reverse order to build a new string. You don't have to understand how this code works to figure out the loop, but it won't hurt you to know that:

- The first line uses the `Mod` operator to divide the number by 10 and assign only the remainder to the `intOneDigit` variable. Because you're dividing by 10, the remainder is the last (right-most) digit of the original number.

- The second line takes the digit obtained by the first line and adds it to the end of the string under construction.

- The third line again divides the number by 10, this time keeping the result of the division in the original variable. This effectively lops off the right-most digit. Note, however, that before the result is assigned to the variable, it is processed by the `Int` function. This is necessary because otherwise, VBA would round off the result — which might change the digits originally entered.

- As the loop loops, `intOriginalNumber` will be 0 after all its digits have been processed (any one digit divided by 10 is less than 1, and the `Int` function drops the fractional part of the result). In VBA-land, zero is False, so the loop ends and the program displays the reversed number.

Other Do statements

Variations on the `Do While...Loop` are easy to understand once you get the basic form. This section discusses three of the alternative `Do` loops. See "When to use Do without While or Until" for the fourth.

Do...Loop While

The difference between the `Do While...Loop` and `Do...Loop While` statements is simple: `Do While...Loop` has the condition at the top of the loop, whereas in `Do...Loop While` the condition comes at the end.

In a `Do While...Loop` structure, the loop is only entered if the condition is True the first time the program reaches it. If the condition is False to start with, the statements in the loop never execute. In a `Do...Loop While` structure, by contrast, the loop always execute at least once, the first time the program runs through the code. Only then is the condition tested, with the loop repeating as long as it remains True. Use a `Do...Loop While` structure when the loop block contains a statement that sets a value in the condition before the condition gets tested.

Another situation that calls for a Do...Loop While structure is when you're performing an action on an item (such as a string or an array) that may have more than one element. If you already know it has at least one element, you want the loop statements to execute at least once and then repeat as many times as needed for the remaining components.

Do Until loops

The Do While...Loop and Do Until...Loop statements are functionally equivalent. That is, you can execute exactly the same statements with either one by modifying the condition expression to perform the opposite test. If the condition for a Do While statement is A = B, a Do Until statement with A <> B would function identically. The Do...Loop While and Do...Loop Until pair are similarly complementary.

Quitting a loop early with Exit Do

At their most elegant, Do loops provide all the information VBA needs to decide whether to execute the loop in the condition expression. Unfortunately, things aren't always so tidy in real-world programming. Sometimes a change in a different condition occurring in the body of the loop demands a hasty exit. That's why VBA has an Exit Do statement. Valid only in a Do structure, Exit Do summarily terminates the loop, passing program execution to the statement that comes after the loop. This example concatenates a string variable to an existing string, but if the variable contains more than one character the loop terminates:

```
Do While strA <= "Z"
    If len (strA) > 1 Then
        Exit Do
    End If
    strB = strB & strA
    strA = GetNextCharacter
Loop
```

Secret

Normally, the Exit Do statement should appear in an If...Then or Select Case statement nested in the loop. That way, the loop runs normally unless some special or aberrant value occurs. However, you can also use Exit Do as a debugging device to bypass the loop temporarily, without having to "comment out" the code.

When to use Do without While or Until

With standard Do...While/Until...Loop statements, you can test a condition at the beginning or end of a loop. But what if you want to test the condition somewhere *within* the loop?

In this situation, use a Do...Loop statement—without While or Until. This technique requires an If or Select Case statement nested inside the loop.

One or more branches of the nested conditional statement include an `Exit Do` statement, allowing the program to terminate the loop when a specified condition is met.

Here's how a `Do...Loop` statement looks in schematic form:

```
Do
(statements to be executed with each pass of the loop)
    If condition Then
        Exit Do
    End If
(more statements to be executed only if loop continues)
Loop
```

As you can see, this technique is appropriate when you want to execute some of the loop statements regardless of whether the condition is met. It's also useful if the loop should terminate under several different conditions.

Frequently, for example, you must validate a user entry based on several criteria. In the following example, a `Do...Loop` structure repeats the loop until the user enters a valid letter answer:

```
Sub GetAnAnswer()

strAnswer = InputBox("Enter your answer (A-E)")

Do
    If strAnswer = "" Then
       strAnswer = InputBox("You made no entry." _
          & " Please type a letter from A to E.")
    ElseIf Len(strAnswer) > 1 Then
       strAnswer = InputBox("Your answer should be" _
          & " only one letter long. Please try " _
          & "again.")
    ElseIf strAnswer < "A" Or strAnswer > "E" Then
       strAnswer = InputBox("You typed an invalid" _
          & " character. Type a letter from A to E.")
    Else
       Exit Do
    End If
Loop

End Sub
```

The program executes the `Exit Do` statement only when all three validation criteria — expressed in the `If` and `ElseIf` clauses — have been met.

Repeating on Count with For...Next loops

When you know how many times a loop should execute before the loop runs, use a `For...Next` loop. You specify how many passes VBA should make through the loop by supplying *start* and *end* values, which can be literal integers, variables, or even complex expressions. As the loop executes, a *counter* variable keeps track of the number of completed cycles. When the counter's value equals that of *end,* the loop is finished.

Simplified, the syntax of a For...Next structure is as follows:

```
For counter = start To end
(statements to be executed during each pass of the loop)
Next counter
```

Keeping it simple for starters, the following example procedure uses the Immediate window to display a message for each repetition of the loop (in the Visual Basic Editor, open the Immediate window by pressing Ctrl+G):

```
Sub CountToTen ()
Dim j As Integer
    For  j = 1 To 10
        Debug.Print "This is pass " & j
    Next j
End Sub
```

In the preceding example, the *start* and *end* values are both literal numbers. When the loop begins, j is set to 1—in other words, the value of *start* is assigned to the *counter* variable. Each time a loop cycle completes, the Next j statement increments j (raises its value by one), and control shifts back to the beginning of the loop. When j finally equals 10, the loop terminates.

Important Tips about For...Next loops

Keep your code easy to understand. You should use 1 as the start value for a For...Next loop unless you have good reason to choose another number. Such good reasons do exist. One is when the value of the counter is used in the loop itself (not changed in the loop, mind you). If the loop takes some action based on consecutively numbered items such as part numbers, you can use the actual values of the items as the start and end values. More commonly, start is often set to 0 when working with arrays, as illustrated in the next section.

Secret

In the Next *counter* statement that ends a For...Next loop, the counter variable's name isn't actually required—the keyword Next by itself automatically calculates the next counter value and sends VBA back to the top of the structure. However, you should definitely train yourself to include the counter in the Next statement. That way, when you nest two or more For...Next loops, you can see at a glance which a given Next statement belongs to.

Caution

Do not change the value of the counter variable within a For...Next loop. Because the counter is just another variable, it's possible, and sometimes tempting, to write code that changes the counter value. Resist the urge—fool with the counter and the loop is likely to skip important steps or go on infinitely.

For...Next loops and Arrays

For...Next loops are perhaps most useful for working with arrays, which are named storage bins for sets of data items. A discussion of For...Next loops would be incomplete without a look at their use with these important data baskets. For example, you can use a For...Next loop to fill an array with a set of calculated values:

```
Dim intArrayOfSquares (14) As Integer
For a = 0 to 14
    intArrayOfSquares (a) = a * a
Next a
```

The example code begins by declaring an array of 15 integer values (15, not 14, because VBA normally numbers the first item in an array 0). It then uses a For...Next loop to assign a value to each item in the array, counting from 0 to 14. Notice that the variable a is used not only as the counter but as the array *index*, pointing to a numbered slot in the array.

Nesting For...Next loops

As with other VBA control structures, For...Next loops can be nested within one another — or within other control structures — as "deeply" as you need to nest them. The following useless fragment of code illustrates the concept:

```
Dim sngR   ' R stands for random number
Randomize ' initialize the random number generator
For A = 1 To 5
    sngR = Rnd ()
    For B = 1 To 5
        Debug.Print sngR * Rnd ( )
    Next B
Next A
```

Tracing the steps VBA follows to execute this code, the code starts by declaring a variable and initializing VBA's random number generator. Next, the outer For...Next loop starts. Here, VBA calls the Rnd function to assign a random number to the sngR variable. Then comes the inner For...Next loop. This loop calculates five other numbers. The results appear in the Immediate window. The inner loop terminates after it completes all five calculations. Now the outer loop takes over again. Obeying the Next A statement, VBA jumps back to the top of the outer loop, which repeats the inner loop for four more passes.

The example I gave may be a trivial one, but it could be extended to perform Genuinely Useful Work. Suppose you wanted to write a multimedia program that selects five CDs at random, playing five random selections from each one. Assuming you have the know-how to write the code that selects CDs and plays individual selections, the preceding example should get you started.

Secret

Nested For...Next loops are also the key to working systematically with multidimensional arrays. Each loop corresponds to one dimension of the array.

Get out now with an Exit For

The `Exit For` statement provides a quick way to terminate a `For...Next` loop before the end of the loop has actually been reached. It's typically used within a conditional statement (`If...Then` or `Select Case`) nested within the main `For...Next` loop.

One use of the `Exit For` escape hatch is to test an array for invalid data, halting whatever process is underway if an aberrant value is detected. As an example, suppose you have learned that a malevolent genius has been able to insert an array containing false information into your price list data. You happen to know he has left behind his trademark. As you update the price information to reflect inflationary price hikes in each array, you want to be sure the price data hasn't been tampered with. This code does both jobs at once:

```
For p = 1 To varArraySize
    If varPriceArray (p) = "Kilroy was here!" Then
        MsgBox "Infested data in this array!"
        Exit For
    End If
    varPriceArray (p) = varPriceArray (p) * sngCOLA
Next p
```

For Each...Next

A variation on the `For...Next` idea, VBA's `For Each...Next` statement performs a set of statements for each object stored in a *collection*. You can read about `For Each...Next` loops in "Using For Each...Next loops to work with collections" in Chapter 22.

Interrupting the Flow with GoTo

If your program is behaving in an unruly fashion, tell it where to go — by transferring execution to another location in the procedure. A `GoTo` statement, combined with a special *label* statement at the destination, enables you to hop at will from place to place within a procedure. A label is a statement that simply marks a location in your code. To enter a label, type in its name (VBA naming rules apply) followed by a colon.

A GoTo example

In this example, a `GoTo` statement jumps out of the main part of the function to the `SpecialValue` label when an unusual value is encountered:

```
Function GoToExample (ItemNumber As Integer)
    Dim intR As Integer
    Select Case ItemNumber
```

```
        Case 2412
            GoTo SpecialValue
        Case Is < CutOffValue
            DoSomething
        Case >= CutOffValue
            DoHardlyAnything
    End Select
    (statements that execute no matter what)
    GoToExample = intR
    Exit Function
SpecialValue:
    DoSomethingSpecial
    GoToExample = -intR
End Function
```

GoTo caveats

Use of the `GoTo` statement is considered inferior programming form. The problem is that it creates "spaghetti code," with the path of execution wandering all over the place. Code containing more than an occasional `GoTo` quickly becomes impossible to read. Whenever possible, you should use control structures to direct program execution.

Occasionally, however, a `GoTo` statement is the most practical way to get your program to do what you want it to. Your brain may be just too tired to come up with the intricate set of nested loops and conditionals required to implement a complex set of criteria. At times like these, `GoTo` can sometimes cut through the maze. Just don't use it too often.

Conclusion

This admittedly bulky chapter took you through a substantial portion of what you need to know to write effective programs in VBA. From the conceptual framework to techniques for working with modules, procedures, and variables, you now have enough skills to create real programs that accomplish substantial tasks. Despite the chapter's girth, you still have more ground to cover before you can fully exploit VBA's potential. In Chapter 22, you learn all about objects in VBA — among other roles they play, objects are the key tools for controlling your Office applications in VBA code.

Chapter 22

Object-Oriented Programming with VBA

In This Chapter

- Essential object concepts
- Properties, methods, and events — important components of VBA objects
- How to work with object models
- Object references to identify the object you want to work with
- Creating your own objects with class modules
- Efficiency with objects using `For`, `Each...Next`, and `With` statements
- Using Collection objects as an alternative to arrays

A core aspect of VBA's identity is that it's an object-oriented software development tool. An understanding of objects is fundamental to VBA programming, especially when you want to create custom dialog boxes or put the features of the host application under your control.

So What's an Object?

Although it's possible to come up with a formal definition of a VBA object, it's a lot easier to understand objects by way of examples and in terms of their functions.

Objects can be components of a VBA application

The easiest way to start thinking about objects is to see them as parts of your VBA application and its documents. A cell in an Excel worksheet is an object, as are named ranges of cells. And so are individual worksheets and complete workbooks, to which all the cells, ranges, and sheets belong. In all Office VBA applications, the toolbars and menus, and the buttons and menu choices they contain, are objects as well.

As is already obvious, VBA objects exist in a hierarchy in which one type of object contains objects of other types. These object hierarchies are the topic of "What's an object model?" the next major section in this chapter. For the time being, though, let's concentrate on understanding individual objects.

Conceptualizing objects can be hard

You may not be able to touch a drawing shape, a worksheet cell, or a toolbar button, but it's fairly easy to think of them as things. In your imagination, at least, you could cut out a circle shape and paste it on another piece of paper. You could write numbers into that worksheet cell, or push that button. In addition to fairly concrete items like these, however, VBA applications offer up all kinds of more abstract objects. Here are some examples:

- Word has a Style object, which represents a combination of formatting characteristics for paragraphs.

- Excel has a CustomView object, representing a workbook custom view (in Excel, a custom view defines the look of the workbook and its print settings).

- Word's FileSearch object "represents the functionality of the Open dialog box," to quote the relevant Help topic. Note that this object doesn't represent the dialog box itself, but its functionality.

- VBA itself has a few objects, which are available in all VBA applications. A Collection object, for example, represents a grab-bag set of variables or other objects that you want to work with as a unit, regardless of their data types.

A practical definition

As you can tell, it's often difficult to imagine a VBA object as a material thing. But that's okay—the more you can let go of such mental models, the more freely you can work the whole range of available objects. The programmer's pragmatic definition of an object is simple, really. An object is a named item that has:

- **Properties.** Settings you can check and change.
- **Methods.** Actions the object can perform when your program asks it to.

And in some cases:

- **Events.** Things that happen to the object, to which it can respond by taking a predetermined action automatically.

If you have any poetic sensibility, the term "objects" may not seem fitting for such richly endowed creatures. Indeed, objects are more like animals than inert lumps. Where a tiger or a whale has characteristic features such as eyes, limbs, and a tail, an object has *properties*. Where a horse or a dog can do tricks on command or run away from danger, an object has *methods* and *events*.

Do you still want a technical definition? Try this one: An object is a named unit within a program that possesses both data and the code that acts on that data. An object is said to *encapsulate* the data and the related code.

Object classes versus specific objects

Here's yet another technicality to keep in mind: There's a distinction between a specific object and the pattern on which the object is based. A particular object represents one specific document, shape, worksheet cell, or what have you. A document object, for example, includes the text of that one document.

An *object class*, on the other hand, can be compared to a set of building plans. You can build many houses from one set of plans, but nobody can live in the plans themselves. In the same way, a class lays down the types of data that can be stored in an object and defines the object's methods, properties, and events. Based on this description, you construct an *instance* of the class — an object — in which you actually store some data. You can create, or *instantiate*, as many objects of a class as you like, each with a separate existence, and each containing different data.

What's an object model?

As you've seen, VBA objects exist in a hierarchical relationship to one another. In addition to having properties, methods, and events of its own, an object at the top of the hierarchy serves as a *container* for one or more other types. These objects in turn each contain other objects, and so on.

For a given VBA application, the specifics of these hierarchical relationships are referred to as the application's *object model*. Often presented graphically, the object model specifies which object contains which other objects. Figure 22-1 shows one such representation of an object model.

As Figure 22-1 makes plain, the *Application object* is at the top of a VBA application's object model. It is the container for all the other objects from the application that you can manipulate. Your own VBA programming *project* is also a container object. It contains all the code *modules* you write and the forms you design, as well as the project's document (Chapter 21 defines and discusses VBA projects in more detail).

Microsoft PowerPoint Objects

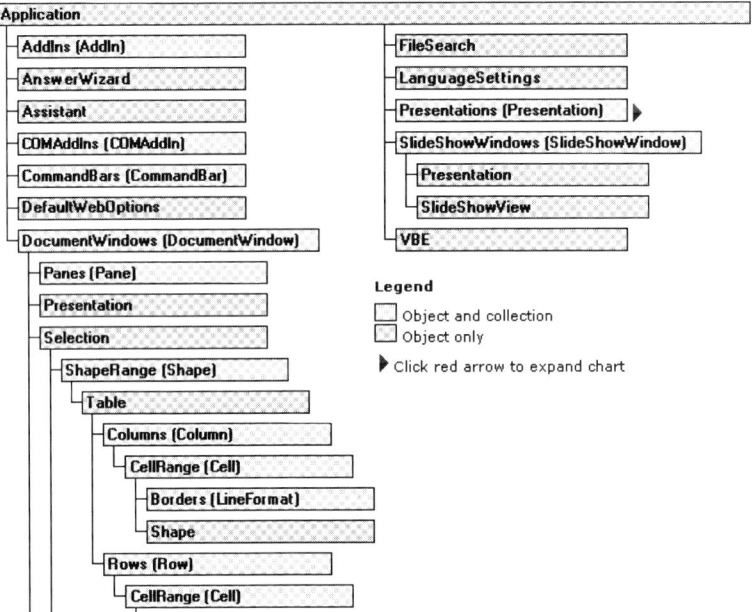

Figure 22-1: A portion of PowerPoint's object model.

Why the object model is important

Because you need to tell VBA which specific object you're working with, a good grasp on the object model of your VBA application is critical to efficient work. Following a chart of the object model such as the one shown in Figure 22-1, you can quickly locate the branch that contains the object you're after. In this example, for instance, you can see that a View object is contained in a DocumentWindow object, itself a member of the DocumentWindows collection. Later in this chapter I tell how to use the relationships between objects described by the object model to identify in your code each specific object you want to work with.

Extending the object model

In the programs you write with VBA, you aren't limited to using the objects in only one VBA application. In fact, you're not even limited to VBA applications per se. Other applications and specialized "components" are fair game, as long as they adhere to Microsoft's *Component Object Model* (COM) standard.

Secret

COM is the technical specification detailing how objects are defined within applications and other software elements, and how those objects are *exposed* so they can be used by other applications. The jargon word *automation* refers specifically to the ability of a COM-based application to be controlled by another program. And by the way, COM isn't specific to VBA or even Visual Basic. Many software development tools such as C++ compilers understand COM and can access objects.

Anyway, all this opens up fantastic possibilities for powerful, customized VBA applications. You can readily (I didn't say "easily") build an application that processes information from Word documents, Excel worksheets, and even non-Office VBA applications such as Visio. Your custom application can show all this information in windows that you have designed, but that use the display capabilities of the individual component applications. Custom application development on this scale is introduced in Chapter 25.

VBA forms are objects

A form is the generic term for any custom window or dialog box you build with VBA. A key understanding to seal into your brain is that VBA forms are themselves objects. That is, they constitute entities that contain both information — representing the layout of the form — and a set of tools for doing things with that information. The official term for a form is UserForm object.

Likewise, a form's controls — each button, checkbox, and other doodad you can see and play with on the form — are also objects. VBA offers a different object type for each type of control.

Forms have properties, methods, and events

Because VBA is a visual design tool, you don't have to write code to create and lay out a form and its controls. But because forms and controls are full-fledged VBA objects, you work with them in your program just as you would any other object. You use:

- *Properties* to change the appearance or behavior of a form or control while your program is running
- *Methods* to make the form or control do something, such as become visible or move to a new location
- *Events* to tell the form or control what to do when the user of your program clicks the mouse or presses a key, or when other events occur

The techniques you use in your code to access a particular form and use its properties and methods are exactly the same as you use for other objects. Chapter 24 delves deeply into the application of these techniques to forms and controls.

Forms have their place in the object model

As self-respecting VBA objects, forms fit comfortably into the object model paradigm. Each UserForm object can belong simultaneously to two collection objects, the VBA project in which the form is stored, and the UserForms collection, which holds all the forms currently loaded by your program. For its part, a UserForm object is a container for a Controls Collection object, which in turn contains all the individual controls you have added to the form. The diagram in Figure 22-2 illustrates these relationships.

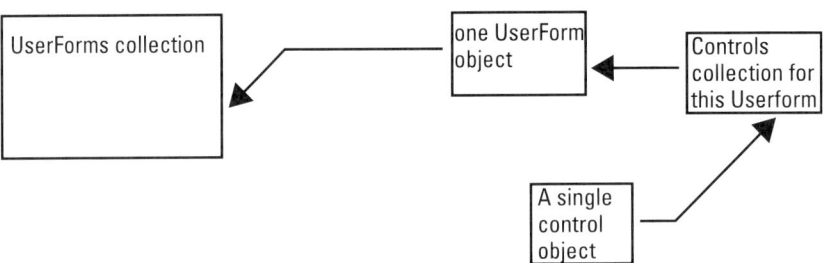

Figure 22-2: This diagram illustrates how control objects reside in control collections, which belong to a UserForm object, which in turn is part of the UserForms collection, which belongs to . . .

Using Objects in Code

Now that the theoretical groundwork has been laid, practical directions for programming with VBA objects are in order. Although the object concept itself can be tough to wrap your mind around, *using* objects is easy. Because objects have names, you always know which one you're working with. In your code, all it takes to identify one of the object's properties or methods is to type the object name, a period, then the property or method name. For example, `MyWorksheet.Calculate` identifies the `Calculate` method of an Excel worksheet object called MyWorksheet.

At this point, though, you may be asking yourself, "But how do I know what the object's name is in the first place?" An excellent question, indeed. For now, though, just assume that it's possible to call an object by name.

What's your object?

Each VBA application has its own different object model (hierarchical set of objects), and each of its objects has its own set of properties, methods, and events. You need a working familiarity with the details of the application's object model to put these objects to work in your programs.

The VBA help file for each Office application includes a topic devoted to a map of the application's object model (refer back to Figure 22-1 for an example). This graphical outline of the object model is the default topic, but if you don't see it when you open Help, look for it in the VBA help system's Contents tab under the title Microsoft Outlook Objects, Microsoft Excel Objects, or what have you.

In the object model map, light blue bars represent single objects, whereas yellow bars represent collection objects. You can jump to the help topics for any object or collection by clicking the corresponding bar in the object model map. Typically, the topic for each object has links to other topics detailing the object's properties, methods, and events.

The Visual Basic Editor's Object Browser is another vital tool for viewing the relationships between the different objects of the application and exploring their properties, methods, and events. Chapter 20 describes the Object Browser in full.

Getting and changing object properties

An object property is a named characteristic of the object. It describes some aspect of the object's appearance, behavior, contents, or "pedigree," if you will. A Document object might have a `Pages` property that tells how many pages are in the document. A Shape object might have a `Fill` property that specifies the shape's color. CommandButton objects (representing buttons on dialog boxes) always have a `Caption` property that contains the text displayed on the button.

Behavior-related properties define the way the object reacts to various stimuli. Controls on forms are objects, and they have properties such as Enabled, which specifies whether the control responds to events such as mouse clicks. Some properties can take on an infinite range of different values. Others are limited to a list of predefined choices, such as Mauve, Teal, and Chartreuse. Many properties can take only two possible settings, such as True or False, Hot or Cold, or Wet or Dry. In any case, you can use simple VBA statements to retrieve the current setting of a given property, and to change the setting to one you prefer.

A VBA program can retrieve the current settings stored in most properties. This allows the program to decide whether or not to take some action, or simply to display the current setting in a window. Conversely, a program can change a property's setting to alter an object's appearance or behavior — but only if the property permits this (many properties can be retrieved but not modified).

What you can't do with some properties

Just knowing how to access a property's value doesn't mean you can. By design, some properties allow you to retrieve their values, but not to change them. These are *read-only* properties. Less commonly, a property is *write-only* — you can set its value, but not retrieve the current setting. However, most properties, are the *read/write* kind — you can both retrieve and change their values.

Property settings are data

Secret

Although a property functions metaphorically to describe some characteristic of the object, you should realize that the setting it contains consists of data—no different in kind from the data you stuff into VBA variables. As such, you can think of a property simply as a more-or-less permanent variable that you don't have to declare.

Once you understand properties this way, it makes sense that each property stores a particular data type, exactly as variables do. Properties that can take only two alternative settings are of the Boolean type. Some properties are strings, some are integers, some are floating-point or decimal numbers, and so on. Properties can even be objects. (See Chapter 21 for information on VBA's available data types.)

Retrieving a property's current setting

To find out, or *get*, the current setting of a given property, use the property as if it were a function or Function procedure. That is, assign the property to a variable in your code. The variable should be of the same or a compatible data type as the property.

In the sample shown here, the object in question represents, let's just say, a question on a computerized test for graduate school admission. The property you're interested in checking is the one that describes how hard the question is on a scale of 1–10.

```
Dim intHowTough As Integer
intHowTough = objTestQuestion.DifficultyLevel
```

The first statement declares a variable to hold the property's current value, whereas the second statement assigns the property to that variable.

So why bother retrieving a property's current value? Often, you use it in a conditional statement to decide whether or not to take some other action, based on the value. (In this case, something like, "If the question's DifficultyLevel is above 8, and if the answer is correct, award double credit" might be in order.) You might also store a property value in a variable so that you can assign the value to the same property of other similar objects.

If you're only going to use the property's value once, you don't need to assign to a variable—you can access it directly in an expression. The example illustrates this practice:

```
If objTestQuestion.DifficultyLevel > 8 Then
    intTestScore = intTestScore + (intPoints * 2)
End If
```

Secret

This is convenient, but remember that your program will slow down if you repeatedly retrieve a property's value. If you need the value more than once or twice, it's better to store it in a variable—VBA can access the value of an ordinary variable more quickly than it can retrieve a property's value.

Changing a property's setting

Remember, properties are just glorified variables. Therefore, you can assign values to them just as you would any other variable — by placing the property name on the left side of an equals sign, and the new value on the right. The statement

```
objMetalTune.GrungeFactor = 999
```

sets the objMetalTune's `GrungeFactor` property — presumably, a measure of distortion, feedback, and extraneous noise — to 999.

```
objMetalTune.Ballad = False
objMetalTune.Title = "I have fleas. Bad."
```

Default properties

Many objects have a default property. You can retrieve or set its value using the object only, without mentioning the property itself by name. Sticking with the last example, suppose the default property for the objMetalTune object is `Title`. In that case, you could simplify the last statement to read

```
objMetalTune = "I have fleas. Bad."
```

Default properties are convenient, as long as you're sure you know which property is the default. If you have any doubt, or if you think you might forget later, it's better to go ahead and type out the property name.

Objects as properties

As I mentioned earlier, a property of one object can identify another object. This arrangement lets your code access the subsidiary objects that belong to a given *container* object, just as you would the container's other properties. For example, in the expression

```
Workbook.ActiveWorksheet
```

`ActiveWorksheet` is a property of the Toolbar object, but its *value* is a worksheet object. Using object properties in this way is the critical technique for identifying the specific objects you want to work with. See "Identifying the object you want to work with" later in this chapter for details.

Climbing the family tree

Just as an object's properties can identify other objects that belong to it, they can also tell you which container objects it belongs to. In Excel, if you have a Chart object stored in a variable and you want to know which document it belongs to, the expression

```
Chart.Parent
```

will return a reference to the correct document. If you need to know which *application* an object belongs to, you can often skip up to the top of the object hierarchy by getting an object's `Application` property:

```
Chart.Application
```

Method acting

A *method* is a named action that an object performs when the method is called. Actually, methods are nothing more than procedures that are tied directly to specific objects. Because the code for each method is part and parcel of the object, the object itself knows what to do when you trigger the method.

Office drawing shape objects, for example, have a `ScaleHeight` method (to change their size in the vertical dimension) and an `IncrementRotation` method (that adjusts their rotation on the page), among others. A worksheet cell object might have a `Calculate` method (that recalculates the cell value) and a `Clear` method (that removes its contents). A document object (representing an entire document) will probably have `Print` and `Save` methods.

Calling methods

To call a method, you type the object's name, a period, and then the method name. Leaving behind metal madness, let's say an object named objJazzTune represents a digital jazz recording in a multimedia program. Most likely, the object has a method called `Play`. Here's how to call the method:

```
objJazzTune.Play
```

The techniques for calling methods are consistent with the ones you use to call procedures and VBA functions, as described in Chapter 21.

Secret

As with properties, many different object classes may have methods with the same names. Objects that contain groups of items or other objects typically have an `Add` method, for instance.

Changing properties with methods

Just so it doesn't surprise you, I should mention that a method can change the value of one or more properties. For example, the objJazzTune object might have a read-only property called `TimesPlayed`, which can only be altered by the `Play` method, but which you can retrieve via a property statement such as `intPlaybacks = objJazzTune.TimesPlayed`. Some objects even have special methods whose sole purpose in life is to set property values.

Events

An event is something that happens to the object, and to which it can respond with some predetermined action (in VBA lingo, when you say an object "has" events, you mean the object can detect and recognize those events). Events include:

- Physical actions the user of your program does, such as clicking or just moving the mouse, pressing a key, or jumping up and down and screaming (okay, so VBA can't recognize "jumping up and down and screaming" events).

- Things that happen to the object under software control. If you're talking about a document object, events might include the opening or closing of the document, or the addition or removal of a page.

Your VBA application specifies which events, if any, a given object can recognize. It's *your* job to write the code that determines what the object does when the event occurs.

The events that you'll most often write code for are the ones that happen to forms, and the controls on them (like buttons and text boxes). When the user of your program clicks the mouse on a certain button, that action has an effect only if you have written code for the button's Click event. Event programming for forms is the subject of Chapter 25.

However, it's often useful to write code for events that occur to other types of objects. In Word, the Application and Document objects recognize events. You can write code that runs automatically when these events occur. The techniques required vary from application to application and sometimes even within the same application, so consult your application's documentation or Help files for details.

Caution

One point may bear clarification: You don't call an event from your own code. Instead, the object automatically takes action when the event occurs.

Identifying the object you want to work with

To do anything useful with an object, you have to tell VBA which object you want to work with. You use an *object expression* for this purpose. This is special kind of VBA expression that uniquely identifies the specific object you're excited about. Behind the scenes, the value that VBA calculates based on an object expression is an *object reference*, a value which you can think of as a street address for the object.

Figuring out the correct object expression you need is most of the battle. Once you've done that, you can make your life much easier by creating a named variable for the object, using the expression to assign the corresponding object reference to the variable. From then on, you can refer to the object by the variable's name in your code.

An *object expression* is a code fragment — an expression — that "points" at a particular object. Using a valid object expression, you can set the object's properties, activate its methods, or assign the object to a variable.

Secret

The ideas covered here are critical to daily work with VBA, yet they're not easy to grasp at first. Because your program can work with many different objects of the same type, a complete object expression must specify all the objects that contain the one you have in mind. It's something like this: Suppose you were told to go get "the boy." You'd immediately ask, "Well, which boy?" If you were told instead to get the oldest boy who lives in the third house on Mayflower Street in the town of Arhoolie in the state of Nebraska in the United States of America, you wouldn't need to ask that question. (Of course, you might ask "Why?")

However, if you're already in the third house on Mayflower Street, and if only one boy lives there, a command such as "feed the boy" is quite adequate. In the same way, if the context is clear, VBA doesn't need the entire list of objects.

Properties can be objects

As I mentioned earlier, a property of one object can be another object. As I've also said, objects exist in a hierarchy, with one object, such as a document, serving as a *container* for other subsidiary objects, such as pages, worksheets, or what have you.

The connection between these ideas is probably obvious: If an object contains subsidiary objects, you can identify a subsidiary object via a property of the first object. The expression you use to specify this property *is* the object expression. For example, consider the following expression, which identifies a specific a object in a Word document:

```
ThisDocument.Sections(2).Range
```

Notice that this object expression contains two periods, not just one. What this means is that `Range` is a property of the second Section object, which is in turn a property of the ThisDocument object.

Getting objects

The diagram shown in Figure 22-3 illustrates the relationship between objects referred to in the preceding object expression.

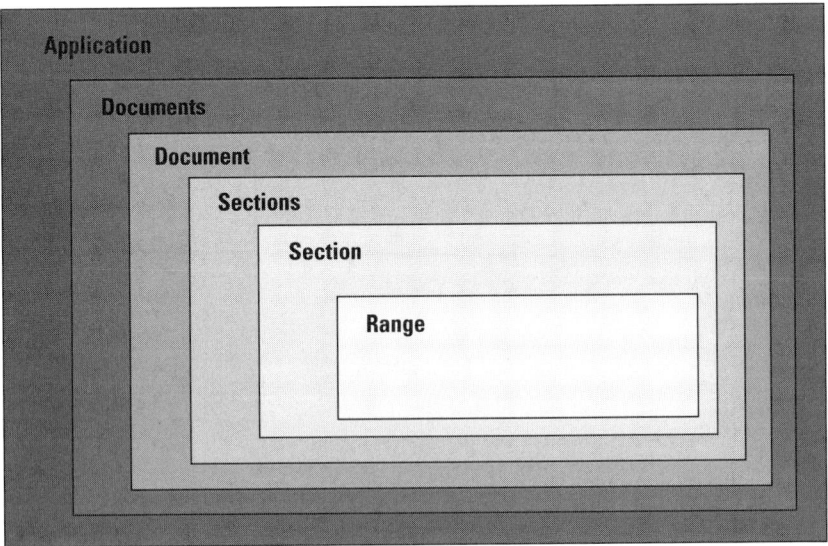

Figure 22-3: This illustration depicts the hierarchical relationship between objects.

The Application object occupies the very top of the object hierarchy in most VBA object models. However, you usually don't need to include it in object expressions — VBA is smart enough to assume you're working with objects from the current application, unless you specify otherwise.

The Application object contains a Documents object, which is a collection representing all the open documents. If you wanted to work with a specific document, you would identify it as a member of the Documents object. For example, `Documents(5)` would represents Document object 5 in the Documents collection. The expression `ThisDocument.Sections(2).Range`, however, starts with the special keyword `ThisDocument`. In many VBA applications, `ThisDocument` stands for the Document object associated with your project.

In Word, each Document object has a `Sections` property. This in turn refers to a Sections collection, an object that represents the set of all the pages in the document. So the first part of the preceding expression — `ThisDocument.Sections` — identifies the particular Sections collection that belongs to the ThisDocument object. Once you've identified the Sections object, you can select a single member of its collection. Thus `Sections(2)` refers to the second section in the document.

Now for the final part of the expression. The tricky part here is that although `.Range` specifies a *property* of the Section object, the value of that property is a Range *object*. The entire expression, then, supplies an object reference to that Range object. Using an expression that threads its way through the object hierarchy like this to a specific object is called "getting an object" in VBA lingo.

Creating object variables

Secret

Nobody likes to type a long, complex object expression like the one discussed in the previous section. If your program uses the same object more than once, you should create a named variable to hold a reference to that object. Then, wherever you would have typed the complete object expression, you can enter the variable name instead.

Besides being shorter, easier to remember, and easier to type than the original object expression, an *object variable* has two other plusses. First, it makes your code run faster. VBA can locate the object directly, rather than having to look up a series of properties in a series of objects. Second, you can use the same object variable to store references to different objects. That way, you can write flexible code that decides which specific object to store in the variable when the program runs.

In outline, the technique for creating an object variable requires two steps:

1. Declare a variable you will use to refer to the object.
2. Assign the object you want to work with to that variable.

The next two sections cover the details on each of these steps.

Declaring an object variable

You declare object variables just as you do variables of other data types. The standard method is with a `Dim` statement (just as with other types of variables, though, you can also use the `Public`, `Private`, or `Static` keywords instead of `Dim` to declare object variables). Here are two examples of object declarations:

```
Dim objGreatBigObject As Object ' A generic object
Dim objShapeObject As Shape ' A drawing Shape object
```

The difference between these two declarations is important. The first statement declares an object variable but doesn't specify the type of object it will contain. You can use this variable to hold different types of objects as the need arises. The second statement declares the particular type, or *class*, of object that you want the variable to store. VBA won't allow you to place other object classes in the variable.

These two types of object declarations are referred to as *late binding*, in which no specific class is specified, and *early binding*, in which you do declare the variable as a definite object class. Whenever possible, you should use early binding, declaring the object variable as a specific class. The benefits of early binding include:

- **Fewer mistakes.** As I mentioned, VBA won't let you assign incorrect objects to the variable. Just as important, by knowing which class of object you're working with, the compiler can check the rest of your code to make sure you use properties and methods that are valid for that class. If you use late binding, the compiler can't perform this check. An error will occur while your program is trying to run if it attempts to use invalid properties or methods.

- **Faster performance.** Because the compiler can determine whether the object has the methods and properties you use in your program, the program doesn't need to pause to check this when it runs.

- **More understandable code.** You can tell by looking at the declaration what class of object the variable is supposed to contain.

In spite of these advantages, there are two situations when it's better to use late binding:

- You may *intend* to use the same variable for different classes of objects. This can be a good idea when the different classes share methods or properties that you need to access in your code. With a variable, you don't need to rewrite code that does the same things using different objects.

- Some objects can't be declared via early binding when they are accessed from another application. Using objects from other applications is an advanced VBA technique that is introduced in Chapter 25.

As you know, a variable of the variant type can hold any type of information, including an object reference. If you declare a variable without explicitly stating its data type, VBA sets it up as a variant. Your program will still work, but it will slow down a bit.

Assigning an object reference to a variable

Once you've declared an object variable, you must fill it with a reference to a specific object before you can use the variable. To do this, assign an object expression to the variable using the Set keyword, as in this example:

```
Set objShapeObject = ThisDocument.Pages(1).Shapes(4)
```

Note that this syntax differs a bit from the way you assign other types of data to variables (see Chapter 21). As with other data types, you place an equal sign between the variable name and the object to be assigned. The only difference is, you must start the statement with the Set keyword.

Emptying an object variable

When you no longer need to access an object, it's good form to break the tie between the object and the variable with which it's associated. This way, you can be sure your code won't mistakenly make changes to the object. The technique is simple. Using a Set statement, just assign the Nothing keyword to the variable as in this example:

```
Set objPriceIsNoObject = Nothing
```

Creating new objects

If the object you want to work with doesn't yet exist, you have to create it. In simple VBA programs, you use the Add method for this purpose. The Add method should work if you're trying to create one of the built-in objects available in your VBA application (the one with which your project is associated).

Using the Add method

Secret

The trick is knowing which object's Add method you should use. What you're looking for is the *container* object in which the object you want to create resides.

For example, let's say you want to create a new Slide object in PowerPoint. Each Slide object is contained in a Slides object, which represents a collection of (one or more) slides. With this in mind, you would choose the Slides.Add method to create a new individual shape. Of course, because you have to identify the specific Shapes object in which VBA should create the new Shape object, the complete statement required would look something like this:

```
ActivePresentation.Slides.Add 1, ppLayoutTextAndClipart
```

Caution

Even if a Slide (singular) object had an Add method (which it doesn't), you wouldn't want to use it. It would create a subsidiary object within the Slide, not another Slide.

When you create an object, create a variable for it

You've gone to the trouble to type out a long object reference — that's what an Add statement amounts to — so you might as well create a variable for the new object at the same time. That way, you can use the variable instead of another lengthy object reference whenever you want to access the object in your code. The two statements here illustrate this technique:

```
Dim objMyBaby As Slide
objMyBaby = ActivePresentation.Slides.Add 1, _
    ppLayoutTextAndClipart
```

Creating objects with New and CreateObject

In other situations, different techniques for creating new objects are required. These alternatives apply when you're creating:

- New copies of an existing form in your own project
- Objects from a *different* application or ActiveX (COM) component
- Specific objects based on classes you write in class modules

Depending on the details of the situation, you may use the New keyword in variable declaration or Set statements, or the CreateObject function to create these objects. Steer clear of the New keyword and the CreateObject function when you're trying to create ordinary objects.

Efficient object coding using With statements

Whether you refer to an object with a short, mnemonic variable or with a lengthy, inscrutable object expression, typing it over and over again gets old in a hurry. But you may not have to. If your program uses the same object in two or more consecutive statements, the With statement allows you to name the object only once. Not only is this easier than retyping the object in each statement, it makes your code easier to understand and faster, too. Here's an example:

```
With objIHaveNoObjection
    .Name = "The Last Straw" ' Set the Name property
    .DisplayName ' Call the DisplayName method
    sngArea = .Area ' Get the Area property's value
    intStretchFactor = .Rotate (60) ' Call the Rotate
    ' method, assigning its return value to a variable
End With
```

As you can see, within the With...End With structure you can mix statements that get and set properties with statements that call methods. Note also that the With structure is not a loop — the statements it contains are executed only once.

Chapter 22: Object-Oriented Programming with VBA

Secret

With structures can be nested. This is perfect when you must perform multiple actions on both an object and one of the objects it contains.

Comparing object references

If you use variables to store object references, there may come a time when you want to know if the object a variable refers to is the same object referred to by another variable, or by an object expression. Use the Is operator in an expression to check whether two object references refer to the same object. The expression's value is True if they do, False if they refer to different objects. Here's some sample code to illustrate how Is works:

```
Dim objObject1 As Object, objObject2 As Object
...
If objObject1 Is objObject2 Then
    MsgBox "It's the same object!"
Else
    MsgBox "They're different objects."
End If
```

Of course, you could also compare an object variable against an object expression with the Is operator, as in the expression used in this line:

```
If objObject3 Is ThisDocument.Pages(2).Shapes(3) Then
```

Caution

Note that you can't use Is (or any other operator) to compare the *contents* of two different objects.

Managing sets of data with Collection objects

A collection is a special type of VBA object. As the name suggests, its role is to simplify working with a set of objects as a group. In the typical collection, all the objects it contains are of the same type. A Shapes collection in an Office document, for example, contains multiple Shape objects, and a Sections collection in Word contains multiple Section objects.

Some collections, however, are less discriminating about which objects they allow in. VBA proper comes with a generic Collection class. From it, you can create your own collection objects, using them to store data and objects of any type in any combination as appropriate. Within some limitations, collections can have significant advantages over arrays.

Secret

A collection can only store a simple list of items, comparable to a one-dimensional array. But because this is the most common type of array, collections can do real service.

Working with Collection objects

What you need to know about Collection objects is how to access the individual objects they contain. You have two options:

- Refer to the object by its "slot" or *index number* in the collection. In Word VBA, `Documents(2)` designates the second Document object in the Documents collection.

- Refer to the object by name. Many objects have names, and if you know the name of the object you want, you can use it in the object expression. For instance, Office command bars (toolbars) have names so an expression such as `CommandBars("Office Secrets toolbar")` identifies a specific command bar in the CommandBars collection.

Caution

Although you can access the item stored in a collection slot with these techniques, you can't use them to place a new value in an existing collection item. The following assignment statement does *not* work:

```
colInventory(1465) = 119
```

The only way to change a value in a generic VBA collection you create yourself is to remove the existing item and add a new one containing the new value. Many built-in collections provided by VBA and Office applications don't have this limitation.

The trade-offs

Once you're comfortable working with VBA objects, you may find Collection objects easier than arrays for handling sets of items. The `Add` and `Remove` methods make resizing the collection effortless. They are also much less likely to result in errors than repeatedly using `ReDim` statements in different parts of your program. (These advantages are especially significant when you must frequently add or remove individual items from the group.)

As a bonus, you can name individual items in the collection so you can retrieve them by name later. This not only gives you an easy-to-remember handle for each element, it makes accessing the data much quicker once your collection contains over about a hundred elements.

Creating Collection objects

Set up a Collection object in your program as you would any other object, using an `As` clause to specify the type of object. As with other objects, you can use either of two variations of the basic technique:

- You can declare a variable name for the object and then use a `Set` statement to create it. Note that you must use the `New` keyword in the `Set` statement to create the new collection:

```
Dim colMixedBag As Collection
...
Set colMixedBag = New Collection ' Create collection
colMixedBag.Add "Howard and Ethel" ' Add a data element
```

- To have VBA create the object automatically the first time you use the variable in your code, you can declare it with the `New` keyword.

```
Dim colSetOfStuff As New Collection
...
' The next statement creates the Collection while
' adding an integer to it.
colSetOfStuff.Add intStuffing
```

Adding data to a collection

Once you've created your collection, use its Add method to fill it with data, just as you would to add objects to your VBA application's built-in collections. The preceding examples show the Add method in action. The complete syntax for the Add method is as follows

```
Add (item[, key][, before index][, after index])
```

The *item* expression is required. It can be a literal value, a variable, an object reference, or a complex expression involving two or more of these components — anything that returns a value VBA recognizes. The remaining terms in the Add method are optional. I won't cover the *before* and *after* terms here, but the *key* term deserves mention.

Although you can refer to an item in a collection by its "slot number," giving the item a meaningful name is important. To do this, supply the name as a string when you add the item to the collection:

```
colFinancials.Add 14323.44, "February sales"
```

The preceding statement adds the value 14323.44 to the colFinancials collection. At the same time, it creates a key, a name, for the item.

The next example boldly adds the built-in Word object ThisDocument (referring to the document containing your VBA project) to a collection and assigns it a key:

```
colGrabBag.Add ThisDocument, "DocKey"
```

Caution

A key isn't just easier to remember than a numeric index — it's the *only* reliable "key" for quick access to an individual item in a collection. Because of the way the Add and Remove methods work, the positions of specific data items in a collection can change. If item 63 becomes item 29, you can still pull out its value if you know its key name.

With collections based on the generic VBA Collection class, the only way to assign a key is with the Add method. To assign a key to an item that doesn't have one, or to change the existing key, you must Add the item all over again and Remove the original copy.

Removing items

To state the obvious, the Remove method deletes an item from the collection. You can identify the object you want to excise by its index number or by its key:

```
colMineral.Remove 2123
```

```
colMineral.Remove "Bauxite"
```

Remember that when you remove an item, VBA fills in the gap, so to speak — the index numbers of all the other items further down in the list decrease by one.

Count-ing your collection

It's easy to lose track of the size of your collection, especially once you `Add` or `Remove` a few items. VBA's generic Collection object has only one property, but it's vital — that's the `Count` property. You can assign it to a variable:

```
intCollectionSize = col20Questions.Count
```

or test it in a conditional expression

```
If colPrices.Count > 1000
    MsgBox "We have too many entries!"
End If
```

Using For Each . . . Next loops to work with collections

Use `For Each...Next` loops to work all of the items in a collection, one at a time. Here's the syntax:

```
For Each objectvariable In collection
(statements to be executed during each pass of the loop)
Next objectvariable
```

One key difference between `For Each...Next` and the standard `For...Next` structure is that you don't have to specify the number of times the loop should execute — VBA figures that out for you. Instead of a counter variable, the `For Each` structure requires an *element* variable that corresponds to the type of object stored in the collection. Of course, you must also indicate which collection you want to work with.

The following simple example of a `For Each...Next` structure works in Word, PowerPoint, or Excel, where the Shapes collection is, of course, a collection of Shape (drawing) objects. The first `For Each...Next` structure simply displays the name of each Shape in the Shapes collection in the immediate window. The second loop looks for a shape named WidgetA and if it finds it, deletes it:

```
' First, place a reference to a document object
' in the someDocument variable.
Dim objS As Shape
For Each objS In someDocument.Shapes
    Debug.Print objS.Name
Next objS
For Each objS In someDocument.Shapes
    If objS.Name = "WidgetA" Then
        objS.Delete
        Exit For
    End If
Next objS
```

The `Exit For` statement lets you leave the loop as soon as you've found the correct item in the collection. If you want to perform some action on every item in the collection, don't include an `Exit For` statement.

Do-It-Yourself Objects: Class Modules

Once you're comfortable using the built-in objects available in VBA, you should eventually begin building your own. While you can perform great feats of legerdemain using standard Sub and Function procedures, compartmentalizing your code into objects can have real advantages. These include:

- By keeping all the code that manipulates a set of data inside a single object, you reduce the opportunities for bugs to creep into your program when you make modifications.
- Your programs are easier to read and understand.
- You can create as many independent copies of an object as you like by writing two quick statements for each copy.
- It can definitely be handy to use the same properties and methods with different object classes. The technical term for this is *polymorphism*.

As you know by now, an object consists of some data (the object's properties) and code that alters that data (its methods). Given that properties are just variables and methods are just procedures, writing the actual code that defines an object is no big deal. But you do have to follow some rules so VBA can figure out what you're trying to do.

Creating class modules

In VBA, a *class* is the pattern upon which an object is based. The class determines which properties, methods, and events the object has, and how each of those components behave. To create a class, you start by inserting a new class module in your VBA project (choose Insert ⇨ Class Module). A class module window looks and works exactly like a code window.

Components of a class definition

The typical class has three main components:

- Private declarations for the variables used internally by the object
- Public property procedures that allow procedures in your standard modules to retrieve or alter current property settings
- Public method procedures that define the actions the object's methods will perform

The simple class definition shown here for a make-believe Thermostat class has all three of these elements. This example does nothing useful, but it does work and it's on the CD-ROM in case you want to try it out. Look in the Excel workbook called VBA examples.xls.

```
Private sngDegrees As Single ' property variable

'Code for the Let Temperature property procedure:
Public Property Let Temperature(ByVal sngInput As _
   Single)
   sngDegrees = sngInput
End Property

'Code for the Get Temperature property procedure:
Public Property Get Temperature() As Single
   Temperature = sngDegrees
End Property

'Code for the CalculateEnergyUse method:
Public Sub CalculateEnergyUse()
   Const cstConversionFactor = 2.45
   Dim dblResult
   dblResult = sngDegrees * 365 * cstConversionFactor
   MsgBox "Annual energy use for this thermostat" & _
      " setting is estimated at " & dblResult & _
      " watts."
End Sub
```

Declaring class variables

Use the Declarations section at the top of the class module to declare any variables you plan to access in more than one property or method. Always declare them as `Private`. After all, the whole point of objects is to ensure that your program can't access the data directly. Variables that you use only in one property or method should be declared there.

At a minimum, you need to declare a variable for each of the object's properties. The variable name should *not* be the name of the property (I'll show you how to define the property's name in a moment). But you can also declare other data that the object uses internally and that won't be accessible to other parts of your program.

Writing property procedures

The secret to endowing an object with a property is write a pair of special procedures, the `Let` and `Get` *property procedures*. Both procedures in each pair should have the same name.

The name of a property is the name you choose for the property's `Let` and `Get` procedures. The name should describe the content or function of the property, of course.

One other point: If you're creating a property representing an object reference, you substitute a `Property Set` procedure for a `Property Let` procedure as half of the property procedure pair. Otherwise, such properties work the same as properties of other data types.

Setting object properties with Property Let procedures

A `Property Let` procedure sets the value of a property. In its simplest form, a `Property Let` procedure takes a value supplied as an argument, assigning that value to a variable that represents the property. To repeat the previous example:

```
Public Property Let Temperature (ByVal sngInput As _
   Single)
      sngDegrees = sngInput
End Property
```

When in the main part of your program you write a statement that sets the property, such as `Thermostat.Temperature = 75` VBA calls the `Let Temperature` procedure with 75 as the argument.

Of course, your property procedures aren't limited to one line of code. You can add statements that check the argument to ensure it falls in a valid range before you assign it to the property. You can also perform other actions depending on the particular argument.

Retrieving object properties with Property Get procedures

A `Property Get` procedure works like a Function procedure, in that it returns a value — the value of the property, of course. As in a Function procedure, you assign the value you want it to return to the procedure name — which also happens to be the property name. Here's the example code again:

```
Public Property Get Temperature() As Single
    Temperature = sngDegrees
End Property
```

Other parts of your program can call the `Get Temperature` procedure to assign its return value to a variable, or test the return value in conditional statements:

```
sngCurrentSetting = Thermostat.Temperature
```

or

```
If Thermostat.Temperature > 80
    MsgBox "Consider turning down the heater!"
EndIf
```

Writing methods

Methods are simply ordinary Sub and Function procedures that you happen to store in a class module. In most cases, of course, a method should do something directly related to the object itself, by manipulating the data stored in the object. VBA automatically associates the methods with their class, so that you can call them from other parts of the program just as you would the methods of built-in objects.

Using your custom objects

You use an object based on one of your own classes in just the same way you would work with the built-in objects of VBA and your application. The steps are:

1. Declare a variable for the object, as in:

   ```
   objCustomThermostat = Thermostat
   ```

2. Use a Set statement to create the actual object you'll be working with:

   ```
   Set objCustomThermostat = New Thermostat
   ```

3. Access the object's properties or trigger its methods using the standard VBA dot syntax, as in:

   ```
   objCustomThermostat.Temperature = 65
   objCustomThermostat.Calcu2lateEnergyCosts
   ```

4. Release memory when finished using the object:

   ```
   Set objCustomThermostat = Nothing
   ```

The VBA examples.xls Excel workbook on the CD-ROM contains a procedure called CustomObjectDemo that illustrates these four steps applied to the Thermostat class.

Conclusion

VBA may not pass muster as a "pure" object-oriented language, but its objects still provide many great benefits to the software developer. Of course, you first have to learn how they work — and that was the subject of this chapter. Chapter 23 takes on the all-important topic of error prevention, detection, and correction.

Chapter 23

Unbreakable Code: Debugging and Error Trapping

In This Chapter

- Essential concepts of bug fixing and error management
- How wonderful it is — when you're hunting bugs — to run in break mode
- All the debugging tools of the Visual Basic Editor, including the Step commands and the Immediate, Locals, and Watch windows
- Sophisticated error-handling techniques to ease the pain when run-time errors occur

Writing VBA code is the easy part. It's getting that code to run, and then to produce the expected results, that takes real work. Hunting down and stamping out bugs is a crucial part of the coding process, and in this chapter you can learn how it's done in VBA. I also cover error trapping, which allows a program to respond gracefully when something goes wrong while it's running.

What Can Go Wrong, Will Go Wrong

Three main kinds of problems can beset the programs you write in VBA or most any language. They are:

- **Compile errors.** Syntax and other errors that prevent the program from running in the first place.
- **Logic errors.** Flaws in the program's design that cause it to do something you don't want it to do, or not to do something you do want it to — the program runs, but it doesn't run correctly.
- **Run-time errors.** These bring the program to a halt while it is running. Run-time errors can result from big-time logic errors, or from encountering unexpected conditions.

Of the three, syntax errors are definitely the easiest to uncover and correct. I mention them only briefly, spending most of my time in this chapter on detecting and eliminating the other two types, the true bugs.

Fixing syntax errors

When you make the first type of mistake, a syntax error, the Visual Basic Editor helps you figure out what you did wrong before you try to run the program. As soon as you type something that the Editor can't figure out, it displays the line in red. Then if you've checked the box labeled Auto Syntax Check in the Editor tab of the Tools ⇨ Options dialog box, you get a message clarifying the problem as soon as you move the insertion point off the line. For example, if you type If x = 3 but forget to type Then, the message is "Compile error: Expected: Then or GoTo." (VBA doesn't catch some syntax errors until you try to run the program.)

Once you know you made the mistake, correcting a syntax error is relatively easy. If you have any doubt about the right way to code what you're trying to accomplish, consult the relevant section here or look up the item in the VBA Help system.

Debugging for VBA programmers

After you get past all the compile errors and your program starts running, it's natural to feel an immediate wave of pride and relief. But when the program reports that 2 + 2 = 22 or all the text in your document turns chartreuse, you know that there's a mistake in your code somewhere.

These are examples of errors in program logic. The program is running, and in fact it is doing exactly what you told it to do. The problem is, what you *told* it to do with the code you wrote isn't what you actually *wanted* it to do. Your job is to track down exactly which statements led to the wrong outcome. This process is called *debugging* your program. The tools and techniques you can use in your debugging campaigns are all cataloged in this section.

Of course, the same debugging techniques you use to stamp out logic errors are vital in preventing the many run-time errors that result from logic errors. But because no program can anticipate every possible circumstance it might face, you should still incorporate code to handle run-time errors in any program destined for others' use.

Test, test, test

It's handy when errors announce themselves by displaying obviously wrong answers or turning things on the screen weird colors. Unfortunately, many logic errors are more subtle, and many run-time errors occur only intermittently. Instead of assuming that your program is going to work properly when freshly hatched, budget plenty of time for testing it under different conditions.

Chapter 23: Unbreakable Code: Debugging and Error Trapping **503**

If the program is supposed to work with different documents, test it by running it with different documents. Try running the program when two or three documents are open in your VBA application — and when no document at all is open. See what happens if you run the program when the document window is in different states (minimized, maximized, or restored). Start the program when different items or groups of items are selected in the document window.

If the program requires input from the user via an input box or custom form, make all kinds of typical and outlandish test entries to see what happens. If the required value is supposed to be an integer, try floating-point, date, and string entries to see how the program responds. Likewise, if the program works with date or time values, see what it does with different dates — including February 29 — and different times of day — including midnight.

If you do find any mistakes, it's time to start debugging in earnest. But if not, don't assume they aren't there — assume instead that they are.

Using break mode for debugging

The key to debugging a program is to use VBA's *break mode*. In break mode, your program has begun running but is suspended at a particular statement in the code. Because the program is still live, you can inspect the current values of all the variables. Beginning from that point, you can use the Step commands to run the program one statement at a time, watching the variables change to see whether you're getting the expected results at each step in the process. Later sections have the details on working with variables and the Step commands.

Figure 23-1 shows a VBA procedure in break mode. With the exception of a yellow highlight and arrow marking the next statement to be executed, the Visual Basic Editor looks almost exactly as it does when you're writing or editing code.

Secret

In fact, in break mode, you can actually edit the code while your program is running, making changes or adding brand new lines as whim or necessity dictates. This isn't at all a frill, but a key debugging feature that you should train yourself to take advantage of — more on this later.

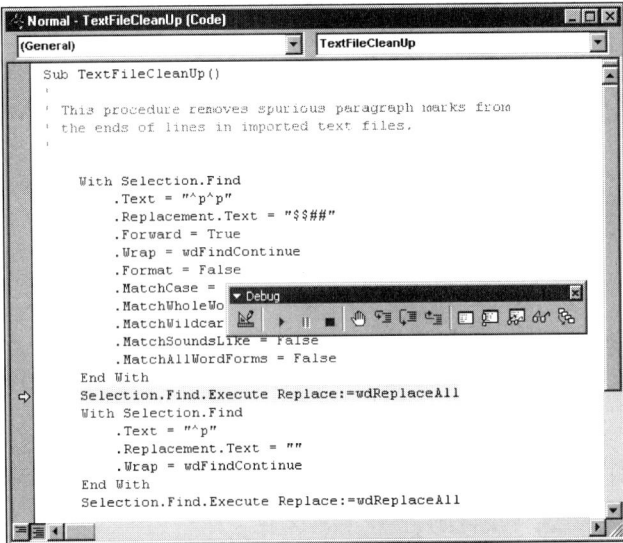

Figure 23-1: A VBA procedure in break mode

Entering break mode

You can use a variety of techniques to put a program into the break mode state of suspended animation. Here's the full list:

- Start the program in break mode from the outset using the Step Into command (see "Steppin' through code").

- Set a *breakpoint* on a line of code. When a running program reaches the statement at the breakpoint, it suspends execution and enters break mode.

- Place a Stop statement in your code. When the program runs, it enters break mode ready to execute the statement following the Stop statement.

- Click the Break button, choose Run ➪ Break, or press Ctrl+Break while the program is running. This is the technique to use to get back control of a runaway program that won't stop on its own. Where you end up when the program enters break mode is anyone's guess, but at least you can see what's going on when you get there.

- Create a Break When True or Break When Changed *watch*. The program enters break mode when the value of the watch expression becomes True or undergoes any change.

One other way a program can enter break mode is when a run-time error occurs. VBA displays a dialog box describing the error (see Figure 23-2). Clicking the End button stops the program altogether, but clicking Debug puts it into break mode. You have some control over which run-time errors trigger break mode in the General tab of the Tools ➪ Options dialog box.

Chapter 23: Unbreakable Code: Debugging and Error Trapping

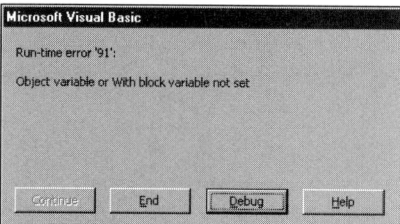

Figure 23-2: A run-time error dialog box

Setting breakpoints

When you suspect a section of code contains a logical error, place a breakpoint just before the miscreant statements. In Figure 23-3, that highlight and the big dot in the margin of the code window show how the Visual Basic Editor represents a breakpoint on the screen.

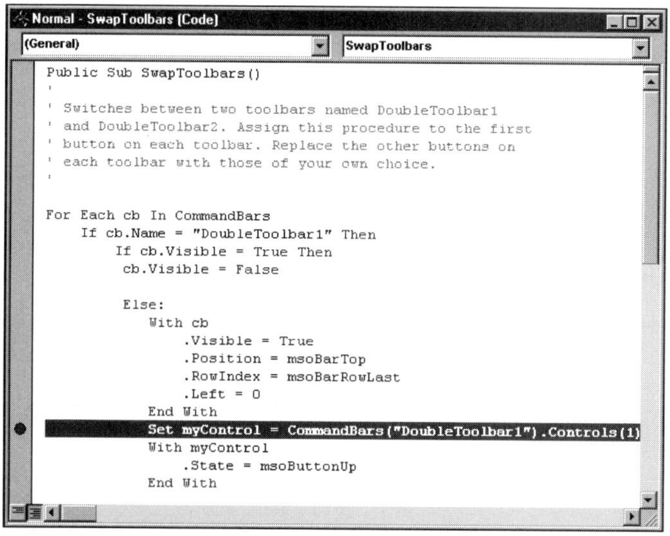

Figure 23-3: When you set a breakpoint, the Visual Basic Editor highlights the line of code before which program execution should stop.

With a breakpoint in place, you can run the program at full speed up to that point, bypassing code that (you hope) works properly. When VBA gets to the statement with the breakpoint, it suspends the program. Once break mode is active, you can examine the variables and then use the Step commands to see how they change as VBA executes each dubious statement one at a time.

To set a breakpoint, all you have to do is click in the margin of the code window next to the target line of code. With the keyboard, put the insertion point on the correct line and press F9.

You can set breakpoints on as many executable statements as you like. However, you can't set breakpoints on comments, of course, nor on statements that VBA doesn't actually execute, such as variable declarations.

Secret

Keep in mind that VBA stops the program and switches into break mode after executing the statement just prior to the breakpoint. In other words, the statement at the breakpoint hasn't been executed yet and will be the next to go when the program continues.

Clearing breakpoints

After you correct the errant code, or give up on fixing it for now, you *clear* the breakpoint to remove it. This allows VBA to execute the program normally the next time you run it. The same techniques you used to set a breakpoint — clicking in the Code window margin, or pressing F9 — will clear an existing one.

To deep-six all breakpoints, choose Debug ➪ Clear All Breakpoints or press Ctrl+Shift+F9. Once you do, they're history — Undo won't restore them.

Knowing where you're at in break mode

When a program is running in break mode, the Visual Basic Editor always highlights the statement that will be executed next. To make sure you get the message, there's an arrow in the Code window margin pointing to the same "next statement." Figure 23-4 provides a reminder of how this looks, though the black-and-white image leaves much to the imagination.

When you have the next statement on the screen, there's no mistaking that highlight. But what happens if you start scrolling to other parts of your code or jump to the Code windows of other modules? You may have trouble finding the next statement again.

Secret

That's where the suitably named Show Next Statement command comes in. When you choose Debug ➪ Show Next Statement, the Visual Basic Editor whisks you straight to the statement in question. Another command lets you select a different statement as the next statement, but I cover that later, in the section "Choosing a different next statement."

Chapter 23: Unbreakable Code: Debugging and Error Trapping

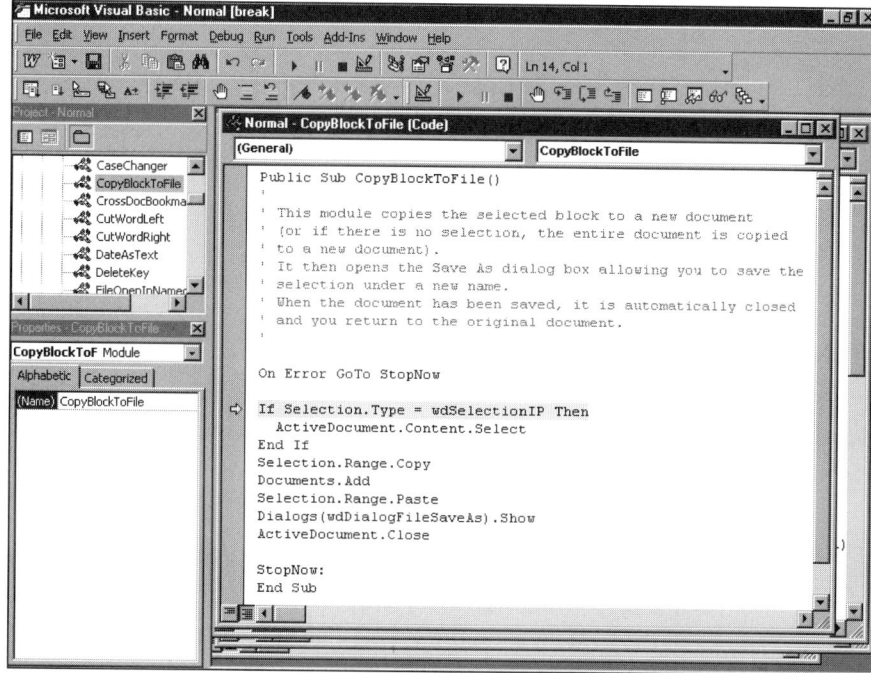

Figure 23-4: You can't miss the statement that's next in line for execution, as long as it's visible on the screen anyway.

A breakpoint alternative: the Stop statement

Breakpoints are super easy to use, but they have one drawback — they're only temporary. When you're debugging a complex program, you may not be able to set things right in a single session. Because breakpoints aren't stored with your code, they'll be gone the next time you open the project in the Visual Basic Editor.

The Stop statement is the solution to this problem. Add it to your code wherever you want the program to switch to break mode. Like any other code you type, Stop statements are saved when you save the project.

Monsieur or Madame, do you crave an example? Allow me to oblige:

```
...
intDataFromMars = GetDataFromMars(1.5454)
Stop
MsgBox "The result is " & intDataFromMars / Z
...
```

You can guess that the Stop statement is being used to probe suspect results displayed in the message box. Once it has been added, the Stop statement forces the program into break mode just after a function procedure has set the value of a variable. You can now look at the values of both variables involved in the next calculation to see which of them seems out of line.

Getting out of break mode

When you're through with break mode, at least for the time being, you can tell VBA to resume normal program execution. Any of the commands you can use to run a program in the first place will work. In break mode, the Run menu item and toolbar button look the same and are in the same places but their names are changed — both are now called Continue. F5 is still the keyboard shortcut. A Continued program will pop back into break mode if it runs into another breakpoint, or if any of the other conditions that activate break mode occur.

To stop running the program altogether, use the Reset command. There's a Reset button and a Reset item on the Run menu, but no equivalent keyboard shortcut.

Steppin' through code

Like all good debuggers, the Visual Basic Editor enables you to run your program one statement, or step, at a time. Slowing things down in this way is a fantastic way to catch the very point at which some logic error knocks a critical value out of whack. It's fun, too.

Secret

To make the best use of this *step execution* technique, you need a way to see the values of your variables as your program modifies them. The Editor's way cool Auto Data Tips feature is always available for this purpose, but the Locals and Watch windows give you more details and enable you to change the values if the need arises. I cover all these features a bit later.

So now about the three Step commands you can use in the Visual Basic Editor: Step Into, Step Over, and Step Out. You can access all three commands via the Debug menu, as buttons on the Debug toolbar, or by way of keyboard shortcuts.

Stepping into code

The Step Into command is the one to use when you want to execute each and every statement in your program in proper sequence. Each time you invoke this command, VBA runs the next statement in your program and then returns to break mode, where you can see what changes have been wrought. Pressing F8 is the most efficient way to invoke the Step Into command.

This command gets its name because it steps into other procedures that your program calls as it runs. When the next statement calls a Sub or Function procedure, invoking the Step Into command opens the called procedure in the Code window, where you can step through it to see what it's doing. This is different from the way the Step Over command works, as you'll see shortly.

Secret

The Step Into command is available even when you're not already in break mode. If you want to step through the program beginning at the beginning, just give the Step Into command to run the first statement and enter break mode. Used in this way, Step Into runs the procedure containing the insertion point, always starting from the procedure's first line.

Stepping over and out

The Step Over command works just like Step Into, with two exceptions:

- Most important, Step Over doesn't step though the individual statements in a called procedure.
- You can't start running a program in break mode with Step Over.

When the next statement calls another procedure, Step Over runs the whole procedure in one gulp, going on to the following statement in the current procedure. This is great when you just want to see whether the procedure as a whole does anything goofy before bothering to check it out in detail. Obviously, stepping over a procedure is also a big timesaver when you're already fairly sure that the procedure works as it's supposed to.

The Step Out command is a handy complement to Step Into. Once you get inside the bowels of a called procedure, you may decide that everything is OK, or you may locate the error and fix it. More embarrassingly, you may just have clicked the Step Into button when you meant to click Step Over (this is the most common scenario in my case).

In any event, there's no point in hanging around to step through the procedure's remaining statements. Use the Step Out command to run the rest of the procedure at top speed. VBA returns you to the procedure from whence you came, highlighting the statement following the procedure call.

Major manipulations during debugging

In break mode, just because you're running your program doesn't mean the program's course is fixed in stone. VBA is sophisticated enough to allow midcourse corrections. Specifically, you can edit the existing code and alter the sequence in which statements get executed.

Adding and editing code in break mode

The Code window's editing features are fully operational during break mode. You can type in new statements, modify existing ones, or delete them altogether. But what's really special is that most of your changes work immediately, becoming part of the running program. For example, you can declare new variables and use them right away in calculations, perhaps in combination with existing variables. Some edits do bring the program to a halt, such as changing a variable to a different type in its declaration.

Choosing a different next statement

Suppose you're stepping through your code in break mode when you realize that the next statement contains a big mistake. Rather than execute the statement and send your program in a tailspin, you can choose to bypass it altogether until you've had a chance to make it right.

The Visual Basic Editor lets you select a different statement almost anywhere in your code as the next statement, using either the keyboard or the mouse. You can jump forward or backward in the code. In addition to letting you skip over foul code, this also lets you repeat statements until you're sure you understand how they work.

Just realize that variables retain the values they have before you make the change. These values may well be very different than what they are when the program reaches the code running normally. If necessary, you can give the variables any value you like using the Immediate, Watch, or Locals windows, described later.

If you can keep all that in mind, here's how to select a different next statement:

- With the keyboard, move the insertion point onto the line containing the statement. Then press Ctrl+F9 or choose Debug ⇨ Set Next Statement.

- With the mouse, drag the yellow arrow pointer in the Code window margin to the new next statement (see Figure 23-5).

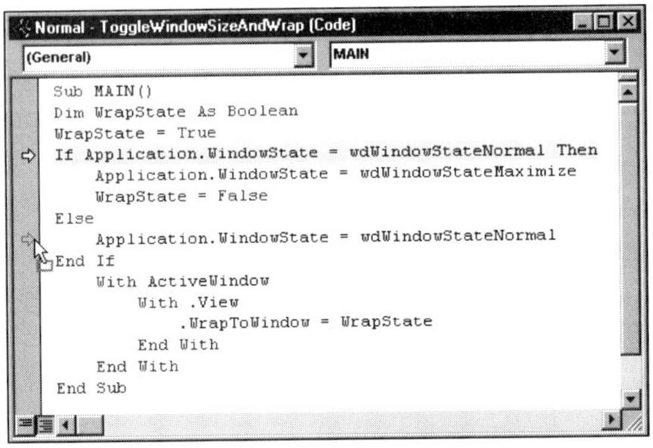

Figure 23-5: Selecting a different next statement lets you repeat blocks of code whose functioning you want to study.

Other Ways to Skip Over Code

You have other options for skipping over code that you know is broken. These methods work whether you're step-executing a program in break mode or editing the code before you run it. One approach is to type in an apostrophe at the beginning of each line you want to skip, turning it into a comment. You can use the Comment Block toolbar button to comment the current line, if you haven't selected anything, or all lines of a selected block of code (see "Long-winded comments" in Chapter 21).

Sometimes an even better way to skip over code is by using line labels in conjunction with temporary GoTo statements. When the following code runs, VBA completely skips all the statements between `GoTo AfterTheSkip` and the statement following the `AfterTheSkip:` label. When you're ready to run the skipped code again, just remove the GoTo statement or turn it into a comment ("comment it out").

```
...
GoTo AfterTheSkip
    A = B + C
    D = A + E/F
    G = B + D
AfterTheSkip:
    MsgBox "Today is " & Format(Now, "dddd")
...
```

Seeing Data Tips

VBA's Auto Data Tips feature enables you to see the current value of any variable wherever it appears in your code. While you're in break mode, hovering the mouse pointer over any variable pops up the Data Tips window, a little box containing the name and current value of that variable. Figure 23-6 shows Auto Data Tips in action.

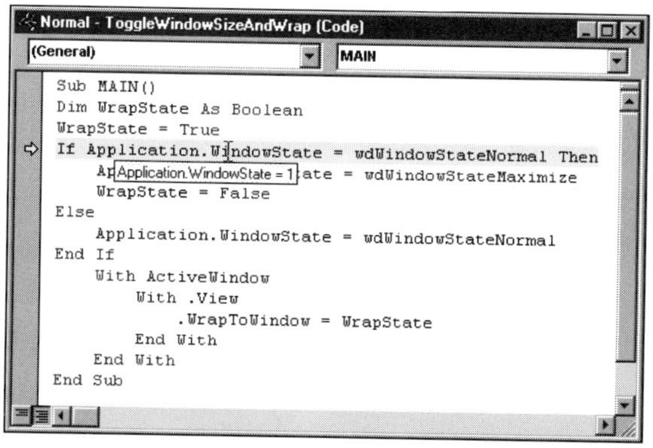

```
Sub MAIN()
Dim WrapState As Boolean
WrapState = True
If Application.WindowState = wdWindowStateNormal Then
    Ap|Application.WindowState = 1|ate = wdWindowStateMaximize
    WrapState = False
Else
    Application.WindowState = wdWindowStateNormal
End If
    With ActiveWindow
        With .View
            .WrapToWindow = WrapState
        End With
    End With
End Sub
```

Figure 23-6: The little Auto Data Tips box shows the value of the variable beneath the mouse pointer.

In case you don't see the Auto Data Tips box when you should, check to be sure its box is checked in the Editor tab of the Tools ➪ Options dialog box.

You can use a different Editor feature to display the type and scope of a variable, though not so automatically. Place the insertion point in or beside the variable name and press Ctrl+I to pop up a Quick Info box containing that information. You don't have to be in break mode to use this feature, which is especially helpful when you're working in the middle of a long program whose variables were declared at the top. Figure 23-7 shows the sort of information you get.

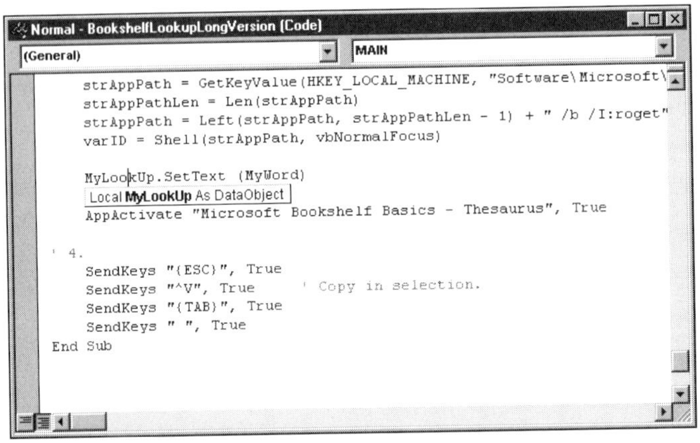

Figure 23-7: Displaying a Quick Info box for a variable.

Immediate Gratifications

Displayed by pressing Ctrl+G, and shown in Figure 23-8, the Immediate window lets you do two things:

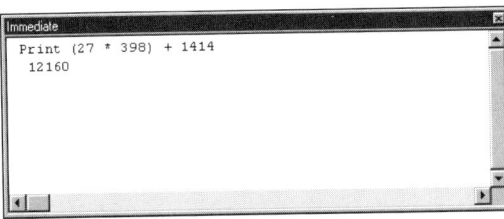

Figure 23-8: The Immediate window in action.

- See the values of calculations and variables using the Debug.Print method.
- Execute individual code statements directly, without running them inside a procedure. To execute a statement in the Immediate window, just type it in and press Enter.

So what good are these talents, you ask? Allow me to list the benefits:

- You can use the Immediate window as a crude calculator. If you type an expression such as

    ```
    Print (27 * 398) + 1414
    ```

    and press Enter, you get the result, well, Immediate-ly. When you work in the Immediate window, you don't have to specify the Debug object.

- You can route intermediate values of variables and expressions at various points in a running program to the Immediate window by placing the Debug.Print method in the program's code (not the Immediate window itself). After the program terminates, you can quickly check to see whether it produced the correct results, without displaying a message box for each value. Figure 23-9 shows an example of this technique.

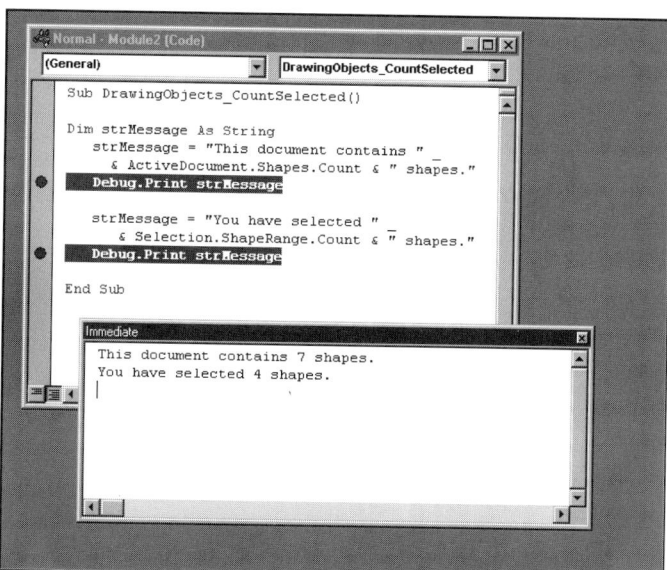

Figure 23-9: Output from a program that uses the Debug.Print method

- During break mode, you can display the value of any variable or object property in the Immediate window with a print statement, or change the value by typing a standard assignment such as:

    ```
    intTheirNumber = 25
    ```

- You can also call Sub and Function procedures just as you normally would. Note that during break mode, statements you execute in the Immediate window can access only those variables, objects, and procedures within the scope of the procedure that's currently executing in the program. In other words, executing a statement in the Immediate window produces the same effect as typing it into the running procedure and executing it there.

From the interesting facts department: You can Ctrl-drag selected text from the Code window to the Immediate window, which means you don't have to retype long expressions or variable names if you want to use them there (if you don't hold down Ctrl as you drag, the code is moved, not copied, to the Immediate window). The F1 key works in the Immediate window as it does in Code windows, displaying Help on whatever keyword the insertion point lies within. However, Auto Data Tips does not function there.

Keeping an Eye on the Locals (Window)

If you have room to display it, the Locals window should be on your screen at all times when you're debugging a program in break mode. Bring it into view by clicking its button on the Debug toolbar, or by selecting the corresponding item on the View menu.

Shown in Figure 23-10, the Locals window automatically displays all the variables accessible in the current procedure, showing their names, values, and data types. The Visual Basic Editor updates the information each time you execute a statement, so what you see in the Locals window always reflects the current values.

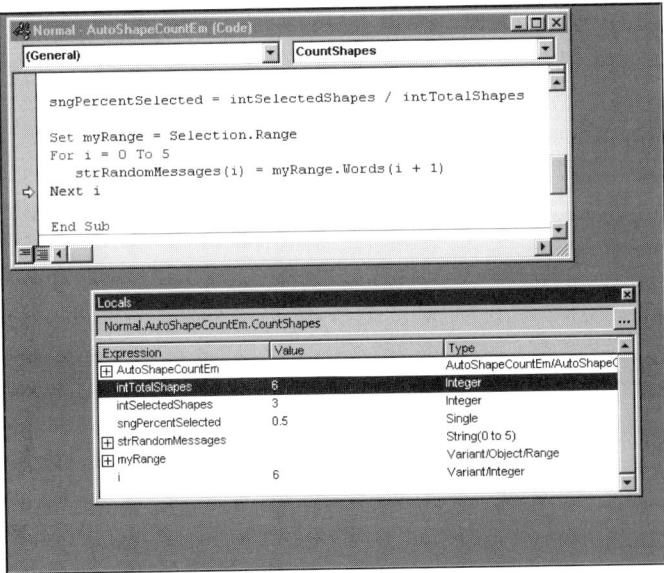

Figure 23-10: The Locals window during break mode.

Local mechanics

Like most Visual Basic Editor windows, the Locals window is dockable by default but can also be displayed as a free-floating separate window. Chapter 20 covers the basics of working with Editor windows.

If you can't see all the information in a column, remember that you can resize the columns. Position the mouse pointer over a column separator in the gray column header just above the main part of the window. When the pointer becomes a double-headed arrow, drag to the left or right to change the widths of the adjacent columns.

If you look back to Figure 23-10, you can see that some rows list individual variables, while others show items such as arrays, variables of user-defined types, and objects. Such items have no values of their own but instead, hold variables and other "container" items. When you begin running a procedure, the Locals window lists them in collapsed form — you can't see the subsidiary items they contain. To expand a collapsed item, click the boxed plus sign to its left.

Secret

Only variables declared (implicitly or explicitly) in the currently running procedure appear already expanded at the top level of the Locals window hierarchy. To see module-level variables accessible to all procedures in the current module, expand the very first item in the Locals window. This item always pertains to the module in which the current procedure is running. You can't work with global variables or those in other projects in the Locals windows.

Why edit variable values?

Before I tell you how to change a variable's value, you should probably know why you might want to. Here are some good reasons:

- A previous line of code has an error in it that assigned an incorrect value to the variable. You've caught the mistake, but you want to continue stepping through the program. Before you go on, change the variable's value to what it should have been, so that the mistake won't affect subsequent statements.

- You want to test various alternative values for the variable without changing your code. You can use the Set Next Statement command to repeatedly pass through the same stretch of code, entering different values in the Locals window each time.

- The values that the program will use when it runs in real life aren't currently available to it. For example, the program may read information from a database or the Internet. In this case, you can supply simulated values via the Locals window.

How to edit variable values

To change the value of a variable in the Locals window, follow these steps:

1. Click twice (don't double-click) directly over the variable's current value in the window to so that only the value is highlighted. Clicking elsewhere on the same row simply selects the whole line.

2. Type in the new value. If you're typing a string value, you must include beginning and ending quotation marks. Similarly, enclose date literals with # characters.

3. If you change your mind, you can cancel your entry and restore the previous one by pressing Esc. Otherwise, press Enter to confirm it. The Editor won't accept an invalid value, and you may get an error message telling you what was wrong with your entry.

You can edit any variable's values, including those of individual members of arrays and user-defined types. Just realize that you have to expand the array or user-defined type variable before you can get to its member data elements. With an object variable, you can't change the object that's assigned to it, but you can edit the object's properties (except the read-only ones). Again, you must expand the object to see the editable items. Figure 23-11 shows expanded array, user-defined type, and object variables.

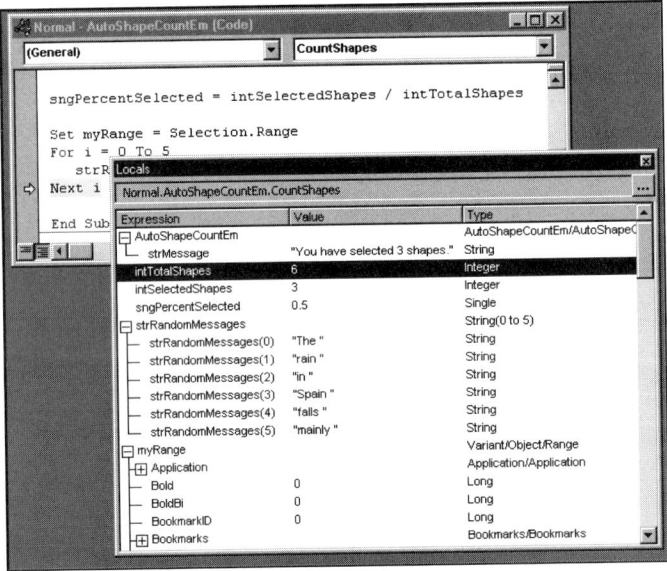

Figure 23-11: The Locals window displays the same procedure shown in Figure 23-10, but items that were collapsed are now expanded.

The Watch Window: A Key Debugging Tool

Once you've mastered the Locals window, working with the Watch window is a piece of pie. It works in essentially the same way, the obvious difference being that *you* get to pick out which values it displays. Figure 23-12 shows the Watch window in action.

Chapter 23: Unbreakable Code: Debugging and Error Trapping

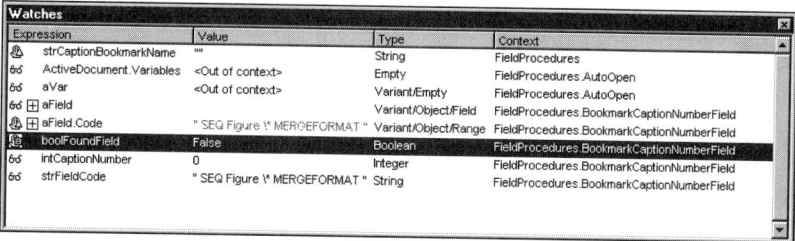

Figure 23-12: The Visual Basic Editor's Watch window

Secret

Use the Watch window when you're debugging larger programs in which many different procedures manipulate global variables. By adding these global variables to the Watch window, you can track their current value no matter what part of the program you're currently stepping through.

The Watch window appears automatically as soon as you define a *watch expression*. If you want more room on the screen, however, you can put it away by clicking the Close button at the upper right.

What else is different compared to the Locals window

Besides the fact that what appears in the window is up to you, the Watch window differs from the Locals window in two other important ways:

- Each line in the Watch window lets you track the value of any valid VBA expression, not just an individual variable. Expressions such as `(X - Y) > 15`, `"The color is " & strColor`, or even `2 + 2` are perfectly acceptable. That's why entries are called watch expressions.

- Because the Watch window can track variables from any module or procedure in the project, it adds a fourth column labeled Context. This column describes the scope in which the window displays a value for the variable or expression. When you're executing a procedure outside the defined context, all you see is "<Out of context>."

Adding watch expressions

If you like having options, you'll love the Watch window — prepare to be overwhelmed by how many different ways you can add watch expressions.

No matter which technique you eventually use, you should start in the Code window by selecting the variable or expression you want to watch. When I say "selecting," I mean selecting the entire item as you would in a word processor, by highlighting it with the mouse or Shift+cursor keys.

However, if you want to watch only an independent variable (in other words, an item that's not an object property or an element in a user-defined type) you don't actually have to select the whole thing—putting the insertion point within the variable name will do.

Now for that "overwhelming" list of techniques. You can add a watch based on the selected expression by:

- Right-clicking the selection and choosing Add Watch to bring up the Add Watch window
- Choosing Debug ⇨ Add Watch, which also displays the Add Watch dialog box
- Clicking the Quick Watch button on the Debug toolbar, or choosing Debug ⇨ Quick Watch. The Editor shows you a confirmatory message describing the watch expression you're about to add, but you can't change anything.
- Dragging the selection to the Watch window. This creates the watch without any intermediate steps.

If you're a diehard do-it-yourselfer, you don't actually need to select anything in the Code window. You can just click the Add Watch button and then type in the expression of interest from scratch in the Add Watch dialog box.

Working with the Add Watch window

Figure 23-13 shows the Add Watch window, which appears when you select Add Watch on the Debug menu, or on the Code window's shortcut menu. Here, you define the details of your watch expression.

The Expression field is, of course, where you specify the expression you want to watch. If you selected the correct variable or expression before you started, you shouldn't have to change anything here. But you can if you want to.

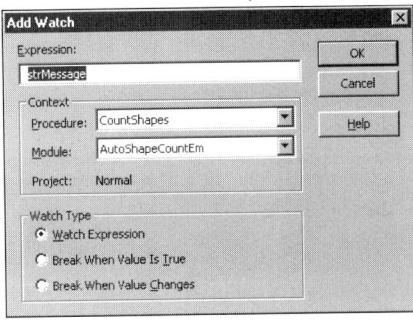

Figure 23-13: The Add Watch dialog box.

The Context section of the dialog box lets you define the procedures in which the Visual Basic Editor actually calculates and displays the value of the watch expression. The values for the Procedure and Module choices are initially set to the procedure in which the variable appeared when you added the watch. If you want to see the value when a different procedure is running, select it by name. If that procedure is in a different module, you must first select its module and then choose the procedure.

Secret

If you want the variable value to remain visible no matter which procedure in a given module is executing, select "(All procedures)," the very first item in the Procedures list. And if you want to see it *always* — throughout the whole program — select "(All modules)" in the Modules list. The broader the scope you select, the longer it takes for VBA to calculate and report the value. Still, being able to track a variable wherever you are in the program is often worth the short wait.

For a normal watch expression, leave the Watch Type set to watch expression. I explain the other choices a bit in "Using watch expressions to define breakpoints" around the next bend.

Editing watch expressions

Secret

The easiest way to modify an existing watch expression is to type changes in the Expression column of the Watch window. Click once on the line containing the expression to select it, and then click again directly on the expression itself to highlight it. You can then edit the expression to taste.

As in the Locals window, you can also change the value of a variable while the program is running. However, you can't change the Context setting for a watch expression in the Watch window.

Instead, you have to bring up the Edit Watch dialog box, a spittin' image of the Add Watch box shown back in Figure 23-13. Edit Watch is a choice on the Debug window and on the shortcut menu for the Watch window. Once the dialog box is open, you can make changes to the expression's context or type or to the expression itself, just as when you originally defined the watch.

Using watch expressions to define breakpoints

Secret

The larger a program gets, the harder it is to keep track of which procedures and statements are changing which variables. Often, you suspect that a variable's final value is incorrect, but you're not sure where to look for the code that caused the problem. In this situation, a breakpoint based on a watch expression can be a lifesaver — or at least a codesaver.

Using the Watch Type option buttons in the Add Watch or Edit Watch dialog box, you can set up two different types of these automatic breaks:

- You can have your program automatically enter break mode as soon as it executes any statement that changes an expression to a nonzero value — in VBA, remember, 0 is False and everything else is True. Select Break When Value Is True for this type of breakpoint.

- You can automatically enter break mode immediately after the program executes any statement that changes the value of an expression. Select Break When Value Changes for this type of breakpoint.

Their special talents notwithstanding, these "breaking" watch expressions still function as ordinary watches in the Watch window. You can distinguish watches of different types, though, by differences in the little icons at the far left of each item. You can sort of see them if you squint real hard at Figure 23-14, but on the screen they're easy to pick out. When a watch-based breakpoint is triggered by a value change, VBA suspends program execution and enters break mode. In the Code window, the statement that caused the change is the one just before the highlighted next statement. The watch expression that triggered the break is highlighted in the Watch window so that you'll know which one did it (see Figure 23-14).

Trapping Wild Bugs with On Error and the Error Object

When something goes unexpectedly wrong while a program is running, the result is often catastrophic. VBA brings the program to a grinding halt, popping up a run-time error dialog box to give you the bad news about what went wrong, tersely. The choices in the dialog box are End (to terminate the program), Debug (enter break mode), and Help (to display a Help topic about the specific error you've run into).

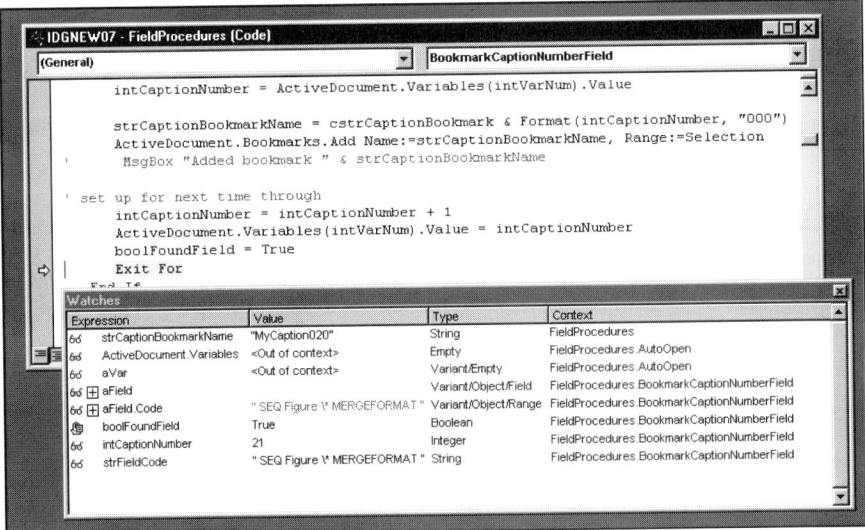

Figure 23-14: A "break when value changes" watch expression on variable intItHappened has just dropped the program into break mode.

None of these options is particularly appealing, especially if you're running the program for real, rather than testing it. It would be far less jarring if your program could detect the error and correct it — or at least sidestep it — before VBA muscles in with that ominous run-time error message. Failing that, you might at least present the user with a more congenial message. All this is possible, but it requires you to add your own error-handling code. This section tells you how.

Where run-time errors come from

As I previously mentioned — but will repeat here because it was so long ago — run-time errors can occur for two reasons:

- A serious error in your program's logic produces a situation that VBA can't deal with. Let's haul out the customary example for one more performance: Suppose you have written a statement in which a value gets divided by a variable. If your code assigns that variable a value of zero, you're sunk — dividing by zero is strictly forbidden and trying to will give your computer a seizure, so VBA stops the program.

- Some unforeseen circumstance has sideswiped your program. For example, a required connection to a database file or Internet set may be cut off, so your program can't retrieve values it needs to do its work.

Either way, the outcome is the same. Protect your program and your users by writing your own error-handling code.

How error-handling code works

To prevent VBA from dealing with run-time errors and take care of them yourself, you must adorn each procedure with an *error handler* — a block of code whose sole purpose is to step in when an error occurs. If something goes wrong as the procedure runs, VBA transfers program execution to the error handler. The code in the error handler can figure out what type of error has occurred and take whatever steps you think the situation warrants.

How to write error-handling code

To add error-handling code to a procedure, you must do three things:

- Add an `On Error` statement at the beginning of the procedure to tell VBA where the error handler code is.

- Type in an `Exit Sub` or `Exit Function` statement following the body of the procedure, just before the error handler code.

- Write the code for the error handler itself.

All the steps are vital — without the initial `On Error` statement, VBA doesn't know the error handler exists.

Writing On Error statements

The On Error statement enables the error handler by telling VBA where to find the error handler in the procedure code. The full statement has the syntax On Error GoTo *label*, where *label* is a label elsewhere in the procedure identifying the first line of the error handler's code.

Here's how it looks in a procedure:

```
Sub ErrorHandlerDemo()
On Error GoTo ErrorHandler
    MamaVariable = DoThisFunction (X,Y,Z)
    PapaVariable = DoThatProcedure
    BabyVariable = MamaVariable + PapaVariable
Exit Sub ' Stop the procedure here if no error has occurred
ErrorHandler:
(error-handling code goes here)
End Sub
```

You should know about two other forms of the On Error statement. They work as follows:

- On Error GoTo 0 disables error handling from this point forward in the procedure and clears the Err object.

- On Error Resume Next causes VBA to ignore the line causing the error, continuing execution with the following line of code. This arrangement is useful if you want to check the Err object just after an error-prone line runs to handle any errors in the body of the procedure.

Adding an Exit statement to the procedure

An error handler is part and parcel of the procedure in which it appears. That means VBA will execute the code in the error handler every time the procedure runs—unless you explicitly tell it not to. Obviously, this isn't right. You want the error handler to run only when an error occurs, and at no other time.

To make this happen, all you need to do is add an Exit statement immediately before the error handler code, as shown in the example in the preceding section, "Writing On Error statements." If you're writing a Sub procedure, the exit statement should be Exit Sub; for a Function procedure, it should be Exit Function.

Writing the error handler

The error handler itself requires several components, described over the next several subsections.

Adding a label

To identify the start of your error-handling code, enter a standard VBA label as the first line of the error handler. As I explained before, the On Error statement for the procedure directs execution to this label if an error occurs. In this example, ThisIsTheErrorHandler is the required label.

```
...
ThisIsTheErrorHandler:
...
    (Error handling statements)
...
End Sub
```

Getting information about and dealing with the error

The body of your error handler has two main tasks: checking to see what type of error has occurred and doing something about it. Although these chores differ conceptually, they go on almost simultaneously in practice.

The standard method for learning what has gone wrong is to use VBA's Err object. If you know that a particular variable has a tendency to go haywire, you might want to check it directly to see whether its value is out of bounds before looking at the Err object. Otherwise, however, the Err object is the ticket.

The Err object is always available in every VBA program. You can use it directly, without creating an instance of it first. VBA automatically stores information about the most recent error in the Err object. All your code has to do is retrieve the Err object's properties, which include Number and Description.

The Number property simply tells you the number of the current error. You can assign it to a variable or use it directly in a conditional statement, as in this example:

```
Sub YetAnotherFineMess()
On Error GoTo ImTryinToThingButNothingHappens
...
(error prone statements)
...
Exit Sub
ImTryinToThingButNothingHappens:
Select Case Error.Number
    Case 7 ' Out of memory error
        (code for handling error number 1)
    Case 11 ' Division by zero error
        (code for handling error number 2)
    ... (and so on)
    Case Else
        (code for handling all other errors)
End Select
End Sub
```

Here, the `Select Case` statement checks the Number property against a series of values for which you've written specific error-handling statements. Such statements might

- Inform the user that something is wrong and ask for instructions via an input box or custom form.
- Try again to get valid data from a source that was unavailable earlier, or try an alternative source.
- Change an errant value to a valid one, recording in a file or via a message box that data had to be changed by brute force to make the thing go.

Obviously, effective use of the Number property requires that you know what each error number means. I don't have space to catalog the possibilities, but you can find information about the most common errors in the Trappable Errors topic of VBA Help (you can locate this topic by starting to type "trappable errors" in the Help window's Index tab).

If your code can't deal with an error — or if you don't want to take the trouble — you can still avoid the standard VBA run-time error message using the Err object's Description property. The following example displays a genteel message:

```
strMyErrMessage = "I'm sorry to inform you that " _
    & "something has gone amiss in this lovely " _
    & "program. According to VBA, the cause of the " _
    & "trouble is "
MsgBox strMyErrMessage & Err.Description
```

Secret

Some VBA applications provide additional objects and functions that provide information about application-specific problems. Microsoft Access, for example, offers a separate Error object.

Resuming program execution

Once your error handler has completed its work, you have a choice: Do you want the procedure to pick up where it left off when the error occurred, or do you want to transfer program execution back to the procedure that called the one where the error occurred?

Place the `Resume` statement in your error handler if you want to jump back into the current procedure. The `Resume` statement comes in several flavors:

- Simply typing `Resume` on its own line transfers control back to the procedure at the statement that caused the error. You should use this version of the statement if you have corrected values used in that statement so that you know an error won't occur again.
- To skip over the statement that caused the error, add a `Resume Next` statement to your error-handling code instead. Execution continues at the statement immediately following the one that caused the error.

- To jump to a particular point in the procedure, enter a `Resume label` statement after the error-handling code. Here, *label* refers to a label somewhere in your procedure, but *not* the label that identifies your error handler. Of course, if you use this version, you must also add the label to the procedure.

Conclusion

Preventing, finding, and correcting errors in your program — and recovering gracefully when they do occur — is a top priority when you set out to develop custom software with VBA. This chapter provided the concepts and techniques you need to become an expert bug fighter.

Chapter 24

Getting Interactive: Custom Dialog Boxes

In This Chapter

- ▶ Using message and input boxes for easy interactions with users
- ▶ Running and printing forms during the design process
- ▶ Inserting a new form and filling it up with controls
- ▶ Using the Properties window — the easy VBA way to set form and control properties
- ▶ Working with key form and control properties
- ▶ Using individual control types, including labels, text boxes, combo boxes, buttons, and more
- ▶ Displaying forms in your VBA programs — and shutting them down when you're through using them
- ▶ Writing event procedures so your form can respond to mouse-clicks, key presses, and miscellaneous other happenings
- ▶ Mastering common challenges in form design

In other programming languages, windows and dialog boxes are the only access points for interaction with a program while it runs. They tend to be less critical in VBA programming, in that you can tack your VBA programs onto the user interface of the underlying VBA application. Even so, plenty of situations in VBA programs call for custom dialog boxes. This chapter covers all the skills you need to construct them.

First, though, I discuss VBA's simpler alternatives: message boxes and input boxes. When these lack the muscle you need, you must design your own *forms*, home-grown dialog boxes that can be as sophisticated as you want to make them. After an introduction covering the basics of form design, the focus shifts to details on individual controls, the gadgets on the form that the user clicks to make things happen. Finally, I explore the all-important topic of writing code to make your forms and their controls do what you want them to.

Simple Interactions with the World

VBA's rich form design tools give you the power to create genuine Windows-style dialog boxes and other windows for your users. But when less will do, less is better. Two VBA functions, `MsgBox` and `InputBox`, provide the basic tools you need to talk to the program's users and to let them talk back. Their basic duties are as follows:

- `MsgBox` displays a message, of course, but it also lets you know which of two or more buttons the user clicked.
- `InputBox` displays a message and a text box where the user can type a response.

Displaying message boxes

The formal syntax for the `MsgBox` function is:

```
MsgBox(prompt[, buttons] [, title] [, helpfile, context])
```

As the brackets indicate, only the *prompt* argument — which specifies the message you want to display — is required.

Specifying the prompt

In its simplest form, the `MsgBox` function acts like a statement. All you do is type it on its own line, supplying the text you want displayed as the single argument, as in:

```
MsgBox "This is a test MsgBox."
```

You can type parentheses around the message, or prompt, but they aren't required when a function is used as a statement — that is, when you don't use the value it returns. The prompt can be literal text, a variable, or any expression:

```
Sub WishCountdown()
   intWishCount = 3
   datWhen = Format(Now, "Short date")
   strInfo1 = "As of "
   strInfo2 = " wishes left."
   MsgBox strInfo1 & datWhen & ", " & intWishCount _
      & strInfo2
End Sub
```

Secret

To display a message on more than one line, separate the lines by adding a the carriage return character (ASCII value 13) to your prompt string, using the `Chr` function. Likewise, you can line up text on two or more lines in columns with Tab characters (ASCII value 9) inserted with `Chr`.

```
Sub LinesAndColumns()
   MsgBox "Here is line one." & Chr(9) & _
      "Column two." & Chr(13) & _
      "Here is line two." & Chr(9) & "Column too."
End Sub
```

Fancier message boxes

Besides displaying text, a message box can show one of several icons and include buttons of several different types. You wrap up your choices for all of these options as a single numeric value, the optional *buttons* argument. By adding an icon, you can make your message box look a little spiffier than the unadorned box. The example in Figure 24-1 carries the critical message icon, which should generate a bit more excitement in the user. The default message box has only an OK button, but you can add buttons labeled OK, Cancel, Yes, No, Abort, Retry, and Ignore in various combinations. A sample of these wares can also be seen in Figure 24-1.

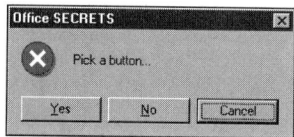

Figure 24-1: A relatively spiffy message box, gussied up with an icon and some buttons.

Calculating a value for the buttons argument

You calculate the value for *buttons* by adding together constants representing the various available choices of icons and buttons. You can calculate the number yourself but it's easier to create an expression using the named constants that VBA has defined for this purpose. Table 24-1 lists each constant with its numeric value and purpose in life. Based on the table, the *buttons* argument in the function call for Figure 24-1's message box should be 531. Instead, you can type the following statement:

```
intA = MsgBox("Pick a button", VbYesNoCancel + _
   VbCritical + VbDefaultButton3, "Office SECRETS")
```

In this example, MsgBox is used as a true function, returning the value of the button clicked by the user into the variable intA — see the next section, "Who's got the button?" Note that VbDefaultButton3, the third of the three constants in the expression for the *buttons* argument, sets up the third button as the default choice (counting from left to right). In this case, that third button is Cancel. If you look closely at Figure 24-1, you can see that the Cancel button "has the focus" — it's highlighted by a dotted line indicating that if you press Space or Enter it will be activated.

Table 24-1 VBA Constants for Message and Input Box Appearance and Behavior

Constant	Numeric Value	What It Does
VbOKOnly	0	Displays OK button only.
VbOKCancel	1	Displays OK and Cancel buttons.
VbAbortRetryIgnore	2	Displays Abort, Retry, and Ignore buttons.
VbYesNoCancel	3	Displays Yes, No, and Cancel buttons.
VbYesNo	4	Displays Yes and No buttons.
VbRetryCancel	5	Displays Retry and Cancel buttons.
VbCritical	16	Displays Critical Message icon.
VbQuestion	32	Displays Warning Query icon.
VbExclamation	48	Displays Warning Message icon.
VbInformation	64	Displays Information Message icon.
VbDefaultButton1	0	Specifies first button as the default.
VbDefaultButton2	256	Specifies second button as the default.
VbDefaultButton3	512	Specifies third button as the default.
VbDefaultButton4	768	Specifies fourth button as the default.

Who's got the button?

The point of buttons in a message box is to give the user some choice. Of course, you need a way to figure out which button that is. That's easy, because the MsgBox function returns an integer value corresponding to the button the user clicks. To minimize the strain on your memory, you can test the returned value against predefined named constants rather than arbitrary numbers. Here are the constants and their "real" values:

Constant	Value
vbOK	1
vbCancel	2
vbAbort	3
vbRetry	4
vbIgnore	5
vbYes	6
vbNo	7

An If...Then statement works well to figure out which button was clicked if your message box has only two buttons, as in this example:

```
If MsgBox ("Go on?", VbYesNo) = VbYes Then
    DoSomething
Else
    DontDoAnything
End If
```

With three buttons to test, you would need an If...Then...Else If... statement.

Adding a title

By default, a message box displays the name of the VBA application you're using in its title bar. You can substitute any title you like by supplying a string for the *title* argument when you call the MsgBox function — refer to Figure 24-1.

Obtaining user input

If you need to know more from the user than which of three options to pursue, you don't necessarily need a form — the InputBox function may be adequate. Here's its formal syntax, minus the more advanced optional arguments:

```
InputBox(prompt[, title] [, default])
```

As illustrated in Figure 24-2, a dialog box displayed by this function provides a text box where the user is asked to type in some piece of presumably crucial information. To bring that information into your program, just assign the return value of the InputBox function to a string variable:

```
strB = InputBox ("Seat preference?", "NYAir", "Aisle")
```

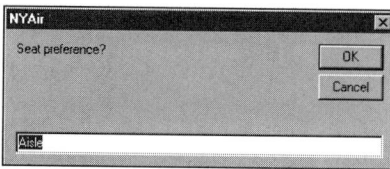

Figure 24-2: Use an input box to obtain information from the user and feed it to your program.

Although an InputBox can collect a much wider range of information than a MsgBox, its basic operations are actually simpler — there are no buttons and icons to fiddle with. The *prompt* and *title* arguments work just as they do in the MsgBox function. You can make it easier for the user by supplying a *default* response — if they like it, they just hit Enter.

Designing Forms

When message and input boxes aren't capable or glitzy enough, create a VBA form instead. Compared to writing code — or even to writing decent English sentences — laying out a VBA form is a piece of cake. Still, some work is involved, and there are a few places where you can get into trouble if you're not forewarned.

Running forms

As you lay out a form, you can "run" it (by pressing F5 or clicking the Run toolbar button) whenever you like. When you run a form, it appears on the screen over your VBA application (that is, the Visual Basic Editor disappears for the moment). You can then test it by clicking its controls to see what happens. Just keep in mind that if the form is part of a larger program, it may not work right if you run it in isolation.

Caution

You must fully select a form before it will run. In the Visual Basic Editor, it's possible to select a form part ways — selection handles appear around its perimeter, but it doesn't run automatically when you press F5. If the Macros dialog box unexpectedly pops up, cancel it and then click anywhere on the form before you try to run it again.

To stop a running form that you haven't equipped with a cancel button, you can click the Close button at the far right side of the form's title bar. Alternatively, press Alt+Tab to get back to the Visual Basic Editor and click the Reset toolbar button.

Forms and controls are objects — and they must be programmed

Secret

Forms and controls are full-fledged VBA objects. That means they have properties, methods, and events. What's special about the properties of forms and controls is that you don't need to set them in code, as this chapter makes plain.

Caution

Keep in mind, too, that you must write code for every control you add to your program, with the exception of some label and frame controls. Forms themselves often require code, too. Be sure to account for this in your thinking about what needs to be done to complete your project.

Planning forms for your program

Laying out forms in VBA is fun and easy, but designing those forms requires some thoughtful planning when you're constructing real programs. Remember that your forms are part of a larger software entity that has a practical mission to accomplish. So before you start fiddling with the forms, spend some time defining a mission statement for the program as a whole and listing tasks the forms have to perform to support that mission. Give some thought to how to group those tasks logically on different forms.

Printing forms during the design process

As you work on laying out forms, it sometimes helps to have paper copies that you can carry around with you as you think about the project. Printed forms are great for scribbling tentative design revisions, and you can pass them around to potential users or other programmers for their reactions.

To print a project's forms in the Visual Basic Editor, start by selecting the form or forms in question. If you want to print only one form, select it in the Project Explorer. If you want to print all the forms in a project, select any form, module, or other component for that project. Now choose File ⇨ Print or press Ctrl+P. Before you OK the resulting dialog box, check the Form Image box. Uncheck the Code box unless you also want a printout of the form's code. Select Current Module if you want just the current form printed, and Current Project if you want to see all the forms on paper.

Laying Out Forms

As Figure 24-3 illustrates, a new form provides a blank canvas for your dabblings in user interface design. You can alter its size and position on the screen, give it a different color, and fill it up with the controls that make it do productive tricks.

Before you create a new form, be sure the correct project — the one where you want the form to live — is active. Use the Project Explorer window to select the correct project.

Creating the form

Create a new form by choosing Insert ⇨ UserForm from the Visual Basic Editor's main menu system or from the Project Explorer's shortcut menu. The new UserForm appears in its own window.

Adding controls from the Toolbox

Once the empty canvas of a new UserForm is on your screen, it's time to start adding controls, the little doodads on the form with which people interact. Controls come from the Toolbox, which should appear automatically when you create a new UserForm (the Toolbox is also shown in Figure 24-3). It graciously hides itself when you click any other window but pops up again when you click the UserForm window. If the Toolbox isn't visible when you need it, choose View ⇨ Toolbox to call it forth.

Part VI: Secrets of VBA

To add a control to your form, click the Toolbox icon for the control you want to add and then drag the mouse over the part of the form you want the control to occupy (Figure 24-4). When you let up on the mouse button, the control appears on the form.

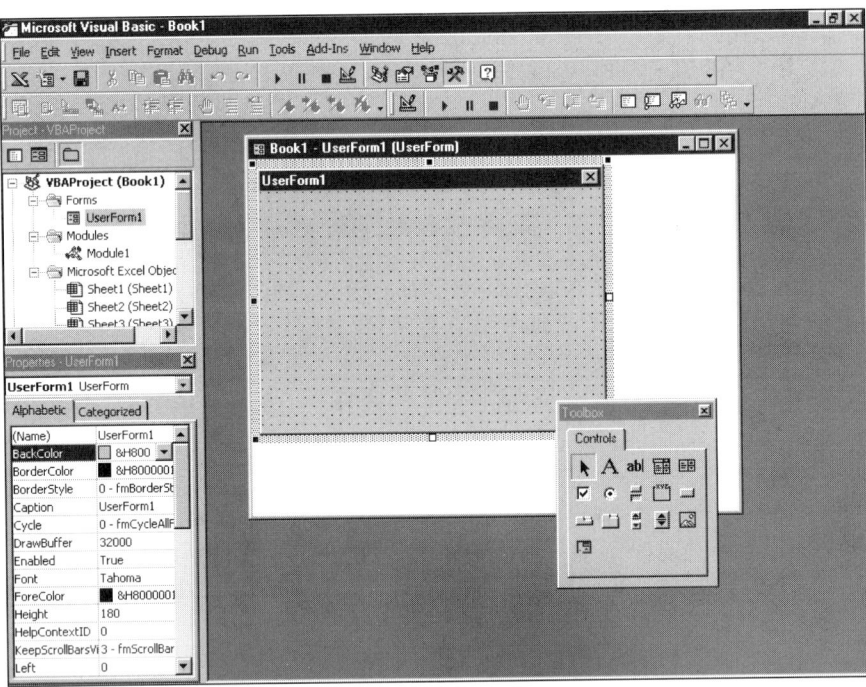

Figure 24-3: A brand-new UserForm. Note the toolbox and its controls.

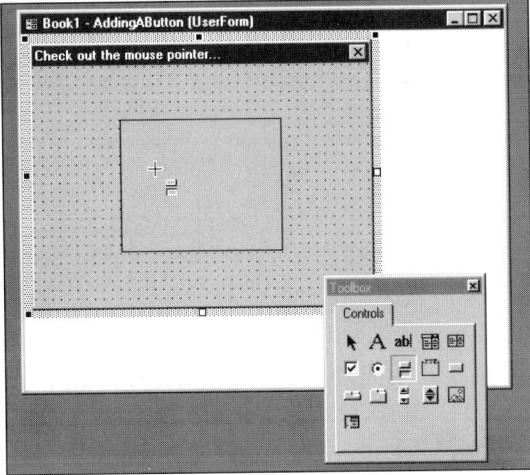

Figure 24-4: Adding a new toggle button control to a form.

Secret Normally, VBA reverts back to the arrow pointer for selecting objects as soon as you've finished adding a new control. If you want to add two or more of the same type of control to a form, double-click the icon for that control in the Toolbox. When you're through, click the arrow icon to stop adding controls.

Working with Form and Control Properties

Because VBA forms and controls are objects, they have properties that determine their appearance and behavior. And as with all object properties, you can examine and change the properties of forms and controls in your code.

For these objects, however, you don't *have* to write code. Instead, the Visual Basic Editor's Properties window lets you easily control many critical characteristics of forms and controls without programming *per se*. As your programs get more sophisticated, you'll want, you'll beg to set properties in code. Even then, though, the Properties window can be the easiest way to control the initial settings for form and control properties.

The Properties window is shown in Figure 24-5. If the Properties window isn't already on your screen, display it by choosing View ➪ Properties Window or by pressing F4.

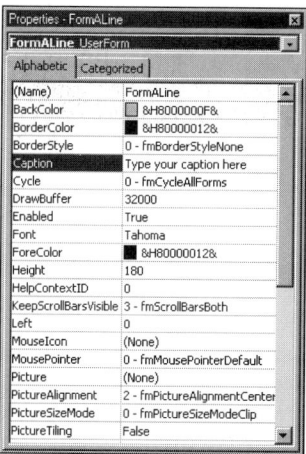

Figure 24-5: The Properties window for a VBA form.

A tour of the Properties window

The Properties window has two outstanding properties of its own:

- It automatically shows the properties of whatever you've selected by clicking it in the UserForm window (a particular control or the form itself).

- You can still work with the properties for any item on the form by selecting the item from the drop-down list at the top of the Properties window. Figure 24-6 shows the drop-down list in action.

Note that the display at the top of the window always shows the name and type of the item whose properties you're currently working with. The bulk of the Properties window is divided into two tabs. Both display exactly the same set of properties, but the Alphabetic tab lists them according to annual income (not really), while the Categorized tab divides them into related groups. Whichever tab you choose, the window works the same way. To the right of the property names, each individual property has a *field* where you can change the property's setting.

Figure 24-6: The drop-down list at the top of the Properties dialog box gives you immediate access to the properties of any item on a form (or the form itself).

Getting Help on properties

If you can't figure out what a given property is for or what settings will work, just ask for Help. Click the property's field and press F1 to display the relevant topic from the VBA Forms Help file.

Changing property settings

Depending on the property, you change the setting in its field in one of three ways:

- By typing in a new setting
- By selecting the new setting from a drop-down list
- By selecting the new setting from a dialog box

Some properties enable you to either type in a setting or select it from a list.

Secret: You can't tell that a property has a drop-down list or a dialog box until you click in the property field. When you do, a button appears in the field, which you can then click. (The button has a downward-pointing arrow for drop-down lists, and three little dots for dialog boxes.)

Don't forget to select the right item

Before you add controls to a form, the form itself is the only item listed in the Properties window. As soon as you've added one or more controls, however, you need to start paying attention to which item (the form or one of its controls) is selected, as indicated by square *handles* on the border of the item.

Caution: One way to select an item in the first place, of course, is just to click it. But that can be a bit tricky. I suggest you make it a habit to select form items a different way, via the drop-down list at the top of the Properties window. The selection handles appear around its perimeter just as if you had clicked it. If you prefer the direct click method, at least practice glancing up at the display at the top of Properties to make sure you've selected the right item.

Key form and control properties

Many properties of forms and controls work identically across different objects and specific properties. For example, you use very similar techniques to change the size of a form and its controls, and all the color-related properties work the same way whether you're setting the color of the form itself, a button control, or some text. This section covers the most important properties common to forms and controls.

The Name is not the Caption

Secret: As you know by now, every object in a VBA program has a name, and forms and controls are no exception. But an object's name doesn't appear anywhere on the form. Instead, you use the name to refer to the object in your code — if, for example, your program needs to activate one of the object's methods or change one of its other properties.

And yes, forms and controls do have a `Name` property. Like the name you assign to any object, a form or control's `Name` property is the name you use in your code. A form or control name must be a valid VBA name (no spaces or punctuation characters allowed — see Chapter 21).

The `Caption` property of a form or control is something else again. A form's caption specifies the text that appears in the title bar, while a control's caption — if the control has one — specifies the text on the surface of a control. You can change the `Caption` property by typing a new text string into the corresponding field in the Properties window. Or in the case of controls, you can click once to select the control and then click again to edit the caption directly on the control.

Sizing and positioning forms and controls

Before you do any serious design work on a form, be aware that like any self-respecting graphics program, the Visual Basic Editor has a *grid*. The grid defines imaginary magnetic lines, vertical and horizontal. When you move or resize any item on a form, the edges automatically snap into place along the nearest grid line. I cover details on the grid in the "Working with the Grid" section later in this chapter.

The easiest property to change on a form or control is its size. Although you can set the Height and Width properties in the Properties window, it's easier to just grab the item by one of its handles. Dragging a bottom or right *side* handle sizes the form in one dimension, whereas dragging the *corner* handle changes the size in both dimensions simultaneously.

Secret

Note that only white handles work for sizing — and most of the handles for a form are black. They black ones don't do anything except set off the form smartly. Forms are always pushed up against the top-left corner of their windows.

Controlling a form's position on the screen

You have full control over where the form initially appears on the screen when you run your program (or the form alone, if you're just testing it). The StartUpPosition property is the key. The default value for this property is 1 - CenterOwner. This means that the form appears in the center of the VBA application's window, regardless of how big it is or where on the screen it's located. If you want your form to appear in the very middle of the screen no matter what the VBA application is doing, set the StartUpPosition property to 2 - CenterScreen instead. And to set its position yourself, choose 0 - Manual and then type in values for the Left and Top properties.

More important appearance-related properties

Other properties that deserve your attention include:

- **Left and Top.** To change a control's position within a form, just drag the control wherever you want it to go. If you're a stickler for details, you can instead type in numeric position values for the Left and Top properties.

- **ForeColor and BackColor.** Set the colors for a form or control.

- **Font.** Lets you select a font from all those installed on your system. To set a default font for all controls on a form, set the *form's* Font property before you add any controls. That way, you don't need to change the Font properties of every control individually.

- **SpecialEffect.** Imparts a subtle but definite impression of depth to the target object in a number of variations.

- **ToolTip.** Specifies the text that appears when the mouse hovers over a control for a second or two.

- `Picture`. Lets you add a graphic to a form or control (see Figure 24-7). Once this picture is in place, use the `PictureAlignment`, `PictureSizeMode`, and `PictureTiling` properties, if available for the object you're working with, to adjust the picture to taste.

Figure 24-7: Pictures added to a VBA form and several of its controls.

Using the Enabled and Locked properties

Two properties, `Enabled` and `Locked`, govern whether a control or an entire form is accessible to the user. Obviously, controls are there so people can use them. There are times, however, when a control should be visible to let the user know it exists, but "grayed out," or *dimmed*, to show that it can't be used at the moment.

The `Enabled` property determines whether the control or form can receive the *focus*, meaning the capability to react to mouse and keyboard actions from the user. Only one object at a time ever has the focus in Windows. To keep you in the know about where the focus goes, Windows places a dotted border around the control that currently has the focus. When `Enabled` is True, the control appears normally and can receive the focus. When `Enabled` is False, Windows displays a dimmed version of the control, which can't take the focus.

If the `Locked` property is False, the control won't respond to mouse-clicks or key presses, regardless of the `Enabled` setting. However, if `Enabled` is True, the control can still receive the focus, and it still looks normal on the screen.

Basic Control Editing

The Visual Basic Editor lets you cut, copy, and paste controls individually or in groups. The standard Windows menu commands and keyboard shortcuts apply. In addition, the standard Office buttons for the Cut, Copy, and Paste commands provide one-click access to these functions. When you paste a control from the clipboard, VBA deposits it in the center of the form, even if that part of the form isn't currently visible. However, if you select a frame or multipage control before doing the paste, the control goes onto the center of that item.

You can delete one or more selected controls without placing them on the clipboard, by pressing the Del key or choosing Edit ⇨ Delete. Note that the Backspace key does not work for this purpose as it does in some other programs.

You can select a group of controls and then move, resize, cut, or copy them as a unit, or apply other formatting commands as described later in this chapter. This is also a great way to efficiently set properties they have in common to the same values. To select multiple controls you can:

- Draw a selection rectangle around the controls that you want in the group by using the Toolbox arrow pointer. If any part of a control is included in the rectangle, that control is included in the selection.

- Click the first control in the group and then Shift+Click a control at the other side of the selection area. All controls between the two are included in the selection.

- Ctrl+Click individual controls to add or remove them to or from the selection.

You can usually reverse the effects of the last formatting change involving controls using the Undo command (Ctrl+Z). Undo doesn't work after you resize a form, nor does it reverse changes you make in the Properties window.

Working with the Grid

The *grid* is an array of horizontal and vertical lines that crisscross your forms. The grid has two functions:

- To visually guide you as you place controls with the mouse. The visual grid comprises those dotted lines that you've probably seen on your forms.

- To automatically align controls to the grid as you move or resize controls. No matter how you move the mouse, the edges of your controls always snap into alignment along one of the grid lines. This ensures a reasonable consistency in your form layout, though it limits your flexibility.

The two functions work independently — you can turn off the visible grid and leave automatic alignment on, or vice versa.

Chapter 24: Getting Interactive: Custom Dialog Boxes

To control the way the grid works, choose Tools ⇨ Options. When the Options dialog box appears, click the General tab to reveal the panel of choices shown in Figure 24-8.

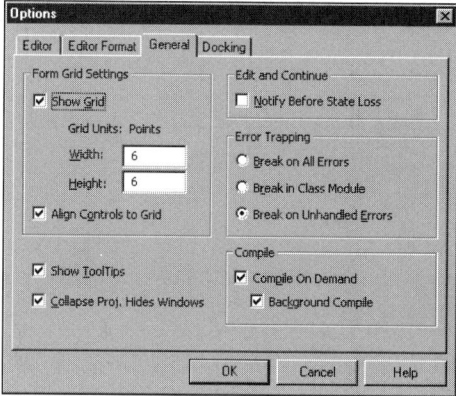

Figure 24-8: Change grid settings on the General tab of the Options dialog box.

Confining your attention to the upper-left part of the dialog box, you can see the few simple grid-related options. They are:

- **Show Grid.** Clear this checkbox to turn off the visual grid, those dotted lines on your forms. This doesn't affect automatic alignment to the grid.

- **Width and Height.** These two boxes let you can control the size of your grid in the horizontal and vertical dimensions independently. The Width setting controls the distance between each pair of vertical grid lines, which in turn affects the horizontal position of controls. Similarly, the Height setting is for the horizontal grid lines but pertains to vertical position.

- **Align Controls to Grid.** When this box is checked, the "snap to grid" function is in force. Clear the box to give yourself complete freedom to position and size controls to any measurements you please. Again, the visual grid can be on when this function is off.

Formatting Controls

Fortunately, VBA provides a stable of tools that help you achieve the goals of symmetry, consistency, and general neatness easily. Although laying out a well-organized form still takes some manual labor, the Visual Basic Editor's automatic formatting features can handle much of the work.

Using the Format menu

The Visual Basic Editor's Format menu (see Figure 24-9) is the control center for commands that affect the layout of controls on a form. Getting on intimate terms with the menu and its multiple submenus will serve you well during the process of forms design.

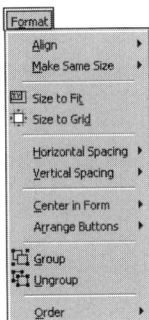

Figure 24-9: The Format menu in the Visual Basic Editor.

The UserForm toolbar

When you're working with a form window in the Visual Basic Editor, the UserForm toolbar comes in handy. If it's not already visible, display it by right-clicking any toolbar and choosing UserForm. Figure 24-10 shows how the UserForm toolbar looks in its floating configuration.

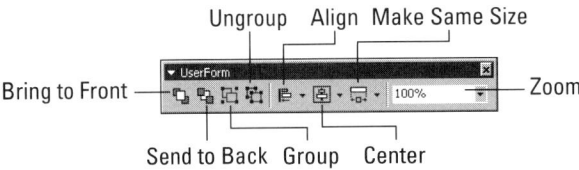

Figure 24-10: The Visual Basic Editor's UserForm toolbar.

Most of the buttons on the UserForm toolbar correspond to items on the Format menu. Some of them are split buttons allowing multiple options. If you click the main part of one of these buttons, VBA immediately activates the option that was last used. To select a different option, click the little arrow and pick it from the list.

Grouping multiple controls

Although it's fairly easy to use the mouse to select multiple controls on the fly, this isn't ideal when you want to work repeatedly with the same set of controls as a unit. By combining all the controls into a *group*, you don't have to reselect the same controls every time you do something to them, and you eliminate the possibility of selection mistakes.

Creating a group is simple. Just select all the controls you want in the group and then click the Group button on the UserForm toolbar, or choose Format ➪ Group.

Secret

Grouping lets you apply formatting commands that normally work on single controls to groups as a whole. If you want to even out the spacing between three rows of buttons, for example, you could convert each row into a group, select all three groups simultaneously, and then use the Horizontal Spacing ➪ Make Equal command (which you can read about later, by the way).

Arranging controls on top of each other

Although it's usually best to avoid overlapping controls, such a design can be vital when you need to change the contents of a form while your program runs. By setting each control's Visible property to True or False as necessary, the program can keep all but one of the overlapping controls invisible at any one time. In the Visual Basic Editor, however, every control is always visible — unless, that is, it's buried underneath other controls on the form. When this happens, you can use the Order commands on the Format menu to rearrange the controls.

Here are suggestions for the use of the Order commands:

- If you can get to a tiny piece of a buried control, click there to select it and then choose Format ➪ Order ➪ Bring to Front to place the control on the very top of the pile. Have at it.

- If the control you want to work with is completely covered up by the ones on top, click the top-most control to select it, and then banish it to the bottom of the pile with Format ➪ Order ➪ Send to Back. Repeat this process until the control you want is on top.

- If you're arranging controls that will actually overlap while the program runs, you may need to use the Bring Forward or Send Backward commands to order them just so. These commands move the selected control by one position in the pile.

Formatting multiple controls

Many of the more advanced commands on the Format menu only work on multiple controls, or on selections that include two or more groups. This section describes each of these commands, after an important digression about which selected item has the power in the relationship.

Designating the dominant control

In some formatting commands involving multiple controls, one control serves as the reference point for the command. This is the *dominant control*, in VBA lingo. For example, when you use one of the Format ⇨ Make Same Size commands to make uniform a set of selected controls, VBA copies the chosen dimension (height, width, or both) from the dominant control to all the other controls in the set. Likewise for the Align command—the other controls in the set line up with the dominant control, which doesn't move. The effects of the Horizontal and Vertical Spacing commands also depend on which control is dominant.

Look at Figure 24-11, where you can see that only one of the selected controls is outlined in *white* sizing handles. That's the dominant control, whose handles are always white. Other controls in the selection have black handles around their margins.

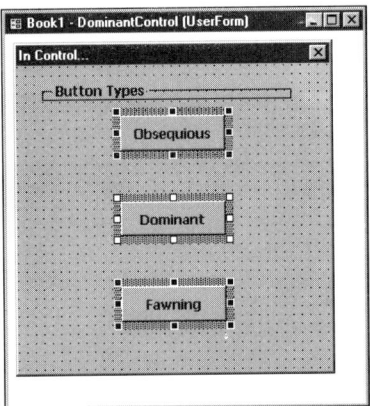

Figure 24-11: The control surrounded by white sizing handles is the dominant control.

Here's how to designate the dominant control while selecting a group:

To	*Use This Technique to Select Controls*
Choose the dominant control by dragging a selection rectangle	Begin dragging the selection rectangle with the mouse pointer closer to the target control than any other.
Choose the first control you click as the dominant control	Shift+Click to select each control in the set.
Choose the last control you click as the dominant control	Ctrl+Click to select each control in the set.
Choose a different dominant control for an existing selection	Ctrl+Click *twice* on the chosen control.

Aligning controls to one another

Even with the grid on, it's common to find that controls that ought to be in a straight line or column actually are staggered. Instead of laboriously lining them up by hand, enlist the Format ⇨ Align commands or their equivalent buttons to do the work for you. You can bring the midline or any edge (top, bottom, left, or right) of each selected control into alignment along either a vertical or horizontal axis.

Making controls the same size

The three Make Same Size commands automatically adjust all selected controls to match the size of the dominant control in the selection. You can bring instant conformity in width, height, or both dimensions.

Adjusting horizontal and vertical spacing

The Horizontal Spacing and Vertical Spacing commands can each change the space between two or more controls in four different ways. Three of these options are most useful (and one is only available) when the selection includes at least three controls. Here's how the choices work:

- **Make Equal.** Evens out the space between three or more selected controls. The controls at either end of the selection stay in place, while the controls in between move. This command isn't available if only two controls are selected.

- **Increase and Decrease.** These commands add or remove space between the selected controls by an amount equal to one grid unit for the dimension you're working with. The dominant control stays in place while the other ones move.

- **Remove.** Moves controls so that there is no space between them, and their edges touch. The dominant control stays in place.

Other formatting choices

For the most part, the other options on the Format menu work on individual controls as well as groups. After selecting one or more controls you can use:

- **Center in Form**, to center the items either vertically or horizontally. Note that if you've selected two or more controls, this command brings all the controls to the midline rather than centering the set as a unit (group the controls first if you want the latter result).

- **Arrange Buttons**, to place one or more selected command buttons at the bottom or right edge of the form. Although Arrange Buttons operates when other controls are included in the selection, only the command buttons move.

- **Size to Fit**, to have VBA resize the control(s) to fit whatever text they currently contain. This command is a one-shot affair — it does not set the `AutoSize` property to True — so the size remains constant if you later change the text in the control.
- **Size to Grid**, to move the edges of the selected control(s) to the nearest grid line.

Secret

The Visual Basic Editor lacks a command to distribute controls evenly along a row or column. However, you can approximate this easily enough with the following steps:

1. Eyeball the controls to arrange them so they're about where you want them.
2. Select the controls and activate the Align Tops command (or any other horizontal alignment option).
3. With all the controls still selected, activate the Horizontal Spacing Make Equal command.
4. Group the selected controls (activate the Group command).
5. Activate the Center in Form Horizontally command.

The preceding steps assume you're distributing the controls along a row. To distribute them vertically instead, substitute the vertical versions of each command in Steps 2, 3, and 5.

Working with Controls

The controls included with VBA offer everything you need for building dialog boxes that look and act like great professional software. This section explores properties common to many controls (but not available for forms) and then covers most of the types of controls individually. Remember that to get a control to do something useful, you must write code for its event procedures as discussed in the "Form Programming" section later in this chapter.

Setting the tab order for controls

A Windows convention is that pressing the Tab key moves the focus from one control to another on a dialog box. By default, every control you add to a VBA form takes its proper place in the *tab order*, the sequence in which controls are selected when the Tab key is pressed. (By the way, Shift+Tab walks through the tab order in reverse.)

Secret

You don't need to run a form to check out its tab order. Pressing the Tab key in the UserForm window selects one control after the next in the same order. Initially, tab order is based on the sequence in which the controls were originally added to the form. What usually happens is that you add controls as you think of them, not in the proper tab order. But you can take direct control of the tab order and even remove controls from the sequence if you like.

The easiest way to change the tab order for a form is with the View➪Tab Order dialog box. To reshuffle the controls listed there, click a control you want to move and then click the Move Up or Move Down button as appropriate. The tab order is actually controlled by each control's `TabIndex` property. The value of `TabIndex` is 0 for the first control in the sequence, 1 for the second control, and so on. If you change one control's `TabIndex` setting, VBA automatically adjusts all the others. To remove a control from the tab order, set its `TabStop` property to False. This doesn't change its position in the tab order, so if you make `TabStop` true again, the control rejoins the sequence right where it was before.

Assigning accelerator keys

Although many people are happy selecting controls with the mouse, some much prefer the keyboard. Be polite — give your users a keyboard shortcut, or *accelerator key*, for each control. When the form is running, pressing Alt followed by the accelerator key moves the focus to the control and may trigger an event (such as the `Click` event).

To make the assignment, type a single character into the Accelerator field in the Properties dialog box. The character should be one found in the control's caption, and it should not duplicate the accelerator of any other control on the same form. VBA automatically underlines the accelerator character for you.

Secret

To add an accelerator to a control that doesn't have a `Caption` property — such as a text box or scroll bar — follow these steps:

1. Create a label for the control (labels are the subject of the next section).
2. Adjust the tab order so that the label comes immediately before the other control.
3. Assign an accelerator to the label.

Secrets of Specific Controls

Each VBA control type is designed for a different task, and each requires a little different handling on your part.

Sending messages with label controls

A *label control* provides a rectangular area on a form where you can display messages. From the viewpoint of a user of your program, a label control isn't much of a control — it doesn't let the user control anything. All it does is display some text, or optionally, a picture. The user can't type over the existing text and can't even copy it to the clipboard.

Still, label controls are vital from the programmer's standpoint because they let you communicate messages to your users. Generally, you use labels to identify controls and their functions, as the example form in Figure 24-12 demonstrates. This is especially useful for controls that don't have their own captions, such as scrollbars, spinner controls, and the like.

The text displayed by a label control is its caption. So to place your own text on the label, change the text in the Caption property in the Properties window.

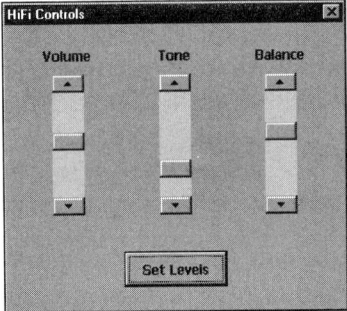

Figure 24-12: Three scrollbar controls, each with an accompanying label.

Automatic label adjustments

Via settings you can make in the Properties window, label controls are capable of adjusting themselves automatically to the text they contain. Options include:

- Leave the WordWrap property set to True, the default, if you want VBA to automatically break the text into separate lines to fit in the available space, much like a word processor does. If you set WordWrap to False, all the caption text remains on one line, even if there isn't enough room to see it all.

- Set the AutoSize property to True if you want the size of the label itself to change so it can fit all the text. If WordWrap is also set to True, the label expands vertically. If you change WordWrap to False, the label widens to accommodate the single line of text.

- Use the TextAlign property to control how text is justified inside the label: on the left, in the center, or on the right.

Changing label text in code

Although users can't change the text in a label control while your program runs, you can. Using the label's Caption property, you need only add a single line of code to modify the text to suit what's currently going on in the program:

```
lblInspirationalMessage.Caption = "Laugh and be happy!"
```

Text boxes let you hear from the user

Use a *text box control* when you want to collect information from the user. Your code can retrieve anything the user types into the text box. Figure 24-13 shows a text box doing its duty.

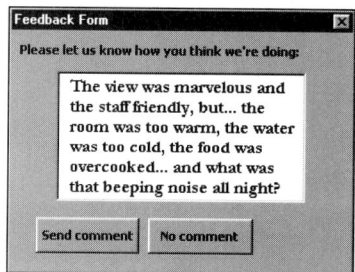

Figure 24-13: Text boxes give users a place to send messages to you.

Use text box controls instead of an `InputBox` when:

- You want a prettier dialog box than the standard `InputBox` function can display.

- You need at least one more control besides the text box in the same dialog box.

- You want to check entries for validity *while they are being typed.* With a text box, you can program an event procedure that gets triggered each time the user presses a key to see whether the key they pressed meets whatever criteria you set up. With an `InputBox`, you can only check the entire entry, and only after the user has closed the box.

Using text boxes as labels

Like labels, text boxes can also display messages from you to the user. Normally, however, the user can edit text in a text box. If you don't want the user to alter to your message, you can ensure they don't by setting the text box control's `Locked` property to True. Just be aware that users will still be able to copy the text to the clipboard, which they can't do with a label. You can prevent *this* by setting the `Enabled` property to False, but then the text appears dimmed (see the discussion of the `Locked` and `Enabled` properties at the beginning of this chapter).

Default text for a text box

You can place a default entry in a text box so that the user doesn't have to type anything if the default is acceptable. To enter the default text, click the text box once to select and then a second time to enter text entry mode, and start typing (don't double-click). Or you can type the text into the `Value` property field in the Properties window. And by the way, text boxes don't have captions. The text string that appears inside a text box is its `Value` property.

What's the secret password?

Passwords are used to protect vital data from unauthorized copying or tampering, and to make people feel that they must be getting something really special if they have to type a password first. Whichever reason appeals to you, it's easy to set up a VBA text box as a password entry field.

With the text box selected in the Visual Basic Editor, locate the `PasswordChar` property in the Properties window. There, type in a single character that you want the text box to display to disguise the actual characters the user types. The text box still records the actual entry, but no one can see it except your program.

Caution

By itself, of course, requiring a password doesn't protect your data. The data themselves and the list of correct passwords must all be encrypted, and your program needs a way to decrypt the data if the user types a valid password.

Retrieving the user's entry

To find out what text the user has entered in a text box, your program should retrieve the box's `Value` property. Typically you would assign the `Value` property to a string variable with a statement such as:

```
strTextBoxText = txtMessageFromUser.Value
```

Text box adjustments

Text boxes have the same `AutoSize`, `WordWrap`, and `TextAlign` properties that labels do, and they work mostly the same way. See the information on these properties in the section on label controls earlier in this chapter. However, the `WordWrap` property doesn't do anything except in multiline text boxes. Read on. . . .

Multiline text boxes

Secret

To get a text box to display text properly, broken up into separate lines to fit in the box, you must set the `MultiLine` property to True. Otherwise, even if `WordWrap` is True, all the text stays on one line, disappearing beyond the edge of the text box.

Text that VBA wraps for you is actually stored behind the scenes as a single line. However, multiline text boxes also permit the user to start a "real" new line, by pressing either Ctrl+Enter, or — if the `EnterKeyBehavior` property is also set to True — Enter alone. That way, a line break can come before the one VBA would have automatically generated. You can also control where lines break using code, as discussed in the section on labels earlier.

Adding scroll bars

Secret

Whatever the settings of the `MultiLine`, `WordWrap`, and `EnterKeyBehavior` properties, a text box can display only so much text. Although a user can always scroll with the arrow keys to see the entire contents, you should add scroll bars to all your text boxes via the `ScrollBars` property. VBA is smart enough to display the scroll bars only when the text box doesn't have enough room to show all its contents.

Get things done with command buttons

When you want something done and you want it done now, nothing gives you the feeling that you're in control like pressing a button and getting an immediate response. The standard issue *command button* is just a gray blob with a bit of explanatory text, such as OK, Cancel, or "Guess Again, Friend." If plain text is too drab for your taste, it's easy to add a little icon graphic to any button. Figure 24-14 demonstrates a variety of command button controls.

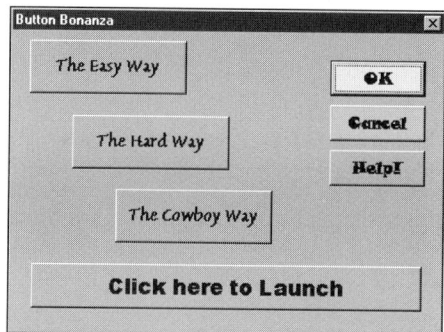

Figure 24-14: Command buttons galore.

Unfortunately, command buttons don't *do* anything to speak of until you program them. Clicking a command button generates a `Click` event, but you have to write code to tell VBA what actions to take when the event occurs.

Selecting a default button

In most dialog boxes, pressing Enter triggers a particular button. This is the *default button*, the one that responds when the user presses Enter, unless the focus has been moved to a different control. To designate a command button as the default button for your form, set the button's `Default` property to True. Of course, only one button on each form can be the default button.

Creating a Cancel button

Secret

If your dialog box can change data or program settings, it's always wise to give users an opportunity to back out before those changes become final. By convention, a button labeled Cancel is this escape hatch. If you're a nonconformist, you might label the button "Never mind" or "Forget it," but concern for the helpless user dictates that you provide a way out, no matter what you call the button.

Also by convention, pressing the Esc key cancels the dialog box, just as if the user had clicked the button in question. Setting a command button's `Cancel` property to True simply means that when the user presses Esc, your program will react as if the button had been clicked. It's up to your code to decide what actually happens when this event occurs.

Caution

To put it more bluntly, setting the `Cancel` property to True does *not* automatically mean that when the user clicks the button, the dialog box is canceled. All it does is connect the Esc key with the button's `Click` event.

Frame controls group other controls

Frame controls are modest but vital components of your VBA forms tool chest. To the eye, a frame is a simple rectangle with a caption embedded in the top side. You place other controls in frame to group them together.

Frames serve two purposes:

- To set off a group of related controls visually, cueing the user that they are in fact related, and lending variety and organization to a large form

- To define a group of option buttons functionally, so that only one of them can be selected at a time

I take up the details on the latter use of frames in the section on option buttons later in this chapter. Here, I stick with the basics on using frames to organize all types of controls.

Placing controls on frames

Once you've added a frame to a form, placing any other control on the frame binds the control and frame together. Now, if you move the frame, the control goes with it, always remaining in the same relative location within the frame.

You can add a control to a frame in two ways:

- By drawing a new control on the frame. Create the new control as you normally would, by clicking the appropriate icon in the Toolbox and then dragging over the target location on your form. In this case, that target location is inside the frame.

- By moving an existing control into the frame. Drag the control with the mouse until the mouse pointer is within the frame boundary. When you let go of the mouse pointer, the frame takes ownership.

Secret

When you successfully stick a control into a frame, the frame border appears selected whenever you select the control. See Figure 24-15.

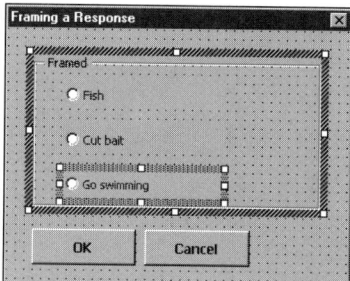

Figure 24-15: Selecting the button inside the frame has selected the frame itself, too.

Removing controls from frames

Breaking the link between a control and its frame is as simple as dragging the control to another spot on the form. As soon as the mouse pointer is outside the frame's border, releasing the button cuts the connection and drops the control into place. Now the two objects (form and control) move independently.

Multipage controls

A *multipage control* reproduces that notebook-tab look found in the dialog boxes used in most commercial Windows software these days. Each page of the control acts like a separate frame. Controls you place on a page become bound to that page and are only visible when the page is displayed. To display a different page, the user clicks the corresponding tab at the top.

Draw a multipage control just as you would any other control. By the way, VBA provides a similar control called a *tab strip*. Tab strips are good when you want the *same* controls to display different information, depending on which tab is selected. They require more programming work than multipage controls and aren't covered here.

Working with properties of multipage controls and their pages

Secret

A multipage control has properties, and so does each page within the multipage. When you want to fiddle with these properties, you have to be sure you're working with the right item. Immediately after you place a multipage control on a form, the multipage as a whole is selected and its properties appear in the Properties window. Later, though, clicking the multipage control selects one of the *pages*, not the multipage control. You can select a different page by clicking the corresponding tab. To select the entire multipage, you must either click the border of the control or use the drop-down list at the top of the Properties window.

Adding controls to a page

To add buttons, frames, and other controls to a page of a multipage control, just draw them on the page as you would on a frame. A key first step, though, is to select the right page before you start plopping down the controls. Again, all you have to do is click the tab for the page you want — the tab controls work even when the form isn't running.

Adding and deleting pages

To add another page to a multipage control, right-click over the tab area and choose New Page from the shortcut menu that pops up. Deleting an existing page is just as easy, except that you have to be very sure to delete the correct page — the Visual Basic Editor deletes the page immediately, without asking for confirmation, and Undo does not work.

Changing the tab text for an individual page

To change the title displayed on a tab, change the caption for that page. One way to recaption a page is by typing the new text in the Caption field in the Properties window. Alternatively, right-click the page's tab in the control and choose Rename from the little shortcut menu to display the Rename dialog box. You can type in the new caption there.

Secret

Don't be confused by the word "Rename" — you really are changing the page's caption, not its name (you need the Properties dialog box to truly rename a page). Anyway, the Rename dialog box also lets you select an accelerator key and enter control tip text, both options that can also be set in the Properties window.

Reshuffling page order

To change the order in which pages of a multipage control are displayed, select Move from the shortcut menu that appears when you right-click over the tab area. In the dialog box shown, click the page you want to move, and then use the Move Up and Move Down buttons to change its position in the lineup.

Picking one item from a group with option buttons

Many choices in life, and in software, are mutually exclusive. When you order a scoop of ice cream, you can pick spumoni or rum raisin or licorice, but not all three at once. When you buy a dress or a pair of slacks, you specify only one out of all the available sizes. And when you marry Ed, you give up on Fred, Ned, and Ted.

In Windows, the most common way to represent mutually exclusive choices like these is with a set of *radio buttons*, the little circular buttons named after the push buttons on car radios. After all, you can only listen to one radio station at a time (unless you're really radical). In VBA, radio buttons are called *option buttons*. Figure 24-16 demonstrates a typical set.

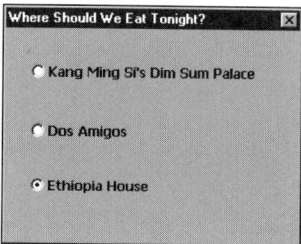

Figure 24-16: Option buttons, also called radio buttons.

And option buttons should always come in sets — after all, the point is to represent one choice among several. Only one button in a set can ever be selected. Clicking one option button turns off the previously selected button automatically.

Grouping option buttons

Don't worry about straining yourself to create a group of option buttons. All you have to do is plop down the buttons on the same part of the form. VBA automatically treats them as a group, and they behave as expected — when one is on, the rest are off — when the program runs.

Secret

But what did I mean by "the same part of the form?" Well, this isn't official VBA jargon, but here's the idea: One part of the form is the form itself — the background canvas, if you will. Each frame control you add creates another part. And each page of a multipage control is also a separate part. You can even place frames within other frames, or on pages of a multipage control — if you do, each subframe constitutes its own part.

Secret

In a form with one or more frames, VBA treats the option buttons that aren't inside any frame as one group, and each frame's buttons as a separate group. If you want to get tricky, the `GroupName` property lets you define more than one option button group in the same part of a form. All you have to do is use the same `GroupName` for all buttons in the group.

Which option button got clicked?

Clicking an option button selects that button but typically causes no other immediate changes. Instead, the dialog box just sits there, allowing the user to think twice and perhaps pick a different option button. Only when the user clicks the OK button is the selection confirmed.

For you as the programmer, the task is to figure out which option button was selected when the confirming event occurred. To do this, you must check the `Value` property for each button in the group. Though there are trickier ways to do this, an `If...ElseIf` statement is a decent solution, as in:

```
If OptionButton1.Value = True Then
    ChosenOption = "Bill"
ElseIf OptionButton2.Value = True Then
    ChosenOption = "Bob"
```

```
ElseIf OptionButton3.Value = True Then
    ChosenOption = "Barney"
Else
    ChosenOption = ""
```

Turning options on or off with check boxes and toggle buttons

Option buttons are great when you're working with multiple, mutually exclusive choices. However, when the number of choices collapses to just two, you should use a checkbox or a toggle button to let the user pick. *Checkboxes* and *toggle buttons* are indicated for any choice involving paired opposites such as Yes or No, On or Off, True or False, and Stay or Leave. In practice, the big difference between checkboxes and toggle buttons is just that they look different.

Grouped checkboxes

Checkboxes are often grouped together to present a list of choices that aren't mutually exclusive. It's like when you go to the store to buy breakfast cereal and come home with one box of Toastie-O's, one of Healthy Cardboard Crunch, and one of Sugar Coated White Flour Kibbles. Figure 24-17 offers several additional examples. Note that each individual checkbox still represents a yes or no choice for the item it pertains to.

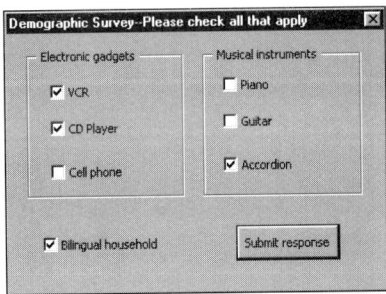

Figure 24-17: Grouped checkboxes let you select multiple items for the same overall option.

For the sake of the user's sanity, you should arrange all the checkboxes in a group together on a form, so that the user can see at a glance they're all related. Frames can help to distinguish these groups.

Secret

Because each checkbox functions independently, you don't need to worry about grouping them together in any other way. If you like, though, you *can* identify them as members of a group by entering the same `GroupName` property for each checkbox in the group. This mainly helps you keep track of which checkboxes belong together in case you reorganize the form.

How to tell whether a checkbox is checked or a toggle button is toggled

As usual, the `Value` property holds the crucial information concerning the user's interaction with these controls. If a checkbox is checked, its `Value` property is True; if it's cleared, `Value` is False. Likewise for toggle buttons: `Value` is True if the button is pushed in, False if not. So code like this retrieves and acts on the current setting:

```
If tglLightSwitch.Value = True
    TurnLightsOn
Else
    TurnLightsOff
End If
```

Selecting options with list and combo boxes

Once there are more than four or five mutually exclusive choices for an item, your dialog box becomes confusingly cluttered if you present all the choices as option buttons. When the choices aren't mutually exclusive, you can get away with maybe 10 or 12 checkboxes, because the user can consider each checkbox on its own merits. Still, a forest of checkboxes won't do.

What's a list box?

The *list box* is Windows' solution to such problems. A list box presents a compact list of named options, allowing the user to select them individually in the list. Obvious examples would be list boxes for picking a salad dressing choice or selecting one of the 50 states.

VBA's list box control lets you set up list boxes with relative ease, although programming is required to add items to the list. A VBA list box can stand in for a framed group of option buttons, allowing the user to choose only one of the listed items. Alternatively, it can function like a set of checkboxes, letting the user pick as many of the options as desired. What a list box can't do is accept entries that aren't in the list. Also, you can't present a VBA list box as a drop-down list on a single line. To overcome these limitations, you need a combo box.

Combo boxes

A *combo box* combines the virtues of a list box with those of a text box. The user can pick a supplied item from the list, but if none of these is appropriate, the user can type in an entry from scratch.

From a user's point of view, combo boxes are usually cooler, because they give you free reign to make your wishes known. From the programmer's standpoint, however, many situations call for limiting user choices to prevent invalid entries. Given that there are only 50 states in the United States, it wouldn't make sense to allow users to make up their own state entries in an address database.

Now that you know what list boxes are, don't use 'em

Secret

My advice is to use combo box controls for all options you present in lists, whether or not the user is allowed to type in entries that aren't on the list. Forget about list boxes.

Here's why: A VBA list box can't display items in a drop-down list. Instead, it's just a rectangular area on the form where the choices are listed. This doesn't really solve the space and clutter problem — if the list contains any significant number of items, it will take up too much room on your form and distract attention when it's not in use. If the number of choices are few enough to make an unobtrusive list, a set of option buttons or checkboxes would work just as well and look more appealing.

Secret

In contrast, combo boxes are much more compact, because they always display only a single choice from those on the list. And when you need it to, a combo box can act just like a list box, not accepting typed entries. All you have to do is set the combo box's `Style` property to 2 (`fmStyleDropDownList`). So why bother with list boxes?

Putting items into a list or combo box

Now for the harder part. You can't use the Properties window to type in the choices that should appear in a list or combo box. Instead, you either have to write code for the control's `AddItem` method or *bind* the control to a *data source*, meaning a list in an Excel worksheet or an Access database.

Secret

To create the list directly in code requires an event procedure for the *form's* `Activate` event. It should contain a series of statements like the ones in this example:

```
Private Sub UserForm_Activate()
    cmbOpinionPoll.AddItem "Overpopulation"
    cmbOpinionPoll.AddItem "Global warming"
    cmbOpinionPoll.AddItem "No time to smell the roses"
    cmbOpinionPoll.AddItem "No roses to smell"
    cmbOpinionPoll.AddItem "Taxes on the rich too high"
    cmbOpinionPoll.AddItem "Too many social services"
    cmbOpinionPoll.AddItem "Inadequate social services"
    cmbOpinionPoll.AddItem "HMOs"
End Sub
```

Chapter 47 on Access forms covers techniques for binding a list or combo box to a data source.

So what option did the user pick?

To retrieve the item that the user has selected or typed in a list or combo box, use the object's `Value` property in your code. This works just like it does in a text box. Just assign the property to a suitable variable (string, numeric, or variant), as in

```
strOpinion = cmbOpinionPoll.Value
```

Selecting values with scroll bars and spin buttons

When you turn up the volume on your stereo or turn down the thermostat on your heater, you're using a real-life control to select a value from a range of possible values. The job of emulating this kind of choice on a form falls to two controls, *scroll bars* and *spin buttons.* Figure 24-18 shows examples.

Of course, scroll bars are most commonly used in Windows for scrolling the visible area of a document or dialog box, when all the information won't fit at one time. But you can think of a scroll bar more generically as a slider control that slides through any range of numeric values. To select a value, the user can drag the scroll box, that squarish thing on the scroll bar itself, or click the arrow controls at either end.

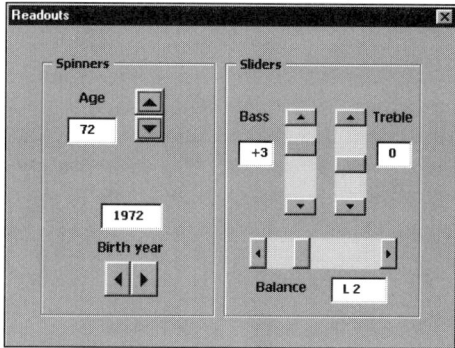

Figure 24-18: Sample scroll bars and spin buttons.

Spin buttons are just scroll bars with the bar removed—only the arrows remain. A spin button doesn't actually spin anything except the numbers it controls.

Drawing the controls

You place scroll bars and spin buttons on your forms just as you do other controls, by clicking the correct icon on the Toolbox and then dragging on the form to place the control. Both scroll bars and spin buttons can be oriented either vertically (with the arrows pointing up and down) or horizontally (left and right). By default, VBA determines the orientation automatically, based on how you draw the control. You can fix the orientation using the Orientation property.

Setting up the controls

After you place a scroll bar or spin button on a form, you have two main tasks to complete to get the control working properly:

1. You must specify the range of values that can be selected with the control.

2. You should provide users with visual feedback about which value they've selected.

Selecting a range of values

Use the `Max` and `Min` properties of a scroll bar or spin button to specify the range of values for the control. Only integer values are acceptable.

Secret

What's weird is that despite their names, these properties refer to locations on the control, not a numeric maximum or minimum. In other words, the `Max` property can take a smaller number than the `Min` property. The `Max` property determines the extreme value by clicking the top arrow on a vertical scroll bar or spin button or the right arrow on a horizontal one. `Min` corresponds to the bottom or left arrow. Setting the `Min` property less than `Max` reverses the polarity of the control, you might say — pressing the down arrow would increase the value.

Giving feedback

Spin buttons and scroll bars aren't very useful unless users know what value they're selecting. Unfortunately, neither control comes with a default gauge. You're stuck with using code to connect the value selected with the spin button or scroll bar to another control's text display. This isn't actually all that tough — you can do it with a single line of code. This example passes the value of a scroll bar to the caption of a label control when the scroll bar control is double-clicked:

```
Private Sub sclWarpFactor_DblClick
    lblScrollBarReadout.Caption = sclWarpFactor.Value
End Sub
```

Note that to provide immediate feedback, the code that displays the selected value in another control should be placed in the `Click` event procedure for the spin button or scroll bar, as in the example (`sclWarpFactor` is the name of the scroll bar control). The next section discusses event programming in detail.

Form Programming

Adding controls to a form is a piece of cake, but getting them to do your bidding takes a little more brain power and programming work. This section cuts through the complexities.

Loading and showing forms

Once you've decided to include custom forms in a VBA program, the first and most fundamental programming problem is how to get your forms on the screen to begin with. Because a VBA program can fall back on the user interface of the underlying application, the program doesn't automatically display a form when it runs. In this respect VBA is different from its cousin Visual Basic, in which the program *is* the form, unless you take extraordinary measures. At any rate, in a VBA program, you must add code to display a form so that it becomes accessible to users.

Displaying a VBA form is a two-step process. You must first *load* the form into memory and then *show* the form on the screen. As a programmer, you can use a single VBA statement to perform both steps. However, it can sometimes be useful to split them up.

Show-ing windows

The ticket to displaying any form is to execute its Show method. If the form is named FormICa, all you need to type is:

FormICa.Show

Note that Show is a method of the UserForm object, so you append it to the form name following a period. If the form in question isn't already loaded into memory, the Show method loads it and then displays it. If the form is loaded but hidden, the Show method just makes it visible.

Loading a form without displaying it

Secret

Use the Load statement to load the form into memory before you actually display it on the screen. Load is not a method, so the syntax is backward compared to Show, as in:

Load FormAlDeHyde

Why load a form without displaying it? Well, if your program uses numerous or complicated forms, this can make your program seem faster to the user. Because a program of any complexity performs lots of miscellaneous initialization procedures (such as reading data from files, calculating initial variables, and creating objects), a waiting period is typical when the program starts up. If you load your forms at that time too, users won't notice the wait as much as they might later on.

Making changes in your form before you display it

You can also load a form — without the Load statement — by entering code statements that manipulate a property or method of the form, or of one of its controls. This technique allows your program to make changes in a form before displaying it on the screen. After all, you may not know how the form (or its controls) should look or act until your program is running.

As a simple example, suppose you want the form's caption to display the date and time. Because you can't predict when someone is going to run your program — and because you probably expect it to run more than once — you need to let VBA figure out the current date and time for you. This simple sample does the trick:

```
Sub DisplayDateCaptionedForm ()
    DateCaptionedForm.Caption = Now
    DateCaptionedForm.Show
```

End Sub

Using a similar approach, you could have the form use a label or text box control to display information about whatever is currently selected in your VBA application. Figure 24-19 shows what you get by running the following PowerPoint procedure, coupled with an appropriate form:

```
Sub DisplayShowSelectionForm()
    Dim ItemCount As Integer, Message As String
    Items = ActiveWindow.Selection.ShapeRange.Count
    Message = CStr(Items) & " objects are selected."
    ShowSelectionForm.lblCountOfItems.Caption = Message
    ShowSelectionForm.Show
End Sub
```

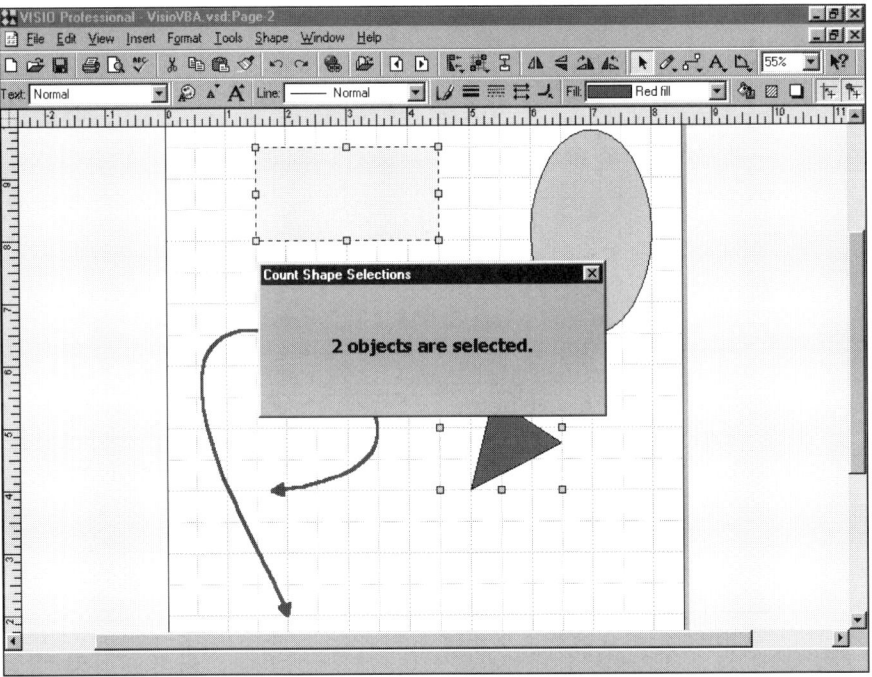

Figure 24-19: This program figures out what to display in the label caption just before you show the form.

Altering a form with the Initialize and Activate events

Another way to make changes in a form before displaying it is to use the form's own Initialize or Activate event. Code you place in these event procedures runs automatically when the corresponding event occurs. Use the Initialize event for code that should run only when VBA first loads the form, and use the Activate event for code that should run every time the form is displayed (including the first time). Writing code for event procedures is discussed in the section "Event Programming for Forms and Controls" later in this chapter.

Modal versus modeless forms

The classic example of a *modal* form is the typical dialog box: When the dialog box is active, you can't work with any other part of the program. You have to close the dialog box in order to work with a different dialog box or directly with a document. When a modal form is active, the only parts of your VBA program that can run are the procedures belonging to the form itself. The form can respond to events, but the rest of your program is suspended, and the underlying application itself is off limits to the user — until the form is closed.

Unlike its predecessors, the version of VBA that comes with Office 2000 gives you a choice between modal and *modeless* behavior for each dialog box. By default, the form's `ShowModal` property is True, meaning the form is modal. Change it to False if you want users to be able to switch back and forth between it and other open forms, and if you want your program — the one that displayed the form — to continue running actively while the form is visible.

Caution

Users of your program won't be able to move between forms unless *all* the open forms are designated as modeless. As soon as your program opens a single modal form, the remainder of the program is suspended until the user closes that form. If the program shows other forms before the modal one, they are visible on the screen but can't be activated.

Referring to forms using variables

Although your code can refer to a form object directly by name, you may prefer to use a variable. If the form has a long name, this can cut down on your typing. It can also help your code run faster when you use forms in different projects. The following procedure illustrates the process. Note that you must declare a form variable based on a specific form, not as a generic UserForm:

```
Sub FormVariableDemo()

Dim frm1 As FormAnOpinion
Set frm1 = FormAnOpinion

' Alter properties and invoke methods via the variable:
With frm1
 .Caption = "All of the above"
 .Show
End With
End Sub
```

Hiding a visible form

Use a form's `Hide` method to close the form so that your program can return to the VBA application's document or activate another form. A statement such as

```
FormErly.Hide
```

does the trick. But you can't use the `Hide` method just anywhere in your program. You must place it in an event procedure belonging to the form. Most often, a `Hide` statement comes at the end of the event procedures for command buttons captioned OK and Cancel. Hiding the form does not remove it from memory. You can redisplay the form at top speed any time you need it with the `Show` method.

Removing a form from memory

If you know your program won't be needing a form again, you can destroy the form altogether, removing it from memory. Just as when you load a form, you use a statement, not a method, to *unload* a form from memory, as in:

```
Unload FormAtion
```

Unloading a form also removes it from the screen, if it was visible.

If you know that a form won't be needed again, you can substitute the `Unload` statement for the `Hide` method in event procedures that close the form (see the previous section).

Event Programming for Forms and Controls

When you activate a `Sub` procedure that doesn't display forms, your code has full control of what the program does and when it does it. Once a form is on the screen, though, your program enters a much more passive state, watchfully waiting for instructions from the user. As the user presses keys or moves or clicks the mouse, each such action generates a software event. In turn, your program registers each event, checking to see whether the form's code contains an event procedure tied to that event. If not, the event passes through your program without a trace. But if the form does have a corresponding event procedure, the program springs to life, faithfully running the procedure.

An event procedure can do anything that any ordinary procedure can. It can calculate variables, manipulate object properties and methods, and even load and display other forms. After the event procedure finishes running, control returns to the form. The program goes back to waiting for the next event to occur.

Common events

VBA forms and their controls are capable of detecting and recognizing a wide variety of different events. Table 24-2 lists commonly useful ones.

Table 24-2 Selected Events for Form and Control Objects

Event(s)	Objects It Applies To	When It Occurs
`Activate`	Forms	Each time the form is activated (receives the focus)
`AddControl`	Forms, frames, and multipage controls	When a control is added to the object while the form is running
`AfterUpdate`	All "action" controls except command buttons (not labels, pictures, frames, or multipage controls)	After VBA has registered a new value for the control, just before exiting the control to move to another one
`Change`	All action controls except labels and command buttons; also mulitpage and tabstrip controls	When the `Value` property of the control changes
`Click`	Forms and all control types	When the user clicks the mouse over the object
`DblClick`	Forms and all control types	When the user double-clicks the mouse over the object
`DropButtonClick`	Combo and text boxes	When the drop-down list drops down (when the user either clicks the drop-down button or presses F4)
`Enter`	All control types	Just before the control receives the focus from another control on the same form
`Error`	Forms and all control types	When an error occurs and error information can't be returned to the program
`Exit`	All control types	Just before the focus moves from the current control to another one on the same form
`KeyUp, KeyDown, KeyPress`	Forms and all control types	When the user presses or releases a key

Continued

Table 24-2 *(continued)*

Event(s)	Objects It Applies To	When It Occurs
`Layout`	Forms, frames, and multipage controls	When the object's size changes
`RemoveControl`	Forms, frames, and multipage controls	When a control is removed from the object while the form is running
`Scroll`	Forms, frames, multipage controls; and text, combo, and list boxes	When the scroll box is repositioned
`Zoom`	Forms, frames, and multipage controls	When the object's magnification (`Zoom` property) changes

Writing and editing event procedures

A form or control *can* respond to lots of different events. But when does it actually respond to a specific event? Only if the form or control in question has an event procedure for that event. Writing an event procedure is called *trapping* the event.

Working in Code windows for forms and controls

Writing an event procedure is just like writing any other VBA code. You simply have to know where to put the statements. Code for an event procedure — and any other code associated with a specific form — belongs in that form's code window in the Visual Basic Editor. Event procedures for all the controls on the form, as well as for the form itself, go in the form's code window.

To write an event procedure for a form or one of its controls, begin by displaying the Code window for the form. Double-clicking the form or control is the quickest way to do so. Alternatively, you can choose View Code from the item's shortcut (right-click) menu.

Next, select the object you're writing the event procedure for — pick it from the Object drop-down list at the top left of the form's Code window (see Figure 24-20). Now select the event you want to write code for. This time, use the Procedure drop-down list at the top right of the Code window.

Beginning work on an event procedure

As soon as you select an event in the Procedure drop-down list, VBA whisks you directly to the event procedure for that event in the Code window. If no code has been previously written for this event procedure, VBA creates a new procedure skeleton for you, placing the insertion point on a blank line between the declaration and the closing statement. If the event procedure already contains code, you're simply placed at the top line of the existing code.

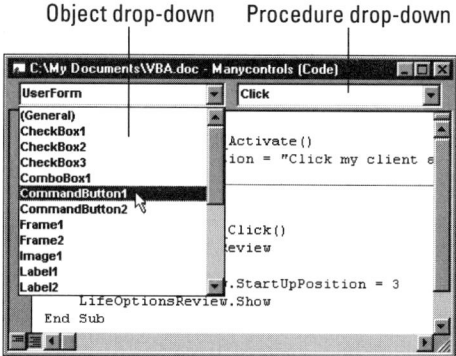

Figure 24-20: Selecting a control in a form's Code window in preparation for writing an event procedure.

Event procedure syntax

The basic syntax for an event procedure is exactly the same as for ordinary Sub procedures you write in VBA modules (see Chapter 20). The only thing unique about an event procedure is its name. For the event procedure to function at all, its name must consist of the name of the object (the form or control), followed by an underscore, followed by the official VBA name for the event. If you have a button named cmdCalculateSquareRoot, the Click event procedure for that button should be named cmdCalculateSquareRoot_Click. You don't usually have to worry about naming an event procedure, because VBA creates the procedure declaration for you when you select the event in the form's Code window.

Caution

The one time you can get into trouble with an event procedure name is when you change the name of the associated object. Let's say you've written an event procedure for the Click event of a button automatically named CommandButton1 by VBA. At this point, the procedure name is CommandButton1_Click. Now you belatedly give the button a more descriptive name, such as cmdTakeOutTheTrash. Unless and until you change the name of the event procedure to cmdTakeOutTheTrash_Click, the button will just sit there mute and unresponsive when the form runs, no matter how many times you click it.

Working with the Click event

Because clicking is so integral an activity in the Windows user interface, you definitely want your VBA forms to respond to mouse-clicks. For most controls, however, you don't have to write any code to make this happen — I'll explain why in a bit. But this is not so for the most important control of all, the command button.

Every command button control definitely must have a Click event procedure, if you want the button to do anything when someone clicks it.

This event procedure simply counts the number of times the user clicks the cmdCountClicks button:

```
Private Sub cmdCountClicks_Click()
' Declaring the intCount variable as Static preserves
'    its value between calls to the procedure
Static intCount As Integer
intCount = intCount + 1
cmdCountClicks.Caption = "You clicked this button " _
    & intCount & " times."
End Sub
```

This code is pretty straightforward. Each time the event procedure runs — which should only occur when the user clicks the button — the value of the intCount variable is increased by one. This value is then used in a string that sets the button's Caption property. By the way, declaring the intCount variable as Static tells VBA to retain the variable's value between passes through the event procedure. If you declared it with a Dim statement, VBA would reinitialize the variable to 0 each time.

Obviously, this example is trivial. Still, it illustrates the way event procedure code looks and acts like any other code.

Often, you don't need to write Click event procedures

Secret

Most VBA controls you can place on a form have (that is, recognize) the Click event. However, except in the case of command buttons, it's usually neither necessary nor wise to write event procedure code for the Click event. The reason: These controls respond to clicks automatically, and in the way you want them to.

For example, say you place some option buttons on a VBA form. When you run the form, clicking an option button selects the one you clicked — no programming is required to make this happen. In like fashion, VBA handles clicks on a toggle button or checkbox automatically, and text box controls automatically respond to clicks by positioning the insertion point at the spot where you click.

What VBA can't do — and what you have to do by writing code — is transfer the setting of the control, after the user has clicked it, to your program. See the sections "Responding to control changes" and "Validating entries" for details on how to do this.

Click events on UserForms

Even forms themselves have Click events. If you want it to, an entire form can act as one big button, so that clicking it anywhere makes something happen in your program. When the program is running, VBA triggers the procedure only if the user clicks over the part of the form that isn't covered by any controls.

Responding to control changes

When users click the up arrow button at the top of a scroll bar or spinner, they deserve some sort of feedback. How much has the value increased by virtue of this click? For that matter, did they actually manage to click the button? Trapping the Change event enables you write code to provide that feedback. The Change event occurs whenever there's a change in the value of the control (that is, when the control's Value property changes). It's most often useful with option buttons, checkboxes, and toggle buttons, as well as with spin buttons and scroll bars.

The simplest response to a Change event is simply to display the changed Value property as the caption of a label. Of course, a Change event procedure can do more with a control's new value than just display it. It can:

- Check to see whether the value meets certain criteria (see "Validating entries" later in this chapter).

- Make calculations based on the value, taking other actions depending on the calculated results.

- Use the control's value to manipulate some other setting, such as the volume on your computer's speaker.

The Change event occurs every time the control's value changes — with *every* mouse click or key press. Sometimes it makes more sense to let the user finish making changes before doing something about those changes. You can use the BeforeUpdate and AfterUpdate events in this situation. The BeforeUpdate event is best used for validating the user's entry in the control and is discussed in "Validating entries" later in this chapter. The AfterUpdate event occurs when the user finishes working with the control and has moved to another control. It's appropriate for performing calculations with the changed value of the original control, or using that value to alter some other setting.

Secret

One caveat: The AfterUpdate event occurs only when the control's setting is changed by the user. If you alter the text in a text box via an assignment statement such as

txtHerTextBox = strNewsFlashScl

you must use the Change event if you want the arrival of the new text to trigger other actions.

Detecting keystrokes

Use the KeyPress, KeyDown, and KeyUp events to respond to the user whacking away at the keyboard. The KeyPress event is good for reading ordinary "typeable" keys when you're processing entries in a text box or combo box. It can also recognize many Ctrl+key combinations and the Backspace key. The KeyDown and KeyUp events, by contrast, detect just about any key combination you throw at them, including convolutions such as Alt+Shift+Ctrl+F9. Although they're harder to work with than `KeyPress`, these events give you more flexibility for creating keyboard shortcuts. For example, you could write a `KeyDown` event procedure to have the Ctrl+Left Arrow and Ctrl+Right Arrow combinations lower and raise the value of a scroll bar or spin button control by 10.

Handling Common Form Programming Tasks

Once you understand how event procedures work, you can put your knowledge to work in building dialog boxes that work the way you want them to and users expect them to. In this section, I've collected a set of tips covering many of the common scenarios in dialog box construction.

Adding a Close or Cancel button

At a minimum, most dialog boxes have one all-important command button: the one that removes the dialog box from the screen. Depending on the way the rest of the dialog box works, this button is typically captioned Close or Cancel, but captions such as Exit, Finish, All Done, or Give Up would also be appropriate. Every form you make needs such a button.

By convention, both Close and Cancel buttons simply hide or unload the form, without doing much else. Here's how to tell which of them your form should have:

- Use a Close button for a form that just displays information or performs tasks immediately, without changing program settings or modifying variables that will be used later in the program.

- Use a Cancel button on a form that does change variables or program settings. When the user clicks the Cancel button, the dialog box closes without recording those changes — everything stays the way it was before the dialog box was displayed. The form should also have an OK button that confirms the changes made.

Easy event procedures for Close and Cancel buttons

Like any other command button, a Close or Cancel button needs a `Click` event procedure to do its job in response to a mouse-click. In most situations, this event procedure requires only a single statement as in these two examples:

```
Private Sub cmdClose_Click()
    Hide ' Object reference to current form implied
End Sub

Private Sub cmdCancel_Click()
    Unload frmOptions
End Sub
```

Of course, event procedures tied to Close or Cancel buttons can do other tasks before closing the form. One simple example would be a statement displaying a message box asking if the user really wants to close (or cancel) the dialog box:

```
Private Sub cmdCancel_Click()
    Message = "Do you really want to close the " _
        & "dialog box and cancel all the changes " _
        & "you've made?"
    If MsgBox(Message, vbYesNo) = vbYes Then
        Hide    ' Hide only if the user clicked Yes
    End If     ' Otherwise do nothing
End Sub
```

The keyboard alternative

Secret

Remember to tie the Close or Cancel button to the Esc key. People are used to pressing Esc to back out of a dialog box, and you shouldn't disappoint them. You don't need to add a `KeyPress` event procedure—simply setting the button's `Cancel` property to True in the Property window does the trick.

Programming the OK button

Suppose someone clicks a dialog box's OK button. The person expects your program to accept the current entries in the form as final, making the specified changes in the program's appearance, behavior, or data. After that, the form should remove itself from the screen.

Gratify these expectations by writing a `Click` event procedure for the OK button. All the code has to do is transfer values from the form's controls to variables in your program, or use the controls' values in conditional statements. The final statement in the procedure should contain the form's `Hide` method or an `Unload` statement. In the following examples, `txtCName` and `txtCAddress` are text boxes. The first two statements transfer their contents to corresponding program variables. Next, the program checks the status of the `tglSend` toggle button and, if it's on, runs a procedure called `SendBillToCustomer`. Finally it `Hide`s the form.

```
Private Sub cmdOK_Click()
    strCustomerName = txtCName.Value
    strCustomerAddress = txtCAddress.Value
    'check toggle button status
    If tglSend.Value = True Then
        SendBillToCustomer
    End If
    Hide
End Sub
```

Validating entries

One of the most common tasks performed in event procedures is validation of entries the user makes via a control. Often, a program can only accept certain values. However, the user is free to enter any text in a text or combo box and to pick almost any number via a slider or spinner. The solution is to add validation code to an event procedure for the control. The code looks at the user's entry, evaluating it to see whether it meets your criteria. If so, the code can store the value or pass it along to another part of your program. If not, you can display a message informing the user of the problem (see Figure 24-21). Alternatively, the code might convert the entry into an acceptable one, say by capitalizing lowercase letters.

Figure 24-21: I used a Change event procedure to check the entry in the text box and display this error message to the user.

Code for validation routines

Validating the value of a control requires you to write `If...Then` statements, `Select Case` statements, or both. This simple example checks a spin button for an unacceptable value:

```
Private Sub spnVolumeControl_Change
    If spnVolumeControl.Value = 11 Then
        MsgBox "11 is not an acceptable setting."
    End If
End Sub
```

Events you can use to validate user entries

It can make sense to perform validation at several different points in the cycle of user and form interactions. Each of these validation points corresponds to a different event procedure on the current control or the form as a whole, as shown here:

Chapter 24: Getting Interactive: Custom Dialog Boxes

When Validation Takes Place	Event Procedure to Use
Each time the value of the control changes	Change event for the control (evaluates the entire value)
Each time a key is pressed	KeyPress event for the control (evaluates the one key just pressed)
When the user finishes working with the control but before moving to another	BeforeUpdate (allows the update to be canceled, returning the user to the control)
When the user closes the form	Click event for the form's OK or Close button

Screening out or changing individual characters

In text box or combo box entries, you may not want to allow certain individual characters anywhere in an entry. Use a KeyPress event procedure to screen them out as the user types them. The following code rejects all characters except letters and numerals:

```
Private Sub txtSerialNumber_KeyPress(ByVal KeyAscii _
    As MSForms.ReturnInteger)
' this whole block is the condition:
If     Chr(KeyAscii) < "0" Or _
    (Chr(KeyAscii) > "9" And Chr(KeyAscii) < "A") Or _
    (Chr(KeyAscii) > "Z" And Chr(KeyAscii) < "a") Or _
    Chr(KeyAscii) > "z" _ Then

    MsgBox "Invalid character!"
    KeyAscii = 0 ' Throw out the character

End If
End Sub
```

Once the If...Then statement detects an invalid character, it displays a message to that effect. Then comes the statement, KeyAscii = 0. KeyAscii is an argument to the KeyPress event procedure, so it works like a local variable in the procedure. Changing its value changes the character code sent to the text box. Because the text box itself won't accept a character code of 0, the character typed by the user vanishes without a trace.

Changing the KeyAscii value also lets you change an invalid entry into a correct one. For example, you could use the following event procedure to display and store all letters typed by the user in uppercase:

```
Private Sub txtSerialNumber_KeyPress(ByVal KeyAscii _
    As MSForms.ReturnInteger)
KeyAscii = Asc(UCase(Chr(KeyAscii)))
End Sub
```

The conversion statement requires three nested functions. Because KeyAscii is a numeric character code, you must first convert it to a string with Chr, then make it uppercase with UCase, and finally convert it back to an integer with Asc.

Delayed validation with the BeforeUpdate event

Sometimes it's preferable to postpone validating the entry until after the user is finished working with it. Some people appreciate being allowed to correct their own mistakes before passing an entry off to the program for a final check — it makes them feel like you're giving them *some* credit in the intelligence department. Another reason to put off validating an entry is because the validation code takes a long time to run.

To check a control's value after the user indicates that work is complete, write a `BeforeUpdate` event procedure. These events occur when the user clicks a different control, presses Tab, or presses the keyboard shortcut for another control. VBA detects the `BeforeUpdate` event just before leaving the original control, which gives you an opportunity to cancel the update and remain there, forcing the user to fix the problem. This example shows how to use the `Cancel` statement:

```
Private Sub txtSerialNumber_Change
    If len(txtSerialNumber.Value) > 5 Then
        MsgBox "Your entry is too long. Try again."
      Cancel
    End If
End Sub
```

Waiting until the form closes

Sometimes it makes sense to postpone validation for a control until the user clicks the OK button to close the entire form. You could do this if the validation criteria depend on the values of other controls. If you go this route, place the validation code in the OK button's `Click` event procedure.

Morphing forms and controls

With event procedures to enliven it, a form can become a dynamic entity that responds to events by changing its own appearance, not just the data in your program. These are key techniques for creating professional-looking forms.

Morphing method 1: Altering control properties

Secret

An easy way to change the appearance of a form is by modifying the properties of the form or its controls in your event procedure code. As you've seen in several previous examples, a basic but very useful application of this idea is to change a label's caption. This lets you send messages to your users based on current conditions.

In the example here, a form has a command button named `cmdClickMe` and a label named `lblLittleMessage`. Clicking the button changes the label's caption. The button's `Click` event procedure looks like this:

```
Private Sub cmdClickMe_Click()

' Declare static integer to count the times
'    the procedure runs
Static X as Integer
```

```
X = X + 1
Select Case X Mod 3
    Case 0
        lblLittleMessage.Caption = Now
    Case 1
        lblLittleMessage.Caption = CStr (X/2 * X)
    Case 2
        lblLittleMessage.Caption = _
            "Life is a series of interruptions."
    End Select
End Sub
```

Of course, you're not limited to changing text on labels. You can modify any property on any of the form's objects, except for read-only properties that are always off limits. Set the `Enabled` property to False when conditions dictate that a control should be unavailable to the user. You can even change the `Value` displayed in a control.

Morphing methods 2: Multiple sets of controls

Secret

Although it's easy to change the appearance of your form in response to events, changing what those controls do takes more work. Suppose your program is supposed to display test questions, get an answer from the user, and then show a message discussing why the chosen answer was right or wrong. You could handle this problem by alternating between two different forms, one for the question and user's answer, the other giving the answer from the program. But consider a slicker method. You could use a single form, displaying one set of controls when the asking the question and another set when providing the answer. This approach involves a little more work, but no rocket science.

An easy way to make one form act as two (or more) is to add a distinct control to the form for every function. You can then use the `Visible` property of each control to hide or display it at your will and pleasure.

Installing and Using New ActiveX Controls

CD

Despite its reputation for software imperialism, Microsoft has taken pains to make its development tools "open." Based on the ActiveX spec, anyone can create new controls that work with just about every Windows-based programming language — including C++, HTML, Visual Basic — and VBA. The benefit to you is that you can add new features by plugging in ActiveX controls that don't come with VBA. Demo versions of some popular ActiveX toolkits are included on the CD-ROM that comes with this book. You can freely mix controls from any source to meet the needs of your programming projects. And all ActiveX controls work in fundamentally the same way as the built-in controls.

Adding new controls to the Toolbox

Before you can use an ActiveX control in your VBA programs, you must install the software for the control onto your computer's hard disk and register the control in Windows. You can register controls in various ways, and the installation step often does it for you. But if you have to do it yourself, the easiest way is in the Visual Basic Editor.

Registering a control

To register a new control, make sure you know the name of the file that contains the control and where it's located on your hard disk. Choose Tools ⇨ References to display the ActiveX references available to your project. In the dialog box, click Browse to display a standard-issue Windows dialog box for opening files. There, select ActiveX controls in the Files of Type combo box. When you locate the file for the control, double-click it to open it. You're returned to the References dialog box, where you should scroll to the item for the control and make sure that its little checkbox is checked. Then close the dialog box.

Next, put the tool in your Toolbox

Once a new control has been registered, the next step is to activate it by placing its icon on the Toolbox. Here's how:

1. Display the Toolbox by selecting any UserForm window or choosing View ⇨ Toolbox.

2. Either right-click the Toolbox and select Additional Controls or choose Tools ⇨ Additional Controls. This brings up the dialog box shown in Figure 24-22.

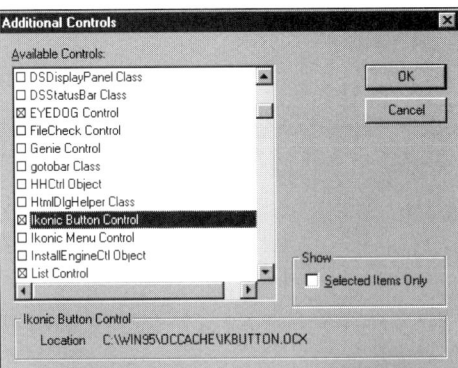

Figure 24-22: Activate new ActiveX controls in this dialog box.

3. Scroll through the list of available controls to locate the one you want to activate. When you find it, check its little checkbox.

Chapter 24: Getting Interactive: Custom Dialog Boxes

4. Close the dialog box. The icon for the newly activated control appears on the Toolbox. Figure 24-23 shows the Toolbox with a bunch of new controls.

Figure 24-23: A customized Toolbox with lots of additional ActiveX controls.

Secret

If you use lots of third-party controls, you can organize them on separate pages of the Toolbox. To add new pages to the Toolbox, right-click over the tabbed area at the top and choose New Page (just like you would with a multipage control on a form). The page that's showing when you activate a control is the one that receives the control's icon.

Using ActiveX controls in your programs

As soon as you have an ActiveX control on the Toolbox, you can add it to your forms just like the stock controls that come with VBA. However, to make the control do something useful, you need to know how its properties and methods work. For that you need the documentation and Help files that come with the control. If the control was properly designed and installed, you should be able to get Help on any of its properties by pressing F1 from when that property is selected in the VBA Properties window.

Some controls are invisible

Secret

Lots of really great ActiveX controls are invisible when your program runs. Rather than directly interacting with the user, such controls perform various actions for you so that you don't have to write your own procedures or create your own objects to get these jobs done. Even though these invisible controls don't show up when your form is actually running, they do appear on the form during the design process.

To use an invisible control in your program, then, you have to add it to a form just as you would any other control. Because the control will never be visible to the user, it doesn't really matter where you stick it on the form. Just put it somewhere where it doesn't overlap other controls.

Conclusion

You can get a lot done in VBA by simply triggering procedures from inside the host application. However, when a VBA program needs user input to accomplish its task, message boxes, input boxes, and custom forms are your communications media. Form design isn't too technically demanding, but it requires that you learn details about the properties and behavior of forms and their controls. Making a form come alive and actually do useful work requires real programming—you must write event procedures for the mouse-clicks and other events you want the form to respond to.

Chapter 25

Building Power Applications

In This Chapter

- Using COM to create custom applications that tap the features of two or more Office applications
- Building COM add-ins to make your Office customizations fast and secure
- Programming the Office Assistant
- Working with Office Developer, the Microsoft toolset for Office VBA programmers
- Protecting the code you've created
- Distributing your solution

If all you ever do with VBA is write individual modules to make your work in Office more efficient, well and good. But VBA is a full-blown software development tool. You can use VBA to create complete custom applications that solve nearly any computing challenges. Your custom VBA software can draw on the power of any combination of the Office applications.

Building Custom Applications with COM Objects

For many custom VBA applications, the goal is to enhance or concentrate the functionality of one of the standard Office applications. For example, you can add a collection of special-purpose financial and reporting functions to an Excel spreadsheet that helps you perform your month-end accounting tasks. You might further enhance such an application by modifying Excel's user interface with new command bars and toolbars. Perhaps you would want to implement a switchboard interface with simple command buttons for inexperienced users who don't want to learn how to navigate the Excel's menu structure. Figure 25-1 illustrates a custom application based on Excel.

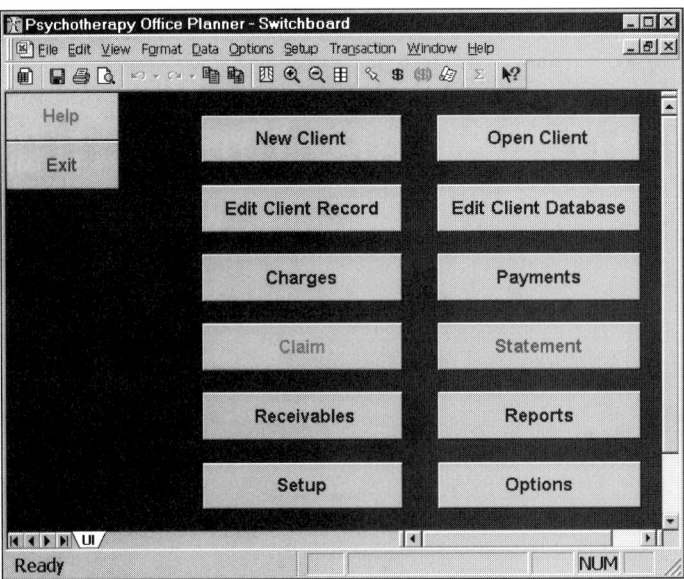

Figure 25-1: A VBA application using a switchboard user interface for less advanced users. Notice the custom command bars at the top of the application window.

But a software world of dazzling variety lies just outside the confines of any particular VBA application — and you're free to travel there with VBA. All the Office applications and accessory components incorporate the COM object model, brazenly exposing their objects so that you can access them in your own programs (see Chapter 22 for the definition of COM). That means you can readily build custom applications that tap the combined firepower of, say, Word, Excel, and Access. For that matter, your VBA apps can draw on the capabilities of any COM-based application, whether it's part of the Office suite or not. If you want to create a Visio organization chart based on personnel data stored in your Outlook folders, you can. Figure 25-2 illustrates a custom Outlook form based on an Excel spreadsheet.

The component object model teaches a developer that great software is built from reusable parts — reinventing the wheel for each application isn't smart, and it's a waste of your time and productivity. Think about the vast array of software functionality Office makes available. Access performs well as a database for large record sets with primary keys and multiple indexes on a table. Excel supports complex statistical and financial formulas that would be hard to duplicate in Access. Word provides text editing and formatting capabilities far beyond those in either Access or Excel. And so it goes. With COM, you can mesh any of these software components to achieve your exact design goals.

In the sample code presented in this section, data stored in Outlook are retrieved and passed for analysis to Excel. The sample code demonstrates many of the concepts you must master to build custom VBA applications.

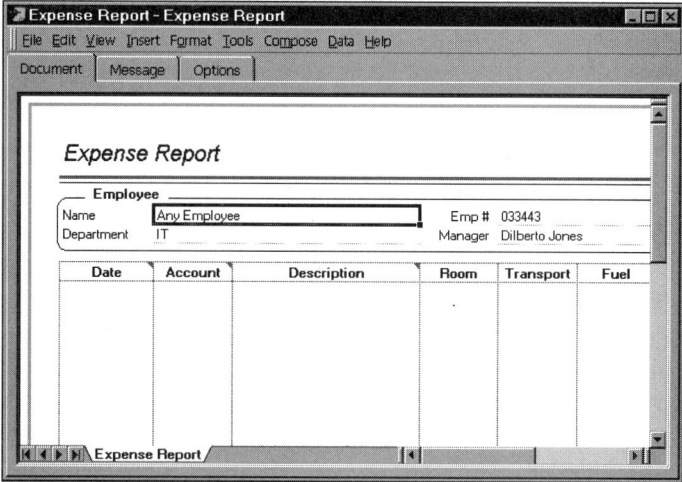

Figure 25-2: A custom Outlook form based on Excel worksheet data.

The Assignment

You're dreaming of that vacation in Hawaii that you've had planned for over a year. You and your team just completed a software project that required several months of 12-hour days and you're really looking forward to a rest. In only a week, you'll be relaxing in the warm waters of the Pacific Ocean! At 4:30 P.M. your boss requests that you drop by for a chat. She informs you that an urgent request has come down from top management that will require an immediate solution.

It seems that management has sponsored a Groupware application in the public folders of your Exchange server that tracks customer contacts, marketing efforts, and sales results in terms of total sales dollars. The bonuses of certain individuals in marketing depend on numbers that have to be extracted from the Customer Contacts public folder, analyzed in Excel, and then presented to management for a final decision by the day on which you're leaving for vacation.

No one else on your team has the time to complete this project. The responsibility has fallen on your shoulders and you don't want to disappoint your boss. All you know about Outlook is that it's your e-mail program. You certainly have no idea about how you're going to move information from an Outlook folder to an Excel spreadsheet. Looks like you're going to endure many more long workdays before you bask in the warmth of the Hawaiian sun.

Defining the problem

Before you start to write a line of code, it's important to define as concretely as possible the problem you need to solve. Unless you understand the problem clearly, you'll thrash around accomplishing little. Taking this advice to heart, you dash off a quick e-mail to your boss requesting additional information on the task. Reading her reply, the challenge comes into focus—they're not requesting the impossible, they just want you to extract information so that the spreadsheet gurus in accounting can work their magic on the numbers. Your task becomes one of moving data from one container application into another.

Once you can summarize the project's overall goal in concrete terms, your next step should be to break it up into a series of specific tasks that your application must perform to meet that goal. Using diagramming software such as Visio—or pencil and paper, if you prefer—sketch out the structure of the application.

Let's assume that your application asks the user, a financial analyst, for a date range and a customer category and then extracts the data from a public Outlook folder to a worksheet. The overall goal is to move the data from one object collection container (an Outlook folder) to a different object collection container (an Excel worksheet).

Fortunately, both of the applications involved are components of Office. Office is built upon ActiveX technology, which has at its foundation the concept of reusable software components defined as objects with properties, events, and methods. Outlook makes available, or exposes, an object model to VBA controller applications such as Excel, where the code will reside.

So in more detail, this problem comes down to determining how to define the objects of Outlook, access those object's properties (their data), and place the retrieved properties into the objects of Excel (sheets, rows, and columns). Once you start thinking in this ActiveX object frame of mind, solving your assignment starts to sound like an exciting adventure rather than a direct path to insomnia.

Getting started

Start a new VBA project by running the Office application that will host the project and opening a new document that will hold the project. In the example code I present a little later, that application is Excel. Then kick-start the Visual Basic Editor by pressing Alt+F11.

Cross-application programming

Maybe it's obvious, but you can only use the objects of another application if that application has been installed on your system. If that requirement is met, working with objects from another COM-based application requires three preliminary steps:

1. In the Visual Basic Editor, add a reference to the external application's object library.
2. Declare variables for the objects you plan to use in the program.
3. Create (instantiate) the objects using the `CreateObject` function.

I have more to say about each of these steps in the next three sections. Please refer to Chapter 22 for the basic techniques you need for working with objects in VBA code.

Adding a reference to the foreign object model

To inform the Visual Basic Editor about an external application's objects model, you add and activate a *reference* to the application's *object library*. In the Visual Basic Editor, choose Tools ➪ References to open the References dialog box (see Figure 25-3).

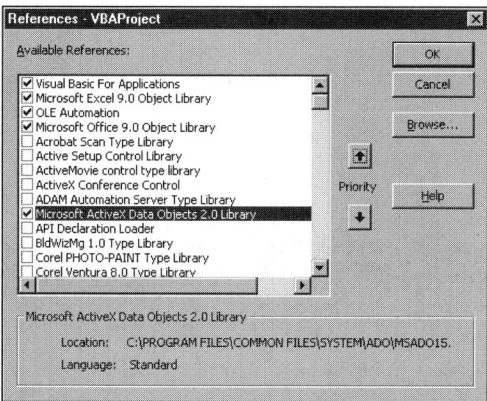

Figure 25-3: Add and activate references to object libraries here.

Outlook's object library should already be listed in the dialog box, assuming you've already installed Outlook on your computer. All you have to do is find it in the Available References list, checking its box to activate it and make its objects accessible. If the object library you want to use isn't listed, add the reference to the list yourself using the Browse button.

Declaring external objects

Use standard VBA syntax to declaring variables for objects from external applications. Use the Object Browser or the external application's Help file to learn what objects it makes available. The following statements from the Declarations section of your module declare variables for the Outlook objects required in the example program:

```
Dim objOutlook As Outlook.Application
Dim objOLNamespace As Outlook.NameSpace
Dim colFolders As Outlook.Folders ' collection of folders
Dim objPeopleFolder As Outlook.MAPIFolder
Dim colPeople As Outlook.Items ' collection of contacts
Dim objPerson As Object ' one individual contact
Dim strName As String
```

Creating the external object

Declaring the objects just announces your intention to use them. You must then actually create the objects you need with Set statements inside a VBA procedure.

Secret

The key to creating an object belonging to an external application is the CreateObject function. CreateObject starts the application, which in turn creates the object. The function's return value is a reference to the object, which you can assign to the appropriate variable. To start the application with a specific file or document, use the GetObject function instead.

Here's a sample procedure for the Excel-Outlook example — all it does is instantiate the needed objects:

```
Sub PeopleWorksheet()

' start Outlook, create an object reference to the application
Set objOutlook = CreateObject("Outlook.Application.9")

' create references to subsidiary Outlook objects
Set objOLNamespace = objOutlook.GetNamespace("MAPI")
Set colFolders = objOLNamespace.Folders   ' all folders
Set objPeopleFolder = colFolders.Item("Personal Folders")

' drill down into folder hierarchy
' reuse some variable names — previous objects no longer needed
Set colFolders = objPeopleFolder.Folders
Set objPeopleFolder = colFolders.Item("Customer Contacts")
Set colPeople = objPeopleFolder.Items

' Call a Sub procedure that puts the Outlook data to work:
OutlookToExcel
End Sub
```

Note that in many situations — including this example — you only need the CreateObject function once. After you create the external application's object, you can access any of its properties and methods. In this case, as is common, those properties include other objects (here, the Folders collection, the Personal folders and Contacts folders, and the collection of items within the Contacts folders).

Secret

Applications you run from within your code via the CreateObject function start up in hidden form — you can't see them on the screen. This is great when you want to use an application's data in your own program without distracting the user. However, sometimes you'll want to see the application in its usual form. Depending on the application, you may have to activate a Display method or set a Visible property to True, with a line of code such as this:

```
objPeopleFolder.Display
```

Using the external objects

At last, you're ready to roll — you can now use the external application's objects in your code, just as if they came from your VBA application:

```
Sub OutlookToExcel()
For each objPerson in colPeople
   With objPerson
' retrieve data from a contact item into variables
       strName = .FullName
       curSales = .SalesTotal
    ... (here's where to put the code that inserts this data
           into your worksheet and analyzes it there)
   End With
Next
End Sub
```

Hawaii here you come.

Secret

Note that this example uses Outlook objects simply to retrieve data from Outlook's data store. However, once you have access to another program's objects in your code, you can trigger any actions they're capable of. You can open, edit, and save documents in the "foreign" application. You can use its data analysis tools, even on data that comes from your VBA code, not the other application.

Building Add-Ins

VBA code running in an ordinary document is fine for personal use, but it's not a very attractive solution for distributing custom applications. By building your own *add-ins,* you can seamlessly blend your VBA customizations with the underlying Office application, making it appear to the user that your enhancements are part and parcel of the original program.

In Office, an add-in is simply a software component that adds functionality to one or more of the Office applications. But add-ins differ from ordinary documents that contain VBA code in two important ways:

- The features provided by an add-in are available to all documents.

- When an add-in is loaded, no document associated with the add-in is accessible to the user. The add-in may make changes to the application's user interface, but the only other way to tell that it's running is to look in the relevant dialog box (usually Tools ⇨ Add-Ins).

Creating application-specific add-ins

In previous versions of Office, an individual add-in could only work with one Office application, and in most cases it consisted of ordinary VBA code that had to be compiled every time the add-in was loaded. You can still create such *application-specific* add-ins, and fairly easily. Here are the basic steps:

1. Create a new document for the add-in.

2. In the new document, add VBA modules and forms, write your code, and test the program. In Access, you need also to add a special table containing Registry information that allows the add-in to be installed.

3. Save the document as an add-in as appropriate for the application (in Word, as a .dot template, in Excel, as an .xla add-in, in PowerPoint, as both a .ppt presentation and a .ppa add-in, and in Access, as an .mda add-in or an .mde database).

4. Install the add-in using the Tools ⇨ Add-Ins dialog box. (In Word, choose Tools ⇨ Templates and Add-Ins and click Add to load the template as an add-in. In Access, choose Tools ⇨ Add-Ins ⇨ Add-In Manager.)

Creating COM add-ins

Office 2000 introduces COM add-ins, a new and more powerful add-in type. A COM add-in is a compiled dynamic link library (DLL) containing special "hooks" that allow it to be loaded by Office. As its name implies, such an add-in works by manipulating the object model of the target Office application through COM technology. COM add-ins have these advantages:

- Because COM add-ins are already compiled, they load and run faster than comparable old-style add-ins.

- A single COM add-in can be shared by more than one Office application when that's appropriate.

- COM add-ins work in Outlook and FrontPage, which don't support application-specific add-ins.

You can create COM add-ins with many different Microsoft programming tools. VBA works, of course, but only if you have Office 2000 Developer (see "Using Office Developer" later in this chapter). Developer includes special software for compiling the add-in code as a DLL and registering the DLL with Windows, and it comes with full instructions for creating COM add-ins using Visual Basic as well as VBA. You can even use Visual C++ or Visual J++ to build COM add-ins.

Using Custom Properties as Document Variables

Plenty of programming situations call for a way to store variable values even when the program isn't running. Take a simple counter, for example. Suppose you want to know how many times one of Excel's toolbar buttons gets clicked over the course of a month. Unless you want to keep Excel running constantly for the entire month, you need to store the current count each time you exit the program, and read it back in the next time you start Excel.

Among the Office applications only Word includes in its object model the tools needed to directly manage persistent variables (via its Variable object). However, custom document properties provide a workaround that fits the bill in Excel and PowerPoint. You can use VBA to create custom document properties, fill them with data, and retrieve that data on demand. And because these properties are part and parcel of the document they're associated with, you don't have to worry about keeping track of them in a separate file — when you save a document, its properties are automatically saved to disk along with the rest of the document. (See Chapter 12 if you need background on document properties and how to work with them in the Properties dialog box.)

To create a new custom document property in Word, Excel, or PowerPoint, use the `Add` method of the document's `CustomDocumentProperties` collection. The following example works in Excel, where the ActiveWorkbook object refers to whatever workbook is currently active when the procedure runs (the comparable objects in Word and PowerPoint are ActiveDocument and ActivePresentation, respectively):

```
ActiveWorkbook.CustomDocumentProperties.Add _
    Name:="Button Count", LinkToContent:=False, _
    Type:=msoPropertyTypeNumber, Value:=0
```

The `LinkToContent` parameter should be False unless you want the value of the property to be based on a range or bookmark. The `Type` parameter determines the data type of the property; valid constants aside from the one shown in valid constants include `msoPropertyTypeBoolean`, `msoPropertyTypeDate`, `msoPropertyTypeFloat`, and `msoPropertyTypeString`.

To retrieve the information stored in a document property, get the Property object's `Value` property with a statement such as:

```
intCurrentCount = _
    ActiveWorkbook.CustomDocumentProperties("Button Count").Value
```

At least two alternative solutions to this problem are available. You can write and read values to the Windows Registry using the `SaveSetting` and `GetSetting` statements, or you can save and read data to separate disk files using the `Put` and `Get` statements.

Programming the Office Assistant

In an Office VBA program, the Office Assistant is at your disposal to dispense information or lead users step by step through tasks that require handholding. As you might expect, you use the Assistant object to display and manipulate the Office Assistant via your VBA code.

Pulling the Assistant's strings

Use the properties of the Assistant object listed in Table 25-1 to control when and how the Assistant appears on screen. Unless you're sure that the Assistant is already turned on, be sure your code sets the `On` property to True before you try to display the Assistant.

Table 25-1   Properties of the Assistant Object

Property	Function	Permitted Value
On	Determines whether the Assistant is available at all. Corresponds to the Use the Office Assistant checkbox in the Office Assistant dialog box.	True or False
Visible	Controls whether the Assistant is visible on the screen.	True or False
FileName	Selects the Office Assistant *actor* that appears on the screen, be it the dog, the paper clip, or what have you.	A valid filename for an Office Assistant actor, including the .acs extension and enclosed in quotes.
Animation	Causes the Assistant to do tricks, that is, to move around on the screen and make noise. You can specify which animation the Assistant performs.	Any of the available constants specifying particular animated animated movements, such as msoAnimationGetArtsy. Use the object browser to list these constants by selecting the MsoAnimationType enumerated type in the Office library.

The code fragment that follows turns on the Assistant, hides it while you change the actor to the Einstein caricature, makes it visible again, and then makes it dance:

```
With Assistant
    .On = True
    .Visible = False
    .FileName = "c:\Program Files\Microsoft Office\Office\genius.acg"
    .Visible = True
    .Animation = msoAnimationEmptyTrash
End With
```

Other properties of the Assistant object let you change in code the same settings available to users in the Office Assistant dialog box. For example, the GuessHelp property corresponds to the Guess Help topics setting in the dialog box. Because most of the controls in the dialog box are checkboxes, the corresponding properties can take values of either True or False. Select the Assistant object in the Object Browser to learn the names of these properties.

Programming the Assistant's balloon

A balloon is that yellow rounded rectangle that appears with the Assistant — it's supposed to represent the Assistant talking to you. Although Office uses the balloon almost exclusively to display Help-related text, you can use VBA to make your own balloons and fill them with stock prices, social commentary, or any information you like. Figure 25-4 illustrates a custom Assistant balloon in action.

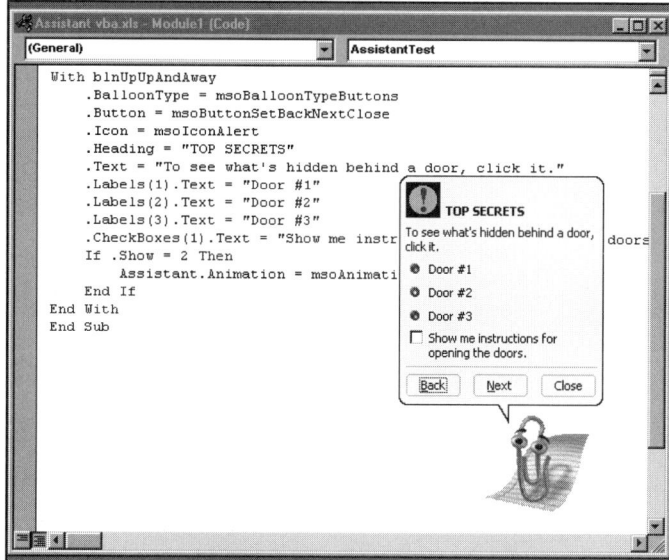

Figure 25-4: You can take control of the content displayed in the Office Assistant's balloon using VBA.

Creating a balloon

The first step on the road to displaying a custom balloon is to create the new, blank balloon object. Curiously, `NewBalloon` is a property, rather than a method, of the Assistant object. At any rate, use a `Set` statement to create the balloon object with code such as:

```
Dim blnUpUpAndAway As Balloon
Set blnUpUpAndAway = Assistant.NewBalloon
```

Once the balloon object is in existence, you can use the properties listed in Table 25-2 to define its contents. At that point, you use the `Show` method to display it to the user.

Table 25-2 Properties of the Balloon Object

Balloon Property	What It Does	Available Settings, Remarks
Mode	Determines whether the user must close the balloon before continuing work with the application.	msoModeModeless (the balloon stays on the screen until the user closes it); msoModeModal (the user must close the balloon); msoModeAutoDown (clicking anywhere on the screen closes the balloon)
BalloonType	Determines whether the labels displayed in the balloon appear as buttons, a numbered list, or bulleted points.	msoBalloonTypeButtons, msoBalloonTypeNumbers, msoBalloonTypeBullets
Icon	Specifies one of the prefab icons available for Assistant balloons.	msoIconNone, msoIconTip, msoIconAlert
Heading	Specifies the text displayed at the very top balloon in bold type.	
Text	Specifies "subheading" text displayed just below the heading and above any labels, checkboxes, or buttons.	
Labels	Lets you access the balloon's labels and specify their text. Labels appear below the text set by the Text property in the format specified by the BalloonType property.	
Checkboxes	Lets you specify text for the balloon's checkboxes and access the user's choice.	
Button	Specifies the number and type of buttons displayed at the bottom of the balloon.	Use one of the MsoButtonSetType constants listed in the Object Browser.

Adding graphics

You can gussy up a custom balloon with one of the stock icons or by including a graphic within a text item. To display an icon, set the Icon property to one of the constants listed in Table 25-2. To display a graphic, designate it as part of the text string used to define the balloon Heading or Text properties, or for one of the labels, as shown in this example:

```
blnUpUpAndAway.Text = "Be Secretive! {bmp c:\secrets.bmp}"
```

Closing balloons

Once your custom balloon is visible on the screen, you'll eventually need a way to remove it. If the balloon is modal (that is, if it's `Mode` property is set to `msoModeModal`, the default), it closes when the user clicks any of its buttons. That includes the buttons at the bottom. If the balloon is modeless, on the other hand, you must use the `Close` method in your procedure to remove the balloon — most often as a response when the user clicks a button such as OK or Cancel.

Working with balloon controls

Just as they do on standard VBA forms, controls on Assistant balloons give users a way to interact with the program. Depending on how you count them, balloons have three kinds of controls: checkboxes, labels (which can act as buttons), and buttons (the ones that appear at the bottom of the balloon).

Adding labels and checkboxes

Every balloon has five labels and five checkboxes. However, unless you specify text for a particular label or checkbox, it doesn't appear on the balloon. To set the `Text` property of a label or checkbox, refer to the item by number in the corresponding collection, as in these examples:

```
With blnUpUpAndAway
    .Labels(2).Text = "You should remember to bring home the milk."
    .Checkboxes(3).Text = "I brought home the milk."
End With
```

Labels can act as buttons, responding when the user clicks them, but only if you set the `BalloonType` property of the balloon to `msoBalloonTypeButtons`. The other available settings for the `BalloonType` property make the labels appear in a bulleted or number list (refer to Table 25-2).

Adding buttons

You specify the number and type of buttons by setting the `Button` property of a balloon object to one of many constants in the `MsoButtonSetType` enumerated type. For example, if you want a balloon with three buttons labeled Abort, Retry, and Ignore, your code should read:

```
blnUpUpAndAway.Button = msoButtonSetAbortRetryIgnore
```

Reading buttons and check boxes

As the programmer, you need a way to tell which button the user clicked and whether each checkbox is checked or not. Here's how. To determine which button was clicked, use the value returned by the `Show` method — it gives you a number representing the clicked button. You can place the value into a variable or use it directly, as in these examples:

```
intButton = blnUpUpAndAway.Show
```

```
Select Case blnUpUpAndAway.Show
    Case msoBalloonButtonOK
        (code to run if the user clicked OK button)
    Case msoBalloonButtonCancel
        (code to run if the user clicked the Cancel button)
    Case 2
        (code to run if the user clicked the 2nd label button)
End Select
```

As the first two `Case` statements show, the Office object library includes named constants that correspond to the value of each type of "regular" button (the type that appear at the bottom of the balloon). You can use the constants to see if one of these buttons was clicked. To detect a click on a label button, just use the label's number, as shown in the third `Case` statement.

To read the current state of the balloon's checkboxes, retrieve the `Checked` property of each box after the user closes the balloon. In the simplest scenario, you'd use a series of `If...Then` statements, one for each checkbox.

```
With blnUpUpAndAway
    If .CheckBoxes(1).Checked Then
        (code to run if checkbox 1 is checked)
    Else
        (code to run if checkbox 1 is not checked)
    End If
    If .CheckBoxes(2).Checked Then
        (code to run if check box 2 is checked)
    Else
        (code to run if checkbox 2 is not checked)
    End If
End With
```

Secret

You can use the balloon's `Callback` property to designate a procedure that processes button clicks. This technique is especially useful—and in fact is mandatory—with modeless balloons that remain open even after the user clicks a button.

Securing Your Code with Digital Certificates

Like anything powerful, VBA can be used for good or ill. As Chapter 13 suggests, VBA procedures can carry viruses that wreak havoc with your system. For that matter, code from a well-intentioned but unskilled programmer sometimes causes serious problems.

New in this version VBA is the ability to identify VBA projects using *digital certificates*. Using Microsoft's analogy, a digital certificate has a function similar to that of a wax seal on an envelope, allowing the recipient to know who sent the project and that its contents haven't been modified. Unlike a seal, however, a digital certificate doesn't assure the recipient that no one else has viewed the project. (To prevent others from seeing your code, follow the steps discussed in "Locking Your Code" later in the chapter.)

A user who opens a file or loads an add-in signed with a digital certificate sees the digital signature, which displays the name of the person who signed it with other identifying information. If everything looks OK, the user approves the code and it becomes active on her system. If the digital signature is missing, however, or if the identifying information is incorrect, the user can choose not to open or load the item.

Caution

Digital signatures are recognized only if Internet Explorer 4 or later is present on the user's system.

As a developer, signing your work digitally requires that you first obtain and install one or more digital certificates on your computer. Digital certificates are issued by commercial certification authorities, to whom you can apply as an individual or organization. If you're a staff programmer, you probably don't have the authority to apply for a digital certificate for your company. Instead, your organization obtains the certificates and sets up a system for administering them, and you request a certificate from whoever is responsible for security in your group.

Anyway, once the digital certificate is in place on your computer, digitally signing the current project is a straightforward process. In the Visual Basic Editor, choose Tools ⇨ Digital Signature. In the resulting dialog box, click Choose to display a list of the certificates in place on your system. Make a selection and OK both dialog boxes to activate the signature.

Caution

When a project carries a digital signature, any change made to the project in the absence of the original certificate invalidates and removes the signature. If you plan to pass on the project in its signed form to someone else, don't modify the project unless you have a copy of the digital certificate on your computer.

In many organizations, only project leaders or other administrative types will actually sign VBA projects. As a team developer in this scenario you would complete a project and forward it to the person with signing authority for final testing, approval, and a signature. Only then would the project be distributed to users.

Locking Your Code

If you are developing custom applications for resale and you want to keep others from unauthorized use of all your hard work, you need to protect the code that you've created, hiding it so that no one can see or modify it. Protecting your code often makes sense when you distribute your application in a corporate environment to keep it from inadvertent or malicious changes. Once your project is debugged and tested, take these steps to protect the code that you've written:

1. Select the Tools ⇨ <ProjectName> Properties command and, in the Project Properties dialog box, switch to the Protection tab.

2. Check the Lock Project for Viewing box to ensure that your code cannot be viewed.

3. Enter a password twice to confirm you've typed it correctly. Don't misplace the password or you will be unable to modify your code at a later date.
4. Click OK.

Once a project is locked, only its name appears in the Project window. Anyone trying to see the project's contents must type in the password to proceed.

You can enter a password without checking the Lock Project for Viewing box. In this case, the password is required to open the Project Properties dialog box, but not to view or modify the project's code or forms.

Using Office Developer

For anyone doing serious VBA development work, Office 2000 Developer is a must. It's a special edition of Office intended for VBA programmers. Table 25-3 lists the tools and other components provided with Office 2000 Developer.

Table 25-3 Tools in Office 2000 Developer

Tool	Function
Package and Deployment Wizard	Creates setup disks for distribution of your application.
Visual Source Safe	Keeps track of versions.
COM Add-In Designer and templates	Converts VBA code into COM add-in DLLs; templates enable you to create COM add-ins using Visual Basic, Java, or C++.
Code Librarian	Allows storage and reuse of code in a searchable database, and includes loads of prefab code in various Microsoft languages.
Error Handler	Automates the addition of standardized custom error-handling routines to your code.
Code Commenter	Adds automatic comment blocks to your code according to your specifications.
String Editor	Assists in writing SQL statements for database access and manipulation.
Data Environment Designer	Provides easier database connections in host applications other than Access.
Data Report Designer	Enables you to design database reports visually without Access.

Tool	Function
Additional ActiveX controls	Includes controls such as a data-aware grid and the Common Dialog control.
HTML Help Workshop	Enables you to create complete HTML Help systems for your custom applications.
Access Run-time	Allows royalty-free distribution of Access applications to users who don't have Access.
Replication Manager	Displays and manages replicated Jet databases on networks or the Internet.

Distributing your solution

To prepare your solution for distribution to other users, use the Package and Deployment Wizard included in Office Developer. The wizard builds the distribution files needed for installing and running the application. A full discussion of the Package and Deployment Wizard is beyond the scope of this chapter, but the following points summarize the steps it walks you through:

- Specifies the files required for your application, including your main application file containing the objects and code that make up your application; data files used by your application; icon, bitmap, sound, or multimedia files; and custom Help files (including ActiveX controls, DLLs, and run-time files).

- Creates shortcuts and Start menu items for Windows.

- Writes the Windows Registry keys (or modifications to existing keys) necessary for your application.

- Identifies redistributable components for your application, such as ODBC drivers.

- Specifies options for a typical, custom, or compact installation.

- Sets options for distribution media (floppy disk, network share point, or CD-ROM).

Building stand-alone Access applications

When you develop custom applications using Excel, Word, PowerPoint, or Outlook, the users of your applications must have Office installed to run them. The situation is different for custom Access apps, if you have Office Developer. By distributing with your application the Access Run Time module, a component of Office Developer, you assure that your apps can run on anyone's computer, regardless of whether Access already resides there. You can freely distribute the database engine provided with either Access, Jet, or MSDE.

Conclusion

Most Office users will never write a single line of VBA code. Unbeknownst to them, however, a powerhouse programming language waits patiently just beyond the familiar confines of Word, Excel, and the other Office applications. This section rends the veil, putting into your hands the fundamental skills you need to take command of the rich VBA programming resources for applications of your own design.

Part VII
Secrets of Word 2000

Chapter 26: Power Customizing

Chapter 27: Expert Editing

Chapter 28: Full-Speed Formatting

Chapter 29: Page Layout and Desktop Publishing

Chapter 30: Getting Organized with Tables and Outlines

Chapter 31: The Book of Numbers

Chapter 32: Creating Long and Technical Documents

Chapter 33: A Dream of Fields

Chapter 34: Word Power Programming

Chapter 26
Power Customizing

In This Chapter

▶ Setting startup options

▶ Customizing the screen for top editing efficiency

▶ Using custom keyboard shortcuts, with special tips on using ordinary keys as shortcut keys

▶ Using templates to keep your own toolbar and keyboard customizations without interfering with group document production

---

Word is easily the most customizable of the Office applications. While all Office programs let you tweak the toolbars and menus to taste, Word goes further, enabling direct control over the shortcut (right-click) menus via drag-and-drop. Many more special options govern the look and function of the program. And you have far more control over keyboard layout and shortcuts than you do in the other Office apps.

Startup Options

Your customization options begin each time you decide to run Word. Word accepts six optional switches on the command line. As listed in Table 26-1, these command line switches determine whether Word creates a blank document when it starts; whether it ignores custom templates and interface settings; which macro it should run (or not run) at startup; and which add-in it should load. This example:

```
winword /a /n
```

would run Word but not load any templates or macros, and not create a new empty document. Chapter 1 discusses the techniques for using command line switches to start Office applications.

Table 26-1   Word Command Line Switches

Command Line Switch	What It Does
/n	Starts Word with an empty window — Word doesn't open a new blank document as it otherwise would.
/a	Starts Word without any templates or add-ins. Word runs with all options, menus, toolbars, and keyboard shortcuts set to their defaults. Don't worry, your customizations aren't lost — they reappear the next time you run Word without the /a parameter.
/m*macroname*	Makes Word run the named macro as soon as the program starts.
/m	Prevents AutoExec macros from running (otherwise, Word automatically runs any macro named AutoExec when it starts).
/l"*addin*"	Loads the named Word add-in (.wll file). Add-ins are special-purpose programs that add new commands or other features to Word. Include the entire path between the quote marks.
/t"*template*"	Opens a new empty document based on the named template. Include the entire path.

Selecting Word Options

Choosing Tools ➪ Options brings up a dialog box full of more than 100 options that control all facets of Word's operations. Figure 26-1 shows the View tab of the Options dialog box. As you can see, and as in the other Office apps, the Options dialog box groups its options on separate tabs — in Word's case, there are ten of them.

I'm not going to cover the available options exhaustively, because many of them are self-explanatory and many others are useful to very few people. In general, I mention specific options at the places in the text where they're relevant to the task at hand. For now, I simply recommend that you set aside a few minutes sometime to acquaint yourself with what the Options dialog box has to offer. Page through all the tabs, using the help tool to explain any choices whose functions aren't clear.

Customizing the Screen

Most Word users quickly get comfortable with the main views: Normal, Print Layout (previously called Page Layout), and Web Layout (formerly Online Layout). Two additional views, Outline and Master Document, are covered in Chapters 30 and 32, respectively. At any rate, the quickest way to "customize" your screen is to switch between these views as your needs dictate. Here's a quick review of the main views with their chief characteristics:

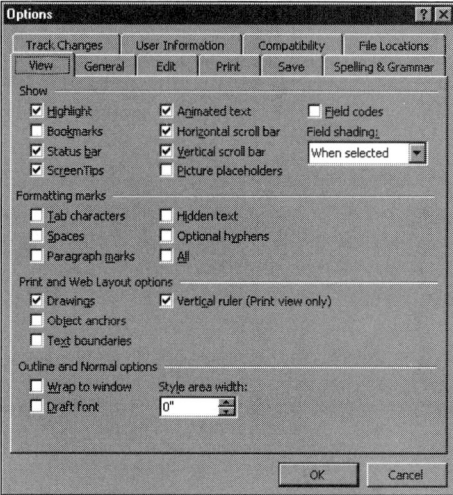

Figure 26-1: Word's Options dialog box, with the View tab (one of 10!) selected.

- **Normal view.** Shows text with character and (most) paragraph formatting. You can also see imported graphics, but not where they will appear in print or on a Web page. Autoshape graphics you draw within Word and columns aren't displayed. Page and section breaks appear as lines.

- **Print Layout view.** Shows the document as it will appear when printed. All graphics, columns, and tables look just as they do on the printed page, allowing for the reduced resolution of the screen. If you zoom out, Word displays the document on convincing-looking "pages."

- **Web Layout view.** Shows the document as it would look in a browser, more or less. All page breaks are removed from the screen (although they're preserved in the document). Some formatting elements available in Print Layout view are limited or missing altogether.

Using the entire screen for your document in Full Screen view

You may know that Word's Full Screen view exists, but I bet you haven't trained yourself to use it. If on-screen space is at a premium, I suggest you make the effort now. Choose View ➪ Full Screen to switch to Full Screen view. This works in Print Preview mode as well, but there, the Print Preview toolbar has a default Full Screen toggle button. You can add this button to other toolbars, of course, using the standard customization methods covered in Chapter 5.

Sure, with today's larger monitors and higher resolutions, more of us can have our cake (scads of toolbars) and eat it too (with plenty of room on the screen left for documents). But lots of folks are still making do with standard 14-inch screens, and notebook users have even less screen real estate to work with.

Full Screen view devotes the entire screen to your document, hiding the menu, the toolbars, the status bar, the scrollbars, and even the title bar at the top of Word's window. The only extraneous item left is a tiny floating Full Screen toolbar. It contains a single escape button that takes you back to the regular window layout. If you prefer, you can dock the Full Screen toolbar along any of the four sides of the Word window, a configuration that keeps it out of the way of your text. But then the toolbar takes up too much space — so I recommend against this setup.

Once the initial anxiety passes (No toolbars?! How can I cope?), you'll find that you still have access to all of Word's power. Of course, all your keyboard shortcuts still work. But so does the top menu bar. All you have to do is open it via a keyboard shortcut (Alt+F for the File menu, for instance). Pressing Alt alone while in Full Screen view displays the menu bar itself.

You can also make the menu bar appear by moving the mouse to the top of the screen. Word is savvy enough to detect the mouse just before it gets to the very top of the screen. In other words, you can station the Office Shortcut bar or the Windows Taskbar up there, even on Auto Hide, and still access the Word menu bar with the mouse.

Adding back window elements to Full Screen view

OK, so that covers the menu bar. But what if you can't be happy unless you can see the ruler, one of the toolbars, or maybe the horizontal scrollbar? No problem — just turn on whatever components you need individually. To display the ruler, choose View ➪ Ruler. If your security blankets are the scrollbars or the status bar, display them by choosing Tools ➪ Options and checking the appropriate boxes on the View tab.

To turn on that certain toolbar, choose View ➪ Toolbars and pick it from a list, or for more choices, pick Customize, and check off the toolbar you want displayed. Full Screen view remembers which toolbars you unhide in this view and displays them again the next time you switch to this view.

But if all you need are 10 or 20 crucial buttons, you can add them to the Full Screen toolbar. Just be aware that you can only customize this toolbar while you're in Full Screen view. To do so, choose Tools ➪ Customize and start adding buttons with the techniques detailed in Chapter 5.

Dumping the Full Screen toolbar

For a perfectly pristine, fully full screen, you can use a VBA macro to remove the Full Screen toolbar when you toggle Full Screen view on and off. You can still return to an ordinary view by pressing Esc. This code you need is listed in the section "Redefining Word's Built-In Commands" later in this chapter.

Customizing tips for special screen situations

The tips here all rely on selections in the View tab of the Options dialog box. Choose Tools ⇨ Options, and then click the View tab to display the relevant set of choices, as shown previously in Figure 26-1.

Toggling the zoom factor

Chapter 3 includes a VBA macro that enables you to flip back and forth between two different magnifications of your document with a single button click. This macro is much more efficient than manually adjusting the zoom setting over and over again.

Maximizing performance

When your main concern is efficient text editing, fine-tuning Word's screen-related options can boost the program's performance. Try the following settings on the View tab:

- **Picture placeholders.** Check this box to have Word display plain rectangles in place of the pictures in your document. This can be a major timesaver while you're working on the text — it takes a lot of computer horsepower to display complex drawings or large bitmaps, particularly if they contain many different colors. When it's time to proof the document as a whole, just uncheck the box again and the pictures will reappear. Obviously, this setting doesn't help if your document has no pictures.

- **Draft font.** Checking this box displays all text in a single plain-looking font in Normal and Outline views. That saves time, because Word no longer spends time figuring out how to display all those different typefaces, sizes, and colors. In draft mode, Word displays all text at the same size, ignores most paragraph formatting, and indicates character attributes like bold, italics, and highlighting by underlining the affected text. But you'll only notice a significant speedup if you're trying to run Word on an old, underpowered PC — fancy screen fonts just aren't a strain for a Pentium.

Minimizing on-screen distractions

Many people find that they write better if they concentrate on document content first, and then go back and format the text so that it looks nice.

- **Draft font.** See the last point in the preceding section. Even if it doesn't appreciably speed up your screen, the Draft font option can still be helpful if you prefer to focus on content alone when you're writing. When you want to work on the document's format, just turn off the Draft font.

- **Animated text.** Text animation may have a place in Web page design and custom applications — although I'm not convinced — but it's definitely annoying when you're writing. Uncheck this box to turn off the special effects without removing the animation.

- **Highlight.** If someone has marked up the document with colored highlights, you may find it difficult to focus on the nonhighlighted text when you have to edit it. Uncheck this box to display everything in plain black and white.

Maximizing screen space, when you don't want to use Full Screen view

The following options in the Window section of the View tab can give you more room for your work:

- **Status bar.** Uncheck this box to hide the status bar, opening up another third of an inch or so (depending on your monitor) for your document.

- **Horizontal scrollbar and Vertical scrollbar.** If you're good with the keyboard, the scrollbars just get in the way. Turn 'em off. Note that the horizontal scrollbar contains the buttons for the various views (Normal, Page Layout, Outline, and Online), but you can change views quickly enough with the View menu or the corresponding keyboard shortcuts (Alt+Ctrl with N, P, O — Word doesn't have a default shortcut for the Online view).

- **Style area.** The little-known style area is a vertical region along the left edge of the window where Word displays paragraph style names. It's handy for scanning visually through a document to see how styles look in use, or to hunt for paragraphs with incorrect styles. On the other hand, it cuts into your usable screen area significantly. The easiest way to remove it is by dragging the vertical line separating it from the document all the way over to the left side of the window. You can also set its size in inches via the Options dialog box — a 0 setting shuts it off. Oh, and by the way — the style area is visible only in Normal and Outline views.

Using Word effectively in a small window

Word processing is best done in the largest possible editing space. If you need to work with other applications, however, you may need to shrink Word's window so that you can see all of your programs at once.

In this situation you are still able to see your text if you check the Wrap to Window checkbox on the Tools ➪ Options dialog box (View tab). Now, instead of truncating each line at the right edge of the window, Word temporarily reformats each paragraph — text that would normally fall past the edge wraps to the next line. The document still prints with the original formatting and returns to its normal appearance on the screen when you uncheck the box.

Switching to Word's Web Layout view turns on the Wrap to Window function automatically. However, Web Layout view has other effects you may not want, such as removing page breaks, and it doesn't resize the window. What you really need is a VBA procedure to switch to a smaller window and change the word wrapping setting in a single step, and then return to the standard wrapping setting when you maximize the window again. Ideally, the macro would take effect when you use the standard Windows buttons for restoring and maximizing an application, but that won't work. Instead, the following macro toggles between the two window configurations. Place it on a toolbar button or give it a keyboard shortcut:

```
Sub ToggleWindowSizeAndWrapToWindow ()
Dim WrapStateAs Boolean
WrapState = True ' Set variable default
If Application.WindowState = wdWindowStateNormal Then
    Application.WindowState = wdWindowStateMaximize
    WrapState = False
Else
    Application.WindowState = wdWindowStateNormal
End If
ActiveWindow.View.WrapToWindow = WrapState
End Sub
```

Activating the Word calculator

This secret isn't primarily a screen customization, but I can't find a better place to discuss it. Word has always had a command for performing calculations on numbers visible on the screen, in your documents. Unfortunately, Word buries this handy command where you're not likely to come across it, in the Customize dialog box. To find and activate the command, choose Tools ➪ Customize and switch to the Commands tab. Select Tools in the Categories list, and then scroll way down in the Commands list until you see the Tools Calculate command. Haul it out and put it on the Tools menu or on a toolbar.

Once the Calculate command is accessible, performing a calculation is as simple as selecting the numbers in your document and clicking the button or menu item. It doesn't matter how numbers are arranged — in a row, in a column, or even within or across paragraphs, separated by any amount of text. The result appears in the status bar and is placed on the clipboard, so doing a quick Ctrl+V deposits it at the insertion point. By default, Word adds the selected numbers, but it will dutifully perform subtraction, multiplication, or division if the appropriate symbol precedes a number in the selected text.

Customizations, Templates, and Documents

Please note that Word can store customizations, including macros, customized toolbars and menus, and keyboard shortcuts, in templates or in documents. Only templates can contain AutoText entries, however. By default, all of these items are placed in the Normal.dot template, making them available in all documents. But if two or more people share the same copy of Word, each can have a different custom setup by maintaining a unique template where these customizations are stored. And if a particular customization is only useful with a specific document, you can store it in that document rather than in a template.

As you might expect, you decide where a new toolbar, macro, keyboard shortcut, or AutoText entry is to be stored when you create it. In Word, the dialog boxes for creating each of these items contain drop-down lists from which you can select a destination: Normal.dot, any other templates currently active or attached to the current document, or the document itself. See the section "Using Word templates" later in this chapter for details on how templates work.

Customizing the toolbars and menus

Chapter 5 covers Office's drag-and-drop techniques for building a made-to-order set of toolbars and menus. Just remember, Office blurs the distinction between toolbars and menus — you can slap buttons on the top menu bar and put menus into the toolbars.

Customizing the shortcut menus

Like other Office applications, Word lets you customize the shortcut (right-click) menus via drag and drop. The process is detailed in Chapter 5. One tip I'll mention here: Place the Cut, Copy, and Paste commands on the Grammar and Spelling shortcut menus. That way, you won't have to stall when you want to edit text that Word thinks is misspelled or grammatically weak.

Customizing the Word keyboard

Keyboard efficiency matters more in Word than in any other Office application. You need both hands on the keyboard for full-tilt typing and editing, and you must break your stride every time you reach for the mouse.

That's why Word, of all the Office applications, gives you the most freedom to customize the keyboard. Do yourself a favor — take advantage of that power. Create a keyboard shortcut for every item you use regularly, whether it's a command, macro, style, font, or AutoText entry; or a character that isn't already available on the keyboard. For that matter, you should change any of the stock shortcuts that you find hard to remember or inconvenient to reach.

Creating and changing keyboard shortcuts

Secret

The Customize Keyboard dialog box described later works for every kind of item to which shortcuts can be assigned, from Word commands to individual special characters. However, you can also assign shortcuts to styles via the Style dialog box and to any single character via the Symbol dialog box. In fact, I recommend you use the latter dialog box (display it by choosing Insert ➪ Symbol) to create shortcuts for individual characters, because it can display all available characters at once and in any font.

To create or redefine a keyboard shortcut, start by choosing Tools ➪ Customize. Word's Customize dialog box no longer offers a Keyboard tab. Instead, you must choose the Keyboard button to bring up the Customize Keyboard dialog box, shown in Figure 26-2.

To assign a keyboard shortcut to a Word command or other function, start by finding the item in the Commands list on the right. Chapter 5 reviews how to navigate the Categories and Commands lists when customizing Office applications.

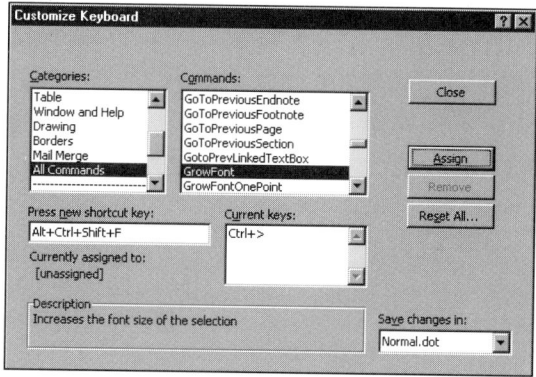

Figure 26-2: The Customize Keyboard dialog box.

When you've selected the item, its existing keyboard shortcuts appear in the Current Keys list at the lower right (who knows — maybe you don't need to create a new shortcut after all). You can have as many keyboard shortcuts as you like for each command, so there's no "pressing" need to delete any of the existing shortcuts. To create a new shortcut, click in the Press New Shortcut field and then type the key or keys you've chosen for the shortcut. The shortcut appears in written form.

Before you choose Assign to create the new shortcut, check to make sure that the keys you've chosen aren't already assigned to some other command. If they are, the message Currently Assigned To: appears just below your entry. You're free to replace the existing assignment, but please don't, unless it's one you're definitely not using already.

Secret

When you choose Assign, the new shortcut is added to the Current Keys list. By the way, the list can hold only eight shortcuts, but shortcuts nine and above will work even though you can't see them on the list.

Choosing keys for shortcuts

When you're cooking up shortcuts, make an effort to be organized — try to assign similar shortcuts to similar commands. You might use the Alt+Ctrl combinations for file- and document-related commands, Alt+Shift combinations for formatting commands, and so on. I realize that there's a problem with this advice: It conflicts with another good idea, that you should stick to Word's default shortcuts whenever possible.

Because few of the defaults follow any sort of recognizable pattern, imposing consistency means sacrificing defaults. The real world is a tough place. In any case, don't neglect any key as a possible shortcut. Except for nonstandard keys — like those Fn keys on most notebook PCs — most keys can be used as shortcuts, alone or in combination with Alt, Ctrl, or Shift. On my computer, Alt+Scroll Lock and Ctrl+Break are valid combinations (you may have different results with these system keys depending on who made the computer and keyboard).

Secret

The Scroll Lock key deserves special mention. Here's a perfectly good key that almost all programs treat as a taboo. In Word, you can use Scroll Lock — all by itself — as a shortcut key, though it takes a little doing. See "Using off-limits keys in custom keyboard shortcuts" later.

Maximum control with two-step shortcuts

Secret

If you're really hungry for more keyboard shortcuts, you'll get all you can eat with Word's two-step shortcuts. In a two-step shortcut, the first key or combination you press initiates the sequence; you press another key combo to complete it. Let's say you set aside F10 as the first key for all your two-step shortcuts. You can now create shortcuts such as F10, 5 (you press F10, then the 5 key), or for that matter F10, F10.

Caution

You can't use the Ctrl or Alt keys in the second step of a two-step shortcut.

Yes, two steps take longer than one, but they're still faster than using the menus or the mouse. Besides, they're often easier (to remember and to press) than some complex combination involving Alt, Ctrl, and Shift. And think of the possibilities they open.

Two-step shortcuts are great for groups of similar commands. Sticking with the F10 example, you could assign F10, F1 through F10, F10 to your most commonly used paragraph styles. You might activate your favorite fonts via F10, 1 through F10, 0 (using the typewriter number keys), while F10, a through F10, z might be given over to special dingbat characters such as ❑. Of course, that still leaves you with F10, A through F10, Z and tons of other combinations with the punctuation keys. By the way, this is the system Word uses for entering accented characters — for example, Ctrl+' followed by e inserts an é into your document.

Using off-limits keys in custom keyboard shortcuts

The Customize Keyboard dialog box refuses to recognize many keys on your keyboard — it just beeps when you type them as part of a new keyboard shortcut. These off-limits keys include all the alphanumeric characters, the punctuation keys, and all of the numeric keypad keys, plus system keys such as Scroll Lock. (Mind you, the Customize dialog box does allow these keys when used in combination with Alt or Ctrl, but not alone.)

Word is trying to protect the novice user from making a mess of the keyboard. I appreciate the thought, but I'm a grown-up now and willing to live with a little risk. I *never* type a reverse apostrophe, hardly ever \ or |, and only occasionally [or] (that is, the square bracket characters located on the pair of keys just to the right of the P key). Therefore, these keys are much more useful to me as ultra-fast, one-key shortcuts to Word commands.

On my keyboard, for example, I use the ` key to swap the last two characters I typed, when I typed them in reverse order — which is pretty darn otfen. The \ key changes the case of the next letter, and the [and] keys cut the word to the left or right of the insertion point, respectively.

Putting the off-limits keys to work just takes a little VBA. Behind the scenes, Word keeps track of each key by a code number. For example, the F1 key is 112, the X key is 88, and the Delete key is 46. You use these key codes in VBA procedures to specify the keys you want to redefine.

Word also supplies named constants for the key codes. Table 26-2 lists the named constants and key codes of some of the keys you can't access in the Customize Keyboard dialog box. As you can see, the table lists only plain and shifted keys. The reason? You don't need VBA if you're using Alt or Ctrl in your shortcut, because the Customize Keyboard dialog box reads any combination that includes either of those keys. (For special projects, you can also redefine the standard alphanumeric and punctuation keys — to learn their key codes and named constants, search for wdKey in the Object Browser.

Table 26-2   Selected Key Codes for Customizing

Key	Key Code Constant	Key Code (Key Alone)	Key Code (with Shift)
5 on the numeric keypad (with Num Lock off)	wdKeyNumeric5Special	12	268
Scroll Lock	wdKeyScrollLock	145	401
`	wdKeyBackSingleQuote	192	—
~	*	—	448
[	wdKeyOpenSquareBrace	219	—
{	*	—	475
\	wdKeyBackSlash	220	—
|	*	—	476
]	wdKeyCloseSquareBrace	221	—
}	*	—	477
Spacebar	wdKeySpacebar	32	288
0 on the numeric keypad	wdKeyNumeric0	96	352
1 on the numeric keypad	wdKeyNumeric1	97	353
2 on the numeric keypad	wdKeyNumeric2	98	354
3 on the numeric keypad	wdKeyNumeric3	99	355
4 on the numeric keypad	wdKeyNumeric4	100	356
5 on the numeric keypad	wdKeyNumeric5	101	357
6 on the numeric keypad	wdKeyNumeric6	102	358
7 on the numeric keypad	wdKeyNumeric7	103	359

Continued

Table 26-2 *(continued)*

Key	Key Code Constant	Key Code (Key Alone)	Key Code (with Shift)
8 on the numeric keypad	wdKeyNumeric8	104	360
9 on the numeric keypad	wdKeyNumeric9	105	361
* on the numeric keypad	wdKeyNumericMultiply	106	362
+ on the numeric keypad	wdKeyNumericAdd	107	363
- on the numeric keypad	wdKeyNumericSubtract	109	365
. on the numeric keypad	wdKeyNumericDecimal	110	366
/ on the numeric keypad	wdKeyNumericDivide	111	367

Note: To specify the keys marked with *, you need the `BuildKeyCode` method of the `KeyCode` argument of the `KeyBindinds.Add` method. Use `wdKeyShift` as Arg1 and the constant for the key immediately above it in the table as Arg2 (see Word VBA Help on BuildKeyCode).

The following sample macro shows how to assign the Scroll Lock key to a command, in this case the Word Count command. The `Add` method of the `KeyBindings` object takes a `KeyCategory` argument for the type of item you're working with (command, macro, style, or what have you). Then come the `Command` and `KeyCode` arguments for the command name and key code, respectively. The example uses the named constant for the Scroll Lock key, but the equivalent numeric key code, 145, would work just as well.

```
Sub AssignWordCountToScrollLock()
    KeyBindings.Add KeyCategory:=, _
        Command:="ToolsWordCount", KeyCode:=wdKeyScrollLock
End Sub
```

If you don't want to type a new macro every time you redefine a key, use the macro listed here and supplied on the CD-ROM that comes with the book. When you run it, it asks you whether the keyboard shortcut you're creating is for a macro or one of Word's built-in commands. Next, you type in the name of the macro or command. You must enter the exact spelling. To find a command's official name, locate it in the Customize Keyboard dialog box, just as if you were going to assign a keyboard shortcut to the command. Finally, type in the code number for the chosen shortcut key — you have to use the number, not the corresponding named constant.

Chapter 26: Power Customizing

```
Sub AssignHiddenKeys()

On Error GoTo BYE

strMacroQuery = "Are you defining a keyboard shortcut " & _
    "for a macro? " + Chr(13) + "If so, click Yes. " & _
    "For built-in commands, click No."
Style = vbYesNo + vbQuestion + vbDefaultButton2
strTitle = "Office Secrets Key Assigner"
strMessage1 = "Type the name of the command or macro " & _
    "you want to assign to a shortcut."
strMessage2 = "Type the code number of the keyboard " & _
    "shortcut key or keys you want to assign."
MacroOrCommand = MsgBox(strMacroQuery, Style, Title)

If MacroOrCommand = vbYes Then
    KeyCategoryName = wdKeyCategoryMacro
Else
    KeyCategoryName = wdKeyCategoryCommand
End If

CommandName = InputBox(strMessage1, strTitle)
KeyValue = InputBox(strMessage2, strTitle)
CodeNumber = Val(KeyValue)

If CodeNumber < 8 Or num > 1919 Then
    MsgBox _
        "Shortcut key code must be between 8 and 1919"
Else
    CustomizationContext = NormalTemplate
    KeyBindings.Add KeyCategory:=KeyCategoryName, _
        Command:=CommandName, KeyCode:=CodeNumber
End If

BYE:
End Sub
```

Shortcuts for standard keyboard characters

Suppose you take my advice and assign the ` key to a shortcut, say one of the speed-up commands suggested in Chapter 27. What happens if one day, ten years from now, you finally need to type a `? No problem — just use the Insert ⇨ Symbol command to place the character you need from the Symbol dialog box into your document.

Secret

For me, the bracket and backslash keys fall into a different category. They're great as shortcut keys, but I do need those brackets in my documents at least three or four times in a blue moon. The solution is to create a shortcut combining Alt or Ctrl with the key in question. The shortcut inserts the original symbol in one step, and is easy to remember because it's based on the symbol's real key. The best way to set up such a shortcut is again the

Insert Symbol command. Choose Insert ⇨ Symbol. In the Symbol dialog box, start by selecting (normal text) in the Font list. Then select the character to which you're assigning the new shortcut and click Shortcut Key. Type the key combination for the new shortcut so that it appears at Press new shortcut key. Combinations with the Alt key usually don't conflict with Word's default shortcuts, which use Ctrl for the most part. To create a shortcut for], for example, enter Alt+] at Press new shortcut key.

Keeping track of keyboard shortcuts

Whether or not you change the default keyboard shortcuts, you should be aware of ways to learn the current shortcuts (default and customized) as you work, and to find out what the current shortcuts are.

Word automatically displays keyboard shortcuts for menu commands on the menus themselves. If you like, you can also see them in the ScreenTips that pop up when the mouse pointer rests over a button for a second or two. To turn this feature on, choose Tools ⇨ Customize, select the Options tab, and check the Show Shortcut Keys in ScreenTips box.

Other tricks for acquainting yourself with keyboard shortcuts include the following:

- To learn the current keyboard shortcuts for any command, macro, or other item, open the Customize Keyboard dialog box and highlight the item in the Commands list. All shortcuts assigned to the item appear in the Current keys box.

- To print a list of all current custom keyboard shortcuts, choose File ⇨ Print and select Key assignments in the Print What field. Only custom shortcuts, not Word's defaults, appear in the printout.

- To create a document containing a table of Word commands with their keyboard shortcuts and menu locations, use the ListCommands command. Select All Commands in the Categories list of the Tools ⇨ Customize dialog box, locate the item for ListCommands, and drag it onto a toolbar or menu.

Redefining Word's Built-In Commands

Secret

Uniquely among the Office applications, Word enables you — invites you, really — to modify the way its own commands work. The trick is simple: You create a VBA macro (a Sub procedure) with the same name as the built-in command you want to alter or replace.

Often, figuring out the name of the command you want to modify is the hardest part of this trick. The sample macro listed here, for example, replaces the built-in View ⇨ Full Screen command, which toggles Full Screen view off and on (for a diatribe on Full Screen view, see "Using the entire screen for your document in Full Screen view" earlier in this chapter).

Unfortunately, Word's official name for this command is ToggleFull, not necessarily your first guess. Unfortunately, I know of no reference list of menu commands with their corresponding official names. You may have to scroll through the list of commands in the Customize dialog box, placing likely candidates on a toolbar and trying them until you hit on the right one.

Once you have found the correct command name, it's on to writing the macro. Typically, you use this technique when you want a built-in command to work just a little differently, not because you want to completely replace the command. For this reason, a macro of this type almost always includes the built-in command as part of its code. For example, the macro shown here toggles Full Screen view on and off sure enough, but also hides the Full Screen toolbar when switching to a Full Screen view.

Now to explain the sample macro. The first executable line (the one beginning with ActiveWindow) is the VBA code corresponding to Word's ToggleFull command. Once that command has done its work, the remaining code steps in to ensure the Full Screen toolbar doesn't appear.

```
Sub ToggleFull()
ActiveWindow.View.FullScreen = Not ActiveWindow.View.FullScreen
    If ActiveWindow.View.FullScreen = True Then
        For Each cb In CommandBars
            If cb.Name = "Full Screen" Then
                cb.Visible = False
            End If
        Next
    End If
End Sub
```

In this type of macro, the macro's name must exactly match that of the command it modifies. In addition, if you're including the original command in your macro, you need the correct VBA syntax for the command. To be sure you get the spelling and code right, have Word start the macro for you, and then add your custom code. Follow these steps:

1. Open the Tools ➪ Macro ➪ Macros dialog box.

2. Select the choice "Word commands" from the Macros In drop-down list.

3. Select the command you want to modify in the long scrolling list in the main part of the dialog box.

4. Returning to the Macros In list, choose the template or document in which you want to store the macro for your modified command. Selecting All Active Templates and Documents stores it in the Normal template.

5. Choose Create. This takes you to the Visual Basic Editor (see Part VI) where the macro has been started for you and already contains the VBA code corresponding to the command you're modifying.

6. Once you've added your custom code, return to Word. Now every time you use the menu item, toolbar button, or keyboard shortcut for that command, your macro runs instead.

Using Word templates

Throughout Office, you use templates to endow new documents with preset layout, formatting, and content that you can then add to or modify. With the template responsible for elements that remain constant from document to document, you can devote your energies to defining the items that make each document unique, and you can be sure that documents based on the same template share consistent common elements.

In Word, however, templates do more. Word templates contain customizations to the program itself, such as custom toolbars and shortcut keys, macros, and AutoText entries. All these customizations are available automatically in documents you base on a template they reside in. What's more — and here's where Word really parts company with its suitemates — Word lets you use multiple templates simultaneously with the same document. Using a hierarchy of templates, you can retain personal customizations to the program while sharing layout and boilerplate content with others in your organization.

Word also enables you to change the templates on which the document is based. This means that in midstream, you can radically alter a document's format, the available customizations, or both. However, content in the new template does not appear in the document.

Word template basics

Among the many details a Word template can store are the following: the settings of the File ➪ Page Setup dialog box; paragraph and character styles; macros; custom toolbars, menus, and shortcut keys; AutoText entries; layout and content of headers and footers; and text, graphics, and other content items. Formatted AutoCorrect entries are stored only in the Normal template, the subject of the next section.

By default, Word templates are stored in the Templates folder, a subfolder of your main Office folder. The General tab of the File ➪ New dialog box lists all the templates — and shortcuts to templates — stored directly in the Templates subfolder. It provides additional tabs for any subfolders and folder shortcuts within the Templates folder, so long as these other folders contain Word templates. You can change the default main, or user, templates folder and specify an additional workgroup templates folder in the Tools ➪ Options dialog box, or via the Office Shortcut bar (see Chapter 2).

Parallel with other Office applications, a Word template is essentially just a standard document stored with the special .dot extension. True, Word templates can contain a few types of information not included in ordinary documents, such as AutoText entries. However, you can use any Word document as a template for the layout, formatting, and content of new documents simply by storing it in one of the templates folders. But documents based on such ersatz templates don't acquire the toolbars, macros, and other customizations of the "template."

Creating and modifying templates

To create a new template, start by setting up a document with the layout, formatting, and content you want in the template. Add new macros, toolbars, and keyboard shortcuts as discussed in the "Customizations, Templates, and Documents" section earlier in this chapter. Then choose File ⇨ Save As. When you select Document Template at Save as Type, Word automatically takes you to your main templates folder. Navigate to one of its subfolders if you wish, name the new template, and save the file. Once a document is saved as a template, you can add AutoCorrect entries as well. To modify an existing template, open it by selecting Document Templates at Files of Type in the File ⇨ Open dialog box. Make any changes you wish and save the file again.

Using the Normal template

In Word, one master template has an all-important role: This is the Normal template, stored in the Normal.dot file. The Normal template governs the layout and content of each new document that appears when you start Word without any startup switches, or click the New toolbar button. You can change the layout and content for these default documents by modifying the Normal template with the technique described in the previous paragraph. In addition, customizations stored in the Normal template are always available no matter what document you're working with and what other template it's based on.

If Word doesn't find the Normal template in any of your templates folders or in the main Office subfolder, it automatically makes a new Normal template containing the default formatting, layout, and program settings. This gives you a quick way to restore the defaults if your experiments produce an ab-Normal template—just rename the current version of Normal.dot or copy it to another folder, and then restart Word.

Scaling the template hierarchy

Because you can use more than one template with a given document, and because the settings stored in these templates may well conflict, Word has to decide which template's settings take priority. The Word template hierarchy has three levels which work as follows:

1. The attached template—the one on which the current document is based—rules supreme. Other settings defined here supersede those in other active templates. Again, you can change the template attached to the document, as the next section discusses in detail.

2. The Normal template occupies the second rank of the template hierarchy.

3. At the bottom of the barrel are any other global templates. Any settings they contain that don't conflict with those in the attached or Normal templates are available. If you load two or more global templates, Word prioritizes them alphabetically.

As an individual user, storing all of your routinely used custom macros, toolbars, and keyboard shortcuts in the Normal template works fine. However, you might consider placing them instead in a separate global template. That way, to revert to Word's default settings you simply unload this template by unchecking its box in the Tools ⇨ Templates and Add-Ins dialog box.

If you use Word in a group, you can individualize it for different users without sacrificing document consistency. Store layout, formatting, and boilerplate text in the Normal template and other templates reserved for this purpose. Whether the group is networked or uses Word on the same computer, these templates should be placed in the workgroup templates folder. There, they will be available to all users for new documents, or to be attached to existing ones. Each user stores personal customizations in a separate template placed in the user templates folder defined for that person. This personalized template can then be loaded as a global template.

Attaching a different template

The template you select when you create a new document is, in Word's jargon, attached to the document. You can attach a different template to change the document's paragraph and character styles, and to make the new template's customizations available when you work with the document.

To change the attached template, choose Tools ⇨ Templates and Add-Ins. In the resulting dialog box (see Figure 26-3), choose Attach to bring up a dialog box displaying the templates in your main templates folder. Select the template you want to attach and choose Open.

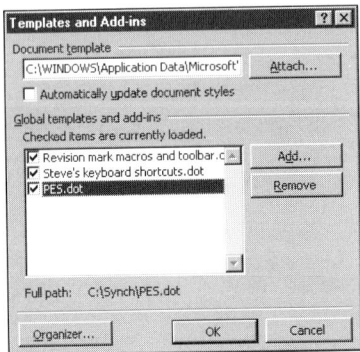

Figure 26-3: Change the document's template in the Templates and Add-ins dialog box.

When you attach a different template, its paragraph and character styles are copied into the document, replacing any existing styles with duplicate names. The template's customizations and AutoText entries become available to the document but aren't copied there. However, text, graphics, and page setup settings in the template do not become part of the document. (If you need content items from the template, you can open the template itself in Word and copy the elements to your document.)

In the Tools ⇨ Templates and Add-Ins dialog box, the setting labeled Automatically Update Document Styles is worth noting. When this box is checked, Word updates the document's paragraph and styles with those currently in the attached template each time you open the document. This is a great way to keep documents automatically consistent with changes you make in your personal or corporate typographic identity by way of template modifications.

To copy individual styles in the reverse direction, from your document to the attached template, use the checkbox labeled Add to Template in the New Style and Modify Style dialog boxes (see Chapter 28), available from the Format ⇨ Style dialog box. By the way, the Automatically Update checkbox in the Modify Style dialog box serves a completely different function than the setting by the same name discussed in the previous paragraph.

Loading global templates

Global templates are those whose AutoText entries, macros, and customizations are available in any Word document. The Normal template is a global template, but as described earlier in this section, it is always loaded and takes precedence over other global templates. You can use any template as a global template with either of the following techniques:

- Load the template manually. Choose Tools ⇨ Templates and Add-Ins, and then choose Add. Select the template and click OK. It should then appear in the large box in the middle of the Templates and Add-ins dialog box.

- Load the template automatically each time Word starts. Copy the template file to the Office startup folder. By default, this is the Windows\Application Data\Microsoft\Word\Startup folder. This is changed from its location in Office 97. You can select a Startup folder of your own on the File Locations tab of the Tools ⇨ Options dialog box.

Add-ins, special-purpose software plug-ins that you can obtain from third-party suppliers or that you can write yourself, are managed the same way as global templates. Chapter 25 introduces the techniques for creating COM add-ins.

Managing styles and customizations across templates and documents

Word's Organizer (see Figure 26-4) lets you rename or delete individual styles, VBA modules and forms, toolbars, and AutoText entries. You can also copy these items from one template or document to another. Note that only templates can store AutoText entries. Note too that you can't work with keyboard shortcuts in the Organizer. You activate the Organizer button from either of two dialog boxes: Tools ⇨ Templates and Add-Ins, or Format ⇨ Style. The Organizer has separate tabs for each of the items you can work with.

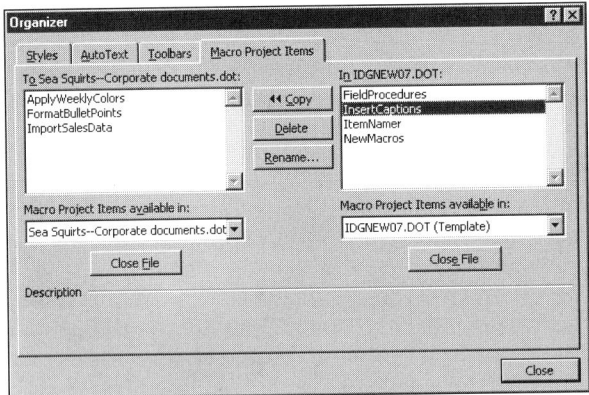

Figure 26-4: The Organizer lets you modify items stored in templates and documents.

Use the two pairs of "available in" drop-down lists and Close/Open File buttons on either side of the Organizer to activate the document or template you wish to work with (before you can open a new file, you must first close the one currently displayed). You can then select the items you want to rename, delete, or copy. The standard Windows Shift+click and Ctrl+click tricks work for selecting more than one item at a time.

If you're copying toolbars, don't forget to copy any macros their buttons depend on as well. Note that you can also use the Visual Basic Editor to copy macros from one document or template to another (see Part VI).

Saving template customizations right now

When you add or change the macros, toolbars, or keyboard shortcuts that reside in a template, Word doesn't save the changes until you exit the program. This means that lots of work can be at risk for quite some time. Although the AutoRecovery feature usually protects you, I recommend saving your templates manually whenever you make important changes. To accomplish this, you must open the Visual Basic Editor by choosing Tools ⇨ Macro ⇨ Visual Basic Editor, or pressing Alt+F11. There, choose File ⇨ Save or click the Save button. This method is labor intensive, but at least it does the job.

If you customize your templates frequently, you need a macro that saves your changes without all those steps. Word includes a SaveTemplate command that you can drag from the Tools ⇨ Customize dialog box (look under All Commands in the Categories list) onto a toolbar or menu. However, this command doesn't save changes to the Normal template.

The following code, available on the accompanying CD-ROM, saves the current document's attached template — even if the template is Normal.dot — and displays a confirmatory message:

```
Sub SaveTemplate()
On Error GoTo SaveTemplate_Err

With ActiveDocument.AttachedTemplate
    .Save
    MsgBox "Saved " & .Name
End With
Exit Sub

SaveTemplate_Err:
    MsgBox Err.Description
    Exit Sub
End Sub
```

Put this macro into Normal.dot or another global document and hook it up to a toolbar button for one-shot access.

Conclusion

Word outdoes all the other Office applications with the depth and sophistication of customizations that are possible. It can be fun to bring such a powerful program under your personal control, but the real reason to learn these techniques is to make your workday more pleasant and to get more done.

Chapter 27

Expert Editing

In This Chapter

- Choosing Word options for efficient editing
- Navigating through documents at top speed with advanced keyboard shortcuts
- Jumping to other locations with Go Back and Go To — and fixing the limitations of these commands
- Locating and changing text and formatting advanced techniques
- Returning instantly to any location in a document with bookmarks
- Speeding text entry with AutoText, AutoCorrect, and AutoFormat as You Type
- Optimizing Word's case-changing command
- Improving on the Spike's capability to collect information from multiple locations

As fancy as you want your documents to look, shaping their content is Word's core function. In your feast of Word secrets, the main course is a generous serving of advanced techniques for locating, entering, and changing the text.

Setting Editing Options

The Options dialog box (Tools ➪ Options) devotes a whole tab to choices related to text editing, as shown in Figure 27-1.

For many of these text editing items, the default settings are fine for almost everyone — you can just forget these options exist. Here are the options you should focus on:

- **When selecting, automatically select entire word.** This box refers to selecting with the mouse, not with the keyboard. It's checked by default, meaning that when you drag over any part of a word, the entire word gets selected. This is great if you have lousy aim with the mouse pointer. The problem is, you can never make a selection that begins or ends in the middle of a word. I would rather have precise control, so I clear (uncheck) this box.

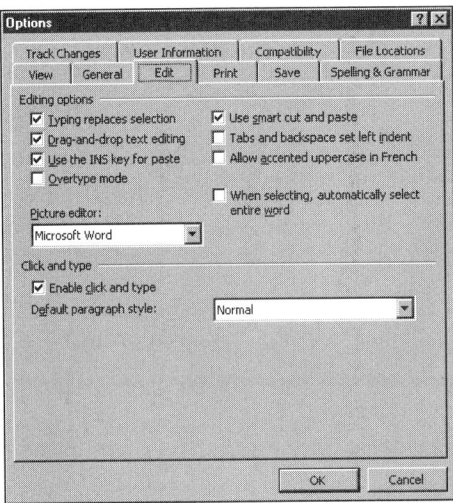

Figure 27-1: The Options dialog box with the Edit tab selected.

If you prefer to leave this box checked, you can override its function whenever you like, selecting only the desired portion of a word by holding down the Alt key while you drag.

- **Use the INS key for paste.** Checking this box turns the Insert key into a shortcut for the Paste command, just like Ctrl+V or Edit ⇨ Paste. Most Word works discourage this use of Insert. They argue that because Ctrl+V works the same in all Windows applications, you might as well stick with it in Word.

  The point is well taken, but here's my counterpoint: Having a one-key shortcut for Paste is great, considering that it's a command you use all the time. And because Insert is just under the cursor keys on a standard keyboard, it's the perfect key for this purpose — as soon as you reach the destination using the cursor keys, a quick tap of your right thumb finishes the paste.

  But what really makes the Insert key sing in this role is to give it a partner: Turn the Delete key into a one-shot Cut command for selected text. Word gives you no such option, but the VBA macro here does the trick. Here's how it works: If there's no selection, the macro deletes the character to the right of the insertion point — in other words, it functions just like Delete does normally. If text is selected, however, the macro cuts the selection, placing it on the clipboard. Once you define the Delete key as the keyboard shortcut for this macro, the cursor pad becomes a cut-and-paste hot-rod:

```
Sub DeleteKey()
If Selection.Type = wdNoSelection Then GoTo DeleteKey
If Selection.Type = wdSelectionIP Then GoTo DeleteKey
        Selection.Cut
        GoTo LeaveOff
DeleteKey:
        Selection.Delete Unit:=wdCharacter, Count:=1
LeaveOff:
End Sub
```

- **Overtype mode.** By default — that is, unless the Use the INS key for paste box is checked — the Insert key toggles between ordinary insert-mode text editing and the overtype mode, where what you type replaces what's already at the insertion point. If you do use Insert as a Paste key, you can activate overtype editing by checking the Overtype mode box. But you can also turn on Overtype mode by double-clicking OVR in the status bar.

- **Tabs and backspace set left indent.** Checked by default for quick adjustments, this setting can cause confusing changes in your document's layout. I recommend you turn it off and set your left indents manually, using the Paragraph format dialog box or the ruler.

Working with Files and Windows

Before you can edit a document, you need to display it on the screen. That's my justification for this brief section on opening and saving document files and working with their windows.

Opening previously used files

The File menu displays up to nine of the last files you opened. To reopen one of these, choose File and pick it from the list or press the corresponding number key.

What if you want to be able to quickly load a specific file, whether you happen to have recently opened it or not? Word's deeply hidden, completely undocumented Work menu enables you to specify files that you always want fast access to. To use the Work menu, you must first add it to a toolbar or another menu. Open the Customize dialog box and switch to the Commands tab. In the Categories list scroll down to and click Built-in Menus. You can then find the Work menu at the very bottom of the Commands list. Drag it to the File menu (or any other menu or toolbar of your choice). Once the Work menu is installed, you can add any file to it by opening the file and then choosing Work ⇨ Add to Work Menu. From then on, you can open that document at any time by choosing it from the list on the Work menu.

Deleting entries on the Work menu list requires a secret keyboard shortcut. Before you open the menu, press Ctrl+Alt+- (that's the hyphen key near

Backspace, along the row of number keys at the top of the main part of your keyboard). The mouse pointer becomes a heavy black horizontal bar. Now open the Work menu and choose the file you want to delete from its list. The Ctrl+Alt+- technique deletes commands from any of the built-in Word menus.

Closing and saving documents: Quick tips

This section covers useful but otherwise unrelated hints on the common operations of closing and saving your documents.

Closing all documents

It's always a good idea to close the documents you aren't using, because they take up memory and thereby slow down your system, and because extra open documents make it harder to switch quickly to the document you want to work with.

To close all open documents at once, hold down Shift while you open the File menu. The Close All command appears on the menu in place of the ordinary Close command. The Close All command is also available in the Customize dialog box, from which you can add it to a toolbar or menu. I've provided a suitable icon on the Office Secrets toolbar, part of Office Secrets.dot on the CD-ROM.

Minimizing file size, maximizing file integrity

The Allow Fast Saves box on the Save tab of the Tools ➪ Options dialog box directs Word to add changes to the end of the disk file each time you save your document. If you clear this box, Word saves the entire file each time. Turning off "fast saves" is slower, of course, but it has two significant advantages:

- It keeps the file to the minimum size possible. Disallow fast saves if you're running short on disk space.

- It ensures that your text appears in the disk file in the same order as it does in the actual document. If something goes wrong with the file so that Word can't open it, you may still be able to retrieve the latest text using Word's "Recover text from any file" import filter, or via a text editor.

Copying a block of text to a new file

Word lets you insert other documents (in any word processing format it can read) into the current document. Use the Insert ➪ File command for this purpose. For some reason, though, it doesn't provide a command for the reverse procedure. In other words, you can't save a portion of the current document as a separate file, at least not without a lot of manual labor. Here's a macro that streamlines the process:

```
Sub CopyBlockToFile ()
On Error GoTo StopNow
If Selection.Type = wdSelectionIP Then
   ActiveDocument.Content.Select
End If
Selection.Range.Copy
Documents.Add
Selection.Range.Paste
Dialogs(wdDialogFileSaveAs).Show
ActiveDocument.Close
StopNow:
End Sub
```

Working with document windows

Switching from one open document or document window to another via the Window menu is fine if you rarely move back and forth between them. If you're a fairly frequent flyer, however, that procedure gets old fast.

Quick cycling through open documents and windows

Word 2000 shortens your travel time from one document to the next by placing a separate item for each open document window on the taskbar. To access a different document window, click its taskbar icon. To switch even faster, use the keyboard: Alt+Tab and Alt+Shift+Tab cycle you in opposite order through all open applications, including each Word window (including Word windows is a new feature).

If you're good with keyboard shortcuts, however, you should also learn and use the Next Window and Previous Window commands — these commands are more direct than Alt+Tab, because you don't have to deal with other applications Ctrl+F6 or Alt+F6 takes you to the next window in this cycle, while Ctrl+Shift+F6 or Alt+Shift+F6 moves you back. You can place these commands on toolbar buttons, too, using the standard techniques for customizing covered in Chapter 5.

Caution

There's only one problem with the Next Window and Previous Window commands: they often work in reverse of the way you'd expect. After you move from one window to another you have to use the Next Window command to get back to the first document again.

Quick access to all open windows

Secret

Using the Window menu to switch gets even older if you open more than nine documents. If the document you need isn't one of the selected nine still on the Window menu, you have to choose the More Windows command at the bottom of the menu and then pick your document from a dialog box. To get around the nine-document limit on the Window menu, assign the WindowList command to a toolbar button. It displays the dialog box showing all your open documents so you don't have to open the Window menu first. Find the

WindowList command in the list of All Commands in the Customize dialog box (Commands tab).

Multiple views of the same document

Remember too that you can view the same document in a split window, or even in two or more windows at the same time. This makes it easier to move or copy items within a long document — you can use drag and drop if you like.

To split a document window into two parts, or *panes*, position the mouse pointer over the split box, a squat gray button located above the top arrow button on the vertical scroll bar. Wait a moment until the pointer changes to a double-headed arrow. Then drag the *split bar*, the horizontal separator between the two panes, downward until the two panes are sized the way you want them. If you've turned off the vertical scroll bar, you can always choose Window ⇨ Split instead to turn on the split bar.

You can adjust the pane size at any time by dragging the split bar up or down. To reunite the windows, double-click the split bar, or drag it up to the toolbar area.

You can move back and forth between the two panes with the mouse, of course. The quick way, though, is to press F6.

To open a new, completely separate window for the document, choose Window ⇨ New Window. When the same document appears in two or more windows, the windows are numbered in the title bar and on the Window menu, as in TopSecret:1, TopSecret:2, and so on.

Advanced Navigation

Before you can make changes in the text, you have to get to where the changes need to be made. That's why editing expertise begins with mastery of all the ways you can get around in a document. While you're probably familiar with basic cursor-movement keys and mouse-navigation techniques, don't neglect the features covered here, including advanced mouse and keyboard skills, the Document Map, browsing by object, and the Go Back and Go To commands.

Mousing around

Review the following quick tips on navigating with the mouse in Office:

- If ScreenTips are turned on in the Customize dialog box, you see the page number and the first heading of the current page as you scroll through a document by dragging the vertical scrollbar's scroll box.

- Clicking in the vertical scrollbar above or below the scroll box scrolls up or down by one screen, just as if you had pressed PageUp or PageDown.

- In Normal view, to scroll left past the left margin hold down Shift while you click the arrow at the left end of the horizontal scrollbar.

- With any three-button mouse, including the Microsoft IntelliMouse, clicking the middle button places Word into a special AutoScroll mode — dragging up or down moves you smoothly through the document until you click the middle button again.

The IntelliMouse has other tricks behind its twitching whiskers. Try the following:

To Perform This Action	Do This with the IntelliMouse
Scroll up or down	Move the wheel forward or back.
Pan smoothly up or down	Move the mouse with the wheel button held down. The farther you move from the point you started, the faster the panning.
Zoom in or out	Hold down Ctrl while moving the wheel forward or back.
Expand or collapse headings (in outline view or the Document Map)	Hold down Shift, point to a heading, and move the wheel forward or back.

Navigating with Document Map

Although it seems to be an unacknowledged imitation of an innovative shareware utility, Word's new Document Map is otherwise a stellar addition to the program. Choose View ⇨ Document Map or click the corresponding button to display Document Map along the left side of your document.

As shown in Figure 27-2, Document Map gives you a quick outline-type overview of the document's organization, showing the headings arranged hierarchically in a narrow, scrollable pane. You can expand or collapse any branch of the outline containing subheadings by clicking the little box beside it. You can control the overall level of detail by right-clicking Document Map and selecting a heading level from the shortcut menu.

But Document Map's real value is as a navigation aid. Click a heading, and Word takes you there instantly. As you move about in the document by any method, Document Map highlights the heading for the section containing the insertion point. To access the Document Map pane via the keyboard, press Shift+F6. You can then navigate with the cursor movement keys. To move in the main document to the heading selected in Document Map, hit Enter.

A paragraph appears in the Document Map only if it has been assigned to a numbered outline level (rather than body text) in the Paragraph dialog box. See the sidebar "Using built-in heading styles and custom outline levels" in Chapter 28.

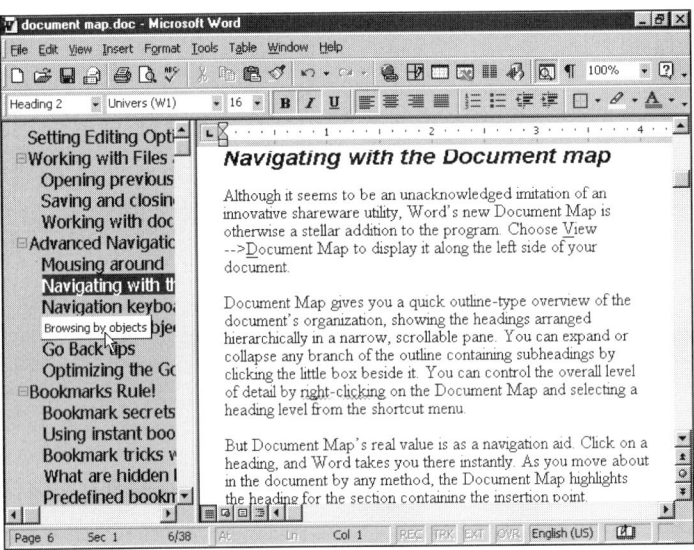

Figure 27-2: Displaying a document with Document Map.

Secret

You can change the look of the headings displayed in Document Map by modifying the Document Map paragraph style in the Format ⇨ Style dialog box.

Navigation keyboard shortcuts

While everyone knows the common navigation keys, it's easy to forget the ones you don't use regularly. Because keyboard navigation is much more efficient than using the mouse, I suggest you keep a cheat sheet handy for those situations when advanced movement commands are called for. Though the best sort of cheat sheet you can make is your own little help box (see "Creating your own Help windows" in Chapter 4), a paper list pinned to the wall will do fine. If you haven't made up your list yet, feel free to consult Table 27-1.

Table 27-1 Advanced Navigation Keyboard Shortcuts

Shortcut	Function in Word 2000
Ctrl+PageUp	Previous browse object (see "Browsing by objects" later)
Ctrl+PageDown	Next browse object
Ctrl+Alt+PageUp	Top of window
Ctrl+Alt+PageDown	Bottom of window

Shortcut	Function in Word 2000
Alt+PageUp	Top of column
Alt+PageDown	Bottom of column
Alt+F1	Next field
Shift+F1	What's This? Help feature
F11	Next field
Shift+F11	Previous field
Ctrl+F6	Next document window
Ctrl+Shift+F6	Previous document window
Alt+Up	In Page Layout view only, previous document object (text column, table cell, footnote, text box, or frame)
Alt+Down	In Page Layout view only, next document object

Browsing by objects

Word lets you browse your document by jumping from one item to the next (or previous) item of the same type with a quick mouse-click. The controls you need are the Previous Object and Next Object buttons, those blue arrow buttons at the bottom of the vertical scroll bar. Introduced in Word 97, they replace the Next and Previous Page buttons found there in earlier versions of the program. (By default, Ctrl+PgUp and Ctrl+PgDn are the keyboard shortcuts for the Previous Object and Next Object browse buttons.)

When you first use Word, the two buttons function to take you to the next and previous pages. Between the buttons, however, the Select Browse Object button lets you choose which type of item to jump to as you browse. Click the button to see a little fly-out graphical menu. If you then select, say, the Browse by Field icon on the menu, clicking an arrow button now moves you directly to the next or previous Word field in your document. For most of the menu choices, the text at the bottom of the menu indicates clearly what happens. A few of the choices need some extra comments, as follows:

- **Go To.** Pops up the Find and Replace dialog box with the Go To tab selected. After you pick an item type in the Go to What box, that item becomes the object for browsing with the Next and Previous object buttons. This lets you browse by objects that aren't on the menu, including bookmarks, equations, and objects (meaning those linked to or embedded in your document, as discussed in Chapter 10).

- **Find.** Displays the Find and Replace dialog box. The text you enter becomes the target for the browse-by buttons.

- **Browse by Edits.** Cycles through the current location of the insertion point and the last three locations where you edited text. This is just like the Go Back command discussed in the next section, except that you can go forward once you've gone back. It does *not* jump to the next revision

Go Back tips

Word's Go Back command can be incredibly handy. In case you haven't made it part of your regular repertoire, Go Back cycles through the last three locations of the insertion point at which you edited text (sensibly, it doesn't return to locations you just visited with the cursor keys without changing anything). Press Shift+F5 to go back.

Go Back is great, though I sure wish Microsoft would give it a longer memory, say for the last five insertion-point locations. Better yet would be an adjustable number — jumpy writers like me would probably set it to ten or more. But you can partially compensate for this deficiency with the instant-bookmark macros I describe later in this chapter.

Secret

Immediately after opening a document you can pick up where you left off in your last editing session by pressing Shift+F5 (Go Back). Word saves with the document only the one editing location last used — the rest of the Go Back information is tossed out. By the way, if this trick doesn't work, it means either the file in question has never been edited or it's stored in a non-Word format such as RTF.

It wouldn't be hard to create a macro that automatically activates the Go Back command whenever you open a document. If you want to get really fancy, design an AutoExec macro (see Chapter 26) that asks you whether you want the insertion point at the top of the document or at the last-used location.

Optimizing the Go To command

Choosing Edit ⇨ Go To or pressing F5 brings up the Go To controls as a tab in the Find and Replace dialog box, which now serves as a master navigation control panel. You can still display the Go To controls quickly by double-clicking the left side of the status bar, in the area where the page and section numbers are displayed. Figure 27-3 illustrates the dialog box with the Go To tab active.

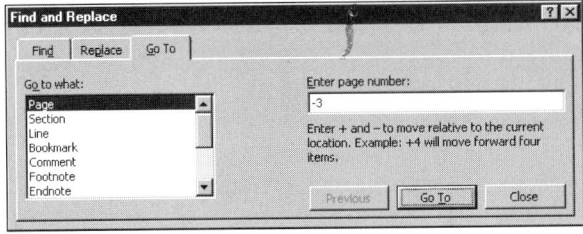

Figure 27-3: The Go To controls are now a tab of the Find and Replace dialog box. Someone must have decided that going to a particular page is sort of like finding a particular chunk of text.

You can use the Go To controls to seek out just about any identifiable landmark in the document. You can, for example, go to the next or previous heading of a particular level (Heading 1, Heading 2, and so on). Just type the level number — to locate the next Heading 3, you would type **3** — and click Next or Previous.

While the Go To command is very powerful, it retains an irritating quirk found in previous versions of Word: The dialog box stays on the screen after you reach your destination, forcing you to press Esc to put it to bed. While this can be handy if you're just inspecting different parts of the document, you usually want to get to Page 18 in a hurry because you have some editing to do there. Having to press Esc can really break your stride. You can fix this only by building a custom GoTo dialog box of your own.

Bookmarks rule!

Bookmarks are a wonderful help when you're editing a long document. Drop a bookmark at any location you expect to revisit later, giving it an appropriately descriptive name. To create a bookmark, open the Insert ⇨ Bookmark dialog box (Ctrl+Shift+F5 is the default shortcut). When you want to return, open the dialog box again, select the bookmark by name from the list, and click Go To — you're there in a flash.

By the way, you can go to any bookmark using the Go To dialog box, described in the previous section. It's easier to press F5 than Ctrl+Shift+F5. Also, the Go To dialog box remembers the last type of item you located. So if you use it for bookmarks repeatedly, they will already be selected in the Go To What list. Then again, if you know the bookmark name, you never need to select Bookmark at Go To What — just type the bookmark name in the Enter field and OK the dialog box.

For mere mortals, bookmarks are simply great navigation aids. But once you start using fields and VBA, you'll find bookmarks are a key element in many automated procedures for manipulating specified text passages and displaying them elsewhere in a document. I cover some of these uses for bookmarks when I detail various advanced techniques.

Bookmark secrets

One complexity of bookmarks is that a given bookmark can identify a location only (this is an empty bookmark) or enclose a text selection within it. For navigation purposes, there's no reason to select text before you drop a bookmark. However, bookmarking a text selection lets you manipulate the bookmarked text on automatic pilot with fields and VBA macros.

Bookmarks are normally invisible, but you can see them by checking the Bookmarks box in the Option dialog box's View tab. If you do, they appear as heavy square brackets enclosing whatever text they identify. Empty bookmarks look like a thick I-beam because the pair of brackets sit on top of one another. Figure 27-4 shows how both types of bookmarks look on the screen.

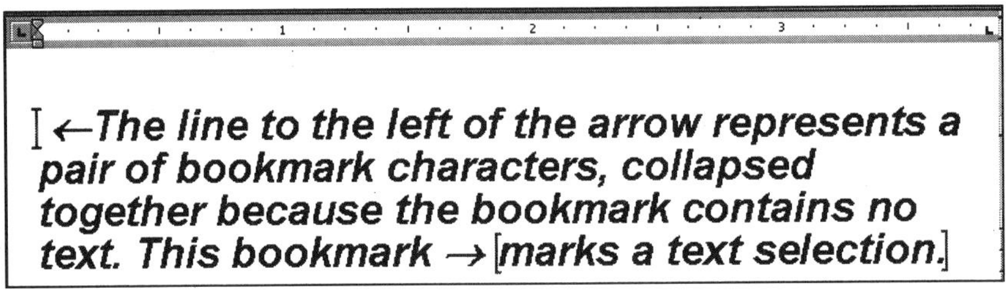

> [←*The line to the left of the arrow represents a pair of bookmark characters, collapsed together because the bookmark contains no text. This bookmark →* [*marks a text selection.*]

Figure 27-4: Word indicates a bookmark onscreen with a pair of bracket-like symbols. On the left is an empty bookmark, with both brackets in the same location. The bookmark on the right marks a text selection with brackets at either end.

When you work with text containing a bookmark, the bookmark behaves as you probably want it to. If you copy text to another location, the bookmark stays in its original spot. If you move the text, however, the bookmark goes along for the ride. Cutting or clearing the text removes the bookmark, but you can't delete it with the Backspace or Delete key. If you copy text to another document, both the original selection and the copy contain the bookmark (each document has its own set of bookmarks). You're free to edit the text within the bookmark itself—text enclosed by the bookmark brackets—whether or not you've displayed the brackets on the screen.

Using instant bookmarks

Word's named bookmarks are perfect for finding your way back to key spots when you work with a document over a period of days or weeks. But they're too much trouble for on-the-fly navigation during the course of a single editing session. For this purpose, you want to be able to drop a temporary bookmark with a single keystroke and return to it just as easily. That way, if you suddenly realize how to handle a writing problem in another part of the document, you're free to follow the muse. Just drop the bookmark, go make the changes, and come right back when you're done.

If you like this idea, what you need is one or more pairs of instant-bookmark macros (VBA procedures). In each pair, the first macro sets a bookmark, the second takes you to it. The macros should be assigned to keyboard shortcuts or toolbar buttons for quick access.

InstantBookmark1Drop:

```
Sub InstantBookmark1Drop()
    With ActiveDocument.Bookmarks
        .Add Range:=Selection.Range, Name:="Instant1"
    End With
End Sub
```

InstantBookmark1GoTo:

```
Sub InstantBookmark1GoTo()
    Selection.GoTo What:=wdGoToBookmark, Name:="Instant1"
End Sub
```

One pair satisfies most people, but you can create as many pairs as you need. If you're making more than one macro pair, the next pair would be called InstantBookmark2Drop and InstantBookmark2GoTo. The code would be identical, except that you would change the name of the macros and change the name of the bookmark to Instant2. Actually, of course, it doesn't matter what you name the bookmark in these macros. Just choose something meaningless, a name that you would never use for a real bookmark. Use a unique bookmark name for each pair of macros, entering the same name in both macros in the pair.

Bookmark tricks with AutoText

Secret

Try this: Select text containing a bookmark, and then create an AutoText or AutoCorrect entry. The bookmark becomes part of the AutoText or AutoCorrect entry (you must save the AutoCorrect entry as Formatted text). Thereafter, each time you insert the entry in your document Word inserts the bookmark too — any previous bookmark by the same name vanishes.

What's this trick good for? Well, instead of having to think up and type in new bookmark names for each document, you might want to create a battery of generic bookmarks and store them as AutoText entries. For example, you could create a Today's Focus bookmark as an AutoText entry that identifies the location in the document where you're currently working.

The only problem is that you can't save a bookmark all by itself as an AutoText or AutoCorrect entry — you must include with it at least one character of text. Otherwise, you could use this trick instead of my "instant bookmark" macro to define on-the-fly bookmarks for navigation (see the previous section).

What are hidden bookmarks?

The Bookmark dialog box offers a checkbox labeled Hidden Bookmarks. Hidden bookmarks are those that Word adds automatically for its own purposes when you insert cross-references, tables of contents, and other such items. If you check this box, you see the automatically generated names for these bookmarks in the list. Figure 27-5 shows the Bookmark dialog box with several hidden bookmarks on display.

Figure 27-5: The bookmarks in the list shown here were all created by Word, which explains why they look like gibberish.

As you can see, the names Word concocts for hidden bookmarks look pretty meaningless to humans. Although you can tell from the first few characters what type of item the bookmark marks, you won't know which specific item it stands for. For example, a "ref" hidden bookmark may represent any one of many captions, footnotes, or other items.

So what can you use hidden bookmarks for? Not much. But you can go to a hidden bookmark, and this gives you one way to hunt down a cross-reference or other such item that you might otherwise miss if you had to page through a long document. By the way, hidden bookmarks are always hidden in the document itself. Even if you make bookmarks visible by checking the relevant box in the View tab of the Options dialog box, you won't see the telltale brackets around the item marked by a hidden bookmark.

Predefined bookmarks — for macros only

Word's predefined bookmarks are even more hidden than the hidden bookmarks just described. Predefined bookmarks mark many locations that you might want to go to in macros, which is where they come in handy. They never appear in the Bookmark or Go To dialog box, but you can go to any predefined bookmark by typing its full name (including the backslash) in either dialog box. For example, the \Sel predefined bookmark takes you to the current selection or the insertion point. To see a list of these bookmarks, look up the topic "Predefined bookmarks" in the Word VBA Help file — you can find it in the Contents tab under Miscellaneous Topics, and the topic on the Bookmark object has a jump to it.

Using hyperlinks as cross-document bookmarks

Secret

When you work with multiple related documents at the same time, it would be nice to flip directly to text passages of interest in one step. Ideally, you wouldn't have to know which document contains the text you want to display. Bookmarks don't give you that ability. Each bookmark is stored with a specific document and is only accessible when that document is already active. There's no one-step way to go directly from one document to a specific bookmark in another document.

But you can accomplish roughly the same goal using Word's hyperlinks. Available throughout Office, hyperlinks are discussed in full in Chapter 14. In brief, hyperlinks work in your documents as they do in your Web browser, taking you immediately to another location. Among other possibilities, this can be a specific spot in a document — any document.

While you can use this technique to give your readers navigational aids within the current document, it's not ideal as a substitute for real bookmarks for your own use while editing. Compared to real Word bookmarks, hyperlinks have the disadvantage that you can only jump to the location they point to from the hyperlink itself — you can jump to a bookmark from anywhere.

The easiest way to create a hyperlink between two Word documents (or within a document) is simply to copy text from the second document. Returning to the location where you want to place the hyperlink, insert the copied text using the Edit ⇨ Paste as Hyperlink command (in Word, hyperlinks are actually fields, and this command inserts the necessary field).

Clicking the hyperlink takes you to the location from which the text was copied.

Secret

Although creating a hyperlink in Word is easy, changing it is a little trickier. Start by clicking *near* the hyperlink, not on it, and then use the arrow keys to move into it. At this point you can edit the text displayed by the hyperlink directly. To change the hyperlink's destination, press Shift+F10 to pop up the shortcut menu and choose Hyperlink ⇨ Edit Hyperlink.

Find and Replace Secrets

I'm sure you know how to hunt down text and to carry out basic find-and-replace operations with the Find and Replace commands. Just remember that these functions are part of the master Find and Replace dialog box that includes Go To, as well (see Figure 27-6). When you press F5 to bring up Go To, the Find tab is just one click away.

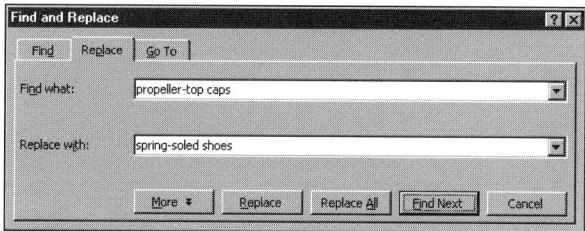

Figure 27-6: The Replace tab on the Find and Replace dialog box. In the default version shown here, you can only enter Find and Replace text — the controls governing advanced features are hidden.

Where are the buttons?

The advanced features of Find and Replace are hidden when you first open the dialog box — you won't see checkboxes for controlling Find and Replace options, nor are the No Formatting, Format, and Special buttons visible. The idea is to protect beginners from too many confusing options. Figure 27-6 shows the Replace tab as it first appears, while Figure 27-7 shows it with the extra buttons. To display the checkboxes and buttons if they're not already visible, choose More. If you want to hide these extremely useful, can't-live-without-them controls, well, that's your business — choose Less.

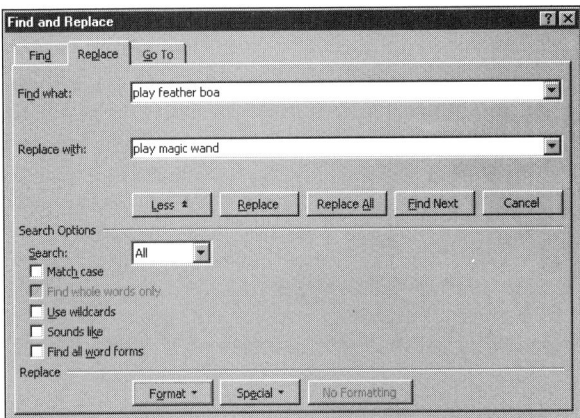

Figure 27-7: The Replace tab of the Find and Replace dialog box shown with its boxes and buttons for advanced features

Caution

Unfortunately, the Find and Replace dialog box always appears without the advanced options the first time you display it during a given session with Word — there's no setting to make the box automatically appear with the advanced options visible. Once you click More, however, those options remain visible until the next time you start the program.

Find and Replace tips

Here are two quick suggestions for making Find and Replace operations more efficient:

- Stop using Find — use Replace instead. All the functionality of the Find dialog box is included on the Replace tab, so you just don't need Find. If you have limited screen space for toolbar buttons, dump the Find button but keep the Replace button.

- Teach yourself to use the Find Next command, and assign it a one-key keyboard shortcut. Find Next is a much better way to zip to the next hit than is the Find Next button on the Replace (or Find) dialog box. The reason is simple — you can see all of the text in the window because there's no dialog box blocking your view.

Secret

The default shortcut for the Find Next command (called Repeat Find in the Commands list) is Shift+F4, hardly the most convenient choice for such a commonly used command. I make mine F3, as do most text editing programs. If you're already stuck on using F3 for AutoText (the default command for the F3 key) consider F8 or F10 as your shortcut for Find Next. After all, most people don't much use the commands — Extend Selection and Activate Menu Mode — that these keys normally trigger. Another good choice would be the

Insert key, if you're not using it for the Paste command (see the "Setting Editing Options" section at the beginning of this chapter).

Caution

Word's Find Next command repeats the last browse-by operation — it doesn't look again for the last Find text. If you search for some text and then browse for other objects, you can't resume searching for the same text without bringing up the Find dialog box again.

Macro VBA

To create a custom command that reliably searches for the Find text you last specified, use the following macro:

```
Sub FindNext()
With Application.Browser
    .Target = wdBrowseFind
    .Next
End With
End Sub
```

As you can guess, substituting .Previous for .Next produces the complementary "search again, in reverse, for the Find text" macro.

Advanced Find and Replace 1: Remember these features

Many competent Word users don't fully appreciate the power lurking under the hood of the Find and Replace commands. Remember that these commands can

- Search for and replace variant forms of the word you enter in the Find What field. If you ask Word to find be and check the Find All Word Forms checkbox, it scoops up *is*, *are*, *was*, *were*, and *been*. If you're replacing a verb, you're usually offered the correct conjugation for the found word. If Word's suggested conjugation isn't correct, you can choose the right one from a drop-down list.

- Search for and replace formatting you specify. If you want to find that one place in the document where you typed *big dog* in bold italics, use the Format button to refine your search criteria. Remember too that you can search for formatting independent of text — just leave Find What blank.

Advanced Find and Replace 2: Using special characters

Find can track down essentially anything in a document. In addition to text and formatting, your potential targets include paragraph marks, tabs, annotations, and line, page, and section breaks. In long documents, getting Word to find these items is much easier and more accurate than visually scanning for them yourself. And with Replace, Word can insert these items or substitute them for others.

Secret

By the way, if you want to find unusual symbols in your document, you can use the Macros8.dot template that came with Word 97. The template includes a macro that lets you insert symbols that you can't type into the Find and Replace dialog box. A similar template called Macros9.dot was included with the first beta version of Office 2000 but was dropped in the second beta — check your disk to see if it has been restored.

Codes for special characters in the Find and Replace dialog box

Table 27-2 lists the codes you must enter in the Find What and Replace With boxes to represent special characters. You can have Word enter these codes for you by picking the special characters by name from a menu. If the More button is visible, choose it. Then choose Special and make your selection from the menu.

Table 27-2 Special Character Codes for Find and Replace

Item	Code to Enter	Availability (Find and/or Replace)
Paragraph mark	^p	Both
Tab character	^t	Both
Annotation mark	^a	Find only
ANSI or ASCII characters	^0*nnn*, where *nnn* is the ANSI or ASCII character code	Both
Any character	^?	Find only
Any digit	^#	Find only
Any letter	^$	Find only
Caret character	^^	Both
Clipboard contents	^c	Replace only
Contents of the Find What field	^&	Replace only
Endnote mark	^e	Find only
Field	^d	Find only
Footnote mark	^f	Find only
Graphic	^g	Find only
Breaks		
Column break	^n	Both
Line break	^l	Both

Item	Code to Enter	Availability (Find and/or Replace)
Manual page break	^m	Both
Section break	^b	Both
Hyphens and spaces		
Em dash	^+	Both
En dash	^=	Both
Nonbreaking space	^s	Both
Nonbreaking hyphen	^~	Both
Optional hyphen	^-	Both
White space (any combination of consecutive spaces, tab characters, and paragraph marks)	^w	Find only

What good are special characters?

Here are a few practical tasks that you can accomplish by finding and replacing special characters.

Reviewing or removing optional hyphens

Optional hyphens can cause unexpected errors in a document, so you should review their placement in each word if you want to be absolutely certain your opus will print flawlessly. Instead of laboriously scanning the document, use Find to locate them for you (don't forget, optional hyphens are invisible unless you turn them on in the Options dialog box's View tab). Or blow 'em away with Replace.

To find all optional hyphens, place their code (^-) as your only entry at Find What. To eliminate optional hyphens from the document, enter ^- at Find What, make no entry at Replace With, and then choose Replace All.

Secret

If you want to search for specific words containing an optional hyphen, your best strategy is not to use the optional hyphen code in the Find What box. If you leave out the optional hyphen code, Find locates all occurrences of the word — including those containing an optional hyphen anywhere in the word. If you do include the optional hyphen code, Word finds the word only when it has the optional hyphen in the same location as you entered it in Find What. Don't know about optional hyphens? See Chapter 29.

Getting rid of manual paragraph indents

Word novices often indent the old typewriter way, pressing Tab or Space when they start a new paragraph. If you have to work on such documents, a replace operation with special characters fixes it up in no time. In the replace dialog box, enter **^p^w^** at Find What and **^p** at Replace With. Choose Replace All and you're done. You can now go back and format the document the proper way.

Finding, adding, or removing page or column breaks

Word lets you insert page and column breaks anyplace in a document you see fit. When you don't want to split up a paragraph over two pages or across two columns, or if you want to reserve space for an illustration that you'll physically paste into the printed document, adding a break is the solution.

But those manual breaks lead to formatting faux pas if later, you insert text toward the beginning of the document, or change margins, paragraph indents, fonts, or just about any other formatting setting. Word repaginates the document as it should, but this renders your manual page and column breaks obsolete. More than likely, you'll end up with pages or columns containing little or no text.

If you know or suspect that a document contains manual breaks, you should inspect them before you print to avoid nasty surprises. Enter the code for each break (^m for page breaks, ^n for column breaks) in turn in the Find What box. Alternatively, you can zap the breaks and start fresh using Replace. After entering the appropriate special character code at Find What, clear the Replace With box and choose Replace All.

You might also have a document that needs manual page or column breaks inserted at predictable locations. Normally, you would want forced page breaks to occur before a new heading, and you can set this up by modifying the heading style by checking the Page Break Before box in the Paragraph Format dialog box.

Occasionally, however, the page break locations are marked by a word or phrase rather than a paragraph style. In this case, you can have Replace insert the breaks for you. Type the text at Find What. At Replace With, type **^&^m**. That ^& code reinserts whatever you type at Find What — without this code, your Replace operation would substitute a page break for the specified text.

Because there's no formatting option to force a column break before a given paragraph, you can't set up styles to automate the task. The method just mentioned works — if you enter **^&^n** at Replace With — but only if there's some repeating unit of text to search for.

Cleaning up plain DOS text files

Word can import ordinary, unformatted text files just fine, but they don't always show up on your screen the way you want them to. The biggest problems are with DOS text files, which contain a paragraph mark (technically, a carriage return and line feed pair) at the end of every line. Real paragraphs are separated by blank lines, so the file contains two paragraph marks in a row between paragraphs.

Chapter 27: Expert Editing   **641**

If you import a DOS text file by selecting Text Files at Files of Type in Word's Open dialog box, each line becomes a separate paragraph. Things will look okay at first, maybe (if space above and space below are both set to 0 in your Normal paragraph style). But when you start editing, you'll know something is wrong.

Look at the sample in Figure 27-8. Text doesn't flow from line to line, because in Word's eyes, you're working with a series of separate paragraphs. Of course, this will be obvious if you have turned Paragraph Marks on.

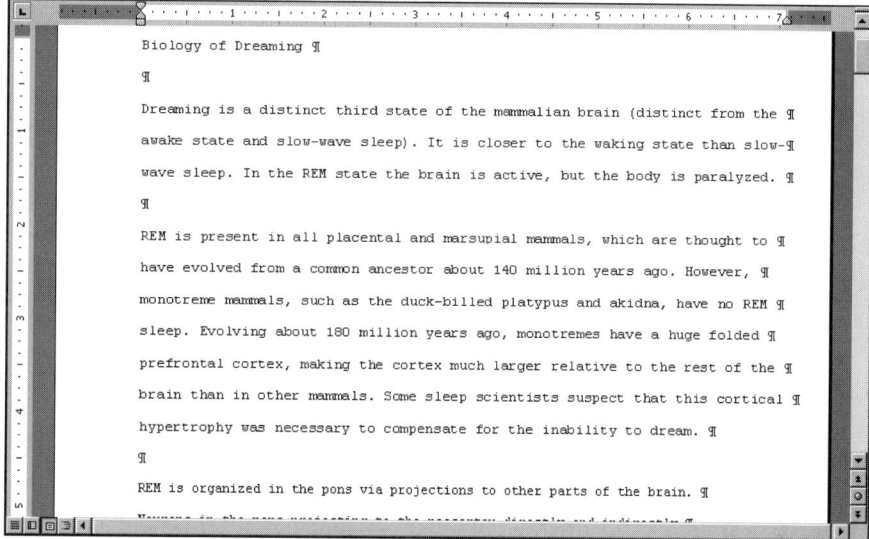

Figure 27-8: A text file opened in Word. Each line ends with a paragraph mark.

You may have somewhat better luck if you import the file using the Text with layout choice — but don't count on it. I find that Word's efforts to autoformat text files usually make the file harder to clean up, stuffing it with unwanted section breaks and assigning multiple paragraph styles.

Secret

So sticking with a text file imported as such — without layout — you need a three-step procedure to find and replace using special characters to clean up the file. To be safe, start by moving the insertion point to the top of your document and then call up the Replace dialog box. For each of the three steps listed here, make the indicated entries and then choose Replace All.

1. First, locate and mark the breaks between real paragraphs:

   Find What: **^p^p** (for two consecutive paragraph marks)
   Replace With: **$$##** (the replace entry can be any sequence of odd characters as long as you're sure they don't already occur in the document).

2. Next, get rid of all those extra paragraph marks falling at the end of lines:

   Find What: **^p**
   Replace With: (make no entry, not even a space)

3. Finally, revive the real paragraph breaks:

   Find What: **$$##**
   Replace With: **^p**

If you expect to import lots of text files, you should convert the preceding steps into a VBA procedure. Here's the code you need:

```
Sub TextFileCleanUp()
    With Selection.Find
        .Text = "^p^p"
        .Replacement.Text = "$$##"
        .Forward = True
        .Wrap = wdFindContinue
        .Format = False
        .MatchCase = False
        .MatchWholeWord = False
        .MatchWildcards = False
        .MatchSoundsLike = False
        .MatchAllWordForms = False
    End With
    Selection.Find.Execute Replace:=wdReplaceAll
    With Selection.Find
        .Text = "^p"
        .Replacement.Text = ""
        .Wrap = wdFindContinue
    End With
    Selection.Find.Execute Replace:=wdReplaceAll
    With Selection.Find
        .Text = "$$##"
        .Replacement.Text = "^p"
        .Wrap = wdFindContinue
    End With
    Selection.Find.Execute Replace:=wdReplaceAll
End Sub
```

Advanced Find and Replace 3: Using wildcards

Rare indeed is the hardy soul who takes advantage of Word's capability to find and replace text that matches an abstract pattern rather than an exact sequence of characters. But this capability can be a huge timesaver for some complex text modifications.

Word now uses the term wildcards for what used to be called pattern matching in early versions. The analogy is to a card game where a deuce can stand in for a range of other cards. In Word, wildcards are special characters you can enter in find and replace operations that represent one or more characters (from a defined range) in the document.

You can only enter the wildcards in the Find What box, not in Replace With. If you think about it, this makes sense—Word can't read your mind and choose from a range of possible characters to insert in the document. However, you can include the text located by the wildcard Find in the Replace entry. That means you can use Replace to revise variable text, which gives this feature its real power.

Of course, you won't be using the wildcards by themselves—they're valuable only when mixed with ordinary characters in a complete expression. As a simple but far-fetched example, say your computer products company has decided to abandon the Macintosh market and climb on the Windows bandwagon. All your new products work just like the old ones did, but you do have to change the names in all your press releases and product information sheets. MacMathWhiz has become PCMathWhiz, MacScanWhiz will now be called PCScanWhiz, and so on.

Wildcards let you make all the changes in one step for each document. In outline, you would simply enter Mac*Whiz at Find What and a corresponding expression at Replace With. The actual process involves a few wrinkles, and they're essentially undocumented. So stick around for the details.

Performing a wildcard Find and Replace

The mechanics of finding and replacing with wildcards are simple. Once you have the Find and Replace dialog box open, your first step is to make sure its advanced options are visible. If you don't see a set of checkboxes and buttons at the bottom of the dialog box, choose More to display them.

All you have to do now is check Use Wildcards. Once the box is checked, Word interprets wildcard characters entered at Find What as such, rather than as ordinary characters. If you don't want to type in the wildcards yourself, choose Special and select them from the pop-up menu.

Replace operations using wildcards

The Word manual and Help files offer scant assistance when it comes to designing useful wildcard-based Replace operations. As I've said, this is where wildcards really shine, but you wouldn't know it from the information Microsoft provides.

In almost every case, you use a wildcard-based Replace operation to *modify* the existing text, not to replace it entirely with something new. Your goal is to change text that may vary with different text that likewise varies, based on what was originally there. That means you need a way to insert portions of the variable text located by Find into the new text inserted by Replace.

In Word, here's how you handle the problem: First, use parentheses to separate the Find What entry into sections based on which portions you want to use in the replacement text. Using the Macintosh-to-PC example introduced earlier, you would make the following entry at Find What:

```
(Mac)(*Whiz)
```

In this example, because everything after the "Mac" should be retained in the new product names, you only need to divide the find text into two sections.

Second, enter your replacement text, referring to the section(s) you want to retain by number. You must enter the backslash character (\) in front of the section numbers. The sample entry would look like this:

PC\2

Secret

Because the sections of a wildcard find entry can include both wildcards and ordinary characters, you can use this procedure to change the order of portions of the find text — even if you use no wildcards at all. Suppose you write a report referring frequently to a Mr. John George. When it turns out that you got his first and last names backward, set things right by entering (John)( )(George) at Find What — that middle section encloses the space between the two names — and \3\2\1 at Replace With.

Wildcard reference

This section collects a miscellany of important tips related to wildcard Find and Replace operations. Table 27-3 lists all the wildcard characters (operators) along with a few other special characters used in conjunction with wildcards. Table 27-4 lists additional characters to use in wildcard Find and Replace operations.

Table 27-3   Wildcards and Other Special Characters Used in Wildcard Find and Replace Operations

To Find	Enter This Wildcard or Character	Sample
Any of the actual characters used as wildcards including ?, *, (,), [,], {, }, <, @, \	\ followed by the wildcard character	\? finds "?"; * finds "*";\\ finds "\"
Any one character but not drug	?	d?g finds dig, dug, and dog
A sequence of characters of any length	*	d*g finds dig, drug, and digressing
Any one character from a specified group	[character list]	d[iu]g finds dig and dug but not dog
Any one character in an ascending alphabetical or numeric sequence	[beginning character-ending character]	do[a-p]e finds dole and dome but not dote or dose
Any one character except those specified	[!character list]	di[!e] finds dig, din, and dip but not die

To Find	Enter This Wildcard or Character	Sample
Any one character except those in a specified sequence	[!beginning character-ending character]	du[!a-f] finds dug and dun but not dub or dud
An exact number of repetitions of the previous character or expression	{n}	20{2}24 matches two and only two additional 0s — it finds 20024 and 20025, but not 2024 or 200024
At least a specified number of repetitions of the previous character or expression	{n,}	20{2,}24 matches two or more additional 0s — it finds 20024 and 2000024 but not 2024
Repetitions of the previous character or expression within a specified range	{n,m}	20{1,3}24 matches 1 to 3 repetitions of 0 — it finds 2024, 20024, and 200024 but not 2000024
One or more repetitions of the previous character or expression	@	dro@l finds drol and drool
The beginning of a word	<	<(de) finds demure and deranged but not sulphide
The end of a word	>	(ed)> finds red and detangled but not educational

Table 27-4   Other Characters to Use in Wildcard Find and Replace Operations

To Perform This Function	Enter These Characters	Sample
Identify sections of a wildcard in a Find What entry	() (parentheses)	The following entry has been divided into three separate sections: (Part No.) (A-)([0-9]{1,})
Include a section of the current wildcard Find entry in the Replace text (you must first have enclosed all the sections of the Find entry in parentheses)	\ followed by section number	The following Replace entry is based on the preceding sample: \1BX-\3. It would convert the text "Part No. A-43254" into "Part No. BX-43254"

Keep this key point in mind: While it may not be obvious, wildcard Finds are always case sensitive. Word looks only for the exact characters you enter in the Find What box, whether you type in real, individual characters or use a wildcard to refer to a range of characters.

Secret

Oddly, Word still doesn't include distinct wildcards for numerals, letters, lowercase or capital letters, or punctuation marks. However, you can create stand-ins for the missing wildcards using the available tools. For example, to hunt down any numeral, you would enter **[0-9]**; to find one or more numerals in succession, enter **[0-9]{1,}**. As detailed in Table 27-3, square brackets are used to match any character in a consecutive sequence, whereas braces (curly brackets) indicate the number of times the previous character must occur for a match to be found.

Watch out for the repeater wildcard, the @ symbol. According to Microsoft, this is supposed to locate any number of occurrences of the preceding character or wildcard expression. If the repeater worked as promised, you could type **[0-9]@** to locate any number from 1 to 999 (even up to 9999999 ... if there are no commas). But it doesn't, at least not when used alone: You must enter it between other characters, or it finds only one matching character at a time. Use {1,} instead, which works as the repeater should.

One last point: You can use most of the codes for special characters such as tabs, page breaks, and so on in wildcard finds. However, the codes for certain items, including paragraph marks, don't work. Fortunately, Word gives you substitute numeric codes for most of these items for use in wildcard find and replace operations — see Table 27-5 for a listing. Note, though, that you can't search for fields if you're using wildcards.

Table 27-5 Substitute Codes to Use in Wildcard Find and Replace

To Find or Replace This Item	Enter This Code
Footnote or endnote mark	^2
Paragraph mark	^13
Section or manual page break	^12
White space	space{1,}

Speeding Text Entry

Word comes with lots of features that accelerate text entry. The most important of these to master is AutoCorrect, covered in full in Chapter 7. However, Word suffers from an embarrassment of riches in this category. Keeping track of which feature performs which function can sometimes be tough. The list that follows summarizes some of the high points:

Feature	Explanation
AutoCorrect	Corrects various common typing errors and converts abbreviations into complete words or phrases.
AutoFormat as you Type	Converts hyphens into dashes and straight apostrophes and quote marks into paired, typographically correct curly marks.

Feature	Explanation
AutoText	Inserts stock text passages from a list or via a toolbar button.
Repeat	When used immediately after typing text, inserts the same text.
Insert Date and Time	Inserts the date, the time, or both in one of many available formats.

AutoText secrets

Over time, Word's AutoText feature has really been beefed up. You can select individual AutoText entries from a toolbar button or from the Insert menu, without having to open the AutoText dialog box. Also appreciated is the capability to group your AutoText entries by category. Word comes with a rich set of prefab AutoText entries for stock phrases such as salutations and closings in letters.

Even better, AutoText is almost as automatic as AutoCorrect. Now, once you've typed the first four letters of an AutoText entry, the AutoComplete feature pops up a little ScreenTip offering the entire item. If that's what you're trying to type, just press Enter to have Word insert the whole word or phrase. If not, just keep typing — Word leaves you in peace.

When to use AutoText

Although I prefer AutoCorrect for most automated text entry chores, AutoText definitely has its place. For one thing, AutoText entries are specific to a template. If the text you reuse varies with the type of document, you can store the appropriate AutoText entries in separate templates (AutoText entries stored with the Normal template are available in all documents, of course). Another AutoText advantage is that you can recall its named entries from menus and toolbar buttons. That means that your shorthand is always readily available, even if you forget a code name.

Including formatting in an AutoText entry

To create a formatted AutoText entry, apply the formatting to text in your document first, select the text, and then open the AutoText dialog box and Add the entry. To include paragraph formatting in the entry, include the paragraph mark in the selection.

You can also include bookmarks in AutoText entries to mark document locations quickly. See "Bookmark tricks with AutoText" in the section on bookmarks.

Using the AutoText menu — watch out for disappearing entries

The AutoText menu (and the AutoText toolbar button, if you choose to display it) lets you access AutoText entries in categories of your choice. Figure 27-9 shows the AutoText menu with several submenus, each offering a collection of related entries.

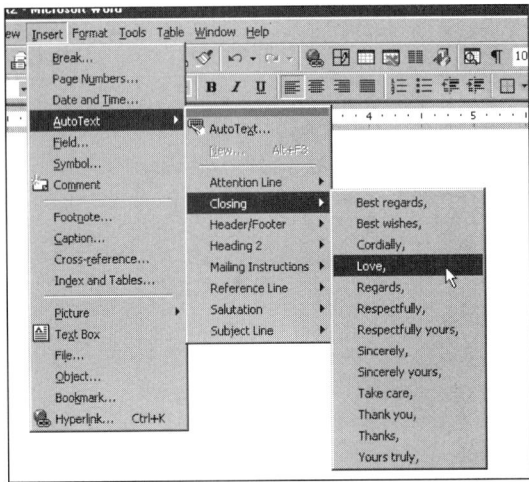

Figure 27-9: When the insertion point is in a Normal paragraph, the AutoText menu shows all your AutoText entries organized into categories as a series of submenus.

Secret

Those submenus are actually the names of paragraph styles, present or past: A Word AutoText entry is associated with the paragraph style in which it was created (Chapter 28 covers paragraph styles in detail). The relationship between specific paragraph styles and AutoText entries can be confusing and problematic, so I try to explain it here. But you can use this relationship to customize the AutoText menu, as described in the next section.

Suppose you happen to be in a Heading 3 paragraph when you create an AutoText entry. From now on, as shown in Figure 27-10, the bottom of the AutoText menu displays that entry, and all others created from Heading 3 paragraphs, whenever you're working in any Heading 3 paragraph.

Caution

Notice, however, that you can no longer access the other AutoText submenus shown in Figure 27-9, nor the entries they contain — they've all disappeared. It turns out that you can only see the submenus when you're working in a Normal paragraph (all AutoText entries are available in paragraphs assigned to the Normal style) or if the paragraph style you're working in has no AutoText entries of its own.

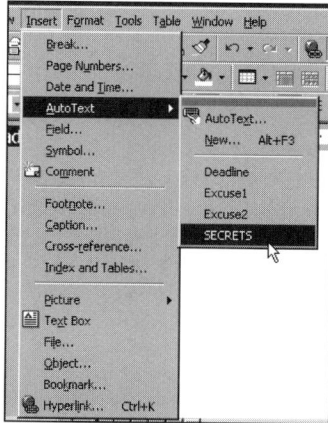

Figure 27-10: The AutoText menu shows entries associated with the current style so that you can access them without opening the AutoText dialog box. If the insertion point is in a paragraph of any style other than Normal, only AutoText entries associated with that style appear on the menu.

With this system, Word's designers have made what I believe is an erroneous assumption. They think that when you're working in a given paragraph, you only need access to AutoText entries associated with that one style. As a result, at times the bulk of your AutoText list is inaccessible via the menu. (When you don't see the entry you want on the menu, you can always insert any AutoText entry by opening the AutoText dialog box and selecting the entry there.) At any rate, be careful when you create an AutoText entry. Check the style of the current paragraph and be sure that you really want to associate the entry with the style.

If you want all your AutoText entries to be available on the menu at all times, always create them from Normal paragraphs. There are tradeoffs: You give up the ability to organize the list, and to include paragraph formatting with the text.

Organizing your AutoText entries using virtual paragraph styles

You can organize the entries on the AutoText menu into submenus with descriptive titles. Here's the technique:

1. For each submenu you want, create a new paragraph style, naming it what you want the AutoText submenu title to be.

2. In a document, assign a paragraph to the new style.

3. Create all your AutoText entries for this category.

4. Now delete the style in the Format ⇨ Style dialog box. Word retains the association between the style's name and the associated AutoText entry, and a submenu with the deleted style's name appears on the AutoText menu. I call the style name a "virtual style," because the AutoText feature thinks it exists but it really doesn't function as a paragraph style.

Deleting the style isn't technically necessary—the associated AutoText entry is still available when you're in a paragraph assigned to the Normal style (or to the new style). It's just that if you don't delete it, you'll be cluttering your template with a style you don't need. To add new entries to the submenu later, you must again recreate the style with the same name, define the new AutoText, and then delete the style once more. Consistent with the previous discussion, you can see the submenus only when you're working in paragraphs assigned to the Normal style, or to a style with no associated AutoText entries.

Creating one-shot AutoText entries

For fastest possible insertion of a specific AutoText entry, assign it a keyboard shortcut or toolbar button. Choose Tools ⇨ Customize to make the assignment—AutoText is one of the items in the Categories list on the Commands tab. But with the improved main AutoText button, it no longer makes sense to set up toolbars with extensive collections of specific AutoText buttons.

Using AutoTextList fields

Secret

A Word field, AutoTextList, provides a document hot spot for inserting one of a variety of preselected words or phrases at that location. The field appears in the document as ordinary text. However, the field is highlighted if field highlighting is turned on, and Word supplies a ScreenTip that tells the reader how to use the field—it appears when the mouse pointer hovers over it for a second or two.

When a reader right-clicks the field, Word pops up a menu listing all the AutoText entries associated with a given paragraph style. When the reader picks one of the entries on the menu, the selected AutoText entry appears in the document in place of the original field text. The item remains a field, however, and can be right-clicked again if the reader wishes to switch to a different AutoText entry.

Obviously, this new feature is best used in templates. In a letter template, for example, you could place one AutoTextList field for the salutation and one for the closing. You would then be able to tailor your tone anywhere from sloppy intimacy to icy formality.

The menu that appears when you click an AutoTextList field is based on a specific paragraph style, chosen at the time the field is inserted. This means you must understand the dirty details about associating styles with AutoText entries, described earlier. The main thing to remember is that you can delete a style once you've created the associated AutoText, which lets you use virtual style names as categories for AutoText entries even in AutoTextList fields. Here's how to insert an AutoTextList field:

1. Choose Insert ⇨ Field.

2. Choose Links and References in the Categories list and then choose AutoTextList in the Field Names list. Word starts the field for you down in the Field codes box.

3. Moving to the Field Codes box, type a message that will appear in your document (on the screen only) to identify the field, surrounding the text within quotation marks. Be sure you type something here or the field will be invisible and unusable when it gets to the document.

4. By default, Word displays AutoText entries associated with the current paragraph style. To specify a different style, type **\s** after the entry followed by the name of the chosen style (real or virtual) in quotes. You can pick styles from a tab on the Options dialog box, but virtual styles aren't included on the list.

5. To change the ScreenTip text, type **\t** at the end of the entry followed by the text (in quotes) you want Word to display when the mouse pointer hovers over the field. The completed entry should look something like this:

   AUTOTEXTLIST "Right-click here" \s "Salutation" \t "Right-click here to choose a salutation from a list"

6. OK the dialog box to insert the field.

Editing AutoText entries

You can delete AutoText entries in the AutoText dialog box, but you can't edit them there. To revise or replace an existing entry, retaining its current name, follow these steps:

1. Insert the entry in a document and make the revisions there. If the new text is radically different than the existing entry, just type the new text into your document.

2. Still in the document, select the revised or new text you now want to use as the AutoText entry.

3. Choose Insert ⇨ AutoText and then click New. The Create AutoText dialog box appears.

4. Here's the key step: Type the exact original name of the AutoText entry you're revising or replacing. When you OK the dialog box, the revision becomes final.

Using AutoText fields to keep documents automatically up to date

It's common to use a repeating passage of text that changes over time. Say you've developed several different documents that quote the company dress code. Your first thought might be to place the dress code in an AutoText entry that you could then insert in any document as many times as necessary. The problem is, fashions change. When the bigwigs revise the dress code, you're going to be stuck with wading through each document to make the updates. But if you insert a field that refers to the dress code

AutoText entry, all you would have to do is make the changes once, replace the existing AutoText entry with them, and then auto-update your documents.

To enter an AutoText field, put the insertion point where you want the entry and choose Insert ⇨ Field to display the Field dialog box (see Figure 27-11). Select Links and References in the Categories list and then AutoText in the list of Field Names. Next, select the specific AutoText entry the field should refer to: Choose Options, pick the field name from the list, and choose Add to Field.

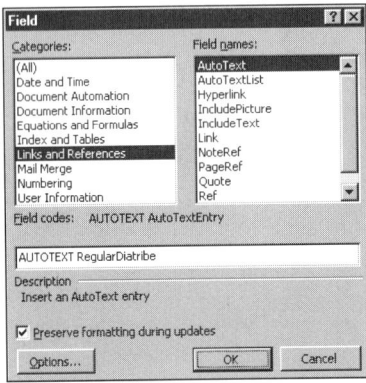

Figure 27-11: Inserting an AutoText field in the Field dialog box.

As soon as you OK the dialog boxes, the AutoText field appears in your document. If field codes are visible (the setting is in the View tab of the Tools ⇨ Options dialog box), you'll see a bracketed expression such as { AUTOTEXT dresscode * MERGEFORMAT }. If you've turned off field codes, the text of the AutoText entry appears instead. You can toggle back and forth between the two views of the entry by placing the insertion point anywhere in it and choosing the ToggleFieldDisplay command (the default shortcut is Shift+F9).

When the dress code policy changes, you must first revise the AutoText entry (see the previous tip, "Editing AutoText entries," for instructions). After that, updating all the documents that contain it will be a breeze. Open each document in turn, press Ctrl+A to select the entire document, and then choose the Update Fields command (F9 by default).

Ditch the Spike for a clipboard enhancement utility

Word's Spike, a special AutoText item, is a neat idea, but it's not implemented well. Unless you need the Spike's services in macros, I recommend that you forget it. The ClipMate utility discussed in Chapter 10 does everything the Spike can, and much more. I highly recommend it. The Clipboard toolbar, new in Office 2000, is another alternative to the Spike; it's discussed in Chapter 10.

In case you're unfamiliar with it, the Spike is a clipboard-like holding station for text and graphics. But unlike the standard clipboard, it can accumulate information from various places in multiple documents — each time you cut a selected item to the Spike, it just adds itself to the bottom of the Spike clipboard without erasing the existing contents. Once you have all the material you want in the Spike, you can place it en masse at any location.

Problems with the Spike

So what's wrong with the Spike? One glaring problem is that you can only cut, not copy, information to it. If you want to assemble a document that summarizes information from several others, leaving the source documents intact, you have to fall back on a repeated sequence of ordinary copy-and-paste operations.

Although you can overcome that weakness with a macro described later in this chapter, the Spike is still a crude tool. All the information you place in the Spike becomes one continuous chunk — you can't reorder it. That means you have to plan carefully the sequence of cuts you make to the Spike, or do a lot of reorganizing once you place the contents in the destination document.

Spike tips

If you do insist on using the Spike, the following points are here to get you started:

- The default keyboard shortcuts for getting your text into and out of the Spike are as follows: Ctrl+F3 cuts selected text to the Spike, while Ctrl+Shift+F3 pastes the Spike contents into your document.

- If you want to set up toolbar buttons for these operations, the commands you need in the Customize dialog box are Spike and InsertSpike. Word doesn't include button bitmaps for either command, so you have to design your own or use them as text buttons.

- Because the Spike is a special AutoText entry, you can also paste its contents via the Insert ⇨ AutoText command.

- AutoComplete works with the Spike too. Just type **spik** and you get a ScreenTip showing you the first two lines of text stored in the Spike. Pressing Enter at this point inserts the Spike contents into your document.

- The Macros8.dot template included with Word 97 comes with a set of secret Spike-enhancing macros. They let you copy items to the Spike, preview its contents, and empty it. Use the Organizer as described in Chapter 26 to copy the Spike and frmpreview macro project items into your Normal.dot or another global template. If you don't have Word 97, check your Office 2000 CD to see whether it contains a Macros9.dot template.

Using Repeat to clone text you just typed

The Repeat feature (F4 is the default keyboard shortcut) is great for repeating Word commands, but did you realize it will repeat what you've just typed? If you need to make several copies of a word, phrase, or sentence, use Repeat to speed the task as follows:

1. Start by moving the insertion point to clear any previously typed text. If the insertion point is already where it should be, just press the left arrow and then the right arrow.

2. Type the text, including a space or paragraph mark at the end to leave room for the next copy. You can use the Backspace key to make corrections. But don't press the cursor keys — if you do, you'll clear the text that Repeat is storing for you.

3. Choose Repeat to place into your document as many copies as you like of the text you typed.

Inserting the current date or time in one step

You're probably familiar with the Insert Date and Time command, located on the Insert menu. When you choose Insert ⇨ Date and Time, the dialog box lets you tell Word to insert the current date, time, or both into your document in one of a host of available formats.

Secret

If you leave the Update Automatically box cleared, Word inserts the date and time information as ordinary text — the date you insert stays the same unless you edit it. If you check the box, however, Word actually inserts a date field, which it updates every time you open or print the document (and whenever you update the field manually). Given that the dialog box doesn't say anything about date fields, this might not be obvious.

The Insert Date and Time command is flexible, but you probably only use one or two date formats most of the time. Wouldn't it be nice to be able to insert a date in a single step, without having to deal with the dialog box? Something you could access via a toolbar button or keyboard shortcut? Word does offer a one-shot Date command and a corresponding toolbar button on the Header and Footer toolbar. You can add this button to other toolbars via the Customize dialog box. But be aware that this Date command has two potential problems.

First, it inserts the date or time using the current default format set in the Date and Time dialog box — this is usually okay, but if you want a button to insert a nondefault format, it won't do the trick. Second, the Date command can only insert the date or time as a field, not as plain text. If you don't want the information to be updated every time you open the document, you're out of luck.

The only real solution is a simple macro, in which you specify which format you want and whether to insert the date or time as a field, or as ordinary text. After you've entered the macro, assign it a custom toolbar button, keyboard shortcut, or both. Here's the macro I use:

```
Sub DateAsText()
Selection.InsertDateTime _
    DateTimeFormat:="MMMM d, yyyy", InsertAsField: = False
End Sub
```

This example inserts a date, in the very standard format "October 12, 1997," as ordinary text. Type **True** instead of **False** if you want your own macro to insert a date field rather than ordinary text. To use a different format, enter the "picture" of the format, just as you would for a date field, in the quote marks. To see a list of these format pictures, choose Insert ➪ Field, select Date in the Field Names list, and choose Options — the list of picture formats is displayed on the General Switches tab. Chapter 33 on Word fields covers the whys and wherefores of picture formats.

Quick Text Changes

All good writers will tell you that writing is rewriting. Whether you're editing for clarity, to make a more powerful argument, or simply to correct minor errors, affording the means to make these changes painlessly is the word processor's greatest strength. Of course, Word's editing functions are so fundamental that you probably have a good grasp on most of them already. But look through the pointers that follow — you may find some new ideas for faster text editing.

Mouse text-selection shortcuts

The mouse makes it easy to select any quantity of text for editing operations such as cutting, pasting, or moving via drag and drop. The standard way to select with the mouse is to drag over the text, and you can extend selections by holding down the Shift key while you click. But just in case you've forgotten them, here are Word's mouse shortcuts for text selection:

This Mouse Action	Selects This Text
Double-click	Entire word
Triple-click	Entire paragraph
Click the selection area (to the left of the text)	Entire line
Click anywhere in a sentence while holding down Ctrl	Entire sentence
Double-click the selection area	Entire paragraph
Triple-click the selection area	Entire document

Don't forget that you can select columnar blocks of text by holding down Alt as you drag. This is sometimes extremely useful, especially when working with tabular material imported from plain text files. Switch to a monospaced font such as Courier for best results before making columnar selections. (With the keyboard, select a columnar block of text by pressing Ctrl+Shift+F8 and then using the arrow keys to define the block. Press Esc to cancel this mode.)

Take advantage of the shortcut menus

Once you've selected a block of text with the mouse, the fastest way to cut or copy it to the clipboard is via the shortcut (right-click) menu. On this point, I recommend adding the Cut, Copy, and Paste commands to the shortcut menu that appears when you right-click a misspelled word. Otherwise, Word forces you to stop and deal with the spelling error before you can cut or copy the word. Chapter 26 explains how to modify shortcut menus.

Using the selection bar

The selection bar is the invisible column between the left edge of the document window and the left margin of the page. To select text with it, point in this area and click once to select a line, twice to select a whole paragraph, or thrice for the entire document. Dragging selects entire lines as you cross over them.

Mouse moves — an alternative to drag and drop

No book revealing Word secrets would be complete without mention of this slick mouse-keyboard maneuver for moving or copying text. To move a chunk of the document, first select the text and then point at the destination and hold down Ctrl while you right-click. To copy, Ctrl+Shift+right-click instead.

A great secret keyboard move technique

Hold down Alt+Shift while you press the up or down arrow to move the paragraph containing the insertion point up or down in the document as a unit. You don't need to select the paragraph first. However, if you do select two or more paragraphs, the whole set of paragraphs moves. This is a really cool way to rearrange paragraphs and an alternative to Outline view for shuffling entire sections.

Keyboard shortcuts for cutting words, lines, sentences, or paragraphs

Selecting text with the mouse is easy, yes, but it slows you down: You have to take your hands off the keyboard. And even with the shortcut menu, cutting a selection is still a two-step procedure. That's why I favor keyboard shortcuts that cut units of text in a single step.

These shortcuts should cut text (rather than copy or delete it) because cutting is the most versatile of the three procedures. If you need the text again at the same or another location, pasting brings it back. Creating a copy of what you cut is as simple as cutting, pasting at the same place, and then pasting again at the new location.

At the very least you should make up a pair of word-cutting shortcuts. The simple macros listed here cut the word (or word fragment) to the left or right of the insertion point, respectively (I mention the lines emphasized by bold type in a moment — when you type them, they appear in the regular VBA font):

```
Sub CutWordLeft()
    Selection.MoveLeft Unit:=wdWord, Extend:=wdExtend
    Selection.Cut
End Sub
and
Sub CutWordRight()
    Selection.MoveRight Unit:=wdWord, Extend:=wdExtend
    Selection.Cut
End Sub
```

Now, where to park these macros on the keyboard? My modest proposal is the two square bracket keys, [and]. You must use the technique described in "Using off-limits keys in custom keyboard shortcuts" in Chapter 26 to assign the bracket keys to the word-cutting macros, because you can't type the brackets in the Customize Keyboard dialog box. But once the shortcuts are in place, you can speed through your text, chopping out words or phrases effortlessly. Most people use brackets only rarely. Still, if you assign the shortcuts Alt+[and Alt+] to the original bracket characters, you can type the brackets immediately when you do need them.

You can create similar macros to cut text in larger chunks moving left or right from the insertion point whole. In each of the preceding macros, the first line (in bold) creates the selection unique to that macro. In your new macros, substitute the following lines for those printed in bold in the version shown earlier:

Unit of Text	Macro's Specific Job	First Line of Macro
Sentence	Cut to beginning of current sentence	`Selection.MoveLeft Unit:=wdSentence, Extend:=wdExtend`
	Cut to end of current sentence	`Selection.MoveRight Unit:=wdSentence, Extend:=wdExtend`
Line	Cut to beginning of current line	`Selection.HomeKey Unit:=wdLine, Extend:=wdExtend`
	Cut to end of current line	`Selection.EndKey Unit:=wdLine, Extend:=wdExtend`
Paragraph	Cut to beginning of current paragraph	`Selection.MoveUp Unit:=wdParagraph, Extend:=wdExtend`
	Cut to end of current paragraph	`Selection.MoveDown Unit:=wdParagraph, Extend:=wdExtend`

Swapping characters

Word still is missing a useful command that was common among many of the old DOS word processors: a function to swap the position of two adjacent characters. It's so easy to mess up and type "teh" when you meant to type "the."

AutoCorrect fixes many common errors of this kind, detecting and setting straight "agian," "esle," and "bakc," as well as "teh." But AutoCorrect only works on the specific sequences of characters in its list, and you can't possibly anticipate all the mistakes you're going to make.

Solve the missing feature problem with a quick little macro called SwapCharacters. It works on the two characters to the left of the insertion point, picking up the closest one and tucking it one position back in the stream of text. If you like this macro, I suggest putting it on a very accessible key.

```
Sub SwapCharacters()
If Selection.Type <> wdSelectionIP Then GoTo NoSwap
    Selection.MoveLeft Unit:=wdCharacter, Count:=1
    Selection.MoveLeft Unit:=wdCharacter, Count:=1, Extend:=wdExtend
    Selection.Cut
    Selection.MoveRight Unit:=wdCharacter, Count:=1
    Selection.Paste
NoSwap:
End Sub
```

Improving on Word's case-changing functions

As befits a sophisticated text editor, Word includes a panoply of functions for changing the case of your text (we're talking about going from BIG LETTERS to baby letters or vice versa). Unfortunately, your access to these functions is restricted.

The standard keyboard layout places a keyboard shortcut for the Change Case command on Shift+F3. Like a good-looking person with bad teeth, this command has a lot of initial appeal but tends to put people off after they take a second glance, for the reasons reviewed in the next section.

How the Change Case command works

As you press Shift+F3 repeatedly, Change Case cycles the affected text through three different case states. But the exact effect varies, depending on whether and how much text is selected first. Now, it's asking a lot to memorize such variations, and this is one of the command's problems. (There are others, as you'll soon see.) Anyway, just so you can look it up for easy reference, Table 27-6 shows how Change Case works.

Table 27-6 Effects of Word's Change Case

Condition		Effect of Change Case (Shift+F3 by Default)
No text is selected	1.	Converts the entire word to UPPERCASE.
	2.	Converts the entire word to lowercase.
	3.	Capitalizes the word containing the insertion point.
Less than a full sentence is selected	1.	Converts the entire selection to UPPERCASE.
	2.	Converts the entire selection to lowercase.
	3.	Capitalizes every word in the selection, changing all other letters to lowercase.
A full sentence or more is selected	1.	Converts the entire selection to UPPERCASE.
	2.	Converts the entire selection to lowercase.
	3.	Capitalizes the first word in every sentence in the selection, changing all other letters to lowercase.

So what else is wrong with the Change Case command? I can list three problems:

- At any one time, Change Case performs only three of Word's five useful case-changing functions (there is a sixth, mentioned later). You can get to

- some of the other options via a dialog box (choose Format ⇨ Change Case), but that route usually takes more time than just retyping the text.
- The Change Case dialog box also leaves out Word's command for capitalizing the first word in the selection, regardless of its sentence location.
- When text isn't selected, Change Case always works on the whole word containing the insertion point. You can't use Change Case to make Powerpoint into PowerPoint (unless you select just the second "p" before pressing Shift+F3).

A better case-changing command

A helpful case-changing macro is included in the Office 2000 Secrets.dot template on the CD-ROM that's included with this book. Here's what the macro does: If no text is selected, it changes the case of the letter at (to the right of) the insertion point — only that letter is affected. If you select text, the macro cycles through the four case-changing functions (if you look at the code, you see that the macro travels the cycle in reverse order, because otherwise two of the functions would produce the same effect).

A quick word about Word's sixth case-changing function, the interesting but nearly useless "toggle case." Use it on the selection PowerPoint, and you would end up with pOWERpOINT. Once in a blue moon you may find a use for this conversion, and if you do, activate it via Format ⇨ Change Case.

Keyboard shortcuts for changing case

Editing often moves a word from somewhere in the middle of a sentence to the lead-off position, and vice versa. Because changing case is such a frequent chore, keep the necessary keyboard shortcut close at hand. I put my case-changing macro on the \ (backslash) key, where it's immediately accessible. As a backup, I assign the | key (Shift+\) as the shortcut for Word's standard Change Case command — that way, I can still capitalize a whole word without selecting it first. See "Customizing the Word keyboard" in Chapter 26 for a discussion of how to create keyboard shortcuts.

Conclusion

When you know how to get around in Word documents, find what you're looking for, and add text faster than greased lightning, you're a Word master in my book, regardless of whether your documents ever win any design awards. This is the one Word chapter to study in detail if you're short on time for learning secrets.

Chapter 28

Full-Speed Formatting

In This Chapter

▶ Reviewing essential background information on Word's formatting system
▶ Using kerning and character spacing effectively
▶ Learning tips on tabs
▶ Using advanced techniques for working with styles

Form and content go hand in hand. Word has a vast array of commands and features that help you present your ideas in inviting, easy-to-read formats.

Formatting Basics: A Quick Review

With a few exceptions, all your formatting decisions in Word can be mapped onto a hierarchy of three levels: character, paragraph, and section formatting.

- **Character formatting** controls the look of individual characters (letters, numerals, punctuation marks, and special symbols). Attributes such as font, size, bold, italics, underline, spacing, color, and special effects all come under this heading. However — and this is a key concept — most characters in a typical document don't carry their own individual formatting information. Instead, their appearance is determined by the paragraph format.

- **Paragraph formatting** specifies all manner of settings that affect the paragraph as a whole, including alignment; indents; tab settings; the space before and after the paragraph and between its lines; and any numbering, bullets, borders, or shading. In addition, every paragraph has a *style* that determines the default appearance of the individual characters. Again, you can override these attributes in a selected passage by applying character formatting, but the paragraph format still sets the look of the text in the rest of the paragraph.

- **Section formatting** controls the basic layout of the document, with settings for paper size and orientation; margins; headers and footers; columns; and related items. A document can have more than one section, and these layout choices can vary from section to section within the same document. Note, however, that you can place text anywhere you want on a page using text boxes and frames, overriding these layout settings. Section formatting and other layout issues are the subject of Chapter 29.

Secret

Don't forget that Word keeps all of the paragraph-formatting information in the paragraph mark, which signifies the end of a paragraph. I discuss the implications of this in the section later on paragraph formatting.

Remember, too, that you can search for and replace any combination of character- and paragraph-formatting options with the Find and Replace commands. If you leave the Find What and Replace With boxes empty, these commands locate and change the formatting only, regardless of the text content.

Methods for applying formatting

There are basically two ways to format text in Word:

- **Direct formatting** refers to the process of applying formatting to a specific paragraph or text selection using the commands on the top part of the Format menu, or via toolbar buttons or keyboard shortcuts.

- **Style formatting** relies on styles, which are collections of many different formatting options that you can apply all at once to a paragraph or text selection. Instead of applying these formatting options directly, you apply the style, which in turn dictates the format. Styles and how to use them are the subject of a complete section later in this chapter.

Displaying formatting information

Secret

For detailed information on the formatting applied to any character, activate the What's This help feature: choose Help ➪ What's This? or press Shift+F1 to add a large question mark to the mouse pointer. Now, clicking over the character you're interested in reveals a balloon box summarizing the text's paragraph and character (*font*) formatting, and where it comes from: a paragraph style, a character style, or direct formatting. Figure 28-1 shows an example. Press Shift+F1 again to toggle the What's This feature off.

Chapter 28: Full-Speed Formatting

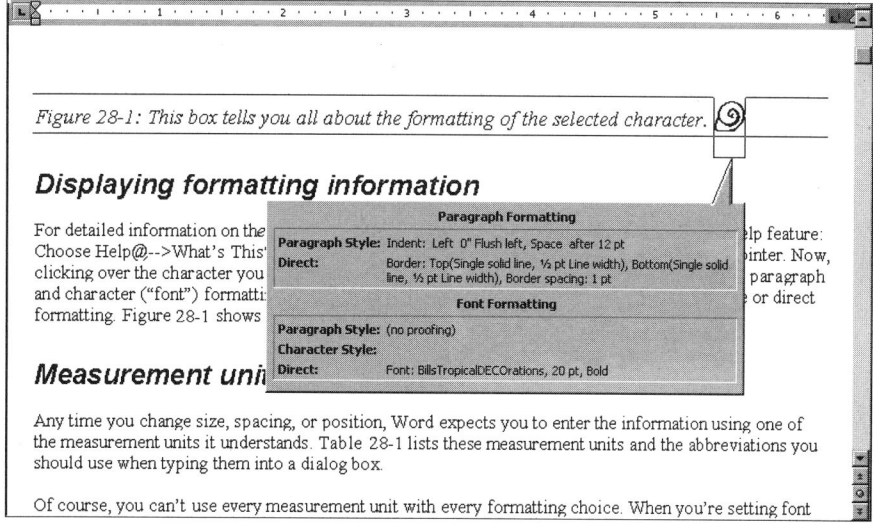

Figure 28-1: This box tells you all about the formatting of the selected character.

Setting the default measurement unit

Word lets you change the measurement system it expects by default in most dialog boxes. If you're more comfortable working in centimeters or picas than in inches, choose Tools ⇨ Options, select the General tab, and pick the units you prefer from the Measurement units list. You'll still be able to type entries in other units by including the correct abbreviation after the numbers (see Chapter 7). Note also that changing the default units doesn't affect the dialog boxes of some format items. In the Paragraph format dialog box, for example, the default spacing units are always points.

Character Formatting

Character formatting refers to changes you make in the appearance of individual characters. Of course, you can apply character formatting to more than one character at a time, but the point is that you're changing the look of the text as separate characters, not by changing the paragraph formatting. Remember, paragraph formatting determines the default appearance of all text that hasn't been altered via character formatting. The mechanics of applying and removing character formatting are Word basics that you've probably mastered. I devote this section to a few fine points.

New font list

New for Office 2000, the Font drop-down list box on the Formatting toolbar now lists the name of each font formatted in that font. The names of symbol (nontext) fonts appear in an ordinary, readable font, but you also get samples of the symbol characters as they actually appear. Figure 28-2 shows the Font list in action.

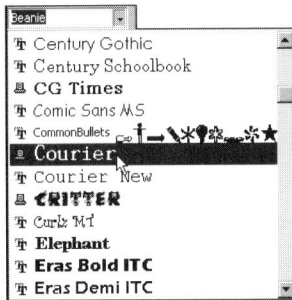

Figure 28-2: The new Font list button shows fonts as they appear in your document.

Performance is the only problem with seeing your fonts before you use them — displaying all those fonts requires more of Word's attention, so scrolling through the list is noticeably slower on a pokey PC. You can shut off the font display and see a simple list of your fonts' names by going to the Options tab of the Tools ⇨ Customize dialog box and clearing the List Font Names in Their Font box.

Tons of character formatting choices

Word's Font dialog box features 11 text effects, 17 underlining styles, and 6 animated-text effects that produce blinking or moving patterns, half of them in color. The most practical of this cornucopia of novelty is the double-strikethrough effect, which is often called for in legal documents.

You can find the animated text effects on their own tab in the Font dialog box. If you discover a use for them, please let me know right away. You may still want to shut them off while you're editing text — use the View tab of the Tools ⇨ Options dialog box.

The fastest way to apply character formatting to the current word

Secret

Even if you're a seasoned Word user, you may have overlooked a one-keystroke shortcut for applying character formatting to individual words (and removing the formatting as well). All you have to do is place the insertion point anywhere within the word and then apply the chosen character format by pressing its keyboard shortcut or clicking the appropriate toolbar button. One key requirement: The insertion point has to be between two letters of the word in question — the technique won't work with the insertion point at the very beginning of the word.

Prior to Word 97, this quick-format method suffered from a bug. With the insertion point between the last two letters of a word, you could apply a character format but you couldn't remove it. That glitch has been removed.

Removing character formats

You can remove all character formats from a selection in one step, by pressing Ctrl+Space. If someone has sprinkled a text passage with bold, italics, and underlining along with a hodgepodge of different fonts, you can return the whole thing to a plain, uniform look by selecting the passage and pressing Ctrl+Space. With character formatting removed, the text takes on the font characteristics specified in the paragraph format.

Ctrl+Space activates this nuke-the-character-formats operation as long as the default keyboard shortcut hasn't been changed. The name for the underlying Word command is ResetChar, in case you need to check on the shortcut assignment, assign a different shortcut, or place the command on a toolbar button.

Using Format Painter

Word's Format Painter duplicates existing formatting at other places in your document. Format Painter is something of a mixed blessing, and you should know about both its benefits and its drawbacks.

Using Format Painter is easy: You copy formatting from one location and paste it to another, replacing the existing formatting at the destination. If the format you're copying is at all complicated, this is a lot quicker than making a whole series of individual formatting changes. Instead of formatting five different paragraphs one at a time with the Arial 13-point bold font, a 2-inch left indent, right tabs at 3 ½ and 5 inches, and a custom bullet character, you only need to make all those changes on the first paragraph. You can then use Format Painter to copy all those settings (and more) from the model paragraph to the other four.

The main problem with Format Painter is that it's so easy to use. You'll find yourself reaching for it when you should be creating a style instead.

Because styles are covered in detail later in this chapter, suffice it to say that they often save you more time in the long run than the Format Painter does, even though they may take some setup work. Once you've created a style and applied it where it belongs in your document, you can make further changes throughout the text by altering the style once (and altering a style is easy, if you know how — see "Creating and modifying styles" later in this chapter). In contrast, if you use Format Painter, you must page through the document manually to make further changes.

Okay, you've been warned. Here's a quick review of how to use Format Painter:

1. Format the original text to taste.

2. Select the original text that has the formatting you want to copy. Key point: If you want to copy the paragraph formatting, include the final paragraph mark in the selection. If you're only copying character formatting, don't — and you only need to select a single character that has the formatting you want to copy (see the Secret at the end of this section).

3. Click the Format Painter button, the one on the Standard toolbar that looks like a paintbrush. Click once if you'll be duplicating the format in only one location, but double-click if you want to reuse the format in two or more locations. The cursor itself changes to a paintbrush.

4. Drag across the text that is to receive the coat of formatting "paint." If you copied the paragraph formatting at Step 2, you don't have to include the paragraph mark at the destination. When you release the mouse button, the destination text appears in the format of the original.

5. If you single-clicked the Format Painter button, you're done. If you double-clicked, the button is still pressed, so you can move to a new location and paint again, repeating the sequence as many times as you like. When you're finally through, click the button again or press Esc.

Word provides keyboard shortcuts for Format Painter. Ctrl+Shift+C copies the formatting of the selected text, whereas Ctrl+Shift+V pastes (paints) the copied formatting elsewhere.

Secret

Be aware that Format Painter copies the character attributes of the first character in the original text selection. If the original text contains a variety of character attributes (such as font, size, italics, or whatnot), only the look of the first character is reproduced at the destination.

Secrets of individual character formats: Quick reference

Secret

Table 28-1 lists useful information about several specific character formats.

Table 28-1   Character Format Specifics

Format	Comment
Bold and italics	Word translates typing conventions that indicate emphasis into the corresponding real-character formatting. It automatically applies bold formatting when you surround a word or phrase with asterisks, and it applies italics to a word or phrase surrounded by underscore characters. For example, *grand ideas* becomes **grand ideas** and __pipe dreams__ becomes *pipe dreams*. You can shut off this feature on the AutoFormat As You Type tab of the Tools ⇨ AutoCorrect dialog box.

Format	Comment
Underlining	The default underlining style, Single, underlines the spaces between words, but not the spaces before or after them. To draw a visible line along an empty space on a line of text, add a border, use a tab with an underscore leader, or type plain-old underscore characters.
Superscripts and subscripts	If you don't like the default formatting applied by the superscript and subscript commands, you can create custom super- and subscripts, adjusting the font size to taste and specifying the text position on the Character spacing tab of the Font dialog box.
Highlighting	The highlighting tool applies a color to the text background to make it stand out. After you click the button, the tool stays active until you start to type or select another command. You can drag over text to highlight it, double-click to highlight a word, or triple-click to highlight the whole paragraph.
Text color	To create white text on a black background, select white as the text color and apply a black highlight.
Hidden text	Text "formatted" as hidden text isn't displayed or printed, unless you check the appropriate boxes in the View and Print tabs of the Tools ⇨ Options dialog box. You can use hidden text to prepare different versions of the same document for different audiences (most people get the regular version, but the elect get the top-secret one). Just remember that it's easy to forget to hide text that's supposed to be invisible and vice versa. Hidden text is perhaps best used in conjunction with a VBA procedure, which can turn on or off blocks of text as dictated by criteria evaluated when the program runs.

Using kerning and character spacing

If you want the best possible look for your printed documents, pay attention to the fine points of spacing between individual characters. Word lets you vary character spacing both uniformly, for all the characters in the passage you're working with, and via kerning, which works on specific pairs of characters and is fully explained later.

Accessing the character spacing settings

Character spacing and kerning are font-related items, so you control them using the Font dialog box. As shown in Figure 28-3, you need the Character Spacing tab to access these controls.

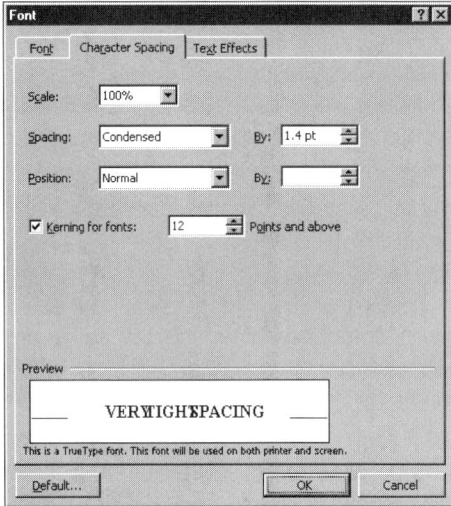

Figure 28-3: Control character spacing and kerning with the Character Spacing tab of the Font dialog box.

As with other character attributes, you can apply character spacing settings by way of a paragraph style. To opt for this route, choose Format ⇨ Style, select a style, and then choose Modify ⇨ Format ⇨ Font to reach the Font dialog box. Alternatively, you can apply these settings directly to selected text as character formatting. In this case, just select the text and choose Format ⇨ Font.

To change character spacing on a uniform basis, use the Spacing controls. With the mouse, you just click the top little arrow at By to expand the space between characters, or click the lower arrow to condense the text spacing. With the keyboard, you need to first choose Expanded or Condensed and then type the amount. In case these terms aren't clear, these changes don't affect the size of the characters themselves, just the space between them.

Spacing tab of the Font dialog box

Turn on kerning by checking the Kerning for Fonts box. Then select a font size at which you want kerning to take effect in the Points and Above box. In other words, Word only kerns text that is at least this size, ignoring smaller passages (see "When to use kerning" later in this chapter). Other options in the Character Spacing tab include:

- Scale, which horizontally stretches or squishes the characters themselves, not just the spaces between them (valid values are between 1% and 600%).

- Position, the control for creating superscripts and subscripts.

When to change character spacing

Uniformly changing the character spacing of an entire paragraph or text selection can be handy when you want to fit a passage into a given space. If one or two lines of your one-page document spill over to the next page, try condensing the character spacing a bit as an alternative to adjusting the margins (or printing both pages). Character spacing adjustments are also useful when you want to achieve a particular density of type. By the way, typographic pros refer to the process of uniformly changing character spacing as adjusting tracking.

Understanding kerning

Kerning is the term for adjustments made to the space between a pair of letters along a line of text. For really polished documents, you should definitely take advantage of this advanced spacing information, which is built into True Type and PostScript (Type 1) fonts. Word knows how to kern, but it does so only if you turn on this feature.

To understand kerning, you first have to understand the way character spacing works normally, before kerning is turned on. Because each font has a different design, the font must specify the width of every character it contains — that is, the space required for the character horizontally, along a line of text. Translated into English, the font is saying something like this: "In this font, a capital A is 2.4 spacing units wide, a lowercase i is 0.9 units wide," and so on. All Windows programs including Word follow these character-width specifications when displaying and printing text. Otherwise, wide letters would bump into each other and narrow ones would have too much space between them.

So why kerning?

However, although this basic spacing information prevents total disaster, it's too inflexible to meet the aesthetic standards of professional typographers. The problem is that the specified width for a character may be just right when that character is paired with some characters but too great when paired with certain others. Look at the following samples:

Unkerned	Kerned
A H A V	AH AV

Because the sides of the H go straight up and down, more or less, the standard widths allowed for the two characters work fine. When the A is paired with a V, however, the characters look too far apart — because their sides slant in the same direction, they have room to cozy up to each other. Kerning does the trick.

When kerning is on, Word looks at each pair of characters in turn. Word checks to see if the font supplies additional spacing instructions for that specific character pair. If found, these kerning instructions override the standard character widths. If not, Word uses the standard widths instead. Exactly which character pairs have kerning information depends on the font.

Some fonts supply no kerning information at all, but others come with kerning settings for hundreds of different character pairs. If you really want to get serious about your typography, you can edit a font's kerning information yourself using various utility programs.

When to use kerning

Kerning makes the most noticeable difference when used with large-size type in titles, headings, and the like. At smaller sizes, it may cause the letters to look too close together, even if the kerning settings seem right. Remember, too, that Word has to work harder to do all that checking and adjusting for every character pair. Kerning small-size text may slow your system down perceptibly, depending on the performance of your computer.

Paragraph Formatting

In Word, a paragraph is a sequence of consecutive characters of any length ending in a paragraph mark. Word places a paragraph mark in your text whenever you press Enter. Actually, a paragraph mark by itself — without any characters between it and the previous paragraph mark — is a perfectly acceptable paragraph, from Word's point of view.

Paragraph formatting constitutes all of the settings that govern the appearance of, yes, the paragraph. You can control a wide range of details including alignment (left, center, right, or justified); indents; tab settings; spacing (before and after the paragraph, and between its lines); numbering or bullets; and borders or shading. Also, by virtue of paragraph styles, paragraph formatting specifies the base format for the paragraph's text, covering aspects such as font, size, color, underlining, boldface, special effects, and so on. You can change any of these details by applying character formatting, but if you remove the character formatting, the text reverts back to the appearance set by the paragraph formatting.

Usually, the best way to control *all* aspects of paragraph formatting is by applying a paragraph style. Styles are covered in their own section later. This section discusses topics that aren't specific to styles, including the all-important paragraph mark, removing changes to the format specified by a style, and many of the individual format options that pertain to entire paragraphs. See Chapter 31 for information on formatting bulleted and numbered paragraphs.

What's so special about the paragraph mark

I've said it before, but I'll say it again: All paragraph formatting is contained in the paragraph mark. Digesting this key concept will help you understand and predict how Word functions when you're editing. Consider the following:

- Given the importance of paragraph marks, many Word experts recommend that you make them visible on the screen so that you know when an editing operation involves one of the marks. I like a "clean screen" so much that I don't do this, but I can understand the point and I thought you should know. The easy way to display paragraph marks is to click the Show/Hide ¶ button, but that turns on all nonprinting characters, which clutters the screen too much. Better to choose Tools ⇨ Options and check the Paragraph Marks check box on the View tab.

- Because you can cut, copy, and paste a paragraph mark (with or without the preceding text), you can transfer paragraph formatting from one location to another through the Clipboard: Select the paragraph mark, choose Copy, select the destination paragraph's paragraph mark, and choose Paste. If you use the mouse, you can accomplish the same task with less work with Format Painter (see "Using Format Painter" earlier in this chapter). Although Word provides keyboard shortcuts for Format Painter, the technique just mentioned may be easier to remember. Besides, experimenting with cutting, copying, and pasting paragraph marks is a good way to understand their function in Word.

- When you combine two consecutive paragraphs that have different formats, the resulting combined paragraph retains the formatting of the first paragraph. To combine two paragraphs, of course, you just press Delete or Backspace to delete the paragraph mark between them. Word copies the formatting to the paragraph mark of the second paragraph, which becomes the mark for the new, combined paragraph. By the way, this isn't how earlier versions of Word worked — your results varied depending on whether you removed the paragraph mark with Delete or Backspace.

Reverting to the paragraph's original format

If you change a paragraph's formatting and later decide you don't like what you've done, use the ResetPara command to restore the original look as determined by the paragraph style. The default keyboard shortcut for this command is Ctrl+Q. Another way to restore the original formatting of a paragraph to that of the assigned style relies on the style drop-down list in the Formatting toolbar. Just select the paragraph and choose the style name (the one already assigned to the paragraph) in the list. When Word asks what you want to do, choose Reapply the Formatting of the Style to the Selection.

Setting indents

Any additional distance from the page margin to the left or right side of a paragraph is an *indent*. (The margin itself is set by section formatting, so it's independent of paragraph formatting.) Actually, Word allows negative indent settings, or *outdents*, which move the sides of the paragraph into the margins.

The standard way to change all indent settings is via the Paragraph format dialog box, shown in Figure 28-4. Word recognizes separate indent settings for the left and right sides of a paragraph. In addition, the first line can have its own setting for the left indent. A *first-line indent* gives you the prototypical paragraph look that you see in most books (but not this one) and many magazines. The other available choice for the first line is a *hanging indent*.

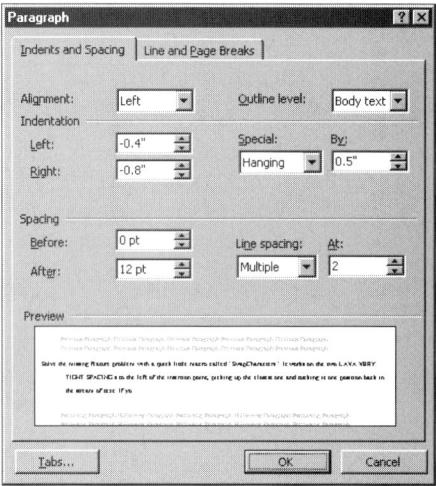

Figure 28-4: The Paragraph format dialog box, where you set all the spacing and break options for the paragraph as a whole

First-line and hanging indents

This paragraph has a first-line indent — the first line is indented farther to the right than the rest of the paragraph. This style of indenting is essential, of course, when you don't provide extra space between paragraphs.

This paragraph has a hanging indent — the first line runs farther to the left than the remaining lines. The most common use of hanging indents is in numbered or bulleted lists, where the numbers or bullets line up to the left of the text proper. Word can format such lists for you, but the standard spacing formula it applies won't always suit you. To change the layout of such paragraphs, you have to mess with the hanging indent setting yourself.

Though it's potentially imprecise, the easy way to create first-line or hanging indents is with the ruler (see the next section). Setting up first-line indents with the Paragraph dialog box (Figure 28-4) is straightforward — choose First Line in the Special box, and then specify the additional indent for the first line in the By box.

However, when you select Hanging in the Special box, the amount you enter in the By box is actually an additional indent setting for all the other lines in the paragraph. In other words, the first line is indented by the amount entered at Left, while the other lines are indented by the total of the Left amount plus the By amount.

Caution

As an alternative to fixed first-line indents, you can use tabs to indent the first line. Some people still are more comfortable with this typewriter-era approach. If you use this method, you must remember to press the Tab key at the start of each new paragraph to add the indent. And if you later decide that the paragraphs shouldn't have first-line indents after all, you must go through the document and remove all the Tab characters. Nevertheless, this is the approach Microsoft takes with its new "click and type" feature. Tabs in general and click and type are covered later in this chapter.

Setting indents with the ruler

You can set indents numerically via the Paragraph format dialog box, and that's the best way to go when you're creating a style. But it's quicker to use the ruler, and the results are fine for short documents when polish isn't critical. To display the ruler, shown in Figure 28-5, choose View ➪ Ruler. Drag the controls at either side of the ruler to set the various indent settings.

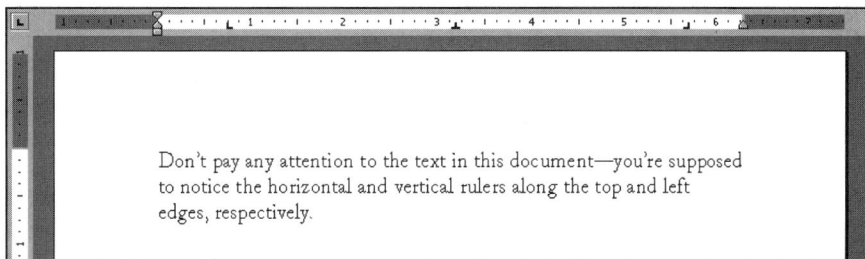

Figure 28-5: Word's ruler controls indenting.

Setting indents with the toolbar or the keyboard

The quickest way to change the left indent is via the Decrease Indent and Increase Indent toolbar buttons. Clicking either button moves the left indent to the next tab stop in the appropriate direction. (Actually, there's an even faster way, via the keyboard, but this technique can cause trouble — see the discussion on setting editing options in Chapter 26.)

Setting indents with tabs

Caution

You can create faux first-line indents just the way you do on a typewriter, by creating a tab stop where you want the indent and then pressing Tab at the beginning of each new paragraph. All pundits recommend against this technique, in that you wind up with a document full of Tab characters that will cause trouble if you decide to change back to nonindented paragraphs. (Chapter 27 tells how to rid a document of all spurious start-of-paragraph tabs in one operation.)

The pundits notwithstanding, Word itself uses this technique in its new "click and type" feature. See "Using click and type to set tabs on the fly" later in this chapter.

A macro for indenting both sides at the same time

When you change a paragraph's left indent, you usually change the right one to preserve a symmetrical look. Indented block quotations, for example, always carry extra indenting on either side. If you use block paragraphs frequently with specific types of documents, you should define appropriate paragraph styles in the templates you use with those documents. In fact, the default Normal.dot template includes a Block Text style that you can modify to suit your requirements (paragraph styles are covered in detail later in this chapter). But if you want a quick way to increase or decrease the indent of any paragraph on both sides, the following macro pair does the trick:

```
Sub IndentBothIncrease()
   CurrentIndent = Selection.Paragraphs.LeftIndent
   Selection.Paragraphs.LeftIndent = (CurrentIndent + 36)
   CurrentIndent = Selection.Paragraphs.RightIndent
   Selection.Paragraphs.RightIndent = (CurrentIndent + 36)
End Sub

Sub IndentBothDecrease()
   CurrentIndent = Selection.Paragraphs.LeftIndent
   Selection.Paragraphs.LeftIndent = (CurrentIndent - 36)
   CurrentIndent = Selection.Paragraphs.RightIndent
   Selection.Paragraphs.RightIndent = (CurrentIndent - 36)
End Sub
```

In VBA, indent settings are always in points (not inches or any other units), so these macros increase or decrease the indents by 36 points — ½ inch — each time you run one. If you prefer smaller or larger increments, change this value.

Advanced line-spacing considerations

If you specify line spacing by number of lines (single, double, and so on) in the Format ⇨ Paragraph dialog box, Word automatically adjusts the spacing between each pair of lines in a paragraph according to the size of the characters on the lower line. If you place even one larger character into a line, Word drops the line down so that the larger character(s) fit with a little headroom. This sounds like a good idea, but variable line spacing is a typographic faux pas. In addition, this problem may occur even if all you do is insert a tall symbol character or simply italicize a word, without changing the font size.

You can force Word to maintain consistent line spacing no matter what the font size by selecting Exactly in the Line spacing box and then typing in the spacing you want. The problem is, the tops of larger characters may then be cut off. It would be nice if Word could overlap the two lines, which I think would generally look better, but it can't. I know of no workaround, though the SYMBOL field discussed in Chapter 33 helps in some situations.

Spacing between paragraphs

Secret

Use the Before and After spacing settings in the Format ➪ Paragraph dialog box to control how much space Word puts between paragraphs. There's nothing tricky about these settings. When Word places a paragraph on a page, it just adds the After setting from the previous paragraph to the Before setting of the current one. The spacing Before is always used, even when the paragraph falls at the top of a page.

Working with the line and page break settings

A word to the wise: Take advantage of the Line and Page Breaks tab of the Paragraph dialog box to prevent document blemishes. This tab was labeled Text Flow in older Word versions, but it hasn't changed otherwise. In brief, the check boxes work as follows:

- **Widow/Orphan Control.** Moves the beginning of the paragraph to the next page if otherwise its first line would be left alone at the bottom of the page or its last line would be left alone at the top of the next page. Best to leave this on, which is the default setting.

- **Keep Lines Together.** This setting would be self-explanatory if it were called "Don't allow paragraph to break across pages." When checked, Word makes sure the entire paragraph is kept together on a single page if at all possible. Use this carefully, because it can cause long stretches of empty space.

- **Keep with Next.** Check here to ensure that the paragraph always falls on the same page as the paragraph that follows. This is a vital setting for most headlines.

- **Page Break Before.** Adds a page break before the paragraph, of course. Check this box for headings of chapters or other major sections that should always start on a new page.

- **Suppress Line Numbers.** Turns off line numbering for the paragraph even when line numbering is on for the whole document. The lines in the paragraph aren't even counted — Word skips over the paragraph and begins counting with the next paragraph that doesn't have this setting on.

- **Don't Hyphenate.** Turns off hyphenation for the paragraph even when hyphenation is turned on for the whole document. Use this for headings that span more than one line and technical material in which hyphens would be confusing.

Tabs

Like other paragraph formatting, tab settings can be applied to one or more selected paragraphs or via a paragraph style. By default, Word places a tab stop every ½ inch within the page margins. You can change the distance between these default tabs by choosing Format ⇨ Tabs and changing the entry at Default tab stops.

Secret

Interestingly, the default tabs are common to all paragraphs in the document, although you can set a different default spacing for every document. In paragraphs where you set tabs individually, Word removes the default tabs to the left of your custom tabs, but the defaults remain active beyond that point.

Default tabs are always ordinary left tabs. Word claims to offer five tab types, but the fifth, bar tabs, doesn't really count. See Table 28-2.

Table 28-2 Types of Tabs in Word

Tab Type	Icon on Ruler	Position of Text Typed at a Tab
Left	L	Extends toward the right from the tab stop.
Center	⊥	Is centered on the tab stop.
Right	⌐	Extends toward the left from the tab stop.
Decimal	⊥·	Extends toward the left from the tab stop until a period is typed, then extends to the right.
Bar	1₁·	No effect (doesn't affect existing tabs) — adds vertical lines at tab stops.

Understanding tab characters

When you're typing text — and if you're not typing inside a table — pressing the Tab key inserts a *tab character* into your document. Invisible in print or in your browser, that tab character appears on your screen when the Show All or Show Tab characters box is checked in the Tools ⇨ Options dialog box (View tab). To insert a tab character inside a table, press Ctrl+Tab.

A tab character tells Word to move the text that follows to the next tab stop position in the paragraph. The tab stop determines where the text settles, not the tab character — so if you change the tab stop, Word moves the text accordingly. The point is, you get to adjust the alignment of your text by altering tab stops, without having to add new tabs.

Caution

If you use tabs to align columnar information and your columns don't line up correctly, the problem is probably simple. Most likely, the tab stops are set too close together for one or more of the lines. Select the entire block of text and reset the tab stops at wider intervals with one of the techniques discussed in the next section.

Setting tabs

The easiest way to set a new tab is with the ruler (which must be visible, of course). Clicking the little black angled icon at the left of the ruler cycles between the four main types of tabs: left, center, right, and decimal. Once you see the icon for the correct tab type, click the lower part of the ruler where you want your new tab to go. The same icon appears there.

Secret

You may have noticed that you can't deposit a tab stop just anywhere along the ruler — Word forces all tabs you drop on the ruler to reside at predetermined intervals. For example, when you're using inches as the measurement system, Word allows tabs only at even $\frac{1}{16}$-inch intervals.

The alternative to the ruler for setting tabs is the Tabs dialog box, which lets you type in each tab's position with numeric precision. In addition, the Tabs dialog box lets you add leaders to your tabs, which you can't do with the ruler. If you call the Tabs dialog box up from the Style dialog box, you won't see the Default tab stops setting.

To change the tab stops for a particular paragraph, display this dialog box by choosing Format ⇨ Tabs. To specify the tab settings for a paragraph style, choose Format ⇨ Style, then New or Modify, and then Format ⇨ Tabs. To set a tab in the Tabs dialog box, type in its position, choose the tab type from the choices listed at Alignment, and choose Set.

Secret

Word measures tab-stop positions from the left margin as set in the Page Setup dialog box, not from the left edge of the page or the left side of the paragraph. The actual locations of your tab stops on the printed page change when you change the left margin setting, but not when you adjust paragraph indents.

Changing and clearing tabs

On the ruler, you can move a tab by dragging its icon and dropping it at the new location. To delete a tab, drag it up or down, off the ruler altogether. Working with the ruler alone, you can't transform a tab — from a left tab into a center tab, for example. Instead, you must first delete the existing tab and then add a new one.

By contrast, the Tabs dialog box makes it easier to change a tab from one type to another than to move it to a new location. To change an existing tab, select it in the list, choose the new type, and then choose Set. However, you can't change an existing tab's location in the dialog box. Instead, you must first remove it (select it and choose Clear) and then set a new tab at the new location. When you've made a muddle of your tab settings, choosing Clear All lets you start with a clean slate. By the way, the easiest way to display the Tabs dialog box is by double-clicking a tab in the ruler. The Tabs dialog box comes up with that tab already selected. Just be careful that you double-click directly on the tab. Otherwise, Word adds a new tab before displaying the dialog box.

Using right tabs

Right tabs deserve a special comment. Use them in left-aligned paragraphs when you want text at the end of two or more lines to align on the right. You can type more text to the right of a right tab, but only by pressing Tab first.

Secret

If you use the Tabs dialog box, positioning a right tab relative to the right side of a paragraph or the right edge of the page requires a little arithmetic. Let's say you want to place a right tab 2 ½ inches from the right page edge. Assume you're using regular letter paper with margins of 1 inch on either side. To figure the entry you should make at Tab Stop Position, you would subtract 3.5 inches (the total of the left margin plus the offset on the right) from 8.5 inches (the total page width), so the tab position should be 5 inches. Here are the formulas you should use to make the calculations.

To place a tab at a location measured from the right edge of the page:

```
Total width of the page -
  (left margin + distance of tab from right page edge)
```

To place a tab at a location measured from the paragraph's right indent:

```
Total width of the page -
   (right margin + left margin +
    offset from the paragraph's right indent)
```

Adding leaders to tabs

A tab leader is a string of repeated characters that fill in the space between a tab stop and any text to the left (or to the left side of the paragraph if there is no other text). Add a leader to a tab by selecting the tab in the Tabs dialog box, choosing a leader character, and then choosing Set. Unlike some desktop publishing programs, Word limits you to just three leader characters: periods, dashes, and underscores. Nevertheless, these should be plenty. A leader helps keep the reader's eye on the right line when a wide gap of empty space separates the text on either side of a tab stop. Leaders are most often used in lists such as tables of contents or other lists, as in this menu excerpt:

> Tofu Turkey (for two) $16.75
>> Our own organic tofu made fresh daily, shaped into a large dome and baked with carrot stick wings, celery legs, and wild rice currant stuffing. Served with onion gravy and cranberries.
>
> Bean Sprout Delight $8.49
>
> Roshi's Repast $15.95

You can add a leader to any tab type (except bar tabs). In lists like the one here, you would typically use a right or decimal tab. Note that Word runs the leader characters right up to the text on either side of the leader. You may want to give the text some breathing room by typing a space or two. On the right side, you could set up a second, leaderless tab to the right of the one with the leader, typing the text at this second tab.

Don't pick up the bar tabs

Don't bother with bar tabs, which simply insert vertical lines at the specified tab stops. They don't affect the location of your text, they don't interfere with any other types of tabs that you intersperse, and you don't even have to press Tab to display the vertical line. They're intended, I gather, to provide a quick-and-dirty way to create a table. However, using a real Word table is actually much easier.

Using click and type for on-the-fly formatting

Caution

Word 2000's new "click and type" feature is supposed to let you add text anywhere on a page simply by double-clicking there and starting to type. Sorry, it just doesn't work that way.

If you understand the "click and type" feature's limitations, it can be handy for quick layout tasks where accuracy isn't a priority. But limitations it has, as follows:

- First, click and type is only available in Print Layout and Web Layout views.

- Second, and more important, click and type only works to the right of one-line paragraphs. Blank paragraphs are okay, as are those that contain no more than one line of text. In other words, you can't click and type to the left or right of an ordinary, multiple-line paragraph, and you can't add click-and-type paragraphs on top of existing text as annotations or the like.

- Third, when you can click and type, the vertical position of your entry always matches that of the paragraph you're clicking beside. You can't add new text between the paragraph and the preceding or following paragraph.

What happens when you click and type successfully depends on whether the existing paragraph beside which you're double-clicking contains text, and where the mouse pointer is at the time. If you start with an *empty* paragraph, here's what you get:

Mouse Pointer Position	Result
About an inch to the right of the blank paragraph	Word adds a first-line indent to the paragraph
Near the center of the page	A centered paragraph
Near the right margin of the page	A right-aligned paragraph

If you double-click anywhere else to the right of a blank paragraph, or click anywhere to the right of a one-line paragraph that contains text, Word sets a custom tab stop where you click. As you type more and reach the end of the line, the insertion point goes back over to the standard left indent as determined by the style you've chosen for click-and-type paragraphs. (You make that choice, by the way, on the Edit tab of the Tools ⇨ Options dialog box.)

You can get an idea of what Word will do when you click and type at a given location by looking at the mouse pointer. When the insertion point is at the end of the paragraph beside which you plan to click and type — *and only then* — the mouse pointer gains an icon that shows the alignment (left, center, or right) of the paragraph or tab you're creating.

Tricks with borders and shading

In earlier versions of Word, borders and shading could only be applied to paragraphs (or tables). Although that has changed, tradition dictates that the topic be covered in the section on paragraph formatting. Outlining a word or paragraph in a box or adding background shading is a piece of cake in Word. It's just as easy to enclose a table in a grid or to add a border around the whole page. Just put the insertion point in the item you want to dress up and choose Format ⇨ Borders and Shading to bring up the dialog box shown in Figure 28-6.

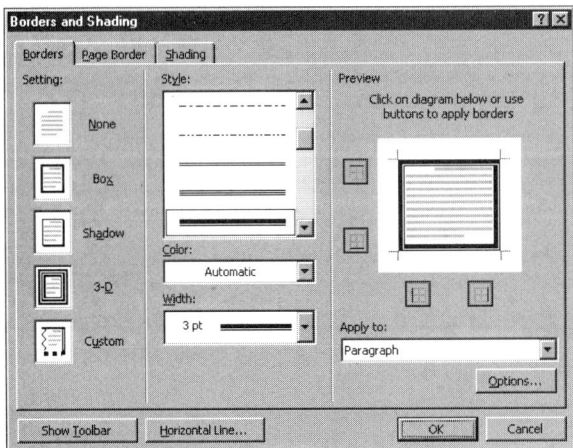

Figure 28-6: The Borders and Shading dialog box

Working with the Tables and Borders toolbar

Alternatively, if the Tables and Borders toolbar is visible, you can select border and shading choices directly from the toolbar. On the toolbar, the Borders button offers a drop-down graphical menu from which you can turn individual borders (top, left, and so on) on or off — see Figure 28-7. If you work frequently with these controls, you can tear off the menu as a separate Borders toolbar (see Chapter 3 for a review of tear-off toolbars).

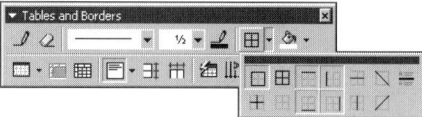

Figure 28-7: The Tables and Borders toolbar showing the tear-off Borders submenu

Border brainstorms

Highlights of Word's raft of border-related options include these:

- Get to know the useful "Setting" buttons in the Borders tab of the Borders and Shading dialog box. These icons show you at a glance the type of border currently in use. Of course, you can also use them to apply preset border effects such as automatic boxes, shadows, and 3-D effects. Don't expect much from the 3-D button — it only seems to work with a few of the Style choices, and even then, the effect is often exceedingly subtle. And don't bother selecting the Custom button — Word selects it automatically if you change any of the border options in the Preview area.

- You can choose from among oodles of border styles, from dots and dashes to wavy lines to fancy designs. To further complicate your choice, each style is available in multiple widths.

- You can tell Word which item you want bordered or shaded: selected text, an entire paragraph, a table cell, or an entire table. Select the item desired at Apply To in the Borders and Shading dialog box.

- Word lets you control the distance of the border from the text it encloses on each of the four sides independently, instead of providing a single setting for all four. Choose Options to display the necessary controls.

- To add a border around the entire page, select the Page Border tab in the Borders and Shading dialog box. The choices are the same as for other types of borders, except that in addition to the standard black-and-white border styles, you can now select colorful artistic borders from the list at Art. But really, a candy corn page border?

- Page borders can be added to the entire document or only to the current section (in three variations) — select your choice at Apply To. Border offset options are available via the Options button. Other options are available from the Custom and Horizontal line buttons.

- In the Shading tab, you can choose whether to apply the shading to selected text or to the entire paragraph. See the "Understanding shading" section later in this chapter.

Text borders

Adding a border around individual words is simply a matter of selecting Text in the Apply To list in the Borders and Shading dialog box. Borders around words always surround the text on all four sides—you can't create a top or bottom border only.

When applied to paragraphs, top and bottom borders always span the entire potential width of the paragraph as determined by the indents.

Automatic horizontal lines in text

In previous versions of Word, you added a rule, or horizontal line, between two paragraphs by giving the bottom paragraph a top border. That technique still works, but it has problems. Far better is Word 2000's new "horizontal line" feature.

The horizontal line command works by creating a separate new paragraph containing the line, which it inserts as a distinct graphical object. You can select the line object by clicking it, and when you do, you see the selection handles that are standard for graphics objects. Figure 28-8 shows an example.

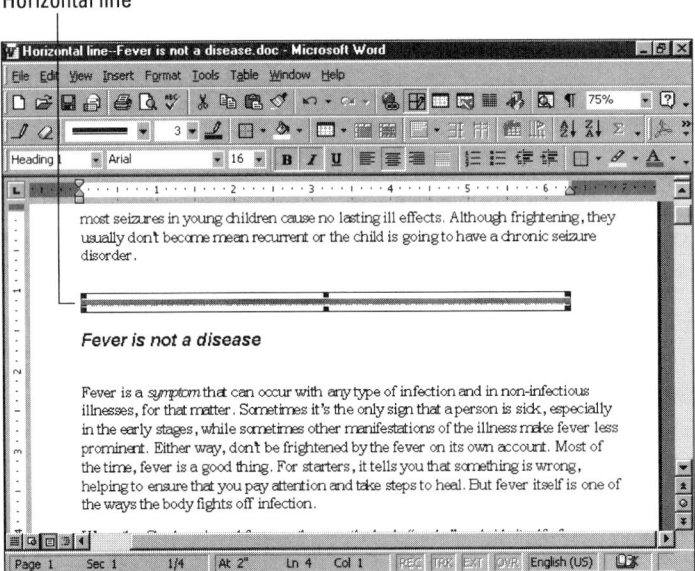

Figure 28-8: Selecting a line inserted with Word's horizontal line feature

Anyway, because the line is a graphical object and isn't attached to other text, you have a lot more control than with a paragraph border. You don't have to worry about deleting it or altering it accidentally when you combine paragraphs, or about adding lines to new paragraphs unintentionally. And you can determine its size, placement, and look, whereas paragraph borders limit you to simple black lines that span the entire paragraph.

Inserting a horizontal line

Before you insert a horizontal line, be sure to move the insertion point to the very beginning of the paragraph that should come after the line. Otherwise, Word breaks the paragraph into two at the insertion point, adding a third paragraph containing the line between them. This is rarely the effect you're after — and it's not the way things work when you add a top border to a paragraph.

The quickest way to drop in a horizontal line is via the corresponding button, a choice on the Borders graphical submenu on the Tables and Borders toolbar. The button you need is shown at the left. Clicking this button inserts a horizontal line like the last one you inserted. If you want to add a different sort of line, you have to:

1. Choose Format ⇨ Borders and Shading.
2. Click Horizontal Line (at the bottom of the Borders tab).
3. Click the line you want from the Clip Gallery window and click the Insert Clip button.

In Step 3, you're working with the standard Clip Gallery but it only shows, well, horizontal lines, a subset of the graphics in the Web Dividers category. Chapter 8 covers the Clip Gallery.

Secret

If you choose the very first clip in the Gallery, you get a plain black line spanning the width of the paragraph. The other, more graphically interesting clips produce a line that's narrower than the originating paragraph and centered above it. As detailed in the next section, you can change these characteristics after you've inserted the line but you can't select them beforehand.

One other point: horizontal lines are bitmap images stored as GIF files. The more intricate designs may look slightly blocky in printed documents.

Reformatting horizontal lines

Once you've added a horizontal line to a document, you're free to modify its size, alignment, and other characteristics. Although you can select the line and resize it via the selection handles, doing so stretches the original image, reducing its sharpness.

The preferred technique for all horizontal line modifications is to use the Format Horizontal Line dialog box, shown in Figure 28-9. Display it by double-clicking the line, or selecting it with the keyboard and choosing Format ⇨ Horizontal Line. The dialog box's main tab lets you set the line's Width and Height and set the horizontal alignment.

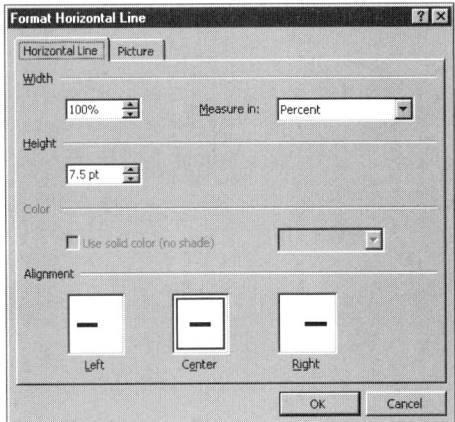

Figure 28-9: The Format Horizontal Line dialog box

The Color controls are only active if you inserted the line using the first Clip Gallery choice, a plain, black line (see the previous section). For these lines, you have the same fill choices as you would for other graphical objects, including gradients, textures, patterns, and bitmaps—Chapter 8 covers these options in more detail.

If you chose any of the other, more graphically complex lines, the Format Horizontal Line dialog box offers a second tab labeled Picture. This contains the same cropping and image control settings found on the Format Picture dialog box, also discussed in Chapter 8.

Borders as an alternative to text boxes

Secret

Word's text boxes and callouts have their place, but the easiest way to enclose a passage of text in a box is to add a border. Select the paragraphs in question, apply a box-style border, and you're done. You can't freely control the box's location on the page, and its width depends on the right indents of the enclosed paragraphs, not on a separate setting. But often, you don't want to modify these characteristics anyway—Word's automatic box looks fine for many purposes, and it's so easy to make, you won't mind giving up a little control. Another big advantage: The boxed text remains part of the main document, instead of being split off into a separate compartment that's harder to edit.

When boxing paragraphs doesn't work

Secret

One of my gripes about Word borders is that you can't use them to enclose text in a box unless *all* the selected paragraphs have the same left and right indents. If you select consecutive paragraphs with different indent settings and apply a box-style border, Word encloses each paragraph in its own box. In other words, bulleted points within a quick border are out.

No workaround appears to be available. Yes, you can insert a separate text box, but that's a lot more trouble than simply selecting the text and hitting the box-style button.

Understanding Shading

Shading applies a shaded background to selected text, paragraphs, or tables. Just so you're clear on this point, it doesn't add a shadow effect around a border (though you can create such shadows by choosing the correct border settings). Moreover, shading does not affect the color of the text itself, only the background.

Secret

Don't blame yourself if you have a hard time understanding the controls in the Shading tab of the Borders and Shading dialog box. What do the terms Fill and Patterns refer to, anyway?

I'll take a whack at this deeply disturbing question. Together, the Fill and Pattern settings let you use two colors as shading. You can mix the colors together in various percentages or arrange them in various small gridlike patterns. If you mix them, the percentage shown in the Style list refers to the percentage of the pattern color (the one you select from the Color list). Therefore, if you choose a 30% style, the shading consists of a mixture of 30 percent of the pattern color and 70 percent of the fill color. Choose None in the Fill grid to vary the intensity of the pattern color by itself. To shade with a solid color, you can either choose a fill color and select Clear in the Style list, or choose None as the fill color and select Solid in the Style list. Got all that?

If you select one of the gray shades as the fill color, don't bother with the Pattern settings — they're set automatically for you (gray shades are actually mixtures of a black pattern color with None as the fill color, but that sure isn't obvious from these settings). To remove shading altogether, you must choose both None in the Fill grid and Clear at Style. Although Word lets you apply shading to selected text, shading is most useful as paragraph formatting. To apply color to text selections, it's easier to use the highlighting tool. Shading does offer more color options, however, and you can select from several simple two-color patterns.

Mastering Styles

Styles are the key to efficient, consistent document formatting. If you learn nothing else about Word, master styles. The control center for styles is the Style dialog box, shown in Figure 28-10. Display it by choosing Format ⇨ Style.

Secret

In the Width section, take note of the Measure In setting. Here, you can select the default measurement unit (inches, millimeters, or what have you) if you want to specify the line's exact width. Alternatively, choose Percent if you want Word to adjust the line width automatically when you change the width of its paragraph.

So what's a style? A style specifies a complete set of formatting choices, all wrapped together in one package. Apply the style to a paragraph or some selected text, and all those formatting choices are applied in one fell swoop. One of the fundamental benefits of styles lies in ensuring consistency in a document's appearance. If you format all the paragraphs by applying styles to them, you can be sure that each paragraph with the same style has the same format.

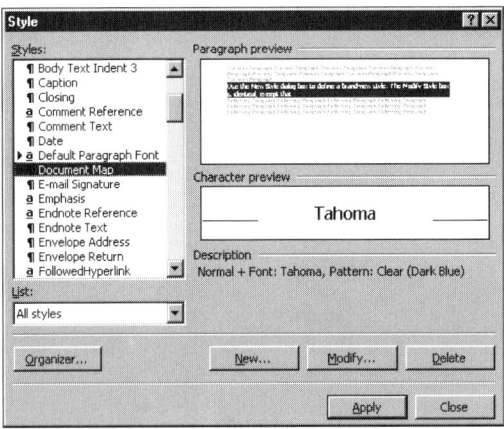

Figure 28-10: The Style dialog box lets you create, modify, delete, and organize the comprehensive formatting specifications Word calls styles.

Obviously, applying a style is much quicker than first selecting a font, then setting the paragraph indents, then adding tabs, and so on. However, an even bigger payoff comes later, when you decide the document needs a face-lift. Instead of laboriously reformatting the entire opus, all you have to do is change the definitions of your styles. Each time you modify a style, all text assigned to it instantly reflects your changes to the style.

Style Factoids

Styles have names. When you apply a style to text, you select the style by name.

Styles belong to the document. The styles available when you first create a document are derived from the template on which the document is based. However, adding new styles or changing the existing ones doesn't affect the template — not unless you specifically instruct Word to copy your changes to the template.

Word's supplied templates (including the default template Normal.dot) come with extensive sets of built-in styles, so you can put styles to work immediately. You can use the Style Gallery command to preview the styles in each template. However, you must first add the Style Gallery command to a menu or toolbar. In the Customize dialog box, find this command in the Format category on the Commands tab (see Chapter 5 on customizing).

The interactions between styles and direct formatting are complex. See "Secrets of overriding styles" later in this chapter.

You can search for and replace styles using the Find and Replace commands.

The language setting, which tells Word which dictionary to use when checking spelling, doesn't affect document appearance, but you can still specify it as part of any style. See Chapter 7.

Paragraph versus character styles

Word provides two kinds of styles, paragraph and character. The paragraph style is by far the most important type, controlling all possible formatting choices pertaining to a paragraph. Of course, it governs the characteristics of the paragraph as a whole, such as indents, line spacing, tabs, and any attached bullet or numbering scheme. In addition, it sets the default character formatting for the entire paragraph, specifying the font, size, color, special effects, and spacing of the individual characters.

In Word, every paragraph has a style. Until you apply a different style, Word automatically assigns the default style, called Normal. (You can and should modify the Normal style in each of your templates to suit the type of document for which the template is intended.) Character styles can also be defined, but they're less useful. Applied to any text selection, a character style specifies all the choices you can make in the Font dialog box. It doesn't affect any unselected text, nor does it alter the format of the paragraph(s) where the selection resides. Character styles come in handy if you have reason to reuse a set of character-formatting choices, but only in portions of a paragraph at a time. When you modify a character style, all text to which you applied the style takes on the new formatting automatically, just as with paragraph styles.

Displaying style assignments and previewing how they look

Secret

As you cursor through a document, the style list in the formatting toolbar always displays the style of the current paragraph (the one where the insertion point is). If you want to keep closer tabs on your style assignments, activate the style area: choose Tools ➪ Options, select the View tab, and then tell Word how much of the screen you want to devote to the style area by making an entry at Style Area Width. The style area appears as a vertical strip at the left of the window in Normal and Outline views only, and lists the style of each visible paragraph.

You can use the Style Gallery to see your document as it would appear if it were formatted with the styles from other templates. Because Style Gallery is no longer on the default menus, you have to add the command to a toolbar or menu via the Customize dialog box using the standard customizing techniques covered in Chapter 5.

Secret

You should switch to the view (Normal or Print Layout) you want to use when previewing the other templates before opening the Style Gallery dialog box.

For each template, the Style Gallery dialog box also lets you view an example document or samples of each style in the template. You can create examples and style samples for your own templates — the trick is to define AutoText entries in each template called Gallery Example and Gallery Style Samples.

To print a listing of the styles in the current document, choose File ➪ Print and select Styles from the Print What drop-down list. For each style, the printout lists the name and summarizes its formatting but doesn't include a sample printed in the style.

Applying styles

The standard way to apply a style is to select it by name from the drop-down Style list in the Formatting toolbar. You don't have to select any text first to apply a style to a single paragraph — just pick the style name in the list and you're done. To apply a paragraph style to multiple paragraphs, or to apply a character format, select the text first.

Opening the Style list with the mouse displays each style name formatted with its own character formatting and paragraph indent and alignment settings — see Figure 28-11. The little gray box to the right of each style name provides additional information: an icon indicating the paragraph alignment; an icon that shows whether the style is a paragraph style (a paragraph symbol) or a character style (an underlined a); and the size of the style's font. If you want to see a simple list of your styles without the formatting and icons, clear the box labeled List Font Names in Their Font on the Options tab of the Tools ➪ Customize dialog box.

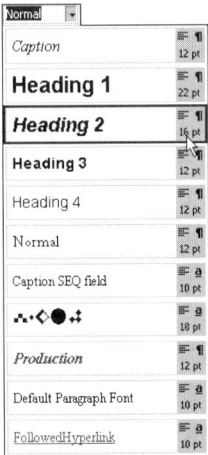

Figure 28-11: When opened with the mouse, the Style drop-down list shows a sample of each style.

Secret

Normally, Word only shows styles already in use in the document in the Style list. To see all styles available in the document's template, hold down Shift when you drop down the list.

The default keyboard shortcut for accessing the Style list is Ctrl+Shift+S. Once you press it, you can use the cursor keys to locate the desired style in the list. If the list is long, save time by starting to type the name of the style you want to apply. After two or three characters, pressing the up or down arrow key will display styles alphabetically close to the one you're after.

If you're a fast typist and the style name is short, you may want to type the whole name, dispensing with the list per se and pressing Enter to apply the style. There's a catch, though — if you mistype the name, Word creates a brand-new style with the misspelled name. (The best way to use this type-the-name technique is described in "Using style aliases" later in this chapter.) Of course, there's nothing wrong with applying a style from the Style dialog box — it just takes too long.

Keyboard shortcuts for applying specific styles

Secret

By far the quickest way to apply a style is via a keyboard shortcut for that one style. Word supplies several default keyboard shortcuts for common paragraph styles:

Style Name	Default Keyboard Shortcut
Normal	Ctrl+Shift+N
Heading 1	Ctrl+Alt+1
Heading 2	Ctrl+Alt+2
Heading 3	Ctrl+Alt+3

These default shortcuts are fine, but they're hardly adequate. If you know you'll be using certain styles regularly, assign them their own permanent keyboard shortcuts. In addition, I recommend you reserve and memorize several "wildcard" keyboard shortcuts for individual styles, assigning them to different styles as your needs dictate. You can choose between two methods for assigning keyboard shortcuts to styles: by selecting Shortcut Key in the New Style or Modify Style dialog box (both of which are covered later in this chapter) or using the Customize Keyboard dialog box described in Chapter 26.

Customizing the shortcut menu to apply specific styles

Short of a keyboard shortcut, the fastest way to apply a specific style is via the shortcut menu (the one that pops up when you click the right mouse button). To add a style to the shortcut menu, customize the menu as described in Chapter 5. Once the little Shortcut Menu toolbar is visible, choose Text ⇨ Text to display the shortcut menu that Word displays when you right-click document text. With the shortcut menu still open for customizing, go back into the Customize dialog box. Switch to the Commands tab, selecting Styles in the Categories list. In the list at Commands, Word displays the styles already in use in the document. You can now drag as many of them as you like to the shortcut menu, one by one.

Secret

For fastest access to the style list (the one found on the formatting toolbar), place it onto the text shortcut menu where it will be just a right-click away wherever you're working. However, you can't drag the style list command from the Tools ⇨ Customize dialog box to the text shortcut menu — once you get it there it only functions to activate the Style dialog box. The trick is to open the Tools ⇨ Customize dialog box, activate the Shortcut Menus toolbar, and then drag the style list button from the Formatting toolbar to the text shortcut menu.

Applying paragraph styles as character styles

If text within a paragraph is selected when you apply a paragraph style, the style acts like a character style: The character formatting from the style is applied to the selection, but the rest of the paragraph retains its existing style. This works no matter which method you use to apply the style.

However, a couple of exceptions exist. The applied style does act as a paragraph style if the selection includes all the paragraph's text, or if the selection includes any portion of two or more paragraphs. In the latter situation, all paragraphs in the selection receive the paragraph style change.

Using Built-in Heading Styles and Custom Outline Levels

Word supplies a total of nine built-in heading styles named Heading 1 through Heading 9. You can and should redefine the *formatting* of these styles to suit your taste and your documents. But don't abandon the built-in heading styles themselves — in general, you should use them for your headings, rather than creating your own styles for that purpose. The case for sticking with the built-in heading styles is strong, in that many Word features require using, or are easier to use with, the built-in styles rather than custom styles.

These features include:

- The Outline and Master Document views
- The Document Map
- Outline numbered lists
- Tables of contents
- Cross-references
- Captions
- The Contents tab in the document's File ⇨ Properties dialog box

> If you insist, you can have most of the benefits of the built-in heading styles with paragraphs of any style. Use the Outline level drop-down list in the Format ⇨ Paragraph dialog box to assign the current paragraph to one of the nine outline levels, equivalent to the nine available built-in heading styles. The paragraph's visible formatting doesn't change, but Word treats it just like a paragraph with the corresponding built-in heading style. To link any style to a given outline level, open the New Style or Modify Style dialog box, choose Format ⇨ Paragraph, and set the outline level there (see "Creating and modifying styles" in this chapter).
>
> The keyboard shortcuts Alt+Shift+left arrow and Alt+Shift+right arrow promote or demote a paragraph from one built-in heading style to the next style in the sequence. By default, buttons for these commands are located on the Outline toolbar (Chapter 30 covers Outline view), but you can place the buttons on any toolbar by dragging them there from the Commands tab of the Customize dialog box. If you use the Promote command on a paragraph of ordinary text, Word applies the Heading 1 style, and you can Demote it from there. If the paragraph has already been assigned to an outline level, the Promote and Demote commands change the level without affecting the paragraph's style or appearance.

Creating and modifying styles

Word provides two main ways to create or modify styles: via the Style dialog box or directly within the document. With either approach, you can build styles by example, copying the formatting from existing document text. Combining the two methods gives you the optimal combination of efficiency and control.

Caution

By default, Word creates styles automatically when it thinks that you've formatted a paragraph for a special function, such as a heading. If it detects that you typed only a few words and then went back and made them large and bold, you are the lucky winner of an automatic Heading 1 style. Fortunately, Word doesn't alter any existing styles, so nothing happens if heading styles are already defined in the document. But unless you like other people messing with your work, turn this feature off. Clear the box labeled Define Styles Based on Your Formatting in the AutoFormat As You Type tab of the Tools ⇨ AutoCorrect dialog box.

A simple tip is in order here: Choose a name for each of your styles based on the style's function rather than its current format. It's much easier to remember when to use "Sonnet Heading" than "Arial 12 pt bold italic with an 18 pt indent."

Creating and modifying styles within a document

The easiest way to define a new paragraph style is by example while working directly within your document. Start by tailoring a sample paragraph to taste. Once the paragraph looks right — after you've selected all the character and paragraph formatting options you want — activate the style list by clicking it or pressing its keyboard shortcut. Type the name you want for the new style directly into the display, and Word records the name and formatting settings as soon as you leave the list. (See "Using style aliases" later in this chapter for tips on choosing style names.)

You can modify an existing style in almost the same way. Find a paragraph to which the style has been applied and alter its formatting as you see fit. Then activate the style list — it still displays the name of the style slated for modification. This time, however, don't type anything. Instead, just press Enter, or open the drop-down list and select the same style name.

Word presents a dialog box asking whether you want to "Update the style to reflect recent changes" (the default) or "Reapply the formatting of the style to the selection." Choose the former option to modify the style with the formatting changes you've made. (Selecting the latter option is one way to restore the original formatting of the paragraph, although the ResetPara command, whose default keyboard shortcut is Ctrl+Q, is more direct.)

The by-example method has two limitations: You can't use it to create character styles, and certain paragraph style options aren't available. Also, you can't change the Normal style with this technique.

Creating and modifying styles with the Style dialog box

Use the Style dialog box (refer back to Figure 28-10) to create and modify styles under the following conditions:

- You're creating a character style. The Style dialog box is the only way to create character styles, although you can modify them in the document with the method just described.

- You want to set two style options that are only available from the Style dialog box: choosing one style on which to base the one you're working with; and choosing another style to follow it automatically. These options are discussed later.

- You want to create or modify a number of related styles at once. Using the Style dialog box makes it easier to keep track of the similarities and differences between the styles so that you can be consistent where you want to be.

Secret

You can create styles in the Style dialog box by example, just as you can when working directly in the document. However, you can't modify styles this way in the Style dialog box.

In the Style dialog box, existing styles are displayed in the list at the left. The List drop-down menu gives you several choices as to which styles you see. You can display all available styles, of course. Other options let you see only styles already in use, or only user styles—those you created from scratch and that didn't come in the default Normal template.

The buttons in the Style dialog box work as their names suggest, though a few comments are in order. First, about those buttons at the bottom:

- The Apply button applies the currently selected style to the paragraph containing the insertion point or to the current text selection. In addition, Word updates the entire document to reflect any style changes you've made.

- If you create or modify one or more styles, the Cancel button changes to Close. Choosing Close leaves the current paragraph unchanged, but Word still updates all text that receives its formatting from the styles you modified.

- The Organizer button is one access point to the Organizer dialog box, which lets you move styles and other items between one document or template and another. The Organizer dialog box is described in Chapter 26.

Using the New Style and Modify Style dialog boxes

Selecting New or Modify displays essentially the same dialog box, shown in Figure 28-12. If you're modifying an existing style, select it from the Styles list before you choose Modify.

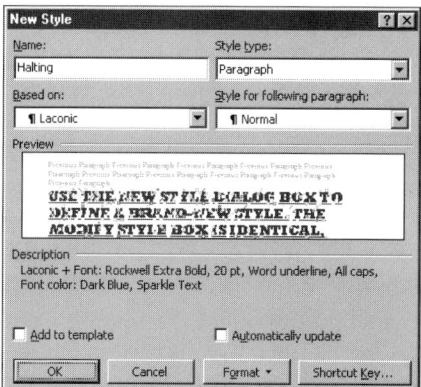

Figure 28-12: Use the New Style dialog box to define a brand-new style. The Modify Style dialog box is identical, except that you can't change the Style type.

I'll tackle the choices in the New Style and Modify Style dialog boxes in order of increasing complexity. First, the easy stuff:

- You can change the name Word displays in the Name box by typing in a new one. Modifying a style via this dialog box is the only way to change its name. See "Using style aliases" later for a style name secret. You can't change the names of some built-in styles.

- To create a character style, select Character in the list at Style Type. Otherwise, ignore this option.

- Check Add to Template to add the style you're working on to the template attached to the document. That way, future documents based on the same template will have access to this style.

- Checking Automatically Update is risky and generally should be done only temporarily, when you're concentrating on finding the right formatting for a particular style. When the box is checked, Word modifies the style definition every time you change its format directly. Throughout the document, all text to which the style is applied changes in lockstep.

Now come the most important choices: those that define the style's format. Curiously, the dialog box doesn't emphasize this. Choosing the nondescript Format button displays an equally nondescript little menu, but it's this little menu that opens the door to all your paragraph and character formatting options. The choices on the Format menu activate the same dialog boxes you use to set character and paragraph formatting directly. When you finish using each box, Word returns you to the New Style or Modify Style dialog box.

Basing a style on another style

The Based On setting is an important key to maintaining a consistent document format and minimizing your work if you decide to change your formatting choices. The style you select at Based On (I'll call it the base style) defines the formatting for the style you're working on, except for those formatting characteristics that you explicitly redefine. If you change anything about the base style, these changes also appear in the style you based on it, unless the style definition specifically overrides them.

For example, say you have an existing style called Base. Base defines a paragraph style that is indented ½ inch on either side with 12-point Garamond as the font, among other formatting choices. Now suppose you create a style called New and base it on Base, specifying only one formatting choice: the bold Font style. If you now increase Base style's indents to ¾ inch and make the font 10-point Arial, paragraphs that have the New style automatically take on ¾ inch indents, and the text appears in bold, 10-point Arial.

This feature becomes vital when you're developing a complex document with many related styles. If you plan the hierarchy of styles based on other styles carefully, you'll be able to make sweeping changes throughout the document by manipulating a style or two at the foundation of the hierarchy.

Caution

When you create a new style, Word chooses the Based On entry for you — it's the same one you made the last time you created a style. This may not be what you intend, and if you don't change the setting it will cause unexpected format changes if you ever redefine the base style. To avoid this, choose the Based On style carefully. To define a style that doesn't depend on another style, select "(no style)" at Based On (it's the top entry in the list).

Specifying the style of the following paragraph

In the New Style and Modify Style dialog boxes, the entry at Style for Following Paragraph sets the style Word assigns to the next paragraph, the one it creates when you press Enter. By default, this is the same style as the one you're creating—when you press Enter, Word starts another paragraph of the same style. After typing a heading, however, you want to follow it with ordinary text, not another heading. When creating or modifying the heading style, you should select Normal at Style for Following Paragraph. Now, pressing Enter at the end of a paragraph assigned to the heading style starts a Normal paragraph rather than one of the same style.

Word's default heading styles already are set up with Normal as the style for the following paragraph. However, because you're not limited to using Normal as the following style, you can automate any repeating sequence of two or more paragraph formats.

Secret

To create a dialog sequence in a screenplay, for example, you might set up a style for each character, adding a customized Outline Numbered scheme to start each paragraph with the character's name. If you set up each style so that the other style is the following paragraph, you can produce the framework for something like the example here just by pressing Enter each time you finish a character's line:

Abelard: I love you, Heloise.

Heloise: Oh, Abelard.

Abelard: Will you be mine, Heloise? (and so on . . .)

Using style aliases

Secret

You can give two names to each style, the regular name and a second one called an alias. Both names work equally well to refer to the style when you apply it using the formatting toolbar's Style list button.

You can define alias names when you create new styles on the fly by typing the name into the Style list on the toolbar, or when creating or modifying styles in the Style dialog box. Either way, all you do is type a comma after the main name, and then the alias, like this:

```
Dialogue, dg
```

So what good are aliases? They're great when you apply styles via the Style list in the Formatting toolbar. Instead of scrolling through the whole list or typing the full style name, all you have to type is the two- or three-character mnemonic alias. Hit Enter, and you've applied the style. The style's lengthier main name still describes its function clearly.

Secrets of overriding styles

When you apply direct formatting, the new format options override those specified by the active style. You can sprinkle direct character formats randomly about a paragraph, overlapping them in whatever combinations suit your communications needs. And you can use direct formatting to radically alter a paragraph as a whole, changing its alignment, indents, spacing, and whatnot.

Things get a little tricky, though, when you apply a different style to text that has received direct formatting. In general, Word retains your direct character formatting—if you italicize a phrase before applying a nonitalic paragraph style, the phrase remains italicized. By contrast, however, applying a character style enforces uniform formatting for all of the selected text, and any direct formatting is removed. This also holds true when you use a paragraph style as if it were a character style, by selecting text before applying it (see "Applying paragraph styles as character styles" earlier in this chapter).

A secret use for character styles

Secret

You can use a character style to display text from somewhere else in the document. This technique is quicker than the alternatives, bookmarks and Ref fields.

Suppose you publish a newsletter and often use pull quotes, brief passages from the body of a story highlighted in a box in larger type. To create an instant pull quote, you would:

1. Define a character style called Pull Quote. In the New Style dialog box, select Default Paragraph Font (a standard character style supplied with Word) at Based On. As long as you don't make any formatting choices, the style won't change the look of your text.

2. Set up the text box for the pull quote (see Chapter 29).

3. In the text box, insert the following field: { STYLEREF "Pull Quote" } between a pair of quotation marks.

4. Find the text you want to lift elsewhere in the document, select it, and apply the Pull Quote style.

5. Back in the text box, update the field. The pull quote should appear. You can now make whatever formatting changes you like (come to think of it, you can create a style for the pull quote to format it automatically).

If you apply the Pull Quote style to more than one selection, the StyleRef field will display the last passage before the text box (that is, the one that is closest to the box, traveling toward the beginning of the document). If none of the passages lies in the upward direction before the text box, the next passage is displayed.

You can use this same basic technique to place a different quote from the document on every page by including the StyleRef field in a header or footer. Once the field is in place, run through the document and apply the Pull Quote style to whatever text you want to display in the header or footer.

When style changes disappear when you reopen a document

If all your custom styles revert to their original settings when you reopen a document, you've just run afoul of what can be a valuable feature — but one that can blow away hours of hard work. Blame it on a setting in the Tools ⇨ Templates and Add-Ins dialog box. The culprit is the box labeled Automatically Update Document Styles.

If this box is checked, Word replaces the style definitions in your document with the ones from the attached template whenever you open the document — even if the template's style definitions haven't changed since last time. This box exists to ensure consistency in the work of teams of people working on documents together. One person can have responsibility for the team template and the styles it contains. With this box checked, any style changes the template-person makes show up in all the team documents automatically, and everyone else can concentrate on content and using the styles properly.

Conclusion

No matter how brilliant your argument, drab or inconsistent formatting can hide its luster. Take advantage of Word's ample stock of text formatting commands to bring out the facts and opinions you want to communicate.

Chapter 29

Page Layout and Desktop Publishing

In This Chapter

▶ Understanding sections

▶ Using advanced techniques with headers and footers

▶ Adding repeating text and graphics anywhere on a page

▶ Understanding desktop publishing techniques, including laying out and formatting columns

▶ Using text boxes to place text anywhere on a page

▶ Wrapping text tightly around irregular graphics

▶ Designing fancy envelopes and labels

For even the simplest document, the overall layout plays a big part in getting your message across — and in getting your audience to read the document in the first place. You must make basic decisions over attributes such as the width of the margins, the number of columns for your text, and the format of the headers or footers. Beyond the basics, Word is capable of amazing feats of page layout and graphic design. In fact, it competes credibly with specialized desktop publishing and Web design software.

Speaking of Web pages, however, you need to know that many of the formatting options Word provides for printed pages aren't available in Web pages. As a simple example, saving a Word document as a Web page creates just that — a *single* Web page. You lose all page breaks in the original document. Chapter 14 delves deeply into Web page design with Word and the other Office applications. In this chapter, the emphasis is on designing pages for print.

Page Layout Secrets

As a crude sort of control over document layout, you can insert manual paragraph, line, and page breaks. To start a new paragraph, of course, you hit Enter. You can also:

Create This Break	By Pressing
Start a new line without creating a new paragraph (manual line break)	Shift+Enter
Create a new page at the insertion point (manual page break)	Ctrl+Enter

If you like taking the long way around, you can insert a manual page break from the Insert ➪ Break dialog box. There, select Page Break. The other choices in this dialog box are covered elsewhere in this chapter.

Beyond these rudiments, *section formatting* controls the basic layout of the document, with settings for paper size and orientation, margins, headers and footers, columns, and related items. A document can have more than one section, and these layout choices can vary from section to section within the same document.

The secret is in the sections

The key to creating a layout of any complexity is to divide the document into sections. In Word, you must create a new section in your document whenever you want to modify the margins, begin or end columns, or switch from one paper size or orientation (portrait or landscape) to another. In fact, you need a new section even if all you want to do is change the page numbering scheme.

Word groups its layout settings in the Page Setup dialog box. Despite the name, these are actually *section* settings for the most part. Although a section often begins on a separate page, a single page can have more than one section — and thus, your "page setup" settings can vary within that one page. Even the simplest document has at least one section, but Word creates the first section for you automatically.

Starting a new section

Word provides two main ways to start a new section:

- To create a new section that inherits the formatting of the current one, use the Insert ➪ Break command. You can then change the layout of either or both sections as you wish. Choosing this command displays a dialog box that lets you choose one of four types of section breaks. Select Continuous to start the new section at the insertion point, without a page break (Word does add a line break, if necessary — any text to the right of the insertion point gets pushed into the new section). The other three choices all start the section on a new page. If you select Even Page or Odd Page, Word numbers the first page of the section appropriately even if it has to add an extra blank page to the end of the previous section. It also applies the appropriate page formatting if you've set up the document for different headers and footers on odd and even pages.

- To create a new section with a layout different from that of the current one, start by selecting layout settings for the new section in either the Page Setup or Columns dialog boxes. Then create the new section by selecting From This Point Forward in the Apply To field. Word inserts a section break at the insertion point, beginning the new section on the next page with the layout settings you chose. Everything before the insertion point remains in the previous section, which retains its original layout.

If you often create multiple-section documents, add toolbar buttons or keyboard shortcuts for the Insert Section Break command available in the Customize dialog box. The Insert Section Break command inserts Next Page section breaks. If you frequently insert other types, you can record macros to insert them in one step.

Using the Page Setup dialog box

Most of Word's essential layout settings are contained in the Page Setup dialog box, shown in Figure 29-1. In general, the available options in the Page Setup dialog box are self-explanatory. A few require some further discussion and are covered in the following sections.

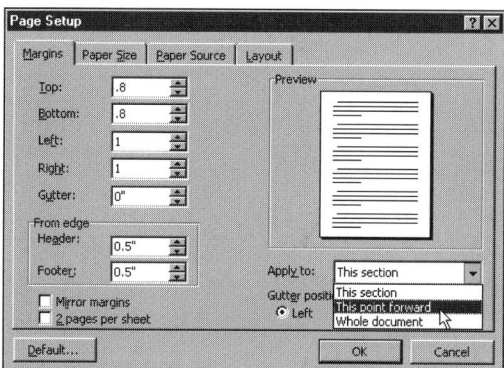

Figure 29-1: The Page Setup dialog box offers many options.

Mirrored margins

To create a book or pamphlet with facing pages that are mirror images of each other in terms of their margins, check the Mirror Margins box in the Margins tab of the Page Setup dialog box. When you do, the Left and Right margin settings become Inside and Outside, reflecting the fact that they change sides depending on whether the page is a left (even) or right (odd) one. If you select mirrored margins, you probably want different headers for odd and even pages (see the discussion of headers and footers later). In addition, if you add a gutter, you should select mirrored margins even if the inside and outside margins will be equal on both sides.

Adding a gutter

The Gutter setting on the Margins tab adds extra space to the margin on one side to allow for a binding, which removes some of the page area from view. Although you could compensate for a binding with the standard margin settings, using a gutter makes it easier to keep track of how the width of the page is apportioned. Word adds the specified gutter to the left margin in documents with unmirrored margins and to the inside margin if the margins are mirrored.

Numbering lines

Secret

Here's a feature you may not have known about, especially if you don't already use Word for legal or technical documents: Word will number the lines in your document. Line numbering is helpful on printed documents that two or more people must communicate about, such as drafts of books. When you want to be sure everyone is "on the same page," referring to a specific line number does the trick.

To turn on line numbering, choose File ⇨ Page Setup and select the Layout tab. Then choose Line Numbers, displaying the Line Numbers dialog box shown in Figure 29-2. Check Add Line Numbering and select the settings you want from the remaining controls in the dialog box. To shut off line numbers for a particular paragraph or a paragraph style, open the Paragraph dialog box and on the Line and Page Breaks tab, check Suppress Line Numbers.

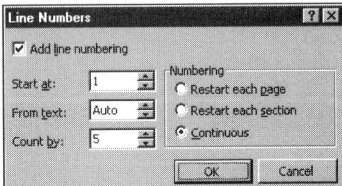

Figure 29-2: The Line Numbers dialog box

Using the Default button

The Default button copies the current settings in the dialog box (from all the tabs) into the template attached to the document. If you like the layout changes you've made to the current document, you may want to use them for similar documents in the future. Clicking this button is easier than opening the template itself, implementing the same changes all over again, and then saving the template.

When you click Default, Word displays a cautionary explanation, considering that the changes you're making will permanently alter many settings. If you go ahead anyway, you have one last escape hatch should you suddenly realize you don't want to lose the original settings in the template. When you close the document, Word asks if you want to save the changes you made to the template. You can choose No to restore the template to its original form.

Working with headers and footers

Headers and footers are areas at the top and bottom of each page that behave in an unusual way: Any text or graphics you place in a header appears on every page the header belongs to. The same goes for footers. While headers and footers are invisible until you put something in them, every document has them. That's why the command you use to work with headers and footers is on the View menu—you're not creating a header or footer, you're viewing one that's already there.

Secret

You can only see headers and footers when you're working in Print Layout view, or in Print Preview. Don't panic if you're not seeing the header or footer you worked so hard to lay out—not, at least, until you've switched to Print Layout view.

The View ➪ Header and Footer command opens both the header and footer for editing, placing the rest of your document off limits for the time being. The document is repositioned in the window to display the header, and the Header and Footer toolbar appears. To jump back and forth between the header and the footer, click the Switch Between Header and Footer button, which shows a page with yellow rectangles at the top and bottom.

Secret

Click Close on the toolbar to put away the header and footer toolbar and return to regular editing. The keyboard shortcut is Alt+C.

Opening headers or footers fast

If you often add text to headers or footers, choosing View ➪ Header and Footer takes too long—especially if you tend to use footers more often than headers, as many people do.

In Print Layout view, double-clicking over the header or footer area opens it immediately—if it already contains content. If you work in other views, or if you want to avoid scrolling to see the target area, you can use the Word commands Header and Footer, and View Footer. Respectively, they open the header or footer directly, without a trip to the menu bar.

CD

You can assign either command to a keyboard shortcut or a toolbar button using the customizing techniques described in Chapter 5 and Chapter 26. If you go the toolbar route, be aware that Word doesn't supply a bitmap image for either command. You can build one of your own—either use the buttons supplied in the custom toolbar that comes with the Office Secrets template found on the CD-ROM that comes with this book, or stick with the text buttons that Word creates for you.

Formatting text in headers and footers

Header text automatically receives the built-in Header paragraph style, while footer text, of course, gets the Footer style. You should modify these styles in your templates to suit the document formats you commonly create. However, you can apply any available style to text in either area. The Header and Footer paragraph styles each have two preset tab stops: a center tab stop in the middle of the page and a right tab stop at the far right. This makes it easy to set up typical headers and footers with elements at the left, center, and right of each page.

Secret

The tab stops don't work in every situation. Sometimes a header or footer contains elements at two or three of the available areas (left, center, or right), with at least one of those elements spilling over onto a second or third line in that same area. In this case, insert a one-row, three-column table into the header or footer.

Header and footer layout facts

Although the point of headers and footers is to reproduce text and graphics on multiple pages, you're not stuck with a uniform header or footer throughout the whole document. In fact, you can have many different headers and footers. Here's how this works:

- The locations of the header and footer are uniform within a section. The From Edge settings for Header and Footer in the Page Setup dialog box apply to the entire section. Respectively, they specify the distance between the top of the page and the top of the header, and between the bottom of the page and the bottom of the footer.

- However, you're allowed some variety within a section: The first page of each section can have a different header and footer than the remaining pages, and you can specify different headers and footers for odd- and even-numbered pages.

- Although each section can have its own headers and footers, the headers and footers remain the same from section to section unless you specifically tell Word to break the link between sections. See the next section, "Varying headers and footers within a document."

The size (height) of a header or footer is determined automatically by the text you place into it, not by any setting you can control in a dialog box. Factors that affect header or footer sizes include the font size and the paragraph spacing settings.

Varying headers and footers within a document

Even if a document is divided into sections, its headers and footers are the same throughout. Changes you make to any header or footer will show up in all the sections (with the caveat that you can have different headers or footers for odd- and even-numbered pages, and for the first page in the document). However, you can break the link between the headers or footers of any two consecutive sections. Once the link is broken, you can format the current header or footer independently of the one in the previous section.

To break the link between the current header or footer and its counterpart in the previous section, click the Same As Previous button on the Header and Footer toolbar so that it doesn't look pushed in. Note that you can only control the link from the current header or footer to the one in the previous section, not the one in the next section. Because headers and footers are consistent within a section, you must insert a section break wherever you want to start a new header or footer, even if the document format doesn't change otherwise at that point. Don't forget that you can use the Show Next and Show Previous buttons on the Header and Footer toolbar to skip from one section's header or footer to the next.

Repeating some elements on all pages and other elements in specific sections

When you break the link between a header and footer and the one in the previous section, Word duplicates existing text and graphics in the header or footer of both changes. Any changes you now make affect only the section you change, but the original elements remain unless you change them. That means that you can build documents in which some elements repeat on all the pages (or over consecutive sections), while others repeat only on the pages of one section. Just add the elements that cross section breaks before you uncouple the relevant headers or footers. Then go ahead and separate the headers and footers and insert the elements that you want in each section.

Placing repeating text or graphics anywhere on the page

To add graphics or text elements that repeat on multiple pages, you insert them while the header and footer are open. However, these repeating elements aren't confined to the top or bottom of the page. Graphics, and text within text boxes or AutoShapes, can be anywhere on the page and still be "in" the header or footer. On the two pages shown in Figure 29-3, the repeating graphical blob — it's actually a 3-D heart shape — and those vertical page references were inserted with the header and footer open for editing.

When you choose View ➪ Header and Footer, Word repositions the document on the screen to make the header area visible, and turns text and graphics in the body of the document gray. What you may not realize is that you can still scroll to the rest of the page using the vertical scrollbar or with the cursor movement keys. If the body text is distracting, you can make it invisible by clicking the Show/Hide Document Text button.

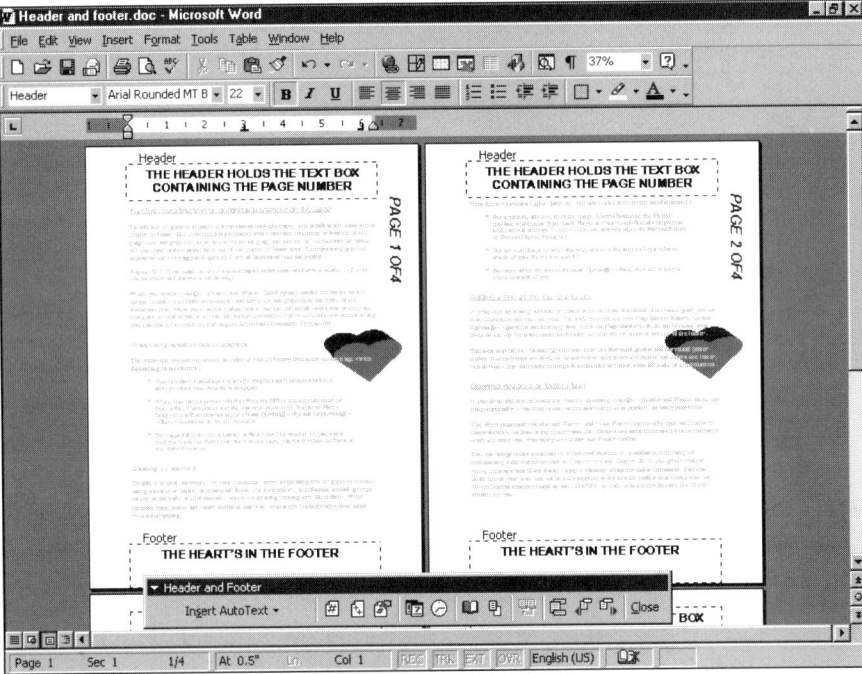

Figure 29-3: These pages show how repeating elements associated with a header or footer can be positioned anywhere on the page.

Positioning repeating text or graphics

The technique you use to position a header or footer element anywhere on the page varies depending on the element. Start by opening the header and footer with the View ⇨ Header and Footer command. The following guidelines then apply:

- You can draw AutoShapes or simple graphics such as boxes or lines directly where you want them to appear.

- When you choose Insert ⇨ Picture and select an image from the Office clip art collection or from a file, Word places it at the insertion point in the active header or footer. Once it's there, drag it to its final destination. Alternatively, select it and choose Format ⇨ Picture or Format ⇨ Object to position it precisely by entering numeric coordinates (see "Floating versus inline graphics" later in this chapter).

- Text typed directly into a header or footer can't be moved. To place text tied to a header or footer elsewhere on the page, insert a text box or frame at the desired location.

Creating a watermark

To add a "digital watermark" to your document, insert a repeating text or graphics element using a header or footer, as described earlier. As a watermark, the element should go right on top of the body of the document, without displacing existing text. By default, Word formats some header and footer elements that way, so that text flows directly over them with no wrapping. To make a watermark lighter (after all, you want to be able to read the document):

- For a picture, select it, click the Image Control button on the Picture toolbar, and choose Watermark for preset watermark-friendly brightness and contrast settings. To enter your own settings, open the Format Picture or Format Object dialog box.

- For an AutoShape or other drawing, select it and then select a light color or shade of gray for the line and fill.

- For text, select the text and choose Format ➪ Font, and then select a light color or shade of gray.

Adding a line at the top of a footer

A crisp line separating a header or footer from the main document often looks good, but the best way to produce one isn't obvious. The trick is to use the Page Border feature. Choose Format ➪ Borders and Shading and then select the Page Borders tab. In the Preview area, click the top for a line under the header, or the bottom for a line at the top of the footer.

The next step is key: Choose Options, select Measure from Edge of Text (not page), and clear the Surround Header and Surround Footer boxes. If these boxes are checked, Word draws lines above the header and below the footer — which won't help the reader distinguish the header or footer from the body of the document.

Customizing the Header and Footer toolbar

Secret

You can customize the Header and Footer toolbar just as you can any other Word toolbar. However, the Header and Footer toolbar appears in the Customize dialog box only when you're viewing a header or footer. To avoid frustration, open a header or footer before you try to customize this toolbar.

Try these customizing suggestions: Create buttons for specific AutoText entries that you often use in headers or footers, and for specific Word fields such as AUTHOR, FILENAME, TITLE, or STYLEREF.

Desktop Publishing with Word

Although specialized page layout software has its place (see sidebar), more than likely, Word has all the desktop publishing power you'll ever need. Nifty multiple-column layouts like the one shown in Figure 29-4 come together easily.

This section brings you up to speed with the skills required. Of course, if your goal is to create documents that look professionally published, you need first-rate typography as well, via character and paragraph formatting. (Don't forget to turn on kerning!) See Chapters 8 and 28 for typographic tips.

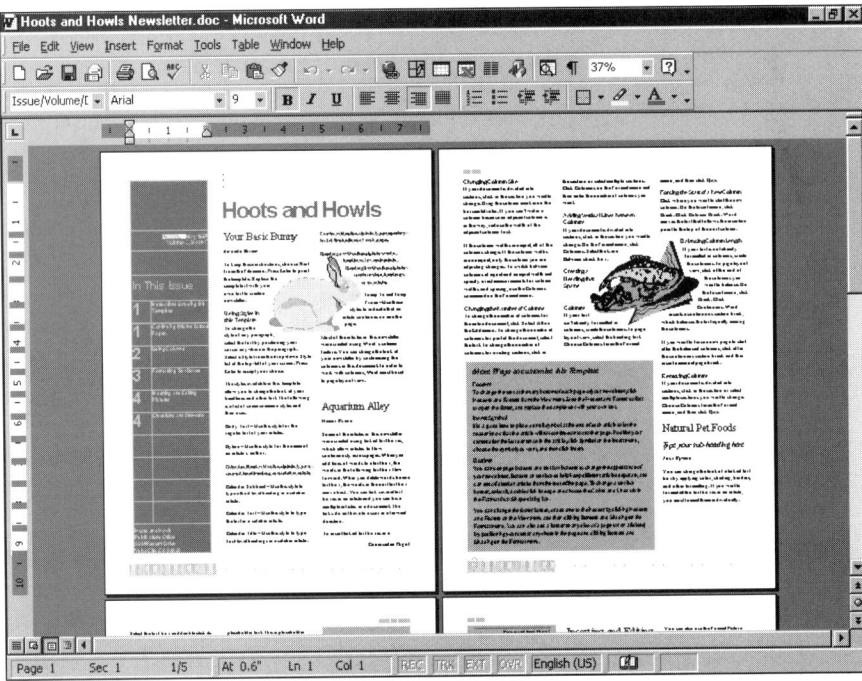

Figure 29-4: A fairly sophisticated newsletter layout produced in Word

When to Use Specialized DTP Software

No mere text editor, Word has formidable design and formatting capabilities. Still, applications that specialize in page layout continue to have an edge for sophisticated projects. Desktop publishing programs have more powerful layout and color tools, they give you more precise control over typographical spacing, and they include better features for managing long and technical documents. In addition, they are designed with the professional printing process in mind, with special options governing color separations and other output details.

Assuming you have the Professional, Small Business, or Premium versions of Office, you already have a page layout program in the form of Microsoft Publisher. While Publisher places a high priority on ease of use, with loads of prefab layouts for ads, brochures, business cards, and the like, it does provide fairly sophisticated layout and output controls. Among graphics arts professionals, the most widely used page layout software is Quark Xpress. Xpress and its closest rival, Adobe PageMaker, excel at design-intensive tasks. By contrast, Adobe FrameMaker's expertise is in long, highly structured documents, although it does include strong layout tools as well. And don't overlook Corel Ventura, which handles both long documents and design-intensive projects with aplomb.

Complex page design in Word

Designing complicated layouts in Word entails all the section-formatting skills covered earlier, as well as facility with formatting columns, text boxes, and graphics. Advanced secrets pertaining to these latter topics are covered in this section.

Working with columns

In Word, columns are a characteristic of section formatting. Each section has a set number of columns, from 1 to 9, throughout the entire section. Setting up a columnar layout is easy, so I'll just remind you of the two available methods:

- You can use the Columns button on the Standard toolbar to change the number of columns in the current section, accepting Word's default settings for the columns' layout.

- You can choose Format ➪ Columns to bring up the Columns dialog box, and fine-tune the layout settings there.

If you take the latter route, the Apply To field lets you decide what portion of your document your new settings will affect. Options include:

- This Section (the current section)
- Whole Document (all sections)
- From This Point Forward (Word creates a new section at the insertion point)
- Selected Text (available if you selected some before you opened the dialog box — Word places continuous section breaks before and after the selection)

Changing column width

Secret

Likewise, you can change column width either by dragging the column marker in the ruler, or by typing in new numbers in the Columns dialog box. Note that dragging the middle of the column marker alters the widths of the columns on either side (the space between the columns stays the same). Dragging the left or right side of the marker adjusts only the column on that side (and changes the space between the two columns). If you hold down Alt and then drag, Word displays the widths of the two columns and the gap between them numerically.

Working with text in columns

Your existing paragraph formatting doesn't change just because you divide the document into columns. The overall indent settings add to the gap between columns to create more white space — for most column paragraphs, you should set the left and right indents to 0, using the intercolumn space to divide the columns. A ½ inch first-line indent that looked fine in the original document will probably look way out of place in a 2-inch column.

To force text following the insertion point to the next column before Word does so automatically, press Ctrl+Shift+Enter, or choose Insert ⇨ Break and select Column Break. However, don't go overboard — specifically, avoid adding a column break at the bottom of each column to even out (balance) the column lengths. Instead, balance columns by placing the insertion point at the end of the last column and choosing Insert ⇨ Break, selecting a Continuous Section Break.

Adding elements that span two or more columns

The easiest way to add a headline or sidebar that crosses column boundaries is to plop down a text box spanning the columns and insert the text into it. That's the way I did it in Figure 29-4. Alternatively, an element that spans the entire width of the page can go into its own section.

Hyphenation: critical for columnar text

With a standard one-column layout, hyphenation is usually only necessary for justified paragraphs. As the column width decreases, however, you'll find hyphenation essential to prevent unsightly irregularity in line length, even on left-aligned paragraphs, and to prevent words from being broken across lines.

In Word 2000, the hyphenation command lives on the Language menu, a submenu of Tools. The Tools ⇨ Language ⇨ Hyphenation dialog box is shown in Figure 29-5. Turning on automatic hyphenation by checking Automatically Hyphenate Document causes Word to hyphenate the entire document immediately. From then on, it also hyphenates any new text you type.

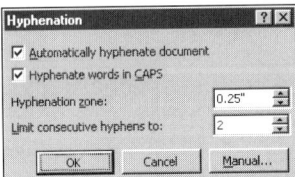

Figure 29-5: Control the document's hyphenation settings in this dialog box.

Even when automatic hyphenation is on, Word skips over paragraphs that you don't want hyphenated. To immunize a paragraph or style against hyphenation, check the Don't Hyphenate box in the Line and Page Breaks tab of the Paragraph dialog box.

"Manual" hyphenation

The Manual hyphenation command on the Hyphenation dialog box is a misnomer — it's more like one of those old VW "automatic stickshifts." If you activate this command, Word stops on each line it thinks requires hyphenation, displaying the ending word with proposed syllable breaks that you can accept or modify.

Secret

Insert an *optional hyphen* to tell Word where to hyphenate a word, if the end of the word would fall past the end of a line (otherwise, optional hyphens remain nonprinting characters). Press Ctrl+- (Ctrl and hyphen together) to insert an optional hyphen. You can see — and delete — optional hyphens by checking the relevant box (or All) in the View tab of the Options dialog box. You can also remove optional hyphens with the Replace command (see "Advanced Find and Replace 2: Using special characters" in Chapter 27). Pressing Ctrl+- is *not* a toggle for optional hyphens — it always adds another one.

In most cases, Word properly handles regular hyphens you've typed, breaking the line after the hyphen if the entire word is too long to fit. If you don't want Word to break a hyphenated word such as CD-ROM, don't use a regular hyphen — press Ctrl+Shift+- to insert a *nonbreaking hyphen*. As far as I know, Word provides no command to prevent an individual nonhyphenated word from being hyphenated, if hyphenating is turned on for its paragraph.

Using text boxes

For the desktop publisher, *text boxes* were the key innovation in Word 97. In earlier versions, text boxes were wimpy — you used a frame to place text into a box separate from the main document, a box you could size and position however you liked. Now, it's better to use text boxes for elements such as sidebars and pull quotes (see Chapter 28 for a tip on automated pull quotes). Frames still exist, but mainly for compatibility with older files.

Text boxes are also available in Excel and PowerPoint; they are covered in Chapter 8, where you can read about the whizzy special effects they make possible. Text boxes in Word, however, have several features that aren't available in the other programs.

For one thing, Word text boxes share the advanced text-wrapping options available for pictures and graphics (see "Wrapping text around graphics" later). For another, you can flip the text vertically. Also, you can place tables, graphics, and other objects inside text boxes (graphics are inserted as inline images — see "Floating versus inline graphics" later in this chapter).

But the most important enhancement is that you can link two or more text boxes so that text flows from one box to the next. This means you can (finally!) set up real newsletter-style layouts, where a story that starts on page 1, column 3, continues on page 4, column 2. In addition, you can set up side-by-side columns that flow independently from page to page, as you find in annotated Bibles and works that include a translation alongside the original version. You can even flow text backward, from page 4 to page 2, if that's how you want to do it. You can extend a chain of text box links as long as you like. When you edit the text anywhere in the chain, Word reflows and reformats it automatically, and you're spared ridiculous amounts of manual copying and pasting.

Creating text boxes in Word

As in other Office applications, you create a text box by clicking the Text Box button on the Drawing toolbar and then dragging to draw the box. However, if you first select some text before you click the button, Word places that text inside a box that it creates automatically. The text is *moved*, not copied, to the box.

The text box toolbar

Word has a special little toolbar for text boxes.

If the toolbar isn't visible, then before you can see and activate a text box, you must select it on the list available by choosing View ⇨ Toolbars. The button at the far right flips the text through all three available orientations. The other buttons are covered next.

Controlling text flow with text box links

To flow text from one text box to another, you need to create a text box link. These are easy enough to make: With the first text box selected, you click the text box link button on the text box toolbar, or, if the toolbar isn't visible, choose the equivalent command on the shortcut menu. The mouse pointer becomes a coffeepot (I guess that's what it is), because you're about to pour text from one box to the next. Click the next text box to establish the link.

The second text box in a link must be empty when you start, as long as it isn't already part of a text link. To extend the chain of text box links, just repeat the process beginning with the second box in the previous link. By the way, Word also refers to a chain of links as a story. Keep in mind that most AutoShape drawings can function as text boxes. If a shape can hold text, it can be part of a text box link.

To break a text box link, click the Break Forward Link button on the Text Box toolbar. This disconnects the current box from the next one in the chain. Text from all the remaining boxes in the chain returns to the current box (but because it can't fit there, it falls off the bottom edge of the box where you can't see it). Breaking a link in the middle of a chain has no effect on the subsequent links — if you add text to the box on the other side of the broken link, the text flows to the remaining boxes downstream.

Navigating through a chain of text box links

Because you can link text boxes anywhere in a document in any order, it could easily become a bother to trace through a chain of linked boxes. Instead, use the Previous Text Box and Next Text Box buttons to beam you directly to your destination.

Editing in linked text boxes

Once an empty text box has been linked to another, you can only edit in the box if it already contains text flowed in from the previous box in the chain. Otherwise, you have to go back through the chain to the last box containing text.

Removing a text box

When you cut or clear a selected text box, the text it contains is cut or cleared as well. If it was part of a chain of text box links, the box is removed from the chain without breaking the chain.

Secret

A roundabout technique lets you remove a text box and return its text to the main document text without manual cutting and pasting. Select the text box. If it's part of a text box link, break the link. Now choose Format ⇨ Text Box and choose Convert to Frame on the Text Box tab. The text appears in your document just before the paragraph that contained the text box's anchor (see "Understanding anchors" later in this chapter for the lowdown on anchors). If the text box was bordered, a border appears around the free text now.

Aligning text boxes with columns

Although you can connect randomly placed text boxes, the most common use for text box links is to create newspaper-style columnar layouts. It's a shame that Word doesn't include a command to automatically line up text boxes with the columns you create via the Format ⇨ Columns dialog box. A manual technique is required. While you can come close by using the mouse to size and position the box, precise placement demands that you use dialog boxes as follows:

1. Open the Columns dialog box and write down the width of each column.
2. Create a text box for each column, positioning it so that the left side of the box is just to the left of the left edge of the column.
3. For each column's text box, select the box and choose Format ⇨ Text Box (or its equivalent on the shortcut menu). In the Position tab, enter **0** at Horizontal and select Column at From to line up the left side precisely with the column edge. In the Size tab, enter the width for that column.

Remember that text boxes have an internal margin by default. If you don't remove this, text in the box won't line up with the column edge even if the paragraphs are set for no indents.

Reordering a chain of text boxes

Reordering a chain of text boxes is a simple, if somewhat labor-intensive, process of breaking existing links and making new ones. Suppose a text box chain flows like this:

⇨ Text Box C ⇨ Text Box D ⇨ Text Box E ⇨ Text Box F ⇨

and you decide it should flow like this instead:

⇨ Text Box C ⇨ Text Box E ⇨ Text Box D ⇨ Text Box F ⇨

Take these steps:

1. Select Text Box C and click the Break Forward Link button. Text Box D and all subsequent boxes in the chain become empty.
2. With Box C still selected, click the Create Text Box Link button. The mouse pointer changes to a pitcher. Click Box E to establish the new link.
3. Select Box E and break its link to Box F. While E is still selected, create a new link to Box D.
4. Select Box D and create a link to Box F.

Text boxes versus frames

Left over from earlier versions of Word, frames are rectangular containers for text and graphics that work differently than text boxes do. Like a text box, a frame *can* have a visible border, but it doesn't have to — you can use the Line Style button on the Drawing toolbar to define a border or turn it off altogether.

At any rate, although text boxes are much more versatile than frames, frames do have a few unique talents. The most important of these is that you can define a frame as part of a paragraph style, meaning that you can frame paragraphs automatically by applying a framed style to them. You also need a frame if you want to include the following in boxed text:

- Comments
- Footnotes or endnotes (not the footnote or endnote text, just the reference to it)
- Certain fields, including: AUTONUM, AUTONUMLGL, AUTONUMOUT (all related to automatic numbering), TC (a table of contents entry), TOC (a complete table of contents), RD (a referenced document), XE (an index entry), TA (a table of authorities entry), and TOA (a complete table of authority)

Secret

Word no longer has a Frame command on the Insert menu — so how do you place a frame in your document? Although the Insert Frame command is missing from the default menus and toolbars, it's still available in the list of Word commands. Use the Customize dialog box to add it to the Insert menu or to a toolbar — Chapter 5 gives details on customizing menus and toolbars — then frame away. If you use frames rarely, you can insert them from the Tools ⇨ Macro ⇨ Macros dialog box. Select Word commands in the Macros In list, choose InsertFrame in the main list, and then click Run.

Secret

You may discover that you need to add comments, footnotes or endnotes, or those fields that don't work in text boxes (just listed) to text that is already in a text box. You must first convert the text box into a frame. Switch to Print Layout or Web Layout view, select the text box, and choose Format ⇨ Text Box. In the Text Box tab, choose Convert to Frame. By the way, Word doesn't convert frames into text boxes when you open a document from an earlier version of the program. In fact, while you can convert text boxes into frames, you can't go the opposite direction.

Automatic side-by-side paragraphs using frames

Because frames can be defined in paragraph styles, they can be used to automatically position boxed text or graphics alongside other text. This is perhaps most useful for creating side headings or graphics (such as the Secret icon in this book) beside body text. Figure 29-6 shows examples of side headings and graphics.

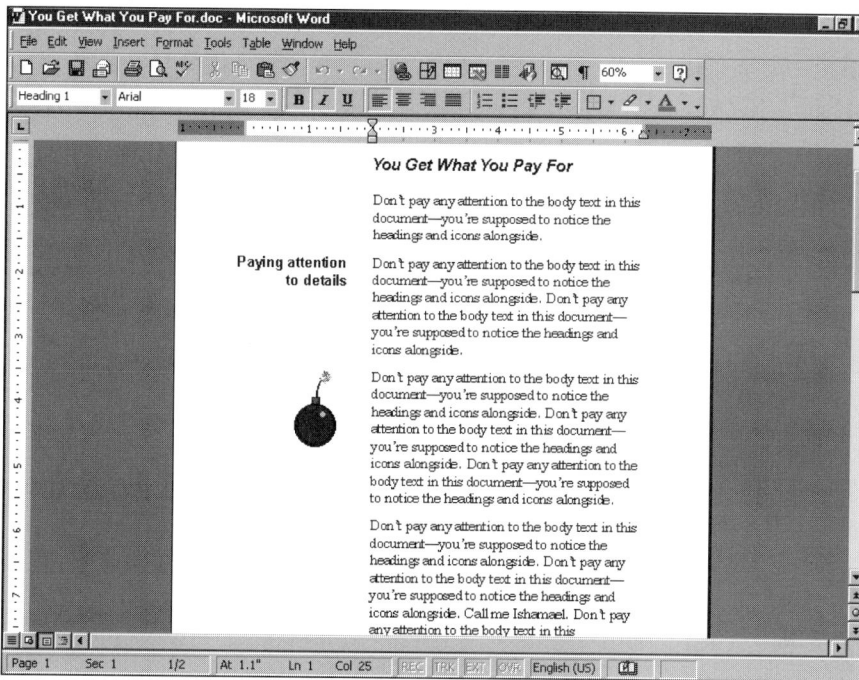

Figure 29-6: This document illustrates side headings and margin icons.

To use side headings, set a wide left margin to leave room for the headings. Then create a side heading style:

1. Choose Format ⇨ Style ⇨ New and name the style Side Heading.

2. In the New Style dialog box, choose Format ⇨ Frame to display the Frame dialog box.

3. Select settings for the horizontal position of the frame that holds the side heading. Set the Relative To setting to Page, and the Distance From Text setting to 0.

4. Set the Vertical Position setting to 0, the Relative To setting to Paragraph, and the Distance from Text setting to 0.

5. Change the Width setting to Exactly and type in the width of the side heading frame in the At box.

6. Leave the box labeled Move with Text checked to have Word move the frame whenever the anchor paragraph moves.

Once the Side Heading style is complete, create your side heading by typing its text in a separate paragraph and applying the style. To place a *graphic* alongside text, just apply the preceding style to an empty paragraph and then insert your picture into the frame. If you use the same graphics repeatedly, turn them into AutoText entries for instant margin icons.

Formatting drop caps

Newsletter and magazine articles often begin with a large initial capital letter, usually referred to as a drop cap. Word makes it easy to set up drop caps in your documents. Just put the insertion point in the paragraph that is to be altered and choose Format ➪ Drop Cap.

In the Drop Cap dialog box, choose the type of effect you want, Dropped or In Margin. You can select any available font for the drop cap, but you can't control its size directly — Word sets that for you based on your entry at Lines to Drop. The Distance from Text setting controls the horizontal distance from the drop cap to the rest of the paragraph (it moves the text if you choose the Dropped effect, the drop cap if you choose In Margin). When you OK the dialog box, Word places the first character in the paragraph in a separate frame, formatting the character according to the settings you selected. If you've selected the first word in the paragraph before calling up the dialog box, Word drops the entire word.

Caution

Drop caps display properly only when you're viewing the document in the Web or Print Layout views.

Working with Graphics

With minor variations, techniques for working with graphics are common to Word, Excel, and PowerPoint — Chapter 8 tells all. Still, Word has a few special tricks up its sleeve that would-be desktop publishers should know. In addition to the techniques covered next, don't forget the tip just mentioned for positioning graphics automatically alongside text.

Floating versus inline graphics

In early versions of Word, the standard way to insert a picture was directly into your text, or inline, so that it acted much like a single character of text. If you wanted more control over its position, you had to draw a frame and insert the picture into that. Nowadays, however, Word frames are almost obsolete, especially as graphics containers. Although you can still insert pictures in line with your text, you can choose instead to let any picture *float*, so that you can move it anywhere you want it on the page (floating pictures remain anchored to a specific paragraph — a wrinkle covered in "Understanding anchors" later in this chapter). AutoShape objects always float, but Word still inserts other pictures and objects inline by default. To make an inline object float, follow these steps:

1. Select the object.
2. Choose Format ⇨ Picture or Format ⇨ *object* — or pick the corresponding Format choice from the shortcut menu. The Format dialog box appears.
3. Switch to the Layout tab.
4. Click any of the graphical buttons for Wrapping Style *except* In Line with Text and then click OK.

Floating a picture is the way to go if your goal is a clean, professional-looking layout. Inline pictures can work well for illustrations in drafts because they move along with the relevant text with no work on your part. The only reason to insert a picture in a frame is if you need to add to it a comment, a footnote or endnote, or one of several special fields. These are the same reasons for using frames instead of text boxes, as discussed in "Text boxes versus frames" earlier in this chapter.

Positioning graphics

You can position a floating picture or other object the easy way (by dragging it with the mouse) or the precise way (by typing numeric coordinates into the Advanced Layout dialog box). I assume you've mastered the mouse technique, but the Advanced Layout box may elude you. To find it, go to the Layout tab of the Format Picture dialog box (Steps 1–3 in the previous section) and click Advanced. As shown back in Figure 8-20, positioning controls are located on the Picture Position tab of the dialog box.

Understanding anchors

Secret

In Word, every graphic object, including text boxes and frames, is anchored to a particular paragraph. The value of the anchor is implied by its name: It enables you to keep the object anchored to its paragraph, no matter where that paragraph winds up in your document.

You can see an object's anchor by clicking the Show/Hide Paragraph Marks button to display all nonprinting characters. When you select the object — and only then — you see a small anchor icon on the top line of the paragraph to which the object is anchored, as shown in Figure 29-7.

Settings on the Picture Position tab of the Advanced Layout dialog box enable you to take advantage of anchors. To require Word to maintain the object's position relative to the paragraph it's anchored to (I'll call it the anchor paragraph), check the Move Object with Text box. Clear this box to position the object in a fixed location, independent of what happens to the text. If you check the Lock Anchor box, the anchor remains on the same page as the paragraph it's currently attached to. With this box cleared, the anchor paragraph changes as you move the object up or down in the document. When it is checked, however, the object always appears on the same page as the anchor paragraph.

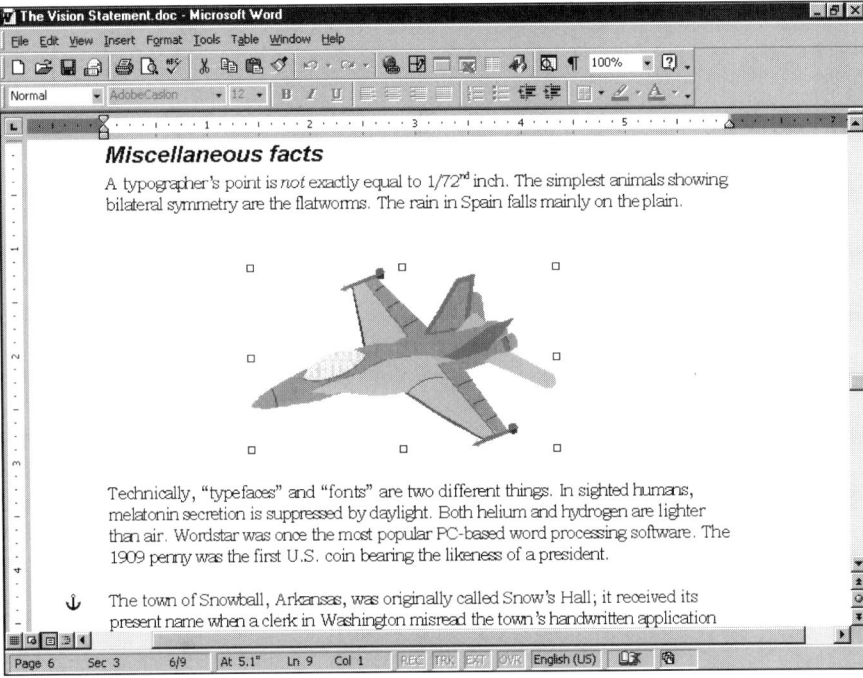

Figure 29-7: The little anchor icon at the left marks the paragraph the selected picture is anchored to.

Wrapping text around graphics

Rudimentary in its early versions, the text-around-graphics wrapping in Word is now truly outstanding. It's fast, flexible, accurate, and modifiable — what more could you ask? Wrapping is available for just about any type of graphic: text boxes; AutoShape objects and other simple shapes; and pictures, whether bitmap or line art. You can choose from a variety of wrapping styles, three of them new in this version. The star of the bunch is the tight wrapping option. Select this style, and text hugs the curves of the picture, cozying in effortlessly to surround the image. The effect looks great.

Rapping about wrapping

To select a wrapping style, you need the Format X (Format Picture, Format AutoShape, Format whatever) dialog box. Display it as follows: Switch to Print Layout view and select the object. Select the relevant Format choice at the bottom of the shortcut menu, or from the Format menu. If the Picture toolbar is active, you can also click the Format Picture button on the Picture toolbar — this works even with graphics that aren't pictures. Once the Format X dialog box appears, select the Layout tab to get to the controls shown in Figure 29-8.

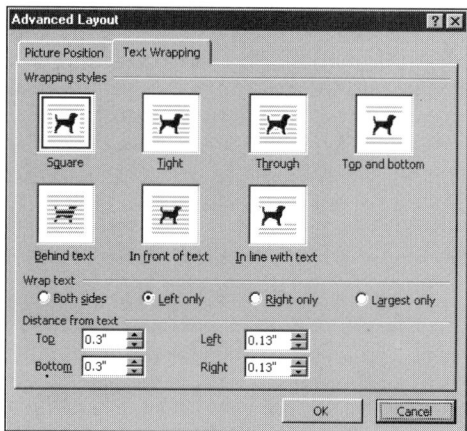

Figure 29-8: Use these controls to tell Word how to wrap text around graphics and text boxes.

Because of the little icons, it shouldn't be too hard to choose the wrapping style option you want.

With the In Line with Text option selected, Word treats the picture exactly like a character of text, allowing just enough room in the paragraph to fit the picture. The picture moves along with the other characters as you insert and delete new text. When this wrapping style is active, none of the other controls in the Layout tab or the Advanced Layout dialog box are available — to access these controls, you must float the picture by choosing any of the other wrapping styles (see "Floating versus inline graphics" earlier in this section).

The other wrapping style choices work as follows:

- The "Square" choice really results in rectangular wrapping.
- Choose Tight for the classy all-around look.
- The Behind Text and In Front of Text buttons make the text appear on top of or underneath the picture.

For two additional wrapping style choices, click Advanced on the Layout tab. The new options work like this:

- The Through setting makes text appear in any large-enough empty areas within the graphic, not just around its edges.
- The Top and Bottom setting creates a textless horizontal swath for your picture across the entire width of the document or column.

If you don't need to change other wrapping settings, you can instead choose the wrapping style via the Picture toolbar. Click the Text Wrapping button and make your selection from the six available styles.

Reshaping the wrapping perimeter

Secret

With the Tight and Through wrapping options, Word generally does a great job of wrapping text closely around the outline of the graphic. But maybe you think you can improve on Word's efforts, moving text just a little closer to that butterfly wing. Select the graphic, click the Text Wrapping button on the Picture toolbar, and choose Edit Wrap Points at the bottom of the menu.

Word redisplays the graphic with a dashed red line to indicate the *wrapping perimeter*, the curve to which nearby text is wrapped. Heavy black dots mark the points where the curve changes direction, as shown in Figure 29-9.

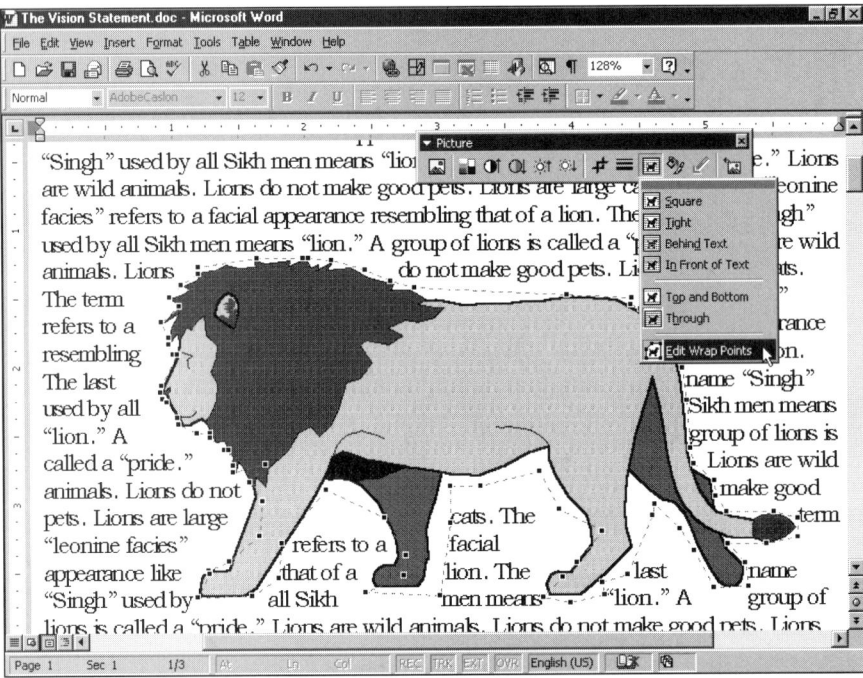

Figure 29-9: That dashed line studded with big black dots is the wrapping perimeter, determining how closely surrounding text can move in on the picture.

Drag the dots to move them, pushing text further away or allowing it to snuggle in closer. If Word hasn't tracked the graphic's outline in sufficient detail, dragging on the dashed line adds a new dot and moves it to a satisfactory location.

Wrapping text manually

Word lets you insert a manual *text wrapping break* when you want text to wrap around only the top part of a picture. In a paragraph that wraps around a picture, place the insertion point where you want the text to stop wrapping. Then choose Text Wrapping Break in the Insert ⇨ Breaks dialog box. The remainder of the paragraph's text jumps down below the picture. A text wrapping break works like a manual line break if the picture's wrapping style is in line with the text, behind text, or in front of text — or if the paragraph doesn't have a picture.

Specialized Desktop Publishing Chores

Although layout programs that specialize in such layout chores as envelopes or labels have their advantages, Word boasts enough design finesse to handle most such projects capably. Tips for laying out envelopes, labels, business cards, and slides are described in this section.

Word comes with wizards for creating envelopes and labels via the File ➪ New dialog box — you can find them on the Letters & Faxes tab. But don't get your hopes up. All they do is offer you a choice between standard or mail merge versions of the item you're creating. Once the Tools ➪ Envelopes and Labels dialog box appears (or the Tools ➪ Mail Merge dialog box, if you selected a mail merge item), you're on your own.

Designing fancy envelopes

Getting Word to print an ordinary envelope is easy: You just fill out the Envelopes tab of the Tools ➪ Envelopes and Labels dialog box with the needed addresses (yours as well as the recipient's). The Options button lets you set fonts and position for the addresses, add a barcode, and control how the envelope feeds in your printer. To print the envelope immediately, you just choose Print.

That's fine for quick envelopes that don't draw attention to themselves. However, if you want your mailing to make a strong statement, choose Add to Document instead of Print. As shown in Figure 29-10, Word inserts the envelope as a separate section at the beginning of the document. Once the envelope is part of the document, you can go to town on the format, changing fonts for any part of either address and adding graphics and text.

Things to know about envelopes:

- Word applies the built-in paragraph styles Envelope Return and Envelope Address to the return and recipient addresses, respectively. Modify these styles in the template to customize the look of future documents' envelopes (whether printed directly or added to the document).

- Word inserts the recipient's address in a separate frame, which you can move around the envelope to the optimum position — you don't have to play with paragraph formatting settings if you don't want to.

- In case you haven't noticed, Word inserts envelopes as page 0. To print the envelope only, you can type **0** in the Pages field of the Print dialog box.

- You don't have to type the recipient's address in the dialog box if it already appears in your document. Just select it in the document or assign the entire address to the bookmark EnvelopeAddress (see Chapter 27 for bookmark tips). If you don't explicitly select or bookmark an address, Word will still display one if it finds one anywhere in the document.

- You can have Word automatically insert a slogan, logo, or any other text or graphic element in every envelope. First, add an envelope to a document. Create and format the text or graphic, and then select it and choose Insert ⇨ AutoText ⇨ New (Alt+F3). Type **EnvelopeExtra1** as the name of the new AutoText entry. You can create a second such element called **EnvelopeExtra2**.

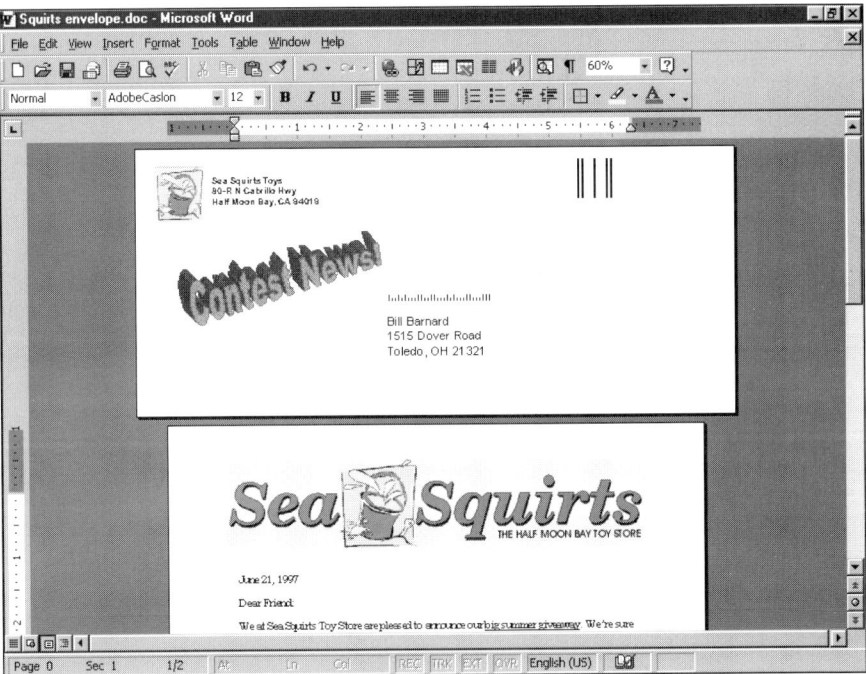

Figure 29-10: An envelope created with the Envelopes and Labels dialog box has been inserted as the first (0th) page of the document.

Designing labels and such

Simple mailing labels, name tags, and other such items are a snap with Word's Tools ⇨ Envelopes and Labels command. After calling up the dialog box, choose the Labels tab. Start by choosing Options to tell Word what type of label stock you're using. You can select from a list of many widely sold label types. If the labels you have aren't on the list, you can design a new label specification to match them. Back in the main dialog box, type the text you want Word to print on each label in the Address field, or insert an address from the Address Book (see Chapter 52). You can then print directly from the dialog box.

Fancy label and business card layouts

While the Envelopes and Labels command works fine for creating ordinary mailing labels and the like, it can't handle more sophisticated layouts without special techniques. Labels that include graphics or 3-D text may better catch the eye of prospective customers. Business cards are an everyday necessity of commerce. Given the ready availability of inexpensive, microperforated business card stock, why not print your own?

If you design and print lots of labels or business cards, get your hands on software specialized for that purpose. If you have any version of Office other than Office Standard, fire up Microsoft Publisher, which has wonderful design and layout tools and templates for most common label formats. Other possibilities include Smart 'n Sticky, a shareware product included on the CD-ROM that comes with this book, and the more sophisticated Bear Rock Labeler from Bear Rock Technologies, www.bearrock.com. One more option is ClickBook, the printing utility I talked about in Chapter 11. With ClickBook, you simply set up a custom page in Word the same size as one label or business card, laying out the label or card on it. When you print, ClickBook duplicates the "page" across as many rows and columns needed to fill the label or business card stock. A demo version of ClickBook is also on the *Microsoft Office 2000 Secrets* CD-ROM.

Ten steps to perfect labels and business cards

For the occasional sophisticated design, however, Word does the job handily. Follow the steps here — the procedure looks long, but the results are great. The technique relies on Word fields, which are covered extensively in Chapter 33.

1. Switch to Print Layout view. Choose Tools ⇨ Envelopes and Labels and select the Labels tab. Using the Options button, select the label format that corresponds to your stock.

2. Place the following field in the Address box: { AUTOTEXT LabelLayout }

   Insert ⇨ Field doesn't work while you're in the dialog box, so you must add the field manually: Press Ctrl+F9 to insert the curly braces, and then type in the preceding field codes inside the braces. You can use any name in place of "LabelLayout," as long as it doesn't conflict with an AutoText entry.

3. Choose New Document. Word creates a one-page document containing a table in the label format you specified. Each table cell represents a single label, and each contains a copy of the AUTOTEXT field you created at Step 2.

4. With the insertion point still at the very beginning of the new document, choose Insert ⇨ Break and select a Next Page section break.

5. Move the insertion point to the top of the document and then choose File ⇨ Page Setup. In the Page Setup dialog box, use the Margins tab to set all the margins, and the header and footer as well, to 0. On the Paper Size tab, define a custom page size that is exactly that of *one* of your labels. Apply these settings to This Section Only. If you get a warning about printable area after OK'ing the dialog box, choose Ignore.

6. Back in the document, you should see a small new first page with the dimensions of one label. Get creative: Compose your label format by adding text and graphics, laying everything out the way you want the printed label to look. An essential point: *Place all your text into text boxes*. Also, be sure not to press Enter to add more paragraphs to the little page.

7. After the layout looks right, select all the objects and choose Draw ⇨ Group on the Drawing toolbar to bind them together as one.

8. With the group still selected, choose Format ⇨ Object. In the Object dialog box, switch to the Layout tab and click Advanced. Now, on the Picture Position tab, check the boxes Move Object with Text and Lock Anchor.

9. With the group *still* selected, choose Insert ⇨ AutoText ⇨ New and type in **LabelLayout** or whatever name you chose in Step 2.

10. Now move back to the original page, the one containing the actual labels. Press Ctrl+A (to select the entire document) and then press F9 to update the fields in your labels.

Whew! On screen, the resulting document should look similar to the one in Figure 29-11. To print your labels, call up the Print dialog box. Enter 2 at Pages, because you don't want to print the little first page. Specify how many label sheets you're printing at Number of copies.

Problems? If the label content doesn't line up correctly in the table, you probably inadvertently added more paragraphs to the little page created in Step 4. To delete the extra paragraphs, click in the top left cell of the table on the main page (page 2) and then press the Backspace key until you can't move the insertion point any farther. Now click the grouped layout and repeat Steps 9 and 10.

The default keyboard shortcut is F9 — see Chapter 33 for other ways to access this command.

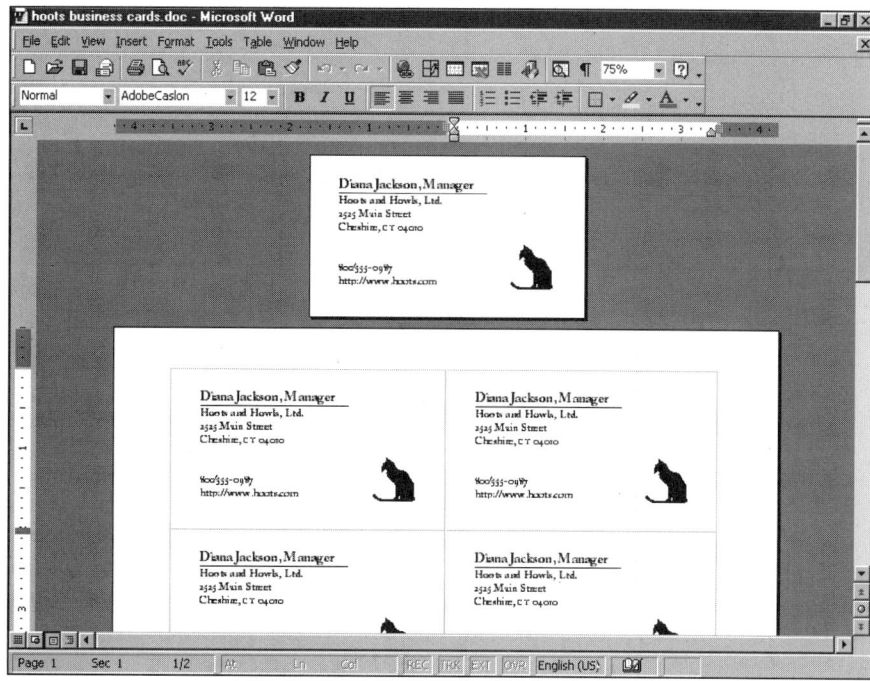

Figure 29-11: Produced using the patented ten-step technique detailed in the text, this document prints a sheet of classy business cards.

Presentations on the cheap: Sharp slides for 50¢ apiece

Sure, PowerPoint slides look great with all those colors and graphics. At five dollars per slide, though, even a modest presentation means you're out some real money if you're footing the tab. If you're willing to forgo the glitz and glitter, you can use Word to make professional-looking slides for less than 50 cents each.

The basic idea is to create a Word file containing a grid of slide-sized text boxes. Type the text for each slide in a separate box. It's okay to add simple line art (AutoShapes), but don't go overboard — you have only two colors to work with, black and white. On disk or by modem, get the file to a service bureau. This is a place that uses high-resolution laser typesetting machines to print desktop publishing files onto the film necessary for commercial printing of books and magazines. Have them output your file as negative film. You shouldn't have to pay more than $20 a page, and a $12-per-page rate isn't hard to find. If even that is too dear, print them yourself on transparency stock you can buy at an office supply store.

On your way back from the service bureau, stop off at a camera store and buy a box of plastic slide mounts. I recommend Hama mounts as easy to use and unlikely to jam. Back at the office, cut the film into individual slides, placing them in the mounts. A good paper cutter helps, but you can do it with scissors. The finished slides look great, with crisp white text and line drawings against a pitch-black background. In fact, audiences who have seen too many busy slides may find them a welcome relief.

To save you the trouble of setting up a text box grid for slides, the CD-ROM bundled with this book includes the Slides.dot template, which contains a prefab grid. After opening a new file based on the template, just type your text into each text box—voilà, instant slides.

Conclusion

Word's collection of page layout and desktop publishing tools provides formidable competition for the dedicated desktop publishing applications. Once you understand how to manage document layout with sections, you can go on to master the fine points of headers and footers, columnar layouts, text boxes, and graphics.

Chapter 30

Getting Organized with Tables and Outlines

In This Chapter

- Drawing sophisticated tables in seconds
- Using advanced techniques for table layout and formatting
- Understanding the ins and outs of working with text in tables
- Managing data in tables: sorting and calculations
- Summarizing commands and techniques
- Writing macros for streamlining outline viewing and printing
- Avoiding the AutoSummarize feature

The story of civilization is the story of the human drive to classify and categorize. At the dawn of a new millennium, Word's tables and outlines are helping millions of us keep the chaos at bay.

Unraveling the Mysteries of Tables

Use Word tables liberally, whenever your document must present a series of similar information items. Building a simple table is oh-so-easy, but as always, Word's power is there when you need it.

Word tables look great in both printed documents and Web pages. Word translates its tables into HTML tables quite accurately, though you should be conscious of some layout limitations in Web pages (see Chapter 14 for details).

Unclassified table secrets

Before the main Secrets parade starts, take the following warm-up of table tips.

Get familiar with your table tools

Word includes a Tables and Borders toolbar with buttons for most of the commands you need when working on tables. Display the toolbar by clicking its button on the Standard toolbar. The button toggles the toolbar off and on.

Also, don't forget that a table's shortcut (right-click) menu offers a broad selection of table-related commands when the insertion point is in a cell.

Installing the secret table macro

If you have Word 97, check out the Table Cell Helper, a modest macro that tells you where in the table the insertion point is located and how many rows and columns the table contains. The readout is in spreadsheet-type coordinates (B:4, for example). You can find this macro in the Macros8.dot template on the CD-ROM for Word 97. Copy it to any template you like using Organizer, covered in Chapter 26. If you don't have Word 97, check your Office 2000 CD-ROM to see if it has a Macros9.dot template.

Selecting table cells

Word 2000's Table menu has a new Select submenu. It's a good thing for people who forget the faster ways to select parts of the table or who have trouble using the mouse with precision.

Once you've started selecting any part of a table, you can extend the selection by holding down Shift and clicking elsewhere in the table. You can't select noncontiguous regions of a table arbitrarily, but the extended selection only includes cells that are at least partly underneath or above the cells you click. To see what I mean, create a table with cells that vary in width from row to row—you'll need the table drawing or cell adjustment techniques discussed later in the chapter. Then start a selection somewhere other than the leftmost column, expanding it into other rows.

Selecting cells

The very fastest way to select a cell and all its contents is to click in the cell three times. This works best in Normal view because you can make your clicks anywhere in the cell. In Print Layout view, you have to click in the top-left corner, or if the cell contains text, over the text. Clicking twice just selects the current word, as it would in ordinary text.

Another mouse technique is to place the pointer anywhere along the left margin of the cell (but inside the cell a little, not over the border). When the pointer becomes an arrow pointing diagonally upward and to the right, you can click to select.

With the keyboard, remember that you use Tab and Shift+Tab to move around in a table from cell to cell, forward and backward, respectively. (To enter a tab character into table text, press Ctrl+Tab.) Tabbing into a cell selects the entire contents of the cell you enter, except the final paragraph mark (the importance of special table paragraph marks is discussed later in this section). To extend such a selection to the paragraph mark and then to subsequent cells in any direction, including their paragraph marks, hold down Shift as you press one of the arrow keys repeatedly.

Selecting rows and columns

Select an entire column by holding the mouse directly over the column top, so that the pointer touches the top border. When the pointer becomes an small black arrow pointing down, click to select, or drag to select adjacent columns.

Select an entire row by placing the mouse pointer alongside the row outside the left border of the table. Click when the pointer is a large white diagonal arrow. Drag using the same arrow to select multiple rows.

Selecting an entire table

To select the entire table, put the insertion point anywhere inside it and choose Table ⇨ Select ⇨ Table. This command used to be easier to find — it was a choice on the Table menu, not on a Select submenu.

The quickest way to select an entire table? Press Alt+5 (the 5 key on the numeric keypad with Num Lock off). If you don't use this shortcut often enough to memorize it, but you still want to make selecting tables easier, place the Select Table command back where it belongs, on the Table menu. Here's how:

1. Start by opening the Tools ⇨ Customize dialog box.
2. Click the Table menu.
3. Click the Select submenu.
4. Hold down Ctrl and drag the Table command back onto the main Table menu underneath the Select submenu. Release the Ctrl key and close the dialog box.

This command also belongs on the Table-related shortcut menus, at least the one called Table Text — the Table Text shortcut menu pops up when you right-click inside a cell with nothing selected, or when ordinary text is selected. Chapter 5 gives the techniques for customizing shortcut menus. By the way, the Select Table command is called TableSelectTable in the All Commands list of the Customize dialog box.

Inserting new tables

When it's time to add a new table to a document, you must choose between at least three divergent roads in the Word woods. The best path depends on the table you're trying to create and your predilections.

Drawing a table

One of the downright coolest features in Word is the table drawing tool. Whether it ends up saving you time is debatable, but it's a lot of fun to use.

If you're sure you can live with a totally uniform table aligned with the left and right margins and with all the rows and columns of equal size, the Insert Table button on the standard toolbar is still the tool to use. But many tables aren't so uniform. That's why the Draw Table tool makes so much sense.

When you click the Draw Table button on the Tables toolbar, the pointer becomes a little pen — see Figure 30-1. Start by dragging diagonally to draw the table perimeter wherever you want it on the page. Then drag vertically or horizontally within the outline to divide the cells. Rows and columns can be any width, and you can subdivide any cell or group of cells in either dimension with a quick swipe of the pen. If you draw a line in the wrong place, erase it with the Eraser tool.

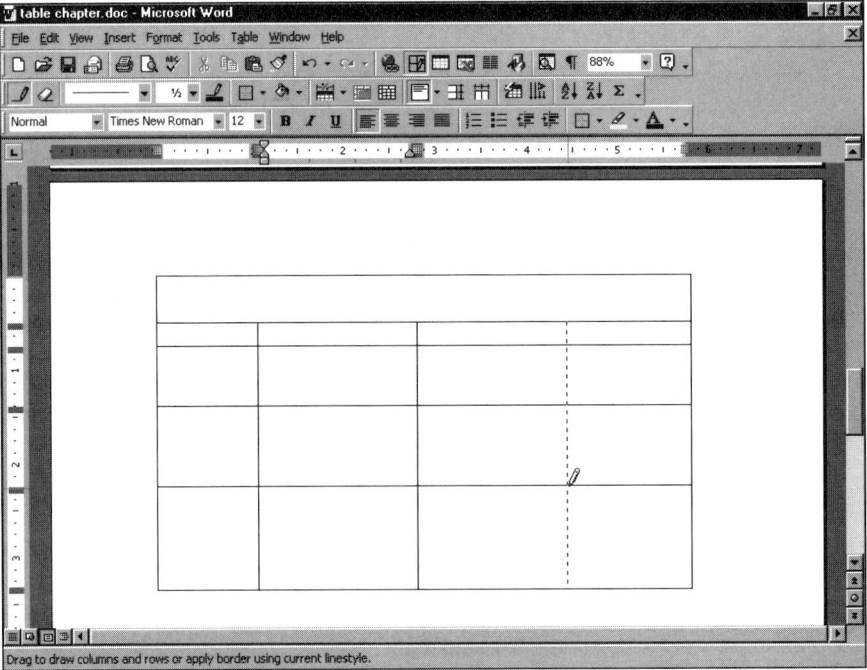

Figure 30-1: Drawing a table

For quick, complex tables, you can't beat the Draw Table tool. But if you're going for a professional look, plan on spending some time fine-tuning the position of the table and the height and width of its cells — freehand sketches rarely produce precisely equal rows, for example. I cover layout tips in "Laying out and formatting tables" later in this chapter.

Quick uniform tables

I already mentioned the Insert Table button, the fastest way to slam down a table. The button resides to the right of the Draw Table button on the Standard toolbar. When you click it, up comes a little grid representing the table-to-be with its rows and columns. Click in this grid where the lower-right "cell" of your table would be, and Word drops a corresponding real table into your document.

Chapter 30: Getting Organized with Tables and Outlines

Secret

But you probably know all that already. The one secret-y thing about the Insert Table button is this: If you *drag* over the dummy table you can expand the grid beyond its usual 4 · 5 dimensions. The only limitation on the table size that you can select using this technique seems to be how far your screen will let you drag the mouse.

Actually, there's something else to know about the Insert Table button: When you select a row, column, or cell, it metamorphoses to become an Insert Row, Insert Column, or Insert Cells button, respectively.

The Insert Table dialog box

If you prefer certain results to quick-and-dirty mouse techniques, Word 2000's new Insert Table dialog box is for you. Shown in Figure 30-2, the dialog box appears when you choose Table ➪ Insert ➪ Table. You can also get to this dialog box by clicking the Insert Table button on the Tables and Borders toolbar. The button in question is actually one of those multipurpose buttons now so common in Office — it may be displaying a different command's icon. In this case you can click the thin strip with the little arrow alongside the proper button to drop down the list of available commands, including Insert Table.

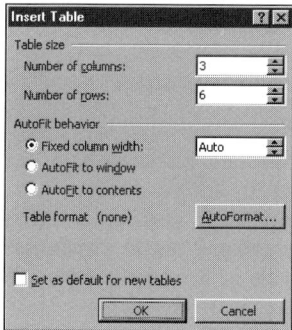

Figure 30-2: The Insert Table dialog box

Obviously, the Insert Table dialog box lets you specify the new table's dimensions. The dialog box also lets you select AutoFit options and access the AutoFormat feature for the new table. AutoFit and AutoFormat are described later in this chapter.

Checking the box labeled Set as Default for New Tables just means that you see the current dimensions and the AutoFit choice the next time you open the dialog box.

Creating and working with nested tables

New in Word 2000 is the ability to handle tables inside tables (within tables inside other tables). You can create these "nested" tables using any combination of the three main table-making commands. Figure 30-3 shows a rather outlandish example.

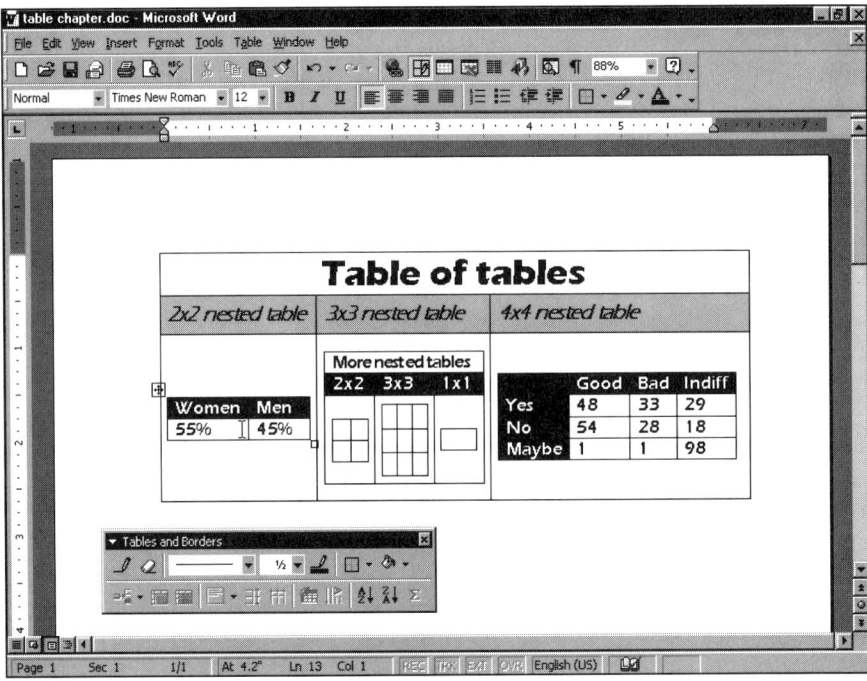

Figure 30-3: The screenshot shows multiple levels of nested tables.

When you're working with nested tables, Word provides visual cues so that you can tell which table the mouse is pointing to. That way, you can be sure you're clicking in the correct table. In Figure 30-3, you can see that Word indicates the table over which the mouse pointer hovers with markers at the top-left and bottom-right corners. The markers are the four-headed arrow in the box and the small square diagonally across from it.

Laying out and formatting tables

You can have Word design a fancy table for you when you insert the table (choose Table ⇨ Insert ⇨ Table, and then click the AutoFormat button) or after the fact (Table ⇨ Table AutoFormat). But while automatic formatting applies shading, text formatting such as bold and italics, and gridlines, it doesn't handle important layout chores such as sizing the rows and columns and positioning the table on the page for the best effect.

Setting table size and position

Word 2000 has gained a great deal of strength when it comes to helping you control the layout of an entire table on a page. You can now drag a table around freely, and you can position it vertically as well as horizontally with numeric precision. And you gain control over other aspects of table layout.

To move or size a table with the mouse, hover the pointer over the table for a second or two. You'll see a move handle at the upper-left corner of the table and a resize handle at the lower-right corner (refer back to Figure 30-3). Drag the move handle to reposition the table, and drag the resize handle to change the overall size of the table.

If you prefer to work by the numbers, the key to controlling table layout is the Table tab of the new Table ⇨ Table Properties dialog box, shown in Figure 30-4 (for a look at another tab of the same dialog box, see Figure 30-7).

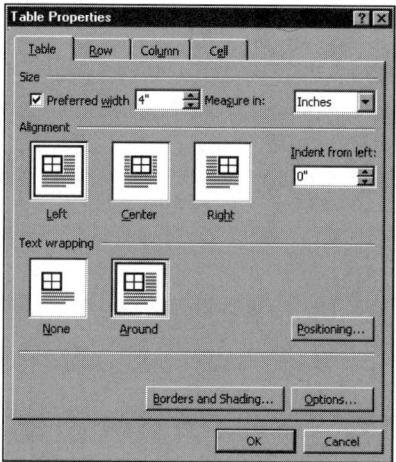

Figure 30-4: The Table tab of the Table Properties dialog box

Your options are as follows:

- You can set the width of the table, either as a percentage of the available page width or in absolute units.

- You can choose how the table should be aligned horizontally: at the left margin, in the center, or along the right margin. If you choose a left-sided table, you also get to specify an indent from the margin.

- You can determine whether text wraps alongside the table or skips over it altogether. If you do activate text wrapping by choosing Around, the Positioning button becomes available. Clicking here pops up the Table Positioning dialog box (Figure 30-5), which gives you the same sort of control you have over the position of graphics elements. Chapter 29 discusses these controls in more detail.

- Use the Options button to control margins inside cells, determine whether Word can break the table into parts if it doesn't fit on the current page, or add space between cells. Figure 30-6 shows a table with excessive amounts of space added between cells, just so you can see what this setting does.

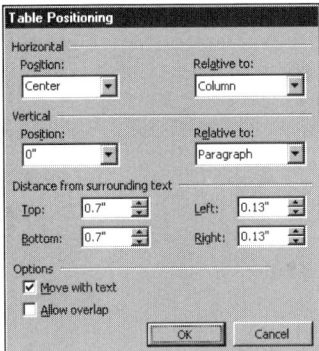

Figure 30-5: You can only get to the Table Positioning dialog box shown here by turning on text wrapping in the Table Properties dialog box.

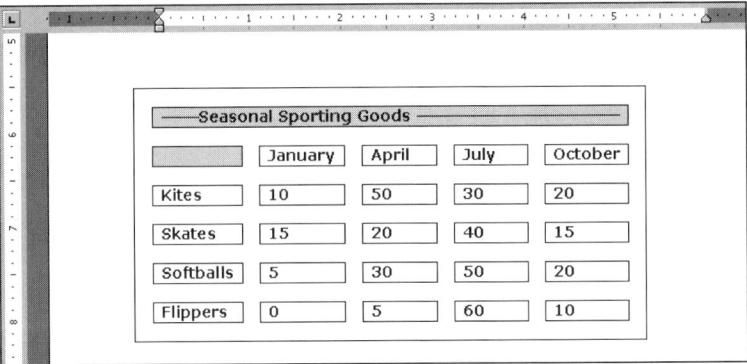

Figure 30-6: A table with lots of space between cells as specified in the Table Options dialog box. Note that Word adds the space between the cell borders.

Adjusting cell height and width

Left to its own devices, Word adjusts the height of table rows according to the text you place in them, leaving column width fixed as it was when you created the table. You're not planning to leave Word to its own devices, are you?

The easy way to modify the row height or column width is by dragging the cell boundaries. To make a row taller or shorter, drag anywhere on the row boundary. One potential source of trouble with this technique: It only works in Print Layout and Web Layout views. Note also that you can't change the height of a single cell with the mouse, or for that matter with any other technique.

Widening or narrowing a column can be a bit trickier. If the column's boundary lines up on two or more consecutive rows, dragging anywhere along the boundary changes the width of all the aligned cells — no problem there. But if you select only specific cells in such a column and drag one of their column boundaries, the boundaries of the unselected cells stay put. Dragging a cell's column boundary that doesn't align with the ones in the rows above or below affects only the boundary for that cell.

If you prefer, you can change row height or column width by dragging the row or column markers in the ruler. Hold down Alt to display the row or column measurements in numeric form while you drag. If these mouse techniques are just too imprecise for your blood, use the Table ⇨ Table Properties dialog box (Figure 30-7) to set the row height and column width numerically. In the dialog box the Row, Column, and Cell tabs let you size the corresponding table elements one at a time. Choose Previous or Next to move from row to row or column to column.

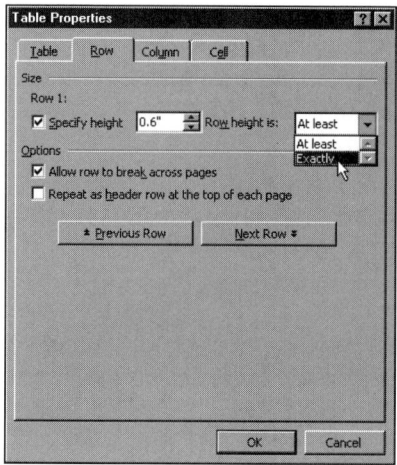

Figure 30-7: Use the Row, Column, and Cell tabs of the Table Properties dialog box to control the size of these table elements.

Secret

To resize multiple rows or columns simultaneously in the dialog box, select them before you choose Table ⇨ Table Properties.

The Cell tab enables you to set the preferred *width* for the cell in the row that contained the insertion point when you opened the dialog box. However, the size you choose may not be the size you get unless you go to the Table Options dialog box and clear the box labeled Automatically Resize to Fit Contents. With that box checked, Word tries to keep the cell width as close as possible to your stated preference, but changes it when necessary as you add or delete text in the table.

Automated column width and row height adjustments

Word 2000's new AutoFit feature includes the existing Distribute commands, which equalize the widths or heights of selected cells. To these, AutoFit adds two commands that adjust column width based on table content or screen size.

Secret

Keep in mind that Word *normally* adjusts row height automatically based on the content of the cells. However, you can fix row height in the Row tab of the Table ⇨ Table Properties dialog box.

Using AutoFit to adjust table size based on content or screen size

Using the two new AutoFit commands for tables, you can tell Word to adjust the column widths in a table automatically, according to changes in the contents of the table or in the width of the screen window. You can turn on either AutoFit setting, or choose a nonautomatic table mode in either of two ways:

- **When you create a table with the Insert Table dialog box** (see Figure 30-2). Pick the setting you want from the choices in the AutoFit Behavior section.

- **Using the AutoFit commands on an existing table.** The commands are available from the Table menu, and in the menu offered on the multipurpose button on the Tables and Borders toolbar (see the section on the Insert Table command earlier in this chapter).

When AutoFit to Contents is turned on for a table, Word automatically adjusts the widths of all columns as you add or delete text or graphics. Word's goal is to make each column as wide as possible. As you type more text in a narrow column, Word narrows other, wider columns. When you delete text from a column, Word narrows that column and gives the space to other columns with more content. Turn on AutoFit to Contents for a new table in the Insert Table dialog box.

For an existing table, place the insertion point or make a selection in any part of the table, and then choose Table ⇨ AutoFit ⇨ AutoFit to Contents or click the AutoFit to Contents button if it's visible. Either way, Word immediately reformats the table. To postpone automatically resizing the table until future edits, check Automatically Resize to Fit Contents in the Table Options dialog box.

The AutoFit to Window setting works when you create a table (with the Insert Table command), dividing the width of the Word window equally among all the columns of your new table. Used with existing tables, the AutoFit ⇨ AutoFit to Window command works as you'd expect only in Web Layout view. With AutoFit to Window on in Web Layout view, Word automatically resets column width every time you change the window size (for example, by clicking the Maximize/Restore button).

A related third command, Fixed Column Width, turns off these Automatic adjustments. Choose this setting in the Insert Table dialog box to create a table whose columns stay the same size as you add or remove content. If you find a column width that works right for an existing table, choose AutoFit ⇨ Fixed Column Width to lock in the current dimensions. You can still adjust column width yourself, but Word won't do it for you any longer.

Chapter 30: Getting Organized with Tables and Outlines

Equalizing cell sizes

To make two or more rows the same height, select the rows and choose Table ➪ AutoFit ➪ Distribute Rows Evenly, or click the corresponding button on the Table toolbar. If you don't specifically select rows, Word equalizes the heights of all the rows in the table.

To equalize cell widths, select two or more entire columns, or adjacent cells in one or more rows. Then choose Table ➪ AutoFit ➪ Distribute Columns Evenly. Word sets cell widths equal within each row. Because column width can differ from row to row, however, the resulting columns may still be of different widths in different rows.

Both of these commands distribute the selected rows or columns evenly within the space they originally occupied, so the perimeter of the selection doesn't change.

Secrets of inserting cells, rows, and columns

Rare is the table that doesn't eventually need more rows or columns. Microsoft has revamped the table insertion commands for Word 2000 so that they work more consistently and flexibly (and don't mysteriously appear and disappear the way they used to). All the commands now appear on a stable submenu at Table ➪ Insert.

The major secret to remember about inserting table rows and columns is this: Word inserts the number of rows or columns that are selected when you use the command. For example, if you select three rows and then choose Table ➪ Insert ➪ Rows (above or below), three blank rows appear in the table. (If nothing is selected in the table, Word inserts a single row or column.)

And it's about time: Word 2000's insert commands for rows and columns finally let you decide where the new rows or columns appear. For rows, you pick whether Word puts them above or below the selection; for columns, whether they're inserted to the left or right of the selection.

To add a row to the *end* of a table, put the insertion point in the bottom right cell and press Tab. Of course, you could also put the insertion point in the final row and choose Table ➪ Insert ➪ Rows Below.

Here's another secret: It may help to know that the Insert Table button on the Standard toolbar can make inserting rows and columns faster. (I'm *not* talking about the multipurpose button on the Tables and Borders toolbar.) When you select rows or columns, the Insert Table button automatically metamorphoses into an Insert Rows or Insert Columns button. When one or more individual cells are selected, the button becomes Insert Cells instead (see the next section).

Inserting cells

The Table ⇨ Insert ⇨ Cells command brings up a little dialog box that lets you add a new, empty cell at the location of the cell that is selected or that contains the insertion point. None of the existing cells are lost. If you choose Shift Cells Down in the dialog box, Word adds a row to the end of the table, pushing the data in all lower cells down. In contrast, choosing Shift Cells Right adds a new cell to the current row only—you don't get a whole new column.

Splitting and merging cells

Secret

The easiest way to split or combine cells is by using the Draw Table and Eraser tools. To break one cell into two, draw a line across the cell with the Draw Table tool. To merge two cells into one, drag the Eraser tool along the boundary between the two cells. Alternatively, of course, you can use Table ⇨ Split Cells.

Deleting versus clearing in tables

Secret

To vaporize table *contents*, select a cell, range, row, or column and press the Delete key. However, if you want to get rid of the cells themselves as well as their contents, place the insertion point in one of the doomed cells, choose Table ⇨ Delete, and pick the appropriate command from the submenu for the element you want to eliminate (rows, columns, or whatever). If you choose Table ⇨ Delete ⇨ Cells, you get a dialog box that lets you decide whether to fill in the gap left by the deleted cell(s) by shifting the remaining cells in the row left, or shifting the remaining cells in the column up.

Actually, it's easier and quicker to remove an entire row or column (cells and contents) by selecting the item and then pressing the Backspace key, or using Cut (Ctrl+X) to send the row or column to the clipboard. To delete or cut a row this way, it's best to select the entire row. If you select something less than an entire row or column, you must clarify what you want Word to erase in the Delete Cells dialog box.

Deleting an entire table via the Table ⇨ Delete submenu is easier in Word 2000 than it used to be. But even quicker is the tried-and-true keyboard technique: Alt+5 to select the table, then Backspace or Ctrl+X.

Moving rows: a way-cool secret

Secret

In a variation on the way they work during ordinary text editing and in Outline view, the Alt+Shift+up arrow and Alt+Shift+down arrow keyboard commands move the current row up or down in the table. Try this, it's fun. If you make a selection first, all rows included in the selection move.

Splitting a table vertically or horizontally

The Table ⇨ Split Table command is good for dividing a table into "table-ettes" by cleaving it at the row containing the insertion point. But what if you want to split a table, making, say, a six-column table into two three-column tables? Here's the simple solution to turn an existing table into two smaller side-by-side tables:

1. Select a set of adjacent columns that you want to break out into a separate table, and use the Cut command to place them on the Clipboard.
2. Place the insertion point below the remaining portion of the table and press Enter to make another new paragraph below.
3. Paste the cut cells into the new paragraph. You should see an empty line between the pasted table and the original one.
4. Use the pasted table's move handle to drag the table up and to the right so that it's beside the original one.

If you want the two smaller tables to stack up vertically, just follow the first three of these steps: Select the columns destined for the second table and cut them to the Clipboard. Move the insertion point to the paragraph mark just past what's left of the original table, hit Enter to give the new table some breathing room, and paste the previously cut columns there.

Perhaps an easier way to create the appearance of two side-by-side tables relies on a false split. All you need to do is place the insertion point in the first column of the right-hand "table" and insert an empty column to create white space between the two parts of the original table. You need to size the new column to taste and apply borders and other formatting so that the two parts of the table look truly independent, as in the example shown in Figure 30-8.

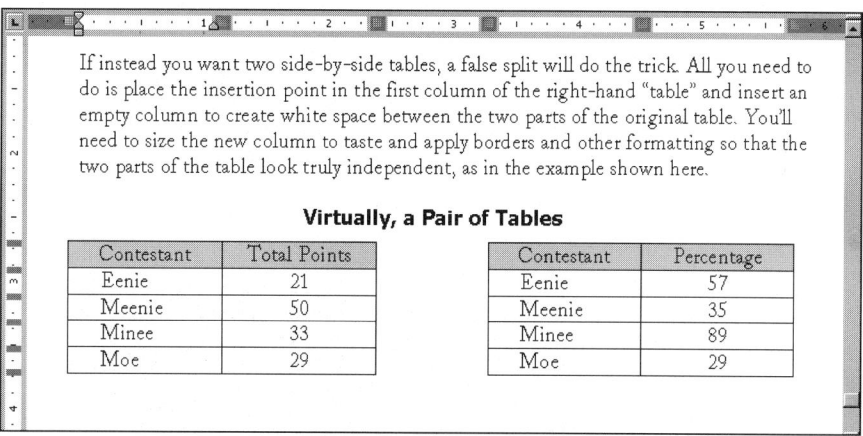

Figure 30-8: This faux pair of tables is actually a single table with an empty middle column.

Setting up headings

If you create a table that spans two or more pages, do your readers a favor and repeat the column headings at the top of the table on each page. Word can duplicate the heading row or rows automatically: At the very beginning of the table, select the top row and any consecutive rows that are to function as headings. Choose Table ⇨ Heading Rows Repeat. That's all it takes. You can turn the headings off by repeating the command. There's an equivalent check box on the Row tab of the Table ⇨ Table Properties dialog box.

Editing and formatting text in a table

Text within a table cell is just like text anywhere else in a document, and you can smother it in character and paragraph formatting of all types, applied directly or via styles. Experiment with borders and shading to make your table stand out suavely.

The paragraph formatting for the final paragraph in a cell is stored in the cell mark, that starlike thing that appears in every cell when you display nonprinting characters. If you cut or copy the paragraph text without its cell mark, it reverts to the Normal style, losing any style or direct formatting you have applied.

Cell alignment

Word gives you push-button control over the top-to-bottom alignment of text within table cells. Select a cell, a range, or the whole table, then bring up the shortcut menu and choose Cell Alignment, followed by one of the alignment icons. Or click the Alignment button on the Tables and Borders toolbar and then pick the desired alignment icon.

Changing text orientation

In the old days, you needed a complex workaround based on frames or text boxes and WordArt to place vertically oriented text in table cells. Although you still need frames to place drawing objects such as WordArt items in a table cell, you can now specify the direction of ordinary table text (normal, vertical reading up, or vertical reading down). Choose Text Direction on the table shortcut menu (which lets you select direction via a dialog box) or click the corresponding button on the Tables and Borders toolbar (which selects the next of the three available directions in turn).

Inserting tabs into table text

Because pressing the Tab key moves you from cell to cell, it won't insert a tab into your table text. Just press Ctrl+Tab instead. Note that if a decimal tab is the only tab in a cell, text automatically aligns there, regardless of the indent settings for the paragraph — you don't need to press Tab.

Converting text to a table, or the other way around

Word provides a two-way conversion between tables and ordinary text. These commands work fine as long as the text you're working with follows a regular pattern and doesn't contain much fancy formatting.

Changing text into a table

To convert ordinary text into a table, start by identifying the units of text that will become the table's rows and columns and deciding how many columns the table should have. If you're working with a crude text-based table, tabs probably separate the columns. But you can just as readily convert consecutive paragraphs into a table, in which case Word will shovel each paragraph in its turn into the next available column.

After making sure that nonprinting characters are visible, you must then scroll through the text to find any irregularities. For example, make sure that every line in a tabular block has one and only one tab for each column. If a line is blank in one or more columns, for example, it may well be missing a tab or two, and the sequence of rows and columns will get thrown off when you do the conversion. Likewise, if you're converting sequential paragraphs into, say, a three-column table, the text should contain three paragraph marks for every row regardless of whether every paragraph mark owns any accompanying text.

Once the text looks clean, select it and choose Table ⇨ Convert ⇨ Text to Table. Word analyzes the selection and decides which characters indicate breaks between the columns, and how many rows and columns will result. You should review these entries and change them if necessary (Word adjusts the number of rows in the table based on the number of columns you specify). The Covert Text to Table dialog box also gives you the same AutoFit and AutoFormat options you have when creating a table from scratch in the Insert Table dialog box, discussed earlier in this chapter.

Changing a table into text

Converting a table into text via the Table ⇨ Convert ⇨ Table to Text command is less error-prone than going the opposite direction. All you have to do is decide which character Word will insert as a column separator when it pours the text into the proper document. Word 2000 lets you choose whether to convert nested tables inside the one you're converting or keep them as tables.

Caution

A word of warning: If you've added any paragraph formatting to the last paragraph in a cell, the conversion strips it out because the cell mark containing the formatting is replaced by a regular paragraph mark. To preserve such formatting, go to the end of each cell and hit Enter to add a new paragraph mark.

Data management in tables

Word can't hold a candle to Excel or Access when it comes to manipulating tabular data, but sometimes you only need a match. Word tables can sort numbers or text, perform simple math, and display information from databases.

Sorting table data

By some standards, Word's table-sorting function is anemic: You can only sort the rows, and you can only sort them according to the contents of two columns. Still, it has enough oomph for many data-management chores. And the sort buttons on the new Tables and Borders toolbar may make the process faster than it used to be.

To perform a sort, place the insertion point anywhere in the column that you want to sort by. For example, if you're sorting a list of people alphabetically by last name, put the insertion point in the Last Name column. If you want to exclude certain rows from the sort, select only the rows you want sorted. And if you want to sort only a particular column, so that the entries in the other columns don't move, select the column.

Choose Table ⇨ Sort to display the Sort dialog box. Here, you can select another column as a secondary sort "key" at Then by. For example, your list of names might well include two or more Smiths or Joneses, so you would select the First Name field at Then By. If you've designated certain rows as headers — with entries such as First Name and Last Name — you don't want them included in the sort, so choose Header Row. Choosing Options brings up a second dialog box that lets you decide whether the sort distinguishes between uppercase and lowercase text and whether to sort only the one column you selected before calling up the Sort dialog box.

Secret

The sort command works on any selected text, even if it isn't neatly tucked into a Word table. If you're sorting a tabular list that isn't a table, you can tell Word which character indicates the separation between columns (usually a tab, but it can be any character you like). You can even rearrange selected paragraphs in alphabetical order according to the first word in each one. See "Sorting a document by headings" later in this chapter for one application of this feature.

Caution

In my experience, the Sort buttons on the Tables and Borders toolbar are unreliable. Use the menu command for surefire sorting.

Math in tables

To perform calculations on the numbers in a table, insert a formula (=) field in the cell where you want the answer displayed. For a quick total of a column or row of values, the shortcut method is to place the insertion point in the cell where the total should go and click the AutoSum button on the Tables and Borders toolbar. Word automatically figures out whether you want to sum the column above or the row to the left. To insert other formulas, position the insertion point and choose Table ⇨ Formula. Word displays the Formula dialog box. Here, you can build your own formula using a small but useful set of functions.

Because formula fields work in tables just as they do anywhere in Word, you can consult the section on the = field in Chapter 33 for reference information. However, there is one formula wrinkle that's unique to tables. Because your table calculations will use values from other table cells, you need a way to refer to specific cells in your formulas. Cells are named and referenced just as in Excel, with letters for the columns and numbers for the rows. However, a cell reference in a Word formula is always an absolute reference — if you move the formula to a different cell, it still bases its calculation on the same cells.

To reference an individual cell in a formula, just type its name, as in C3 or H12. Use the following methods to reference multiple cells:

Chapter 30: Getting Organized with Tables and Outlines

To Reference This	Use This Format or Term
A range of cells	C4:C8 or C4:F4
A group of separate cells	D2,E4,F6
All cells above in the same column	ABOVE
All cells below in the same column	BELOW
All cells to the left in the same row	LEFT
All cells to the right in the same row	RIGHT

Inserting an Excel worksheet

If you need more powerful computations than Word's formula fields can provide, insert an actual Excel worksheet directly into your document. You can insert one from scratch using the Insert Microsoft Excel Worksheet button on the Standard toolbar, or you can bring in an existing worksheet "live" by inserting it as an object. When you double-click the worksheet, Excel's menus and toolbars appear.

Working with Outlines

Outlining in Word is so simple that I don't think it needs much explanation. The main thing to remember is that Word's outlines are simply ordinary documents viewed in a different light. When you activate Outline view, the various headings are displayed in a hierarchically indented layout that makes it easy to see which heading signifies which level. To focus on a given level or on the hierarchy, you can hide (or collapse) subsidiary headings and body text below any heading, or below all headings of a certain level.

If you're tempted to use Outline view simply to get a bird's-eye view of your document to see its structure or find a certain section more easily, try Word's Document Map feature, described in Chapter 27.

Word normally bases the outline on the built-in heading styles, Heading 1 through Heading 9. However, you can assign a specific outline level to any paragraph directly, or via a custom style. See the sidebar "Using Built-in Heading Styles and Custom Outline Levels" in Chapter 29.

Caution

You should also keep in mind that when you move, cut, copy, or delete a heading in Outline view, all its subsidiary text goes along for the ride. This makes deleting (or clearing) text in Outline view quite dangerous — Undo protects you from catastrophe.

Table 30-1 summarizes the main commands and techniques you can use in Outline view.

Table 30-1 Outline View Commands and Procedures

To Perform This Task	Use This Command	Button	Keyboard Shortcut If Available
Collapse or expand all body text (all paragraphs except Heading 1 through Heading 9).	Click the All button on the Outlining toolbar.		Alt+Shift+A
Collapse or expand to given heading level.	Click the corresponding button (Show Heading 1, Show Heading 4, and so on).		
Collapse subsidiary text under a specific heading.	Double-click the plus sign beside the heading, or select the heading and click Collapse.		Alt+Shift+Gray minus (on numeric keypad)
Expand subsidiary text under a specific heading.	Double-click the plus sign beside the heading, or select the heading and click Expand.		Alt+Shift+Gray plus (on numeric keypad)
Show or hide text formatting.	Click the Show Formatting button.		Gray forward slash (on numeric keypad)
Promote a paragraph one level.	Click the Promote button.		Shift+Tab or Alt+Shift+left arrow
Demote a paragraph one level.	Click the Demote button.		Tab or Alt+Shift+right arrow
Promote or demote a paragraph to a specific level.	Drag the plus or minus sign at the left of the paragraph left or right to the desired indentation.		
Demote a paragraph to body text (Normal style).	Click the Demote to Body Text button.		Ctrl+Shift+N
Move a heading with its subsidiary text up in the document.	Drag the plus or minus sign at the left of the heading up, click the Up button.		Alt+Shift+up arrow

To Perform This Task	Use This Command	Button	Keyboard Shortcut If Available
Move a heading with its subsidiary text down in the document.	Drag the plus or minus sign at the left of the heading down or click the Down button.		Alt+Shift+down arrow
Cut, copy, or delete a heading and all its subsidiary text.	Click the plus sign beside the heading and choose Cut or Copy, or press Delete.		

Automatically collapsing body text

If you use Outline view primarily to see and work with your document's structure, displaying body text just obscures the forest for the trees. The first time you switch to Outline view, Word displays the entire document, so you have to shut off body text manually. In a big step forward, however, Word now retains the outline setting you last used during the current editing session.

If you use Outline view frequently, you may want to avoid the inconvenience of shutting off body text yourself. To do so, create a macro (VBA procedure) named ViewOutline that switches to Outline view and shuts off the display of all paragraphs except headings. The code is simple:

```
Sub ViewOutline()
With ActiveWindow.View
    .Type = wdOutlineView
    .ShowHeading 9
End With
End Sub
```

Because the macro has the same name as the standard Word command for switching to Outline view, it steps in when you choose View ⇨ Outline or use the corresponding keyboard shortcut, Ctrl+Alt+O. It even works when you click the little Outline View button to the left of the horizontal scroll bar.

Sorting a document by headings

Secret

If you're preparing a glossary or an alphabetically arranged reference of any type in Word, you don't need to worry about keeping everything in correct order while you write each article or chapter. Instead, use the Heading 1 style for your article headings, placing the alphabetical or numeric label at the beginning of each heading. When it comes time to bring order out of chaos, switch to Outline view and click the Show Heading 1 button, collapsing the whole document so that only the Heading 1 paragraphs are visible. Now select the entire document (Ctrl+A) and choose Table ⇨ Sort. As the headings magically rearrange themselves, all the subsidiary text follows along with them.

A macro for printing outlines

When you're in the throes of editing, keeping a printed copy of the document's outline at hand can help you stay focused and organized. Although you can print an outline by switching manually to Outline view and choosing File ⇨ Print, the following macro does the job for you, returning you to your previous view as soon as Word sends the outline to the printer. Assign the macro to a toolbar button or menu for quick access:

```
Sub PrintOutline()
With ActiveWindow.View
    intType = .Type
    .Type = wdOutlineView
    .ShowHeading 9
    Dialogs(wdDialogFilePrint).Show
    .Type = intType
End With
End Sub
```

AutoSummarize? Don't Get Your Hopes Up

Caution

Someday, maybe, we'll have computers that think like people. Word's AutoSummarize command is another tiny step in that direction, I guess, but it succeeds only in reminding us people that we still have some talents that machines can't emulate. Anyway, the AutoSummarize feature is supposed to be able to read through a document and pick out the key points, copying them to the top of the document or another document altogether. In my trials, the results were meaningless snippets of headings and body text, basically useless to anyone.

To be fair, Microsoft warns that you may have to "fine-tune" the summary, and if they mean by that "throw the whole thing out and do it yourself," well, consider yourself an informed consumer. My advice: If you need to create a document summary, make a copy of the document and use Outline view to pare away the details.

Conclusion

Using tables and outlines helps you structure your thoughts and keeps your documents neat and tidy. Word makes working with these organization aids a pleasant, productive process, so be sure to take advantage of these features. But wait until the post-millennium before you let Word summarize your documents for you — believe me, if AutoSummarize worked properly, I'd be using it at this very moment.

Chapter 31

The Book of Numbers

In This Chapter

- Numbering pages, chapters, and sections using advanced techniques
- Knowing when to use automatic numbered and bulleted lists, and when not to
- Customizing bullets to spice up your documents
- Setting up complex numbered lists with ease (well, at least without major stress)

Whether you're a tax collector, lawyer, or engineer, if you have a passion for numbering things, Word lets you scratch that itch in oh-so-many ways. Whether you need a simple list or a complex, multilevel numbering scheme, whether you want to print page numbers, part numbers, or serial numbers, Word gives you the tools.

Bulleted lists are covered in this chapter, too. Though they are number-less, they belong here because of their similarity to numbered lists, both in the function they serve in a document and in the techniques you need to use them in Word.

Word 2000 further refines its numbering features compared to earlier releases of the program. The most important advance is that Word can now produce multilevel numbering and bulleting semiautomatically. Along with the new capabilities introduced with Word 97 — being able to mix two or more numbering schemes in a single document, and to interweave multiple schemes at will — these features give Word the capacity to handle most any numbering chore.

Numbering Pages and Sections

Placing page numbers in a Word document is easy, but getting their look and location right can be a little tougher. Fortunately, Word makes the process of customizing page number entries painless. On the other hand, the provisions for inserting section numbers remain rudimentary.

Keep in mind that all page numbers calculated by Word are actually PAGE fields (Chapter 33 covers fields). If you have field code display turned on, you see this:

{ PAGE }

instead of the number. The Page Numbers command on the Insert menu and the Page Numbers button on the Header and Footer toolbar both insert these PAGE fields. Though Word doesn't have any menu commands or buttons for inserting section numbers, you can add the current section number anywhere you like by inserting a SECTION field. Choose Insert ⇨ Field, and then select Section in the Field names list.

Don't believe every page number you see. Word updates all PAGE fields automatically every time it repaginates, but before repagination occurs, the displayed page numbers may be inaccurate. This is especially likely if background (automatic) repagination is turned off. The Background Repagination check box is located on the General tab of the Options dialog box.

Custom page numbering using Insert Page Numbers

The standard Insert Page Numbers command, displayed by choosing Insert ⇨ Page Numbers, is actually pretty flexible. The initial Page Numbers dialog box lets you put the page numbers in any of several standard locations and decide whether the page number shows on the first page. If you choose the Format button, the Page Number Format dialog box shown in Figure 31-1 gives you more options: You can control the numbering style (1, 2, 3 versus i, ii, iii, and so forth), whether Word displays chapter as well as page numbers, and whether the page numbering should restart at each section break. This is plenty for many documents.

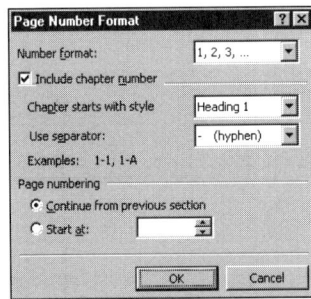

Figure 31-1: You can display the Page Number Format dialog box from the Page Numbers dialog box or by clicking the Format Page Number button in the Header and Footer toolbar.

If the standard choices don't suit your needs, Word provides tools for creating just about any conceivable custom page number layout. But it's easy to get confused once you leave the built-in options behind.

To customize the page numbers inserted with the standard Insert Page Numbers command, you need to know two things: First, the page numbers are placed into a separate frame, albeit a small one; and second, that frame is linked to the document's header or footer.

Items that are linked to a header or footer repeat on every page, which is what you want a page number to do. But because of that link, you can only reformat, move, or delete the page number when you're viewing the header or footer the frame belongs to. Because the standard page numbers live in a separate frame and aren't placed directly into the header or footer, they can be hard to work with. If you decide to change the page number's location, you have to drag the frame where you want it — you can't use paragraph formatting to do the trick. If you want to change the character formatting, you have to drag the mouse pointer directly over the frame — you can't select a page number by clicking to the left.

Using the Insert Page Numbers command for fancy page numbers

Though the Insert Page Numbers command is usually used for quick-and-dirty page numbers, you can use it to create fancier ones, too. Again, this command inserts page numbers in frames, which you can position anywhere on the page. Say you want frilly numerals along the outside edges of each page, so that facing pages are mirror images of one another, as shown in Figure 31-2. Start by choosing File ➪ Page Setup, and then check the Different Odd and Even box in the Layout tab.

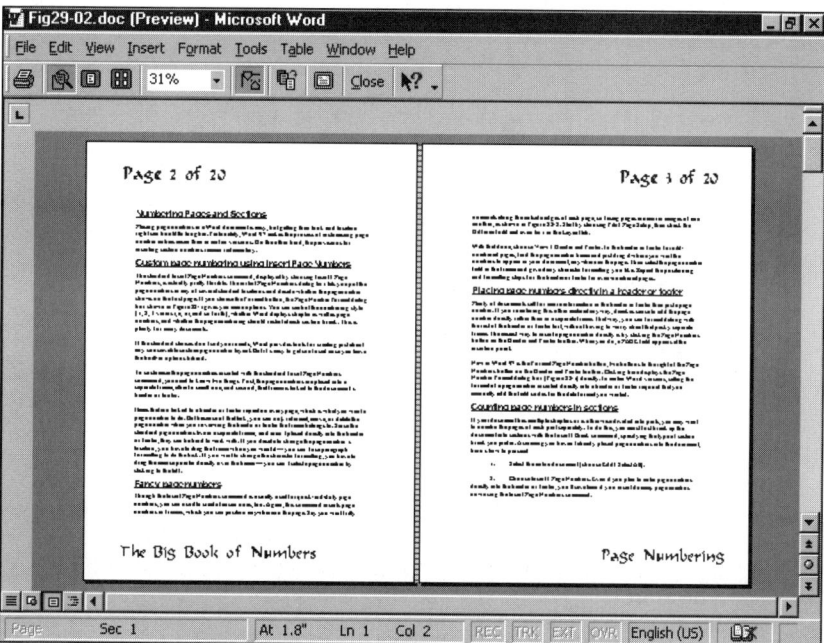

Figure 31-2: If you're producing a book or pamphlet, you must set up the document layout to use different odd and even headers and footers if you want to display page numbers on the outside edges of facing pages, as shown here.

With that done, choose View ⇨ Header and Footer. In the header or footer for odd-numbered pages, find the page number frame and just drag it where you want the numbers to appear in your document, anywhere on the page. Then select the page number field in the frame and give it any character formatting you like. Repeat the positioning and formatting steps for the header or footer for even-numbered pages.

Placing page numbers directly in a header or footer

Plenty of documents call for more information in the header or footer than just a page number. If you're entering this other material anyway, it makes sense to add the page number directly rather than in a separate frame. That way, you can format it along with the rest of the header or footer text, without having to worry about that pesky separate frame. The easiest way to insert a page number directly is by clicking the Page Numbers button on the Header and Footer toolbar. When you do, a PAGE field appears at the insertion point.

Be aware also of the Format Page Number button, located two buttons to the right of the Page Numbers button on the Header and Footer toolbar. Clicking here displays the Page Number Format dialog box (earlier Figure 31-1) directly. In earlier Word versions, setting the format of a page number inserted directly into a header or footer required that you manually add the field codes for the date format you wanted.

Counting page numbers in sections

If your document has multiple chapters or is otherwise divided into parts, you may want to number the pages of each part separately. To do this, you must first break up the document into sections with the Insert ⇨ Break command, specifying the type of section break you prefer. Assuming you haven't already placed page numbers into the document, here's how to proceed:

1. Select the entire document (choose Edit ⇨ Select All).

2. Choose Insert ⇨ Page Numbers. Even if you plan to enter page numbers directly into the header or footer, you'll save time if you insert dummy page numbers now using the Insert Page Numbers command.

3. Click Format to open the Page Number Format dialog box. Type **1** in the area labeled Start At to reset the page counter for the first page in each section. OK this dialog box.

4. Choose a location for the page number with the Position and Alignment settings. If you plan to place your own page numbers directly in the header or footer, it doesn't matter what you select here.

5. OK the Page Numbers dialog box. Word inserts the page numbers in a frame linked to the header or footer, resetting the page counter at the start of each selected section.

Now you can refine the layout and appearance of your page numbers. Choose View ⇨ Header and Footer to access the page number in its frame. You can move the frame around or change the character formatting of the number itself. On the other hand, if you want to insert your own page numbers directly into the header or footer, your first step is to select and delete the frame. Then you can click the Page Number button to add a new page number where you want it in the header or footer.

Considering that you're bothering to count the pages in each section, you probably want the page number entry to read something like Section 3, Page 15 or simply 3.15. Word doesn't provide a button for inserting section numbers. To add a SECTION field, you must choose Insert ⇨ Field and select Section in the Field Names list, or add the field manually (see Chapter 24). By default, layout changes you make in the header or footer of any section ripple throughout the document. See Chapter 29 if you want different header or footer layouts in each section.

Skipping page numbers

It's a rare problem, but sometimes you need to skip page numbers in a document. The solution is to insert a section break at the top of the page that interrupts the page number sequence. With the insertion point still in the new section, call up the Format Page Number dialog box (discussed in "Placing page numbers directly in a header or footer" earlier). Use the Start At box to restart the page counter at the correct number.

Including the total page count with page numbers

The Header and Footer toolbar now has a button for inserting the total document page count. This button makes it easy to design fancier page numbering entries such as "This is Page 29 of a Grand Total of 355 Pages." If you're satisfied with generic, less bombastic entries, you can produce a shorter entry with the same information in one step using another new button on the Header and Footer toolbar, Insert AutoText. Choosing Insert ⇨ AutoText ⇨ Header/Footer ⇨ Page X of Y produces an entry in the form "Page 5 of 6."

Removing page numbers

To delete page numbers from your document, you must remove them from the header or footer to which they are linked. In simple documents, deleting the number from any header or footer removes the numbers on every page. But this won't work if:

- You've set up the document with different headers and footers on odd and even pages (on the Layout tab of the Page Setup dialog box).

- You've activated a different header and footer for the first page (also via the Layout tab).
- You've broken up the document into two or more sections — and if you've severed the link between the sections (by deselecting the Same as Previous button on the Header and Footer toolbar).

In any of these situations, you have to remove the numbers separately from each independent header or footer. Navigate in turn to each part of the document, open the header or footer containing the page number, and delete the number. Remember, you can't see header or footer text clearly except in Print Preview. If you really want to make sure that all the numbers are gone, you should browse through your document in Print Preview.

Printing both section and document page numbers

In technical documents it's often considered good form to print two page numbers per page: one showing the current page's number in the current section, the other showing its number in the entire document. Though Word provides no command to perform this task automatically, you can accomplish it with calculation fields. I suggest two alternatives; neither technique is perfect, but both get the job done.

As a preliminary to either technique, make sure all sections are set to start numbering with page 1. You can do this with just two commands: First, use Select All to select the entire document; and then choose Insert ⇨ Page Numbers, click the Format button, and in the Page numbering area choose Start At and enter **1** in the adjacent field. (Don't forget that this procedure adds a frame containing a page number field to the footer, which you'll probably want to remove — see the preceding section, "Removing page numbers.") With either technique, be sure you update all of the fields in the document before you print it. Select the entire document and choose the Update Field command, which is conveniently available on the shortcut menu.

Note that complex techniques aren't necessary if you simply want to list the total pages in the document or a given section. In this case, use the fields { DOCPROPERTY "Pages" } or { SECTIONPAGES }, respectively.

Using bookmarks to mark section breaks

In the first method you must add a bookmark to every section break in the document. Starting with the insertion point at the beginning of the document, use the Find command to hunt down the section breaks by entering **^b** at Find What. When you choose Find Next, Word locates and selects the next section break. With the section break still selected — and without selecting any adjacent text — insert a bookmark to mark it. Using a consistent naming scheme and keeping the names short will help later on. I suggest Sec1, Sec2, and so forth.

In the header or footer where you want the page number to print, enter a standard page number field { PAGE } to place the section page number. In the first section, the document page number will be the same, so just insert a second PAGE field. In each subsequent section, however, you need a calculation field to display the document page number.

For the second section, this field would be { ={PageRef Sec1}+{Page}}. It adds the page count for section 1 to the page number of the current section. For section *n*, the required field would be { ={PageRef Sec1}+{PageRef Sec1} . . . +{PageRef Sec*n*-1}+{Page}}.

Now for the caveats: As you get into section 3 and beyond, it becomes a real bother to type all those PageRef items within each calculation field. And I shudder to think of the grunt work that would be needed if you swapped Section 18 with Section 2. You can avoid the latter problem by waiting until the document is otherwise final before inserting the calculation fields. But if you create such documents with any regularity, the time spent in developing a macro to automate the whole process is quickly repaid.

Using document variables to calculate the overall page number

The alternative method relies on a pair of variables to store the page count of the document. Begin by defining them in two fields at the very beginning of the document: {SEQ endpagecount \h \r {SectionPages} } and {SEQ startpagecount \h \r0}. The first of these fields simply places the page count of the first section in the endpagecount variable. The second field sets startpagecount to 0 (even though this is page 1). The \h switch hides the fields so they won't appear in your document text. Then enter two more fields at the start of each section except the first. Here they are:
{SEQ startpagecount \h \r {=[SEQ endpagecount \c} } }{SEQ endpagecount \h \r {={SectionPages}+{SEQ startpagecount \c} } }.

Here, the first field transfers the page number for the first page in the section from the accumulated count for all previous sections. The second field adds that value to the page count in the current section, giving the document page number of the last page in the section. Finally, set up your headers or footers to display the page numbers. Just as with the bookmark technique, a standard page number field displays the section page number in your header or footer. To output the document page number, add this field as well: {={SEQ startpagecount \c}+{Page}}.

Unlike the bookmark method, this approach enables you to use the same header or footer for all the sections. Its biggest problem is those hidden fields — you're apt to delete them because you can't see them. For safety's sake, turn on the display of field codes (the default keyboard shortcut is Alt+F9, or you can check the proper box in the View tab of the Options dialog box). Word still won't print the hidden fields.

Numbering chapters and sections

In longer documents that are divided into chapters, you can use several techniques to number the chapters and use those chapter numbers in headers, footers, and cross-references in the text.

The orthodox chapter numbering technique

The technique Word offers for chapter numbering works if all your chapters are contained in a single document file, or if you're using a master document to join the document files containing the individual chapters (see Chapter 32 for info on master documents). Start by making sure that all the chapter titles are assigned to the same paragraph style, which must be one of the built-in styles intended for headings (Heading 1, Heading 2, and so on). You must then actually number each of the chapter titles using the Bullets and Numbering command. You can apply a number to each title one at a time, but the easier way is to have Word do the numbering for you. From the Outline Numbered tab of the Bullets and Numbering dialog box, click Customize to display the dialog box shown in Figure 31-3.

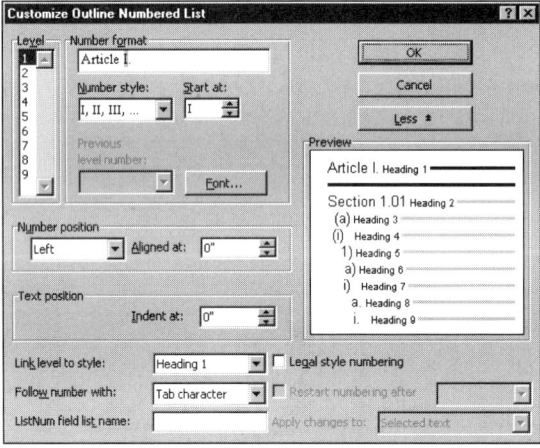

Figure 31-3: Use this dialog box to customize outline numbering schemes.

Using this dialog box, follow the steps described in "Numbering nonconsecutive paragraphs throughout a document" later to link the style you've used for the chapter titles to a numbering level. As soon as you OK the two dialog boxes, Word numbers all the chapter titles. If you want Word to automatically number sections as well as chapters, use the same technique for your section and subsection heading styles.

Alternative chapter numbering methods

Because I tend to store each chapter in a separate document file, and because I don't often use the master document feature, Word's regular chapter numbering feature doesn't work for me. Instead, I use a custom document property called *Chapter number* to store the number. (Chapter 12 covers document properties.) If you use this technique, first add the Chapter number property to the template you plan to use for all your chapter documents, and *then* start writing. Each time you start a new chapter document, open the File ⇨ Properties dialog box, switch to the Custom tab, and type in the correct value for the Chapter number property.

To place the current chapter's number anywhere in the document, you can use the following VBA procedure to insert the necessary field.

```
Sub InsertFieldForChapterNumber()
Selection.Fields.Add Range:=Selection.Range, _
    Type:=wdFieldEmpty, Text:= _
    "DOCPROPERTY ""Chapter number"" ", _
    PreserveFormatting:=True
End Sub
```

You can insert a reference to a *different* chapter using an INCLUDETEXT field. First, select and bookmark the chapter number where it appears in the other chapter. If you inserted the chapter number via a field, bookmark the field. (Remember the bookmark name.) Then insert the INCLUDETEXT field where you want the cross reference to appear. It should look similar to this example:

```
{ INCLUDETEXT "c:\\my documents\\Puzzles.doc" "ChapterNumber" \! }
```

Enclose the file containing the referenced chapter number in quotes, using double backslashes instead of single ones in the path. Then comes the name of the bookmark. The \! switch locks the field results so that the chapter number always appears as it does in the cross-referenced chapter.

With all your chapter number cross references in place, renumbering your chapters won't cause much grief. Open each chapter and change its custom Chapter number property. Then select the whole document and update the fields. If you've included cross references to other chapters, you need to update all the chapters a second time to ensure that these cross references are correct.

Including chapter numbers in headers or footers

Readers of complicated documents will appreciate it if you include the chapter number along with the page number in the header or footer, as in II-127 or 15.3.

To do this with the standard technique, you begin by numbering the chapters with the steps presented in "The orthodox chapter numbering technique" section earlier in this chapter. Then use either standard method for inserting page numbers (see "Custom page numbering using Insert Page Numbers" and "Placing page numbers directly in a header or footer" earlier). Get to the Format Page Number dialog box and check the Include Chapter Number box, and then choose the correct heading style from the list just below the box. You're in business.

Other ways to insert chapter numbers

You can also display the chapter number or title in the header or footer (or anywhere else) using the Insert ➪ Cross-Reference command. If you're inserting a chapter number, choose Heading number (no context) in the list at Insert Reference To in order to see only the chapter number.

If you include all the chapters in a single document, creating a single section for each chapter offers another route to inserting the current chapter in your document — in a header or footer, for example. Just insert a SECTION field where you want the chapter number to go. This technique gives you more control over the location and format of the chapter number, and you may even find it easier than the method just described.

Secrets of Numbered and Bulleted Lists

Unless you're a real writer — you know, an essayist, novelist, or poet — simple numbered and bulleted lists are bread-and-butter staples in your word-processing kitchen. As a Secrets reader, you probably know how to prepare them already.

Just in case you don't, I review the steps in this section. First, though, an important technoid point bears mentioning: The numbers and bullets that Word adds are part of the paragraph format. When you apply either to a paragraph, Word doesn't insert a numeral or bullet character into the text. Instead, the program adds the numbering or bullet information — including the specific numbering scheme or bullet character you choose — to the paragraph format.

Among other things, this means that you can't click alongside or select a paragraph number or bullet. When you cursor through a numbered list, you'll see that the insertion point skips over the numbers as though they are protected by a force field. It also means that when you copy the paragraph mark of a numbered paragraph and paste it elsewhere, Word numbers the destination paragraph automatically.

What's new, and newish, in Bullets and Numbering

Before we go any further, it's time to list the major changes in Word's list-numbering features. Because many of the important refinements occurred in Word 97, I've included them along with the brand-new features in Word 2000:

- Word 2000 adds automatic, *multiple-level* numbering and bullets — previously, it could only automate single-level lists.

- You can now use graphical bullets in any document, not just Web pages.

- You can set up outline-style numbering using any paragraph style, not just the built-in heading styles.
- You have complete control over customized outline-style numbering schemes.
- In each new paragraph in a numbering sequence, you can tell Word whether to continue the sequence in order or restart it at a specified number.

Creating numbered and bulleted lists

Permit me to remind you that Word provides three alternative methods for creating numbered and bulleted paragraphs. For the first two, you place the insertion point in the target paragraph, or select a group of paragraphs, and then either:

- Click the appropriate button, Numbering or Bullets.

Or:

- Choose Format ➪ Bullets and Numbering and select the bullet or number format you want from the resulting dialog box (Figure 31-4). This is the option to use when you want direct, certain control over the format of your numbering scheme (as in 1., 2., 3. . . ., I., II., III. . . ., or even (A), (B), (C) . . .) or bullets (such as ●, •, or ¤).

To use the third alternative, just place the insertion point on a blank line, and:

- Let Word format your list automatically as you type them — I devote considerable hot air in this chapter to details on automatic lists.

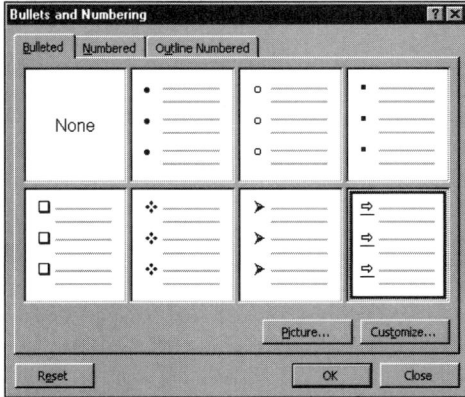

Figure 31-4: The Bullets and Numbering dialog box. Select a format for bulleted lists from the Bulleted tab, one of three tabs.

Using the Bullets and Numbering buttons

Secret

When you apply bullets to a paragraph with the Bullets toolbar button, the bullet character you get is the last one you used. Likewise, when you click the Numbering button, the paragraph receives the numbering scheme you last applied.

Removing numbering and bullets

Two quick ways to turn off paragraph numbering or bullets are:

- Select the paragraphs (for a single paragraph, just place the insertion point in it) and click the appropriate button.
- Click just to the left of the first character in the paragraph (not counting the number or bullet) and press Backspace.

Why you should use automatic numbered and bulleted lists

To activate the automated, as-you-type method for adding simple numbered and bulleted lists, check the Automatic Numbered Lists and Automatic Bulleted Lists boxes in the AutoFormat As You Type tab of the Tools ➪ AutoCorrect dialog box.

I recommend this method because it's so easy. Not only are you spared from the extra steps of selecting the paragraphs, but you don't need to call up and fiddle with a dialog box to choose the format for your numbering system or bullets.

Instead, here's all you need do:

1. On a blank line, type the "number" for your first point, as in (**1**), **I.**, or **A)** — you must either include punctuation after the number or press Tab in Step 2. Or type a bullet character (see "Characters to type for automatic bullets" later in this chapter).
2. Press Space or Tab.
3. Type the paragraph text.
4. Hit Enter.

Word starts the next point in the sequence with the appropriate, correctly formatted number or bullet. From then on, you can add more numbered or bulleted paragraphs by simply pressing Enter after typing some text in the current paragraph. Word also applies this formatting to the original paragraph, converting the numbers or bullet character you typed there into the automatic kind.

Secret

To finish the list, hit Enter a second time after the last point to start a new ordinary paragraph. Alternatively — and this is new in Word 2000 — you can press Backspace to "delete" the number or bullet character. What this actually does is turn off the numbering or bulleting setting in the paragraph format.

Remember, the number or bullet character Word displays is actually part of the paragraph formatting, not the document proper. Therefore, it can't be directly edited. The automatically formatted paragraphs use an indent setting to imitate any spaces or tabs you typed in front of the number or bullet. In addition, Word copies any character formatting, such as bold or italics, that you applied to the number or bullet characters you originally typed.

Secret

Even if you've turned automatic bulleted lists off, Word automatically adds bullets to each new paragraph you insert after a bulleted paragraph. Automatic bulleting really refers to the way Word recognizes certain ordinary characters typed at the beginning of a paragraph and adds a bullet to the paragraph automatically.

Multiple-level automatic numbering and bullets

Many numbered and bulleted lists are organized hierarchically. The classic multiple-level list is the standard outline format you learned in grade school:

I. Main point
II. Second main point
    a. Subsidiary point 1
        i. Sub-subsidiary point 1
        ii. Sub-subsidiary point 2
    b. Subsidiary point 2
III. Third main point

Word's automatic numbering and bulleting has been beefed up to create such lists with a minimum of effort on your part.

Start an automatic multiple-level list with the technique outlined in the previous section: Type a number or bullet character, press Space or Tab, type the text for the first item, and then hit Enter. At the start of the new paragraph, Word places the appropriate number or bullet for the same level of the hierarchy.

If the new paragraph is supposed to be at the same level as the previous paragraph, all you have to do is type the text. If you want to change the level, press Tab to demote the paragraph to a lower level in the outline, or Shift+Tab to promote it. Finish the list the same way you would a single-level list, by pressing Enter twice.

When not to use automatic numbering and bullets

When shouldn't you use on-the-fly numbering and bullets? Only when you're creating unusually fancy numbered or bulleted lists. Word's attempt to manage lists automatically will almost certainly screw up any complicated format you design, so turn off the autonumber and bullets feature.

Don't be scared of autonumbering

If you're used to older versions of Word, you may be avoiding the automatic numbering and bullets features for fear of bugs. It's time to put away your worries.

Before Word 97 came along, applying numbers to a list after you typed it (not to on-the-fly lists) could erase parts of the text. This would happen to any paragraph that started with a number or a letter followed by punctuation. The problem has been fixed.

Using automatic lead-in emphasis

In numbered and bulleted lists, the first phrase or sentence of each point often gets special formatting to make it stand out. Here's an example:

- **New features.** This year, Tony's Toy Turtles are made of wood, not plastic, and they now have moveable, jointed feet.
- **New price.** We've rolled back the suggested retail price to $25.99.
- **New possibilities.** Tony's Toy Turtles go where your imagination goes!

Secret

When automatic numbering and bulleting is on, Word detects such "lead-in emphasis" in the first point and automatically turns on the same formatting at the beginning of each subsequent numbered or bulleted point. When you conclude the lead-in text by typing a punctuation mark — dashes, colons, and semicolons work as well as periods, question marks, and exclamation points — Word reverts back to the standard formatting for the paragraph's style.

Creating empty numbered or bulleted lists semi-automatically

Automatic numbering or bulleting only works if you type something — anything other than spaces or tab characters — in the paragraphs. In other words, you can't create an empty list of numbered or bulleted points and then go back and fill in the list.

The closest you can get to that ideal is to place a single character in each paragraph, perhaps an x. If you're using as-you-type automatic numbering, you type the initial number or bullet character, press Space or Tab, and then type x, finally pressing Enter to finish the line. On the next line, because Word has entered the number or bullet already, all you have to do is type another x. If you'll be applying the numbers or bullets using the toolbar buttons or the dialog box, begin by entering a series of paragraphs each containing an x. Select the group of paragraphs and then apply the numbers or bullets. With either method, once the numbers or bullets are in place, you're free to erase those x's, if you really must have an empty list.

Characters to type for automatic bullets

For bullets, you don't actually type the bullet symbols at the beginning of the first bulleted point. Instead, you type one or two ordinary keyboard characters and Word converts it (or them) into a corresponding bullet. Table 31-1 shows the characters to type to get different types of automatic bullets.

Table 31-1   Word Creates Automatic Bulleted Lists

For Bullets Like These	Type As the First Characters on the Line	Followed By
•	o (the letter)	tab
•	*	space
➢	>	space or tab
-	- (hyphen)	space or tab
–	– (en dash)	space or tab
■	-- (two hyphens)	space or tab
—	— (em dash, not entered with AutoFormat as you type)	space or tab
⇨	=> (equal sign followed by right triangle bracket)	space or tab
→	->	space or tab

Maintaining a consistent format: Paragraph styles for automatic numbering and bullets

Because Word stores numbering and bullets as part of the paragraph format information, they can be added to paragraph styles. You should create such styles if you're producing a polished document and want to be sure that numbered lists on page 12 have the same layout as numbered lists on page 45. Of course, when you use styles to apply bullets and numbers, you have to forgo the convenience of the as-you-type method, but this is a small sacrifice for a professional look.

You can add a number or bullet format to a paragraph style in the Modify Style dialog box. The quicker alternative: Format a paragraph in the document to your liking, reapply the same style name in the style list on the formatting toolbar, and then choose Reapply the Formatting of the Style to the Selection? when Word gives you that option.

Assign keyboard shortcuts to the numbering and bullets commands

If you do any amount of business writing, bulleted and numbered lists are an almost daily chore. For faster editing, I recommend you assign keyboard shortcuts to the commands that toggle numbers and bullets on or off. The commands you need are FormatNumberDefault and FormatBulletDefault. Once you've made the assignments, pressing the shortcut keys does exactly the same thing as clicking the corresponding toolbar button.

Bullet-specific secrets

Although bulleted and numbered items share much in common, you should know a few particulars about each type of list.

Any character can be a bullet

One reason to apply bullets via the Bullets and Numbering dialog box rather than automatically is to access alternative bullet symbols. You're limited to the choices shown in Table 31-1 when you use as-you-type, automatic bullets. With the dialog box, you can select any character from any active font as the bullet. From the main dialog box select an existing bullet format and click Customize and then Bullet. (Don't bother with the Font button unless you want to change the bullet's size or character format — you can select a bullet character from any installed font using the character chart that appears when you click Bullet.) Once you've custom "bulletized" the first paragraph in your list, Word automatically adds the same custom bullet to subsequent paragraphs until you press Enter twice.

While most of the standard bullets are drawn from the Symbol font, many other dingbat fonts have suitable symbols. The Windows font Wingdings is a good place to start looking. Monotype Sorts (equivalent to the PostScript font Zapf Dingbats) has a wide selection of more conservative symbols; Sorts comes with Office and should already be installed on your system. For more unusual collections of bullets, try U-Design's series of specialty fonts, which includes offerings such as Bill's Big Bullets, Bill's Peculiars, and Bill's DECOrations (www.gs1.com/utf/utf.htm). Wacky bullets are fun, but just remember that the whole point of the bullet is to draw attention to the text it marks. If the bullet itself attracts too much attention, you're defeating the purpose.

Using graphical bullets

Word 97 introduced graphical bullet "characters" — bitmaps, really — but restricted their use to Web pages. In Word 2000, you can use these "picture bullets" easily, in any type of document.

To add a graphical bullet to one or more paragraphs, open the Insert ⇨ Bullets and Numbering dialog box. After selecting the Bulleted tab, click Picture. Word presents the Clip Gallery (see Chapter 8) with a selection of small images suitable for bullets. Pick the one you want and then click Insert Clip to add it to the selected paragraphs. Word formats the paragraphs just as it does for ordinary bulleted paragraphs. Subsequent new paragraphs pick up the picture bullet, too, until you press Enter twice.

Caution

You can't assign picture bullets to the bullet styles available in the Bullets and Numbering dialog box. Also, the bitmap bullets look great within Word and when displayed in your browser, but because they are bitmaps they don't print quite as sharply as ordinary bullets.

Numbering secrets

Some situations demand complex numbering schemes. This section offers tips on solving numbering problems Word users occasionally encounter.

Creating automatic numbered lists that start with zero

Word lets you use zero to start a sequence of autonumbered points, but only if you

(0) Punctuate it, as in this example (instead of (0), you could have typed 0. but not 0 alone); and

(1) Follow it with a tab, not a space.

Numbering nonconsecutive paragraphs in sequence

Communication experts insist that numbered lists should be simple, but they probably haven't tried writing step-by-step instructions for Word. When you must cover lots of options and caveats, a point can get too long. To break up the layout, you must resort to unnumbered paragraphs between the numbered points.

If the list is short, the best way to do this is with Word's as-you-type automatic numbering (otherwise, see the next section). The key to making the list work properly is to type all the paragraphs in the list before you mess with the numbering scheme. In other words, let Word add numbers even to those paragraphs that shouldn't have them — don't hit the Backspace key to remove a number.

Once all the paragraphs have been entered, go back and remove the numbering where you don't want it. To do this, place the insertion point in the paragraph and click the Numbering button (so that it's no longer pressed in). If you have assigned the equivalent commands, FormatNumberDefault, to a keyboard shortcut, you can press the appropriate shortcut keys instead.

When you remove paragraph numbers with this method, Word maintains the links between the paragraphs in the list. In fact, you can go back and add or delete entire paragraphs without disrupting the sequence. If you don't have as-you-type numbering turned on, there's another way to accomplish the same effect. Type all the points to be numbered first, select the entire list, and click the Numbering button. Now go back and turn numbering off for any specific paragraphs you like.

Because you're going to open the Bullets and Numbering dialog box at some point, I'm obligated to mention that it provides still another method for properly maintaining a numbering sequence in a list containing unmarked paragraphs. The key control is the radio button Continue Previous List. I'll say no more, because this method is harder to use. It may be helpful if you need to interweave two or more numbered lists, but I recommend outline numbering in that situation — and that's the topic of the next section.

Numbering nonconsecutive paragraphs throughout a document

When you need to alternate numbered and unnumbered paragraphs, Word's automatic numbering is fine if the list is short. When the numbering scheme extends over pages or chapters, however, automatic numbering becomes unwieldy. Word finally has a viable alternative solution that lawyers will love.

The key is to associate a numbering sequence with a particular paragraph style. In Word 95 you could number paragraphs with this technique, but you had to use the built-in heading styles (Heading 1, Heading 2, and so on). This meant you couldn't use them to organize your document in Outline view unless you wanted all your headings numbered. Word now lets you assign any paragraph style to a numbering level, removing the previous limitations. Some setup work is required, but nothing onerous:

1. Select and redefine a style you want to use for the numbered paragraphs, or create a new one for this purpose. (One called Numbered Paragraphs would be in order, don't you think?) Choose formatting options for the style that blends harmoniously with the intervening text.

   You can use the Normal style for numbered paragraphs if most of your document's paragraphs will be numbered. But heed this important caveat: Remember that the default heading styles are all based on Normal. This means that all your headings will be numbered too, unless you modify each heading style so it is based on None, or on some other style.

2. Choose Format ⇨ Bullets and Numbering and then select the Outline Numbered tab. In the dialog box pick any of the numbering layouts you don't plan to use for other documents and click Customize. When you finally arrive at the Customize Outline Numbered List dialog box (earlier Figure 31-3), click More to reveal additional options you need for the task at hand.

   All the options in the dialog box pertain to the number level that is currently selected in the skinny Level box at the top left. Ordinarily you will be using the level 1, which should already be selected, so you won't need to change the setting there.

3. After you choose the number format options you like, the key step is to associate the selected level with the paragraph style you chose in Step 1. Pick the style from the list at Link Level to Style. OK the dialog boxes in succession until you return to your document.

From now on, whenever you apply the chosen style to a paragraph, Word gives the paragraph the next number in the sequence. It doesn't matter how many plain paragraphs separate it from the last numbered item, and you can edit to your heart's content — each time you add or remove numbered paragraphs or change their order, Word updates the numbering sequence for the whole document.

Numbering blocks of repeated text: Serial numbers, ticket numbers

With some printing jobs, the ultimate output is a series of items that are identical except for a number. If you're printing tickets for a drawing, each ticket needs its own number. If you're printing product labels, you may want to put a unique serial number on each one. Of several possible solutions, here's the easiest one, in my opinion. It uses Word's Envelopes and Labels feature to duplicate the text and relies on a couple of fields to provide the numbering. Start by choosing Tools ⇨ Envelopes and Labels. Select the Labels tab to display the Envelopes and Labels dialog box.

Type the repeating text in the Address field. Though you can't format the text using Word's toolbars and main menu in the Labels dialog box, you still have access to formatting commands via the shortcut menu and keyboard shortcuts. I cover techniques for more sophisticated formatting control in a moment.

To place the serial number in the text, you must use a Word field. Press Ctrl+F9 to insert the special pair of curly braces required for a field. The completed field should look like this:

```
{ SEQ counter }
```

where *counter* is any variable name you like — I'll use SerialNumber for the discussion here. Now select an output layout by clicking Options. OK the layout dialog boxes as necessary until you're back at the main Envelopes and Labels dialog box.

Assuming you want to print more than a single page's worth of your repeating text, you must now click New Document. This creates a one-page document containing a table whose dimensions match your layout settings. Word pours your repeating text into each cell, but you won't see the results of the fields until you update them.

To create additional pages, start by inserting a section break at the end of the document (choose Insert ⇨ Break and specify Next Page). Now select the entire document and copy it to the clipboard. With the insertion point at the end of the document (just past the section break), paste repeatedly until you have enough pages for the number of tickets you need. To update the fields, select the entire document and press Alt+Shift+U. Check the numbering sequence. If everything looks right, you're ready to print.

Starting a numbering sequence with a number other than 1

With the preceding procedure, the numbering sequence in the output always starts with 1. A bit more work is required to start with another number (perhaps you want people to think you've already sold lots of tickets). Follow the steps just described until you have finished making copies of the original page. Before updating the fields, move the insertion point to the very beginning of the document (at the top left of the first table cell). Your task here is to insert a field to set your counter.

This time, the Field dialog box is accessible, so you don't have to type in the entire field manually unless you prefer that route. Choose Insert ➪ Field and then select Numbering in the Categories list and Seq in the Field Names list. Now type SerialNumber (or the name you chose for the number variable) in the Field Codes box.

Click Options and choose the Field Specific Switches tab. Here, click \h and then \r to add these two switches to the field. The \h switch hides the new field so that it doesn't appear in the printed document, while the \r switch sets the counter. Finish the field by typing in a value one less than the number you want to print on the first ticket (if you want the first ticket numbered 101, type 100 here). The completed field contents should look like this:

```
{SEQ counter \h \r 100}
```

OK the dialog box to enter the new field in the document. Now when you update the field, the numbers throughout the document will reflect the new starting value.

Bookmark tricks with repeating text

Suppose you need bullets or special tab settings in your repeating text. Or what if the repeating text changes with each printing, as it would if you were printing tickets for a monthly concert? You can use the same basic technique to format the repeating text or to build a template for your repeating-text document that eliminates future hassles with the Envelopes and Labels dialog box.

The basic idea is this: Enter a REF (reference) field in the Address area of the Labels dialog box instead of typing the repeating text directly. This REF field takes the form { REF *bookmark* }, where *bookmark* is a bookmark name you create for the repeating text. You still need to insert separately the SEQ field that numbers each repeated item.

With the Address entry complete, click New Document. To set up the repeating text, create a separate section for it before or after the body of the document. After typing the text, format it to taste and then bookmark it, selecting all the text, including the final paragraph mark, before you choose Insert ➪ Bookmark. Give the bookmark the same name you used earlier in the REF field.

Now, when you update the fields, Word fills each cell with a copy of the formatted bookmarked text and a unique number. When you print, don't waste paper — use the Pages field to exclude the page containing the bookmarked text. If you expect to reuse the same layout with other text, you should save the document as a template. Each time you open a new document based on the template, you can print as soon as you revise the bookmarked text and update the fields.

Including multiple outline numbers on a single line

With the combination of its classy automatic numbering system and a special field type, LISTNUM, Word lets you set up more complex numbering formats than ever before. For example, in many legal documents, a new subpoint and a new sub-subpoint begin on the same line, while the sub-subpoints that follow are listed separately.

Check out this example, based on Word's new built-in legal-style numbered list:

> Article I.
>
> . . .
>
> > Section 1.01(a) . . .
> >
> > > (b) . . .
> >
> > Section 1.02 (a) . . .
> >
> > > (b) . . .
> > >
> > > (c) . . .
>
> Article II.

Note the two lines that begin with "Section." Both list sub-subpoint (a) on the same line rather than pushing it down as in a more generic outline format. But on the following line, the next sub-subpoint appears alone.

To generate this type of numbering scheme, start by applying a built-in scheme to your text using the Outline Numbered dialog box. At this point, you should have a conventional outline going, with only one level shown in each paragraph:

> Article I.
>
> . . .
>
> > Section 1.01
> >
> > > (a) . . .
> >
> > Section 1.02
> >
> > > (a) . . .
> > >
> > > (b) . . .
>
> Article II.

To place those missing (a)'s on the same line as the section numbers, you have to manually insert a LISTNUM field on each incomplete line. Position the insertion point where the (a) should go and:

1. Choose Insert ⇨ Field.
2. Choose Numbering in the Categories list.
3. Double-click ListNum in the Field Names list (or choose it and then choose OK).

How the LISTNUM field works

By default, each LISTNUM field in the same paragraph inserts the formatted number (or other list item) at the next lower level. To see how this works, select and copy the field and paste it repeatedly at the insertion point. If necessary, turn off field codes display. You should see something like this, depending on which numbering scheme you started with:

```
Section 2.01 (a) (i) 1) a) i) a. i.
```

If you insert LISTNUM in consecutive paragraphs that aren't already numbered, you get the next number in the sequence at the current level.

Conclusion

This chapter definitely qualifies as a course of delicacies for the Word secrets gourmand. You may not use the techniques described here every day, but there will come a time when you need these fancy techniques for numbering pages, chapters, sections, lists, and special items.

Chapter 32

Creating Long and Technical Documents

In This Chapter

- Understanding how captions work, and an improved way to add captions
- Cross-referencing any document element
- Customizing indexes and tables of contents using fields
- Understanding the pros and cons of the Master Document feature for building long documents
- Using tips and tricks for group document development

From the very first version (for DOS, I mean), Microsoft Word has aspired to be a serious publishing tool, not just a word processor. Though the early attempts fell way short of that goal, thousands of person-years of intensive development have paid off: Microsoft has built a software juggernaut that can handle very long and very complicated documents with a minimum of grunt work on your part.

In this chapter, I lump various features that are likely to come in handy when you finally get around to editing that annotated version of *War and Peace*. But if your plans are less expansive, don't pass up this chapter — most of the features described here are useful in shorter, simpler documents as well.

Adding Reference Information

When you put together a document of any complexity, the body of the document needs lots of support in the way of reference elements such as cross-references, numbered captions, footnotes and endnotes, indexes, and tables of contents. Word has an amazingly rich set of tools for adding these items painlessly, and for keeping their text and numbers up to date semiautomatically as you make changes in the document. Yet despite all the effort Microsoft has invested in its flagship application, rough edges remain. But you can smooth out a few of them.

Inserting captions

The Insert ⇨ Caption command sounds promising. It's a real challenge to come up with pithy, informative descriptions for figures and tables, and I would love to delegate the task to my computer. Figure 32-1 shows the Caption dialog box. I forgot to add this to the table chapter. If you click that little + icon in the upper-left corner of the table and then right-click, you can add a caption to a table.

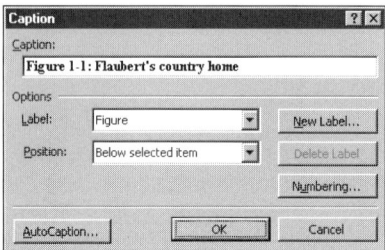

Figure 32-1: The Caption dialog box

Alas, the Caption command doesn't write your captions for you. Instead, it simply gets you started, placing a caption label (as in Figure 32-1) at the insertion point and applying the Caption paragraph style to your text.

But what makes Word's captions so useful is that the numbers in that caption label are fields. You can add captions anywhere in the document in any order; as soon as you update the fields, Word numbers all your captions in proper sequence. Another nice touch is that you can tell Word where the caption should go, above or below the selected item. But even better is the AutoCaption feature. When you turn on AutoCaption for a particular item type, Word starts a new paragraph with a caption label formatted to your specifications every time you insert an item of that type. Items you can autocaption include pictures, tables, and any object type you can link or embed in the document via OLE. If the item is a picture or a linked or embedded object, Word places the caption in a text box sized to match the object.

Problems with the caption command

So much for the sweetness and light. Unfortunately, the Insert Caption command has its dark side:

- Although you can include the chapter number in a caption label (as in "Figure 23-2"), this feature suffers from the same limitations as its counterpart in the Page Numbers Format dialog box. It only works if you use one of the built-in heading styles for your chapter title and number that style via the Format ⇨ Bullets and Numbering command. If you use a style called Chapter Title instead of Heading 1 to announce new chapters, you're sunk.

- For some reason, Word won't add a period or colon for you at the end of an automatic caption. Many caption labels have the form Figure 23-3: or Figure 23-4., but Word forces you to type the extra punctuation every time.

Better captions

If you're willing to give up automatic captions, an AutoText or AutoCorrect entry overcomes the limitations of the Insert Caption command. You can even use the command to get you started:

1. Place the insertion point into a blank paragraph and choose Insert ⇨ Caption.

2. Choose the label you want and select a numbering scheme, but don't activate chapter numbering. Choose OK to insert the caption into your document.

3. Place the insertion point in the caption label, just in front of the number field. Here, insert a field for the chapter number. Here are two of several possible solutions:

   If you use a single document to hold all the chapters in your book, you can number the chapter title paragraphs using an autonumbered paragraph style (see Chapter 31). In this case, you would use a STYLEREF field to enter the chapter number in your caption via a reference to that style of the chapter title paragraphs. The field you need looks like this: { STYLEREF "Chapter Title" \s }. (Put the name of the paragraph style inside the quotes.)

   If your chapter titles are numbered "by hand" (you just typed the number where it belongs in your document), use a Ref field such as { REF ChapterNumber }. You must also assign a corresponding bookmark — in this case named ChapterNumber — to the chapter number where you typed it into your text.

4. Type a hyphen (-) after the field you entered at Step 3, and then go to the end of the label inserted by Word at Step 2. Type a colon or a period if you want.

5. At this point, you may want to change the Caption paragraph style to a custom style specific for this type of caption, such as Table Caption, Equation Caption, and so on.

6. Select the entire caption label, including the paragraph mark. Assign it to an AutoCorrect entry (such as fg) or to a named AutoText entry (go with AutoText if you want to assign it to a button).

From then on you can insert a complete caption into any document by typing the AutoCorrect abbreviation or inserting the AutoText entry. If you later add, delete, or reorder your chapters, you have only to update the fields in the document to correct all your captions. (If you type in the chapter numbers yourself as discussed in Step 3, you must first locate and change the bookmarked chapter numbers.)

Secret

What is a caption, really? In Word's eyes, it is any paragraph containing an SEQ field that refers to one of the labels listed in the Caption dialog box. The paragraph's style doesn't matter.

Fording cross-references

Word's cross-referencing feature will save you truckloads of time in big documents, once you learn how to use it. There's nothing to be afraid of, really.

Creating a cross-reference

In outline, the mechanics of setting up a cross-reference are easy. Choose Insert ⇨ Cross-Reference, make a few selections from the dialog box shown in Figure 32-2, and click OK. Voilà, instant cross-reference.

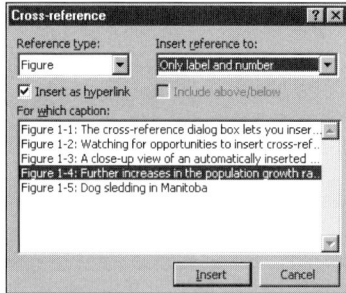

Figure 32-2: The Cross-Reference dialog box

Ah, but the devil is in the details. What's confusing are all those choices in the dialog box. The following explanations may help:

- **Reference Type.** Select the type of item you want the cross-reference to refer to — a figure, a table, or what have you — not the type of reference, whatever that would mean. But even this clarification is a bit misleading: In many cases, what you're really selecting is the type of caption to refer to, not the underlying item type. For example, when you select Figure, you're telling Word you want to cross-reference a figure caption, not the graphic it describes. You'll see why this matters in a moment.

- **Insert Reference To.** Choose the information you want to place at the insertion point. The function of this field would have been clearer if Microsoft had labeled it "Insert the Following Information" or just "Insert."

- **Insert as Hyperlink.** If this box is checked, as it is by default, you can click the cross-reference to move directly to the item it references. This makes the cross-reference command the easy way to build hypertext documents (hyperlinks are covered in Chapter 12).

- **Include Above/Below.** See "Creating above and below references" next.

- **For Which Caption (or Other Item Type).** This area contains a list of all the items of the selected Reference type, from which you can pick the one item you want to cross-reference. Just be aware that when you have selected a type of caption, what you see is a list of captions, not a list of the actual pictures, tables, or equations they describe. If you haven't inserted a caption, you can't cross-reference the corresponding item. And if you choose, say, Table as the Reference type, but you haven't captioned any tables, the box will be empty no matter how many tables your document contains.

By the way, the cross-reference feature works fine with captions inserted using the alternative method described in "Better captions" earlier.

Creating "above" and "below" references

You can have Word automatically add "above" or "below" to a cross-reference, depending on the relative location of the cross-referenced item, as in "Please see Figure 23-2 above." When you update the cross-references, Word makes sure that the correct term (above or below) is inserted in your text, even if the cross-referenced item has been moved. If the Include Above/Below box is available, checking it adds an above/below cross-reference to the other information selected via the Insert Reference To field. If the box is grayed out, you need to insert two cross-references to build an entry like the example at the beginning of this paragraph: first, one for the main cross-reference information, and then another to the same caption or other object with above/below selected in the Insert Reference To field.

More cross-reference arcana

Secret

If your document contains numbered paragraphs, you can insert a cross-reference consisting of the number of any numbered paragraph. In legal documents, for example, cross-references such as ". . . exceptions noted in paragraph I.A.2.e . . ." are common.

Set up paragraph number cross-references by selecting Numbered Item or Heading in the Reference Type field of the Cross-Reference dialog box. Among the items that then appear in the Insert Reference To field, three create these paragraph number cross-references (see Table 32-1). The actual appearance of the cross-reference in your document depends on which item you choose. It may also depend on the relative locations of the current paragraph and the paragraph you're cross-referencing.

Say you're working in paragraph c of section 3 and you want to cross-reference paragraph b in the same section. If you select the Paragraph Number item, the cross-reference appears as b in the document. If you cross-reference paragraph e in section 2 instead, you would get 2e as the cross-reference. On the other hand, if you select Paragraph Number (Full Context), the two cross-references would read 3b and 2e, respectively.

Table 32-1 Options for Paragraph Number Cross-References

Choice in Insert Reference To	Cross-Reference Inserted in Document	Example		
		Number of referenced paragraph	Number of paragraph where cross-reference appears	How cross-reference appears in document
Paragraph or Heading number	The paragraph's own number, along with enough of the complete number sequence specifying its location in the outlined numbered list to identify it	I.A.2.b.	I.A.2.d.	b
		I.A.2.b.	I.A.5.g.	2.b
		I.A.2.b.	III.C.3.b	I.A.2.b
Paragraph or Heading number (no context)	Only that paragraph's number no matter what its location in the outline numbered list	I.A.2.b.	III.C.3.b	b
Paragraph or Heading number (full context)	The full number sequence that specifies the paragraph's location in the outline numbered list	I.A.2.b.	I.A.2.d.	I.A.2.b.

Cross-references to nonheader paragraphs

Secret

Word's cross-reference command can cross-reference text based on the style it is formatted with, but only if that style is one of the built-in header styles. To cross-reference text based on another style, use a STYLEREF field. See "A secret use for character styles" in Chapter 28 for one suggestion on using STYLEREF fields.

Adding footnotes and endnotes

Adding a footnote or endnote to a document couldn't be easier: Choose Insert ⇨ Footnote and complete the dialog box. When you choose OK, Word inserts a *reference mark* (the number or symbol in the body text that signifies an associated note) and places the insertion point into a special area at the bottom of the window where you can type in the note text.

If you're working in Normal, Outline, or Web Layout view, this area is a separate pane, with its own scroll bars. In Print Layout view, you work with the notes directly on the document, but Word keeps them where they belong (at the bottom of the page or at the end of the document). When you insert a footnote, you can choose whether to restart the note numbering scheme on every page or with every section, or to number the footnotes continuously throughout the document. Indicate which of those options you want by choosing Options from the Footnote and Endnote dialog box.

You can insert a note directly, bypassing the Footnote dialog box, with a keyboard shortcut. By default, Alt+Ctrl+F inserts a footnote, Alt+Ctrl+E, an endnote.

Resting the mouse pointer over a footnote or endnote reference mark displays a ScreenTip containing the note text, right there in the document. The only reason to reopen the footnote or endnote pane is to edit or format the note text.

About footnotes and endnotes in Web pages

Secret

When you save a Word document containing footnotes or endnotes as a Web page, Word converts the reference marks into bona fide HTML hyperlinks. Each reference mark, of course, is linked to its note text at the bottom of the page — which in turn is linked back to the reference mark. Regardless of whether the notes are officially footnotes or endnotes, they all wind up at the end of the Web document, because Word converts the entire document, no matter how long it is, into a single Web page.

Using symbols instead of numbers for reference marks

Select the number format for footnotes and endnotes and their reference marks by choosing Options in the Footnote and Endnote dialog box. If your document includes both footnotes and endnotes, they should have different number formats or your readers won't know which is which.

In documents that have both types of notes, symbols (such as *, †, ‡, and §) are often used for the footnotes and numbers for the endnotes. You find these symbols as the last option in the Number Format list in the Note Options dialog box. If you select symbols, choose Restart Each Page unless you're sure the document or section will have no more than eight to ten footnotes or endnotes. Alternatively, you can assign each note individually to any character or symbol you like. Type the character at Custom Mark or choose Symbol and select any character from any active font.

Locating a footnote fast

Use the Browse Object command (see Chapter 27) to locate the next or previous note in a hurry. To jump to a specific footnote by number, choose Edit ➪ GoTo, select Footnote at Go to What, and type in the footnote number you want to track down.

The footnote or endnote pane contains all notes of the relevant type. Use the cursor keys or vertical scrollbar to scroll through the notes. As you move from note to note, Word keeps the text in the main document window synchronized — you can always see the line containing the current note's reference mark.

Editing and formatting footnotes and endnotes

You can use all of Word's editing and formatting commands on footnote or endnote text — you just have to get to the text in the first place. In Print Layout view, you can just scroll to the note in question and edit away. In Normal and Outline views, you must open the note pane to edit footnotes or endnotes. Do so by double-clicking the reference mark or by choosing View ⇨ Footnotes. Know these things about the note pane:

- If a document has both footnotes and endnotes, switch between them by choosing the desired item in the drop-down list at the top of the note pane.

- You can set the note pane to a different zoom factor than the main document pane.

- You can change the height of the note pane (and in the opposite direction, that of the main document pane) by dragging the thin horizontal separator between them.

Moving, copying, and deleting footnotes and endnotes

Secret

A reference mark is more than just a superscripted number or symbol — it contains the note's text. So when you want to move, copy, or delete an entire note, work with the reference mark. Select the mark (this is easiest with the keyboard) and then choose Cut or Copy to move it and its text to the clipboard, or hit Delete or Backspace to remove the note.

More about formatting footnotes and endnotes

Word automatically applies the Footnote Text or Endnote Text paragraph style to the note text. It applies a character style, Footnote Reference or Endnote Reference, to the reference mark. So if you want to reformat note text or reference marks, just change the relevant style or styles. You can control the position of your footnotes via the Note Options dialog box. From the Footnote and Endnote dialog box, choose Options. At Place At, select Bottom of Page to place footnotes at the bottom of the page, or select Beneath Text to place them right under the last line of text, wherever on the page that occurs.

Secret

You can also modify several elements that Word displays and prints in conjunction with footnotes and endnotes. These include the *separator*, by default a short line above the first note; the *continuation separator*, a longer line that appears on the second page when a note is split over two pages; and the *continuation notice*, a message Word adds to the second page of a two-page note.

To choose the element you want to modify, select it from the drop-down list at the top of the note pane (you must be in Normal or Outline view to see this list). You can add text or other characters or delete the special line characters used to form the separators.

Bibliographic references by the book

The InsertFootnote macro that comes with Word transforms the standard Insert ➪ Footnote command into a wizard that formats bibliographic references to conform with either of two widely used guidelines for such things — the Modern Language Association (MLA) standards and *The Chicago Manual of Style*. This macro is one of several included in the Macro8.dot template, which is discussed in Chapter 27.

Once you've installed the InsertFootnote macro, choosing Insert ➪ Footnote displays the standard Footnote and Endnote dialog box as usual — but when you choose OK, the Footnote Wizard appears. In the first of a series of panels, one of which is shown in Figure 32-3, you're prompted to choose a reference type (book, magazine, or whatever). In subsequent panels, you're asked to type in the appropriate information (author, title, date, and so on), and to select which of the two formats you want the reference to appear in. When you've completed the sequence, the wizard inserts the completed reference as a footnote or endnote.

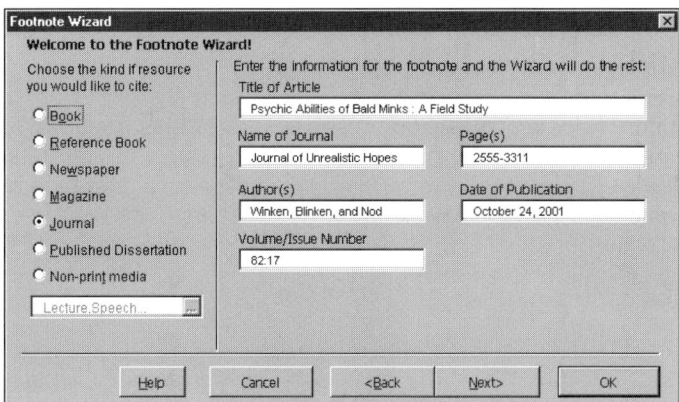

Figure 32-3: Complete this panel in the Footnote Wizard for a semiautomated bibliographic reference.

Secret

If your documents regularly require bibliographic references, do yourself a big favor and buy specialized software to keep track of your database of such references. Papyrus, a leader in the field, lets you search the database by keyword, author, journal, and other criteria. Better yet, it can export the references you select to your Word documents already formatted according to the demands of a particular journal or publisher. As of this writing, Papyrus is still only available as a DOS program, yet it does the job well — and a Windows version is finally expected to arrive by the beginning of the new millenium (Research Software Design, 503-796-1368, www.rsd.com).

Referring more than once to the same note

Secret

In scientific and technical papers, it's common to refer to the same journal or book more than once. Because Word always numbers footnotes and endnotes in sequence, you need another tool to insert a duplicate reference mark.

The solution is a cross-reference to the note. A cross-reference to a footnote or endnote is actually a NOTEREF field, inserted automatically by Word. You can confirm this by selecting the cross-reference and choosing Toggle Field Codes from the shortcut menu. You'll see something like { NOTEREF _Ref371563450 \h }.

By default, a NOTEREF field inserted by the Cross-Reference command functions as a hyperlink—that's the function of that \h switch in the field code. Clicking the cross-reference number takes you directly to the original reference mark. If you don't want the hyperlink, delete the switch. Also by default, a NOTEREF field takes on the formatting of the text where you insert it—in other words, it isn't superscripted. To make the cross-reference look like the other reference marks, add the \f switch within the field code. This applies the character formatting of the Footnote Reference or Endnote Reference style.

Adding indexes, tables of contents, and other reference tables

Though the software technology involved isn't all that complex, I'm still amazed by Word's capability to create instantly complete indexes, tables of contents, and other such tables, with the correct page numbers all perfectly in place. Of course, what really counts is that these features save you great gobs of time.

The key to advanced work with any of these items is to understand that the index or table you see in your document, no matter how lengthy, is a little bitty Word field. Many formatting options can be controlled via field switches, and you can update the whole index or table at any time to bring it in sync with any changes made to the document.

By the way, I use the term *reference tables* throughout this section to refer to tables of contents, figures, equations, and so forth.

Editing and formatting indexes and reference tables

Once you've created an index or reference table, you can customize its text and appearance in three main ways:

- By editing and formatting the text of the index or table entries directly. But take note of the caveats in "Updating an index or reference table" next.

- By modifying the style(s) Word applies automatically to each entry (paragraph) in the item. For indexes, these styles are Index 1, Index 2, and so on. For tables of contents, they are TOC 1, TOC 2, and so on. All entries in a table of figures get the Table of Figures style (what else?).
- By changing switches in the TOC field. Remember, indexes and reference tables are fields. If you toggle the field display on so you can see the field code, a default index field takes this form:

{ INDEX \c "2" };

A typical table of contents field looks like this:

{ TOC \o "1-3" };

And a table of figures looks like this:

{ TOC \c "Figure" }.

Consult Chapter 33 for information on the relevant field switches.

Updating an index or reference table

The page numbers listed in an index or reference table are valid when Word first inserts the item, but they can get out of whack as soon as you edit your text or change any aspect of the formatting. Because Word doesn't update these items automatically, it's up to you to do the job.

Because indexes and reference tables are just fields, you use the standard Update Field command to make them fresh again. To update a specific item, park the insertion point anywhere within the index or reference table and press F9 or select Update Field from the shortcut menu. To update all indexes, references, and other fields in the document, select the whole document first and then press F9. To ensure that printed documents contain the current page numbers, you can tell Word to update fields whenever it prints. Choose Tools ⇨ Options, and on the Print tab, check the Update Fields box.

Caution

When you update an index or reference table, or if Word does so at print time, you get two options about what to update: just the page numbers, or the entire item. Be cautious! If you have edited or reformatted the text of the index or reference table, you will lose those changes if you ask for a full update. On the other hand, if any referenced items in the document proper have been added, deleted, or changed, those changes won't make it into the index or table if you only update the page numbers.

Creating an index

Indexing a book is hard, hard work. Choosing what to index, deciding on succinct index entries to refer to complex ideas, and ensuring consistency are all tough challenges. If you can hire a pro, do so.

Caution

Word solves some of the mechanical problems involved in marking index entries, and it keeps the index itself up-to-date as edits or format modifications change the document's page breaks. But the Index command has some real shortcomings. Count the cost before you undertake to index a document of any length, and consider buying a third-party utility that does a better job.

I don't have space to review the indexing technique in detail. In outline, it's quite simple: You mark index entries in your documents using the dialog box shown in Figure 32-4. When all the index entries are in place, you choose Insert ⇨ Index and Tables, select the Index tab, select formatting options, and choose OK.

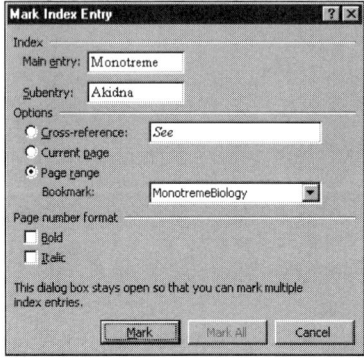

Figure 32-4: The Mark Index Entry dialog box

Quick tips on marking index entries

Here are a few pointers for marking index entries:

- For fast access to the Mark Index Entry dialog box, use the keyboard shortcut Alt+Shift+X, or assign the MarkIndexEntry command to a toolbar button.

- To include document text in an index entry, just select the text. When you open or return to the Mark Index Entry dialog box, the text appears at Main entry.

- To identify an entry as the major discussion of a particular topic, check the Bold or Italic page number format boxes at the bottom of the dialog box.

- In the document, index entries are XE fields. You can add these "by hand" for more control if you like. XE fields are formatted as hidden text, so you can't see them unless nonprinting characters are displayed.

- You can create index entries automatically based on a list of terms in another file. This doesn't usually save much time — believe me, I've tried. But if you choose AutoMark in the Index and Tables dialog box, Word asks you to open the *concordance file* containing a list of the terms you want indexed. To create such a file, type each word to be indexed on its own line. To create an index entry different from the term being indexed, type the term, press Tab, and then type the text for the index entry.

What Word's indexing can't do

Caution

The deficiencies of the Index command? Read 'em and weep:

- Word doesn't remember previous index entries when you mark new ones. Once you've created an index entry, Word should list it the next time you open the Mark Index Entry dialog box, so you can select it as is without the hassle of retyping the entry, and avoiding the introduction of typing errors or minor variations.

- You can't enter page range references directly. To create an entry that covers a range of pages (as in "Indexing problems, 500-502"), you must first insert a bookmark that spans the entire range and then choose Page Range in the Mark Index Entry dialog box, selecting the proper bookmark from the list.

- Word can't list page numbers in "See also" entries. You can set up cross-references to other entries, but if you do, no page number will appear. Often that's okay, but when it's not you have to create a second entry for the page number and then edit the index to remove redundant text.

- You're allowed only two levels in an index: main entries and subentries in the Mark Index Entry dialog box. Sure, an overly complex index can confuse the reader, but sometimes three or four levels are necessary. The illustrated sample in the Index dialog box shows three levels, a bit of a foolie, yes? Worse, there are nine index styles, leading you to believe that you can index away to your heart's content. And trying to format as Index 3 puts in a section break — who needs that annoyance?

You can add levels manually by manipulating the index entry fields or reformatting the index, but either workaround is cumbersome and error-prone.

For serious indexing, get help from other software

There's no avoiding it: You need additional or alternative software if your documents require indexes of much sophistication. Sonar Bookends (Virginia Systems, 804-739-3200, `www.virginiasystems.com`) is an automated indexing utility that works well with Word. It can index all words in your document that occur less than a specified number of times — that way, the index doesn't include words like "the" — or it can read in a list of index terms you supply, creating index entries when it finds them in the document. A document describing Sonar Bookends is included on the CD-ROM that comes with this book.

You should also consider switching from Word to an industrial-strength desktop publishing program. Adobe FrameMaker and Corel Ventura Publisher have stronger indexing features.

Creating a table of contents or other reference table

Choose Insert ⇨ Index and Tables to create a table of page number references: a table of contents or a table of elements such as figures, equations, or, for that matter, tables. In the resulting dialog box select the tab for the type of table you're creating, Tables of Contents or Tables of Figures. Use the latter choice for tables of any document element you have captioned, such as tables or equations.

Tables of contents differ from tables of figures mainly in that TOCs can have up to nine different levels, each appearing with its own format (via a paragraph style) in the finished table. If you need a hierarchical reference table for any other type of item, create it as a table of contents rather than a table of figures. (Behind the scenes, both tables of contents and tables of figures are TOC fields; they just use different field switches.)

Secret

After inserting a table of contents, you may find that the pagination of your document is affected by the presence of the TOC itself. If that happens, it's likely to throw off the page number references in the TOC. To square things again, select the whole TOC and use the Update Field command. See "Updating an index or reference table" earlier in this chapter.

Basing a table on styles or fields

Word generates these tables based on the location in your document of two items: paragraphs with specific styles, and fields marking table entries. You can tell Word to include either or both of these items when constructing any one table. By default, tables of contents are based on styles only, and tables of figures, on fields. To change these settings, choose Options from the appropriate tab in the Index and Tables dialog box, checking or clearing the boxes for styles and fields in the dialog box that appears, shown in Figure 32-5.

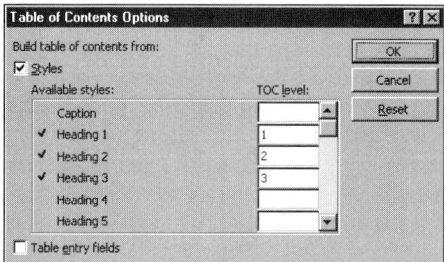

Figure 32-5: This dialog box lists options for tables of contents. Word offers similar choices in the Options dialog box for tables of figures.

Using styles

When you base a table on styles, Word turns each paragraph formatted with any of the specified styles into a table entry. The entire text of the paragraph is included in the table. To base a table on styles, you must first apply one of the specified styles to each paragraph that is to appear in the table (Word includes the entire text of the paragraph as the table entry). For tables of contents it's easiest to use styles. If you use Word's standard heading styles in a consistent fashion for your headings and subheads, you're all set to generate a table of contents.

If your headings have other styles instead, that's fine, too, as long as you're up for a little customizing. After choosing Insert ⇨ Index and Tables, select the Tables of Contents tab, set Show Levels to 1, and then choose Options. In the resulting dialog box (Figure 32-5), locate the styles for your headings and assign each to a level (1 through 9). You can specify as many styles as you like for each level. This is great if you applied different Foreword Title, Chapter Title, and Appendix Title styles but want all these titles to appear at the same level in the finished table.

You can use styles to create tables of figures and the like, too. This works fine if you create and apply a different style for the captions of each item type (figures, tables, equations, and whatnot). This will be the case if you create captions using the technique described in "Better captions" earlier.

If you add captions with the Insert ⇨ Caption command, however, you need fields.

Using fields

To create a table using fields, you must put a TC or SEQ field into the document at each location you want to list in the table. Placing the field is easy enough:

- Word inserts an SEQ field with each caption you create using the Insert ⇨ Caption command or via the technique recommended in "Better captions" earlier. Tables of figures are based on SEQ fields by default.

- To insert a TC field, press the keyboard shortcut Alt+Shift+O or select it from the Insert ⇨ Field dialog box. (Watch out: TC fields are hidden text, so you can only see them if you have nonprinting characters turned on.) To base a table of contents or figures on TC fields, check Table Entry Fields in the Options dialog box.

SEQ fields are inserted by Word when you add captions with Insert ⇨ Caption. If you use this command, fields are better than styles for tables of figures. Insert ⇨ Caption applies the same paragraph style to all captions (the Caption style, of course). For this reason, a table of "figures" based on the Caption style lumps in entries for tables, equations, and so on. By contrast, Word inserts a different type of SEQ field for each kind of item you caption, and your tables are confined to one item type.

TC fields can be useful because they let you specify the text you want for each table entry. If you create a table of contents using styles, all the text from each heading paragraph appears in the table. Because you can edit entries in the finished table directly, TC fields aren't strictly necessary to get the table into shape. Still, you must repeat these edits each time you update the table, increasing the likelihood of errors. Chapter 33 has the lowdown on SEQ and TC fields.

About tables of authorities

Space limitations prevent coverage of tables of authorities, more-complicated reference tables used primarily in legal documents. Suffice it to say that the basic techniques are much like those used for the other types of reference tables covered earlier. The keyboard shortcut for marking a table of authorities entry is Alt+Shift+I.

Building Long Documents

Constructing a book-length document is always an ambitious undertaking, but Word can handle much of the heavy lifting. You can choose between two basic strategies for the overall project:

- You can store the entire book in a single Word document.
- You can store each chapter or section of the book in its own file, combining them all with the Master Document feature.

Secret

Keeping the entire book in one document has genuine advantages. What could be simpler? You only have to keep track of a single file. No special steps are required to create cross-references, a table of contents, or an index. Potential drawbacks? Navigating a 1,000-page document may take a little longer, though you probably won't notice if your computer is reasonably fast. If the one file gets damaged, the entire project may be lost, so backing up becomes even more critical. And as the document gets larger, it may not fit on a floppy disk and it may take too long to send via modem. But don't reject this approach out of hand — many Word experts prefer it.

The Master Document feature is designed to manage multiple separate chapter files as a single document, and it does the job reasonably well. But it introduces complexities that can confuse and delay you. Anyway, if you're serious about long documents, you should learn enough about master documents to see if they make sense for you. A master document is a Word document in its own right, in which you can place text if you like. But a master document functions mainly as a container for a series of subdocuments, separate documents containing the component chapters.

When you need to edit a chapter, you open it separately. When you want to create cross-references, reference tables, or an index, you work in the master document. When it's time to print your whole opus, the master document numbers the pages sequentially throughout all the subdocuments. You can also use the master document to reorganize the entire document, dividing or combining subdocuments or moving material between different subdocuments.

Creating a master document

You can create a master document from scratch, outlining the main headings of the book and then having Word divide your outline into separate subdocuments for you. Alternatively, you can import existing documents into a master document. Either way works fine, and you can combine both techniques if you like.

Caution

Before you start work, settle on a single template you'll use for all the subdocuments and for the master document itself. Otherwise, you're liable to cause conflicts that can spoil your printed results. Decide on the styles you're going to use for titles and headings — the discussion in Chapter 28 about built-in heading styles applies here, too.

Also, create a new folder for the project and keep the master document and all the subdocuments there for the duration. Don't move subdocuments after you've added them to a master document — the master document can't track them down.

To create the master document, start a new document and choose View ➪ Master Document. What you see is the familiar Outline view, modified only by the presence of the Master Document toolbar. Type in the book's title at the top of the outline, assigning it to the Heading 1 style if you're using Word's built-in heading styles.

Creating a master document from scratch

If you plan to create subdocuments from scratch, type in their titles next as Heading 2 styles. You can go ahead and develop the complete outline of your book now, or stop at this point and fill in the contents of each subdocument when you edit it separately later. When you're ready to divide the outline into subdocuments, collapse the outline if necessary so that you can see the chapter titles, select them all, and then click the Create Subdocument button on the Master Document toolbar. Word breaks the document up, placing each chapter title and all its subsidiary text in a separate subdocument. When you save the master document, Word saves the new subdocuments as separate files, assigning a name to each file based on the first few characters of the chapter titles.

Linking existing documents to a master document

To add an existing document to a master document, start by placing the insertion point where the document belongs in the master document outline. Click the Insert Subdocument button on the Master Document toolbar and locate and open the file.

Caution

Be sure that the insertion point isn't an existing subdocument — because any Word document can function as a master document, you can create subdocuments within subdocuments, and so on.

Splitting and merging subdocuments

When a change of editorial vision demands substantial reorganization of a book-length project, reordering, removing, combining, or dividing subdocuments may be necessary.

The easiest way to manage such operations is to use the standard outlining procedures to drag a heading and its subsidiary text where you want it to go:

- To move an entire subdocument to a new position in the outline, drag its square icon at the far left of the window.

- To combine any part of a subdocument into another subdocument, select and drag the relevant heading markers, dropping them inside the destination subdocument.

- To remove a subdocument, placing its contents back in the master document, drag the main subdocument heading marker, dropping it at its destination *between* subdocuments.

- To divide a subdocument into two, drag the portion you want to place in a new subdocument into the main master document, between existing subdocuments. With the heading or headings still selected, click the Create Subdocument button.

You can also use the Master Document toolbar to perform these same functions, but working directly with the outline is usually quicker. When you save the master document after merging two or more subdocuments, Word saves the merged contents in the file of the first merged subdocument. The files of the other subdocuments involved in the merger aren't deleted, but they are no longer in use, so you can delete them if you wish. Likewise, when you place the contents of a subdocument into the main master document, its file is no longer used and can be deleted.

Creating reference tables, indexes, and cross-references in long documents

Work with your master document to insert or update reference tables, indexes, and cross-references in your book-length project. As should be obvious, you must create reference tables or indexes pertaining to the entire document by inserting them into the master document. You can insert the table or index anywhere, in the master document proper or in any of the subdocuments.

To cross-reference items in subdocuments, start by opening the master document. Switch to Normal view, where you can scroll the entire "virtual" book even though it is made up of separate document files. You can now insert your cross-references, which will rely on hidden bookmarks that belong to the master document rather than to the subdocument in which they reside. When it's time to update the table of contents, index, or cross-references, do so from within the master document, even if the item occurs in a subdocument. Otherwise, Word won't be able to identify referenced items that reside in other subdocuments.

Group Document Development

Word has bunches of features designed to facilitate document creation, review, and revision by teams of writers, editors, and know-it-all bosses. Many of these features are equally useful for individuals who want to keep track of the changes made to a document over time.

The Reviewing toolbar (Figure 32-6) collects buttons pertaining to document review and group document development. Word displays the Reviewing toolbar automatically when you edit a comment, but you can choose View ⇨ Toolbars to activate it at any time. Buttons on the toolbar give fast-track access to commands for finding and editing comments, tracking and reviewing document changes, highlighting text, saving multiple versions of the document, and sending it in an e-mail message to a collaborator.

Figure 32-6: Activate the Reviewing toolbar for quick access to commands used in collaborating on documents.

Inserting comments

When you hand a paper document to someone for a critique, you expect to get the pages back all covered with questions, corrections, suggestions, and personal reactions. There's nowhere to attach a paper clip or sticky note to a Word document, but Word's Comments feature serves the same purpose, without all the smudges and wrinkles.

To insert a comment, select the text you want to comment on and then choose Insert ⇨ Comment or press Alt+Ctrl+M (if you don't select text first, Word applies the comment to the word containing the insertion point). Type the comment in the pane Word opens for that purpose at the bottom of the window.

Word indicates the comment in your document in two ways, but what you see on the screen depends on settings on the View tab of the Tools ⇨ Options dialog box. If hidden text is displayed, you see the comment mark, consisting of brackets around the initials of the "commentator" and the comment number. If ScreenTips are visible, the commented text is shaded light yellow, becoming bright yellow when you activate the comment.

These cues simply alert you to the presence of a comment. To read the comment itself, just hold the mouse pointer over the text to which the comment is attached, and the comment itself appears in one of those yellow ScreenTip boxes. The ScreenTip also lists the reviewer's name for reference. Figure 32-7 shows an example. For this to work, ScreenTips must be displayed as just described.

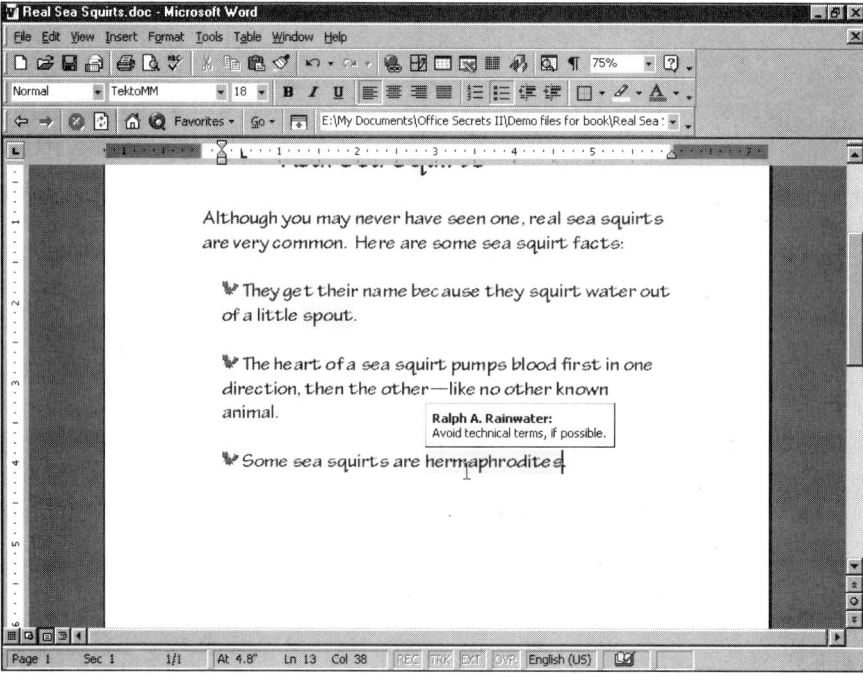

Figure 32-7: Here's a sample comment displayed as a ScreenTip over the text it refers to.

Secret

You can record spoken comments if your computer has a sound card with a microphone, and you can write them by hand if you're set up for pen input. See Chapter 3 for info on using voice and pen technology with Office.

Finding and working with comments

To jump instantly from comment to comment, use the Browse Object command described in Chapter 27, or click the Previous Comment and Next Comment buttons on the Reviewing toolbar.

Alternatively, you can open the comment pane by double-clicking the comment mark or by choosing Edit Comment from the shortcut menu or the Reviewing toolbar. Once the pane is open, you can scroll through all the comments in the document. The comment pane is synchronized to the main document pane above, so that Word always displays the associated document text for the comment you're currently viewing. To display only the comments of a particular comment maker, choose that person from the list at the top of the pane.

You can edit a comment in the comment pane, of course, but you can also change character or paragraph formatting, directly — perhaps to add highlighting — or by applying styles. By default, Word applies the Comment Text paragraph style to comments. (By the way, comment marks receive the Comment Reference character style.) Ctrl+Home and Ctrl+End take you to the beginning or end, respectively, of the current comment. To delete a comment, right-click in the text it pertains to and select Delete Comment from the shortcut menu or click the Delete Comment button.

Printing comments

Comments normally don't print, but you can get them onto paper by checking Comments in the Print Options dialog box. Word prints the comment marks (and all other hidden text) where they belong in the document, and it prints the comments themselves at the end of the document, beginning on a separate page.

Changing identifying information for comments

Word displays comments with the name and initials of the person who made them. This information comes from the User Information tab of the Tools ➪ Options dialog box. If someone else uses the same computer to comment on the document, that person should change the User Information so that Word can keep track of who made which comments. Better yet, each person using the PC should have his or her own Windows user profile. That way, that person's user information is automatically activated whenever they log into Windows and start Word.

Reviewing documents

When you work with somebody else on the same document, each of you needs to know when changes have been made, and by whom. The functions on Word's Tools ➪ Track Changes submenu fit the bill. In previous versions, these functions were located in the Revisions dialog box, but they worked the same way.

You can have Word identify changes made to a document in two main ways: by turning on the Track Changes command, so that changes are recorded while the document is being edited; or by comparing the current document to another version. With either approach, changes are marked in the document the same way.

Secret

When you print a document containing tracked changes, the changes can appear in the printout if the Track Changes in Printed Document option is on. The check box for this option is located in the Tools ➪ Track Changes ➪ Highlight Changes dialog box.

Tracking changes during editing

To have Word track and display the changes you make as you (or someone else) edit the document, click the Track Changes button on the Reviewing toolbar so that it looks pressed in. The default keyboard shortcut for this command is Ctrl+Shift+E. Repeating the command turns off change-tracking. You can also choose Tools ➪ Track Changes ➪ Highlight Changes and check or clear the Track Changes While Editing box. You can set up documents you send to reviewers so that Track Changes is turned on automatically. See "Setting up a document to be reviewed" later in this chapter.

Comparing two copies of a document

To have Word mark the differences between two copies of the same document, start by opening the copy in which you want the changes to be marked (see the next discussion). Choose Tools ⇨ Track Changes ⇨ Compare Documents. Word displays an Open dialog box with which you can track down and open the second copy. When the comparison is complete, the differences between the two documents appear in the first copy, marked according to the settings in the Track Changes tab of the Options dialog box.

Choosing the order of a document comparison

In general, you should start with the newer copy, considering that text marked as an insertion by the comparison was, in fact, inserted after the original copy was saved (and likewise with deletions). If you prefer to keep the earlier copy as the main version of the document, you can start with it and work in the other direction. Just keep in mind that "insertions" now indicate text that has been removed in the newer copy. However, you may find the Merge Documents command more helpful in this situation (see "Merging changes from another copy" later in this chapter).

If you don't know which copy is more recent, you can check the date/time of the file itself, or if both copies have been modified since they parted ways, you can start with either one. If you're trying to figure out which copy is current, run the comparison and then look for a text passage that you're sure was present only in the newer copy. If the passage is marked as an insertion, the newer copy is the one you opened first. If it is marked as a deletion, you started the comparison with the original copy.

How Word marks changes

Once Word has identified changes with either of the preceding techniques, it marks them so that they stand out in your document. By default, inserted text is marked with underlining, and deleted text is marked with the strikethrough format. Both types of changes are displayed in a color chosen for you by Word based on which author made the change. In addition, all lines containing changes are marked by a thin vertical line at the left of the window. Note that Word displays a little box showing who made a change when you point at it with the mouse.

If you care to, you can change the defaults governing tracked changes on the Track Changes tab on the Tools ⇨ Options dialog box. Good reasons to change these settings include these:

- **To minimize distracting colors.** Letting Word pick the color ensures that each reviewer's changes get a unique color. If the riot of color blows your mind, select a specific color to use for all changes. You can still see who made the changes by holding the mouse pointer over a section until a ScreenTip appears (the author of each change is also listed in the Accept or Reject Changes dialog box).

- **To mark deletions without displaying the deleted text.** This is a commonly used convention in legal documents. At Mark for Deleted Text, choose # or ^. The chosen character appears instead of the text. You can restore the actual text by again selecting Strikethrough. By the way, the Hidden option hides the deleted text whether or not hidden text display is turned on.

- **To track formatting changes.** By default, formatting changes are "marked" in ordinary text. Select a different color, mark, or both to see them.

- **To change the location of that vertical line indicating changed lines.** Alternatives to the default (Left Border) include None, Right Border, and Outside Border. The last choice places the line in the left margin of even-numbered pages and in the right margin of odd-numbered pages, but only if you have set up different odd and even pages in the Page Setup dialog box. In Normal view, the line always appears on the left.

Hiding and displaying changes

Sometimes you need to work with a document containing many tracked changes without being distracted by Word's on-screen marking of additions and deletions. You can turn off the *display* of tracked changes while Word continues to track new changes you make. Choose Tools ➪ Track Changes ➪ Highlight Changes. In the resulting dialog box, clear the box labeled Highlight Changes on Screen, but leave the Track Changes While Editing box checked.

The following simple VBA procedure toggles the on-screen display of tracked changes on and off. Assigned to a toolbar button, it's a lot handier than opening the Highlight Changes dialog box.

```
Sub RevisionMarksToggleDisplay()
    With ActiveDocument
        .ShowRevisions = Not (.ShowRevisions)
    End With
End Sub
```

Accepting and rejecting changes

It's all well and good to keep track of the changes made to a document, but eventually the moment of truth arrives: Which changes are you going to keep? I'll leave the tough decisions to you. The mechanics are simple: Using the Reviewing toolbar, click the Next Change or Previous Change button to locate a change. Inspect the changed text and then click the Accept Change button to confirm the change or the Reject Change button to rescind it. Note that when you accept a deletion, the text marked as deleted disappears from your document. The same is true when you reject an insertion.

Secret

The Accept Change and Reject Change buttons only work if you select text first, and then only if the selection begins with a tracked change. In a document with lots of changes that require review one at a time, this behavior can mean a great deal of time and effort for you in making precise selections. The following VBA procedures accept or reject all changes in a selection, regardless of where the selection starts or ends. As a bonus, if no text is selected, they accept or reject all changes in the current paragraph.

Macro VBA

```
Sub RevisionsAcceptInSelection()
   With Selection
      Set myRange = .Range
      If .Type = wdSelectionIP Then
         myRange.Expand Unit:=wdParagraph
      End If
      myRange.Revisions.AcceptAll
   End With
End Sub
Sub RevisionsRejectInSelection()
   With Selection
      Set myRange = .Range
      If .Type = wdSelectionIP Then
         myRange.Expand Unit:=wdParagraph
      End If
      myRange.Revisions.RejectAll
   End With
End Sub
```

The Reviewing toolbar is convenient for accepting and rejecting changes, but for more control choose Tools ➪ Track Changes ➪ Accept or Reject Changes. Like the toolbar buttons, the Accept or Reject Changes dialog box lets you find and accept or reject individual changes, but it also tells you who made each change without any mouse action on your part. You can view the document as if the changes had all been accepted or rejected, and you can Accept All or Reject All to cut the review process short.

Merging changes from another copy

When you want to incorporate changes made by another person in a separate copy of the document, the Tools ➪ Merge Documents command is an alternative to a document comparison. This command imports marked changes from the other copy, including any comments it contains.

Caution

The Merge Documents command is much more persnickety than Compare Documents — it works only if Track Changes has been turned on during all edits of both copies of the document. If you plan to merge, make sure your reviewers turn on Track Changes before they add or delete anything — and be sure you do, too.

To perform the merge, open your copy of the document. Choose Tools ➪ Merge Documents to display an Open dialog box. As soon as you have opened the other file, Word displays your original copy with the imported change marks. You can now go on to review them as described in the previous section.

Using versions

Beginning with Word 97 you can store multiple versions of a given document in one big file. The Versions feature lets you keep track of who was responsible for each saved revision, when it was saved, and what it contains. Retaining intermediate versions of a document isn't just a boon for obsessive administrators. If you suddenly realize that after all, you need that big section you deleted three revisions ago, you don't need to panic — just pull the version containing the section out of storage.

Of course, you can maintain multiple versions of a document using Save As, storing each version in a separate file. But this is cumbersome and it litters your hard disk with large numbers of files whose purpose is quickly forgotten. In addition, this method wastes disk space, because there is bound to be a lot of redundant information in all those copies of the document. By contrast, when you save multiple versions in the same file, Word stores only the differences between the versions, not a complete copy of each version (nevertheless, a file containing versions is still significantly larger than a standard file).

Secret

By the way, you can insert into your document a field that shows the date and time that the document was last saved as a quick way to identify the version of a printed document. After opening the Insert ⇨ Field dialog box, select SaveDate in the Field Names list. Typically you'll place the field in a header or footer.

Saving versions

You can save the current state of the document as a separate version at any time. Choose File ⇨ Versions to display the dialog box shown in Figure 32-8. To save a new version, choose Save Now and type in identifying comments in the secondary dialog box for that purpose.

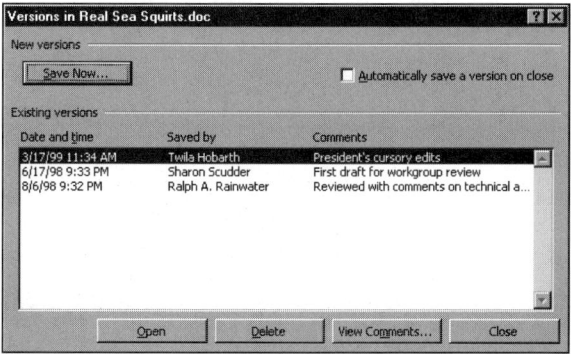

Figure 32-8: Use the Versions dialog box to view and manage versions stored together in a single file.

You can also have Word save a new version each time the document is closed. This is a good way to handle revisions made by multiple authors, especially when an audit trail is required. Just check the Automatically Save a Version on Close box in the Versions dialog box. You can't add your own comments to versions saved automatically.

Working with earlier versions

Once you have saved one or more versions of a document, the Versions dialog box displays information about each version, including who saved it, the time it was saved, and any comments that were entered (you can see the entire comments text by choosing View Comments). To work with an earlier version, double-click it in the dialog box. Word displays the current document and the selected version in separate, horizontally tiled windows. You can only open one previous version at a time. You can edit the earlier version, but you can't save the changes in the current document — instead, you must use Save As to save it in a new file.

Secret

It's a good idea to save a version in its own file if you plan to send a document to a reviewer, so that the reviewer only gets to see the one version that's fit for semipublic consumption. You must also convert a version as a separate file when you want to compare the current version to an earlier one. If you start the comparison from the earlier version instead, you don't need to create a new file first.

To delete a version you no longer need, select it in the Versions dialog box and choose Delete.

Setting up a document to be reviewed

Before you distribute a document to others for review, make some basic preparations to ensure that you send out only the information, and so that you can easily incorporate changes made by the reviewers.

After opening the document, choose File ➪ Versions to see if the file contains multiple versions, and if so, save separately only the version you want to send out. (See the Secret in the preceding section.) Then comes the important step: controlling the kinds of changes your reviewers can make.

Choose Tools ➪ Protect Document to display the Protect Document dialog box. To enforce activation of the Track Changes function, so that Word marks every insertion and deletion the reviewer makes, choose Tracked Changes. To allow the reviewer only to add comments, preventing any changes to the document itself, choose Comments. Then enter a password so the reviewer can't change these settings — and write down the password now, so you won't be locked out when you get the file back.

Network considerations in group document development

Chapter 18 discusses Office features for sharing documents on networks and via e-mail. If your organization uses Exchange Server, you can also take advantage of Outlook's features for tracking e-mail documents, summarized in Chapter 51. Word itself has little specific support for network document development. Documents being edited by one user can be viewed but not edited by others. The document protection options just discussed apply here, although they aren't specific to networks.

Conclusion

Aside from its underpowered indexing feature, Word is big and brawny enough to produce documents of just about any length or complexity. Use the skills this chapter presents to add all the elements a long document requires, including captions, cross-references, and tables. And if the project is too big for one person, bring in the cavalry on the backs of Word's group document development features.

Chapter 33

A Dream of Fields

In This Chapter

- Learning what fields are good for
- Working with field-related keyboard shortcuts for fast action with fields
- Inserting, formatting, and displaying fields
- Getting to know many of Word's most useful fields

Fields are magic codes inserted in your document that instruct Word to carry out some special function. The typical field functions as a kind of text-making machine — Word translates the field's instructions into text that appears in your document. One key benefit is that the resulting text isn't static but reflects prevailing conditions at the time Word performs the translation. Take a simple date field, for example. On each different day that Word processes the field, it displays that day's date in the document.

This type of field can perform far more complex tasks, such as gathering all the headings in your document into a formatted table of contents. But some fields perform other kinds of wizardry without directly inserting text into the document. Fields are most commonly used in headers and footers. As Chapter 31 points out, the Header and Footer toolbar has buttons for inserting common fields. In addition, the same toolbar's AutoText menu offers prefab selections that insert useful combinations of text and fields into your headers and footers.

VBA can probably accomplish everything that fields can, and VBA is certainly the tool to use if the document tasks you're automating are of any complexity. But fields often give you a shorter route to the destination, they're less demanding in terms of memory and system resources, and they don't take you out of the document to a separate software universe. But it's not an either-or proposition — you can manipulate fields with VBA to capitalize on the strengths of each.

A thorough elucidation of fields would fill up the entire Word section in this book. If you need more information than is provided here, consult the Help files.

Working with Fields

Behind the scenes, Word relies on fields to perform many of the functions you use regularly. But Word lets you work directly with fields if you so choose, editing the fields it has inserted or creating new fields from scratch.

Keyboard shortcuts for field commands

Word's default menus and toolbars offer little help for field explorers, but all the field-related commands are available via default keyboard shortcuts. Most of these involve the F9 key, though F11 plays a role too. If you forget any of the items listed in Table 33-1, just keep pressing various combinations of Ctrl, Alt, and Shift with F9 until you get the desired results, relying on Undo to reverse accidental unlinking.

Table 33-1   Keyboard Shortcuts for Fields

Shortcut	Name	Function
F9	Update Field	Causes Word to reevaluate the current field or all fields in the current selection, bringing the results up to date.
Ctrl+F9	Insert Field	Inserts a new empty field, signified by heavy curly braces.
Shift+F9	Toggle Field Code	Toggles the display of field codes versus field results for the current field, or for all fields in the current selection.
Alt+F9	View Field Codes	Toggles the display of all fields in the document.
Ctrl+Shift+F9	Unlink Fields	Converts the current results of the selected fields to ordinary text. No further updating of the original fields will then be possible.
Alt+Shift+F9	Do Field Click	Activates button fields such as MACROBUTTON or GOTOBUTTON, as if you had clicked them with the mouse.
F11	Next Field	Jumps to the next field in the document.
Shift+F11	Previous Field	Goes back to the last field.
Ctrl+F11	Lock Field	Locks the field so that it can't be updated.
Ctrl+Shift+F11	Unlock Field	Unlocks a locked field so that it can again be updated.

Using field commands on toolbars and menus

Although keyboard shortcuts are the fastest way to access field-related commands, they only work if you memorize them. Until then, you can use the shortcut menu that appears when you right-click a field to get to two important field-related commands: Update Field and Toggle Field Codes. Consider adding the remaining field commands to one or more shortcut menus or to a regular menu or toolbar.

Figure 33-1 shows my modified version of the Insert menu, complete with a whole special section devoted to the field commands. In the same illustration, the main menu bar has buttons for the same commands.

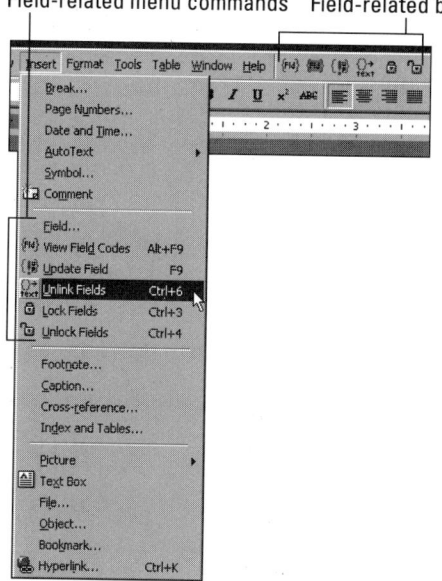

Figure 33-1: Field commands placed on a menu and toolbar for easy access

Drag the field-related commands from the Tools ⇨ Customize dialog box (Commands tab) to the destination toolbar or menu using the techniques laid out in Chapter 5. With a few exceptions, the items you select in the dialog box are the same as the command names, as listed in Table 33-1 (but without any spaces). The exceptions are:

For This Command	Select This Item in the Customize Dialog Box
Toggle Field Codes	ToggleFieldDisplay
Insert Field	InsertFieldChars (note that the command called InsertField in the dialog box brings up the Insert Field dialog box, rather than immediately placing a new blank field in the document)
Previous Field	PrevField

How fields work

Each field can appear in your document in one of two forms: as a field code (the instructions used to specify the field and its options) or as field results (the information Word derives according to the field code instructions). It's an either/or kind of thing: Either you see the field code or you see the field results, not both at the same time. Here's an example of a field code:

{ DATE \@ "dddd, MMMM dd, yyyy"}

And here's how the same field looks when its results are displayed instead:

Sunday, August 17, 1999

A field's results are expected to change over time. To display the correct current results, you must update the field (see "Updating fields" later in this chapter).

Field anatomy

A field code consists of three main elements, as shown in this example:

{ REF CurrentTopic * Caps }

- The field characters are the pair of bold, curly braces that enclose the rest of the field code.

- The field type is the name of the field. This name gives at least a hint of its function. In the example, the field type is REF, which stands for reference (to a bookmark).

- The instructions are various items that follow the field type and further define what the field should do and how the results should look in your document. The example field has two instructions, CurrentTopic and * Caps. CurrentTopic is the name of the bookmark the field refers to. The * Caps instruction capitalizes the first letter of each word in the bookmarked text. Instructions that begin with a backslash are called switches, because they switch on optional functions or formatting.

Fields can often be nested, meaning that you can include one field as part of the instructions within another field. This enables you to build fields that carry out very sophisticated procedures to finally produce the results you want.

Inserting fields

You have three main ways to insert fields into your documents:

- You can have Word do it for you behind the scenes, based on selections you make in various dialog boxes.

- You can build the field code with Word's help, using the Insert ⇨ Field dialog box. See the next section.

- You can insert the field manually, pressing Ctrl+F9 to place an empty field — with the requisite pair of heavy curly braces — into your document. You then type in the entire field code yourself. Note that you can't create a field by simply typing in the braces — even if you format them in bold, Word still treats them as ordinary text.

Inserting fields with the Insert ⇨ Field command

Choosing Insert ⇨ Field brings up the dialog box shown in Figure 33-2. Here, Word guides you in putting together a field code that produces the results you're after, but don't expect wizard-like pampering: You still have to know when and how to use field code components, and you're not protected from errors that give the wrong results, or none at all.

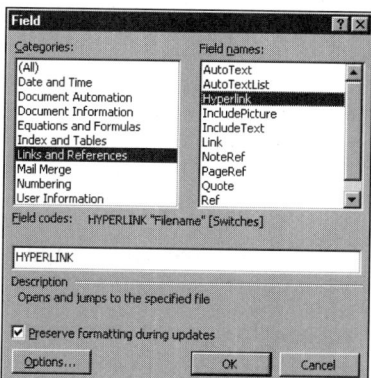

Figure 33-2: The Insert ⇨ Field dialog box

To assemble a field in the dialog box, your first step is to select the right field type by name in the Field Names list. If you know which category your field belongs to, selecting that first in the Categories list reduces the names you have to look through. Otherwise, just leave "(All)" selected at Categories.

As you move through the list of field names, Word automatically transfers the selected field name to the one-line Field Codes box below. It also displays a schematic of the complete field code required and offers a description of what the field does. At this point, you can follow the schematic, typing in any instructions yourself. However, you can choose Options to get further aid with some instructions you can include in the field code, as described in the next section. Unfortunately, Word can't help with many of the required instructions, and you must type them in yourself.

Selecting field code options

The Field Options dialog box shown in Figure 33-3 presents whatever options are relevant to the field you're assembling. The term "options" may be misleading, because some of the instructions available in the dialog box are required or the field won't produce any results. Some fields have two or more types of options, which are listed on separate tabs of the dialog box. If you don't see the option you're looking for, try another tab.

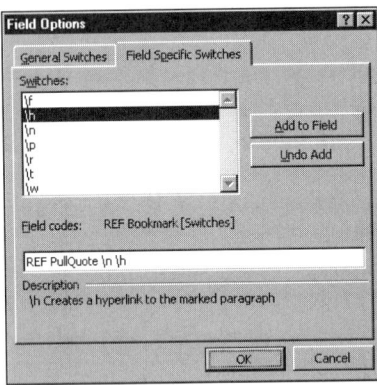

Figure 33-3: This dialog box lets you select from options that pertain to the field you've chosen.

As you move through a list of options, you may see a description of the currently selected option at the bottom of the dialog box. In other cases, though, the description just gives you a general idea of what this type of option does. To insert an option into the developing field, select it and choose Add to Field. The Undo Add button only undoes the last option added.

Caution

Be sure to follow the field code pattern Word suggests, because the dialog box won't ensure that you add options where they belong. Also, you should know that some options are incompatible with each other, yet Word lets you enter them in the same field anyway. Finally, some options require you to type in additional information, but Word doesn't prompt you to do so.

Secrets of field instructions

Whether you generate a field in the Field dialog box or type it in all by yourself, the order of the instructions makes a difference, so follow the correct syntax. You should leave at least one space between each instruction except the switches (Word identifies them by the backslash character). Instructions containing spaces should be enclosed in quotation marks, but you can usually omit the quotation marks otherwise.

Toggling between field codes and field results

Because information is what you're after, the finished document normally displays and prints the field results. Before the document is finished, however, you can switch back to the field codes to ensure that the field is set up to produce the right information. Switching back and forth between codes and results is also a good way to learn how fields work. You have several ways to switch back and forth between field codes and field results. If you want to see all the field codes in the document, press Alt+F9, or check Field Codes on the View tab of the Tools ⇨ Options dialog box. To toggle between field codes and results for a specific field, or for all the fields in a selection, press Shift+F9 instead.

By the way, if for some reason you want to print field codes with your document, check the Field Codes box on the Print tab of the Tools ⇨ Options dialog box. You can access these same choices via the Options button on the Print dialog box.

Selecting a field

You don't have to fully select a field to work with it (for example, to update it or to toggle the display of field codes). It's enough to position the insertion point anywhere within the field or just to the left of the first character. On the other hand, the field remains unselected if the insertion point is immediately to the right.

Updating fields

Keep in mind that Word doesn't automatically update fields, except when you open a document or (optionally) when you print it. Before you can believe the results of a field in your document, you have to update the field yourself. Unfortunately, the UpdateField command isn't on any of Word's regular menus; the corresponding button is found only on the Database toolbar, which isn't normally visible. But Word does give you two quick ways to access the UpdateField command: via the shortcut menu or the default keyboard shortcut, F9. (By the way, to ensure that all fields contain updated values in the printed version of a document, check the Update Fields box on the Print tab of the Tools ⇨ Options dialog box.)

Locking a field to prevent updating

Sometimes you don't want a field to be updated. As a simple example, you might delete some text from the field results. If the field gets updated, your edits would be nullified. You can lock the field to prevent updates by pressing Ctrl+F11. To unlock it, press Ctrl+Shift+F11.

Converting fields into plain text

If you're sure that you'll never again want to update the results of a field, unlink the field. This command converts the current field results into ordinary text. Aside from Undo, there's no going back. The keyboard shortcut is Ctrl+Shift+F9.

Working with field results

When you display a field's results, the results look and behave almost like ordinary text. I say "almost" for two reasons:

- The field results may be shaded in gray, depending on the Field Shading setting in the View tab of the Tools ⇨ Options dialog box. I prefer the "When selected" choice for this setting — it's good to know when the insertion point is within a field rather than ordinary text, but shading fields all the time is distracting.

- Although you can edit the text of the field results, you'll find the editing process quirky. Specifically, with the insertion point just to the right of the field, pressing Backspace once simply selects the field, and pressing it again deletes the entire field. Be aware that any changes you make in the text will be wiped out if you update the field, or if Word does so at print time.

Formatting field results and field codes

You can format a field's results or any portion thereof just as you would ordinary text. If you select the entire field before making a formatting change, the new format survives after the field is updated. On the other hand, an update nullifies formatting applied to selected text within the field results.

When the field code is visible, you can format selections within it. These changes do endure following an update. In combination with the * charformat switch described later, this is one way to control the appearance of the entire results. You can control other types of formatting with switches in the field itself. Read on.

Controlling the display of field results with switches

Although many switches are specific to individual field types, you can use four in many different fields:

- In fields that give text results, the Format switch (*) controls capitalization of text. In fields that give numeric results, it controls the way Word displays the numbers (as Roman numerals, written out as text, and so on). The Format switch can also be used to preserve or apply character formatting to the field results.

- The Numeric Picture switch (\#) controls other aspects of the appearance of numeric field results.
- The Date-Time Picture switch (\@) controls the way Word displays date and time information in field results.
- The Lock Result switch (\!) keeps Word from updating a field when it is included in another field of one of the following types: BOOKMARK, INCLUDETEXT, or REF. These fields are used to reference information in other locations, and if you include this switch, the information they report will always match the results of the included field as displayed in the original location.

Except for Lock Result, these switches must be followed by an additional instruction that tells Word which of the available options you want to activate.

Using the Format switch to control capitalization, number schemes, and character formatting

Select from the following additional instructions for the Format switch.

To control capitalization (in fields that give text results):

* caps	Capitalizes the first letter of each word.
* firstcap	Capitalizes only the first letter of the field results.
* lower	Displays the field results in all lowercase.
* upper	Displays the field results in uppercase.

To control number display:

* alphabetic	Displays each numeral as a corresponding letter of the alphabet.
* arabic	Displays ordinary numbers. This is the default.
* cardtext	Writes out the numbers in words.
* dollartext	Writes out the amount as you would on a check.
* hex	Displays the amount in hexadecimal notation (base 16).
* ordinal	Displays the number in ordinal form (1st, 2nd, 3rd . . . 999th).
* roman	Displays the number in Roman numerals.

To control character formatting (you can enter either of these switches even if you have used one of the * switches just listed):

* mergeformat	Preserves any character formatting you have applied to the field result during field updates. If you don't include this switch, character formatting is removed when Word updates the field.
* charformat	Applies the formatting of the first letter of the field type to the entire field result.

Using the Numeric Picture switch

The Numeric Picture switch (\#) lets you control how Word displays numeric results, in terms of the number of decimal points, whether or not commas are included in large numbers, whether a dollar sign is added, and how negative numbers are listed. Following the \# switch itself, combine the following instructions to taste:

Instruction	*Results Displayed*
,	Adds commas between groups of three digits (as in 12,345). When added to a field by Word, this instruction contains additional # characters, but they aren't necessary.
0	Rounds the value to the nearest integer, with no decimal places.
0.00	Rounds the value to the number of decimal places specified (in this example, two). When you select a decimal format, the field results always display all the specified decimal positions, even those whose value is 0.
% or $	You can include these symbols (or any text for that matter) by typing them into the field code where you want them to appear in the results.

To tell Word to use different formatting for negative numbers, type a semicolon after the numeric picture for positive numbers, and then enter the picture for the negative ones. Some examples should clarify how to use these instructions:

Numeric Picture	*Example Results*
\# $,0.00;($,0.00)	$112.52 (positive number) ($45.68)
\# $0	$65
\# ,0.000%	6,324.445%

Using the Date-Time Picture switch

Normally, fields that display date or time information do so using the format set as the default in the Insert ⇨ Date and Time dialog box. And if no default is set there, you get the format set in the Windows Control Panel on the Date tab in the Regional Settings Properties dialog box.

The Date-Time picture switch (\@) lets you take complete control. The field results can list, in any order, the named day of the week, the numeric day of the month, the month, the year, the minute, and the hour. You can include punctuation or even extra text, to produce automatic results such as, "It was in the year 1999. The day was Monday, February 15. The time was 5:00 AM." Table 33-2 lists the elements you use in date-time pictures to specify various date- and time-related results in fields. Examples of date-time pictures include the following:

Switch	Sample Result
\@ "yyyy"	1999
\@ "dddd, MMMM d"	Monday, September 22
\@ "h in the AM/PM"	6 in the PM

Unfortunately, I don't know of a way to include apostrophes within a date-time picture. That's why the last example doesn't read "6 o'clock PM."

Table 33-2 Components Available for Use in Date-Time Pictures

Entry in the Date-Time Picture	Field Results Displayed
Month (uppercase M)	
M	Number of the month, without a leading 0 (zero) if it's a single-digit month
MM	Number of the month, with a leading 0 (zero) if it's a single-digit month
MMM	The three-letter abbreviation of the month
MMMM	The month's full name
Day (lowercase d)	
d	Day of the month, without a leading 0 (zero) if it's a single-digit day
dd	Day of the month, with a leading 0 (zero) if it's a single-digit day
ddd	The three-letter abbreviation of the day of the week (Mon, Tue, and so on)
dddd	The day of the week spelled out in full

Continued

Table 33-2 *(continued)*

Entry in the Date-Time Picture	Field Results Displayed
Year (lowercase y)	
yy	The last two digits of the year (works for both 20th and 21st century dates). The result includes a leading 0 (zero) for the years 01 through 09.
yyyy	The full year as a four-digit number
Hours (H or h): Use lowercase h for 12-hour time, uppercase H for 24-hour time (military time)	
h or H	The hour, without a leading 0 (zero) if it's a single-digit hour
hh or HH	The hour, with a leading 0 (zero) if it's a single-digit hour
Minutes (lowercase m)	
m	The minute, without a leading 0 (zero) if it's a single-digit minute
mm	The minute, with a leading 0 (zero) if it's a single-digit minute
AM/PM	
AM/PM	AM or PM in uppercase
am/pm	am or pm in lowercase
A/P	A or P in uppercase
a/p	A or P in lowercase

Using VBA with Fields

Word's VBA library includes plenty of support for fields. This section offers a quick but deep look at the most important VBA objects, methods, and properties related to fields.

Field-related objects, properties, and methods

- You access the individual fields in a document, range, or selection object using the Fields collection of the object in question. An individual field is represented by a Field object, of course. Return a particular Field object from a Fields collection using the field's index number. Check out these examples:

```
Set FirstField = ActiveDocument.Fields(1)
' Fields(1) refers to the first field in the document,
' FirstField now refers to that field object.
Set SomeField = Selection.Fields(3)
' Fields(3) refers to the third field in the selection.
```

- Use the `Count` property of a Fields collection when you want to know how many fields the collection contains, as in:

```
intHowManyFields = SomeRange.Fields.Count
```

- You can determine what sort of field you're working with using the Field object's `Type` property. Word supplies a named constant for each field type (for instance, `wdFieldAutoText`, `wdFieldRef`, and so on — the complete list appears in the "Add Method (Fields Collection)" Word Help topic). See the next line of code for an example.

- A Field object's `DoClick` method activates the field, as if it had been clicked. The following line of code executes the `DoClick` method if the field is a Hyperlink:

```
If AField.Type = wdFieldHyperlink Then AField.DoClick
```

- The `Next` and `Previous` properties for a Field object return the next and previous fields in the Fields collection. After this example executes, the variable `FieldDay` refers to the next field (you don't have to search through the collection for the next field, because a Field object itself knows where the next field is):

```
Set FieldDay = FieldDay.Next
```

To examine or use a field's *result*, use its `Result` property. This property returns a Range object, not text, so you must use the range's `Text` property to place those results in a string variable:

```
strResultory = LeftField.Result.Text
```

- Other `Field` properties include `ShowCodes`, which you can use to switch between the field's results and code in your document, and `Locked`, with which you can lock or unlock the field. Both can be either True or False.

- Use the `Add` method on a Fields collection to insert a new field into the document. The method takes arguments specifying the location for the field — via a Range object — and the type of field (see the previous discussion on the `Type` property). The first line of this example ensures that the new field doesn't replace any existing text:

```
Selection.Collapse Direction:=wdCollapseStart
ActiveDocument.Fields.Add _
    Range:=Selection.Range, Type:=wdFieldDate
```

- To delete a field, use the `Delete` method directly on the Field object in question, as in these examples:

```
OutField.Delete  ' OutField refers to a Field object
ActiveDocument.Fields(5).Delete
' Deletes the fifth field in the Fields collection
```

Here are some other useful field-related methods:

Method(s)	Use	Applies to (Field Object or Fields Collection)
`Select`	Selects the field.	Field object
`Cut, Copy`	What you'd expect.	Field object
`Update`	Updates the results of the field.	Both
`Unlink`	Converts field results to ordinary text.	Both
`ToggleShowCodes`	Toggles field code display for all fields.	Fields collection

A procedure for finding fields

Word's Find command and Browse By feature can both locate fields in your document, but they do so indiscriminately — they locate the next field of any type. To hunt down fields of a specific type, use the following VBA procedure. In the `Do...Loop` statement near the end of the procedure, for `wdFieldRef` substitute the `Type` property constant appropriate for the type of field you want to search for.

```
Sub Field_FindNextOfOneType ()
Dim FoundFieldFlag As Boolean
Set thisDoc = ActiveDocument
Set FieldRange = thisDoc.Range(Start:=Selection.Start, _
End:=thisDoc.Content.End)
If FieldRange.Fields.Count >= 1 Then
    Set SearchFields = FieldRange.Fields
    Set CurrentField = SearchFields(1)

' Check to make sure that the insertion point isn't
' already at a field
    Selection.Collapse
    Selection.NextField
If Selection.Start = FieldRange.Start Then
    If FieldRange.Fields.Count >= 2 Then
        Set CurrentField = SearchFields(2)
    Else
        Exit Sub
```

```
        End If
    End If
    Do Until (CurrentField Is Nothing)
        If CurrentField.Type = wdFieldRef Then
            CurrentField.Select
            FoundFieldFlag = True
            Exit Do
        End If
        Set CurrentField = CurrentField.Next
    Loop
End If
If Not FoundFieldFlag Then
    MsgBox "Your field type not found."
End If
End Sub
```

If you're a little more ambitious, you could wrap up this procedure in a little dialog box (UserForm) using a list box to enable the user to choose the type of field to search for.

A Field Guide to Fields

This section provides brief but critical reference information on some of the most useful Word fields. The section begins with a big table (see Table 33-3 that follows) of the fields available for working with information in the current document. The remainder of the chapter covers many other important fields individually, in alphabetical order.

The discussion of each field begins with a schematic of the field's syntax. *Instructions enclosed in brackets are optional.* As a rule of thumb, you can omit the quotes surrounding an item in an instruction if the item contains no spaces. After the syntax comes an introduction explaining the field's purpose and use. In most cases, the functions of each of the individual instructions are detailed in a table after the field's purpose and use are explained.

Document information fields

Table 33-3 lists the many fields you can use to extract information from the document itself. References to the dialog box tabs (as in "the Statistics tab") refer to those on the File ➪ Properties dialog box.

Table 33-3 Word's Document Information Fields

Field Name	Description	Syntax	Details	Comments, Samples
Author	Inserts the document author's name as listed on the Summary tab of the Properties dialog box.	{ AUTHOR ["Author's name"] }	If no one has typed in another name, the author name is on the User Information tab of the Tools ⇆ Options dialog box. Author's name. To change the author name, enter the new name in quotation marks here. The entry replaces the existing one in the Properties dialog box.	{ AUTHOR " { FILLIN "Please enter the author's name: " } " } This field asks the user to type in. The name is printed in the document and is added to the Properties dialog box (File menu).
Comments	Inserts the text in the Comments box on the Summary tab.	{ COMMENTS ["New Comments"] }	New Comments. To change the current comments, place the new ones in quotation marks here.	
CreateDate	Inserts the date and time the document was first saved under the current name (from the Created box on the Statistics tab).	{ CREATEDATE [\@ "Date-Time Picture"] }	See "Using the Date-Time picture switch."	This deposition taken { CREATEDATE \@ "MMMM d, yyyy" }.
DocProperty	Inserts specified document information from the Properties dialog box.	{ DOCPROPERTY "Property"}	Property. Enter the name of any property listed in the Properties dialog box (including custom properties). You can list only one property per field.	Contact: { DOCPROPERTY Project }
EditTime	Inserts the time in minutes that the document has been open for editing since it was first created, or since it was saved under a new name (Statistics tab).	{ EDITTIME }		

Chapter 33: A Dream of Fields

Field Name	Description	Syntax	Details	Comments, Samples
FileName	Inserts the document's filename (General tab).	{ FILENAME [\p] }	\p. Includes the full path with the filename.	
FileSize	Inserts the document's size in bytes (Statistics tab).	{ FILESIZE [\k] [\m] }	\k displays the file size in kilobytes (KB). \m displays the file size in megabytes (MB).	
Info	Inserts specified information from the Properties dialog box.	{ [INFO] *Property* ["*NewValue*"] }	*InfoType*. The property type. *NewValue*. You can change the entry for any of the following properties, AUTHOR, COMMENTS, KEYWORDS, SUBJECT, and TITLE, by placing the new value in the field.	Similar to DocProperty, but enables you to change some properties
Keywords	Inserts contents of the Keywords box from the Summary tab.	{ KEYWORDS ["*NewKeywords*"] }	*NewKeywords*. To change the current keywords, place the new ones in quotation marks here.	
LastSavedBy	Inserts the name of the person who last saved the file, as listed on the Statistics tab.	{ LASTSAVEDBY }	Despite the name, this field reports the current entry at Author on the Statistics tab, whether or not the document has been saved since the author's name was changed.	
NumChars	Inserts the number of characters in the document (Statistics tab).	{ NUMCHARS }		Use the following field to calculate the average word length: { = { NUMCHARS } / { NUMWORDS } }

Continued

Table 33-3 *(continued)*

Field Name	Description	Syntax	Details	Comments, Samples
NumPages	Inserts the total number of pages in the document (Statistics tab).	{ NUMPAGES }	Use this field with the PAGE field to create entries such as Page 3 of 300. If the document begins on a page number other than 1, calculate the total page count with this field: { = (StartingNumber - 1) + { NUMPAGES } }	
NumWords	Inserts the total number of words in the document (Statistics tab).	{ NUMWORDS }		
PrintDate	Inserts the date and time when the document was last printed (Statistics tab).	{ PRINTDATE \@ "Date-Time Picture" }	See "Using the Date-Time picture switch."	
RevNum	Inserts the number of times the document has been saved. (Statistics tab).	{ REVNUM }	This field is worthless! You're supposed to save your documents frequently, not just when you consider a "revision" complete. If you follow this advice, this field actually reports "number of times I felt that it was prudent to save the document."	
SaveDate	Inserts the date and time a document was last saved ("Modified" on the Statistics tab).	{ SAVEDATE \@ "Date-Time Picture" }	See "Using the Date-Time picture switch."	
Subject	Inserts contents of the Subject box (Summary tab).	{ SUBJECT ["NewSubject"] }	*NewSubject*. To change the subject as listed in the Properties dialog box, add the new subject here in quotation marks (up to 255 characters).	You can use a FILLIN field to ask the person working on the document to enter a new subject: { SUBJECT " { FILLIN "Enter the document subject" } " }

Field Name	Description	Syntax	Details	Comments, Samples
Template	Inserts the filename of the document's template (Summary tab).	{ TEMPLATE [\p] }	\p includes the full path with the template's filename.	
Title	Inserts the document title, as listed in the Summary tab.	{ TITLE ["*NewTitle*"] }	*NewTitle*. To change the title as listed in the Properties dialog box, add the new subject here in quotation marks.	
UserAddress	Inserts the address from the Mailing Address box on the User Information tab in the Tools ⇨ Options dialog box.	{ USERADDRESS ["*NewAddress*"] }	*NewAddress*. To place an address (or any text) you specify in the document, enter it here in quotation marks. The entry can include line and paragraph breaks. It does not affect the information in the User Information tab.	
UserInitials	Inserts the user initials from the Initials box on the User Information tab (in the Tools ⇨ Options dialog box).	{ USERINITIALS ["*NewInitials*"] }	*NewInitials*. To place initials (or any text) you specify in the document, enter them here. The entry does not affect the information in the User Information tab.	
UserName	Inserts the user name from the Name box on the User Information tab (in the Tools ⇨ Options dialog box).	{ USERNAME ["*NewName*"] }	*NewName*. To place a name (or any text) of your choice in the document, enter it here. The entry does not affect the information in the User Information tab.	

= (Formula or Calculation) Field

Field syntax: { = Formula [\# Numeric Picture] }

Use an = field in the body of a document or in a table to calculate a mathematical expression.

Formula is any mathematical expression Word can interpret, which can be quite complex. The expression can contain numbers as such, of course. But it can also include other fields that give numeric results (not the least of which are nested = fields), bookmarks that refer to numbers in the document, and (when you use it in a table) references to cells that contain values. And while Word doesn't have Excel's mathematical prowess, it does offer an impressive list of mathematical operators and functions you can use to manipulate these numeric values (see Tables 33-4 and 33-5). See "Using the Numeric Picture switch" earlier for the number format choices you can use with the \#Numeric Picture switch to display the field's results.

Table 33-4 Operators Available in = Fields

Operator	Description
+	Addition
−	Subtraction
*	Multiplication
/	Division
%	Percentage
^	Powers and roots
=	Equals, equal to
<	Less than
<=	Less than or equal to
>	Greater than
>=	Greater than or equal to
<>	Not equal to

Table 33-5 Functions Available in = Fields

Function	Result
ABS(x)	Absolute value of x
AND(x,y)	True (1) if both x and y are true, otherwise False (0)
AVERAGE(x,y,z . . .)	Arithmetic mean of x + y + z + . . .
COUNT(x,y,z, . . .)	Number of items listed
DEFINED(x)	True (1) if x is a valid expression, False if Word can't calculate the value of x
False	False (0)
IF(x,y,z)	y, if x is True; otherwise z
INT(x)	The integer portion of x
MAX(x,y,z . . .)	The largest item listed
MIN(x,y,z . . .)	The smallest item listed
MOD(x,y)	The remainder of x divided by y
NOT(x)	False (0) if x is True, otherwise True (1)
OR(x,y)	True (1) if either x or y is True, False if both x and y are False
PRODUCT(x,y,z . . .)	Product of x times y times z . . .
ROUND(x,y)	x rounded to y decimal places
SIGN(x)	1 if x is positive, 0 if zero, −1 if negative
SUM(x,y,z . . .)	Sum of x + y + z . . .
True	True (1)

See Chapter 30 for information about referring to cells in = fields used within tables.

Using Excel instead

It's easier to insert an Excel worksheet (or a portion thereof) into your document than to create a Word table using = fields for your calculations. Creating formulas of any complexity without Excel's help is bound to waste time and lead to errors. Use the = field only if Excel isn't installed on your system for some reason or if you're sending the document to someone who doesn't have Excel.

Using bookmarks in formulas

Any portion of the expression calculated by an = field can be a bookmark that refers to a value somewhere else in the document. The bookmarked text can be a single number, a field that produces a numeric result, or even a complete expression. Examples include { = 4*Bookmark }, { = Max(33, Bookmark, 78)+Bookmark2 }, and even { = Bookmark }.

To place a mathematical expression in your document for bookmarking purposes, just type it in as it would appear inside the = field. If you bookmark a sequence of numbers or numeric expressions separated only by commas or spaces, Word adds them together to calculate the value of the bookmark.

Ask

Field syntax: { ASK *Bookmark* "*Prompt*" [\d "*Default*"] [\o] }

Each time an ASK field gets updated, it displays a little dialog box asking the reader of the document to type in a response. When the reader clicks OK, Word stores the typed text in a bookmark. If you want to display the newly bookmarked text, you must insert another field (a REF field) to do so. Alternatively, you can use the bookmarked information in other fields. For example, you can ask the reader to type in a number and use the entry in a calculation performed by an = field.

Instruction	Function
Bookmark	This is the bookmark name that will be assigned to the entry typed by the reader in the dialog box.
"*Prompt*"	This is text to be displayed as instructions to the reader in the dialog box, such as "How many were going to St. Ives? Please enter a number from 1-100."
\d "*Default*"	Use this switch to provide Word with a default response that it can use if no entry is made in the dialog box. If you don't include this switch, Word suggests the previous entry, if any. If an undefined entry would cause trouble in other fields referring to the bookmark, you can specify a blank entry as the default by entering only a pair of quotation marks after the \d.
\o	When an ASK field resides in a mail merge main document, its dialog box normally appears every time a new data record is merged. If you include the \o switch, however, Word displays the dialog only once and uses that response in every document created during the mail merge.

AutoNum, AutoNumLgl, AutoNumOut

These fields are holdovers to ensure compatibility with earlier Word versions. Use ListNum instead.

AutoText

Field syntax: { AUTOTEXT *AutoTextEntry* }

This field inserts the text or graphics stored in *AutoTextEntry* into your document. Use it when you expect a component of the document to change over time. When the item does change, just redefine the AutoText entry and update the fields for an instant revision.

AutoTextList

Field syntax: { AUTOTEXTLIST "*LiteralText*" [\s "*StyleName*"] [\t "*TipText*"] }

This field builds and displays a drop-down list of AutoText entries drawn from the current template. You can limit the list to AutoText entries associated with a particular character or paragraph style.

Instruction	Function
LiteralText	This is text that displays in the document before the user displays the drop-down list. If the text contains spaces, enclose it in quotation marks.
\s "*StyleName*"	To limit the AutoText entries displayed in the list to those associated with a particular style, enter the style's name here. If no entries are associated with the style, Word displays all AutoText entries.
\t "*TipText*"	Lets you specify ScreenTip text for the field.

Barcode

Field syntax: { BARCODE "*Address*" [\b] [\u] [\f "*char*"] }

This field inserts a postal barcode based on an address that you type in or that is marked by a bookmark (in which case *Address* is the bookmark name and must be followed by the [\b] switch). Don't insert this field manually — use the Tools ⇨ Envelopes and Labels dialog box instead, selecting the appropriate check boxes for your barcodes. However, if you want to base the barcode on a bookmarked address, you'll need to edit the resulting field to add the bookmark name followed by the \b switch.

"Bookmark"

This is just an alternative version of the REF field type — see the discussion on that field.

Compare

Field syntax: { COMPARE *Expression1 Operator Expression2* }

This field compares two numeric expressions or character strings with a single-minded purpose: to determine whether or not they are equivalent. The field result is 1 if the comparison is true, zero if it is false. The COMPARE field is almost always nested within an IF field, so that some action can be taken based on the result of the comparison.

Instruction	Function
Expression1 and *Expression2*	These are the expressions or character strings to compare. See the section on the = field for a discussion of the forms numeric expressions can take. If you're comparing strings of characters with the = or < > operators, you can use wildcard characters in *Expression2*: ? stands for any character, *, for any string. In this case, or if an expression contains spaces, you must enclose it in quotation marks.
Operator	May be any of the comparison operators in Table 33-4 (equal to, less than, less than or equal to, greater than, greater than or equal to, or not equal to).

Date

Field syntax: { DATE [\@ "*Date-Time Picture*"] [\l] }

The DATE field inserts the current date, time, or both. See the discussion in "Using the Date-Time Picture switch" earlier.

Instruction	Function
\@ "*Date-Time Picture*"	Use this switch to specify a custom date and time format.
\l	Inserts the date and time information in the same format last selected in the Insert ⇨ Date and Time dialog box.

DDE and DDEAuto

Field syntax: { DDE *Application Document* [*PlaceReference*] }
Field syntax: { DDEAUTO *Application Document* [*PlaceReference*] }

Not for the faint of heart, these fields set up dynamic data exchange (DDE) links with information in a document from another application. When the field gets updated, any revisions in the specified information appear in your document (DDEAUTO fields update themselves automatically).

Instruction	Function
Application	This is the name of the other application as it is known to Windows.
Document	This is the name of the item containing the information. This is usually a filename, but it may be another named item known to the other application. To list a filename with its path, replace single backslashes with double backslashes, and enclose the name in quotation marks if it contains spaces.
PlaceReference	This is the name used in the other application to identify the specific information you want the field to obtain. One example would be a named range in an Excel worksheet.

Eq

Field syntax: { EQ [*Switches*] }

The EQ field places a formatted mathematical equation into your document. I mention it only to warn you off — please don't use this field, because the equation editor that comes with Office is a much more capable tool (see Chapter 8 for a brief introduction).

Fill-in

Field syntax: { FILLIN ["*Prompt*"] [\d "*Default*"][\o] }

This field works much like the ASK field. The difference is that instead of creating a bookmark that you can reference in other fields, a FILLIN field simply displays the reader's entry.

GoToButton

Field syntax: { GOTOBUTTON *Destination DisplayText* }

Now that Word has hyperlinks for instant point-to-point navigation, GoToButton fields are less valuable. To add a graphical button that the reader can push to another location, you can now insert a hyperlink onto an AutoShape or a control from the Control toolbox. Unlike hyperlinks, however, GoToButton fields can jump by number to a specific page, line, section, footnote, or comment — you don't need to bookmark these locations first.

You can use a GoToButton field to jump to any item that has been cross-referenced by a page number, or to any footnote. Instead of entering a literal page number or footnote number, insert into the field a cross-reference (itself a field) after the appropriate code letter, as in these examples:
{GOTOBUTTON "p{ PAGEREF _Ref375226869 }" "Jump to Table 12.12"}
{GOTOBUTTON "f { NOTEREF _Ref375225952 }" "Push here to jump to relevant footnote" }.

Instruction	Function
Destination	This is either a bookmark name or a code indicating by number a line, page, section, footnote, or comment. For example, you would enter p4 to jump to page 4. Use l (the letter "el") to jump to a specified line number, s for a section, f for a footnote, and a for a comment.
DisplayText	Type the text that should serve as the jump button, or insert an INCLUDEPICTURE field to display a graphic button. The text or graphic must appear on one line in the field result; otherwise, an error occurs. You can also enter a field that gives text.

Hyperlink

Field syntax: { HYPERLINK "*Destination*" [\h] [\l] [\m] [\n] [\s] [\t] }

Hyperlinks are covered in Chapters 6 and 14, but details on the field instructions are given here. *Destination* is the name of the file or URL you want to jump to. Single backslashes in a path name should be entered as double backslashes here. Enclose the destination in quotation marks if it contains spaces.

Instruction	Function
\h	Instructs Word not to add the link to the history list.
\l	Sets the specific target location in the destination file, typically a bookmark.
\m	Adds server-side image map coordinates.
\n	Opens the destination in a new window.
\s	This switch should not be added manually. Word supplies it when you create a hyperlink via dragging and indicates a location that doesn't have a bookmark.
\t	Another switch you shouldn't add manually. T is for the target when Word redirects a link.

If

Field syntax: { IF *Expression1 Operator Expression2* "*TrueText*" "*FalseText*" }

An IF field gives one of two possible results depending on the outcome of a test you set up within the field. Typically, at least one of the expressions compared in an IF field is based on another field or fields. That way, the outcome of the IF comparison varies depending on the current values of the nested fields. As a simple example, you would use the following field to insert in your document either "long" or "short," depending on whether the current document is longer than 30 pages.

```
{ IF {NUMPAGES}> 30 long short }
```

Expression1 and *Expression2* can also include numbers, mathematical formulae, bookmark names, and text (character strings), as well as nested fields that return a value. If you're comparing strings of characters with the = or <> operators, *Expression2* can contain wildcard characters: ? stands for any character, *, for any string. If you use a wildcard, or if a text expression contains spaces, you must enclose it in quotation marks. Text comparisons are case sensitive. If either expression is based on a field, include a format switch (*) in that nested field to ensure that the field results are capitalized like the other expression (see "Using the Format switch" earlier in this chapter).

Operator can be any of the comparison operators. Insert a space before and after the operator. *TrueText* and *FalseText* are the results you want the field to display, depending on whether the comparison is true or false. The final result of an IF field can be based on multiple comparisons if you include nested COMPARE or IF fields. Another trick is to test two COMPARE fields simultaneously using nested = fields based on the AND or OR functions.

IncludePicture

Field syntax: { INCLUDEPICTURE "*FileName*" [\c *Converter*] [\d] }

Use this field to insert a graphic file. The best use for INCLUDEPICTURE is as a nested field in GOTOBUTTON and MACROBUTTON fields, where it serves to insert a graphical button for the reader to press.

Instruction	Function
FileName	Enter the name of the graphics file with the full path, replacing single backslashes with double backslashes. Enclose the whole thing in quotation marks if it contains spaces.
\c Converter	Specifies the graphics filter Word should use to display the image, omitting the .flt extension. This switch is rarely necessary.
\d	If you include this switch, the graphic is not stored in the document.

Index

Field syntax: { INDEX [\b *Bookmark*] [\c *Cols*] [\d "*Separator*"] [\f "*GroupID*"] [\g "*Separator*"] [\h "*Heading*"] [\l "*Separator*"] [\p "*Range*"] [\r] [\s *Sequence*] }

This is one powerful little field. Each time you update it, it combs through the document collecting index entries (XE fields) and assembling them into a complete index, which it then displays.

Instruction	Function
\b *Bookmark*	Limits the index to just the bookmarked text.
\c *Cols*	*Cols* is a number between 1 and 4 specifying the number of columns for the index.
\f "*GroupID*"	Limits the index to XE fields containing an \f switch with the same *GroupID*. The \f switch lets you create separate, special-purpose indexes (for example, Index of Authors, Index of Song Titles).
\h "*Heading*"	Inserts *Heading* text between alphabetical sections in the index, formatted with the Index Heading style. If *Heading* contains any single letter (with or without surrounding punctuation), the letter is replaced by the correct letter for each section. Insert a blank line between sections with the switch.
\p "*Range*"	Limits the index to the letters specified by *Range*. For example { INDEX \p x-z } creates an index listing only entries that start with X, Y, and Z. Use an exclamation point for entries beginning with symbols.
\r	Places subentries on the same line as the main entry, with a colon between main entries and subentries and semicolons between subentries.

The remaining switches specify separators between numbers.

ListNum

Field syntax: { LISTNUM "*Name*" [\l] [\s] }

See Chapter 31 for a discussion of this field type.

Instruction	Function
\l	Specifies the level in the named list for the current field, overriding the automatic sequence Word would otherwise use.
\s	Specifies the starting value.

MacroButton

Field syntax: { MACROBUTTON *Macro DisplayText* }

This field places the macro named *Macro* directly into the document where the reader can run it by double-clicking the field results or by pressing Alt+Shift+F9. *DisplayText* is what appears in the document as the button.

You can type in text or enter a field that gives text or graphics as its result (see the previous entry "IncludePicture"). The text or graphic must appear on a single line in the results.

Print

Field syntax: { PRINT "*PrinterInstructions*" [\p *Rectangle* "*PS*"] }

This field sends control codes to the printer when you print the document. If you're a PostScript or PCL wizard, here's your magic wand. Use the \p switch to send PostScript code: Specify the drawing rectangle at *Rectangle*, and then list the PostScript instructions in quotation marks at *PS*. To print PostScript "on top" of the rest of the document, check the Print PostScript Over Text box in the Print tab of the Tools ⇨ Options dialog box.

Quote

Field syntax: { QUOTE "*MyText*" [\@ "*Date-Time Picture*"] }

This field inserts *MyText* into the document. You can type text directly into a document, of course. The real value of this field lies in its ability to reformat dates calculated numerically by other fields nested inside it. See "Using the Date-Time Picture switch" for details on how to specify date formats.

In the following example (based on one in the Word help file), the IF nested field calculates next month's number (1 if next month will be January, 5 if it will be May). The QUOTE field converts those results to text, displaying the next month's name. Pretty slick.

{ QUOTE { IF { DATE \@ M } = 12 1 {= { DATE \@ M } +1 } }/1/99 \@ MMMM }

Ref

Field syntax: { [REF] *Bookmark* [\f] [\h] [\n] [\p] [\r] [\t] [\w] }

This field inserts the text or graphics marked by the specified bookmark. Ref fields are so often useful that Word doesn't even make you include the "REF" within the field brackets—all you need to type is the bookmark name inside a pair of field brackets. (Such fields without an explicit "REF" are also called BOOKMARK fields.) The only time you must include "REF" in the field is when the bookmark name is the same as another field type (such as Page or Time). You can only reference bookmarks in the active document—use INCLUDEPICTURE or INCLUDETEXT to insert bookmarked information from another document.

Instruction	Function
\f	If the bookmark marks a footnote, endnote, or comment number, the REF field inserts a copy of the note or comment, and the correctly numbered reference mark.
\h	Makes the field a hyperlink to the bookmarked information.
\n	If the bookmark is a numbered paragraph, includes only the paragraph number of the bookmarked paragraph, without any context information. See the section "More cross-reference arcana" in Chapter 32 for an explanation of context information.
\p	Displays "above" or "below" based on the location of the field relative to the bookmarked information. When used with the \n, \r, or \w switches, "above" or "below" appears at the end of the field result.
\r	If the bookmark is a numbered paragraph, includes the paragraph number of the bookmarked paragraph in its relative context in the numbering scheme.
\t	Removes alphabetic text from the paragraph number produced with the \n, \r, or \w switches (a reference to a paragraph numbered "Subsection 2.23" becomes "2.23").
\w	If the bookmark is a numbered paragraph, includes the complete paragraph number of the bookmarked paragraph, in its full context in the numbering scheme.

Section

Field syntax: { SECTION }

This field inserts the number of the current section of the document.

SectionPages

Field syntax: { SECTIONPAGES }

The SECTIONPAGES field inserts the total number of pages in a section. When using this field, you should restart page numbering from 1 in each section after the first section.

Seq

Field syntax: { SEQ *ID* [*Bookmark*] [*Switches*] }

Use SEQ fields to set up a sequential numbering scheme for any items you want to count. Use LISTNUM fields instead to number paragraphs in complex lists. The Insert ⇨ Caption command inserts SEQ fields, but it makes other changes in your document. So when you need SEQ fields for more complicated jobs, you should insert them yourself (see Chapter 31 for an example). SEQ fields in headers, footers, comments, and footnotes are numbered separately from those in the body of the document.

Instruction	Function
ID	A name you choose for a given set of numbered items. It must start with a letter.
Bookmark	Includes a bookmark name to refer to an item elsewhere in the document. For example, to cross-reference an illustration, mark the SEQ field numbering for that illustration with the bookmark "Pic2," and then insert a cross-reference to it using { SEQ illust Pic2 }.
Switches	
\c	Repeats the last number in the sequence — good for listing numbered items in headers or footers.
\h	Hides the field result. This is useful when you want to refer to the SEQ field by number in a cross-reference but don't want the number given by the SEQ field itself to appear. For an example of this switch in action, see "How to print both section and document page numbers" in Chapter 29.
\n	Default setting. Inserts the next number in the sequence.
\r *n*	Restarts numbering at *n*.

Set

Field syntax: { SET *Bookmark* "*Information*" }

Use a SET field to set up an invisible bookmark that you can then use in other fields, or in VBA procedures. SET fields produce no visible results, so if you want to display or print the bookmarked information, you'll need a REF field.

Instruction	Function
Bookmark	This is the name for your new bookmark.
Information	This is the information to be bookmarked in the form of text or a nested field. Use quotation marks if the information contains spaces.

StyleRef

Field syntax: { STYLEREF *Style* [\l] [\n] [\p] [\r] [\t] [\w] }

A STYLEREF field displays text formatted with the specified style, which should be listed in quotation marks if it contains spaces. This field is often useful in headers and footers, where it searches the current page, displaying the text passage to which *Style* is applied. That lets you include the current main heading in a header or footer. With the \l switch you can also set up dictionary-style headers or footers listing the first and last entries on the page. Other neat uses for STYLEREF fields are covered in Chapters 29 and 31.

The placement of the STYLEREF field in your document is important. When placed in document text, or within footnotes, endnotes, or comments, it first searches backward in the document (not the note or comment text) for the nearest preceding occurrence of *Style* text. If none is found in that direction, it then searches forward from the field.

In headers and footers, the field's behavior varies depending on whether you're printing the document or just displaying it on screen. During printing, it starts by searching the current page from top to bottom. If it finds no *Style* text there, it starts from the top of the current page and works backward to the beginning of the document, and then searches from the bottom of the current page to the end of the document. For ordinary display, the search starts at the beginning of the current section rather than the current page and continues to the end of the document.

Instruction	Function
\l	Inserts the last passage of *Style* text on the current page, instead of the first *Style* text.
	The remaining switches work the same way as their counterparts in REF fields.

Symbol

Field syntax: { SYMBOL *ANSICode* [\f "*Font*"] [\h] [\s *Points*] }

This field inserts a character or text specified by its number in the ANSI character set (*ANSICode*). You can insert special characters much more easily with the Insert ⇨ Symbol command or via keyboard shortcuts, but there's one excellent reason to use this field: It lets you place the symbol into a line without changing line spacing. While you accomplish a similar end by setting the paragraph line spacing to an exact value, doing so prevents Word from adjusting the spacing when you change font size.

Instruction	Function
ANSICode	The ANSI code for the symbol you want to insert, in decimal or hexadecimal notation. To use a hexadecimal value, enter it in the format 0x*nn*, where *nn* are the hexadecimal numerals.
\f "*Font*"	Tells Word which font to use to display the character. If you omit this switch, Word uses the current font.
\h	Inserts the symbol without changing the paragraph's line spacing. This can chop off the top of tall characters, but used with care it prevents unsightly variations.
\s *Points*	Specifies the font size — in points, of course.

TC

Field syntax: { TC "*EntryText*" [\f *GroupID*] [\l *Level*] [\n] }

This is one of two Word fields related to tables of contents (see TOC for the other). A TC field marks a table of contents entry if you don't want to use the standard, automated method for creating a table of contents (from headings). Place the TC field just before each heading or other passage you want to include in the contents. TC fields are hidden text, appearing in the document only if you display their codes.

Instruction	Function
EntryText	Specifies the entry's text as it will appear in the table of contents.
\f *GroupID*	Marks the entry as belonging to the Type group. You can then use the \f switch in the TOC field to build a reference table consisting only of entries belonging to the Type group.
\l *Level*	Specifies the level for this entry. For example, the field { TC "Entering Data" \l 4 } marks a level-4 entry, and Word applies the built-in style TOC 4 to that entry in the table of contents. If no level is specified, level 1 is assumed.
\n	Omits the page number for the entry.

TOC

Field syntax: { TOC [\a *ID*] [\b *Bookmark*] [\c *ID*] [\f *GroupID*] [\l *Levels*] [\n *Levels*] [\o "*Headings*"][\p "*Separators*"] [\s *ID*] [\d "*Separators*"] [\t "*Style,Level, Style,Level, . . .*"] [\w] [\x] }

A TOC field inserts a finished table of contents or other reference table in your document based on headings or other styles, or on TC fields. Although you can insert a TOC field via the Insert ⇨ Index and Tables dialog box, you often need to add or edit switches to customize the results.

Instruction	Function
\a *ID*	Creates the table of contents from paragraphs in which SEQ fields of type *ID* reside. Only the text you typed in the document is listed in the table of contents — not the sequence number itself, or any other text inserted by the SEQ field. Usually used to create tables of figures, equations, and so on, as described in Chapter 32.
\b *Bookmark*	Limits the table of contents to entries taken only from the bookmarked part of the document.
\c *ID*	Like \a, except that the sequence number and text inserted by the SEQ field are included in the table of contents, along with the paragraph text in which the SEQ field resides.

Continued

Instruction	Function
\f *GroupID*	Bases the reference table on TC fields. If you include a *GroupID*, the table is limited to TC fields with the corresponding letter.
\l *Levels*	Builds a table of contents from TC fields that assign entries to one of the specified levels. For example, { TOC \l 1-4 } builds a table of contents from TC fields that assign entries to levels 1–4 in the table of contents. TC fields that assign entries to lower levels are skipped.
\n *Levels*	Omits page numbers from the specified range of level numbers (as in \n 4-5), or from the entire table of contents if you don't specify a *Level*.
\o "*Headings*"	Bases the table of contents on paragraphs formatted with built-in heading styles (Heading 1, Heading 2, and so on). *Headings* is optional, specifying a numeric range (as in \o "1-4"). If you leave out the range, the table of contents includes all heading levels listed.
\p "*Separators*"	Specifies up to five characters separating each entry and its page number. The default is a tab with a leader of periods.
\s *ID*	Displays the number of the last SEQ field of type *ID*, placing it before the page number. You can use this switch to create Chapter Number–Page Number references in the table of contents, as long as the chapter numbers in the document are actually SEQ field results.
\d "*Separator*"	Used with the \s switch to specify up to five characters that separate the sequence numbers from the page numbers. Word inserts a hyphen by default.
\t "*Style, Level, Style, Level, . . .*"	Creates the table of contents based on paragraphs formatted with specific named styles. The number after each *Style* item specifies the level for text of that style. You can combine the \o and \t switches in the same TOC field.
\w	Preserves tabs within reference table entries.
\x	Preserves line breaks within reference table entries.

XE

Field syntax: { XE "*Entry*" [\b] [\f *GroupID*] [\i] [\r *Bookmark*] [\t "*Text*"] }

An XE field marks a location that is to be referenced in an index. Don't create these fields from scratch — you should get Word to make them for you, via the Mark Index Entry dialog box. But you have to edit them in at least two situations: if you want to create two or more specialized indexes in the same document, or if you want an index with more than two levels, main entries and subentries. XE fields are hidden text, invisible unless field codes are displayed.

Instruction	Function
Entry	This is the text that actually appears in the index. To specify subentries, place a colon between the subentry and the main entry, or the previous subentry, like this: "Washington, George:Fables about:Cherry tree, chopping down." The Mark Index Entry dialog box only has room for main entries and subentries, but you can add up to nine levels this way. In the resulting index, each level receives the corresponding built-in paragraph style (Index 1, Index 2, and so on).
\b	Displays the entry's page number in bold.
\f *GroupID*	Specifies that the entry is part of the *GroupID* group. See the earlier section on the INDEX field.
\i	Displays the entry's page number in italics.
\r *Bookmark*	Lists in the index the range of pages marked by the *Bookmark* instead of a single page number.
\t "*Text*"	Displays *Text* in the index instead of a page number.

Conclusion

Not for the timid or lazy, Word fields demand a significant intellectual investment. Once tamed, however, fields can be useful servants in your quest to build sophisticated documents with smarts of their own.

Chapter 34
Word Power Programming

In This Chapter

- An overview of the Word object model
- Key Word objects: documents, windows, selections, ranges, and the Find object
- Ranges versus selections — when to use which of them for working with text
- Crucial methods and properties for manipulating text in your code
- How to find and replace text in Word VBA

The VBA concepts and techniques covered at length in Part VI apply in all Office applications. Still, each app has its own object model through which you access the specific features of that program. In the Office suite, Word's object model offers the richest array of programming treasures. Understanding Word objects such as Range and Find can be a challenge, but getting the hang of them is crucial if you're going to be constructing VBA routines of any power in Word. That's where this chapter comes in.

Word's object model encompasses so many objects and collections that you'd need a sizeable wall poster to portray the object hierarchy in graphical form. Obviously, I can only cover a fraction of the objects, properties, and methods you can tap for your own programs. This chapter turns the spotlight on the most important Word VBA techniques. You should turn to the Help files for details once you grasp these fundamentals.

Understanding the Application Object

As in the other Office applications, the root object in Word's object model is Application. In other words, all other Word objects are contained by the Application object. Because the Application object is so central to VBA programming in Word, you don't need to explicitly mention it when working with many important Word objects. However, you shouldn't forget its role, because you need it to work with properties and methods of the application itself, as well as to include in some object references. For example, the following statement triggers the `ListCommands` method of the Application object:

```
Application.ListCommands ListAllCommands:=True
```

Secret

By the way, the `ListCommands` method creates a new document and places in it a table containing the keyboard shortcuts and menu locations of all Word commands. When you supply True as the value of the `ListAllCommands` argument, the new document contains both custom keyboard and menu assignments. Switch to False if you only want to see custom assignments in the table.

Accessing Word Documents in VBA

If the VBA procedure you're writing acts directly on a document, you must specify that document object in your code. Often, you can do so implicitly, using the Selection object, covered later in this chapter. But in other situations you must identify the target document explicitly.

Working with the active document

Secret

The typical VBA procedure in Word performs its magic on the document that's currently being edited. Use the ActiveDocument object to specify this *active document*. The statement

```
ActiveDocument.Close
```

closes the active document, of course. The point is, you don't need to write any code to figure out which document is the one being edited at the time the procedure runs — just use the ActiveDocument object.

Specifying a particular document

If you need to work with a particular document that isn't necessarily active, you must specify it as a member of the `Documents` collection. This collection contains all the documents currently open in Word. As with the generic VBA collection, you can refer to an individual document in the collection by its title, which in this case is its filename (use the filename only, not the complete path). Here's an example:

```
Documents("Toy Store Newsletter.doc")
```

Because you may not know the filename of the target document in advance, and because the user can change the document's filename, you may want to create a variable to hold the name. You can then use the variable to specify the document object, as in `Documents(strDocName)`.

You can also refer to a document by index number. The object reference

```
Documents(3)
```

specifies the third document in the `Documents` collection. As simple as this technique may be, it's of limited value — typically, you don't know the index number of the document you want to work with. One use for it is to learn the name of an open document. The following statement places the second open document's filename in a variable:

```
strDocName = Documents(2).Name
```

Creating, opening, activating, and closing documents

To create a brand-new document, use the Add method of the Documents collection. Used without arguments, the Add method starts a document based on the Normal template. To specify another template, add its full path as the argument as in

```
Documents.Add template:= _
"C:\Windows\Application data\Microsoft Office\Hidden templates"
```

To open an existing document, you need the Open method, again a method of the Documents collection. Of course, you have to include the complete path of the document file, as in

```
Documents.Open FileName:="C:\Toys\Toys for infants.doc"
```

Activate a document that's already open with the Activate method. Suppose you want your VBA program to activate a specific document that may or may not be open already when the program runs. Use code similar to the following to activate the document if it's already open, or to open it if not:

```
Sub DocActivateOrOpen()
Dim docFileName As String, docPath as String
docFileName = "Pull toys.doc"
docPath = "C:\Toys\"
For Each targetDoc In Documents
    If targetDoc.Name = docFileName Then targetDocIsOpen = True
Next targetDoc
If targetDocIsOpen = True Then
    Documents(docFileName).Activate
Else
    Documents.Open FileName:=docPath & docFileName
End If
End Sub
```

Working with document sections

Because each Word document has one or more sections, you would expect Word VBA to provide a Sections collection and individual Section objects to work with these elements. One important use of Section objects is to access their headers and footers (via the HeaderFooter object). You can add new sections to a document using the Add method of the Sections collection or the InsertBreak methods of a range or selection.

Opening Windows with VBA

Each open document has at least one window, but a Word user can open as many windows as desired for any given document. Each of these windows is an object in its own right. In the Word object model, the Application object has a Windows collection containing all the windows of all open documents. In addition, each Document object has its own separate Windows collection that contains only the windows for that document.

You have two main reasons to work with Window objects in Word: to control the appearance of the window and to manipulate document content via the Selection object. The Selection object is the topic discussed in the next section; here, I focus on the technique for specifying a particular window and on introducing the properties you can use to alter window appearance.

Specifying windows in code

The easiest window to work with in code is the one that's currently being edited when the procedure runs. Use the ActiveWindow object to specify this window.

To designate a specific window in code, identify it as a member of one of the Windows collections. You don't have to name the Application object when you work with the global Windows collection, but when you access a specific document's Windows collection, a reference to that document is required. You can identify the window by its name or index number in the collection. A window's name is the same as the name of the document it displays — except that, if more than one window is open for the same document, add a colon and the window number after the document name.

The following are typical object references for Window objects:

Reference	Comments
`Windows("Document4")`	Valid if Document4 has only one open window
`Windows("Kites, tops, and skip ropes.doc:3")`	Specifies the third window of the named document
`Documents("Window display.doc").Windows(2)`	Specifies the second window of the named document's Windows collection

Working with window panes

A Word window has at least one *pane*, but it can have more than one. When you split a window vertically using the Window ⇨ Split command, the top and bottom portions of the window are separate panes. The areas where Word displays headers, footers, footnotes, endnotes, and comments are also panes.

If you have to access the appearance settings or the selection in an individual pane, you must first identify the target Pane object in your code. Refer to it by index number in its window's `Panes` collection. However, you can omit pane references when you simply want to work with the main part of the window (or the top pane if the window is split) — that's the default pane.

Changing window appearance

Window objects offer a host of properties representing the state of all the elements you see on the screen that are pertinent to an individual window. A number of these properties act as toggles — their values can be either True or False. For example, to turn on the Document Map for the active window, enter this statement in your code:

```
ActiveWindow.DocumentMap = True
```

Use similar statements to turn on or off properties such as `DisplayScreenTips` or `DisplayVerticalScrollBar`. Remember that the keyword `Not` reverses the current value of a Boolean variable or property. It's the easiest way to toggle such properties, as shown here:

```
ActiveWindow.DisplayRulers = Not ActiveWindow.DisplayRulers
```

The `Left`, `Top`, `Height`, and `Width` properties let you set the size and location of a nonmaximized window.

Using the View object

Many aspects of the appearance of a window or pane are governed by a subsidiary object, View. A few of the View object's many properties include these:

Property of View Object	What It Does
Type	Corresponds to the selection at the top of the View menu (Normal, Outline, Print Layout, and so on). To change the view type, use one the following predefined constants: `wdMasterView, wdNormalView, wdOutlineView, wdPrintView, wdWebView,` or `wdPrintPreview.` For example, the statement `ActiveWindow.View.Type = wdPrintPreview` switches the ActiveWindow to the Print Preview view.
FullScreen	Controls whether the window is displayed in standard or full-screen view (see Chapter 26 for information on full-screen view).
TableGridlines	Determines whether table gridlines are visible or not.
ShowAll, Show . . .	`ShowAll` determines whether all nonprinting characters are visible — it corresponds to the setting of the All check box on the View tab of the Tools ⇨ Options dialog box. You can turn on or off the display of each individual type of nonprinting characters, as well as other items such as text highlighting and boundaries with various properties that start with `Show`, such as `ShowBookmarks` and `ShowHighlight`.

Zooming in code

To control the window's magnification, you need to drill down still deeper into the object hierarchy to the Zoom object, and then modify its `Percentage` property. Here's an example:

```
ActiveWindow.View.Zoom.Percentage = 135
```

If you want to preset the zoom factor for a view type that isn't currently displayed, include the constant for its type as an argument to the `View` property, as in

```
ActiveWindow.View.Zoom.Percentage = 75
```

The next time the user switches to that view, the document appears at the specified zoom percentage.

Alternatively, you can use the `PageFit` property of the Zoom object to duplicate the Page Width and Full Page choices in Word's Zoom toolbar button. With either of these settings active, Word rezooms the document whenever the window size changes, ensuring that the correct fit is maintained. This statement is equivalent to selecting Page Width in the Zoom button:

```
ActiveWindow.View.Zoom.PageFit = wdPageFitBestFit
```

The Full Page choice is only available in Print Layout view, but you can duplicate it with the following code:

```
Windows("Document1").View.Zoom.PageFit = wdPageFitFullPage
```

To shut off automatic rezoom, set the `PageFit` property to `wdPageFitNone`.

Working with the Selection Object

In Word VBA, the Selection object refers to whatever is currently selected in a window pane. That's right, the Selection object belongs to a window pane, not a document, because a document can have more than one open window, each window can have more than one pane, and each of these contains a selection. (Although a Selection object technically belongs to a window pane, it's okay to think of it as belonging to a window instead, unless you specifically want to work with the selection in a special pane such as a header or footer.)

Although you can manipulate selections in your code through the Selection object, it's often better to use a Range object instead. See the section "Working with Text in Word VBA" later in this chapter for a discussion of when to use each of these objects.

Secret

The content of a selection can be a block of text, a table, a text box, a graphic, or anything else you can select with the mouse or keyboard. Key point: If nothing is selected, the Selection object represents the current location of the insertion point.

Although every window pane contains a selection, you only need to refer explicitly to the target window if the selection you want *isn't* in the main pane of the active window. To work with the selection in the main pane of whatever window is active when the procedure runs, just use the Selection object by itself. For example, you can use the following statement to replace the active window's selection with the text in quotes:

```
Selection.Text = "My dog has fleas."
```

If you want to refer to a selection in one of the windows that isn't active, you must specify the window in full. Here's an example:

```
Documents("Sea chanties.doc").Windows(2).Selection.Text = _
    "My bonnie lies over the ocean."
```

Secret

Because the Selection object can refer to many different types of content, it's always best to check to see what type of content is selected before you perform some action on it. Otherwise, you risk unexpected results or errors. Use the Selection object's `Type` property to provide this information. For example, the following code tests the selection to be sure it's a regular text selection of one or more consecutive characters before proceeding to cut the selection to the clipboard:

```
With Selection
If .Type = wdSelectionNormal Then
    .Cut
End If
```

The `DeleteKey` procedure listed in Chapter 26 shows another example of the `Type` property in use. You can use the following selection constants in such tests:

Selection.Type Constant	What Is Selected
`wdNoSelection`	No selection at all
`wdSelectionBlock`	A vertical block of text
`wdSelectionColumn`	A table column
`wdSelectionFrame`	A frame
`wdSelectionInlineShape`	A graphic residing in text
`wdSelectionIP`	Just an insertion point — nothing is actually selected
`wdSelectionNormal`	A standard selection consisting of consecutive text characters
`wdSelectionRow`	A table row
`wdSelectionShape`	A floating graphic, not in-line with text

Understanding Range Objects

When you're editing a document yourself, you must position the insertion point or make a selection before adding, deleting, or formatting the text. In VBA, however, Word's Range objects free you from that necessity. A Range object simply specifies a continuous block of text of one or more characters anywhere in a document. Range objects are completely independent of the insertion point or highlighted selection the user sees in the document window. Once you've created a Range object, you can then manipulate the text it encompasses with VBA equivalents for all of Word's powerful editing commands, just as you can with Selection objects.

You can specify Range objects in your code in two ways:

- By accessing predefined ranges via the `Range` property
- By defining ranges yourself using a Document object's `Range` method

Using the Range property

An open Word document already contains Range objects corresponding to many document elements. Each paragraph defines a range, as does each table, individual table cell, comment, and footnote, to name just a few examples. You can think of these ranges as existing only in a sort of virtual reality until you access them using the Range property of the object in question. For example, to specify the Range object represented by the first paragraph in the active document, you would use the following object reference:

```
ActiveDocument.Paragraphs(1).Range
```

Because these predefined ranges already exist in Word's mind, you can use object references to them directly, without assigning them to object variables. This is the way to go if you need a given range for a single operation. The following statement copies the document's second table to the clipboard using the Range object's Copy method:

```
ActiveDocument.Tables(2).Range.Copy
```

When multiple consecutive statements use the same range, you can use a With... block to speed up code entry and the program. Here, this technique is used with a range representing the document's third section to sort the paragraphs in the range and then make the first sentence bold:

```
With ActiveDocument.Section(3).Range
    .Sort SortOrder:=wdSortOrderAscending
    .Sentences(1).Range.Bold = True
End With
```

Secret

The preceding example illustrates how a Range object typically contains other objects which themselves encompass ranges. The statement on the third line accesses the range corresponding to the first sentence in the original range, and then makes that sentence bold. Note too that you can't apply formatting directly to objects such as words, sentences, or paragraphs — you must use their Range properties.

If you plan to use the range in multiple statements that *aren't* consecutive, go ahead and assign the range to an object variable. Again, doing so makes your code easier to type and your procedure a bit faster.

Secret

Selection objects also have the Range property. That fact makes it easy to use the properties and methods belonging to Range objects on existing selections. This example assigns the selection's range to a variable, moves the selection, and then converts the text of the original range to all lowercase characters:

```
Set deRange = Selection.Range
Selection.Move Unit:=wdParagraph, Count:=3
deRange.Case = wdLowerCase
```

Defining your own ranges using the Range method

When existing objects don't contain the text you want to work with, create your own Range object. You can define as many Range objects as you need in any open documents. The technique relies on the document's Range method, which requires you to specify the new range's starting and ending points in terms of character position in the document. Check out this example:

```
ActiveDocument.Range (Start:=10, End:=20)
```

Secret

The preceding expression is an object reference to a range beginning with the 11th character and ending with the 20th character in the document. The "character position" values actually refer to the place just to the left of a given character where the insertion point would go. A value of 0 corresponds to the location immediately to the left of the first character in the document, and a value of 10 to the spot just past the 10th character and just left of the 11th character. Word counts *all* characters in the document, including hidden and nonprinting characters, whether or not they're currently visible.

To create a range that is just a location and contains no text, set the Start and End values to the same number. To include the entire document in the Range object, use the document's Range method with no arguments, or use the document's Content property.

Secret

It's easy enough to create a Range object — as long as you know the values for the starting and ending characters you want to include in it. The trouble is, you rarely want to work with an arbitrary number of characters at an arbitrary location in your document. More often, you're interested in text at meaningful places in the document. You might want to begin a range at an existing bookmark, at the start of the current selection or an existing range, or at a particular word or phrase that you know is somewhere in the document.

To define a range based on some such item, use the Start or End properties of a Selection, Range, or Bookmark object to learn the character position value you need. If you want to create a 10-character range starting at a bookmark named ForgetMeNot, these statements do the trick:

```
With ActiveDocument
Set myBkMark = .Bookmarks("ForgetMeNot")
Set homeOnTheRange =.Range (Start:= myBkMark, End:= myBkMark + 10)
End With
```

Here's another example showing how you can use the Range property to locate a paragraph, focus in on a particular word it contains, and then use the beginning of the word as the start of a new range. Here, the End argument is omitted, so the range extends from that point to the end of the document:

```
With ActiveDocument
    Set firstWord = .Paragraphs(160).Range.Words(3)
    Set RangeTop =.Range (Start:= firstWord.Start)
End With
```

As discussed in the section later in this chapter, using Find with a range or selection redefines the object to encompass only the text it finds. So after Find locates a phrase in a range or selection, the Start or End properties for the same range or selection now identify the start and end positions of the found text.

Working with Text in Word VBA

Range and Selection objects are the starting points for almost everything you can do to text in Word VBA. Some text manipulations can be applied to documents as a whole, but in general, you need a range or selection before you can make changes.

Range and Selection objects have a great deal in common, but they also have important differences. Both represent continuous sequences of characters, upon which you can perform all kinds of editing magic. They share the majority of their properties and methods. However, some properties and methods are unique to selections and some to ranges. The big differences, of course, are that a Selection object corresponds to a window pane's one visible selection — which can be text, graphics, or other items — but Range objects exist independently of the selection, always consist of text, and can be accessed in any number.

Secret

Use the Selection object when your procedure depends on the user to identify the text to be manipulated, or when you want to show the user the text being changed. Range objects are better otherwise. They make your program faster and less distracting to the user — Word updates the screen every time the selection changes, but it leaves the screen alone when modifying a range. In addition, range modifications politely leave the user's selection undisturbed.

Selecting ranges, and creating ranges from selections

Despite their differences, Selection and Range objects can be created easily from one another. This capability is key. Many important editing functions work only with ranges. Contrariwise, the only way to display the contents of a range to the user is by selecting the range. Use these simple techniques:

- To select a range, use the range's `Select` method. For a range object called `RangeR`, the code would be `RangeR.Select`.

- To access a range representing the same contents as a selection, use the selection's `Range` property, as in `Selection.Range`.

Secret

Remember, if a text-related method calls for a range but you want to use it on the selection, just type `Selection.Range.MethodName` in your code.

Redefining ranges and selections

Word VBA offers scads of methods for moving and resizing ranges and selections. I cover some of the most important of these in this section, but you can find more with careful study of the Help files.

Expanding a range or selection

The `Expand` method makes an existing range or selection bigger by tacking on at its end a unit of text. The unit can be a character, word, or paragraph, or any of a number of other predefined chunks. You can only add one of the specified units at a time, however, and you can't add units to the beginning of the range or selection. To add to the selection the word that immediately follows it, use the following statement:

```
Selection.Expand(wdWord)
```

You can use any of the following constants to expand the object: `wdCharacter`, `wdWord`, `wdSentence`, `wdParagraph`, `wdSection`, `wdStory`, `wdCell`, `wdColumn`, `wdRow`, `wdTable`, and (for Selection objects only) `wdLine`. `wdWord` (the default).

Perhaps confusingly, Selection objects (but not ranges) also have an `Extend` method. This method turns on Word's extend mode, which extends the selection when the user moves the insertion point. Each time your program calls the `Extend` method the selection grows by a larger unit of text to encompass in sequence the current word, sentence, paragraph, section, and document. If you specify a character argument, as in `Selection.Extend("C")`, the selection extends to the next occurrence of that character instead.

Moving a range or selection

Word VBA permits you to redefine the beginning and end of a range or selection at will. Just be aware that the methods that include "Move" in the name change the location of the range or selection—they don't actually move the text contained in the object.

The `Move` method alters the range or selection by first collapsing it so that it marks a location only and no longer contains any text. This location is the starting position of the original object. The method then moves this collapsed object according to your instructions. After the move is complete, you can use the `Expand` or `MoveEnd` methods to make the object encompass text.

The following example moves the named range backward in the document by two paragraphs. Note that you use a named constant for the `Unit` argument (see the earlier section "Expanding a range or selection" for a list of these constants). The `Count` argument is a positive integer if you want to move forward in the document (toward the end) and negative to move backward. If the range or selection isn't already collapsed, or if it falls inside a unit, the beginning or end of the current unit is counted as the first one of the move. In this example, no parentheses appear around the arguments because the method's return value—how many units were actually moved—isn't used here.

```
onTheRange.Move Unit:=wdParagraph, Count:= -2
```

The `MoveStart` and `MoveEnd` methods work like `Move`, except that they only change the starting or ending position of the range or selection. The statement

```
Selection.MoveStart Unit:=wdWord, Count:=3
```

moves the beginning of the selection three words closer to the end of the document. Note that if you move the object's starting point past the end, Word collapses the range or selection and moves it as specified. Vice versa when moving the object's end before the start.

Yet another pair of methods, `StartOf` and `EndOf`, move or extend the start or end position of a range or selection. `StartOf` moves the start of the object backward to the start of the current unit, while `EndOf` moves the end of the object forward to the end of the current unit. With either method you can use the `Extend` argument to control whether Word moves both the start and end positions simultaneously, collapsing the object or only the side being moved. If the side of the object being moved is already at the side to which you're moving, nothing happens. Here's an example:

```
Selection.StartOf Unit:=wdSentence, Extend:=wdMove
```

Use the `wdMove` constant to collapse the object or `wdExtend` to move only the specified side.

Collapsing a range or selection

Often you must *collapse* a range or selection to a single position that doesn't enclose any text. In technical terms, a collapsed range or selection is one in which the start and end are the same. One situation where collapsing these objects is critical is when you want to insert a field, table, or other item before or after a selection or range without replacing the object's text. (You *can* insert plain text, new paragraphs, and some other items at a noncollapsed range or selection.)

Use the `Collapse` (what else?) method to collapse a range or selection. You can collapse the object to the original starting or ending position, as you prefer, using the optional `Direction` argument. The first of the following examples collapses the selection to its start, while the second collapses a range object to its end:

```
xSelection.Collapse
Selection.Collapse(Direction:=wdCollapseEnd)
```

Secret

If you collapse a range that ends with a paragraph mark to its end (using `wdCollapseEnd`), Word places the collapsed range *after* the paragraph mark (that is, the collapsed range is located at the start of the next paragraph). If you want to insert something in front of the original range's paragraph mark, you must first move the range backward with the `MoveEnd` method via a statement such as this:

```
someRange.MoveEnd Unit:=wdCharacter, Count:=-1
```

Deleting, copying, and pasting text

Erasing all the text in a range or selection is easy — just use the object's `Delete` method. You can use the `Cut` method instead if you want to remove the text and place it on the Windows clipboard. Of course, the `Copy` method puts the text on the clipboard without affecting the text in the range or selection.

You can insert text placed on the clipboard into any range or selection with that object's `Paste` method. If the destination object isn't already collapsed, the pasted text replaces the text in the object — just the way the Paste command works in Word.

Although using the clipboard to transfer text from one location to another is a familiar method, it's not the most efficient one. A better approach is to use the `Text` or `FormattedText` properties of the destination range or selection. Set these properties equal to the range or selection containing the text you want to transfer and you're in business. The destination object should be collapsed unless you want the transferred text to replace the object's existing text.

The following example transfers the text from the selection to a collapsed range based on a bookmark (the fourth line actually performs the transfer). Only the text itself, without any formatting, gets copied to the new location.

```
With ActiveDocument.Bookmarks("TheBookmark")
    Set RangeY = ActiveDocument.Range(Start:=.Start, End:=.Start)
End With
RangeY.Text = Selection.Text
```

To transfer all the formatting along with the text, just substitute the `FormattedText` property for the `Text` property on both sides of the equal sign.

Inserting new text

The easiest text-adding technique to remember is to set the `Text` property of a range or selection to the text you want to insert. The following statement illustrates this:

```
Range2.Text = "Hey, ho, nobody home"
```

Just remember that setting the `Text` property replaces the existing text, if any, in the range or selection. Collapse the object first unless that's your intention.

Use the `InsertBefore` or `InsertAfter` methods of a range or selection object to insert text at a specific location in a document without destroying the object's existing text. These methods place the new text immediately before the start or after the end of the object in question, respectively. Word includes the inserted text in the selection or range.

With either method, the only argument is the text you want to insert. The following example inserts a new paragraph containing the text "Diary entry" at the beginning of the selection (note the use of the VBA constant `vbCr` to insert a paragraph mark). It then adds a paragraph stating today's date at the end. If you select an entire paragraph before running this code, the date paragraph appears after the paragraph mark in the selection:

```
Dim strInsertText As String
Selection.InsertBefore "Diary entry" & vbCr
strInsertText = "Today" & Chr(146) & "s date is "
strInsertText = strInsertText & Format(Now, "Long date") & ". "
Selection.InsertAfter strInsertText & vbCr
```

The example shows how inserted text can include string variables and VBA functions that return strings, as well as literal text and VBA constants. See Chapter 21 for information on working with strings in VBA.

Secret

The easiest way to add a new, empty paragraph to a document is to insert a paragraph mark (represented by the constant vbCr) with the Text property or InsertBefore/InsertAfter methods. The Add method used on a Paragraphs collection also works, but it's more cumbersome. Use it only if you want to place the new paragraph within a range or selection rather than at the beginning or end.

Formatting text

Several key properties of a range or selection are your gateways to changing the appearance of the text. These properties correspond to the items in Word's Format menu, and they function as follows:

This Property	Gives Access To
Font	Subsidiary properties for each aspect of character formatting, such as Name, Size, and Bold. For some reason, you can directly access the most common character formatting properties on Range objects, without going through the Font property, but not on selections.
ParagraphFormat	Subsidiary properties for each aspect of paragraph formatting, such as LeftIndent and LineSpacing.
Style	The name of the character or paragraph style applied to the range or selection.
Borders	The borders around the text.
TabStops	Types and locations of tab stops. You can access this property only through Paragraph objects, not directly via ranges or selections.

Finding and Replacing in Word VBA

Although it sounds like an imperative, Find is an object in Word VBA. Find objects belong to ranges and selections. Locating text or formatting with a Find object requires the following steps:

1. Access the Find object for a particular range or selection. If you want to search the entire document, use the Document object's Content property to access the corresponding range, as in

    ActiveDocument.Content.Find

2. Set the Find object's properties corresponding to what you're looking for and how you want to look for it.

3. Trigger the Find object's Execute method.

Here's an example of the technique:

```
With OpenRange.Find
    .ClearFormatting
    .Text = "pogo sticks"
    .Execute
End With
```

Secret

For properties you don't explicitly set, the Find object takes on the options that were last used or that are currently set in Word's Find and Replace dialog box. That's why you should always include the .ClearFormatting method when you're starting a new search — it removes any formatting that may have been previously specified from the search request.

Working with found text

The Execute method's job is to locate the first occurrence of the search text or formatting in the specified range or selection. Once the Execute method runs, your first programming concern is to see whether it found the text you were looking for. Use the Find object's Found property with an If...Then statement to perform this test, as in this sample code skeleton:

```
If .Found = True Then
    (take action on the found text)
Else
    (display an appropriate message)
End If
```

Secret

If the Execute method does find the search text, the original range or selection is redefined so that it encompasses the found text. This is a key point, because it means you can work directly with that text through the original object's properties and methods. In the following code, an expansion of the first example in this section, the statement .Parent.Italic = True refers to the parent of the Find object, that is, the range called OpenRange. If that statement runs, OpenRange now encompasses only the found text — so only that text will be formatted in italic.

```
With OpenRange.Find
    .ClearFormatting
    .Text = "pogo sticks"
    .Execute
    If .Found = True Then
        .Parent.Italic = True
    Else
        MsgBox "No pogo sticks found."
    End If
End With
```

Replacing text or formatting

Secret

The Replacement object belongs to (that is, is a property of) the Find object. To code a search and replace operation, you set properties and trigger methods of the Replacement object.

The following example replaces all occurrences of the word "pogo sticks" with "skateboards." The selection changes when the find criterion is found because the Find object is accessed from the Selection object:

```
With ActiveDocument.Content.Find
    .ClearFormatting
    .Text = "pogo sticks"
    With .Replacement
       .ClearFormatting
       .Replacement.Text = "skateboards"
    End With
    .Execute Replace:=wdReplaceAll
End With
```

Note that the Execute method can take a Replace argument, used to control whether all occurrences of the found text, or only the first, get replaced.

Finding and replacing formatting

To search for text that's formatted a certain way, use the Find object's format-related properties. These are identical to the properties you use to work with formatting of a range or selection, as discussed in "Formatting text" earlier in this chapter. You use these same properties on the Replacement object if you want to specify formatting for the replacement text.

To search for *any* text with particular formatting, set the relevant Find properties and then set the Text property to an empty string using a pair of adjacent quotation marks. To change the formatting of found text without altering the text itself, use an empty string for the Text property of the Replacement object. The following code searches for paragraphs currently assigned to the Drab style and applies the Frilly style to them instead:

```
With Selection.Find
    .ClearFormatting
    .Style = "Drab"
    .Text = ""
    With .Replacement
       .ClearFormatting
       .Style = "Frilly"
       .Text = ""
    End With
    .Execute Replace:=wdReplaceAll
    .ClearFormatting
    .Replacement.ClearFormatting
End With
```

Secret

Including the two format-clearing statements in your procedures *after* the `Execute` method is a good idea. Otherwise, the next time the user opens the Find and Replace dialog box, she'll have to clear formatting options manually.

Using Document Variables

Unique among the Office applications, Word enables you to define in your code special *document variables* that it records with an individual document for later use. Document variables make it possible to store values used by a procedure between editing sessions.

Create and access document variables as members of the document's `Variables` collection. Like ordinary variables, document variables have names. The following statement places the value of a document variable called `Henry` into an ordinary variable called `FriendOfAnais`:

```
FriendOfAnais = ActiveDocument.Variables("Henry").Value
```

To create a new document variable, use the `Variables` collection's `Add` method as shown here:

```
Documents("Document1").Variables.Add _
    Name:="TimesThisMacroHasRun", Value:=0
```

Because you get an error if you try to add a document variable that already exists, the safe way to create variables is by checking to see if the variable name already exists. If so, you can retrieve the value; if not, you can create the variable and assign it an initial value. The following code illustrates this technique:

```
For Each DocVar In ActiveDocument.Variables
    If DocVar.Name = "LastCaption" Then DocIndex = aVar.Index
Next DocVar
If DocIndex = 0 Then
    ActiveDocument.Variables.Add Name:="LastCaption", Value:=1
    CaptionCounter = 1
Else
    CaptionCounter = ActiveDocument.Variables(DocIndex).Value
End If
```

Secret

Even though the object models of the other Office applications don't explicitly provide document variables, you can commandeer custom document properties for the same purpose. See "Using Custom Properties as Document Variables" in Chapter 25.

Conclusion

VBA enables you to bend all of Word's awesome editing power to your own ends. You can use it to take complete control of Word's configuration options and user interface, to boot. Full mastery of the Word object model takes time and practice, but you can already do some heavy lifting with the techniques detailed in this chapter.

Part VIII

Secrets of Excel 2000

Chapter 35: Power Customizing

Chapter 36: Advanced Navigation and Selection

Chapter 37: Essentials of Editing, Formatting, and Printing

Chapter 38: Formulas and Functions

Chapter 39: Charting New Territory

Chapter 40: Analyzing Data

Chapter 41: Debugging Your Worksheets

Chapter 42: Excel Power Programming

Chapter 35

Power Customizing

In This Chapter

- ▶ Controlling startup options with command line switches and startup folders
- ▶ Customizing the screen on a worksheet-by-worksheet basis
- ▶ Saving customized worksheet views for instant reuse
- ▶ Recording and running Excel macros
- ▶ Using templates to eliminate repetitive chores and ensure consistent workbooks

Excel may offer fewer customization options than Word, but you still have extensive control over the way the program operates, how it looks on the screen, and perhaps most important, what information, formatting, and special features it adds automatically for you in new workbooks.

Startup Options

Your control over Excel's operation begins even before you have the program open on your screen.

Controlling startup behavior with command line switches

As with other Office applications, you can use command line switches to control what happens when Excel starts. Table 35-1 lists the available command line switches.

Add command line switches in the Shortcut tab of the Properties dialog box for the Excel program (or Windows shortcuts to the program). You can find details on the technique in the corresponding "Startup Options" section in Chapter 1.

Table 35-1 Excel Command Line Switches

Command Line Switch	What It Does	Notes
"*path\file name*"	Opens the named workbook.	The enclosing quotes are required only if the path or filenames include spaces. You can omit the path in several situations: if the file is stored in the same folder as the Excel shortcut or in the folder from which you start Excel in DOS, if the file is stored in the default folder specified in the General tab of the Tools ➪ Options dialog box, or if it's stored in the folder specified in the Start In box in the Properties dialog box's Shortcut tab.
/r "*path\filename*"	Opens the named workbook as a read-only document.	See the preceding notes.
/e	Starts Excel without showing the startup window and without a new blank workbook.	
/p "*path\folder name*"	Sets the working folder, in which Excel will open and save documents.	The folder you name in the command line switch overrides the setting selected as the Default file location on the General tab of the Tools ➪ Options dialog box.

Opening workbooks automatically with startup folders

If you routinely use one or more workbooks, you can have Excel open them for you when you start the program. Just put shortcuts to the workbooks (or the workbooks themselves) into the XLStart folder located in the \Application Data\Microsoft\Excel folder, located in the main Windows folder (for single-user machines) or your profile folder (if you work on a shared computer).

If another folder suits you better, or if you want to automatically open worksheets stored elsewhere on your network, specify the location by typing its full path in the Alternate Startup File Location box. This setting is on the

General tab of the Tools ⇨ Options dialog box. Each time it starts, Excel opens the documents in *both* startup folders, the alternate folder and the XLStart folder. The alternate folder is a good place to put shared workbooks so that each user doesn't require a separate copy.

You can place workspace files in either startup folder to have a group of workbooks open simultaneously just as you last used them (workspace files are covered in Chapter 36). Just be sure to place only the workspace file in the startup folder, and not shortcuts to the workbooks within it.

Excel templates stored in either startup folder appear in the General tab of the File ⇨ New dialog box, right along with templates in the Templates folder.

Secret

Note that Excel will attempt to open *every* file it finds in the startup folders, be it word processing documents, sound recordings, or whatever — so place only workbooks, workspaces, and their shortcuts in these folders.

Setting Excel Options

As in Word and PowerPoint, Excel's Tools ⇨ Options dialog box is the central control panel for configuring the program. As shown in Figure 35-1, the settings in the Options dialog box are organized into eight tabs. I cover many of these options later, but a few bear mention here.

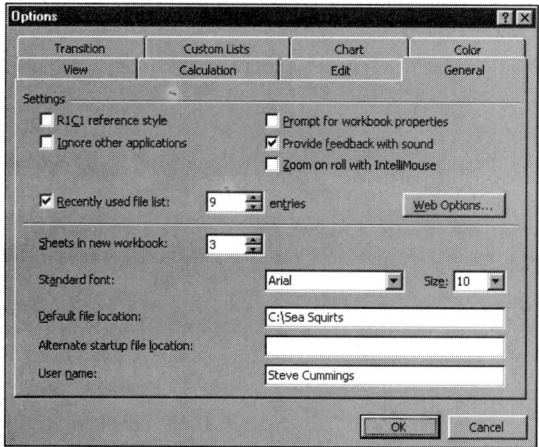

Figure 35-1: Excel's Tools ⇨ Options dialog box. This illustration shows the General tab.

The General tab offers miscellaneous settings affecting overall program operation:

- I recommend maxing out the Recently Used File List setting to 9. Being able to reopen files with a quick menu choice instead of going to the Open dialog box is a real boon.

- Note that you can change the number of blank worksheets Excel places into each new workbook you create, to a maximum of 255. Consider changing this setting to 1 — for many uses, a single sheet is plenty; it saves memory and disk space, and you can always add extra sheets as you need them.

- The User Name you specify here applies to your other Office applications as well.

The settings on the Transition tab are mainly designed to ease the process of switching from Lotus 1-2-3 to Excel. Because Excel has long since won the spreadsheet wars, few people now need these options. But the Save Excel Files As setting will be useful if you share files with others who use an earlier version of Excel or a different program.

Putting on a Pretty Face: Customizing the Screen

The View tab of the Tools ⇨ Options dialog box contains most of the controls you need to customize the way Excel looks. Most settings are self-explanatory. A few comments should suffice:

- To control which elements of the Excel user interface appear on the screen, use the settings at Show and Window options. The two Show choices apply throughout Excel, no matter which window you have open. The Window options settings, however, apply only to the current worksheet or chart sheet, or to the current workbook (in the case of the two scroll bar boxes and the Sheet Tabs box).

- The Objects section governs the visibility of charts, graphics you create with the Drawing toolbar, clip art and other pictures, text boxes, and buttons. Select the Show Placeholders button to display charts and imported pictures (only) as gray rectangles to speed up scrolling. Other objects remain visible. The Hide All button, on the other hand, hides all types of objects both on your screen and in printed worksheets.

- Check Page Breaks to display dotted lines indicating the current page breaks for printing, whether or not you've changed the ones Excel sets automatically. This doesn't affect the display of page breaks in Page Break Preview mode (see Chapter 37).

- If the Zero Values box is checked, you see a 0 in each cell containing a zero value. Otherwise, Excel displays the cell as empty, even if you explicitly entered the numeral 0.

- To change the color of the *worksheet* (not workbook) gridlines, choose from the drop-down menu at Color, at the bottom of the View tab.

Working with the color palette

Excel limits you to a selection of 56 distinct colors that you can apply to just about anything that appears in a worksheet. However, you're welcome to customize this color palette, replacing any of the individual colors with any available on your system.

Use the Color tab of the Tools ⇨ Options dialog box to modify the color palette. To specify a new color, select one of the colors and choose Modify to bring up the requisite dialog box. The colors selected at Chart Fills and Chart Lines define the first 8 colors Excel automatically applies to these chart elements. The remaining 40 colors are available for general use. The Reset button restores all 56 colors to their default hues.

Excel stores the current color palette with the workbook. You can copy the palette from any open workbook using the drop-down list at Copy Colors From. To change the default palette used in new workbooks, change the color palette in your default or custom workbook template.

When you apply a color to a worksheet element, you're actually assigning one of the palette's numbered slots — not a color per se — to the element. Change a palette color, and all elements to which that palette slot have been assigned change color accordingly. When you copy elements between workbooks with different palettes, their colors change as well.

Secret

You can apply the 16 Chart Fills and Chart Lines colors to nonchart worksheet elements. The catch is, these colors aren't displayed on the drop-down color menus of the Fill Color and Font Color buttons (Formatting toolbar). To apply the chart-related colors, you must make a worksheet selection, choose Format ⇨ Cells, and choose a color from the Font, Border, or Pattern tabs (use the latter tab to select a cell shading color).

Using Full Screen view

If you want more room to see the numbers, choose View ⇨ Full Screen to hide the title bar, the toolbars, and the status bar. Full Screen view works differently in Excel from the way it does in Word. For one thing, it doesn't remove the menu bar. On the other hand, Excel doesn't require a macro to hide the Full Screen toolbar, which is small but potentially annoying. Just click the Close box in the toolbar's upper-right corner to put it to sleep. Also, pressing Esc doesn't return you to Normal view. Instead, you have to choose Close Full Screen on the Full Screen toolbar, or again choose View ⇨ Full Screen.

Storing a view of the current workbook

Save a *view* to record a worksheet's current look so that you can return it to those settings by opening the view later. In addition to the settings on the

View tab of the Tools ➪ Options dialog box, a view can store hidden rows, columns, and sheets; filter settings; and print settings.

After setting up the worksheet the way you want it to look for future use, choose View ➪ Custom Views. When you then choose Add to create a new view, the dialog box shown in Figure 35-2 appears. Enter a name for the view and check or clear the boxes for optional components of the view. If you do include print settings, the view records the print area, or, if none is defined, the entire sheet.

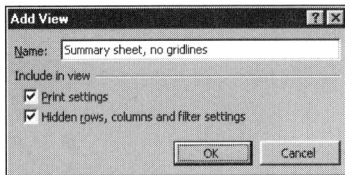

Figure 35-2: Define a new view in this dialog box.

Custom views define settings for an individual worksheet. When you open a view from any worksheet in the same workbook, Excel activates the worksheet for which you defined the view.

Recording and Using Macros

Macros are great for automating repetitive tasks and extending Excel's functionality. Chapter 5 explains how to record macros in Office, so I confine myself (if only that were possible!) to Excel-specific issues here.

In case you missed Excel 97, macros are no longer stored directly on worksheets, but out of sight in Visual Basic modules attached to a workbook.

Defining a keyboard shortcut for the macro

You can assign a keyboard shortcut for a new macro directly from the Record Macro dialog box (Figure 35-3). Excel limits you to keyboard shortcuts that combine Ctrl with a lowercase or uppercase letter (Ctrl+Shift+the letter). In other words, macro shortcuts are case sensitive. You can't use numbers, punctuation marks, or other symbols in a macro keyboard shortcut. Alt and the function keys are off limits, too.

To change the keyboard shortcut assigned to a macro, open the Tools ➪ Macro ➪ Macros dialog box and choose Options.

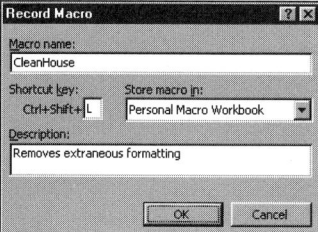

Figure 35-3: About to record a new macro, you use this box to name the macro, assign a keyboard shortcut, and pick a storage location.

Storing a macro

Use the drop-down list at Store Macro In to select the destination for a new macro. If you want the macro to be available always, no matter which workbooks are open, pick "Personal Macro Workbook." When Excel exits, the macro is saved in the personal.xls workbook file in your XLStart folder. Excel opens personal.xls automatically each time it starts up, but as a hidden workbook (for more on the XLStart folder, see "Opening workbooks automatically with startup folders" earlier in this chapter).

Alternatively, you can select "This workbook" in the Store Macro In field to record the macro in the current workbook, or "New workbook" to have Excel create a workbook from scratch and place the macro there. If you make the latter choice, just be aware that Excel doesn't announce the new workbook's arrival and doesn't identify it as a special macro workbook. The new workbook is simply listed on the Window menu as Book1.

Storing macros in a separate new workbook makes sense for special-purpose macros that you plan to use with more than one workbook but don't want available in all workbooks.

Caution

Excel doesn't automatically save workbooks in which you place macros. To protect your work against unforeseen system crashes, get in the habit of saving the workbook containing a new macro immediately after you record it. If you stored the macro in the Personal Macro Workbook, you must unhide the workbook (Window ➪ Unhide) before you can save it.

Recording absolute versus relative cell references

Before recording a macro, decide whether you want it to record absolute or relative cell references. By default, Excel keeps track of absolute references, the actual row and column locations you select while recording the macro. When you run a macro recorded with absolute cell references, it selects these same cells no matter which cell is selected when you start the macro.

To record relative cell references instead—relative to the cell selected when you run the macro—click the Relative Reference button on the Stop Recording toolbar. Clicking it again turns absolute cell references back on. Excel graciously enables you to record a combination of absolute and relative cell references. All you have to do is toggle the Relative Reference button at the appropriate steps as you record the macro. Just remember, when the button is pressed in, the macro is recording relative references.

Running macros

When you run a macro, it acts on the current worksheet, even if the macro is stored in another workbook.

Use the Run button in the Tools ⇨ Macro ⇨ Macros dialog box to start any macro stored in the Personal Macro Workbook or any of the open workbooks. Use the Macros In drop-down list to control which workbooks' macros appear in the dialog box.

You can assign a macro to a button, to another control, or to any graphic object, so that the macro runs when you click the item (use the Forms toolbar to add controls to your worksheet). Excel asks you to specify or record a macro when you add a button. To assign macros to other controls or graphics, choose Assign Macro from the item's shortcut menu. You can then assign an existing macro or record a new one.

Secret

Macros can also be assigned to menus and toolbar buttons. The basic procedure for customizing toolbars applies (see Chapter 5), with this wrinkle: When you select Macros in the Commands tab of the Customize dialog box, the available macros themselves don't appear in the Commands list.

Instead, you're offered two items, Custom Menu Item and Custom Button. Drag either of these items to a desired location on a toolbar or menu. Then right-click the new item and select Assign Macro at the bottom of the shortcut menu.

Secret

To make any macro faster, turn off screen updating while the macro runs. To do this, you need to edit the macro's VBA code as discussed at the beginning of Chapter 42.

Saving Custom Toolbar Layouts

Use the techniques laid out in Chapter 3 to customize toolbars in Excel. Then to store a custom toolbar for future use, use the techniques described here.

Creating global custom toolbars

Secret

Excel automatically saves the customizations you make to your toolbars and menus in a configuration file named Excel.xlb. By default, the toolbar file is stored in your \Application Data\Microsoft\Excel folder, but the location can be changed via a system policy file (see Chapter 17) or via the Registry.

If you want to be able to switch between two or more alternate toolbar setups no matter which workbook is open, follow these steps:

1. After setting up the toolbars to suit your preferences, exit Excel. This is the only way to save the setup.

2. Using My Computer, Explorer, or DOS, rename the Excel.xlb toolbar file (if you want to start a new toolbar setup from scratch) or make a copy under a new name (if you want to base a new setup on this one). You can use any descriptive name you like, but keep the file's .xlb extension.

3. Restart Excel, which opens with the default toolbars and menus. You can now create an alternative set of customizations. When you next exit the program, Excel again saves these in Excel.xlb.

To activate a customized toolbar setup, just use the File ⇨ Open command to open it. Excel reverts to the toolbar configuration in the standard toolbar file each time you start the program unless you make further changes. If you want Excel to start up with one of your alternate toolbar configurations, copy that file to Excel.xlb.

Attaching custom toolbars to a workbook

You can attach custom toolbars to a particular workbook so that these toolbars are always available when the workbook is open. Open the Customize dialog box and choose Attach on the Toolbars tab. The resulting dialog box lets you copy currently active custom toolbars to the active workbook. Custom toolbar setups can also be stored in templates, by saving a workbook to which they've been attached as a template (read on).

Using Excel Templates to Store Customizations

Chapter 13 outlines the way templates work in Office applications, but a few specifics pertaining to Excel deserve coverage here. Excel templates can contain the following:

- The number of sheets in a workbook, and their names and types
- Formatting for individual cells and entire sheets, cell styles, page formats, and custom print areas

- Repeating text or values, including page headers and row and column labels
- Protected and hidden sheets, rows, columns, or cells
- Settings from the Tools ⇨ Options dialog box
- Custom toolbars, macros, hyperlinks, and ActiveX controls

Secret

Excel claims to support both workbook and worksheet templates. However, worksheet templates are simply workbooks containing only one sheet — there are no other differences between the two types. You can use worksheet templates for workbooks and workbook templates for worksheets.

Creating and saving workbook templates

To create a new template, all you do is save a workbook in one of the folders Excel recognizes. Obviously, you should set up the workbook with all the formatting, content, and customizations you want in your template before saving it as such. To create a *worksheet* template, you just create a one-sheet workbook.

You can recognize an Excel template by its .xlt extension, and the File ⇨ Save As dialog box lists a Template choice in the Files of Type box. However, you don't need to select this before saving the new template. All that really matters is where you save a workbook destined for template-hood.

- To create a new *default workbook* template, save the workbook in the XLStart folder or the alternate startup folder using the name book.xlt. Excel uses this template as the basis for new workbooks it opens when you start the program or when you click the New button.

- To create a new *default worksheet* template, save a one-sheet workbook in one of the startup folders using the name sheet.xlt. Excel uses this template for new worksheets inserted into the current workbook using the Insert ⇨ Worksheet command.

- To create any other template, save the workbook (or a shortcut to it) in the Templates folder (located in the main Office folder) or any of its subfolders. Templates stored in the Templates folder appear on the General tab of the File ⇨ New dialog box. Those stored in subfolders appear on separate tabs.

Inserting a new worksheet based on a custom template

The worksheet added by the Insert ⇨ Worksheet command is always based on the default worksheet template. To insert a sheet based on a different template, right-click the worksheet tab where you want the new sheet to be inserted. Choose Insert from its shortcut menu to display the available templates. It's OK to choose a workbook template here, but doing so inserts however many sheets the template contains.

Conclusion

This chapter discussed the nuances of customizing Excel to make it truly your own. For more extensive customizations, you have to delve into VBA programming, covered in Chapter 42.

Chapter 36

Advanced Navigation and Selection

In This Chapter

- ▶ Using precision navigation tricks to move anywhere in a worksheet
- ▶ Naming cells and ranges for fast navigation—and easy reference in formulas
- ▶ Selecting the right combination of cells, ranges, or worksheets
- ▶ Speeding data entry into individual cells and ranges, including automatic filling with customized lists
- ▶ Validating data at entry time to prevent errors

Moving around in worksheets, selecting cells of interest, and filling them—these are the basics, right? So what's the big deal?

In a word: efficiency. Navigating your worksheet and selecting cells is probably the single most important thing you'll ever do in Excel. Because these are the tasks you'll be performing almost constantly, you need to learn tricks to get them done as quickly and painlessly as possible.

On the Move

Face it: With 16,777,216 cells to play in, worksheets can get pretty large. And that's only counting one sheet in your workbook! There's gotta be an easy and fast way to get around.

Knowing your place

It doesn't take a rocket scientist, or a whole village, to figure out which is the *active cell*, the one in which you can type or edit data. The active cell has a thick black border, and Excel puts its address up to the left of the formula bar in the Name box. But there's another way to know where you are: Excel gives a subtle highlight to row and column headings of the selected area, so a quick glance tells you the current range.

Keyboard navigation

As soon as your worksheet fills more than a single window, you feel a hunger for quick ways to travel to the cell you want to work with. Table 36-1 should give you something to chew on.

Table 36-1   Keyboard Shortcuts for Navigation

To Go Here	Press This Key Combination	Notes (If Applicable)
Active cell	Ctrl+Backspace	Use this shortcut if the active cell has scrolled off the screen.
Next unlocked cell	Tab	
Beginning of current row	Home	
Last column containing any filled cells in the current row	End, then Enter	
Beginning of the worksheet	Ctrl+Home	
Last worksheet cell	Ctrl+End; or End, then Home	Cell at intersection of last row and column used.
Last filled cell in current block	Ctrl+Arrow key; or End, then arrow key	Repeat to jump over the blank cells to the next filled cell in the same row or column. See the section "Making a run for the border," in this chapter.
Up or down one screen	Page Up or Page Down	
Left or right one screen	Alt+Page Up or Alt+Page Down	
Upper-left corner of the window	With Scroll Lock on, Home	
Lower-right corner of the window	With Scroll Lock on, End	
Next or previous worksheet	Ctrl+Page Up or Ctrl+Page Down	
Next or previous workbook or window	Ctrl+Tab or Ctrl+Shift+Tab	
Next or previous pane	F6 or Shift+F6	

Making a run for the border

Spreadsheets are made up of filled-in cells and empty cells. And usually, filled-in cells come clumped together. Empty or full, there are many times when you want to reach the edge of one of these areas. From either the mouse or the keyboard, some easy tricks are at hand.

Secret

With your hand on the mouse, you'd be surprised how much agility you have in moving the active cell. Let's say you're in the heart of a large worksheet, and you want to find the next empty cell in the current column. By merely double-clicking the bottom border of the active cell, you immediately jump to the bottom of the current block of filled-in cells. The selected cell lies now just above that empty cell you were looking for. If you had double-clicked the *right* border of the active cell, you would have jumped to the *right* border between filled and empty cells in the current row, and so on.

The same holds true when you're in the middle of a blank area. Double-click the active cell's edge to jump in that direction to the place where blank cells meet filled-in cells. (You have to point directly over the cell outline, so that the mouse pointer becomes an arrow.)

You can use this trick in several ways. From inside a block of filled-in cells, double-click a cell's top edge to see the heading for that column. Double-click its right edge to see the totals for that row. Or if you're out in the middle of a field of blank cells, double-click in the direction of your data to find its closest border.

If you have any previous spreadsheet experience, you're no doubt aware of the keyboard equivalent for this trick: Press Ctrl+arrow to quickly accomplish the same task. If you're in the middle of a table of data and you press Ctrl+down arrow, you immediately jump down to the last row. (Caveat: If Transition Navigation Keys are activated on the Transition tab in Tools ⇨ Options, these keys work slightly differently.)

Border crossings have never been so easy. (No passports or visas required.)

Jumping to a defined name

Any cell or range of cells can be given a name that you can jump to instantaneously. Using range names, you never again have to scroll around thinking, "Now where did I put that table . . . ?" Excel treats names exactly as it does all other cell addresses.

To add a name, position yourself in a cell, select a significant range of data, or make a nonadjacent selection (see "Making multiple selections" later in this chapter). Now click the Name box on the left side of the formula bar (it should currently show the address of the active cell). Type a name that's easy to remember — naming do's and don'ts are covered in the "Naming conventions" section — and press Enter. From now on, you can refer to the cells in the range by name rather than address.

Named ranges are valuable enough for clarifying the purpose of important regions of your worksheets. But learn to put them into action for super-fast navigation. From wherever you are in the workbook (even on a different sheet), click the down-arrow button next to the Name box to drop down the list of named ranges defined for the workbook. Figure 36-1 shows the list in action. Now click your destination range, and Excel transports you there faster than Scotty could beam you. (If the Formula bar is hidden for some reason, you can also press F5 to bring up the Go To dialog box and double-click the destination range name.)

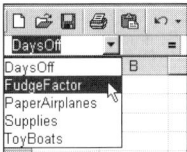

Figure 36-1: Selecting a named range from the Name box transports you to the range instantly.

Named ranges have other uses besides navigation. You can refer to them in formulas, which are discussed in Chapter 38. You can also print a named range by selecting it via the Name box, then opening the File ⇨ Print dialog box and choosing Selection in the Print What area.

Secret

When the worksheet is zoomed out to 39 percent or less, Excel indicates explicitly defined ranges with a border and the name in blue. The border and the name do not print, and they are not displayed when the zoom is above 39 percent.

Naming conventions

Though you *can* use up to 255 characters, I suggest something that's easily visible in the Name box. The first character of a name must be a letter or an underscore, and spaces and most other punctuation are not allowed (you can use underscores or periods as word separators). Of course, Excel won't accept names that are identical to cell addresses. Case is significant, and I recommend using an initial cap (see the debugging tip in "Using lowercase is a capital idea" in Chapter 41).

Managing named ranges

Secret

Manage named ranges using the Insert ⇨ Name ⇨ Define dialog box (see Figure 36-2). To assign an existing name to a different range, make the change in the Refers To box—you can type in the new cell reference or use the Collapse Dialog button as discussed in "Selecting from within a dialog box" later in this chapter. You can't directly rename a range. Instead, you must select the range name, click it when it appears at Names in Workbook, edit it to taste, click Add—and then delete the original range name.

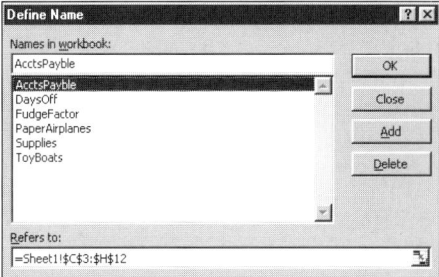

Figure 36-2: The Define Name dialog box enables you to add, modify, and delete named ranges.

Naming cells automatically based on row and column labels

Secret

Why go to the trouble of creating range names for the rows and columns in your worksheet when you've already labeled them on the worksheet itself? Excel can create the names for you from existing row and column labels. Select a range that includes both data and the row and column labels, and choose Insert ⇨ Name ⇨ Create to display the dialog box shown in Figure 36-3.

Figure 36-3: Creating names using existing row and column labels

In the Create Names dialog box, Excel makes an educated guess as to where the ranges you want to define are located on the worksheet. Confirm that it's chosen the same rows or columns that you've intended, and click OK. When you do so, Excel creates new names based on the headings of the chosen rows or columns, substituting any impermissible characters with underscores. Note that the resulting named ranges encompass only the cells containing data, not the cells with the labels themselves.

You can also create a name that represents the same cell or range of cells on more than one sheet in the workbook. (See Chapter 38, "Formulas and Functions," for more information on 3-D references.)

Going out for a scroll

Though defined names make it simple to navigate a large spreadsheet, at times you may need to take a scroll and look around. Knowing a few simple tips makes it easy.

Using the mouse to scroll through your worksheet is as simple as using a scroll bar. When you drag the scroll box to move a larger distance, a ScreenTip appears showing you how far you've gone. (In a very large worksheet, hold down Shift while dragging to scroll faster — much faster — through the sheet.) The size of the scroll box shows proportionally what percentage of the entire worksheet you see on the screen. The position of a scroll box indicates the relative location of the top line of the screen within the worksheet.

Dragging the vertical scroll box displays which row number would be at the top of the screen if you stopped at this moment. And likewise, dragging the horizontal scroll box displays the letter of the column that would be at the left of the window. Long distances are now a cinch to navigate.

Secret

When you use keys on your keyboard to scroll around, the active cell moves as you're scrolling. As long as the Scroll Lock key is turned off (which it is by default), keys such as Page Up, Page Down, and the arrow keys move the active cell. However, if you want to scroll through the spreadsheet and *preserve* your selection, make sure that Scroll Lock is turned *on*. When it's on, you can use these keys as much as you like without affecting the current selection. When you're ready to return, press Ctrl+Backspace to bring the current selection back into view.

The Scroll Lock key also enables a few selection shortcuts, as listed in Table 36-1. (If you're not sure of Scroll Lock's status by looking at the keyboard, look in the status bar at the bottom of the Excel screen. When you see the letters "SCRL," you know Scroll Lock is on.)

Controlling selection direction

Secret

So which way does the cell selection travel when you type an entry and hit Enter? It's totally up to you. Go to Tools ⇨ Options and look at the Edit tab. If you check Move Selection after Enter, you can decide if the selection should move down, right, up, or left. Or clear the box to turn off this feature completely — if you do, you stay in the current cell when you press Enter.

Navigating by IntelliMouse

Smarter than the average mouse, the Microsoft IntelliMouse has a repertoire of quick scroll and zoom functions that are sweet music if your worksheets are large. Table 36-2 summarizes these talents.

Table 36-2 Use these IntelliMouse Functions to Get Where You're Going Faster

What to Do	How to Do It
Scroll up or down	Turn the wheel up or down.
Pan the worksheet	While holding down the wheel button, drag toward a window edge. The farther you drag, the faster the worksheet pans.
Pan automatically	Click the wheel button and then move towards a window edge. To return to normal operations, click any mouse button. This works with any three-button mouse.
Zoom in or out	Hold down Ctrl while turning the wheel up or down.
Show or hide detail in outlines	Point to a cell containing an outline, hold down Shift, and then turn the wheel up or down.

Secret

The quick zoom feature may be worth the investment in an IntelliMouse. To jump to a different location on a worksheet, roll the wheel back until you see the destination, click there, and then roll the wheel forward for a comfortable magnification. If you use the IntelliMouse mostly for zooming, set it up so you don't need to hold down Ctrl to zoom. Go to the General tab on the Tools ⇨ Options dialog box and check the box labeled Zoom on roll with IntelliMouse.

Navigating to other worksheets

This is really very basic, but in case you're just now graduating from one of those old DOS-based spreadsheet programs, Excel lets you keep multiple worksheets in the same workbook. To move from one worksheet to the next, click the named tab for the destination sheet (the tab controls are at the lower left of the window). If all the tabs aren't visible, you can use the scrolling buttons to the left of the tabs to bring the one you want into view. Ctrl+Page Up and Ctrl+Page Down are the keyboard shortcuts for moving from one worksheet to the next.

Secret

For even faster worksheet-hopping in workbooks with lots of worksheets, right-click over the scrolling buttons to the left of the worksheet tabs and choose the destination sheet from the shortcut menu. This doesn't work when you right-click the tabs themselves — in that case, you get a menu that lets you insert, delete, copy, move, and rename sheets.

By the way, the Contents tab of a workbook's Properties dialog box lists the included sheets by name. Because you can access the Properties dialog box from the shortcut menu for a worksheet file in Explorer or My Computer, this can help you get more information on workbooks when you're nosing around your hard disk outside of Excel.

Using workspace files

Use a *workspace file* to open a group of work*books* (not just multiple sheets in the same workbook) all at once. The workspace file records the window size and location of each workbook in the group. However, it doesn't contain the workbooks themselves, which you continue to edit and save individually once you open them via the workspace file.

To create a workspace file, open the workbooks you want it to include and arrange them on the screen to taste. Choose File ⇨ Save Workspace. Excel saves the file with the .xlw extension. Use the standard File ⇨ Open command to open workspace files, which are displayed by default in the Open dialog box's file list. As with individual workbooks, you can have Excel open a workspace file automatically whenever you start the program by placing the file in the XLStart folder described in Chapter 35 (only the workspace file needs to be there, not the component workbooks).

The Art of Natural Selection

Selecting cells is critical in anything you do in Excel. You need to select data before moving it, copying it, bolding it, shading it, or adding a polka dot background.

The typical user selects ranges with a simple drag of the mouse. You may be thinking to yourself, "Of course! What could be easier?" But the truth of the matter is, the larger the range, the more that dragging becomes a drag.

Shift magic

There's much more magic to the Shift key than merely creating capitals or bleeping unmentionables (#@$%^&*!). If you hold down Shift whenever you move the cursor, you also extend the highlight. Say you're using the arrow keys to move to a cell nearby. Hold down Shift while you're arrowing, and voilà! The highlight goes along for the ride. All the cells you've passed have been selected.

You can also add Shift to a simple mouse-click. How often do you need to select an area that's larger than the screen, so you drag down past the last visible row, only to find you're suddenly scrolling way past the speed limit and now have to drag upward and, oops, too far in the other direction, and back down, and #@$%^&*! . . . ? You get the picture.

Next time, use the shift-click trick: Click without the Shift key in the top corner of the desired range. Now *using the scroll bar only*, scroll down until the bottom of the range comes into view. Press Shift while you click the opposite corner. If the range isn't exactly the right size, keep Shift down while you reclick. It's as easy as that.

You'd be surprised how often you can add the Shift key while moving around on the keyboard. Here are just a few more examples:

- **With the Go To box.** While sitting in a cell, bring up the Go To box (choose Edit ⇨ Go To, or press Ctrl+G or F5). Enter a cell address in the Reference box, and hold down Shift as you press Enter or click OK. The selected range now spans from the original cell to the new address you typed.

- **With the Name box.** While sitting in a cell, click the Name box on the left side of the formula bar. Type the address of a new cell, and hold down Shift as you press Enter. The entire range is selected.

- **While double-clicking a cell border.** As mentioned under "Making a run for the border," you can double-click a cell's border to jump to the edge of the current region. While you're doing so, merely hold down Shift to carry the highlight along with you. It's a quick way to select a large area.

Experiment on your own and you'll find some other handy examples. With one named range selected, try holding down Shift while you specify another in either the Go To box or the Name box. Even multiple selections become easy.

Making multiple selections

Don't forget that Excel lets you make multiple, or *nonadjacent*, selections; that is, you can select cells or ranges that are not adjacent to each other (see Figure 36-4). Once you've selected the first cell or range you want in the normal fashion, hold down Ctrl and select some more. This is a great way to add formatting to cells that aren't sitting together.

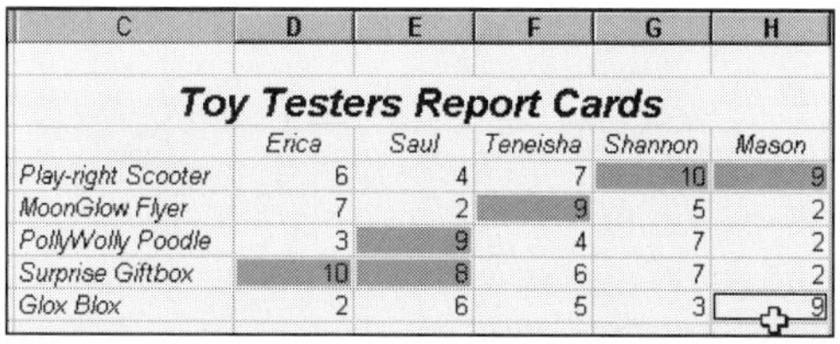

Chapter 36: Advanced Navigation and Selection

Figure 36-4: Using the Ctrl key, I made a multiple selection of only those toys that scored 8 or above. Now I can make them bold to make them stand out.

Back to square one

When you're done with the selected area, you can collapse the selection to just the top-left cell in the selection by pressing Shift+Backspace. If you're working with a multiple selection, the active cell is the top left cell of the block that was last added to the selection. Ctrl+Backspace, by contrast, brings the current selection back into view no matter where you've scrolled.

Selecting from within a dialog box

There are *many* occasions when you need to specify a specific cell reference in a dialog box. It could be a single cell or a range of cells. And of course, the easiest way to do this is to click inside the dialog box's field and click or drag the worksheet. But as dialog boxes offer more increased functionality, they also become bigger and cover more screen area. Arranging the box on your window so you can see it, without it obscuring the area to select, can get pretty tricky.

Dialog box fields that accept range references are called *range selection boxes.* You can type a range into a range selection box or enter the range by dragging on the worksheet with the dialog box as is. But learn to take advantage of the Collapse Dialog button on the right side of each range selection box (Figure 36-5 shows the button). Clicking the button hides all of the dialog box except its title bar and the range selection box you're working with, as shown in Figure 36-6. You have complete freedom (and space!) to select the area you choose. As you do, your selection is echoed in the range selection box. When you're done, you can restore the entire dialog box by clicking the corresponding Expand Dialog button.

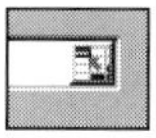

Figure 36-5: Click the Collapse Dialog button shown here to hide unnecessary parts of a dialog box while you're selecting a range.

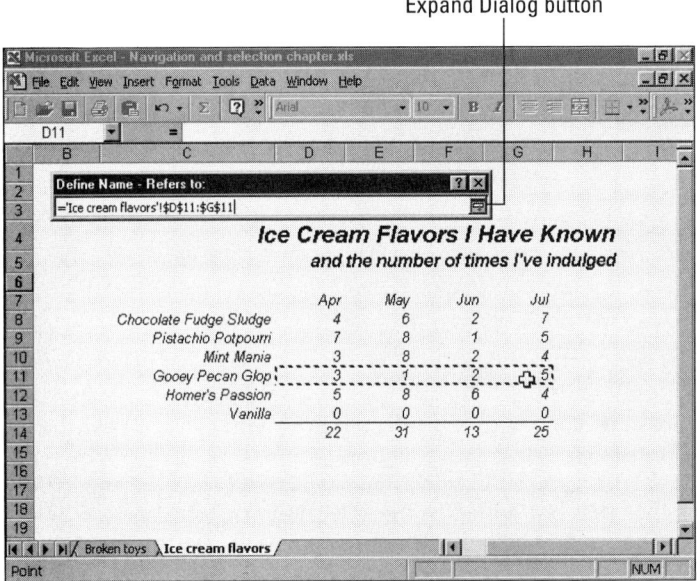

Figure 36-6: Selecting a range while working in a dialog box. Most of the box has been hidden to make it easier to see the worksheet while selecting.

Navigating inside a selection

Once you've gone to all the trouble to select some data, you'll often want to move around inside without disturbing the selection. Don't use arrows, Home, End, or click — the selection will disappear. Instead, try these:

Enter	Moves cell by cell in the direction set on the Edit tab of the Tools ⇨ Options dialog box.
Shift+Enter	Moves cell by cell in the opposite direction as Enter.
Tab	Moves right.
Shift+Tab	Moves left.
Ctrl+period	Jumps to each corner.

A table of selection shortcuts

Equivalent commands for most of the choices in Table 36-3 can also be found in the Edit ⇨ Go To ⇨ Special dialog box, but the shortcut keys get the job done faster. Here's a plug for my personal favorite: If you don't use any other shortcut in this table, make sure you check out how enormously handy Ctrl+* can be.

Table 36-3 Keyboard Shortcuts for Selecting Specific Items in Excel

Range to Select	Keyboard Shortcut	Mouse Action	Notes (If Applicable)
Entire worksheet	Ctrl+A	Click the Select All button at the upper-left corner of the worksheet.	
Whole column	Ctrl+Space	Click the column letter.	
Whole row	Shift+Space	Click the row number.	
Create or extend selection	Shift+cursor movement keys in Table 36-1	Shift-click.	
Current region	Ctrl+* (hold down Shift if you use the asterisk on the 8 key)	Click the Select Current Region button:	Selects the rectangular area of filled cells that includes the active cell, bordered by blank rows or columns. To place the Select Current Region button on a toolbar, drag it from the Commands tab of the Customize dialog box (select Edit in the Categories box).
Filled cells in current column up or down	Ctrl+Shift+up or down arrow	Shift-double-click on the top or bottom of active cell.	Selects from the current cell to the next empty cell in the current column.
Filled cells in current row left or right	Ctrl+Shift+left or right arrow	Shift-double-click on the left or right side of active cell.	Selects to next empty cell in the current row.
Last filled cell in the active cell's column or row	End, then Shift+arrow key		
Last cell in the current row	End, then Shift+Enter (same as End, then Shift+Right arrow)		Doesn't work if Transition Navigation Keys is checked on the Transition tab of the Tools ⇨ Options dialog box.
Upper-left corner of the window	With Scroll Lock on, Shift+Home		In the subsequent entry for Last filled cell, note different response to Shift+Home after pressing End.

Continued

Table 36-3 *(continued)*

Range to Select	Keyboard Shortcut	Mouse Action	Notes (If Applicable)
Lower-right corner of the window	With Scroll Lock on, Shift+End		
Last filled cell (lower-right corner of the worksheet)	End, then Shift+Home		
Visible cells	Alt+Semicolon		Selects nonhidden cells in the existing selection.
Current array	Ctrl+/		Selects array containing active cell.
Row differences	Ctrl+\		Selects cells in current row whose contents are different from active cell. If multiple rows are selected first, the comparison cell for each row is in the column of the active cell.
Column differences	Ctrl+|		Selects cells in current column whose contents are different from active cell. If multiple columns are selected first, the comparison cell for each column is in the row of the active cell.
Cells with comments	Ctrl+Shift+O (letter O)		
Direct formula precedents	Ctrl+[	Click the Trace Precedents button on the Auditing toolbar:	Select cells referred to by formula in active cell. Display the Auditing toolbar by checking its box in the Customize dialog box.
Direct and indirect precedents	Ctrl+Shift+{		As in the preceding entry, but also selects cells referred to by the direct precedents.
Direct formula dependents	Ctrl+]	Click the Trace Dependents button:	Selects cells with formulas that refer to active cell.

Range to Select	Keyboard Shortcut	Mouse Action	Notes (If Applicable)
Direct and indirect dependents	Ctrl+Shift+}		As in the preceding entry, but also selects cells that refer to the direct dependents.
All sheet objects	Ctrl+Shift+Space		You must select at least one object first.

Very Cool: Automatic Calculations on Selected Cells

Whenever you select two or more cells containing numbers, the status bar at the bottom of the screen shows the sum of the values in the selection (text is ignored). Even multiple, nonadjacent selections are allowed (see "Making multiple selections" earlier in this chapter). Right-click the status bar to change the type of calculation Excel displays.The shortcut menu for the status bar lets you select the type of calculation Excel displays there when two or more cells containing numeric values are selected.

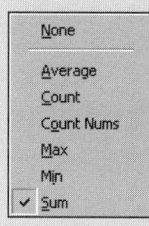

Details of Data Entry

If you filled every cell on an entire worksheet with the maximum number of characters, you'd have typed 536,870,912,000 characters from your keyboard (more, if you made any mistakes). Multiply that by the number of sheets in your workbook, and you end up with one mighty sloooow-calculatin' worksheet, not to mention your probable carpal tunnel syndrome.

While you're not likely to do this, your worksheets undoubtedly have large amounts of significant data. The more efficiently you lay them out, the more efficiently they reflect the correct results. You need data entered to your exact specifications. And . . . you need it by yesterday. With some shortcuts in hand, it can be done.

Single cell entries

You probably enter most of your data by typing it one chunk at a time. The tips in this section should make this basic chore much easier.

Getting it right the first time

Back in the olden days, after entering a number into a worksheet cell, you needed to then go somewhere else to apply the appropriate format. Nowadays, spreadsheets can sense what you want the moment you type in the data. Dates and times are recognized automatically. Enter one and it's formatted for you. Same with numbers containing commas, dollar signs, or percent signs. For the most part, Excel knows just what you mean. (Excel depends upon the Regional Settings you've set in the Windows Control Panel when it chooses default formats for your numbers, dates, and times. From the Control Panel folder, open Regional Settings and confirm that everything is set correctly.)

Caution

Occasionally, you may be intending one thing while Excel is assuming another. These times are predictable and easy to get around. For example, if you type **1/4** into a cell, Excel thinks, "Ah, hah! A slash — it must be a date," and immediately returns 4-Jan, the default date format. But you had intended to specify one quarter. A quick workaround is to always precede fractions with a zero. Type **0 1/4** and Excel will place 1/4 in the cell and display 0.25 in the formula bar. Or just train yourself to enter fractions as their decimal equivalents.

Eastern zip codes are another example. Excel can't believe we'd want a number to include a leading zero. So we get around that by telling Excel it's text. Precede the number with an apostrophe (for example, '05454) and the number is displayed just as any other piece of text (it's even left-aligned, but you can quickly right-align it if you'd like). An important caveat is in order, however: Excel treats text composed of numerals differently than real numbers for calculations and sorts. If you want to be able to sort a zip code list correctly, you must precede *all* the entries with an apostrophe, not just the ones that start with 0.

Secret

One other little tidbit: To enter a hard carriage return in a cell, press Alt+Enter where you want the line to break. This automatically turns on the Wrap Text format (otherwise found on the Alignment tab of the Format ⇨ Cells dialog box) and adjusts the row height so that the text can fit.

Copying data from neighboring cells

Copying from neighboring cells can come in handy more often than you'd think. When you need to do it, here are the tricks to use:

- Press Ctrl+D to copy the contents and formatting of the cell directly above (you're copying in a downward direction).
- Use Ctrl+R to copy from the cell directly to the left (you're copying toward the right). This also copies both contents and formatting.
- Ctrl+' copies only the formula from the cell directly above. No formatting comes across.
- Ctrl+" copies only the resulting value from the cell above. Again, no formatting.

Confining data entry to a range

If you know that your data belongs only within a specific range of cells, select the whole range before you start entering the data. As you fill each cell and press Enter, Excel respects the range boundaries. By default, pressing Enter moves the active cell down one row in the same column, until you're at the bottom of the range. When you then press Enter, the active cell pops up to the top of the next row. And when the active cell gets to the bottom right of the selected range, pressing Enter takes you back to the top left.

You can also move around inside a selection without using the other keyboard shortcuts described in "Navigating inside a selection" earlier in this chapter. And by the way, you can change the direction in which Excel moves the active cell within the range on the Edit tab of the Tools ➪ Options dialog box.

Taking advantage of AutoComplete

Secret

Using AutoComplete, Excel guesses at what you're typing in a cell. If the first few characters you enter in a cell match an existing entry in that column, Excel completes the entry for you. To accept, merely press Enter. To reject, continue typing. It's that easy.

Well in fact, that's not true. It's actually *easier*. If you're *really* lazy, you can press Alt+down arrow to display a small list of existing entries in that column. Click the one you want and you're done. You can also right-click a cell in the column (even if it's completely empty) and choose Pick from List on the shortcut menu. Figure 36-7 illustrates how all this works.

Figure 36-7: Either choose Pick from List on the right-click menu or press Alt+down arrow to choose from a list of existing entries in the current column.

Caution

AutoComplete works only with entries that contain text or a combination of text and numbers. Numbers, dates, and times are not completed.

You can turn AutoComplete off (though who'd want to?) as follows: Go to Tools ➪ Options, and on the Edit tab, clear Enable AutoComplete for Cell Values.

Entering nondynamic dates and times

Although the =NOW function displays the date and time dynamically (that is, it's constantly updating), you may have occasion to enter the date and time as static text. You can do this easily with two shortcuts. Press Ctrl+; to enter the current date as text, and Ctrl+: to enter the current time. When you do so, the formula bar remains active, in case you'd like to add anything to the cell. (Remember that these entries are static, and they don't update when you calculate the worksheet.)

Home on the range

As worksheets grow and become more complex, patterns begin to emerge. You might have found a formula that works on an entire series of values (calculating a row or column in a database). Or maybe your data calls for some sort of logical progression of values, perhaps a progression that you've designed. Either way, the bases are covered.

Filling a range with a single entry

Secret

Let's say that an entire row or column of your database has the same calculation — a sum, perhaps. As long as the formula doesn't change, you should only have to type it one time.

The important thing to remember here is to *select the entire range first*. Before typing a single character, select all the cells you want to fill. (For some great tips on selecting, see the previous section.) Now begin typing the formula or value into the active cell (residing anywhere within the selection). As you know, if you merely press Enter, the data goes into the active cell, and the cursor moves down. Instead, press Ctrl+Enter. The data is filled immediately into the entire selection.

The preceding tip could easily be my favorite one in the whole chapter. It's fast, easy, and powerful. And it works great on multiple selections, too.

AutoFilling a list of entries

Secret

Few things get as many oohs and aahs in Excel as the AutoFill feature. It is without a doubt the most powerful way to fill a range of cells with a single drag. With each fill, not only do you have several built-in lists to choose from, but you can even customize your own.

At the bottom-right corner of the selection, be it a single cell or a range, you see a small black square. This is called the *fill handle*. When you position the mouse pointer on top of the fill handle, it changes to a black cross. You are now ready to autofill. By merely dragging the fill handle in any direction, you begin to fill the adjacent cells with a logical progression. The way in which they're filled depends upon the cells initially selected and the kind of progression you've chosen.

Chapter 36: Advanced Navigation and Selection

Secret

If you don't see the fill handle even on a selection of a single cell, go to Tools ➪ Options. On the Edit tab, make sure the Allow Cell Drag and Drop box is checked. (Note that you cannot autofill from a multiple selection.)

Sample AutoFill progressions

If the initial selection is a single cell that Excel recognizes (such as a date or time), the neighboring cells are filled in a very logical fashion. If it's a string that Excel doesn't recognize, it does a simple copy.

Initial Selection	Filled Cells
January	February, March, April
Jan	Feb, Mar, Apr
Monday	Tuesday, Wednesday, Thursday
Mon	Tue, Wed, Thu
Week 1	Week 2, Week 3, Week 4
Quarter 1	Quarter 2, Quarter 3, Quarter 4, Quarter 1
Qtr 1	Qtr 2, Qtr 3, Qtr 4, Qtr 1
9:00	10:00, 11:00, 12:00
1997	1997, 1997, 1997
Potato	Potato, Potato, Potato

If the initial selection is *more than one cell*, you've specified a trend. Excel calculates the trend and extends it for you.

Initial Selection	Filled Cells
3, 6	9, 12, 15
2/23/97, 2/24/97	2/25/97, 2/26/97, 2/27/97
Jan, Apr	Jul, Oct, Jan
1997, 1998	1999, 2000, 2001
Jan-96, Apr-96	Jul-96, Oct-96, Jan-97

Other AutoFill options with the shortcut menu

Other date and time progressions are also possible. When you drag the fill handle with the *right* mouse button, the AutoFill shortcut menu appears (see Figure 36-8). Depending upon the initial selection, a variety of these choices is available.

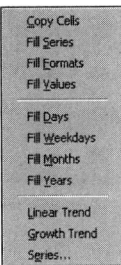

Figure 36-8: The AutoFill shortcut menu

Notice that autofilling can be used to copy *formatting only*. Also notice that you can choose between a linear trend and a growth trend. A linear trend extends the selection arithmetically "3, 6" to "3, 6, 9, 12, 15." A growth (geometric) trend would appear as follows: "3, 6, 12, 24, 48."

A quick tip to remember is that if a simple autofill doesn't give you what you intended (for example, it copies when you wanted a progression, or vice versa), hold down Ctrl while you drag the fill handle. You'll get the opposite of the default action.

Creating custom AutoFill lists

AutoFill's magic capabilities can be extended to include lists of your own design. These can include anything from names of people within your group, to product part numbers, sales regions, or all seven dwarves. (Quick! How many can you name?)

Custom lists can be defined in one of two easy ways. If the list you want to define already exists somewhere on your spreadsheet, select it and go to the Custom Lists tab of the Tools ⇨ Options dialog box, shown in Figure 36-9. The Import List from Cells field at the bottom shows the reference to your list. If it's not correct, or if you haven't yet selected the proper range, you can make changes or reselect on your worksheet now. Once the reference is correct, click the Import button. You'll see your new list appear to the left under Custom lists.

If the list you want doesn't already reside on a worksheet, you can type one in from scratch on the Custom Lists tab. Click in the List Entries field, and start typing. Click Add when you're done. The List Entries field is also where lists can be updated and maintained. (Note that you can't make any changes to Excel's built-in lists.)

You can use custom lists to define the order in which Excel's Data ⇨ Sort command sorts a selected range.

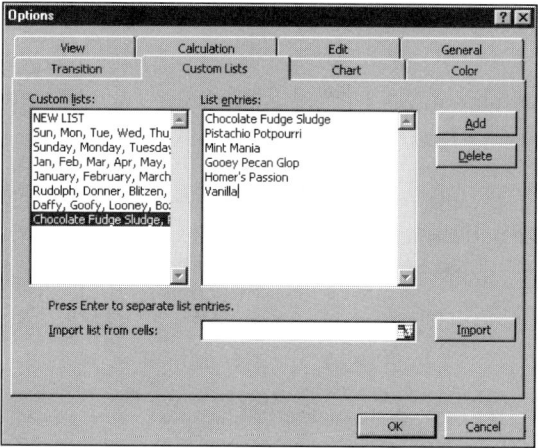

Figure 36-9: The Custom Lists tab of the Tools ⇨ Options dialog box

Using AutoFill to clear entries ("Auto-unfilling"?)

As described earlier, autofilling involves dragging a fill handle outside of the selection to extend a logical progression. But you can also use it to clear existing entries. When you drag the fill handle over the face of the selection, the area becomes shaded. Let go and the cells are cleared. (Identical to the Delete key on the keyboard, this method clears contents, but not formatting.)

Using AutoFill to insert or delete cells

When coupled with the Shift key, the fill handle can be used to insert blank cells into the spreadsheet (same as Edit ⇨ Fill), or to delete cells from the worksheet (same as Edit ⇨ Delete). Depending upon the initial selection, you can use this method to insert or delete a single cell, a range of cells, or entire rows and columns.

Beginning with a single cell or a range, you can shift-drag to insert new cells in neighboring rows or columns (cells are shifted in the same direction as your drag). The number of cells inserted matches the dimension of the initial selection. If you begin with a selection of whole rows or columns, you can shift-drag the fill handle to insert more of the same.

Deleting cells is done in a similar fashion. However, as in the clearing process described previously, you shift-drag over the face of selected cells. Excel deletes the shaded cells and shifts cells in the same direction as you drag to fill the space.

Entering data in groups of worksheets

When workbooks contain worksheets with similar designs (for example, each shows the same accounting data for a different region), any changes made to formatting or layout must be made to all sheets in the same way. When worksheets are grouped together, changes made to one worksheet affect the entire group.

Worksheets are grouped using the worksheet tabs at the bottom of the screen. You can select tabs exactly the way you would select cells on the sheet itself:

- To select sheets that are all in a row, click the first tab, and shift-click the last one.
- To select sheets that aren't adjacent, click the first tab, and Ctrl-click each other one.
- To select all the sheets in the workbook, merely right-click anywhere on the tabs, and choose Select All Sheets from the shortcut menu.

When sheets are grouped, [Group] appears in the menu bar, and each selected sheet tab becomes white. Once you've created a group, any edits made to the active sheet are reflected on all the sheets in the group *in exactly the same location*. Figure 36-10 shows this.

\ Survived dates / Broken toys / Playgroups \ Ice cream flavors /

Figure 36-10: Use Ctrl to select worksheets individually and create a group.

When sheets are grouped, you can also take *existing* values or formats from the active sheet, and fill the rest of the sheets in the group. Select the values or formats you want to fill, and choose Edit ⇨ Fill ⇨ Across Worksheets. You can then choose whether you want to fill Contents, Formats, or both.

Want to print a particular set of sheets in the workbook? Group just those, go to File ⇨ Print, and select the Active Sheets button at the bottom.

Secret

Finally, to ungroup a group of worksheets, click the tab for any worksheet that isn't in the group. If you can't see the tabs for any ungrouped worksheets, right-click the tab for any sheet in the group and choose Ungroup Sheets.

Data validation

If you're working on a spreadsheet that compiles data from many sources, chances are you're not the only person who contributes to it. Of course *you* know what kind of data goes where and how to enter it, but how can you guarantee that the others are entering data properly? And how can you guarantee that the current temp will do your job correctly, while you're off being interviewed for "Lifestyles of the Rich and Famous"?

When you want to make sure that correct data is entered on a worksheet, you can specify specific constraints for cells or cell ranges. You can restrict the data to a particular type (such as whole numbers, decimal numbers, or text) and set limits on the valid entries. These limits can depend upon data being entered, or a calculation in another cell. You can specify certain messages to pop up on the screen to aid users. After data has been entered and calculated, you can audit the worksheet to find and correct data that isn't valid.

Setting the constraints

Select the cell or cells that need validation, and choose Data ➪ Validation. On the Settings tab, shown in Figure 36-11, choose the type of data to be entered under Allow. You can constrain the entry to be a whole number, decimal, date, or time, or to have a specific length. Once you've done so, you can use the Data field to further limit the data to those that fall within a particular range.

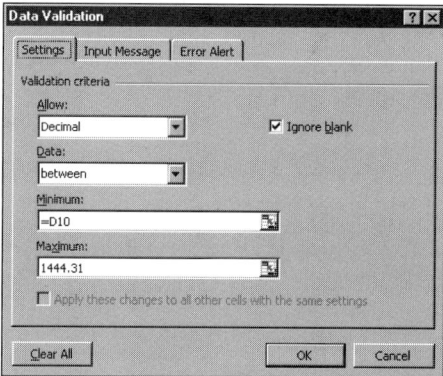

Figure 36-11: The Settings tab of the Data Validation dialog box

You can restrict the valid entries for a cell to come from a list of your own design. From short lists ("low, medium, high") to long lists (every game in which Jerry Rice has made a touchdown), you tailor it to your exact specifications. Choose List, and type in the entries or select a range on the spreadsheet. Then at any time, a user can drop down the valid choices and select one. Or the entry may depend upon a calculation that doesn't reside on the worksheet. Merely select "Custom" in the Allow list and specify the formula in the Formula field.

Displaying an input message

An input message can be displayed whenever a user selects or clicks the cell. You can use this message to explain the cell's constraints and offer help on entering data. To set up a message, choose the Input Message tab in the Data ➪ Validation box. Enter a message of up to 255 characters, and a title that appears in bold. Even if you leave the Input Message field blank, a default message still appears when a user selects a restricted cell. To turn off all Input messages, clear the Show Input Message When Cell Is Selected box.

An input message can also be displayed on a nonrestricted cell. Under the Settings tab, select "Any Value" at Allow. Enter a message on the Input Message tab. The message is displayed until the user moves to another cell.

Displaying an error message

An error message can be displayed whenever a user enters invalid data in the cell. To set up a message, choose the Error Alert tab in the Data ⇨ Validation dialog box. As with the input message, you can enter a message of up to 255 characters, and a bolded title. A default error message alerts the user even if you've left this field blank, but you can turn off all error messages by clearing the Show Error Alert After Invalid Data Is Entered box at the top. As invalid entries may still find their way onto your worksheet, take a look at the section on "Auditing Data Validation errors" in Chapter 41.

Can't remember which cells are restricted?

You can easily find all the cells with the same restrictions as the active cell, or all the cells that have restrictions of any kind.

Bring up the Edit ⇨ Go To box (shortcut: F5), and choose Special. Turn on Data Validation down at the bottom. Choose All to find all cells on the worksheet that have data validation applied. Choose Same to find cells with the same validation as the active cell.

Secret

Data validation attributes can be copied and pasted just like other cell formatting. After copying a cell with the restrictions you want, right-click the destination, click Paste Special, and choose Validation.

AutoCorrecting as you go

The beauty of AutoCorrecting is twofold: common spelling errors are corrected as you type them, and long entries can be linked to shortcuts that immediately expand. The downside is that you must define these words in advance. But the convenience definitely makes it worthwhile. Chapter 8 has detailed information on AutoCorrect.

Conclusion

If you want to manipulate more than one number in an Excel worksheet, you have to be able to move from cell to cell. The advanced navigation skills uncovered in this chapter will get you there fast. Likewise, there's more to selecting cells than first meets the eye; you can find here the lore you need to deal with every selection situation.

Chapter 37

Essentials of Editing, Formatting, and Printing

In This Chapter

- Rearranging information in and among worksheets
- Unhiding hidden columns
- Formatting commands for perfect-looking cells
- Creating custom number formats: the whys, wherefores, and how-tos
- Tapping the power of conditional formatting to vary the look of cells, depending on the values they contain
- Using styles to quickly apply multiple format choices
- Working with cell comments to annotate your data and formulas
- Printing tips

How many times have you entered data and had it look perfect the very first time? (Okay, now uncross your fingers and answer the question again.) All cells need some basic editing and formatting to give them that *savoir faire*. It takes very little to create a professional-looking spreadsheet. And if you change your mind, you can now undo or redo up to 16 previous actions.

Rearranging Information

Excel is chock-full of power tools for moving data around in and among your worksheets.

Life's a drag

When you position the mouse pointer on top of a selection's border (multiple selections not included), and the pointer turns into an arrow, you're ready for a move or copy. Simply drag the border to move, or press Ctrl and drag to copy. When you do so, you'll be followed by an outline of the selected area and a ScreenTip showing the address of the destination. But you already knew that. Read on — your powers are just beginning.

Right on the button

Dragging a selected area with the right mouse button gives you a shortcut menu with a powerful array of options, as shown in Figure 37-1.

Figure 37-1: Drag with the *right* mouse button to get this list of choices.

- **Move/copy.** The first two choices are identical to the classic drags described previously. Move Here is the same as a simple left-button drag, and Copy Here is the same as a Ctrl-drag.
- **Selected attributes.** You can choose to copy only specific attributes of a selection, such as the resulting value of a formula (Values Only), or the formatting (Formats Only). (To copy other attributes, see "Pasting particular cell attributes" later.)
- **Links.** Link Here creates in each target cell a simple formula referring to the value of the corresponding cell in the original selection (for example, =B7). As a result, Excel updates the value displayed in the target cell when the source changes. Create Hyperlink Here inserts a hot spot where the user can click to be immediately transported to the site of the original selection (see Chapter 14).
- **Inserting by shifting cells.** While moving or copying a selection, you can insert it *between* existing cells to avoid pasting over data. The four choices on the menu let you determine the direction in which existing cells are shifted to make room for new cells. The next section tells how to do the same thing without the menu.

Inserting within an existing range

When doing a move or copy, you can shift existing cells to the right or down to make room for the new range. All you need do is hold down Shift while you move a cell or selected range by dragging its border. When you drop the selection at its destination, Excel *inserts* it between existing cells. A gray line tells you whether you're inserting into a column (existing cells are shifted down) or into a row (existing cells are shifted to the right). As a bonus, a ScreenTip shows you the new address. If you're doing a copy, hold down Ctrl as usual, and add Shift to it to insert the copied cells.

Going to another sheet in the workbook

Just because your destination is a different worksheet doesn't mean you have to give up dragging and dropping. You still have tricks to use. Hold down Alt and drag the selection onto the destination's sheet tab at the bottom of the screen. When the sheet tab lights up, that sheet is active. Drag back up to your destination, and drop it into place.

Resizing rows and columns

You can change the height of any row or the width of any column by typing in a new measurement. Use the Format ➪ Row ➪ Height and Format ➪ Column ➪ Width commands. If you select multiple rows or columns first, the new size applies to all the selected items.

Resizing rows or columns with the mouse is easy. Here's the technique when you're working with rows: Place the mouse pointer in the row heading and point to the boundary between the target row and the next one down. When the pointer becomes a thick horizontal line with arrows extending up and down, hold down the mouse button to see the row's current height in a ScreenTip, and drag to change the height.

The method is essentially the same for columns, but you hold the pointer over the boundary between the target column and the one to the right, and the pointer is oriented vertically. If you select more than one row or column before you resize, you can drag over any heading border within the selection. All the selected rows or columns take on the new size.

Hiding rows and columns

To hide one or more adjacent rows or columns, select them in the appropriate heading. Then right-click anywhere over the selection and choose Hide. The hidden rows or columns disappear from view, but their contents remain intact and can be used in formulas. Use this trick to prevent underlying data from distracting you as you view calculation results.

Finding and unhiding a hidden column

You're a pretty bright person. You know that "ABCEFG" is not the same alphabet they taught you in school. So what's it doing right there on your spreadsheet? Well, this could only mean one thing: a hidden column. And you'd like to *un*hide it, but . . . you just can't seem to get the pointer in there to touch it. . . .

Secret

There are two quick tricks for unhiding hidden rows or columns with the mouse. Using the previous example of a hidden column D, the first technique requires you to select columns C:E by dragging over their column headings. Now right-click anywhere within the selection and select Unhide. Column D immediately appears.

The second trick is even fancier, a variation on the technique you probably already use for resizing columns (and rows) with the mouse.

Let's say that your row headings show "123789," and you just want to see row 6. As far as you're concerned, rows 4:5 can remain hidden. In this case, the first trick just won't cut it. Try this: Position the mouse pointer in the row heading over but a little below the boundary between the two rows that adjoin the hidden rows (in this case, the boundary between 3 and 7). When you get the pointer in just the right place, it changes to *two* horizontal lines attached with arrows pointing up and down. Hold down the mouse button right in that spot, and you see a ScreenTip showing the height of the lowest of the hidden rows (in this case, 6). Initially, of course, this height is 0.00, but as you drag downward to unhide row 7, the height readout changes accordingly. Figure 37-2 shows this tip in action on a hidden *column*.

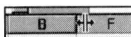

Figure 37-2: The mouse pointer changes to show you've found a hidden column.

Formatting

Over the years Excel has gained sophisticated graphical and layout features so that now you rarely need a separate desktop publishing or drawing program to gussy up your spreadsheets. Most of the formatting commands can be found on the Formatting toolbar, shown in Figure 37-3.

Figure 37-3: Use the Formatting toolbar for your most common format changes.

Here you can choose a typeface and point size; bold, italicize, and underline; left-align, center, right-align, or center across columns; apply a number format of currency, percent, or comma; increase or decrease decimal places; increase or decrease indents; add a border; add a background fill or font color; and apply a style (whew). These formats were put on the toolbar because they're just the most common—there are *many* more to choose from. And if that's not enough, you also have freedom to create your own customized formats.

Custom number formats

When you choose Format ⇨ Cells and look at the Number tab (see Figure 37-4), you find twelve different categories of built-in formats, including options for currency, percentages, scientific notation, zip codes, phone numbers, and social security numbers. Whereas these formats will meet your need in a great majority of cases, you still may need to customize your own from time to time. That's when some fancy footwork comes in.

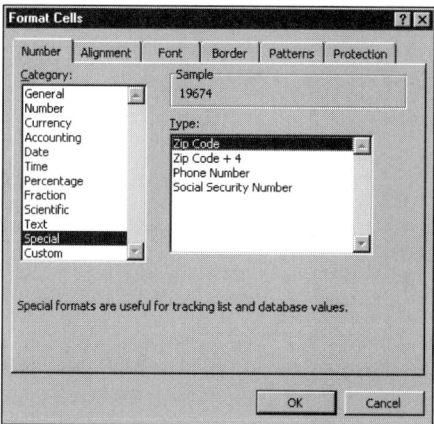

Figure 37-4: Use the Format ⇨ Cells dialog box to apply existing formats, or to customize your own.

The number format you apply does not affect the actual value that Excel uses for calculations. The actual value displayed in the formula bar is the one Excel computes with.

Rounding

Although Excel's formats give you *carte blanche* when it comes to choosing decimal places, commas, and so forth, no built-in formats will round numbers to the nearest specified whole number (larger than one). The ROUND function does the trick, but you can accomplish a similar effect with a custom number format.

On the Number tab of the Format ⇨ Cells dialog box, choose the last category in the list, "Custom," to enter a number format code for your custom format (see Figure 37-5). At Type, enter the following codes for the specified rounded results:

#,	(Rounds to the nearest thousand, excluding insignificant zeroes.)	54,223 becomes 54
#,",000"	(Rounds to the nearest thousand, including insignificant zeros.)	54,223 becomes 54,000
0.0,,	(Rounds to the nearest million, including one decimal place.)	54,789,223 becomes 54.8

See the Help topic "Custom number, date, and time format codes" for a list of custom codes and their meanings. You can find this topic by searching for "number formats" in the Help Index tab.

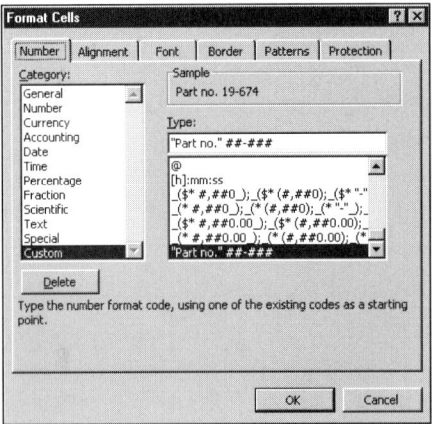

Figure 37-5: Creating a custom number format

Using special currency symbols

To specify a currency symbol in a custom number format, you can easily enter a code using your numeric keypad. First make sure that your Num Lock key is turned on (Excel shows the word NUM in the status bar). Then hold down Alt and type the following code using the keypad. When you lift up, the symbol appears.

The following symbols can be inserted into the Type field when creating a custom format, or directly onto your spreadsheet. For more about inserting special characters, see Chapter 7.

¢ (cents)	0162
£ (British pounds)	0163
¥ (Japanese yen)	0165

Aligning data

You want your numbers to fall in line just so, in nice crisp rows and tight columns, right? Excel has the tools you need to make sure everything lines up and, for that matter, that it fits in the available space.

Alignment options

On the Alignment tab in the Format ⇨ Cells dialog box (Figure 37-6), you find options to align cell data horizontally, vertically, and at an angle.

Secret

If you choose to left-align horizontally, you'll also be able to specify an indent (indenting within a cell was finally allowed in Excel 97). You can also set the data at an angle from 0–90° (but not if you specify an indent or choose the "Fill" or "Center across Selection" options in the Horizontal field). If the cell has borders, they're rotated to the same degree as the rotated text.

Chapter 37: Essentials of Editing, Formatting, and Printing

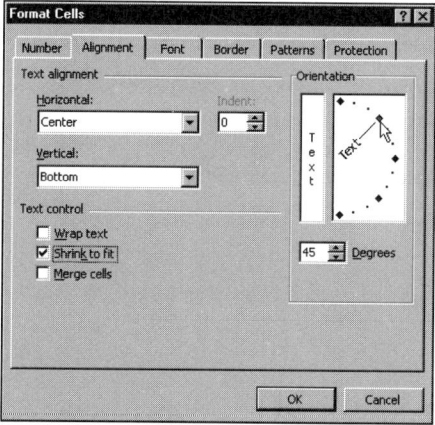

Figure 37-6: Use this tab on the Format ⇨ Cells dialog box to control alignment within a cell.

If the cell fits . . .

Secret

When not all the contents are visible in a cell, you may choose to have the font size adjusted instead of resizing the column width. You now have that choice. Turn on Shrink to Fit in the Alignment box, and Excel will adjust the font size automatically. If you later change the column width, Excel readjusts the font.

Remember that if Excel displays a bunch of number signs in a cell (as in #####), the cell contains a number that is too wide to display with the current formatting choices within the column. Widening the column displays the number correctly.

Got the urge to merge (cells, that is)?

Cells can be merged *both* horizontally and vertically. With the data in the upper-leftmost cell, select as many cells across and/or down as you want to merge, and click the Merge and Center button on the Formatting toolbar. Figure 37-7 shows the results of one such merger.

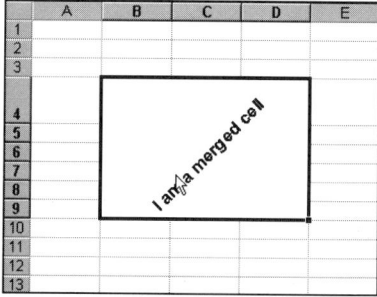

Figure 37-7: With data in cell B4, select B4:D9 to create this mega-merger.

Excel places the contents from the upper-left corner into a single resulting merged cell. The cell address of the merged cell is that of the upper-left cell in the original selection.

Secret

Merged cells retain their original alignment, which could result in a small amount of text sitting in the corner of a very large cell. It's usually a good idea to center the text both horizontally and vertically after merging. Go to the alignment tab of the Format ⇨ Cells dialog box (see Figure 37-6).

Caution

Only the data in the upper-left cell of the selection survives after a merge. You get a warning message if Excel finds data elsewhere in the selection. To include all data in the range in the merged cell, move it into the upper-leftmost cell.

AutoFormatting

Not very artistic? Have Excel do the formatting for you. You can apply one of 16 built-in table designs, called AutoFormats. The design uses distinctive formats for the various elements of the table, such as column and row labels, summary totals, and detail data. Click anywhere in the table, and take a look at the options in the Format ⇨ AutoFormat dialog box (Figure 37-8). You can browse through the 16 different designs, and choose one to decorate your data. Excel is aware of row and column totals and will format those differently from the detail data.

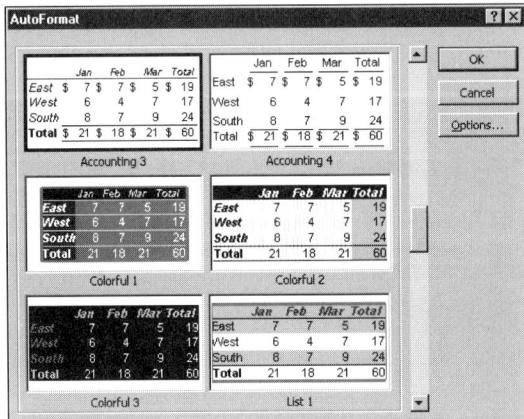

Figure 37-8: Use this dialog box to select among 16 built-in table designs.

The Options button lets you choose only a portion of the formatting; let's say you like the fonts but not the background colors. Clear the Patterns check box and away go all the shades. To remove the AutoFormatting, go back into the AutoFormat dialog box and choose None at the bottom.

Conditional formatting

Secret

You can monitor the values of particular cells by applying conditional formats. As the results change, the formats automatically change too. You can set certain formats to appear when values fall outside of a set range, or when a particular formula meets certain conditions.

Select the cells you want to monitor, and go to Format ⇨ Conditional Formatting (the dialog box is shown in Figure 37-9). To use cell *values* as the formatting criteria, choose "Cell Value Is" in the box labeled Condition 1. Then select a comparison phrase and type a value in the appropriate box. You can compare the values to either a constant or a formula, but you must include an equal sign (=) before any formula.

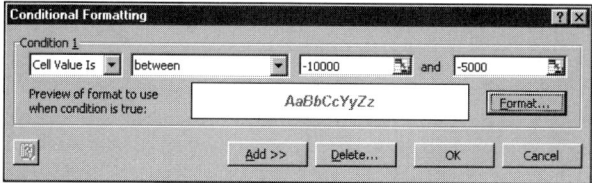

Figure 37-9: You can conditionally format cells based upon their values.

You can also evaluate data using a *formula* as the criteria. Choose "Formula Is" in the Condition 1 box, and enter the formula in the box on the right. The formula must evaluate to a logical value of True or False.

After you've specified a condition, choose Format to define the formatting Excel will apply if the condition is met. A sample shows up in the dialog box. (Note that you can't change row height or column width conditionally.) To apply a second condition, click Add. You can specify up to three conditions.

When the appropriate conditions are met, Excel automatically applies the formats you've set. If none of the conditions are met, the cell takes the formats it had before you added Conditional Formatting. If you specify multiple conditions and more than one condition is met, Excel applies only the formats for the first true condition.

Finding cells with conditional formatting

Excel can find cells with conditional formatting for you. Use the Edit ⇨ Go To dialog box (shortcut: F5). In the dialog box, choose Special, and turn on Conditional Formats near the bottom. Choose All to find all cells on the worksheet that have conditional formatting applied. Choose Same to find cells with the same conditional formatting as the active cell.

Copying conditional formatting

There's a special trick to copying just the conditional formatting of a cell. Select the cells to receive the formatting, plus one cell that already has the conditions you want to copy. Go to Format ⇨ Conditional Formatting and click OK.

Pasting particular cell attributes

Instead of copying the exact contents of cells, you can copy specific attributes only, such as the resulting value of a formula, formatting, comments, data validation restrictions, and so on.

The Paste Special command

After copying the cells with the desired attributes, go to the destination and bring up the Paste Special dialog box. You can either drop down Edit ➪ Paste Special or right-click the destination's upper-left corner and choose Paste Special from the shortcut menu. As shown in Figure 37-10, Excel's Paste Special dialog box lets you choose from a variety of cell attributes to apply, including: formulas with or without formatting; resulting values; formatting only; comments; or validation restrictions. You can also, among other things, transpose the new range (rows become columns and vice versa), or create a hot link between source and destination.

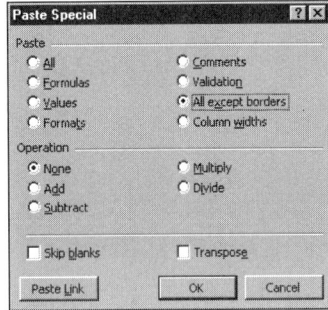

Figure 37-10: Have it your way using the Paste Special dialog box.

The Format Painter button

When formatting is all you're concerned with, Format Painter is a quick and easy way to transfer the font, borders, alignment, and so on from a cell to another location. Excel's Format Painter works much like the one in Word. Select a cell with the attributes you'd like to copy and click the Format Painter button on the toolbar. The mouse pointer shows a small paintbrush attached to it. With a click (for one cell) or a drag (for several cells), "paint" over the range to be formatted. It adopts the original cell's format instantly.

Format Painter can also be used for multiple pastes. Double-click the button to paint as many different cells and ranges as you like. When you're done, press Esc to get out of paint mode.

Autofilling values or formats

Secret

Using the fill handle is another way to copy specific cell attributes. As the section on AutoFill in Chapter 36 points out, selecting a cell and dragging the fill handle with the *right* mouse button displays a shortcut menu asking which attributes you'd like to copy to the neighboring cells (refer back to Figure 36-7). Note the Fill Formats choice, which copies formatting only.

The List AutoFill feature

New for Excel 2000, List AutoFill automatically copies the existing format from a list or table when you add new rows or columns. Let's say you build a table with a standard background shade, font, and other formatting in each column. When you add a new row to the table, Excel automatically duplicates the column formatting in the new row. But if all this "help" bugs you, clear the box labeled Extend List Format and Formulas in the Edit tab of the Tools ⇨ Options dialog box.

Applying multiple formatting options quickly with styles

Much like Word, Excel lets you apply a group of predetermined formatting choices all at once to a cell or range by specifying a named *style*. Excel styles can govern any combination of the following formatting attributes: number formatting, alignment, font choice, borders, pattern or shading, and cell protection (this last one isn't a format per se, but it's one of the characteristics you can control with a style).

To apply a style to a range, or to create or modify styles, choose Format ⇨ Style. In the resulting dialog box, select a style and choose OK to apply it to the selection. Note that the types of formatting options (font, borders, and so on) governed by a style depend on which of the boxes in the dialog box are checked. You can check or clear these boxes at will to control which of the style's presets Excel actually applies to the selection. You should realize, however, that Excel automatically remembers the changes, retaining them the next time you use the style.

To modify the formatting choices themselves, select the style and choose Modify. You get the standard Format Cells dialog box. To add a new style, type a new name first, and then choose Add. The Merge button lets you copy styles from other worksheets.

Secret

Why Excel omits the Style drop-down list button from the default Formatting toolbar is beyond me. But you can put it there, or on any other toolbar that's convenient. In the Customize dialog box, select Format on the Commands tab, and then drag the Style list button to its new home. You can then apply styles without having to call up the dialog box.

Formatting shortcut keys

Table 37-1 lists some keyboard shortcuts to format your worksheets in Excel.

Table 37-1   Formatting Shortcut Keys

To Do This...	Press This...
Display the Format ⇨ Style dialog box	Alt+' (apostrophe)
Display the Format ⇨ Cells dialog box	Ctrl+1
Apply the General number format	Ctrl+Shift+~ (tilde)
Apply the Currency format with two decimal places (negative numbers appear in parentheses)	Ctrl+Shift+$
Apply the Percentage format with no decimal places	Ctrl+Shift+%
Apply the Exponential number format with two decimal places	Ctrl+Shift+^
Apply the Date format with the day, month, and year	Ctrl+Shift+#
Apply the Time format with the hour and minute, and indicate A.M. or P.M.	Ctrl+Shift+@
Apply the Number format with two decimal places, 1000 separator, and – for negative values	Ctrl+Shift+!
Apply an outline border	Ctrl+Shift+&
Remove all borders	Ctrl+Shift+_ (underscore)
Toggle bold formatting	Ctrl+B
Toggle italic formatting	Ctrl+I
Toggle underlining	Ctrl+U
Toggle strikethrough	Ctrl+5
Hide rows	Ctrl+9
Unhide rows	Ctrl+Shift+(
Hide columns	Ctrl+0 (zero)
Unhide columns	Ctrl+Shift+)

Adding Comments

Some entries on your spreadsheet just plain need extra explanation: where the data came from, how a certain value was calculated, tips for entering data into this cell, or why this month there's less money allocated to home care and more money allocated to Jelly Bellies. If you want to say this about that, attach a comment.

Attaching a comment to a cell

Couldn't be easier. Right-click the cell and choose Insert Comment. As shown in Figure 37-11, a little yellow sticky appears with your name. Speak your mind, and when you're done, click outside the comment box.

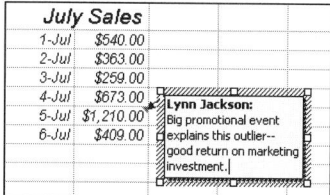

Figure 37-11: A comment helps to explain why one value is so different from the others.

A small red triangle (a *comment indicator*) appears in the cell's upper-right corner to indicate an attached comment. To see the comment box, merely rest the mouse pointer over the cell.

If you tend to be long-winded, you'll probably need to adjust the size of the comment box. Only the first four lines show up by default. Right-click the cell again, and choose Edit Comment. Small white handles appear around the comment box. Drag the handles to resize. Note that, as with cell formatting, comments in the selected cell or range are not deleted when you press Delete, whereas cell contents perish.

Viewing comments

By default, comment indicators appear in cells, and comments show up when you rest the mouse on top. If you'd like to change this default, you can under the View tab of Tools ➪ Options. Here's where you decide if you want to see neither indicators nor comments, indicators only, or both.

The easiest way to control the display of some but not others is to use the View ➪ Comments command. When you do, every comment on the spreadsheet is revealed, and the Reviewing toolbar appears. From here you can cycle through each comment one by one; edit, hide, or delete; and choose ones to send via e-mail.

Secret

You can also hide a particular comment by right-clicking the cell and choosing Hide Comment. If you've hidden certain comments and now decide to display them all, click View ➪ Comments twice.

Editing comments

To change a comment, right-click the cell it's attached to and choose Edit Comment. If you're a keyboard hotshot, the faster equivalent is Shift+F2.

Finding comments

You can quickly select all cells with comments by pressing F5 (shortcut for Edit ➪ Go To) and choosing Special, then Comments. All cells with attached comments are selected. To find a comment with a particular word or words, specify Comments in the Look In field of Edit ➪ Find.

No comment at this time

To delete a comment from a cell, right-click the cell and choose Delete Comment. (The same option also appears on the Reviewing toolbar, and under Edit ➪ Clear.) To remove all the comments from the entire worksheet, select them using F5 (as described previously), go to Edit ➪ Clear, and choose Comments.

Secret

If you click a cell and press the Delete key, Excel removes the cell contents, but not comments or other formatting.

A Couple of Quick Printing Tips

Secret

Be sure you learn to use the Page Break Preview option. Located on the View menu, it lets you clearly see and easily modify the boundary between one printed page and the next. Just drag those heavy blue lines to change the page break locations. This is a major improvement over the old way of having to go back and forth to the Print Preview mode to see where the page breaks fell. In Print Preview, you can't edit the worksheet, and the way it's broken up into separate pages makes it harder to tell whether the pages are breaking at the correct places.

Remember, too, that you can print only a selected region of the worksheet. Open the File ➪ Print dialog box and choose Selection in the Print What area before you OK the box. To print a named range, first select it via the Name box, and then print the selection. To print a particular set of sheets in the workbook, group them first (see "Entering data in groups of worksheets" in Chapter 36). Then go to File ➪ Print, and select the Active Sheets button at the bottom.

You can control whether Excel prints individual worksheet objects — such as graphics, buttons, text boxes, pictures, and OLE objects — using the Format Object dialog box. The Properties tab has a Print Object check box. Excel won't print any objects if you hide them all via the View tab of the Tools ➪ Options dialog box.

Conclusion

Even when it comes to the fundamentals of editing, formatting, and printing, Excel is loaded with special features that can speed your work and bring you the worksheet look you want. Mastery of the "advanced basics" in this chapter gives you the tools you need for building complex Excel applications and lovely worksheet presentations.

Chapter 38

Formulas and Functions

In This Chapter

▶ Understanding the difference between underlying cell values and the results displayed when Excel calculates a formula
▶ Using the Formula palette to enter and edit formulas
▶ Finding a formula's precedent cells with Range Finder
▶ Calculating across multiple worksheets with 3-D references in formulas
▶ Using date functions for the coming millennium, and last year, too
▶ Using data tables for really cool, really quick calculations based on variable inputs

Formulas are the basis for all of your work in Excel. After all, the reason you bought the program in the first place is because your slide rule just won't cut it anymore, right? The more you know about formulas, the more powerful your spreadsheets become.

Formulas often contain functions — functions are the source of their power. Functions perform predefined calculations using specific values. Excel has more than 200 built-in functions available for you to use. If you require a particularly complex calculation and the existing functions don't meet your needs, you can even create your own.

The Secret Formula

As time goes on and Excel becomes more sophisticated, formula creation just becomes easier. The program now includes more handholding than ever before. The key to success with formulas is to understand the essentials behind how Excel calculates, and to know when to ask for help (and where to get it).

Automatic versus manual calculation

Anytime you change or edit your spreadsheet, Excel recalculates your formulas to keep them up to date. Whenever possible, Excel recalculates only those cells dependent on values that have changed. This type of calculation helps to save time by avoiding unnecessary number crunching. But unless you specify otherwise, Excel always completely recalculates when a workbook is opened or saved.

Secret

The Calculation tab on the Tools ⇨ Options dialog box enables you to control whether Excel performs its calculations automatically or manually. When set to manual calculation, you can get around in complex worksheets more quickly, but you have to remember that the values you see may not be current. Another option, Automatic except Tables, is useful when a worksheet contains data tables of any size, which typically demand lots of Excel's attention during recalculations (data tables are discussed in "Creating dynamic data tables" later in this chapter).

With manual calculation on, press F9 to calculate all open worksheets, or Shift+F9 to calculate the active worksheet only. If you do choose manual calculation, you'll most likely want to check the box labeled Recalculate before Save to guarantee your data will be updated when you save.

Note that all open workbooks use the same calculation mode (automatic or manual). The calculation mode is not saved with workbooks or with templates.

How does Excel calculate formulas?

Regardless of how a cell has been formatted, Excel normally uses the underlying stored values for all calculations. No matter how many decimal places you've hidden or shown, or how many other cosmetic changes you've made, Excel relies upon the stored values. Remember that fact when you see a crazy sum like this:

Check the underlying values. They might look something like this:

Secret

To force Excel to calculate using the values displayed in your worksheet rather than the underlying stored values, go to the Tools ⇨ Options dialog box and check the Precision as Displayed box on the Calculation tab. You can set this option independently for each workbook.

Viewing formulas instead of results

To see the contents of all the formulas on your worksheet, press Ctrl+backquote (the backquote character [`] is located on the same key as the tilde [~] character). Every column on your worksheet widens, and every formula cell displays its contents. This shortcut is a toggle; each time you press it, the screen toggles between formula display and result display. Ctrl+backquote is the shortcut for selecting Tools ⇨ Options, going to the View tab, and turning on Formulas.

The one great commandment for creating formulas

The most important thing to remember when creating a formula is that *it must begin with an equal sign*. This is so important, in fact, that Microsoft has put a big, bold equal sign right there on the Formula bar where you can't miss it. It's called the Edit Formula button. Click the Edit Formula button to insert an equal sign and begin a formula. Of course, you can just type an equal sign instead as the first character in a cell. Either way, Excel activates the Formula palette.

Using the Formula palette

Even sophisticated users who don't need baby formulas can benefit from the Formula palette. In short, it's a tool that helps create or edit a formula and provides information about functions and their arguments. When you start or edit a formula by clicking either the Edit Formula button on the Formula bar or the Paste Function button on the Standard toolbar, a drop-down list of functions replaces the Name box at the left of the Formula bar. The palette appears below the Formula bar when you click the Edit Formula button.

Normally — when you're not in the process of entering a function — the palette shows the calculated result of the formula you've entered so far. The true magic comes when you begin to use functions. To insert a function in your formula, you can either choose one from the drop-down list on the left or simply type one in. When you do, the palette displays a description of the function and provides a field for each argument (see Figure 38-1). You need only click a field to read a description of that argument.

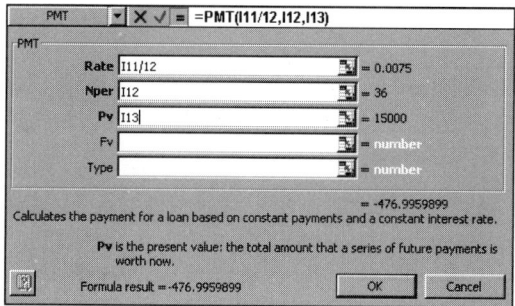

Figure 38-1: Using the Formula palette to get help with each argument of the PMT function

As you enter information, you see the current result of this function, and the current result of the entire formula (which may involve many other parts). Excel may even fill in quote marks for you when it knows you need them.

Secret

Keyboard access to the Formula palette is available but not direct — the palette doesn't appear automatically when you type an equal sign (=) to start a formula or F2 to edit one. Instead, you have to press Ctrl+A after typing a valid function name (before you type any parentheses). Pressing Ctrl+Shift+A after typing a function name inserts the function's argument list and parentheses but doesn't display the Formula palette. Although the drop-down function list appears in place of the Name Box when you're editing a formula with the keyboard, you can't use the keyboard to pick functions from the list — use Insert ➪ Function instead.

Smooth operators for your formulas

A formula can consist of nothing more than an equal sign followed by a value as in =2 or =TRUE or, using a function, =DATE(). But garden variety formulas consist of at least two numbers or cell references strung together by *operators*. Excel calculates the result of the formula by performing the operations specified by these operators on the values they connect.

In a formula containing more than one operator, Excel follows a predetermined scheme to decide the order in which to make its calculations. Even if you commit this *operator precedence* scheme to memory — and I've never been able to — you can and should use parentheses to group values with their operators in your formulas. Instead of =**2*3+5**, for example, type =**(2*3)+5** or =**2*(3+5)**, whichever is correct. That way, you can see at a glance which operations should be done first, and you can be sure Excel follows your intentions.

Secret

Excel and VBA share many of their operators (see Chapter 21). However, each has a different set. VBA has the Mod operator and a whole set of logical operators not found in Excel (Excel's Mod *function* performs the same calculation as the Mod operator, but it isn't an operator). On the other hand, VBA lacks Excel's operators that work on cell references, of course, as well as its percent and exponentiation operators.

Of course, the characters +, –, *, and / are the operators for addition, subtraction, multiplication, and division, respectively. Other operators available in your Excel formulas include:

Arithmetic Operators

This Operator	Performs This Function	Example
%	Percent	A5% (result is 1/100th the value of cell A5)
^	Exponentiation	4 ^ 3 (4 raised to the 3rd power — result is 64)

Comparison Operators (Same as in VBA)		
Text Operator	Performs This Function	Example
&	Concatenates two values into a single text string.	"Foot" & "ball" (result is "Football")

Referring to cells and ranges in your formulas

Let's review, class: To refer to a cell in a formula, just type its address. If you put the formula =A1 into cell B2, cell B2 shows the current value of cell A1 whenever Excel recalculates the worksheet.

Another super basic point: You don't need to type in the address of a referenced cell yourself. Whenever you're editing a formula, clicking or dragging on a worksheet places the address of the cells you touched into the formula automatically.

Referring to ranges of cells

Excel provides special operators to refer to multiple cells in your formulas. The most common is the range operator, : (colon). The reference B4:U8 is not only a cute way to refer to your appetite before dinner but also defines a rectangle of cells spanning B4 at the top left and U8 at the bottom right. Here are the available cell reference operators:

Reference Operators (Combine Ranges of Cells for Calculations)		
Operator	Type of Cell Reference	Example
:	Range — creates a reference to all cells between and including two other references.	A3:C19
,	Union — creates a reference to all cells included in two other references (either single cell or range references).	A3:C19,D34:D39
(a single space)	Intersection — creates a reference to any cells common to two other references.	X10:X20 W5:X11

The union and intersection operators are probably most useful when used with named ranges, because then it's easier to understand the range you're trying to target. More on this in the next section.

Referring to named cells and ranges

Chapter 34 introduced the concept of and the techniques for naming cells, individually or as ranges. Although named ranges are great for navigation, they're maybe even better when used in your formulas. Instead of typing an obscure, arbitrary code you just enter the name as in:

```
= (Height + Weight)/ShoeSize
```

You don't have to remember where the target cells reside in your workbook, and the formula remains understandable when you return to it 10 minutes (or 10 days) later.

Cooking with automatic ranges

Actually, you can start using range names even before you tell Excel to create them in the Name box or the Create Names dialog box (Figure 36-3). Existing row and column labels give you automatic license to refer in your formulas to the cells within those columns and rows.

Caution

Unfortunately, you can't *navigate* to automatic range names with the Name box or the Go To dialog box — you can only use them in formulas. I bring them up here because they are range names of a sort, and that's the topic of this section.

With that caveat in mind, Figure 38-2 shows my dating diary for three months. Though no names have been defined on the worksheet (if you looked in the Insert ⇨ Name ⇨ Define dialog box you'd find it empty), I immediately begin entering formulas using both my dates' names and month names. =APR BOZO or =SUM(LOONEY) yield the results 6 and 9, respectively. Though the example is simple, the point applies to worksheets of any size and formulas of any complexity.

Dates I've survived			
	Apr	May	Jun
Daffy	3	2	4
Goofy	2	5	6
Looney	0	1	0
Bozo	1	0	3
Nerdy	5	1	2
Perky	2	6	2

Figure 38-2: Excel creates range names automatically from row and column labels.

An important distinction to remember: Automatic names derived from row and column labels are available to *that worksheet only*. Names that you explicitly define are available to any sheet within the workbook.

Using range operators with named ranges

Although they can make formulas look unduly complex when used with ordinary cell or range references, the union and intersection range operators come into their own when teamed with named ranges.

Consider the little worksheet table shown in Figure 38-2 and the automatic range names Excel recognizes based on its row and column headings.

Suppose I want to know how many dates I lived through with Perky back in May. Using the intersection operator — which is just a space — I can write the following formula to read the table for me, without looking up any cell coordinates:

```
=Perky May
```

The union operator is probably less often useful. Still, if for some reason I had to know the total number of dates I had in May *and* the dates I had with Perky during the entire 2nd quarter, my formula would be:

```
=SUM(Perky, May) - Perky May
```

The second term keeps Excel from counting the Perky dates in May twice.

Relative versus absolute references

By default, cell references are *relative*. If the address of the cell to which you referred changes, Excel automatically changes the formula to preserve the reference. If, say, you cut cell A1 and paste it into cell C5, cell B2's formula automatically becomes =C5.

In similar fashion, sort of, if you *copy* cell B2 to cell B3, B3's formula becomes =D5. Note that in this case, the cell you're referring to hasn't changed at all. But Excel assumes you want to create a table, and because you copied the formula to the next column, Excel thinks you would want the formula in the new cell to refer to the cell one column over from the original cell.

Relative references are great, most of the time — they enable you to reorganize your worksheets on the fly without having to retype every formula. However, sometimes your formula should always point to the same cell, even if the formula's cell changes. To create an *absolute* cell reference, add a $ character before the row and column coordinates as in =$A$1. Then, if you copy the formula to another column, the formula will still be =$A$1. You can add the dollar sign to only one of the coordinates, as in $A1 or A$1, if you want the reference to remain absolute in only one dimension.

Even with absolute references, Excel still updates your formulas if the referenced cell changes its address. You can prevent this — but you would rarely want to — with the Indirect function.

Cell references outside the current worksheet

When you're editing a formula, Excel lets you create cell and range references using point and click, even when the referenced cells lie in other sheets or other workbooks. Still, it's good to know how such out-of-sheet references look.

To refer to a cell or range in another worksheet in the same workbook, precede the cell address(es) with the sheet's name followed by an ! (exclamation mark). If the name contains spaces, enclose it in single quote marks, as in: =SUM('Spring sales'!C2:D5).

To enter a reference to another open workbook, list the workbook in square brackets, followed by the sheet name, the exclamation point, and then the cell reference. This time single quote marks should go before the opening bracket and before the exclamation point if the names include any spaces. Here's an example: =SUM('[Toy sales 1999]Spring sales'!R20:T35). When you close the alien workbook, Excel adds its complete path to the reference.

Finding formula precedents with the Range Finder

No, *precedents* are not what we elect every fourth November, nor even what you receive on your birthday. They're the cells referred to by a formula. Precedent cells contain data that the formula uses for calculation. Excel now makes it easy to locate a formula's precedents, and to control the relationships among them.

When you edit formulas on a worksheet, Excel gives visual cues to formulas and their precedents. This is the job of the Range Finder. Click a formula in the Formula bar, and each reference in the formula is highlighted with a different color. The precedent cell or cells on the worksheet are highlighted with a matching color.

To change a cell or range reference, simply use the drag handle in the lower-right corner of the highlighted border to select more or fewer cells. Drag the border itself to select a completely different range of cells. (See Chapter 39 on charting to learn more about the Range Finder.)

Working with 3-D references

Workbooks are designed to hold several worksheets for a reason: The worksheets have some relationship to each other. So it follows that you may need to analyze data in the same cell or range of cells on adjacent sheets within the workbook. To do so, you can use a 3-D reference. 3-D references come in two varieties: formulas or defined names. They're just as easy to create as the 1- or 2-D kind, and they can be great time-savers.

Using 3-D formulas

A 3-D formula comprises: first a range of sheet names from the current workbook, then an "!" as a delimiter, and finally a cell or range reference. When calculating the formula, Excel includes the cell reference from each and every worksheet within the range. Let's say you have a workbook with the four sheets whose tabs and names are shown in Figure 38-3. Each worksheet has exactly the same layout, but different data. A 3-D formula like this:

=SUM(North:South!J54)

returns the sum of cell J54 on the first three worksheets.

Figure 38-3: A typical use of different worksheets: sales data for each of four regions

Too much typing?

An easy way to create a 3-D formula is to use good ol' point 'n' click. Position yourself in the cell where you want the formula, and try this:

1. Type = (an equal sign), the name of the function, and an opening parenthesis.
2. Click the tab for the first worksheet in the range.
3. Hold down Shift and click the tab for the last worksheet in the range.
4. Select the cell or range to be calculated.

Excel drops the corresponding 3-D reference into your formula. You can now complete the formula.

Defining 3-D range names

A range name represents a single cell or group of cells on a worksheet. A 3-D range name represents a group of cells that reside on *different* worksheets. One name may refer to cells residing on several sheets in a workbook. The only restriction is that the named cell or range must be the same for each sheet.

1. Go to Insert ➪ Name ➪ Define.
2. In the Names in Workbook field, type any name you like.
3. Type = (an equal sign) in the Refers To field.
4. At the bottom left of the Excel window, click the tab for the first worksheet in the range.
5. Hold down Shift and click the tab for the last worksheet in the range.
6. Select the cell or range of cells to be referenced. (You can do this on any one of the worksheets.)
7. Choose Add to define the name, and stay in the box for more definitions or click OK to define the name and exit.

A few warnings

Be careful when you move or copy sheets within the workbook. Always be aware of how it might affect any 3-D references. Using the scenario referenced in the discussion of Figure 38-3, here are some situations to be aware of:

- If you insert a worksheet between North and South (via a move or copy), the inserted worksheet's data will also be included in the formula or name.
- If you move West to a location somewhere *outside* the range, Excel removes the values from the formula or name.
- If you move either North or South to another location in the same workbook (such as after East), Excel adjusts the formula or name to accommodate the new range of sheets between them.

Performing complex calculations: VBA versus formulas

Keep in mind that Excel considers the first and last worksheets in the range (in this case, North and South) as the "anchors."

In a real sense, adding formulas to a worksheet is a form of programming. After all, you're creating a customized piece of computer software — your worksheet automatically changes the results it calculates according to the current values of other cells.

Secret

As long as your formulas are fairly simple, you can ignore VBA and enter your calculating "programs" — formulas — directly into worksheet cells. As your skills and ambitions grow, however, you require formulas of greater complexity. At some point, it may make sense to design your computations as VBA modules instead of Excel formulas.

VBA lets you do anything you can do with Excel, and more (all of Excel's built-in functions are accessible in your VBA procedures). Here's an analysis of the trade-offs:

Advantages of Excel Formulas	Advantages of VBA
Immediacy. Just type the formula into a worksheet cell.	**Room.** Whereas an Excel formula is limited to 255 characters, VBA routines can be as long as you want to make them.
Worksheet-specific debugging tools. Features like the Range Finder and the Auditing toolbar help you understand your formulas and home in immediately on potential problems with cell references.	**Clarity.** Because you have plenty of room, you can separate the steps of a complex calculation on individual lines of your VBA procedure and add line-by-line comments. Confined to your worksheet, you either have to build highly complex formulas that are very difficult to understand or break them up into separate cells, making the flow of computation hard to follow.
	Powerful, full-featured debugging tools. Your ability to set break points, monitor watch values, and trace through the computation step by step makes a VBA procedure *much* easier to debug than a comparable Excel formula.
	Strong error handling features. A VBA program can respond much more flexibly if the routine encounters an error such as a reference to an empty cell.

Using Functions in Your Formulas

An Excel function calculates a value for you. You use functions in your formulas sometimes to perform complex calculations that would take much more work if you constructed them from scratch, and sometimes to obtain values you just couldn't get otherwise.

Given Excel's vast wealth of functions, and the way you can combine them into highly complex formulas, I could never introduce them all to you, let alone cover the ways in which they solve real-life problems. What I can do is give you a decent introduction to the techniques required to use them effectively, and list the types of functions Excel provides with some representative examples in each category.

Secret

If you plan to build dynamic worksheets that adapt their behavior to changing conditions, plan to master the IF function. I discuss it in "Using the IF function" later in this chapter.

Function anatomy

A function consists of the function name followed by paired parentheses, which contain the function's *arguments*, if it has any. A function may have any number of arguments, and some have none. Here are some examples:

Function	Value It Returns
NOW()	The current date and time
COLUMNS(range)	The number of columns in range
MEDIAN(number1, number2...)	The median of the numeric values specified in the argument list
PMT(rate,nper,pv)	The payment amount for a loan expressed as a negative number. The arguments specify the interest rate, the number of payments, and the loan amount.

Entering functions

You can enter a function into a formula using any of the following techniques:

- Select a function from the drop-down function list at the left of the Function bar — it replaces the Name box when you're editing a formula. Once you've chosen a function name, use the Formula palette to enter its arguments (see "Using the Formula palette" earlier in this chapter).

- Click the Paste Function button or choose Insert ➪ Function to display the Paste Function dialog box, shown in Figure 38-4. After you've selected a function, the Formula palette appears.

- Type the function name directly into your formula. If you know how to use its arguments, just go ahead and type an opening parenthesis, the list of arguments, and the closing parenthesis. If you're hazy on the arguments, press Ctrl+A to display the Formula palette after typing the function name (don't type parentheses).

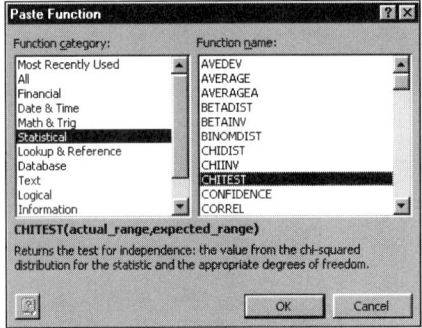

Figure 38-4: You can choose functions to insert into your formulas via this Paste Function dialog box.

Nesting functions

A formula can consist solely of a single function, as in =NOW() or =PMT(7%/12, 60, 20000). Often, however, you include one or more functions mixed with cell references and values you type in. Functions can even be *nested* inside other functions — in other words, you can use the result of one function as an argument in another function. Here's a simple example:

=ABS(SUM(C2:C20))

Here, the SUM function sums the values in cells C2 through C20. That value becomes the argument for the ABS function, which returns the absolute value of the sum. You can nest functions up to seven levels deep.

Creating custom functions

Secret

With VBA, you can create custom functions to use in formulas (and call from within other VBA procedures) just as you do the built-in ones. Custom functions are a great way to condense and simplify complex formulas that you use repeatedly. I cover the basic techniques for building and using custom functions in Chapter 42.

Using the IF function

If you forego VBA, the IF function is an absolute necessity for creating worksheets that adapt to current conditions automatically. Here's its basic form:

IF(logical_test, truevalue, falsevalue)

The IF function's first argument, logical_test, should be an expression that can be evaluated as either TRUE or FALSE. Expressions such as B9<6 (meaning, "the value of cell B9 is less than 6") and Q10<>R15 ("Q10 is not equal to R15") are typical examples of such expressions. The next two arguments determine what value the IF function returns. If the logical_test expression is TRUE, the function returns truevalue; if logical_test is FALSE, the function returns falsevalue. The return values can be numbers or text.

Now for an example:

=IF(TodaysSales > 1000, "Celebrate", "Ordinary day")

This formula places the text "Celebrate" in its cell if the value in another cell named TodaysSales is greater than 1000. If not, the cell containing the formula reads "Ordinary day."

Though simple in concept, IF becomes a very powerful tool when applied to changing data and coupled with other functions. In particular, it's often very useful to nest IF functions. See if you can follow the logic here:

=IF(Jackpot>3000000,IF(WEEKDAY(TODAY())=7,"Wednesday special bonus!","Big jackpot"),"Meager winnings")

In this example, the outer IF function tests to see whether Jackpot is greater than $3 million. If not, the formula produces the discouraging message, "Meager winnings." However, if the threshold for big jackpots was passed, the inner IF takes over—because it is the truevalue argument for the outer IF, its value becomes the final result of the formula. The inner IF checks to see whether today is a Wednesday and if so, posts a special Wednesday message. Otherwise it gives a run-of-the-mill message touting the large payout.

A survey of Excel functions

Secret

Although Excel has far too many functions for me to cover in detail, you deserve at least a quick tour of the calculating power that's yours for the asking, if you know where to look. You owe it to yourself to become familiar with the array of chores these functions can perform—you don't want to spend valuable time creating a formula of your own when a built-in function could give you the same results.

Excel's functions are grouped into categories. This section lists the categories and describes a few representative functions in each one — but remember, Excel has many more functions than I show here. By the way, many functions are identical or very similar to comparable functions in VBA.

Information functions give you information about the kind of data stored in cells. The IS... functions return TRUE if the cell contains the specified type of data, and FALSE if not.

Information Functions

Function	Value It Returns
CELL	Information you specify about a given cell (such as its value, formatting, data type, or color)
COUNTBLANK	The number of blank cells in the specified range
INFO	Specified information about your computer (the current path, how much memory is available, and many other info items are available)
ISBLANK	TRUE if the specified cell is blank
ISEVEN	TRUE if the specified cell contains an even number
ISTEXT	TRUE if the specified cell contains text
TYPE	A number representing the type of data the specified cell contains

The most important function in the logical functions group is the all-important IF, which returns one of two values depending on whether its first argument is TRUE or FALSE. The remaining logical functions return TRUE or FALSE, depending on the values of the arguments. These arguments are themselves logical values. For example, an argument might be a statement such as 2+2=4, which has the value of TRUE.

Logical Functions

Function	Value It Returns
AND	TRUE if *all* the arguments are TRUE, otherwise FALSE
IF	The first of two values you specify if the test argument is TRUE, otherwise the second value
NOT	TRUE if the input argument is FALSE, FALSE if the input is TRUE
OR	TRUE if *any* of the arguments are TRUE, FALSE if none are TRUE

Date and time functions let you write formulas that update themselves based on the current date and time and let you make calculations with dates.

Like VBA, Excel uses a special *serial number* (the date value) to store and manipulate dates. You can use the DATE function to convert a "human" date into a date value. Functions such as DAY, YEAR, and MONTH convert date values into human dates.

Date and Time Functions

Function	Value It Returns
DATE	The date value for a date specified as a year, month, and day
DAY	An integer corresponding to the day of the month specified by the input date value (similar functions are YEAR, MONTH, HOUR, MINUTE, and SECOND)
NOW	The date value for the current date and time according to your PC. Use TODAY to return only the date, and TIME for only the time.
WEEKDAY	The day of the week for a specified date value
WORKDAY	The date value for the next workday after a specified start date
YEARFRAC	The decimal fraction of the year represented by the interval between two dates. Good for prorating employee benefits.

Lookup and reference functions locate cells in a worksheet range or identify values in an array. The functions in the database category are somewhat complementary and may be easier to use if you set up your worksheet properly.

Lookup and Reference Functions

Function	Value It Returns
CHOOSE	The value at a specified position in a list
COLUMNS	The number of columns in a range. ROWS gives the number of rows, of course.
INDEX	The value of a specified cell within a range, or the cell address
INDIRECT	The value of another cell whose address is given by the cell you specify in the arguments. Use this when you want your formula always to refer to the same cell address, even if the original contents move to another address because the cell is moved or if you insert or delete rows or columns.
MATCH	The relative *position* of an item you're searching for in a range (not the item's value)
OFFSET	A cell or range reference that is a specified number of rows and columns from another cell or range

Math and trigonometry functions perform a wide variety of mathematical computations.

Math and Trigonometry Functions

Function	Value It Returns
ABS	The absolute value of the input value
COS	The cosine of the input value. Excel includes a complete set of basic trigonometric functions.
FACT	The factorial of the input number
LOG	The logarithm of the input number in the specified base (use LN to return the natural log)
PI	The value of pi
PRODUCT	The product of all the input values (you can input a range of cells, just as with the SUM function)
QUOTIENT	The integer portion of the result of a division (Analysis ToolPak required)
RANDBETWEEN	A random integer between two specified numbers (Analysis ToolPak required)
ROMAN	The roman numeral equivalent of the input number
ROUND	The input number rounded off to a specified number of digits
SIGN	1 if the input number is positive, 0 if the number is zero, or –1 if the number is negative
SQRT	The square root of the input value
SUMPRODUCT	Multiplies together corresponding elements in two or more arrays and then sums all of the products.
TRUNC	The integer portion of the input value, truncating any decimal portion

Text functions alter text strings in all sorts of useful ways, or they create text from numbers.

Text Functions

Function	Value It Returns
CLEAN	The input text stripped of all nonprinting characters
DOLLAR	Converts a numeric value to text formatted as currency with the decimals rounded to two places.

Function	Value It Returns
LEFT	A specified number of characters starting at the left side of the input string. (MID and RIGHT extract characters from the middle and right side of the input string.)
LEN	The number of characters in the input text string
LOWER	The text converted to lowercase. UPPER performs the opposite conversion.
TEXT	Converts a number into corresponding text, formatted according to a pattern you specify (similar to VBA's FORMAT function).
TRIM	The text with all extra spaces removed (single spaces between words are preserved)

As befits the essential business software tool, Excel has hordes of functions for calculating loans, investments, and the like.

Financial Functions

Function	Value It Returns
ACCRINT	The accrued interest for an interest-paying security (requires Analysis ToolPak)
DB	The depreciation of an asset using the fixed-declining balance method
DISC	The discount rate for a security (requires Analysis ToolPak)
FV	The future value of an investment, assuming a constant interest rate
INTRATE	The interest rate for a security. Use RATE for an annuity.
IPMT	The interest payment for an investment or loan
IRR	The internal rate of return
PMT	The payment for an investment or loan including interest and principal
PV	The present value of an investment
YIELD	The yield on an interest-paying security

Not for the mathematically challenged, Excel's 80-or-so statistical functions can handle all manner of complex statistical analyses. I've listed a few of them here that even math boneheads may find useful, plus a smattering of the more arcane.

Statistical Functions

Function	Value It Returns
AVERAGE	The arithmetic mean of the arguments
CHITEST	The test for independence based on the chi-squared (^{2}) distribution
CONFIDENCE	The confidence interval for a population mean
COUNT	The number of cells containing numeric values within the input range
FISHER	The Fisher transformation
FREQUENCY	An array containing the frequencies within which values occur in specified ranges of values
LARGE	The value in a series that occupies a specified rank (to identify, say, the third-best selling CD during the third quarter). SMALL gives the inverse result.
MAX	The largest value in a series. MIN gives the smallest value.
MEDIAN	The median of the argument values
MODE	The value in a series that occurs most often
NORMDIST	The normal distribution
STDEV	An estimate of the standard deviation

Many functions in the large engineering functions category are definitely left to the engineers and their work with imaginary numbers and the like. But the category also includes convenient functions for converting between different number systems (like decimal, hex, and binary) and the one-size-fits-all CONVERT, which recognizes and converts around 40 different measurement units. All engineering functions require the Analysis ToolPak.

Engineering Functions

Function	Value It Returns
BIN2DEC	The decimal equivalent of a binary number. Similar functions handle other number system conversions.
CONVERT	The input quantity expressed in another system of measurement units. If you need to know how many atomic units 10 slugs equals, this is the function for you. Parsecs not included.
IMAGINARY	The imaginary coefficient of a complex number

Many people use Excel as a flat-file (nonrelational) database manager, storing database records in worksheet rows and fields in the columns (the column labels function as field names). The dozen or so functions in the database and list management functions category help you analyze such data. Typically, you specify the range containing your database, the field you want to work with, and selection criteria.

Database and List Management Functions	
Function	**Value It Returns**
DCOUNT	The number of records (cells) matching your criteria
DMAX	The maximum value of those records matching your criteria
DSUM	The sum of the values in a field for all records matching your criteria

Formula Tips and Tricks

The rest of this chapter is devoted to some extremely useful tips for working with formulas in general. A related tip is worth mentioning here: To learn how cell formatting can be set to change based upon the results of a particular formula, see the section "Conditional formatting" in Chapter 37.

Defining named constants

Secret

The standard method for defining a constant is to place its value into a cell and then refer to that cell when you need to use the variable in your formulas. That way, if the "constant" changes, you can type a new value in the cell to recalculate all the dependent results automatically. If the value is truly a constant, however, you can define it as a name that exists only in Excel's mind-space, not in a worksheet cell.

Choose Insert ➪ Name ➪ Define. In the Define Name dialog box, type in the name for the constant, and then type its numeric value in the field labeled Refers To, erasing the existing contents (don't precede the value with an equal sign). From then on you can use the named constant in any formula.

The new millennium

By now, everybody knows about the "Y2K problem," the fact that many computer programs will interpret two-digit years for the new millenium as twentieth century dates. Excel may be Y2K "compliant," but it still has to make assumptions about which century you intend when you enter two-digit years. Here are the default rules it follows:

- 00 through 29 signify the years 2000 through 2029. If you enter 2/23/14, Excel assumes the date is February 23, 2014.

- 30 through 99 signify the years 1930 through 1999. If you type 2/23/54, Excel assumes the date is February 23, 1954.

Out-of-range date arguments

Some Excel date functions permit arguments outside the expected range. This allows for some fancy footwork to create handy results. You can find the dates before and after the current month by using numbers outside of the range 1–31. The "zeroth" date of one month (the day before the first, of course) gives you the last date of the previous month. You can also do the same with months and years. Here are some examples:

=DATE(98,3,0)	February 28, 1998
=DATE(99,0,3)	December 3, 1998
=DATE(99,2,30)	March 1, 1999
=DATE(96,13,32)	February 1, 1997
=DATE(99,-2,-3)	September 27, 1998

Programmers, especially, may find this handy when designing loops.

Creating dynamic data tables

A *dynamic* data table is by far one of the most powerful devices I've found in Excel. It combines two wonderful features (data tables and the DSUM function), and it has a million and one uses.

Analyzing variable inputs with data tables: Feature 1

A data table shows the results found when a range of different values is substituted into a formula. It provides a shortcut for calculating multiple variations, and it's a good way to compare the results you can expect under different conditions. Data tables can have either one or two variables (called *input cells*). A simple example of a one-variable data table is shown in Figure 38-5.

	C10	=EFFECT(A2,C5)*C4	
	A	B	C
1		**Interest analysis**	
2	4.50%		
3			
4		Initial investment	$12,000
5		Compounding periods	12
6			
7			
8			
9	Nominal interest rate	Effective annual rate	Interest earned
10		4.59%	$551.28
11	5.00%	5.12%	$613.94
12	5.50%	5.64%	$676.89
13	6.00%	6.17%	$740.13
14	6.50%	6.70%	$803.66
15	7.00%	7.23%	$867.48
16	7.50%	7.76%	$931.59
17	8.00%	8.30%	$995.99

Figure 38-5: A data table comparing annual returns based on seven different interest rates

Using the EFFECT function, the data table in the example takes a variety of nominal interest rates and returns the corresponding effective yearly rates. That result is then used to compute the yearly return on the investment. Though your data table may be completely different, the setup will be similar:

1. List the values to be substituted into the formula in a column. In the example, the nominal interest rates are in A11:A17.

2. The formula itself goes into the cell one column to the right and one row higher than the first variable value. The values will be returned below this formula. Enter the formula as you normally would, but at the place in the formula where the variable belongs, type a cell reference as a placeholder (this is called the *input cell*). Actually, it doesn't matter which cell reference you use here, as long as the cell isn't in the table itself — the value it contains is used as an input to the formula only in this cell and doesn't affect the results displayed in the table itself. In the example, the formula =EFFECT(A2,C5) was placed in B10. A2 is the input cell (placeholder), while C5 contains an actual value to be used in the formula, the number of compounding periods.

   You can place additional formulas to the right of the first one. In the example, the second formula in C10 calculates the ending balance:

   = EFFECT(A2,C5)*C4

   and again uses A2 as the input cell (C4 holds the value of the initial investment). Note that all formulas in a data table must refer to the same input cell.

3. Select the entire area of the table (A10:C17 in the example) and choose Data ⇨ Table. Go to the Column input cell field and click the input cell (in this case, C5). Understand that all you're doing here is identifying which cell reference in the formula Excel should replace with variable values from the table (again, the calculations ignore the actual value in the input cell). When you choose OK, the range B11:C17 is instantly filled with the resulting values.

Though you can't change any part of a data table (the resulting values are presented in an array), you can adjust any of the values in the first (variable) column or the values of any other cells referred to in the formula. In the example, for instance, you might fiddle with the initial investment or number of compounding periods.

Secret

The cells containing the formulas—B10 and C10 in the example—will, of course, still display their original results. If you prefer to hide such cells, you can either color the text to match the background, or use a custom number format of ";;;" (three semicolons).

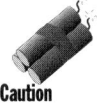

Caution

Workbook calculation may take more time when you're using data tables. If it's a problem, go to the Calculation tab of the Tools ➪ Options dialog box and turn on Automatic except Tables. Hereafter, press F9 or Shift/F9 to manually update any tables.

Two-variable data tables

Though you can't change a data table's calculated values, you can of course adjust the values in the first (variable) column or the values of any other cells referred to in the formula. In the preceding example, for instance, you might fiddle with the initial investment or number of compounding periods. But for really powerful analysis, construct a two-variable data table. The example shown in Figure 38-6 illustrates the concept by extending the earlier example to show the effects on effective yield of changing the number of compounding periods as well as the interest rate.

A7 = =EFFECT(A2,A3)*C4

	A		B	C	D
1			*Interest analysis*		
2		4.50%			
3		1			
4			*Initial investment*	*$12,000*	
5					
6				**Compounding periods**	
7		$540.00	**1**	**12**	**365**
8	**Nominal**	5.00%	$600.00	$613.94	$615.21
9	**interest**	5.50%	$660.00	$676.89	$678.43
10	**rate**	6.00%	$720.00	$740.13	$741.98
11		6.50%	$780.00	$803.66	$805.83
12		7.00%	$840.00	$867.48	$870.01
13		7.50%	$900.00	$931.59	$934.51
14		8.00%	$960.00	$995.99	$999.33

Figure 38-6: A two-variable data table

To construct a two-variable data table, place one series of variable values down the leftmost column of those you plan to use in the table, and the other across the top row. Enter the formula in the top-left corner cell of the table. The formula should contain two input cells (placeholders), one for the variables listed in the left column, the other for the values in the top row.

Once again, the cell references you use for the input cells don't matter (except that they should be different).

A look at the formula used in the example should help clarify things. The formula used is =EFFECT(A2,A3), where A2 is the input cell for the variable column values and A3 is the input cell for the row variables.

Once the variables and formula are in place, select the whole table, choose Data ➪ Table and enter the correct references in the Row input cell and Column input cell fields (A3 and A2, respectively).

Using DSUM for selective sums: Feature 2

The DSUM function sums the values in a specified column of a table, according to criteria you've defined. Unlike data tables, it returns only a single value, but it's just as useful. The simple DSUM shown in Figure 38-7 adds up all of Bloe's sales during the specified period. His total of $133 (D15) was calculated using this formula:

=DSUM(B2:D11, "Amount", C14:C15)

	A	B	C	D
1				
2		Day	Rep	Amount
3		10/18/99	Joe	$ 50.00
4		10/20/99	Bloe	$ 41.00
5		10/21/99	Joe	$ 88.00
6		10/24/99	Schmoe	$ 93.00
7		10/28/99	Schmoe	$ 57.00
8		10/31/99	Bloe	$ 92.00
9		11/1/99	Joe	$ 50.00
10		11/1/99	Schmoe	$ 20.00
11		11/3/99	Moe	$ 46.00
12				
13				
14			Rep	
15			Bloe	$133.00
16				

Figure 38-7: Using the criteria in cells C14:C15, the DSUM in D15 sums the sales for one particular rep.

Excel searches the specified range (B2:D11), and sums the values from a particular column ("Amount") that meet the criteria (C14:C15). You could click C15 and type a different rep's name to immediately get results for that rep in D15.

Putting data tables and DSUMs together

Let's say you had 25 rep names in the preceding example. You could be inefficient and sloppy, and tediously enter 25 DSUM formulas to keep track of all their totals. Or you could be a totally cool Excel whiz and create a data table, using the DSUM function as the pivotal formula to calculate the sales total for each rep. To combine these two features, build a one-variable data table that includes the reps' names in the first column. While I used the EFFECT function last time, this time I'll use a DSUM. I use a data table to put it all in motion and sum all the reps at once.

Using this example, I'll build a table that adds the sales of Joe, Bloe, Schmoe, and Moe. In Figure 38-8, you can see the new data table directly below the data. The reps' names for the table reside in C14:C17 with the table Excel has built right alongside in D14:D17. Note also that the two cells containing the DSUM criteria argument are still there but they've moved from C14:C15 in Figure 36-7 to C20:C21.

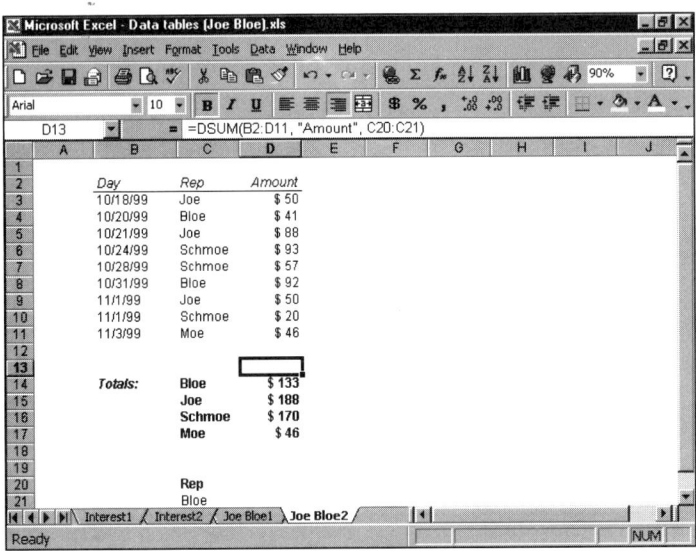

Figure 38-8: Using a dynamic data table to total the sales of several reps at once

Because the data table covers C14:D17, the formula for the table belongs in cell D13 — look back to the beginning of the "Creating dynamic data tables" section if you've forgotten how that works. In the illustration printed here, the formula is =DSUM(B2:D11,"Amount",C20:C21). Just as in Figure 38-7, this DSUM is looking at the table in B2:D11 and adding the values in the column "Amount" that match the "Rep = Bloe" criteria, although this time the criteria appear in cells C20:C21. By the way, the formula is there in D13, all right. It's just that you can't see it in the picture — I've colored it white to keep my spreadsheet clean. However, D13 is selected so that if you look in the Formula bar you can see the formula there.

Now, let's get fancy. Of course I want the DSUM to use the criteria of "Bloe," but I *also* want to use the criteria of "Joe," "Schmoe," and even "Moe." That's where the data table comes in. With my DSUM formula sitting in D13, I selected

C13:D17. (The label in B14 is outside of the data table.) Then I went to Data ⇨ Table, clicked in the Column input cell field, and clicked in C21. Cell C21 is the one that I want to vary: first I want to use the criteria of "Joe," and then "Bloe," and so on. I clicked OK, and voilà! My results instantly appeared.

Although the example table is small, the technique applies to real-life databases you maintain in Excel — a table with many more rep names would be just as easy to create. Once you catch on to the way they work, you should be able to think of loads of useful applications for dynamic data tables.

Conclusion

This chapter took you beyond the basics of writing formulas and using functions in Excel, with a medley of secrets and high-end tricks you can use in building custom calculations. Now that you've peeked behind the curtain, you can apply formulas and functions with greater skill and efficiency as you develop real-life worksheets.

Chapter 39

Charting New Territory

In This Chapter

- Learning how to speak Chart-ese
- Comparing the fourteen different chart types
- Creating embedded charts and chart sheets
- Changing the chart type
- Adjusting chart data with the Range Finder
- Using Goal Seek to adjust a single data point
- Changing a chart's orientation

Charts are indispensable for their ability to illustrate your data in a graphical fashion. While you can investigate details by scrutinizing the individual values in your worksheet, a chart shows you the big picture, clarifying the way the numbers change from month to month, region to region, or person to person.

Charts are pretty and lively, too. That's reason enough to use them liberally in the otherwise drab and orderly universe of the Excel worksheet.

Remember, you can place Excel charts in any of your Office documents. Again, I recommend that you use Excel charts for all your charting needs and ignore the Microsoft Graph application that also comes with Office. See "Just a suggestion: Don't use Microsoft Graph" in Chapter 8 for a full discussion.

Chart Speak

Before we start, let's agree on some lingo: A *chart* is the graphical representation of your data. It has a *hot link* to your data, meaning that as the data changes, Excel immediately updates the chart. You may also hear people call a chart a *graph*—the two terms mean exactly the same thing.

Each single value on the chart is called a *data point*. Data points can come in many different varieties, such as columns, bars, lines, pie slices, and even ice cream cones! (Yes, you can import clip art and use it to represent data points.) A group of related data points is called a *data series*. All data points within a single data series are formatted with the same colors and patterns. Data series' names and colors are shown in a key called the *legend*. (Pie charts are examples of charts with only one data series.)

The *category axis*, running horizontally along the bottom of the chart, is also called the *x-axis*. It separates data into groups based on such things as months or regions. The *value axis*, running vertically along the left, is called the *y-axis* in a 2-D chart, and the *z-axis* in a 3-D chart. It defines the values shown by data points. The area bounded by the axes is called the *plot area*. A 3-D chart also has a *series axis* (in 3-D charts, the y-axis is synonymous with the series axis). The series axis runs from the front to the back of the plot area. (Pie and doughnut charts, because of their circular shapes, do not have axes.)

An *embedded chart* is in the form of an object that resides on the worksheet. You can manipulate it like a picture and embed it on any sheet in the workbook. A *chart sheet* is a separate sheet in the workbook containing only the chart. Both maintain a hot link to your data.

Choosing a Chart Type

Excel offers 14 basic built-in chart types from which to choose, each one with several of its own variations. Can't decide? Click the chart toolbar to instantly change from one to another:

- A *column chart* shows data changes over a period of time. It helps compare individual values and percentages to the whole in a vertical format. Variations include *clustered columns* and *stacked columns*.

- A *bar chart* also shows data changes over a period of time. It helps compare individual values and percentages to the whole in a horizontal format. Variations include *clustered bars* and *stacked bars*.

- A *line chart* shows trends in data over time. Lines are displayed in a horizontal format. Variations include *stacked lines* and *lines with markers*.

- A *pie chart* shows the ratio of each point within a single data series to the total. Variations include *bar of pie* and *exploded pie* (sponge not included).

- A *doughnut chart* is similar to a pie chart, but it can contain more than one data series. Variations include *exploded doughnut*. (Note: Using a pie chart and a doughnut chart at the same time can cause unwanted intestinal distress.)

- An *area chart* emphasizes the degree of change over time and the relationship of data points to the whole. Variations include *stacked area*.

- A *surface chart* shows trends and finds optimum combinations between different sets of data. Variations include *wireframe* and *contour*.

- An *XY* or *scatter chart* plots data points against each other to portray differences in trends. It is often used to illustrate uneven intervals or clusters. Variations include *connecting lines* (with or without data point markers).

- A *bubble chart* is a type of XY (scatter) chart that compares sets of at least three values. Each data point has at least two values, and the size of the bubble represents the value of a third.
- A *radar chart* compares the changes in values relative to a center point. Variations include *filled radar* and *radar with markers*.
- A *stock,* or *high-low-close, chart* illustrates stock prices and scientific data. Variations include *open high-low-close* and *volume high-low-close*.
- *Cone, cylinder,* and *pyramid charts* are column charts with special shapes.

Most of these chart types offer 3-D variations. And as if these choices weren't enough, Excel complicates your life further with a host of options for custom chart formats — fancier variations on the standard 14 chart types. You can save your own custom-formatted charts for reuse.

A fifteenth chart type, the *PivotChart* report, is a new animal in Excel 2000. It's a hybrid PivotTable and chart, and you need special techniques to create it. Chapter 38 covers PivotTables and PivotCharts.

Worksheets à la Chart

A chart can be either embedded on a worksheet or stored on a separate chart sheet by itself. Both methods offer a simple creation process, and umpteen formatting options.

Using the Chart Wizard

The simplest way to create a chart is with the Chart Wizard. Once you've entered your data, click the Chart Wizard button and sit back as Excel asks you everything it needs to know. The four-step process guides you through selecting a chart type (see Figure 39-1), specifying the source data, adding special options, and choosing a location for the chart (embedded site or new chart sheet).

Note that an embedded chart must be created from adjacent selections within the source data. If you need to pull data from multiple areas, you can add it afterward by copying and pasting.

If you've chosen an embedded chart, a chart object appears on the worksheet you chose in Step 4 of the wizard. You can move it or resize it (using the black handles around the edges) to your heart's content. If a chart sheet is more your style, a new sheet is inserted in your workbook with your new chart filling the window.

You can create a chart sheet without the Chart Wizard by selecting the source data and pressing F11. There's no default keyboard shortcut to create an embedded chart.

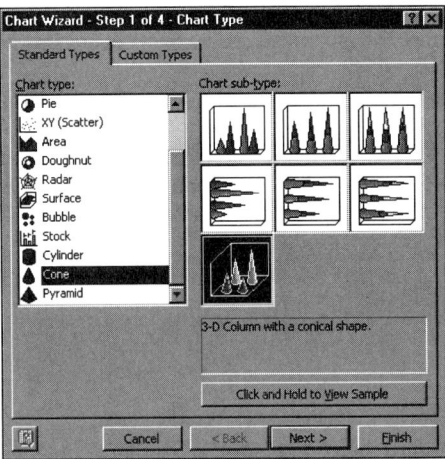

Figure 39-1: Step 1 of the Chart Wizard lets you choose a chart type and then select from among the built-in subtypes. Or you can create your own customized chart type.

Viewing chart items

Rest the mouse pointer over any chart item to see its name appear in a ScreenTip. If you rest it over a data point, you'll see its series name and value. If you don't see the ScreenTips, go to Tools ⇨ Options and look at Chart Tips on the Chart tab. The Show Names and Show Values boxes must be checked.

The name box on the formula bar shows the currently selected chart element. Click any chart element to select it. You can also select chart elements using the arrow keys. If you're working with an embedded chart and the worksheet data is in view, you also see the corresponding values highlighted when you select a data series. And thanks to Range Finder, it's all color-coded. (For more on Range Finder, read "Finding formula precedents with the Range Finder" in Chapter 38.)

Changing the Chart Type

If you don't see the chart toolbar on the screen, right-click any existing toolbar and choose Chart. Clicking the Chart Type button drops down a graphical menu of 18 different chart types as shown in Figure 39-2. Click one, and your chart instantly changes.

If you'd like to view more options, right-click the chart and choose Chart Type, or use the Chart ⇨ Chart Type command. You see a dialog box similar to Step 1 of the Chart Wizard. Here you can peruse the various chart types. For a preview, use the button labeled Press and Hold to view a sample.

Figure 39-2: The menu displayed by the Chart Type button

Adjusting Data

Although you can, you don't need to return to the source data to make changes. Changes can be made right on the chart itself, so you can watch how other values are affected. Imagine you worked for the federal government and had to chart those inflation indexes that come out every month. Given that Washington economists are always releasing revised figures, you would need a way to modify your charts as the "facts" change. With Excel, all it takes is a simple drag to remedy the situation.

Dragging points on the chart

Data marker is the term for any chart element that depicts an individual data point or value, such as a bar, pie slice, or bubble. Some line charts have visible rectangles marking each data point, but if not, each location that represents a value in the source data is a data marker.

At any rate, the quickest way to change the value of a marker in a 2-D column, bar, pie, doughnut, line, XY (scatter), or bubble chart is to drag the data marker. Figures 39-3 and 39-4 show this technique in action on a sample chart. When Excel detects such changes to a chart, Excel instantly updates the underlying values on the worksheet.

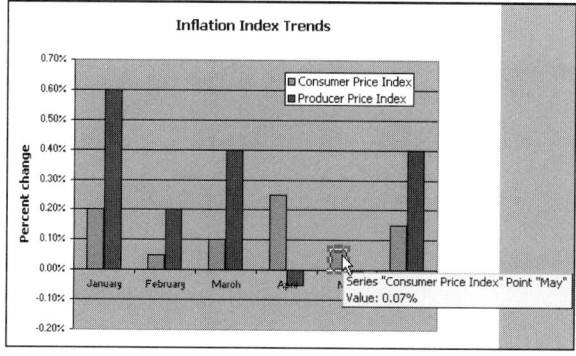

Figure 39-3: A sample chart before a data marker is resized with the mouse. The data marker in question has been selected, though this isn't necessary.

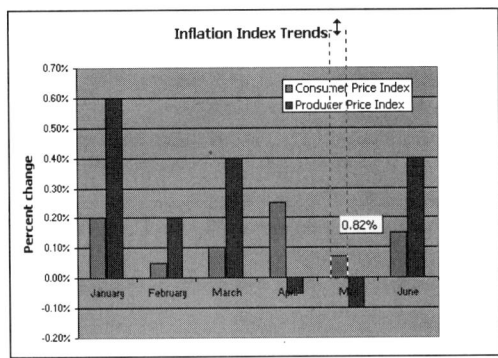

Figure 39-4: Dragging the data marker to a new position to change a value in the chart

To change a chart item, click the data series containing the data point you want to manipulate, and then click again until the specific data point is selected. You can tell it's selected by the presence of handles around its outline. Then drag the *largest* handle to change the data point's value. On columns and bars, the handle you want is at the top center. On pies and doughnuts, it's on the outer edge. You'll know when you've found it because the mouse pointer becomes the familiar double-edged arrow.

As you drag the marker, a ScreenTip displays the changing value. You know exactly when you've reached your destination. If the data marker was based on a cell containing a fixed value, the cell's value changes accordingly. If the cell contains a *formula*, however, you have a bit more work to do, as discussed in the next section.

Goal-seeking using charts

Adjustable data points are not limited to those represented by constant values. Formula values can be changed, too. But formulas are often dependent on other cells in the spreadsheet (their precedent cells). When this is the case, you turn to goal-seeking, the process whereby Excel varies the value in a precedent cell until the dependent formula returns the result you want.

On the chart

Select the data point you want to change (as described previously). Drag the largest handle to the approximate value you'd like it to be, and let go (a little tip displays the changing value). When you do, the Goal Seek dialog box immediately appears.

The cell that contains the formula appears in the Set Cell field, and the value you want the formula to reflect appears in the To Value field. Adjust either of these, as necessary, and in the By Changing Cell field, tell Excel which precedent cell you'd like to change. (Though the formula may have more than one precedent cell, you can adjust the value of only one.)

On the worksheet

To change values generated from worksheet formulas in 3-D, surface, radar, and area charts, you can use the Goal Seek feature right on the worksheet. To do so, select the formula to be changed, and choose Tools ⇨ Goal Seek. Follow the same procedure that you did for goal-seeking on the chart.

Modifying a chart's source data range

Secret

Just to prove *nothing* is set in stone, you can even change the source data of an already-existing chart. Want to add or subtract data? Want to add or subtract labels or categories? Want to change the range altogether? Here's how.

Modifying embedded charts with the Range Finder

On an embedded chart sheet, use Range Finder. Arrange the chart and the worksheet data so that both are easily in view. As you click different chart elements, you see the corresponding data highlighted by the Range Finder as shown in Figures 39-5 and 39-6. The monochrome screen shot doesn't show it, but category names are outlined in purple, series names in green, and data values in blue. To add or subtract adjacent cells to a range, simply drag the handle in the lower-right corner of the highlighted border to select more or fewer cells. To select a completely different range of cells altogether, you can even drag the border itself.

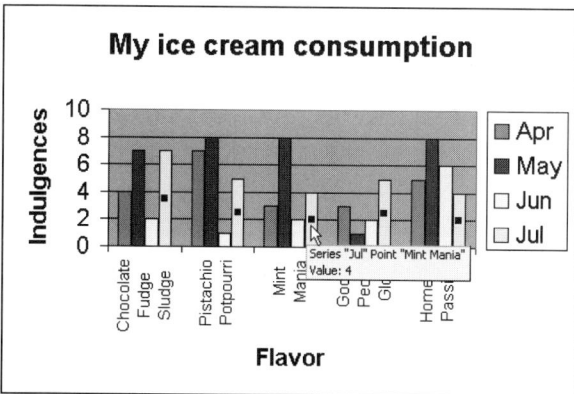

Figure 39-5: In this sample chart, the July series has been selected. Excel highlights the corresponding worksheet data, shown in Figure 39-6.

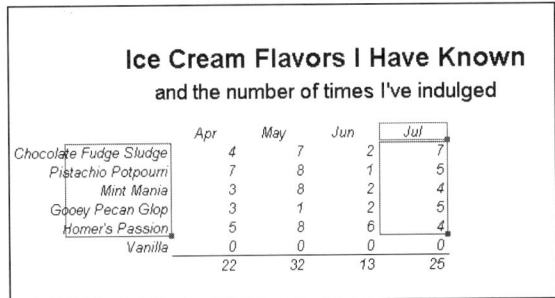

Figure 39-6: The chart in Figure 39-5 is based on this worksheet. As shown here, Excel's Range Finder highlights data corresponding to selected chart elements.

Changing source data on a chart sheet

The Range Finder works on embedded charts only. To adjust the data on a chart sheet, right-click the chart and choose Source Data, or use the Chart ⇨ Source Data command.

Including multiple selections in a chart

Yes, it's true. A chart *can* be made from nonadjacent areas of data. If you're starting from scratch (for example, the chart doesn't exist yet), make your multiple selection as you normally would and start the Chart Wizard. To add a nonadjacent area to an existing chart, copy it to the clipboard, activate the chart, and paste it in. Excel can usually sense where the data should be added, but if you need to make some adjustments, right-click the chart and choose Source Data, or use the Chart ⇨ Source Data command.

Changing a chart's orientation

By default, Excel uses the leftmost column of your worksheet data for category names, and the topmost row for series names. Each column of data is considered to belong to one data series. To change the way data series are plotted, click the By Row or By Column tool on the chart toolbar. (You can also right-click the chart and go to Source Data.)

Formatting Charts

You can format *any* chart element either by right-clicking it and choosing Format, or simply by double-clicking it. A custom-tailored dialog box will appear, depending on which item you clicked. (If you're not sure what you clicked, check out the formula bar.)

Notice that data series, data labels, and the legend all have individual elements that can be selected after clicking the group. (Try clicking the legend first and then clicking a single colored marker to see what I mean.) And you'll be pleased to know that after selecting an element, you can make changes straight from the plain ol' Formatting toolbar.

Dabbling with your data

You have so many different ways to represent your chart data, it will truly bring out the artist in you. I'll share some goodies with you, but there's so much more to tell that I recommend you spend time double-clicking different items and browsing dialog boxes.

Displaying worksheet figures

The first thing that you might want to do with your chart data is to display the numbers at the bottom of the chart, showing the part of the worksheet from which it's derived. Figure 39-7 illustrates how a chart with an attached *data table* looks. Right-click the chart outside the plot area and choose Chart Options (you can also use the Chart ⇨ Chart Options command). Go to the Data Table tab and turn on Show Data Table. The data used to create the chart is placed directly below it; you can format the data table just like any other chart element.

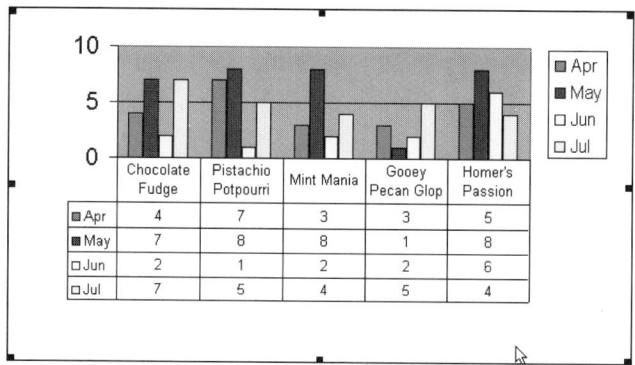

Figure 39-7: A chart with an attached data table

Secret

When you hide or filter worksheet data, the corresponding chart doesn't show it either. By default, charts show only visible rows and columns. If you'd like your chart to display all the data, go to Tools ⇨ Options. On the Chart tab, turn off Plot Visible Cells Only.

Controlling the way empty cells are plotted

Secret

If the values in a complex chart contain zeroes or blank cells, you can specify how these values are plotted. Click anywhere on the chart and select Tools ⇨ Options. Under Plot Empty Cells As, specify whether you want to leave gaps (creating a segmented line), treat the blanks as zeros (causing the line to drop), or interpolate (filling the gaps with connecting lines).

Choosing colors and patterns for chart elements

Who said chart elements have to be one solid color? A few clicks can create an eye-catching display. And if your heart so desires, every data point in the chart can have a different design. The Format Data Series dialog box offers a dazzling array of choices (see Figure 39-8). To change an entire data series, double-click any marker in the series. To change a single data point, first click the series and then either double-click the point or right-click the point and choose Format Data Point from the shortcut menu. In this case, the dialog box you see is titled Format Data Point, of course. Similar dialog boxes are available for the plot area (the portion on which the data markers appear) and the chart area (the background for the entire chart) by double-clicking these elements.

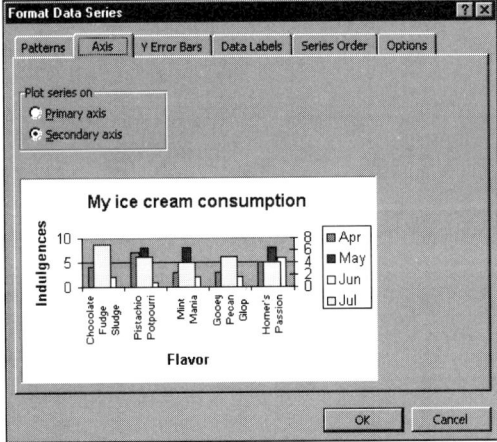

Figure 39-8: The Format Data Series dialog box

When it comes to basic visual effects, the Format dialog box works just like the similar ones for formatting all Office graphics objects (see Chapter 8). On the Pattern tab, go straight to the Fill Effects button. The four tabs in the resulting Fill Effects dialog box (see Figure 39-9) — Gradient, Texture, Pattern, and Picture — are as much fun as a game. A gradient allows the color to flow through the marker, and a texture adds a fancy touch. You can even add a gradient to a texture (talk about cool). When you're in a splashier mood, try a pattern.

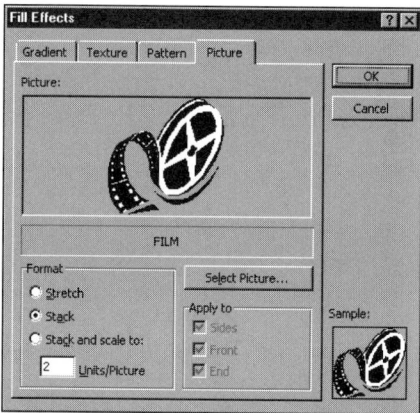

Figure 39-9: You can select pictures to represent data points in the Fill Effects dialog box, activated from the Format Data Series dialog box.

For a completely different effect, go to the Picture tab (it's the one shown in Figure 39-9), and navigate your way to that clip art you've been saving. Click Select Picture and find a simple object (a dollar bill is a classic example, especially in a 3-D line chart). Once you've chosen one, you can Stretch it (for example, a single dollar bill is stretched out to match the size of a marker) or Stack it (several dollar bills are stacked to match the marker). If you're working in a 3-D chart, you can even specify which sides of the markers should be formatted.

Adding pictures this way works for column, bar, area, bubble, 3-D line, and filled radar charts. To use a picture as a data marker in 2-D line, XY (scatter), and unfilled radar charts, copy the picture onto the clipboard, click the data series, and paste it in.

You can also add a picture or textured background to the chart area, the plot area, or the legend, and in 3-D charts, to the walls and floor. Right-click the element you want to work on, select Format from the shortcut menu, and off you go.

Timelines on the x-axis

X-axes often show timelines. And on occasion, the time units are not equidistant from each other (for example, Feb, May, Oct, Nov). When Excel sees times on the category axis, it automatically uses a type of axis called a *time-scale axis*. A time-scale axis places categories at *equal* intervals, which in the preceding example would cause blank gaps.

If you prefer to place the categories spaced next to each other, you can change from a time-scale axis to a standard category axis. Right-click the chart outside the plot area and choose Chart Options (or go to Chart ⇨ Chart Options). On the Axes tab, you'll see an option to change from Time-Scale to Category.

Adding trendlines

A *trendline* is the graphical representation of the direction or course of the data in a data series. Trendlines can be used for regression analysis, by extending the data forward or backward to indicate trends. They can also show a moving average, which smooths out fluctuations to show a clear pattern. (Trendlines can be added to all data series but those in 3-D, stacked, pie, doughnut, or radar charts.)

Right-click a data series and choose Add Trendline (or go to Chart ➪ Add Trendline). On the Type tab, select the type of line you want. You can also customize a Polynomial's Order (the highest power for the independent variable) and a Moving Average's Period (the number of periods used during calculation). You can find the equations for calculating trendlines in Help.

Secret

A moving average on an XY (scatter) chart is based on the order of the x-axis values. To get the result you want, you might need to sort the values before adding the moving average.

Displaying ranges of error

Data series can display error bars, a graphical representation of potential error or uncertainty relative to each data point within the series. You can add error bars to y-axis values on column, bar, line, and area charts. For XY (scatter) and bubble charts, you can add error bars to y-axis values, x-axis values, or both. (A caveat: Except on bubble charts, Excel doesn't allow error bars on 3-D charts.)

Double-click a data series. If you're using one of the preceding chart types, you'll see the appropriate Error Bars tab on the Format Data Series dialog box. Here's where you determine the type of display and the method used to determine the range of error. You can even define your own custom error settings. In the Plus and Minus fields, either specify a worksheet range to use as error amounts or enter the values you want to use, separated by commas. To delete error bars for a data series, click one and press Delete. When you delete one error bar, all error bars for the entire series are deleted.

Toying with your text

What good is a chart without some helpful explanation? Empty columns and lines mean nothing without clarification. It's up to you to make your chart user-friendly. You can do that in several ways. Just remember to keep it simple: No more than two or three fonts per chart should do the trick. (For more tips on stylish text, see Chapter 7.)

The two flavors of text

Chart text comes in two flavors: text that comes from the source data on the worksheet, and embellishments you add later. Both are easy to manipulate, but it's important to know how they differ.

Text that comes from the worksheet

Upon chart creation, Excel captures certain text items from the worksheet source data. These items include things like row and column headings (which become category and series names), and the heading directly above the data (which becomes the chart title). Though you can format as much as you like right on the chart, if you want to change the *wording* of this text, you should probably go back to the worksheet to do it, in order to maintain the link.

Text that you add later

Added embellishments can include things such as axis titles, chart titles, data point labels, and text boxes. The first three are labels that are affixed to a particular chart element (axis, chart area, and data series or point, respectively). You can add them simply by formatting that element. A text box is a free-floating piece of text that can be positioned anywhere on the chart. It's often used in conjunction with an arrow to point out a noteworthy characteristic, such as the month you actually sold more widgets than schmidgets.

Secret

The easiest way to create a text box is to just select the chart (unnecessary on a chart sheet) and start typing, pressing Enter when you're finished. As you type, the text appears in the Formula bar, but when you press Enter, Excel deposits it in a box in the middle of the chart. You can reposition and format the new text box as you please. Alternatively, you can use the Drawing toolbar to add text boxes (see Chapter 8).

Rotating chart text

Most chart text can be rotated or angled to some degree. This not only adds some interest, but it could be of great help when you're trying to fit everything into a limited space. The chart title, axis titles, and data point labels can all be angled at any increment from 90° to –90°. They can also be vertically aligned so that they're read from top to bottom. Double-click any text item and go to the Alignment tab to see your choices. If you're looking for a quick fix, click either of the Angle Text buttons on the chart toolbar to quickly rotate the selected text up or down by 45°.

Secret

You can rotate text boxes using the Alignment tab of the Format box, but the toolbar buttons are unavailable. You cannot rotate legend text.

Scaling fonts and preventing scaling

Secret

Normally, fonts in a chart scale proportionally when you resize either an embedded chart or the chart area of a chart sheet. To keep the font sizes constant, right-click the chart area (outside the plot area and near the border) and choose Format Chart Area. On the Font tab, clear the Auto Scale check box.

Perspective and rotation

Sometimes, a chart needs more pizzazz even after you've chosen the perfect colors and fiddled with the fonts. Excel's 3-D and rotation options may be what you need to make the chart stand out.

Wanting a new perspective?

Three-dimensional charts can be manipulated in many different ways to suit your taste. The most common way to give one a new look is to rotate it. All 3-D charts are easily rotated in the Chart ⇨ 3-D View box. But you can also rotate one by dragging it.

Click the edge of the plot area to select the corners of the chart (make sure it says "Corners" in the formula bar). Drag a corner handle to adjust the elevation and rotation of the 3-D view. You might want to drag slowly until you get the hang of it.

Secret

If you get into trouble, go back into the 3-D View box and click the Default button. Then slowly try again. To view an outline of the data markers as you rotate the chart, hold down the Ctrl key. Rotation is not the only option available.

For a new look, you can also:

- **Change the height and perspective.** The 3-D View box lets you try out a host of different angles from which to view the chart. (The Perspective option is not available for 3-D bar charts.)

- **Change the chart depth, gap depth, and gap width.** Double-click a data series and go to the Options tab. Here's where you have complete control over the spacing between markers and categories. (You can change the chart depth in 3-D charts with axes, the gap depth in 3-D perspective charts, and the gap width in 3-D bar or column charts.)

2-D pie and doughnut rotations

The order in which Excel plots data series in pie and doughnut charts is determined by the order of the data on the worksheet. If you'd like to change the rotation, you've got 360 angles from which to choose.

Double-click the data series you'd like to change, and go to the Options tab. In the Angle of First Slice box, specify any value from 0° to 360° for the angle of the first slice. A sample box shows you a preview.

Mixing Different Data Types in the Same Chart

Just as people come in all shapes and sizes, so does data. And Excel gives you the flexibility to mix data to create more complex charts (see Figure 39-10 for an example). Combination charts and charts with secondary axes are often used to emphasize certain information.

Figure 39-10: A sample combination chart

Using combination charts

A combination chart has at least one data series with a different chart type (you may have also heard this called an *overlay*). A common use for this is to plot actual values in columns, and as a contrast, add a line series showing the average values. To change the type of a data series, right-click the series and go to Chart Type. You can also select a series and use the drop-down list on the Chart toolbar.

Charts with secondary axes

When you have different kinds of data to show in the same 2-D chart (such as cost and quantity), you can plot one or more on a secondary value (y) axis. Double-click the data series you want to plot along a secondary value axis, and go to the Axis tab. Click Secondary Axis to plot this series separately from the others. The secondary axis appears on the opposite side of the chart and can be formatted completely independently from the primary value axis. Data markers associated with the secondary axis are positioned in front of other markers.

Saving Chart Options to Use Again

Once you've gone to all the trouble of creating the chart of your dreams, you'll probably want to use it again next time. You have a couple of different ways to save your work.

With the chart selected, go to Chart ➪ Chart Type. On the Custom Types tab, click the Set as Default Chart button. You'll then be asked to supply a name and a description for this type of chart. Once the default is set, all new charts will appear in this style. You can also save this chart formatting *without* making it the default, which enables you to select it only when you're ready to use it. On the Custom Types tab, go to the Select From box, and click User-defined. Click the Add button to define your new type. At any time, you can choose this chart type from the custom list.

Conclusion

Excel makes it so easy to create charts that you can sprinkle them into your Office documents freely, wherever numeric information resides. And with the tips and tricks of this chapter in your repertoire, you can fine-tune your charts so that they perfectly clarify the relationships and trends hidden in the data—and so they look great, besides.

Chapter 40

Analyzing Data

In This Chapter

▶ Filtering data in lists and tables
▶ Using PivotTables for dynamic data summaries
▶ Tapping the power of Excel add-ins
▶ Sharing workbooks

Entering data onto the spreadsheet and arranging it is merely part of the preparation process. Now we get down to the heart of the matter, my friend. It's time to analyze, scrutinize, poke, peek, and otherwise examine your data in many different ways. Let's find the proverbial bottom line. Excel has many ways to probe through the data you've entered; I show you a few of the more efficient ones.

Filtering Data

Any list or table can be used as a database (no special definitions are needed). When you perform database tasks, such as finding, sorting, or filtering data, Excel automatically treats the information as a database and assumes that the columns are the fields and the rows are the records. Filtering data in lists is one of the most common uses of Excel. With just a few simple clicks, you can easily display the records that match any criteria.

AutoFilter

The AutoFilter feature is a quick way to find a subset of the data in a list. To prepare to AutoFilter a list or table, click anywhere inside it and choose Data ➪ Filter ➪ AutoFilter. Excel treats the cells of the first row in the list or table as column labels (field names) and places small arrow buttons next to each one.

Click any arrow to drop down a list of conditions for that column (see the example in Figure 40-1). The available choices work as follows:

- To display only the records (rows) that equal a particular value, click that value in the list.

- Choose Blanks at the bottom of the drop-down list to see only the blank cells in the list. Once you've found any blank records, it's a cinch to delete them. A NonBlanks choice is also available.

- To display a certain number of top or bottom values in a list of numbers, click Top 10. You can then specify how many top or bottom values you want to see.

- If these choices aren't enough, you can create fully customized filter conditions by choosing Custom in the drop-down list, as detailed in the next section.

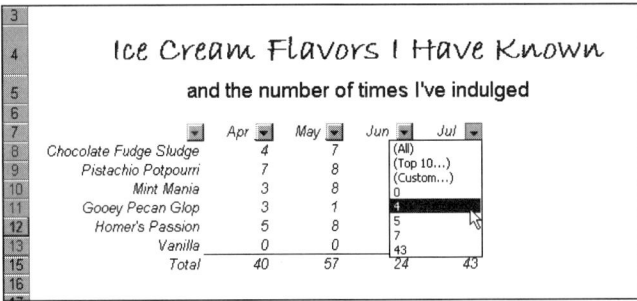

Figure 40-1: When AutoFilter is turned on, column names provide drop-down lists of built-in filtering options.

Miscellaneous AutoFilter facts:

- Once you've filtered a list, Excel displays filtered row numbers in blue, and AutoFilter arrows that are in use (that is, those you've actually used to filter the data) also turn blue.

- You can filter values in more than one column at the same time. After filtering the list in one column, click the arrow in another column to restrict the filter even further.

- When a list or table has been filtered, the AutoSum command totals only the visible rows.

- To remove a filter from a column, click the arrow again and choose All (it's at the top of the drop-down list and you may have to scroll up to see it). Turn off AutoFiltering altogether by again choosing Data ➪ AutoFilter.

Secret

Note that you can apply filters to only one list on a worksheet at a time. To begin filtering a different list on a worksheet, turn off the existing filter, and then turn on the new filter.

Creating custom filters

By using custom filters, you can set two criteria in the same column or apply a comparison operator other than "equals." Click the arrow in the column you want to filter, and click Custom. The first field is a drop-down list of 14 different comparison operators, ranging from "is greater than" to "begins with" to "does not end with" and everything in between (see Figure 40-2). In the second field, you enter the value that completes the condition.

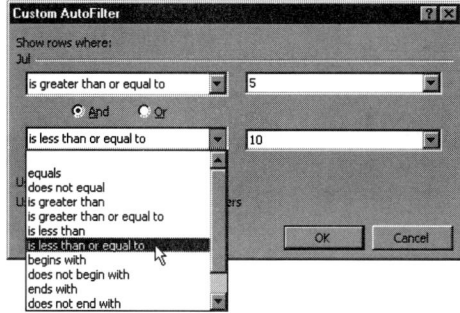

Figure 40-2: In the Custom AutoFilter dialog box, you can filter a list using one or two specifications.

To further restrict the filter, you can also enter a second criterion. Choose either And or Or, and enter another condition. AutoFilter displays all records that match *both* conditions ("And"), or all records that match *at least one* condition ("Or").

Secret

To find blank or nonblank fields with the custom filter box, use "equals" as the criterion to find blanks, and "does not equal" to find nonblanks. Leave the field to the right blank.

Using advanced filters

If you need to apply more than two conditions to a column, use calculated values as your criteria, or if you need to copy records to another location, you can use advanced filters. Using the Data ⇨ Filter ⇨ Advanced Filter dialog box, you can extract data the old-fashioned way. Enter a criteria range directly on your spreadsheet. You can use as many conditions as you need, and you can apply complex criteria or calculated values (see Help for some examples). In the Advanced Filter box, specify the list range, the criteria range, and an optional extract range (you can also filter the list in place).

Removing filters

To remove all filters of any kind, use Data ➪ Filter ➪ Show All.

Saving filters in shared workbooks

Each user of a shared workbook can save his or her own filter settings. On the Advanced tab of the Tools ➪ Share Workbook box, look under Include in Personal View. Make sure the Filter Settings check box is selected. (For more on shared workbooks, see "Sharing Workbooks" later in this chapter.)

Handy Functions for Manipulating Lists

Many wonderful functions let you manipulate data in lists. Here are just a few:

- **COUNTBLANK.** Counts the number of blank cells in the specified range.
- **COUNTIF.** Counts the number of cells in a range that meet a single criterion.
- **SUMIF.** Totals the cells in a range that meet a single criterion. (This rivals the new Conditional Sum wizard—I happen to think SUMIF is faster and easier to use.)

These functions combine very neatly with automatic row or column names, discussed in "Cooking with automatic ranges" in Chapter 38.

Pivot Tables and Pivot Charts

A *pivot table* is an interactive table that quickly summarizes large amounts of data. You can rotate the rows and columns to see different summary views, filter the data by displaying different pages, or display details for any data field. You can also have Excel produce a complementary chart from a pivot table automatically.

Other neat pivot table features include:

- One-click updating of table data and headings when the source data change
- Formatting that stays in place even when you refresh a table or change its layout
- Data that sorts automatically and maintains its sort order (including dates)
- The capability to specify precedence for multiple calculations
- Dynamic sorting or hiding of items based on items in the table

You construct a pivot table based on an existing database. The data can come from Excel, stored in a worksheet database-style—with rows as the records and labeled columns as the fields. Alternatively, you can draw on an external database, such as an Access table.

It's much easier to see how pivot tables work by experimenting with one than by reading about them. If you're trying to see whether a pivot table would help you understand your own real-life database, I strongly encourage you to make a copy of your workbook and use the copy to try out these techniques now. If you prefer, you can use the database in the sample worksheet on the CD-ROM, PivotTableSecrets.xls.

Prior to Excel 97, pivot tables were called cross-tab tables. You can easily convert a cross-tab table to a pivot table. After selecting a cell on the sheet where the cross-tab table resides, start the PivotTable Wizard. The wizard tells you what to do to complete the conversion.

You can't create pivot tables or change the layout of existing pivot tables in shared workbooks.

When to use pivot tables

In general, it's appropriate to use a pivot table when you use your database to summarize and consolidate information from detailed records so you can see larger trends. A pivot table can summarize data using functions such as Sum, Average, or Count. You can also automatically include subtotals, grand totals, and calculated fields of your own.

The worksheet shown in Figure 40-3 offers an example of a database that's prime for pivot table–making. As in the sample, such a database normally includes fields of *both* of the following types:

- **Numeric information.** Fields for quantity, cost or price, weight, size, or some other measured amount. These are the details you want to summarize.

- **Categorical information.** Fields defining the categories into which you summarize the numeric information on a category-by-category basis.

	A	B	C	D	E	F
1						
2		Toy type	Eco rating	Quality	Unit sales	Cost
3	Bite-size Amy doll	Doll	Fair	Superior	63	$10.50
4	WhistleStop Train Set	Models	Good	So-so	96	$29.85
5	Pogo sticks	Sports	Fair	Superior	33	$15.00
6	MeltAway Action Figures	Action	Excellent	Shoddy	52	$5.75
7	Softball Set	Sports	Fair	So-so	27	$8.00
8	Plastic Squeezer Alien	Novelty	Poor	Shoddy	44	$2.25
9	Bean bag Walrus	Plush	Fair	So-so	104	$6.00
10	Wooden Blocks	Construction	Good	Superior	65	$19.00
11	Fins of the Fifties	Models	Poor	So-so	38	$12.43
12	Salty the Seal	Plush	Good	Shoddy	78	$4.95
13	Eat 'em up aliens	Novelty	Excellent	Superior	262	$1.30
14	PivotTable PlaySet	Construction	Good	Shoddy	1	$295.00

Figure 40-3: The worksheet shown here contains a database suitable for summarizing with a pivot table.

Of course, categorical information is often expressed numerically, especially when the categories represent rankings on a scale. For example, ratings such as "Good," "Better," and "Best" could just as well be represented by numbers 1, 2, and 3. Such fields can be used in pivot tables as either kind of information. Another wrinkle: You can always use a pivot table to summarize categorical information by simply counting the number of records in each category.

Creating a pivot table

If the target database is in a worksheet, activate the sheet and click anywhere in the database. Choose Data ⇨ PivotTable and PivotChart Report to start the PivotTable Wizard. It walks you through the creation process:

1. Begin by specifying the type of source data and type of report. You can create a pivot table from information on a single worksheet, information on several worksheets, another pivot table, or an external database. If you want a pivot chart as well as a pivot table, click the appropriate button and see the section "Creating pivot charts" later in this chapter.

2. Depending upon your answer in Step 1, the wizard helps you specify the data's exact location. In the case of worksheet data, if the active worksheet contains a suitable database, Excel selects it for you but you can adjust the range or choose another one as necessary.

3. All you need to do in Step 3 is decide whether the table should appear in its own new worksheet or in an existing sheet. (However, you can use the Layout and Options buttons to control the organization and look of the table as discussed later in "Using the PivotTable Wizard.") Click Finish to complete the wizard.

These first three steps produce only the skeleton of the pivot table, which appears in your workbook as shown in Figure 40-4. The real fun starts when you actually lay out the information the way you want to see it in the table.

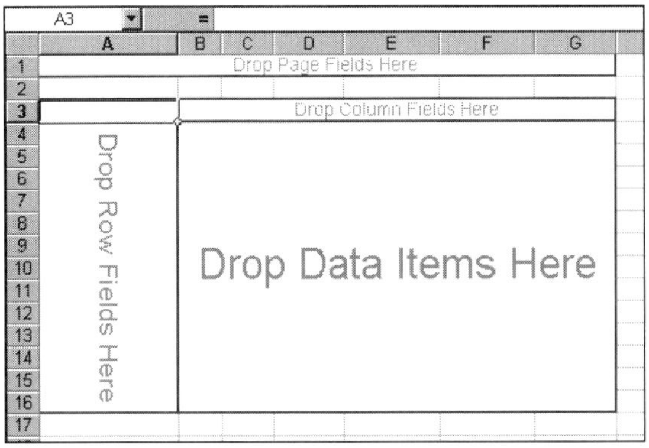

Figure 40-4: The outline of a new pivot table appears like this in your worksheet, ready for you to lay out its fields.

Laying out fields

Note the PivotTable toolbar, also visible in Figure 40-4. Along with the graphical buttons along the top, the toolbar includes a labeled button for each field (column) in the original database. As shown in Figure 40-5, all you have to do is drag these buttons to the desired locations on the pivot table outline.

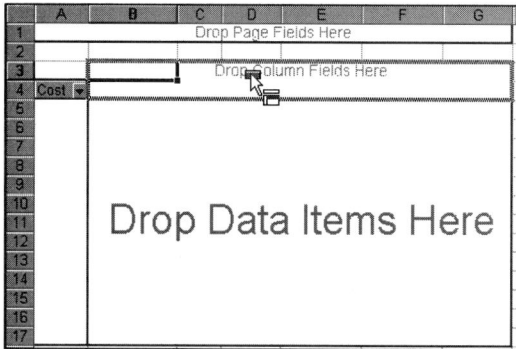

Figure 40-5: Laying out a pivot table is as easy as dragging each field name button to its respective position in the diagram.

You can drag fields to any of these destinations in the pivot table:

- **Column and row axes.** Fields in the column and row areas specify how the table is to summarize the data.

- **Data area.** This area is for the data you want to summarize.

- **Page field area.** Fields in the page field area determine which categories show up in the table at all. If you want to be able to limit the entire table to a particular category, place the field for this category in the page field area. (The page field area may not appear in a new pivot table. You can use the PivotTable Wizard to add a page field area to a pivot table that doesn't have one and place fields in it — see "Using the PivotTable Wizard" later in this chapter.)

Secret

So which fields go where? Until you become pivot table adept, you can use this simple rule for making effective tables: *fields containing numeric values go in the data area, while fields that define categories belong in the rows and columns and the page area.* Text fields that contain unique entries rather than category information can be placed usefully in the data area if you want to count the number of records in the categories defined by other fields. At a minimum, you must place at least one field in the data area, and one in either the row axis or the column axis.

Don't be concerned in the slightest about getting the layout perfect the first time. You can reorganize the table just as easily as you laid it out initially, as detailed in the section "Pivoting the data" later in this chapter.

Pivot table anatomy and physiology

Figure 40-6 shows a completed pivot table after fields from the sample database have been laid out. The final rows and columns (the ones labeled "Total" or "Grand Total") contain the overall summary calculations for the fields in the data area.

	A	B	C	D	E	F
1	Toy type	(All)				
2						
3	Sum of Unit sales	Eco rating				
4	Quality	Excellent	Fair	Good	Poor	Grand Total
5	Shoddy	52		79	44	175
6	So-so		131	96	38	265
7	Superior	262	96	65		423
8	Grand Total	314	227	240	82	863

Figure 40-6: A completed pivot table, before additional formatting has been applied

By default, the calculations shown in a pivot table are simple sums of the values for numeric data, and simple counts of the number of items for text. You can change the calculations performed for each data field using the technique covered in "Controlling summary calculations" later in this chapter.

A pivot table has a button for each field in the table, except that you get only one button for the data area no matter how many fields it contains. Each button is titled with the field name. Clicking the arrow on the button opens a drop-down list that lets you select the elements that are to appear in the table (see Figure 40-7). This is a great way to focus in on a specific category of information.

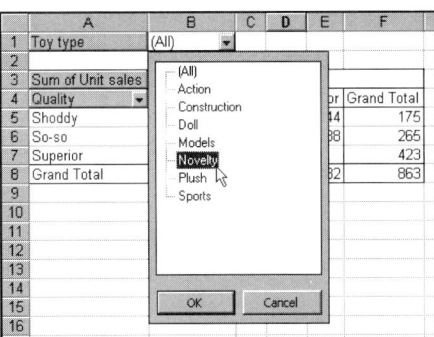

Figure 40-7: Use a field button's drop-down list to limit the table to items matching specific categories in the field.

If a piece of data within the table looks suspicious, or if you're just curious about how it was derived, double-click it. A separate worksheet opens showing the source data for that item. If this doesn't work, right-click the table, choose Table Options, and check Enable Drilldown.

Pivoting the data

They don't call it a "pivot" table for nothing. By dragging fields to different parts of the table, you can view your data from different perspectives. Excel automatically reformats the table according to the field locations, relabeling column and row headings according to the current fields in those areas.

To remove a field altogether from the page, row, or column areas, just drag its button out of the pivot table. If you remove all the fields in either the row or column area, the table's data disappears — you see the empty skeleton again. Don't worry — as soon as you add back one or more fields into the empty area, the table comes to life again.

Secret

If you've placed only a single field in the data area, its name appears in the top-left corner of the table and you can drag it off the table from there. However, you can't drag individual fields out of the data area when it contains two or more fields. Instead, remove them from the table by clicking the Data drop-down button (it will be labeled with the field name if the data area contains only one field). In the pop-up list of fields, clear the check box for the field you want to remove. Alternatively, you can remove all data fields by dragging the item labeled Data Off of the Table and then add back fields individually.

Using the PivotTable toolbar and shortcut menu

Once you create a pivot table, the PivotTable toolbar remains on the screen until you dismiss it. However, while you can always use it to activate the PivotTable Wizard, the toolbar is otherwise active only when you select some portion of an existing pivot table. Then the toolbar's buttons become available.

Secret

Actually, though, you only need the toolbar when you're laying out fields on the worksheet — you have to be able to drag those field buttons from the toolbar to the table. For almost all other pivot table operations you can rely on the table's right-click (shortcut) menu.

Fine-tuning pivot tables

Once you've decided on your table's basic layout, you have a host of options for controlling how it summarizes the data, displaying additional calculations, and making the table pretty.

Working with field options

To fine-tune the way your pivot table handles an individual field, right-click the field heading in the table and choose Field Settings in the resulting shortcut menu. Alternatively, you can just double click, row, column, and page fields. The PivotTable Field dialog box appears, as shown in Figure 40-8.

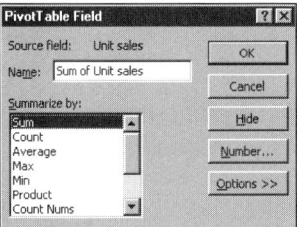

Figure 40-8: Fields in a pivot table can be customized using the PivotTable Field dialog box. Numeric fields include a Number button for formatting numbers.

If the field contains numeric data, you'll see a Number button that lets you control the formatting. On fields in the row, column, and page areas, the Advanced button gives you further display and sort options.

Controlling summary calculations

Use the list in the middle of the PivotTable Field dialog box to control which calculations appear in your pivot table. For data fields, you're choosing the calculation displayed in the cells in the body of the table. You can pick only one calculation for data fields. For row, column, and page fields, you're determining the calculation displayed in special "subtotal" rows or columns. These subtotals only appear when you place two or more fields in one area (row, column, or page). You can select as many subtotal calculations as you like for fields in the row, column, and page areas.

Creating calculated fields and items

Excel's 11 built-in calculation types available in the PivotTable Field dialog box cover most situations. But when these don't meet your needs, you can create custom calculations. A *calculated field* summarizes data from existing fields based on a formula that you design and can be used just like other fields in the table, while a *calculated item* appears within a field in the row, column, or page areas and is based on the data that field contains. The calculations become a part of the pivot table, and afterward, you can display a list of the custom formulas you've used.

To create a custom calculation, right-click a field name or item, choose Formulas, and choose either Calculated Field or Calculated Item (one or both appear, depending upon your selection). In creating your formula, you can use operators and functions just as you do in other worksheet formulas, though you can't refer to cells or ranges. When you OK the dialog box, Excel places the new field in your table and puts a corresponding button on the PivotTable toolbar for future use.

To view a list of custom formulas, right-click again, and choose Formulas ⇨ List Formulas. The formulas appear on a new worksheet.

Comparing fields

Another option lets you compare the values of the current field with those in a different field. Bring up the PivotTable Field dialog box for an item in the data area and click the Options button. Now select the type of comparison you want under Show Data As. In the Base Field and Base Item boxes, choose which field and individual item you want to base the comparison on.

Refining pivot table layout

Secret

Suppose you just want to reorder a pivot table's rows or columns, perhaps because the headings represent rankings that should appear in rank order rather than alphabetically. To move a row or column heading, activate the cell and then drag its *border* to the new location.

To *merge* two or more row or column headings into a group:

1. Select the headings you want to include. You can hold down Ctrl while you click to select nonadjacent headings.

2. Right-click a selected cell and choose Group and Outline ⇨ Group from the shortcut menu. Excel adds a new heading labeled Group1 or the like to your table.

3. To consolidate the entries from the rows or columns in the group, right-click the group heading and choose Group and Outline ⇨ Hide Detail.

Using the PivotTable Wizard

Although you can lay out fields on the pivot table itself, you can also do so in the PivotTable Wizard when you're creating the table in the first place, or later, to modify the layout of an existing table. To use the wizard for layout, click the Layout button on the wizard's third panel. (You're taken immediately to this panel when you activate the wizard for an existing pivot table — to do so, right-click anywhere in the table and choose Wizard from the shortcut menu.)

The Layout dialog box displays a diagram of the pivot table structure, with page, row, column, and data areas, along with a series of buttons representing the fields. Drag the fields of interest to the diagram, just as you would on the actual table. Because the diagram doesn't display data, you may find it easier to make layout modifications here, especially when the table includes many fields. And you may need the Layout dialog box to use the page area — the page area is always visible here, even if it isn't displayed on the pivot table itself.

Using the PivotTable Options dialog box

Clicking Table Options on a pivot table's shortcut menu brings up a big dialog box (Figure 40-9) stuffed full of formatting options. The box also includes options dealing with the table's underlying data. You can also get to this dialog box from the third panel of the PivotTable Wizard.

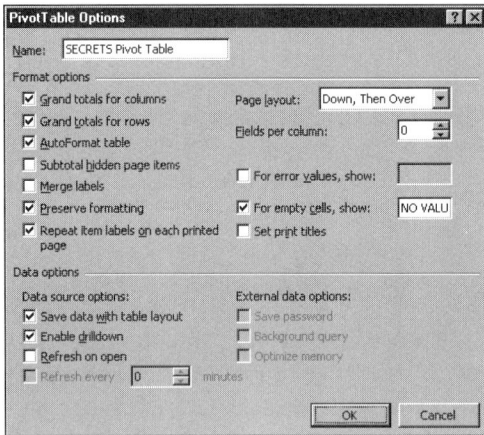

Figure 40-9: From the PivotTable Options dialog box, you can define how error values and blank cells are displayed (among other things).

Handling blank cells and error values

Use the PivotTable Options dialog box to control what Excel does with blank cells and error messages. To change how errors are displayed, select the For Error Values, Show box, and enter the value you want to display instead of errors. To change how empty cells are displayed, select the For Empty Cells, Show box, and enter the value you want to display in empty cells. In either case, your entry can be a zero, a word, or no value at all. The changes you make affect the entire pivot table. If you don't check the Error Values box, Excel displays a default message.

Secret

By default, a pivot table does not display field items that have no associated data. To show these items, right-click the Field button and go to Field. Select the Show Items with No Data box.

Formatting pivot tables

The easiest way to give your table a classy format is with one of the AutoFormat choices available via the Format Report button, available on the PivotTable toolbar or shortcut menu. You can apply any of 21 different formats in report or table styles. Use the None option at the bottom of the format list to remove automatic formatting.

Creating pivot charts

You can chart your pivot table summaries instantly, either by selecting PivotChart during Step 1 of the PivotTable Wizard, or from an existing pivot table (choose PivotChart from the table's shortcut menu or click the Chart Wizard button on the Standard or PivotTable toolbar).

Pivot charts work almost exactly like pivot tables, only graphically. Once you have one in your workbook, you can play around with its layout and control the data it displays just as you can a pivot table. Looking at Figure 40-10, you can see the sample chart has the field buttons just like those in pivot tables in addition to a conventional legend.

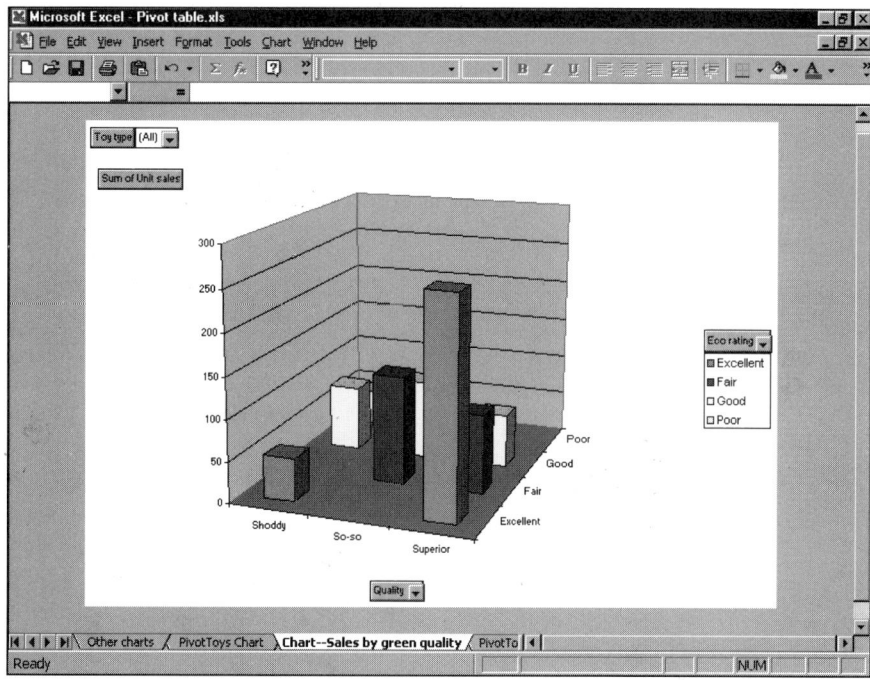

Figure 40-10: A pivot chart based on the pivot table shown in Figure 40-6

Some of the modifications you can make to pivot charts include:

- Dragging fields on or off the chart or to different locations inside it
- Selecting items from the field button drop-down lists to control which data the chart displays
- Altering field options via the PivotTable Field dialog box (display it by double-clicking a field button)

The chart remains connected to the table from which you created it, so these changes appear on the table as well. Of course, you can format the chart visually just as you would an ordinary chart—see Chapter 39 for details.

Working with Add-ins

Add-in programs are optional components that add functionality to Excel. Although some add-ins are installed automatically when you install Excel, others must be installed separately by you.

After installing an add-in onto your hard drive, use the Tools ⇨ Add-Ins command to load the add-in into Excel. This makes the feature available and adds any associated commands to the menus. The Tools ⇨ Add-Ins dialog box (Figure 40-11) is very easy to use: If the add-in is listed in the box, you know it's been installed onto your hard drive. If it has a check next to it, you know it's been loaded into Excel.

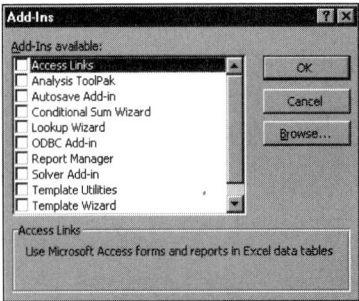

Figure 40-11: These Add-Ins have been installed but not yet loaded into Excel.

Some add-ins may delay the time it takes to launch Excel. To conserve memory, you might want to unload add-ins that you don't use often. (Unloading an add-in removes its features from Excel, but the program remains on your PC so that you can easily reload it.)

The sections that follow offer quick looks at some add-ins that are especially helpful in analyzing data. If you can't find one of the commands or features mentioned, go to Tools ⇨ Add-Ins to install the appropriate add-in program.

Lookup Wizard add-in

Use the Lookup Wizard add-in when you need to determine the current value of an item in a list. Suppose you keep track of your pet store's canine menagerie in a simple Excel list. Each row of the list (which is basically a table) shows a dog breed in the first column and how many of them you have on hand in the second column, which is labeled In Stock.

What you want is a way to find the current number of beagles on hand. The list is long and it's too much trouble to comb through it yourself. Besides, another worksheet needs to know how many beagles are in stock so that it can calculate how many beagle puppies to buy each month. Whenever you update this second worksheet, it must have access to current information even if the beagle row has changed places in the list.

To count your hounds reliably, use the Lookup Wizard. Follow these steps:

1. Start by selecting the entire list, including the row and column labels.

2. Choose Tools ⇨ Wizard ⇨ Lookup. In the first of four wizard windows, confirm the list range.

3. Specify the labels for the row and column containing the information you seek. In the example, you would pick the label for the beagle row and the label for the In Stock column.

4. Tell the wizard how you want to enter the results — as a formula in a single cell, or as the formula along with the column labels (the parameters) used to do the lookup.

5. The last step is really easy: Just designate the cell or cells where Excel should enter the lookup formula (and the parameters if you chose to include them in Step 4). You can switch to a different worksheet to deposit the cell(s) there. The formula cell displays the results of the lookup, of course, so you simply see the same value as in the list. If you choose to include parameters, their cells simply contain the selected row and column labels.

Whenever Excel recalculates the formula, the current value from the inventory list is transferred to the target cell. Because the formula sniffs out the desired information in the list based on row and column labels, not on predefined cell coordinates, you always get the correct answer — even if beagles have moved up one row in the list after your store stopped carrying basset hounds.

If you chose not to include parameters, the formula used for the lookup includes the literal characters of the row and column labels you selected. If you opted to include cells for the parameters, however, the formula refers to the current contents of those cells. That means you can type a different breed name in the row label parameter cell and instantly see how many afghans, poodles, or spaniels are in stock.

Analysis ToolPak add-in

The Analysis ToolPak is a set of 19 data-analysis tools that assist in complex statistical and engineering analyses. You provide the data and parameters for each analysis; the tool calculates the results and displays an output table. Some tools generate charts in addition to tables.

To use the Analysis ToolPak, you must first install it by checking its box in the Add-ins dialog box (see previous Figure 40-11). Then choose Tools ➪ Data Analysis to display the Data Analysis dialog box. Select an analysis tool from this dialog box. When you then choose OK, a dialog box with options relevant for that tool appears.

Solver

The Solver is another add-in for those who need advanced data analysis. It calculates solutions to what-if scenarios based on variable cells. Unlike Goal Seek, which finds a single value, Solver can find multiple values and enables you to define constraints. (When you use Solver, the cells involved must be related through formulas on the worksheet.)

When using Solver, you specify the target cell whose formula result you want to optimize. You then designate the cells to be changed (up to 200) — those that are related, either directly or indirectly, to the target cell. You can apply constraints to restrict the values in the cells or their relationships. Solver changes the values in the input cells to produce the desired result in the target formula cell.

To use Solver, choose Tools ➪ Solver and fill in the dialog box shown in Figure 40-12. For a bit of general information about the algorithm used by Solver, choose Help in the Solver Parameters dialog box.

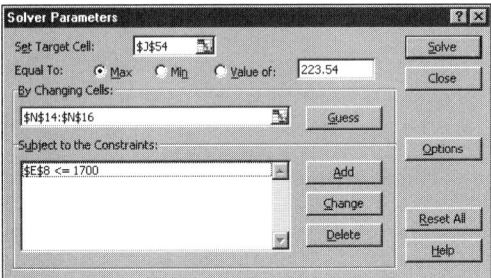

Figure 40-12: Cells N14:N16 contain values that drive the formula in cell J54. Use Solver to vary them until J54 equals the target value of 223.54.

Secret

For nonlinear problems, it can be helpful to experiment with different starting values for the input cells, especially if Solver has found a solution that is significantly different from what you expected.

Secret

Use Goal Seek when you know the desired result of a formula, but not the input value from a single cell that the formula needs. Use Solver when you need to change the values in several cells and have multiple constraints for those values.

Template Wizard with Data Tracking add-in

The Template Wizard with Data Tracking helps you create custom templates or electronic forms that record worksheet entries in a database for tracking and analysis. You use the wizard to produce the template or form, and link it to a database. The database can exist in Excel, Access, FoxPro, dBase, or Paradox. When you or others create a new workbook based on the template, the information you enter is saved as a new record in the database. You can then use the forms to gather data from various users and send the data to a database without retyping. You can also create reports from the saved data or use it as you would any other database.

To create the template, first open an existing workbook that's organized and formatted so that you can easily fill in the data you want entered in the database. Then begin the wizard by choosing Data ➪ Template Wizard. The database must come from a program for which you have installed the necessary ODBC driver and other data access components.

Built-in forms for data tracking

Excel includes some built-in templates that automate common tasks (such as an expense report, an invoice, and a purchase order). These templates can be used with the Template Wizard add-in. To use one of the built-in templates, go to File ➪ New and double-click a template on the Spreadsheet Solutions tab. You can personalize the templates with your company name and logo, but the VBA code they contain is locked and can't be modified.

You can obtain additional Excel templates on Microsoft's Web site. These are designed for tasks such as planning personal finances.

Sharing Workbooks

"Share and share alike," your mother used to say. Well, I'm not sure if she was referring to Excel spreadsheets, but I'm sure she'd be proud. Now, everyone in your group can edit workbooks at the same time, by creating a shared workbook.

You can allow others to review and edit a workbook simultaneously. During the process, their changes are highlighted (in different colors, of course), change histories are tracked, and comments are stored. And if you decide to, you can put limits on access.

To open a workbook for sharing, open the workbook and go to Tools ➪ Share Workbook. On the Editing tab, select Allow Changes by More Than One User. The list on the Editing tab shows the current users for this workbook. If you've just enabled sharing right now, the only user shown is you. You can return to this box at any time to see who is currently working on this shared workbook.

When you filter data in a shared workbook and set print options, your settings are saved independently of those made by other users. Whenever you open the shared workbook, your personal settings appear. (See the section "Filtering Data" earlier in this chapter.)

Many Excel features are off limits in shared workbooks. You can't delete worksheets, merge cells, or define conditional formats. Nor can you insert or delete blocks of cells; insert or modify charts, pictures, objects, or hyperlinks; or create or modify macros. For a list of such commands, look up the "Limitations of shared workbooks" Help topic.

Keeping track of changes

Excel keeps track of all changes made to a shared workbook and which user made the changes. Whenever a change is made, Excel identifies it using the name in the Tools ➪ Options box (look in the User name field on the General tab). You can later view a complete history of every change, including information about those that conflict.

You can keep a history in two ways: by highlighting changes directly on the worksheet, or by maintaining a separate History worksheet.

Secret

If you protect a workbook for sharing, others cannot remove it from shared use or turn off the change history. In this way, you guarantee that all changes are tracked. Use the Tools ➪ Protection ➪ Protect Shared Workbook command.

Highlighting changes on the sheet

Individuals can highlight their changes right on the sheet, making them easily visible. To highlight changes to the current workbook, open the Tools ➪ Track Changes ➪ Highlight Changes dialog box, shown in Figure 40-13. Turn on Track Changes While Editing. This also turns on sharing and the change history, if they're not already on. The Highlight Changes on Screen field shows the changes as you make them. List Changes on a New Sheet saves the changes to the change history (discussed in the next section).

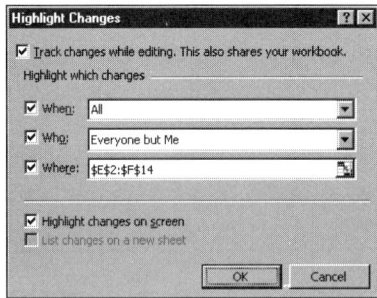

Figure 40-13: You can track changes while editing to keep a record of all your edits.

When a change is made to a cell, the cell is outlined in color, and a small indicator is placed in the upper-left corner. Changes are color-coded according to the user. Rest the pointer over a highlighted cell to see a small note with the user's name, the date, the time, and the change that was made.

You can also choose to highlight changes for a certain time period, for certain users, or on a particular part of the worksheet (see Figure 40-13). When highlighting changes, Excel does not track certain things, such as formatting.

Keeping a change history

You can view a complete list of changes to the workbook by maintaining a History worksheet. The History sheet (called the Conflicts sheet prior to Excel 97) includes information on who made the change, when and where it was made, what data was changed, and how conflicts were resolved. The column labels have filter arrows that you can use to find specific information.

To keep a change history, you must first save the workbook in shared, protected form with the command previously described. Then, go to Tools ➪ Track Changes ➪ Highlight Changes. Turn on List Changes on a New Sheet. A sheet named History is added to the workbook.

When viewing the History sheet, you can filter the information in several ways. Each column heading has a filter arrow, with a drop-down list. Any column can be filtered to show changes made by particular users on particular dates. You can review changes in the order that they were made, or view changes to particular areas of the worksheet.

Information about how conflicts are resolved is also available on the History sheet. You can find information about any changes that are replaced by other changes, and print the change information.

The History worksheet shows only the changes that have been saved. To include all changes from your current session, save the workbook before viewing the History sheet.

Merging changes

When you save a shared workbook, you can have your changes replace any conflicting changes made by others, or you can review each change and decide whether to accept it.

Updating settings

If you plan to merge copies of a shared workbook, you must prepare some settings ahead of time. Select Tools ➪ Share Workbook. On the Advanced tab, you determine how long changes are tracked, when they're updated, and how conflicting changes are resolved.

In order to merge changes, each copy of the shared workbook must track changes from the day when the copies were created, through the day when they're merged. If the number of days specified is exceeded, you can no longer merge the copies. (If you aren't sure how long the review will take, enter an unusually large number of days.)

On the verge of a merge

Open the shared workbook into which you want to merge changes. Choose Tools ➪ Merge Workbooks. If prompted, save the current version. In the dialog box that appears, select the copies that have changes to be merged and click OK.

Excel incorporates changes from all shared copies selected and resolves conflicts according to the settings on the Advanced tab of Tools ➪ Share Workbook. Even cell comments from different users are identified by individual user names and merged into a single comment box.

The entire process is recorded on the History sheet for viewing any time. Revisions by different users are color-coded. When it's done, you can have the final word by going to Tools ➪ Track Changes, Accept or Reject Changes. Excel steps through every change, displays it for you, and allows you to give your yay or nay. (On the History worksheet, rejected changes display "Undo" or "Result of rejected action" in the Action Type column.)

Secret

You can use this feature with the Windows Briefcase to work on a shared workbook when you aren't connected to your network. When you reconnect, simply merge your changes back into the copy of the network version (see Chapter 13).

Conclusion

No short section on Excel can hope to plumb its wealth of data analysis features. Still, learning the tricks covered here for filtering, summarizing, and searching your data will prepare you to tackle even more advanced tasks. And if you're not up to the challenge alone, get help by sharing your workbooks with others using Excel's gifts for collaboration.

Chapter 41

Debugging Your Worksheets

In This Chapter

- Tracing formula precedents and dependents using the Auditing toolbar and keyboard shortcuts
- Translating cryptic cell error messages
- Finding precedent cells containing errors with the Trace Error button
- Detecting accidental circular references in your worksheets (and fine-tuning the ones you put there on purpose)
- Using Formula AutoCorrect to catch syntax errors as you make them
- Miscellaneous tips on detecting errors in your worksheets

Want more control over what's going on behind the scenes? I have a few tricks here that are guaranteed to make you feel like a power user.

Using the Auditing Toolbar

If you didn't know that Excel has an auditing toolbar, that's probably because it isn't listed on the shortcut menu you see when you right-click a toolbar. To display it, select Tools⇨Auditing⇨Show Auditing Toolbar. On it you find some indispensable surprises (see Figure 41-1).

Figure 41-1: The Auditing toolbar is a handy little gadget.

Depending on You

The Doobie Brothers were actually singing about an important topic concerning the cells on your worksheet. On whom do they depend? Who depends on them? Excel gives you several quick and easy ways to find out.

Cell *precedents* are the cells that provide data to the formula in the active cell. These precedents contain the input values that the formula needs (for more on cell precedents, see Chapter 35). Cell *dependents* are those that depend on the value in the active cell. The active cell provides data to them. The diagram in Figure 41-2 shows a very simple example. To help debug problems on your worksheet, Excel provides tools for tracing precedents and dependents.

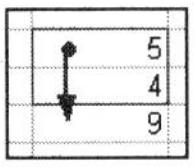

Figure 41-2: The sum of "9" depends upon the two values above it. "9" is the dependent cell, and "5" and "4" are the precedent cells.

Tracing with the Auditing toolbar

On the Auditing toolbar, the first four buttons give you the ability to show and hide *tracer arrows* on your worksheet. When you click the Trace Precedents button, blue tracer arrows indicate cells that are precedents of the selected cell. Cells off the current worksheet are indicated by arrows with a small worksheet icon. When you click the Trace Dependents button, blue tracer arrows indicate cells that are dependent on the selected cell.

In each case, the arrow shows the direction of the reference (see Figure 41-3).

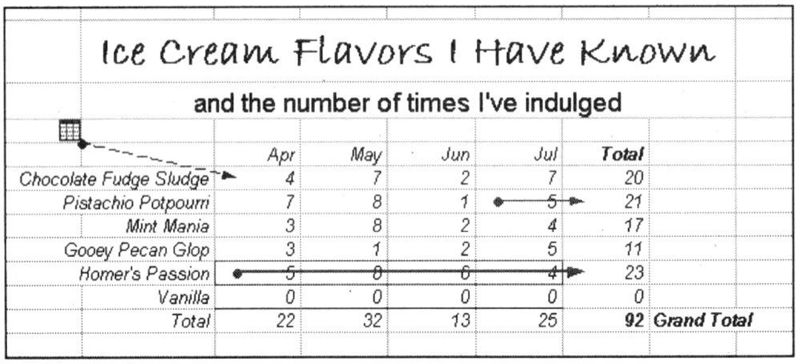

	Ice Cream Flavors I Have Known				
	and the number of times I've indulged				
	Apr	May	Jun	Jul	Total
Chocolate Fudge Sludge	4	7	2	7	20
Pistachio Potpourri	7	8	1	5	21
Mint Mania	3	8	2	4	17
Gooey Pecan Glop	3	1	2	5	11
Homer's Passion	5	8	6	4	23
Vanilla	0	0	0	0	0
Total	22	32	13	25	92 Grand Total

Figure 41-3: With a single click, you can trace one dependency (as in Pistachio Potpourri) or several dependencies (as in Homer's Passion). Chocolate Fudge Sludge's April value came from another worksheet.

Each time you click a button, one level of precedents or dependents is shown. The first time you click the Trace Precedents button, for example, Excel locates and displays the immediate precedents (the "parents" of the active cell). With each additional click, successive levels of indirect links — grandparents, great-grandparents, and so on — are shown by additional arrows.

If you want to find the cell at the other end of a tracer arrow, you can simply double-click anywhere along the arrow. This also works for cells on other worksheets or in other workbooks. Double-click the arrow, and in the Go To box that appears, double-click your destination.

A few caveats on tracing precedents and dependents

Caution

You can't trace the following referenced items with the auditing tools: text boxes, embedded charts, pictures, pivot tables, named constants, and dependent cells residing in a closed workbook. Also, because tracer arrows are graphical objects, you won't see them if objects are hidden on the worksheet. If they aren't visible, check the View tab in the Tools ➪ Options dialog box. Under Objects, make sure that Show All is selected.

Removing tracer arrows

Select a formula cell and click the Remove Precedent Arrows button to remove the arrows that point from its precedent cells. Select a precedent cell and click the Remove Dependent Arrows button to remove the arrows that point to its dependent cells.

If several levels of links are shown, they are removed one level at a time. The first time you click the button, the arrow indicating the most indirect link is removed, and so on. To remove all tracer arrows, click the Remove All Arrows button.

The double-click trick

Secret

Interested in precedents only? A simple double-click might do. Open the Tools ➪ Options dialog box. On the Edit tab, look at the Edit Directly in Cell field. If it's checked and you like it that way, this trick won't work for you — use one of the other methods mentioned in this section. But if you're willing to turn it off in favor of a great shortcut, do so and read on.

Once you've turned off in-cell editing, you can double-click any formula to immediately select all the precedent cells. This is an extremely efficient way to get an immediate look at what the formula is doing. Because functions are a kind of formula, I use it liberally on my SUM formulas. I frequently double-click a SUM to get a reminder of what I'm summing. As a bonus, if you double-click a formula with a remote reference (that is, a reference to another workbook), the workbook opens and the precedent cell is selected.

For keyboard users

Here are shortcuts for you, too. Feast your fingers on these:

Press This	To Do This
Ctrl+[	Select direct precedents of the active cell.
Ctrl+Shift+[	Select direct and indirect precedents of the active cell.
Ctrl+]	Select direct dependents of the active cell.
Ctrl+Shift+]	Select direct and indirect dependents of the active cell.

Cell Errors

Cell errors are usually traceable. If you understand what the error means, it's an easy fix.

Understanding cell error messages

Error messages in cells can be awfully cryptic. Let's review a few of the meanings:

Error	Meaning
#DIV/0!	The formula is dividing by zero.
#N/A	A value is not available to the function or formula.
#NAME?	Text in the formula is not recognized. (For more on the #NAME? error, see "Error checking on the fly" later.)
#NULL!	The formula refers to an intersection of two areas that do not intersect.
#NUM!	A problem occurs with a number in the formula or function.
#REF!	A cell reference is not valid.
#VALUE!	The wrong type of argument or operand is used.
#####	The formatted number is too wide to display within the column. (This is the only error that is not traced with the Auditing toolbar. Simply widen the column to fix it.)

Tracing errors

Sometimes the source of cell errors is immediately obvious. If it's not, select the cell that has the error, and click the Trace Error button. Red arrows point to *formulas* that cause error values; blue arrows point to cells containing *values* that create errors.

To select and display the cell at the other end of an arrow, double-click the arrow. If more than one error path exists, Excel stops tracing at the branch point when you use Trace Error. To continue tracing, click Trace Error again.

Auditing Data Validation errors

If you've used Data Validation to constrain entries in a cell, chances are you defined error messages to pop up for incorrect entries. But invalid entries can still find their way onto your worksheet.

Input and error messages only appear when a user is typing *directly* into the cell. Copying, autofilling, formulas, and macros can also alter worksheet information, and these incorrect entries don't produce error messages. But rest assured they can easily be tracked down. (This is the one time you'll be *pleased* to have an audit!)

When you audit a worksheet for incorrect entries, Excel identifies *all* cells containing values outside the limits you've set using Data Validation. To trace these errors, you need merely turn to a button on the Auditing toolbar. On the toolbar, click the Circle Invalid Data button. Excel immediately checks the worksheet and places red circles around the first 255 cells containing data that do not meet the criteria you set with Data Validation. Once the errors have been found and corrected, click the Clear Validation Circles button to erase the red circles.

Caution

The auditing buttons are not available on a protected worksheet.

Identifying circular references

A *circular reference* is a formula that directly or indirectly refers back to itself. Excel cannot automatically calculate all open workbooks when one of them contains a circular reference. While many of them happen by accident, some scientific and engineering formulas require circular references to perform their calculations.

When a circular reference occurs, Excel alerts you with a message and the Circular Reference toolbar. If you didn't mean to create one, you can use the toolbar to track it down and correct it. If you intended to create one for a specific process, you can control how the reference is calculated.

Accidental circular references

When a circular reference occurs, Excel automatically displays an alert, opens the Circular Reference toolbar, and places blue auditing arrows in the cells involved (see Figure 41-4).

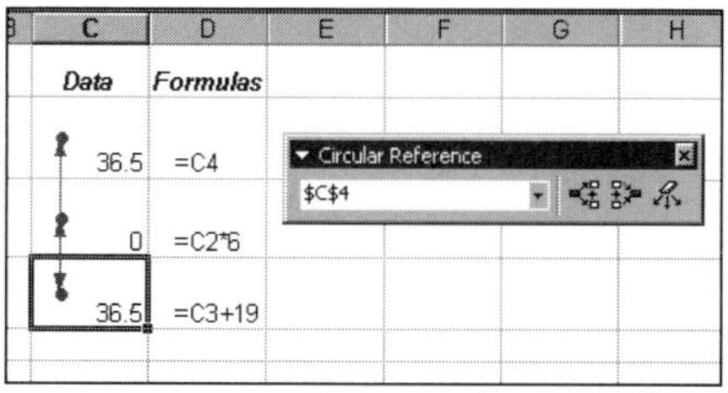

Figure 41-4: The Circular Reference toolbar and blue auditing arrows alert you to the location of circular references.

If you're familiar with the Auditing toolbar, you'll recognize the Trace Dependents, Trace Precedents, and Remove All Arrows buttons on the Circular Reference toolbar. Use these buttons to display tracer arrows. You can move between cells in a circular reference by double-clicking the arrows, or by choosing them from the toolbar's drop-down list. As you move to each cell in turn, you can redesign the logic to break the circular reference.

Another visual cue can be found in the status bar. You'll see the word *Circular* followed by a reference to one of the guilty cells. If the status bar message appears without a cell reference, it means the error is found on a different sheet in the workbook.

You can display the Circular Reference toolbar manually. Right-click any toolbar, and choose Customize. On the Toolbars tab, select the Circular Reference check box.

Intentional circular references

If you're using a scientific or engineering formula that requires a circular reference, it might be helpful to know how Excel treats them, and how to control the process by which Excel calculates results that depend on circular references.

Secret

To have Excel calculate circular references, you must go to the Calculation tab of the Tools ⇨ Options dialog box. There, check the Iteration box. When you turn iteration on, Excel iterates (that is, repeatedly calculates the worksheet) the number of times specified at Maximum Iterations, or until all values in the circular reference change by less than the value at Maximum Change, whichever comes first.

Finding errors in logic

While tracer arrows and validation circles are a fast, efficient way of finding errors, what they can't find is errors in your logic. But if some values on your worksheet seem fishy, you can take a closer look at your formulas to see whether they're really doing what you intended them to do.

By default, your worksheet displays formula *results*; to see the contents of a formula, you must click it and look in the formula bar. But debugging is laborious when you can only see one formula at a time. Why not look at them all at once?

Secret

I know what you're thinking. The best of all possible worlds would be being able to see *both* formulas and results at once. Try this: Go to Window ⇨ New Window. Another window containing the current worksheet opens. Now arrange both windows on the screen with Window ⇨ Arrange. You can choose either a one-on-top-of-the-other arrangement (Vertical) or a side-by-side arrangement (Horizontal). (If other worksheets are open, you may want to temporarily hide them with Window ⇨ Hide, and then rearrange the two windows of the worksheet you're debugging.)

Once the two windows are arranged on the screen, show formulas in one and results in the other. This way, you can discover at a glance the logic behind your formulas. The results should look something like the picture in Figure 41-5.

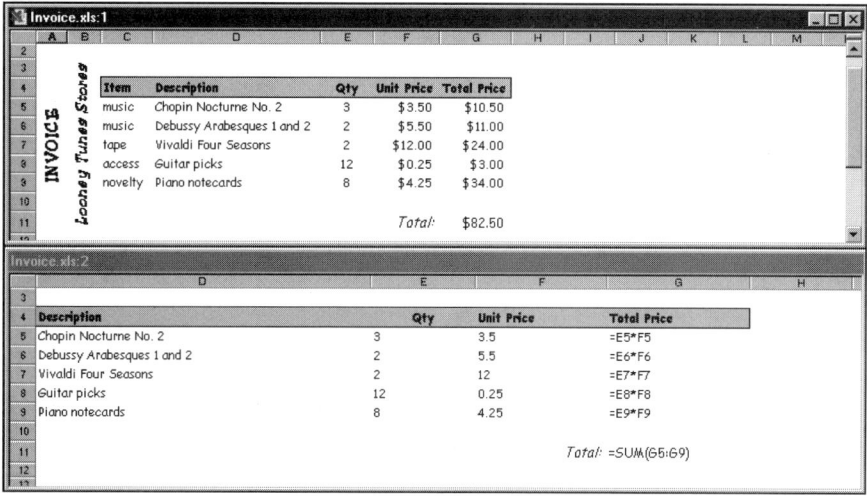

Figure 41-5: While both windows display the same worksheet, the top window shows results and the bottom window shows formulas.

Error checking on the fly

If in the best of all possible worlds you can find your errors at a glance, in the best of all possible universes your mistakes would be fixed for you as you made them. As detailed in Chapter 7, the AutoCorrect feature corrects errors in spelling and punctuation in text you enter on your worksheets. Excel's Formula AutoCorrect feature automatically catches the most common mistakes when creating a formula. And the following few extra tips show that sometimes just knowing how Excel thinks can give you the edge.

Formula AutoCorrect

So you know your way around Excel pretty well, and you've typed a gazillion formulas before, so you tend to do it pretty fast. Well, even the most experienced make mistakes sometimes. Thanks to Formula AutoCorrect, now you can continue to make them. Excel catches many of the most common formula errors, bringing them to your attention (see the list in Table 41-1). You can then accept or reject the suggested correction, which appears in an alert message (see Figure 41-6). For example, if you end a function with an extra parenthesis, Excel finds the extra parenthesis and proposes the correction. In some cases, such as when a parenthesis is missing in a simple formula, Excel corrects the problem without bothering you with a message.

Table 41-1 Thirteen Boo-boos You Can Keep on Making, Thanks to AutoCorrect

Common Error We've All Made	How Excel AutoCorrects the Problem
Missing parenthesis	Creates a matching pair.
Missing quote mark	Creates a matching pair.
Cell reference as row-col instead of col-row	Changes the reference to col-row.
Semicolon instead of colon	Replaces the semicolon with a colon.
Colon in the wrong place	Moves the colon to between two cell references
Extra space in cell reference or number	Removes the space.
Two decimal points together	Removes the second decimal point.
Two operators together	Removes the second operator.
Extra operator at the beginning or end	Removes the operator.
"=>" "=<" or "><"	Reverses the operator symbols.
Commas in values over 999	Removes the commas.
Letter X instead of *	Replaces the X with *.
Implied multiplication, as in: =2(a+b)	Inserts *, as in =2*(a+b).

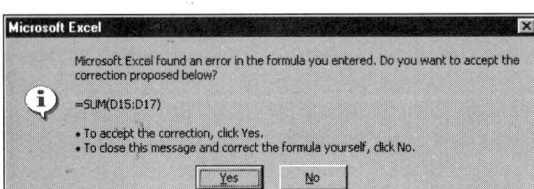

Figure 41-6: Excel displays an alert message when you make one of the 13 boo-boos listed in Table 41-1.

Playing the parentheses match game

Ever been haunted by the infamously cryptic message "Parentheses don't match"? Parentheses are the bane of most users who type formulas, and when they don't match, it's always been up to *us* to figure out which one is missing.

Not anymore. Excel now displays parentheses in color as they are entered. While the outermost pair is in black, the inner pairs are displayed in a series of up to seven different colors. Not only that, but as you type a closing parenthesis, the pair is momentarily highlighted. If the parentheses are already entered, move the cursor across one to highlight the pair. It couldn't be simpler to see how they match up.

As mentioned in the preceding section, Formula AutoCorrect catches several common parentheses errors. It's actually difficult now to create an error that Excel can't help you with (I tried). But these tips will help you if and when you do.

Using lowercase is a capital idea

Secret

Another common error message, #NAME?, can actually be pretty obscure. If you've just entered a complex formula full of functions and defined names, which one is causing the problem? To avoid puzzling over the source of the message, take advantage of Excel's built-in error checking. You can do this by regularly entering all formulas in lowercase, and giving all defined names an initial cap.

When you enter a formula, Excel goes through an error-checking routine. At this time, it does two things:

- It bumps all recognized function names to uppercase.
- It converts all recognized defined names to the case in which they were defined.

If you've defined names with an initial cap but regularly type in lowercase, #NAME? errors are a cinch to track down. When you see one, simply check the formula for a name still in lowercase — that's the one Excel couldn't recognize (see Figure 41-7).

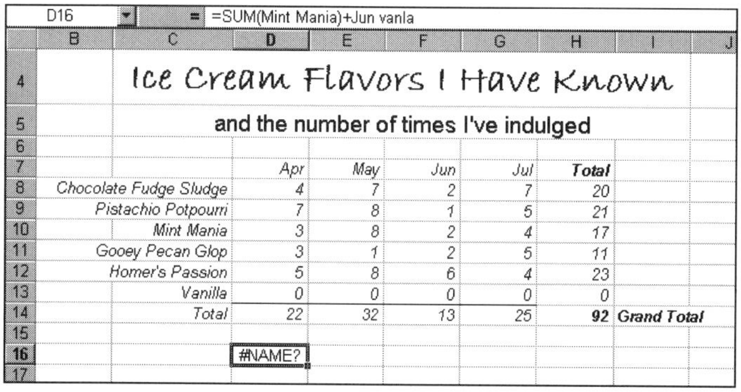

Figure 41-7: Excel capitalized the known function SUM, and gave initial caps to the known range names Mint Mania and Jun. Because "vanla" remains in lowercase, I know that's the unrecognized name.

Using the formula bar as a calculator

Secret

Complex formulas can pass Excel's error checkpoints but still deliver wrong or suspect results. One way to investigate potential problems is to calculate formulas one portion at a time. In the formula bar, select one piece of the formula. (Make sure that it can stand on its own — parentheses should still be paired.) Press F9. Only that portion is calculated, and the result appears in the formula bar. You can do this to other parts of the formula, if more detective work is required. By seeing how Excel interprets each piece, you can more easily track down where the error lies.

Caution

After calculating the desired portion, press Esc to restore the original formula.

Conclusion

Columns of official-looking numbers impress some people, but much more compelling are columns of *accurate* numbers. Excel's many tools for detecting and correcting worksheet errors should be standard-issue weapons in your number-crunching armamentarium.

Chapter 42

Excel Power Programming

In This Chapter

▶ Understanding Excel's object model
▶ Manipulating cells using range objects
▶ Creating your own functions for use in worksheet formulas
▶ Cannibalizing built-in Excel functions for your VBA code
▶ Working with Excel events

If you've ever written a worksheet formula, you're already a programmer of sorts, so don't think VBA is beyond you. Once you get used to working in the Visual Basic Editor instead of directly on your worksheets, you're likely to find that writing VBA code is actually easier than writing formulas, in that you can spread out in an editing window and add explanatory comments to your code. But VBA also offers the power to create customized spreadsheet-based applications that perform feats of calculation and automatic formatting that you could never achieve without it. Just be sure to ground yourself in the VBA fundamentals covered in Part VI before you get too ambitious with the monster Excel coding techniques presented here.

Navigating the Excel Object Model

To write VBA code for Excel, you need a basic grasp of the hierarchy of Excel objects and how to identify those objects in your code. At the top of the hierarchy sits the Application object, representing the functionality of the whole Excel program.

Secret

To make many Excel VBA programs run faster, turn off screen updating. By default, Excel displays each and every change made to your workbook as VBA code runs. This leads to a significant drag on performance. Use the Application object's `ScreenUpdating` property to shut off this behavior with the following statement:

```
Application.ScreenUpdating = False
```

It's considered good form to set the `ScreenUpdating` property back to True at the end of the procedure.

When you set the `ScreenUpdating` property, you must name the Application object explicitly. Generally, however, you can use the Application object's properties directly. For example, the `ActiveSheet` property of the Application object refers to the worksheet or chart sheet that's currently active (in the currently active workbook, of course). To refer to this sheet in your code, you can simply use `ActiveSheet` rather than `Application.ActiveSheet`.

The Workbooks collection of the Application object contains all the workbooks currently open. Use the workbook name in parentheses to identify the specific workbook you want to refer to. The following example activates a particular workbook:

```
Workbooks("Consolidated toy statistics.xls").Activate
```

Individual worksheets are also objects in their own right, of course. They belong to the Worksheets collection and must be specified as such. The expression `Worksheets("Sheet3")` refers to the sheet named Sheet3. Similarly, an individual Chart object for a chart housed in its own separate sheet is a member of the Charts collection. Refer to it via an expression such as `Charts("Parts Chart")`. Charts embedded on worksheets are another matter—coding techniques for them are beyond the scope of this book.

The route to the screen appearance of your workbooks (and sometimes to their contents) is through Window objects. These are members of the Application object's Windows collection. Refer to a window by specifying the filename of the workbook it contains as an index into the Windows collection, as shown here:

```
Windows("Toy Sales Trends.xls")
```

If more than one window is open for the workbook, place a colon and the window number after the workbook name, as in `Windows("Toy Sales Trends.xls:2")`.

Working with Cells in Code Using Range Objects

Surprising fact: Excel doesn't have a Cell object. So remember this basic coding principle: To refer to cells in your VBA code, use the Range object. In Excel, a Range object can encompass one or more cells and can even include more than one noncontiguous area of the sheet.

Excel's Range object has similarities to Word's object of the same name, but there are significant differences, of course. As in Word, a VBA program can refer to as many Range objects as needed. You're not confined to working with the user's visible selection, and you don't need to select an area to act on it in code.

Specifying a Range object

Excel provides several methods for identifying a range of one or more cells that you want your code to act on. You can use:

- **Standard cell references.** So-called A1-style cell references are probably the easiest way to get started with Range objects. To specify a range, enclose the reference in quotation marks and parentheses following the `Range` keyword, as in these examples:

  ```
  ActiveSheet.Range("B3")
  Worksheets("Sheet2").Range("M5:S20")
  ```

- **Named ranges.** If your worksheet contains named ranges, you can base VBA Range objects on them, as shown here:

  ```
  Worksheets("Budget Summary").Range("Interest payments")
  ```

  To name a range in your code, set the range's `Name` property with a statement such as:

  ```
  Range("A3:B4").Name = "SalePrices"
  ```

- **Shortcut notation.** Because Range objects are used so frequently, Excel lets you omit the `Range` keyword when you specify a Range object with A1 notation or by name. To use this trick, place the cell reference or range name in square brackets, as in these examples:

  ```
  ActiveSheet["A1:Z26"]
  ["Quarterly subtotals"]
  ```

- **The `Cells` property of a Worksheet object.** This technique is important to master because it's the best way to define a range based on variables rather than fixed cell addresses. The basic idea is to list the row and column coordinates of the range numerically. See "Using the Cells property to define a range" later in this chapter.

- **The `Selection` property.** Use the `Selection` property when your code needs to work with the range corresponding to the user's selection. See "Working with selections" later in this chapter.

- **The `ActiveCell` property.** Use the `ActiveCell` property to access the range representing the active cell of a given window. Used without an object qualifier (or equivalently, as a property of the Application object), the `ActiveCell` property refers to the active window:

  ```
  ValueStorageBin = ActiveCell.Value
  ```

- **The `Rows` or `Columns` property of a Worksheet object.** Access a range encompassing an entire row or column via the `Rows` or `Columns` property of the worksheet, using the index number of the target row or column (you can't address columns by their letter designation). The following example defines a range covering column E, the fifth column:

  ```
  Workbooks("IOU.xls").Worksheets("Sheet Shootout").Columns(5)
  ```

- **Object references you define.** Because a range is an object, you can set a named object reference to it and then access the range using the reference's name. This technique is faster and easier than repeatedly specifying the original range. After setting the `RanGer` object reference as shown in the following example, you can then use its properties in expressions such as `RanGer.Value`. Here's the code fragment:

```
Dim RanGer As Range
Set RanGer = Worksheets("Sheet1").Range("B12:H13")
```

Using the Cells property to define a range

Used without coordinates, the `Cells` property of a Worksheet object refers to a range encompassing *all* the cells of that worksheet. Similarly, the `Cells` property of the Application object (`Application.Cells`) refers to all the cells of whatever worksheet is currently active.

If you want to home in on a more localized range, the `Cells` property requires that you specify row and column coordinates numerically, rather than using a letter name for the column. The following example refers to a range encompassing cell E3:

```
Worksheets("Old news").Cells(3,5)
```

What's really confusing is that the row coordinate comes first, then the column coordinate — the opposite of A1 notation. In the preceding example, the second value in the cell reference refers to the row number, row E being the fifth row. Because this system is counter-intuitive, you should only mess with it when you need its special virtue. Because both coordinates are numeric, it's easy to specify them with variables. Variable coordinates allow your program to decide as it runs where the target range is located based on typed user input, a calculation, or the like. The following example decides which row to select from depending on the current month of the year:

```
CurrentMonth = Month(Now())
aGoal = Worksheets("Monthly Projections").Cells(CurrentMonth, 8)
```

Secret

The syntax required to refer to a range covering more than one cell is tricky, as shown in this example:

```
Worksheets("Sheet1").Range(Cells(3, 5), Cells(3, 6))
```

Acting on cells en masse

You can change a characteristic of an entire range in a single step using the properties of the range. The following line of code changes the font size for all the cells in the range:

```
Worksheets("Sheet1").Range("B12:H13").Font.Size = 14
```

Of course, you can and should use `With` structures when you need to work with a number of properties or methods of the entire range, as shown here:

```
With someRange  ' a previously defined object reference
    .Value = 20 ' sets the value of all the cells to 20
    .Font.Name = "Garamond"
    .Font.Italic = True
    .Locked = True
    someRangeName = .Name ' store the range name
End With
```

Acting on individual cells in a range

Although you can assign all cells in a range to a single value with one statement as in the preceding example, Excel provides no one-step method for modifying existing values in a multicell range. A statement such as `someRange.Value = someRange.Value + 10` won't work. Instead, you must cycle through all the cells in the range individually using a `For Each...Next` loop. With this technique, you don't need to know how many cells the range contains. The following code does work:

```
For Each aCell In Selection
    aCell.Value = aCell.Value + 10
Next
```

Often you need to examine the individual cells within a range before deciding whether or how to act upon them. Based on the current value of the cell, your code may decide to change to the cell format, change the value itself, or use the value in some other computation. Again, use a `For Each...Next` loop. Here's an example:

```
For Each aCell In Worksheets("Sheet2").Range("A5:B10")
    If IsNumeric(aCell) Then
        Select Case aCell
            Case 5 To 10
                aCell.Font.Underline = xlUnderlineStyleSingle
            Case 10 To 20
                aCell.Font.Italic = True
            Case Is > 20
                aCell.Font.Bold = True
        End Select
    End If
Next
```

Working with selections

A user interacting with a worksheet must select one or more cells before she can edit or format them. However, selecting cells isn't necessary in VBA, because you can use Range objects to identify the cells you want to work with. But VBA does provide selection-related tools for two reasons: so that your code can tell which cells the user has selected, and so that your code can show the user where something important is happening on the worksheet.

Identifying the current selection

Many times custom code must act like most of Excel's built-in commands, affecting the cells the user has selected. To access the range corresponding to the user's selection, use the Selection property of the Application object or a Window object. The Application object's Selection property returns the range for whatever is selected on the worksheet that's currently active. The following two statements are equivalent:

```
Application.Selection.Value = 20
Selection.Value = 20
```

Use a window's Selection property to ensure that you always refer to the object selected on that particular window, regardless of which window is currently active. The following example demonstrates this technique; it also shows how you can set an object reference to the range representing the current selection so that you can reuse the same range in the future:

```
Dim SelRange As Range
Set SelRange = Windows("Toy Inventory.xls").Selection
With SelRange
    .CheckSpelling
    .AutoFit
    .Copy
End With
```

Selecting a range

When your VBA program makes a change to the worksheet that you want the user to notice, use the Select method to move the selection to that range, chart, or what have you. The Select method applies to just about any worksheet object available in Excel — it's available for Chart objects and all of their components (each part of a chart is also a separate VBA object); for Shape (drawing) objects; and, of course, for Range objects.

To select a range, you must first activate its worksheet, then use the Select method for the Range object, as shown in this example:

```
With Worksheets("Love Statistics")
    .Activate
    .Range("BrokenHearts").Select
End With
```

By the way, the Select method for Worksheet objects apparently does nothing more than activate the specified worksheet and doesn't change the existing selection there. In other words, it's equivalent to the worksheet's Activate method. Similarly, you can use the Activate or Select methods to activate a chart sheet, but neither method actually selects the chart. Here's an example:

```
Charts("Customer Demographics").Select
```

To select chart components or embedded charts, use the Select method on the object in question.

Activating a specific cell

To set the active cell for user input, use the `Activate` method of the Range object corresponding to that cell. If the activated cell is within the current selection, the entire range remains selected. The following example works that way:

```
Worksheets("DoNothingTillYouHearFromMe").Activate
Range("A1:E7").Select
Range("C4").Activate
```

If the activated cell is outside of the selection, the selection moves to the new active cell.

Determining the selection type

Code designed to work on selected cells is likely to fail if you try to apply it to a chart instead. That's why you should generally check to make sure the current selection contains the type of object the code expects before doing anything with the selected object. Use VBA's `TypeName` function to return a string containing the object type of the selection. You can use this string in `If...Then` or `Case Select` structures to decide what to do with the selected object, if anything:

```
With Selection
Select Case TypeName(Selection)
    Case "Range"
        .Value = 2001
    Case "ChartArea"
        .Interior.ColorIndex = 3  ' 3 = bright red
    Case "Nothing"
        MsgBox "Nothing is selected"
    Case Else
        MsgBox "I refuse to recognize this selection type!"
End Select
End With
```

Programming Custom Worksheet Functions

You should consider working in VBA even if Excel's built-in data analysis tools seem to meet all your needs. The reason: With VBA, you can create custom worksheet functions that have big advantages over the formulas you type directly into cells.

Custom functions do enable you to carry out calculations and other operations that you just can't accomplish using formulas based on the built-in functions. But even if you could write a formula to get the same results, a custom function has the major benefits of being easier to write, easier to test, and easier to understand later on. Instead of the cramped confines of the formula bar, you have the entire code window to work with and can break up complex logic onto separate lines. Equally important, you can (and should) include explanatory comments directly beside the code they pertain to.

Writing custom worksheet functions

Custom Excel functions are simply ordinary VBA function procedures. All the details on function procedures and their syntax laid out in Chapter 21 apply. In brief, a function procedure begins with a declaration of its name and ends with an End Function statement. Somewhere in between you need a statement that assigns a value to the function's name — that value is the one the function returns. Here's a trivial example showing these rudiments:

```
Function MemoryAvailable()
    MemoryAvailable = Application.MemoryFree
End Function
```

This function simply returns the amount of memory in bytes that's currently available to Excel. Note that the function takes no arguments, because it merely retrieves the quantity of available memory from your system. Here's another slightly more complex Excel function that does take arguments:

```
Function CheckForValue(aRange, Value)
For Each objCell In aRange
   CheckForValue = False ' default return value is False
   If objCell.Value = Value Then
      CheckForValue = True
      Exit For
   End If
Next objCell
End Function
```

This function checks a range of cells for a specific value. If the value is present anywhere in the range, the function returns True; if not, it comes back False. When you trigger this function you must supply the two arguments: the range and the value you want to look for.

Running custom functions

One way to run custom functions, of course, is the regular VBA way: by calling them from within a Sub procedure. That technique is covered in Chapter 21.

To insert the return value of a custom function into a worksheet, use your function just as you would one of the built-in functions: Type the function's name in a cell after an equal sign. After the name, type a pair of parentheses, adding inside them any arguments to the function. You need the parentheses even if there are no arguments, as in this example:

```
=MemoryAvailable()
```

Just as is true of built-in functions, a custom function can be part of a more complex cell formula, as in these simple examples:

```
=MemoryAvailable() & " bytes are now available"

=IF(CheckForValue(B8:B18,C8)),"Value found","Value not found")
```

Using the Formula palette with custom functions

What's really cool is that the Formula palette recognizes custom functions. If you don't remember what arguments your function requires, or whether it takes any arguments at all, no matter — the Formula palette shows you exactly what's required (see Figure 42-1).

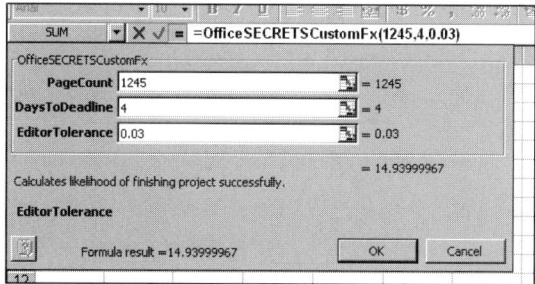

Figure 42-1: Using the Formula palette to enter the arguments for a custom function

If you don't remember the name of your custom function in the first place, choose More Functions from the drop-down Functions list. In the resulting Paste Function dialog box, choose User Defined at the bottom of the Function category list. You can then select from among the available custom functions.

Secret

You can add a description of your custom function that appears in the Paste Function dialog box when the function is selected. To create the description, choose Tools ➪ Macro ➪ Macros and type the function name in the Macro Name box (functions don't appear in the macro list). Now click Options and enter a description of the function in the appropriate field.

Accessing custom functions in other workbooks

If the custom function you want to use is stored in the current workbook, you only need to type its name in your cell formulas. To use a function stored in a different *open* workbook, precede the function name with the workbook's name and an exclamation point as in this example:

```
=SECRETfunctions.xls!TopSecretFunction(C4:D6,M9)
```

To access functions stored in a workbook that isn't open, or that might not be open the next time you need them, set up a VBA reference to the workbook. Choose Tools ➪ References. If the workbook isn't already listed in the resulting dialog box, click Browse to locate it and add it to the list. If the box beside the workbook isn't already checked, check it to activate the reference. You can then use the functions it contains by name only, without specifying the workbook they come from.

Testing your custom functions

When an error occurs in a custom function that you've placed in a worksheet formula, you don't get the benefit of VBA's normal error messages. Instead, all you see is a vague error message such as #VALUE! in the cell containing your function. When you're building a custom function, use the following tricks to help you test and debug the function:

- Before you place the function into a worksheet, test it by calling it from a Sub procedure. This way, you gain direct access to VBA's error messages and debugging tools. If the function requires cell references, you must use the Range object when you call the function, as in this example:

```
Sub FxTester()
    ReturnVal = CheckForValue(Range("B8:B13"), Range("C8"))
    MsgBox ReturnVal
End Sub
```

- With the function in a worksheet formula, set a breakpoint in the function's code in the Visual Basic Editor. Whenever Excel recalculates the worksheet, your function runs. As soon as VBA reaches the line of code that has the breakpoint, you're taken into the Editor, ready to debug.

Fancier functions

Don't hesitate to write functions that give you exactly the output you want — why leave anything to a formula when you can do all the work in the function itself? This modification of the CheckForValue function (presented earlier in "Writing custom worksheet functions") returns an explanatory text string rather than merely True or False:

```
Function CheckForValue2(aRange, Value)
For Each objCell In aRange
    CheckForValue2 = "Search value " & Value & " not found"
    If objCell.Value = Value Then
        CheckForValue2 = "Search value " & Value & _
            " found in Cell " & objCell.Address
        Exit For
    End If
Next objCell
End Function
```

If the modified function finds the target value anywhere in the range, it returns a string such as "Search value 3.57 found in Cell $F$83"; if not, it comes back saying "Search value 3.57 not found."

Using Built-In Functions in Your Code

Whether you're writing a custom function or a Sub procedure, don't be bashful about calling on the wealth of calculating and data analysis power offered by Excel's built-in functions. Using them in your own code is simple:

You just call them as methods of the WorksheetFunction object. For example, suppose you're writing a procedure that makes a calculation based on an average of the values in a worksheet range. To obtain the average, you would use code similar to the following:

```
OnAverage = WorksheetFunction.Average(Range("B8:B13"))
```

Caution

Some of Excel's built-in functions are off-limits in VBA. These are the functions that duplicate VBA's own built-in functions, which are introduced in Chapter 21.

Programming for Excel Events

Writing code for events often assumes a more important role in Excel than it does in the other Office applications. That's because a spreadsheet's whole mission involves responding to changes made by the user. Changing the value of a single cell can produce ripple effects throughout an entire workbook as Excel recalculates dependent formulas and charts. As a VBA programmer, you can intercept the events that drive this process to enhance and supplement Excel's built-in responses.

Choosing the right object

Before you start writing event code, one of your first considerations is deciding which object should respond to the event. Four Excel objects recognize events: charts, individual worksheets, workbooks, and the entire Excel application. If you want to write code that responds to events occurring to a specific chart, your code belongs in the chart's event procedures. However, for events that occur in response to worksheet changes, you have choices to make.

Although some Excel events are recognized only by a particular object, many are passed up the object hierarchy from the Worksheet object to the Workbook and Application objects. For example, a change occurring on a worksheet triggers the Worksheet object's Change event, which in turn triggers the SheetChange event for both the Workbook object and the Application object. With this arrangement in mind, you must decide whether your code belongs in the event procedure for the worksheet, the workbook, or the application. The choice shouldn't be too difficult:

- If you want the code to run only in response to changes occurring on a single worksheet, it belongs in that worksheet's event procedure.

- If you want your procedure to run when a change happens to any worksheet in a particular workbook, put the code in the workbook's event procedure.

- If your code should be active throughout all open workbooks, it belongs in the application's event procedure.

Starting an event procedure

The fundamental technique for writing an event procedure for one of Excel's objects is no different than writing event code for a VBA form or control. Chapter 24 has the details, but the basic steps are the following:

1. Display the code window for the object.

2. Select the object by name from the Object drop-down list at the top left of the code window.

3. Select the event for which you want to write code from the Procedure drop-down list at the top right of the code window. When you do, the skeleton for your chosen event procedure appears in the window.

Aside from writing the code itself, the only tricky part can be to bring up the object's code window in the first place (Step 1). For Worksheet and Workbook objects, and for Chart objects that occupy separate sheets, you face no special challenges: Just select the object in the Project Explorer and click the View Code button. Objects appear by their names, which you can change in the Properties window.

Secret

The situation is more challenging when it comes to charts that are embedded in worksheets and the Excel application object. You must write special class modules to make these objects available in the Project Explorer. I don't have space in this book for the details on how to do this, but you can find them in the Help system.

Reacting to worksheet changes

If your goal is to make things happen as the user interacts with the worksheet moment by moment, the tools you need are the `Change`, `Calculate`, and `SelectionChange` events (for Worksheet objects) and the corresponding `SheetChange`, `SheetCalculate`, and `SheetSelectionChange` events (for Workbook and Application objects). To fire custom procedures when worksheets themselves or charts are activated or deactivated, use the `Activate` and `Deactivate` events.

The Change and SheetChange events

The `Change` and `SheetChange` events are triggered every time the value of any cell or cells change via a user action or the updating of a link. Changes in calculated values don't trigger the event, however. The corresponding event procedures let you zero in on the specific cells whose value has changed. The following example checks the changed values — which are contained in the range called `Target` — to see if they fall within a specified range. Those that do, receive highlighting in the form of a large, bold, green font:

```
Private Sub Worksheet_Change(ByVal Target As Range)
    For Each oCell In Target
        If oCell > 4 And oCell < 11 Then
```

```
            With oCell.Font
                .Bold = True
                .Size = 16
                .Color = RGB(0, 255, 0) ' green
            End With
        End If
    Next oCell
End Sub
```

Note that `Target` can include more than one cell — it's a range, after all — because operations such as filling, clearing, and pasting can be performed on more than one cell at a time. For this reason, your `Change` event procedure should include a `For Each...Next` structure whenever you want it to act on the contents of an individual cell or cells, as shown in the preceding example.

Secret

Actually, the `Change` and `SheetChange` events may fire even if a value doesn't change. These events are bound to occur once the user starts editing a cell (by clicking in the formula bar or pressing F2), even if the user stops the edit without making any changes (by pressing Enter, clicking the Enter check button, or clicking the worksheet). The events don't fire if the user abandons the edit by pressing Esc or clicking the Cancel button.

The Calculate and SheetCalculate events

The `Calculate` event, recognized by both Worksheet and Chart objects, happens whenever Excel updates a worksheet or chart. The `SheetCalculate` event for the Workbook and Application objects occurs in response. If automatic calculation is on, these events fire immediately when any cell value changes — meaning that it occurs in tandem with the `Change` event. When you switch to manual calculation, the calculate events only occur when the user presses F9 to initiate the recalculation.

Use event procedures for the `Calculate` and `SheetCalculate` events to modify the worksheet according to the results of a calculation. For example, if you know that recalculation may change the items in a sorted list, you might want the `Worksheet_Calculate` event procedure to resort the list following the calculation. Because these event procedures don't tell you which cells changed after a calculation, you must place into your code the addresses of the cells you want to change.

The SelectionChange and SheetSelectionChange events

Excel registers a `SelectionChange` event for the worksheet every time the active cell moves or a selection expands or contracts. Parallel `SheetSelectionChange` events also occur for the Workbook and Application objects. You can use the event procedures for these events to provide feedback about the current selection. In the following simple example, the `SelectionChange` event is used to display the address of the active cell in the current worksheet's top-left cell, and to place the worksheet name and the selection's address in the status bar. Note how the `Sh` argument enables you to identify and work with the current worksheet:

```
Private Sub Workbook_SheetSelectionChange(ByVal Sh As Object, _
    ByVal Target As Excel.Range)
        Sh.Range("A1") = ActiveCell.Address
        Application.StatusBar = Sh.Name & ":" & Target.Address
End Sub
```

Getting a little fancier, you might instead have a selection change trigger some response (say, displaying a custom dialog box) only if the new selection encompasses a specified cell or range:

```
Private Sub Worksheet_SelectionChange(ByVal Target As Excel.Range)
    If Target.Address = "$B$2" Then
        MsgBox "You found the SECRETS cell!"
    End If
End Sub
```

Programming dynamic charts

Because Excel chart objects recognize a multitude of events, many of them mouse-related, you can think of them as big ActiveX controls parked in your workbooks. Charts recognize the `Activate`, `Deactivate`, and `Calculate` events. Other chart events you can write code for include:

- **`DragOver` and `DragPlot`.** Occur when cells are dragged over a chart embedded in a worksheet, and when they are dropped onto the chart, respectively.

- **`MouseDown`, `MouseUp`, and `MouseMove`.** Occur in response to mouse actions.

- **`Select`.** Occurs when any part of the chart is selected. Your code can determine the type of element and the specific element that was selected, and respond accordingly.

- **`SeriesChange`.** Occurs when the user changes a value on the chart by manipulating the chart itself (rather than by changing the underlying value in the worksheet).

Conclusion

Much more can be said about the intricacies of Excel programming, but this chapter provides a serviceable foundation. With the tools and techniques discussed here, your forays into designing dynamic custom spreadsheets should be quickly productive.

Part IX
Secrets of Access 2000

Chapter 43: Getting Inside Access

Chapter 44: Fundamentals of Access

Chapter 45: Secrets of Database Application Design

Chapter 46: Working with Data Using VBA

Chapter 47: Designing Access Forms

Chapter 43

Getting Inside Access

In This Chapter

▶ Understanding Access — about the different tasks
▶ Controlling Access's startup behavior
▶ Adding and removing components
▶ Creating macros the Access way
▶ Assigning keyboard shortcuts using the AutoKeys macro group
▶ Optimizing database performance using the Performance Analyzer and Windows Registry settings

Everyone knows Access has something to do with databases, but beyond that the picture gets a bit fuzzy. You can't blame us users for our confusion — it's inherent in Access itself. Access plays a variety of roles, and some of these overlap extensively with the territory of other products. This chapter sets out to clarify the mission Microsoft has set for its Office database component. It then goes on to deal with issues of setup, customization, and housekeeping that need discussion but that don't pertain directly to database management — which is the focus of the remaining chapters in this section.

Getting a Grip on Access

Access has at least five major mandates. It can serve as:

- **An ad hoc database manager.** Via the menus and toolbars, you can have direct, hands-on access to data drawn from a wide variety of sources on your own PC or anywhere on the network.

- **A powerful reporting tool.** Even if you rely on a non-Access application for entering and extracting data, you may want to turn to Access's reporting capabilities when it's time to analyze those data in presentable form. Access reports are easier to put together and look nicer than those available in many applications.

- **A workshop for building dynamic Web pages.** New features make it easy to construct Web pages that automatically reflect changes in the underlying database. Chapter 15 has details.

- **A complete development environment for producing finished database applications.** Although other development tools can create smaller, faster, or glitzier applications, you can build complete, full-featured database applications — including true client/server applications — with Access alone. If you have Office Developer, you can distribute these applications to users who don't have their own copies of Access.

- **An application prototyping tool.** Even if you decide to use Visual Basic, C++, or some other tool for your finished applications, Access offers an easy-to-use test bed for building working prototypes in a hurry.

Understand that these functions are somewhat independent. You can, for example, use Access for ad hoc database management by way of the menus and toolbars and never worry about application design and VBA programming. Conversely, if you're an application developer, you may largely ignore the Access menus and toolbars in favor of custom ones you create for the users of your application.

Power Customizing

Access enables you to reconfigure its toolbars and control what happens when the program starts, just as in the other Office applications. Scratch a little deeper, though, and you'll find a daunting array of technical settings to play with in pursuit of optimal database performance. Fortunately, Access provides some help in knowing which lever to pull, and when.

Controlling startup behavior

First things first. Access provides a number of settings and special command line switches that determine how the program (or your database application) works when you start it.

Using command line startup options

As with other Office applications, Access lets you use startup (command line) switches and other options in Windows shortcuts or typed at the DOS prompt to control its operations. See Table 43-1 for a list of the available switches. The section in Chapter 1 called "Command Line Options for Starting Office Apps" covers the techniques required to set up a Windows shortcut via the Properties dialog box.

Table 43-1 Access Command Line Options

Command Line Entry	What It Does
"*database*"	Opens the named database. You must include the path unless the database is in the default folder specified in the General tab of the Tools ⇨ Options dialog box. You can omit the quotation marks in this and all switches if the item name contains no spaces.
"*database*" /excl	Opens the database in exclusive mode, so that no one else can open it as long as you're using it. Obviously, you shouldn't use this switch if others need concurrent access to the database. Shared mode is the default.
"*database*" /ro	Opens the specified database in read-only mode — you can view and query the data, but you can't change it.
/user "*user name*"	Logs in with the user name given.
/pwd *password*	Starts Access with *password* so that you don't have to type it in.
/profile "*user profile*"	Activates the options in the named user profile, overriding the standard Windows Registry settings. You can create user profiles with the Developer Edition of Office.
"*original database*" /compact "*compacted database*"	Compacts the original database and then closes Access. If you omit a name for the compacted database, Access compacts the original database using its original name and folder. The compacted database is placed in your default database folder unless you include a different path with its name.
"*database*" /repair	Repairs the named database and then closes Access.
"*old database*" /convert "*output database*"	Converts a Version 1.*x* or 2.0 database (old database) to an Access 95 database (output database) and then closes Access.
/x *macro*	Runs the named macro as soon as Access starts. See "Running VBA procedures at startup" later in this section for a tip on using this capability. Remember also that Access automatically runs a macro at startup if you name it AutoExec.
/cmd "*ReturnValue*"	Specifies ReturnValue as the value returned by the Command function in VBA. This switch must be the last one used.
/nostartup	Suppresses the Startup dialog box when Access starts.
/wrkgrp "*workgroup information file*"	Loads the named workgroup information file.

For example, the following command line entry starts Access, loads a database called Waterfowl — the one that tracks your inventory of ducks, geese, and swans — and runs a macro called Get Today's Price (the entire item should be entered on one line):

```
"C:\Program Files\Microsoft Office\Office\MSAccess.exe
C:\Inventory\Waterfowl.mdb" /x "Get Today's Price"
```

You can create as many shortcuts as you like — one for each of your databases, if that suits you.

When you open a database by naming it in a Windows shortcut or on the command line, Access can display a Windows bitmap graphic instead of the box you usually see. Once you locate, scan, or "paint" the image, place it in the folder where the database is stored and give it the same name as the database (a startup bitmap for the preceding example should be named `Waterfowl.bmp`).

To specify a forward slash (/) or semicolon (;) on the command line, type the character twice. For example, to specify the password ;mjs/md on the command line, the command line should read `MSAccess /pwd ;;mjs//md`.

Running VBA procedures at startup

Although Access doesn't offer a command line option to run a specific VBA procedure when a database opens, you can accomplish this in either of the following ways:

- Create a macro that includes a RunCode action. Then use the /x command line switch to run the macro when Access starts.

- Design a form that specifies the VBA procedure as its `OnOpen` event. Then set it as the startup form on the Tools ⇨ Startup dialog box, described in the next section.

Controlling database startup behavior

To control how a specific database behaves when it is opened, as well as other aspects of its behavior, choose Tools ⇨ Startup. One setting in the Startup dialog box (Figure 43-1) lets you set the startup form, the form that appears as soon as the database opens. Another lets you shut off the initial display of the standard Database window, the default Access control center. (To restore the Database window, choose Window ⇨ Unhide. The functions of the Database window receive attention in Chapter 44.)

Most of these startup settings are primarily intended for customizing the look and behavior of a database application that you distribute to others. Unless you take special measures, however, they can be overridden by holding down Shift when the database is opened.

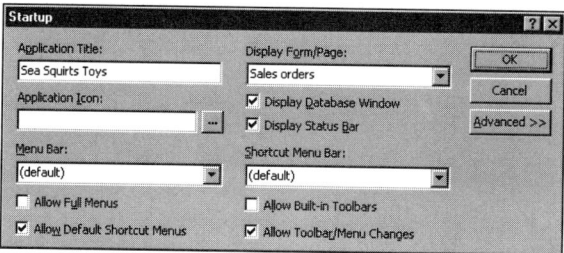

Figure 43-1: Use the Startup dialog box to set options governing how a database behaves when first opened.

Customizing the Interface and Other Options

The standard methods available throughout Office for customizing menus and toolbars work just fine in Access to let you create a database home of your dreams. In common with its mates, Access even lets you customize the individual shortcut menus that appear when you right-click an item. Chapter 5 covers the Office customizing techniques you need.

Along with all the other Office applications, Access provides control over many program settings on the Tools ⇨ Options dialog box. When you're getting started, be sure to look at the choices available on the Keyboard, View, and General tabs.

Creating Macros in Access

Like the other Office applications, Access lets you perform a series of actions with a single custom command using a macro. Access is decidedly unlike the other applications, however, in the way it handles macros. The key point is that Access macros are not VBA procedures, as they are elsewhere in Office. Access also lacks a macro recorder — you must build macros by entering commands in a special dialog box.

Secret

Among the actions that a macro can perform are RunCommand, which executes one of many available built-in Access commands; RunCode, which runs a VBA procedure; and RunMacro, which runs another macro.

To assign a set of actions to a macro:

1. In the Database window, select the Macro tab and then New to display the Macro window shown in Figure 43-2.

2. In the Action column, enter the series of actions you want this macro to carry out, one action per row. In each row, select an action from the drop-down list (see the Secret later in these steps). If the action allows or requires additional arguments, Access displays appropriately labeled fields at the bottom of the dialog box. There, you can select them from drop-down lists or type them in.

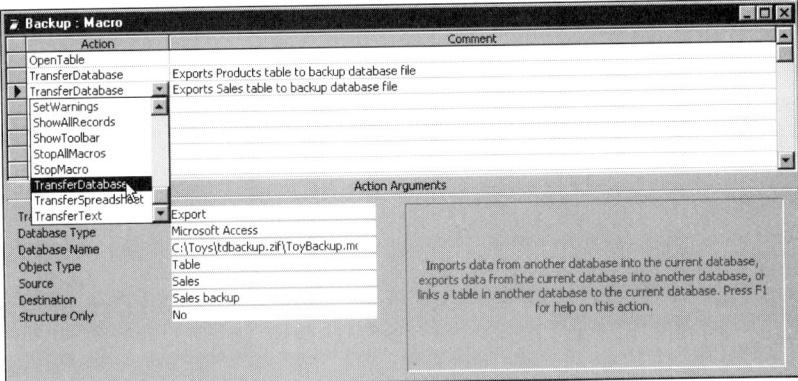

Figure 43-2: Assigning Access commands to a macro

3. To specify when the macro should be available, enter an expression in the Condition column. If this column isn't visible, click the Conditions button on the Macro Design toolbar. To get help creating the condition, click the Build toolbar button or right-click in the column and choose Build from the shortcut menu.

4. Save the macro by clicking the Save button, pressing Ctrl+S, or choosing File ➪ Save. Access asks you to name the macro now.

To run a macro, double-click it in the Macros tab or select it and choose Run. You can also access it from the Tools ➪ Macros ➪ Run Macro dialog box, assign it to a keyboard shortcut as detailed later, or place it on a toolbar button or menu with the techniques discussed in Chapter 5. To run a macro automatically when you open a database, name it AutoExec or use the /x command line switch described in Table 43-1.

Creating macro groups

You can define two or more separate macros in a single macro window and store them together under one name. Access refers to a macro that contains more than one individual macro as a *macro group*. The macros in the group still run independently. This technique enables you to organize related macros in sets rather than keeping track of many separate macro objects. A special macro group is required if you want to assign macros to keyboard shortcuts. To create a macro group, just start a new macro as you normally would. Once the Macro window appears, display the Macro Name column by clicking the Macro Names button on the toolbar.

You can now type a name for the first macro in the group in the Macro Name column. Go on to specify the actions the macro should perform in the Action column in this and subsequent rows, adding conditions in the Condition column as appropriate. However, leave the Macro Name column empty in the remaining rows for this macro. When you're finished defining the first macro in the group, start the second by typing its name in the Macro Name column on the next blank row. Continue adding macros in this fashion to complete the macro group.

Access refers to individual macros in a macro group by way of a compound name combining the macro group name and the macro name separated by a period, as in

```
GeneralMacros.PrintCurrentRecord
```

Double-clicking a macro group runs only the first macro in the group. To run any of the others, choose Tools ⇨ Macros ⇨ Run Macro and then select the macro from the list where it appears in the format just described.

Customizing the keyboard with macros

As Figure 43-3 shows, the two "keys" to defining custom keyboard shortcuts in Access are these:

- Set all of them up as macros in one special macro group you name AutoKeys (the previous section covers macro groups in detail).
- Type the keyboard shortcut's abbreviation as the name for each macro in the AutoKeys group. Table 43-2 lists the permissible keys and their abbreviations.

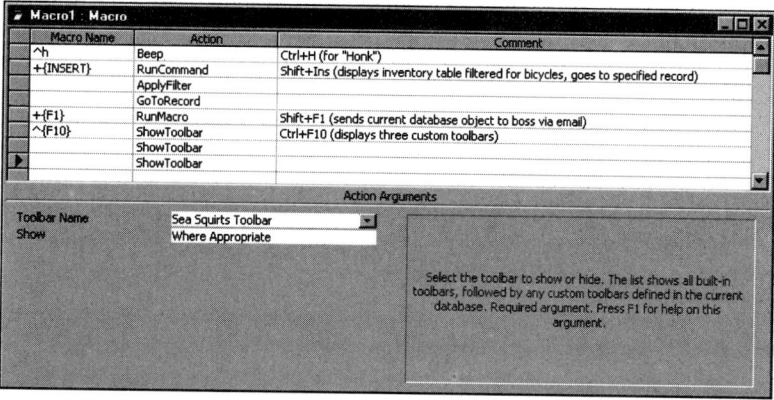

Figure 43-3: Assign macros to keyboard shortcuts by creating the macros in the AutoKeys macro group.

As soon as you've created and saved the macros in the AutoKeys group, Access activates the key assignment. If you assign actions to a shortcut already used by Access (for example, Ctrl+P for File ⇨ Print), your shortcut replaces the default in all windows in the current database.

Table 43-2 Permissible Keys for Keyboard Shortcuts for Naming Macros in AutoKeys Group

Key or Key Combination	Entry in Macro Name Column	Example (If Applicable)
Insert	{INSERT}	
Delete	{DEL}	
Function key	{Function key abbreviation}	{F9}
Ctrl+Insert, Delete, or any letter, number, or function key	^key	^r (Ctrl+r) ^{F3} (Ctrl+F3)
Shift+Insert, Delete, or any function key	+key	+{F6} (Shift+F6) +{DEL} (Shift+Del)

Another, more powerful way to control the keyboard in Access when you're working with a form is to use the KeyDown and KeyPress events for the form or any single control, assigning a custom response to the event.

Adding and Removing Components

Access comes with an assortment of add-in tools that perform all kinds of useful functions. Use the Add-in Manager, available on the Tools menu, to install or remove add-ins. You can create and install your own add-ins, which are actually just specialized Access databases. Categories of Access add-ins include:

- **Wizards.** These tools ask you a series of questions and, based on your input, create a database object, such as a datasheet table, query, form, or report.
- **Builders.** These are modules that help simplify tasks by walking you through the steps of assembling, or building, complex expressions or database components.
- **Managers.** These help you handle housekeeping chores associated with Access components. The Add-in Manager is itself an add-in!

Choosing a Database Engine

Access itself functions mainly as a sort of customer service representative, showing you what's available in terms of commands and data, and taking your orders from the menus, the toolbars, and the keyboard. In other words, Access proper is a database *front end*, the part you and other users interact with. However, Access knows its limits. When it comes to the heavy labor of inserting and extracting information in the database, Access turns to a separate piece of software, a *database engine*—also referred to as the *back end*.

The Jet engine

The default database engine for Access is Microsoft Jet. Standard Access database files (extension .mdb) are actually Jet files and can be opened and manipulated by any development tool that can activate the Jet engine, including Visual Basic and C++. Via special drivers, Jet can also access other types of data residing on your PC, such as dBase, Excel, and Outlook files. Jet is a sophisticated relational database manager, and it works well for databases that serve individual users and small groups.

Alternatives to Jet

But Jet has its limitations, and Microsoft is in the process of easing it out in favor of newer technology. Access 2000 now ships with a new engine, fittingly enough called Microsoft Data Engine (MSDE). In essence, MSDE is a workstation version of SQL Server, Microsoft's flagship database product intended for "enterprise-level" applications. You can use MSDE for development work on a single PC and then switch to SQL Server itself when you're ready to deploy your database application on a larger scale — the only modification you need to make is to change the connection from MSDE to SQL Server. (Although SQL Server is referred to as a database server rather than an engine, the two terms mean essentially the same thing, except that a server is typically located on a different computer.)

You have still more options for the back end of your database project. Using the ODBC or OLE DB standards discussed in Chapter 46, Access can get at data in everything from dBase to high-end databases such as Oracle and Sybase (Jet is still necessary when you're working with data tables stored in formats such as dBase on your own PC or your network).

Considerations in choosing an engine

If you've decided to use Access to work with corporate data stored on a server in an Oracle database, you don't have to worry about choosing a back end — it has to be Oracle. For projects you start on your own PC, however, you face a choice between Jet and MSDE. As you consider the strengths of each alternative, keep in mind that you can't go too far wrong — Access includes a utility that converts Jet databases into equivalent MSDE/SQL Server databases (see "Upsizing a database from Jet to SQL Server" later in this chapter).

Jet advantages

Jet's main advantages are seniority and simplicity. Applications developed for Jet in previous versions of Access will run in Access 2000 without modification. Because Jet has been the standard Access database engine for a long time, many database developers know it well. Compared to MSDE, Jet requires less memory and much less disk space, so it's definitely the way to go if your computer is limited in either of these resources. And Jet is also decidedly easier to use — it offers fewer technical settings to bedevil you. If you know for sure that the database you're building will never need to run on a large network and doesn't need to perform 24 hours a day, use Jet.

When to go with MSDE

Starting every new Access database project using MSDE can save you trouble down the road — assuming that your organization uses SQL Server as its organization-wide database. Because MSDE projects transfer to SQL Server with minimal changes, you can scale up your project almost instantly to many more users and much larger datasets. Like other high-end database managers, MSDE and SQL Server offer many sophisticated features designed to support the hard-core networked database requirements — and not available in Jet. These advantages are discussed in the next several sections.

Caution

As strong as the case for MSDE seems to be, don't install it on your system unless you have plenty of disk space. It consumes over 100 megabytes without any of its optional features.

Network performance

On a heavily trafficked network, the volume of data sent back and forth across the network is a critical factor in the performance each user experiences. Unlike Jet, SQL Server is a true client/server database manager. When the user wants to work with a particular set of data, the user's application (the client) sends a request for that data to the server. Because this query is executed by the server, which returns only the desired data, a relatively small amount of data has to be sent over the network — especially if queries are carefully designed to home in on specific information.

By contrast, when Jet is used on a network, it functions as a file server. It sends all the raw data required to run a user's query across the network back to the user's PC, where the user's copy of Jet executes the query. If the database is of any size, network performance sags.

Data Integrity and Reliability

MSDE and SQL Server log transactions as they occur — Jet does not. If the network goes down or the power goes out, MSDE restores the data to the last known state based on its transaction log. By contrast, Jet can't recover automatically from such errors. You have to use backup files to restore a damaged database, and if you made your last backup yesterday, you're out a full day's worth of important business records.

Security

MSDE and SQL Server rely on Windows NT security, which you should already have in place for a solid network. Because Jet's security features are independent of the operating system, they have to be administered separately, costing you time and tribulation.

Scalability

MSDE and Jet are comparable in terms of the amount of data (2GB files) and number of users (in practical terms, only a few) they can handle. But with adequate hardware, SQL Server demolishes these limits, allowing a practically unlimited number of simultaneous users and terabytes of data.

Database administration support

MSDE enables you to conduct administration and maintenance while the database is open and being used. Aside from the obvious convenience, this means that the database can stay online 24 hours a day. With Jet, you have to shut down the database to repair, compact, or replicate it.

How to select an engine — creating a database project

You must decide which engine you're going to use, Jet or MSDE/SQL, at the time you create each new database. Notice the choices on either side of the File ⇨ New dialog box, shown in Figure 43-4. (You can get to this box by choosing the second option, Access database wizards, pages, and projects, in the dialog box that appears each time you start the program.)

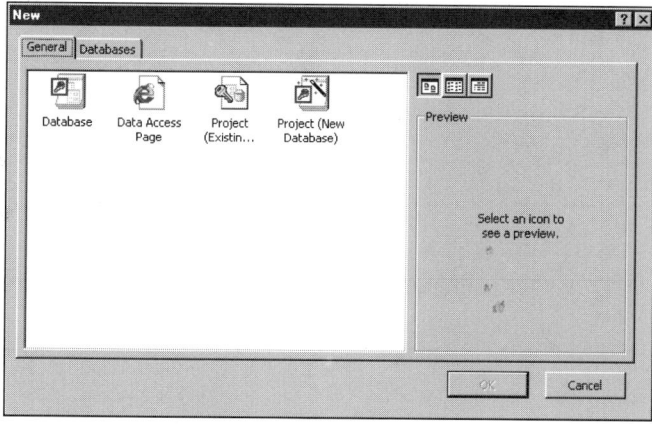

Figure 43-4: Select the engine for a new database in the New dialog box.

Although I use the term *database* in its general sense, Access gives it a much more restricted meaning: an Access 2000 *database* corresponds to a Jet file. The alternative choice, a *project*, is the front end for an MSDE or SQL Server database. Double-click the Database icon to start a Jet database, or one of the Project icons to create a new project. Project files contain Access-specific items such as forms, reports, and VBA code, but no tables or queries. Instead, the queries (called *views* in MSDE) and tables are housed in the MSDE or SQL Server database file, where they can be called on by the Access project. (I discuss database components such as tables, queries, and reports in Chapter 44.)

Secret

Multiple projects can manipulate the same MSDE or SQL Server database. If the database you want to work with in your project already exists, start a new project by double-clicking Project (Existing Database). If you want to create a new database at the back end along with the front-end project, use Project (New Database) instead.

Once you've chosen the type of database you're creating, Access database or project, Access wants you immediately to name and save a skeleton file for the item. Jet databases are stored with the .mdb extension, projects, with the .adp extension. As soon as you save a new Jet database, the database window, Access's central control panel, appears on your screen. If you've elected to create a project, however, you see instead the SQL Server Database Wizard dialog box (if you're starting a new database) or the Data Link Properties box (if you're creating a project for an existing MSDE/SQL Server database). These dialog boxes are shown in Figures 43-5 and 43-6.

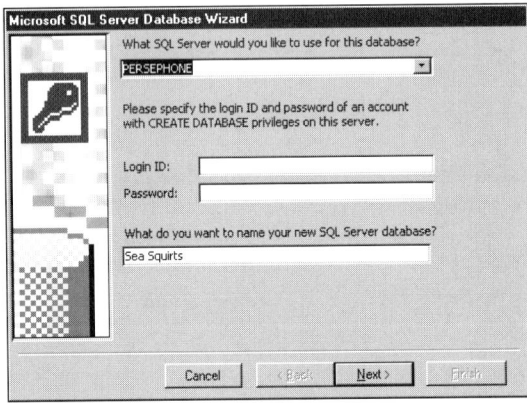

Figure 43-5: Use this wizard to start a new project and create a new MSDE or SQL Server database in the process.

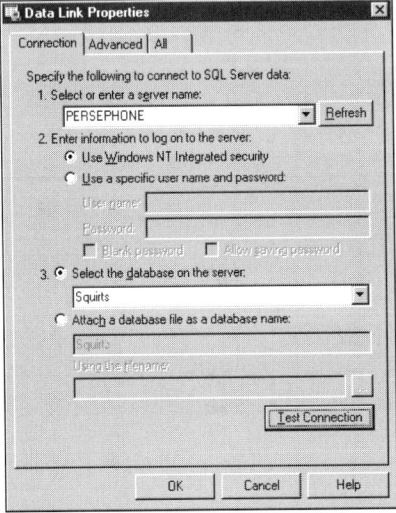

Figure 43-6: Select an existing MSDE or SQL Server database for a project by specifying the server and the database name in this dialog box.

Upsizing a database from Jet to SQL Server

Suppose you decide to stick with Jet as your database engine and later find that you need to move the data or your entire database application to a large network. Fortunately, you don't need to recreate the database from scratch using SQL Server. Instead, call on Access's Upsizing Wizard to convert the existing Jet database for you. If you simply want to place the data itself on the server, you're only a few mouse-clicks and some finger tapping away from the goal. You may run into more complications if you're converting a full-fledged VBA application to an Access project — but these should be minimal if you wrote the application using ADO as your database object library. You face somewhat more work if the code is based on DAO, but at least you don't have to redesign all of the tables, queries, reports, and what not. (ADO and DAO are discussed in Chapter 46.)

To activate the Upsizing Wizard, choose Tools ⇨ Database Utilities ⇨ Upsizing Wizard. In a series of panels, you're asked to specify options for the conversion, including which tables to include in the upsized database and how their attributes, such as default values and validation rules, are to be handled. In a key step, the dialog box shown in Figure 43-7 lets you choose between three upsizing methods.

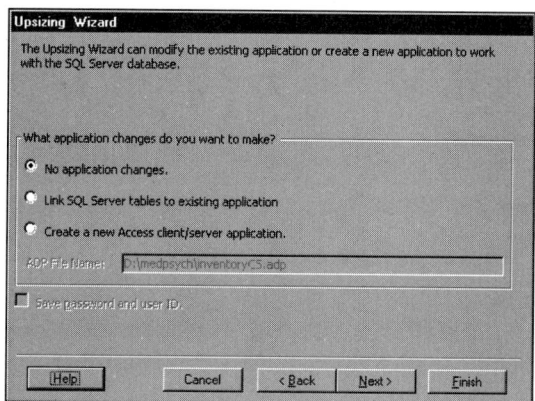

Figure 43-7: In this step of the upsizing processing, you choose the type of conversion the wizard makes.

The three upsizing methods are as follows:

- **No application changes.** This choice simply copies the data to equivalent tables in an MSDE/SQL Server database. Use this choice to make your Jet data available on the network — presumably someone else is responsible for creating the front-end application for accessing the data, or perhaps you plan to use a tool other than Access to develop your own.

- **Link SQL Server tables to existing application.** If you select this option, the wizard creates equivalent tables in an SQL Server and then links your current Jet-based application to them. This usually isn't optimal, in that you gain none of SQL Server's performance, security, and scalability advantages. However, the tables are on the network where they can be readily accessed and maintained.

- **Create a new Access client/server application.** Choose this option to translate the existing database into a complete Access project, with the data stored in MSDE/SQL Server and the .adp project file on your computer. You must specify a name for the project file.

Working in Access

Access's user interface parallels those of the other Office applications. Just be aware that Access provides an extensive set of keyboard shortcuts for navigating in database windows and editing data. I mention many of these individually in the chapters that follow, but I recommend that you refer from time to time to the comprehensive listing in the Keyboard Shortcuts Help topic.

Expanding entries for easy editing

Secret

One trick you really must master is *zooming* so that you can much more easily edit the information in a field, text box, or property setting. Although you can edit these items directly, you often can't see the entire entry at once, and the text may be displayed in a tiny font. To edit the entry in a separate, comfortably large box, click the item or move into it with the keyboard and then press Shift+F2. In property sheets, you can right-click the setting and choose Zoom from the shortcut menu. Charitably enough, the Zoom box lets you select any font at any size for editing purposes.

Renaming database items

Access 2000 is the first version of the program to automate the process of renaming items in a database. If you rename a table, report, form, query, or what have you, references to that item in other database objects must change accordingly—otherwise, the other objects won't know where to find the data they need. In the past, you had to manually change all those references yourself. Now, Access can do it for you if the feature called Name AutoCorrect is turned on.

Name AutoCorrect is on by default in Access 2000 databases, but you must activate it yourself on databases converted from older versions. You can find the controls on the General tab of the Tools ⇨ Options dialog box—they're in the upper-right corner of the window. Note that the first of the three relevant check boxes lets you have Access keep track of the changes you make, whether or not Name AutoCorrect is actually turned on via the second check box. If you check the first box and not the second, you can make extensive changes in a large database without having to wait for Access to fix each one. You can then go back and turn on Name AutoCorrect to fix all the broken references.

Note that Name AutoCorrect doesn't correct references in your VBA code to the objects whose names you've changed. A product called Speed Ferret can do that for you (Black Moshannon Systems, www.moshannon.com).

Optimizing Performance

Let's start with some of the more obvious ways you can improve the performance of Access on your system:

- **Equip your computer with plenty of memory.** Microsoft recommends a minimum of 24MB on Windows 95 or 98, and 40MB on an NT (Windows 2000) workstation. More is almost mandatory and improves performance dramatically.

- **Keep your swap disk tuned.** Windows can usually manage its swap file (virtual memory) without your help. All you need to do is set aside plenty of free space on the hard disk containing the swap file. Regularly delete files you're not using or move them to storage disks. Defragmenting the swap file hard disk every now and then can't hurt.

- **Tweak virtual memory settings.** In some cases, you may want to take a more active role in managing virtual memory. Change the virtual memory settings by starting the System applet in the Windows Control Panel, selecting the Performance tab, and choosing Virtual Memory (click the Change button in NT). Increasing the minimum size for virtual memory can help, especially if your computer has barely enough RAM or you run multiple large applications simultaneously with Access. If a specific disk has more space than the one currently being used for virtual memory, tell Windows to switch to it.

- **Run your databases in exclusive mode.** If only one person will be using a database at any given time, opening it in exclusive mode not only locks other users out but also improves performance. To place a database in exclusive mode, open it by starting Access with the /excl command line switch described in Table 43-1. If Access is already running, check the Exclusive box in the File ➪ Open dialog box when you open the database. If you work on a single-user machine, it makes sense to set the default for all databases to exclusive mode by selecting the Exclusive radio button on the Advanced tab of the Tools ➪ Options dialog box.

- **Compact your databases regularly.** Compacting databases is discussed in the section "Housekeeping in Access" later in this chapter.

Using the Performance Analyzer

The Performance Analyzer is a powerful tool for improving a database's performance. It analyzes the entire database or any selected component looking for suboptimal settings and data storage techniques. After reporting its findings to you, it can carry out its recommendations at your command.

To use the Performance Analyzer, open the database to be analyzed. Then, on the Tools menu, choose Analyze ⇨ Performance. From the Performance Analyzer dialog box, select the tab that corresponds to the type of database object you want to analyze, or switch to the All Object Types tab to see all the objects in alphabetical order. Then check off the specific objects of interest, or choose Select All to analyze every object on the current tab.

After the Performance Analyzer completes its work, a second dialog box displays the Analyzer's findings. These are divided into three categories of optimizations: Recommendations, Suggestions, and Ideas. When you click an item in the list, information about the proposed optimization appears at the bottom of the dialog box (see Figure 43-8).

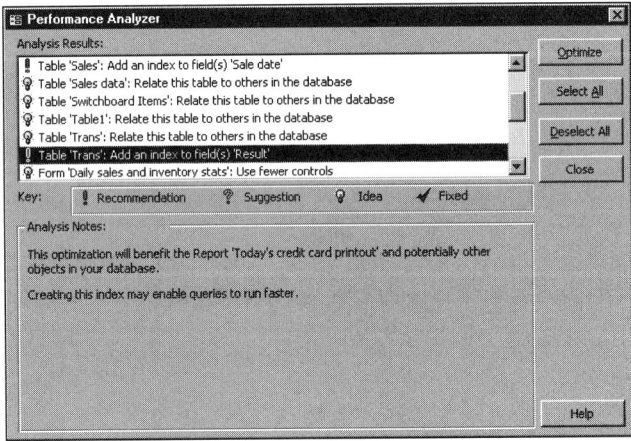

Figure 43-8: This window reports the results of the Performance Analyzer's snooping.

As a rule of thumb, you should always accept optimizations in the Recommendations category. These are changes that can have no bad side effects and are virtually guaranteed to boost performance. Suggestions are optimizations that may have minor negative consequences. The Analysis Notes portion of the dialog box provides a risk/benefit analysis for the selected suggestion.

Access can make the changes advised under Recommendations and Suggestions for you. Select any combination of these optimizations and then choose Optimize. When the work is complete, the item is marked as Fixed. Optimizations listed under Ideas require manual implementation. Instructions appear in the Analysis Notes portion of the dialog box when you select the item.

Tweaking Jet settings in the Windows Registry

Basic database functions take far more time than displaying forms and activating menu choices, especially as your database grows. Therefore, focus your attention on optimizing Jet if you want the best performance from your Access databases. The Windows Registry contains a panoply of arcane settings that govern Jet's functions. When Jet is first installed, default values for these settings are placed in the Registry key:

`\HKEY_LOCAL_MACHINE\SOFTWARE\Microsoft\Jet\4.0\Engines\Jet 4.0`

In most situations, the defaults give optimum or near-optimum performance. Under certain circumstances, though, tweaking these settings can provide dramatic performance improvements — although tweaking them the wrong way can cause equally dramatic performance declines. As long as you back up the Registry before making changes, you can experiment with the settings to see whether and how much they benefit you.

Because Access isn't the only software that uses Jet, and because the ideal settings may vary from database to database, you may not want to change the main Jet settings. Fortunately, you can create alternate Jet settings that override the main ones only under certain conditions.

For example, to deploy an Access-specific set of Jet settings, use the Registry Editor to create (if necessary) and edit the following key:

`\HKEY_LOCAL_MACHINE\SOFTWARE\Microsoft\Office\9.0\Access\Jet\4.0\Engines\Jet 4.0`

There, create and edit keys and values for the main settings you want to change. Alternatively, you can use Windows user profiles to record Jet settings that apply only when that profile is in use. User profiles were intended to allow different people to keep customized versions of Windows on the same computer. However, they can just as easily be used to activate alternative configurations for the same person. If you know that a certain huge database needs all the firepower you can throw at it, you can set up a special user profile for that database, or a profile that you use whenever you need maximum warp from the Jet engine. As shown in Table 43-1, include the `/profile` option on the command line or in a Windows shortcut to start Access with a specific user profile.

Jet's Registry settings can also be modified with VBA code, at least if you're programming with DAO. Use the DBEngine object's `SetOption` method. Because changes you make with this method affect only the current instance of the DBEngine object, this is an ideal way to control Jet's operations for a specific database.

The remainder of this section surveys the specific Registry changes most likely to give you better database performance.

Threads

Windows is a multithreaded operating system: It allows a single application program to launch and manage multiple independent processes, or *threads*. Jet makes enthusiastic use of threads to conduct a variety of critical tasks simultaneously, for all intents and purposes.

The Threads setting in the Registry determines the maximum number of simultaneous threads that Jet can launch. The default setting of three is usually adequate, but increasing it can be useful when you're running an application that processes data intensively. Don't specify a setting higher than five or six — above that, no further performance boost accrues, and other applications will go wanting.

MaxBufferSize

The MaxBufferSize setting specifies a maximum for the size of the buffer in which changes to your data are temporarily stored. As soon as the buffer overflows, Jet writes the changes to the database file, reducing the buffer's size back to or below the maximum value. When Access is installed, MaxBufferSize is set to 0. When MaxBufferSize is 0, Jet uses its own internal formula to determine the maximum buffer size. Here's the formula:

$$((\text{RAM in K} - 12{,}288)/4 + 512K)$$

No matter how little memory your system has, Jet's minimum value for this setting is 512K. If your system has a barely adequate amount of RAM, you probably ought not to raise this default. However, if your system has 64MB of RAM or more, boosting the MaxBufferSize setting may give you a speed gain with large, busy databases. Values of up to 8MB are worth trying, but more than that won't help. Enter the new setting in the Registry as an integer. For example, to change the setting to 1MB, enter **1024**.

FlushTransactionTimeout

You can experiment with raising the FlushTransactionTimeout setting to see if this speeds up network database updates. The default setting of 500 milliseconds works well with faster networks and on individual PCs, so it shouldn't be changed unless your network is slow. This parameter determines how long Jet waits during periods of inactivity before it writes database changes out of its buffer to the database disk file. The waiting period doesn't apply if the cache exceeds the buffer size specified by the MaxBufferSize setting.

Refresh Interval and PageTimeout

If you work in a multiuser environment, you can play with settings that shift the balance between performance and the timeliness of your data. In Access, the Refresh Interval setting on the Advanced tab of the Tools ➪ Options dialog box governs how often Jet looks to see whether other users have modified records in datasheets and forms. If it detects changes at this point, it places the new data into memory. Decrease the setting if it's crucial that your data always be up to date. Increase the setting if performance is more important. Valid values in seconds are between 1 and 32766. Jet has its own setting for Refresh Interval, stored as the PageTimeout Registry key. However, the setting in Access overrides this entry.

By the way, you can do a manual refresh at any time by pressing F9, and your VBA code can initiate one using the `Refresh` method. Refreshing a database only updates the fields within records, not the changes to entire records, such as additions and deletions. If you want a full update, you must requery the records (Shift+F9 does that).

LockDelay

On certain types of networks, if Access fails to lock a page in a shared database, it tries again after a waiting period set by the LockDelay Registry value. This setting applies only when the network doesn't handle lock retries for you. Networks of this type include the peer-to-peer networking included with Windows 95. Major league network systems such as NT Server and NetWare manage lock retries themselves, so the LockDelay setting is ignored.

The default setting of 100 milliseconds typically works well, unless many records are being locked. In that case, raising the LockDelay setting prevents pointless retries and allows Access to attend to other chores instead.

MaxLocksPerFile

Decrease the MaxLocksPerFile setting to prevent errors or apparent system crashes caused when the network server can't respond to the number of locks Jet places on a file. When Jet reaches the number of locks set by MaxLocksPerFile, it writes the data currently in memory to disk and frees the existing locks. When it picks up processing the operation, it can start requesting new locks from scratch. Reducing this value causes more frequent disk writes and thus slows performance, but may be necessary to prevent the system from grinding to a halt altogether.

The default setting is 9,500. You should use a setting no greater than the server maximum. Although Novell servers can handle up to 10,000 locks, the effective maximum can be lower because multiple databases can be accessed concurrently via a single connection.

RecycleLVs

Long value (LV) pages represent disk space used to store large items such as Memo and OLE object fields and the definitions for forms and reports. In a shared database, when data changes and an LV is discarded, the RecycleLVs setting controls when that disk space becomes available for reuse. If the setting is 0 (the default), all users have to close the database before the discarded pages can be reused. If the setting is 1, discarded pages are made available as soon as Jet recognizes that only one user is currently accessing the database. Use the 0 setting when performance is your priority, and the 1 setting if you want to minimize the size of the database and reduce the frequency with which you must compact it. This setting has no effect on databases opened in exclusive mode.

Optimizing Network Performance

The client/server architecture of an Access - SQL Server database application is designed for efficient performance on a network. Of course, you can take steps to optimize performance for your specific application. One essential for maximum network speed is to minimize the amount of data sent and the number of trips back and forth between the server and user workstations. See to it that the server processes the data whenever possible — it should be considerably faster than any workstation. And optimize the database itself. Consider these suggestions:

- **Create *stored procedures* for any SQL statements that you expect to regularly execute.** Stored procedures are stored in the SQL Server database, where they can be activated by your application. Because they're compiled in advance, they execute faster than ordinary SQL statements.

- **Have the server sort records before it sends them to the requesting workstation.** You can accomplish this via stored procedures or SQL statements you place in a form or report's RecordSource property.

- **Limit the number of records users can retrieve at any one time.** Rather than allowing the user to call up an entire table, design your application so that it focuses on records matching certain criteria. The smaller the number of records that have to move across the network, the faster your application seems to run — and the faster the network as a whole performs. To achieve this goal, use views, stored procedures, server filters, and WHERE clauses in SQL statements built into your code or the RecordSource properties of forms and reports.

- **Tweak the SQL server database for top performance.** Some suggestions: Turn on referential integrity to keep the relationships between tables intact as you modify the data. Define each field's data type and size so that it is no larger than necessary to hold the data you expect to store in it. Create indexes for all fields used in sorts and joins, and for which criteria are set. Indexes make queries run much faster, so be sure to create them for fields used in queries you run frequently or that retrieve large sets of records.

Housekeeping in Access

Like most databases, Access files require periodic maintenance to keep them running efficiently. When you delete data from an Access database file, the file doesn't get smaller. Instead, Access just marks the data as deleted, leaving useless holes in the file. In the meantime, all new records are added at the end of the file. Note that modifying records actually causes the database file to get larger because Access deletes the old versions and adds new ones. In addition, performance is impaired because the records gradually get all jumbled up, resulting in a small-scale fragmentation problem analogous to the type that afflicts hard disks.

Access can reuse the space occupied by deleted records, but only after the file is *compacted*. Access 2000 can automatically compact a database at the time you close it, if it determines that doing so would recover a significant amount of disk space. To turn on this feature, check the Compact on Close box in the General tab of the Tools ➪ Options dialog box. If you don't turn this option on, or if you keep the database open for long periods while many deletions and edits are made, you can compact the database manually by choosing Tools ➪ Database Utilities ➪ Compact Database.

You can compact both Access (Jet) databases and MSDE/SQL Server projects. However, the benefits of compacting are much greater with Access databases, because compacting doesn't affect tables, views, and other objects that are actually stored in SQL Server.

Secret

The compacting process attempts to repair any defects found in an Access database. If your database is acting strangely, compacting it may fix the problem. Also, be sure to compact both copies of a replicated database.

Conclusion

Access is probably the most complex of the Office applications, and it certainly provides for the widest range of arcane technical customizations. The effort you spend in learning to adjust these settings properly will pay off in faster results, especially as your databases grow larger. In the mean time, use startup options and macros to set the Access juggernaut on the course you choose.

Chapter 44

Fundamentals of Access

In This Chapter

- Understanding how relational databases work
- Planning a database from concept to field details
- Working with the Database window and object views
- Creating tables, defining fields, and building (s)table relationships
- Designing queries and reports

This chapter offers an intensive course in database management with Access. There is much more to learn, of course, but when you master the concepts and techniques covered here you can confidently set out to cruise the information sea.

Database Concepts: The Short Course

Rare is the Secrets reader who is unfamiliar with the basic concepts of databases. A quick review will suffice before we turn to practical Access techniques. While the term database can refer to any collection of information, it's typically applied when the information in question consists of items that share common elements repeating in a regular pattern. That is, the information is structured. The standard example of a structured data collection is a set of Rolodex-style file cards. All the cards contain the same types of information (name, address, and so on), but the details vary on each card.

Tables: Where the data dwells

Like all such database software, Access presents each set of structured data in a *table*. The table has rows, each of which corresponds to one item — this might be a person, company, product, part, order, or what have you. Each such item is called a *record*.

The table also has columns, each of which lists an individual detail about each item. If the records represent people, the table might have columns for name and street address, among others. The information details represented in the columns are the record's *fields*.

Any given database can, and usually should, have more than one table. If you're building an order-entry database, for example, you will need one table for the customers, one for their orders, and one for the ordered items, at the very least.

The alternative, mixing all these kinds of information in a single table, leads to massive inefficiencies — you would have to duplicate all the information about the ordering customer and each product ordered in every record you add to the database. With Access, you would only store a customer's information once in a separate table. When that customer places an order, you can link the customer's record to the order to show who bought what and when. This capability to link separate tables qualifies Access as a *relational database* in my book, even though some experts argue the point on technical grounds.

Queries: Honing in on the data you want to see

Queries enable you to extract specific data you want from your Access tables. The most common type, the *select query,* collects records containing fields that match criteria you specify. A query presents its findings in a table of its own, with the information arranged as you see fit. Once you design a query, you can reuse it at any time to access the information in your database that currently matches those criteria. And you can base a form, report, or data access page on a query to determine which information appears on that item.

While you're designing an Access query, it appears as a special window containing tools for specifying the fields and criteria that define the query. However, Access queries are actually just graphical representations of SQL (structured query language) statements. You can convert an Access query into the equivalent SQL statement if you like, and you can even dispense with the query window and write the SQL code directly.

Forms, pages, and reports: Tools for presenting and interacting with the data

On the screen, you use *forms* to work with the raw information provided by tables and queries in a more attractive, easier-to-read format. You can select specific fields you want to display, use controls such as drop-down lists and check boxes to display them, and have the form make calculations based on the other information shown. You can add other controls such as push buttons that let the user control what information the form displays, adorn the form with formatted text and graphical touches, and customize the overall layout of all of these items. The most basic kind of form simply shows the fields from one record of one table so that you can focus on that item.

However, a single form can combine information from more than one record and more than one table to show all the data you care about.

Data access pages are the Web equivalent of forms — they're the medium through which an Internet or network user of your database gets at the information of interest. Like forms, pages can display exactly the information you wish them to, all presented in a neatly formatted design. And compared to ordinary Web pages, data access pages are much more alive. Although you can convert an Access query into a static, unchanging Web page, a data access page lets the user interact with the information, requesting specific records at will.

When you want to print information from your database, you use *reports*. Much like a screen form, a report lets you choose criteria for the information that it extracts, and it lets you add text and graphical elements to describe and highlight the information. *Report snapshots* let you distribute Access reports in electronic form, so that they can be viewed by others — even those who don't have Access.

Making things happen with macros and modules

You can analyze data well enough by viewing the database objects (the tables, forms, queries, and reports) and manipulating them with Access's menu commands. If you want Access to do more of your work for you, however, you can write *macros* and VBA *modules* to perform particular sequences of commands. The macros and modules you write are stored with your database along with the other objects it contains.

You're free to run a macro or module whenever you like, but you can set things up so that Access launches it automatically when a specific *event* occurs. Events are actions such as mouse-clicks, key presses, or changes in database content. In other words, you can program Access so that it automatically responds to user actions or new information.

Although they can function quite similarly, macros and modules are fundamentally very different in concept. Chapter 45 discusses these differences in detail and helps you choose between the two technologies for your own applications.

Database objects

All of the elements discussed so far — tables, forms, queries, reports, data access pages, macros, and modules — are, in Access jargon, database *objects*. Whether that term is fitting I'll leave to you to decide, but it does give you a convenient way to refer to the disparate elements of an Access database.

Planning a Database

The first step in creating a new database — one you should take even before you start Access — is to plan the database design. Start by putting into words the tasks you want to be able to accomplish with the database.

If you run a small business, for instance, you know you're going to want to keep track of your customers. But think in detail about what you might want to do with that information. Would you like to be able to send mailings to select customers, such as those who haven't made purchases for more than a year, or those who have purchased a particular item or service in the past? Be as detailed as you can be about these requirements.

With your statement of objectives in hand, get down to details by figuring out how to meet them. List the specific information items you'll need to store in your database and decide which database objects you must create to hold them.

Start from the finish line

This process can't be strictly linear, because the content, function, and layout of the various objects are interrelated. However, one way to proceed is to start by designing (on paper) the final output elements — on-screen forms, Web pages, and printed reports. From these, you can abstract the specific answers you need from your database — you'll need to plan queries to provide these answers. When you know all these details, you'll know what you need when it comes to the fundamental database building blocks — the tables and their fields.

As you sketch the designs of the reports and screens, write down all the individual information items each one contains on a master list. This list gives you a good starting point for determining which fields belong in the database. Just keep in mind that you will probably need additional fields that don't appear on any report. Also, some items on your reports may not be fields, but calculated values.

Now rearrange the list, grouping related items together. The tables you need are likely to correspond to these groups.

Designing tables and organizing fields

Table design is probably the most difficult aspect of database planning to get right. The rule of thumb is that all the fields in a table should pertain to one kind of thing, or *subject*, as Microsoft puts it. A table's subject might be people, products, places, or events, but not "people and the products they bought" or "events and the people who attended."

Sometimes it's hard to know whether a particular bit of information pertains to one subject or another. Clearly, the decision on which table a field belongs in is somewhat arbitrary and depends on the particulars of the information. For example, is a phone number a characteristic of a person, like her age or shoe size, or does it deserve to be considered a separate subject?

In the old days, when everybody had only two phone numbers, one for work and one for home, it would have been safe to put corresponding fields directly into the People table. Now, many people may have two home lines, a dedicated fax line, a car phone, a pager, and sometimes more besides. Other people don't work and have just one home number. Depending on how urgently you need to reach people, it's starting to look as if a separate Phone Number table would be a good idea.

Consider the following guidelines when deciding how to organize the information items on your master list, assigning them to fields on specific tables:

- If an information item can have only one entry per record, it *may* be appropriate for inclusion as a field on the table that holds those records. A person's last name and a building's street address fit this criterion quite well. If the item represents a varying number of entries, such as orders placed by a customer, it belongs in its own table.

- If the information item is associated with other items that describe or qualify it, that information item is a subject in its own right and probably should have its own table. A modern phone number, for instance, should be described by type (fax, pager, or what have you).

Of course, Access doesn't force you to place each subject in its own table. If you only want to record one phone number for each person, you could decide to place a pair of corresponding fields directly into the People table, one for the number and the other for its type (work or home).

Designing table relationships

Once you have a rough idea of which tables you need and the fields they should contain, your next step is to define the relationships between the tables. In Access, you must define these relationships explicitly before you can work with the data in separate tables together.

Continuing the earlier example, let's say you have a People table and a Phone Numbers table. Obviously, a table consisting only of phone numbers isn't going to do you any good at all unless you like to make random phone calls. You need some way to know which phone number belongs to which person.

The classic solution to this problem is to identify or add a pair of fields, one in each table, that contain the same information. The names of the two *related* fields don't have to match, but the data they hold does.

Because some people have identical names (did you know there's a national Jim Smith club?), you can't reliably identify the owner of a phone number by name. In such situations — when a table contains no definitely unique field — you must create a field in both the People and Phone Number tables for a unique identifying number. Then, when you're looking at a person's record in the People table, Access can use this ID number field to locate phone number records that contain the same number in their related field.

With these ideas in mind, figure out how each pair of tables you've come up with are related, and specifically, which fields you should use to identify that relationship. As you evaluate the relationship between each pair, categorize it in one of the following types:

- **One-to-many.** In this type of relationship, a record in one table can have more than one matching record in the other table, but each record in the second table matches only one record in the first. For instance, a customer can place many orders, but each order is placed by only one customer. The Customers and Orders tables therefore have a one-to-many relationship.

- **Many-to-many.** Here, each record in one table can match to multiple records in the other. In the example of people's phone numbers, each person can have more than one phone number. But the opposite is also true — because some people live or work at the same locations, a phone number can have more than one person. Thus, the People and Phone Number tables have a many-to-many relationship.

- **One-to-one.** In a one-to-one relationship, one, and only one, record in one table matches one, and only one, record in the other. If you find such a relationship in the tables you've designed, you should reevaluate the way you've organized them. Usually, items in a one-to-one relationship go in the same table. However, sometimes it makes sense to carve out such items as a separate table, perhaps to make a table with many fields more manageable.

Defining fields in detail

With the overall organization of your database taking shape, you can now focus on the details of each field's definition. For each field, you must do the following:

- Come up with a short but memorably descriptive name. Access allows up to 64 characters (including spaces) for a field name.

- Decide on the data type for the field. Table 44-1 lists your options.

- Determine acceptable values for the field. Access can perform data validation — that is, it can check entries to make sure they match criteria you've defined. For example, for the Age field from a Grown-ups table, the range of permissible values would be "greater than 17."

- Decide on how you want the field data to appear in tables and fields. In Access, a field's *format* can be used to separate parts of the entry in a field making the information easier to read without changing the stored data. As a simple example, raw numbers such as 123456 might be formatted to read 123,456.
- Write all these choices down for use when you create the table.

Table 44-1   Access Field Data Types

Data Type	Type of Data Stored
Text	Letters, numerals, and punctuation to a maximum of 255 characters. Use the Text type for numbers, such as phone numbers and zip codes, that won't be used in calculations.
Memo	Letters, numerals, and punctuation to a maximum of 64,000 characters
Number	Numeric values for calculations, except monetary amounts
Date/Time	Dates and times, of course. Use the Date/Time data type rather than Number so that dates and times will be sorted properly.
Currency	Dollars and cents, pounds or yen, and so on. Access doesn't round off calculated currency values. The currency symbol and other formatting shown in the field are based on the selected currency type in the Regional Settings applet of the Control Panel.
AutoNumber	A number that Access enters automatically in sequence each time you add a new record
Yes/No	1 or 0 only (interpreted as logical values Yes/No, True/False, On/Off)
OLE object	Any OLE object up to 1 gigabyte in size (Chapter 10 covers OLE)
Hyperlink	A URL or UNC path hyperlink containing up to 64,000 characters

Planning queries

Making sense of all the raw information stored in a table requires effective use of queries. During the planning stage, just write out the questions that need to be answered in ordinary English. If your database tracks dairy products and you want to know the price of eggs in Wisconsin, you'll need a query to extract that information.

Designing forms, data access pages, and reports

Although you can view, enter, and manipulate data effectively in the default table view, designing on-screen forms for these tasks improves efficiency and accuracy and makes the experience more fun. Likewise, if you're publishing database information on the Web, presenting that information as data access pages enables users of your Web site to work with just the data they need to see.

During the design phase, your job is to determine which forms and pages you need and to lay them out on paper, at least roughly. A form or page in Access has a defined area in which you can see and edit each piece of information. These areas, of course, correspond to fields in your database. A form or page can include fields from more than one table as long as you have created relationships between the tables. In addition to fields, items you can place on a form or page include text for labels and instructions; calculations based on field values; controls such as buttons, check boxes, and drop-down lists; and graphics and OLE objects. Sketch each form, placing the fields and other items in logical order.

Access Boot Camp: Database Construction Techniques

With the plan for your database in hand, you've earned the right to let Access show you what it can do on the open road. The rest of this chapter is devoted to a whistle-stop tour of the fundamental Access objects and features you'll need to manage databases with this rich piece of software.

Using the Database window

When you run Access without specifying a database to open, it prompts you to open or create one. What you see when you eventually open an existing database or create a new one varies a great deal, depending on which database you open or which template you use as the starting point for a new database.

If the designer of the database or template hasn't changed the default setup, the first thing that appears on your screen is the Database window. In a completed database application, however, the Database window is often hidden from view, replaced by a *switchboard* form that provides buttons for activating functions specific to the application.

Shown in Figure 44-1, the Database window consists of a main panel in which you can see and work with the seven types of database objects. The Objects bar at the left of the window determines which objects appear in this main area. By clicking a button in the Objects bar, you can display all of the objects of a given type together or access customized groups containing any mix of objects you want to work with together. If you click the Forms item, for example, the Database window displays any Forms objects that currently exist in the database.

Much as in My Computer or Explorer, you can change the way the window displays objects (as large or small icons, and so on) using toolbar buttons.

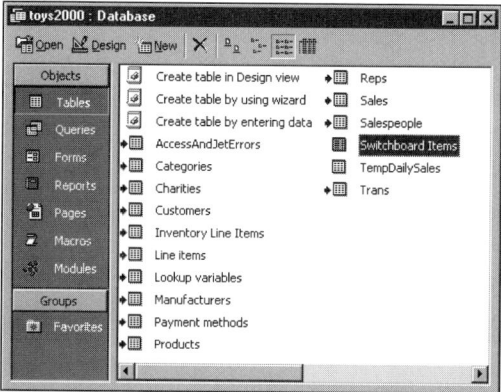

Figure 44-1: Use the Database window as your springboard to database objects in Access.

Secret

Although each type of database object serves a different purpose — and its icon is unique — you work with objects in the Database window in the same basic ways. Use the window's four main buttons as follows:

- Choose New to create a new object. Alt+N works too, but don't press Ctrl+N — that starts a new *database*, not a new object. The New command isn't available when you're working in a group. However, you can always create a new object of *any* type by choosing from the Insert menu.

- Select an object and choose Design to modify it. The corresponding keyboard shortcuts are Ctrl+Enter or Alt+D.

- Select an object and choose Open, Preview, or Run to activate it (the button label varies depending on which tab you're using). Double-clicking the object or selecting it and pressing Enter accomplishes the same thing.

- Right-click an object and choose Create Shortcut from the resulting menu to place a shortcut to that object on the Desktop, on the Start menu, or in any folder. When you activate the shortcut in Windows, Access runs and opens the selected table, form, or what have you.

Secret

You can make the Database window work like a browser, so that pointing to an object selects it and single-clicking an object opens or runs it. Go to the View tab of the Tools ➪ Options dialog box and select Single-Click Open. Also, you can jump to an object in the current list by starting to type its name. As you type each character, Access selects the first object that matches your entry.

With the exception of the Run choice for macros and modules, each of these actions opens a separate window containing the object. You can open multiple objects, each in its own window, and navigate from window to window using the mouse, the Window menu, or the keyboard shortcuts shown in Table 44-2. As you open windows and switch between them, Access changes the menu and toolbars according to which type of object the active window contains.

Caution

Closing the Database window closes the entire database. If you want the Database window out of your way, *don't* click the Close button — minimize the window, or choose Window ➪ Hide.

Table 44-2 Keyboard Shortcuts for Navigating in Access

To Do This	Press This Keyboard Shortcut
Rename the selected object	F2
Select the next or the previous tab	Ctrl+Tab or Shift+Ctrl+Tab
Enter Design view for the selected database object	Ctrl+Enter or Alt+D
Create a new object	Alt+N
Switch to the next window	Ctrl+F6
Switch to the previous window	Ctrl+Shift+F6

Working with views

With the exception of macros and modules, you can display all Access database objects in at least two different *views* (three, if you count Print Preview). The views available depend on the type of object you're working with, as follows:

- Use *Design view* to define fields for a table, set up a query, lay out a form or report, or write a macro or module.

- *Datasheet view* presents information in a *datasheet*, a spreadsheet-like grid containing the data from a table, form, or query. If you view a form in Datasheet view, you see only data from the table on which the form is primarily based (the one listed as the form's `RecordSource` property), even though the form may include fields from other tables.

- *Form view*, of course, displays a form as a working unit.

- *SQL view* for queries displays the SQL (Structured Query Language) code that the query runs to retrieve or modify data.

- *Print Preview* is available for all objects. The *Layout Preview* (available only when you're working with a report in Design view) also lets you see the report as it will print but prepares the preview faster, because it displays only a sample of your data and doesn't carry out underlying queries in full.

Secret

The quickest way to switch between available views is via the object's shortcut menu. To bring up the shortcut menu for the entire object — as opposed to the menu for a component such as a field, column, or control — right-click the title bar of the object's window. The available views are listed at the top of the menu.

You can also switch between views using the View menu or the View button, which appears at the far-left side of the default toolbar when a table, query, form, or report window is active.

When you first use the View button, you may find its behavior a bit strange. It's not telling you which view you're looking at now, but rather, which one you would switch to if you clicked it. The View button is a split button. If more than one view is available for the current object and the one you want isn't showing, you can click the thin rectangle to the right of the button image to list all the available views and make your selection there.

Creating and working with tables

The first practical step in building a new database is to add its tables, defining the fields each one contains. If you have planned the database before starting work, as I previously recommended, you can focus on the mechanics at this point.

Starting from the Table item on the Database window, creating a new table is as simple as double-clicking one of the "Create table" icons. You can open the new table in either Datasheet or Design view, or you can use a wizard to build the table for you based on your input. Alternatively, you can hit the New button or press Alt+N to bring up the dialog box shown in Figure 44-2. In addition to the same datasheet, Design view, and wizard choices you get with the icons, this box also lets you add existing tables from another source to the current Access database via the Import Table or Link Table options.

Two words to the wise are in order here. First, about the wizard: The wizard is only useful if you need one of its predefined tables. These cover all kinds of common subjects (in the database sense of that term defined earlier), such as products, people, and personal collections and activities. They define appropriate fields for you, cutting your work to a minimum. But if the table you're creating is on a different subject, it's probably easier to start from scratch than to modify a wizard's table.

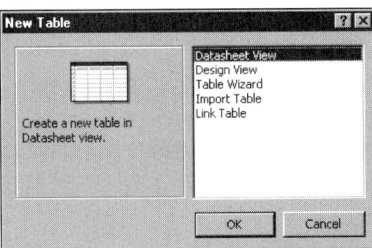

Figure 44-2: Access offers these choices when you create a new table. Note that the default choice at the top opens the new table in Datasheet view.

My second point is a simple piece of advice: I recommend using Design view for new tables if you're not using the wizard. Note that Access selects Datasheet view as the default in the New Table dialog box. It's easy to create and reorder fields in Datasheet view, and Access figures out what type of field you've created based on the data you enter. However, you must use Design view to take control over the fields in detail. Why not start there, especially if you've gone to the trouble of planning the table in detail beforehand?

Defining fields in Design view

Figure 44-3 shows an example of a table in Design view. The top part of the window consists of a listing of the fields in the table by name, and in the order in which they appear in the table.

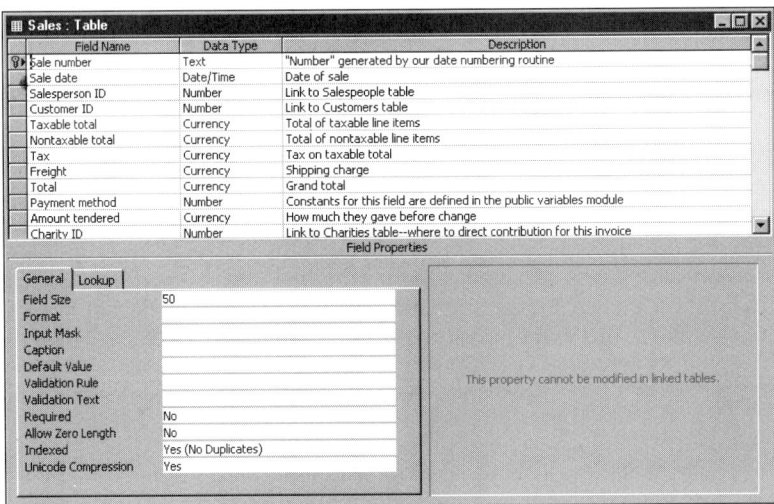

Figure 44-3: A table as it appears in Design view

To create a new field:

1. Type in its name.

2. Move to the Data Type column and select the correct type from the drop-down list (as elsewhere in Windows and Office, you can drop the list down by pressing F4). If you haven't planned the field definitions in advance you can refer back to Table 44-1 for a listing of data types.

3. Add a description of the field in the appropriate column, if you like.

That was the easy part. The lower half of the Design View window, used to define field properties, is where you'll need your wits about you.

Working with field properties

For each field, the Field Properties area lists the properties you can set that are available for the field's data type. Although the available properties vary between types, most of them are common to all types of fields. As you move among the properties, the pane to the right displays a help message describing their functions. The help message should suffice for some of the items, but you'll need more background for others. I provide some critical pointers here, and you can always press F1 to get detailed information on the current property.

Although you can define a property by typing an entry, Access often helps you enter the setting. When you move to most properties, a drop-down list button, a *builder* button, or both appear. You can then select an entry from the drop-down list or click the builder button to get help constructing an expression.

Formatting a field

Use the field's Format property to define the appearance of data displayed in the field — the format has no effect on the stored value of the data. When you enter data into a field, the format takes effect only when you save the data. You can choose from a predefined format appropriate for the field's data type from the drop-down list, or you can type in a custom format.

- In Number and Currency fields, the General format is the default, even if you don't select it — it makes no change to the way the number is entered. If you choose the Standard, Percent, Fixed, or Currency formats, you can override the default for the number of decimal places displayed — which is 2 — by typing in a number in the Decimal Places property.

- By default, Date/Time fields are displayed in the format selected in the Windows Control Panel.

- For Yes/No-type fields (representing *Boolean* data) that allow only one of two choices, you can select any of three standard formats: Yes/No, True/False, or On/Off. You can also create formats of your own for custom two-choice fields. For example, to have Access display either In or Out for a field of this type, you would type the following:

  ;"In";"Out"

- Text and Memo fields have no standard formats.

Defining an input mask

Use an *input mask* to control the way data is entered in the first place. The Input Mask property can include characters that separate portions of an entry, such as the dashes in a social security number. In addition, it controls which type of character can be typed into the field (letter or number) and which characters are required or optional. By default, these extra characters aren't stored in the table data.

Secret

Access supplies input masks for common fields such as phone numbers. Click the builder button beside the Input Mask property to display the Input Mask Wizard shown in Figure 44-4. You can select one of the prefab input masks or choose Edit List to redefine them.

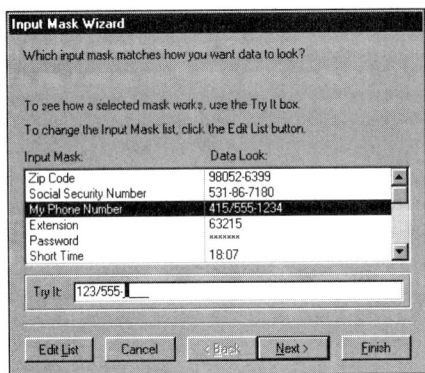

Figure 44-4: This wizard lets you select from a variety of predefined input masks.

Defining validation rules

The Validation Rule and Validation Text properties tell Access to check entries in the field to ensure they meet your specifications. For instance, you can require that entries fall into a certain alphabetic or numeric range.

Enter the validation rule itself into the property by the same name. You can click the builder button to run the Expression Builder, shown in Figure 44-5. The Validation Text property is for a message that Access should display when someone types data that violates the rule into the field.

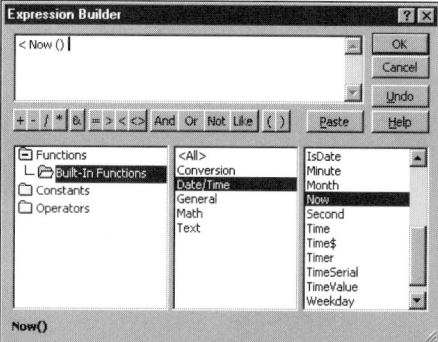

Figure 44-5: Use the Expression Builder any place in Access you need to define criteria or create a calculation.

Secret

You can also set up record validation rules that can test one field against another, for example, to confirm that the area code entered is valid for the listed city. Set up record validation rules on the Properties sheet for the table as a whole. Another tip: To see whether the data currently stored in a table meet the validation rules you've set up, choose Edit ⇨ Test Validation Rule while in table Design view. Access checks through the table and reports its findings.

Working with fields in Design view

You can perform the following actions with fields in a table's Design view:

- To move a field in the list, click the field's row header to select it, release the mouse button, and then drag the field to its new location.

- To insert or delete fields (rows), right-click over the field and choose the appropriate command from the shortcut menu.

- To add a new field from one of the prefab tables supplied with Access, right-click where you want the field to be inserted in the list, and then choose Build from the shortcut menu.

Specifying a primary key field

A table's *primary key* is the field or set of fields that enables Access to identify a record as unique. Access uses the primary key to *index* the table so that it can find the records you want quickly when you query or report on the database. Although Access doesn't force you specify one, you should.

If you know that a field in the table will have a unique value in every single record, you can use that field as the table's primary key. Otherwise, you should add a field of the AutoNumber data type as the primary key. Access automatically numbers each record you add in sequence in this field, ensuring a unique value. To set a field as the primary key, right-click it and choose Primary Key, or select the field and choose Edit ⇨ Primary Key.

Working with tables in Datasheet view

Use Datasheet view to display a table as such (see Figure 44-6). Here you can enter or edit table data, but you can also redefine the table if you like. Each row represents a record, and each column represents a field. The last row in the table is marked with a star, indicating the place to start a new record.

Figure 44-6: A table displayed in Datasheet view

The controls at the bottom left of the Datasheet view window let you quickly move among the records. The display there shows the number of the current record. Click this area and type in a record number to jump to that record. Starting from the left, the first four arrow buttons take you to the first, previous, next, and last records, respectively. The fifth button, the one with the star, goes beyond the last record, starting a new one.

 Access 2000 datasheets based on tables now let you display matching records in a subsidiary datasheet. If the table you're working with has a primary key, the first column in its datasheet consists of expand indicators, little boxes containing plus signs. Click the expand indicator of a chosen record for an instant display of records matching that primary key value from the related table.

Selecting and editing data in tables

For operations such as cut-copy-paste edits, you can select individual characters, all the contents of a single field, entire rows and columns, or a whole table. To select a single record (row), click its *record selector*, the gray box at the far left of the table. An arrow or other icon appears in the record selector of the selected record. To select a single column (field), click its *field selector*, the column heading. For many operations on single rows or columns, however, you need only click anywhere in a row or column. To select multiple rows or columns, drag in the row or column header area. To select the whole table, click the box at the top-left corner of the table. To select a block of fields, Shift+click first at one corner of the block and then at the opposite corner diagonally.

Secret

Once a field contains data, moving to it with the arrow keys selects the entire field. To edit the individual characters, press F2. You can change this behavior by opening the Tools ➪ Options dialog box, switching to the Keyboard tab, and selecting either of two buttons, Go to Start of Field or Go to End of Field. If you make this change, press F2 after entering a field to select the whole field.

Controlling table structure and appearance

Mouse acrobatics and shortcut menus provide the fastest means for manipulating a table's organization or looks in Datasheet view. Try the following techniques:

- To insert a new field in the table, right-click in the column and choose Insert Column from the shortcut menu. The new column appears to the left of the one you started with. In similar fashion, insert a new record by right-clicking the row header and choosing New Record. The new record appears at the bottom of the table.

- To move a column (field) with the mouse, click the column header, release the mouse button, and then drag the column header to its new location.

- You can move columns with the keyboard. After moving to the column to be moved, select the whole entry (if it isn't already selected) by pressing F2. Press Ctrl+Space to select the column, using the arrow keys to select additional columns if desired. Then press Ctrl+Shift+F8 to turn on Move mode and execute the move with the arrow keys. Press Esc to finish up.

- To resize a column, move the mouse pointer to the column's left boundary in the column header so that the pointer becomes a double-headed arrow. Then drag the boundary. You can use a parallel technique to resize all the rows at once, but you can't change the heights of individual rows. To set the row or column size to a specific measurement, choose Row Height or Column Width from the appropriate shortcut menu.

- Freeze one or more selected columns to keep them visible at the left of the window as you scroll the table horizontally. Select the columns, right-click the column heading of the selection, and choose Freeze Columns.

- You can hide one or more selected columns by choosing Hide Columns from the shortcut menu. The Unhide Columns selection is on the shortcut menu for the whole table, produced by right-clicking the title bar of the table window.

- Change the font for the table as a whole using the Font choice on the table's shortcut menu (right-click the table's title bar) or on the main Format menu. To alter the table's appearance in other ways, choose Datasheet from either menu. The Datasheet Formatting dialog box, shown in Figure 44-7, lets you turn gridlines on or off, select table color, and activate 3-D effects.

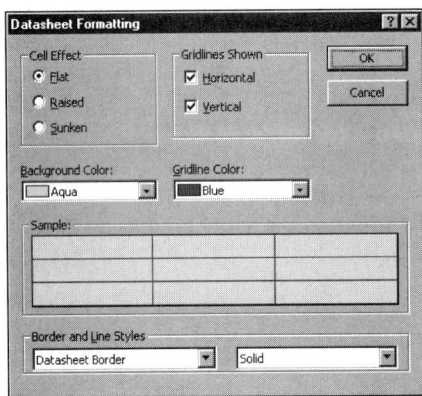

Figure 44-7: Use the Datasheet Formatting dialog box to alter a table's overall appearance.

Defining relationships between tables

Individual tables can hold a lot of information, but the key to a database's real power lies in the relationships between the tables. To set up these relationships in Access, close any open tables, and then choose Tools ➪ Relationships or click the Relationships button on the Database toolbar.

The Relationships window (see Figure 44-8) provides a big workspace where the links between your tables can be comfortably defined, viewed, and edited in graphical fashion. Each little box in the window is a *field list* and represents a table in the database. The primary key field is shown in bold (tables without primary keys can't be related to other tables or shown in the Relationships window). Queries, which define new tables, can also be related to tables or other queries.

Add tables to the window by clicking the Show Table button or choosing the corresponding item on the shortcut menu. The Show Table dialog box appears automatically if no relationships have been defined for the database. After selecting the tables you want to work with, you can go to work on connecting them using drag and drop.

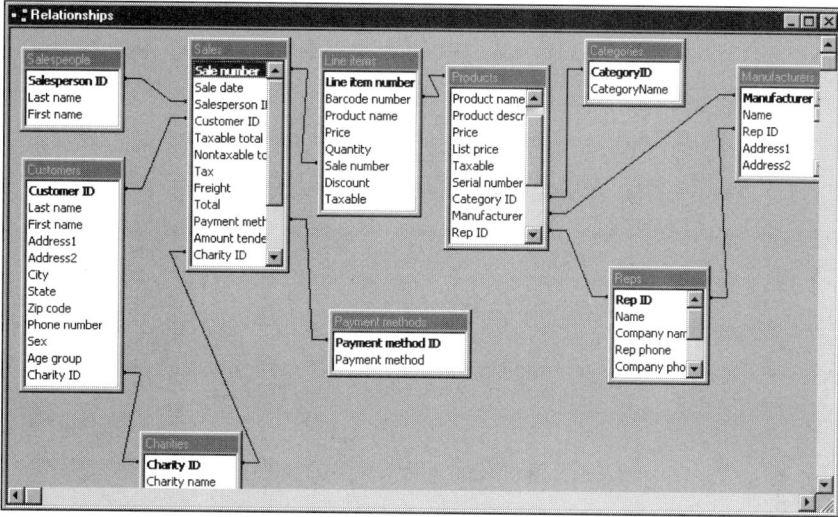

Figure 44-8: Define relationships between tables graphically in Access using this window.

Setting up and editing relationships

To define a relationship, you just drag a field name from one table's field list and drop it on a field name in the other table's list. In the usual case — when defining a one-to-many relationship — you drag the primary key of the first table to the matching field that contains the same information in the second, the foreign key.

When you release the button, a dialog box describing the relationship appears. If you goofed on the fields you intended to connect, you can correct the mistake here. Once you choose Create, Access draws a line between the two fields to indicate the relationship. If you can drag the field lists around on the window, this *relationship line* is redrawn accordingly. To edit an existing relationship, double-click its relationship line.

Defining many-to-many relationships

Secret

Access doesn't provide for direct many-to-many relationships between two tables, even though they occur in many real-life situations (see "Designing table relationships" earlier in this chapter for a definition of the concept). To work around this problem, you must create a third table called a *junction table* and relate it to both of the other tables.

The junction table requires only two fields, defined to match those of the primary keys in each of the original tables. The junction table's primary key must be set to *both* of these required fields. To set a primary key to multiple fields, hold down Ctrl while you select the fields, and then choose Edit ⇨ Primary Key.

The People and Phone Numbers tables discussed earlier in this chapter provide a good example of a many-to-many relationship — a person can have many different phone numbers, and a phone number can connect you to many different people. If the People table's primary key is the Person ID field, in the Phone Numbers table you might use the Phone Number field itself as the primary key. However, if you want to allow for situations where one phone number serves as both a voice and fax line, the primary key would be a Phone Number ID field.

Assuming you take the latter course, the junction table required would include two fields, Person ID and Phone Number ID. Together, these two items establish a unique entry — no person has more than one copy of a specific phone number. After you've created the junction table, you can set up the many-to-many relationship. In the Relationships window, define one-to-many relationships between each of the original tables and the junction table, using the primary keys to connect them.

Getting Answers

Unprocessed, raw information in a set of big tables is essentially useless. The whole point of database software is that it helps you dig through that data to find the specific facts you need, organized as required by your project.

Finding, sorting, and filtering data

The simplest data manipulations require very little work but produce quick, often very useful results.

Finding and replacing data

Access can perform word processing functions — like find and replace operations on your data. Searching for data with this technique is much slower than using a query, but it works fine with smaller tables and is very convenient. To look for a needle in a data stack, open a table, query, or form and press Ctrl+F or choose Edit ⇨ Find. The settings you make in the Find dialog box are critical to locating the data you want. In the Match list, select Any Part of Field if you're not sure whether the items you're seeking occupy entire fields or just parts of fields.

Be sure to check the setting of the Look In box. Your selection here determines whether your search is confined to the field that was active when you opened the dialog box or covers the entire table, query, or form. As in other Office applications, Access tries to shield you from too many choices in the Find and Replace dialog box.

Secret

If you feel bold, click More to display additional options. The function of one of these choices may not be obvious: When the Search Fields as Formatted box is available, check it if you want to match the Find What entry to the field data as displayed, instead of to its stored value.

Sorting and filtering

To sort the records in a table, query, or form according to a field, right-click in the field and choose Sort Ascending or Sort Descending from the shortcut menu. These quick commands let you sort on multiple fields in a table or query, but only if they're adjacent — you have to select them as a group. To restrict the items displayed in a table, query, or form to those matching a given value or expression, right-click in the field and choose one of the following Filter options from the shortcut menu:

- Filter by Selection and Filter Excluding Selection use the value of the current field (or block of fields, if more than one is selected) as the filter criterion. Say you have a large table of dogs and you've just clicked in the Breed column in a field containing "Poodle." If you filter by selection, the table will shrink to show only the poodle records.

- Filter For lets you type in a value or enter an expression for the filter.

Other filtering techniques are available. Choose Records ⇨ Filter ⇨ Filter by Form to open a special window based on the original object. Here, you can type or select filter criteria into any of the fields. If you want to specify additional sets of filter criteria — to display records matching any of the criteria sets — click the Or tab at the bottom of the window and type in the new criteria. When you've completed the entries, click the Apply Filter button on the toolbar.

For more sophisticated sort and filter operations, choose Records ⇨ Filter ⇨ Advanced Filter/Sort.

Creating queries

Queries are your core tool for industrial-strength information-retrieval operations. Queries can also act upon your data, adding or deleting records or creating brand-new tables under your instructions.

Secret

A query is a specification from which Access creates a temporary table each time you run the query. The point I'm making is that you can use queries anywhere you use tables — as the basis for forms, data access pages, reports, and even other queries.

Types of queries

The basic query is the *select query*. Based on criteria you specify, it extracts data from one or more tables and places the information in a datasheet. You can include calculations and totals of various types in the query, such as a count of the records with the name Fido in the Dog's Name field or an average of the values in all the Owner's Age fields. You can edit the items in the resulting datasheet, and your changes update the corresponding fields in the original tables.

A *parameter query* is just a select query based on criteria that you define when the query runs. The query displays a special dialog box in which you type the information for the criteria. The obvious example is a query based on a range of dates that you specify on an ad-hoc basis when you run the query.

To total, average, or count the values in a field grouped by the contents of another field, create a *crosstab query*. It's a lot easier to see how this works than to explain it, so I offer Figure 44-9 for your perusal.

Figure 44-9: A small, sample crosstab table

Secret

You can get the same information more easily and with greater flexibility using a PivotTable. PivotTables are an Excel feature, but they're also available in Access via the PivotTable Wizard. Run the wizard from the New Form dialog box (note that you start a new *form,* not a query). Excel PivotTables are covered in Chapter 40.

Action queries alter multiple records in one step. Use one of these when you want to raise prices across the board or add a prefix to all part numbers for a certain product line.

An *SQL query* is based on an SQL (Structured Query Language) statement. Actually, Access uses SQL statements to implement all queries, as you can see if you use View ⇨ SQL View to look at any query. In an SQL query, *you* write the SQL statement.

Designing a query

If all you want to do is look at the data in a selection of fields, the Query Table Wizard is probably the easiest way to set up your query. When it comes to finding specific information of interest, however, the wizard leaves you high and dry.

In Design view, a query window is split horizontally across the middle, as shown in Figure 44-10. The top part shows the field lists for all the tables available in the query, and the lower part contains the actual query specifications. You can add additional tables to the upper part by clicking the Show Table button on the toolbar.

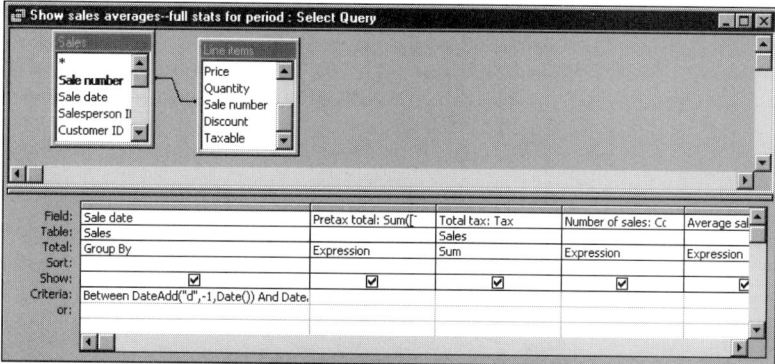

Figure 44-10: Defining a query in Design view

The *design grid* occupies the lower half of the query window. Each column represents a field used to select records for inclusion in the query. To enter a field in the query, you drag it from one of the field lists into a column.

Secret

Drag the asterisk (*) from the top of a field list to a query column to include all the fields in the query with special updating features activated. From now on, when you add or delete fields in the underlying table, these changes appear automatically in the query results datasheet. However, you can't select individual fields to show or hide, and you must add individual fields to the design grid if you want to use them to sort or filter the query results.

The remaining rows in the design grid work as follows:

- Use the Sort row to define fields on which the query datasheet will be sorted. If you sort on more than one field, Access performs the sorts in the order in which the fields appear in the design grid, working from left to right. You can move the column for a field by dragging it to a new location after first clicking the heading to select it.

- Check the box in the Show row if you want that field to appear in the query results — at times, you use a field to determine which records appear in the query, but you don't want to see that field's data.

- Place in the Criteria row any criteria that records must match to appear in the query results. If you want to show records that match any of several different criteria sets, use additional rows labeled Or below the Criteria row to define each alternative set.

Distributing reports

At its most basic, an Access report is a printed version of a table or query with fancier formatting. In addition to the control reports give you over layout, they let you include subtotals and other kinds of calculations and add decorative elements to make the high points stand out.

As always, the easiest way to create a report is to rely on a wizard. Included in the selection of wizards in the New Report dialog box are two that create an entire report for you. If you select either of the AutoReport wizards, all you have to do is specify a table or query to report on, and Access does the rest. Obviously, these AutoReports are lacking in originality. To stamp a report with your personal touch, work on it in Design view.

If you want to distribute a report electronically instead of on paper, convert it into a report snapshot. Report snapshots are covered in Chapter 15 in the section on Web page design, but you can make available a report snapshot file to interested parties on disk or via e-mail as well as on the Web.

Working with reports in Design view

Design view shows the underlying structure of the report. As you can see in Figure 44-11, reports have five main sections. Items you place on the report print differently, depending on which section you put them in. The sections work as follows:

- **Report Header.** This section prints at the top of the first page of the report only. Place the report title and banner ornaments here.

- **Page Header.** Items in the report header are printed at the top of each page. Although the header is typically used for column headings, it can also include information such as page number, date, author, and the like.

- **Detail.** Field data appear in this section, which is printed once for each record in the table or query on which the report is based.

- **Group Header.** If you plan to group together items in the report by date, salesperson, or region, for example, use the group header to label the start of each group. To set up the groups, use the instructions in "Grouping items in reports" later in this chapter. (In Design view, group headers and footers are labeled with the name of the fields on which the groups are based — you won't see an area labeled Group Header.)

- **Group Footer.** See the preceding description of the Group Header section. To print summary calculations such as subtotals and counts at the end of a group of records, place them in the group footer section.

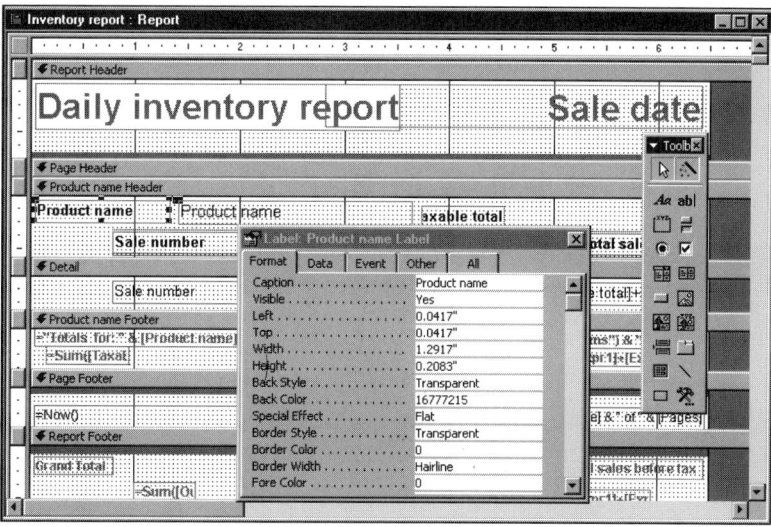

Figure 44-11: The report design takes shape in this window.

- **Page Footer.** Appearing at the bottom of every page, this is where you'd usually insert the page number, date, and author information.
- **Report Footer.** Here's a tricky one. Although the report footer section falls at the bottom of the report in Design view, it's actually printed above the page footer on the final page of the report. Overall summary information such as grand totals should appear here.

Adding fields and other items to the report

Just as in a form, every item on a printed report is represented by a corresponding control on the screen version of the report (Chapter 47 covers Access controls). Besides the text box controls that display field data in the Detail section of the report, most reports rely primarily on simple text label controls.

To add a text box bound to a field, drag it from the field list for the underlying table or query onto the report design. You can place fields in any section of the report, but they should usually go in the Detail section. Use label controls to display text that you define. These are ideal for the report title and group and column headings.

Use unbound text box controls to set up calculations in the group footer and report footer sections, and for variable items such as the page number in the page headers and footers. After adding the text box to the report, type the expression for the calculated value into the Control Source property.

For example, the expression =Now() yields the current date and time; the expression ="Page " & [Page] & " of " & [Pages] produces a "Page 2 of 4" printed result; and the expression =Sum[Daily Sales] totals the values in the Daily Sales field.

Grouping items in reports

You can group and subgroup a report based on up to ten different fields or expressions. For example, a main group might include all the orders from a region of the country. Subgroups within the main group could list the orders from a particular state, and sub-subgroups might divide those into the individual cities' orders.

Set up such groups by clicking the Sorting and Grouping toolbar button to define the grouping criteria. In the Sorting and Grouping dialog box, use the Field/Expression column to select the field you want to group, or type an expression defining the criterion (for example, as a range of values). Choose Ascending or Descending in the Sort Order column to control the order in which items print within the group.

Setting a grouping criterion isn't enough to produce a group in your report. For each criterion, you must also activate a group header or footer (or both) by setting the corresponding item or items to Yes in the Group Properties section of the Sorting and Grouping dialog box.

When you do this, the corresponding header or footer area appears in the report in Design view. You can now add controls to it, including text boxes that calculate subtotals, averages, and counts for the group — see the previous section for tips on creating such controls.

Creating and Using Forms and Data Access Pages

Because effective forms are such a key ingredient in successful database applications, and because designing them is not a trivial task, I'm devoting all of Chapter 47 to the topic. There, you learn the steps required to create and lay out a form and fill it with the data you want to see. Chapter 47 also covers specifics on the controls Access provides for forms and reports, and the differences between them and standard VBA controls. Consult Chapter 15 for details on designing data access pages and using them for interactive database access in a complete Web site.

Conclusion

Access is a huge program, and a little chapter like this can hardly do it justice. With the skills covered here, however, you'll be able to manage substantial databases and extract vital information from them.

Chapter 45

Secrets of Database Application Design

In This Chapter

- Understanding database applications
- Deciding whether to use Access macros or VBA to automate your application
- Building database applications without Access — when to consider this alternative
- Planning custom switchboard forms, menus, and toolbars
- Distributing finished Access applications

Once you've mastered the core database tools discussed in Chapter 44, you're likely to find yourself hankering after better ways to harness all that power under the Access hood. After all, Access is much more than a database program — it offers a complete development environment for building custom applications.

Actually, Access offers *two* distinct application development environments. You can put together full-blown applications using macros alone to automate the commands available from the toolbars and menus. Alternatively, you can cut your ties to the Access user interface and turn to VBA for the ultimate in programming power. This chapter dishes out the pros and cons of each of these options.

Secret

Microsoft's Web site offers loads of detailed articles on Access development topics. Go to www.microsoft.com/accessdev/.

Understanding Access Applications

In concept, an Access application is a complete piece of software that performs a set of related data-management tasks, presenting its functions to the user with toolbars and forms that are custom-tailored to the job at hand. Of course, there's no need to quibble about when a database becomes an application. The point is simply that applications are more ambitious and more highly customized than the type of database in which you manage information via the standard Access user interface commands.

When the typical Access application starts up, a special *switchboard* form appears in place of Access's default Database window (see Figure 45-1 for an example). Acting as a central control panel for the application, a switchboard provides a set of buttons or other controls that activate custom commands or branch to other forms that display data for review, editing, and querying. At the same time, the application's custom toolbars and menus replace the standard ones normally available in Access. They may even display and hide themselves automatically as the user moves from form to form.

Figure 45-1: A custom application's switchboard form, the first item displayed when the application starts up

Although you can build applications for your own use, they are more often intended for distribution to others. By packaging the data together with push-button controls for specific tasks, you enable users to get their work done without having to know much at all about Access itself.

Planning and implementing the application

The planning process described in detail in Chapter 44 assumes even greater importance and requires more attention when you set out to build a complete application. The design of the underlying database's building blocks — its tables, fields, forms, queries, and reports — will be crucial to the application's success. In addition, however, you need to think carefully about what automated commands your users will need and how to present them on switchboards, menus, and toolbars.

As you plan, it's vital to think about the application as a series of *events* that may happen in any order. Clicking a button with the mouse and opening or closing a form are examples of events. In Access applications, as in VBA programs, such events trigger all custom features. If you want to let the user run a certain query, you might set up your application so that the query runs when the user clicks a particular button. Your application plan must provide the macro or VBA code to activate the query when the button gets clicked.

Choose the right tool: Access macros versus VBA

To repeat a key point, Access macros are *not* the VBA-based macros found in Word, Excel, and PowerPoint. Because you can use either tool to create custom applications, an important step in planning a new application is to decide which is right for your needs.

Differences between macros and VBA

In brief, the differences between macros and VBA procedures are as follows:

- Access macros automate a series of *actions*, most of which correspond to commands you can perform in the Access user interface (via a menu or toolbar button). You can open tables, run queries, display forms, print reports, and so on. Chapter 43 covers the basics of writing Access macros.

- VBA procedures in Access are like those you write in any of the other Office applications. The only thing unique about them is that they can make direct use of the programming objects that belong to Access itself. VBA isn't tied to the Access user interface, so its ways of looking at and working with databases can be very different, and more powerful, than the way the user interface works.

Secret

Despite these real differences, the division between macros and VBA isn't airtight. A macro can run VBA function procedures, and Access VBA code can use the methods of the DoCmd object to execute macro actions. And don't overlook Access's capability to convert macros to VBA procedures. To make the conversion, start by selecting the macro object in the database window (don't open it). Alternatively, if the macro is connected to a form or report, you can open the form or report in Design view. Then choose Tools ➪ Macro ➪ Convert Macros to Visual Basic.

When to use macros, when VBA

How to decide between macros and VBA? In a nutshell, macros are easier but VBA is much more powerful.

Secret

Here's my advice: Unless you're sure macros are sufficient for all your applications, skip macros. Yes, the learning curve for VBA is steeper, and it may take longer to finish your first applications. But the investment is worth it. The skills you pick up as you build simple applications apply directly to the more complicated ones you're surely going to want later. And if you find your "simple" application needs more features than you expected, coding it in VBA means you won't have to start from scratch to add them.

Actually, Access doesn't force you to choose between macros and VBA — you can use both in a single application. If you're willing to learn both tool sets, you can have the best of both worlds.

Advantages of macros

Now for some details. Macros are easier to use than VBA for two main reasons. First, if you're familiar with the Access user interface, building an application using macros is a simple extension of skills you already know. Most macro actions are equivalent to commands you use regularly. In addition, Access gives you plenty of hand-holding as you construct a macro, providing fill-in-the-blank fields for the arguments needed for each action in the Macro window.

Macros have other advantages besides ease of use. Their strengths include:

- You can define keyboard shortcuts for the entire application — as opposed to individual forms — only with macros, not with VBA. Chapter 43 covers this technique.
- Macros are faster and require less memory than VBA modules. For a given form or report you realize this advantage only if *no* VBA code is attached to the object (see "Maximum efficiency with minimum VBA code" later in this chapter).

Advantages of VBA

VBA has many advantages over macros. Compared to macros, VBA code is:

- **Easier to maintain.** As an application becomes more complex, VBA makes it much easier to keep track of the flow of your program because you can work with a variety of related procedures in the same module. Because the VBA code for a form, report, or data access page is part of the object, the code accompanies the object if you move it to a different database.
- **Easier to debug.** Access's Visual Basic Editor includes the advanced debugging tools covered in Chapter 23. Access provides no similar features for macros.
- **More flexible.** Although macros can test conditions and perform different actions accordingly, VBA's complete set of control structures is much more sophisticated. Combined with your ability to specify the arguments for a VBA procedure while the program runs, your programs can respond much more flexibly to current conditions than macros ever could.
- **Better at computations.** VBA lets you code custom functions to perform sophisticated, tailor-made calculations on numbers or text.
- **Better at handling errors.** Macros give you a generic error message when an error occurs. With VBA, *you* can decide what happens when an error occurs — your code can attempt to correct the problem, and it can display custom error messages with detailed information.

VBA offers one other big benefit: You can use the Visual Basic language to write database applications in any Office application, or in the stand-alone version of Visual Basic. Once you're familiar with database objects and their methods and properties, you can work with them in any Visual Basic environment — and as discussed in the next section, a Visual Basic environment other than Access may be the right choice.

When *not* to use Access for database applications

Because Access is Office's database program, it seems only logical that you would use Access to build custom database applications. However, it turns out that there are good reasons to consider other options.

What you have to keep in mind is that Access itself doesn't actually manage your database. That role belongs to the database engine, the software responsible for storing and retrieving data. (The database engines available for use with Access, Jet, and MSDE/SQL Server are discussed in "Choosing a Database Engine" in Chapter 43.) Access's real job is simply to provide a means for you to interact with the underlying database engine. The Access user interface is full of creature comforts such as its graphical query designer and its customizable forms and reports, all of which make it easy to request the data you want to work with and control how you want to see the data displayed. But as nice as those tools are, they are quite separate from the database engine that actually does the grunt work of locating and extracting the data you're interested in. Figure 45-2 illustrates this separation of roles schematically.

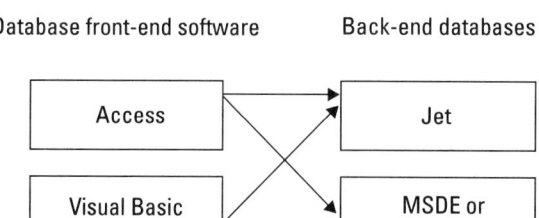

Figure 45-2: This illustration shows how you can pair different database front ends with different database engines.

The point is that because the database user interface and the database engine are distinct pieces of software, you can use tools other than Access to tell the engine what you want it to do. That's exactly what you're doing when you build a database application in VBA. Even if you code the application inside Access, your VBA code speaks to the database engine not through Access, but through a completely independent software component such as ADO or DAO (these components and their acronyms are defined in Chapter 46).

Database application development options

So if Access isn't your only option for control of the database engine, what tool should you use to code your database applications? Your choices and their respective benefits include:

- **Access.** VBA applications built from inside Access can make direct use of Access objects such as forms and reports. Because Access forms and reports have built-in database functionality, they can shorten the development cycle significantly over generic VBA. Also, Access is the best choice for applications that you create for personal use, when you expect to be adding new features frequently as the need arises and your time permits.

- **Another Office application such as Word or Excel.** In many custom applications, database access is only part of the function. If your planned application requires significant word processing or number crunching features, creating it in Word or Excel lets you take direct advantage of that program's resources. Through ADO or a similar component, your VBA code can still retrieve, display, and manipulate database data. And the application will be smaller, faster, and less complicated than if you use COM to automate Access from, say, Word (or automate Word from Access). Unaided, VBA forms and reports aren't database-aware, but the code required to manually connect a form to data isn't all that daunting. Besides, you can buy Office Developer or third-party toolkits to bind controls and forms to data. And you can transfer your work directly to other VBA applications because it won't be dependent on Access-specific forms.

- **Visual Basic proper (not VBA).** Visual Basic is a great tool for database development. Your Visual Basic code can connect to databases via ADO just as in VBA, and Visual Basic forms are database-aware much as those of Access are. An application created with Visual Basic has two big advantages over one created within a VBA program like Access, Word, or Excel. First, it's always a lot faster, because Visual Basic applications are compiled rather than interpreted when you run them. Second, you can freely distribute the application to others — they don't need a copy of the host VBA application. The only real drawback is that you have to buy Visual Basic.

Why Access still may have a role

Even if you decide to forego Access as your development environment, Access is still a great tool for the database application developer. Using its comfortable commands, you can quickly build the tables and queries that constitute the database. You can write and test your VBA code in Access and move it to the final environment when everything is working right. And you can quickly prototype the application's forms.

The only problem is that you can't export those forms to the final application. To belabor the point, Access forms are incompatible with both standard VBA UserForms and the forms used by Visual Basic. However, you can overcome this limitation, at least to a degree, with a commercial utility called Access Upsizer (n-Dimensional Software, 888-270-6346). Access Upsizer converts Access applications to equivalent VBA projects, converting the forms to Visual Basic forms (not VBA UserForms).

Applications by Magic: Using the Database Wizards

The easiest way to create a working application is to let Access do it for you. The wizards supplied with Access demonstrate the power and benefits of applications, but the applications they create for you are useful in their own right, too. Included in the collection that comes with Access are wizards for common business database tasks, such as contact management and inventory control, and wizards for keeping track of personal information, such as your video collection or your fitness workouts.

To use the wizards, click the New button on the toolbar (only available when the Database window is active) or choose File ⇨ New. In the resulting New dialog box, double-click Database to create a new Jet-based database, or double-click Project (New Database) to create an MSDE/SQL Server project. Again, the section "Choosing a Database Engine" in Chapter 43 discusses the differences between Jet and MSDE.

You can also use the wizards on the Databases tab of the New dialog box to create new Jet databases. When you open a wizard, it walks you through a series of panels in which you can choose which fields to include in the application and set basic formatting options for your forms and reports. Based on your choices, the wizard creates the database objects your application needs, plugging in Visual Basic procedures where necessary. All of the objects and the code are available for you to play with, so you can study how Access put the application together. You can customize or add to the existing objects as you see fit.

Realistically, of course, even the most wonder-working wizard can't anticipate your specific information-management needs. After you've generated a few sample applications with the wizards, you're going to want to dig in and create your own.

Building Custom Applications in Access

In outline, the process of constructing an application in Access is really pretty simple. You start by creating a set of basic database building blocks, and then you connect them together to form the application.

Designing the user interface

As an Access application developer, one of your important tasks is to craft a customized user interface that looks inviting and unique and at the same time serves its function efficiently. Fortunately, you can devote most of your attention to aesthetics and the behind-the-scenes functionality of your application — the mechanics of building a customized user interface are straightforward. By taking advantage of the drag-and-drop customization features of Office, you can put together your forms, toolbars, and menus with a minimum of hassle.

Setting up switchboards

Chapter 47 discusses the basics of creating forms in Access. The layout techniques described there also apply when you're building switchboards and other forms used not to display data, but to activate other features of the application.

The only thing special about such forms is that they aren't associated with any table or query in the database. When you create a form of this type in the New Form dialog box, just leave blank the line that asks you to select a table or query for the form. You can now use the form as a primary element in your custom user interface without worrying about its connection to your data.

Using the Switchboard Manager

Secret

Choose Tools ⇨ Database Utilities ⇨ Switchboard Manager to start the Switchboard Manager, a utility that creates functioning switchboard forms (see Figure 45-3). The forms you wind up with look much like those built by the wizards for the sample applications that come with Access. They're nice, and perfectly serviceable, but not very distinctive. You can edit them with the form design tools discussed in Chapter 47.

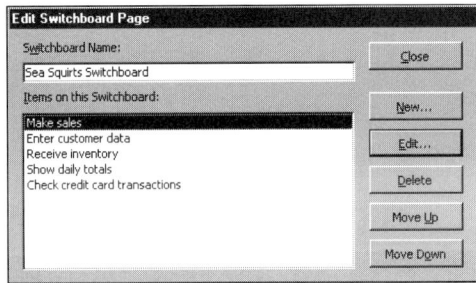

Figure 45-3: The Switchboard Manager add-in creates generic but attractive switchboard forms for you.

Setting your startup form

The switchboard or other form that you want users to see when they first run your application is the *startup form.* Specify the startup form in the Display Form/Page drop-down list of the Tools ⇨ Startup dialog box.

Customizing command bars for your application

The basic techniques for creating custom toolbars, menu bars, and buttons in Access are the same ones you can use in any Office application (see Chapter 5). However, Access gives you more direct control over technical settings for these items than do the other Office applications.

Creating new menu bars, toolbars, and shortcut menus

When you're constructing a custom application, you should create custom toolbars from scratch rather than modify the existing toolbars.

Although you can create custom toolbars in the other Office applications, Access alone lets you change a toolbar's properties without VBA code. To do this, go to the Toolbars tab of the Tools ⇨ Customize dialog box and choose Properties. A secondary dialog box appears. Here, selecting a toolbar from the drop-down list lets you modify its settings (see Figure 45-4).

Figure 45-4: You can view and alter basic toolbar properties from this dialog box.

The Toolbar Properties dialog box gives you control over whether the toolbars in your application can be customized, moved, docked, hidden, and so forth. If you're working on a custom toolbar, rather than one that's built in, you can also control the type of toolbar you're building.

Attaching custom toolbars and menu bars to forms and reports

Secret

You can designate any of your custom toolbars as a menu bar by using the Type drop-down list in the Toolbar Properties dialog box. You can then attach it — loosely speaking — to a form or report, or make it the default menu bar for the whole database. To set up a menu bar for a form or report, assign it to the `Menu Bar` property in the Properties sheet for that object, working in Design view. From then on, every time the object is activated in your application, the specified menu bar appears at the top of the screen, just below the title bar, replacing the global one.

And speaking of global menu bars, you can set up a custom menu bar for the whole database in the Tools ⇨ Startup dialog box. The menu bar you select there will be visible instead of Access's default bar except when the current form or report has been assigned a different menu bar.

Regular, non-menu toolbars can also be attached to a form or report, this time using the object's `Toolbar` property. When the user of your application switches to that object, the specified toolbar appears, not Access's default for that object type. With a form, for example, the Form View toolbar would no longer be visible; instead, the specified custom toolbar would appear.

Creating custom shortcut menus

Secret

In the Toolbar Properties dialog box, designating a custom toolbar as a Popup Type box converts the toolbar into a shortcut menu, ready to receive new right-click commands. While the Customize dialog box remains open, it appears on the Custom menu of the Shortcut Menus toolbar, where you can add menu items to it. Why the term Popup is used here instead of shortcut menu is beyond me.

Adding custom commands to the toolbars

Just as Word lets you assign individual fonts to toolbar buttons, Access is set up so that you can easily fill your toolbars with buttons that display specific tables, queries, forms, and reports. Click one of these custom buttons, and the associated object will open immediately. Just as in Word, you can place your macros on toolbar buttons, too.

Using the Customize dialog box, switch to the Command tab and locate the items labeled All Tables, All Queries, and so on, on the menu. Then just drag one of those objects up to its resting point on the toolbar.

Secret

Opening a database object by clicking a toolbar button amounts to the same thing as opening it in the Database window. You can't control which view it opens in, or carry out any other actions in the process. To get the results you want, create an appropriate macro and assign *it* to the toolbar.

Working with properties for command bar controls

Access gives you direct, dialog box–style control over a number of settings pertaining to individual *controls* on the command bars, including menu items and toolbar buttons. In the other Office applications, you would need VBA code to modify these options. With the Customize dialog box open, right-click a button or menu item and then choose Properties at the bottom of the shortcut menu. The Properties dialog box shown in Figure 45-5 appears.

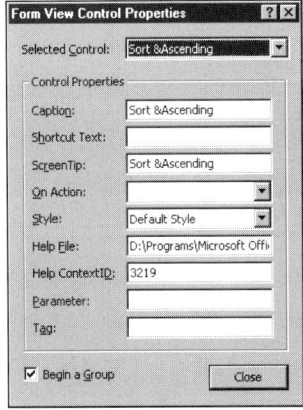

Figure 45-5: Use this Control Properties dialog box to specify settings for toolbar buttons and menu items in your custom applications.

Chapter 45: Secrets of Database Application Design

Access is the only Office application that doesn't force you to use VBA to specify the text displayed alongside a control when it's used as a menu item. This text is usually used to list the corresponding keyboard shortcut for the control. In Access, type the text of your choice into the Shortcut Text. Similarly, the ToolTip item lets you enter custom text that will appear when the user rests the mouse pointer over the control.

Assigning VBA functions to toolbar buttons

Combined with the Control Properties dialog box (Figure 45-5), a special toolbar item called Custom Command gives you one-click access to any Visual Basic function procedure. To set this up, start by writing the function using the Visual Basic Editor. This technique only works with functions, not with Sub procedures, so be sure you use the correct syntax.

Once the function is complete, open the Customize dialog box. At the very top of the Commands list, you should see Custom command (if not, be sure File is selected in the Categories list). Drag the Custom command onto a toolbar. Right-click it and choose Properties to bring up the necessary dialog box. Now you can type in an expression that runs the function in the On Action field. If your function is called StayAlert, for example, you would enter =StayAlert( ).

Setting startup options and securing your custom interface

Use the Tools ⇨ Startup dialog box to take full control of what users see when they run your application and what tools they have access to. To ensure a fully customized environment, clear all of the check boxes in the Startup dialog box and specify your own menu bar, shortcut menu, and display form.

Clearing the Display Database Window box, for example, prevents the appearance of the generic Access main window — hardly an appropriate focus of attention when you're trying to grab attention for your own screens. To prevent users from activating the Database window by way of the keyboard, you must also clear the box labeled Use Access Special Keys (choose Advanced if you don't see that box).

Even with these measures in place, anyone with a little experience can open up your application and get at Access itself. For example, users could make changes to the toolbars, just as you can when you run Access without special customizations. They could display or hide custom toolbars, position them on the screen where they wanted them, and freely customize them by adding or deleting buttons — or entire toolbars, for that matter.

To lock the user interface so that it can't be changed, follow these three steps:

1. Position each of the application's toolbars where they belong. Now use the settings in the Toolbar Properties dialog box (earlier Figure 45-4) to allow or prevent users from moving, resizing, or docking each toolbar.

2. Open the Tools ⇨ Startup dialog box and uncheck Allow Toolbar/Menu changes. This prevents access to the Customize menu bar and to the View ⇨ Toolbars menu and keeps the current toolbars on the screen no matter what. It doesn't prevent users from moving, resizing, or docking the toolbars.

3. So far, so good. Now you need a way to keep users from changing that setting you just made in the Startup dialog box. That requires password protection via user-level security, covered in Chapter 13.

Maximum efficiency with minimum VBA code

Secret

Although it's often necessary and desirable to write VBA code, you can sometimes get by without it — and there are good reasons to minimize your use of code in an Access application. One reason, of course, is to protect your free time. VBA, powerful as it is, demands a lot from the programmer. In addition, though, VBA imposes a performance penalty on your application and increases its size.

After all, most of the work in a typical application involves setting up simple connections between user interface elements, such as buttons, and ordinary database objects, such as forms or queries. Much of the time, all you want a control to do is take you to another object in the database. In this situation, lightweight forms will suffice — you don't need VBA. Likewise, VBA code may not be necessary for large-scale updates and deletions of records in the database. Instead, you can construct an action query as one of the objects in your database and then call it from a lightweight form.

Using lightweight objects

A *lightweight* form or report is simply one that has no attached VBA module. That doesn't mean the form is crippled. As Chapter 47 makes clear, it can still display field data by way of controls that are bound to fields in the database. In addition, controls can be assigned hyperlinks that navigate to and open other database objects without the aid of VBA. Alternatively, you can use macros to perform actions such as hiding or displaying custom toolbars when the form is opened or just about any other event occurs.

Compared to an object that includes a VBA module, a lightweight form or report takes up less room on a disk and loads into memory faster. Unless you really need the advanced features of VBA, it can make sense to avoid adding a module to the object.

Checking for attached VBA modules

Secret

You can tell whether a form or report has an attached module by looking at the `HasModule` property in the object's Properties sheet. The `HasModule` property is near the bottom of the Other tab.

Caution

Don't use the View ⇨ Code command to find out whether the object has an attached module. This command creates a module if one didn't exist already. Even an empty module is a drag on performance and consumes an additional chunk of memory.

Deleting attached VBA modules

Once a form or report has an attached module, it remains in place until you explicitly set the `HasModule` property back to No. When you do, the module and all the code it contains are permanently deleted.

Using action queries to minimize VBA coding

Many situations require operations on a number of records as a group. At the beginning of each month, for example, you may want to place all the records entered the previous month in a separate archive table for safekeeping. Instead of coding this task in VBA, where it would require a substantial chunk of code, you should use an action query.

As the name implies, action queries don't just retrieve data, they perform some action on the data they find. In this case, you would use query Design view to set up a query that filters records by entry date, using the previous month as the criterion. Instead of hard-coding the month, you would enter in the query's Criteria row an expression such as this one:

```
Month([DateField])= If(Month(Now())=1,12,Month(Now())-1)
```

where `DateField` is the name of the field containing the dates you want to screen the records by. You would then choose Query ⇨ Make-Table Query. Enter the name of the archive table you wish to create, and you're ready to run the query. It culls the previous month's records from the complete database, exporting them to a new table.

Once the query is ready, you can assign it to a control on your application's switchboard or another similar form. In the macro window, use the `OpenQuery` action to activate the query, specifying its name as the `Query Name` property. You may want to precede the `OpenQuery` action with the `SetWarnings` action to turn off the cautionary message that Access otherwise displays when executing an action query. After the macro is saved, you can use the Properties dialog box to assign it to any of the events recognized by a form or report or one of their controls.

Writing VBA code in Access

While the techniques described so far are adequate for many simple applications, Visual Basic code is always available should you need its power. Part VI covers the basic concepts and skills you need to write VBA modules for every Office application. Although the core elements of Visual Basic hold throughout Office, all VBA applications including Access have their own set of objects. In Access, the most important of these are its form, report, and data access page objects, and the objects for the individual controls on these items. Chapter 47 discusses techniques for working with these items in Access VBA.

Distributing the Application

After you've completed the construction of the application building blocks, added the connecting code, and tested all of its components thoroughly, you're ready to distribute your magnum opus to an eager public. The following sections cover issues to consider when preparing the completed application for distribution.

Splitting a Jet database for network use

In most organizations, the typical database application is intended for use by multiple individuals and on a number of different PCs. If you're sending out your project to more than one person, and if the group has a reliable network, your best bet is usually to set up the application in two parts — one on each person's computer, the other on a network server. In this scenario, each person has a separate copy of the user interface portions of the application — all of the custom forms and toolbars — as well as functional items such as queries, macros, and modules. The database itself — the tables and the data they contain — are stored on a network server where they're accessible to everyone.

Breaking up an application this way makes sense for several reasons. For one, network data are usually more secure, and the backup schedule can be supervised more closely. In addition, because everyone is working with the same copy of the database, you don't have to worry about maintaining, and keeping synchronized, several separate sets of data.

Another advantage in splitting up a database is that the application becomes easier to distribute. Those big tables need to be placed on the server only once. Updating and upgrading the rest of the application should be relatively easy, because in a database of any size, the user interface portion makes up a relatively small amount of the total bulk of the software.

Access supports this split-database configuration by design. In the case of Access projects based on MSDE/SQL Server databases, data are always stored separately from the project itself. For its part, a Jet-based Access application can be readily linked to tables located on any accessible disk drive, server, or Internet site. If you're linking to external tables that already exist, use the File ➪ Get External Data ➪ Link Tables command to locate and link the outside tables to the current database. On the other hand, if you want to place tables from the current database into a different file, use Access's Database Splitter.

Before you break up your completed application, you should decide where on the network your data tables should go. Then, with a good network connection, choose Tools ➪ Database Utilities ➪ Database Splitter. The Database Splitter Wizard steps you through the procedure, asking you where it should store the new back-end database. Soon, it starts the process of dividing the raw data tables from the rest of the current database (the front-end portion of the application) and placing them in the new database. If everything goes well, it updates the front-end database with links to the tables in their new location. The application now consists of two separate database files, but it works exactly as it did as a single file.

Database replication

When it's not possible or practical to connect all your users to the same server, Access provides database replication as a way to keep everyone on the same page. A replicated database is simply a set of two or more copies of the same information, set up so that they can be kept synchronized as the data in each copy changes.

One of these *replicas* serves as the Design Master, the only copy in which changes to the overall database design can be made. But everyone with the application can change, add to, or delete records. Each time the databases are synchronized, changes made to any replica database are duplicated in all the others. The process is incremental — only changed data are transferred from one database to the other — so it's relatively quick.

Replication is preferred over splitting a database when connections to the network are slow or intermittent, such as when the company sales force connects its laptops to the main network. If each laptop user has a copy of the entire database, each has access to reasonably current data at all times and can still plug into the network for a quick incremental update anytime.

The replication commands are on the Tools ➪ Replication submenu. After using the Create Replica command to get things started, you convert that new database to a Design Master. The Design Master can then be used to make further replicas for other users.

Securing your files

When your database application is fully tested, consider saving it as an .mde file. This process strips out the Visual Basic source code after first compiling it. Although the application runs the same — better in fact, because it uses less memory — no one can see your programming work or modify the design of components such as forms and queries.

To save an application as an .mde file, choose Tools ➪ Database Utilities ➪ Make MDE file. You get to name the new .mde file, of course. Access doesn't alter the original File, which you should keep somewhere safe yet accessible for the inevitable day you need to make upgrades.

Conclusion

Despite the depth and complexity of the Visual Basic development system, creating fully functioning, highly productive database applications is a goal well within the reach of a *Microsoft Office 2000 Secrets* reader. If you start with a set of well-crafted tables and queries and spend some time designing clean-looking information forms, the rest is easy. All you need to do is add a few switchboards, plugging them into your database objects with some simple navigational actions. Add some custom menus and toolbars, and you have a customized database power application you can call your own.

Chapter 46

Working with Data Using VBA

In This Chapter

- Understanding database programming technology
- Choosing a database object model
- Writing database code using ActiveX Data Objects
- Getting up to speed with SQL

Although this chapter resides in the Access section, its scope extends way beyond Access alone. Through VBA, *any* Office application can make full use of information housed in databases on your own PC, a network server, or the Internet. This chapter covers VBA coding techniques for managing data that work in all Office applications. Refer back to Chapter 42 for a full discussion of the options you have for working with databases, including Access alone, Access supplemented by VBA, VBA in other Office applications, and stand-alone Visual Basic applications.

An Introduction to VBA Database Programming

Before you can start writing database code, you need a bit of background on the technology and terminology involved. This brief section provides those basics.

Using DoCmd in Access

You should know about one difference between Access and the other Office applications when it comes to VBA. It's this: Access includes an entirely separate system for VBA database programming based on the DoCmd object. The DoCmd object encapsulates all the commands available from Access's menu system. With it, you can open tables, run queries, run reports, display forms, and fiddle with the user interface . . . in other words, anything a user can do sitting in front of the computer.

If you're an Access veteran without much previous programming experience, the DoCmd object provides a familiar handhold as you transition to VBA. The problem with DoCmd is that it confines you to Access, while with standard VBA your skills translate directly to all other Visual Basic environments.

Even if you opt for "pure" VBA, you still can't do entirely without the DoCmd object for applications you create in Access. Perhaps because Access forms aren't standard VBA forms, the Show method doesn't work—instead, to display forms in an Access VBA application, you must use the OpenForm method of the DoCmd object.

SQL and VBA

The Structured Query Language (SQL) is the reigning standard for database queries—every data management system from Access to Oracle recognizes SQL. SQL is the key to getting things done in a database application. SQL statements enable you to select, modify, or delete specific sets of records that you choose.

So how do SQL and VBA complement one another? It's through VBA—working through one of several database object models—that you execute those SQL commands. And once an SQL command has produced a set of records from the database for use by your application, VBA takes over, enabling you to display and modify the retrieved information.

As befits its fundamental importance, SQL rates a full section of its own later in this chapter. The techniques for incorporating SQL statements into your VBA code are covered both there and before that, in the section "Writing Database Code with ADO."

All about database objects

Choosing VBA for your database work leads directly to yet another decision point: Which *database object model* are you going to use? VBA alone doesn't provide a means for you to access and manipulate databases. Coupled with a database object model, however, VBA becomes an extremely capable database-programming tool.

The job of a database object model is to turn databases and their components—tables, queries, and reports—into objects that behave just like the other objects you use in VBA. That is, you manipulate them using their properties, methods, and events (see Chapter 22). Because the database is "packaged" as a set of objects, you don't have to muck around with the details of the database's structure. Additionally, you can use the same set of objects to manipulate many different types of databases.

In recent years Microsoft has developed and promoted several of these database object models, resulting in a confusing array of acronyms. The three main options are DAO, RDO, and ADO.

DAO (Data Access Objects)

DAO was the default object model for database programming in Office 95 and 97. It provides a complete set of objects for working with all types of databases, whether they are local (on your own PC) or remote (somewhere else). DAO enables access to different types of databases simultaneously — for example, a custom application might blend together information residing in Access, dBase, and Oracle databases. One problem with DAO is that it provides slightly different object models for local and network data access. By itself, DAO isn't designed for industrial strength client/server applications, although DAO becomes much more potent in that area with the help of ODBCDirect (described in the next section).

RDO (Remote Data Objects)

The RDO object model was designed for accessing SQL databases located on a server and isn't appropriate for use with desktop-type databases such as Jet, dBase, or Paradox. RDO is provided with the high-end Enterprise versions of Microsoft development tools. Advanced features of RDO include disconnected recordsets (the capability to work with records without maintaining a constant connection to the server) and asynchronous queries (which lets the application regain control while the query is still running).

ADO (ActiveX Data Objects)

ADO is intended to be the object model of choice from here on out, superseding and improving upon both DAO and RDO. ADO provides a single, simpler, and more consistent object model for working with both local and remote data. It includes all the major-league features needed for large-scale networked applications with many simultaneous users, yet it works well for single-user desktop projects as well. And unlike DAO and RDO, ADO also can access non-SQL data — meaning it can easily tap storehouses of data such as Outlook that don't recognize SQL.

So which object model do you use?

The simple message here is that you should use ADO for all new database applications. Office 2000 does include an updated version of DAO, which means you can run and enhance any older DAO-based applications you still use. But ADO's advantages are clear-cut, and besides, it's the only object model Microsoft plans to develop and fully support (for now, at least — the way these folks work, I won't be surprised if the next release of Office comes with something called DOA).

Some related database technologies

You're going to see several other terms in connection with Office database programming, so you'd better know a little about them. *ODBC* (Open Database Connectivity) is an older Microsoft programming standard for accessing all kinds of structured data via SQL. ODBC was designed with the programming habits of its day in mind, so it requires you to use C/C++ function calls—not something you want to play around with in VBA. But because ODBC has been around for years, ODBC drivers are available for almost every database type imaginable. I should also mention that RDO relies on ODBC, translating ODBC function calls into objects that Visual Basic programmers can readily use.

ODBCDirect is part of DAO. ODBCDirect is a software layer that converts ODBC function calls into DAO objects, enabling you to use DAO to access any database for which you have an ODBC driver. (Although ODBCDirect is based on RDO, it doesn't provide all the features available via RDO itself.) Prior to the invention of ODBCDirect, Access developers could connect to ODBC databases through Jet. However, doing so slowed things down and didn't provide the advanced server-related features available via ODBC.

OLE DB is a new Microsoft specification for data access roughly comparable to and replacing ODBC. Based on COM rather than SQL, OLE DB should in theory enable simpler and more flexible access to any type of information that can be represented in tabular form. That information might be stored in a desktop database, an SQL-based database on a server, a collection of e-mail messages, or a geographical, map-based data system. ADO relies on OLE DB rather than ODBC to present database objects to the programmer. However, because specific OLE DB Providers (drivers) aren't yet available for all data sources, ADO comes with an additional component called the ODBC Provider that can connect any ODBC database through OLE DB to ADO.

Writing Database Code with ADO

Although designing the right SQL statements can be tough, writing database code with ADO itself isn't all that difficult. You have only three main objects to master—Connection, Recordset, and Command—and their properties and methods are implemented logically.

Error handling

Although I don't spotlight the critical role of error handling code in this chapter, the omission is only because space is limited. Be sure to include an error handler in every database procedure you write. Chapter 23 has details on constructing error handlers in VBA.

Creating a reference to ADO in your project

Before you can use ADO and its objects in a VBA program, you must first establish a reference to the ADO software, or type library, in your project. In the Visual Basic Editor, choose Tools ⇨ References and check the box for

Microsoft ActiveX Data Objects 2.x Library (as I write this, the current version of ADO is 2.1). Unless you plan to use both ADO and DAO in the same project — not generally a good idea, but perhaps necessary if you're mixing old code with new — be sure to clear all boxes for Microsoft DAO (you may have several DAO versions on your computer).

Caution

If you do combine DAO and ADO in the same project, you must preface all references to ADO objects with the object identifier ADODB, as in ADODB.Connection. Because similar DAO and ADO objects have the same names, VBA needs to know which object model you mean. You can omit the identifier in projects that don't refer to DAO.

Establishing the connection

Your first order of business in accessing a given *data source* (a database or other repository of data) is to establish a *connection* to that data source. You can think of the Connection object as the communications pipeline between your program and the data.

Connecting to the open database in Access

Secret

This is really important! If you're using Access to write ADO code, you don't need to create a new Connection object to work with the Jet database that's already open in Access. That's because Access sets up the necessary Connection object for you automatically. Use the Connection property of Access's CurrentProject object to reference the database as a connection. This code fragment shows how to do it:

```
Dim conADOConnection As Connection
Set conADOConnection = CurrentProject.Connection
```

In similar fashion, you can easily connect to the underlying SQL Server database in an Access project, as long you're writing code in that project in Access. In this case, you need the BaseConnectionString property of the CurrentProject object, as illustrated in the following example:

```
Dim conADO As New Connection
conADO.ConnectionString = CurrentProject.BaseConnectionString
```

Creating Connection objects

Under any other circumstances, you must create the Connection object yourself. To create a Connection object, just declare the variable name for your object and then *open* the connection. The Open method takes as its argument a *connection string* containing various parameters that specify the OLE DB Provider you're using and the specific data source you're accessing. Alternatively, you can first set properties of the Connection object corresponding to the items in the connection string, and then use the Open method by itself. Check out these two equivalent examples, which both create a Connection object for the same Jet database:

```
' Example 1
Dim conADOConnection As New Connection, strConnect As String
strConnect = "Provider=Microsoft.Jet.OLEDB.4.0;" _
    & "Data Source=C:\Data\Toys"
conADOConnection.Open strConnect

' Example 2
Dim conADOConnection As New Connection
With conADOConnection
    .Provider = "Microsoft.Jet.OLEDB.4.0"
    .Properties("Data Source") = "C:\Data\Toys"
    .Open
End With
```

The parameters required by the Open method vary depending on the Provider you're using — consult the Help system, Microsoft's Web site, and Office Developer documentation for details. The following example is for SQL Server:

```
Dim conADOConnection As New Connection, strConnect As String
strConnect = "Provider=SQLOLEDB;Data Source=Hecate;" & _
    "Initial Catalog=toys;User ID=sa;Password=;"
conADOConnection.Open strConnect
```

If you're working in Access, ADO falls short of a universal data management solution. Access projects can connect only to SQL Server/MSDE databases, and not to other OLE DB Providers. Also, creating a connection to an SQL Server database using Access VBA requires different parameters than those used in other development environments. In Access, the Provider property must be set to MSDataShape, whereas the Data Provider property is the one you set to SQLOLEDB.

Connecting on the fly

Secret

Unlike DAO and RDO, ADO enables you to work with database objects without first creating a Connection object — you can associate those objects with a connection when it's time to fill them with real data. Alternatively, you can create a connection implicitly in the process of defining a Recordset or Command object. However, creating the Connection object explicitly makes your code easier to follow and enables you to associate the same connection with multiple other objects.

Working with Recordset objects

Get closely acquainted with Recordset objects — you use them constantly for fundamental data operations. As the name implies, a Recordset object is a container for records drawn from a data source. As befits a container, the same Recordset object can hold different records at different times.

Creating a recordset

Once you've declared a variable for a recordset, you can immediately start working with the object's properties. At this point, however, it only exists in a sort of virtual form. To fill the empty container with actual records, you use any of the following techniques:

- The Recordset object's own Open method
- The Execute method of a Command object
- The Execute method of a Connection object

Creating recordsets using the Open method

The simplest technique for creating a recordset is by way of the Open method of the Recordset object itself. The Open method works well when you're using simple SQL Select statements to request the records of interest. The following code shows how to set up a recordset using the Open method:

```
Dim conMan As New Connection
Dim rstMan As Recordset
Dim strSQL As String
... (Code creating the conMan connection object goes here)
strSQL = "SELECT * FROM Toys" ' select the entire Toys table
Set rstMan.ActiveConnection = conMan
rstMan.Open strSQL, , adOpenForwardOnly, adLockReadOnly, adCmdText
```

Note how the preceding sample code associates a connection with the recordset by setting the recordset's ActiveConnection property. Note, too, how options governing the recordset's behavior are included as arguments to the Open method.

Creating recordsets using the Command object

SQL SELECT statements only take you so far — in client/server applications, efficiency often dictates that you obtain recordsets by executing stored procedures (queries). When such procedures require parameters, creating a Recordset object using a Command object is the way to go.

Set up the Command object first, setting its ActiveConnection property to the desired connection and feeding it your SQL string. You can then turn your attention to the Recordset object. In this case, you must set its options as properties first. You then fill it with records by setting it to the results of the Command object's Execute method. Here's an example:

```
Dim conTest As New Connection
Dim cmdTest As New Command
Dim rstTest As Recordset
Dim strSQL As String
... (Code creating the conTest connection object
... and defining the strSQL string goes here)
' Create the command object:
  With cmdTest
    Set .ActiveConnection = conTest
```

```
        .CommandText = strSQL
        .CommandType = adCmdText
    End With
rstTest.CursorType = adOpenForwardOnly
rstTest.LockType = adLockReadOnly
Set rstTest = cmdTest.Execute()
```

Creating recordsets using the Connection object

The final technique for creating recordsets involves the Connection object's Execute method. This approach is simpler than using the Command object but still enables you to access stored procedures, though if they require parameters you have to include these in your SQL string. The following code is illustrative:

```
Dim conVert As New Connection
Dim rstVert As Recordset
Dim strSQL As String
... (Code creating the conVert connection object
... and defining the strSQL string goes here)
rstVert.CursorType = adOpenForwardOnly
rstVert.LockType = adLockReadOnly
Set rstVert = conTest.Execute(strSQL)
```

Creating a connection on the fly

If you know you're going to need a connection for only one recordset, creating the connection first offers no particular advantage. Instead, you can include the connection string as the second argument of the Recordset object's Open method, as shown in this sample code:

```
Dim rstInPeace As New Recordset
Dim strSQL As String, strConnect As String

strSQL = "SELECT * FROM Bicycles" ' Retrieve all records
' code assigning the connection string to strConnect goes here
rstInPeace.Open strSQL, strConnect, adOpenForwardOnly
```

Setting Recordset options

You have control over the type of recordset you create via various settings that determine the cursor type, lock type, and so on. You specify the settings you want in one of two forms, depending on the technique you use to create the recordset: as arguments to the Recordset object's Open method, or as properties of the Recordset object. The code fragments in the previous sections demonstrate both forms.

Choosing a cursor type

In database parlance, a *cursor* refers to the functionality required to navigate through a set of records. The cursor type you choose for a Recordset object determines how free the user is to work with the records it contains and whether changes made by other users automatically appear in the recordset. Use the CursorType property or the corresponding argument of the Open statement to specify your choice. Table 46-1 lists the available options. The default cursor type is Forward-only.

Table 46-1   Cursor Types Available for ADO Recordset Objects

Cursor Type	Constant for CursorType Property	Definition
Forward-only	`adOpenForwardOnly`	Allows movement through the recordset only in the forward direction, either by a specified number of records or to the last record. Changes made by other users don't appear until the recordset is closed and reopened. This type offers the fastest performance but is only appropriate when you need to run through the records only once.
Static	`adOpenStatic`	A fixed recordset that can't be updated and doesn't reflect changes made by other users until it is closed and reopened. It allows free movement. Good for finding data and creating reports, and faster than the Keyset and Dynamic types.
Keyset	`adOpenKeyset`	A recordset whose records and their values can be changed, in turn changing the corresponding items in the underlying data source. The recordset doesn't reflect changes made by other users, however.
Dynamic	`adOpenDynamic`	Like a keyset-type recordset, except that it does reflect changes made by other users to the underlying data.

Choosing a cursor location

The Resultset object's `CursorLocation` property lets you specify whether the cursor resides on the client (user's) computer or on the server. Set it to either `adUseClient` or `adUseServer`, respectively. In general, you should use client-side cursors with SQL Server and other networked databases, and server-side cursors with Jet databases. You can set a default cursor location for all the recordsets of a connection via the Connection object's `CursorType` property.

Locks

The `LockType` property for a Recordset object determines how your program responds when two or more users try to edit the same record at the same time. The default setting is adLockPessimistic, which prevents you or anyone else from making changes to the records. If you want to be able to edit the recordset, you must set the `LockType` property to one of the other settings shown in Table 46-2.

Table 46-2   Lock Options for ADO Recordset Objects

Lock Type	Constant for LockType Property	Definition
No locks	`adLockOptimistic`	Multiple users can edit the same record at the same time, but they receive notice that the changes they make may conflict with another user's changes (records are locked only when the `Update` method is in progress, and then only one at a time). Good for single-user databases, and in multiuser databases when the most recent information is assumed to be always correct and complete.
	`adLockBatchOptimistic`	Same as the preceding, except that records are locked when they are being updated in batches (groups) instead of individually.
Read only (all records)	`adLockReadOnly`	All records are locked while the recordset is open — no one can edit them. Other users can still retrieve the records.
Read only (edited records)	`adLockPessimistic`	The page of records containing the one currently being edited is locked and can't be changed until the user moves to another record.

Checking for records

Assuming you encounter no errors as VBA creates your Recordset object, the first action you take with it should be to verify that it contains records. If not, you can let the user know there are none to work with. The trick here is to check the recordset's BOF (beginning of file) and EOF (end of file) properties — if they're both True, the recordset is empty. The best way to do that is with the logical And operator, which returns True only if two Boolean values are both True, as shown here:

```
If rstY.BOF And rstY.EOF Then
    MsgBox "No records in this recordset!"
End If
```

Caution

The promising-sounding RecordCount property is not a reliable way to check for the number of records in a recordset.

Moving through recordsets and locating specific records

ADO lets you navigate through a recordset fairly freely. For simple positioning, use the MoveFirst method to jump to the first record in the recordset, MoveLast to get the final record, and MoveNext and MovePrevious to step through records one at a time. The Move method lets you jump a specified number of records forward or backward in the recordset. For example, the statement rstZ.Move -3 moves three records back.

If you know you're going to want to return to a specific record later, set a bookmark for that record. While you're working with the record, assign the Recordset object's Bookmark property to a variable (use a variant) as in this example:

```
varBookmark1 = rstA.Bookmark
```

You can then jump back to that bookmark later by reversing the assignment:

```
rstA.Bookmark = varBookmark1
```

The Seek method and the four Find methods (FindFirst, FindLast, FindNext, and FindPrevious) enable you to track down a specific record based on its contents. Because Seek locates the target record using an index, it's faster than the Find methods — but the database must be indexed on the field containing the data you're looking for.

Adding and deleting records

Use a Recordset object's AddNew method to tack on a new record to the recordset and move to the new record. If you've already created a Recordset object called rstIng, the statement rstIng.AddNew is all you need to add a new record. You can then go on to fill up the record's fields (see "Changing field data" later in this chapter). If you prefer, however, you can specify field values at the time you create the new record. The `AddNew` method enables you to specify the fields and the values they are to contain, as shown in this example:

```
With rstIng
    .AddNew Array("Name", "Age","Gender"), Array("Ann", 42, "F")
End With
```

As the example shows, you supply the arguments to the `AddNew` method as a pair of arrays, the first containing the field names, the second, their values. In the example, I used the VBA `Array` function to create an array on the fly from literal strings. You could instead use variables representing arrays you previously created. At any rate, using this technique to supply field values at the time you add a new record means you don't need a separate line of code for each field.

The `Delete` method, of course, deletes the current record.

Reading field data

Working with the current value of a specific field in your code is as simple as reading the field's `Value` property. Specify the field either by name or index number, as shown in the examples here. Note that `Value` is the default property, so it isn't required in your code:

```
If rstYGate.Fields("Service visits").Value > 10
    MsgBox "This unit needs a major overhaul!"
End If

strCurrentFieldData = rstYGate.Fields(3)
```

Because the `Fields` collection is the default collection of a Recordset object, you actually aren't required to mention it by name. To refer to a field, just precede its name by an exclamation point, using brackets around names that include spaces. Here are two examples:

```
rstYGate!Date = #5/15/2000#

With rstYGate
    intItems = ![Oil cans]
End With
```

Changing field data

Changing (updating) field values in particular records is simpler in ADO than its predecessors. All you have to do is specify the new value and then move to a different record, as in this example (assume the `rstBucket` Recordset object is already open and filled with records):

```
With rstBucket
    .Fields(0).Value = "Love"
    .MoveNext
End With
```

Alternatively, if you don't want to move off of the current record, you can write changes to the database using the `Update` method. In the example that follows, I've taken advantage of the default status of the `Fields` collection and `Value` property to minimize the code I had to write:

```
With rstBucket
    !Volume = 8.93
    .Update
End With
```

Like the `AddNew` method, `Update` lets you supply a set of new field values with a pair of arrays, as shown here:

```
With rstBucket
    .Update Array("Name", "Rank","Cereal brand"), _
        Array("Lola", "Lt. Colonel", "Sugar Showers")
End With
```

Repeating operations on multiple records

Use a `Do` loop to perform a test or operation on multiple records in a recordset, as in this example:

```
'Loop through the recordset
    With rstInPeace
        Do Until .EOF
            Debug.Print.Fields(0)
            .MoveNext
        Loop
    End With
    Set rstInPeace = Nothing
End Sub
```

Using the Command object

In ADO, a Command object represents a command, such as an SQL statement or stored procedure, that is to be carried out by the data source. You can use Command objects to retrieve records as Recordset objects, and to have the data source carry out operations such as updates and deletes on multiple records. (The code samples shown in this section demonstrate the latter operations; for an example involving recordsets, see the section "Creating recordsets using the Command object" earlier in this chapter.)

Don't be shocked if you can't use the Command object with a particular data source. OLE DB Providers aren't required to implement the Command object, and those that do aren't required to handle parameters.

About stored procedures

Stored procedures are queries and other operations that you or someone else define in advance (usually using SQL) and store at the data source. Access queries are examples of stored procedures. Although you can design an Access query visually on a grid, it represents an SQL statement, which you can see by switching to SQL view. The query is stored as part of the .mdb database file that it pertains to. Network databases such as SQL Server also permit you to define similar stored procedures.

Because a stored procedure is all ready to go, you only need to know its name — you can forget about the complexities of the query definition in your code. More important, stored procedures run faster and are more reliable over a network than equivalent SQL statements. On the downside, the SQL for a stored procedure isn't part of your program's code, so you can't modify it or even examine it there.

Setting up a Command object

To set up a Command object, start by declaring a variable for it and instantiating the actual object. You can then use its properties to associate it with a connection, to define the command you want to run — in the form of an SQL statement or the name of a stored procedure — and to specify the type of command. With all that out of the way, use the Command object's Execute method to actually run the command. Here's an example demonstrating these steps using an SQL update query. Note the CommandType property, which you must set to adCmdText to pass an SQL statement to the data source:

```
Dim conSecrate As Connection
Dim cmdSecret As Command
Dim prmDate
(code to set up the conSecrate Connection object goes here...)
Set cmdSecret = New Command
With cmdSecret
   .ActiveConnection = conSecrate
   .CommandText = _
      "UPDATE Bicycles SET OnSale = True WHERE Category = 4;"
   .CommandType = adCmdText
   .Execute
End With
```

Using command parameters

If the command requires input *parameters* (values that must be supplied when it runs, such as a date range or search criteria), you must also define individual Parameter objects, appending each to the Command object's Parameters collection. The example shown here illustrates how this works, and shows how to use a Command object to execute a stored procedure rather than an SQL statement:

```
Dim conSecrate As Connection
Dim cmdSecret As Command
Dim prmDate
(code to set up the conSecrate connection goes here...)
Set cmdSecret = New Command
With cmdSecret
```

```
      .ActiveConnection = conSecrate
      .CommandText = "qryDeleteOldRecords"
      .CommandType = adCmdStoredProc ' in Jet, adCmdTable
End With

Set prmDate = New Parameter
With prmDate
   .Name = "Date"
   .Value = InputBox "Enter the cut-off date."
   .Type = adDate
   .Direction = adParamInput
End With
With cmdSecret
   .Parameters.Append prmDate 'Adds the parameter just defined
   .Execute ' Executes the command
End With
```

Secret

If you're running a query stored in a Jet/Access database, use `adCmdTable` as the `CommandType` property for the Command object — *not* `adCmdStoredProc`, which is the choice for SQL Server and many other database servers.

Many data sources — but Jet isn't one of them — also support output parameters for stored procedures. These are named items that hold values returned by the procedure.

Working with SQL

It's easy enough to open a recordset using ADO, but filling it with the right records can be a more daunting project. If you're going to build serious database applications, you have to learn to write SQL code — or how to use tools that write it for you.

Avoiding SQL

Inserting SQL statements in VBA code is something like interrupting a letter with snippets of Greek, or calculus, or music notation. Although SQL is a much smaller and more narrowly focused language than Visual Basic, many VBA programmers find it difficult to use just because it's so different. Given this reality, you may want to rely on development tools that compose SQL based on your picks from lists of fields, criteria for selecting particular records, and actions you want the query to perform.

Access's query designer, described in Chapter 44, is one such tool. Once you've designed and tested an Access query, you have two choices for connecting a Command object in your VBA code to the query: The Command object can run the query as a stored procedure, or you can copy and paste the SQL code generated by the query designer into your code. To use the latter technique, design and test the query in Access and then choose View ⇨

SQL View to display the corresponding SQL statement. Copy it to the clipboard, switch to VBA, and paste it — between a pair of quote marks — into the statement that sets the `CommandText` property for the Command object. For details on executing SQL statements or stored procedures, see the section "Using the Command object" earlier in this chapter.

The Access query designer is fine so far as it goes, but it can't handle every situation. It won't build sophisticated query types such as union queries and subqueries. Of course, its stored queries work only with Jet databases (however, other databases come with similar visual query design tools). You can try using the Access query designer to generate SQL for use with a non-Jet database, but keep in mind that different databases use different versions of SQL, so you may have to hand-tweak the code.

Understanding SQL dialects

Although SQL is nearly universal as the query language for database management, many databases speak unique SQL dialects. Jet, for example, provides several nonstandard SQL enhancements but doesn't implement certain other features found in the standard version. For the discussion in this chapter, I'm sticking with Jet's version of SQL simply because it's the one everyone can use with Office. If you use a different database system, you may need to make adjustments to conform to its SQL dialect.

Inserting SQL statements in VBA code

The examples in the earlier section "Writing Database Code with ADO" should make plain how to place SQL statements into a VBA procedure. The key is to remember that VBA treats SQL statements as text strings, not as part of the code itself. These strings receive special handling when interpreted as arguments to the `Open` or `Execute` method of ADO objects, but until then, they're just ordinary VBA strings of text characters.

Which means, then, that you must enclose every SQL statement within a pair of double quote marks. Whether you're setting a Command object's `CommandText` property or entering an argument to a Recordset object's `Open` method, use the quote marks. Again, you can find a number of examples in the ADO section earlier in this chapter. And don't miss the related Secret in "Refining the recordset: Setting criteria" later in this section.

Writing SELECT statements

I covered the mechanics of creating ADO Recordset objects earlier in this chapter. Here, the focus is on the SQL code you need to specify which records belong in your recordsets. Because it performs precisely this task, the `SELECT` statement is the workhorse of SQL.

The simplest form of the SELECT statement retrieves all the records from a single table. The following example returns all the fields and all the records from the Toys table:

SELECT * FROM Toys

Because this statement contains no additional criteria, all records from the Toys table are included in the returned recordset. The asterisk indicates that the recordset is also to contain all fields in the chosen table.

Secret

SELECT statements retrieve records from the database, but don't change the stored data. To make such changes, you must modify the values in the recordset's fields and then save your changes, or use SQL UPDATE or DELETE statements.

Relating multiple tables in SELECT statements

A single SELECT statement can query more than one table. Simply listing the tables from which you want to select records in the FROM clause works, as shown here:

SELECT * FROM Toys, Clerks

However, the recordset returned by this simple listing of tables isn't likely to be very useful. Nothing connects the two tables together, so the database doesn't know which record in the first table belongs with which record in the second. As a result, you get for each record in the first table as many new records as there are records in the second table.

To relate two tables together properly, perform a *join* in the SELECT statement. An *inner join*, the most common type, creates a record in the recordset from matching pairs of records in the source tables. The match is based on values in a specified field the two tables have in common. The following statement creates a recordset listing the manufacturer's rep for each toy in the inventory:

SELECT Toy, Rep FROM Toys INNER JOIN Reps ON Toys.ID = Reps.ToyID

To create an inner join, place the INNER JOIN term between the two tables in the FROM clause. Follow this with an ON clause, which specifies the fields that should contain values to be compared. Normally, the field names in the ON clause are separated by an equal sign, indicating that selected records have to have identical values in the two fields (other comparison operators are permitted).

Choosing fields

To specify a subset of particular fields, name them explicitly as in this example:

SELECT Toy, InStock, OnOrder FROM ToyInventory

If a field or table name contains spaces or punctuation, place square brackets around the name, as shown here:

```
SELECT Toy, [List Price], [Sale Price] FROM ToyInventory
```

By default, the `Name` property of each Field object in the recordset returned by the `SELECT` statement is the name of the corresponding field in the original table. You can assign different field names (*aliases*) in the recordset using an `AS` clause for each field you want to rename:

```
SELECT Toy AS ToyName, InStock AS OnHand, OnOrder FROM ToyInventory
```

If you're retrieving records from multiple tables and want to select fields that have the same name in more than one table, precede each field name with the source table's name. Here's an example:

```
SELECT ToyInventory.Name, Clerks.Name FROM ToyInventory, Clerks
```

Creating calculated fields and values

You can build a recordset containing new fields whose values are calculated from the underlying values in the underlying database. In your `SELECT` statement, define the calculated fields using expressions based on VBA operators and functions. For example, let's say you want to list what prices would be if you put everything on sale at 10 percent off the regular price.

```
SELECT Toy, (Price * .9) AS SalePrice FROM ToyInventory
```

Note that when you define a calculated field, you must include an `AS` clause to create an alias (name) for the field in the recordset. The parentheses aren't necessary but help to clarify the calculation you're performing. You can use more than one field in the expression that creates a calculated field, as in `(Price * InStock) AS InventoryValue`.

As another example, suppose that for some reason you wanted a recordset listing all your clerks' names in uppercase without changing the way the names are recorded in the database. The following statement would do the trick:

```
SELECT UCase(Name) AS [Clerk's name] FROM Clerks
```

Using SQL *aggregate functions*, a `SELECT` statement can return a recordset consisting of a single summary value such as the number of records containing an entry in a given field:

```
SELECT Count(Recyclable) AS [Can recycle] FROM Toys
```

or the average of all values for a field:

```
SELECT Avg(Price) AS [Average Price] FROM Toys
```

You can then transfer the value of this one record's one field to a variable in your code for use in other calculations or to display on a form:

```
intRecylableCount = rstRecyclableToys![Can recycle]
```

Aggregate functions include Count, Avg, Sum, Min, Max, and a few statistical functions.

Selecting records with the DISTINCT, DISTINCTROW, and TOP predicates

Use the DISTINCT, DISTINCTROW, and TOP SQL *predicates* in a SELECT statement as simple tools for specifying a subset of the underlying database. Place these special words directly after SELECT, as shown in Table 46-3.

Table 46-3 SQL Predicates for Selecting Records

Predicate	Use	Example
DISTINCT	Selects only one record when the underlying data has two or more records containing the identical data in the named field(s).	SELECT DISTINCT Address FROM Members Returns a recordset containing only one record for each address, even when the Members table contains more than one record per address.
DISTINCTROW	Selects all unique records based on all fields. If two records differ by only one character, both will be included; if they're identical in all fields, one will be omitted.	SELECT DISTINCTROW Name, Address FROM Members Returns a recordset with Name and Address fields. The recordset may contain duplicate records, but only when other fields in the underlying table differ.
TOP *n*	Selects a specified number of records at the top or bottom of a range determined by an ORDER BY clause.	SELECT TOP 10 ToyName FROM Toys ORDER BY UnitsSold Returns a recordset containing the 10 best-selling toys. To identify the 10 worst sellers, you would add ASC (ascending) following the UnitsSold field name.

Refining the recordset: Setting criteria

To restrict a recordset to a range of records meeting some criteria, add a WHERE clause to the SELECT statement, as shown in these examples:

```
SELECT * FROM Toys WHERE Price <= 20
SELECT Customer, Date FROM Sales WHERE Date = #10/24/2000#
SELECT Name, Rank, CerealNumber FROM Kids WHERE Rank = 'Queen'
SELECT Name, Age, [Shoe Size] FROM Kids WHERE Age Between 3 And 6
```

As you can see, a WHERE clause follows the FROM clause and includes an expression specifying the criteria that records have to meet to make it into the recordset. As you can also see, these expressions aren't quite like VBA expressions. For one thing, text strings are enclosed by single quote marks, not double ones. For another, you can specify ranges with the Between...And construct, which doesn't exist in VBA. Also, the Like operator functions differently in SQL than it does in VBA.

You can combine multiple expressions using logical operators (And, Or, and so on).

```
SELECT * FROM Toys WHERE Price > 20 And Category = 'Action Figures'
```

Secret

In VBA code, it's proper form to use single quotes to specify a string within an SQL statement—which in its entirety is a VBA string inside double quotes. For example you might set up a Command object like this:

```
strSQL = "SELECT Name FROM Kids WHERE Hates = 'Brocolli'"
cmdEr.CommandText = strSQL
```

Often, especially in WHERE clauses, you need to base a portion of an SQL statement string on a variable—for example, if you're performing a query based on the user's entry in a text box on a form. Compose the string by concatenating the variable with the rest of the string. If the variable represents a string, remember to tack on the single quotes before and after the string, as in this example:

```
strSQL = "SELECT Name FROM Kids WHERE Hates = ' " _
    & frmInputForm.TextBox1 & "'"
```

Grouping records

The GROUP BY clause enables you to combine records having the same values in specified fields, converting them into a single record in the resulting recordset. Typically, this clause is used when you want a recordset that summarizes the underlying data. For example, you might want to know how many records there are in the database for each value of a given field. Try this example:

```
SELECT Category, Count([Category]) AS [Number of Items] FROM Toys
    GROUP BY Category;
```

The result of this statement is a recordset that might look something like this:

Category	Number of Items
Action Figures	42
Dolls	37
Games	29
Plush	23
Puzzles	17
Sporting Goods	31

You can use other SQL aggregate functions such as Max or Avg to produce other kinds of summaries.

Further filtering with the HAVING clause

A HAVING clause follows a GROUP BY clause and sets criteria for the grouped records. It works like the WHERE clause and can be used alone, or in combination with WHERE to further limit the returned records. In this example, the HAVING clause includes only categories that have at least five records meeting the criteria set by the WHERE clause (a price tag greater than $100):

```
SELECT Category, Count(Category) As [Number of Items] FROM Toys
   WHERE Price > 100 GROUP BY Category
   HAVING Count(Category) > 4
```

Sorting with the ORDER BY clause

Use an ORDER BY clause to sort the records returned by a SELECT statement according to the values in one or more fields. It belongs at the end of the statement, as in this example:

```
SELECT Toy, Price, InStock FROM ToyInventory ORDER BY Toy
```

The resulting recordset lists the toys in alphabetical order by their names.

To list them by price instead, sorted alphabetically by name when items have the same price, you'd use the following statement. As it demonstrates, you can sort on multiple fields simply by listing the fields in the order in which you want the sort to happen:

```
SELECT Toy, Price FROM ToyInventory ORDER BY Price DESC, Toy
```

By default, sorts are performed in ascending order. To specify a sort order for a field explicitly, add DESC (for descending) or ASC (for ascending) following the name of the field. The previous example produces a recordset with the highest-priced items listed first.

Performing bulk updates and deletions in SQL

The UPDATE and DELETE statements enable you to change or remove a group of records in the underlying data source with one command. These statements work directly on the source database — you don't have to first retrieve a recordset, modify its records, and then update the database with your changes. Consider this example, useful if you decide to raise your prices by 10 percent in a particular merchandise category:

```
UPDATE Toys SET Price = Price * 1.1 WHERE Category = 'Trains'
```

The name of the table you're working on follows immediately after the UPDATE term. Then comes the SET clause, in which you assign a new value to one or more fields in the target table. Finally, an optional WHERE clause enables you to specify criteria limiting the change to specified records. The `WHERE` clause works just as it does in `SELECT` statements.

The `DELETE` statement is even simpler than the `UPDATE` statement, because all it does is remove whole records. The following example deletes records for all toys that aren't in stock and haven't been reordered:

```
DELETE FROM Toys WHERE InStock = 0 And OnOrder = 0
```

To delete entries for a field rather than an entire record, use an `UPDATE` statement with a `SET` clause that sets the value for that field to `Null`.

`UPDATE` and `DELETE` statements produce irreversible changes in the underlying database — you can't undo their results. Be sure to back up your data before running such a statement.

Conclusion

Although many fat books have been devoted exclusively to database programming, this brief tour of the realm should quell any anxiety you have about getting your hands deep into the rich loam of ADO and SQL. No matter which Office application you choose as your launch pad, the techniques covered here are enough to construct serious custom database applications using VBA.

Chapter 47

Designing Access Forms

In This Chapter

▶ Understanding the unique strengths of Access forms — and how those strengths can be liabilities for database developers

▶ Working with form components and form views

▶ Laying out forms

▶ Binding a form to data

▶ Adding and laying out controls

▶ Using subforms to display relational data automatically

Although you can work directly with the information in your tables and queries, an Access database becomes much more, well, accessible when equipped with forms for viewing and editing its information. If you're designing a full-scale database application, custom forms provide the user interface for your program. But even if you use Access more casually, creating a few forms can help you focus on individual records, break up the monotony of table rows and columns, and give you push-button access to macros and VBA procedures. Equally important, forms are one of the most effective ways to work with data relationally — that is, with related data from different tables at the same time.

From the designer's perspective, reports have a lot in common with forms. Of course, their mission is different. Reports only present information — they don't allow the user to fiddle with the data. Also, although you can view a report within Access, the real point is to get the information to other people, either in print or electronic form. Nevertheless, you use essentially the same techniques to lay out reports and hook them up to Access data as you do for forms. There are a few differences, but I don't have space to cover reports explicitly here.

Access Forms: A World Apart

Like most other VBA applications, Word, PowerPoint, and Excel rely on the UserForms discussed in Chapter 24 for on-screen interactions with users of your custom programs. Not so Access, which goes its own way when it comes to forms. From the user's point of view, an Access form works and looks very much like a VBA UserForm — after all, both are Windows dialog boxes, with the typical buttons, text boxes, and other controls. But behind the scenes, and during the design process, Access forms differ significantly from UserForms.

As you may know, VBA UserForms and the forms you can build in the stand-alone version of Visual Basic are distinct as well. Well, Access forms aren't Visual Basic forms, either.

About bound forms

The most important difference between an Access form and a VBA UserForm is this: An Access form and the controls it contains can be *bound* readily to data, data in the form of a specific table, query, or SQL statement. When a record on a bound form changes, that change is saved in the database table to which the form is bound, whether it's bound directly or through an intermediary query or SQL statement. Access forms also have the innate capability to navigate through a bound set of records automatically. When the user moves from one record to the next, the form's controls immediately fill with the corresponding values from the new record. Ordinary VBA UserForms don't have this capability. However, you can add it with the data controls that come with Office Developer and in many third-party toolkits (check out the CD-ROM that comes with this book for samples).

Form design tools — Access versus VBA

Access's design tools don't work quite like those for VBA UserForms — contrast the Format menus from the Visual Basic Editor and Access as shown in Figure 47-1 and the Toolbox and Properties windows for the two environments, shown in Figure 47-2. Access is slightly less capable when it comes to laying out controls. For example, you can't center selected controls on an Access form or automatically line up their centers, capabilities you do have with UserForms. However, Access 2000 finally lets you group controls to move or resize them as a unit.

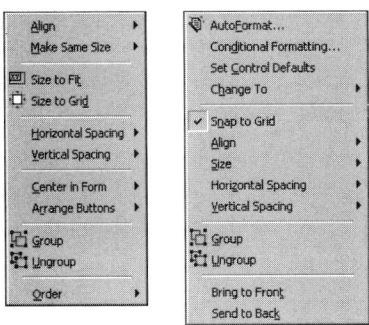

Figure 47-1: On the left is the Format menu of the Visual Basic Editor; on the right, the Format menu in Access.

 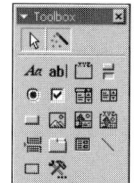

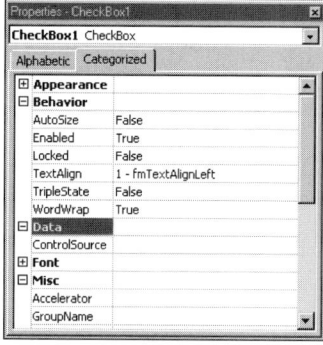 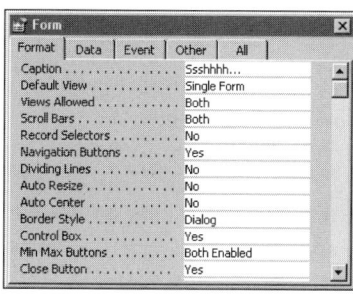

Figure 47-2: The Toolbox and Properties windows of the Visual Basic Editor (on the left) and Access (on the right)

Access offers a different set of stock controls than are available for VBA UserForms — you can see for yourself if you look closely at the Toolbox windows in Figure 47-2. The controls that the two environments do share differ as well. These variations are subtle, consisting primarily of differences in the names and behavior of the controls' properties. If you're accustomed to working with UserForm controls, you'll have to make some minor adjustments when you're building Access forms.

Access's unique forms affect your development plans

Secret

Before you jump into building a whole set of neat forms in Access, be sure you understand the implications of Access's nonstandard forms. The fact that you can't reuse Access forms in Visual Basic or VBA is truly a Big Deal — it may lead you to abandon Access as a development tool for production database applications!

If you're sure that you *never* will want to convert your Access application to Visual Basic — for faster performance and easier distribution — feel free to go hog wild with Access forms. If there's a chance that you might eventually want to convert, be sure to count the cost of reengineering the application's forms. In an application with many complex forms, recreating them from scratch in Visual Basic could take many hours. If you decide to use Access for prototyping purposes only, minimize the time you spend laying out forms. Stick with simple, quick-and-dirty form layouts, even if they're ugly. (To get help in converting an existing Access application to Visual Basic, try Access Upsizer — see www.ndimensional.com for details.)

Designing Access Forms

To start a new Access form, select the Forms in the Objects bar and click New. In the New Form dialog box, select the object (table, query, or view) on which the form will be based. This step is important, because it binds the form to the object you select — that is, the fields you can attach to the form and that depend on the underlying table. However, if you're creating a form to serve as a switchboard, with buttons that activate other functions and database objects, or if you're going to connect the form to data via VBA code, you can leave this item blank.

The New Form dialog box also asks you to choose from several methods for starting the form. These include:

- To start laying out a form from scratch, choose Design View.
- The Form Wizard can build fairly complete working forms for you with a minimum of effort on your part.
- The AutoForm wizards are even less trouble — just double-click the layout you want and you have an instant form.
- If your form requires a chart or pivot table, the appropriate wizards prepare it for you.

Even if you have the wizards do some of the work for you, you're going to wind up in Design view soon enough. That's where you get full control over a form's layout and functionality. When you open a form in Design view (see Figure 47-3), it appears on the screen marked with a grid of lines and dots to assist you in aligning items you place upon it. The Control Toolbox opens beside the form.

Using form views

You can work with forms in three views, as follows:

- *Design view*, illustrated in Figure 47-3, is for laying out the form.
- *Form view* displays the working version of the form so that you can view, enter, and edit data.
- *Datasheet view* doesn't display the form at all, really — instead, it displays the data bound to the form in a plain tabular format, like a table or query datasheet. This view isn't particularly pretty, but it's a good way to get at a large number of records at one time.

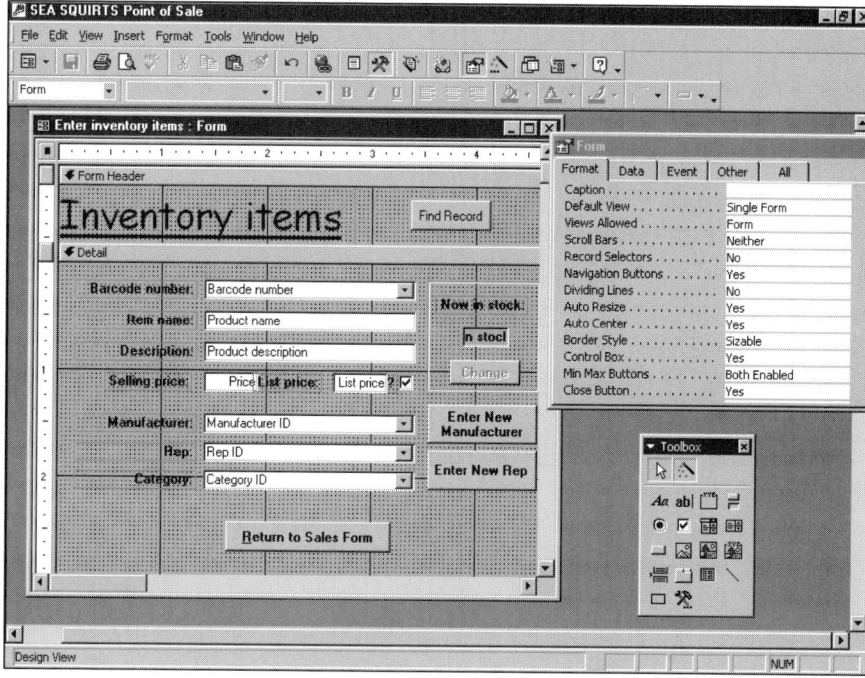

Figure 47-3: Laying out an Access form

Double-clicking an existing form in the database window opens it in Form view. To open a form in Design view, select it and click Design. To switch between views when a form is already open, use the choices at the top of the View menu. Alternatively, you can click the desired choice on the View split button (if it's visible) or right-click the form's background or title bar and choose from the shortcut menu.

Secret

If you're displaying a pop-up form in Form view, the only way to return to Design view without closing the form first is via the right-click (shortcut) menu.

Access form anatomy

Access forms have one or more separate *sections*. These include:

- **Detail section.** Always present, the detail section is the main part of an Access form — and the only part visible when you create a new form from scratch in Design view. The detail section is usually used to show records from the table, query, or view on which the form is based. It can display a single record at a time (in single form view) or act as a scrollable window showing all the records in the underlying object (in the continuous form or datasheet views).

- **Form header.** The form header appears at the top of the form window. Its contents remain constant as you move from record to record in Detail view. Headers are usually used to display items such as the form title, a company logo or other graphic, and column headings for fields in tabular layouts in continuous form or datasheet views.
- **Form footer.** Similar to the header, the footer remains static as you flip from record to record. It's a good place to park buttons (such as OK and Cancel) and other action-oriented controls.
- **Page header and footer.** These sections appear only on printed copies of the form, at the top and bottom of every printed page, respectively. Use them to print a title or description, the page number, or the date.

Other optional elements present in Access forms but not found in VBA UserForms include:

- **Navigation buttons.** Located at the bottom edge of a form, these buttons enable you to move quickly to other records by typing in a record number or clicking a button.
- **Record selectors.** Displayed in a gray bar along the left edge of the form, a separate record selector is visible for each record showing. If the form is set to single form view you see only one record selector, but in continuous form view you see as many as there are records. A heavy arrowhead appears in the record selector of the selected record until you start to edit it, at which point it's replaced by a pencil graphic.

Adding and deleting sections, buttons, and selectors

To add a header or footer to a form, choose View ⇨ Form Header/Footer or View ⇨ Page Header/Footer. Note that you can't add or remove a header or footer individually — it's a both or neither proposition.

Secret

To effectively remove a header or footer without deleting its counterpart, resize the section to a height of zero. You can do this with the mouse (see the "Sizing forms" section) or by setting the Height property in the Properties window.

Secret

Although the header/footer commands are on the View menu, they function to add or delete sections from the form, not just to display or hide them. When you turn off a header/footer, Access irreversibly deletes the affected sections and their controls.

To turn navigation buttons and record selectors on or off, set the corresponding options in the Properties box.

Selecting forms and their sections

As you saw previously in Figure 47-3, each section is set off by a horizontal *section bar* running across the form.

Secret

To select an entire form, click the *form selector*, the box at the top left of the form where the vertical and horizontal rulers intersect. The form is selected when a heavy black square appears in the selector. If the rulers aren't visible and you don't want to display them, choose Edit ⇨ Select Form or press Ctrl+R. To select an individual section, click its section bar so that it turns black.

Working with form properties

Many attributes govern the appearance and function of the form and any of its controls. For unfettered access to these attributes, use the Properties dialog box (also called the Properties sheet) associated with the form or the control you are working with. To display the Properties dialog box — if it isn't already visible — click the Properties button on the Form Design toolbar — the button should appear pressed in. Alternatively, you can right-click any item in the form and choose Properties from the shortcut menu. Although it's visible in earlier screen shots, the Access Properties dialog box is shown again in Figure 47-4.

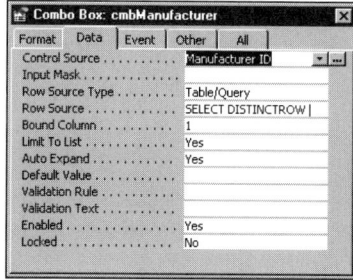

Figure 47-4: Edit properties for a form or control in this dialog box.

Once the Properties dialog box is visible, its contents change accordingly as you select different items on the form. Fortunately, you can get help on any property by placing the insertion point in its field and pressing F1. Also, you can select entries for many properties by choosing an option from a drop-down list or clicking the builder button (see the first Secret in "Binding a form to data" later in this chapter).

Sizing forms

Access forms are truly weird, and frustrating, when it comes to the size they occupy on the screen. In Form view, users can resize forms at will with the mouse, assuming you've designed the form to allow this. But if you value a well-proportioned application, at times you will want to preset and lock in a form's size. This section provides an introduction to the peculiar machinations required.

Secret

Although Access lets you set a form's dimensions in Design view, the size you set there doesn't control what you see in Form view. Instead, the Design view size determines how much area you have for placing controls. A form often appears larger than that in Form view, but any extra room it occupies will be empty. (The size of each section, however, *is* fixed by its size in Design view.)

Sizing a form in Design view

I'll start with the easy part—how to control a form's size settings in Design view. The obvious way to resize a form is with the mouse, but you can also set a form's size in the Properties dialog box. To control width, arrange the form's window so that you can see the right border of the form. Point to the right border so that the mouse pointer becomes a double-headed arrow, and then drag to the new width. If you want to specify the width with numeric precision, select the form itself and change the value of its Width property on the Format tab.

Changing a form's height is a bit more complicated. The form itself doesn't have a Height property. Instead, the overall height depends on the sum of the heights of each of its sections. To change a section's height with the mouse, point to the *bottom* border of the section and drag it up or down. Alternatively, you can select a section and type in a value for its Height property in the Properties box.

Controlling the size of a form as it appears in Form view

The following Secret contains the key fact to know about the size of forms in Form view.

Secret

The size of a form as it is displayed in Form view always corresponds to the dimensions of the form's window—not the form itself—in Design view. The relationship works both ways. You can control the size of a form in Form view by resizing the form's window in Design view. Vice versa, when you resize a form in Form view and switch back to Design view, you'll find that Access has resized the form's window to match.

In Design view, if you leave empty space between the borders of the form itself and its window, Access fills in any empty space when you open the form in Form view. If you make the form window narrower or shorter than the form itself, Access displays the form accordingly, adding scroll bars so that you can reach the parts that aren't visible. Now for another Secret.

Secret

You can't make a form display at the correct height in Form view by visually matching its window to the form's bottom border in Design view—the displayed form will always be taller than you expect. The reason: The section bars lower the position of the bottom border in Design view. Those bars aren't visible in Form view, so the form is actually shorter than it appears in Design view.

You've heard all the bad news. Fortunately, you can match the displayed form size to the dimensions of the form itself in a roundabout way. That's the third Secret.

Secret

To display a form at the dimensions specified in Design view, set the Auto Resize property to Yes (the default), close the form, and then *reopen it directly from the database window*, without opening it in Design view first (double-click the form item in the database window to open it directly). To resize a form already open in Form view, select it and choose Window ⇨ Size to Fit Form. If you then switch back to Design view, you'll see that Access has resized the form's window accordingly. Click the Save button to be sure that Access stores the window size — and don't change it, or you'll have to repeat the process.

Locking in form size

If you don't want users to be able to resize a form, change the form's Border Style property to something other than Sizable. If you don't want them to be able to maximize or minimize the form, choose None or Dialog for the Border Style, or set the Min Max Buttons property to an option other than Both Enabled.

Controlling form appearance with AutoFormat

The AutoFormat command is the easiest and most efficient way to alter a form's look. AutoFormats work much like styles in Excel or Word — they apply a predetermined set of appearance attributes. You can choose an AutoFormat when you create a form via the Form Wizard. But let's assume you're already working with a form in Design view and decide to change its appearance. Although you can alter the properties that specify fonts, colors, and other characteristics individually, it's quicker to apply an AutoFormat.

To get the ball rolling, select the entire form, one of its sections, or one or more controls — Access applies your AutoFormat choice only to the selected items. Then click the AutoFormat button on the Form Design toolbar, or choose Format ⇨ AutoFormat. In the resulting dialog box, select the format you want to use and click OK. Use the Options button to restrict the attributes (properties) you want to alter. Figure 47-5 shows the AutoFormat dialog box with the Options check boxes turned on.

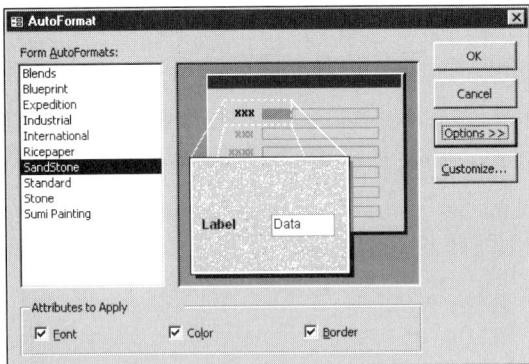

Figure 47-5: Apply a form AutoFormat from this dialog box, using the boxes at the bottom to control which form properties receive AutoFormats.

Once you've developed a form design you like, consider saving it as a custom AutoFormat for reuse on other forms. With the form whose properties you want to memorize open in Design view, open the AutoFormat dialog box and click Customize.

Binding a form to data

A form's `RecordSource` property is the key to binding the form to a specific set of records in your database. Once the form has been bound to a recordset, and you've fleshed it out with controls bound to individual fields in that recordset, the form automatically displays all the records without any programming on your part.

When you specify a table, query, or view at the time you create a form, Access automatically sets the `RecordSource` property accordingly. To set it or change it yourself, select the form, open the Properties dialog box, and enter the name of a table, query, or view, or type in an SQL statement directly (Chapter 46 introduces SQL statement syntax). If you're creating a full-fledged database application in VBA, you can set the form's `RecordSource` property in your code rather than in the Properties window with a statement such as

```
Forms!frmToyInventory.RecordSource = "Inventory"
```

If you're writing code in the form's own code module, it's easier to use the keyword `Me` to refer to the current form, as in this example (which assumes you've already assigned a valid SQL statement to the `strSQL` variable):

```
Me.RecordSource = strSQL
```

Secret

When you're typing a lengthy setting in the `RecordSource` property (or the `ControlSource` property for a control), press Shift+F2 to open the Zoom window, in which you see and edit the entire entry at once. Alternatively, click the builder button to edit the entry in the Expression Builder window, which lets you construct expressions by selecting items from lists of database objects, functions, and keywords.

Secret

Remember that for top performance it's always best to bind a form or control to a narrowly defined query or SQL statement, rather than to an entire table. These performance benefits are especially critical on a network, where connecting to an entire table across the network would slow you way down.

Working with controls

Until you add controls to it, a form is just an empty box. You must add controls to make it come alive with fields from your database, information text, and buttons and other controls to make things happen.

Adding fields and controls to a form

You can place controls on an Access form in two ways: by adding fields from the underlying set of records to which you've bound the form, or by dropping them on the form from the Toolbox.

If your form is bound to data, Access's field list displays the names of the fields in the underlying recordset. All you have to do is drag fields from the field list to the form. If the field list isn't visible, click the Field List button to display it. Upon arrival, a dragged-in field appears in a text box, with a label containing the field's caption or name to its left. The new text box is automatically bound to the data in that field — when you display the form in Form view, the text box shows the data for that field from the current record.

Secret

You can drag multiple fields to the form at once. Select adjacent fields as a group by Shift+clicking, or select individual fields by Ctrl+clicking. Select the whole shooting match by double-clicking the field list's title bar.

To add other types of controls, whether or not you want to bind them to data, drag the controls from the Toolbox to the form. Once a control is on the form, you can bind it to a field using its `ControlSource` property. Just select the field from the drop-down list in the Properties box (some types of controls can't be bound to data). To display a calculated result, set the `ControlSource` property to an expression. You can include bound field names and controls in such expressions. For example, suppose the form is bound to a table containing a `CurrentSales` field, and `FantasyMultiplier` is the name of an unbound text box control. The following expression calculates your hoped-for results each time the user types a new entry in the unbound control:

```
=[CurrentSales] * [FantasyMultiplier]
```

Secret

Don't try to set a control's `ControlSource` property to an SQL statement — Access doesn't allow this. If you want to bind a control to data not available in the table or query bound to the form, go back and fix yourself a query that does contain the field you need — along with the other fields needed by the form. Then bind the new or revised query to the form.

Unbound controls also make nice ornaments on your forms and can be used to display information under your application's control. They can also function as triggers for macros, hyperlinks, or VBA code (see Chapter 14 for the scoop on using hyperlinks in Access).

Formatting controls

To work with a control, click it to select it. After selecting it, you can move it around or resize it by dragging its handles, and you can cut or copy it with the usual Windows techniques. Shift+click two or more controls to select them all. Two or more selected controls can be aligned to one another, matched in size, and spaced evenly using commands on the Format menu.

Secret

There is one aspect of control layout that might throw you initially. Each control has a *label*, a box containing text that tells the user of the form what the control is for. The label is considered part of the control, so Access makes it easy to work with both label and control together. For example, if you click the control and then choose Edit ⇨ Cut, both items are placed on the clipboard. Likewise, Access makes it easy to move both label and control together. However, you can also move them independently, and you can cut or copy the label by itself. After you have selected a control or its label, the mouse pointer changes to an open hand when it's over the perimeter of the selected item, and not over one of the resize handles. Dragging now moves both control and label. To move just one of these items, drag over the heavier move handles at the top-left corner of each item. The mouse pointer becomes a pointing hand when you can drag a label or control by itself. To cut or copy the label independently, click the label to select it first.

Setting default properties for controls

If the defaults for a control's properties don't suit your needs, you're not stuck with them. Once you have formatted a control and set up its other properties to suit your project, you can reuse these settings as the default for controls of the same type that you add from now on. To set new default properties, select the control that has the properties you want and choose Format ⇨ Set Control Defaults.

Converting controls

Access lets you convert some types of controls into others, preserving as many of their properties as possible. Text boxes, for example, can become labels, list boxes, or combo boxes, while you can change option buttons into check boxes or toggles. To convert a control, select it and choose Format ⇨ Change To to open a submenu of the available conversion options.

Making controls responsive without VBA

VBA isn't always necessary to provoke a response from a control — you can instead assign control events to macros or hyperlinks. For example, say you design a simple database with two main forms: the EggSales form is for displaying and entering records, and the PriceOfEggs form displays the results of a query. Now you create a third form to serve as the switchboard, placing on it a command button for each of the other forms.

For the sake of variety, you decide to use both the hyperlink and macro techniques to connect the switchboard buttons to their respective forms. In Design view, you would start by placing the two command buttons on the switchboard form. Here's how you would then proceed:

- To assign a hyperlink, select the first button. In the Properties dialog box, use the `Hyperlink Subaddress` property to specify the target for the hyperlink. In this case, type **Form EggSales**. If typing makes you anxious, click the builder button beside either hyperlink property to bring up the Insert Hyperlink dialog box. There, you can pick any object in the database by choosing Object in This Database and selecting the object from the graphical list (see Figure 47-6).

- To use the macro technique, first write and save a macro called See Price of Eggs consisting of one action, OpenForm. After setting the action's Form Name property to PriceOfEggs, close the macro window. Then, back in your switchboard form, select the second button, go to the Event tab on the Properties dialog box, and in the `On Click` property, choose the name of your macro from the drop-down list (see Figure 47-7).

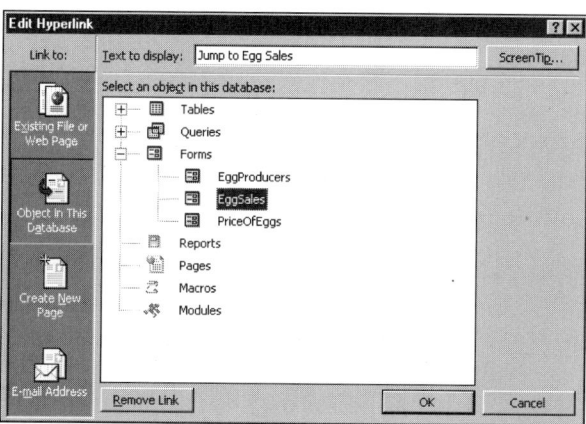

Figure 47-6: Assigning a hyperlink that calls up another form to a command button

Chapter 43 discusses how to write macros in Access, and Chapter 14 contains an extended discussion of hyperlinks.

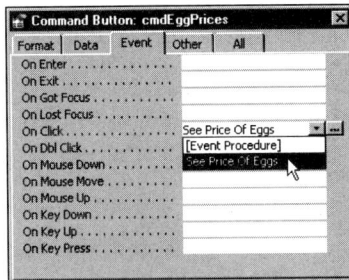

Figure 47-7: Assigning a macro to a button's On Click property

Working with forms in VBA code

You can use VBA to retrieve or set almost any property available in the Properties dialog box, and some others besides. Some advanced programmers believe you should always set all properties in code, to ensure that your program behaves properly even if a user makes changes in Design view.

Because most form-related VBA code belongs in event procedures for the form and its controls, you should familiarize yourself with form events. Important form events include Open, Load, Activate, and Current, which occur in that order when you open a form for the first time. At the time you close a form, the Unload, Deactivate, and Close events occur. Look in the Help system to learn how these events differ from one another and when to use each one.

Writing event code

Access controls and forms respond to events such as mouse-clicks in the same way that standard VBA controls do (see Chapter 24). Here's how to write event code in Access:

1. Open the form in Design view.
2. Select a control (by clicking it) or the form itself (by clicking the form selector or pressing Ctrl+R).
3. Switch to the Event tab of the Properties dialog box for the item you've selected.
4. Click in any of the available events for the item and then click its builder button (the one with three dots to the right of the field).
5. Double-click the Code Builder choice.
6. Access displays the module window for the form with a new procedure started for the event type you chose. You can now add the code for the procedure.

Referring to forms and controls in Access VBA code

One notable contrast in syntax between regular VBA and the Access dialect of VBA is the way you refer to forms and controls in code. In Access, you're supposed to use the exclamation point operator to refer to these objects, as in:

```
Forms![An Access Form]!AnAccessButton
```

Note that when you refer to a form or control whose name contains spaces, you must enclose the name in brackets.

When you're working in the Code window for a form, you can refer to any of its controls directly, without mentioning the Forms collection or the form itself by name. For example, to change the `Enabled` property of a button, the following two statements are equivalent:

```
Forms!UniForm![Big Button].Enabled = False
```

```
[Big Button].Enabled = False
```

The preceding code fragment also illustrates the use of the dot operator (.) in Access to refer to properties of forms or controls. In code for standard VBA UserForms, by contrast, you identify objects as well as their properties using the dot operator, as in this example:

```
LittleForm.LittleButton.Enabled = True
```

Use the `Me` operator to refer to the current form when you write procedures that can be run by more than one form. The statement

```
DoSomethingNow Me
```

runs the `DoSomethingNow` procedure, passing to that procedure an object reference to the current form.

Working with subforms

A relational database manager earns its title because it can link data stored in one table to related data in another table. When you want to display related data on a form, a subform embedded in the form is very often the best means to that end. Subforms display the "many" side of a one-to-many database relationship.

Take the sample point-of-sale form shown in Figure 47-8. The form is bound to the Sales table, which records all the details of each individual sale such as the sale number, the date, and dollar total. Corresponding controls for many of these fields appear on the main part of the form. However, because a single sale may encompass any number of distinct items, the list of individual items sold is stored in a separate table, Sale Line Items. For each record, this table records the sale number, the name of the item, the quantity sold, the sale price, and what not. The subform, that grid in the middle of the form, is bound to that Sale Line Items table.

But what makes a subform really useful is that the main form and the subform are linked to one another by a common field. You may have recognized that in this example the Sales and Sale Line Items tables can be linked through the sale number field, which the two tables have in common. That is, by matching the sale number of a record in the Sales table to sale numbers in the Sale Line Items table, Access can find all the items purchased in that sale. And because the subform and the main form are linked in the same way, the subform automatically displays the related line items as you move from one sale to another in the main form.

A technical note: In reality, a subform is simply a regular Access form. Subforms appear as separate items on the Forms panel of the database window, and you can open them in their own windows. What makes a subform special is that it's embedded into another form by a subform control.

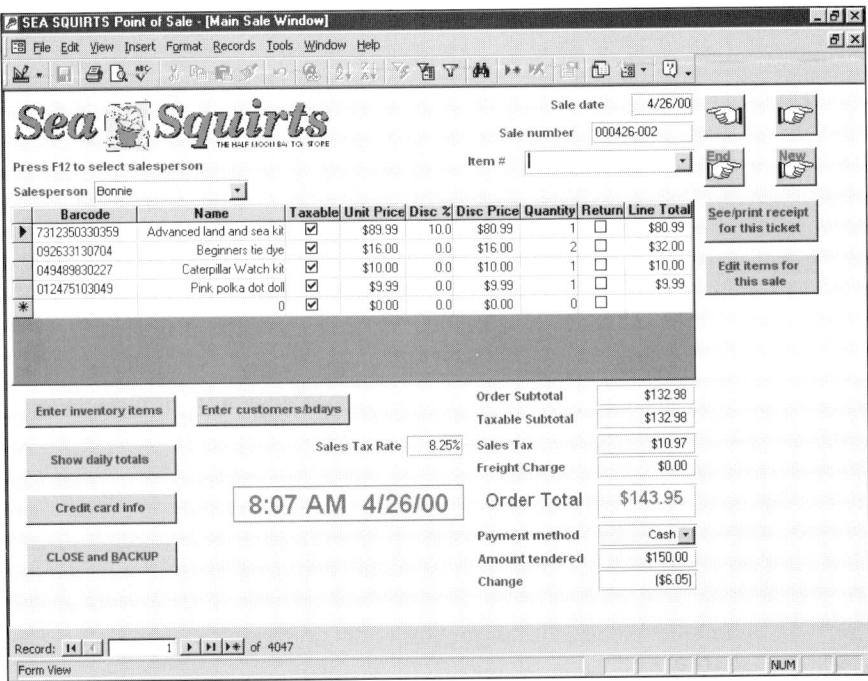

Figure 47-8: A form from a real-life point-of-sale application developed in Access. The grid in the center is a subform.

Adding subforms to forms

Because a form and its subform require a relationship between the tables on which the two forms are based — directly or indirectly through a query — you should specify that relationship in the Tools ⇨ Relationships window. This step isn't absolutely necessary, but it ensures that Access is able to automatically link the two forms by the correct fields.

Note that you don't need to place the fields you use to link the two forms on either form. Often, these fields contain arbitrary ID numbers that are of no interest to the user and that the user shouldn't change.

Using the Form Wizard to build a new form containing a subform

If you're just starting work on a new form, the Form Wizard can put together a form containing a subform for you. In the New Form dialog box, select the table or query forming either side of the one-to-many relationship. In the first of the wizard's dialog boxes, pick the fields from that table that you want to see on the form. Next, remaining in that dialog box, select the table or query forming the other side of the relationship, and pick out the fields from that object that you want. Move to the wizard's next dialog box. Here, you tell Access which table or query belongs on the main part of the form (the one you want to view by) — in the example I'm using, that would be the Sales table. Complete the dialog box by choosing Form with Subform(s), and then work your way through the remaining wizard boxes.

Creating a new subform on an existing form

You can add a subform to an existing form at any time, of course. To create the subform, open the main form in Design view and click the Subform/Subreport control in the Toolbox. Click in the form to place the control where you want it. Assuming the Control Wizards button is pressed, a wizard starts up to guide you through the process of setting up the subform.

Converting an existing form into a subform

If you prefer to do without the wizard's help, follow these steps:

1. Create a form for the subform. Set its Default View property to continuous form or datasheet, so that it will show all the records that match the current record on the main form, and then save and close the form.

2. Open the main form and situate it so that you can also see the Database window. Drag the subform from the Database window to the main form. Assuming the two forms have matching fields, Access automatically links the subform to the main form.

To redefine a subform, use the following properties on the Data tab for the subform control:

- **SourceObject.** The name of the form that you want to function as the subform.

- **LinkChildFields** and **LinkMasterFields.** The names of the fields in the subform and main form, respectively, that Access uses to link the two forms together. To select the fields from a list, click the builder button on either of these properties.

Working with subforms in code

There's a simple secret to accessing a subform and its properties and controls from the VBA code for the main form: Use the Form property of the subform control that contains the subform. Suppose the subform shown in Figure 47-8 resides in a control called LineItemsSubform. If you're working in the Code module for the main form, you can retrieve the number of records shown in the subform with a statement such as this:

```
intRecords = LineItemsSubform.Form.RecordsetClone.RecordCount
```

Note that the object expression begins with the name of the *control*, not the form that control displays. Then comes the Form property, producing a reference to the form object. From that point, you can access any form properties. Don't refer directly to the form on which the subform is based.

If you need to write code for the subform itself or its controls, open the form in its own window (select it in the Database window and choose Design). Add the event code there. If you want events on the subform to trigger changes on the main form, refer to the main form in full. The following sample event procedure activates the SaleItem control on the main form as soon as the value in a subform control changes:

```
Private Sub Price_AfterUpdate()
    Forms!Sales!SaleItem.SetFocus
End Sub
```

Conclusion

Access's form design tools make it easy to build intelligible, attractive view ports into large, complicated databases. Just keep in mind that a decision to use them for forms of any complexity commits you to Access as your database development platform, unless you're willing to toss out hours of hard work.

Part X
Secrets of PowerPoint 2000

Chapter 48: Powerful Presentations

Chapter 49: Deeper PowerPoint Secrets

Chapter 48

Powerful Presentations

In This Chapter

▶ Planning your presentation

▶ Ensuring consistency within and between your presentations

▶ Starting a new presentation

▶ Working with the PowerPoint user interface

▶ Modifying the layout of individual slides

▶ Adding and formatting text

▶ Including graphics and multimedia in your presentation

Arguably today's premier presentation software, PowerPoint turns out attractive, professional-looking slide shows and electronic presentations with a minimum of hassle. Over and above its rock-solid, basic slide layout and editing features, it can endow your presentations with a raft of special animations and multimedia effects. But don't be put off by the glitzy stuff — PowerPoint ably handles mundane but essential chores such as printing your speaker's notes and audience handouts.

By the way, a quick word on PowerPoint terminology is in order at the outset. A PowerPoint document is referred to as a *presentation*, even if it isn't currently being presented to anyone. A PowerPoint *slide show* displays a presentation's slides one by one, without the distractions of the screen tools used to design the presentation.

Planning Great Presentations

Spending time planning before leaping in with both feet is critical for a successful presentation. Important factors to consider during the planning process include:

- **Your message.** Start by identifying the core ideas that you want to communicate and organizing the facts you will use to support them. You can think intelligently about the text, images, sounds, or other items you actually need in order to convey the information most clearly.

- **Your audience.** The most important consideration in planning a presentation is knowing who you're presenting it to. Is this a technical-minded crowd responsive to factual details presented in a serious tone? Or will the audience be partying during your presentation and looking to you for more good times?

- **Your medium.** Obviously, if you plan to present your work on conventional photographic slides or overhead projector transparencies, you won't be incorporating animation and multimedia special effects. An 8-by-10-foot projection screen effectively conveys much more information than a cramped laptop display, so you can include more detail on each slide. (By the way, if you are preparing a presentation for a conventional slide projector, don't miss the tip in Chapter 29 on using Word for inexpensive slide presentations.) Performance considerations become critical if you're going to offer your presentation over the Web, so minimizing the complexity of your slides becomes an especially high priority.

- **Room size and lighting.** All things being equal, the larger the room, the larger the type and images you should use (and the less information you should squeeze onto each slide). If the lights will be dimmed during your talk, consider going with light-color slide backgrounds to help lighten the room and enable your audience to see you and, ideally, pay more attention to what you're saying.

The virtues of simplicity

Keep your slides simple. You can commit no greater sin in the presentation world than bombarding your audience with so much information that the slides look like an eye chart — and leave your audience needing an eye doctor.

You certainly face that danger with PowerPoint. You can sculpt slides with richly detailed backgrounds, captivating graphics, and lists of multiple bullets, each branching into further subcategories — and then add sound, animation, and video. Unfortunately, piling these elements on can be as attractive as a resume with 30 different fonts, à la the dreaded ransom note style.

Content is king. When designing a presentation, focus on driving the key points into the minds of your audience as your priority.

Ensuring consistent presentations

Variety is the spice of life, but too much spice causes indigestion. Typically, a presentation audience appreciates a surprise when it occurs within a stable framework of design elements that repeat from slide to slide. Consistency from one presentation to the next makes sense, too, helping you create a professional identity, a sort of visual trademark. Three PowerPoint features help give your slides thematic consistency: masters, color schemes, and templates. All are covered in the "Developing Custom Layouts and Formats" section of Chapter 49.

Starting New Presentations

Unlike Word and Excel, PowerPoint doesn't create a blank document for you when you start the program directly (rather than by opening an existing presentation). Before you can get to the toolbars and menus, PowerPoint asks *you* to create a new presentation or open an existing one (see Figure 48-1).

Figure 48-1: The PowerPoint dialog box asks you to start or open a presentation whenever you run the program without specifying an existing document.

If you select a new blank or design template presentation (see the section after next, "Choices for new presentations"), PowerPoint asks you to create the first slide, choosing from one of 24 *AutoLayouts*. Figure 48-2 shows the familiar New Slide dialog box. An AutoLayout choice dictates the number of layout elements or *placeholders*, the type of information each placeholder will contain (text, charts, tables, and so forth), and their arrangement relative to one another.

Disabling the Startup and New slide dialog boxes

If you're used to starting programs before opening documents, PowerPoint's insistence that you open or create a presentation is a nuisance, especially if you almost always create the same type of presentation.

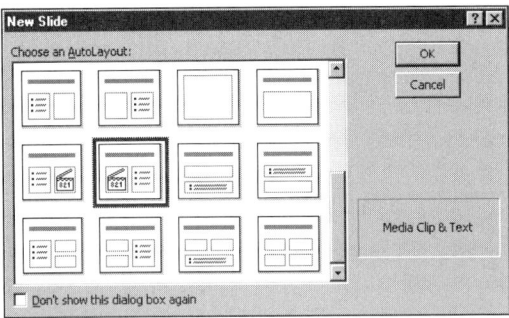

Figure 48-2: The choices on the New Slide dialog box are called AutoLayouts. Scroll the list to see all 24 AutoLayouts.

Secret

To quell the nagging, clear both the PowerPoint (startup) dialog and New Slide dialog check boxes in the View tab of the Tools ⇨ Options dialog box. You can also check the choice labeled Don't Show This Dialog Box Again in either dialog box to suppress that box from now on. With both dialog boxes turned off, PowerPoint creates an empty new presentation for you each time you start the program, with no intervention from you. If you want to customize the presentation PowerPoint starts with, use the tip in "Changing the default presentation" in Chapter 49. Once the PowerPoint or New Slide dialog box has been turned off, reactivate either or both using the View tab of the Tools ⇨ Options dialog box.

Choices for new presentations

Whether you respond to the PowerPoint dialog box usually shown when you start the program, or later choose File ⇨ New, PowerPoint offers you three ways to create a new presentation. You can:

- Activate the AutoContent Wizard (available in the General tab of the File ⇨ New dialog box). Based on your responses, it builds a wide range of boilerplate presentations with skeletal, fill-in-the-blanks content.
- Select a template on which to base the new document.
- Start a blank presentation, one devoid of background color or graphics.

Buttons for these choices are obvious in the PowerPoint dialog box, but when you begin a new presentation with the File ⇨ New command, it isn't clear how they differ.

Secret

There's a reason for that. All three options are just variations on a theme — in each case, you're simply selecting a template (see Chapter 13 for an overview of templates, and see "Working with templates in PowerPoint" in Chapter 49 for PowerPoint-specific details).

Creating Great Slides and Presentations

Although computer books can't impart artistic talent, the general tips on design in Chapters 7 and 8 and the discussion of planning earlier in this chapter should improve your layout horse sense. Once you have your design ideas in mind, you can turn to this section for loads of little tips and background facts that make it easier to bring the slides you imagine into electronic reality.

Working with the PowerPoint user interface

For starters, a quick run-through of a few general user interface topics is in order.

Working with views

PowerPoint's View menu offers three ways to see your presentation while you edit it, plus a Slide Show view to display the slides alone:

- **Normal.** Divided into three resizable panes, Normal view is your main presentation editing tool. The upper-right pane displays a single slide and enables you to edit the slide's contents. The pane on the left shows you a scrolling list of all your slides and their text in outline form. You can edit as well as browse slide text in the outline — see "Reviewing and editing slide text in the outline pane" for details. The pane at the bottom lets you type in your speaker's notes using a simple word processor.

- **Slide Sorter.** Displays thumbnail miniatures of all the slides in the presentation. As described in Chapter 49, you can assign special animation effects with the Slide Sorter toolbar — if you do, corresponding icons and notations appear below slides with the effects.

- **Notes Page.** Displays an editable print preview of your speaker's notes. PowerPoint creates a separate page of notes for each slide with a copy of the slide as well as the note text. You can move the slide and text box around on the page, and you can add more text boxes and graphics, but you can't change the slide content in this view.

- **Slide Show.** The Slide Show view is crucial for testing and giving presentations, but you can't edit slides while you're showing them. See "Performing Your Presentation," the final section of Chapter 49.

Take note of the five little buttons at the bottom left of the PowerPoint window (shown in Figure 48-3, just to the left of the horizontal scrollbar):

Figure 48-3: The buttons at the bottom left of the PowerPoint window

Clicking these buttons gives you an alternative way to switch between different views, but the choices are a bit different than on the View menu. You don't get a button for the Notes Page, and two other views are available, Outline and Slide. Both of these are simply variations on Normal view. In Outline view, PowerPoint enlarges the outline pane on the left to the maximum size allowed, consigning the slide to a small corner. In Slide, on the other hand, the slide takes up most of the window.

To display the Slide master, which determines basic design choices such as the fonts and color scheme used in all slides, Shift+click the Slide View button. Shift+click either the Outline View button or the Slide Sorter View button to see the Handout master, where you can lay out the printed copies of your slides for distribution to your audience (masters are covered in Chapter 49). Shift+clicking the Slide Show button — the rightmost of the five — displays the Set Up Show dialog box.

Zooming in PowerPoint

Don't forget that PowerPoint lets you change the magnification at which you view your slides. Even when the entire slide fits into the window at a reasonable enlargement, it can pay to zoom in still further (with the Zoom toolbar button) for detail work. The default zoom setting, Fit, lets PowerPoint adjust magnification automatically so that the entire slide always fits as you resize its pane.

Working with the slide miniature

PowerPoint automatically displays the current slide in a small floating window when you zoom in to see details of the slide or your notes (see Figure 48-4). If the miniature gets in your way, just click its Close button to put it away.

You can preview a slide's animation effect, if any, using the Slide Miniature window. Right-click the window and choose Animation Preview. If the window isn't already visible, choose Slide Show ➪ Animation Preview.

Previewing in black and white

If you plan to print handouts and notes on a black-and-white printer, use the Grayscale Preview command to see how your presentation looks in a noncolor version. It's available on the Standard toolbar or by choosing View ➪ Black and White.

You can control how PowerPoint converts colors into shades of gray. Once you've turned on the Grayscale Preview mode, right-click any slide to pop up its shortcut menu and choose a conversion option from the Black and White submenu. Your choice applies to all slides in the presentation.

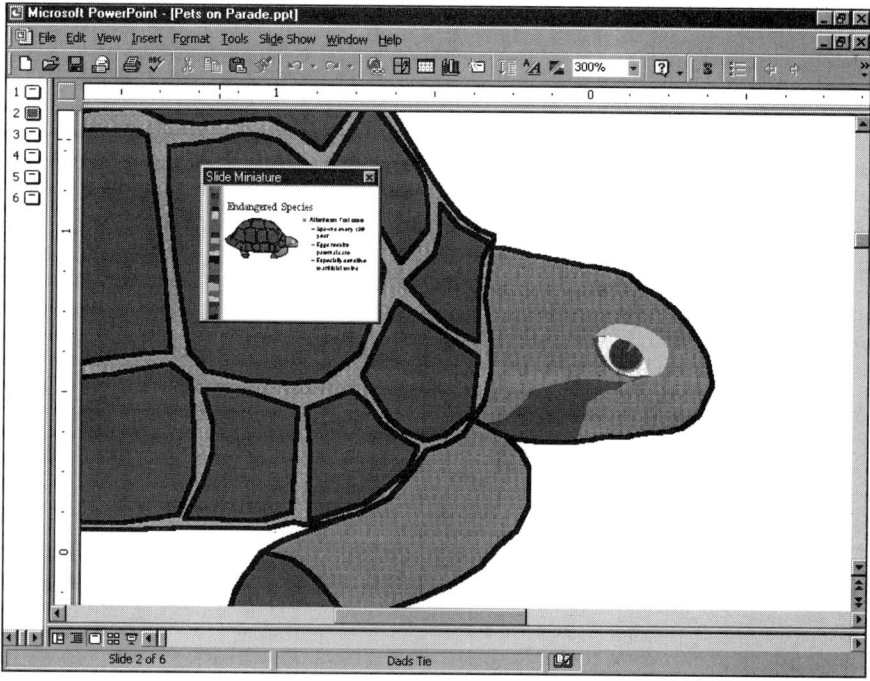

Figure 48-4: The Slide Miniature window shows a thumbnail version of the current slide.

Arranging slides in a presentation

Use Slide Sorter view or the outline pane to shuffle the slides in your presentation. In Slide Sorter view, just drag and drop slides where you want them to fall in the presentation sequence. In the outline pane, drag the icon for the entire slide to the destination (for a discussion of the icon, see the section "Reviewing and editing slide text in the outline pane" later in this chapter). You can cut, copy, and paste selected slides in either view. Select a slide in Outline view by clicking its icon. In Slide Sorter view, you can select nonadjacent slides by pressing Ctrl and clicking.

Modifying the layout of individual slides

You can resize, move, or delete with reckless abandon any placeholder whose content you can change (on nonmasters, that means you can't alter the date, slide number, or footer placeholders). If you need a place for additional text, add it via a text box. PowerPoint text boxes are special because they automatically contain outlined text (see "Working with outlined and bulleted text in masters" in Chapter 49).

Aligning objects with guidelines

Like any self-respecting graphics program, PowerPoint includes optional guides that help you align objects visually or automatically. When guides are visible, dragging an object in a guide's vicinity makes its corner or center (whichever is closer) line up with the guide.

To see the default guides, choose View ⇨ Guides. You can drag a guide to wherever it will do you the most good, or drag it off the slide altogether if you want to delete it. To create an additional guide, hold down Ctrl while you drag one of the existing ones. You don't need to delete the guides to hide them — just choose View ⇨ Guides again to toggle them off.

Using the pasteboard

Secret

If you're making extensive edits to a slide's graphics, use the blank area surrounding the slide as a temporary parking place for objects you might want to reuse. Figure 48-5 shows this technique in action. To place an object on this pasteboard, just drag it off the slide and drop it there. As always, pressing Ctrl while dragging makes a copy of the objcct, whether you're dragging it to or from the pasteboard. Unfortunately, the pasteboard moves with the slides when you scroll — when you move to a new slide, you can't access an item you parked alongside another one.

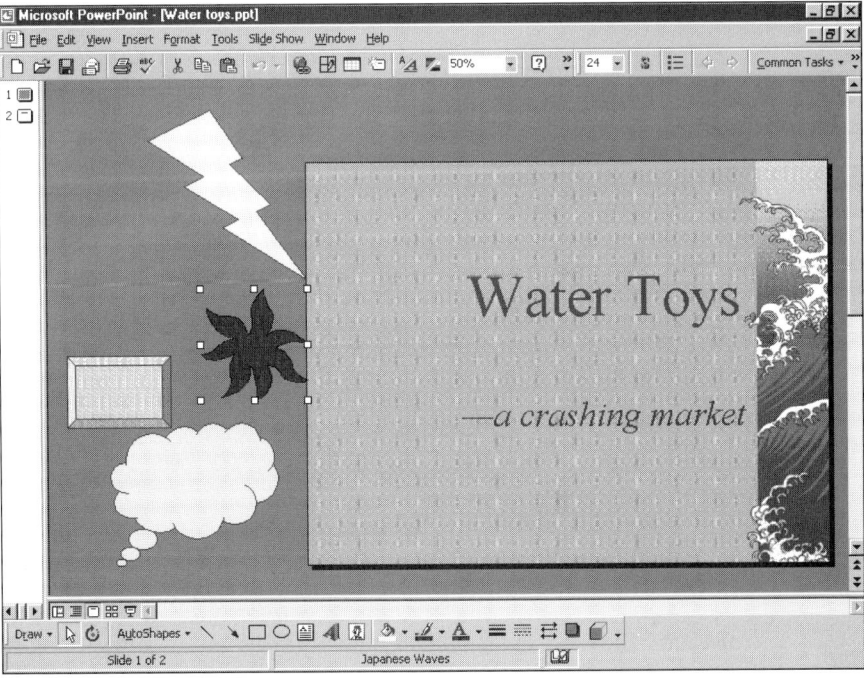

Figure 48-5: Design elements have been parked temporarily on the pasteboard for easy access as slides take shape.

Adding and formatting text

In PowerPoint, text must have a receptacle. You can only type text into placeholders, text boxes, or AutoShapes, not directly onto the slide background.

Editing and navigating text on slides

PowerPoint inserts dummy text into each empty placeholder on a new slide. The dummy text disappears as soon as you add any text of your own. When you're working inside a text placeholder, you can use the arrow keys to move around and the standard Windows Shift+arrow keys to select text. Cut, Copy, and Paste work as expected, of course.

Secret

However, cursor movement keys often function differently in PowerPoint than they do in Word or other word processors. Table 48-1 lists the important keyboard navigation commands. Note, too, that if you have an IntelliMouse, you can use the wheel to scroll through the slides in Normal, Outline, or Slide view.

Table 48-1 Text Navigation Keys on Slides

To Do This	Press These Keys
At all times	
Move to the next or previous slide	Page Down or Page Up
Move to the next text placeholder and select the text within it; if at the last placeholder in the slide, insert a new slide	Ctrl+Enter
When text editing isn't active inside a text placeholder	
Move to the first or last slide	Shift+Home or Shift+End
Select the next or previous text placeholder on the current slide	Tab or Shift+Tab
When a text placeholder is selected, but text editing isn't active inside it	
Select the placeholder's text	Enter (you can then use the arrow keys to move to a specific location in the text)
Unselect the placeholder	Esc
When text editing is active inside a text placeholder	
Move up or down a line	Up or Down arrow. Home and End also work, when pressed with the insertion point at the beginning or end of a line.

(continued)

Table 48-1 *(continued)*

To Do This	Press These Keys
When text editing is active inside a text placeholder	
Remove the insertion point and select the placeholder	Esc
Demote or promote the current bulleted point to the next lower or higher level in the outline	Alt+Shift+Right arrow or Alt+Shift+Left arrow. Tab or Shift+Tab also works when pressed at the beginning of the paragraph.

Reviewing and editing slide text in the outline pane

You can edit your presentation's text in the outline pane rather than on the slide itself. Editing in the outline pane lets you develop content for the entire presentation in one editing window, and it enables you to focus on organization and ideas without distracting layout concerns. Figure 48-6 shows the outline pane at work. Icons and an outline layout make the presentation's organization easy to understand. Each slide has a number and a shadowed slide icon. The text in bold alongside these symbols is the slide's title and appears in the title placeholder. PowerPoint identifies each additional text placeholder on the slide with a boxed number.

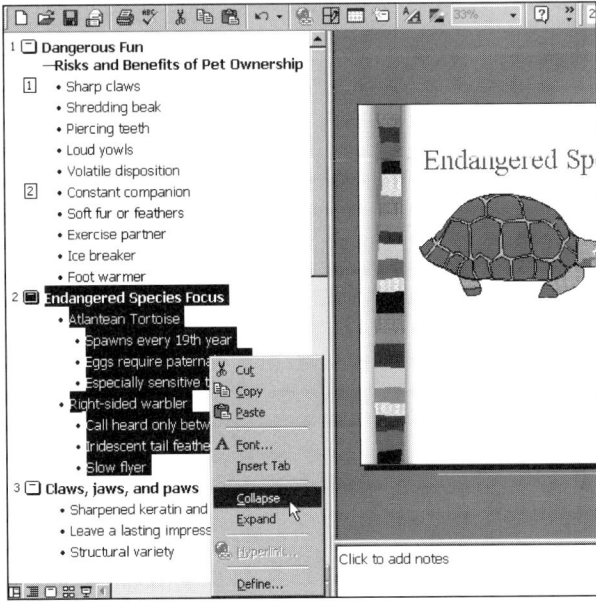

Figure 48-6: PowerPoint's Outline view lets you work with multiple slides in text format.

The outline pane works much like Word's Outline view (Chapter 30). You can:

- Collapse or expand any selected slides of the outline to show only the slide titles or all of the subsidiary points. Select the slides you want to work with — you have to Shift+click each slide individually — and then right-click over the selection. On the resulting shortcut menu, choose Collapse or Expand.

- Demote or promote bulleted items in the outline. Drag them to the right or left or use the Demote and Promote buttons (the ones with the big green arrows) on the Formatting toolbar. If you don't see these buttons, right-click any toolbar to turn on the Outlining toolbar — which offers many other outline-related buttons as well.

- Reorder bulleted points or entire slides by dragging them up or down.

The Alt+Shift+arrow combinations provide keyboard alternatives for the latter two types of mouse moves. In general, editing keys work in the outline pane like they do when you're working directly with your slides (see Table 48-1). One exception: Page Up and Page Down move you up and down through the outline a page at a time, rather than to the previous or next slide.

The difference between text placeholders and text boxes

When the text placeholders specified by a slide layout aren't enough, you can add as many text boxes as you need via the Drawing toolbar or the Insert ➪ Text Box command. But text boxes aren't quite like text PowerPoint placeholders. For one thing, they and their content don't appear in the outline pane. For another, although they do take on the slide's default font, they don't pick up the custom bullets specified by the slide's template. Chapter 8 covers text boxes in depth.

Bookmarking text in PowerPoint

You can use a custom document property to jump to a specific text location in a PowerPoint presentation. This trick is sort of like a one-legged version of the bookmark feature in Word.

First create the custom property, linking it to the content you want to be able to jump to. To do that, select the text you want to bookmark — you can't bookmark an unselected insertion point — and choose File ➪ Properties. On the Custom tab, type in or select a property name and check the Link to Content box.

Thereafter you can move immediately to the bookmarked text. Choose Edit ➪ Go to Property, select the name of the custom link, and then choose Go To.

Turning slide titles into a summary slide

To make a summary or agenda slide based on the titles of others already in the presentation, switch to Slide Sorter or Outline view. There, select the slides whose titles you want to pilfer and click the Summary Slide button on the Slide Sorter or Outlining toolbar. The result is a new slide, containing a bulleted list of the selected slides' titles. PowerPoint inserts it into the presentation just before the first slide of those you selected.

Splitting and merging slides

To divide up an overly long text passage over two slides, use Outline view. Place the insertion point where you want the break and press Enter. Now, without moving the insertion point, click the Outline Promote button until you see a new slide icon. You can then give it a title.

Similarly, you can combine two slides into one, incorporating the text of the second slide into the body text of the first. In the outline pane, begin by moving the slides to be merged so that they're in consecutive order in the presentation, with the one that will receive the merged text first. Select the title of the second slide and click the Demote button or press Alt+Shift+Right arrow. After you OK a warning message, PowerPoint merges the slides.

Importing text from an outline

You can also import text formatted as an outline from just about any kind of file and have PowerPoint convert the outline into slides automatically. Choose Insert ⇨ Slides from Outline to create new outline-based slides in an existing presentation. Alternatively, if you're starting a new presentation, you can base it on an outline by choosing File ⇨ Open and selecting All Outlines in the Files of Type box. Each top-level heading becomes the title for a new slide, with the points beneath it entering the slides as body text, indented according to their outline level in the original file.

As you would hope, this technique works especially well with outlines created in Word. Paragraphs assigned to the Heading 1 style in a Word document become titles of PowerPoint slides, Heading 2 paragraphs get converted to the top level in bulleted lists, and so forth. If you're currently working with the document in Word, you can jump-start the presentation by choosing — in Word — File ⇨ Send To ⇨ Microsoft PowerPoint.

Formatting text

Text formatting works in PowerPoint as it does elsewhere in Office, with a few wrinkles:

- The Formatting toolbar has a button for Shadow Format Text. (No such button is even available in Word, although Word does let you apply shadow formatting via the Font dialog box.)

- For fast modifications of font size, use a pair of buttons on the Formatting toolbar: Increase and Decrease Font Size. You can make similar quick adjustments of line spacing for paragraphs with the Increase and Decrease Paragraph Spacing buttons, but you have to add them to a toolbar first. For more precise work, use the Font and Line Spacing commands on the Format menu.

- You can add or remove the bullet from any paragraph with the Bullet button. To change the bullet character or its size or color, right-click the paragraph and choose Bullets and Numbering from the shortcut menu. You can select any character from any available font as a bullet or choose a graphic from the Clip Gallery. To create an automatically numbered list, pick one of the number formats from the Numbered tab of the Bullets and Numbering dialog box.

- In an ordinary text placeholder containing outline-formatted text, use the Promote and Demote buttons to change the outline level of the current paragraph. Alternatively, you can use two pairs of keyboard equivalents: Tab and Shift+Tab, or Alt+Shift with the left and right arrow. If the text is bulleted, its bullet character changes accordingly. (By the way, Alt+Shift+up arrow or down arrow moves the current paragraph up or down as a unit, as in Word.)

Setting paragraph indents

Secret

PowerPoint has a ruler much like Word's, and you need it to indent paragraph text. Display the ruler by choosing View ⇨ Ruler. Then use the techniques detailed in "Setting indents with the ruler" in Chapter 28 to change the indents of the paragraph containing the insertion point.

Adding text animation

PowerPoint lets you fiddle with text animation effects in a seemingly infinite number of permutations. I recommend that you stick with one or two relatively simple methods except when you want to draw attention away from the speaker and to the screen.

The quick way to experiment is with the Animation Effects toolbar, or via the Slide Show ⇨ Preset Animation submenu. If you really want to blow an afternoon, open the Slide Show ⇨ Custom Animation dialog box. Shown in Figure 48-7, this dialog box is also available from a button on the Animation Effects toolbar.

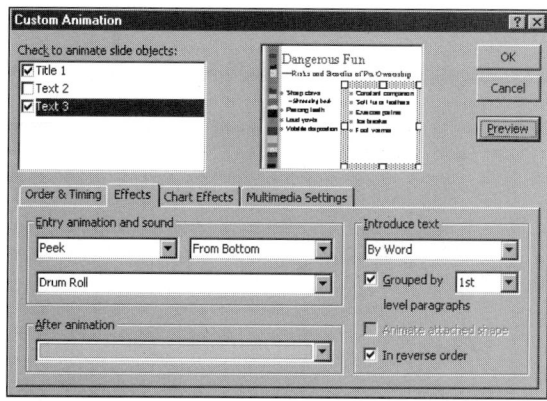

Figure 48-7: Control animation effects for individual elements on each slide using this dialog box.

Checking spelling

As discussed in Chapter 7, PowerPoint now shares the Office spell checker with Word and its other sisters and brothers. And like Word, PowerPoint checks your spelling on the fly if you leave the Spelling box checked in the Tools ⇨ Options dialog box (the Spelling tab). You see little wavy red lines under words that aren't in the dictionary.

Getting suggestions on style and clip art

In PowerPoint 2000, the Office Assistant serves as a consultant on stylistic matters, not just as a front-person for the Help system. While you work, this Presentation Assistant feature analyzes the current slide for amateurish inconsistencies in text layout, capitalization, and punctuation. It also checks for items in the Clip Gallery having keywords that match terms in the slide content. Stylistic transgressions and matching clip items trigger a little light bulb graphic on the slide. Click it to display the Assistant's explanatory message with a list of possible responses (see Figure 48-8).

Secret

To turn on or off the style analysis and clip art suggestions, click the Assistant and choose Options to display the Office Assistant dialog box. Here, check or clear the box labeled Using Features More Effectively.

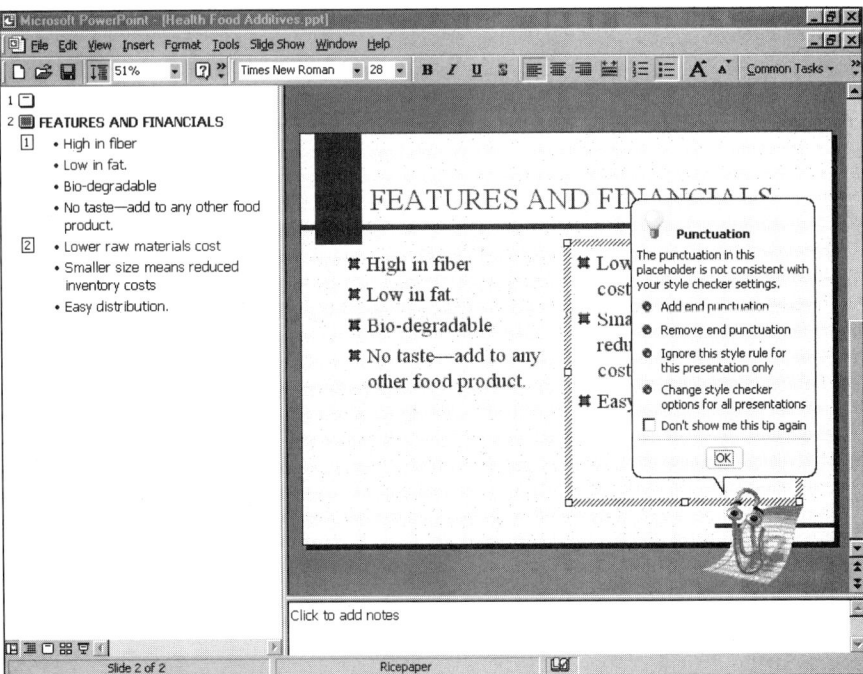

Figure 48-8: PowerPoint's Presentation Assistant identifies stylistic faux pas and gives you choices for handling them.

Use the Style Options dialog box shown in Figure 48-9 to set the rules PowerPoint uses for analyzing style. To display this box, go to the Spelling and Style tab of the Tools ⇨ Options dialog box and click the Style Options button. The dialog box has two tabs, Case and End Punctuation and Visual Clarity. Both choices refer to text — whatever the name suggests to you, the Visual Clarity options govern text-related issues such as minimum font size and maximum number of bullets per slide.

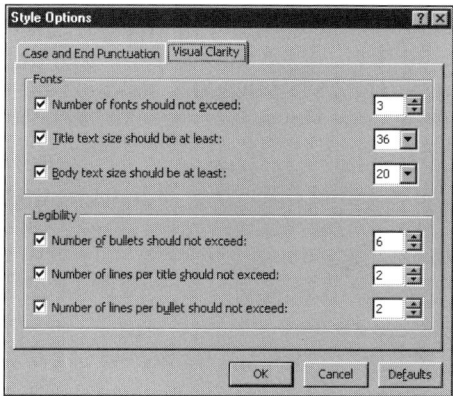

Figure 48-9: Change Visual Clarity settings for the Style Checker with this tab on the Style Options dialog box.

Adding graphics, charts, and tables

Because PowerPoint presentations typically rely so heavily on graphic elements, be sure to draw on the information presented in Chapter 8 to supplement the PowerPoint-specific techniques covered here. You can draw shapes (line art), add AutoShapes, or insert clip art, pictures, maps, and charts, or any other object in your PowerPoint documents. Note that like Excel, PowerPoint's Autoshapes menu offers a Connectors submenu. These shapes are lines that connect two objects on a slide and that stay attached when you move the objects.

Creating tables in PowerPoint

You can now create new tables from scratch within PowerPoint. For a simple table, choose Insert ⇨ Table and specify the table's dimensions in terms of rows and columns. To get creative, display the Tables and Borders toolbar which looks and works much like its counterpart in Word. Click the Draw Table button (the one that looks like a pencil) to lay down the table divisions freehand.

Secret

Click the menu button labeled Table on the Tables and Borders toolbar to reveal a laundry list of table-related commands. If you work regularly with PowerPoint tables and don't want to keep the toolbar visible always, Alt+Ctrl+drag a copy of this menu to the main menu bar for immediate access at any time.

Inserting Word tables and Excel charts

Although you can create tables in PowerPoint, you may prefer to rely on Word's more powerful table editing and formatting features. After you perfect the table in Word, select it, copy it to the clipboard, and then switch to PowerPoint and paste it onto a slide. The same simple technique works for Excel charts as well.

The simple clipboard method doesn't create a hot link to the original table or chart. If you want to be able to edit the item using the originating program, or if you want changes in the source document to appear automatically in your slide, you must insert or link the item as discussed in Chapter 10.

Copying formats

When you want to duplicate a set of formatting options you've already applied to an item on a slide, use PowerPoint's Format Painter. This feature works much like the comparable command in Word. Select the text or picture with the formatting you want to copy, and then click the Format Painter button. All you have to do then is drag over the text or click the picture that you want to receive the same formatting.

Adding action buttons, interactive controls, and hyperlinks

Secret

Make your PowerPoint presentations interactive. You can insert an *action button* on any slide by choosing the desired button from the Draw toolbar's AutoShapes ➪ Action Buttons menu. You can tear off the Action Buttons submenu as a separate toolbar if you use these buttons a lot — see Chapter 3 for the scoop on tear-off menus. Figure 48-10 shows what you'll see.

Figure 48-10: The Action Buttons submenu

You "draw" and modify these buttons on a slide just as you would any other AutoShape, using the techniques covered in Chapter 8. The available buttons have descriptive names such as Home, Next, and End, many of them with corresponding default actions—Home takes the viewer to the first slide in the presentation, for example. However, as soon as you draw a button, a dialog box appears in which you can specify many other possible actions, such as playing a multimedia clip or hyperlinking to another presentation, to a document from another application, or to a Web site. To display this dialog box later, right-click the button and choose Action Settings from the shortcut menu (note that *any* AutoShape can become an action button by right-clicking the shape and choosing Action Settings).

The Action Settings dialog box has two tabs, letting you specify two different actions for each button: one occurs when the viewer clicks the action button, the other when the mouse pointer is simply held over the button. Typically, the mouse-over action plays a sound or runs a macro.

As in other Office documents, you can also add hyperlinks and dialog box–type interactive controls to any PowerPoint presentation. Hyperlinks, covered in detail in Chapter 14, can be placed into any area that holds text. To add controls to a slide, display the Control Toolbox by selecting it on the View ⇨ Toolbars menu (see Chapter 9 for information on controls).

Multimedia madness

When does it make sense to add video and sound to a slide show? Only when they actually clarify your presentation. Using them just because you can is at best annoying and at worst a superlative means of obfuscating your point. Er, muddying your message. Over my protests, add your multimedia objects via the Insert ⇨ Movies and Sound submenu. You can insert existing video clips or sound recordings, record your own sounds, or have PowerPoint play a specified audio CD track.

Secret

To optimize video performance, place the clips themselves—not just shortcuts—in the PowerPoint folder.

Controlling playback of multimedia clips

Use the Play Options, Action Settings, and Custom Animation dialog boxes to control when and how your multimedia clips play, and how they interact with the slide show itself. All of these dialog boxes are available from the shortcut menu that appears when you right-click a clip's icon.

- The Play Options dialog box lets you decide whether a clip plays only once or in a continuous loop until you stop it. You can select which tracks of a CD should play and for how long, and you can control whether a video clip rewinds after it's through playing.

- The Action Settings dialog box has two tabs that let you control whether or not the clip plays when you click it, or when you just hold the mouse over it. (You can always play a clip by double-clicking it.)

- Use the Timing and Play Settings tabs in the Custom Animation dialog box to play the clip automatically when its slide is displayed, or to control when it plays in the sequence of animations — whether the slide show waits for it to finish or whether it continues playing after other slides are displayed.

Recording a sound track

As an alternative to adding individual sound clips to particular slides, you can record a continuous soundtrack. Use the Slide Show ⇨ Record Narration command. This is especially valuable for presentations that you don't give live, such as those you post to the Web or an intranet. Be forewarned, though, that you'll need great gobs of disk space for a narration of any length, particularly if you record at high fidelity.

Using the ValuPack add-ins

The ValuPack folder on the Office CD-ROM includes several software goodies designed to enhance multimedia PowerPoint presentations. These include:

- **The Custom Soundtracks add-in.** Install this add-in and you'll be able to record and play back MIDI soundtracks without burdening your presentation files with the huge .wav files required to store recorded audio. Look in the \MusicTrk subfolder.

- **The RealAudio and ActiveMovie add-ins.** These add-ins let you stream multimedia presentations across a network by converting them to the Progressive Networks RealAudio format or the ActiveMovie Stream Format (ASF) format, respectively. Each add-in places a corresponding "Publish To" command on the Tools menu. Find them in the \RealAud, \Amovie, and \ASF subfolders.

- **The PowerPoint Animation Player.** This browser plug-in for Internet Explorer Version 3.0 and Netscape Navigator 2.x+ lets you play PowerPoint Animation (.ppz) presentations inside these browsers. It's stored in the \PPTAnim subfolder.

Conclusion

With the concepts and techniques explored in this chapter, you can plan effective presentations and produce top-notch individual slides. Chapter 49 discusses advanced topics such as customizing, templates, and macros, and it covers the steps required to create and give a complete PowerPoint slide show.

Chapter 49

Deeper PowerPoint Secrets

In This Chapter

- Customizing PowerPoint with the Options dialog box
- Understanding PowerPoint templates and macros
- Developing custom layouts and formats
- Putting together a complete presentation
- Performing your presentation and sending it to others

Although PowerPoint fits comfortably right out of the box, a little touch-up tailoring can make it hug you like Spandex. PowerPoint still lags behind Word and Excel in customizing features, but you should definitely take advantage of the options you do have.

Working with the Options dialog box

As in other Office applications, the Tools ⇨ Options dialog box (Figure 49-1) is the control center for tweaking PowerPoint to your personal preferences. The default settings for many of the items in the dialog box are usually appropriate, but some adjustments may make sense based on the way you work.

Here are some settings you should consider changing:

- Tired of having to choose the type of new presentation each time you start PowerPoint without specifying an existing presentation? Use settings on the View tab to eliminate the dialog boxes you normally get (refer back to the "Starting New Presentations" section in Chapter 48 for details).

- When you give a slide show using an overhead projector or large-screen equipment, check the End with Black Slide box on the View tab. This gives a clear-cut visual ending to the presentation and serves as a cue to bring up the lights.

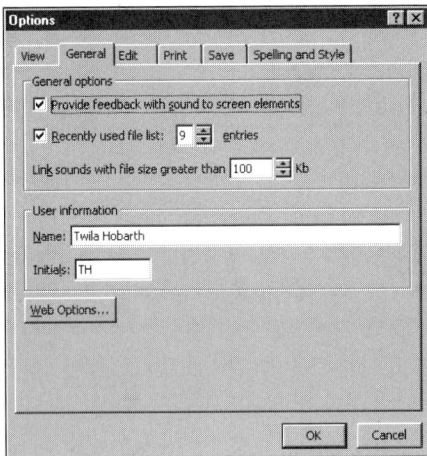

Figure 49-1: The General tab on PowerPoint's View ⇨ Options dialog box

- On the Edit tab, increase the entries number for the Recently Used File list setting to its maximum, 9. Also, use the Maximum Number of Undos box to increase the number of consecutive changes PowerPoint will remember and reverse — why stop at 20? The highest value allowed is 150.

- Sharing files in an office with multiple versions of PowerPoint requires that everyone settle on a lowest-common-denominator file format. The Save tab lets you change the default file format for saving PowerPoint files to one used by any previous version back to 4.0. One interesting choice is the dual 95 and 97-2000 format, which lets users of both versions open presentation files, although the files are larger and they can't be modified by PowerPoint 95 users. Another is Web page, good for those who use PowerPoint primarily to create Web-based presentations.

Using macros in PowerPoint

PowerPoint has a macro recorder like the ones in Word and Excel. Chapter 5 covers the process of customizing Office applications by recording macros that you assign to toolbar buttons or menu items. Just be aware that in PowerPoint, the Record Macro dialog box doesn't let you assign a new macro to a toolbar button, menu item, or keyboard shortcut. Customizing the keyboard is out in PowerPoint, but you can place a macro on a button or menu using the Tools ⇨ Customize dialog box.

Where to store PowerPoint macros

As in Word and Excel, you can store a PowerPoint macro in a particular document (presentation), or in a template on which other documents are based. Note, however, that to store a macro in a template, you must have opened that template separately with the File ⇨ Open command. In other words, the templates on which your presentations are based don't appear in the Store Macro In box when you record a new macro. PowerPoint templates are covered in the section "Working with templates in PowerPoint" later in this chapter.

Why record a PowerPoint macro?

Even if you're a heavy PowerPoint user, you're likely to find macros of value only occasionally. Of course, a recorded macro is a good way to give text or graphics a set of formatting choices all at once — after all, PowerPoint lacks styles. You can also use PowerPoint macros to insert text you use repeatedly, especially if it requires special formatting. Although the AutoCorrect feature is often more convenient (see Chapter 7), it requires you to memorize an abbreviation for your boilerplate text. By contrast, you can assign a macro to a toolbar button or menu.

Developing Custom Layouts and Formats

The final appearance of an individual slide depends on several interrelated factors. The template on which the entire presentation is based governs the initial layout, background, and repeating graphics elements for the *master* for that type of slide. However, you're free to modify the master's layout at will, and these changes affect all the slides in the presentation based on that master. Similarly, the AutoLayout chosen for that specific slide dictates which placeholders are present on the slide to begin with and how they're arranged. Although you can't alter the AutoLayouts themselves, you can go on to move, resize, or delete any of the placeholders on the resulting slide, and you can insert additional text boxes, graphics, and other objects.

Working with masters

Each presentation has one or two master slides, the *slide master* (always) and the *title master* (optional). In addition, it has a *handout master* and a *notes master* for the printed portions of the presentation. Masters govern the basic layout and text formatting of the items based upon them. Slide and title masters also contain the backgrounds, graphics, and other objects that appear on all the slides they govern. The title master — if there is one — only controls the slides based on the first of the 24 AutoLayouts, the one named Title Slide. All other slides, including the title master itself, are based on the slide master.

Editing masters

Use the View ⇨ Master submenu to display and modify any of the four masters. Shift-clicking the Slide Sorter View or Outline View buttons at the left of the status bar displays the Handout master. If the presentation doesn't have a title master, you can add one by choosing Insert ⇨ New Title Master. Figure 49-2 shows a slide master. The dotted rectangles are the text placeholders. A background graphic has been added to the slide.

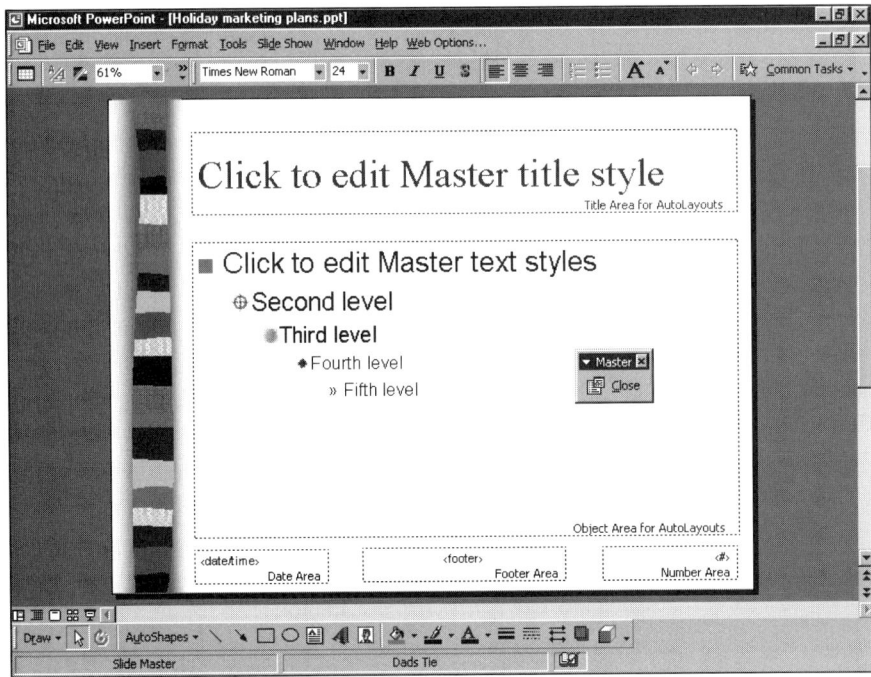

Figure 49-2: Viewing the slide master

Any change you make to a master is reflected on each slide that is based on it. For example, if you change the font of the slide title text in the slide master, the same change will automatically ripple through the title master and all your slides. If you make the same change on the title master, the font change only appears on slides based on the Title Slide AutoLayout.

Secret

However, once you change an element on a particular slide, that element retains its independent formatting when later you make changes to the masters. To restore the connection between the master and the slide, reapply its AutoLayout using the Slide Layout command, available on the Format menu or the Common Tasks toolbar.

Laying out and formatting text on masters

Although the 24 AutoLayouts provide placeholders for various types of information in various combinations, the slide and title masters only display text placeholders. PowerPoint creates the AutoLayout variations automatically, based on the sizes and positions of the placeholders in the master. A master can have up to five text placeholders: title, text, date, slide number, and footer. To remove a placeholder, just select it and press Delete. Use the Format ➪ Master Layout dialog box to restore any of these items you've removed. You're free to move the text placeholders around on the master and to resize them.

Secret

Although you can type text and change its formatting inside any of a master's placeholders, PowerPoint handles the title and text placeholders differently than the others. The text you type into either of these placeholders on a master never appears on slides based on the master — instead, you get a message telling you to click them to add your own text. That part's easy to figure out. What may not be so obvious is that although PowerPoint lets you format selected text in a master's title and text placeholders, that formatting applies to *all* text in the box.

The date, slide number, and footer placeholders act differently. Text you type into them appears on every slide and can't be changed. You can format the text on a letter-by-letter basis, however, and these formats do appear in slides based on the master. (For tips on formatting text in PowerPoint, refer to "Adding and formatting text" in Chapter 48.)

Working with outlined and bulleted text in masters

Secret

The title and text placeholders differ in one important respect: Text in the title placeholder is formatted in ordinary paragraphs, while that in the text placeholder is automatically set up as a hierarchical outline. Working in the master's text placeholder, you can control the default text format for each level of the outline.

On a typical slide, of course, the body text consists of a series of *bulleted* outline points. The Bullet command on the shortcut menu for any PowerPoint text lets you choose which bullet symbol to use for the paragraph, if any; how big it is; and its color. Keep in mind that although you can add a bullet to any paragraph (in a master or on an individual slide), only the paragraphs in a text placeholder can be promoted and demoted in the outline.

Creating repeating slide elements by adding them to a master

You can place any content item on a master, including text boxes; shapes from the Drawing toolbar; clip art and other pictures; and multimedia and other objects. Any item you place on a master appears in the background on all the slides it controls — unless you turn off the entire background using Format ➪ Background (see "Mixing slide designs within a presentation" later in this chapter).

Working with color schemes

Each presentation, and the template it's based on, has up to nine distinct color schemes. You work with the color schemes by choosing Format ⇨ Slide Color Scheme. The resulting dialog box is shown in Figure 49-3.

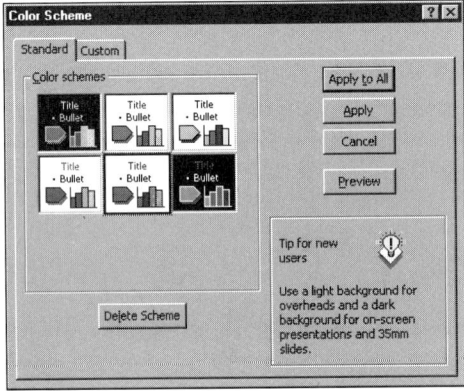

Figure 49-3: Choose and customize color schemes in this dialog box.

How color schemes work

Although PowerPoint uses one color scheme for all new slides you add, you can apply any of the other schemes to any slide without otherwise altering its look. If you design your color schemes carefully, you can apply the alternate schemes to vary the colors of individual slides and still preserve a chromatic unity. Of course, when you change the color scheme of a master, all the slides based on it change accordingly.

In more detail, a color scheme sets the eight colors PowerPoint applies automatically to the various elements of a slide: text, background, filled objects, and the like. You can override these defaults by selecting the item and choosing the appropriate formatting command.

However, the colors you select for the scheme also appear on the color menus displayed by the Fill Color, Line Color, and Font Color dialog boxes, making it easy to change an element's color and still stay coordinated with the color scheme. (You can still apply other colors by choosing More Colors from these menus.) Applying the Automatic color choice to an element restores the default set in the color scheme, and if you later change the color scheme, the element's color changes to match.

To apply a different color scheme to the selected slide or slides, select it in the Standard tab of the Color Scheme dialog box and choose Apply. Apply to all changes the color scheme for the entire presentation. You can see how your slide will look with a new color scheme before leaving the dialog box by choosing Preview. If you like the original scheme better, just click Cancel in the dialog box.

Customizing color schemes

You can customize any of the existing color schemes by selecting it first in the Standard tab, and then switching to the Custom tab, where its colors are now shown for the individual slide elements — background, text, and so forth. As you choose new colors for these elements, a dummy slide reflects your changes. You can apply a custom scheme on a one-shot basis or click Add as Standard Scheme to place it on the Standard tab for future use.

Note that when you use this technique to save a modified color scheme, PowerPoint does *add* your scheme to the Standard tab rather than replace the scheme you started with. To effectively *replace* the original scheme, you must then delete it by selecting it in the Standard tab and choosing Delete Scheme.

Working with templates in PowerPoint

Just as in the other Office applications, you use templates in PowerPoint to define a set of formatting, layout, and content choices ahead of time for new presentations. See Chapter 13 for background on how Office templates work.

Secret

The PowerPoint documentation and Help file make a distinction between two types of templates, *design templates* and *content templates*. Actually, though, the only thing that distinguishes the two is what you choose to save in them. Design templates store formatting, color schemes, and background graphics, whereas content templates store those elements, plus text and graphics content for one or more individual slides. Note that this is just how templates work in Word or Excel — in Word, for example, you can save a template containing only formatting choices, or one that also includes prefab text and graphics. But the Word and Excel documentation doesn't distinguish between these variations.

Creating new templates

To create your own template, start a new presentation or open an existing presentation. Make whatever changes you like to the color scheme, the slide master, or the content of individual slides. When everything looks right, choose File ⇨ Save As. Select "Design Template" in the Save as Type box, and select a folder for the new template.

But what folder should you use? An obvious choice is your user templates folder, or one of its subfolders. By default, the user template folder is Application Data\Microsoft\Templates in your main Windows folder (in single-user versions of Windows) or in the Profiles\Administrator folder (in multiuser installations). However, if you want to stick to the organization system Office uses, place templates containing no content (design templates) in the Presentation Designs folder, a subfolder of the Templates folder in the main Office folder.

Once you create a template you can add it to the AutoContent wizard. Start the wizard by choosing File ➪ New and double-clicking AutoContent Wizard in the General tab. When the wizard appears, click Next to access the Presentation Type panel. There, click the presentation category to which you want to add your template, and then click Add and select the template. From then on you can create new presentations based on the template using the wizard.

Changing the default presentation

Ordinarily, PowerPoint opens a completely blank, design-less presentation when you click the New button, or when starting the program if you opt to shut off the startup dialog boxes (see Chapter 48). Fortunately, however, you don't have to start from scratch every time with a completely empty, unadorned presentation — you can change the default template.

Secret

To define a custom default template, open or create the presentation you want to use for this purpose, removing any content that you don't want to reuse. When you're happy with your work, choose File ➪ Save As and select "Design Template" in the Save as Type box, which should take you automatically to the user templates folder. Once you're there, type **Blank Presentation** in the Save As box and click Save. Alternatively, you can use an existing template as the default by simply copying it to the user templates folder and renaming it to Blank Presentation.pot. To return to a truly blank, empty presentation as your default, just delete or rename the Blank Presentation.pot file.

Applying another template to an existing presentation

You can radically alter an entire presentation's look without changing its content by applying a different template, replacing the current masters and color schemes with those stored in the other template. To bring up the Apply Design dialog box, double-click over the middle part of the status bar, which lists the name of the current template. Alternatively, you can click Apply Design Template on the Common Tasks toolbar or choose Format ➪ Apply Design Template.

Secret

PowerPoint implies that only so-called design templates should be applied to an existing presentation. Actually, you can use any template you like, or for that matter, any presentation — no matter how stuffed full of content it happens to be. PowerPoint only applies the design elements of the chosen template or presentation to the existing presentation — all content stays behind in the template.

Mixing slide designs within a presentation

Although technically you're limited to only one template per presentation, you can use various techniques to create slides with markedly different designs than those the masters impose.

Changing the background of selected slides

To create a slide that departs from the masters' dictates, the first step is to remove the design elements that come from the masters. Use the Format ⇨ Background command for this purpose. In the dialog box shown in Figure 49-4, first check the box labeled Omit Background Graphics from Master. Although this instruction strikes me as ambiguous, what it means is that on this slide only, you're turning off the repeating elements found on the master.

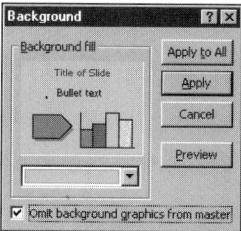

Figure 49-4: Use this dialog box to control the background of one or more slides.

Now you're free to choose a different background using the untitled drop-down color menu in the Background dialog box. Your new background can take the form of a solid color or any of the special fill effects described in "Filling objects" in Chapter 8. By drawing new graphics or inserting pictures, you can completely overhaul the slide's layout in no time.

Inserting slides from another presentation

Suppose you want to insert an existing slide — including its design — into another presentation. Because PowerPoint doesn't let you mix templates, simply copying the slide doesn't work — upon arrival, a copied slide's content is preserved, but its design conforms to the template in the destination presentation.

Secret

With a bit of trickery, however, you can use the clipboard to mix slide designs in a single presentation. Rather than pasting a copied slide as such, you can use the Paste Special command to transfer slide designs as OLE objects or as pictures. In either case, the copied slide can still be edited. Here's how to proceed:

1. Open both presentations, and close all other presentations so that you have plenty of elbow room.

2. Choose Window ⇨ Arrange All to place the two windows side by side.

3. Using Normal view, go to the presentation containing the slide you want to use elsewhere. In the outline pane, select the slide you want to transfer by clicking to its left, and copy it to the clipboard.

4. Move to the destination presentation, the one into which you want to insert the copied slide. Create a new blank slide where you want the copied slide.

5. Important: Click the destination slide itself — don't select it in the outline pane.

6. Choose Edit ⇨ Paste Special. In the resulting dialog box choose Microsoft PowerPoint Slide Object (if you want to embed or link the slide) or Picture (if you want to transfer it as a collection of drawing objects).

The copied slide arrives in the presentation at half size and in the middle of the slide onto which you've pasted it. To make it an exact fit, right-click it and choose Format Object or Format Picture. In the Format dialog box, use the Position tab to set the Horizontal and Vertical position to 0" from the top-left corner, and use the Size tab to scale the slide to 200% at both Height and Width.

With all that out of the way, you can edit the pasted slide to taste. If it's an embedded object, double-clicking it lets you edit it as you would any other slide — the only problem is that its text doesn't show up in the outline pane. If it's linked, double-clicking the slide opens it in its own window for editing. To edit a pasted picture, you must first convert it into a drawing object. Double-click the picture and answer Yes when you're asked to make the conversion. You can now use the standard Office drawing tools to make changes to any element, including graphics that were originally part of the master.

Transferring slide designs via disk files

Secret

PowerPoint lets you save any slide as a single graphic in formats such as GIF, JPEG, PNG, and Windows metafile (.wmf) files. While this can be useful for transferring slides to other applications that don't speak the PowerPoint tongue, it also gives you an alternative method for using the design of one presentation in another.

Start by selecting a slide with the layout elements you want to place in other presentations. The slide shouldn't contain any text or other content unless you want to transfer it, too.

Choose File ⇨ Save As and select "Windows Metafile" at Files of Type. PowerPoint asks whether you want to export all the slides or just the current one. (If you select the former option, it creates a *folder* with the name you enter in Save As and then exports the individual slides there as Slide1.wmf, Slide2.wmf, and so on.)

Now you can open the other presentation. Choose Insert ⇨ New Slide and select the completely blank AutoLayout at the bottom right of the New Slide dialog box. When you insert the new slide, it won't have any placeholders but it will have any background elements specified by the template. Open the Format ⇨ Background dialog box. Using the technique mentioned in

"Changing the background of selected slides" earlier in this chapter, shut off the master's repeating elements, and then use the Picture tab on the Fill Effects dialog box to import the .wmf file of choice.

Inserting Content from Another Presentation

If you simply want to merge the contents of one or more slides into an open presentation, you can accomplish this goal either with the Slide Finder, or via drag-and-drop.

To use the Slide Finder:

1. Start by selecting the slide after which you want the imported ones to appear.

2. Choose Insert ⇨ Slides from Files to display the Slide Finder dialog box, shown here.

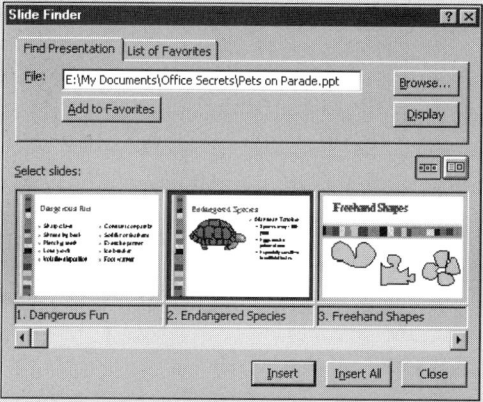

The Slide Finder dialog box

3. On the Find Presentation tab, use the Browse button to locate the presentation document containing the slides you want to insert. If you think you will use this presentation again, click Add to Favorites; if you want to use a presentation you used previously, switch to the List of Favorites tab to select it.

4. To help you find the right slides, the Display button shows zoomed-out views of the individual slides from the selected presentation. Those two funny-looking buttons off to the right switch between a view that shows three tiny slide previews with their titles below, and one that shows a list of all the slide titles with one slightly larger slide preview.

5. Click Insert or Insert All to insert the chosen slides into your presentation. The Slide Finder stays open until you click Close.

It's probably just as easy to open both presentations in tiled windows (use Window ⇨ Arrange All) and then move or copy slides from one to the other by dragging and dropping. A plain drag moves the slide, while a Ctrl-drag copies it. Or you can right-drag and pick from the little menu that appears when you drop the slide on the destination window.

Putting Together a Complete Presentation

Once you have the layout and content of all the individual slides firmed up, it's time to fine-tune the presentation as a whole.

Checking your work with slide shows

As you work, run test slide shows frequently to check on the sequence of slides and the effectiveness of any special effects. Use Slide Show ⇨ View Show or View ⇨ Slide Show to get the show on the road with equal effect. As a further alternative, you can click the Slide Show button, the farthest right of the group of buttons at the left end of the horizontal scroll bar. Switch from slide to slide by clicking the mouse or pressing Enter.

Reordering and hiding slides

To shuffle slides around within a presentation, drag them to where you want them to go in Outline view (by using the slide icon) or in Slide Sorter view (by dragging the slide thumbnail). See Chapter 48 for more on these views.

To temporarily hide a slide so that it doesn't appear in the slide show, choose Slide Show ⇨ Hide Slide. In Slide Sorter view, hidden slides are marked with an appropriate icon. PowerPoint still displays the slide in other views. (You can display a hidden slide during a slide show by pressing H.)

Animating slide transitions

If the text animations described in Chapter 48 aren't enough, PowerPoint lets you add animated effects to the transitions between entire slides. For example, you can have the next slide replace the current one not all at once, but starting at the edges and working to the middle.

Use the Slide Show ⇨ Slide Transition dialog box (Figure 49-5) to select from among 40 or so different variations, and to pick sounds to accompany these transitions. Alternatively, switch to the Slide Sorter view and select transition options from the drop-down lists on the Slide Sorter toolbar.

My rule of thumb is to stick with one transition effect, at most, throughout the presentation, except when I deliberately want to disrupt the flow to make a particularly important point or let a little levity leak in.

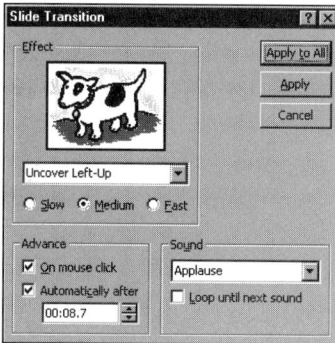

Figure 49-5: Select animations and sound effects for transitions from one slide to the next in this dialog box.

Setting slide show timings

You can give a PowerPoint presentation interactively, but sometimes it makes sense to have it run automatically, changing from slide to slide at prearranged intervals. You can set these intervals in one of two ways: manually, by entering the number of seconds that should pass before showing each slide in succession, or semiautomatically, by recording the timings you use as you rehearse the presentation.

Setting timing manually

To set slide timings manually, go to Normal or Slide Sorter view and select the slide to receive the timing setting. Choose Slide Show ➪ Slide Transition. In the Advance area of the resulting dialog box, select Automatically After, and enter the number of seconds you want the slide to remain visible. For more flexibility, you can have PowerPoint display the next slide either when you click the mouse *or* automatically according to your timing, whichever comes first. Choose Apply to activate the new settings.

Recording timings during rehearsal

Choose Slide Show ➪ Rehearse Timings to record the timings you actually use in rehearsing your presentation. This command starts the slide show and displays a little dialog box (see Figure 49-6) where you can monitor the elapsed time as you control the pace of the show. You're supposed to narrate each slide as you plan to during the real presentation, clicking the arrow button or pressing Enter to advance to each slide in turn. PowerPoint keeps track of the time between clicks for you.

Figure 49-6: Recording timings during a slide show rehearsal

After the presentation is complete, PowerPoint tells you how long the entire slide show took and lets you decide whether to keep your timings. If so, it plugs the values into the same Slide Transition dialog box you can access manually, which means you can use the other settings there to decide whether clicking the mouse advances the slide show. If you plan to use this technique, be sure to try at least a few practice runs first. Even if you plan to take full manual control over the final presentation, recording your rehearsed timings can be valuable.

Creating custom shows

Because it's common to have to give the same presentation many times with minor variations, PowerPoint now lets you create "custom slide shows" based on a subset of the slides in a presentation. If you have short and long versions of the same talk, you probably use most of the same slides for both versions. Instead of keeping the slides in two separate files that are more alike than different, you can select the specific slides you want to specify custom shows containing whichever specific files you need.

Use the Slide Show ➪ Custom Shows dialog box for this purpose. Choose New to set up a new custom show definition. In the Define Custom Show dialog box that next appears (see Figure 49-7), pick out the specific slides you want in the custom show. You can reorder the slides within a custom show using the arrow buttons at the far right of this dialog box. To play a custom slide show, select it in the Slide Show ➪ Custom Shows dialog box and choose the Show button.

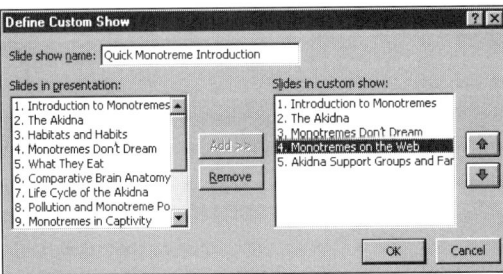

Figure 49-7: Manage custom slide shows with this dialog box.

Overall slide show setup options

Choose Slide Show ➪ Set Up Show to display a dialog box of options governing the overall characteristics of your presentation. The Show type settings govern the window size, the looping pattern, and whether animations and narrations are played. Use the Slides settings to specify whether the presentation includes all slides in the document, a range of slides, or a specific custom show. The pair of Advance slides radio buttons can override the timings settings for all slides in the presentation.

A few other slide show options are located on the View tab of the Tools ⇨ Options dialog box. Here, you can control:

- Whether PowerPoint displays a shortcut menu when you right-click during a slide show. The shortcut menu is discussed in "Running a slide show from your computer" later in this chapter.

- Whether you see a special button at the lower-left corner of every slide. If the button is visible, clicking it displays the slide show shortcut menu. Again, see "Running a slide show from your computer."

- Whether all slide shows end with a "black slide," that is a blank, black screen. Check this box to signal the end of the show without redisplaying PowerPoint itself with all its menus and toolbars — usually not the smooth, professional effect you want to leave your audience with.

Performing Your Presentation

With your presentation complete, the day looms when you'll actually have to give it publicly. In preparation for that fateful moment, you should of course give the finished presentation a dry run with an on-screen slide show.

When at last you're satisfied with your work, your final preperformance task is to convert the presentation to the form in which it will actually be given. If you need to image it on slides or transparencies, you send the presentation file to your company's graphics department, or to an outside service bureau. If you'll be taking it on the road, distributing it to others, or setting it up to run unattended on another computer, you need to bundle it up with any linked files and if necessary, the PowerPoint viewer. And if the presentation is destined for the Internet or a company intranet, you must save the slides as Web pages using the techniques discussed in Chapter 14.

Sending a presentation

If your presentation can stand on its own without your spoken accompaniment (or with a recorded narration), you can send it to others for viewing at their convenience. If the recipient has a copy of PowerPoint, you can send your presentation on a floppy, attach it to an e-mail message, or send it via e-mail from within PowerPoint using the File ⇨ Send To ⇨ Mail Recipient command. If the recipient doesn't have PowerPoint, or if the presentation includes linked files, use the Pack and Go Wizard to prepare it, as described later in "Creating transportable presentations with the Pack and Go Wizard." Alternatively, you can distribute the presentation as a set of Web pages, as discussed in Part IV.

Distributing the PowerPoint viewer

Microsoft permits you to distribute freely the PowerPoint viewer, a hefty chunk of software that runs PowerPoint presentations. It's for those who don't own PowerPoint itself, or who don't have it installed on their traveling computer. It works with presentations stored in most PowerPoint formats, including those of versions 2.0 to 4.0 and 95 (for Windows) and Versions 3.0 to 4.0 (for Macintosh).

Secret

The easiest way to distribute the PowerPoint viewer is by including it in a presentation prepared with the Pack and Go Wizard. However, this version doesn't work with Windows 3.1. A viewer that does have that capability is available and may be located on your Office CD-ROM—check for a folder called PPt4View. Otherwise, you can get it from Microsoft's Web site.

Saving a presentation as an automatic slide show

Secret

Saving a document with the extension .pps makes PowerPoint open it as a slide show that starts immediately when the file is double-clicked in Windows. This can be a good choice when you're distributing it to others and want them to be able to see the show with a minimum of hassle. To save a presentation as an automatic show in the File ⇨ Save As dialog box, choose "PowerPoint show" at Save as Type.

Note that when you use the File ⇨ Open command to open a slide show file with PowerPoint already running, the document appears on the screen as an ordinary presentation. And by the way, you can right-click *any* PowerPoint presentation in Windows and choose Show from the shortcut menu to start it as a slide show.

Running a slide show from your computer

When you deliver a slide show directly from your computer in real time, you can use the keyboard or the mouse to switch slides. With the mouse, just click the current slide once to advance to the next one, or to start the next animated effect, if there is one in line. With the last slide on display, clicking the mouse terminates the show.

Using the slide show shortcut menu

To jump to a specific slide out of sequence, display the slide show shortcut menu. You can accomplish this in several ways, depending on your settings on the View tab of the Tools ⇨ Options dialog box: by right-clicking the current slide, clicking the pop-up menu button at the lower left of the slide, if visible, or pressing Shift+F10 (this last technique always works). Aside from the expected Next and Previous, the shortcut menu's navigation choices are located on the Go submenu. Here, use By Title to pick any slide in the current show, or use Slide Navigator to select from all slides in all the custom shows (see "Creating custom shows" earlier in this chapter).

The shortcut menu also lets you display the Meeting Minder (covered later in the chapter) and your speaker notes and enables you to change the appearance and function of the mouse pointer.

Navigation keys during slide shows

Caution

Any of the following keys displays the next slide or animated effect: N, Space, right arrow, down arrow, Page Down, or Enter. To go back to the previous slide, press P, left arrow, up arrow, or Page Up.

One caveat: None of these methods will work until the current slide has finished loading. The way to tell? When the Scroll Lock light on your keyboard comes on, you can advance to another slide.

With the last slide visible, any of the keys for advancing to the "next" slide ends the show. To end a slide show at any time, press Esc.

Pausing a slide show

Secret

Suppose someone asks a question and you feel an uncommon moment of eloquence coming on. To get the full attention of your audience, consider temporarily shutting off your slides. The easy way to create such a pause is by pressing B (for black) or W (for white) to blank the screen. Pressing the same key again restores the slide you were showing. You can use this trick to end the show with a blank screen — but PowerPoint now lets you end all shows that way, by checking the End with Black Slide box on the View tab of the Tools ➪ Options dialog box.

Scribbling on your slides

PowerPoint lets you write all over your slides during a slide show to add emphasis to the information and energy to your presentation. Activate the pen mouse pointer during a slide show by pressing Ctrl+P or by displaying the shortcut menu and choosing Pointer Options ➪ Pen. With the pen active, drag over a slide to mark or write on it. To erase your doodles, just press E. You can control the color of the scribblings via Pointer Options ➪ Pen Color.

Keeping track of discussions during a presentation

If you're seeking feedback from your audience, use the Meeting Minder to record what happens during the presentation: who said what, what decisions were made, and which tasks were assigned to whom. During a show you can pop up the Meeting Minder box by right-clicking the current slide and choosing Meeting Minder from the shortcut menu. Alternatively, you can bring it up before the show starts from the Tools menu. The Meeting Minutes tab lets you record free-form text, while the Action Items tab is for listing specific to-do items that emerge from the discussion. After entering an action item, click Add to append it to the list.

Secret

PowerPoint automatically creates a new slide based on your action points, placing it at the end of the presentation. In other words, the slide show finishes with a neat summary of what needs to be done and who is responsible for doing it. Just remember that you must close the Meeting Minder dialog box to make the current list of action items appear on the final slide.

Other slide show keys

Press S to alternately show or hide the mouse pointer during a slide show. Pressing H displays the next slide, if that slide has been hidden — otherwise, it has no effect.

Printing handouts, outlines, and speaker's notes

In PowerPoint, *handouts* are printed copies of your slides intended for distribution to your audience. Depending on the layout you select, a handout contains two to nine slides per printed page. PowerPoint handouts contain only the slides themselves, not your speaker's notes. Of course, you can also print the notes; they appear on paper with the corresponding slide. And you can print the Outline view of your presentation. If you choose this option, the printout contains the same level of detail your outline has on the screen.

To print any of these items, choose File ➪ Print and use the Print What box to select the item you want to print. If you're printing handouts, use the Slides per Page and Order controls to specify how densely you want to cram the printed slides on paper, and in what order. Use the File ➪ Page Setup dialog box to control the orientation (landscape versus portrait) of your printouts. You can't select different orientation settings for notes than for handouts, so you must revisit this box if you plan to print your notes vertically but your handouts "long-wise."

Creating portable presentations with the Pack and Go Wizard

The Pack and Go Wizard (Figure 49-8) walks you through the steps necessary to take a presentation with you and ensures that you have all the files you need to give the presentation elsewhere. Start the process by choosing File ➪ Pack and Go. The wizard asks you to specify a destination drive, which can be a floppy or other portable disk or a network drive. If the entire presentation doesn't fit on one disk, PowerPoint prompts you to insert new ones as necessary. The wizard gives you the option of including linked files and embedded True Type fonts, as well as including the PowerPoint viewer, on your travel disk. To unpack the presentation, run the Pngsetup program created by the wizard on the destination computer.

Chapter 49: Deeper PowerPoint Secrets

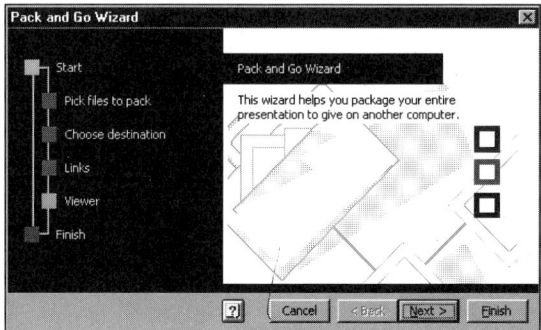

Figure 49-8: Bundling up a presentation for the road with the Pack and Go Wizard

Choosing a display device

If you're running Windows 98 or Windows 2000 (NT 5.0), and if your computer has more than one display device — say, a monitor and a projector — you can control which device displays the slide show. To select the device, choose Slide Show ➪ Set Up Show. Then use the Show On drop-down list to tell PowerPoint where to display the show.

Live online collaboration

PowerPoint's new online collaboration feature enables you to broadcast interactive presentations over the Internet or a corporate intranet. Members of your audience can add on-screen annotations that can be seen by all participants, or even edit the presentation itself. Online collaboration is based on and requires Microsoft NetMeeting, discussed in Chapter 18. Choose Tools ➪ Online Collaboration to get things going.

Conclusion

Although a less complicated piece of software than Word, Excel, or Access, PowerPoint offers an unmatched combination of features for building and presenting the perfect slide show, electronic or otherwise. The options described in this chapter help you fine-tune PowerPoint's behavior to meet your presentation-development needs. In addition, the techniques covered here provide the skills you need for creating custom layouts and putting together complete presentations — and ultimately, for getting your ideas across to your audience.

Part XI

Secrets of Outlook 2000

Chapter 50: Outlook Overview

Chapter 51: Managing E-mail in Outlook

Chapter 52: Managing Tasks, Schedules, Contacts, and Miscellany

Chapter 50

Outlook Overview

In This Chapter

- Choosing or creating an Outlook user profile
- Working with the Outlook bar, Outlook Today, folders, and views
- Entering information items on forms and directly on views
- Managing Windows files in Outlook
- Keeping house in Outlook
- Customizing views and forms

Outlook is a productivity enhancement and information-management tool for both personal and workgroup use. Outlook gives you features aplenty for keeping track of your own e-mail messages, appointments, meetings, tasks, and contacts (it replaced Schedule+ from Office 95). It enables you to store and recall random facts, too, and can even substitute for Explorer as a disk- and file-management utility.

Because most people work in groups, Outlook is designed from the ground up to facilitate information exchange and group collaboration throughout an organization. Outlook lets managers assign tasks and schedule meetings and appointments for members of the workgroup and then monitor meeting attendance and task completion.

As the client (individual user) portion of Microsoft's emerging groupware solution, Outlook is at its most powerful when used in conjunction with Exchange Server. But if your organization doesn't run Exchange, don't let that stop you from using Outlook — some of the more arcane networking features will be unavailable, but you can still tap a wealth of information-management power.

Though Outlook delivers plenty of power right out of the box, you're not locked into the stock forms supplied with the product. With its extensive customization features, you can build a productivity command center tailored to your information management needs. If the options on the toolbars aren't enough, Outlook's Visual Basic interface lets you put its resources to work in custom applications using the techniques covered in Part VI.

Getting Started with Outlook

Outlook's e-mail and groupware features rely on the messaging capabilities built into Windows. If you go with Outlook's Internet Only configuration, or if you don't use Outlook for e-mail at all, setting up the program is straightforward. If you're working on a network with the Corporate or Workgroup configuration, you must choose or set up a *user profile*, a collection of settings that defines the way Windows messaging applications function. For one thing, the user profile specifies where (that is, using which *information services*) the program stores and retrieves data. User profiles were introduced with the Microsoft Exchange client included with Windows, but Outlook uses them too when it's configured for network use.

If you have previously set up a user profile for Exchange or a previous version of Outlook, Outlook 2000 uses it automatically. If not, a wizard leads you through the process of creating a new profile. To use Outlook successfully, you must configure your user profile properly. Because understanding and configuring user profiles and information services is challenging, I postpone a discussion of the necessary steps until Chapter 51. If you're anxious to get started with Outlook, it's OK to accept the default profile configuration choices that the wizard suggests for now.

Startup Switches

Table 50-1 lists the command line switches available for controlling how Outlook behaves when you start it. Using these switches, you can create as many Outlook shortcuts as you need for fast access to specific folders or items. See Chapter 1 for information on how to use command line switches with Office applications.

Table 50-1 Outlook's Command Line Startup Switches

Command Line Switch	Function
`"outlook:`*folder name*`"`	Opens the named Outlook folder. For example, the switch `outlook:calendar` runs Outlook, opening the Calendar folder. The quotation marks are necessary only if *folder name* contains spaces. To open a subfolder, use the switch `"outlook:`*folder name*`\`*subfolder name*`"`.
`"outlook:`*mail folder*`/~`*subject*`"`	Opens the specific message identified by *subject* from the named mail folder (inbox, outbox, sent, or items).

Command Line Switch	Function
`"outlook:contacts/~Contact name"`	Displays the specific named contact. If the contact is stored in another folder, substitute that folder name for `contacts` in the switch shown.
`/folder`	Opens Outlook but hides the Outlook bar.
`/profiles`	Makes Outlook prompt you to select a profile at startup, if you're using the Corporate or Workgroup e-mail configuration.
`/profile profile`	Opens Outlook using the specified profile.
`/select path/folder`	Outlook opens displaying the contents of the named disk or network folder for file management in Outlook, without the Outlook bar (see "Using the semisecret Outlook file manager" in the section on the Outlook bar).
`/c MessageClass`	Opens an Outlook form for entering an information item. Specific `MessageClass` options for the standard forms are listed later. To open a custom form, enter its message class as listed in the Publish Form As dialog box (see "Saving a form in a forms library" later in this chapter).
`/c ipm.note`	Opens a new e-mail message. E-mail is the default message class — `/c ipm` gives the same results as `/c ipm.note`.
`/c ipm.post`	Opens a post or folder.
`/c ipm.appointment`	Opens a new appointment.
`/c ipm.task`	Opens a new task.
`/c ipm.contact`	Opens a new contact.
`/c ipm.activity`	Opens a new journal entry.
`/c ipm.stickynote`	Opens a new note.
`/a path/file name`	Includes the specified file as an attachment to one of the previously specified message classes. If you don't specify a message class, the file is attached to a new e-mail message.

Customizing Outlook

In common with the other Office applications, Outlook places most of its customizing settings on the Tools ➪ Options dialog box and enables you to customize its menus and toolbars.

Using the Tools ➪ Options dialog box

As shown in Figure 50-1, the Outlook 2000 version of this dialog box is better organized than the one in Outlook 97, but learning its many controls may keep you plenty busy.

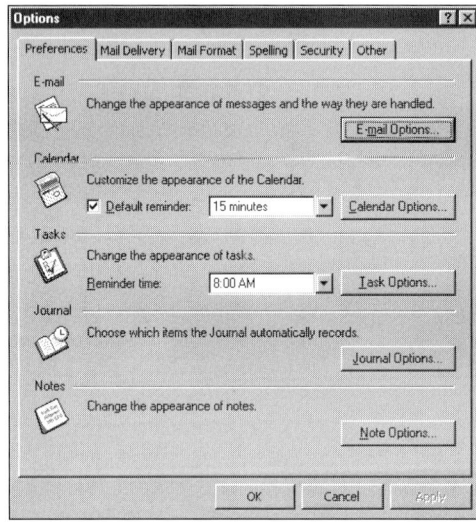

Figure 50-1: The Preferences tab on Outlook's Tools ➪ Options dialog box

Your choices in the Options dialog box occupy six or seven separate tabs, as follows:

- **Preferences.** This tab offers basic settings controlling the look of Outlook items and includes options governing contact and journal items.
- **Mail Delivery** and **Mail Format.** The settings on these tabs pertain mostly to e-mail and are covered in Chapter 51.
- **Spelling.** Options governing Outlook's spell-checker reside on this tab. See "Spell-Checking in Outlook" later in this chapter for details.
- **Security.** This tab has controls that can help protect you and your organization from unauthorized access to mail and sensitive data.

- **Other.** Though burdened with an uninspired name, this tab houses some key Outlook settings. Take special note of the Advanced Options button—many of the settings in the dialog box it produces are useful.

- **Fax (not shown in Figure 50-1).** If you've set up Outlook for the Internet Only e-mail configuration, Office installs Symantec WinFax Starter Edition the first time you create a new fax message (by choosing File ⇨ New ⇨ Fax Message). Once the software is installed, the Fax tab appears on the Options dialog box. Settings here enable you to modify the cover page sent with your faxes and to control your modem's behavior when sending and receiving fax transmissions.

Customizing Outlook toolbars

Outlook lets you add and remove toolbars at will using the same techniques you use in the other Office applications. The simplest way is to right-click any toolbar to display a shortcut menu. You can select any other toolbar you want to display or hide. New in Outlook 2000 is the capability to customize the toolbars themselves, again using the methods common throughout Office (see Chapter 5).

Secret

I recommend that you keep the Advanced toolbar on your screen. Its buttons offer one-click access to many commonly used menu commands, as well as to some functions that aren't on the menus at all.

Working with Outlook Folders

Right out of the starting gate, Outlook is set to manage your information with its collection of built-in folders. Access the contents of individual folders by clicking their icons in the Outlook bar on the left of the screen, shown in Figure 50-2.

Although you can add folders of your own at any time, Outlook's default folders include the following:

- **Outlook Today.** Strictly speaking, the top Outlook folder isn't a folder at all, but a panel that collects important information from multiple folders.

- **Inbox, Outbox, and Sent Items.** These folders list e-mail messages you've received, written, and already sent, respectively. Only the Inbox folder appears by default in the Outlook Shortcuts group, the primary group on the Outlook bar (see "Working with Outlook bar groups" later in this chapter).

- **Calendar.** As initially configured, this folder displays events scheduled for the day, a small monthly calendar for access to other days, and a To Do list.

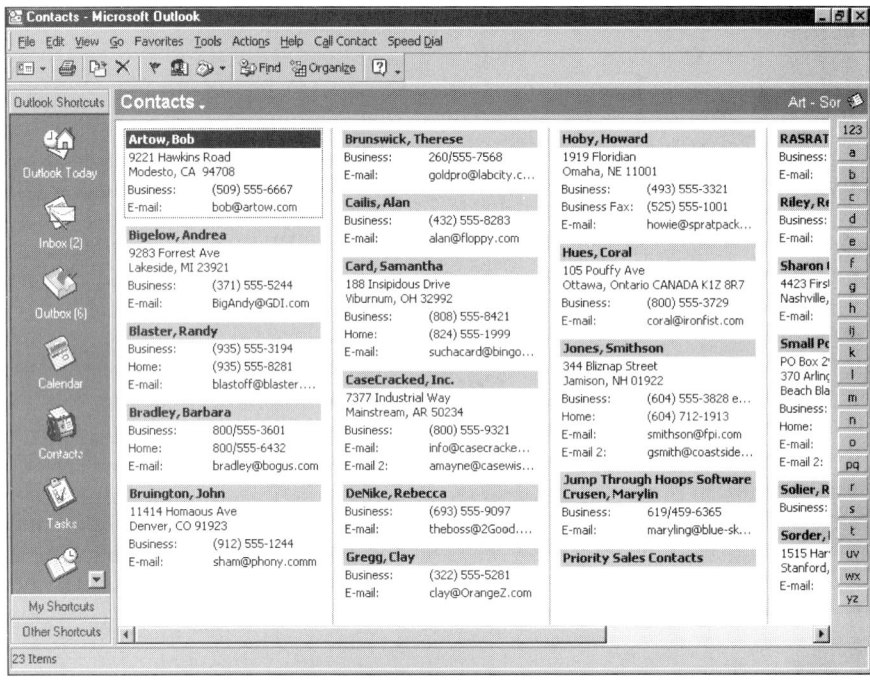

Figure 50-2: The Outlook window, showing the Outlook bar on the left with large icons

- **Contacts.** Your little black book. This folder collects names, addresses, and other critical information about the important people in your world. You can have Outlook dial any number or send mail to any e-mail address listed in a contact.

- **Tasks.** This folder displays tasks you have defined for yourself or that have been assigned by the powers that be. You can change the priority of any task on the list or double-click it to obtain or modify details.

- **Journal.** This folder records activities of all types. You can use it to track interactions with your contacts or to keep a record of which Office documents you open and when, all automatically.

- **Notes.** This folder stores random notes. From here, you can post individual notes on your screen in their own windows as electronic sticky notes.

- **Deleted Items.** Outlook moves items deleted from all other folders here, where you can retrieve them until you empty this folder. See "Outlook Housekeeping Secrets" for details on using the Deleted Items folder.

If you have been using Exchange for e-mail, the corresponding Inbox and Outbox folders in Outlook contain messages you've previously composed, sent, and received. Otherwise, these folders are empty when you first start Outlook, except for a message or two from Microsoft.

Secret The Outlook folders do *not* correspond to folders on your hard disk, and their contents are not individual files. Instead, Outlook stores all of your information in one gigantic mailbox file specified in the properties for your Personal Folders information service.

Selecting a folder

The quickest way to get around the Outlook folders is to simply click an icon in the Outlook bar. Boom — up pops the corresponding folder. Depending on factors such as your screen resolution and the Outlook window size, the default folder icons may not all fit in the Outlook bar. Use the arrow buttons at the top and bottom to scroll the bar. To squeeze in more icons, right-click in the bar and choose Small Icons from the shortcut menu. To widen or (more likely) narrow the Outlook bar, drag the divider separating the Outlook bar and the main part of the screen.

To turn the Outlook bar off, choose Hide Outlook Bar from its shortcut menu. With the Outlook bar hidden, you can use one of three other options to select and display folders:

- Open the View menu and choose the folder you want.
- Click the button giving the current folder's name at the left side of the Folder Banner, the bar that runs across the main part of the Outlook window just below the toolbars. Clicking the folder name drops down the *folder list* in a separate pane between the main work area and the Outlook bar (see Figure 50-3). You can select the folder you want to open by clicking it in the folder list. Drag the divider between it and the main area to resize the list.

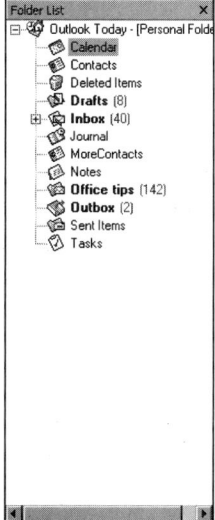

Figure 50-3: One way to switch to other Outlook folders is with the folder list.

- Click the Folder List button on the Advanced toolbar button (or choose View ⇨ Folder List) to display the folder list.

Once you've switched to at least one other folder, you can use the Back and Forward arrow buttons on the Advanced toolbar to retrace your steps in either direction, just as you would move among Web pages you've visited in your browser. The Back button is a split button — clicking the narrow bar on its right side produces a little menu of the folders you've previously visited, enabling you to select the one you want to return to.

Secret

If you right-click a folder in the Outlook bar or the folder list, you can choose Open in New Window on the shortcut menu to display the folder in a separate Outlook window. Unlike the Outlook bar, where you can control which folders are displayed and how they're grouped, the folder lists and the View menu both display all the Outlook folders.

Creating new folders

To create a new Outlook folder, choose File ⇨ New ⇨ Folder, or right-click the Folder Banner and choose New Folder. In the Create New Folder dialog box, select the level in the folder hierarchy where the new folder should go using the folder list at the bottom of the dialog box. Use the Folder Contains drop-down list to specify the type of Outlook folder you want — contacts, calendar, mail items, and so on.

Using Outlook Today

The Outlook Today "page" is a simple but effective summary view of your daily activities. It lists the appointments and tasks you've scheduled, displays an inventory of your mail folders, and lets you look up names in your Contacts folder quickly. Figure 50-4 shows Outlook Today in action.

Because Outlook Today is designed for ease and simplicity, I don't need to say much about it. Keep in mind these few points:

- Outlook Today works like a browser. To view an item listed on the page, just click it once. Clicking a calendar or task item displays the item details in a separate window. Clicking a heading such as Calendar or Tasks displays the corresponding folder.

- Contacts aren't listed in Outlook Today, but you can still look them up: Type a portion of the person's name in the Find a Contact box that appears in the Standard toolbar when you display Outlook Today. When you press Enter, Outlook displays the matching contact in a separate window. If more than one contact matches your request, you see instead a box listing all the matches from which you can choose the correct one.

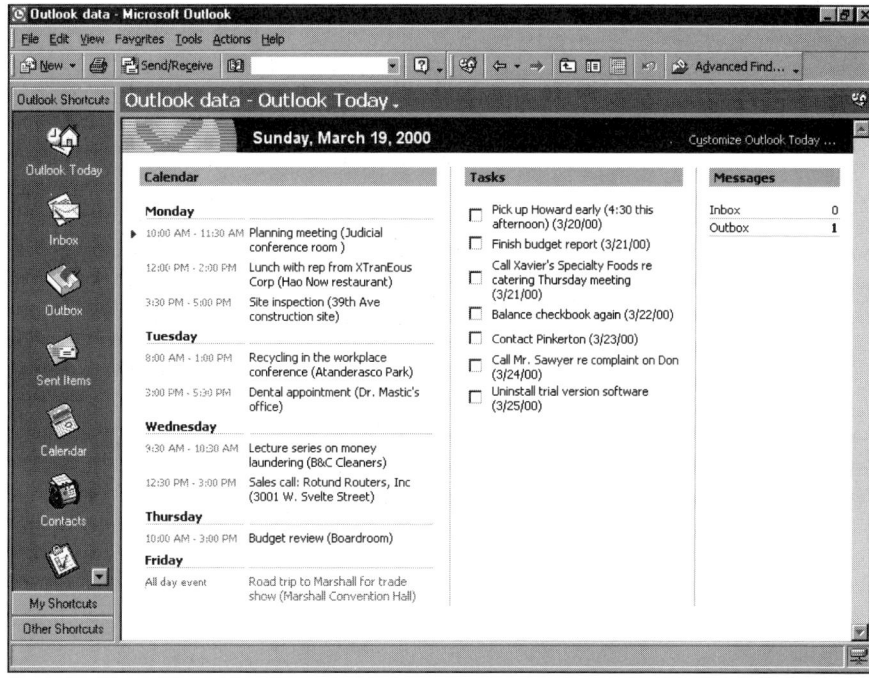

Figure 50-4: Outlook Today lets you see the challenges that face you today at a glance.

- You control Outlook Today's behavior by clicking Customize Outlook Today. The resulting page has a box you can check to ensure that Outlook Today is the first thing you see whenever you start the program. Other options govern what you see in each of the three main headings (Mail, Calendar, and Tasks) and Outlook Today's style, that is, its overall look.

Using and Customizing the Outlook Bar

Once you've gotten the hang of the Outlook bar — which should take about a minute — you can customize it to your needs. By adding, moving, or removing shortcuts for folders and other items, you can create an environment that fits your personal information management needs:

- To add a folder or other shortcut to the Outlook bar, right-click over the bar (but not over an icon) and choose Outlook Bar Shortcut. Use the Look In list in the resulting dialog box to display Outlook's special folders or the folders available on your system (including network-accessible folders).

- Reorganize your shortcut icons by dragging them to new positions on the Outlook bar.
- To delete any unwanted shortcuts, right-click the icon and choose Remove from Outlook Bar. You're deleting the icon from the Outlook bar, not the underlying folder or other item, and you can restore the shortcut by adding it again any time.

Working with Outlook bar groups

By default, Outlook arranges the shortcuts on the Outlook bar into three *groups*: Outlook, My Shortcuts, and the highly informative Other Shortcuts. As you would expect, though, you can reorganize the filing system, creating, renaming, or deleting groups as need or whimsy dictates.

As shown in Figure 50-5, the Outlook bar includes a button for each group at the top or bottom of the bar. To view the shortcuts of a different group, just click the corresponding button. Note that by default, the only mail-related shortcut in the Outlook group is Inbox. Switch to the My Shortcuts group by clicking its button to display all the folders associated with your e-mail messages, including Inbox (again), Outbox, and Sent Items.

Figure 50-5: A close-up of the Outlook bar showing the Group buttons

To add a new group, right-click the Outlook bar and choose Add New Group. Outlook adds a button for the group below the existing ones. After naming the new group, click its button to display the empty group (Outlook slides all the other group buttons to the top or bottom of the Outlook bar). You can now add Outlook bar shortcuts to the new group.

To remove a group from the Outlook bar, right-click a group button and choose Remove Group. Or with the doomed group active, right-click an empty area of the Outlook bar, again choosing Remove Group. You can rename a group by choosing Rename Group from its shortcut menu.

Using the semisecret Outlook file manager

Secret

Open the Other Shortcuts group by clicking its button to display three icons corresponding to portions of your computer's file hierarchy: My Computer, Personal (or My Documents), and Favorites. Clicking (only once) any of these icons opens Outlook's "secret" file manager window. Though it may look a little different from My Computer or Explorer, it offers the same basic feature set, and then some.

Shortcut menus are active, as is network drive mapping. Double-clicking a disk or folder icon opens the item. As in My Computer, you can control whether the item opens in the same window or a separate one—in Outlook, use the Tools ⇨ Options command. You can also traverse the disk and folder hierarchy using the tree view available in Outlook's folder list. You can add a disk drive or file folder to the currently active group in the Outlook bar by right-clicking the item in the main window and choosing Add to Outlook bar from its shortcut menu; or just drag the folder and drop it on the Outlook bar.

Secret

Not only can you launch programs from the main window, you can now drag them to the Outlook bar. This means that you can easily add one-click access to frequently used applications from within Outlook.

Secret

The Keywords field in the Outlook file manager applies to Office documents. The field displays the contents of the Keywords item in the document's File ⇨ Properties dialog box.

Working with Views

When you open an Outlook folder, the program presents the information it contains in one of many possible *views* available for the folder. A view defines the way Outlook displays the information in a folder. You can change the view at any time, modify existing views, or create new ones of your own.

The Outlook Calendar's standard view is the Day/Week/Month view. When you switch to the Calendar folder, notice that separate sections of the window display appointments, a monthly calendar (the *Date Navigator*, which in the maximized Outlook window actually shows two months), and a list of tasks (the *TaskPad*, located in the lower-right corner). The Day/Week/Month view has several viewing options of its own. To see a week's or month's worth of appointments at once, choose Week or Month from the View menu, or click the corresponding toolbar buttons. Figure 50-6 shows the Calendar folder in the Week view.

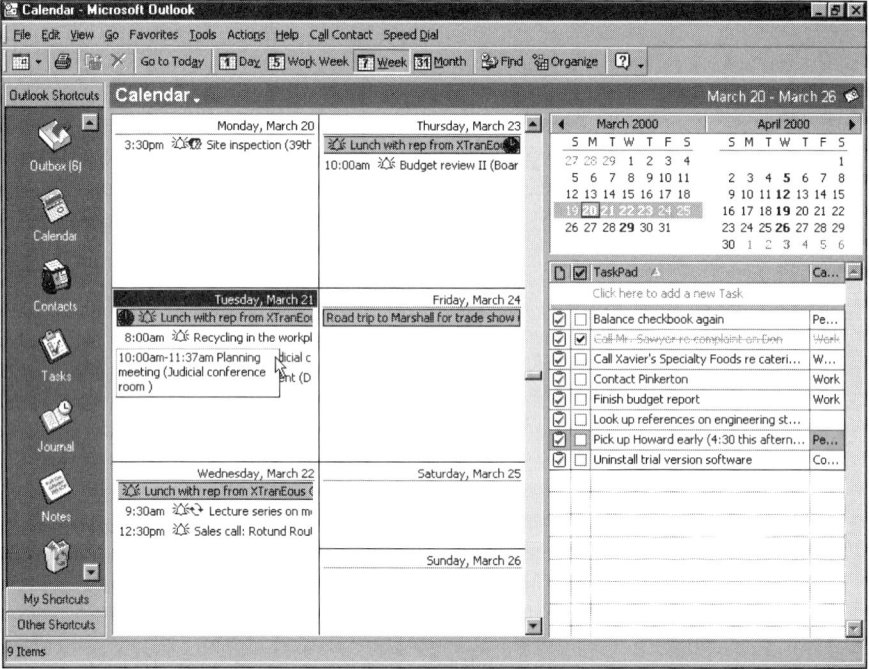

Figure 50-6: The Calendar folder's Week view, one of the options for a Day/Week/Month view

This view provides a pretty fair time-management tool. You can see details of your schedule and To Do list, while the two-month calendar alerts you to all days with scheduled events and appointments by displaying them in bold type. However, my main point is that this is only one way to look at your date-related information. In Figure 50-7, for example, I selected the Active Appointments view for the Calendar folder. The window now displays details about future appointments in tabular form. This view can help you locate an appointment quickly, without bothering to search in your monthly, weekly, or daily calendar.

Switching views

To switch between the available views for the current folder, choose View ➪ Current View and select the view you want by name from the submenu. If you frequently alternate between different views, get in the habit of using the Current View list button—it's on the Advanced toolbar, which I recommend you keep on your screen. Alternatively, you can add the Current View list box from the Tools ➪ Customize dialog box to the main menu bar. You can add or modify the views in each available folder using the techniques laid down in "Customizing Views" later in this chapter.

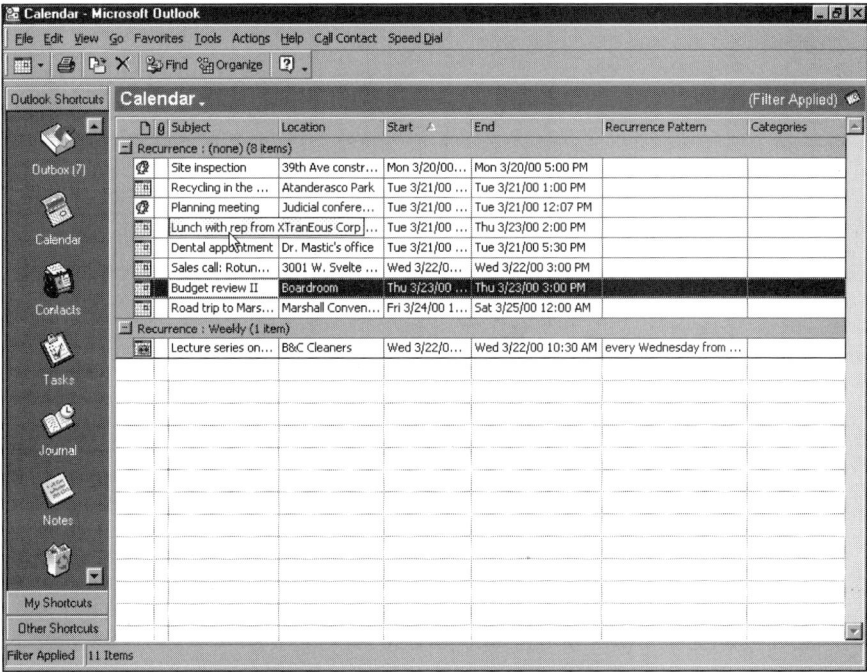

Figure 50-7: The Calendar, now showing Active Appointments view

Types of Outlook views

Probably the most commonly used Outlook views are *table views*. They display information in tabular form, organized with items in the rows and specific fields of information in the columns.

But Outlook offers four other view types. You've already crossed paths with *Day/Week/Month views,* which show items by date and time on a calendar. *Timeline views* also present chronological information, but along a horizontally scrolling bar. *Card views* show information about each item in a rectangular block rather than a row. *Icon views* are the simplest type; they only show an icon for each item in the view. A view's name usually doesn't tell you which type of view it is — you have to display the view to see. You can change the view type for any view, as detailed in "Customizing Views" later in this chapter.

Adding and Editing Information Items

Outlook lets you enter or edit individual items of information — mail messages, contacts, tasks, and so on — either by typing directly into a view or by opening a separate *form* for that specific item.

Secret

By the way, you can move or copy information items between Outlook folders by dragging them from a view to the destination folder in the folder list. Dragging with the left button moves the item. When you drag with the right button, you get a little menu asking whether you want to move or copy the item.

Working with items directly on a view

The easiest way to add new information items is to type them directly into a view. Outlook enables this in most calendar views, and table views provide a special top row for entering new items. To activate this row if it's not visible, check the box labeled Show "New Item" Row in the Other Settings dialog box, available from the View Summary dialog box covered in the "Customizing Views" section. You can't add new items directly on other views. Calendar, table, and card views permit editing of the existing information, unless you have cleared the Allow In-Cell Editing box in the Other Settings dialog box. To edit an item in any view that permits editing, just click the field you want to change.

Secret

Keyboard editing tricks in table views: Move from field to field with the Tab key and then press F2 to edit the existing entry, or just start typing to erase the current contents. If you're in a field offering several preset choices — such as the Flag Status field in contact views — pressing F2 or Space drops down the list of choices. You can then use the Up and Down arrow keys to make your selection. Use Space to check or clear check boxes.

Secret

Some fields can't be edited at all. However, if you can't type in *any* field, go to the Other Settings dialog box (View ➪ Current View ➪ Customize Current View ➪ Other Settings). There, check the Allow In-Cell Editing box. However, you can't directly edit Notes in any view, even if you turn on in-cell editing.

Deleting items from a view

To delete an item by moving it to the Deleted Items folder, highlight it and click the Delete button (the one with the artistic X), press Ctrl+D, or drag the item to the Deleted Items folder. Depending on the view you're working in, the Del key alone may or may not perform the same chore. You can delete any item listed in a view permanently, without moving it to the Deleted Items folder, by highlighting it and pressing Shift+Del.

Entering and editing items on forms

Although entering new items in the main Outlook window is convenient, Outlook doesn't permit it in all views. Besides, space is cramped and you have access only to a subset of the available fields. To add a new information item no matter what view you're using, enter it on a form designed for that purpose. You have many choices for starting new items, but the fastest ways are to double-click the view window or press Ctrl+N. Either action opens the default item form for the current folder. (Some folders let you add variations on the standard item type. In the Calendar folder, for example, you add appointments, or events, and meeting requests on different — if very similar — forms.) Other methods for adding new items via forms include these:

- Click the New button at the far left of the toolbar. Clicking the main part of this button opens a new default item form. To add an item to another folder, click the right portion of the button, the thin bar with the arrow — this drops down a menu of all item types.

- Choose New from a view's shortcut menu or from the menu specific to the open folder (such as Journal, Calendar, or what have you) to open a new default item form. If the folder permits more than one item type, the menu lists those alternatives, too.

- Choose File ⇨ New and select any item type from the submenu.

To edit an existing item on a form, double-click it, or select it and press Ctrl+O or Enter.

Working with forms

The supplied forms for entering and editing information items are clearly organized, and I'm sure you can figure out how to fill them in without my help. Just be aware that most forms have two or more tabbed pages, and you may find just the right basket for a particular detail on one of the pages that isn't showing when you first open the form. Of course, Outlook's form designers couldn't think of everything. If you need to add special fields for the information you require, you can customize the existing forms or create your own from scratch (see "Customizing Forms" later in this chapter).

Assigning categories to items

Categories are keywords that can help you organize information you store in Outlook. You can use them to help you find, sort, filter, or group items in any folder.

Categories can help you get over your anxiety about keeping similar yet distinct groups of items in the same folder. For example, instead of creating separate folders for personal and business contacts, you can place both in your main Contacts folder and then create two distinct views filtered by category to display them separately.

To assign a category to an item visible in a view, right-click the item and choose Categories from its shortcut menu. Most forms have a Categories button on the first page that takes you to the same Categories dialog box. You can add and delete Outlook categories using the Master Category list, accessible from the Categories dialog box.

Customizing Views

Outlook doesn't just give you plenty of alternative prefab views; it lets you customize the existing views or develop your own views from scratch. The multitude of options may make your head swim, so ready your cranial flotation device.

Creating new and modified views

The rest of this section describes the specific techniques you can use to customize views. First, though, you should know that Outlook 2000 automatically saves any changes you make to a view. This leads me to a simple point: If you want to preserve the current view for later use, start with a new view before you begin your customizations.

Secret

Assuming you want to base your changes on the view you're currently using, the technique for creating a copy of the current view is as follows:

1. Choose View ⇨ Current View ⇨ Define Views to display the Define View dialog box, shown in Figure 50-8.

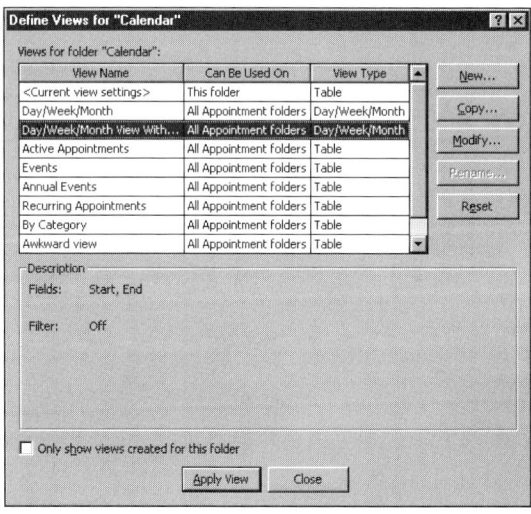

Figure 50-8: Use Outlook's Define Views dialog box to create, copy, and modify views.

2. Leave selected the top choice in the Views list, "Current view settings," and click Copy.

3. Outlook presents a little Copy View box asking you to name the copied view and designate where it will be available. Make your selections and click OK.

4. Outlook presents the View Summary dialog box for accessing all the controls pertaining to view layout and content. As discussed in the next section, this box gives you access to all of Outlook's view customizing commands. But if you want to use the copied view immediately, just click OK at this point to return to the Define Views box, and there click Apply View to activate the view.

After you've added a new view, it appears by name on the View ⇨ Current View submenu.

If you want to start work on a custom view from scratch, open the Define Views dialog box and click New. In this case, you must select the type of view you want to build (see "Types of Outlook views" earlier in this chapter) in addition to choosing a name and specifying the view's availability.

Caution

Once you've created a view, you can't change its type or where it can be used.

Secret

The Current View list box provides a faster alternative to the Define Views dialog box for creating new groups, and it works just as well as the View Í Current View submenu for switching from view to view. Here's how it looks:

The Current View list box should be on the Advanced toolbar. If you don't find it there, you can add it to any toolbar from the Tools ⇨ Customize dialog box. You can create new views simply by typing a new name into the Custom View list box. When you press Enter, Outlook presents the Copy View dialog box so that you can name the view. The copy begins life with the same settings as the view you started from.

Defining views comprehensively

The View Summary dialog box, shown in Figure 50-9, is a master control panel for customizing views. You can display it:

- From the Define Views dialog box (refer back to Figure 50-8), by selecting a view and clicking Modify. This technique lets you customize any view.
- By choosing Views ⇨ Current View ⇨ Customize Current View.
- By right-clicking the column heading of the current view and choosing Customize Current View.

The View Summary dialog box contains buttons that in turn display the dialog boxes for specific customizing functions, such as Group By, Sort, and Filter. However, you can perform many of these same functions more quickly with other techniques described in the relevant sections that follow.

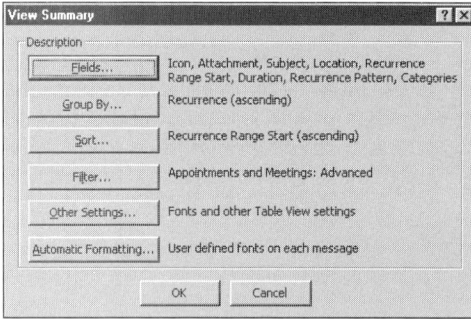

Figure 50-9: The View Summary dialog box is an access point for all functions governing views.

Adding and reorganizing fields in a view

Customizing the existing fields works much like customizing toolbars in the other Office applications. To move a field, drag it horizontally to a new location. To remove a field, drag it vertically until you see a big black X and then release the mouse button. To add a field, however, you need the Field Chooser, shown in Figure 50-10. Display it by choosing Field Chooser from the shortcut menu you get by right-clicking a column header.

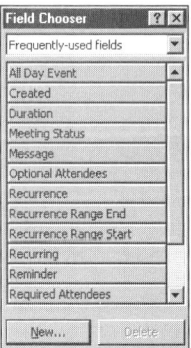

Figure 50-10: The Field Chooser dialog box

The Field Chooser provides a collection of buttons based on the existing fields in your Outlook folders. To add a field to the view, just drag its button from the Field Chooser to the desired location along the column heading area. You can use the drop-down list at the top of the dialog box to select the type of fields displayed.

The Field Chooser also gives you a fast way to add new fields to the folder represented in the view. Choose New, enter a name for the field, and specify its type and format. When you return to the Field Chooser, the new field shows up under the heading "User-defined fields in this folder." You can then add it to the view. In doing so, you make it part of the folder, available for use in other views and in custom forms.

The Show Fields dialog box (available from the View Summary dialog box discussed in the previous section) is an alternative to the Field Chooser. Show Fields offers a simple list of fields that you can copy to or remove from the current view. It also lets you reorder the view's fields.

Filtering a view

Filtering a view lets you limit the displayed information to items matching particular criteria. Click Filter in the View Summary dialog box to bring up the dialog box shown in Figure 50-11. The choices in the Filter dialog box depend partly on the folder that you're working with. In general, you can filter a view based on text present in one or more fields, or by people associated with the item (for example, those who have been invited to a meeting).

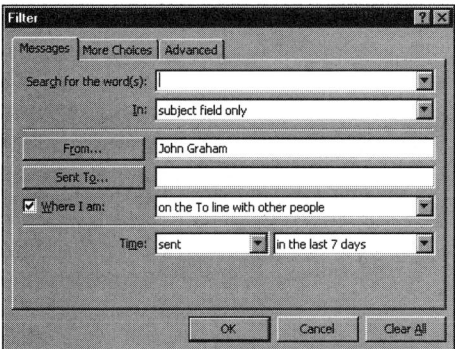

Figure 50-11: Use the Filter dialog box to focus in on items of particular interest in an Outlook view.

You can use additional filtering options based on the categories you can associate with items in Outlook (see "Assigning categories to items" earlier in this chapter). Switch to the More Choices tab and choose Categories to select from those available. This tab has miscellaneous filtering options that are often useful, such as "Only items that are unread."

If you're still hungry for more filtering choices after that big meal, you're bound to reach satiety with the dessert offered on the Advanced tab. Here, you can build complex sets of filtering criteria using conditions for the contents of every field in Outlook individually.

To add a criterion for filtering, select the field from the submenus in Field and then choose appropriate conditions and values from the subsequent boxes. Appropriate conditions (and often values) for each field have been predefined, so you won't have to worry about writing these from scratch. Many of Outlook's stock views are based on advanced filters, and it may pay to start a custom filter by modifying what's already been done for you.

Sorting a view

To sort a view on any field, right-click the column heading for that field and choose Sort Ascending or Sort Descending. Quicker still, click the column heading for the field to sort it in ascending order, and click it again to reverse directions. Fancier sorts can be had using the Sort dialog box. Click Sort in the View Summary dialog box to display it. Here, you can select up to four separate fields for four separate sorting levels.

Grouping related items

To group related items together visually, *group* them by a field. When you right-click a column heading and choose Group by This Field, Outlook puts together an outline-like representation of the information. Each unique value from the chosen field is displayed as a main heading, with all the items containing that value grouped together beneath it. As with a tree-type folder list in Explorer (or Outlook, for that matter), you can display or hide the individual items under each heading by clicking its little +/– icon to the left.

For more complex groupings (showing groups within groups within groups), click in the column heading area and choose the Group By box. Outlook adds an empty area just above the items. You can now drag column headings up into this Group By box, arranging them in the order you want the groupings. For a nongraphical alternative, click the Group By button in the View Summary dialog box.

Formatting choices

Outlook's formatting tools for views are "satisfactory," I guess you might say. Although you can pick fonts and specify field alignment and field size options, don't expect to create fancy custom formats within a view.

The formatting options are grouped in various menu choices and dialog boxes. To control column size and alignment, right-click over the column headings and make your selections from the Best Fit and Alignment choices, or choose Format Column for a dialog box. To select fonts for the column headings and item details, click Other Settings in the View Summary dialog box.

Limitations on customizing views

View types vary regarding how many customization options they offer, but you always have some choices. In Day/Week/Month views, for example, you can switch between the daily, weekly, and monthly calendars, filter the items displayed, and specify the intervals for dividing your daily schedule.

Outlook Housekeeping Secrets

Although Outlook excels at organizing large amounts of information, the sheer volume of material you have to deal with can become overwhelming. You have to be able to find the particular information you need, when you need it. And one of your main tasks is to throw out the stuff you don't need on a regular basis, so that you can find the stuff you do need — and so that your hard disk doesn't become clogged with old e-mail you no longer need.

Using the Organize command

Outlook's Organize command helps you locate information via visual cues and place related information in appropriate folders. Choose Tools ⇨ Organize or click the Organize button to display a special pane above the items in the current folder. Here, you can click the various options listed on the left to display commands that make your information easier to work with. The options available depend on the type of folder you're working with. They include:

- **Using Folders.** Enables you to move a selected item to another folder, presumably one where it better belongs.

- **Using Categories.** Enables you to assign categories to the selected items, and to create new categories. You can accomplish the same tasks via the Edit ⇨ Categories command, or with the Categories item when you're editing individual information items.

- **Using Views.** Lets you switch to another view for the current folder. The Change Your View list is equivalent to the View ⇨ Current View submenu.

- **Using Colors.** Available only for mail folders, this option lets you choose colors for mail items according to the people they're sent to or received from.

The Junk E-mail option, also exclusively for mail folders, is covered in Chapter 51.

Pay attention to the upper-right corner of the Organize pane as you switch between the options. It offers buttons that let you access more advanced commands and settings related to the option you're working with (the buttons are labeled with text only, not icons). To close the Organize pane, click the big X in the far upper-right corner of the pane or click the Organize button again.

Finding information

Outlook can search for information you want to locate in two main ways: the easy way, and the powerful way. For the easy way, click Tools ➪ Find or click the Find button on the Standard toolbar. A special pane appears at the top of the folder window offering one simple control: a Look For box in which you type your search request. The text on the left side of the Find pane tells you which fields Outlook searches — but you also can check or clear a box that determines whether the search also covers the body of the item.

When Outlook completes the find operation, matching items appear in the folder window, though the view changes automatically as appropriate. When you're finished working with the search results, click Clear Search below the Look For box to return to the original view.

When you want more control over your search operations, click the Advanced Find button at the top right of the Find pane, or if the Find pane isn't open, choose Tools ➪ Advanced Find. You can add the Advanced Find button to a toolbar from the Tools ➪ Customize dialog box, but if you want it to display an icon rather than text, you have to create your own picture for it (see Chapter 5).

The Advanced Find dialog box, shown in Figure 50-12, is a compact but sophisticated search tool. Type or select search criteria in the controls of any of the three tabs and then click Find Now to begin the search. The dialog box expands downward with a list of the items found by the search. You can double-click an item to open it in its own window.

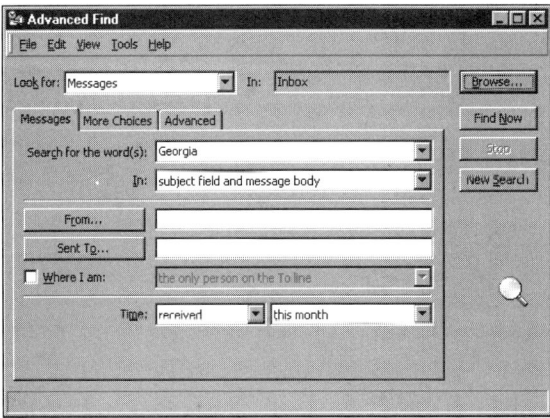

Figure 50-12: Use the Advanced Find dialog box to create complex Outlook searches.

I don't have space to detail how to use each of the myriad Advanced Find options individually, but you can figure them out with a few trial searches. The first tab provides the search choices most commonly used for the type of item you're working with. When you change the item type in the Look For box—"Any type of Outlook item" is one of the available types—the tab's title and fields change accordingly. The controls on the More Choices tab are a bit more stable, but not entirely—they change if you select Files in the Look For box. The Advanced tab lets you create search criteria based on any field associated with the items you're searching.

Secret

Outlook's Advanced Find dialog box offers an alternative to the search tools available in Windows and Office for locating files on disk or your network—and you don't have to run Outlook to use it. To search for files according to any combination of hordes of different characteristics, select Files in the Look For box. To activate Advanced Find when Outlook isn't open, click the Windows Start button and then choose Find ⇨ Using Microsoft Outlook.

Deleting items permanently

Remember that deleting an item moves it to the Deleted Items folder but doesn't actually erase the item altogether. To empty the Deleted Items folder manually, you have to choose Tools ⇨ Empty "Deleted Items" folder. To set Outlook so that it empties the folder automatically when you exit the program, check the appropriate box on the Other tab of the Tools ⇨ Options dialog box.

Secret

To delete an Outlook item permanently without moving it to the Deleted Items folder, select the item and press Shift+Del or hold down Shift while you click the Delete toolbar button. To retrieve a deleted item from the Deleted items folder, right-click it and choose Move to Folder from the shortcut menu.

Archiving Outlook information

Archiving means moving information out of the folders you normally use and into a special folder for storage. To archive manually, choose File ⇨ Archive. In the dialog box shown in Figure 50-13 select the folder you want to archive, choose a cutoff date, and select a destination file.

It's often handy to let Outlook automatically do your archiving. To turn on AutoArchive, open the Tools ⇨ Options dialog box, switch to the Other tab, and click AutoArchive. Use the settings on the resulting AutoArchive dialog box to switch on the process, specify how often it takes place, and select a default archive file. You must then activate AutoArchive on a folder-by-folder basis. Open each folder in turn, using the AutoArchive tab on the File ⇨ Folder ⇨ Properties dialog box to tell Outlook how old items should be to be automatically archived.

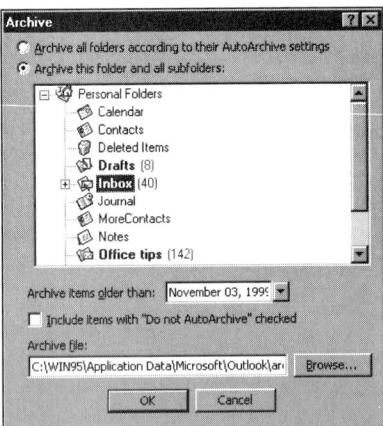

Figure 50-13: Archive outdated information using this dialog box.

Compacting your Outlook folders

Secret

As you delete unwanted items from your personal folders file, Outlook doesn't necessarily free up disk space accordingly. To reclaim at least some of this real estate, you must *compact* the file. To do so, choose View ➪ Folder List so that the folder list is visible (refer back to Figure 50-3). Right-click the very first item, Outlook Today, and choose Properties for "Personal Folders" from the resulting shortcut menu. In the Personal Folders Properties dialog box, click Advanced, and in the subsidiary dialog box click Compact Now. If you use the Corporate or Workgroup e-mail configuration, you can also access the compact command via the Tools ➪ Services command (choose Microsoft Exchange Server).

Spell-Checking in Outlook

Outlook can check the spelling in any of your individual information items, including e-mail messages, appointments, contact entries, and tasks. However, only text in the body of the item, not in the individual fields, is checked.

Outlook uses the Office spell-checking engine, so the details spelled out in Chapter 7 apply as much here as in Excel or Access. Just be aware that you can only check spelling of a single Outlook item at a time, and only when that item is open in its own window. To check the spelling of an item, locate the item in its Outlook folder, double-click the item to open it, and then choose Tools ➪ Spelling from the item's own menu to start the check.

Customizing Forms

As you know, Outlook opens a distinct window, or form, for each information item you work with individually, be it an e-mail message, contact, meeting or appointment, task, or journal entry. If the forms supplied with Outlook don't meet your needs, customize them.

Opening a form for customizing

Use the following steps to ready a form for customization:

1. Open the existing form on which you want to base your custom version, just as if you were creating a new information item of that type.

2. On the *form's* menu, choose Tools ➪ Forms ➪ Design This Form. As shown in Figure 50-14, the form window now includes new menu items, toolbars, and tabs. You use them to shape your custom form.

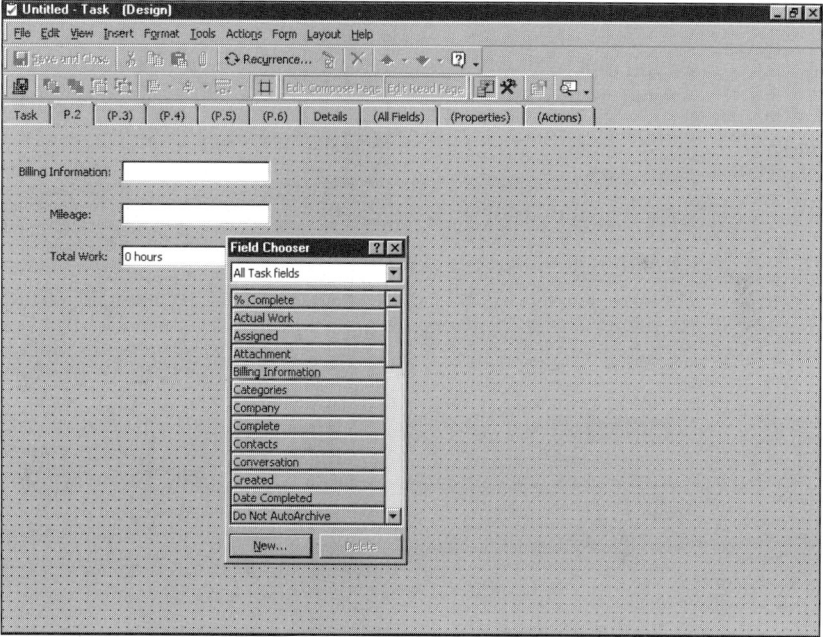

Figure 50-14: The standard Task form is displayed ready to be customized in design mode.

Working with form pages in design mode

In addition to its standard, prefab pages, an Outlook form has five customizable pages (six for a message form). When you first open a form in design mode, the customizable pages are labeled P.2, P.3, and so on. These labels are in parentheses, indicating that the pages are hidden when you display the form for normal use in editing information. To add or modify the contents of a customizable page, start by displaying it (click the page's tab). Outlook displays the page as a blank grid on which you place new fields and buttons, and it shows the Field Chooser window from which you can drag the fields you want to display on the page.

Caution

You can't modify a form's prefab pages. However, you can create a custom form with a customizable page that duplicates the fields on the prefab tab, and then hide the prefab one.

One prefab page, All Fields, is common to all form types. This page gives an unobstructed view of all the available fields via a big table. For efficiency's sake, some users may prefer to enter information in the table instead of on the other, more elegantly designed pages. Note, though, that the All Fields page is hidden in most of the standard Outlook forms (you can tell because its name is in parentheses in design mode). If you want this page to appear in a form, you must display the page as described in "Displaying, hiding, and renaming pages," which follows, and then publish the custom form.

Working with special design mode pages

To the right of the tabs for the pages that actually appear on your form when it's in use are two additional pages exclusively for the design process. These are:

- **Properties.** Use this page to define the custom form's properties. If you're creating lots of different forms, you can use the Category and Sub-Category fields to organize them hierarchically. The Contact field lets you add the name of the form's designer or anyone else that users of the form should contact if they have questions.

- **Actions.** This page enables you to add to the form a command that automatically opens another form, usually to reply or respond to the arrival of the form from another user. Use the New, Properties, and Delete buttons at the bottom of the page to add new, modify, and remove actions, respectively.

Displaying, hiding, and renaming pages

To hide or display a page in the normal view of the form (not while designing it), toggle the Form ⇨ Display This Page command. When a page is hidden, its name appears in parentheses. To rename a page, choose Form ⇨ Rename Page and type in the new name.

Adding fields and controls to a custom page

To add content to a custom page, drag fields from the Field Chooser onto the page. You can select from fields associated with items in the current folder and from fields from other folders as well.

To add controls (radio buttons, check boxes, combo boxes, and so on), display the Control Toolbox by choosing Form ➪ Control Toolbox or clicking the corresponding button, the one with the wrench and hammer. Chapter 24 explains how to write code to make controls do useful work, but in Outlook you must use VBScript rather than VBA for this purpose. To get started, select the control and choose Form ➪ View Code.

Just as in the Visual Basic Editor, you can use the toolbar buttons or Layout menu commands to align, group, and order the fields and controls you add. To modify characteristics of an individual field or control, right-click it and select Properties from the shortcut menu. Also on the shortcut menu, the Advanced Properties choice displays a list of properties in tabular form. You can leave the latter dialog box open while you select different items on the page.

Adding default information to a custom form

Information you type into the fields on a custom form will be saved with the form. If you want to supply yourself (or other Outlook users) with default content, just add it before saving the form.

Saving forms

Once you've customized a form, you're faced with a decision about how to save the new version. You have three choices:

- You can save it as an individual item in the corresponding Outlook folder.
- You can save it as a separate template or message file.
- You can save it in an Outlook forms library, which makes it easy to access from anywhere in Outlook.

These choices aren't mutually exclusive — you can save a custom form with all three methods if you feel the urge.

Saving a form as an information item

Whether or not you're working in design mode, a form's File ➪ Save command saves the custom form as a single item in the Outlook folder associated with that form type. If you ever plan to use the custom form again, save it as a template or in a forms library, too.

Secret

Because plans change, though, there may come a time when you want to use a "one-time" custom form for a second item. The quickest way is to make a copy of the original item on a view. Use the Edit menu Copy and Paste commands or their keyboard equivalents, Ctrl+C and Ctrl+V. As detailed in the next section, you can't save a second copy of the same item using the File ⇨ Save As command.

Saving a form as a separate file

Use the Form's Save As command to save a form and any accompanying information in a separate file—not in one of the special Outlook folders—in one of four formats. As usual, you use the Save as Type box to select the format you want in the Save As dialog box.

The first two of the available formats are plain text and rich text, both of which are useful if you want to transfer the *information* in the form to someone who doesn't own Outlook or Exchange. To save the *form* itself as well as its contents in a separate file, save it as an Outlook template (.oft) or message (.msg) file. Outlook templates are covered briefly in "Using Outlook forms" later in the chapter. The message format is used by both Outlook and Exchange for storing information in separate files. Either are good formats in which to send someone else a copy of the form on a floppy disk when the recipient isn't on your network.

Saving a form in a forms library

Outlook provides two separate but equally effective ways to store custom forms for reuse: as templates—as just described—and in a *forms library*. These libraries house stockpiles of custom forms for your own use (in the personal library) or for use throughout an organization (in the organization library).

To store a custom form in a forms library, choose Forms ⇨ Publish Form As or click the corresponding toolbar button. In the dialog box shown in Figure 50-15, Outlook asks you to supply a name for the new form (this is the name that will appear on its title bar, unless you've changed the Form caption on the form's Properties page).

In addition, you must decide where the form should be stored by choosing Look In:

- **Personal Forms library.** A choice in the Forms Library drop-down list, the Personal Forms library stores forms for your use only.

- **Organization Forms library.** This library resides on a network server and stores forms accessible throughout the organization. It's available in the Look In list only if your PC is on a network.

- **Outlook folders.** Select a specific Outlook folder in which to store the form. If you don't see the folder you want in the list, click Browse and locate it in the tree-type list that appears.

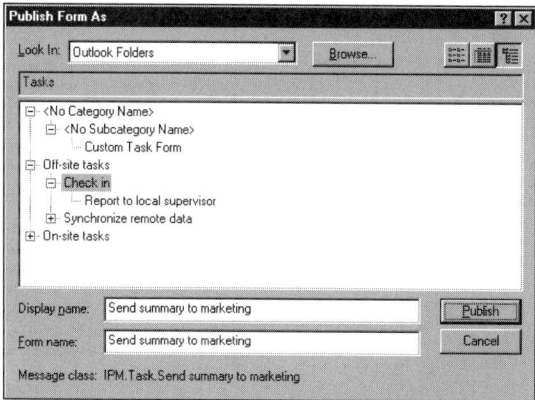

Figure 50-15: Store custom forms using the Publish Form As dialog box.

Secret

Note the *message class* that appears in the Publish Form As dialog box after you've identified where you're going to store the form and under what name. You can open the new form from a Windows shortcut by entering this text on the command line (see Table 50-1).

Caution

The name you assign to a custom form appears in the form's title bar only after you save a new item based on the form. When you first create the item, Outlook displays only the name of the generic item type on which the custom form is based (note, message, contact, or what have you).

Using Outlook forms

To create a new Outlook item based on a custom form or template, choose File ➪ New ➪ Choose Form (or the equivalent command, Tools ➪ Forms ➪ Choose Form). When Outlook displays the Choose Form dialog box, use the Look In drop-down list to select from the available form libraries, Outlook folders, and template locations.

Forms stored as such are kept together in libraries, while templates are form designs stored in separate files with the .oft extension. Previous versions of Outlook came with many decorative templates for e-mail messages — the choices included Urgent, Rain, and Hightech. Although my prerelease copy of Outlook 2000 doesn't have these templates, take a few minutes to see what, if any, prefab templates may be included with your software. Outlook supplies its templates in two forms: as Outlook (.oft) templates and as standard Word (.dot) templates.

Conclusion

Behind its simple facade, Outlook is incredibly rich with options for tracking personal information. Fortunately, you don't need to master all options to make effective use of the Outlook tools.

Chapter 51

Managing E-mail in Outlook

In This Chapter

▶ Setting up Outlook for e-mail

▶ Adding and configuring mail accounts

▶ Working with messages in Outlook folders

▶ Using not-so-obvious shortcuts for sending new messages

▶ Making Word your e-mail editor — pros and cons

▶ Customizing Outlook's e-mail settings

Although Outlook is many things, most people will come to know and love this powerhouse information-management software as an e-mail organizer. Okay, so maybe you don't love software. Outlook will earn your respect, anyway.

Setting Up Outlook for E-mail

In case you never had the privilege, take my word for it: Setting up Outlook 97 for e-mail was a major hassle, full of arcane complexities. Microsoft has since completely overhauled the setup process, to the point that it's now quite straightforward — especially if you use Outlook e-mail via the Internet, rather than with network mail service such as Microsoft Exchange or Lotus Notes.

Unless you're upgrading from a previous version, Outlook asks you to choose an *e-mail configuration* (also called an *e-mail service option*) the first time you start the program. Your choices are simple. Select Internet Only if you only send and receive e-mail on the Internet, and or Corporate or Workgroup if you're in an organization that uses a network mail service, even if you also use Internet e-mail. From here on, the setup process diverges.

Setting up for Internet-only e-mail

Your main task in configuring Outlook 2000 for Internet e-mail is to create and specify settings for at least one mail *account*. Each Outlook account corresponds to a particular e-mail address on a particular Internet server to which you connect via a particular method. If you have multiple e-mail addresses, or if you connect to your mail server over a LAN at some times but by modem at others, you can create as many Outlook accounts as you need.

Choose Tools ⇨ Accounts to get to the Internet Accounts dialog box, shown in Figure 51-1. As an alternative route to the same box, click the Accounts button on the Mail Delivery tab of the Tools ⇨ Options dialog box.

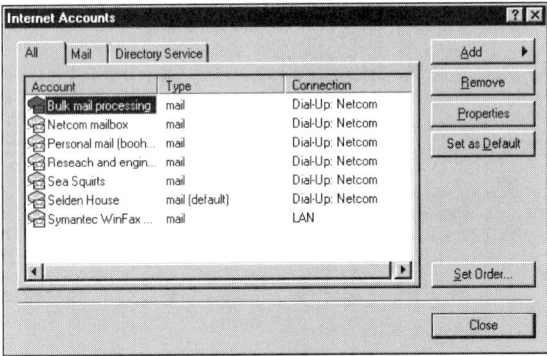

Figure 51-1: Create and modify Internet e-mail accounts in this dialog box.

Creating and modifying e-mail accounts

Before you start a new Outlook e-mail account, you should gather a few pieces of vital information. You need the e-mail address for the account, the server names and types, and your logon name and password. With these facts handy, start the account by clicking the Add button in the Internet Accounts dialog box and selecting Mail from the little menu that pops up. From this point, all you have to do is fill in the blanks in the series of simple dialog boxes you see.

To make changes to an existing Outlook account, select the account in the Internet Accounts dialog box and click Properties. A tabbed dialog box presents an array of pertinent settings, including those you worked through when creating the account. The General tab lets you give the account a name you see in Outlook, different from the user name that recipients see when they get messages from you. You can also specify a return address for an account other than the one used to send messages. The Advanced tab mostly contains technical settings that probably won't require your intervention. However, if you want automatic backups of your messages, or if you want to pick them up from more than one computer, you can check the box Leave a Copy of Messages on the Server.

Managing your accounts

If you create more than one mail account, you have some choices to make about how to use them together. A mandatory task is to set a default account — the one from which messages are sent unless you specify otherwise. Use the Set as Default button in the Internet Accounts dialog box.

The typical Outlook user relies on one or two accounts on a daily basis, using other accounts only under special circumstances. That's why you can designate the accounts with which Outlook's standard Send/Receive command transfers mail. To change an account's status, start from the Tools ⇨ Accounts dialog box, selecting the account. Click Properties, and on the General tab of the Properties dialog box, check or clear the box Include This Account in Send and Receive All. If you clear the box so that the account isn't included, you can still use it to send and receive mail — see "Mailing on specific accounts" later in this chapter.

Setting up for networked e-mail services

If you've chosen the Corporate or Workgroup e-mail configuration, the setup process is a bit complicated. The key is to create and configure one or more *user profiles*, which contain the settings governing the operation of Windows messaging software — Microsoft Exchange client, Outlook, and all applications based on MAPI (the Messaging Application Programming Interface).

Among other settings, a user profile defines the set of *information services* you can use with that profile. As the term is used here, an information service is a software plug-in providing the specifications the application must have in order to exchange information with another information-management entity. The latter might be an e-mail server on a network or the Internet, but it can also be a set of folders or an address book file on your own computer. So to set up your user profiles properly, you must know which information services to add and how to configure each individual information service.

User profiles also specify where your incoming mail is to be stored, the order in which the available information services should process your outgoing mail, and the address lists you can use for addressing new messages you write.

Getting started with user profiles

When you first start Outlook in the Corporate or Workgroup configuration, the Outlook Setup Wizard helps you select a user profile (if your system already has one or more) or walks you through the two simple steps required to create a new profile. If you're creating a new profile, the wizard first asks you to choose from the available information services option (you can modify your choice later) and then to name the new profile.

Creating and deleting user profiles

To create or delete a user profile later, you must use the Mail applet in the Windows Control Panel. (You can't create or delete profiles when Outlook is running, but you can add, remove, and modify the information services associated with the current profile.) Here's how to create or delete a profile:

1. Open the Control Panel's Mail applet.
2. Click Show Profiles.
3. Click Add to start the Setup Wizard, or select an existing profile and click Remove to delete it.

Using user profiles

A specific user profile is activated whenever you start Outlook or another MAPI application. To use a different profile, you must follow these steps:

1. Open the Tools ⇨ Options dialog box, switch to the Mail Services tab, and in the Startup Settings area, choose the new profile at Always Use This Profile. Alternatively, select Prompt for a Profile to Be Used.
2. *Log off* from the current user profile by choosing File ⇨ Exit and Log Off rather than the standard Exit command.
3. Restart Outlook. If you told Outlook to prompt you for a profile, you must pick one before the program runs.

Alternatively, you can choose a default profile in the Windows Control Panel's Mail applet. Open the applet, click Show Profiles, and select the profile you want at the bottom of the Mail dialog box.

Modifying a user profile

Use the dialog box shown in Figure 51-2 to modify the settings for a user profile.

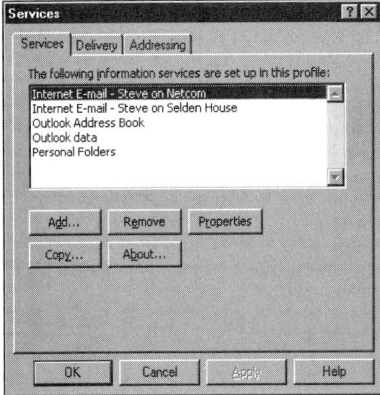

Figure 51-2: The dialog box shown here contains settings for the user profiles Outlook uses in its Corporate or Workgroup e-mail configuration.

Display this dialog box with either of the following techniques:

- From within Outlook, choose Tools Í Services to reconfigure the current profile.
- From the Control Panel, open the Mail applet to see the settings for the default profile. To work with another profile, click Show Profiles, select the desired profile, and then click Properties.

The dialog box offers three tabs, as follows:

- The Services tab lets you add or remove information services, as described in the next section.
- Use the Delivery tab to route your incoming mail and determine which information service has first dibs on processing outgoing mail.
- On the Addressing tab, the Show This Address List First field selects the default list of contacts from which you can select recipients for your e-mail messages. The When Sending box lets you determine the order in which Outlook consults your address lists to determine the correct e-mail address when you type in a name yourself, rather than selecting it from an address list.

Working with information services

Outlook and Windows come with lots of information services. Depending on your system, the list includes Internet E-mail, Microsoft Mail, Exchange Server, LDAP Directory, Lotus cc:Mail, and the Outlook address book and personal folders. Other services are available from Microsoft and third-party sources.

To add a service, click Add in the Services tab of the dialog box shown in Figure 51-2. Windows may need to copy support files from the Office CD, so be sure you have it handy. As the setup process proceeds, you'll see a dialog box containing settings that are relevant for the service you're adding. In the case of the Internet e-mail service, these settings are identical to the ones you work with for accounts in Outlook's Internet Only e-mail configuration (see "Creating and modifying e-mail accounts" earlier in this chapter).

Working with Messages in Your Mail Folders

Like your typical e-mail software, Outlook organizes your messages into Inbox, Outbox, Sent Items, and Deleted Items folders. You can display messages in any of these folders in a multiplicity of views depending on your needs at the moment. Remember that by default, only the Inbox and Deleted Items folders appear in the Outlook Shortcuts group.

You open a message by double-clicking it or selecting it and pressing Enter. If you're using Word as your e-mail editor, the message appears in a modified version of the same word processor you use for your most complex documents (see "Using Word as your e-mail editor" later in this chapter). If not, Outlook displays the message in its built-in e-mail editor, a less powerful program than Word, perhaps, but quicker to load.

Using AutoPreview to peek inside your messages

Outlook's AutoPreview feature lets you read a bit of your mail before you open it. If you're like me, many's the time you've received messages that you regretted wasting time opening. With AutoPreview, you can quickly scan your messages for meaningful content and choose whether to read them right away, read them later, or simply discard them. Figure 51-3 illustrates AutoPreview in action on my Inbox.

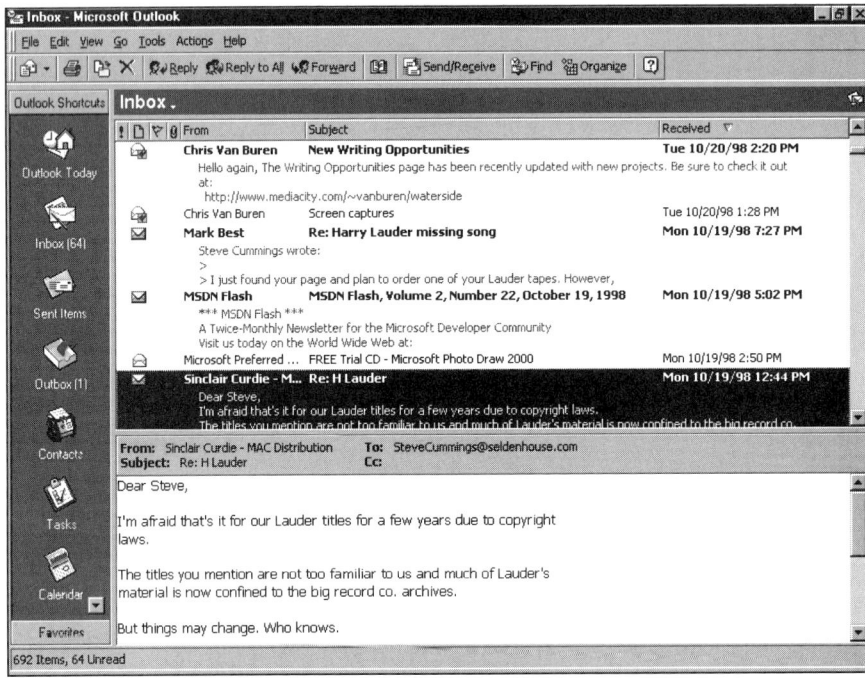

Figure 51-3: Inbox messages displayed with AutoPreview and the Preview pane both turned on

Secret

To toggle AutoPreview on or off, click the AutoPreview toolbar button on the Advanced toolbar (the button with the magnifying glass). This only works, however, if the AutoPreview feature is enabled—it is enabled by default, but someone may have turned it off. To control this and other AutoPreview settings, choose View ➪ Current View ➪ Customize Current View and click the Other Settings button. The resulting dialog box has a section in which you can decide which messages Outlook previews, and what font it should use for the AutoPreview text.

Viewing mail with the Preview pane

Even better than AutoPreview for making your mail easier to read is the Preview pane. With the Preview pane activated, Outlook displays the text of a selected e-mail message in a separate area at the bottom of the window. This is a much faster way to read your mail than opening each message in an individual separate window. Though the Preview pane takes up space you could use for displaying more messages, that price is well worth its benefits, in my view. Figure 51-3 shows the Preview pane in operation.

If the Preview pane isn't already visible, display it by choosing View ⇨ Preview Pane. If you don't find a corresponding toolbar button, you can go to the Commands tab of the Tools ⇨ Customize dialog box to make one. Select View in the Categories list and then, when you locate the Preview Pane command, drag it onto a suitable toolbar. If you want a graphical image on the button, you have to create your own icon using the techniques discussed in Chapter 5.

Other facts you need to know about the Preview pane include:

- You can resize the pane by dragging up or down the bottom border of the main part of the window. Wait until the mouse pointer becomes a double-headed arrow.

- Right-clicking over the top border of the Preview pane itself brings up a short shortcut menu. Use the commands here to close the pane, hide or display header information for the current message, select a font for the text in the pane, and bring up a dialog box of additional options (see the next tip).

- As long as the box for Single Key Reading is checked in the Preview Pane options dialog box, you can use Space to scroll through the current message displayed in the pane, and then move on to the next message when you get to the end. Train yourself to use this handy shortcut.

- You can use the Edit ⇨ Copy command or Ctrl+C to place the text from the Preview pane on the clipboard. To select text in the Preview pane, press Tab to select the pane, and then press Ctrl+A to select the entire message. Alternatively, use the standard Windows text navigation commands to get to the information you want to select. To select a block of text, hold down Shift as you move to the end of the block. You can make selections with the mouse as well — to select the whole message, right-click the Preview pane and choose Select All.

- If the message you're viewing includes attachments, a button showing a paperclip appears at the right edge of the Preview pane header (see Figure 51-3). Click here to open the attached document immediately — if the document type is acceptable — or to see a box asking whether you want to open the attachment or save it on disk. (To ensure that you're always asked whether to open or save the attachment, use the File Types tab in the View ⇨ Options dialog box in Explorer or My Computer. There, pick the file type you want and click Edit and then check Confirm Open After Download.)

Selecting a view

Outlook provides many alternative views for the mail-related folders via the View ➪ Current View menu. Here are a couple to try:

- **By Follow Up Flag.** Displays messages flagged for some follow-up action at the top of the folder, with the accompanying message and due date visible in each item. See "Flagging messages" later in this chapter.

- **Message Timeline.** Shows graphically when your messages came in or went out.

Flagging messages

Outlook lets you mark messages that require some kind of further attention with a little red flag icon. You see this icon for all flagged items in any view that includes the corresponding column in the heading. The standard flag type is Follow Up, but you can select from several others.

To flag an e-mail message, choose Flag for Follow Up from the Actions menu or the message's shortcut menu. The dialog box that pops up lets you choose the type of flag you want to apply and a date when you want to be reminded about the pending concern. To mark a message flag as completed, check the Completed box in the same dialog box.

Managing your mail with the Rules Wizard

The Rules Wizard lets you set up automatic handling procedures for e-mail messages. For example, when a message arrives from a certain person, you can have Outlook shunt it into a special folder, play a distinctive sound, or display an appropriate message — or do all of these things. To set up custom rules, choose Tools ➪ Rules Wizard or, if the Organize pane is active and you're working with the Using Folders options, click the Rules Wizard button at the top right.

The main Rules Wizard dialog box displays existing rules and lets you create, delete, and modify individual rules and rearrange their order — the order in which Outlook applies the rules can be important if a message meets the criteria for two different rules. Clicking Create or Modify starts the Rules Wizard proper (Figure 51-4), which walks you through the steps of specifying the rule.

Secret

Use the Run Now button in the Rules Wizard dialog box to test your new rules immediately, so you're sure that they work properly.

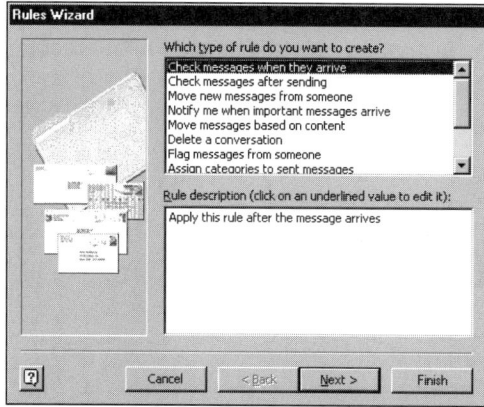

Figure 51-4: Use this box to start defining a new mail-handling rule.

Managing your junk mail

Outlook now includes unobtrusive (and ineffective, unfortunately) junk mail filters. Although I keep the junk mail filters turned on, I can't tell you why — in my experience they often incorrectly identify spam messages as desirable and vice versa.

The junk mail filters work by identifying visually messages that are from a known spam purveyor or an unknown source, or that contain suspect content. The filter attempts to differentiate between generic spam and X-rated ads separately, assigning each type of detritus its own color. If you want to take chances on missing important mail, you can even set up an automatic rule to route the presumed trash to a special folder, or delete it altogether, before you ever see it — use the Rules Wizard, described in the previous section.

Secret

Outlook classifies incoming messages as junk mail or adult on the basis of criteria stored in the filters.txt file stored in the \Office\1033 subfolder of the main Office folder (for English-language content). You can get additional filters from www.microsoft.com/outlook.

Writing Messages

To start a new e-mail (or fax) message from within Outlook, use any of the methods to create new items described in Chapter 50. If you already have one of the mail-related folders open (Inbox, Outbox, Sent Items, or Deleted Items), the fastest way is to press Ctrl+N or click the New Message button.

Secret

Outlook's drag-and-drop capabilities shine when you're viewing a folder containing contact items and want to send a message to someone in the database. Just drag the person's contact item over to any of the mail-related folders — Inbox will do — and Outlook starts a new message with that contact's address already filled in. When you're in another folder, you can choose Tools ⇨ Address Book to start the Address Book, pick a name from the list there, and click the Send Mail button to open a new message to the person. Chapter 52 has more info on the Address Book.

Outlook supplies an assortment of *stationery* for use with HTML-formatted messages that produce fancy, preformatted e-mail. See "Understanding message formats" later in this chapter.

Using special commands for messages

A message appears in its own window, of course, complete with its own menu items and toolbar buttons — they're different from the ones you see in the main Outlook window (Figure 51-5). The same e-mail-related toolbars appear whether you write messages with Outlook's built-in e-mail editor or Word — Outlook blends them in with Word's regular user interface. In Word, however, only Word's main menu bar, not Outlook's, is visible (see "Using Word as your e-mail editor").

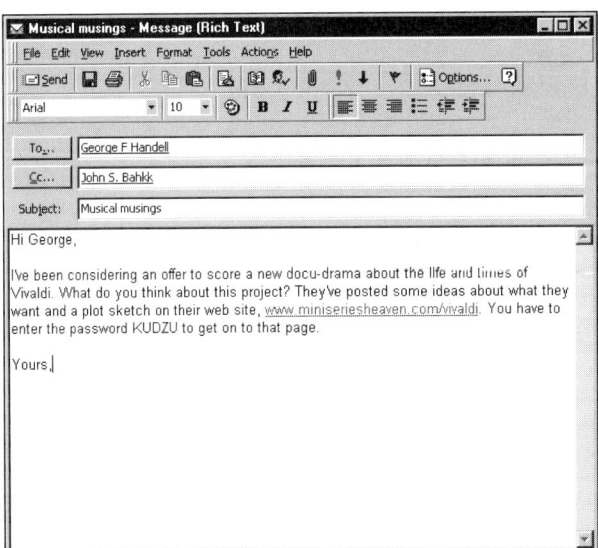

Figure 51-5: Writing an e-mail message in the Outlook editor

Special elements of note include the following:

- Click the Send toolbar button to save your message and close it, storing it in the Outbox until it's actually sent.

- The Save button (and menu command) saves the message but doesn't close it. If you're working in Outlook's e-mail editor, the message is saved in the Outbox folder but is marked as unsent. Even if you close the message manually, it won't be sent until you reopen it and click Send. When you're working in Word, the Save button saves the document in Word format, not as a message.

- The File ⇨ Save As command lets you save the message in a separate file. The file formats you can choose depend somewhat on whether you're using Word as your editor, and on what message format you're working with — plain text, Rich Text, or HTML. If you're using the Outlook editor, you can save a message as text, as an Outlook template or message, or in Rich Text Format or HTML, whichever of these formats is in effect at the time. With Word, you can save it in any available format.

- When you're not using Word as your e-mail editor, the Mail Format tab of the Tools ⇨ Options dialog box lets you define and select text signatures for the Outlook editor. Outlook automatically adds the selected signature to the end of every message. To create or modify signatures, click Signature Picker. For directions on inserting signatures in Word e-mail messages, see "Using Word as your e-mail editor" later in this chapter.

Addressing a message

To address a message, you can type in names yourself or choose one from your Address Book by clicking the To and Cc buttons.

Secret

It may seem easier to pick your recipient's e-mail address from a list, but with Outlook, typing may be more efficient. Enter a portion of the name, and Outlook tries to find a matching name in the Address Book, filling in the e-mail address if it's successful. To address the message to multiple recipients, separate their addresses with a semicolon in the To and Cc fields.

Picking addresses from your contact list

When you click the To or Cc button in a message header, Outlook displays the Select Names dialog box (Figure 51-6). This box lists the names and e-mail addresses from your Outlook folders that contain contact information. If you have more than one such folder, you must select the one you want to draw from in the drop-down list just above the main list of names. (Note that folders containing contact items appear in the Select Names dialog box only if the box for Show This Folder as an E-mail Address Book is checked in the Properties dialog box for the folder.) To address a message to more than one recipient, you can Shift+click or Ctrl+click to select multiple names and then click To, Cc, or Bcc to identify them all as recipients.

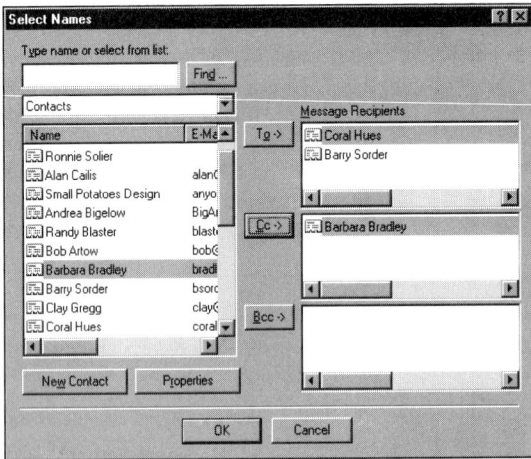

Figure 51-6: The Select Names dialog box displays names from your contact folders for quick selection of e-mail addresses.

Hiding names of other recipients

Addressing a message using the Bcc (blind carbon copy) field prevents recipients from seeing the addresses of the other recipients. If the Bcc field isn't visible in your e-mail message item, choose View ⇨ Bcc Field to display it. It's always available as an addressing choice in the Select Names dialog box. This is a courtesy to the person reading the mail (because it keeps the message header free of clutter) and the other recipients (whose privacy is protected a bit, although a savvy recipient can still recover their addresses).

Mailing to the masses with Outlook

Secret

You can mail a message to a whole slew of recipients in one step, more or less, once you've created a *personal distribution list.* With the list in place sending any message to the distribution list sends a copy to everyone on the list.

To create a personal distribution list, follow these steps:

1. Choose File ⇨ New ⇨ Distribution list. An Outlook item for the distribution list opens, as shown in Figure 51-7.

2. Type a name for the distribution list.

3. Click Select Members to add recipients from your contacts folders, or Add New to include a recipient who isn't listed in Outlook (you can add the new recipient to your Contacts folder, but you don't have to).

4. Click Save and Close to store the list. Outlook places it in your Contacts folder, where its name is listed in bold type in the Full Name field.

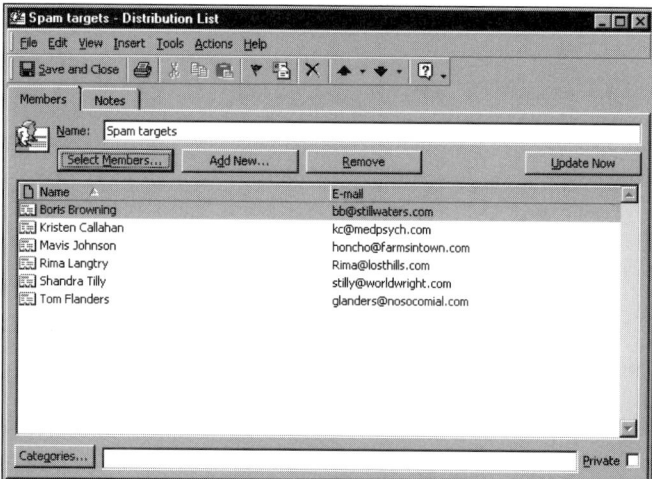

Figure 51-7: Create a group for mass mailing in this dialog box.

You can address a message to a distribution list using Outlook's standard addressing techniques. With the Contacts folder open, right-click the list item and choose New Message to Contact to start a new message to the list. Working within a message item, you can type the distribution list's name in the To or Cc fields, or click the associated button and choose the list from the Select Names dialog box — distribution lists appear in bold type.

You can also create distribution lists in the Address Book, although they're called *groups* there. In the Address Book window, click the New button and choose New Group. The Properties dialog box for the new group appears. Type in a name for the group. Click Select Members to pick out the contacts you want to include using the same dialog box shown previously in Figure 51-6. OK both boxes to finish defining the group.

Secret

To send a message to an ad hoc group, start in your contacts folder and select multiple addresses for the mailing by Shift+clicking (to select a range of consecutive items) or Ctrl+clicking (to select contacts one by one). If all the contacts are members of a single category, you don't need to select them — just display the contact list in the By Category view. Now drag, starting from any of the selected contacts or from the category heading, onto a mail folder icon on the Outlook bar. After you approve a warning, Outlook displays a new message with the To field filled with the e-mail addresses of all those contacts.

Selecting an account for an Internet e-mail message

If you're using Outlook in its Internet-only e-mail configuration, you can control which account handles each message. Unless you tell it to do otherwise, Outlook sends each new message you write from the default account you set in the Tools ⇨ Accounts dialog box. Here's how to send a message using one of your other accounts: Have the message open in its own window. There, choose File ⇨ Send Using to bring up a submenu listing all your accounts. Select the desired account and you're done.

Caution

If you select a nondefault account for sending a message, remember that back in Outlook itself, the standard Send/Receive command sends that message only if you have included the account in that command (see "Managing your accounts" near the beginning of this chapter). If you haven't, you need to send the message by using the Tools ⇨ Send command (which sends the selected message) or by picking the account from the Tools ⇨ Send/Receive submenu, as discussed in "Sending and Receiving Messages" later in this chapter.

In the Corporate or Workgroup configuration you can't assign individual messages to specific services. Instead, the order in which services are listed in the Delivery tab of the Tools ⇨ Services dialog box determines the sequence in which those services process outgoing messages. In many cases, the first service sends out all the mail. To bypass the order set in the dialog box, use the Tools ⇨ Send/Receive submenu to select a specific service.

Using message options

Don't neglect the Options button for individual messages. Figure 51-8 shows the resulting dialog box.

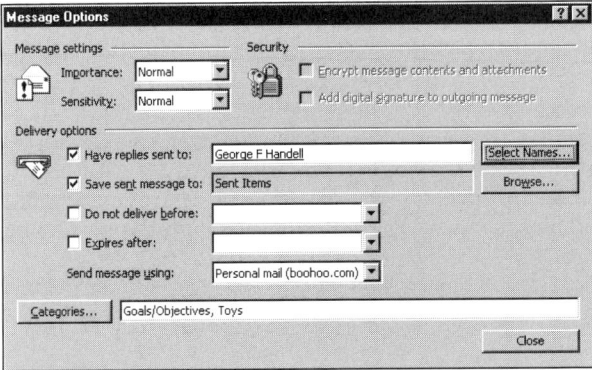

Figure 51-8: The Message Options dialog box lets you control settings for individual messages.

Use the Message Options dialog box to:

- Assign importance and sensitivity ratings.
- Specify a folder in which your copy of the message should be saved after it's sent.
- Indicate who should receive replies to your mail.
- Postpone delivery of the message until a specified time (useful when you need to record an idea but want to control when it arrives).
- Assign Outlook categories to the message.
- Set Security options for the message.

Understanding message formats

The lowest common denominator for e-mail messages is plain text (also known as ASCII). However, Outlook can send and display e-mail messages stored in the Rich Text Format (see Chapter 7), as HTML (see Chapter 14), or as Word documents. Rich Text Format preserves the full formatting of your text, including fonts, paragraph indents, bullets, and so on. HTML, of course, is the formatting language of the Web, and it can also store complex formatting.

Secret

To select a default format for new messages, go to the Mail Format tab on the Tools ⇨ Options dialog box and select a format in the Message Format area near the top. To create a new message in a specific format, choose Actions ⇨ New Mail Message Using and select the format from the resulting submenu. If you're already composing a message, you can switch to another format by choosing the one you want from the Format menu.

Caution

The ability to use Rich Text Format and HTML sounds great, but it takes two to format — your recipient must also be using Outlook or another e-mail program that supports the format you've chosen. If Outlook sends a Rich Text or HTML message to a recipient whose software can't understand the format, one of two things may happen. If you're lucky, the message will show up as ordinary text — the formatting will be missing, but at least the information will be readable. More likely, however, the receiving software will let the formatting codes through. Your recipient will see a more or less unreadable message and may end up mad instead of impressed. (If the recipient is savvy and wants to read your message anyway, it can be exported to a separate file, which can then be opened in a word processor, such as WordPad, that can import Rich Text Format files, or a browser).

Secret

If the Rich Text, HTML, or Word format works for most of your recipients but not for everyone, you can force Outlook to send messages to certain people in plain text format — if you're using the Internet-only configuration. Open the contact item for the person. There, check the box Send Using Plain Text located on the right side of the window just under the e-mail address box. In the Corporate or Workgroup configuration, your choice is reversed. If you want to see that Outlook always sends messages to a certain recipient in Rich Text format, regardless of the default message format setting, open the contact item and double-click the e-mail address itself. In the resulting dialog box, check the Always Send box.

To set a default background graphic and font for new messages, open the Mail Format tab of the Tools ➪ Options dialog box, set the message format to HTML, and then select a stationery choice either from the drop-down list or by clicking Stationery Picker. To select different stationery when you start a new message, choose Actions ➪ New Mail Message Using and select the stationery choice Different Stationery, None, or Other Options.

Using Word as your e-mail editor

You can specify Word as the editor for the e-mail messages you write, and for viewing incoming messages. Obviously, Word has far more editing and formatting power than ordinary e-mail editors, and all of that power is at your disposal when you edit e-mail with Word.

To make Word your e-mail editor, open the Tools ➪ Options dialog box, switch to the Mail Format tab, and check the relevant box near the top. The remaining options change to reflect your selection.

Specify settings for Word e-mail messages by going to the General tab of the Tools ➪ Options dialog box (in Word) and clicking the E-mail Options button. As shown in Figure 51-9, the resulting dialog box has two tabs.

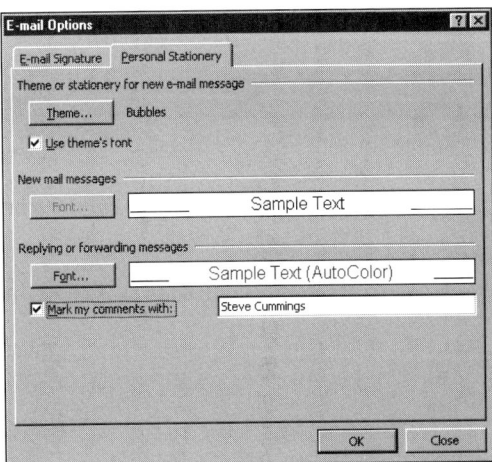

Figure 51-9: Set e-mail options for Word messages in this dialog box, available from the General tab of Word's Tools ➪ Options dialog box.

The two tabs work as follows:

- Use the E-mail Signature tab in the E-mail Options dialog box to create signatures for e-mail messages and designate default signatures that appear automatically when you start a new message. Once you've defined a signature, you can also insert it anywhere in a message by choosing Insert ⇨ AutoText ⇨ E-mail Signature and selecting the signature from the submenu.

- The Personal Stationery tab of the E-mail Options dialog box lets you select formatting options for new e-mail messages. You can choose a complete format by selecting a theme (themes are discussed in Chapter 14), or you can just pick fonts for the text of your messages.

Word also includes the following features specifically useful for e-mail editing:

- By default, Word displays messages with the text wrapped to the window no matter how long the lines are formatted to print.

- Word's on-the-fly spell checker works when you compose e-mail messages just as it does in other Word documents — you see those wavy red lines under misspelled words.

- If the message you're reading is a response to someone else's message (and in turn, that message responded to an earlier one), the View ⇨ Document Map command displays names of all the authors of the messages in the chain. You can click a name to jump directly to the corresponding message, if it's available to your system.

- Right-click a name in the body of a message and choose Who Is from the shortcut menu to display that person's listing in the Address Book.

Including other information with e-mail messages

Like all modern e-mail software, Outlook lets you *attach* other files to your e-mail messages. With a message open, click the Insert File button or choose Insert ⇨ File. Alternatively, drag and drop the attachment file from a file-management window (My Computer, Explorer, or a file-management view in Outlook) into the body of the message. Don't forget that you can also send any open Word, PowerPoint, or Excel document as an e-mail message attachment from within those applications. Choose File ⇨ Send To ⇨ Mail Recipient.

To send an Outlook item of any type (such as a contact or task item) to a person who also uses Outlook, right-click the item and choose Forward from the shortcut menu, or press Ctrl+F. This starts a new e-mail message with the item attached. If you started the message already, choose Insert ⇨ Item instead, or drag the item onto the body of the message. The recipient just drags the item from the message onto the icon for the Outlook folder where it belongs.

Secret

Using cut and paste or drag and drop, you can attach documents or other files of any type to *any* Outlook item, not just to messages. For that matter, you can add them directly to mail-related folders.

Working with encoding formats for e-mail attachments

Originally designed to handle sequences of ordinary text, e-mail systems must take special measures to send files. Files attached to or inserted in an e-mail message must be encoded in ordinary text characters for the trip and then decoded and converted back into files on the recipient's computer. Outlook and other e-mail programs handle the encoding and decoding process automatically. Your only worry is to ensure that the mail programs at the sending and receiving ends use the same encoding formats.

Two encoding formats are in widespread use: UUENCODE and MIME. They enable you to send e-mail messages containing embedded objects and files inserted at specific points in the message, not just attached at the end.

MIME, Outlook's default, is generally preferable and is the only choice if you're sending HTML messages. However, if your recipient's software understands only the UUENCODE format, you must set up Outlook accordingly.

To set the default encoding format for Outlook, Exchange, and all other MAPI e-mail applications, open the Tools ⇨ Options dialog box. If Outlook is running in the Corporation or Workgroup configuration, switch to the Internet E-mail tab and select MIME or UUENCODE and set the relevant options for your selection. If you're using the Internet-only configuration, click Settings on the Mail Format tab to accomplish the same end.

Even when both the sending and receiving programs are using the same encoding format, attached or inserted files still won't get through unless both sides use the same character sets for the encoding/decoding process. This is most likely going to be a problem when you are communicating internationally. Use the same dialog boxes just described to change the character sets for default and individual messages.

Sending and Receiving Messages

The standard way to manually send the messages in your Outbox and check for new incoming mail is by clicking the Send/Receive button on the Standard toolbar. The keyboard shortcut for this command is F5. If you're using the Corporate or Workgroup configuration, Outlook displays a nondescript message letting you know that it's busy sending and receiving information. With the Internet-only configuration, however, you get the dialog box shown in Figure 51-10, as Outlook connects to your network or dial-up service provider and transfers messages.

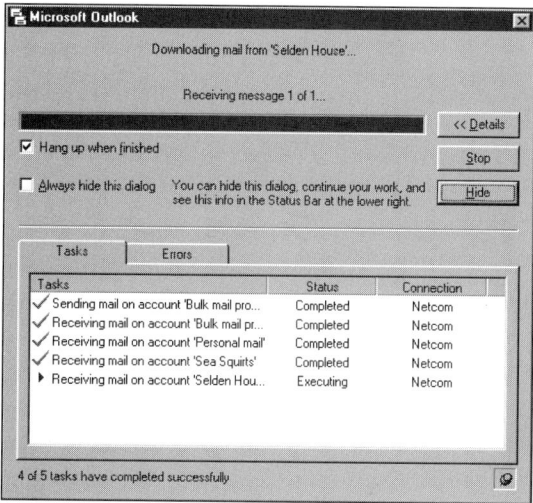

Figure 51-10: Outlook displays the progress of a mail session in this dialog box.

Working with the mail dialog box

Figure 51-10 shows the mail dialog box (I call it that, anyway) in its expanded version. Click the Details button to display or remove the lower portion of the box. Other items on this dialog box work as follows:

- The top part of the dialog box is for messages from Outlook. When an account is connected and Outlook is actively sending or receiving messages, this area tells you how many messages need to be processed and displays progress graphically along the horizontal bar.

- The tabbed box below shows pending mail tasks. It lists a separate task for each send or receive operation on each account included in the current mail operation. You see a send task only for those accounts for which you have unsent outgoing mail. As each task is completed, Outlook displays a message and icon indicating whether the task is executing, was completed successfully, was canceled, or experienced an error. If you do get errors, you can see details on them in the Errors tab.

- If you're mailing via a dial-up connection — that is, using a modem — the Hang Up When Finished box lets you decide whether to disconnect automatically after completing the mailing or to stay online so that you can surf the Web or do another mailing.

- You can put away the mail dialog box and go back to Outlook by clicking Hide. The mailing operation continues, and Outlook uses the status bar to keep you informed of its progress with the mailing as you work with other folders and items.

- If you never want to be bothered with the mail dialog box again, click the box Always Hide This Dialog.

Sending an individual message

Suppose you want to send a key message you just wrote, but your Outbox is full of other messages that are in progress and not quite ready to send. Or suppose you assigned a message to an account that Outlook leaves out when you trigger the standard Send/Receive command. To send a message individually, select it in your Outbox (or another appropriate mail folder) and choose Tools ➪ Send.

Mailing on specific accounts

Important, well-connected people often maintain many different e-mail accounts. Because checking all those accounts at the same time can tie up your PC for too long, Outlook gives you a way to send and receive mail on any one account whenever you like. Just choose Tools ➪ Send/Receive and select the desired account from the resulting submenu.

Mail-handling options for networked computers

If your computer is connected to a network, Outlook can automatically send and receive your mail on a schedule. To control if, and how often, automatic mail handling kicks in, open the Tools ➪ Options dialog box. If you're using the Internet-only e-mail configuration, go to the Mail Delivery tab and check or clear the box labeled Check for New Messages, and set the interval in minutes. With the Corporate or Workgroup configuration, you need to use the Internet E-mail tab instead. In this case, you can have Outlook check for messages on a schedule even if you use a dial-up Internet connection.

Most people prefer having a few moments to review the content in their minds before letters go out. But if you like to live dangerously, you can set Outlook so that it sends each message instantaneously, as soon as you click Send on the message's own toolbar. Check the Send Messages Immediately box on the Mail Delivery tab of the Tools ➪ Options dialog box. This choice seems to be available only when the Internet-only e-mail configuration is active.

Customizing Outlook's E-mail Settings

Choose Tools ➪ Options to examine and change your e-mail settings in Outlook. The hordes of relevant options are listed on the Preferences, Mail Delivery or Mail Services, Mail Format, and Other tabs. Many of them have been covered elsewhere in this chapter, but here are some additional pointers:

- On the Preferences tab, click E-mail Options to check out the options for including the text of an original message when you reply to or forward it (Figure 51-11). Try the "Include and indent original message text" and "Attach original message text" choices. The latter is the most courteous and probably the best: It lets recipients read the original if they want to but lets them trash it without reading it if they prefer.

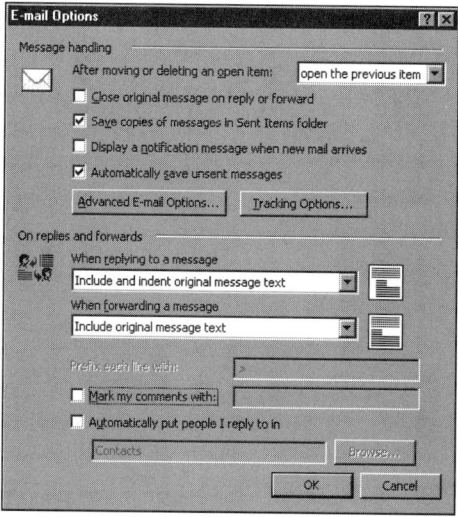

Figure 51-11: This dialog box offers many but by no means all of Outlook's e-mail-related settings.

- On the same E-mail Options dialog box shown in Figure 51-11, click Tracking Options to see some powerful settings for working with receipts so that you and your correspondents can know who got what mail, when. Unfortunately these features only work if your organization uses Exchange Server.

- The choices on the Spelling tab are straightforward. Your big decision is whether or not you want every message spell-checked before it goes out.

Conclusion

That concludes this Secrets-oriented run-through of Outlook's e-mail features. Chapter 52 concludes the Outlook story, with an exploration of the features related to contacts, task lists, and scheduling.

Chapter 52

Managing Tasks, Schedules, Contacts, and Miscellany

In This Chapter

▶ Managing your to-do list for maximum productivity

▶ Scheduling appointments, meetings, and all-day events

▶ Keeping track of important people

▶ Stashing and retrieving miscellaneous information

Even if you don't use Outlook for e-mail, you shouldn't overlook its other talents. This one program can keep track of your to-do list, schedule your appointments and meetings, maintain your collection of names, addresses, and other people-type information, and store any random facts, opinions, quotes, and discussion topics you care to preserve. What's more, it knows how to follow the connections between these disparate items. That way you can, say, quickly recall the vital statistics of the people who will be at your next meeting. Clearly, you should be on familiar terms with this software.

This chapter assumes you know the basic techniques for creating new Outlook items of any type. Those techniques are outlined in Chapter 50.

Keeping Up with Your Tasks

Outlook is a strong to-do list manager, helping you keep track of what you're supposed to be doing and when you're hoping to get it done. You enter to-do items, or tasks, individually and then use various folders and views to remind yourself of the pending chores. You can set each task's priority, organize related tasks by assigning them to categories, and have Outlook notify you in advance of your deadlines.

Viewing your tasks

Three Outlook folders display pending tasks: Tasks, Calendar, and Outlook Today. The Tasks folder shows the most detail, of course, but the two other folders have their place. Outlook Today is a quick way to review the tasks you need to complete in the context of pending appointments and meetings and a summary of your unread and unsent mail. Still, I find the TaskPad (Figure 52-1) on the daily and weekly calendars more useful, because it shows *all* your pending tasks along with highly relevant details about your schedule, and because you can use it to add and edit tasks.

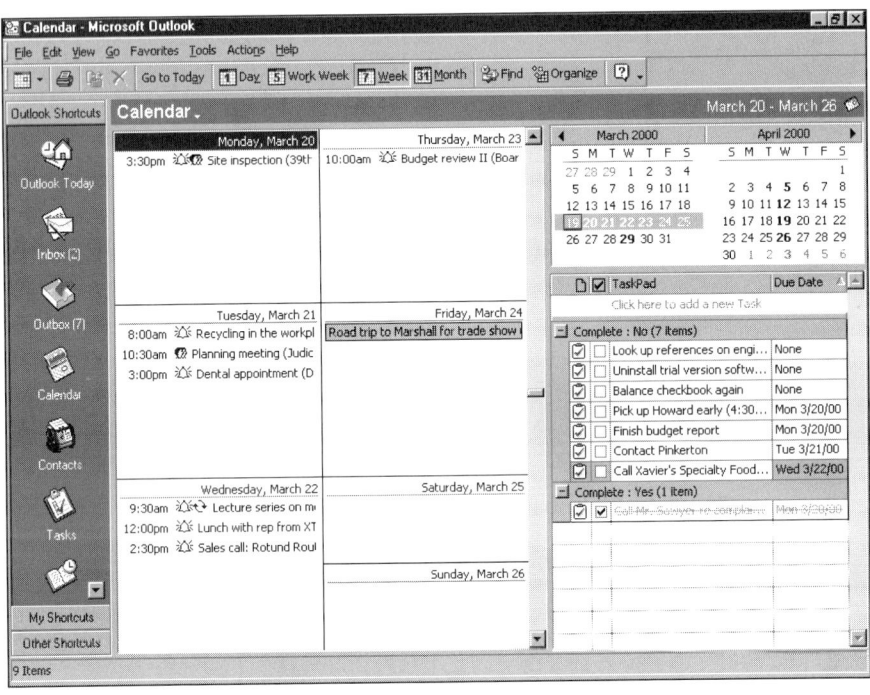

Figure 52-1: The TaskPad occupies the lower right of the Calendar folder's Work Week view.

Secret

Outlook's default task views display completed as well as incomplete tasks. This is distracting, so move the completed tasks to the bottom of the list or hide them altogether. To sort the list, click the Complete check box icon in the column heading, or if it's not visible, click Sort in the View Summary dialog box (View ⇨ Current View ⇨ Customize Current View) and choose Complete in the Sort By field. To hide completed items, click Filter in the View Summary dialog box, switch to the Advanced tab, type **Complete** in the Field box and then choose "Equals" in the Condition box and "No" at Value. Note that you can't sort or filter the TaskPad in a Calendar view from the View menu. You must right-click the gray bar at the top of the TaskPad and choose Customize Current View from the resulting shortcut menu.

Secret

I also recommend sorting your task list by date in *ascending* order. That way tasks without due dates fall at the top of your list, where they won't get lost. They're followed by those with the earliest due dates, keeping tasks whose deadlines have already passed near the top of the list. If you sort on both the completion status and the due date, enter **Complete** as the first criterion in the Sort dialog box, followed by choosing Due Date in the Then By box.

Setting task-related options

Outlook scatters its settings related to tasks in several locations, all accessible from the Tools ➪ Options dialog box. Here's where to find them:

- **Reminder Time.** On the Preferences tab, enter the time when you want to receive your reminders of the tasks due today.

- **Color Options.** Click Task Options on the Preferences tab to display a little dialog box that lets you choose font colors for overdue and completed tasks.

- **Miscellaneous Options.** Switch to the Other tab and click Advanced Options to see the corresponding dialog box. Then click Advanced Tasks. The first check box, Set Reminders, creates an automatic reminder for each new task based on the preset reminder time discussed earlier. The remaining two options pertain to tasks you assign to others and are covered in "Delegating work" later in this chapter.

- **Reminder Options.** From the Advanced Options dialog box, click Reminder Options to access default settings pertaining to the reminders for task and calendar items. You can decide whether to see a reminder notice, hear an alert, or both, and you can select the sound file for the alert.

Completing tasks

Cataloging your chores is a dandy activity, but what really counts is finishing them. When you accomplish a task, grant yourself a moment of Great Satisfaction and then get it off your to-do list so that you can move on to the next one. Outlook gives you many different ways to mark tasks as complete. If the check box for the Complete field is visible in the current view, just check it. If not, right-click the task and choose Mark Complete from the shortcut menu. If you're working with the task in its own window, click the Mark Complete button, or choose Actions ➪ Mark Complete.

When you mark a task as complete, Outlook doesn't delete the item. Instead, it displays the finished task in gray, strikethrough text. If you've sorted your task list as I suggest, completed items immediately fall to the bottom of the list where you can view them or mark them as not complete, if necessary.

Entering tasks

Outlook is set up to accept great detail about each task you add to your to-do list. But that doesn't mean you need to supply all those details. Let me warn you, by the time you fill out a task form, you might be able to finish the task itself. Often, a simple undated memory jogger is enough. Just type a description of the task in the so-called Subject field and you're done.

However, when you're juggling lots of different responsibilities, and especially when you manage the work of others, you may really need some of the other task fields. Some comments on them follow:

- **Priority.** You can select High, Normal, or Low. To make your task list more useful, try to restrain your impulse to mark every other task as a high-priority item.

- **Due Date.** Entering a due date enables you to sort your task list by deadline. Of course, many important tasks don't have fixed due dates. Tasks for which you don't enter a due date fall at the bottom of the list if you sort the list in ascending date order as I recommend.

- **Start Date.** Entering a start date is useful when you're planning future activities. You can then set the reminder to the start date to help you remember to actually start the task. If you enter both the start date and due dates, the task shows up on the Task Timeline view as a horizontal band, which is especially helpful when planning interrelated tasks for larger projects.

- **Recurring.** Because many tasks are monthly, weekly, or even daily obligations, Outlook lets you set them up as recurring tasks. Outlook does have a field named Recurring, but you don't change it directly. Instead, with a task's own window open, click the Recurrence button to display the dialog box shown in Figure 52-2. Here, tell Outlook how often the task recurs; what day of the week, month, or year it falls on; and how long it will continue to recur. By the way, to identify recurring tasks in a table view, add the Recurring field to the column heading.

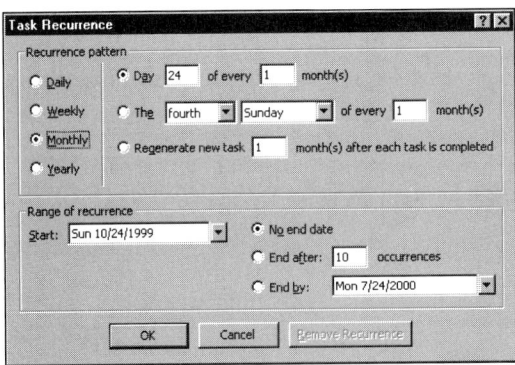

Figure 52-2: Set options for a recurring task in this dialog box.

■ **Status, % Complete, and the fields on the Details tab.** Use these fields if you're keeping track of someone else's work or if someone else is tracking you. Otherwise, skip 'em.

Managing projects — you're mostly on your own

A simple to-do list is great for remembering a series of unrelated tasks. When you're working on a project of any complexity, however, Outlook offers limited help. The program does enable you to assign tasks to others and follow their progress, as discussed in the next section. But unfortunately, Outlook can't identify relationships between tasks. For example, you need to know when you can't start work on a task until another task has been completed, but Outlook doesn't highlight this sort of dependency.

About the best you can do is to group a set of related tasks by assigning them to a category. You can then use the group by or filter features (see "Grouping related items" in Chapter 50) to display the tasks in that category together. Whether tasks are grouped or filtered, the Task Timeline view can give you at least a rough idea of how each task fits into the schedule for your project — see Figure 52-3 for an example. For serious project management, get specialized software such as Microsoft Project.

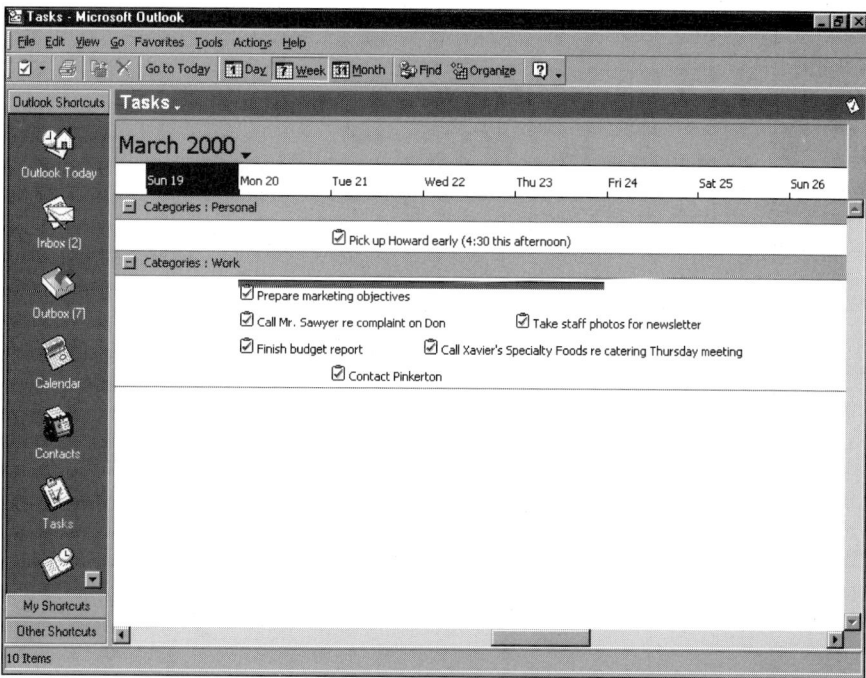

Figure 52-3: Displaying a group of tasks in the Task Timeline view

Delegating work

If you manage the work of other people, you can use Outlook to assign tasks to your colleagues and subordinates, and to keep track of their work. To assign a new task to someone, create a new *task request* by clicking the right portion of the New split button and choosing Task Request from the drop-down menu. Alternatively, you can convert an existing task to a task request by opening the item and clicking the Assign Task button. A task request differs from a standard task item in a few details, as follows:

- You enter the recipient's name in the To field.

- A couple of extra check boxes appear above the main text box. Check Keep an Updated Copy if you want to have Outlook automatically update your copy of the task information as the assignee changes it. Click Send Me a Status Report if you want to be notified when the task has been completed. You can control the default settings for these items in the Advanced Tasks dialog box, available from the Other tab of the Tools ⇨ Options dialog box when you click Advanced Options and then Advanced Tasks.

- A Cancel Assignment button appears on the toolbar. Click here to convert the task request into a regular task for yourself.

Secret

Task requests you send to others appear in your task list, but you can't make changes except to delete them. Only a task's *owner*—the person who has accepted responsibility for it—can update the task information. To view only those tasks you've assigned to others, choose View ⇨ Current View ⇨ Assignment.

Responding to task requests

When a task request from someone else comes in, respond to the request by opening the item and clicking Accept or Decline as you see fit. You can send a simple notification of your decision by clicking Send the Response Now, or you can provide more details—perhaps concerning what you expect in return—by clicking Edit the Response.

Outlook even lets you pass an incoming task request on to someone else further down the pecking order. Ignoring the Accept and Decline buttons, choose Actions ⇨ Assign Task to convert the item into a task request for someone else. This redelegation process can go on indefinitely. Assuming everyone in the sequence has checked the Keep an Updated Copy and Send Me a Status Report boxes, each person receives updates when the one who ultimately accepted the task makes changes.

Scheduling Appointments, Meetings, and Events

Use Outlook's Calendar folder to keep track of activities that happen at specific times. Outlook makes a distinction, at least in name and by icon, between *appointments,* where the focus is on you and your schedule, and *meetings,* involving other people. *Events* are all-day affairs of either type. Such hair-splitting notwithstanding, you use the same Outlook form to work with all three types of items.

Most of the built-in views available for the Calendar folder look like standard paper calendars (see Figure 52-4). You can switch among them using the relevant toolbar buttons (they have little calendar icons). If your schedule is sparsely populated, you may prefer the Active Appointments view, which simply lists all appointments and meetings scheduled for today or later.

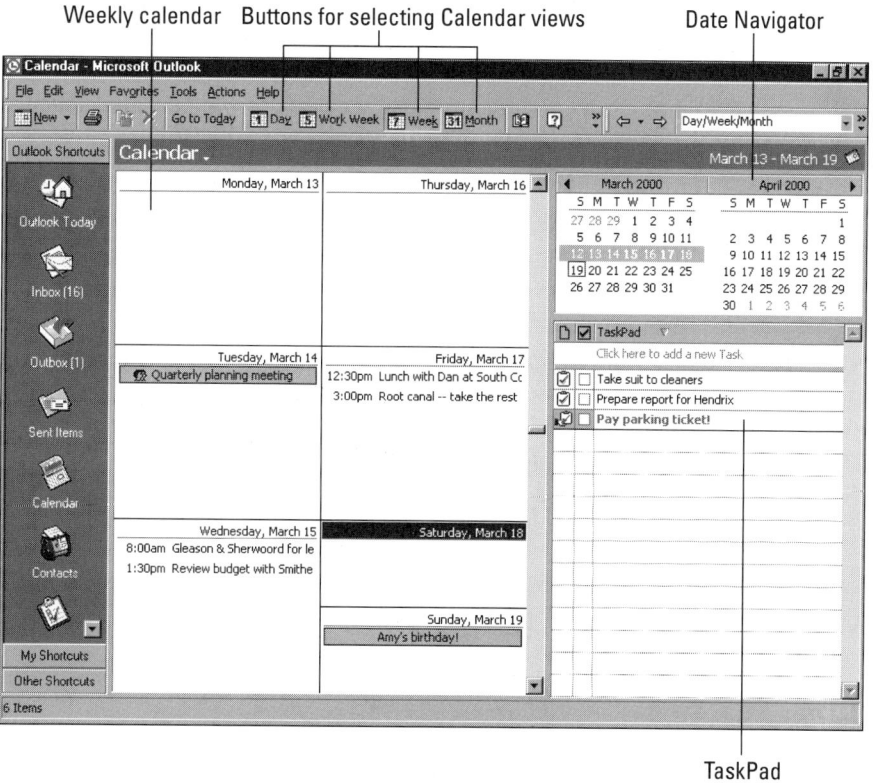

Figure 52-4: Outlook's Calendar in Week view

Secret: You can control the number of days Outlook displays at a time via hidden keyboard shortcuts: Press Alt with the corresponding number key. Alt+3, for example, gives a view showing three days. Press Alt+0 to see 10 days — but don't expect to see much of any one day. Alt+- gets you to the Week view, and Alt+= displays the Month view.

Navigating in the Calendar

In all calendar-type views except Month, the Date Navigator is the quick ticket to your destination date. If the date you want to display is already visible in the Navigator, click it to display it in Day view. To see more than one day, drag over the range of dates you want to display, or click the first date and then Shift+click the last date in the range. You can switch to Week view for a particular week by clicking the left margin of the week in question.

Secret: You can even display two or more nonconsecutive dates: In the Navigator, Ctrl+click each date in turn.

Secret: If you select Month view from the View menu or by clicking the toolbar button, the Date Navigator and TaskPad disappear. You can trick Outlook into retaining them by drag-selecting an entire month in Date Navigator.

If the Date Navigator isn't showing the dates you're interested in, you need other navigation tricks. Your choices include the following:

- **Use the scroll bar.** I prefer this method. As you drag the scroll bar thumb, a screen tip shows you what date you've reached. Don't worry if you can't scroll far enough into the future — click the bottom scroll bar arrow to advance further.

- **Use Date Navigator.** Click the month name at the top of the Navigator to jump to a new month by picking from a list. Or click the arrows to move one month at a time. This works great for short hops but is time consuming if you're headed for a different year.

- **Type in the target date.** Choose View ⇨ Go To ⇨ Go to Date or just press Ctrl+G to bring up a little dialog box into which you can type the destination date. Outlook doesn't require a complete date — entries such as 2005, mar 19, or sep produce the expected results.

Secret: You may have already noticed the Go to Today button, but it's easy to miss. Click it (or press Alt+A) to jump directly to today's date.

Adding new calendar items

The simplest way to create a new calendar item is to enter it directly on the calendar. In the Day or Work Week views, drag over the calendar to select the block of time for your appointment, meeting, or nap. Then just start typing the item description, pressing Enter when you finish. The resulting item is an appointment, in Outlook terms. In the Week or Month views, click the day for the new item, or drag across two or more days to select them, and then start typing. You get an event.

For access to more item details, right-click the selection and choose New Appointment, New All Day Event, or New Meeting Request. The new item opens in its own window. If you chose an appointment or meeting, the start and end times are already set to those of the selection, if there was one. If you chose an event, the All Day Event box is checked, and the time fields for the start and end times are hidden.

Secret

You can convert any ordinary meeting or appointment to an event, or vice versa, by opening the item and checking or clearing the All Day Event box. Note that "all day" events can span more than one day. In the calendar proper, they appear in a bar at the top of the day or days when they occur.

Moving calendar items

You can edit an item's start and end time and even change its date by opening the item and modifying the appropriate fields. A quicker approach, though, is to alter the item in place. Drag the top or bottom borders of the item to change the start or stop time (in Month view you can drag the left and right borders of event items). Drag the item as a whole to quickly reschedule the entire item, even to another day.

Secret

If you want to move an item to a day that isn't visible on the main calendar, drag it to the Date Navigator and drop it on the target date.

Scheduling meetings

In Outlook, an appointment becomes a meeting as soon as you include people from your Contacts folder in the event. To do so, click the Invite Attendees button. A field and button labeled To appear beneath the item's tabs, intended for the e-mail addresses of the people who you want at the meeting. You can now type in their names or click the To button to select them from your contacts.

Once your meeting time is set, and after you've typed in a description of the meeting and any other appropriate message in the body of the Appointment tab, click Send to save the meeting on your schedule and simultaneously send it as an e-mail message to all the attendees. If you later change the meeting item, click Send Update to inform the participants.

If the attendees' schedules are accessible via a network connection, you can use the Attendee Availability tab to schedule a meeting time that works for everyone. Outlook automatically displays the schedules of all attendees, with colored bars to represent times that the participants aren't available. It's easy enough to eyeball a time when no one has a conflict, but you can click the

AutoPick arrows to have Outlook find a suitable time for you. The next section explains how Outlook users can make their schedule information available for meeting planning.

Setting Calendar options

With the exception of options for default reminders, all Outlook settings pertaining to the calendar are accessible on the Preferences tab of the Tools ⇨ Options dialog box. On the Preferences tab itself you can set a default for how far in advance of an appointment or meeting you would like Outlook to send you a reminder. To get to the other settings, click Calendar Options. The dialog box shown in Figure 52-5 appears.

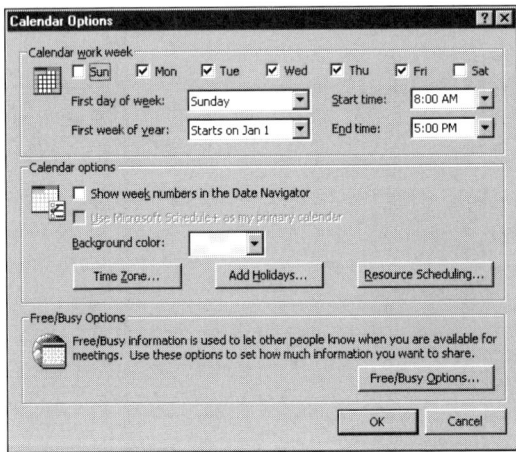

Figure 52-5: Use this dialog box to set options related to your calendar and group scheduling.

Let's cover the simple items first:

- The first group of boxes enables you to define your own work week for the Work Week view — handy if you have an unorthodox schedule.

- If you check the box labeled Show Week Numbers in the Date Navigator, the week-of-the-year numbers appear everywhere the Date Navigator does. That is, you see them not only in the Calendar folder, but anywhere in Outlook that you can pick a date from the little pop-up calendar.

- Click the Add Holidays button to import calendar items for predefined holidays. In the little dialog box that appears you get to choose holidays for a number of countries and religions.

Working with time zones

Clicking the Time Zone button gives you an alternative to the Windows Date/Time Properties (available in the taskbar tray) for selecting the current time zone. The choice you make in the top Time Zone field does apply to your whole system, not just in Outlook. If you check Show an Additional Time Zone, Outlook displays a second set of times in the Day and Work Week views so that you can see at a glance when a meeting would occur in the second zone. If you travel back and forth between the two zones, clicking Swap Time Zones is a quick way to adjust your system each time you arrive.

Resource options

You can ignore the options revealed by the Resource Scheduling button unless it's your job to coordinate meetings — you know, if you're the one who keeps the schedules for the meeting rooms, who arranges for catering, and that sort of thing. Each of the options on this dialog box instructs Outlook how to process automatically the meeting requests you receive. Note that if you check the first box but not the second, you could wind up sending automatic acceptance messages even when your schedule shows a conflict.

Publishing schedule information

If you schedule meetings for other people or attend meetings that other people schedule for you, use the Free/Busy Options button to set up Outlook to share scheduling information. Figure 52-6 shows the Free/Busy dialog box.

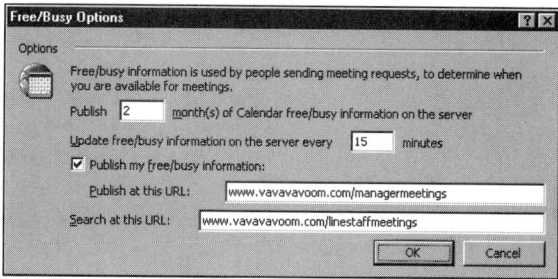

Figure 52-6: This dialog box controls settings governing the sharing of schedule information.

If you want (or are required) to make your schedule accessible to others so that they can schedule meetings for you, all but the last of the fields in the Free/Busy dialog box pertain to you. You can make any appropriate entries in the first two fields. However, all will be for naught unless you also check the Publish box and type in the URL for the Internet or intranet server to which your schedule information should be sent.

The final field is for meeting schedulers. If you're using the Attendee Availability page of an Outlook meeting item to schedule a meeting, the address at Search is where Outlook checks for the attendees' schedules.

Tracking Important People

Outlook's Contacts folder lets you store as much information as you care to collect about all the people who matter to you: your friends, relations, customers, suppliers, competitors, and consultants, be they financial or spiritual. A contact item can contain anything from a name and telephone number to tens of fields containing details of all aspects of the person's professional or personal life.

You shouldn't have any problems entering a new contact. In any table view, you can type the basic information directly into the top line, and in any view, the New Contact button produces a blank contact item in its own window. One shortcut can save a few seconds of typing time: To create a new contact item for a person from the same company as an existing contact, select the contact and then choose Actions ⇨ New Contact from Same Company.

In the Contact window, the General tab contains the critical contact information. A few pointers may help here:

- Outlook is smart enough to understand most names and addresses without requiring you to break them into separate fields for first and last name or city and state. Just type in the full name or address in the appropriate field. If making an unusual entry, however, you can click the Full Name or Address button to fill in individual fields for each portion of the name or address.

- Although you can sort your contact list by any field, Outlook uses the File As field to establish its default sort order. Outlook automatically transfers the name entry here, rearranging it so that the last name comes first. You can select other File As alternatives from the drop-down list or type in an entry of your own.

- Before you start typing an address, be sure to use the drop-down list beside the Address field to designate the type of address (business, home, or other).

Be sure to check out the wealth of built-in fields provided for contact items. Commonly, valuable fields are placed on the Details tab, but you can find hordes more on the All Fields tab (choose All Contact Fields in the Select From list to see them all).

Contacting your contacts

Once you've entered a contact into your list, you can put the information you entered into action immediately. After selecting a contact, try these moves, all of which you can make from the Actions menu:

- **Dial the contact.** Choose Call Contact and select a number from the submenu. In the New Call dialog box, confirm the number and click Start Call. Of course, your modem needs to be hooked up to the phone line.

- **Send e-mail to the contact.** Choosing New Message to Contact starts an e-mail message with the To field filled in for you.

- **Create a letter to the contact.** The New Letter to Contact choice starts Word and activates the Letter Wizard, transferring information from your contact to the appropriate places in the Wizard dialog box.

Other choices on the Actions menu let you create meetings and tasks involving the selected contact.

Secret

To check out the contact's Web page, select the item and press Ctrl+Shift+X. You can add the corresponding Explore Web Page command to any menu or toolbar from the Advanced category in the Tools ⇨ Customize dialog box (Commands tab).

Working with Address Book

The Address Book that comes with Office is not really a part of Outlook but a separate little program that's also distributed with Outlook's little sibling, Outlook Express. At any rate, you can use the Address Book to store and access contact information throughout Windows, even when Outlook isn't running — or for that matter, even if you never install Outlook. Figure 52-7 shows the Address Book.

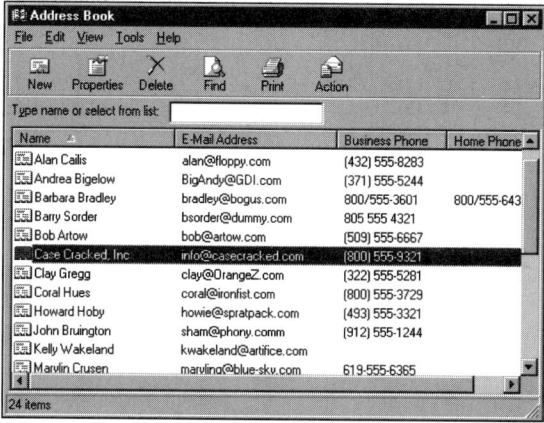

Figure 52-7: The Address Book program gives you access to your contacts when Outlook itself isn't running, or when you're using another Outlook folder.

The names and addresses stored in the Address Book can come from either of two sources: Outlook's Contacts folder or the Address Book's own database file. To switch between these two sources, choose Tools ⇨ Options on the Address Book's menu and click the appropriate button.

In Outlook, you activate the full Address Book program by choosing Tools ⇨ Address Book. This command is available in all Outlook folders. If Outlook isn't running, you can bring up the Address Book from the Windows Start menu (use Start ⇨ Programs ⇨ Internet Explorer to get to it). The Address Book also appears, though in different form, when you click the To button in an Outlook e-mail message, and in Word, when you click the appropriate button in the Letter Wizard or the Envelopes and Labels dialog box.

Although the Address Book stores and displays essentially the same information as your Contacts folder does, that information is organized quite differently. The list of contacts in the main Address Book window offers a few basic fields, and you can get more details by holding the pointer over a selected item for a second or so. To see the full entry for a contact, though, you select the item and click the Properties button. As you can see in Figure 52-8, the resulting dialog box doesn't look much like an Outlook Contact window.

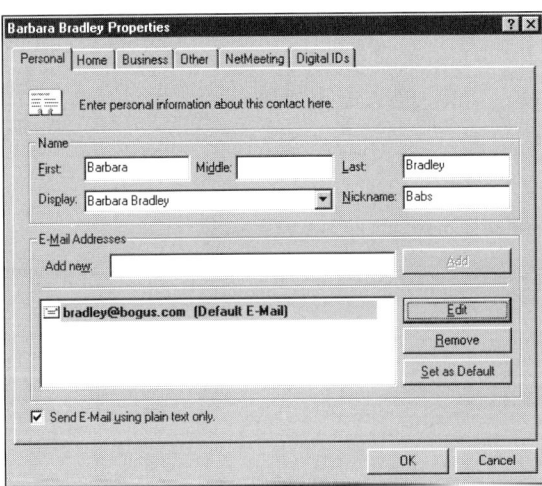

Figure 52-8: View and edit contact fields for the Address Book in this dialog box.

Speed dialing with Outlook

Outlook includes a built-in speed dialer for frequently called numbers. Once you set it up, you can dial any stored number by selecting it from a menu — without having to open the Contacts folder and track down the person you want to call.

Secret

Setting up the speed dialer takes a little work. Although it's available in the stock Outlook menus via the Actions ⇨ Call Contact submenu when you're working in the Contacts folder, you can't use it when you have other folders open. To remedy this situation, choose Tools ⇨ Customize, switch to the Commands tab, and select Tools in the Categories list. Scroll down in the

Commands list until you find the Speed Dial item, and then drag it out onto the menu bar or any toolbar you always keep visible.

Once the Speed Dialer menu item is out where you can get to it easily, click it and choose None. This produces the New Call dialog box. Here, you can type in any number and have Outlook dial it for you. Instead, however, click the misleadingly labeled Dialing Options button. Most of the resulting dialog box (Figure 52-9) is devoted to slots for your speed dial numbers. Type in names and numbers in the fields at the top, clicking Add to enter each one. After you OK the dialog boxes, the names and numbers appear on the Speed Dial menu. Select one, and Outlook dials it for you.

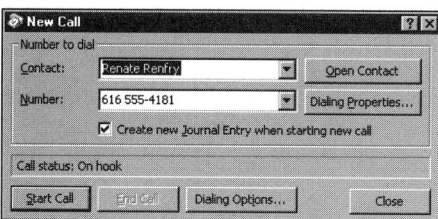

Figure 52-9: Set up speed dial entries in this dialog box.

Storing Miscellaneous Information

I don't have a whole lot to say about Outlook's Notes folder — this is one Office feature that is sweet and simple. Just keep in mind that the Notes folder exists, and that its "sticky notes" are a wonderful way to store and access bits of information that don't fit neatly into the rows and columns of a standard database table. A few more bits of information about Outlook notes should suffice, as follows:

- A note's title, or *subject* in Outlook jargon, is the first line you type. You see the subject when you view the note in its folder, but the rest of the text is visible only when you open the note.

- Because each open note occupies a separate window, you can access it directly via the taskbar or Alt+Tab without returning to the main Outlook program first. And by the way, open note windows stay open when you close Outlook for ready access when you want to conserve your system memory and resources.

- The standard Find command for notes only lets you search for text in the subject line. You have to use Advanced Find to track down text in the body of the note.

- You can drag and drop other items from other Outlook folders into an open note.

Although Outlook notes are great so far as they go, they really can't hold a candle to those of the finest in "sticky note" software, the superb DeskNotes. DeskNotes is included on the CD-ROM that accompanies this book. And don't overlook venerable Info Select, by far the best software for organizing and quickly searching random textual information on an ad hoc basis (Micro Logic Corp., www.miclog.com).

Conclusion

This tour of Outlook's work-flow and information management features should convince you that Outlook has storage cubbies for just about everything. Because you need help remembering what you're supposed to be doing or when you should be at your next meeting, because you need to keep track of the people who figure large in your life, and because you need a place to squirrel away random bits of information, you need Outlook.

Appendix

What's on the CD-ROM

The *Microsoft Office 2000 Secrets* includes a CD-ROM created exclusively for this book. The CD pulls together a variety of great programs and utilities for Office users, along with a smattering of other interesting software. Included are add-in tools and practical applications designed specifically for Word, Excel, and Access, along with file management and system utilities that are useful with Office in general. All these items have been selected on the basis of their quality, applicability to Office tasks, and originality. Refer to the page at the end of the book for installation instructions.

Software Included on the CD-ROM

This section lists many of the individual software titles included on the *Microsoft Office 2000 Secrets* CD-ROM, each in its appropriate category. The titles are shareware or trial version products unless otherwise noted. Additional programs may have been added to the CD-ROM after the book went to press. Check the ReadMe.txt file in the root directory.

Word enhancement

Office Toys. A compact toolbar and two menus provide a slew of useful shortcuts and add-on features for Word, which make full use of the programmable Office Assistant technology available in Office 2000.

Excel enhancements

Power Utility Pak. This top-notch Excel cornucopia contains 30 utilities, 40 custom functions, and a variety of enhanced shortcut menus.

SmartChecker. Reads the contents of your Excel worksheet back to you using your sound card for proofreading purposes.

Access enhancements

Cary Prague Freeware and Demos. These items are published by Cary Prague Books and Software — Cary is the author of the *Microsoft Access 2000 Bible* (IDG Books Worldwide) and other Access books. Check Writer is a complete freeware application that lets you write and print your checks.

Other products include Cool Combos and the demo versions of the Yes! I Can Run My Business and the EZ Access Developers Suite.

Internet tools

GrabNet. Lets you store and organize information culled from Web pages.

InfoCourier and WebCourier. Convert HTML files into stand-alone hypertext documents for distribution.

WebWhacker and Grab-a-Site. Offline Web browsers, these programs save entire Web sites to your hard disk so that you can later view them at high speed. Grab-a-Site includes more extensive Web site management tools.

System utilities

ClipMate. Dramatically enhances the Windows clipboard — a necessity for anyone doing serious editing with Office or any Windows program.

DeskNotes. This is a truly great "sticky notes" program for Windows.

Keyboard Express. This elegant keyboard macro program lets you insert words, phrases, and longer passages into your documents with a minimum of typing.

Macro Express and Macro Magic. Two strong macro utilities for automating tasks in Windows and in applications that don't have VBA, these programs record mouse actions as well as keystrokes.

Multi-App. Lets you associate multiple applications with any file type, so that you can use any of these applications to open a file by right-clicking it in My Computer or Explorer.

PowerDesk. This is a supercharged replacement for Windows Explorer, and then some.

Recent Documents 97. Organize and manage your Documents folder so that the documents you use regularly are always at hand.

Second Copy. Automates backup of your disks and synchronizes desktop and notebook versions of your document files — you may find this program easier to use than the Windows Briefcase.

ShortKeys. Otherwise similar to Office's AutoCorrect, this utility is available in all Windows programs.

SmartSum. This robust onscreen calculator prints and talks (through your sound card).

SmartWheel. Adds functionality to the Microsoft IntelliMouse and compatibles in applications that don't directly support their special features.

Text Find. Searches for text in multiple files simultaneously. Text Find is easier to use and has more features than the Office file-finding tools.

ZipMagic and FreeSpace. Both products compress data so that it takes much less space on your disk, but in such a way that the information remains immediately available — no "unzip" step required. ZipFolders turns standard Zip files into folders that you can use just as you do ordinary folders, while FreeSpace lets you select specific files for compression and does other tricks to increase disk space.

ZTree for Windows. For those who cut their computer teeth in character mode, ZTW pays magnificent 32-bit homage to the classic file manager of the DOS era, XTree. Enjoy long filename support and other enhancements. Do try out this program!

Printing utility

ClickBook. Conveniently print documents as booklets or in condensed formats that fit multiple pages on a single sheet of paper.

File compression utilities

WinZip. If you prefer to work with ZIP archives directly, this is a must-have utility.

ZipFolders. Lets you work with ZIP archives as if they were ordinary folders, copying files in and out of them using standard Windows and DOS functions.

Zip-n-Go. This is another complete ZIP file manager.

Graphics editors

IconForge. This is a full-featured editor for creating and modifying icons. An accompanying freeware product, ActivIcons, lets you change your Windows system icons easily.

Paint Shop Pro. This comprehensive bitmap graphics software package enables you to create and edit bitmap art with a gallery of special effects at your fingertips. It opens and converts between all major formats. As a bonus, it includes great screen capture functions that surpass those of many specialized screen capture programs.

Smart 'n Sticky. This is label design and printing software.

Help tools

EasyHelp/Web. Use Word to build custom Help files for Office or your own Office applications in the WinHelp format, and generate HTML files at the same time.

EasyHTML Help. Use Word to build custom HTML Help files.

Font managers

Font Namer. This freeware application lets you rename your fonts so that the names appear as you want them to in your Windows applications.

MyFonts. Use this terrific font management system for TrueType and Type 1 fonts to organize your fonts into related groups, activate and deactivate them, and view and print samples in many different formats.

Software development tools

ProtoView and Sheridan Software toolkit demos. This includes demo versions of many great ActiveX controls for use in your VBA projects.

Business solutions

Debt Analyzer 97. Helps you to keep track of loans, bills, and mortgages, and figures out the best way to pay off what you owe to keep money in your own pocket instead of burning it as interest.

Zip Code Explorer and Zip Express. These two utilities are for looking up U.S. Zip Codes and associated information.

Microsoft Office 2000 Secrets macros and templates

Included on the *Microsoft Office 2000 Secrets* CD-ROM is a Word template (Office 2000 Secrets.dot) containing the macros that appear in the book. If you don't want to type in the macros yourself, use the Organizer in Word to copy them from the Secrets template to your own templates or documents. To work with the Organizer, choose the Organizer button on the Tools ⇨ Templates and Add-Ins dialog box (see Chapter 26).

Other template files include:

- **Slides.dot.** This is a template for making 35mm slides.
- **Secrets.xlt.** This contains Excel macros mentioned in the book.

Electronic Version of *Microsoft Office 2000 Secrets*

This Adobe Acrobat PDF version of the complete *Microsoft Office 2000 Secrets* book enables you to use Word to search for topics in the book while you work. Now you can run Word and find answers to your questions at the same time. Start the Adobe Reader and open the .PDF file, or double-click the .PDF file to launch the Adobe Reader and open the electronic version of the book. For information about other Office 2000 titles that IDG Books Worldwide offers, visit the company's Web site at www.idgbooks.com.

IDG Books Worldwide: HTML version of the Internet Directory from *Internet Bible*

This file doesn't have anything to do with Office per se, but it's really cool. It provides almost 1,000 Web site links, organized in about 140 categories. You can use it as an Internet directory to research topics that you want to know more about. For information about other Office 2000 titles that IDG Books Worldwide offers, visit www.idgbooks.com.

MindSpring: Internet Services

MindSpring is an Internet service provider. If you don't have an Internet account, run this software to walk through a very easy process of getting one. Keep in mind that you will pay a monthly service fee for MindSpring service, just as you would for any other Internet service. MindSpring's Web site is www.mindspring.net.

Netscape Communicator v. 4.5

Netscape's Web browser is still the most popular browser today. Netscape Navigator is the browser component of Communicator 4.5, which supports several HTML-related features that have been added to the new Word HTML format, such as cascading style sheets. A number of plug-ins for Netscape Navigator to update Netscape Communicator are available at home.netscape.com/smartupdate/.

About Shareware, Freeware, and Trial Version Software

Few programmers are willing to give away the fruits of their labor. Although a couple of freeware titles are included on the CD-ROM, most of the programs fall in the try-before-you-buy shareware category.

As you're probably well aware, shareware is a proven distribution method for software developers with limited resources. The idea is simple: You try out the software for a limited period. Then, if you decide to continue using it, you're duty-bound to pay a registration fee to the developer. When you register, you get additional benefits such as technical support, a printed manual, and automatic upgrades, depending on the product. If you play by the rules, this is a great system for both parties. You get a chance to see whether the software fits your needs before you pay for it, and the developer can place the software before a large potential market without having to pay for advertising and packaging.

Some developers don't like the shareware term, because it implies that they are sharing their software with you when they want you to buy it (or, to be technically correct, to license it). For this reason, you may see terms such as "trial software" in the documentation for some of the programs included on the *Microsoft Office 2000 Secrets* CD-ROM. Aside from the terminology change, however, the arrangement is the same as for shareware.

Freeware refers to programs provided at no charge. However, sometimes there are strings attached. For example, you may be granted unlimited personal use of a freeware product, but commercial use may require a fee. Consult the documentation with each program.

All the software included on the CD-ROM is copyrighted, including freeware, shareware, and trial version software. This means that you can't sell it, and you can't take it apart and use it as the basis for other projects.

Technical Support

If by some chance you wind up with a defective CD-ROM, return it to IDG Books Worldwide for a replacement. For questions about a specific piece of software, however, you should consult the publisher of that program. Contact information for each program is usually listed in a Readme or other text file, or in the program's Help file.

Index

Numbers and Symbols

3-D effects for graphic objects, 152–154
3-D perspective in Excel charts, 943–944
3-D references in Excel formulas, 912–914
* (asterisks) as wildcards, 240
= (equals sign) in formula fields, 742, 816–818, 907
? (question marks) as wildcards, 240

A

absolute cell references in Excel, 861–862, 911
Access, 993–1013
Access VBA code, 1093
  add-ins, 1000
  custom VBA applications in, 595
  customizing
    interface, 997
    keyboard shortcuts, 999–1000
    overview of, 994
    startup options, 994–997
  in developing database applications, 1046
  DoCmd object in, 1057–1058
  document security in, 266–267
  document templates in, 261
  Format menu, 1080
  hyperlinks in
    formatting, 285
    placing on controls, 287
    storing in table fields, 286
  importing Web pages into, 91
  macros in
    assigning actions to, 997–998
    creating macro groups, 998–999
    customizing keyboard shortcuts with, 999–1000
    overview of, 997
    versus VBA macros, 1043–1044
  optimizing performance
    by compacting databases, 1012–1013
    of Jet in Windows Registry, 1009–1011
  on networks, 1012
  overview of, 1007
  with Performance Analyzer, 1008
  overview of, 993, 1013
  pasting data into and out of, 186
  pasting Word text into, 185
  printing in, 213–214
  startup
    with command line switches, 994–996
    controlling database behavior at, 996–997
    running VBA procedures at, 996
  toolbars, 67
  uses for, 993–994
  views
    Datasheet view, 1025, 1030–1032
    Design view, 1025, 1026–1029, 1037–1039
    Form view, 1025
    for forms, 1025, 1082–1083
    Layout view, 1026
    overview of, 1024–1025
    Print Preview view, 1026
    SQL view, 1026
    switching between, 1025
  Visual Basic Editor in, 384–385
  writing VBA code in, 1054
Access custom applications, 1041–1056
  See also custom Office applications
  Access database wizards for, 1047
  Access macros versus VBA macros in, 1043–1044
  customizing command bars and menus, 1048–1051
  distributing, 1054–1055
  overview of, 1041–1042, 1056
  planning, 1042
  saving, 1056
  setting startup options, 1051–1052
  setting up switchboards, 1042, 1048
  tools for developing, 1045–1046
Access databases, 1015–1040
  compacting after edits, 1012–1013
  data access pages, 310–318, 1017, 1022
  Database window for, 1022–1024
  defined, 1003
  engines for
    choosing, 1000, 1001
    in creating database projects, 1003–1004
    Jet.Standard Access engine, 1001–1002
    Microsoft Data Engine, 1001–10003
    overview of, 1045
    SQL Server and, 1001, 1002
  fields
    creating, 1026–1027
    data types for, 1021
    defined, 1015
    defining, 1020–1021
    formatting, 1027–1028
    freezing, 1031
    hiding, 1031
    input masks, 1028
    inserting, 1031
    modifying, 1029
    moving, 1031
    planning, 1018–1019
    primary key fields, 1029
    properties of, 1027
    resizing, 1031
    validation rules, 1028–1029
  filtering data, 1035
  finding and replacing data, 1034–1035
  keyboard shortcuts for navigating, 1024
  macros and, 1017, 1043–1044
  overview of, 1015–1017
  planning
    data access pages, 1022
    data types, 1021
    field definitions, 1020
    forms, 1022
    overview of, 1018
    queries, 1021
    reports, 1022
    table and field design, 1018–1019
    table relationships, 1019–1020
  publishing as interactive Web pages, 310–318

(continued)

Access databases (continued)
  queries of
    action queries, 1053
    defined, 1016
    designing, 1037–1038
    overview of, 1035
    SQL and, 1071
    types of, 1035–1036
  renaming items in, 1006–1007
  replicating, 1055
  reports
    versus Access forms, 1079
    adding fields and items to, 1039
    creating report snapshots, 311
    defined, 1017
    distributing, 1038
    grouping items in, 1040
    lightweight reports, 1052
    planning, 1022
    sections in, 1038–1039
  sorting data, 1035
  splitting for network use, 1054–1055
  startup options, 996–997
  tables
    creating, 1025–1026
    defined, 1015
    displaying, 1030
    editing data in, 1030–1031
    formatting, 1032
    modifying fields in, 1031–1032
    planning design of, 1018–1019
    relating with SQL statements, 1073
    relationships between, 1019–1020, 1032–1034
    selecting data in, 1030–1031
  terminology, 1015–1017
  upsizing from Jet to SQL Server, 1005–1006
  VBA modules and, 1017
  views, 1024–1025
  zooming entries for editing, 1006
Access forms, 1079–1096
  See also forms; VBA
  adding fields, 1089
  adding sections and elements, 1084
  AutoFormatting, 1087–1088
  binding to data, 1088–1089
  bound forms, 1080
  compatibility software for, 1046
  controls
    adding, 1089–1090
    assigning hyperlinks to, 1091
    assigning macros to, 1091–1092
    converting type of, 1090
    default properties, 1090
    formatting, 1090
    referring to in Access VBA, 1093

  defined, 1079–1080
  deleting sections and elements, 1084
  designing, 1082–1083
  lightweight forms, 1052
  navigation buttons, 1084
  overview of, 1016–1017, 1040, 1079, 1096
  planning, 1022
  properties, 1085
  record selectors, 1084
  referring to in Access VBA, 1093
  versus reports, 1079
  sections in, 1083–1085
  selecting forms and sections, 1084–1085
  sizing, 1085–1087
  subforms
    converting forms into, 1095
    creating, 1095
    defined, 1094
    linking to forms, 1094–1095
    overview of, 1093–1094
    in VBA code, 1096
  versus VBA forms, 1080–1081
  views for, 1082–1083
  Visual Basic and, 1081–1082
  writing VBA event code for, 1092
action buttons, 139, 1114–1115
active documents
  See also controls; documents; forms
  ActiveX controls in, 175–178
  AutoShape controls in, 173, 174–175
  defined, 171
  in Excel, 173, 174
  specifying in Word VBA, 834
  types of controls in, 172–173
  uses for, 171–172, 178
  in Word, 173–174
ActiveX controls
  See also ADO; controls
  adding to forms, 577
  adding to Toolbox, 576–577
  automating, 389
  COM and, 389
  defined, 173, 387
  design mode and, 177
  inserting, 176–177
  in interactive Web pages, 321–322
  invisible controls, 577
  overview of, 175, 387–389, 575
  property options, 177
  registering, 576
  types of, 175–176
  with and without VBA code, 178
Add method, 491–492, 495
Add or Edit Discussion Servers dialog box, 369

Add or Remove Buttons command, 69–70
Add Toolbar dialog box, 24–25
Add View dialog box, 860
Add Watch dialog box, 518–519
Add Web Folder dialog box, 362
Add/Modify FTP Locations dialog box, 364
add-ins
  for Access, 1000
  COM add-ins, 385, 585
  for custom Office applications, 585–586
  for Excel data analysis, 959–963
  for PowerPoint presentations, 1116
Add-Ins dialog box in Excel, 960
Additional Controls dialog box, 576
addresses, Internet, 88
addressing Outlook e-mail messages, 1179–1181
ADO (ActiveX Data Objects) model, 1060–1071
  See also VBA database programming
  Command objects, 1069–1071
  connecting to data sources, 1061–1062
  creating references to, 1060–1061
  defined, 383–384, 1059
  error handling, 1060
  Recordset objects, 1062–1069
    adding records, 1067–1068
    changing field data, 1068–1069
    checking for records, 1067
    creating, 1063–1064
    cursor options, 1064–1066
    deleting records, 1067–1068
    locating records, 1067
    lock options, 1066
    loop operations on, 1069
    overview of, 1062
    reading field data, 1068
    setting options for, 1064–1066
Adobe Type Manager (ATM) software, 120, 122
Advanced Find dialog box in Outlook, 1160–1161
Advanced Layout dialog box, 169, 719
alias names for Word styles, 695
aligning
  graphic objects, 154–155, 1106
  text boxes into columns, 713
  text in table cells, 740
  VBA controls, 545
Alignment tab of Format Cells dialog box in Excel, 894–895
Allow Fast Saves option, 624
Analysis ToolPak add-in, 961
anchoring
  graphic objects, 717–718

Index **1215**

scripts, 320–321
animation in PowerPoint presentations, 1111, 1128–1129
Application objects, 387, 489, 833–834
Archive dialog box in Outlook, 1162
arguments
   See also VBA code
   advantages of, 426
   date arguments, 924
   defined, 426
   overview of, 412–413
   in Sub procedures, 424
   versus variables, 426
Arial Unicode MS font, 16
arithmetic operators, 444–445, 908
arrays
   See also VBA code
   array dimensions, 454
   versus Collection objects, 494
   declaring, 454–455
   defined, 453
   dynamic arrays, 455
   fixed arrays, 455
   `For...Next` loops and, 471–474
   indexes for, 455–456
   overview of, 453–454
art. *See* graphics
Ask fields, 818
ASP (Active Server Pages) data format, 312–313
assignment statements, 428–429, 440, 441
asterisks (*) as wildcards, 240
ATM (Adobe Type Manager) software, 120, 122
auditing Excel data validation errors, 970–971
Auditing toolbar in Excel, 967–969
Auto Data Tips window, 511–512
Auto Fit into Title Bar Area option, 21
Auto Hide option, 21
AutoComplete feature in Excel, 881
AutoCorrect feature, 112–120
   See also text
   adding special characters to, 118–119
   adding words to, 117
   in creating captions, 771
   default symbol substitutions, 114–115
   defined, 646
   em and en dashes in, 119–120
   in Excel, 888
   expanding abbreviations with, 114
   lists, 112, 113, 116–117
   overview of, 112–113
   settings, 112, 113

   sharing between Office apps, 114
   turning off automatic exceptions, 116
   turning off and on, 117–118
   undoing changes made by, 115
AutoFill feature in Excel
   clearing entries with, 885
   creating custom AutoFill lists, 884–885
   deleting cells with, 885
   formatting with, 899
   inserting cells with, 885
   overview of, 882–883
   shortcut menu, 883–884
AutoFilter feature in Excel, 947–948
AutoFormat feature
   in Access, 1087–1088
   in Excel, 896
   in Word, 646
AutoLayouts in PowerPoint, 1101–1102, 1120–1121
automatic calculations in selected Excel cells, 879
Automatic color option, 84
automatic error checking in Code windows, 408
Automatic Update options for Word styles, 694, 697
AutoNum fields. *See* ListNum fields
AutoPreview feature in Outlook, 1174
AutoRecover feature in Word, 238
AutoShapes
   See also graphic objects
   action buttons, 139, 1114–1115
   adding text to, 143
   assigning actions to, 173, 174–175
   changing to other, 142
   connectors, 139
   formatting text in, 144
   inserting in documents, 138
   More AutoShapes command, 138
   overview of, 136
   reshaping, 141
   as VBA controls, 173, 174–175
AutoSummarize command in Word, 248, 746
AutoText feature, 647-653
   See also editing in Word
   in creating captions, 771
   creating one-shot entries, 650
   editing entries, 651
   including formatting in, 647
   inserting AutoTextList fields, 650–652
   menus, 648–650
   organizing entries, 649–650
   overview of, 647
   Spike clipboard tool, 652–653
   updating documents with, 651–652
AutoText fields, 819
AutoTextList fields, 819

B

Back button on Web toolbar, 92, 93
background color in windows, 83–84
Background dialog box in PowerPoint, 1125
banners in Web pages, 341
Barcode fields, 819
batch files in Internet Explorer, 97
Binder, 249-258
   See also document management
   adding sections to binders, 252
   binder sections, 252–254
   creating binder headers and footers, 255–257
   creating binders, 251
   document security in, 266
   document templates in, 261
   File menu, 252–253
   Go Menu, 253
   overview of, 249–251
   printing binders, 255–257
   printing in, 214
   running, 251
   saving binders, 255
   Section menu, 253
   setting options for, 257–258
   templates for, 261
Bookmark fields. *See* Ref fields
bookmarks
   See also navigation
   in AutoText or AutoCorrect entries, 633
   creating, 631
   creating hyperlinks as, 634–635
   in Excel, 284
   in [=] (formula) fields, 818
   going to, 631
   hidden bookmarks, 633–634
   instant bookmarks, 632–633
   in navigation, 631, 632
   for page section breaks, 752–753
   for PowerPoint text, 1109
   predefined bookmarks for macros, 634
   for repeating text in lists, 766
   in VBA code, 409–410
   viewing, 631–632
Bookshelf reference tool, 112
Boolean data type, 449, 450
Borders and Shading dialog box, 680, 685
borders in Word, 680–682, 684, *See also* frames; shared borders
break mode. *See* debugging VBA code
Briefcase utility, 262–263

Index

browsers. *See* Web browsers
bulleted lists. *See* numbering, Word
Bullets and Numbering dialog box in Word, 757
Bullets toolbar button, 758, 761
business cards, 723–725
Button Editor, 72–73
buttons
   See also icons; toolbar buttons
   action buttons, 139, 1114–1115
   ActiveX control buttons, 175–176
   adding to message boxes, 529–531
   Close button, 41
   Design Mode button, 177
   in Internet Explorer, 92
   in Office Assistant balloons, 591–592
   in Outline view, 744
   on Outlook bar, 1148
   in PowerPoint window, 1103–1104
   radio buttons, 554–556
   split buttons, 41
   toggle buttons, 556, 557

C

calculations
   See also Excel formulas
   automatic, in selected Excel cells, 879
   in `Calculate` events, 989
   with Calculator tool in Word, 605
   creating calculated fields, 1074–1075
   in pivot tables, display options for, 956
   using Excel formula bars for, 976
   of Word page numbers, 753
Calendar folder. *See* Outlook
Calendar Options dialog box, 1200–1201
callouts, 143–144
Cancel buttons, 551–552, 570–571
Caption dialog box, 770
`Case` clause tests, 465–466
`Case Else` clauses, 465
case in Excel formulas, 975
`Cells` property in Excel, 980
`Change` events in Excel, 988–989
`Change` events of VBA forms, 565, 569, 572
Change Case command in Word, 659–660
character formatting. *See* formatting in Word
Character Spacing tab of Font dialog box, 667–668
Chart Wizard, 933–934
charts. *See* Excel charts
Chat windows in NetMeeting, 373

check box controls, 591–592
Circular Reference toolbar, 971–972
`Click` events of mice, 565, 567–568, 570–571
class modules
   See also modules; VBA objects
   classes defined, 479, 497
   components, 497–498
   creating, 497
   custom objects in, 500
   declaring class variables, 498
   defined, 419, 422
   as objects, 497
   writing methods, 499–500
   writing property procedures, 498–499
clearing
   See also deleting; removing
   breakpoints in debugging VBA, 506
   versus deleting, 738
   Excel entries, 885
   paragraph tabs, 677
"click and type" feature in Word, 679–680
ClickBook printing utility, 216–218, 723
Clip Gallery
   See also graphic objects
   importing images into, 162
   inserting pictures from, 158, 160, 165
   organizing clips in, 161
   overview of, 138
Clip Properties dialog box, 161
clipboard
   See also sharing information
   Clipboard toolbar, 180–182
   copying and pasting hyperlinks via, 282
   enhancing with ClipMate utility, 182
   overview of, 180
   Paste as Hyperlink command, 184
   Paste Special command, 183–184
   pasting data into and out of Access, 186
   pasting Excel or Access tables into Word, 185
   pasting Word text into Access data, 185
   when to use, 180
Close button, 41, 570–571
Code windows. *See* Visual Basic Editor
collaborating on documents
   See also documents, long; sharing documents on networks
   in Excel, 368, 963–966
   long documents, 787–795

   accepting changes, 791–791
   comments in, 787–789
   comparing document copies, 790
   hiding and displaying changes, 791
   marking changes, 790–791
   merging changes, 792
   overview of, 368
   rejecting changes, 791–791
   reviewing documents, 787, 789–792, 794
   saving versions of documents, 793–794
   tracking changes while editing, 789
   on networks
      with Discussions feature, 368–370
      in online meetings, 373–374
      subscribing to change notices, 370
      tools for, 368
   in PowerPoint, 368, 1135
Collapse Dialog button, 875
Collection objects
   accessing objects in, 493–494
   adding objects to, 495
   versus arrays, 494
   changing values in, 494
   counting objects in, 496
   creating, 494–495
   defined, 493
   `For Each...Next` loops and, 496–497
   removing objects from, 495
color options
   for Excel charts, 940
   for graphics and line art, 150–152, 157
   for HTML Help system, 54
   for PowerPoint presentations, 1122–1123
   for ScreenTips, 84
   transparent color, 164
   for window backgrounds, 83–84
Color Scheme dialog box in PowerPoint, 1122
colored Excel parentheses, 974–975
columnar layouts. *See* page layout in Word
COM (Component Object Model)
   ActiveX automation and, 389
   add-ins, 385, 585
   building custom applications with, 579–581, 585
   extending VBA object model with, 480–481
combo box controls, 557–558
command button controls, 551–552

Index **1217**

command line switches
  See also switches
  in Access, 994–996
  in Excel, 855–856
  in Outlook, 1140–1141
  overview of, 7–8
  in Word, 599–600
Command objects in ADO, 1069–1071
commands
  adding to Drawing toolbar, 156–157
  adding to toolbar buttons, 70–71
  built-in, for VBA code, 456–458
  creating keyboard shortcuts for, 82–83
  customizing with macros, 61–65
  customizing in Word, 612–613
  in Outline view, 744–745
Commands tab of Customize dialog box, 70–71
comments
  adding to VBA code, 432–434
  attaching to Excel cells, 901
  deleting, 902
  editing, 788–789, 902
  finding, 902
  identifying author of, 789
  inserting, 787–788
  jumping to, 788
  overview of, 900
  printing, 789
  viewing, 901
compacting
  Access databases, 1012–1013
  Outlook folders, 1162
Compare fields, 820
comparison operators, 445–448, 909
compiler options statements, 429
Complete Word feature, 412
concatenation operators, 444, 445, 448
condition expressions, 460–461
conditional statements, 458, 461–466. *See also* VBA code
Confirm Data Source dialog box, 191
constants
  See also VBA code
  benefits of, 443
  declaring, 442–443
  defined, 442
  for Message and Input boxes, 529–530
  named constants in Excel formulas, 923
  representing attributes with, 443–444
  for Selection objects, 840
Contacts folder. *See* Outlook
container objects, 387, 485

Contents and Index command, 56–57
control structures. *See* VBA code
Control Toolbox. *See* Toolbox
controls, Access form
  See also Access forms
  adding, 1089–1090
  assigning hyperlinks to, 1091
  assigning macros to, 1091–1092
  converting type of, 1090
  default properties, 1090
  formatting, 1090
  placing hyperlinks on, 287
  referring to in Access VBA, 1093
controls, VBA form, 541–60
  See also ActiveX controls; forms, VBA
  accessing overlapping controls, 543
  adding from Toolbox, 533–535
  aligning, 545
  arranging buttons, 545
  assigning accelerator keys to, 547
  AutoShapes as, 173, 174–175
  Cancel buttons, 551–552
  centering, 545
  combo boxes, 557–558
  command buttons, 551–552
  defined, 171
  designating dominant controls, 543–544
  distributing evenly, 546
  editing, 539–540
  formatting, 541–546
  frame controls, 552–553
  grouping, 542–543
  grouping option buttons, 555
  label controls, 547–548
  list boxes, 557–558
  multipage controls, 553–554
  multiple sets of in one form, 575
  in Office Assistant balloons, 591–592
  option buttons, 554–556
  overview of, 546
  scroll bars, 559–560
  selecting, 544
  setting tab order for, 546–547
  sizing, 545, 546
  spacing, 545
  spin buttons, 559–560
  text boxes, 549–551
  toggle buttons, 556, 557
  types of, 172–173
controls, Web Component, 305–306
converters, file, 188, 189–190, 194–195
converting
  embedded objects into linked objects, 201
  fields into plain text, 804

  tables into text, 741
  text boxes into Word frames, 714
  text into Word tables, 740–741
  type of Access controls, 1090
  between VBA data types, 448
copying
  binder sections, 254
  custom Outlook forms, 1166
  Excel data, 880, 889–890, 897–898, 899
  footnotes and endnotes, 776
  graphic objects, 140
  images to toolbar buttons, 73
  Outlook information, 1152
  toolbar buttons, 68
copying and pasting
  See also clipboard; cutting and pasting
  browsed VBA code, 406
  files in Open and Save As dialog boxes, 236
  hyperlinks via clipboards, 282
  paragraph marks, 671
  text in Word VBA, 845–846
counter variables, 472
crash handling, 237–238
Create Hyperlink dialog box in FrontPage, 337–338
Create Name dialog box in Excel, 871
cross-references in Word documents, 772–774, 778, 786
cross-tab tables. *See* pivot tables
Currency data type, 436, 449, 450
currency symbols, 894
cursor options for ADO Recordset objects, 1064–1066
Curve tool, 146
Curved Segment option for freeform shapes, 149
Custom Animation dialog box, 1111
custom dialog boxes. *See* forms
Custom Header dialog box, 256
Custom Installation Wizard, 7
Custom Lists tab of Options dialog box in Excel, 884–885
custom Office applications
  579–596, *See also* Access custom applications
  in Access, 595
  building with Component Object Model, 579–581, 586
  creating add-ins for, 585–586
  custom document properties as variables, 586–587
  distributing, 595
  locking code, 593–594
  Office 2000 Developer tools for, 594–595
  overview of, 579–581, 596

(continued)

custom Office applications
(continued)
  programming Office Assistant, 587–592
  securing code with digital certificates, 592–593
  steps in creating
    adding references to external objects, 583
    creating external objects, 584
    declaring variables for external objects, 583
    defining problem, 581–582
    overview of, 582–583
    using external objects in code, 584–585
Custom tab of Properties dialog box, 248–249
Customize dialog box, 70–74
Customize Keyboard dialog box, 606–607
Customize Outline Numbered List dialog box, 754
customizing, FrontPage themes, 338
customizing Access
  See also Access custom applications
  interface, 997
  keyboard shortcuts, 999–1000
  overview of, 994
  startup options, 994–997
customizing Office, 61–84
  See also Microsoft Office 2000
  commands with macros, 61–65
  HTML Help system, 57–59, 587–592
  installation in organizations, 7
  keyboards, 82–83
  menus
    adding graphic images to, 79, 80
    creating, 79
    display options, 77–78
    menu items, 78–79
    moving with mouse, 78
    overview of, 76–77
    renaming, 80
    restoring original menus, 82
    saving and reusing custom menus, 82
    shortcut menus, 80–81
  Office Assistant, 587–592
  overview of, 61, 84
  ScreenTip color, 84
  Shortcut bar toolbars, 25–27
  toolbar buttons
    adding, 25, 69–71
    adding space between, 26, 68–69
    assigning hyperlinks to, 75–76
    changing width of, 69, 75
    copying, 68
    copying images to, 73
    customizing, 71–74
    deleting, 27, 69
    displaying hidden buttons, 25–26
    displaying ScreenTips for, 74–75
    displaying text and images on, 72
    editing images on, 72–73
    hiding, 25–26
    importing images for, 73
    for inserting graphics, 75–76
    moving, 26, 68
    naming, 74–75
    removing space between, 68–69
    renaming, 26
    saving and reusing custom buttons, 82
  toolbars
    in Access, 67
    creating, 24–25, 67
    customizing, 66–67
    deleting, 26
    displaying, 66
    in Excel, 67
    hiding, 66
    overview of, 65
    placing, 66
    renaming, 26
    reordering, 25
    restoring deleted toolbars, 26–27
    restoring original toolbars, 65
    saving and reusing custom toolbars, 82
    solving space problems of, 67–68
  window background color, 83–84
customizing Outlook
  e-mail settings, 1188–1189
  forms, 1163–1167
  Outlook bar, 1147–1149
  overview of, 1142–1143
  views, 1154–1159
customizing Word, 599–619
  activating Calculator tool, 605
  commands, 612–613
  Full Screen view, 601–602
  Headers and Footers toolbar, 707
  keyboard shortcuts
    accessing, 612
    changing, 606–607
    choosing keys for, 607–608
    creating, 606–607
    for keyboard characters, 611–612
  overview of, 606
  printing, 612
  showing in ScreenTips, 612
  two-step shortcuts, 608
  using off-limits keys in, 608–611
  with Options dialog box, 600–601
  overview of, 599, 619
  screen view options, 601–602, 603–605
  shortcut menus, 606
  startup options, 599–600
  templates
    attached templates, 615, 616–617
    creating, 615
    global templates, 615–616, 617
    hierarchy of, 615
    modifying, 615, 617–618
    Normal templates, 615
    overview of, 614
    saving, 618–619
    storing customizations in, 605
  toolbars and menus, 606
cutting and pasting
  See also clipboard; copying and pasting
  files in Open and Save As dialog boxes, 236
  paragraph marks, 671
  text in Word VBA, 845–846
cutting text, keyboard shortcuts for, 657–658

D

DAO (Data Access Objects) model, 1059
data access pages, 314–318, 1017, 1022
data analysis. See Excel data analysis
Data Link Properties dialog box in Access, 1004
data source drivers, 191
data tables in Excel, dynamic, 924–927
data types in Access databases, 1021
data types for variables
  See also variables; VBA code
  Boolean data type, 449, 450
  converting between, 448
  Currency data type, 436, 449, 450
  Date data type, 451–452
  Decimal data type, 436, 449
  default values of, 441–442
  defined, 435–436
  Double data type, 436, 449
  listed, 436–437

Index

numeric data types, 449–450
properties as, 484
pros and cons of using, 437
Single data type, 436, 449
Variant data type, 448–449
Data Validation dialog box in Excel, 887
data validation in Excel, 970–971
database objects, importing, 191–192
Database toolbar, 200
Database window in Access, 1022–1024
databases. *See* Access databases; VBA database programming
Datasheet Formatting dialog box, 1032
Datasheet tab of Options dialog box, 8–9
Datasheet view in Access, 1025, 1030–1032
date arguments in Excel formulas, 924
Date data type, 451–452
Date fields, 820
dates and times in Excel, static, 882
Date-Time Picture switch, 807–808
DDE and DDEAuto fields, 820–821
DDE (Dynamic Data Exchange), 191
debugging Excel worksheets, 967–976
  auditing data validation errors, 970–971
  with Auditing toolbar, 967–969
  case in formulas and, 975
  cell error messages in, 970
  colored parentheses and, 974–975
  finding logic errors, 972–973
  with Formula AutoCorrect, 973–974
  identifying circular references, 971–972
  keyboard shortcuts for, 969
  overview of, 976
  removing tracer arrows, 969
  tracing cell errors, 970
  tracing cell precedents and dependents, 967–969
  by using formula bar as calculator, 976
debugging VBA code, 501–525
  in Auto Data Tips window, 511–512
  in break mode
    adding code, 509
    choosing next statements, 510–511
    clearing breakpoints, 506
    defined, 503–504
    editing code, 509
    entering, 504

getting out of, 508
locating next statements, 506–507
setting breakpoints, 505–506, 519–520
skipping faulty code, 510–511
Step commands and, 508–509
`Stop` statements, 507–508
error types, 501–502
  in Immediate window, 512–514
  in Locals window, 514–516, 517
  logic errors, 501, 502
  overview of, 501, 525
  in Quick Info window, 512
  run-time errors, 501, 502, 521
  with Step commands, 508–509
  syntax errors, 501–502
  by testing procedures, 502–503
  in Visual Basic Editor, 415
in Watch window
  adding watch expressions, 517–519
  defining breakpoints, 519–520
  editing watch expressions, 519
  versus Locals window, 517
  overview of, 516–517
  writing error-handling code
    `Exit` statements, 522
    labels in, 523
    `On Error` statements, 522
    overview of, 520–521, 523–524
    `Resume` statements, 524–525
    run-time errors and, 521
Decimal data type, 436, 449
declaration statements, 428, 434–440
Declarations section in VBA modules, 419, 421–422
declaring
  See also variables
  arrays, 454–455
  class variables, 498
  constants, 442–443
  object variables, 489–491
  variables, 434–440, 498
Define Custom Show dialog box, 1130
Define Name dialog box, 284, 870
Define Views dialog box, 1154–1155
deleting
  See also clearing; removing
  versus clearing, 738
  comments, 902
  database data in bulk, 1077–1078
  database records, 1067–1068
  elements from Access forms, 1084
  Excel cells, 885
  files, 236
  footnotes and endnotes, 776
  frames, 295
  hyperlinks, 281

items from Outlook views, 1152
in Outlook permanently, 1161
Outlook user profiles, 1172
paragraph marks in Word files, 671
restoring deleted toolbars, 26–27
retrieving deleted Outlook items, 1161
tabs from Word files, 677
text in Word VBA, 845
toolbar buttons, 27, 69
toolbars, 26
dependent cells in Excel formulas, 967–969
Design Mode button, 177
Design view in Access, 1025, 1026–1029, 1037–1039
desktop
  See also screen options; user interface
  accessing from Shortcut bar, 28
desktop publishing. *See* page layout in Word; publishing Web pages
DHTML effects in Web pages, 342–345
dialog boxes, collapsing, 875–876
dictionaries. *See* spell-checking
digital cameras, 162
digital certificates, 592–593
digital watermarks, 707
`Dim` declaration statements, 434, 438
Discussions feature, 368–370
displaying
  See also viewing
  Access database tables, 1030
  changes in long documents, 791
  docked toolbar buttons, 38–39
  error bars in Excel charts, 942
  hidden toolbar buttons, 25–26
  menus, 77–78
  OLE objects as icons, 201
  Outlook forms, 1164
  paragraph marks in Word files, 670–671
  ScreenTips for toolbar buttons, 74–75
  style assignments, 687
  text and images on toolbar buttons, 72
  toolbars, 36–37, 66
  worksheet figures in Excel charts, 939
`Do...Loop` statements, 467–471
docked toolbars
  See also toolbars
  accessing hidden buttons on, 38–39
  changing from floating to, 40

(continued)

docked toolbars *(continued)*
   docking Shortcut bar, 20, 21
   moving, 38
   overview of, 37
docking Visual Basic Editor
     windows, 398–399
DoCmd object in Access, 1057–1058
document management, 223–270
   with Binder, 249–258
      adding sections to binders, 252
      creating binder headers and
         footers, 255–257
      creating binders, 251
      File menu, 252–253
      Go Menu, 253
      overview of, 249–251
      printing binders, 255–257
      running, 251
      saving binders, 255
      Section menu, 253
      setting options for, 257–258
      templates for, 261
      working with binder sections,
         252–254
   crash protection options, 237–238
   document security
      in Access, 266–267
      in Binder, 266
      in Excel, 265–266
      file-opening restrictions,
         232–233
      locking fields, 803
      locking VBA code, 593–594
      in Outlook, 267–268
      overview of, 264
      passwords, 265–267
      preventing updates, 803
      protecting from macro viruses,
         268–270
      recovering from accidental
         erasure, 270
      third-party software for, 268
      in Word, 265
   finding documents
      with Find dialog box, 241–243
      with Find Fast indexing utility,
         244–246
      with Open dialog box, 239–241
      overview of, 239, 246
      by tracking properties, 247–249
   in Open dialog box
      adding to Favorites with,
         234–235
      displaying files using
         wildcards, 240
      displaying subfolder files in,
         232
      file-opening options, 232–233
      finding files with, 239–241
      selecting multiple files in, 226
      sorting file list in, 232

   in Open and Save As dialog
      boxes, 225–241
      adding FTP sites to, 364
      buttons in, 227–229
      Details view buttons, 230–232
      File Name boxes in, 239–241
      filtering file lists in, 239–240
      keyboard shortcuts in, 226–227
      managing files with, 236
      opening to folders in, 235–236
      overview of, 225–226
      Preview view buttons, 229–230
      Tools menus, 233–234
   overview of, 223, 258, 270
   of properties, 247–249
   in Save As dialog box, 225–241
      crash protection options,
         237–238
      saving files with custom
         extensions, 237
      saving files in other formats,
         236
      setting save options, 237–238
      synchronizing shared documents,
         262–264
   using templates, 259–262
Document Map in navigation,
     627–628
documents
   See also active documents;
      sharing documents on
      networks
   creating, 224
   document windows, 34
   editing in Internet Explorer, 95
   inserting Excel charts in, 167
   inserting hyperlinks in, 85
   opening, 224–225
   opening from Internet Explorer,
      94–95
   in Web sites, working offline on,
      363
documents, long, 769–795
   captions in, 770–772
   collaborating on, 787–795
      accepting changes, 791–791
      comments in, 787–789
      comparing document copies,
         790
      hiding and displaying changes,
         791
      marking changes, 790–791
      merging changes, 792
      networks and, 795
      rejecting changes, 791–791
      reviewing documents, 787,
         789–792, 794
      saving versions of documents,
         793–794
      tracking changes while editing,
         789

   cross-references in, 772–774, 778,
      786
   footnotes and endnotes
      bibliographic references in, 777
      cross-referencing, 778
      editing and formatting, 776–777
      inserting, 774–775
      locating fast, 775–776
      moving, copying, deleting, 776
      multiple references to same
         note, 778
      numbers in, 775
      reference marks in, 774, 775
      symbols in, 775
      in Web pages, 775
   indexes
      creating, 779–780
      editing and formatting, 778–779
      indexing software, 781–782
      marking index entries, 780–781
      overview of, 778, 786
      updating, 779
      in Word, deficiencies of, 781
   master documents
      creating, 785
      linking documents to, 785
      merging subdocuments, 786
      overview of, 784
      splitting subdocuments, 786
   overview of, 769, 795
   strategies for, 784
   tables of authorities, 784
   tables of contents and figures
      creating, 782–784
      editing and formatting, 778–779
      field settings, 782, 783–784
      overview of, 778, 786
      style settings, 782–783
      updating, 779
domain names, 88
DOS text files, removing paragraph
     marks from, 640–642
Double data type, 436, 449
dragging and dropping
   See also copying and pasting;
      moving
   Excel data, 889–891
   hyperlink content, 282
   Outlook information, 1152
   printing by, 209, 216
   in sharing information, 186–188
Draw Marquee command in Word,
     156
drawing. *See* graphic objects
Drawing Grid dialog box, 142
Drawing toolbar, 137, 156–157
Drop Cap settings, 716
DSUM function in Excel, 927–929
Dynamic Data Exchange (DDE), 191
dynamic Excel charts, 990
dynamic Excel data tables, 924–927

Index

E

Edit File Type dialog box, 231
Edit tab of Options dialog box in Word, 621–623
editing
  See also modifying
  Asian documents, 15–16
  data in Access tables, 1030–1031
  documents in other languages, 14–16
  file type descriptions, 230–232
  freehand shapes, 146–149
  HTML code in Web pages, 290
  hyperlinks, 281
  Office documents in Internet Explorer, 95
  OLE objects and links, 201–202
  Outlook data, 1151–1153
  PowerPoint text, 1107–1109
  values in variables, 515–516
  VBA code, 509
  VBA controls, 539–540
  watch expressions, 519
  Web pages in FrontPage, 337
  Web pages opened in Internet Explorer, 96
  Web PowerPoint presentations, 302
editing in Word, 621–660
  Allow Fast Saves option and, 624
  with AutoText feature, 647–653
    creating captions, 771
    creating one-shot entries, 650
    editing entries, 651
    including formatting in, 647
    inserting AutoTextList fields, 650–652
    menus, 648–650
    organizing entries, 649–650
    overview of, 647
    Spike clipboard tool in, 652–653
    updating documents with, 651–652
  Change Case command and, 659–660
  comments, 788–789, 902
  custom dictionaries, 107
  field results, 804
  find-and-replace operations, 635–646
    adding page or column breaks, 640
    cleaning up DOS text files, 640–642
    Find command and, 636
    Find Next command and, 636–637
    finding all word forms, 637
    finding formatting, 637
    found text, 848
    overview of, 635
    removing optional hyphens, 639
    removing page or column breaks, 640
    replacing text or formatting, 849
    for special characters, 637–642
    using wildcards, 642–646
    viewing advanced options, 635–636
    in Word VBA, 847–850
  footnotes and endnotes, 776–777
  hyperlinks, 635
  indexes, 778–779
  keyboard shortcuts for
    changing case, 660
    cutting text, 657–658
    moving or copying text, 656
    rearranging paragraphs, 656
    swapping adjacent characters, 658
  navigation and, 626–635
    via bookmarks, 631–635
    with Document Map, 627–628
    with Go Back command, 630
    with Go To command, 630–631
    keyboard shortcuts for, 628–629
    with mouse, 626–627
    with Next Object button, 629
    overview of, 626
    with Previous Object button, 629
    with Select Browse Object button, 629–630
  overview of, 621, 660
  in Print Preview mode, 207–208
  setting options for, 621–623
  shortcuts for
    accessing open windows, 625–626
    closing documents, 624
    copying blocks of text, 624–625
    cycling through document windows, 625
    deleting files from Work menus, 623–624
    multiple views of same document, 626
    opening files, 623
    selecting text, 655–656
    in shortcut menus, 656
  speeding up text entry
    with AutoText feature, 647–653
    of dates and times, 654–655
    with Repeat feature, 654
    tools for, 646–647
  table text, 740–741
  tables of contents, 778–779
  text box text, 712

Web pages, 292–293
EditPoints command, 156
em and en dashes, 119–120, 123
e-mail
  See also Outlook e-mail
  features, 86, 98
  requirements, 98
  sharing documents via, 365–367
E-mail Options dialog box in Outlook, 1189
E-mail Options dialog box in Word, 1184–1185
`Enabled` property, 539
engines. *See* Access databases
envelopes, 721–722
environment variables, 356–357
Eq fields, 821
equals sign (=) in formula fields, 742, 816–818, 907
equation applets, 166–167
error bars in Excel charts, 942
error checking in Code windows, 408
error handling in ADO, 1060
error messages in Excel, 888, 958, 970
errors. *See* debugging
event procedures, 564-575
  See also forms, VBA
  for altering control properties, 574–575
  for Close and Cancel buttons, 570–571
  for control `Change` events, 565, 569, 572
  defined, 423, 564
  for Keystroke events, 565, 569–570
  listed, 565–566
  for mouse `Click` events, 565, 567–568, 570–571
  for OK buttons, 571
  starting in Excel, 988
  syntax, 567
  for validating user entries, 572–574
  writing, 566–567
events
  choosing objects for, 987
  defined, 481
  of VBA objects, 481, 486–487
  worksheet change events, 988–990
  writing code for, 487
`Exit` statements, 522
`Exit Do` statements, 470
`Exit For` statements, 474
Excel, 855–990
  See also debugging Excel worksheets

(continued)

Excel *(continued)*
  collaboration features, 368, 963–966
  comments
    attaching to cells, 901
    deleting, 902
    editing, 902
    finding, 902
    overview of, 900
    viewing, 901
  copying data in, 889–890, 897–898, 899
  creating bookmarks in, 284
  data entry, 879–888
    with AutoComplete, 881
    with AutoCorrect, 888
    with AutoFill, 882–885
    clearing entries, 885
    confining to ranges, 881
    copying data from other cells, 880
    deleting cells, 885
    error messages in, 888
    filling ranges with single entries, 882
    in groups of worksheets, 886
    input messages in, 887–888
    inserting cells, 885
    keyboard shortcuts, 880, 882, 886
    overview of, 879–880
    single cell entries, 879–882
    of static dates and times, 882
    validating, 886–888
  in developing database applications, 1046
  document security in, 265–266
  document templates in, 260
  dragging and dropping data, 889–891
  [=] (formula) fields and, 817
  formatting in, 892–900
    alignment, 894–895
    applying with styles, 899
    with AutoFill feature, 899
    with AutoFormat feature, 896
    conditional formatting, 897
    currency symbols, 894
    custom number formats, 892–894
    with Format Painter, 898
    with Formatting toolbar, 892
    hyperlinks, 284–285
    keyboard shortcuts, 900
    with List AutoFill feature, 899
    merging cells, 895–896
    overview of, 892
    with Paste Special command, 898
    rounded off numbers, 893–894
    shrinking text to fit cells, 895

  forms in, 173, 174
  hiding rows and columns, 891
  HTML Help system in, 51
  hyperlinks in, 284–285
  inserting worksheets into Word tables, 743
  naming cells and ranges, 869–871
  navigation
    active cells and, 867
    with IntelliMouse, 872
    keyboard shortcuts for, 868, 869
    to named ranges, 869–871
    to other worksheets, 873
    overview of, 867
    by scrolling, 871–872
  object model hierarchy, 977–978
  printing in, 213, 902
  publishing spreadsheets as Web pages, 306–310
  resizing rows and columns, 891
  selection
    automatic calculations in, 879
    controlling selection direction, 872
    from within dialog boxes, 875–876
    keyboard shortcuts for, 874, 875, 876–879
    multiple selections, 874–875
    navigating inside selections, 876
    overview of, 873
    with Shift key, 874
  sharing workbooks
    highlighting changes, 964
    keeping change histories, 964–965
    merging changes, 965–966
    overview of, 368, 963
    saving filters in, 950
    tracking changes, 963–964
  toolbars, 67
  unhiding hidden rows or columns, 891–892
  VBA forms in, 173, 174
  worksheets
    change events of, 988–990
    displaying figures in, 939
    formatting text in, 943
  workspace files, 873
Excel, customizing, 855–865
  attaching custom toolbars to workbooks, 863
  command line switches and, 855–856
  macros
    absolute cell references in, 861–862
    assigning keyboard shortcuts to, 860–861

    overview of, 860
    relative cell references in, 861–862
    running, 862
    storing, 861
  opening workbooks on startup, 856–857
  overview of, 855
  saving custom toolbars and menus, 862–863
  screen options
    color, 859
    Full Screen view, 859
    overview of, 858
    saving workbook views, 859–860
  setting general options, 857–858
  startup options, 855–857
  and storing in templates, 863–865
Excel charts, 931–946
  changing
    chart type, 934–935
    data in, 935–938
    formulas in, 936–937
    orientation of, 938
    source data of, 937–938
  combination charts, 945
  creating, 933–934
  data markers in, 935–936
  embedded charts, 932, 933, 937–938
  formatting
    3-D perspective, 943–944
    added text, 943
    adding pictures, 941
    adding trendlines, 942
    colors and patterns, 940
    data, 939–942
    displaying error bars, 942
    displaying worksheet figures, 939
    overview of, 938–939
    preventing scaling, 943
    rotating chart text, 943
    rotating charts, 944
    scaling fonts, 943
    text, 942–943
    timelines on x-axis, 941
    worksheet text, 943
  inserting in Office documents, 167
  inserting in PowerPoint presentations, 1114
  versus Microsoft Graph charts, 167
  mixing data in, 944–945
  overview of, 931, 936
  saving custom charts, 945–946
  with secondary axes, 945
  terminology, 931–932
  types of, 932–933

Index

viewing chart items, 934
Excel data analysis, 947–963
  add-ins
    Analysis ToolPak, 961
    Lookup Wizard, 960–961
    overview of, 959–960
    Solver, 961–962
    Template Wizard with Data Tracking, 962–963
  filtering data
    with advanced filters, 949
    with AutoFilter feature, 947–948
    with custom filters, 949
    overview of, 947
    removing filters, 950
    saving filters in shared workbooks, 950
  in lists, functions for, 950
  overview of, 947
  in pivot charts, 950, 958–959
  in pivot tables
    anatomy of, 954
    calculation display options, 956
    compare fields option, 957
    creating, 952–955
    custom calculations, 956
    defined, 950
    empty cell display options, 958
    error message display options, 958
    field options, 955–956
    formatting, 958
    layout options, 953, 957
    overview of, 950–951
    pivoting data, 955
    PivotTable toolbar, 955
    PivotTable Wizard, 957
    setting options, 955–958
    shortcut menu, 955
    when to use, 951–952
  tracking with built-in templates, 963
Excel formulas, 905–929
  3-D formulas, 912–913
  automatic versus manual calculation, 905–906
  case in, 975
  in charts, changing, 936–937
  creating, 907
  creating dynamic data tables, 924–927
  date arguments out-of-range, 924
  defining 3-D range names, 913
  defining named constants, 923
  equals signs (=) in, 907
  Formula palette, 907–908
  functions in
    anatomy of, 915
    built-in functions, 986–987
    custom functions, 916
    database management functions, 923
    date and time functions, 918–919
    DSUM function, 927–929
    engineering functions, 922
    entering, 915–916
    financial functions, 921
    IF function, 917
    information functions, 918
    list management functions, 923
    logical functions, 918
    lookup functions, 919
    math functions, 920
    nesting, 916
    overview of, 915, 917–918
    reference functions, 919
    statistical functions, 921–922
    for summing list data, 950
    text functions, 920–921
    trigonometry functions, 920
  versus modules, 914
  operators for, 908–909
  overview of, 905, 929
  referring to cells and ranges in
    3-D references, 912–914
    absolute references, 911
    finding precedent cells, 912
    named cells and ranges, 910–911
    outside current worksheets, 911–912
    overview of, 909
    ranges of cells, 909
    relative references, 911
  underlying values in, 906
  versus VBA modules, 914
  viewing, 906–907
  "Y2K problem" and, 923–924
Excel VBA, 977–990
  for custom functions
    accessing in other workbooks, 985
    overview of, 983
    running, 984–985
    testing, 986
    using Formula Palette with, 985
    writing, 984, 986
  for dynamic charts, 990
  for events
    choosing objects for, 987
    overview of, 987
    starting event procedures, 988
    worksheet change events, 988–990
  Excel built-in functions and, 986–987
  Excel object model hierarchy and, 977–978
  overview of, 977, 990
  Range objects of cells
    acting on single cells, 981
    activating specific cells, 983
    changing cells en masse, 980–981
    defining with Cells property, 980
    overview of, 978
    selection tools for, 981–983
    specifying, 979–980
executable statements, 429
expand indicators, 5, 401
explicit declarations, forcing, 437–438
exporting
  See also sharing information
  Favorites from Internet Explorer, 97
  file conversion software and, 194–195
  generic file formats and, 193–194
  overview of, 192–193
Expression Builder in Access, 1028–1029
expressions of objects, 487, 488–489
expressions in statements, 441
Extensible Markup Language (XML), 274

F

Favorites in Internet Explorer, 97
faxing, 218
Field dialog box in Word, 801
Field Options dialog box in Word, 802
fields, Access database
  adding to forms, 1089
  adding to reports, 1039
  creating, 1026–1027
  data types for, 1021
  defined, 1015
  defining, 1020–1021
  formatting, 1027–1028
  freezing, 1031
  hiding, 1031
  input masks, 1028
  inserting, 1031
  modifying, 1029
  moving, 1031
  planning of, 1018–1019
  primary key fields, 1029
  properties of, 1027
  resizing, 1031
  validation rules, 1028–1029
fields, Word, 797–831
  adding field commands to toolbars and menus, 799–800
  Ask fields, 818
  AutoText fields, 819

(continued)

fields, Word *(continued)*
  AutoTextList fields, 819
  Barcode fields, 819
  Compare fields, 820
  components, 800
  converting into text, 804
  Date fields, 820
  DDE and DDEAuto fields, 820–821
  defined, 797
  document information fields,
    811–815
  Eq fields, 821
  field codes
    defined, 800
    formatting, 804
    options, 802
    toggling between field results
      and, 803
  field instructions, 802
  field results
    Date-Time Picture switch,
      807–808
    defined, 800
    display option switches,
      804–808
    editing, 804
    Format switch, 804–806
    formatting, 804
    Numeric Picture switch, 806
    shading, 804
    toggling between field codes
      and, 803
  Fill-in fields, 821
  finding, VBA procedure for,
    810–811
  [=] (formula) fields, 742, 816–818
  GoToButton fields, 821–822
  Hyperlink fields, 822
  IF fields, 822–823
  IncludePicture fields, 823
  Index fields, 823–824
  inserting, 801
  keyboard shortcuts for, 798
  ListNum fields, 767–768, 824
  locking, 803
  MacroButton fields, 824–825
  methods of, 808–810
  overview of, 797, 831
  Print fields, 825
  properties of, 808–810
  Quote fields, 825
  Ref fields, 825–826
  Section fields, 826
  SectionPages fields, 826
  selecting, 803
  Seq fields, 826–827
  Set fields, 827
  StyleRef fields, 827–828
  Symbol fields, 828
  tables of contents for, 782,
    783–784
TC fields, 829
TOC fields, 829–830
  updating, 803
  using VBA in, 808–811
  VBA objects and, 808–810
  XE fields, 830–831
file conversion software, 188,
  189–190, 194–195
file formats, generic, 193–194
file manager window in Outlook,
  1149
File menu in Binder, 252–253
File Types tab of Options dialog
  box, 230–231
Fill-in fields, 821
fills for graphic objects, 151–152,
  157, 941
filtering
  Access data, 1035
  Excel data, 947–950
  junk e-mail in Outlook, 1177
  Outlook data, 1157–1158
Find command, 636
Find dialog box, 241–243
Find Fast indexing utility, 244–246
Find Next command, 636–637
Find and Replace dialog box,
  630–631, 635–636
find-and-replace operations,
  635–646
  See also editing in Word
  in Access databases, 1034–1035
  adding page or column breaks,
    640
  cleaning up DOS text files,
    640–642
  Find command and, 636
  Find Next command and, 636–637
  finding all word forms, 637
  finding formatting, 637
  found text, 848
  overview of, 635
  removing optional hyphens, 639
  removing page or column breaks,
    640
  replacing text or formatting, 849
  for special characters, 637–642
  using wildcards, 642–646
  viewing advanced options,
    635–636
  in Word VBA, 847–850
finding
  See also tracking
  comments, 902
  container objects, 485
  footnotes and endnotes, 775–776
  Outlook information, 1160–1161
  precedent cells in Excel formulas,
    912
  records, 1067
finding documents
  with Find dialog box, 241–243
  with Find Fast indexing utility,
    244–246
  with Open dialog box, 239–241
  overview of, 239, 246
  by tracking properties, 247–249
floating graphics, 716–717
floating toolbars, 20, 39, 40
FlushTransactionTimeout setting
  for Jet engine, 1010
`For...Next` loops, 471–474
`For Each...Next` loops, 474,
  496–497
folders
  See also Outlook
  in FrontPage, 329–330, 335
  Web Folders, 361–363
Font dialog box, 667–668
fonts
  120-134, *See also* text
  expert sets of, 132–133
  families of, 132
  font manager software, 121–122
  in HTML Help system, 54
  ligature style, 132
  "old-style" numerals, 133
  OpenType fonts, 120–121
  overview of, 120
  rules for, 134
  scalable fonts, 120–121
  scaling in Excel charts, 943
  small caps style, 133
  sources for, 133
  special characters, inserting,
    129–131
  special characters, listed,
    122–129
  TrueType fonts, 120–121
  Type 1 fonts, 120–121
  viewing lists of, 664
  in Word, for character formatting,
    664
footers. *See* headers and footers
Footnote Wizard, 777
footnotes and endnotes
  See also documents, long
  cross-referencing, 778
  editing and formatting, 776–777
  inserting, 774–775
  locating fast, 775–776
  moving, copying, or deleting, 776
  multiple references to same note,
    778
  numbers in, 775
  reference marks in, 774, 775
  symbols in, 775
  in Web pages, 775
[=] (formula) fields, 742, 816–818
form letters, sending via mail
  merge, 202–203

Index **1225**

Form view in Access, 1025
Format Cells dialog box in Excel, 893–895
Format Data Series dialog box in Excel, 940
Format dialog box, 168–169
Format Horizontal Line dialog box, 683–684
Format menu, 542, 1080
Format Painter
  in Excel, 898
  in PowerPoint, 1114
  in Word, 665–666
Format switch, 804–806
formatting
  AutoShape text, 144
  graphic objects, 168–170
  Outlook e-mail messages, 1184
  Outlook views, 1158
  PowerPoint text, 1110–1111
  text in text boxes, 144
  VBA controls, 541–546
formatting in Access
  fields, 1027–1028
  form controls, 1090
  hyperlinks, 285
  tables, 1032
formatting in Excel, 892–900
  alignment, 894–895
  applying with styles, 899
  with AutoFill feature, 899
  with AutoFormat feature, 896
  charts
    3-D perspective, 943–944
    added text, 943
    adding pictures, 941
    adding trendlines, 942
    colors and patterns, 940
    data, 939–942
    displaying error bars, 942
    displaying worksheet figures, 939
    overview of, 938–939
    preventing scaling, 943
    rotating chart text, 943
    rotating charts, 944
    scaling fonts, 943
    text, 942–943
    timelines on x-axis, 941
    worksheet text, 943
  conditional formatting, 897
  currency symbols, 894
  custom number formats, 892–894
  with Format Painter, 898
  hyperlinks, 284–285
  interactive Web pages, 309–310
  keyboard shortcuts, 900
  with List AutoFill feature, 899
  merging cells, 895–896
  overview of, 892

  with Paste Special command, 898
  pivot tables, 953, 957, 958
  rounded off numbers, 893–894
  text to fit cells, 895
Formatting toolbar in Excel, 892
formatting in Word, 661–697
  See also page layout in Word
  applying, 662
  borders, 680–682, 684
  character formatting, 663–670
    applying, 664–665
    defined, 661, 663
    with Format Painter, 665–666
    kerning option, 668–670
    keyboard shortcuts in, 664–665
    removing, 665
    spacing settings, 667–669
    types of, 664, 666–667
    viewing font lists, 664
  "click and type" feature, 679–680
  direct formatting method, 662, 695–696
  displaying format information, 662–663
  field codes, 804
  field results, 804
  footnotes and endnotes, 776–777
  frames, 296
  hyperlinks, 284–285
  indexes, 778–779
  overview of, 661–662, 697
  paragraph formatting, 670–685
    border options, 680–682, 684
    defined, 661, 670
    heading styles, 690–691
    horizontal lines, 682–684
    indents, 671–674
    line and page breaks, 675
    line spacing, 674
    paragraph marks and, 670–671
    resetting original formatting, 671
    shading options, 680–681, 685
    spacing between paragraphs, 675
    tab settings, 675–679
  paragraph indents
    for both sides at once, 674
    first-line indents, 672–673
    hanging indents, 672
    setting options for, 671–674
    Tab indents, 639–640, 673
  paragraph marks
    cutting, copying, and pasting, 671
    deleting, 671
    displaying, 670–671
    removing from DOS text files, 640–642
  paragraph styles, 687, 690, 696, 761

  paragraph tabs
    adding leaders to, 678
    bar tabs, 678–679
    changing, 677
    clearing, 677
    overview of, 675–676
    right tabs, 677–678
    setting, 676–677
    types of, 676
  section formatting, 661–662, 700–701
  setting default measurement units, 663
  styles, 685–697
    adding to shortcut menus, 689–690
    adding to templates, 694
    alias names for, 695
    applying, 688–690
    Automatic Update options, 694, 697
    basing on other styles, 694
    character styles, 687, 690, 696
    creating and modifying, 691–695
    defined, 662, 685
    displaying style assignments, 687
    from within documents, 691–692
    format options, 694–695
    heading styles, 690–691
    keyboard shortcuts for, 689, 691
    with Modify Style dialog box, 693–695
    naming, 691, 693, 695
    with New Style dialog box, 693–695
    for next paragraphs, 694–695
    overriding, 695
    paragraph styles, 687, 690, 696
    previewing, 687
    printing style listings, 688
    problem of disappearing styles, 697
    with Style dialog box, 692–693
    for tables of contents, 782–783
  tables of contents and figures, 778–779
  VBA text, 847
formatting Word tables
  with AutoFit feature, 735–737
  with AutoFormat command, 732
  cells, rows, and columns, 737–738
  column width, 734–737
  deleting versus clearing, 738
  headings, 739
  keyboard shortcuts in, 738
  merging cells, 738

(continued)

formatting Word tables *(continued)*
  moving rows, 738
  row height, 734–737
  size and position, 732–734
  splitting cells, 738
  splitting tables, 738–739
  text in cells, 740–741
forms, Outlook
  actions, 1164
  adding default information, 1165
  adding fields and controls, 1165
  customizing, 1163–1167
  displaying, 1164
  editing items on, 1153
  entering items in, 1152–1153
  forms libraries, 1166
  hiding, 1164
  opening in design mode,
    1163–1164
  properties, 1164
  renaming, 1164
  saving custom forms, 1165–1167
  templates for, 1166, 1167
forms, VBA, 527–578
  See also Access forms; active
    documents; controls, VBA
    form
  versus Access forms, 1080–1081
  adding Close or Cancel buttons,
    570
  captions, 537
  changing before displaying,
    561–562
  creating, 58, 533
  defined, 173, 481
  designing, 532–533
  enabling, 539
  event procedures for, 564–575
    altering control properties,
      574–575
    Close and Cancel buttons,
      570–571
    control Change events, 565,
      569, 572
    defined, 564
    Keystroke events, 565, 569–570
    listed, 565–566
    mouse Click events, 565,
      567–568, 570–571
    OK buttons, 571
    syntax, 567
    for validating user entries,
      572–574
    writing, 566–567
  events of, defined, 481
  in Excel, 173, 174
  Format menu, 1080
  grid settings, 540–541
  hiding, 564
  input boxes in, 528–531, 549

laying out, 533–535
loading, 560–561
locking, 539
message boxes, 528–531
methods of, 481
modal forms, 563
modeless forms, 385, 563
naming, 537
as objects, 481–482
overview of, 383, 527, 578
positioning, 538
printing, 533
property options, 481, 535–539
referring to using variables, 563
running, 532
showing, 560–562
sizing, 538
unloading from memory, 564
validating user entries, 572–574
VBA code and, 532
in VBA object model, 481–482
in Word documents, 173
in Word Web pages, 297–299
Formula AutoCorrect, 973–974
formula bars, 976
Formula Palette, 907–908, 985
formulas. *See* Excel formulas
Forward button on Web toolbar, 92,
  93
frame controls, 552–553
Frame Properties dialog box, 295
frames in Word documents
  See also shared borders
  anchoring, 717–718
  converting text boxes into, 714
  for positioning items in side
    headings, 715–716
  versus text boxes, 714
frames in Word Web pages
  adding to frames pages, 295
  creating frames pages, 294–295
  defined, 293–294
  deleting from frames pages, 295
  formatting, 296
  Frames toolbar and menu, 294
  initial pages in, 295
  inserting hyperlinks in, 296–297
  naming, 295
  properties options, 295
Free/Busy Options dialog box in
  Outlook, 1201
Freeform tool, 146
freehand shapes. *See* graphic
  objects
FrontPage, 323–345
  creating Web pages in, 336–343
    adding hyperlinks, 337–338,
      339–340
    applying DHTML effects,
      342–345

    applying themes, 338
    duplicating content, 341–342
    editing pages, 337
    Include Page command in,
      341–342
    inserting hit counters, 341
    inserting navigation bars,
      339–340
    inserting page banners, 341
    inserting site maps, 342
    inserting tables of contents,
      342
    inserting Web Components,
      341
    overview of, 336
    previewing pages, 343
    shared borders in, 338–339,
      340, 341
  creating webs in, 327–336
    adding pages, 328
    creating subwebs, 335–336
    designing navigation structure,
      330–333
    importing files into, 336
    managing hyperlinks, 333–334
    naming pages, 329
    navigating files and folders,
      329–330
    overview of, 327–328
    private folders in, 335
    publishing webs, 343–345
    titling pages, 329
    tools for, 325–326
    webs defined, 325
  folders and files in, 329
  Office apps and, 323–324
  overview of, 323–325, 345
  Server Extensions, 323
  terminology, 325
  user interface, 324
  views
    Folders view, 329–330
    Hyperlinks view, 333–334
    Navigation view, 330–333
    overview of, 326–327
  windows, 327
FTP (File Transfer Protocol) sites,
  88, 364–365
Full Screen View in Word, 33–34,
  601–602
Function procedures
  See also procedures; VBA code
  in assignment statements, 441
  calling, 425
  defined, 419, 422, 423, 425
  versus functions, 425
  versus Sub procedures, 425
functions in Excel formulas, 915–923
  anatomy of, 915
  built-in functions, 456–458,
    986–987

Index **1227**

custom VBA functions
   accessing in other workbooks, 985
   overview of, 916, 983
   running, 984–985
   testing, 986
   using Formula Palette with, 985
   writing, 984, 986
database management functions, 923
date and time functions, 918–919
DSUM function, 927–929
engineering functions, 922
entering, 915–916
financial functions, 921
for [=] (formula) fields, 817
versus Function procedures, 425
IF function, 917
information functions, 918
list management functions, 923
logical functions, 918
lookup functions, 919
math functions, 920
nesting, 916
overview of, 915, 917–918
reference functions, 919
statistical functions, 921–922
for summing list data, 950
text functions, 920–921
trigonometry functions, 920

G

General tabs
   of Options dialog box in Excel, 857–858
   of Options dialog box in PowerPoint, 1117–1118
   of Options dialog box in VBA, 541
   of Project Properties dialog box in VBA, 402–403
GIF images, 288–289
Go To statements, 474–475
Go Back command, 630
Go menus, 92, 94, 253
Go To command, 630–631
Go To tab of Find and Replace dialog box, 630–631
Gopher, 88
GoToButton fields, 821–822
Gradient tab of Fill Effects dialog box, 151–152
grammar checking in Word, 110–111
graph applets, inserting, 166–167
graphic objects, 135–170
   adding
      to documents, 137
      to Excel charts, 941
      to menus, 79, 80
      to Office Assistant balloons, 590–591
      to PowerPoint presentations, 1113
   aligning, 154–155
   anchoring, 717–718
   AutoShapes
      action buttons, 139, 1114–1115
      adding text to, 143
      assigning actions to, 173, 174–175
      caution, 138
      changing, 142
      connectors, 139
      formatting text in, 144
      inserting in documents, 138
      More AutoShapes command, 138
      overview of, 136
      reshaping, 141
   as bullets, 762
   callouts, 143–144
   in Clip Gallery
      importing images into, 162
      inserting pictures from, 158, 160, 165
      organizing clips in, 161
      overview of, 138
   copying, 140
   creating with Drawing toolbar, 137, 156–157
   creating with PhotoDraw, 165
   displaying on toolbar buttons, 72
   editing
      freehand shapes, 146–149
      graphic hyperlinks, 281
      on toolbar buttons, 72–73
   equation applets, 166–167
   filling with color or texture, 151–152, 157
   floating versus inline graphics, 716–717
   formatting, 168–170
   freehand shapes
      closing open shapes, 149
      Curve tool, 146
      editing, 146–149
      Freeform tool, 146
      opening closed shapes, 149
      Scribble tool, 146
      tangent handles on, 147
      tools for drawing, 145–146
   graph applets, 166–167
   grid settings for, 142
   grouping, 155
   importing bitmap pictures, 164–165
   importing for toolbar buttons, 73
   inserting
      from Clip Gallery, 158, 160, 165
      as embedded OLE objects, 166
      from files, 158, 165
      from scanners or digital cameras, 162
      toolbar buttons for, 75–76
   line style and color options, 150–151, 152, 157
   linking to files, 166
   map applets, 166–167
   measurement units and, 169–170
   modifying
      freehand shapes, 146–149
      line art, 165
      overview of, 162–163
      with PhotoEditor, 162
      with Picture toolbar, 163–164
   moving, 139–141
   multimedia clips, 1115–1116
   Office drawing tools, 135, 145–146
   OLE objects, 165–166
   ordering, 155–156
   organization chart applets, 166–167
   overview of, 135, 159–160, 716
   pictures, defined, 157–158
   positioning, 715–716, 717
   resizing, 140, 141
   rotating, 141
   selecting for edits, 139, 140
   setting defaults for, 157
   sound clips, 167
   special effects
      3-D effects, 152–154
      overview of, 136
      setting defaults for, 157
      shadows, 152–153
   text boxes, 143–144
   transparent color option, 164
   video clips, 167
   in Web pages
      GIF and JPEG images, 288–289
      overview of, 288
      saving in PNG format, 289
      vector graphics, 289
   WordArt, 149–150
   wrapping text around, 718–721
grids
   creating Word tables using, 730–731
   defined, 540
   for drawing, 142
   in VBA forms, 540–541
   in Visual Basic Editor, 538
grouping
   Access macros, 998–999
   Access report items, 1040
   in data access pages, 315–317
   graphic objects, 155
   Outlook items in fields, 1158
   records, 1076–1077
   VBA controls, 542–543, 555

H

Header and Footer toolbar, 703, 707
headers and footers
   See also page layout in Word
   adding horizontal lines in, 707
   for binders, 255–257
   digital watermarks and, 707
   formatting text in, 703–704
   placing page numbers in, 750, 755–756
   repeating text or graphics and, 705–706
   varying within documents, 704–705
   viewing, 703
headings
   formatting in tables, 739
   positioning alongside text, 715–716
   sorting outlines by, 745
   styles for, 690–691
Help
   See also debugging; HTML Help system
   in Object Browser window, 406
   with VBA form properties, 536
hiding
   Access database fields, 1031
   binder sections, 254
   document changes, 791
   Excel rows or columns, 891–892
   floating toolbars, 39
   FrontPage navigation structure, 333
   Office Assistant, 55
   Outlook forms, 1164
   parts of dialog boxes, 875–876
   PowerPoint slides, 1128
   Shortcut bars, 21
   toolbar buttons, 25–26
   toolbars, 36–37, 66
   VBA forms, 564
   windows in Visual Basic Editor, 397
Highlight Changes dialog box, 964
history pane in Internet Explorer, 97
hit counters in Web pages, 341
horizontal lines in Word documents, 292–293, 682–684, 707
HTML Help system, 49–60
   accessing, 52, 56–57
   Answer Wizard tab, 53
   color and font settings for, 54
   Contents tab, 53
   customizing
      accessing custom help, 59
      creating Help windows, 57–58
      with Help authoring software, 58–59
      Office Assistant, 587–592
      for Excel, 51

Index tab, 53
installing, 49
navigating help topics, 53
Office Assistant
   customizing with VBA, 587–592
   defined, 54
   displaying tips at startup, 56
   hiding, 55
   immobilizing, 56
   overview of, 52
   properties of, 587–588, 590
   Respond to F1 key option, 55
   roles of, 54–55
   setting options for, 55–56, 57
   turning off, 49, 57
opening outside Office, 53–54
overview of, 49, 50, 60
storing help files, 50
toolbar buttons, 52
using with multiple Office apps, 53
versus WinHelp, 50–51
HTML (Hypertext Markup Language)
   defined, 88
   DHTML effects in Web pages, 342–345
   HTML forms controls, 173
   Web pages and, 275
HTTP (Hypertext Transfer Protocol), 88
Hyperlink fields, 822
hyperlinks, 278–288
   in Access, 285, 286–287
   assigning to Access controls, 1091
   assigning to toolbar buttons, 75–76
   as controls, 172–173
   creating
      by copying and pasting, 282
      by dragging and dropping, 282
      to existing documents, 280–281
      with Insert Hyperlink dialog box, 283–284
      overview of, 279–280, 635
      to specific locations, 281–284
   defined, 278
   deleting, 281
   editing, 281, 635
   in Excel, 284–285
   following, 279
   formatting, 284–285
   FrontPage site maps of, 342
   inserting
      in AutoShapes, 174
      in FrontPage Web pages, 337–338, 339–340
      in Office documents, 85
      in Web page frames, 296–297

   managing in FrontPage webs, 333–334
   navigating, 93–94
   to Office documents from Internet Explorer, 96
   Paste as Hyperlink command, 184
   in PowerPoint, 285, 287–288, 1115
   ScreenTips for, 279
   in Word, 284–285
Hyperlinks view in FrontPage, 333–334
hyphenation settings for columnar layouts, 710–711

I

icons
   See also buttons
   changing on Shortcut bar, 27–28
   displaying OLE objects as, 201
   in documents for non-OLE files, 199–200
   in file management dialog boxes, 90–91
   refreshing on Shortcut bar, 23–24
   for system policies, 353, 355
IDC/HTX (Internet Database Connector/HTML extension) data format, 312–313
IF fields in Word, 822–823
IF function in Excel formulas, 917
If...ElseIf statements, 463
If...Then statements, 461–462, 463–464
If...Then...Else statements, 462, 463
images. *See* graphic objects
IMEs (Input Method Editors), 15–16
Immediate window, debugging VBA code in, 512–514
importing
   See also sharing information
   bitmap pictures, 164–165
   database objects, 191–192
   file converters and, 188, 189–190, 194–195
   files into FrontPage webs, 336
   generic file formats and, 193–194
   images into Clip Gallery, 162
   images for toolbar buttons, 73
   overview of, 188
   problems with, 190
   text from PowerPoint outlines, 1110
   Web pages into Access, 91
Include Page command, 341–342
IncludePicture fields, 823
indent settings. *See* formatting in Word
indenting
   PowerPoint text, 1111

Index

removing manual Tab indents, 639–640
VBA code, 431
Word paragraphs, 671–674
Index fields, 823–824
indexes
See also documents, long; Find Fast utility
for arrays, 455–456
creating, 779–780
editing and formatting, 778–779
indexing software, 781–782
marking index entries, 780–781
overview of, 778, 786
updating, 779
in Word, deficiencies of, 781
information resources. See resources; telephone numbers; Web site addresses
inline graphics, 716–717
input box controls, 528–531, 549
input masks, 1028
Input Method Editors (IMEs), 15–16
Insert Date and Time command, 654
Insert Hyperlink dialog box, 279–280, 283–284, 296–297
Insert menu, 198–200
Insert Page Numbers command, 748–750
Insert Table dialog box in Word, 731
installing
file format converters, 189–190
HTML Help system, 49
multiple language support, 12
Office 2000, 3–7
Office on networks, 349–351
Office Server Extensions, 358
Table Cell Helper macro, 728
IntelliMouse, 42, 627, 872
interactive documents. See active documents; controls; forms; Web pages, interactive
interface. See user interface
Internet, 85–88.
See also Web; World Wide Web
Internet Accounts dialog box, 1170
Internet e-mail in Outlook, 1169–1171, 1182
Internet Explorer (IE)
See also Web browsers
batch files, 97
buttons, 92
editing Office documents in, 95
editing Web pages opened in, 96
Favorites, 97
file management with, 97
history pane, 97
hyperlinking to Office documents, 96
keyboard shortcuts, 92, 96

opening Office documents from, 94–95
overview of, 87
shortcut menus, 97
start and search pages, 93
version 5, language support and, 12
InterPrint printing utility, 218
intranets, 87

J

JavaScript, 318–320
Jet.Standard Access engine
See also Access databases
advantages of, 1001–1002
in creating database projects, 1003–1004
defined, 1001
splitting Jet databases on networks, 1054–1055
upsizing databases to SQL Server from, 1005–1006
Window Registry settings, 1009–1011
JPEG images, 288–289
jumps, 53.
See also hyperlinks

K

kerning text, 668–670
Keystroke events, 565, 569–570
keyboard layouts for multiple language support, 13–15
keyboard shortcuts
accessing in Word, 612
for all commands, 82–83
for applying styles, 689, 691
assigning to controls, 547
assigning to macros, 860–861
for automatic bullets, 760–761
changing, 606–607
for changing case, 660
choosing keys for, 83, 607–608
compiling, 35–36
for controlling toolbars, 35
for copying text, 656
creating in Word, 606–607
for cutting text, 657–658
for cycling through document windows, 625
in debugging Excel worksheets, 969
for deleting items on Work menus, 623–624
for DOS-type paths, 241
for em and en dashes, 119–120, 123
in Excel data entry, 880, 882, 886
in Excel formatting, 900

for formatting characters, 664–665
in Internet Explorer, 92, 96
for keyboard characters, 611–612
for moving text, 656
for navigating in Access, 1024
for navigating in Excel, 868, 869, 876
for navigating in Word, 628–629
in Outline view, 744–745
in Outlook, 1152
overview of, 35
in PowerPoint, 1107–1108, 1133, 1134
printing, 612
for rearranging paragraphs, 656
for saving documents, 236
in ScreenTips, 612
for selecting in Excel, 874, 875, 876–879
for selecting multiple files, 226
for special characters, 123, 126–129
for swapping adjacent characters, 658
two-step shortcuts, 608
using off-limits keys in, 608–611
in Visual Basic Editor, 395–396, 397
in Word, overview of, 606
for Word fields, 798

L

Label button on Control Toolbox, 58, 176
label controls
adding to Office Assistant balloons, 591
overview of, 547–548
text boxes as, 549
label layouts, 722–724
languages. See multiple language support
LapLink program, 264
Layout view in Access, 1025
layouts. See page layout in Word
ligatures, 132
line art. See graphic objects
line breaks in Word, 675, 699–701
line continuation characters in VBA code, 432
Line Numbers dialog box, 702
line spacing in Word paragraphs, 674
links. See jumps; hyperlinks; OLE
Links dialog box, 201–202
ListCommands method, 833–834
List AutoFill feature in Excel, 899
list box controls, 557–558
List Constants feature, 412

List Properties and Methods
    feature, 411–412
ListNum fields, 767–768, 824
Locked property, 539
Locals window, debugging VBA
    code in, 514–516, 517
locating. *See* finding
lock options for ADO Recordset
    objects, 1066
LockDelay setting for Jet engine,
    1011
locking
    fields to prevent updating, 803
    VBA code, 593–594
logical operators, 445, 446, 460–461
Lookup Wizard add-in, 960–961
loop control structures
    See also VBA code
    defined, 458, 466
    Do...Loop loops, 467–471
    For...Next loops, 471–474
    For Each...Next loops, 474,
        496–497
    nesting, 467, 473
    for Recordset objects, 1069
    types of, 466

M

macro virus protection, 268–270
MacroButton fields, 824–825
Macros9.dot templates, 638, 653
macros, Access
    assigning actions to, 997–998
    assigning to controls, 1091–1092
    creating macro groups, 998–999
    customizing keyboard shortcuts
        with, 999–1000
    overview of, 997, 1017
    versus VBA macros, 1043–1044
macros, VBA
    absolute cell references in,
        861–862
    versus Access macros, 1043–1044
    assigning keyboard shortcuts to,
        860–861
    assigning to AutoShapes, 174
    defined, 385, 423
    deleting from documents, 270
    disabling automatic execution of,
        269
    in Macros9.dot templates, 638, 653
    overview of, 61–62, 860
    in PowerPoint, 1118–1119
    for printing shortcuts, 208–209
    recording, 62–63, 861–862
    relative cell references in,
        861–862
    running, 64–65, 862
    storing, 861
mail. *See* Outlook e-mail

mail merge software, 202–203
Map Network Drive dialog box,
    357–358
MAPI (Messaging Application
    Programming Interface), 365
mapping network drives, 357–358
maps
    inserting map applets in
        documents, 166–167
    inserting site maps in Web pages,
        342
    navigating with Document Map,
        627–628
    of object models, viewing,
        482–483
margins, 701–702
Margins tab of Page Setup dialog
    box in Word, 701
Mark Index Entry dialog box, 780
marking
    See also bookmarks
    document changes, 790–791
    index entries, 780–781
master documents, 784-6, *See also*
    documents, long
masters, PowerPoint presentation,
    1119–1121
math formulas, inserting in Word
    tables, 742–743
MaxBufferSize setting for Jet engine,
    1010
MaxLocksPerFile setting for Jet
    engine, 1011
measurement units, 169–170, 663
Meeting Minder in PowerPoint,
    1133–1134
meetings online, 371–374
menus
    See also shortcut menus
    adding field commands to,
        799–800
    adding graphic images to, 79, 80
    adding script commands to, 320
    of Chart Type button, 934–935
    converting into toolbars, 40
    creating, 79
    customizing
        caution about, 79
        display options, 77–78
        menu items, 78–79
        overview of, 76–77
        restoring original menus, 82
        saving custom menus, 82
        in Word, 606
    File menu in Binder, 252–253
    Go menus, 92, 94, 253
    moving, 78
    navigating on, 78
    renaming, 80
    Section menu in Binder, 253
    in Visual Basic Editor, 394, 395

merging
    changes in shared workbooks,
        965–966
    changes in Word collaborations,
        792
    Excel cells, 895–896
    PowerPoint slides, 1110
    Word subdocuments, 786
message box controls, 528–531
Message Options dialog box in
    Outlook, 1182–1183
Messaging Application
    Programming Interface
    (MAPI), 365
methods
    See also VBA objects
    of built-in objects, 457
    calling, 486
    changing properties with, 486
    defined, 481, 486
    of field objects, 808–810
    Range method, 841–842
    of VBA forms, 481
    writing, 499–500
mice
    See also shortcut menus
    Click events, 565, 567–568,
        570–571
    IntelliMouse, 42, 627, 872
    navigating with, 626–627
    settings, 41
    tips, 40–41
    types of, 41–42
Microsoft Active Server Pages
    Output Options dialog box,
    313
Microsoft Data Engine (MSDE),
    1001–1003
Microsoft Graph, 167
Microsoft NetMeeting, 371–374
Microsoft Office 2000
    See also custom Office
        applications; customizing
        Office
    command line switches, 7–8
    Developer tools, 594–595
    e-mail features and requirements,
        98
    HTML format features, 4, 9–10
    innovations, 3–4
    installation
        customizing in organizations, 7
        Install on First Use option, 6
        overview of, 3, 4–5
        repairing, 6
        setting options for, 5–6
    Internet features, 85–86
    "localized" versions of, 11
    measurement units in, 169–170
    Office Resource Kit (ORK), 17
    Options dialog boxes, 8–9

overview of, 3, 18
resources, 17–18
text converters, 189–190
versions of, 4
Web sites, 18, 43
Microsoft Office Language Settings dialog box, 13
Microsoft Office Shortcut bar. *See* Shortcut bar
Microsoft Outlook dialog box, 1186–1187
Microsoft Script Editor, 318, 319
Microsoft SQL Server Database Wizard, 1004
Microsoft Windows language support, 11–12, 13–14
MIME encoding format, 1186
modal forms, 563
modeless forms, 385, 563
Modify Style dialog box in Word, 693–695
modifying
  See also editing
  Access fields, 1029, 1031–1032
  graphics
    line art, 165
    overview of, 162–163
    with PhotoEditor, 162
    with Picture toolbar, 163–164
  Outlook e-mail accounts, 1170
  Outlook user profiles, 1172–1173
  themes in FrontPage, 338
  Word styles, 691–695
  Word templates, 615, 617–618
modules
  See also class modules; VBA code
  adding to projects, 421
  class modules, 419, 422
  Declarations section, 419, 421–422
  defined, 385, 419, 420
  versus Excel formulas, 914
  planning, 420–421
  standard modules, 419, 422
More AutoShapes command, 138
More Buttons pop-up menu, 38–39
moving
  See also dragging and dropping
  Access fields, 1031
  docked toolbars, 38
  floating toolbars, 39
  footnotes and endnotes, 776
  graphic objects, 139–141
  menus, 78
  Outlook information, 1152
  sections to other binders, 254
  Shortcut bar, 20
  text ranges or selections, 844–845
  toolbar buttons, 26, 68
MS Query program, 191–192

MSDE (Microsoft Data Engine), 1001–1003
multiline text boxes, 550
multimedia in PowerPoint presentations, 1115–1116
multiple language support, 10–17
  adding locales, 14
  editing documents in other languages, 14–16
  elements in, 10–11
  entering accented characters, 14–15
  Input Method Editors and, 15–16
  installing, 12
  Internet Explorer 5 and, 12
  keyboard layouts for, 13–15
  limitations in, 11–12
  overview of, 4
  setting options for, 13–14
  spell-checking in other languages, 108–109
  switching locales, 13–14
  for Unicode characters, 16–17
  Visual Keyboard utility and, 15
  in Windows 95/98, 14
My Documents folder, renaming, 235

N

named Excel cells and ranges, 869–871, 910–911
named Excel constants, 923
naming
  elements in VBA code, 429–431
  frames, 295
  FrontPage Web pages, 329
  items in Access databases, 1006–1007
  menus, 80
  My Documents folder, 235
  Outlook forms, 1164
  projects, 403
  toolbar buttons, 26, 74–75
  toolbars, 26
  VBA forms, 537
  Word files, 236
  Word styles, 691, 693, 695
navigating
  HTML Help topics, 53
  hyperlinked documents, 93–94
  keyboard shortcuts for, 92, 96
  linked text boxes, 712
  menu items, 78
  in VBA Code windows, 409
navigating in Access, 1024, 1084
navigating in Excel
  active cells and, 867
  to cell borders, 869
  inside selections, 876
  with IntelliMouse, 872
  keyboard shortcuts for, 868, 869

  to named ranges, 869–871
  to other worksheets, 873
  overview of, 867
  by scrolling, 871–872
navigating in FrontPage, 330–333, 339–340
navigating in PowerPoint, 1107–1108, 1133
navigating in Word
  See also bookmarks; editing in Word
  via bookmarks, 631–635
  with Document Map, 627–628
  with Go Back command, 630
  with Go To command, 630–631
  keyboard shortcuts for, 628–629
  with mouse, 626–627
  with Next Object button, 629
  overview of, 626
  with Previous Object button, 629
  with Select Browse Object button, 629–630
nesting
  control structures, overview of, 459
  Excel functions, 916
  If...Then control structures, 463–464
  loop control structures, 467, 470–471, 473
  Word tables, 731–732
NetMeeting software, 371–374
Netscape Navigator, 87
network e-mail in Outlook, 1171–1173, 1188
networks, Office on, 349–358
  See also sharing documents on networks
  installing, 349–351
  installing Office Server Extensions, 358
  mapping network drives, 357–358
  overview of, 349, 358
  sharing Access databases, 1012, 1054–1055
  sharing document templates, 262
  system policies and
    controlling features with, 352
    creating, 354
    defining individual policies, 355–356
    network requirements for, 352
    overview of, 351–352, 356
    specifying types of, 355
    System Policy Editor, 352–354
    using environment variables as, 356–357
  Web documents in
    adding shortcuts to Web Folders, 362

(continued)

networks, Office on *(continued)*
    finding with Web Find Fast tool, 363–364
    managing in Web Folders, 361–363
    overview of, 361
New Call dialog box in Outlook, 1205
New dialog box in Access, 1003
New Slide dialog box, 1101–1102
New Style dialog box in Word, 693–695
New Table dialog box in Access, 1025–1026
Next Object buttons, 629
Normal templates in Word, 615
Normal views
    in PowerPoint, 1103
    in Word, 601–602
Notes Page view in PowerPoint, 1103–1104
Number tab of Format Cells dialog box in Excel, 893–894
numbering, Word, 747–768
    in footnotes and endnotes, 775
    numbered and bulleted lists, 756–762
        adding to paragraph styles, 761
        automatic lists, 758–761
        bookmarking repeating text, 766
        bullet character options, 762
        Bullets toolbar button, 758, 761
        creating, 757–761
        empty lists, 760
        keyboard shortcuts for, 760–761
        lead-in emphasis in, 760
        legal-style lists, 767–768
        multiple-level automatic lists, 759
        new features in, 756–757
        numbering as-you-type, 763
        numbering blocks of repeated text, 765–766
        numbering nonconsecutive paragraphs, 763–764
        numbering not starting with 1, 763, 765–766
        Numbering toolbar button, 758, 761
        outline list numbers, 767–768
        overview of, 756, 768
        removing numbering and bullets, 758, 763
        serial or ticket numbers, 765–766
    overview of, 747
    pages and sections, 748–756
        bookmarking section breaks, 752–753

calculating page numbers, 753
in chapters, 754–756
counting section page numbers, 750–751
fancy numbers, 749–750
including total page count, 751
with Insert Page Numbers command, 748–750
overview of, 747–748
placing in headers or footers, 750, 755–756
printing section and page numbers, 752–753
removing page numbers, 751–752
skipping page numbers, 751
numbers in Excel, formatting, 892–894
numeric data types, 449–450
Numeric Picture switch, 806

O

Object Browser window, 404–406
Object dialog box, 199
Object list box in Code windows, 409, 566–567
object variables
    See also variables; VBA objects
    creating, 489–491, 492
    declaring, 489–491
    emptying, 491
    object references in, 487, 491, 493
objects. *See* graphic objects; OLE; VBA objects
OCR (Optical Character Recognition) software, 46–47
ODBC (Open Database Connectivity) standard, 1059–1060
ODBCDirect, 1060
Office applications. *See* custom Office applications; *individual applications*
Office Assistant
    See also HTML Help system
    customizing balloons
        adding controls, 591–592
        adding graphics, 590–591
        closing, 591
        creating, 589
        properties, 590
    defined, 54
    displaying tips at startup, 56
    hiding, 55
    immobilizing, 56
    overview of, 52
    properties of, 587–588, 590
    Respond to F1 key option, 55
    roles of, 54–55
    setting options for, 55–56, 57

turning off, 49, 57
Office Assistant dialog box, 55–57
Office Server Extensions (OSE), installing, 358
Office Web Components, 305–306, 341
OK buttons, 571
"old-style" numerals, 133
OLE DB specification, 1060
OLE (Object Linking and Embedding)
    See also sharing information
    converting embedded objects into linked objects, 201
    defined, 195
    displaying objects as icons, 201
    editing links, 201–202
    editing objects, 201–202
    embedding objects, 197–198
    inserting objects, 166, 198–200
    linking versus embedding, 195–196
    linking objects, 198
    overview of, 165–166
    pasting objects, 197, 200
    pros and cons of, 196
On Error statements, 522
online meetings, 371–374
Open Database Connectivity (ODBC) standard, 1059–1060
Open dialog box, 225–241
    See also document management
    adding FTP sites to, 364
    adding to Favorites with, 234–235
    buttons in, 227–229
    Details view button, 230–232
    displaying files using wildcards, 240
    displaying subfolder files in, 232
    File Name box in, 239–241
    file-opening options, 232–233
    filtering file lists in, 239–240
    finding files with, 239–241
    keyboard shortcuts in, 226–227
    managing files with, 236
    opening to folders in, 235–236
    overview of, 225–226
    Preview view button, 229–230
    selecting multiple files in, 226
    sorting file list in, 232
    Tools menu, 233–234
operators
    See also VBA code
    arithmetic operators, 444–445
    comparison operators, 444, 445, 446–448
    concatenation operators, 444, 445, 448
    defined, 444
    in Excel formulas, 908–911
    for [=] (formula) fields, 816

Index

logical operators, 445, 446, 460–461
precedence in, 444–446
`Option Explicit` statements, 437–438
option button controls in VBA, 554–556
Options dialog boxes
  in Access, 8–9
  in Excel, 857–858, 884–885
  in Explorer, 230–231
  in Outlook, 1142–1143
  in PowerPoint, 1117–1118
  in VBA, 541
  in Word, 600–601, 603–604, 621–623
Options tab of Customize dialog box, 74
organization chart applets, inserting, 166–167
Organize command in Outlook, 1159
Organizer, Word, 617–618
orientation
  of Excel charts, 938
  in printing, 205
OSE (Office Server Extensions), installing, 358
outlines, Word
  commands for, 744–745
  heading styles for, 690–691
  keyboard shortcuts, 744–745
  levels in, 690–691
  overview of, 743
  printing, 746
  shutting off body text, 745
  sorting by headings, 745
outlines of PowerPoint presentations, 1108–1109
Outlook, 1139–1168, 1191–1206
  adding information, 1151–1153
  Calendar folder
    adding items to, 1198–1199
    appointments, 1197
    defined, 1143, 1197
    events, 1197
    meetings, 1197
    moving items in, 1199
    navigating in, 1198
    resource options for meetings, 1201
    scheduling meetings, 1199–1200
    setting options for, 1200–1201
    sharing schedules, 1201
    time zone options, 1201
    views, 1197–1198
  categorizing information, 1153
  Contacts folder
    Address Book, 1203–1204
    contacting contacts, 1202–1203
    defined, 1143, 1202
    entering contacts, 1202
    overview of, 1202
    speed dialing contacts, 1204–1205
  customizing, 1142–1143
  default folders, 1143–1145
  Deleted Items folder, 1144, 1161
  document security in, 267–268
  editing information, 1151–1153
  folders
    creating, 1146
    default folders, 1143–1145
    folder list, 1145–1146
    saving forms in, 1165
    selecting, 1145–1146
  forms
    actions, 1164
    adding default information, 1165
    adding fields and controls, 1165
    customizing, 1163–1167
    displaying, 1164
    editing items on, 1153
    entering items in, 1152–1153
    forms libraries, 1166
    hiding, 1164
    opening in design mode, 1163–1164
    properties, 1164
    renaming, 1164
    saving custom forms, 1165–1167
    templates for, 1166, 1167
  Journal folder, 1144
  keyboard shortcuts, 1152
  main window, 1144
  Notes folder, 1144, 1205
  organizing
    archiving information, 1161–1162
    compacting folders, 1162
    deleting permanently, 1161
    finding information, 1160–1161
    with Organize command, 1159
    overview of, 1159
    retrieving deleted items, 1161
  Outlook bar, 1143–1144, 1147–1149
  Outlook file manager window, 1149
  Outlook Today "page," 1143, 1146–1147, 1192
  overview of, 1139–1140, 1168, 1191, 1206
  printing in, 209, 213
  speed dialer, 1204–1205
  spell-checking in, 1162
  startup command line switches, 1140–1141
  TaskPad, 1192
  tasks
    accepting, 1196
    assigning, 1196
    completing, 1193
    declining, 1196
    delegating, 1196
    entering, 1194–1195
    managing, 1195
    overview of, 1191
    recurring tasks, 1194
    setting options for, 1193
    viewing, 1192–1193
  Tasks folder, 1143, 1192
  templates, 260, 1166, 1167
  toolbars, 1143
  views
    Active Appointments view, 1150, 1151
    adding fields to, 1156–1157
    Card views, 1151
    copying custom forms in, 1166
    creating and modifying copies of, 1154–1156
    customizing, 1154–1159
    Day/Week/Month views, 1149–1150
    deleting items from, 1152
    editing items in, 1152
    filtering, 1157–1158
    formatting, 1158
    grouping items in fields, 1158
    Icon views, 1151
    overview of, 1149
    reorganizing fields in, 1156–1157
    sorting, 1158
    switching, 1150
    table views, 1151
    Timeline views, 1151, 1195
    Week views, 1149, 1197–1198
  Visual Basic Editor in, 385
Outlook e-mail, 1169–1189
  accounts
    creating, 1170
    defined, 1170–1171
    mailing on specific accounts, 1188
    managing, 1171
    modifying, 1170
    selecting, 1182
  adding information services, 1172, 1173
  addressing messages
    from contact lists, 1179–1180
    hiding names using Bcc field, 1180
    overview of, 1179
    from personal distribution lists, 1180–1181
  attaching files to, 1185–1186

(continued)

Outlook e-mail *(continued)*
  customizing settings, 1188–1189
  filtering junk mail, 1177
  formatting messages, 1184
  mass mailings, 1180–1181
  messages in mail folders
    flagging, 1176
    managing, 1176–1177
    opening, 1173
    overview of, 1173
    previewing, 1174–1175
    views for, 1176
  overview of, 1169
  receiving messages, 1186–1188
  Rules Wizard, 1176–1177
  sending messages, 1186–1188
  setting up
    Internet e-mail, 1169–1171, 1182
    network e-mail, 1171–1173, 1188
    overview of, 1169
  user profiles
    creating, 1172
    deleting, 1172
    modifying, 1172–1173
    overview of, 1171
    using, 1172
  writing messages
    addressing messages, 1179–1181
    attaching files, 1185–1186
    encoding formats and, 1186
    with message commands, 1178–1179
    message options, 1182–1183
    overview of, 1177
    selecting accounts, 1182
    starting, 1177–1178
    text formats for, 1183–1184
    using Word as e-mail editor, 1184–1185
overriding styles, 695

P

Pack and Go Wizard in PowerPoint, 1134–1135
Package and Deployment Wizard, 594, 595
page banners in Web pages, 341
page breaks in Word, 675, 699–701
page layout in Word, 699–726
  adding digital watermarks, 707
  business cards, 723–725
  columnar layouts
    adding elements spanning, 710
    changing column width, 709
    formatting text in, 709–710
    graphics or headings along sides of, 715–716
    hyphenation settings, 710–711
    methods for, 709
    in newspaper-style, 711, 713
  default settings, 702
  Drop Cap settings, 716
  DTP software and, 707–708
  envelopes, 721–722
  frames
    anchoring, 717–718
    converting text boxes into, 714
    positioning text boxes and graphics using, 715–716
    versus text boxes, 714
  graphic objects
    anchoring, 717–718
    floating versus inline graphics, 716–717
    overview of, 716
    positioning, 715–716, 717
    wrapping text around, 718–721
  headers and footers
    adding horizontal lines in, 707
    digital watermarks and, 707
    formatting text in, 703–704
    placing page numbers in, 750, 755–756
    repeating text or graphics and, 705–706
    toolbar, 703, 707
    varying within documents, 704–705
    viewing, 703
  inserting breaks manually, 699–701
  labels, 722–724
  line numbering settings, 702
  margin settings, 701–702
  overview of, 721
  section formatting in, 700–701
  text boxes
    aligning into columns, 713
    anchoring, 717–718
    converting into frames, 714
    creating, 712
    creating slides with, 725–726
    editing text in, 712
    versus frames, 714
    linking, 712
    navigating linked boxes, 712
    for newspaper-style layouts, 711, 713
    overview of, 144, 711
    positioning in frames, 715–716
    removing, 713
    reordering chains of, 713–714
    text flow in, 711, 712
    toolbar, 712
Page Number Format dialog box, 748
Page Setup dialog box in Outlook, 213
Page Setup dialog box in Word, 701
PageTimeout setting for Jet engine, 1010–1011
paragraph breaks, manual, 699–701
Paragraph Format dialog box, 671–672
paragraph formatting. *See* formatting in Word
Parameter Info window in Visual Basic Editor, 413
parent webs, 335
parentheses in Excel, colored, 974–975
passwords
  in document security, 265–267
  for text boxes, 550
  for VBA projects, 403
Paste button, 197–198
Paste Function dialog box in Excel, 916
Paste as Hyperlink command, 184
Paste Special command, 183–184, 197, 200, 898
pasteboard in PowerPoint, 1106
Pattern fill effect, 152
patterns for Excel charts, 940
Pen Comment command, 46
pen technology, 44–46
Performance Analyzer in Access, 1008
phone numbers. *See* telephone numbers
PhotoDraw program, 165
PhotoEditor program, 162
Picture fill effect, 152
Picture tab of Fill Effects dialog box in Excel, 941
Picture toolbar, 163–164
pictures. *See* graphic objects
pivot charts, 950, 958–959
pivot tables, 950–959
  See also Excel data analysis
  anatomy of, 954
  calculation display options, 956
  compare fields option, 957
  creating, 952–955
  custom calculations, 956
  defined, 950
  empty cell display options, 958
  error message display options, 958
  field options, 955–956
  formatting, 958
  layout options, 953, 957
  overview of, 950–951
  pivoting data, 955
  setting options, 955–958
  shortcut menu, 955
  when to use, 951–952
PivotTable dialog boxes, 955–958
PivotTable toolbar, 955

PivotTable Wizard, 957
Place A Call dialog box, 371–372
PNG (Portable Network Graphics) format, 289
pointing devices, 41. *See also* mice
Policy Template Options dialog box, 354
polymorphism, 497
pop-up jumps, 53
PowerPoint
    collaboration features, 368, 1135
    document templates, 261
    hyperlinks in, 285, 287–288
    printing in, 212
    views, 1103–1104
PowerPoint dialog box, 1101
PowerPoint presentations, 1099–1116
    adding
        action buttons, 1114–1115
        controls, 1115
        graphic elements, 1113
        hyperlinks, 1115
        multimedia clips, 1115–1116
    aligning objects, 1106
    arranging slides, 1105
    AutoLayouts, 1101–1102, 1120–1121
    copying formats, 1114
    creating, 1102
    creating custom shows, 1130
    creating tables in, 1113–1114
    defined, 1099
    disabling startup dialogs, 1101–1102
    help from Presentation Assistant, 1112
    inserting Excel charts, 1114
    inserting Word tables, 1114
    keyboard shortcuts, 1107–1108, 1133, 1134
    merging slides, 1110
    modifying slide layouts, 1105–1106
    pasteboard for, 1106
    performing
        choosing display devices, 1135
        distributing PowerPoint viewer, 1132
        in live online collaborations, 1135
        navigation keys in, 1133
        overview of, 1131
        pausing, 1133
        portable presentations, 1134–1135
        printing audience handouts, 1134
        printing outlines, 1134
        printing speaker notes, 1134
        recording audience discussions, 1133–1134
        scribbling on slides, 1133
        sending to others, 1131–1132
        shortcut keys in, 1134
        shortcut menu in, 1132–1133
        on your computer, 1132–1134
    placeholders in, 1101, 1109
    planning, 1099–1101
    previewing in black and white, 1104
    recording sound tracks for, 1116
    rehearsing slide show timings, 1129–1130
    saving as automatic slide shows, 1132
    saving as Web pages, 299–302
    shortcut menu, 1132–1133
    slide miniature window and, 1104, 1105
    splitting slides, 1110
    starting new presentations, 1101–1102
    summary slides, 1109–1110
    test running, 1128
    text
        animating, 1111
        bookmarking, 1109
        editing, 1107–1109
        formatting, 1110–1111
        importing from outlines, 1110
        indenting paragraphs, 1111
        navigating, 1107–1108
        spell-checking, 1112
        text placeholders versus text boxes, 1109
        viewing text outlines, 1108–1109
    zooming in, 1104
PowerPoint presentations, customizing, 1117–1131
    animating slide transitions, 1128–1129
    changing default settings, 1117–1118
    changing slide backgrounds, 1125
    color schemes, 1122–1123
    hiding slides, 1128
    inserting slides from other presentations, 1125–1127
    with macros, 1118–1119
    masters
        bulleted text in, 1121
        editing, 1119–1120
        formatting text on, 1120–1121
        laying out text on, 1120–1121
        outlined text in, 1121
        overview of, 1119
        repeating elements by adding to, 1121
        types of, 1119
    mixing slide designs, 1124
    overview of, 1135
    reordering slides, 1128
    setting slide show timings, 1129–1130
    slide show setup options, 1130–1131
    templates in
        applying to existing presentations, 1124
        changing default templates, 1124
        creating, 1123–1124
        types of, 1123
    transferring slide designs via disk files, 1126–1127
precedence in operators, 444–446
precedent cells in Excel formulas, 912, 967–969
predicates, SQL, 1075
Preferences tab of Options dialog box in Outlook, 1142–1143
Presentation Assistant in PowerPoint, 1112
Preview pane in Outlook, 1175
previewing
    Outlook e-mail messages, 1174, 1175
    PowerPoint presentations, 1104
    print jobs, 206–207
    scripts, 321
    Web pages in FrontPage, 343
    Word styles, 687
Previous Object buttons, 629
Print fields, 825
Print Layout view in Word, 601–602
Print Preview mode in Word, editing in, 207–208
Print Preview view in Access, 1025
printing, 205–219
    in Access, 213–214
    audience handouts, 1134
    in Binder, 214
    binders, 255–257
    with ClickBook utility, 216–218
    collate option, 210–211
    comments, 789
    with drag and drop, 209, 216
    editing in Word Print Preview, 207–208
    in Excel, 213, 902
    by faxing, 218
    with InterPrint utility, 218
    macros for, 208–209
    orientation, 205
    in Outlook, 209, 213
    overview of, 205, 219
    page and section numbers, 752–753
    in PowerPoint, 212, 1134

(continued)

printing *(continued)*
  previewing, 206–207
  with Print button, 208
  with Print dialog box, 208, 209–211
  Print to File option, 211, 214–216
  setup options, 209–210
  from shortcut menus, 209, 216
  with SuperPrint utility, 218
  unopened documents, 209
  utilities for, 216–218
  VBA forms, 533
  in Word, 211–212
  Word keyboard shortcuts, 612
  Word outlines, 746
  Word style listings, 688
private declarations, 438
private folders in FrontPage webs, 335
private procedures, 427, 428
procedures
  See also VBA code
  arguments and, 426
  defined, 419
  defining scope of, 427
  Event procedures, 423
  for finding fields, 810–811
  Function procedures, 419, 422, 423, 425
  overview of, 422
  private procedures, 427, 428
  Property procedures, 423, 498–499
  starting, 422–423
  Sub procedures, 419, 422, 423–424
  writing, 422–426, 498–499
Procedures/Events list box in Code windows, 409, 566–567
Programs toolbar, 28
Project Explorer window in Visual Basic Editor, 399–403
Project Properties dialog box, 402–403
projects
  adding modules to, 421
  defined, 419, 420
  protecting, 403
  renaming, 403
  saving, 399
  setting properties, 402–403
properties
  of Access fields, 1027
  of Access forms, 1085
  of ActiveX controls, 177
  changing with methods, 486
  of Office Assistant balloons, 590
  of Outlook forms, 1164
  of projects, 402–403
  of text boxes, 550
  of VBA forms, 481, 535–539

of VBA objects
  changing settings, 483, 485
  as data types in variables, 484
  default properties, 485
  defined, 481
  of field objects, 808–810
  finding container objects via, 485
  as objects, 485, 488
  Range property, 840–841
  read-only properties, 483
  retrieving, 483, 484
  write-only properties, 483
  of windows in Word VBA, 837
Properties dialog boxes, accessing, 7–8
Properties windows
  in Access, 1080–1081
  for VBA forms, 535–536, 1080–1081
  in Visual Basic Editor, 414–415
Property procedures, 423, 498–499
Protection tab of Project Properties dialog box, 403
protocols, Internet, 88
public declarations, 438
Publish Form As dialog box in Outlook, 1166–1167
Publish Web dialog box in FrontPage, 344–345
Publish as Web Page dialog box, 300–301, 306–308
publishing Web pages
  Access databases as, 310–318
  Excel spreadsheets as, 306–310
  in FrontPage webs, 343–345
  overview of, 302–303
pull quotes, 696

Q

queries, Access database
  action queries, 1053
  defined, 1016
  designing, 1037–1038
  overview of, 1035
  SQL and, 1071
  types of, 1035–1036
question marks (?) as wildcards, 240
Quick Info feature in VBA, 412–413, 512
Quote fields, 825
quotes, pull, 696

R

radio button controls, 554–556
Range method of Word objects, 841–842
Range property of Word objects, 840–841

ranges of Excel cells
  acting on single cells in, 981
  activating specific cells, 983
  changing en masse, 980–981
  defining 3-D range names, 913
  defining with `Cells` property, 980
  named ranges, 910–911
  overview of, 909, 978
  Range Finder for, 912, 937–938
  range operators, 909, 910–911
  range selection boxes, 875
  selection tools for, 981–983
  specifying, 979–980
RDO (Remote Data Objects) model, 1059
`Resume` statements, 524–525
read-only properties, 483
Record Macro dialog box in Excel, 860–861
record selectors in Access forms, 1084
recording macros, 62–63, 861–862
records. *See* VBA database programming
RecycleLVs setting for Jet engine, 1011
Ref fields, 825–826
references, object, 487, 491, 493
references in Excel formulas
  See also Excel formulas
  3-D references, 912–914
  absolute references, 911
  finding precedent cells of, 912
  to named cells and ranges, 910–911
  outside current worksheets, 911–912
  overview of, 909
  to ranges of cells, 909
  reference operators in, 909–911
  relative references, 911
references to ADO objects, 1060–1061
references in Word documents. *See* documents, long
Refresh Interval setting for Jet engine, 1010–1011
refreshing Shortcut bar icons, 23–24
registering ActiveX controls, 576
Registry, Windows, 1009–1011
Rehearsal dialog box in PowerPoint, 1129–1130
relationships between Access tables, 1019–1020, 1032–1034
relative cell references in Excel, 861–862, 911
Remote Data Objects (RDO) model, 1059
removing
  See also clearing; deleting
  bullets from lists, 758, 763

character formatting, 665
Excel filters, 950
Excel tracer arrows, 969
numbering from lists, 758, 763
objects from collections, 495
page numbers, 751–752
paragraph marks, 640–642
Tab indents, 639–640, 673
text boxes, 713
Replace tab of Find and Replace dialog box, 635–636
replacing. *See* find-and-replace operations
replicating Access databases, 1055
reports, Access
See also Access databases
versus Access forms, 1079
adding fields and items to, 1039
creating report snapshots, 311
defined, 1017
distributing, 1038
grouping items in, 1040
lightweight reports, 1052
planning, 1022
sections in, 1038–1039
Reset command, 65, 82, 671
resizing. *See* sizing
resources
See also telephone numbers; Web site addresses
on Office 2000, 17–18
on VBA, 390
Respond to F1 key option for Office Assistant, 55
reviewing document collaborations, 787, 789–792, 794
Reviewing toolbar in Word, 787
right-click menus. *See* shortcut menus
rotating
Excel chart text, 943
Excel charts, 944
graphic objects, 141
text in text boxes, 144
Row tab of Table Properties dialog box in Word, 735
RTF (Rich Text Format), 193, 194, 1183
rulers for setting paragraph indents, 673
Rules Wizard in Outlook, 1176–1177
running
Binder, 251
custom Excel VBA functions, 984–985
macros, 64–65, 862
VBA forms, 532

S

Save As dialog box, 225–241
See also document management
adding FTP sites to, 364
buttons in, 227–229
crash protection options, 237–238
Details view button, 230–232
File Name box, 239–241
filtering file lists in, 239–240
keyboard shortcuts in, 226–227
managing files with, 236
opening to folders in, 235–236
overview of, 225–226
Preview view button, 229–230
saving files with custom extensions, 237
saving files in other formats, 236
setting save options, 237–238
Tools menu, 234
saving
binders, 255
copies of binder sections, 254
custom Access applications, 1056
custom buttons, 82
custom Excel charts, 945–946
custom menus, 82
custom Outlook forms, 1165–1167
custom toolbars, 82
documents in networks, 360
Excel custom toolbars and menus, 862–863
Excel filters in shared workbooks, 950
graphics in PNG format, 289
Outlook forms in folders, 1165
PowerPoint presentations as Web pages, 299–302
projects, 399
screen layouts in VBA, 399
search criteria, 243
Word documents as Web pages, 274
Word templates, 618–619
scaling fonts in Excel charts, 943
scanners, 162
scope
in declaring variables, 438
of procedures, 427
screen options
See also desktop; user interface
in Excel, 858–860
saving screen layouts, 399
in Word, 601–602, 603–605
ScreenTips
changing color of, 84
for hyperlinks, 279
overview of, 36
showing Word keyboard shortcuts in, 612
for toolbar buttons, displaying, 74–75

Scribble tool, 146
Script Editor, Microsoft, 321
scripts in Web pages
See also Web pages, interactive
adding script commands to toolbars and menus, 320
editing, 321
identifying, 320
inserting, 321
JavaScript, 318–320
overview of, 318
previewing, 321
script anchors, 320–321
VBScript, 318–320
in Word Web pages, 298
scroll bars
adding to text boxes, 551
as VBA controls, 559–560
scrolling in Excel navigation, 871–872
`SelectionChange` events in Excel VBA, 989–990
search pages, setting, 93
searching
See also finding
in Object Browser window, 406
Second Copy utility, 264
Section fields, 826
Section menu in Binder, 253
SectionPages fields, 826
sections
in Access forms, 1083–1085
in Access reports, 1038–1039
in binders, 252–254
in data access pages, 314–316
in Word documents, 750–753
security, document
See also document management
in Access, 266–267
in Binder, 266
in Excel, 265–266
file-opening restrictions, 232–233
locking fields, 803
locking VBA code, 593–594
in Outlook, 267–268
overview of, 264
passwords, 265–267
preventing file updates, 803
protecting from macro viruses, 268–270
protecting VBA projects, 403
recovering from accidental erasure, 270
securing code with digital certificates, 385, 592–593
third-party software for, 268
in Word, 265
Segment options for freeform shapes, 148–149
`SELECT` statements. *See* SQL
`Select Case` statements, 464–465

Select Browse Object button, 629–630
Select Multiple Objects command, 156
Select Names dialog box in Outlook, 1179–1180
selecting
   Access forms and sections, 1084–1085
   binder sections, 253–254
   data in Access tables, 1030–1031
   in Excel
      automatic calculations when, 879
      controlling selection direction, 872
      from within dialog boxes, 875–876
      keyboard shortcuts for, 874, 875, 876–879
      multiple selections, 874–875
      navigating inside selections, 876
      overview of, 873
      with Shift key, 874
   fields, 803
   graphic objects, 139, 140
   multiple files at once, 226
   objects, Excel VBA for, 981–983
   Outlook folders, 1145–1146
   records, 1075
   table elements, 728–729
   text, shortcuts for, 655–656
   VBA controls, 537, 544
Selection objects in Word VBA, 839–840, 843
Seq fields, 826–827
Server Extensions, FrontPage, 323
Services dialog box in Outlook, 1172–1173
Set fields, 827
Set Transparent Color tool, 164
SheetCalculate events in Excel VBA, 989
SheetChange events in Excel VBA, 988–989
SheetSelectionChange events in Excel VBA, 989–990
shading
   field results, 804
   in Word documents, 680–681, 685
shadow effects for graphic objects, 152–153
shapes. *See* graphic objects
shared borders in Web pages, 338–339, 340, 341.
   See also borders; frames
sharing documents on networks, 359–375.
   See also collaborating on documents

and collaborating on
   with Discussions feature, 368–370
   in online meetings, 373–374
   subscribing to change notices, 370
   tools for, 368
between different versions of Office, 374–375
via e-mail, 365–367
on FTP sites, 364–365
via online meetings, 371–374
opening documents, 360
overview of, 359, 360–361, 375
saving documents, 360
synchronizing documents, 262–264
Web documents, 361–364
workgroup template folders for, 262, 365
sharing Excel workbooks
   highlighting changes, 964
   keeping change histories, 964–965
   merging changes, 965–966
   overview of, 368, 963
   saving filters, 950
   tracking changes, 963–964
sharing information, 179–203
   See also Binder; custom Office applications; forms
   via clipboard
      Clipboard toolbar, 180–182
      ClipMate utility, 182
      overview of, 180
      Paste as Hyperlink command, 184
      Paste Special command, 183–184
      pasting data into and out of Access, 185–186
      when to use, 180
   by dragging and dropping, 186–188
   by exporting, 192–195
   by importing
      database objects, 191–192
      file converters and, 188, 189–190, 194–195
      generic file formats and, 193–194
      overview of, 188
      problems with, 190
   via Object Linking and Embedding
      converting embedded objects into linked objects, 201
      defined, 195
      displaying objects as icons, 201
      editing objects and links, 201–202
      embedding objects, 197–198

      inserting objects, 166, 198–200
      linking versus embedding, 195–196
      linking objects, 198
      overview of, 165–166
      pasting objects, 197, 200
      pros and cons of, 196
   overview of, 179, 203
   by sending form letters using mail merge, 202–203
Shift key in Excel selection, 874
Shortcut bar, 19–29
   See also toolbars
   accessing, 23
   accessing Windows desktop from, 28
   changing button icons on, 27–28
   changing default folders from, 28–29
   components, 20–21
   customizing toolbars on
      adding buttons, 25
      adding space between buttons, 26
      creating toolbars, 24–25
      deleting buttons, 27
      deleting toolbars, 26
      displaying hidden buttons, 25–26
      hiding buttons, 25–26
      moving buttons, 26
      renaming buttons and toolbars, 26
      reordering toolbars, 25
      restoring deleted toolbars, 26–27
   docking, 20, 21
   fitting into title bar area, 22–23
   floating, 20
   hiding, 21
   moving, 20
   overview of, 19–20, 29
   Programs toolbar on, 28
   refreshing icons on, 23–24
   viewing toolbars on, 21
shortcut menus
   See also menus
   adding styles to, 689–690
   for AutoFill, 883–884
   for automatic spell-checking, 109
   customizing, 80–81, 606
   for editing freehand shapes, 148, 149
   for Excel pivot tables, 955
   in Internet Explorer, 97
   for moving and copying Excel data, 890
   overview of, 40–41
   in PowerPoint, 1132–1133
   printing from, 209, 216
   in Project Explorer window, 402

Index

in Word, 606
in Word editing, 656
Shortcut Menus toolbar, 80–81
shortcuts. *See also* keyboard shortcuts
shortcuts to Web, adding to Web Folders, 362
shortcuts in Word
   for accessing open windows, 625–626
   for closing documents, 624
   for copying blocks of text, 624–625
   for cycling through document windows, 625
   for deleting files from Work menus, 623–624
   for multiple views of same document, 626
   for opening files, 623
   for selecting text, 655–656
   in shortcut menus, 656
Single data type, 436, 449
site maps, 342
sizing
   Access fields, 1031
   Access forms, 1085–1087
   Excel rows and columns, 891
   floating toolbars, 39
   graphic objects, 140, 141
   VBA controls, 545, 546
   VBA forms, 538
Slide Finder dialog box, 1127
Slide Show view, 1103–1104
slide shows. *See* PowerPoint presentations
Slide Sorter view, 1103–1104
slides, creating with Word text boxes, 725–726
small caps, 133
Solver add-in, 961–962
Solver Parameters dialog box, 962
sorting
   Access records, 1077
   data in Access databases, 1035
   data in Word tables, 741–742
   Outlook views, 1158
sound
   adding to documents, 167
   applying to Office interface events, 167
   sound tracks for PowerPoint presentations, 1116
Sounds Properties dialog box, 43
spacing
   toolbar buttons, 68–69
   VBA controls, 545
   in Word paragraphs, 674, 675
special characters
   See also symbols
   adding to AutoCorrect, 118–119

em and en dashes, 119–120, 123
inserting, 129–131
keyboard shortcuts for, 123, 126–129
listed, 122–129
wildcards, 642–646
special characters, finding and replacing, 637–642
   codes for, 638–639
   optional hyphens, 639
   overview of, 637–638
   page or column breaks, 640
   paragraph marks, 640–642
   Tab indents, 639–640
special effects. *See* graphic objects
speech-recognition software, 44, 45
speed dialer in Outlook, 1204–1205
spell-checking, 101–110
   See also text
   automatically as you work, 109–110
   correcting misspellings, 103–104
   dictionaries in
      custom dictionaries, 105–107
      exception dictionaries, 107–108
      for other languages, 108
      overview of, 105
   Ignore and Ignore All options, 103
   in other languages, 108–109
   in Outlook, 1162
   overview of, 101–103
   in PowerPoint, 1112
   turning off for specific text, 104
   in Word, 101–102, 107, 108–110
Spike clipboard tool in AutoText, 652–653
spin button controls, 559–560
split buttons, 41
splitting
   Access databases for network use, 1054–1055
   Code windows, 410, 411
   PowerPoint slides, 1110
   subdocuments, 786
   Word tables, 738–739
Spreadsheet Property Toolbox, 306, 310
SQL (Structured Query Language), 1071–1078.
   See also VBA database programming
   Access query designer and, 1071
   bulk updates and deletions in, 1077–1078
   defined, 1058
   dialects, 1072
   inserting in VBA code, 1072
   predicates, 1075
   `SELECT` statements, 1072–1077
      for choosing fields, 1073–1074

      for creating calculated fields, 1074–1075
      for grouping records, 1076–1077
      overview of, 1072–1073
      for relating multiple tables, 1073
      for selecting records, 1075
      for setting recordset criteria, 1075–1076
      for sorting records, 1077
   SQL Server, 1001, 1002
   SQL view in Access, 1026
standard modules, 419, 422
start pages, setting, 93
startup options
   for Access databases, 994–997
   for custom Access applications, 1051–1052
   in Excel, 855–857
   in Outlook, 1140–1141
   in Word, 599–600
statements. *See* VBA code
static declarations, 439
Step Into, Over, and Out commands, 508–509
`Stop` statements, 507–508
storing
   custom dictionaries, 106
   Excel customizations, 863–865
   help files, 50
   hyperlinks in Access fields, 286
   macros, 861
   Word customizations, 605
Straight Segment option for freeform shapes, 149
string variables, 452–453
Style dialog box in Word, 685–686, 692–693
Style drop-down list in Word, 688–689
Style Options dialog box in PowerPoint, 1113
StyleRef fields, 827–828
styles, Excel, 899
styles, Word. *See* formatting in Word
Sub procedures, 419, 422, 423–425
Submit controls, 298
SuperPrint utility, 218
switchboards in Access, 1042, 1048
switches
   command line switches
      in Access, 994–996
      in Excel, 855–856
      in Outlook, 1140–1141
      overview of, 7–8
      in Word, 599–600
   controlling field display with, 804–808

(continued)

1240 Index

switches *(continued)*
  Date-Time Picture switch, 807–808
  Format switch, 804–806
  Hyperlink field switches, 285
  Numeric Picture switch, 806
Symbol dialog box in Word, 118–119
Symbol fields, 828
symbols
  See also special characters
  AutoCorrect default substitutions for, 114–115
  currency symbols in Excel, 894
  in footnotes and endnotes, 775
  in Macros9.dot templates, 638
synchronization software, 262–264
Synchronize command, 363
system policies
  See also networks
  controlling features with, 352
  creating, 354
  defining individual policies, 355–356
  network requirements for, 352
  overview of, 351–352, 356
  specifying types of, 355
  System Policy Editor, 352–354
  using environment variables as, 356–357

T

tab settings. *See* formatting in Word
Table Cell Helper macro, 728
Table of Contents Options dialog box, 782
Table Positioning dialog box in Word, 733, 734
Table Properties dialog box in Word, 733, 735
tables, Access database
  creating, 1025–1026
  defined, 1015
  displaying, 1030
  editing data in, 1030–1031
  formatting, 1032
  modifying fields in, 1031–1032
  relating with SQL statements, 1073
  relationships between, 1019–1020, 1032–1034
  selecting data in, 1030–1031
tables, creating in PowerPoint presentations, 1113–1114
tables, Word, 727–746
  adding to Web pages, 292
  converting text into, 740–741
  creating
    by drawing, 729–730
    with Insert Table dialog box, 731

using grids, 730–731
editing text in, 740–741
formatting
  with AutoFit feature, 735–737
  with AutoFormat command, 732
  cells, rows, and columns, 737–738
  column width, 734–737
  deleting versus clearing, 738
  headings, 739
  keyboard shortcuts in, 738
  merging cells, 738
  moving rows, 738
  position, 732–734
  row height, 734–737
  size, 732–734
  splitting cells, 738
  splitting tables, 738–739
  text in table cells, 740
inserting
  in documents, 729–731
  Excel worksheets into, 743
  math formulas in, 742–743
  in PowerPoint presentations, 1114
  Tab stops in text, 740
installing Table Cell Helper macro, 728
nesting, 731–732
overview of, 727, 746
selecting table elements, 728–729
sorting data in, 741–742
tools for, 727–728
tables of authorities, 784
Tables and Borders toolbar in Word, 680–681
tables of contents
  creating, 782–784
  editing, 778–779
  field settings, 782, 783–784
  formatting, 778–779
  inserting in Web pages, 342
  overview of, 778, 786
  style settings, 782–783
  updating, 779
tables of figures, 778–784
tangent handles on freehand shapes, 147
Task Recurrence dialog box in Outlook, 1194
tasks. *See* Outlook
TC fields, 829
TCP/IP (Transmission Control Protocol/Internet Protocol), 88
telephone numbers
  BlueSky Software (RoboHelp), 59
  BlueSquirrel, 216
  Data Junction, 194
  McAfee Software, 270

n-Dimensional Software (Access Upsizer), 1046
for resources on VBA, 390
Symantec, 270
Vector Research Corporation (UNIA mouse), 41
Virginia Systems (Sonar Bookends), 781
Telnet, 88
Template Wizard with Data Tracking add-in, 962–963
templates
  in Access, 261
  adding styles to, 694
  for binders, 261
  creating Web pages with, 290
  in Excel, 260
  Macros9.dot template, 638, 653
  in Outlook, 260, 1166, 1167
  for Outlook forms, 1166, 1167
  in PowerPoint, 1123–1124
  saving Excel customizations in, 863–865
  of system policies, 352–354
  template folders for workgroups, 262, 365
  tracking Excel data with, 963
templates, Word
  attached templates, 615, 616–617
  creating, 615
  customizing, 614–619
  global templates, 615–616, 617
  hierarchy of, 615
  modifying, 615, 617–618
  Normal templates, 615
  overview of, 614
  saving, 618–619
  storing customizations in, 605
Templates and Add-ins dialog box, 616–617
text, 101–134
  adding scrolling text to Web pages, 293
  adding to AutoShapes, 143
  AutoCorrect feature, 112–120
    adding special characters to, 118–119
    cautions, 114, 117, 119
    default symbol substitutions, 114–115
    defined, 646
    em and en dashes in, 119–120
    expanding abbreviations with, 114
    lists, adding words to, 117
    lists, overview of, 112, 113
    lists, using multiple, 116–117
    overview of, 112–113
    settings, 112, 113
    sharing between Office apps, 114

Index

turning off automatic exceptions, 116
turning off and on, 117–118
undoing changes made by, 115
Bookshelf reference tool for, 112
built-in thesaurus in Word, 111–112
displaying on toolbar buttons, 72
editing on hyperlinks, 281
fonts, 120–134
   expert sets of, 132–133
   families of, 132
   font manager software, 121–122
   ligature style, 132
   "old-style" numerals, 133
   OpenType fonts, 120–121
   overview of, 120
   rules for, 134
   scalable fonts, 120–121
   small caps style, 133
   sources for, 133
   special characters, inserting, 129–131
   special characters, listed, 122–129
   TrueType fonts, 120–121
   Type 1 fonts, 120–121
formatting in AutoShapes, 144
formatting in Excel charts, 942–943
grammar checking in Word, 110–111
layout, rules for, 134
overview of, 101
in PowerPoint presentations
   animating, 1111
   bookmarking, 1109
   editing, 1107–1109
   formatting, 1110–1111
   importing from outlines, 1110
   indenting paragraphs, 1111
   navigating, 1107–1108
   spell-checking, 1112
   text placeholders versus text boxes, 1109
   viewing text outlines of, 1108–1109
special characters, adding to AutoCorrect feature, 118–119
spell-checking, 101–110
   automatically as you work, 109–110
   correcting misspellings, 103–104
   creating exception dictionaries, 107–108
   custom dictionaries, 105–107
   dictionaries, overview of, 105
   dictionaries for other languages, 108

Ignore and Ignore All options, 103
in other languages, 108–109
overview of, 101–103
turning off for specific text, 104
in Word, 101–102, 107, 108–110
in Word VBA
   copying or cutting, 845
   creating ranges from selections, 843
   deleting, 845
   formatting, 847
   inserting, 846–847
   pasting, 846
   redefining ranges and selections, 843–845
   selecting ranges, 843
   transferring, 846
wrapping around graphic objects in Word, 718–721
text box controls
   See also controls, VBA form
   adding scroll bars to, 551
   default text for, 550
   versus input box controls, 549
   as label controls, 549
   multiline text boxes, 550
   passwords for, 550
   properties of, 550
   retrieving user entries from, 550
text boxes, Word
   See also page layout in Word
   aligning into columns, 713
   anchoring, 717–718
   converting into frames, 714
   creating, 712
   creating slides with, 725–726
   editing text in linked boxes, Word, 712
   versus frames, 714
   linking, 712
   navigating linked boxes, 712
   for newspaper-style layouts, 711, 713
   overview of, 143–144, 711
   positioning in frames, 715–716
   removing, 713
   reordering chains of, 713–714
   text flow in, 711, 712
   versus text placeholders in PowerPoint, 1109
   toolbar, 712
texture fills for graphic objects, 151–152, 157
themes, applying to Web pages, 292, 338
Themes dialog box in FrontPage, 338
thesaurus in Word, 111–112
threaded document discussions, 369

Threads setting for Jet engine, 1010
timelines in Excel charts, 941
title bar area, 22–23
titling
   message boxes, 531
   Web pages, 274, 329
TOC fields, 829–830
toggle button controls, 556, 557
toolbar buttons, 68–76
   adding, 25
   adding space between, 26, 68–69
   assigning hyperlinks to, 75–76
   changing width of, 69, 75
   copying images to, 73
   customizing, 68–76
   deleting, 27
   displaying hidden buttons, 25–26
   displaying ScreenTips for, 74–75
   displaying text and images on, 72
   on docked toolbars, accessing, 38–39
   editing images on, 72–73
   hiding, 25–26
   in HTML Help system, 52
   importing images for, 73
   for inserting graphics, 75–76
   moving, 26
   naming, 26, 74–75
   overview of, 40
   on Picture toolbar, 163–164
   removing space between, 68–69
   renaming, 26
   saving custom buttons, 82
Toolbar Properties dialog box in Access, 1049–1050
toolbars
   See also Shortcut bar
   3-D Settings toolbar, 152–154
   adding field commands to, 799–800
   adding script commands to, 320
   Auditing toolbar in Excel, 967–969
   Clipboard toolbar, 180–182
   controlling with keyboard shortcuts, 35
   converting submenus into, 40
   creating, 24–25, 67
   customizing, 65–68, 606
   Database toolbar, 200
   deleting, 26
   DHTML Effects toolbar, 342–345
   displaying, 36–37
   docked toolbars
      accessing hidden buttons on, 38–39
      changing from floating to, 40
      docking Shortcut bar, 20, 21
      moving, 38
      overview of, 37
   Drawing toolbar, 137, 156–157

(continued)

Index

toolbars *(continued)*
  floating toolbars
    changing from docked to, 40
    overview of, 39
    Shortcut bar as, 20
  Formatting toolbar in Excel, 892
  Frames toolbar, 294
  Full Screen toolbar in Word, 602
  Header and Footer toolbar, 703, 707
  hiding, 36–37
  interactive spreadsheet toolbar, 310
  Navigation toolbar, 332–333
  Online Meeting toolbar, 372
  in Outlook, 1143
  overview of, 36
  Picture toolbar, 163–164
  PivotTable toolbar, 955
  placing, 66
  renaming, 26
  reordering, 25
  restoring deleted toolbars, 26–27
  restoring original toolbars, 65
  Reviewing toolbar in Word, 787
  saving custom toolbars, 82
  ScreenTips option for, 36
  Shadow Settings toolbar, 152–153
  Shortcut Menus toolbar, 80–81
  solving space problems of, 67–68
  Tables and Borders toolbar, 680–681
  text box toolbar, 712
  Views bar in FrontPage, 326–327
  in Visual Basic Editor, 394–395
  Web toolbars, 91–93
  Web Tools toolbar, 298
Toolbox
  in Access, 1080–1081
  adding ActiveX controls to, 576–577
  adding controls from, 533–535
  buttons on, 58, 175–176
  in VBA, 1080–1081
Toolbox, Spreadsheet Property, 306, 310
tracking
  See also finding
  changes in shared Excel workbooks, 963–964
  changes while editing documents, 789
  documents via properties, 247–249
  Excel data with built-in templates, 963
transparent color, 164
trendlines in Excel charts, 942
troubleshooting. *See* debugging

U

undoing AutoCorrect changes, 115
Unicode characters, 16–17
updating
  databases with SQL, 1077–1078
  documents with AutoText, 651–652
  fields, 803
  indexes, 779
  shared documents, 262–264
  tables of contents, 779
Upsizing Wizard in Access, 1005
URLs (Uniform Resource Locators), 88
User and Group Permissions dialog box, 267
user interface, 31–47
  in FrontPage, 324
  keyboard shortcuts, 35–36
  mouse
    IntelliMouse, 42
    right-click menus, 40–41
    settings, 41
    tips, 40–41
    types of, 41–42
  OCR software and, 46–47
  overview of, 31
  pen technology and, 44–46
  screen
    document windows, 34
    full screen view, 33–34
    zooming in and out of, 31–33
  sound settings, 43
  speech-recognition software and, 44, 45
  toolbars
    accessing hidden buttons, 38–39
    buttons, 40
    changing type of, 40
    converting submenus into, 40
    displaying, 36–37
    docked toolbars, 37
    floating toolbars, 39
    hiding, 36–37
    moving, 38
    overview of, 36
    ScreenTips option, 36
  in Visual Basic Editor, 393–396
user profiles in Outlook e-mail, 1171–1173
UserForm toolbar, 542
UserForms, VBA. *See* forms, VBA
UUENCODE encoding format, 1186

V

validating
  Access field values, 1028–1029
  Excel data entries, 886–888
  user entries, 572–574

variables, 434–442
  See also VBA code
  versus arguments, 426
  assigning values to, 440
  counter variables, 472
  custom document properties as, 586–587
  data types for
    Boolean data type, 449, 450
    converting between, 448
    Currency data type, 436, 449, 450
    Date data type, 451–452
    Decimal data type, 436, 449
    default values of, 441–442
    defined, 435–436
    Double data type, 436, 449
    listed, 436–437
    numeric data types, 449–450
    pros and cons of using, 437
    Single data type, 436, 449
    Variant data type, 448–449
  declaring
    class variables, 498
    data types in, 435–437
    forcing explicit declarations, 437–438
    multiple variables on same line, 439–440
    object variables, 489–491
    overview of, 434–435
    private declarations, 438
    public declarations, 438
    specifying scope in, 438
    static declarations, 439
  default values in, 441–442
  defined, 434
  editing values in, 515–516
  in expressions, 441
  object variables
    creating, 489–491, 492
    declaring, 489–491
    emptying, 491
    object references in, 487, 491, 493
  referring to VBA forms using, 563
  string variables, 452–453
  using in Word VBA documents, 850
  variable statements, 447–448
Variant data type, 448–449
VBA code, 417–475
  See also debugging VBA code; variables
  in Access, 1054, 1093
  ActiveX controls and, 178
  adding comments to, 432–434
  arguments
    advantages of, 426
    date arguments, 924
    defined, 426

overview of, 412–413
in Sub procedures, 424
versus variables, 426
arrays
  array dimensions, 454
  versus Collection objects, 494
  declaring, 454–455
  defined, 453
  dynamic arrays, 455
  fixed arrays, 455
  For...Next loops and, 471–474
  indexes for, 455–456
  overview of, 453–454
commands for, built-in, 456–458
constants
  attributes and, 443–444
  benefits of, 443
  declaring, 442–443
  defined, 442
  for input boxes, 529–530
  for message boxes, 529–530
control structures, 458–475
  anatomy of, 459
  Case clause tests, 465–466
  condition expressions in, 460–461
  conditional statements, 458–466
  defined, 458–459
  Do...Loop statements, 467–471
  Exit Do statements, 470
  Exit For statements, 474
  For...Next loops, 471–474
  For Each...Next loops, 474, 496–497
  If...ElseIf statements, 463
  If...Then statements, 461–462, 463–464
  If...Then...Else statements, 462, 463
  loops, 458, 466–474
  nesting, 459, 463–464, 470–471, 473
  Select Case statements, 464–465
  With statements, 459
Function procedures
  in assignment statements, 441
  calling, 425
  defined, 419, 422, 423, 425
  versus functions, 425
  versus Sub procedures, 425
functions for, built-in, 456–458
Go To statements, 474–475
hierarchy, 419
indenting, 431
inserting SQL statements in, 1072
line continuation characters in, 432
locking, 593–594
making legible, 431–432
modules
  adding to projects, 421
  class modules, 419, 422
  Declarations section, 419, 421–422
  defined, 385, 419, 420
  versus Excel formulas, 914
  planning, 420–421
  standard modules, 419, 422
naming elements in, 429–431
operators
  arithmetic operators, 444–445
  comparison operators, 444, 445, 446–448
  concatenation operators, 444, 445, 448
  defined, 444
  logical operators, 445, 446, 460–461
  precedence in, 444–446
procedures
  arguments and, 426
  defined, 419
  defining scope of, 427
  Event procedures, 423
  for finding fields, 810–811
  Function procedures, 419, 422, 423, 425
  overview of, 422
  private procedures, 427, 428
  Property procedures, 423, 498–499
  starting, 422–423
  Sub procedures, 419, 422, 423–425
  writing, 422–426, 498–499
programs defined, 420
programs sample, 417–419
projects defined, 419, 420
securing with digital certificates, 592–593
statements
  assignment statements, 428–429, 440
  built-in statements, 456–458
  compiler options statements, 429
  declaration statements, 428, 434–440
  defined, 419
  Dim declarations, 434, 438
  executable statements, 429
  expressions in, 441
  operators in, 444–448
  Option Explicit declarations, 437–438
  types of, 421, 428–429
Sub procedures
  arguments in, 424
  calling, 424
  defined, 419, 422, 423–424
  versus Function procedures, 425
using objects in, 482
writing, 380–382
VBA database programming, 1057–1078
  with ADO, 1060–1071
    Command objects, 1069–1071
    connecting to data sources, 1061–1062
    creating references to, 1060–1061
    defined, 1059
    error handling, 1060
    Recordset objects, 1062–1069
    stored procedures and, 1069–1070
  ADO Recordset objects
    adding records, 1067–1068
    changing field data, 1068–1069
    checking for records, 1067
    creating, 1063–1064
    cursor options, 1064–1066
    deleting records, 1067–1068
    locating records, 1067
    lock options, 1066
    loop operations on, 1069
    overview of, 1062
    reading field data, 1068
    setting options for, 1064–1066
  DAO model, 1059
  database object models for, 1058–1059
  DoCmd object in Access and, 1057–1058
  ODBC standard and, 1059–1060
  ODBCDirect and, 1060
  OLE DB specification and, 1060
  overview of, 1057, 1078
  RDO model, 1059
  with SQL, 1071–1078
    Access query designer and, 1071
    bulk updates and deletions in, 1077–1078
    defined, 1058
    dialects, 1072
    inserting in VBA code, 1072
    predicates, 1075
  with SQL SELECT statements
    for choosing fields, 1073–1074
    for creating calculated fields, 1074–1075
    for grouping records, 1076–1077
    overview of, 1072–1073
    for relating multiple tables, 1073

(continued)

VBA database programming *(continued)*
  for selecting records, 1075
  for setting recordset criteria, 1075–1076
  for sorting records, 1077
VBA macros. *See* macros, VBA
VBA objects, 477–500
  application objects, 387, 489, 833–834
  class modules
    classes defined, 479, 497
    components, 497–498
    creating, 497
    custom objects in, 500
    declaring class variables, 498
    as objects, 497
    writing methods, 499–500
    writing property procedures, 498–499
  code as, 497
  Collection objects
    accessing objects in, 493–494
    adding objects to, 495
    versus arrays, 494
    changing values in, 494
    counting objects in, 496
    creating, 494–495
    defined, 493
    `For Each...Next` loops and, 496–497
    removing objects from, 495
  container objects, 387, 485
  creating, 491–492
  defined, 477–479
  events, 481, 486–487
  fields and, Word, 808–810
  form objects, 481–482
  identifying objects to work with, 487–488
  methods
    of built-in objects, 457
    calling, 486
    changing properties with, 486
    defined, 481, 486
    of field objects, 808–810
    Range method, 841–842
    of VBA forms, 481
    writing, 499–500
  object expressions, 487, 488–489
  object models
    Application objects, 489, 833–834
    defined, 387, 479–480
    extending with COM, 480–481
    forms in, 481–482
    hierarchy in, 488–489
    importance of, 480
    viewing maps of, 482–483
  object references, 487, 491, 493

  object variables
    creating, 489–491, 492
    declaring, 489–491
    emptying, 491
    object references in, 487, 491, 493
  overview of, 386–387, 388
  properties
    changing settings of, 483, 485
    as data types in variables, 484
    default properties, 485
    defined, 481
    of field objects, 808–810
    finding container objects via, 485
    as objects, 485, 488
    Range property, 840–841
    read-only properties, 483
    retrieving, 483, 484
    write-only properties, 483
  selection tools for, 981–983
  using in code, 482
  `With` statements and, 492–493
VBA UserForms. *See* forms, VBA
VBA (Visual Basic for Applications)
  See also custom Office applications; Visual Basic Editor
  ActiveX technology and, 387–389
  built-in commands in, 456–458
  COM add-ins and, 385
  defined, 379, 417
  in developing database applications, 1046
  features in Office 2000, 383–385
  functions
    in assignment statements, 441
    built-in functions, 456–458
    versus Function procedures, 425
  history of, 382
  as industry standard, 382
  information resources on, 390
  macro recorders and, 385–386
  in Office apps, 384
  overview of, 391
  purpose of, 382, 385
  uses of, 386
  viewing examples on CD-ROM, 379
  versus Visual Basic, 382, 383
VBScript, 318–320
vector graphics, 289
Versions dialog box in Word, 793–794
vertex, 146
video clips, 167
View Summary dialog box in Outlook, 1155–1156
View tab of Options dialog box in Word, 600–601, 603–604

viewing
  See also displaying
  Excel chart items, 934
  Excel comments, 901
  Excel formulas, 906–907
  headers and footers, 703
  maps of object models, 482–483
  PowerPoint text outlines, 1108–1109
  Shortcut bar toolbars, 21
  Visual Basic Editor windows, 397
views
  See also Access; Outlook; windows
  in Access databases, 1024–1025
  in PowerPoint, 1103–1104
  overview of, 326–327
views in FrontPage
  Folders view, 329–330
  Hyperlinks view, 333–334
  Navigation view, 330–333
  overview of, 326–327
views in Word
  customizing, 601–602, 603–605
  Full Screen view, 33–34, 601–602
  Normal view, 601–602
  Outline view, 743–745
  Print Layout view, 601–602
  properties of in VBA, 837–838
  Web Layout view, 601–602
VIM (Vendor Independent Messaging), 365
virus protection, 268–270
Visual Basic
  Access forms and, 1081–1082
  versus VBA, 382, 383
Visual Basic Editor, 393–415
  See also VBA
  in Access, 384–385
  Code windows, 407–413
    arguments and, 412–413
    automatic error checking in, 408
    bookmarking code, 409–410
    Complete Word feature, 412
    creating, 407
    entering code in, 407–408
    features for, 410
    list boxes, 409
    List Constants feature, 412
    List Properties and Methods feature, 411–412
    navigating in, 409
    opening, 407, 566–567
    overview of, 407
    Quick Info feature, 412–413, 512
    splitting, 410, 411
  formatting controls, 541–546
  grids, 538
  keyboard shortcuts, 395–396
  menus, 394, 395

Object Browser window
  accessing code, 406
  browsing objects, 405–406
  copying and pasting browsed code, 406
  defined, 404
  Help, 406
  opening, 404
  searching for objects in, 406
in Outlook, 385
overview of, 379–380, 383, 393, 415
Parameter Info window, 413
Project Explorer window
  buttons in, 401
  components in, 400–401
  defined, 399
  navigating, 401
  nodes in, 401
  opening, 400
  protecting projects, 403
  renaming projects, 403
  saving projects, 399
  setting project properties, 402–403
  shortcut menu, 402
Properties window, 414–415
Quick Info window, 413, 512
saving screen layouts, 399
toolbars, 394–395
user interface, 393–396
windows
  Code windows, 407–413
  for debugging code, 415
  docking, 398–399
  hiding, 397
  keyboard shortcuts for switching, 397
  nondockable windows, 398–399
  Object Browser window, 404–406
  overview of, 396–397
  Parameter Info window, 413
  Project Explorer window, 399–403
  Properties window, 414–415
  Quick Info window, 413, 512
  viewing, 397
Visual Clarity tab of Style Options dialog box, 1113
Visual Keyboard utility, 15
VML (Vector Markup Language), 289

W

Watch window
  See also debugging VBA code
  adding watch expressions, 517–519
  defining breakpoints, 519–520
  editing watch expressions, 519
  versus Locals window, 517
  overview of, 516–517
watermarks, digital, 707
Web browsers
  See also Internet Explorer
  capabilities of, 276–277
  choosing, 87
  Netscape Navigator, 87
  opening Excel Web pages in, 310
  opening Web pages from inside, 94–95
  opening Web pages into, 89
  previewing Web pages in, 274
  specifying target browsers in Word, 292
  viewing Web PowerPoint presentations in, 302
Web Components, 305–306, 341
Web Find Fast tool, 363–364
Web Layout view in Word, 601–602
Web Page Wizard, 291–292
Web pages, 273–303
  See also FrontPage; Web sites
  accessing
    with Back and Forward buttons, 92, 93
    from Go menus, 92, 94
    from inside browsers, 94–95
    opening into browsers, 89
    opening in Office apps, 89–91
    from Web toolbars, 91–93
  changing titles of, 274
  editing HTML code in, 290
  editing in Internet Explorer, 96
  footnotes and endnotes in, 775
  graphics in
    GIF and JPEG images, 288–289
    overview of, 288
    saving in PNG format, 289
    vector graphics, 289
  HTML and, 275
  hyperlinks in
    in Access, 285, 286–287
    creating, 279–284
    defined, 278
    deleting, 281
    editing, 281
    in Excel, 284–285
    following, 279
    formatting, 284–285
    inserting in frames, 296–297
    navigating, 93–94
    in PowerPoint, 285, 287–288
    ScreenTips for, 279
    in Word, 284–285
  importing into Access, 91
  overview of, 98, 273–274, 303
  previewing in browsers, 274
  publishing, 302–303
  saving PowerPoint presentations as, 299–302
  saving Word documents as, 274
  setting options for, 275
  setting start and search pages, 93
  in Word
    adding scrolling text, 293
    adding tables, 292
    applying themes, 292
    building frames, 293–297
    creating, 290–292
    editing, 292–293
    hyperlinks in, 284–285
    inserting horizontal lines, 292–293
    overview of, 290, 699
    specifying target browsers, 292
  Word forms in
    adding Submit controls, 298
    creating, 298
    empowering with scripts, 298
    formatting using tables, 298–299
    overview of, 297
  XML (Extensible Markup Language) and, 274
Web pages, interactive, 305–322
  ActiveX controls in, 321–322
  overview of, 305, 322
  publishing Access databases as
    creating data access pages, 313–318
    creating report snapshots, 311
    creating server-side pages, 312–313
    data formats for, 312–313
    exporting dynamic data, 313
    exporting static data, 310–311
    overview of, 310, 313–314
    storing data on Web servers, 312
  publishing Excel spreadsheets as
    choosing elements to convert, 307–308
    formatting interactive pages, 309–310
    overview of, 306–307
    publishing interactive data, 308–309
  scripts in
    adding script commands to toolbars and menus, 320
    editing, 321
    identifying, 320
    inserting, 321
    JavaScript, 318–320
    overview of, 318
    previewing, 321
    script anchors, 320–321
    Script Editor, 318, 319
    VBScript, 318–320
  Web Component controls in, 305–306

Web site addresses
  of author, 18
  Bear Rock Technologies, 723
  BlueSquirrel.com, 216
  DataViz Conversions Plus software, 194
  EasyHelp/Web software, 59
  of font sources, 133
  Micro Logic Corporation (Info Select), 1206
  Microsoft Access development, 1041
  Microsoft Outlook filters, 1177
  for Office information, 18
  Office Update tool, 43
  Properties Plus utility, 233
  QualiType Font Handler/Font Sentry programs, 122
  for third-party security software, 268
  Traveling Software.com, 264
  for VBA information, 390
  Virginia Systems (Sonar Bookends), 781
  for virus disinfection software, 270
  Zenographics.com, 218
Web sites
  See also FrontPage; Web pages
  browser capabilities and, 276–277
  determining location of, 276
  managing files in with Web Folders, 361–363
  Office automatic subfolders and, 278
  planning file structure for, 277
  working offline on files in, 363
Web Subscriptions feature, 370
Web toolbars, 91–93
webs, 325, *See also* FrontPage
Whiteboard in NetMeeting, 373–374
With statements, 459
width
  in columnar layouts, 709
  of toolbar buttons, 69, 75
wildcards, 240, 642–646
windows
  document windows, 34
  in FrontPage, 327
  in Visual Basic Editor
    Code windows, 407–413
    for debugging code, 415
    docking, 398–399
    hiding, 397
    keyboard shortcuts for, 395–396, 397
    nondockable windows, 398–399
    Object Browser window, 404–406
    overview of, 396–397
    Parameter Info window, 413
    Project Explorer window, 399–403
    Properties window, 414–415
    Quick Info window, 413, 512
    viewing, 397
  in Word VBA
    changing properties of, 837
    overview of, 836
    specifying in code, 836
    views, properties of, 837–838
    window panes, 837
    zooming in code, 838
Windows Registry, 1009–1011
WinHelp versus HTML Help, 50–51
With statements, 492–493
Word, 599–851
  See also customizing Word
  AutoSummarize command, 248, 746
  bookmarks in, 283–284
  Calculator, 605
  collaboration features, 368
  command line switches, 599–600
  in developing database applications, 1046
  document security in, 265
  document templates in, 260
  editing in Print Preview mode, 207–208
  forms in, 173
  grammar checking, 110–111
  hyperlinks in, 284–285, 635
  language settings, 108–109
  as Outlook e-mail editor, 1184–1185
  pasting Excel or Access tables into, 185
  pasting Word text into Access, 185
  printing in, 211–212
  spell-checking, 101–102, 107, 108–110
  thesaurus, 111–112
Word VBA, 833–851
  Application objects, 833–834
  documents
    activating, 835
    active documents, 834
    creating, 835
    document sections, 835
    opening, 835
    specifying, 834–835
    using variables in, 850
  finding and replacing in, 847–850
  overview of, 833, 851
  Range objects, 840–843
  Selection objects, 839–840, 843
  text
    copying or cutting, 845
    creating ranges from selections, 843
    deleting, 845
    formatting, 847
    inserting, 846–847
    pasting, 846
    redefining ranges and selections, 843–845
    selecting ranges, 843
    transferring, 846
  windows
    changing properties of, 837
    overview of, 836
    specifying in code, 836
    views, properties of, 837–838
    window panes, 837
    zooming in code, 838
Word Web pages, 290–299
  adding scrolling text, 293
  adding Word tables, 292
  applying themes, 292
  building frames in, 293–297
  creating with templates, 290
  creating with Web Page Wizard, 291–292
  editing, 292–293
  forms in
    adding Submit controls, 298
    creating, 298
    empowering with scripts, 298
    formatting using tables, 298–299
    overview of, 297
  hyperlinks in, 284–285
  inserting horizontal lines, 292–293
  overview of, 290, 699
  specifying target browsers, 292
WordArt, 149–150
workgroup template folders, 262, 365
worksheets. *See* Excel
workspace files, Excel, 873
World Wide Web, 7, 87.
  See also Internet; Web
wrapping text around graphic objects, 718–721
write-only properties, 483
writing
  custom Excel VBA functions, 984, 986
  event code, 487
  event procedures, 566–567
  methods, 499–500
  procedures, 422–426
  property procedures, 498–499
  VBA code, 380–382

X

XE fields, 830–831
XML (Extensible Markup Language), 274

Y

"Y2K problem", Excel formulas and, 923–992

Z

zooming
    customizing with VBA code, 838
    in editing Access data, 1006
    with IntelliMouse, 42
    macro for toggling settings, 32–33
    overview of, 31–32
    in PowerPoint, 1104

IDG Books Worldwide, Inc.
End-User License Agreement

READ THIS. You should carefully read these terms and conditions before opening the software packet(s) included with this book ("Book"). This is a license agreement ("Agreement") between you and IDG Books Worldwide, Inc. ("IDGB"). By opening the accompanying software packet(s), you acknowledge that you have read and accept the following terms and conditions. If you do not agree and do not want to be bound by such terms and conditions, promptly return the Book and the unopened software packet(s) to the place you obtained them for a full refund.

1. **License Grant.** IDGB grants to you (either an individual or entity) a nonexclusive license to use one copy of the enclosed software program(s) (collectively, the "Software") solely for your own personal or business purposes on a single computer (whether a standard computer or a workstation component of a multiuser network). The Software is in use on a computer when it is loaded into temporary memory (RAM) or installed into permanent memory (hard disk, CD-ROM, or other storage device). IDGB reserves all rights not expressly granted herein.

2. **Ownership.** IDGB is the owner of all right, title, and interest, including copyright, in and to the compilation of the Software recorded on the disk(s) or CD-ROM ("Software Media"). Copyright to the individual programs recorded on the Software Media is owned by the author or other authorized copyright owner of each program. Ownership of the Software and all proprietary rights relating thereto remain with IDGB and its licensers.

3. **Restrictions On Use and Transfer.**

    (a) You may only (i) make one copy of the Software for backup or archival purposes, or (ii) transfer the Software to a single hard disk, provided that you keep the original for backup or archival purposes. You may not (i) rent or lease the Software, (ii) copy or reproduce the Software through a LAN or other network system or through any computer subscriber system or bulletin-board system, or (iii) modify, adapt, or create derivative works based on the Software.

    (b) You may not reverse engineer, decompile, or disassemble the Software. You may transfer the Software and user documentation on a permanent basis, provided that the transferee agrees to accept the terms and conditions of this Agreement and you retain no copies. If the Software is an update or has been updated, any transfer must include the most recent update and all prior versions.

4. **Restrictions On Use of Individual Programs.** You must follow the individual requirements and restrictions detailed for each individual program in the "What's on the CD-ROM" appendix of this Book. These limitations are also contained in the individual license agreements recorded on the Software Media. These limitations may include a requirement that after using the program for a specified period of time, the user must pay a registration fee or discontinue use. By opening the Software packet(s), you will be agreeing to abide by the licenses and restrictions for these individual programs that are detailed in the "What's on the CD-ROM" appendix and on the Software Media. None of the material on this Software Media or listed in this Book may ever be redistributed, in original or modified form, for commercial purposes.

5. **Limited Warranty.**

    (a) IDGB warrants that the Software and Software Media are free from defects in materials and workmanship under normal use for a period of sixty (60) days from the date of purchase of this Book. If IDGB receives notification within the warranty period of defects in materials or workmanship, IDGB will replace the defective Software Media.

    (b) IDGB AND THE AUTHOR OF THE BOOK DISCLAIM ALL OTHER WARRANTIES, EXPRESS OR IMPLIED, INCLUDING WITHOUT LIMITATION IMPLIED WARRANTIES OF MERCHANTABILITY AND FITNESS FOR A PARTICULAR PURPOSE, WITH RESPECT TO THE SOFTWARE, THE PROGRAMS, THE SOURCE CODE CONTAINED THEREIN, AND/OR THE TECHNIQUES DESCRIBED IN THIS BOOK. IDGB DOES NOT WARRANT THAT THE FUNCTIONS CONTAINED IN THE SOFTWARE WILL MEET YOUR REQUIREMENTS OR THAT THE OPERATION OF THE SOFTWARE WILL BE ERROR FREE.

    (c) This limited warranty gives you specific legal rights, and you may have other rights that vary from jurisdiction to jurisdiction.

6. **Remedies.**

    (a) IDGB's entire liability and your exclusive remedy for defects in materials and workmanship shall be limited to replacement of the Software Media, which may be returned to IDGB with a copy of your receipt at the following address: Software Media Fulfillment Department, Attn.: *Microsoft Office 2000 Secrets*, IDG Books Worldwide, Inc., 7260 Shadeland Station, Ste. 100, Indianapolis, IN 46256, or call 1-800-762-2974. Please allow three to four weeks for delivery. This Limited Warranty is void if failure of the Software Media has resulted from accident, abuse, or misapplication. Any replacement Software Media will be warranted for the remainder of the original warranty period or thirty (30) days, whichever is longer.

- **(b)** In no event shall IDGB or the authors be liable for any damages whatsoever (including without limitation damages for loss of business profits, business interruption, loss of business information, or any other pecuniary loss) arising from the use of or inability to use the Book or the Software, even if IDGB has been advised of the possibility of such damages.
- **(c)** Because some jurisdictions do not allow the exclusion or limitation of liability for consequential or incidental damages, the above limitation or exclusion may not apply to you.

7. **U.S. Government Restricted Rights.** Use, duplication, or disclosure of the Software by the U.S. Government is subject to restrictions stated in paragraph (c)(1)(ii) of the Rights in Technical Data and Computer Software clause of DFARS 252.227-7013, and in subparagraphs (a) through (d) of the Commercial Computer — Restricted Rights clause at FAR 52.227-19, and in similar clauses in the NASA FAR supplement, when applicable.

8. **General.** This Agreement constitutes the entire understanding of the parties and revokes and supersedes all prior agreements, oral or written, between them and may not be modified or amended except in a writing signed by both parties hereto that specifically refers to this Agreement. This Agreement shall take precedence over any other documents that may be in conflict herewith. If any one or more provisions contained in this Agreement are held by any court or tribunal to be invalid, illegal, or otherwise unenforceable, each and every other provision shall remain in full force and effect.

SPECIAL OFFER FOR IDG BOOKS READERS

FREE GIFT!

FREE
IDG Books/PC WORLD CD Wallet
and a Sample Issue of
PC WORLD

THE #1 MONTHLY COMPUTER MAGAZINE

How to order your sample issue and FREE CD Wallet:

- ✉ Cut and mail the coupon today!
- ☎ Call us at 1-800-825-7595 x434
  Fax us at 1-415-882-0936
- ☞ Order online at
  www.pcworld.com/resources/subscribe/BWH.html

The IDG Books Worldwide logo is a trademark under exclusive license to IDG Books Worldwide, Inc., from International Data Group, Inc.

FREE GIFT/SAMPLE ISSUE COUPON

Cut coupon and mail to: PC World, PO Box 55029, Boulder, CO 80322-5029

YES! Please rush my FREE CD wallet and my FREE sample issue of PC WORLD! If I like PC WORLD, I'll honor your invoice and receive 11 more issues (12 in all) for just $19.97—that's 72% off the newsstand rate.

NO COST EXAMINATION GUARANTEE.
If I decide PC WORLD is not for me, I'll write "cancel" on the invoice and owe nothing. The sample issue and CD wallet are mine to keep, no matter what.

PC WORLD

Name
Company
Address
City   State   Zip
Email

Offer valid in the U.S. only. Mexican orders please send $39.97 USD. Canadian orders send $39.97, plus 7% GST (#R124669680). Other countries send $65.97. Savings based on annual newsstand rate of $71.88.   7BXP7

SPECIAL OFFER FOR IDG BOOKS READERS

Get the Most from Your PC!

Every issue of PC World is packed with the latest information to help you make the most of your PC.

- Top 100 PC and Product Ratings
- Hot PC News
- How Tos, Tips, & Tricks
- Buyers' Guides
- Consumer Watch
- Hardware and Software Previews
- Internet & Multimedia Special Reports
- Upgrade Guides
- Monthly @Home Section

YOUR FREE GIFT!

As a special bonus with your order, you will receive the IDG Books/ PC WORLD CD wallet, perfect for transporting and protecting your CD collection.

The IDG Books Worldwide logo is a trademark under exclusive license to IDG Books Worldwide, Inc., from International Data Group, Inc.

SEND TODAY

for your sample issue and FREE IDG Books/PC WORLD CD Wallet!

How to order your sample issue and FREE CD Wallet:

✉ Cut and mail the coupon today!
   Mail to: PC World, PO Box 55029, Boulder, CO 80322-5029

☎ Call us at 1-800-825-7595 x434
   Fax us at 1-415-882-0936

☞ Order online at www.pcworld.com/resources/subscribe/BWH.html

PC WORLD

my2cents.idgbooks.com

Register This Book — And Win!

Visit **http://my2cents.idgbooks.com** to register this book and we'll automatically enter you in our fantastic monthly prize giveaway. It's also your opportunity to give us feedback: let us know what you thought of this book and how you would like to see other topics covered.

Discover IDG Books Online!

The IDG Books Online Web site is your online resource for tackling technology — at home and at the office. Frequently updated, the IDG Books Online Web site features exclusive software, insider information, online books, and live events!

10 Productive & Career-Enhancing Things You Can Do at www.idgbooks.com

- Nab source code for your own programming projects.
- Download software.
- Read Web exclusives: special articles and book excerpts by IDG Books Worldwide authors.
- Take advantage of resources to help you advance your career as a Novell or Microsoft professional.
- Buy IDG Books Worldwide titles or find a convenient bookstore that carries them.
- Register your book and win a prize.
- Chat live online with authors.
- Sign up for regular e-mail updates about our latest books.
- Suggest a book you'd like to read or write.
- Give us your 2¢ about our books and about our Web site.

You say you're not on the Web yet? It's easy to get started with IDG Books' *Discover the Internet,* available at local retailers everywhere.

CD-ROM Installation Instructions

The *Microsoft Office 2000 Secrets* CD-ROM contains an electronic version of the book and a Web site directory, along with a set of outstanding shareware, demos, and more.

Most of the directories or subdirectories contain installation files with an .exe file extension. You can display the directories and files using Windows Explorer and then by double-clicking any .exe file to launch the install program for the file you want to copy to your hard drive. Each installation file asks if you want a Start menu shortcut created for you.

Please read the "What's on the CD-ROM" appendix for a complete guide to using the CD-ROM.